2nd Workshop on Natural Language Generation, Evaluation and Metrics (GEM 2022)

Abu Dhabi, United Arab Emirates and Online
7 December 2022

ISBN: 978-1-7138-9111-6

Printed from e-media with permission by:

Curran Associates, Inc.
57 Morehouse Lane
Red Hook, NY 12571

Some format issues inherent in the e-media version may also appear in this print version.

Printed with permission by Curran Associates, Inc. (2024)

Association for Computational Linguistics
209 N. Eighth Street
Stroudsburg, Pennsylvania 18360

Phone: 1-570-476-8006
Fax: 1-570-476-0860

acl@aclweb.org

Additional copies of this publication are available from:

Curran Associates, Inc.
57 Morehouse Lane
Red Hook, NY 12571 USA
Phone: 845-758-0400
Fax: 845-758-2633
Email: curran@proceedings.com
Web: www.proceedings.com

GEM 2022

2nd Workshop on Natural Language Generation, Evaluation, and Metrics

Proceedings of the Workshop

December 7, 2022

Introduction

Welcome to the second workshop on Natural Language Generation, Evaluation, and Metrics (GEM), to be held on December 7, 2022 as part of EMNLP in Abu Dhabi. The workshop aims to bring together researchers interested in model audits, new evaluatyion approaches and meta evaluations. The workshop is privileged to present several invited talks this year and the results of the shared task on generation with limited resources.

We are grateful to the program committee for their careful and thoughtful reviews of the papers submitted this year. Likewise, we are thankful to the shared task organizers for their hard work in preparing the shared tasks. We are looking forward to a workshop covering a wide range of topics, and we hope for lively discussions.

GEM Workshop Organizers.

Organizing Committee

Organizers

Antoine Bosselut, EPFL
Khyathi Chandu, Meta AI
Kaustubh Dhole, Emory University
Varun Gangal, Carnegie Mellon University
Sebastian Gehrmann, Google Research
Yacine Jernite, Hugging Face
Jekaterina Novikova, Winterlight Labs
Laura Perez-Beltrachini, University of Edinburgh

Program Committee

Reviewers

Tosin Adewumi, Ameeta Agrawal, Fatih Amasyali, David Aparicio, Samuel Arcadinho, Shima Asaadi

Simone Balloccu, Indrajit Bhattacharya, Şafak Bilici, Bernd Bohnet

Samuel Cahyawijaya, Pengshan Cai, Eduardo Calò, Ronald Cardenas, Boaz Carmeli, Silvia Casola, Khyathi Raghavi Chandu, Elizabeth Clark, Jordan Clive

Kordula De Kuthy, Mingkai Deng, Yuntian Deng, Daniel Deutsch, Mark Dingemanse, Esin Durmus, Ondřej Dušek

Moussa Kamal Eddine

Federico Fancellu, Raquel Fernandez

Albert Gatt, John Glover, Olga Golovneva

Tahmid Hasan, Behnam Hedayatnia, David M. Howcroft, Shulin Huang, Rudali Huidrom

Nikolai Ilinykh

Yacine Jernite, Mayank Jobanputra, Shailza Jolly

Emil Kalbaliyev, Mihir Kale, Marzena Karpinska, Noriaki Kawamae, Dimitar Kazakov, George Kour, Sergey Kovalchuk, Kalpesh Krishna, Rishu Kumar, Vanya Bannihatti Kumar

Harsh Lara, Alberto Lavelli, Hwanhee Lee, Jing Yang Lee, Yinghui Li, Paul Pu Liang, Andreas Liesenfeld, Sijia Liu, Yinhong Liu, Yixin Liu, Zhengzhong Liu, Ehsan Lotfi

Shirong Ma, Aman Madaan, Khyati Mahajan, Abinaya Mahendiran, Andreas Marfurt, Simon Mille, Sebastien Montella

Tapas Nayak, Vitaly Nikolaev, Tadashi Nomoto

Salomey Osei

Alexandros Papangelis, Cheoneum Park, Eunil Park, Tatiana Passali, Diogo Pernes, Sandro Pezzelle, Maja Popović, Jiashu Pu

Vipul Raheja, Anand A. Rajasekar, Vikas Raunak, Ehud Reiter, Leonardo F. R. Ribeiro, Daniele Riboni, Giuseppe Riccardi, Michael Ridenour, Terry Ruas

Rifat Shahriyar, Tianhao Shen, Anna Shvets, Arabella Sinclair, Marco Antonio Sobrevilla Cabezudo, Somayajulu Sripada, Yixuan Su, Barkavi Sundararajan

Bowen Tan, Katherine Thai, Craig Thomson, Grigorios Tsoumakas

Ashish Upadhyay

Jan Philip Wahle, Shira Wein, Michael White, Genta Winata, Zixiu Wu

Yadong Xi, Deyi Xiong, Xinnuo Xu, Yumo Xu

Li Yangning

Alessandra Zarcone, Jiawei Zhou, Yongxin Zhou, Qi Zhu

Keynote Talk: Challenges in evaluating safety for LLMs

Emily Dinan
FAIR (Meta AI)

Abstract: While research on large language models (LLMs) continues to accelerate, much recent work has called attention to anticipated risks and harms from their use in society. We will discuss challenges in evaluating the relative safety of these models as well as current approaches for doing so. Finally, we will highlight avenues for future research into evaluating and mitigating these harms.

Bio: Emily Dinan is a Research Engineer at FAIR (Meta AI) in New York. Her research interests include conversational AI, natural language processing, and safety and responsibility in these fields. Recently she has focused on methods for preventing conversational agents from reproducing biased, toxic, or otherwise harmful language. Prior to joining FAIR, she received her master's degree in Mathematics from the University of Washington.

Keynote Talk: Instructable and Collaborative Language Models

Timo Schick
FAIR (Meta AI)

Abstract: Textual content is often the output of a collaborative writing process — which includes writing text, making comments and changes, finding references, and asking others for help —, but today's NLP models are only trained to generate the final output of this process. In this talk, we will discuss an alternative approach where models are trained to imitate the entire writing process. We will look at examples of how this enables models to plan and explain their actions, to correct their own mistakes, and to better collaborate with humans. We will also discuss how to make such models better at following human-written instructions.

Bio: Timo Schick is a research scientist at FAIR working on few-shot learning in NLP. Previously, he did his PhD at the Center for Information and Language Processing (CIS) in Munich and worked in industry as a data scientist for several years. Timo's current research focuses on instruction-based learning and teaching language models to collaborate with other entities.

Keynote Talk: Reflections on Trusting Untrustworthy Language Generators

Sean Welleck
University of Washington

Abstract: In his 1984 Turing Award Lecture "Reflections on Trusting Trust", Ken Thompson famously said "You can't trust code that you did not totally create yourself". These words are especially relevant today, as powerful and flexible language models generate natural language and code that is increasingly human-like. However, these same systems challenge our trust, exhibiting odd degeneracies, amplifying biases, and producing flawed reasoning. In this talk, I will introduce two directions for harnessing the potential of these language models while mitigating the risks. First, I will discuss unlearning: removing undesirable behaviors by integrating feedback and learning. Second, I will discuss how integrating language models with trustworthy symbolic systems can open the door to tackling challenging mathematical reasoning tasks. Join me as we explore the path towards trusting untrustworthy language generators.

Bio: Sean Welleck is a Postdoctoral Scholar at the University of Washington and the Allen Institute for Artificial Intelligence, working with Yejin Choi. His research focuses on algorithms for natural language generation and machine reasoning, with the aim of minimizing the effort needed to trust the output of AI systems. He has developed unlearning, decoding, and evaluation algorithms for controllable neural language generation, and methods for integrating language models with symbolic systems, with a particular focus on mathematical reasoning. He received his Ph.D. from New York University, where he was advised by Kyunghyun Cho. Outside of his research activities, he hosts the Thesis Review Podcast and enjoys running long distances.

Table of Contents

Program

Wednesday, December 7, 2022

09:00 - 10:30	*Opening Remarks and Keynote (Sean Welleck)*
10:30 - 11:00	*Coffee Break*
11:00 - 12:30	*Talk Session*
12:30 - 14:00	*Lunch Break*
14:00 - 15:30	*Poster Session*
15:30 - 16:00	*Coffee Break*
16:00 - 17:00	*Keynote (Timo Schick)*
17:00 - 18:30	*Talk Session*
20:00 - 21:00	*Virtual Keynote (Emily Dinan)*
21:00 - 22:30	*Virtual Poster Session*

Improving abstractive summarization with energy-based re-ranking

Diogo Pernes[ϡ,ɱ] **Afonso Mendes**[ϡ] **André F. T. Martins**[ψ,♀,♭]
[ϡ]Priberam [ɱ]Universidade do Porto
[ψ]Instituto de Telecomunicações [♀]LUMLIS (Lisbon ELLIS Unit), Instituto Superior Técnico [♭]Unbabel
Lisbon, Portugal
diogo.pernes@priberam.pt,
amm@priberam.pt, andre.t.martins@tecnico.ulisboa.pt.

Abstract

Current abstractive summarization systems present important weaknesses which prevent their deployment in real-world applications, such as the omission of relevant information and the generation of factual inconsistencies (also known as *hallucinations*). At the same time, automatic evaluation metrics such as CTC scores (Deng et al., 2021) have been recently proposed that exhibit a higher correlation with human judgments than traditional lexical-overlap metrics such as ROUGE. In this work, we intend to close the loop by leveraging the recent advances in summarization metrics to create *quality-aware* abstractive summarizers. Namely, we propose an energy-based model that learns to re-rank summaries according to one or a combination of these metrics. We experiment using several metrics to train our energy-based re-ranker and show that it consistently improves the scores achieved by the predicted summaries. Nonetheless, human evaluation results show that the re-ranking approach should be used with care for highly abstractive summaries, as the available metrics are not yet sufficiently reliable for this purpose.

1 Introduction

In recent years, abstractive methods have greatly benefited from the development and widespread availability of large-scale transformer-based language generative models (Vaswani et al., 2017; Lewis et al., 2020; Raffel et al., 2020; Zhang et al., 2020), which are capable of generating text with unprecedented fluency. Despite the recent progress, abstractive summarization systems still suffer from problems that hamper their deployment in real-world applications. Omitting the most relevant information from the source document is one of such problems. Additionally, factual inconsistencies (also known as *hallucinations*) were estimated to be present in around 30% of the summaries produced by abstractive systems on the CNN/DailyMail dataset (Kryscinski et al., 2019). This observation has motivated a considerable amount of research on strategies to mitigate the hallucination problem (Falke et al., 2019; Cao et al., 2020; Zhao et al., 2020; Zhu et al., 2021), but the improvements achieved so far are mild. This is partly due to the difficulty of evaluating the quality of summaries automatically, leading to the adoption of metrics that are often insufficient or even inappropriate. Despite its limitations, ROUGE (Lin, 2004) is still the de facto evaluation metric for summarization, mostly due to its simplicity and interpretability. However, not only does it correlate poorly with human-assessed summary quality (Kané et al., 2019), but it is also unreliable whenever the reference summary contains hallucinations, which unfortunately is not an uncommon issue in widely adopted summarization datasets (Kryscinski et al., 2019; Maynez et al., 2020). For these reasons, the development of more reliable evaluation metrics with a stronger correlation with human judgment is also an active area of research (Kryscinski et al., 2020; Scialom et al., 2021; Deng et al., 2021).

In this work, we propose a new approach to abstractive summarization via an energy-based model. In contrast to previous approaches, which use reinforcement learning to train models to maximize ROUGE or BERT scores (Paulus et al., 2018; Li et al., 2019), our EBM is trained to re-rank the candidate summaries the same way that the chosen metric would rank them – a much simpler problem which is computationally much more efficient. This way, we are distilling the metric, which presents as a by-product an additional advantage: a quality estimation system that can be used to assess the quality of the summaries on the fly without the need of reference summaries. It should be remarked that any reference-free metric, can be used at inference time for re-ranking candidates from any abstractive summarization system, hence improving the

Proceedings of the 2nd Workshop on Natural Language Generation, Evaluation, and Metrics (GEM), pages 1 - 17
December 7, 2022

quality of the generated summaries. Our re-ranking model can therefore leverage the advantages of recently proposed evaluation metrics over traditional ones, which are essentially two-fold: i) being able to better capture high-level semantic concepts, and ii) in addition to the target summary, these metrics take into account the information present on the source document, which is crucial to detect hallucinations. We demonstrate the effectiveness of our approach on standard benchmark datasets for abstractive summarization (CNN/DailyMail, Hermann et al. (2015), and XSum, Narayan et al. (2018)) and use a variety of summarization metrics as the target to train our model on, showing the versatility of the method. We also conduct a human evaluation experiment, in which we compare our re-ranking model trained to maximize recent transformer-based metrics that aim to measure factual consistency and relevance (CTC scores, Deng et al. (2021)). Our proposed model yields improvements over the usual beam search on a baseline model and demonstrates the ability to distill target metrics. However, the human evaluation results suggest that re-ranking according to these metrics, while competitive, may yield lower quality summaries than those obtained by state-of-the-art abstractive systems trained with augmented data and contrastive learning.

The remainder of the paper is organized as follows: in Section 2, we discuss the related work; in Section 3, we do a brief high-level description of neural abstractive summarization systems and how different candidate summaries can be generated from them; in Section 4, we describe our methodology in detail, as well as the summarization metrics that we shall use to train our re-ranking model; Section 5 presents the experimental results of our model and baselines, which include both automatic and human evaluation; in Section 6, we discuss the limitations of our approach and point some directions for future work, and we conclude this work with some final remarks in Section 7.

2 Related work

In the context of natural language generation, the idea of re-ranking candidates has been studied extensively for neural machine translation (Shen et al., 2004; Mizumoto and Matsumoto, 2016; Ng et al., 2019; Salazar et al., 2020; Fernandes et al., 2022), but only seldom explored for abstractive summarization. Among the former, the approach by Bhattacharyya et al. (2021) is the most similar to ours as they also resort to an energy-based model to re-rank the candidates. However, they do not apply their method to abstractive summarization and their training objective is different than the one we shall define for our model: at each training step, they sample a pair of candidates, and the model is trained so that the difference between the energies of the two candidates is at least as large as the difference of their BLEU scores (Papineni et al., 2002). Thus, their approach only exploits the information of two candidates at each training step. Recently, improved learning objectives such as contrastive losses have been proposed to enhance the quality of the predicted summaries, especially their factual consistency. Tang et al. (2022), Cao and Wang (2021), and Liu et al. (2021) used data augmentation to generate both factual consistent and inconsistent sentences and used these in a contrastive learning objective to regularize the transformer learned representations. In a different line of work, Cao et al. (2020) and Zhao et al. (2020) trained separate models on the task of correcting factual inconsistencies in the predicted summaries. Zhu et al. (2021) presented a model that learns to extract a knowledge graph from the source document and uses it to condition the decoding step. Goyal and Durrett (2021) trained a model to detect non-factual tokens and used it to identify and discard these tokens from the training data of the summarizer. Aralikatte et al. (2021) modified the output distribution of the model to put more focus on the vocabulary tokens that are similar to the attended input tokens. Despite being sensible ideas, these techniques mostly focus on redefining the training objective of the model and disregard the opportunity to improve the summary quality at inference time, either by redesigning the sampling algorithm or using re-ranking. In a somewhat similar direction to ours, a contemporary work (Liu et al., 2022) proposes using a ranking objective as an additional term on the usual negative log-likelihood loss. Similar to us, Liu and Liu (2021) and Ravaut et al. (2022) propose to use a trained re-ranker in as post-generation step. The former use a contrastive objective to learn a re-ranker that mimics ROUGE scores. The latter employs a mixture of experts to train a re-ranker on the combination of ROUGE, BERT and BART scores.

3 Abstractive summarization systems

A typical abstractive summarization model approximates the conditional distribution $p(y \mid x)$, of summaries y given source documents x, and works auto-regressively, exploiting the chain rule of probability:

$$p(y \mid x) = \prod_{i=1}^{l+1} p(y^{(i)} \mid x, y^{0:(i-1)}), \qquad (1)$$

where $y^{(0)}$ is a start-of-sequence token, the following $y^{(1)}, \dots, y^{(l)}$ are the tokens in the summary, from the beginning to the end, and $y^{(l+1)}$ is an end-of-sequence token. Typically, the parameters of this model are estimated under the maximum likelihood criterion, by minimizing the negative log-likelihood loss for a training dataset $\{(x_i, y_i)\}_{i=1}^{n}$ containing source documents x_i paired with the respective reference summaries y_i.

Usually, the decoding process aims at finding the most likely sequence y^* for the given x, i.e. $y^* \triangleq \arg\max_y p(y \mid x)$. Since searching for the most likely sequence is intractable due to combinatorial explosion, mode-search heuristics like greedy decoding and beam search are used in practice. Even if one could find the optimal sequence, it is not guaranteed that this would be the best summary for the given document. A primary reason for this is that the distribution learned by the model is only an approximation of the true conditional distribution, and preserves some background knowledge acquired during the unsupervised pre-training of the underlying language model. This is responsible for the presence of additional information in the summary that was not in the source document, which is the most frequent form of hallucination in summarization (Maynez et al., 2020). Another source of problems is the noise in the training datasets, which are often scrapped automatically from the web with little human supervision (Kryscinski et al., 2019).

In essence, finding the optimal training objective and decoding algorithm to obtain the best summary remains an open problem. We take a step in this direction by sampling a set of candidate summaries $\{\hat{y}_1, \hat{y}_2, \dots, \hat{y}_k\}$ and then using a re-ranking model to choose the best one. To ensure diverse candidates, we experiment with diverse beam search (Vijayakumar et al., 2016), a modification of traditional beam search including a term in the scoring function that penalizes for repetitions across different beams.

4 Energy-based re-ranking

4.1 Formulation

Formally, a summarization metric is a function $\phi : \mathcal{X} \times \mathcal{Y}^2 \mapsto \mathbb{R}$ that takes as input the source document $x \in \mathcal{X}$, the human-written reference summary $y \in \mathcal{Y}$, and the generated summary $\hat{y} \in \mathcal{Y}$, and outputs a scalar, usually in the unit interval, measuring the quality of the generated summary. Without loss of generality, throughout this work we assume that higher values of the metric indicate a better summary (as evaluated by the metric). Then, for a given summarization metric ϕ, our goal is to find a reference-free function $E : \mathcal{X} \times \mathcal{Y} \mapsto \mathbb{R}$ with parameters θ such that, for two candidate summaries $\hat{y}$ and $\hat{y}'$ for the same document x with reference summary y, $E(x, \hat{y}; \theta) < E(x, \hat{y}'; \theta)$ if and only if $\phi(x, y, \hat{y}) > \phi(x, y, \hat{y}')$. In the spirit of energy-based models (LeCun et al., 2006), E should assign *low energy* wherever $p(y \mid x)$ is high and *high energy* wherever $p(y \mid x)$ is low, but does not need to be normalized as a proper density. More precisely, E should satisfy $p(y \mid x) \propto \exp(-E(x, y; \theta))$. Under this perspective, at training time, ϕ works as a proxy for the true conditional distribution, which is unknown. At inference time, sampling summaries directly from the distribution defined by the energy-based model is a non-trivial task since this model is not defined auto-regressively (Eikema et al., 2021), unlike standard encoder-decoder models for summarization. Hence, we use its scores to re-rank candidate summaries previously obtained from a baseline summarization model.

4.2 Training and inference

We assume to have access to a training data set $\mathcal{D} = \{(x_i, y_i, \hat{\mathbf{y}}_i)\}_{i=1}^{n}$, where x_i and y_i are respectively the i-th source document and the corresponding reference summary and $\hat{\mathbf{y}}_i = \{\hat{y}_{i,1}, \hat{y}_{i,2}, \dots, \hat{y}_{i,k}\}$ is a set of (up to) k candidate summaries sampled from a baseline summarization model, such as BART (Lewis et al., 2020) or PEGASUS (Zhang et al., 2020). Several techniques have been proposed for training energy-based models that avoid the explicit computation of the partition function $Z(x; \theta) \triangleq \int_{\mathcal{Y}} \exp(-E(x, y; \theta))\, \mathrm{d}y$ and its gradient, which are usually intractable (Song and Kingma, 2021). Here, given this data and the metric ϕ, we adopt the ListMLE ranking loss (Xia et al., 2008) as the training objective. Specifically, the model is trained to minimize:

$$\mathcal{L}_{\phi}(\theta) \triangleq -\mathbb{E}_{(x,y,\hat{\mathbf{y}})\sim\mathcal{D}} \log \prod_{i=1}^{k} \frac{\exp(-E(x,\hat{y}_i;\theta)/\tau)}{\sum_{j=i}^{k} \exp(-E(x,\hat{y}_j;\theta)/\tau)}, \tag{2}$$

where $\tau > 0$ is a temperature hyperparameter and the candidates $\hat{y}_1, \hat{y}_2, \ldots, \hat{y}_k$ are sorted such that if $i < j$ then $\phi(x, y, \hat{y}_i) \geq \phi(x, y, \hat{y}_j)$.

To gain some intuition about this loss function, let us define: i) r_i as the random variable corresponding to the i-th ranked summary in a list of k candidates $\hat{y}_1, \hat{y}_2, \ldots, \hat{y}_k$ and ii) the probability that r_1 takes the value $\hat{y}_1$ as:

$$P(\mathrm{r}_1 = \hat{y}_1 \mid x) \triangleq \frac{\exp(-E(x,\hat{y}_1)/\tau)}{\sum_{j=1}^{k} \exp(-E(x,\hat{y}_j)/\tau)}, \tag{3}$$

where we have omitted the parameters θ for brevity. Assuming that the first $i-1$ candidates are ranked correctly, the probability that the i-th candidate is also ranked correctly is the probability that it is ranked first in the list $\hat{y}_i, \hat{y}_{i+1}, \ldots, \hat{y}_k$, thus:

$$\begin{aligned} P(\mathrm{r}_i = \hat{y}_i \mid x, &\mathrm{r}_{1:(i-1)} = \hat{y}_{1:(i-1)}) = \\ &= \frac{\exp(-E(x,\hat{y}_i)/\tau)}{\sum_{j=i}^{k} \exp(-E(x,\hat{y}_j)/\tau)}. \end{aligned} \tag{4}$$

It then follows from the chain rule that the probability that all the k candidates are ranked correctly is:

$$\begin{aligned} &P(\mathrm{r}_{1:k} = \hat{y}_{1:k} \mid x) = \\ &= \prod_{i=1}^{k} P(\mathrm{r}_i = \hat{y}_i \mid x, \mathrm{r}_{1:(i-1)} = \hat{y}_{1:(i-1)}) \\ &= \prod_{i=1}^{k} \frac{\exp(-E(x,\hat{y}_i)/\tau)}{\sum_{j=i}^{k} \exp(-E(x,\hat{y}_j)/\tau)}. \end{aligned} \tag{5}$$

Hence, $P(\mathrm{r}_{1:k} \mid x)$ is a distribution over all the possible permutations of the k candidates and the minimization of the loss $\mathcal{L}_{\phi}$ maximizes the likelihood of the correct permutation, i.e. of the permutation induced by ranking the candidates $\hat{y}_1, \ldots, \hat{y}_k$ according to the metric $\phi(x, y, \cdot)$. At inference time, given an unsorted list $\hat{\mathbf{y}}$ of k candidate summaries for the document x, we choose the candidate $\hat{y}^*$ that is the most likely to be the top-ranked:

$$\hat{y}^* \triangleq \arg\max_{\hat{y}\in\hat{\mathbf{y}}} P(\mathrm{r}_1 = \hat{y} \mid x) = \arg\min_{\hat{y}\in\hat{\mathbf{y}}} E(x, \hat{y}). \tag{6}$$

Thus, our energy based-model aims at ranking a set of candidates the same way that the metric ϕ would rank them, but it does this without having access to the reference summary y. Therefore, this is a way to distill the information contained in the metric into a single and reference-free model that can rank summary hypotheses on the fly.

4.3 Adopted metrics

So far, the definition of summarization metric we have provided was generic, so now we focus on describing the particular metrics we have used to train our model. Summarization metrics can be divided into two groups: *reference-dependent* and *reference-free*, depending on whether ϕ actually needs the reference summary or not. In the latter case, $\phi(x, y, \hat{y}) \equiv \varphi(x, \hat{y})\ \forall y$, for some function φ. Thus, reference-dependent metrics are mostly used to evaluate and compare summarization systems, whereas reference-free metrics can also be used to assess summary quality on the fly. Therefore, training our energy-based model using reference-dependent metrics provides an indirect way to use these metrics for the latter purpose as well.

Automatically assessing the quality of a summary is a non-trivial task since it depends on high-level concepts, such as factual consistency, relevance, coherence, and fluency (Lloret et al., 2018). These are loosely captured by classical metrics (Kané et al., 2019; Kryscinski et al., 2019) such as ROUGE, which essentially measure the n-gram overlap between $\hat{y}$ and y. However, in recent years, the availability of powerful language representation models like BERT (Devlin et al., 2019) permitted and motivated the development of several transformer-based automatic metrics.

There are a few metrics based on question generation (QG) and question answering (QA) models (Wang et al., 2020; Durmus et al., 2020). Among these, QuestEval (Scialom et al., 2021) exhibits the strongest correlation with human judgment. This metric uses a QG model to generate questions from both the source document x and the candidate summary $\hat{y}$ and a QA model to get the answers from both, which are then compared to produce a score in the unit interval. In addition to the QA and QG models, QuestEval uses an additional model to determine the importance weight of each question generated from x. Although being reference-free, this metric is computationally expensive, so it is important to investigate whether our model can produce a similar ranking more efficiently.

Following a different paradigm, Deng et al.

(2021) proposed a set of metrics for natural language generation tasks, named CTC scores, which are based on the notion of *information alignment*. They define the alignment of a document a to a document b, denoted $\text{align}(a \to b)$, as a vector with the same length as a where the i-th position is a scalar in $[0, 1]$ representing the confidence that the information in the i-th token of a is grounded in b. For summarization tasks, two alignment-based metrics are proposed, one for factual consistency and the other for relevance, both achieving state-of-the-art results in correlation with human judgment. A generated summary $\hat{y}$ is consistent with its source document x if all the information in $\hat{y}$ is supported by x, hence the consistency score is:

$$\text{CTC}_{\text{consistency}}(x, \hat{y}) \triangleq \text{mean}(\text{align}(\hat{y} \to x)). \tag{7}$$

For relevance, the authors argue that, besides being consistent, $\hat{y}$ should contain as much information as possible from the reference summary y, so they define the relevance score as:

$$\text{CTC}_{\text{relevance}}(x, y, \hat{y}) \triangleq$$
$$\triangleq \text{mean}(\text{align}(\hat{y} \to x)) \times \text{mean}(\text{align}(y \to \hat{y})). \tag{8}$$

Clearly, both metrics produce a score in the unit interval, being consistency reference-free and relevance reference-dependent.

5 Experiments

5.1 Datasets

We evaluate our model and the baselines in two benchmark datasets for abstractive summarization: CNN/DailyMail (Hermann et al., 2015) and XSum (Narayan et al., 2018), both containing news articles paired with their respective reference summaries. In XSum, each summary consists of a single sentence, while in CNN/DailyMail it can consist of three sentences or more. XSum is also known to be more abstractive and to have more hallucinations than CNN/DailyMail (Narayan et al., 2018; Maynez et al., 2020).

5.2 Baselines

A BART model (Lewis et al., 2020) trained on the usual maximum likelihood objective is our baseline. Summaries are sampled from this model using the usual beam search. In addition, we also compare our model with the following state-of-the-art methods: BRIO, by Liu et al. (2022), which employs a ranking loss as an additional term on the training of the abstractive system; CLIFF, by Cao and Wang (2021), which uses data augmentation techniques and contrastive learning to enhance the factual consistency of the summaries; DAE, proposed by Goyal and Durrett (2021), which detects and discards non-factual tokens from the training data; FASum, by Zhu et al. (2021), which incorporates knowledge graphs also to enhance factual consistency; SummaReranker, by Ravaut et al. (2022), which employs a mixture of experts to train a re-ranker on the combination of various metrics. In Appendix B, we also experiment training the re-ranking model with the max-margin objective proposed by Bhattacharyya et al. (2021) for machine translation and we present the results obtained by using a perfect re-ranker for $\text{CTC}_{\text{consistency}}$ and QuestEval, which is feasible since these metrics are reference-free.

5.3 Implementation details

Our energy-based re-ranking model (EBR-ListMLE) consists of a BERT that receives as input a pair $(x, \hat{y})$, of source document x and candidate summary $\hat{y}$, and outputs the corresponding energy score $E(x, \hat{y})$. Candidates are sampled using diverse beam search (Vijayakumar et al., 2016) on a BART encoder-decoder fine-tuned on the respective summarization dataset. Further implementations details are provided in Appendix A. For reproducibility purposes, our code and trained models are also publicly available[1]. Regarding the baselines, we use the official source code and model checkpoints for CLIFF and DAE. The latter is only evaluated on the XSum dataset since there is no checkpoint available for CNN/DailyMail. For the same reason, BRIO is only evaluated on CNN/DailyMail. For FASum, we use the released predicted summaries directly since this is the only resource available.

5.4 Metrics

We train our model using the metrics discussed in section 4.3 as the target metric ϕ. Specifically, we experiment with ROUGE-L, QuestEval, $\text{CTC}_{\text{relevance}}$, and $\text{CTC}_{\text{relevance}} + \text{CTC}_{\text{consistency}}$. ROUGE scores, QuestEval and CTC scores each belong to a different evaluation paradigm and so it is interesting to investigate their effect on our re-ranking approach. It is important to point out

[1] https://github.com/Priberam/SummEBR

that $\text{CTC}_{\text{consistency}}$ is a reference-free metric whose computational complexity is similar to that of our re-ranker, so it is pointless to train our model based on that metric alone. Instead, we report the results using this metric directly for re-ranking in Appendix B. However, combining (i.e. summing) it with $\text{CTC}_{\text{relevance}}$ yields an interesting metric as it takes into account two fundamental attributes of a summary: factual consistency and relevance. QuestEval is also reference-free but it is much more computationally intensive as it requires a question generation and a question answering step. Thus, we train our model with this metric and report the computational times for comparison. For evaluation, in addition to the aforementioned metrics, we also report results for ROUGE-1, ROUGE-2, and FactCC (Kryscinski et al., 2020), which is a metric based on NLI scores.

5.5 Automatic evaluation

5.5.1 Comparison with the baselines

The results obtained by our model and baselines are presented in Table 1. We used 8 candidates for the re-ranking models and beam search with 8 beams for the baselines. The effect of using different number of candidates for re-ranking is studied in Appendix C. It is noticeable that the best results for all the metrics are obtained by the EBR models, except for the ROUGE scores, where BRIO, CLIFF, and SummaReranker often outperform our models. SummaReranker is likely the strongest competitor with our models, achieving close-to-best ROUGE scores in both datasets and outperforming the BART baseline in most of the remaining metrics. Surprisingly, DAE and FASum score below BART in the vast majority of the automatic metrics. Unfortunately, the authors of DAE do not provide results for any of these metrics. Regarding FASum, the authors do provide the ROUGE scores for their model but they evaluate factual consistency using a custom metric, for which they did not release the implementation.

Among the re-ranking models, the best result for a given metric is obtained when the model is trained to re-rank according to that metric, as expected. It is also interesting to observe that training for a given metric generally yields improvements in the remaining metrics as well. This might be an indication that the ranking model learns a useful measure of summary quality, rather than exploiting possible loopholes of the metrics. The best model overall is arguably EBR-ListMLE trained for $\text{CTC}_{\text{consistency}} + \text{CTC}_{\text{relevance}}$, achieving close to best results in all the metrics except ROUGE scores, which are known to correlate less strongly with human judgment.

We also compared the inference time of our model with the computation time of the two reference-free metrics, $\text{CTC}_{\text{consistency}}$ and QuestEval[2]. We performed this experiment by sampling 1000 (document, summary) pairs from the test set of the CNN/DailyMail dataset and computing the scores one by one (i.e. without mini-batching) using our model and each of the metrics. The results are in Table 2. The computation time of $\text{CTC}_{\text{consistency}}$ is comparable to, but larger than, that of our EBR, with the difference explained by the fact that the former is based on a RoBERTa-large model (Zhuang et al., 2021) and the latter uses BERT-base. As argued before and confirmed by these results, the computation of QuestEval takes two orders of magnitude longer, which motivates distilling this metric into an EBR.

5.5.2 Cross-model experiments

An interesting question to investigate is whether our model is learning a general approximation of the target metric ϕ, rather than just learning to recognize features that correlate with ϕ but are specific to the summarization system that generated the candidates. For this purpose, we experiment using a different abstractive summarizer to generate the test candidates than the one that was used to generate the training candidates. Specifically, we apply the same EBR models as in Section 5.5.1, which were trained using summaries sampled from BART, to re-rank summaries obtained from PEGASUS (Zhang et al., 2020). Like before, we obtain 8 candidate summaries for each source document using beam search. In this experiment, our baseline is PEGASUS with no re-ranking. The results are in Table 3 and confirm that our EBR models have learned to mimic the respective metrics faithfully. The best score for each of the metrics is achieved by the EBR model that was trained for that metric. Moreover, when evaluated with different metrics, these models tend to surpass the PEGASUS baseline in the vast majority of the cases.

	CNN/DailyMail							XSum						
	R1	R2	RL	QE	Cons	Rel	FCC	R1	R2	RL	QE	Cons	Rel	FCC
BART	43.64	20.75	40.52	43.28	95.01	61.75	55.68	42.67	19.42	34.48	28.27	83.18	52.23	26.28
BRIO	**47.97***	**24.06***	**44.86***	43.49	89.61	60.75	33.05	–	–	–	–	–	–	–
CLIFF	43.86	20.88	40.63	43.28	94.68	60.38	55.85	44.50	**21.41**	36.41	29.34	82.57	51.92	24.86
DAE	–	–	–	–	–	–	–	37.61	14.19	28.84	29.20	79.45	51.05	19.46
FASum	40.40	17.68	37.26	42.87	94.30	57.91	51.20	30.22	9.97	23.69	24.35	75.45	39.42	26.96
SummaReranker	45.07	21.73	41.87	43.61	95.07	62.49	54.50	**44.93**	21.40	**36.76**	28.76	83.00	52.75	26.27
EBR [RL]	44.90	21.58	41.75	43.60	95.01	62.16	54.95	43.63	20.28	35.78	28.55	84.47	52.92	**27.21**
EBR [QE]	44.07	21.13	40.94	**44.27***	95.71	62.48	59.23	42.94	19.42	34.62	**29.89**	83.34	52.50	26.34
EBR [Rel]	44.04	20.98	40.85	43.78	95.93	**63.40**	60.28	43.39	19.75	35.03	28.60	85.49	**54.80**	26.28
EBR [Cons+Rel]	43.88	20.87	40.69	43.79	**96.15**	63.32	**61.67***	43.28	19.72	34.92	28.66	**86.03***	54.74	27.12

Table 1: Results of our models and baselines on each of the automatic evaluation metrics. Bold font indicates best result, and the second best results are underlined. A * mark indicates that the difference to the second best result is statistically significant (approximate permutation test at 95%). In the re-ranking models, the metric in brackets indicates the target metric ϕ used to train the re-ranker. (R1: ROUGE-1, R2: ROUGE-2, RL: ROUGE-L, QE: QuestEval, Cons: $\text{CTC}_{\text{consistency}}$, Rel: $\text{CTC}_{\text{relevance}}$, FCC: FactCC)

	EBR	$\text{CTC}_{\text{consistency}}$	QuestEval
Time	1	1.83	114.98

Table 2: Relative computation times of the reference-free scorers when scoring 1000 (document, summary) pairs from CNN/DailyMail. The absolute computation time for EBR was 23s.

5.6 Human evaluation

Even though the results on automatic evaluation are promising, directly optimizing a metric is risky as none of these metrics correlate perfectly with human judgment. For this reason, it is crucial to conduct human evaluation. Specifically, we asked the judges to do pairwise comparisons between the summaries generated by three models: BART, CLIFF, which was the strongest published baseline at the time we conducted this study, and our EBR trained for $\text{CTC}_{\text{consistency}} + \text{CTC}_{\text{relevance}}$ and re-ranking candidates from BART. We chose these metrics for the EBR since they exhibit stronger correlation with human judgment than the remaining (Deng et al., 2021) and explicitly account for two key attributes of a summary: factual consistency and relevance. For each source document, we presented three pairs of summaries consecutively, which correspond to all the pairwise combinations of the summaries generated by the three systems. Then, we asked the judges to rank the summaries in each pair according to three criteria: factual consistency, relevance, and fluency. For each criterion, the judges had to evaluate whether the first summary was better than, tied with, or worse than the second summary. The names of the systems that generated each summary were not shown to the judges and the order at which summaries were presented was randomized. We randomly sampled 30 source documents from the test set of CNN/DailyMail and another 30 from the test set of XSum, so each judge was asked to compare 180 pairs of summaries. A screenshot and description of the user interface of the evaluation form is provided in Appendix D.1. We recruited two judges for this task, who are specialists in linguistics. The results are presented in Table 4. The first observation is that our EBR model succeeds at improving the quality of the candidates sampled from BART on the CNN/DailyMail dataset in all the three criteria. On XSum, the improvements are marginal or even absent, except on the fluency dimension. The EBR model itself has lower confidence on the predictions made on the XSum dataset: as shown in Figure 1, the EBR model generally assigns higher energy to the XSum summaries than to the CNN/DailyMail summaries. The fact that our model improves fluency, which it was not trained for, may indicate that there is an implicit bias in our model and/or in the the target metrics ($\text{CTC}_{\text{consistency}}$ and $\text{CTC}_{\text{relevance}}$) towards more fluent summaries. Surprisingly, the comparison of our model with CLIFF contradicts the results of the automatic evaluation (Table 1), especially on the XSum dataset. Three reasons could explain this phenomenon: i) the small number of documents used for human evaluation when compared to the size of the whole test set, ii) the EBR failing to re-rank the candidates according to the target metrics on these documents, and iii) limitations of the metrics themselves. In order to investigate which is true, we computed the actual values of $\text{CTC}_{\text{consistency}}$ and $\text{CTC}_{\text{relevance}}$ on the examples from XSum used for human evaluation. Regarding $\text{CTC}_{\text{consistency}}$, the summaries of EBR

[2]We used an 80-core CPU Intel Xeon Gold 5218R @ 2.10GHz with 800GB of RAM and a GPU NVIDIA A100 with 80GB of memory.

	CNN/DailyMail							XSum						
	R1	R2	RL	QE	Cons	Rel	FCC	R1	R2	RL	QE	Cons	Rel	FCC
PEGASUS	43.19	20.64	36.74	41.22	92.27	59.09	41.13	46.64	23.79	38.53	28.55	82.02	53.32	24.10
EBR [RL]	**44.35***	**21.37***	**37.66***	41.60	92.54	59.50	42.45	46.74	**24.28***	**39.16***	28.52	82.01	51.87	**26.04***
EBR [QE]	43.70	21.04	37.17	**42.28***	93.30	60.04	45.31	46.43	23.58	38.40	**29.82***	82.72	53.38	22.94
EBR [Rel]	43.51	20.80	36.80	41.62	93.38	**61.05***	44.19	**46.92**	23.70	38.50	28.78	83.18	**55.33***	22.57
EBR [Cons+Rel]	43.36	20.76	36.75	41.74	**93.82***	60.98	**46.10***	**46.92**	23.79	38.61	28.82	**83.82***	55.26	23.60

Table 3: Results of the cross-model experiment in which EBRs trained with summaries from BART are tested on re-ranking summaries from PEGASUS. Bold font indicates best result. A * mark indicates that the difference to the result of PEGASUS is statistically significant (approximate permutation test at 95%). In the re-ranking models, the metric in brackets indicates the target metric ϕ used to train the re-ranker. (R1: ROUGE-1, R2: ROUGE-2, RL: ROUGE-L, QE: QuestEval, Cons: $\text{CTC}_{\text{consistency}}$, Rel: $\text{CTC}_{\text{relevance}}$, FCC: FactCC)

	CNN/DailyMail			XSum		
	FC	R	F	FC	R	F
CLIFF is better	.17	.33	**.33**	**.25**	**.32**	**.27**
Tie	.65	.24	.40	.63	.63	.68
BART is better	**.18**	**.43**	.27	.12	.05	.05
EBR is better	**.13**	**.30**	**.24**	**.15**	.12	**.30**
Tie	.80	.52	.58	.72	.77	.63
BART is better	.07	.18	.18	.13	.12	.07
EBR is better	.12	**.45**	**.32**	.10	.08	.07
Tie	.68	.20	.42	.63	.63	.88
CLIFF is better	**.20**	.35	.27	**.27**	**.28**	**.08**
Agreement	.50	.63	.54	.56	.58	.87
Strong disag.	.01	.11	.08	.01	.00	.00

Table 4: Proportion of times that each model was considered the best for the human judges in each pairwise comparison according to each criteria (FC: factual consistency, R: relevance, F: fluency). Rows "Agreement" and "Strong disag." show, respectively, the proportion of times that the two judges agreed and chose opposite options on the pairwise comparisons.

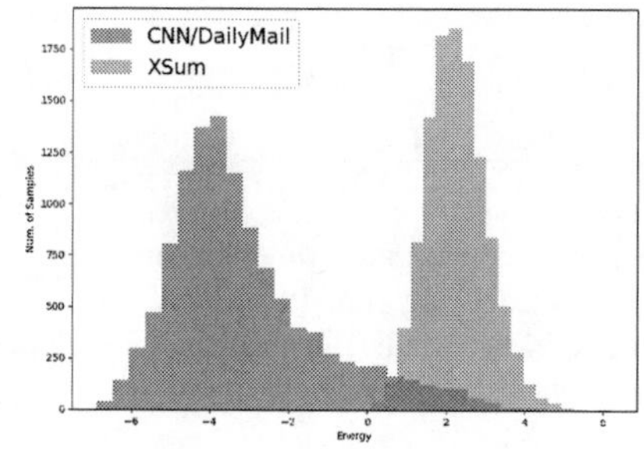

Figure 1: Energy histogram of the candidate summaries chosen by the EBR model on CNN/DailyMail and XSum.

achieve a better score than those of CLIFF in 22 cases (out of 30), with an average score of 83.9% vs. 80.2% for CLIFF. For $\text{CTC}_{\text{relevance}}$, EBR wins against CLIFF in 20 cases, with average scores of 54.3% and 49.9%, respectively. We have also inspected the particular examples (shown in Appendix D.2) where the judges agreed that CLIFF summary was better than the EBR summary on the factual consistency dimension. This happened only in three cases, but in all of them the EBR summary has obvious hallucinations and the CLIFF summary does not. Nonetheless, in two of them, the $\text{CTC}_{\text{consistency}}$ scores of the EBR summaries are larger than those of the CLIFF summaries, which confirms the flaws of the metric.

6 Limitations and future work

Despite the improvements attained by our EBR model, its applicability is fundamentally dependent on the availability of reliable automatic evaluation metrics. Unfortunately, the correlation of these metrics with human judgment is still imperfect, especially for highly abstractive summaries. In addition, transformer-based metrics are currently only available for English. Finally, their backbone models are trained on news data, which hampers the reliability of these metrics in other domains. It is, therefore, crucial to continue the pursuit for more reliable metrics and to extend them to more languages and domains.

7 Conclusion

We proposed an energy-based re-ranking model that can be trained to rank candidate summaries according to a pre-specified metric, leveraging the recent advancements in automatic summarization metrics to enhance the quality of the generated summaries. The experiments show that the proposed re-ranking model succeeds at distilling the target metrics, consistently improving the scores of the generated summaries. However, these improvements not always agree with the human evaluation, especially in the more abstractive setting (XSum), due to flaws of the adopted target metrics (CTC scores). Nonetheless, the proposed approach is flexible in the sense that we can train it with any target metric and apply it in conjunction with virtually any abstractive summarization system.

Acknowledgments

This work is supported by the EU H2020 SELMA project (grant agreement No. 957017).

References

Rahul Aralikatte, Shashi Narayan, Joshua Maynez, Sascha Rothe, and Ryan McDonald. 2021. Focus attention: Promoting faithfulness and diversity in summarization. In *Proceedings of the 59th Annual Meeting of the Association for Computational Linguistics and the 11th International Joint Conference on Natural Language Processing (Volume 1: Long Papers)*, pages 6078–6095, Online. Association for Computational Linguistics.

Sumanta Bhattacharyya, Amirmohammad Rooshenas, Subhajit Naskar, Simeng Sun, Mohit Iyyer, and Andrew McCallum. 2021. Energy-based reranking: Improving neural machine translation using energy-based models. In *Proceedings of the 59th Annual Meeting of the Association for Computational Linguistics and the 11th International Joint Conference on Natural Language Processing (Volume 1: Long Papers)*, pages 4528–4537, Online. Association for Computational Linguistics.

Meng Cao, Yue Dong, Jiapeng Wu, and Jackie Chi Kit Cheung. 2020. Factual error correction for abstractive summarization models. In *Proceedings of the 2020 Conference on Empirical Methods in Natural Language Processing (EMNLP)*, pages 6251–6258, Online. Association for Computational Linguistics.

Shuyang Cao and Lu Wang. 2021. CLIFF: Contrastive learning for improving faithfulness and factuality in abstractive summarization. In *Proceedings of the 2021 Conference on Empirical Methods in Natural Language Processing*, pages 6633–6649, Online and Punta Cana, Dominican Republic. Association for Computational Linguistics.

Mingkai Deng, Bowen Tan, Zhengzhong Liu, Eric Xing, and Zhiting Hu. 2021. Compression, transduction, and creation: A unified framework for evaluating natural language generation. In *Proceedings of the 2021 Conference on Empirical Methods in Natural Language Processing*, pages 7580–7605, Online and Punta Cana, Dominican Republic. Association for Computational Linguistics.

Jacob Devlin, Ming-Wei Chang, Kenton Lee, and Kristina Toutanova. 2019. BERT: Pre-training of deep bidirectional transformers for language understanding. In *Proceedings of the 2019 Conference of the North American Chapter of the Association for Computational Linguistics: Human Language Technologies, Volume 1 (Long and Short Papers)*, pages 4171–4186, Minneapolis, Minnesota. Association for Computational Linguistics.

Esin Durmus, He He, and Mona Diab. 2020. FEQA: A question answering evaluation framework for faithfulness assessment in abstractive summarization. In *Proceedings of the 58th Annual Meeting of the Association for Computational Linguistics*, pages 5055–5070, Online. Association for Computational Linguistics.

Bryan Eikema, Germán Kruszewski, Hady Elsahar, and Marc Dymetman. 2021. Sampling from discrete energy-based models with quality/efficiency trade-offs. *arXiv preprint arXiv:2112.05702*.

Tobias Falke, Leonardo F. R. Ribeiro, Prasetya Ajie Utama, Ido Dagan, and Iryna Gurevych. 2019. Ranking generated summaries by correctness: An interesting but challenging application for natural language inference. In *Proceedings of the 57th Annual Meeting of the Association for Computational Linguistics*, pages 2214–2220, Florence, Italy. Association for Computational Linguistics.

Patrick Fernandes, António Farinhas, Ricardo Rei, Perez Ogayo José G. C. de Souza, Graham Neubig, and André F. T. Martins. 2022. Quality-aware decoding for neural machine translation. In *Proceedings of the meeting of North-American Association for Computational Linguistics*.

Tanya Goyal and Greg Durrett. 2021. Annotating and modeling fine-grained factuality in summarization. In *Proceedings of the 2021 Conference of the North American Chapter of the Association for Computational Linguistics: Human Language Technologies*, pages 1449–1462, Online. Association for Computational Linguistics.

Karl Moritz Hermann, Tomas Kocisky, Edward Grefenstette, Lasse Espeholt, Will Kay, Mustafa Suleyman, and Phil Blunsom. 2015. Teaching machines to read and comprehend. *Advances in neural information processing systems*, 28.

Hassan Kané, Yusuf Kocyigit, Pelkins Ajanoh, Ali Abdalla, and Mohamed Coulibali. 2019. Towards neural similarity evaluator. In *Workshop on Document Intelligence at NeurIPS 2019*.

Diederik P Kingma and Jimmy Ba. 2014. Adam: A method for stochastic optimization. *arXiv preprint arXiv:1412.6980*.

Wojciech Kryscinski, Nitish Shirish Keskar, Bryan McCann, Caiming Xiong, and Richard Socher. 2019. Neural text summarization: A critical evaluation. In *Proceedings of the 2019 Conference on Empirical Methods in Natural Language Processing and the 9th International Joint Conference on Natural Language Processing (EMNLP-IJCNLP)*, pages 540–551, Hong Kong, China. Association for Computational Linguistics.

Wojciech Kryscinski, Bryan McCann, Caiming Xiong, and Richard Socher. 2020. Evaluating the factual consistency of abstractive text summarization. In *Proceedings of the 2020 Conference on Empirical Methods in Natural Language Processing (EMNLP)*, pages 9332–9346, Online. Association for Computational Linguistics.

Yann LeCun, Sumit Chopra, Raia Hadsell, M Ranzato, and F Huang. 2006. A tutorial on energy-based learning. *Predicting structured data*, 1(0).

Mike Lewis, Yinhan Liu, Naman Goyal, Marjan Ghazvininejad, Abdelrahman Mohamed, Omer Levy, Veselin Stoyanov, and Luke Zettlemoyer. 2020. BART: Denoising sequence-to-sequence pre-training for natural language generation, translation, and comprehension. In *Proceedings of the 58th Annual Meeting of the Association for Computational Linguistics*, pages 7871–7880, Online. Association for Computational Linguistics.

Siyao Li, Deren Lei, Pengda Qin, and William Yang Wang. 2019. Deep reinforcement learning with distributional semantic rewards for abstractive summarization. In *Proceedings of the 2019 Conference on Empirical Methods in Natural Language Processing and the 9th International Joint Conference on Natural Language Processing (EMNLP-IJCNLP)*, pages 6038–6044, Hong Kong, China. Association for Computational Linguistics.

Chin-Yew Lin. 2004. ROUGE: A package for automatic evaluation of summaries. In *Text Summarization Branches Out*, pages 74–81, Barcelona, Spain. Association for Computational Linguistics.

Wei Liu, Huanqin Wu, Wenjing Mu, Zhen Li, Tao Chen, and Dan Nie. 2021. Co2sum: Contrastive learning for factual-consistent abstractive summarization. *arXiv preprint arXiv:2112.01147*.

Yixin Liu and Pengfei Liu. 2021. SimCLS: A simple framework for contrastive learning of abstractive summarization. In *Proceedings of the 59th Annual Meeting of the Association for Computational Linguistics and the 11th International Joint Conference on Natural Language Processing (Volume 2: Short Papers)*, pages 1065–1072, Online. Association for Computational Linguistics.

Yixin Liu, Pengfei Liu, Dragomir Radev, and Graham Neubig. 2022. BRIO: Bringing order to abstractive summarization. In *Proceedings of the 60th Annual Meeting of the Association for Computational Linguistics (Volume 1: Long Papers)*, pages 2890–2903, Dublin, Ireland. Association for Computational Linguistics.

Elena Lloret, Laura Plaza, and Ahmet Aker. 2018. The challenging task of summary evaluation: an overview. *Language Resources and Evaluation*, 52(1):101–148.

Joshua Maynez, Shashi Narayan, Bernd Bohnet, and Ryan McDonald. 2020. On faithfulness and factuality in abstractive summarization. In *Proceedings of the 58th Annual Meeting of the Association for Computational Linguistics*, pages 1906–1919, Online. Association for Computational Linguistics.

Tomoya Mizumoto and Yuji Matsumoto. 2016. Discriminative reranking for grammatical error correction with statistical machine translation. In *Proceedings of the 2016 Conference of the North American Chapter of the Association for Computational Linguistics: Human Language Technologies*, pages 1133–1138, San Diego, California. Association for Computational Linguistics.

Shashi Narayan, Shay B. Cohen, and Mirella Lapata. 2018. Don't give me the details, just the summary! topic-aware convolutional neural networks for extreme summarization. In *Proceedings of the 2018 Conference on Empirical Methods in Natural Language Processing*, pages 1797–1807, Brussels, Belgium. Association for Computational Linguistics.

Nathan Ng, Kyra Yee, Alexei Baevski, Myle Ott, Michael Auli, and Sergey Edunov. 2019. Facebook FAIR's WMT19 news translation task submission. In *Proceedings of the Fourth Conference on Machine Translation (Volume 2: Shared Task Papers, Day 1)*, pages 314–319, Florence, Italy. Association for Computational Linguistics.

Kishore Papineni, Salim Roukos, Todd Ward, and Wei-Jing Zhu. 2002. Bleu: a method for automatic evaluation of machine translation. In *Proceedings of the 40th Annual Meeting of the Association for Computational Linguistics*, pages 311–318, Philadelphia, Pennsylvania, USA. Association for Computational Linguistics.

Romain Paulus, Caiming Xiong, and Richard Socher. 2018. A deep reinforced model for abstractive summarization. In *International Conference on Learning Representations*.

Colin Raffel, Noam Shazeer, Adam Roberts, Katherine Lee, Sharan Narang, Michael Matena, Yanqi Zhou, Wei Li, and Peter J Liu. 2020. Exploring the limits of transfer learning with a unified text-to-text transformer. *Journal of Machine Learning Research*, 21:1–67.

Mathieu Ravaut, Shafiq Joty, and Nancy Chen. 2022. SummaReranker: A multi-task mixture-of-experts re-ranking framework for abstractive summarization. In *Proceedings of the 60th Annual Meeting of the Association for Computational Linguistics (Volume 1: Long Papers)*, pages 4504–4524, Dublin, Ireland. Association for Computational Linguistics.

Julian Salazar, Davis Liang, Toan Q. Nguyen, and Katrin Kirchhoff. 2020. Masked language model scoring. In *Proceedings of the 58th Annual Meeting of the Association for Computational Linguistics*, pages 2699–2712, Online. Association for Computational Linguistics.

Thomas Scialom, Paul-Alexis Dray, Sylvain Lamprier, Benjamin Piwowarski, Jacopo Staiano, Alex Wang, and Patrick Gallinari. 2021. QuestEval: Summarization asks for fact-based evaluation. In *Proceedings of the 2021 Conference on Empirical Methods in Natural Language Processing*, pages 6594–6604, Online and Punta Cana, Dominican Republic. Association for Computational Linguistics.

Libin Shen, Anoop Sarkar, and Franz Josef Och. 2004. Discriminative reranking for machine translation. In *Proceedings of the Human Language Technology Conference of the North American Chapter of the Association for Computational Linguistics: HLT-NAACL 2004*, pages 177–184, Boston, Massachusetts, USA. Association for Computational Linguistics.

Yang Song and Diederik P Kingma. 2021. How to train your energy-based models. *arXiv preprint arXiv:2101.03288*.

Xiangru Tang, Arjun Nair, Borui Wang, Bingyao Wang, Jai Desai, Aaron Wade, Haoran Li, Asli Celikyilmaz, Yashar Mehdad, and Dragomir Radev. 2022. CONFIT: Toward faithful dialogue summarization with linguistically-informed contrastive fine-tuning. In *Proceedings of the 2022 Conference of the North American Chapter of the Association for Computational Linguistics: Human Language Technologies*, pages 5657–5668, Seattle, United States. Association for Computational Linguistics.

Ashish Vaswani, Noam Shazeer, Niki Parmar, Jakob Uszkoreit, Llion Jones, Aidan N Gomez, Łukasz Kaiser, and Illia Polosukhin. 2017. Attention is all you need. *Advances in neural information processing systems*, 30.

Ashwin K Vijayakumar, Michael Cogswell, Ramprasath R Selvaraju, Qing Sun, Stefan Lee, David Crandall, and Dhruv Batra. 2016. Diverse beam search: Decoding diverse solutions from neural sequence models. *arXiv preprint arXiv:1610.02424*.

Alex Wang, Kyunghyun Cho, and Mike Lewis. 2020. Asking and answering questions to evaluate the factual consistency of summaries. In *Proceedings of the 58th Annual Meeting of the Association for Computational Linguistics*, pages 5008–5020, Online. Association for Computational Linguistics.

Fen Xia, Tie-Yan Liu, Jue Wang, Wensheng Zhang, and Hang Li. 2008. Listwise approach to learning to rank: theory and algorithm. In *Proceedings of the 25th international conference on Machine learning*, pages 1192–1199.

Jingqing Zhang, Yao Zhao, Mohammad Saleh, and Peter Liu. 2020. Pegasus: Pre-training with extracted gap-sentences for abstractive summarization. In *International Conference on Machine Learning*, pages 11328–11339. PMLR.

Zheng Zhao, Shay B. Cohen, and Bonnie Webber. 2020. Reducing quantity hallucinations in abstractive summarization. In *Findings of the Association for Computational Linguistics: EMNLP 2020*, pages 2237–2249, Online. Association for Computational Linguistics.

Chenguang Zhu, William Hinthorn, Ruochen Xu, Qingkai Zeng, Michael Zeng, Xuedong Huang, and Meng Jiang. 2021. Enhancing factual consistency of abstractive summarization. In *Proceedings of the 2021 Conference of the North American Chapter of the Association for Computational Linguistics: Human Language Technologies*, pages 718–733, Online. Association for Computational Linguistics.

Liu Zhuang, Lin Wayne, Shi Ya, and Zhao Jun. 2021. A robustly optimized BERT pre-training approach with post-training. In *Proceedings of the 20th Chinese National Conference on Computational Linguistics*, pages 1218–1227, Huhhot, China. Chinese Information Processing Society of China.

A Further implementation details

A.1 Hyperparameters

To generate the training data for the re-ranking model, we sample 8 candidate summaries for each source document using diverse beam search with a diversity weight of 0.8. The candidates are then ranked according to the desired metric ϕ and the BERT model is fine-tuned on this data for up to 4 epochs, with a batch size of 24, and using the Adam optimizer (Kingma and Ba, 2014) with a learning rate of 5×10^{-5}. We use $\tau = 1$ (equation (2)) in all experiments. We keep the model that achieves the highest normalized discounted cumulative gain in a validation set. To generate the candidates at inference time, we set the diversity weight to zero since results in a separate validation set showed that this option yields the best results in most cases (see Appendix A.2). The models are implemented using the HuggingFace library on top of PyTorch. We also use HuggingFace publicly available checkpoints for the BART summarizers (`facebook/bart-large-cnn` and `facebook/bart-large-xsum`) and for BERT (`bert-base-uncased`).

A.2 Choice of the diversity weight

Although we have used diverse beam search to generate the candidate summaries for training, we decided to stick to *vanilla* beam search for testing. This choice was made based on the results presented in Table 5. For this experiment, we have used a held-out development set from the validation set of CNN/DailyMail and we registered the results achieved by our EBR model and by an oracle re-ranker with diversity weights ranging from 0 to 0.8. According to all the metrics except ROUGE-L, setting the diversity weight to a positive value has a negative effect on the quality of the generated hypotheses since even an oracle re-ranker would have better results when the diversity weight is

	Diversity weight	RL	QE	Cons	Rel
EBR-ListMLE [RL]	0	43.50	**43.57**	**95.32**	**63.28**
Oracle [RL]		46.95	43.37	95.26	64.54
EBR-ListMLE [RL]	0.2	**44.96**	42.83	90.61	59.54
Oracle [RL]		49.89	42.48	90.72	61.39
EBR-ListMLE [RL]	0.5	44.98	42.83	90.47	59.53
Oracle [RL]		50.58	42.44	90.71	61.61
EBR-ListMLE [RL]	0.8	44.92	42.81	90.32	59.42
Oracle [RL]		50.72	42.38	90.59	61.65
EBR-ListMLE [QE]	0	42.59	**44.17**	**95.93**	**63.59**
Oracle [QE]		42.55	45.72	95.72	63.19
EBR-ListMLE [QE]	0.2	44.01	43.92	92.57	60.82
Oracle [QE]		43.80	45.60	91.84	59.98
EBR-ListMLE [QE]	0.5	**44.08**	44.08	92.69	60.97
Oracle [QE]		43.92	45.84	91.87	60.15
EBR-ListMLE [QE]	0.8	43.95	44.09	92.70	60.87
Oracle [QE]		43.74	45.88	91.81	60.00
EBR-ListMLE [Rel]	0	42.67	**43.70**	**96.11**	**64.53**
Oracle [Rel]		44.32	43.52	96.24	66.40
EBR-ListMLE [Rel]	0.2	43.83	43.24	93.77	62.26
Oracle [Rel]		46.04	42.87	93.56	64.52
EBR-ListMLE [Rel]	0.5	**43.87**	43.32	94.03	62.51
Oracle [Rel]		46.40	42.92	93.72	65.10
EBR-ListMLE [Rel]	0.8	43.79	43.29	94.06	62.47
Oracle [Rel]		46.40	42.82	93.69	65.18
EBR-ListMLE [Cons+Rel]	0	42.49	**43.69**	**96.35**	**64.45**
Oracle [Cons+Rel]		44.09	43.57	96.56	66.27
EBR-ListMLE [Cons+Rel]	0.2	**43.62**	43.24	94.21	62.25
Oracle [Cons+Rel]		45.30	43.00	94.42	64.20
EBR-ListMLE [Cons+Rel]	0.5	43.50	43.24	94.52	62.44
Oracle [Cons+Rel]		45.56	43.09	94.67	64.74
EBR-ListMLE [Cons+Rel]	0.8	43.43	43.21	94.56	62.46
Oracle [Cons+Rel]		45.42	43.02	94.70	64.79

Table 5: Results (in %) for different diversity weights in a held-out validation set of CNN/DailyMail. (RL: ROUGE-L, QE: QuestEval, Cons: $\text{CTC}_{\text{consistency}}$, Rel: $\text{CTC}_{\text{relevance}}$)

zero. Thus, we decided to set it at this value for the subsequent experiments with the test set.

B Ablation study

We now study the effect of training our EBR model using the max-margin loss proposed by Bhattacharyya et al. (2021) for machine translation. In addition, we also compare our models with perfect re-rankers for the two reference-free metrics: QuestEval and $\text{CTC}_{\text{consistency}}$. The results are in Table 6, where we also reproduce the results from our models presented in Table 1 for easier analysis. The comparison between the max-margin loss (EBR-MM) and ListMLE (EBR-ListMLE) shows that the latter tends to perform slightly better, although in the majority of the cases the difference is not statistically significant. It should also be remarked that re-ranking with the $\text{CTC}_{\text{consistency}}$ metric directly (Perfect Re-Rank [Cons]) yields competitive results too: it is the best on this metric in both datasets and it is close to the best model on $\text{CTC}_{\text{relevance}}$ in XSum. Re-ranking with QuestEval (Perfect Re-Rank [QE]) generally produces inferior results and, as shown previously in Table 2, has the additional inconvenience of being much slower.

C Effect of varying the number of candidates

Figure 2 shows the effect of varying the number of candidate summaries on the performance of our EBR models and BART baseline. The candidates were obtained using beam search with the number of beams equal to the number of candidates. The figure also shows the performance of the perfect re-ranker (Oracle), which defines the upper bound on the performance of the EBR.

Increasing the number of candidates leads to improvements in the performance of the EBR model when evaluated with the same metric it was trained to maximize. However, for ROUGE-L, these improvements are only marginal. Moreover, the performance gap between the Oracle and EBR tends to increase as well, especially in the reference-dependent metrics (ROUGE-L and $\text{CTC}_{\text{relevance}}$). The BART baseline also benefits from having larger beam sizes according to all metrics except ROUGE-

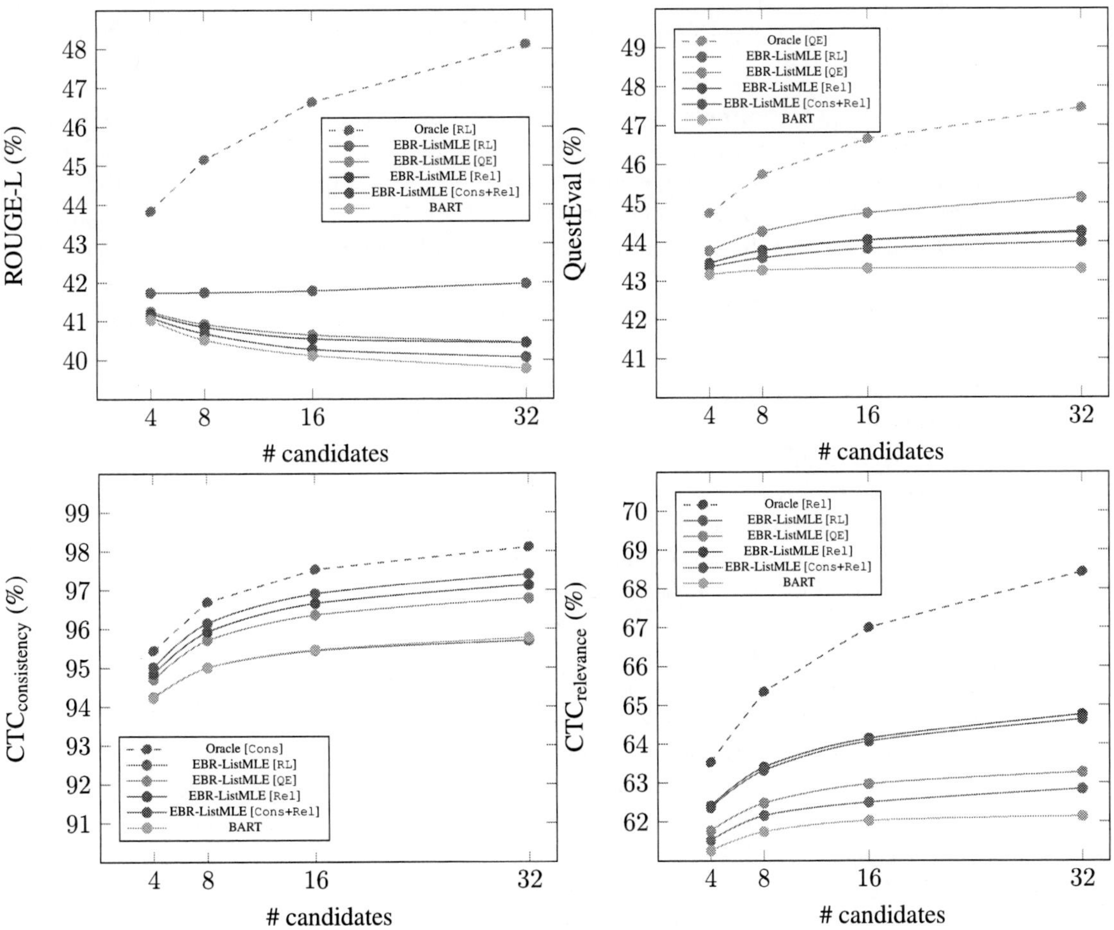

Figure 2: Performance of the models on the CNN/DailyMail dataset according to the indicated metrics for different numbers of candidate summaries. (RL: ROUGE-L, QE: QuestEval, Cons: $\text{CTC}_{\text{consistency}}$, Rel: $\text{CTC}_{\text{relevance}}$)

	CNN/DailyMail							XSum						
	R1	R2	RL	QE	Cons	Rel	FCC	R1	R2	RL	QE	Cons	Rel	FCC
Perfect Re-Rank [QE]	43.91	20.99	40.76	**45.74***	95.46	62.06	58.26	42.81	19.33	34.53	**32.28***	83.31	52.57	26.58
Perfect Re-Rank [Cons]	43.43	20.59	40.29	43.68	**96.69***	62.60	61.36	43.02	19.58	34.76	28.70	**87.64***	54.33	**27.61***
EBR-MM [RL]	44.49	21.35	41.32	43.72	95.23	62.22	56.89	**43.86**	**20.30**	35.72	28.68	83.32	52.85	25.98
EBR-MM [QE]	44.07	21.13	40.93	44.22	95.70	62.54	59.49	42.85	19.42	34.54	29.63	83.37	52.58	25.86
EBR-MM [Rel]	43.92	20.87	40.72	43.79	95.78	63.20	59.84	43.44	19.83	35.03	28.79	84.82	54.54	25.67
EBR-MM [Cons+Rel]	43.75	20.78	40.56	43.78	95.98	63.10	60.75	43.31	19.76	34.95	28.83	85.42	54.50	26.38
EBR-ListMLE [RL]	**44.90**	**21.58**	**41.75***	43.60	95.01	62.16	54.95	43.63	20.28	**35.78**	28.55	84.47	52.92	27.21
EBR-ListMLE [QE]	44.07	21.13	40.94	44.27	95.71	62.48	59.23	42.94	19.42	34.62	29.89	83.34	52.50	26.34
EBR-ListMLE [Rel]	44.04	20.98	40.85	43.78	95.93	**63.40**	60.28	43.39	19.75	35.03	28.60	85.49	**54.80**	26.28
EBR-ListMLE [Cons+Rel]	43.88	20.87	40.69	43.79	96.15	63.32	**61.67***	43.28	19.72	34.92	28.66	86.03	54.74	27.12

Table 6: Results of our models (EBR-ListMLE) and baselines on each of the automatic evaluation metrics. Bold font indicates best result, and the second best results are underlined. A * mark indicates that the difference to the second best result is statistically significant (approximate permutation test at 95%). The metric in brackets indicates the target metric ϕ used to train the re-ranker. (R1: ROUGE-1, R2: ROUGE-2, RL: ROUGE-L, QE: QuestEval, Cons: $CTC_{consistency}$, Rel: $CTC_{relevance}$, FCC: FactCC)

L. Nonetheless, BART performs consistently worse than our EBR models according to all the metrics. Interestingly, increasing the number of candidates degrades ROUGE-L scores for all the models, except for EBR trained using this metric as the target.

D Human evaluation: further details

D.1 Evaluation form interface

The human evaluation form was built using the Google Forms platform. Figure 3 presents a screenshot of the user interface. As we can observe, the interface was divided into seven sections. The first one provides instructions to the user and a brief definition of each of the three evaluation criteria: "(1) - Factual consistency: A factually consistent summary should only contain exact, undistorted information that is present in the source text. No external information should be added."; "(2) - Relevance: A relevant summary should provide the most important information presented in the source text."; "(3) - Fluency: A fluent summary should be clear, grammatically correct, and sound like human-written text.". The three subsequent sections present the source text followed by the two anonymized summaries. Finally, the last three sections contain the multiple choice questions for each of the evaluation criteria. This seven-section pattern repeats itself for all pairwise comparisons in the evaluation form.

D.2 Detected factual inconsistencies

In Table 7 we show a few documents together with the summaries obtained from the baseline BART obtained with the usual beam search and the summaries chosen by the EBR model. Table 8 shows the examples from XSum used in the human evaluation questionnaire where the two judges agreed that the CLIFF summary was better than the EBR summary, regarding factual consistency. In two of the three examples, the $CTC_{consistency}$ metric wrongly assigns a larger score to the EBR summary than to the CLIFF summary. Interestingly, though, the EBR model would prefer the CLIFF summary over the BART summary in two of the three cases.

	Text	Cons	E
Source (CNN/DM)	Kell Brook has finally landed the Battle of Britain he craved, but will take on Frankie Gavin rather than bitter rival Amir Khan. Just sixty four days after the first defence of his IBF belt against Jo Jo Dan, Brook will return to action on a packed pay-per-view show on May 30 at the O2 in London. The welterweight bout has been added to a card that includes world title challenges for Kevin Mitchell and Lee Selby while Anthony Joshua faces his toughest test to date against Kevin Johnson. Kell Brook poses outside London's O2 Arena where he will fight Frankie Gavin on May 30. Brook posing on the train as he headed to London for the announcement of his fight. Brook (left) was back in action as he beat Jo Jo Dan for the IBF World Welterweight title in Sheffield last month. Brook poses with Gavin inside the O2 arena after announcing their world title fight. Brook had been desperate to face Khan at Wembley in June but his compatriot ruled out a fight until at least later in the year. (...)		
BART	Kell Brook will fight Frankie Gavin at the O2 in London on May 30. The welterweight bout has been added to a card that includes world title challenges for Kevin Mitchell and Lee Selby. Anthony Joshua faces his toughest test to date against Kevin Johnson. Click here for more boxing news.	88.6%	0.09
EBR	Kell Brook will fight Frankie Gavin on May 30 at the O2 in London. The welterweight bout has been added to a card that includes world title challenges for Kevin Mitchell and Lee Selby. Anthony Joshua faces his toughest test to date against Kevin Johnson. Brook had been desperate to face Amir Khan at Wembley in June.	**97.3%**	**−3.67**
Source (CNN/DM)	Aston Villa match-winner Fabian Delph was left pinching himself after booking his side's place in the FA Cup final at the expense of Liverpool. Villa skipper Delph set up Christian Benteke's equaliser after Philippe Coutinho opened the scoring for the Reds and then rounded off a superb afternoon by sweeping home nine minutes into the second half to secure a 2-1 victory. Delph's strike means that Tim Sherwood's charges will return to Wembley to face holders Arsenal in next month's showpiece and the former Leeds midfielder says it will be a dream come true. Fabian Delph fires past Liverpool keeper Simon Mignolet to book Aston Villa's place in the FA Cup final . Delph celebrates with team-mate Ashley Westwood after his 54th minute strike . Delph (left), Gabriel Agbonlahor (centre) and Grealish savour the winning feeling in the Villa dressing room . 'I can't wait for the final. To walk out as captain is going to be the highlight of my career. So happy days, I'm happy for the boys,' he told BT Sport 1. (...)"		
BART	Aston Villa beat Liverpool 2-1 in the FA Cup semi-final at Wembley. Fabian Delph scored the winning goal in the 54th minute. Tim Sherwood's side will now face Arsenal in next month's showpiece. Delph says the final will be the highlight of his career.	85.3%	1.22
EBR	Aston Villa beat Liverpool 2-1 in the FA Cup semi-final at Wembley. Fabian Delph scored the winning goal in the 54th minute. Tim Sherwood's side will now face Arsenal in next month's final. Delph says to walk out as captain in the final will be the highlight of his career.	**85.5%**	**0.73**
Source (XSum)	The UN has said media restrictions and violence meant the environment was not conducive to free, credible elections. Unrest started in April after President Pierre Nkurunziza said he would run for a third term - something protesters say is illegal. The president says he is entitled to a third term because he was appointed for his first term, not elected. The presidential election is scheduled for 15 July. East African leaders have called for a further two-week delay. Africa news highlights: 7 July The electoral commission spokesman told the BBC turnout for the parliamentary poll had been low in the districts of Bujumbura where there had been protests, but that in some provinces outside the capital it was as high as 98The ruling party - the CNDD FDD - was ahead in every province of the country, Burundi's electoral commission announced. They won 77 out of 100 elected seats in parliament, AFP news agency says. (...)		
BART	Burundi has held parliamentary elections, two months after the UN suspended its observer mission to the country.	80.6%	3.68
EBR	The ruling party in Burundi has won parliamentary elections, the first since a wave of protests began in April.	**83.7%**	**2.57**
Source (XSum)	Many Sephardic Jews were killed, forced to convert to Christianity or leave at the end of the 15th Century. Parliament paved the way for a change in citizenship laws two years ago, but the move needed Cabinet approval. From now on, descendants of Sephardic Jews who can prove a strong link to Portugal can apply for a passport. Proof can be brought, the government says, through a combination of surname, language spoken in the family or evidence of direct descent. Thousands of Sephardic Jews were forced off the Iberian peninsula, first from Spain and then from Portugal. Some of those who fled to other parts of Europe or to America continued to speak a form of Portuguese in their new communities. The Portuguese government acknowledges that Jews lived in the region long before the Portuguese kingdom was founded in the 12th Century. (...)		
BART	Portugal has approved a law that will allow descendants of Jews who fled the country to become citizens.	86.8%	1.48
EBR	The Portuguese government has approved a law that will allow descendants of Jews who fled to Portugal to become citizens.	**93.1%**	**1.15**

Table 7: Examples where the judges agreed that one of the summaries was better than the other on the factual consistency dimension. Consistent and inconsistent segments are highlighted in green and red, respectively. Columns Cons and E show the $\text{CTC}_{\text{consistency}}$ (in %) and the energy score (output of the EBR model) on each of the summaries, respectively. (Remember that for E lower is better.)

	Text	Cons	E
Source	Lance Naik (Corporal) Hanamanthappa Koppad was tapped under 8m of snow at a height of nearly 6,000m along with nine other soldiers who all died. Their bodies have now been recovered. The critically ill soldier has been airlifted to a hospital in Delhi. "We hope the miracle continues. Pray with us," an army statement said. The army added that "he has been placed on a ventilator to protect his airway and lungs in view of his comatose state". (...)		
CLIFF	An Indian soldier who was injured in an avalanche on the Siachen glacier in Indian-administered Kashmir last week is in a "comatose state", the army says.	81.5	**1.66**
EBR	A soldier who was trapped in an avalanche on the Siachen glacier in Indian-administered Kashmir last week has been declared dead, the army says.	**85.7**	1.82
Source	They were among four people who were on Irish Coastguard Rescue 116 helicopter when it crashed on Tuesday. The funeral for pilot Captain Dara Fitzpatrick was held on Saturday. The search, which has been impeded by adverse weather, will also focus on finding the wreckage of the helicopter. The priority for those involved in the multi-agency operation has been to recover the bodies of chief pilot Mark Duffy and winchmen Paul Ormsby and Ciarán Smith. (...)		
CLIFF	The search for the bodies of three crew members who died in a helicopter crash off the coast of the Republic of Ireland has resumed.	**89.4**	**3.24**
EBR	The search for two coastguard crew missing since a helicopter crash off the County Mayo coast has resumed.	79.9	3.51
Source	In the Yemeni capital, Sanaa, where the threat of attack is considered greatest, the UK, France and Germany have also shut their embassies. The British embassy has emptied completely, with all remaining British staff leaving the country on Tuesday, while the US air force flew out American personnel. So just what is it about al-Qaeda's branch in Yemen that triggers such warning bells in Washington? Al-Qaeda in the Arabian Peninsula (AQAP), al-Qaeda's branch in Yemen, is not the biggest offshoot of the late Osama Bin Laden's organisation, nor is it necessarily the most active - there are other, noisier jihadist cells sprawled across Syria and Iraq, engaged in almost daily conflict with fellow Muslims. But Washington considers AQAP to be by far the most dangerous to the West because it has both technical skills and global reach. (...) According to the US think-tank the New America Foundation, US drone strikes in Yemen have soared, from 18 in 2011 to 53 in 2012. A drone strike on Tuesday reportedly hit a car carrying four al-Qaeda operatives. (...)		
CLIFF	The US has stepped up its drone strikes on al-Qaeda in the Arabian Peninsula (AQAP), a branch of the group that it considers the most dangerous to the West.	76.8	3.57
EBR	The US has ordered all its diplomats to leave Yemen, saying it is under "heightened" US security concerns.	**80.3**	**2.25**

Table 8: Examples from XSum where the two judges agreed that CLIFF was better than EBR on the factual consistency dimension. Consistent and inconsistent segments are highlighted in green and red, respectively. Columns Cons and E show the $\text{CTC}_{\text{consistency}}$ (in %) and the energy score (output of the EBR model) on each of the summaries, respectively. (Remember that for E lower is better.)

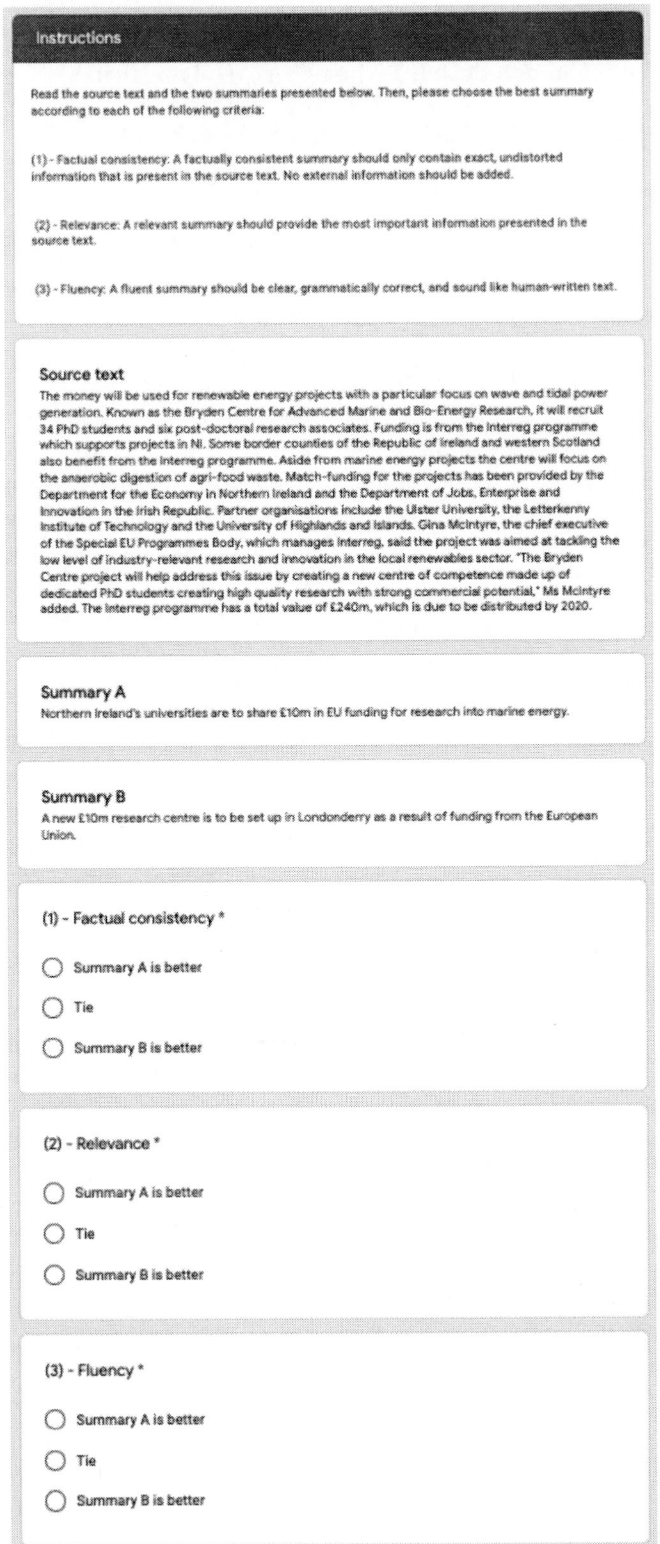

Instructions

Read the source text and the two summaries presented below. Then, please choose the best summary according to each of the following criteria:

(1) - Factual consistency: A factually consistent summary should only contain exact, undistorted information that is present in the source text. No external information should be added.

(2) - Relevance: A relevant summary should provide the most important information presented in the source text.

(3) - Fluency: A fluent summary should be clear, grammatically correct, and sound like human-written text.

Source text

The money will be used for renewable energy projects with a particular focus on wave and tidal power generation. Known as the Bryden Centre for Advanced Marine and Bio-Energy Research, it will recruit 34 PhD students and six post-doctoral research associates. Funding is from the Interreg programme which supports projects in NI. Some border counties of the Republic of Ireland and western Scotland also benefit from the Interreg programme. Aside from marine energy projects the centre will focus on the anaerobic digestion of agri-food waste. Match-funding for the projects has been provided by the Department for the Economy in Northern Ireland and the Department of Jobs, Enterprise and Innovation in the Irish Republic. Partner organisations include the Ulster University, the Letterkenny Institute of Technology and the University of Highlands and Islands. Gina McIntyre, the chief executive of the Special EU Programmes Body, which manages Interreg, said the project was aimed at tackling the low level of industry-relevant research and innovation in the local renewables sector. "The Bryden Centre project will help address this issue by creating a new centre of competence made up of dedicated PhD students creating high quality research with strong commercial potential," Ms McIntyre added. The Interreg programme has a total value of £240m, which is due to be distributed by 2020.

Summary A

Northern Ireland's universities are to share £10m in EU funding for research into marine energy.

Summary B

A new £10m research centre is to be set up in Londonderry as a result of funding from the European Union.

(1) - Factual consistency *

- Summary A is better
- Tie
- Summary B is better

(2) - Relevance *

- Summary A is better
- Tie
- Summary B is better

(3) - Fluency *

- Summary A is better
- Tie
- Summary B is better

Figure 3: Evaluation form

Task-driven augmented data evaluation

Olga Golovneva[*1,2], **Pan Wei**[1], **Khadige Abboud**[1],
Charith Peris[1], **Lizhen Tan**[1], **Haiyang Yu**[*1,3]

[1]Alexa AI, Amazon, Cambridge, MA
[2]FAIR Labs, Meta, Washington, DC
[3]Google, New York, NY

olggol@meta.com, {panwei, abboudk, perisc, ltn}@amazon.com, yuhaiyang@google.com

Abstract

The main focus of data augmentation research has been on the enhancement of generation models, leaving the examination and improvements of synthetic data evaluation methods less explored. In our work, we explore a number of sentence similarity measures in the context of data generation filtering, and evaluate their impact on the performance of the targeted Natural Language Understanding problem for the example of intent classification and named entity recognition tasks. Our experiments on ATIS dataset show that the right choice of filtering technique can bring up to 33% in sentence accuracy improvement for targeted underrepresented intents.

1 Introduction

Recent advances in transfer learning methods have been a driving force in the progress of many Natural Language Understanding (NLU) tasks. These methods typically involve pre-training of a large-scale language model, followed by the task-specific fine-tuning (Peters et al., 2018; Devlin et al., 2019). Although these approaches have helped achieve state-of-the-art results on a variety of supervised learning tasks, they do not directly address the problem of task-specific annotated data sparsity. This is where data augmentation techniques come in to play, boosting model performance for a given supervised task by generating novel data points that are similar in characteristics to the available data.

The main thrust of data augmentation research has been focused on improving generation models (Yu et al., 2017; Golovneva and Peris, 2020; Kim et al., 2020; Liu et al., 2020; Sun et al., 2020; Anaby-Tavor et al., 2020), while comparatively little work has been done on comprehensively evaluating and filtering high-quality synthetic utterances. Current approaches suggest the use of a combination of automated metrics that evaluate utterances at the word or embedding level (Sharma et al., 2017; Liu et al., 2020).

Popular word-based evaluation approaches are based on comparing n-grams in the original and generated text, and were originally developed for machine translation evaluations. Among them commonly used scores are Bilingual Evaluation Understudy (BLEU) score (Papineni et al., 2002), Recall-Oriented Understudy for Gisting Evaluation (ROUGE) (Lin, 2004), and Metric for Evaluation of Translation with Explicit ORdering (METEOR) (Lavie and Agarwal, 2007). Both BLEU and ROUGE-N are based on comparing the n-gram overlap of the reference and generated texts and counts the number of token matches, with the difference being that ROUGE is recall-focused whereas BLEU is precision-focused. METEOR uses a set 1-gram mappings between the reference and generated text to get a weighted F-score, and adds a penalty function for incorrect word order.

Word-based sentence evaluation can give low scores for predictions with high lexical variation, but these predictions are not necessarily poor quality. To address that, one could use embedding similarity (Sharma et al., 2017), that will measure the semantic similarity between the reference and prediction based on the cosine similarity between word and sentence embeddings.

While high-quality generated data should be similar to the source data at hand, it is also important for this data to be novel. To measure the diversity of the generated text, one can use self-BLEU (Zhu et al., 2018) score, which is computed by averaging the BLEU scores of each generated utterance using the rest of the generated text as the reference set. Furthermore, in an effort to address the diversity-quality trade-off of synthetically generated data, (Montahaei et al., 2019) propose joint diversity-quality metrics: MS-Jaccard similarity calculated as the average n-gram Jaccard index of the generated text, and Frechet BERT Distance

[*]Work done during the authors' tenure at Amazon.

Proceedings of the 2nd Workshop on Natural Language Generation, Evaluation, and Metrics (GEM), pages 18 - 25
December 7, 2022 ©2022 Association for Computational Linguistics

(FBD) calculated as the Frechet distance between the generated text distribution and the reference set distribution while using BERT's feature space for the text.

Some approaches have been made to create a statistical model that would serve as an independent data evaluator. In their work, (Lowe et al., 2017) propose an RNN-based Automatic Dialogue Evaluation Model (ADEM) that predicts human evaluation score for the generated utterance. The drawback of this approach is that it requires additional data collection to train the model.

Despite a variety of approaches to annotated data evaluation, there is no golden standard, moreover, they often disagree on evaluation (Bhandari et al., 2020). However, the real value of the generated data can be only evaluated through the downstream task, for example by estimating how much performance improvement synthetic data can bring to the targeted supervised NLU task.

In our work, we are connecting automated data evaluation with the downstream tasks, and apply it as a filtering mechanism to generated utterances. Instead of attempting to build correlations with expensive human evaluations, we indirectly evaluate the quality of the generated data through the performance of the intent classification (IC) and named entity recognition (NER) tasks on the widely used Air Travel Information System (ATIS) dataset (Hemphill et al., 1990).

In summary, our contributions are as follows:

1. We propose a novel synthetic text data evaluation framework by adapting different word-based and embeddings-based similarity measures for post-generation quality evaluation linked to the performance improvement of the targeted NLU problem on the example of IC and NER tasks.

2. We propose a way to adapt a classification model, which can serve as an independent data evaluator and does not require additional data collection.

3. We adapt generation models to produce labeled data with and without delexicalization.

4. We conduct experiments on ATIS dataset, a standard benchmark dataset for intent classification and slot labelling. Our experimental results show that proposed methods help to improve generated data quality which reflects in model performance improvements.

2 Synthetic data evaluation

Data sparsity is a common issue in multiple areas of NLU research. It is often a difficult and costly exercise for researchers to secure the required amounts of high-quality annotated data to train their models. In our work, we aim to generate synthetic data that can be used to improve NLU model training. We use the original training data along with intent and slot labels as a source to the data generation model. Each utterance $u = w_0, w_1, ..., w_n$ of length n is represented as a sequence of tokens, where w_0 is utterance's intent, and w_i $(i = 1..n)$ denotes the ith slot of the utterance. In this paper, we will use sentence and utterance interchangeably. Once data is generated, we use several text evaluation metrics to filter out high-quality utterances that will potentially bring greater benefit for the model.

2.1 Word-based sentence similarity

To evaluate the quality of the synthetic utterances through word similarity, we calculate the n-gram BLEU scores of the generated sentence pairing with each sentence in the original training data with the same intent. We also calculate the maximum of the n-gram BLEU scores with all other intents, then assign the difference between these two scores as our $maxBLEU$ score for the generated sentence. This score considers both the similarity of the generated utterance to within-intent source data and the dis-similarity to out-of-intent utterances. For each generated utterance u for intent j, we calculate the in-intent BLEU score $BLEU_j = BLEU_N(u, U_j)$ where $N = \min(4, length(u))$, U_j is the reference set of source utterances in intent $j \in I$, and calculate the out-of-intent BLEU score as the maximum BLEU scores across all other intents. Finally our quality score for the generated utterance is given by the difference:

$$maxBLEU = BLEU_j - maxBLEU_N(u, U_i)_{i \in I, i \neq j} \quad (1)$$

Instead of maximization, we can also use average operation to estimate the out-of-intent score to get the $avgBLEU$ score:

$$avgBLEU = BLEU_j - meanBLEU_N(u, U_i)_{i \in I, i \neq j} \quad (2)$$

maxBLEU score will show how the generated utterance is similar to the closest intent, other than the generated one j, while avgBLEU score reflects how much close the utterance is to all other intents on average. Inherently, the maxBLEU and avgBLEU scores are similarity measures, while we aim to preserve both the similarity and dissimilarity within/out-of-intent that is in the original source data. The Jaccard distance on the other hand measures both the similarity and the diversity of the the data (Montahaei et al., 2019):

$$JD(S_{u_i}, S_{u_j}) = 1 - \frac{|S_{u_i} \cap S_{u_j}|}{|S_{u_i} \cup S_{u_j}|} \quad (3)$$

where u_i, u_j denote two different sentences/corpora, $S_{u_i} = w \in u_i$ denotes the set of words in the sentence u_i. We apply intra-group similarity check by using Jaccard distance check, the steps are as follows:

1. for each intent j in the reference, calculate the pairwise distance between each utterance and take the mean as the intent threshold, t_j;

2. for each generated utterance u, based on its first generated token (i.e. the intent k it is predicted to be), calculate the Jaccard distance between uand all sentences in the reference intent group it falls into, if $mean(JD(u, u_m)_{u_m \in U_k}) < t_k$, then the generated sentence will be retained.

2.2 Embedding-based sentence similarity

In additional to token/ngram-based utterance similarity check, we also utilize word embedding which takes semantic context information into account for word similarity. For a given utterance, we construct a sentence embedding by averaging the embeddings of words composing in the sentence as in embedding similarity (Sharma et al., 2017). To compare the utterances, we use the popular cosine distance

$$CD(u_i, u_j) = 1 - \frac{\bar{e}_{u_i} \cdot \bar{e}_{u_j}}{\|\bar{e}_{u_i}\| \|\bar{e}_{u_j}\|} \quad (4)$$

where $\bar{e}_{u_i}$, $\bar{e}_{u_j}$ denote the average sentence embedding for sentences u_i, u_j respectively.

With this definition, we apply the same intra-group similarity check algorithm as mentioned in the previous session to filter the generated sentences. In our experient, we use the pre-trained fastText English embeddings (Grave et al., 2018).

2.3 Independent evaluator

Finally, we use a machine learning model to evaluate synthetic data quality. Unlike ADEM model (Lowe et al., 2017), our evaluator, similar to the filtering method used in (Anaby-Tavor et al., 2020), does not aim to predict human evaluation scores. Instead, it acts as an independently trained discriminator that assigns the probabilities for the utterance to be real. For our evaluator, we first train a BERT-based intent classification model on the train partition of ATIS. To account for the data imbalance, we add class weights calculated based on class frequencies to the cross-entropy loss. This model is then used to evaluate each synthetic utterance u. An utterance is considered as legitimate and added to the augmented set only if the model confidence on predicting intent $w_0 = i, i \in I$, is greater than pre-defined threshold t_i. Each threshold is calculated as follows:

$$t_i = \begin{cases} \max(p_j), & \forall j \neq i, j \in J, |J| > 1 \\ \min(p_i), & \text{if } J = \{i\} \end{cases} \quad (5)$$

where $J \subset I$ is a set of all hypotheses for utterances that in the reference belong to the intent $i \in I$.

3 Experiments

In this section, we describe experimental setup, evaluation metrics and provide the summary of the experimental results.

3.1 Data

In our experiments, we use the Airline Travel Information System (ATIS) dataset imported from the Microsoft Cognitive Toolkit (CNTK). ATIS is a standard benchmark dataset widely used for intent classification and slot filling tasks. It consists of a set of spoken utterances in the context of airline information, classified into one of 26 intents with 127 slot labels. Table 1 shows train, dev and test sizes per intent. We note that the intent distribution of ATIS is highly imbalanced with over 70% of the data belonging to the one intent (*atis_flight*) while others intents have very low number of utterances sometimes within only one subset, train, dev or test.

3.2 Delexicalization

Similar to (Yu et al., 2020), in order to reduce noise and add more variety to the generated data, we experiment with using delexicalized utterances.

Table 1: Utterance count in training, development and test partition of ATIS dataset per intent.

intent	train	dev	test
atis_flight	3309	357	632
atis_airfare	385	38	48
atis_ground_service	230	25	36
atis_airline	139	18	38
atis_abbreviation	130	17	33
atis_aircraft	70	11	9
atis_flight_time	45	9	1
atis_quantity	41	10	3
atis_flight#atis_airfare	19	2	12
atis_city	18	1	6
atis_airport	17	3	18
atis_distance	17	3	10
atis_capacity	15	1	21
atis_ground_fare	15	3	7
atis_flight_no	12	0	8
atis_meal	6	0	6
atis_restriction	5	1	0
atis_airline#atis_flight_no	2	0	0
atis_aircraft#atis_flight#atis_flight_no	1	0	0
atis_cheapest	1	0	0
atis_ground_service#atis_ground_fare	1	0	0
atis_airfare#atis_flight_time	0	1	0
atis_airfare#atis_flight	0	0	1
atis_day_name	0	0	2
atis_flight#atis_airline	0	0	1
atis_flight_no#atis_airline	0	0	1

We preprocess the data by replacing slot values (some consisting of multiple tokens) with their corresponding slot labels, before feeding it into our data generation model. Once we obtain the generated data, we re-fill the slot labels present in these utterances with randomly sampled slot values which correspond to the label. The utterances thus created are used for the downstream tasks.

The following are the detailed steps together with examples:

- Use original training data to create catalogs, that for each label will contain a list of corresponding slot values extracted from catalogs, e.g.: {city_name: [london, denver, new york, boston]};
- For input data in generation model, anonymize slot values with slot labels, e.g. from "buy a ticket to denver" to "buy a ticket to city_name". This will help the generation model focus on carrier phrase and learn syntactic variations, rather than semantic similarities between slot values, as well as help to reduce the amount of noise in generated data, such as when model incorporates meaningless or confusing parts of the slot values (for example, "find the ticket price from new to san");
- Generate data using data generation model, e.g. generate sentence like "*atis_airfare* find the ticket price from city_name to city_name" with intent appended to the beginning of the utterance;
- Fill the slot value with catalogs by random sampling, e.g. from generated utterance "find the ticket price from city_name to city_name" we backpropagate to "find the ticket price from new york to boston".

3.3 Data generation

For data generation, we use the Sequence Generative Adversarial Networks (SeqGAN) model developed by (Yu et al., 2017). Generative Adversarial Nets (GANs) consist of two competing networks, generator and discriminator. Generator network implicitly learns data distribution through the feedback it receives from discriminator network, that is trained to distinguish fake and real data points. Unlike classic GANs, SeqGAN specifically addresses the issues of discrete tokens generation through a stochastic policy in reinforcement learning that will guide token-by-token sequence generation. The discriminator judges at sequence-level with the intermediate state-action value calculated using Monte Carlo (MC) search. While (Yu et al., 2017) applied the MC search at sequence-level, (Golovneva and Peris, 2020) expanded this work to apply the reinforcement learning reward as an average of the token-level rewards. Their results showed significant improvement in accuracy metrics for domain classification, intent classification, slot F1 and Frame accuracy in their task mimicking the bootstrapping of a new language. We use their methods as a basis for our data generation tasks here. It is worth noting, that synthetic data evaluation approach does not depend on the method chosen for data augmentation, but is driven by the downstream supervised NLU tasks.

Table 2: Performance results for stack-propagation model on ATIS dataset: baseline.

method	slot F1	intent acc	sentence acc
baseline, published	95.900%	96.900%	86.500%
baseline, in-house	96.031%	96.678%	89.212%

Table 3: Performance results for stack-propagation model on ATIS dataset in terms of slot F1 score, intent accuracy (acc), and sentence acc. All metric values are calculated using the average of multiple trials, and t-test is used to determine whether the results are statistically significant or not. In the table, the results with * are statistically significant with $p < 0.1$, and best performing model for each metric is highlighted in bold. Utterance counts are provided for train and dev partitions combined. Data were generated with (wd) and without (nd) delexicalization.

method	# gen utt	# utt after filter	total # utt	slot F1	intent acc	sentence acc
baseline			4,978	96.031%	96.678%	89.212%
no filtering, nd	7,519		12,497	95.996%	91.601%	85.330%
maxBLEU, nd	7,519	2,637	7,615	96.172%	96.529%	**89.959%***
weighted BERT, nd	7,519	2,503	7,481	95.983%	**97.088%**	89.586%*
jaccard, nd	7,519	3,317	8,295	**96.308%**	96.267%	89.436%
avgBLEU, nd	7,519	3,099	8,077	95.948%	96.417%	89.205%
cosine, nd	7,519	1,992	6,731	95.900%	95.633%	88.578%
BERT, nd	7,519	4,739	9,717	94.882%	96.081%	83.763%
no filtering, wd	9,591		14,569	90.488%	86.338%	70.549%
maxBLEU, wd	9,591	1,152	6,130	95.926%	96.715%	89.287%
weighted BERT, wd	9,591	4,885	9,863	96.044%	96.939%	89.548%*
jaccard, wd	9,591	3,348	8,326	95.998%	96.753%	89.474%
avgBLEU, wd	9,591	3,499	8,477	95.056%	95.529%	88.026%
cosine, wd	9,591	1,834	6,812	95.755%	96.305%	88.578%
BERT, wd	9,591	5,332	10,310	94.134%	96.001%	83.521%

3.4 Model Architecture

For IC and NER tasks, we select one of the recent state-of-the-art models, that achieved high performance in intent classification and slot labeling tasks on the ATIS dataset. A Stack-Propagation Framework with Token-Level Intent Detection proposed by (Qin et al., 2019) for joint intent detection and slot filling, that explicitly use intent information for slot labeling task. Unlike multitask framework, where two tasks share only encoder, stack-propagation explicitly provides features from one task (IC) to another (NER). Additionally to account for contextual information, BiLSTM encoder is enriched with self-attention.

3.5 Baseline

We evaluate model performance according to the three metrics: intent accuracy for IC task, micro-averaged slot F1 for NER prediction, and overall sentence accuracy which is the relative number of utterances for which the intent and all slots are correctly identified. First we train the model on non-augmented ATIS dataset, and average results over 3 runs. As shown in the Table 2, results published by (Qin et al., 2019) on application of a Stack-Propagation Framework to ATIS dataset are consistent with our results.

3.6 Results

In Table 3, we provide a summary of all experimental results which include data counts both pre- and post-filtering and final metric values. Using SeqGAN model described in Section 3.3) we generate two sets of 9600 utterances, one with delexicalization and one without. The generated data sets are approximately twice the size of the original training partition. Although we use training data for all intents as an input to the data generation model, we only augment utterances for underrepresented intents, which excludes the biggest *atis_flight* intent. We then remove any generated utterances which do not start with a valid intent. This led to 7519 and 9591 augmented sentences with and without delexicalization respectively. We apply our six filtering mechanisms as described in Section 2. based on the following approaches: maxBLEU, avgBLEU, Jaccard distance, cosine distance, BERT-based evaluator with and without class weight added to the loss function. We use the resulting filtered sets as augmentation for each experiment and present results of our quality evaluation tasks (IC and NER) in Table 3.

Our results show that three filtering methods consistently outperform the baseline, regardless of whether delexicalized or not, when considering the overall sentence accuracy metric. These are maxBLEU and Jaccard scores, as well as BERT model with class weights. The overall highest improvement in sentence accuracy in observed when using maxBLEU with no delexicalization.

Contrary to expectations, we do not see much improvement offered by the use of delexicalization, with delexicalized augmentation outperforming non-delexicalized augmentation only in the case of Jaccard-based filtering. Filtering using the word-based sentence similarity methods - maxBLEU and Jaccard - show similar results, while the BERT-based classifier with weighted loss function outperforms on intent classification task. This is most likely due to the fact that the classifier was trained on the intent classification task at the slot value level, so it can be expected to be better at filtering those sentences where true sentence intent does not match the first token of the generated sequence, while it does not capture the correctness of the labels. maxBLEU shows better performance than aveBLEU, likely due to it being better at detecting and filtering those generated utterances that belong to a wrong intent. maxBLEU filtering without delexicalization produces the best overall sentence accuracy. In particular, in Table 4 we see up to 33% in overall sentence accuracy improvement for targeted underrepresented intents.

Table 4: Sentence accuracy comparison between in-house baseline and model with training data augmented by filtering generated data with maxBLEU score criteria. Per-intent performance shows significant improvements on intents with small amount of training data.

intent	# test utt	baseline	maxBLEU
atis_flight	632	94.357%	**94.568%**
atis_airfare	48	97.222%	**97.917%**
atis_airline	38	92.105%	**93.860%**
atis_ground_service	36	66.667%	66.667%
atis_abbreviation	33	76.768%	**87.879%**
atis_capacity	21	**84.127%**	82.540%
atis_airport	18	59.259%	**62.963%**
atis_flight#atis_airfare	12	41.667%	**47.222%**
atis_distance	10	40.000%	**43.333%**
atis_aircraft	9	**81.481%**	74.074%
atis_flight_no	8	100.000%	100.000%
atis_ground_fare	7	66.667%	66.667%
atis_city	6	**88.889%**	61.111%
atis_meal	6	55.556%	**77.778%**
atis_quantity	3	77.778%	**88.889%**
atis_day_name	2	0.000%	0.000%
atis_flight_time	1	33.333%	**66.667%**
atis_flight#atis_airline	1	**33.333%**	0.000%
atis_flight_no#atis_airline	1	33.333%	33.333%
atis_airfare#atis_flight	1	0.000%	0.000%

We run additional experiments to demonstrate that the maxBLEU filtering allows us to obtain higher quality utterances than simple random sampling. We randomly sample utterances from our GAN-generated dataset to match the utterance count yielded by maxBLEU filtering and add those to the original training set as shown in Table 5. We then train our NLU models on this dataset and obtain metric values for comparison. The results show that in all evaluations obtained using a train set augmented with maxBLEU filtered data significantly outperform those obtained using a train set augmented with random-sampled data (t-test $p < 0.1$). This shows that the maxBLEU filtering method helps in choosing utterances of significantly higher quality when compared to simple random sampling.

Table 5: Comparing maxBLEU filtering with random sampling.

method	slot F1	intent acc	sentence acc
rand sample, nd	95.910%	94.401%	86.861%
maxBLEU, nd	**96.172%**	**96.529%**	**89.959%***

4 Conclusions

We have explored a number of different approaches for augmented data evaluation, that we used as a filter for generated data. We evaluated the effectiveness of the evaluations metrics based on the selected targeted supervised NLU tasks, intent classification and named entity recognition. Experiments show that the maxBLEU filtering method without delexicalization produces the best overall/sentence accuracy, while weighted BERT-based classifier and Jaccard distance provide the best performance in terms of intent accuracy and slot F1 scores, respectively. Filtering through word-based sentence similarity measures - maxBLEU and Jaccard - show consistent improvement across all metrics, while BERT-based classifier with weighted loss function filtering significantly outperforms on intent classification task. We relate it to the fact that being trained on the intent recognition task on full sentences, the classifier network can capture the correctness of the utterance intents, while it underperforms on evaluating the correctness of the labels.

References

Ateret Anaby-Tavor, Boaz Carmeli, Esther Goldbraich, Amir Kantor, George Kour, Segev Shlomov, Naama

Tepper, and Naama Zwerdling. 2020. Do not have enough data? deep learning to the rescue! *Proceedings of the AAAI Conference on Artificial Intelligence*, 34(05):7383–7390.

Manik Bhandari, Pranav Narayan Gour, Atabak Ashfaq, and Pengfei Liu. 2020. Metrics also disagree in the low scoring range: Revisiting summarization evaluation metrics. In *Proceedings of the 28th International Conference on Computational Linguistics*, pages 5702–5711, Barcelona, Spain (Online). International Committee on Computational Linguistics.

Jacob Devlin, Ming-Wei Chang, Kenton Lee, and Kristina Toutanova. 2019. BERT: Pre-training of deep bidirectional transformers for language understanding. In *Proceedings of the 2019 Conference of the North American Chapter of the Association for Computational Linguistics: Human Language Technologies, Volume 1 (Long and Short Papers)*, pages 4171–4186, Minneapolis, Minnesota. Association for Computational Linguistics.

Olga Golovneva and Charith Peris. 2020. Generative adversarial networks for annotated data augmentation in data sparse nlu. *Computing Research Repository*, arXiv:2012.05302.

Edouard Grave, Piotr Bojanowski, Prakhar Gupta, Armand Joulin, and Tomas Mikolov. 2018. Learning word vectors for 157 languages. In *Proceedings of the Eleventh International Conference on Language Resources and Evaluation (LREC 2018)*, Miyazaki, Japan. European Language Resources Association (ELRA).

Charles T. Hemphill, John J. Godfrey, and George R. Doddington. 1990. The ATIS spoken language systems pilot corpus. In *Speech and Natural Language: Proceedings of a Workshop Held at Hidden Valley, Pennsylvania, June 24-27,1990.*

Y. Kim, S. Won, S. Yoon, and K. Jung. 2020. Collaborative training of gans in continuous and discrete spaces for text generation. *IEEE Access*, 8:226515–226523.

Alon Lavie and Abhaya Agarwal. 2007. METEOR: An automatic metric for MT evaluation with high levels of correlation with human judgments. In *Proceedings of the Second Workshop on Statistical Machine Translation*, pages 228–231, Prague, Czech Republic. Association for Computational Linguistics.

Chin-Yew Lin. 2004. ROUGE: A package for automatic evaluation of summaries. In *Text Summarization Branches Out*, pages 74–81, Barcelona, Spain. Association for Computational Linguistics.

Mingtong Liu, Erguang Yang, Deyi Xiong, Yujie Zhang, Yao Meng, Changjian Hu, Jinan Xu, and Yufeng Chen. 2020. A learning-exploring method to generate diverse paraphrases with multi-objective deep reinforcement learning. In *Proceedings of the 28th International Conference on Computational Linguistics*, pages 2310–2321, Barcelona, Spain (Online). International Committee on Computational Linguistics.

Ryan Lowe, Michael Noseworthy, Iulian Vlad Serban, Nicolas Angelard-Gontier, Yoshua Bengio, and Joelle Pineau. 2017. Towards an automatic Turing test: Learning to evaluate dialogue responses. In *Proceedings of the 55th Annual Meeting of the Association for Computational Linguistics (Volume 1: Long Papers)*, pages 1116–1126, Vancouver, Canada. Association for Computational Linguistics.

Ehsan Montahaei, Danial Alihosseini, and Mahdieh Soleymani Baghshah. 2019. Jointly measuring diversity and quality in text generation models. In *Proceedings of the Workshop on Methods for Optimizing and Evaluating Neural Language Generation*, pages 90–98, Minneapolis, Minnesota. Association for Computational Linguistics.

Kishore Papineni, Salim Roukos, Todd Ward, and Wei-Jing Zhu. 2002. Bleu: a method for automatic evaluation of machine translation. In *Proceedings of the 40th Annual Meeting of the Association for Computational Linguistics*, pages 311–318, Philadelphia, Pennsylvania, USA. Association for Computational Linguistics.

Matthew Peters, Mark Neumann, Mohit Iyyer, Matt Gardner, Christopher Clark, Kenton Lee, and Luke Zettlemoyer. 2018. Deep contextualized word representations. In *Proceedings of the 2018 Conference of the North American Chapter of the Association for Computational Linguistics: Human Language Technologies, Volume 1 (Long Papers)*, pages 2227–2237, New Orleans, Louisiana. Association for Computational Linguistics.

Libo Qin, Wanxiang Che, Yangming Li, Haoyang Wen, and Ting Liu. 2019. A stack-propagation framework with token-level intent detection for spoken language understanding. In *Proceedings of the 2019 Conference on Empirical Methods in Natural Language Processing and the 9th International Joint Conference on Natural Language Processing (EMNLP-IJCNLP)*, pages 2078–2087, Hong Kong, China. Association for Computational Linguistics.

Shikhar Sharma, Layla El Asri, Hannes Schulz, and Jeremie Zumer. 2017. Relevance of unsupervised metrics in task-oriented dialogue for evaluating natural language generation. *ArXiv*, abs/1706.09799.

Lichao Sun, Congying Xia, Wenpeng Yin, Tingting Liang, Philip Yu, and Lifang He. 2020. Mixup-transformer: Dynamic data augmentation for NLP tasks. In *Proceedings of the 28th International Conference on Computational Linguistics*, pages 3436–3440, Barcelona, Spain (Online). International Committee on Computational Linguistics.

Boya Yu, Konstantine Arkoudas, and Wael Hamza. 2020. Delexicalized paraphrase generation. In *Proceedings of the 28th International Conference on Computational Linguistics: Industry Track*, pages

102–112, Online. International Committee on Computational Linguistics.

Lantao Yu, Weinan Zhang, Jun Wang, and Yong Yu. 2017. Seqgan: Sequence generative adversarial nets with policy gradient. In *Thirty-First AAAI Conference on Artificial Intelligence*, pages 2852–2858. AAAI Press.

Yaoming Zhu, Sidi Lu, Lei Zheng, Jiaxian Guo, Weinan Zhang, Jun Wang, and Yong Yu. 2018. Texygen: A benchmarking platform for text generation models. In *The 41st International ACM SIGIR Conference on Research & Development in Information Retrieval*, SIGIR '18, pages 1097–1100, New York, NY, USA. Association for Computing Machinery.

Generating Coherent Narratives with Subtopic Planning to Answer How-to Questions

Pengshan Cai,[1] Mo Yu,[2] Fei Liu,[3] Hong Yu[1,4]

[1]Manning College of Information & Computer Sciences, University of Massachusetts, Amherst

[2]Wechat AI, Tencent

[3]Department of Computer Science, Emory University

[4]CHORDS, University of Massachusetts, Lowell

Abstract

Answering *how-to* questions remains a major challenge in question answering research. A vast number of narrow, long-tail questions cannot be readily answered using a search engine. Moreover, there is little to no annotated data available to help develop such systems. This paper makes a first attempt at generating coherent, long-form answers for *how-to* questions. We propose new architectures, consisting of passage retrieval, subtopic planning and narrative generation, to consolidate multiple relevant passages into a coherent, explanatory answer. Our subtopic planning module aims to produce a set of relevant, diverse subtopics that serve as the backbone for answer generation to improve topic coherence. We present extensive experiments on a WikiHow dataset repurposed for long-form question answering. Empirical results demonstrate that generating narratives to answer *how-to* questions is a challenging task. Nevertheless, our architecture incorporated with subtopic planning can produce high-quality, diverse narratives evaluated using automatic metrics and human assessment.[1]

1 Introduction

How-to question (e.g., "How to turn off news notification on my phone?") is an important question type. To find answers, most people resort to internet search. However, the answers usually scatter in different web pages, making the search time-consuming and inefficient. To remedy this issue, Wikihow.com offers a platform for experts to share their answers to *how-to* questions. Despite its valuable content, the total volume of Wikihow articles is still limited. By far, Wikihow has only collected around 74K articles, too few when compared to other open-collaborative databases (e.g. over 6M articles in Wikipedia, over 90M items in Wikidata). As a result, it would be valuable to both editors

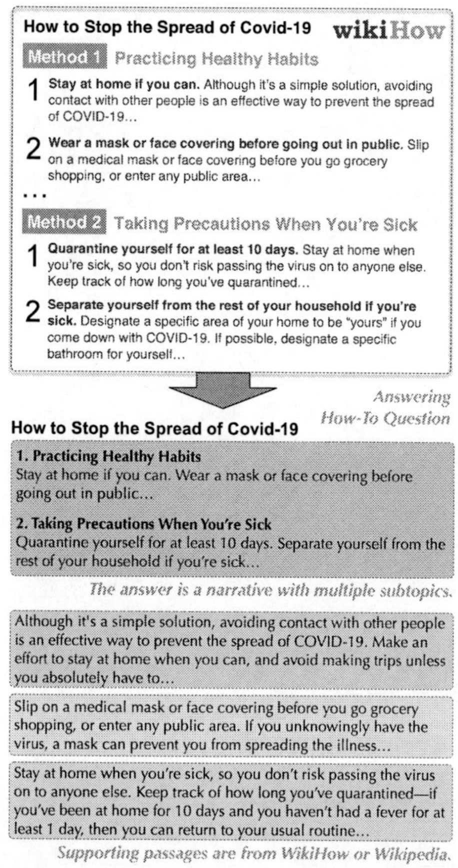

Figure 1: An example *how-to* question, its long-form answer and supporting passages.

and readers if NLP technology could be applied to automatically generate Wikihow entries to provide high quality answers to *how-to* questions.

Recent advances in generative QA researches have made it possible to generate answers to non-factoid questions (Tan et al., 2018; Nishida et al., 2019; Izacard and Grave, 2020). However, they have two limitations in generating an Wikihow entry: First, Wikihow presents answers in a hierarchical structure: an answer usually contains several sections, each led by a succinct subtopic. This

[1]We have made our dataset and source code available at https://github.com/pengshancai/how-to-QA

Proceedings of the 2nd Workshop on Natural Language Generation, Evaluation, and Metrics (GEM), pages 26 - 42
December 7, 2022 ©2022 Association for Computational Linguistics

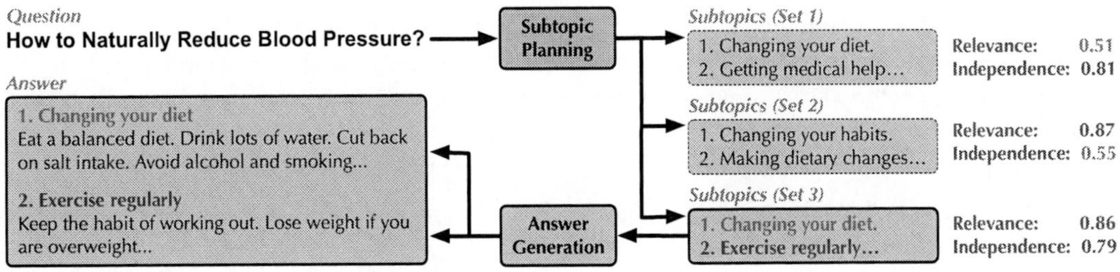

Figure 2: An overview of our *Arc-P* architecture for answering how-to questions. Given a question, our **subtopic planning module** generates multiple sets of subtopics using a sampling approach. It then automatically selects an optimal set of subtopics by measuring their *Relevance* and *Independence* (section 2.4). The selected subtopics are finally sent to the **answer generation module** to provide guidance to narrative generation.

structure helps readers with an overview of the answer scope before locating the details (Hearst and Pedersen, 1996). On the contrary, answers generated by current QA models are usually unstructured. Second, an informative and detailed answer is usually a long sequence of text. Due to exposure bias (He et al., 2019), long text generation suffers from the risk that the quality of generated text deteriorates as its length increases.

In this paper, we present a two-step approach to answering *how-to* questions. For each question, our **subtopic planning** module first generates several subtopics to cover different aspects of the question. Based on each subtopic, our **answer generation** module then generates a paragraph of text to elaborate the subtopic. Compared to previous generative question answering methods, our architecture has two advantages: (1) Subtopic planning allows presenting answers in a well-organized structure, which helps our readers to easily grasp the general idea of the answer, offering an easy-to-follow reading experience. Moreover, by generating answers from various subtopics, our architecture is able to provide answers with higher diversity in content. (2) Our architecture decreases the risk of exposure bias in the generated texts, by breaking down the answer into multiple shorter subsections instead of directly generating a long paragraph. In this way, it improves the generated answer's quality.

The quality of subtopics is crucial for the generation of long-form, explanatory answers. While a set of good subtopics can improve answer generation, a set of bad subtopics may digress the answer from the question. We observe two types of common mistakes in subtopic planning: (1) **Irrelevant subtopics**: a generated subtopic is not closely related to the question. For example, in Figure 2, the subtopic *Getting medical help* in the first subtopic set is not related to the question *how to naturally reduce blood pressure*; (2) **Redundant subtopics**: two or more generated subtopics to the same question have semantic overlap. For instance, in the second subtopic set in Figure 2, the subtopic *Making dietary changes* is included in the subtopic *Changing your habits*. This may further lead to repetition in subsequent answer generation.

We deal with these problems with an additional subtopic set selection step in the subtopic planning module. The key idea is to first generate multiple subtopic sets, and then evaluate their *relevance* and *independence* to select one optimal subtopic set for next-step processing. Specifically, we measure these two quantities in the vector space: We use a paragraph encoder (which in our work is the Dense Passage Retrieval model (Karpukhin et al., 2020)) to map the question and all the generated subtopics into a common embedding space. We then measure *relevance* and *independence* according to the subtopic vectors' relative distances and their distances to the question vector.

The contributions of our paper include:

- A novel *how-to* question answering architecture based on subtopic planning;
- An efficient vector-space model to evaluate and select high-quality subtopics to a question in terms of *relevance* and *independence*;
- Extensive experiments with human study that both prove the effectiveness of our methods and explore factors affecting the quality of *how-to* question answering results.

2 Model

2.1 General Architectures

A **retrieve-generate paradigm** consists of a retriever and a generator. Given a query x, the retriever first collects K supporting paragraphs

$P = \{p_1, ..., p_K\}$ from a large text corpus. The supporting paragraphs are expected to include external knowledge relevant to to x. The generator then outputs the result y based on x and P. We consider the following two architectures:

1) **Arc-Direct** (*Arc-D*) directly generates the answer from the question by applying the *retrieve-generate paradigm*;

2) **Arc-Planning** (*Arc-P*) (Figure 2) is composed of a subtopic planning module and an answer generation module. It generates an answer in a two-step manner: First, the subtopic planning module decomposes q into a set of N subtopics $S = \{s_1, ..., s_N\}$, for each subtopic $s_i, i \in \{1, ..., N\}$, the answer generation module generates a paragraph of explanation to the subtopic. We present all the subtopics and their explanation as the final answer. Both subtopic planning and answer generation modules apply the *retrieve-generate paradigm*. Specifically, during subtopic planning, all the subtopics are generated in one single sequence, and divided by a special separation token. During answer generation, supporting paragraphs for each individual subtopic are retrieved based on the question and the subtopic.

2.2 Retriever

We use dense passage retriever (DPR) (Karpukhin et al., 2020), a neural retrieving model as our retriever. DPR is composed of a query encoder E_X and a paragraph encoder E_P. E_X and E_P respectively encodes the query and potential paragraphs into vectors in a common embedding space, the relevance score of x and p is calculated as the inner product between two vectors.

$$sim(x, p) = E_X(x)^T E_P(p) \quad (1)$$

After gaining the relevance score of x to each paragraph in the large text corpus, we rank the paragraphs according to their relevance score, the top K paragraphs are selected as supporting paragraphs to x. Note that we use the same DPR retriever to retrieve supporting paragraphs for both question queries and subtopic queries. This embeds questions and subtopics in the same space, thus enables measuring the semantic relevance of a question and its subtopics as will be described in Section 2.4.

2.3 Generator

We employ BART-LARGE (Lewis et al., 2020a), a seq2seq Transformer model (Vaswani et al., 2017) pretrained with a denoising objective as our generator. The generator takes as input a concatenation of the query x and its relevant paragraphs P and outputs a sequence of words $y = \{y_1, ..., y_L\}$, where L is the length of y. Formally,

$$p(y|x, P) = \prod_{l=1}^{L} p(y_l|x, P, y_{1:l-1}) \quad (2)$$

We leverage BART to decode multiple subtopics, conditioned on the question and its supporting paragraphs. All subtopics of a question are concatenated to form the target sequence. To predict the l-th word of the sequence, our generator computes a probability distribution over the vocabulary tokens $p(w|q, P, y_{1:l-1})$. Instead of the argmax inference

$$y_l = \arg\max_{w} p(w|x, P, y_{1:l-1}), \quad (3)$$

we perform sampling from the top-*k* most probable tokens to obtain

$$y_l \sim p(w|x, P, y_{1:l-1}). \quad (4)$$

Our subtopic planning module attempts to generate multiple sets of subtopics using a sampling method. The method is advantageous over greedy decoding, which tend to produce high-likelihood rather than diverse sequences (Ippolito et al., 2019). The sets of subtopics will be subsequently measured by their *relevance* and *independence* to identify an optimal set of subtopics.

2.4 Subtopics Selection

While the generators are able to generate locally fluent text, they do not guarantee global semantic optimality (Holtzman et al., 2020, 2018). Specifically, during experiments, we observed that for the same question, the quality of different subtopic sets generated using *top-k* sampling from the same question vary greatly (Section 3.4). In this section, we explore the following question: How to automatically single out a high quality subtopic set from various generated ones.

By observing the subtopic planning results, we realize there exist two types of common mistakes in subtopic planning: 1. The subtopics is irrelevant to the question. 2. Subtopics have semantic overlap with each other.

We present a simple yet effective method to filter subtopics which may lead to the above mistakes. To this end we reuse the trained DPR retriever to measure the generated subtopic sets from two perspectives: 1. *Relevance*: How relevant each subtopic is to the question and 2. *Independence*: How much overlap the subtopics have with each other.

Formally, given a question q and a subtopic set S, we first transform q and each subtopic s_i in S into vectors $E_X(q)$ and $E_X(s_i)$ in the DPR embedding space. We define the neighbors of x, denoted as $\mathcal{N}_M(x)$, as the top M paragraphs whose DPR embeddings are closest to $E_X(x)$, where M is a human specified hyper-parameter.

Measuring relevance: We measure the relevance of a question q and a subtopic s_i as follows:

$$\text{relv}(q, S) = \frac{\sum_{s_i \in S} \# \left(\mathcal{N}_M(q) \cap \mathcal{N}_M(s_i)\right) / M}{|S|} \tag{5}$$

where $\#(\cdot)$ refers to the number of elements within a set. A higher relevance score indicates more paragraphs relevant to the question also relates to the subtopic, implying their semantic relevance.

Measuring Independence: We measure the independence of a set of subtopics as follows:

$$\text{indp}(S) = Avg\left(1 - \frac{\#(\mathcal{N}_M(s_i) \cap \mathcal{N}_M(s_j))}{M}\right) \tag{6}$$

A high independence score indicates a paragraph relevant to one subtopic may not be related to the other subtopics, implying low semantic overlap among subtopics.[2]

Selecting subtopics: A set of good subtopics needs to be balanced in both relevance and independence. As a result, we select a set of subtopics with the maximum independence subject to the minimum relevance of the subtopics greater than a human specified threshold τ.

2.5 Training

Retriever. When retrieving supporting paragraphs for a question q, we use the question itself as the query. When retrieving supporting paragraphs for a subtopic s, we use the concatenation of the q and s as the query. We train the retriever by optimizing the negative log likelihood loss:

$$L_R = -\log \frac{e^{\text{sim}(x,p^+)}}{e^{sim(x,p^+)} + \sum_{j=1}^{n} e^{\text{sim}(x,p_j^-)}} \tag{7}$$

where x is a query, positive paragraph p^+ is a gold supporting paragraph related to x, negative paragraphs $\{p_1^-, ..., p_n^-\}$ are randomly sampled from paragraphs unrelated to x.

Generator. After finished training the retriever, we use the retriever to collect supporting paragraphs as a part of training data to the generators[3]. When training the generator of both *Arc-D* and *Arc-P*'s subtopic planning module, we use the concatenation of the question and supporting paragraphs as input. When training the generator of *Arc-P*'s answer generation module, we use the concatenation of the question, subtopic and supporting paragraphs as input. We minimize the following maximum-likelihood objective function:

$$L_G = -\sum_{l=1}^{L} \log(p(y_l^* | x, P, y_{1:l-1}^*)) \tag{8}$$

where $y^* = \{y_1^*, ..., y_L^*\}$ is the ground-truth output sequence.

3 Experiments

3.1 Datasets

We build a dataset *HowQA* by reformatting *HowSum* (Koupaee and Wang, 2018), a summarization collected from *Wikihow*. Overall, our *HowQA* contains 72.4K Wikihow articles, we randomly split them into training/validation/test sets. As shown in Figure 1, each Wikihow article contains one *How to* question and several subtopics, each subtopic is followed by a few description paragraphs. Each paragraph starts with a summary sentence which summarizes the meaning of the rest of the paragraph. We collect all the summary sentences as the *explanation* to the subtopic, and the rest of the paragraphs as *gold supporting paragraphs* to the subtopic. We consider two large text corpora as source of supporting paragraphs: A. Wikihow training set; B. Wikipedia[4]. *HowQA* is used for training and testing both retriever and generator. We show the statistics of our *HowQA* in Table 1[5]

[2]We use the overlap of neighbors instead of the vector cosine similarity to calculate *relevance* and *independence* as the former directly reflects the overlap of potential supporting paragraphs input to the generator.

[3]We use the retrieved supporting paragraphs instead of gold supporting paragraphs as this better mimics the situation in test time, where gold supporting paragraphs are unavailable.

[4]We use Wikipedia as it is a trustworthy information source for a knowledge intensive task like ours. By default, results reported in the experiment are based on using Wikihow training set as the supporting paragraph corpus unless stated otherwise.

[5]See Appendix for implementation and evaluation details.

Dataset	# Questions	# Subtopics (Explanations)	# Supporting Paragraphs
Train	69,990	214,549	1,074,129
Validation	1,200	3,692	18,423
Test	1,231	3,770	18,680
Avg Length of Subtitle			4.02
Avg Length of Explanation			35.14
Avg Length of Wikihow-train Paragraphs			68.89
Avg Length of Wikipedia Paragraphs			100.00
# Paragraphs in Wikihow-train			1.1M
# Paragraphs in Wikipedia			21.0M

Table 1: Statistics of our *HowQA*.

3.2 Evaluation Metrics

Automatic Metrics. We evaluate our overall performance with two sets of metrics: (1) Surface-form coverage metrics, including ROUGE-1, ROUGE-2, ROUGE-L and METEOR that are commonly used in automatic summarization and machine translation. These metrics measure how many words in the groundtruths are covered by the generated answers; (2) Diversity metrics (Li et al., 2016; Hua et al., 2019a) is calculated by the number of distinct unigrams (distinct-1), bigrams (distinct-2) and trigrams (distinct-3) in the generated answers. The values are scaled by the length of the answer to avoid favoring long text. The best-performed system should have both high coverage and diversity scores.

For the study of retrievers, we evaluate two common document retrieval metrics: (1) Hit@10 (Bordes et al., 2013), i.e., the proportion of gold supporting paragraphs ranked in the top 10; (2) Mean reciprocal rank (MRR) (Radev et al., 2002).

Human Evaluation Metrics. We note that surface-form coverage metric may not necessarily reflect the quality of generated answers. It is limited in a situation when there are multiple ways to decompose a *How-to* question into subtopics. For instance, for the question "How to deal with loneliness", one subtopic set may emphasize embracing and enjoying loneliness, another may focus on encouraging social interaction and improving social skills. Both subtopic sets make good sense, their contents vary greatly. We thus resort to human judges to evaluate the quality of our answers.

Specifically, we collected our evaluation results using Amazon Mechanical Turk[6]. We randomly sample 90 questions from our test set. To evaluate **answer generation**, we present judges with several answers generated by different methods to the same question, and let judges rank their preference for the answers from the best to the worst. We report the average ranking for each model and pairwise preference for each pair of model. To evaluate **subtopic selection**, we ask our judges to evaluate subtopic sets from three perspectives: (1) *Relevance:* How close is each subtopic set related to the question; (2) *Independence:* How independent is each subtopic to the other subtopics in the same subtopic set; (3) *Overall Preference:* How do judges like the subtopic set. The grading scale for each perspective is from 1 to 3. For both tasks, each result is evaluated by ten individual judges.

3.3 Overall Performance with and without Subtopic Planning

In this section, we explore the effects of subtopic planning by comparing the overall answer generation performance of *Arc-D* and *Arc-P*. Evaluation results show that our proposed *Arc-P* gives clear advantage in both automatic and human evaluation.

• **Surface-form Coverage.** From Table 2 we observed that *Arc-P* achieves better performance than *Arc-D* in ROUGE and METEOR. This demonstrates our *Arc-P* generates better answers than *Arc-D* in terms of coverage of the original answer.

• **Content Diversity.** Table 2 shows the diversity degree of *Arc-D*, *Arc-P* and the golden answers. *Arc-P* significantly outperforms *Arc-D* in all distinct-1, 2 and 3. This proves that by answering questions from various perspectives, *Arc-P* is able to generate answers that are more diversified in content. However, there still exists gaps between *Arc-P* and the gold answer, this implies our generated answers still do not match human written answers in content diversity.

• **Human Evaluation.**[7] Given a question, we ask human judges to rank their preference for the gold answer and answers generated by *Arc-D* and *Arc-P* respectively. From Table 3 we observed human judges prefer answers from *Arc-P* much more than *Arc-D*'s. Comparing to *Arc-D*, our *Arc-P* wins on more than 72% of the cases. This demonstrates the effectiveness of subtopic planning.

The results also show that neither *Arc-D* nor *Arc-P* is comparable to human performance. A closer investigation of the machine generated answers

[6]We require our judges to have at least 100 previous jobs and greater than 95% acceptance rate.

[7]We present more examples and analysis in the appendix.

Models	Coverage				Diversity		
	ROUGE-1	ROUGE-2	ROUGE-L	METEOR	Distinct-1	Distinct-2	Distinct-3
Arc-Direct	26.13	6.37	25.54	16.64	57.85	73.64	78.42
Arc-Planning	**28.3**	**7.11**	**25.63**	**17.47**	**62.45**	**83.60**	**89.88**
Gold Answers	n/a	n/a	n/a	n/a	68.51	90.61	94.52

Table 2: Performance of *Arc-D* and *Arc-P* in answer generation. *Arc-P* achieves higher ROUGE and METEOR score.

Single Model	Average Rank ↓
Arc-D	2.48
Arc-P	**1.87**
Gold	**1.65**
Model Pair	**Prefer Rate ↑**
Arc-P > Arc-D	**72.22%**
Arc-P > Gold	**40.66%**
Arc-D > Gold	23.55%

Table 3: Average ranking of each model and pairwise preference rate between each pair of models.

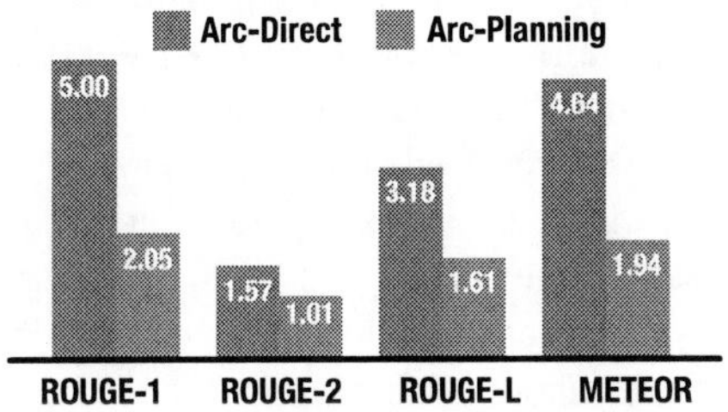

Figure 3: Score difference between part1 and part2.

Subtopic Set	R-1	R-2	R-L	METEOR
Low relv	27.53	6.59	24.83	17.27
Low indp	28.12	6.98	**25.64**	**17.57**
Selected	**28.3**	**7.11**	25.63	17.47
Oracle	28.93	8.11	25.96	19.87

Table 4: Automatic evaluation scores of answer generation when using different subtopic sets. *Selected* refers to the best subtopics set by our selecting metrics, *Low relv* and *Low indp* respectively refers to choosing the subtopic set with the lowest relevance and independence scores, *Oracle* refers to the oracle subtopics in Wikihow articles.

Subtopic Set	Relevance	Independence	Overall
Low relv	2.15	2.21	2.12
Low indp	2.30	2.07	2.02
Selected	**2.39**	**2.30**	**2.25**
Oracle	2.40	2.32	2.29

Table 5: Human evaluation scores for each subtopic set.

show that they sometimes make obvious logical mistakes. For example, for the question *How to Use Google Shopping Express*, the machine presents a generated fake sign-up URL.

Analysis of Degradation in Long Generation. We conduct analysis on *Arc-P*'s effectiveness. Our hypothesis is that by generating diverse answers, all parts of an answer from *Arc-P* convey useful information. To verify this, we design the following experiment: For each generated answer from *Arc-D* and *Arc-P*, we cut the answer into two parts of equal length from the middle. We then calculate each part's ROUGE and METEOR score to the golden standard. Figure 3 presents the score differences between part1 and part2. The performance gaps from *Arc-D* are significantly large, implying our *Arc-P* effectively avoids the performance degradation in long-form text generation, and generates answers of more consistent quality.

3.4 Effects of Subtopic Selection

In this section we analyze the effect of our subtopic selection algorithm in Section 2.4. We compare the qualities of our selected subtopics (*Selected*) with two variations: (1) selecting subtopic sets with lowest relevance (*Low relv*) and (2) selecting subtopic sets with lowest independence (*Low indp*). Similar to our overall evaluation, we conduct both the automatic evaluation and human evaluation as below:

Automatic Evaluation. Table 4 shows the performance of *Arc-P*'s answer when using different subtopic selections. We find that *Selected* gives better performance than *Low relv*. This implies irrelevant subtopics deteriorate the quality of subsequent answer generation. However, *Selected* shows similar performance to *Low indp* under the automatic metric. Considering the large performance gap from human evaluation, this confirms the problem of these coverage-based metrics that they overlook the semantic repetition of generation results.

Human Evaluation. Table 5 presents human evaluation results of the subtopic planning module of *Arc-P*. We observed score difference between *Selected*, *Low relv* and *Low indp*. This proves there exists quality discrepancy between different subtopic sets generated from the same question using *top-k* sampling. Specifically, *Low relv* and *Low indp* achieve the worst performance in *Relevance* and *Independence* respectively, this implies

	Category	R-1	R-2	R-L	METEOR	Portion (%)
WORST	*Work World*	25.17	4.27	22.1	16.52	1.72
	Health	25.72	5.97	25.24	16.94	14.21
	Holidays and Traditions	25.82	5.37	24.07	14.82	0.81
	Education and Communications	26.01	5.72	24.26	16.83	8.46
	Work World	26.01	3.93	26.56	15.64	0.7
BEST	*Cars & Other Vehicles*	30.15	8.11	26.17	18.32	1.7
	Youth	31.27	7.69	28.46	**21.22**	3.21
	Personal Care and Style	31.45	9.11	**28.67**	19.23	6.73
	Pets and Animals	32.52	9.96	26.99	20.13	6.6
	Food and Entertaining	**32.58**	**10.49**	27.17	19.49	8.03

Table 6: Performance of different categories. The performance between categories vary greatly (e.g. The highest difference in ROUGE-1 is over seven points). The training data portion for each category also varies greatly.

our vector space based metric is consistent with human rankings, and could distinguish unrelated and semantically overlapped subtopics. Moreover, *Selected* outperforms both *Low relv* and *Low indp* in all three metrics, and even achieves similar performance to *Gold*. This demonstrates our subtopic selection methods could effectively select subtopic sets with a higher quality.

3.5 Effects of Question Categories

Wikihow classifies all questions into 20 categories. We show in Table 6 the performance of 5 categories with the highest ROUGE-1 F1 score and 5 categories with the lowest[8]. From the table we have the following observations: 1. There exists a great discrepancy between performance of different categories. 2. Generally, if a category contains more data in the training set, it is more likely to demonstrates better performance. 3. However, a few categories with more training data (e.g. *Education and Communications*) achieved much lower performance than categories with less training data (e.g. *Cars and Other Vehicles*). We argue this is because in some categories, the answers to questions follow some specific routines. While in other categories, there is no answer routine to follow. For example, the category *Cars and Other Vehicles* contains many questions about installing car parts, e.g. *how to install a car starter, How to install a car stereo*, etc. The answer to these questions usually starts with removing the old car parts (Set the parking brake, stall the car, take out the old car parts, etc.) On the contrary, the category *Education and Communications* contains many primary/middle school math questions e.g. *How to calculate volume, how to divide double digits*, etc. The answers to these questions do not follow any pattern, and can not be answered routinely.

[8]We omit categories with <10 instances in the test set.

3.6 Effects of Other Factors

Effects of Retriever . We compare DPR with three other retrievers: 1) *TF-IDF* (Wu et al., 2008) measures the relevance between a query and a paragraph by the weighted sum of overlapped words between the query and the paragraph. 2) *None-RTV* use only the query as input to the generator; 3) *Oracle-RTV* uses the gold supporting paragraphs in oracle Wikihow article as supporting paragraphs; For each question, We rank all the supporting paragraphs in test set. We demonstrate the retrievers' performance in Table 7. We present in Table 8 the ROUGE and METEOR scores when using different retrievers to collect supporting paragraphs. For both architectures, *Oracle-RTV* outperforms *TF-IDF* and *DPR* by large margin, *TF-IDF* and *DRP* also outperforms None-RTV significantly. However, even *DPR* achieves much better performance than *TF-IDF* in retrieving evaluation, we do not notice prominent difference in answer generation. This implies the quality of supporting paragraphs has limited effects on generation results.

Retriever	Hits@10	MRR
TF-IDF	39.18	69.11
DPR	**54.67**	**87.76**
Oracle-RTV	100.00	100.00

Table 7: Performance of retrievers.

Effects of supporting paragraphs corpora. According to Figure 4, We do not observe explicit difference when using *Wikihow-train* and *Wikipedia* as corpus. However, we note that compared to Wikipedia, Wikihow-train is much smaller in volume. Thus in practice, Wikihow-train is a better choice for corpus as it takes less retrieving time.

Retriever	R-1	R-2	R-L	METEOR
		Arc-Direct - Answer Generation		
TF-IDF	26.4	6.41	25.53	17.15
DPR	26.13	6.37	25.54	16.64
None-RTV	17.65	4.53	18.52	8.02
Oracle-RTV	41.92	16.51	39/63	27.61
		Arc-Planning - Answer Generation		
TF-IDF	27.89	6.71	25.02	17.3
DPR	28.3	7.11	25.63	17.47
None-RTV	21.11	3.97	19.33	13.2
Oracle-RTV	46.45	18.94	43.05	32.32
		Arc-Planning - Subtopic Planning		
TF-IDF	23.0	7.89	23.79	17.13
DPR	23.04	7.8	23.57	16.59
None-RTV	16.36	4.68	17.17	11.39
Oracle-RTV	27.13	10.75	28.23	19.24

Table 8: Performance of answer generation when using different retrievers. Even though *DPR* outperforms *TF-IDF* by over 10 points in both Hit10 and MRR (Table7), their answer generation results are not prominently different.

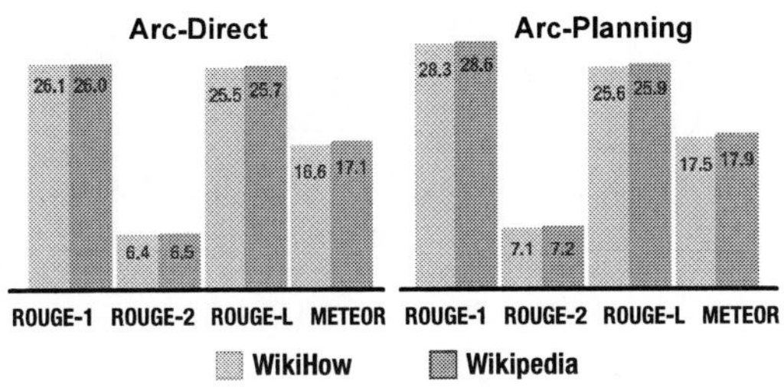

Figure 4: Performance of answer generation when using different supporting paragraph corpora. We find that the difference is not prominent.

4 Related Works

Question Answering Datasets Recent years has witnessed great advances in open domain question answering. However, most question answering datasets (Yang et al., 2018; Joshi et al., 2017; Rajpurkar et al., 2016; Dunn et al., 2017) are designed for factoid questions, i.e., questions that start with 'what', 'when', 'who', 'where', 'which', etc. and they require only extractive answers, i.e., the answers are spans of source text.

There exist several non-factoid question answering datasets (Dos Santos et al., 2015; Yang et al., 2015; Cohen et al., 2018; Nakov et al., 2017; Hashemi et al., 2019; Fan et al., 2019). Most of these datasets are proposed for the purpose of passage retrieval and re-ranking, i.e., the proposed tasks are ranking the provided evidence passages according to their relevance to a given question. No answer generation is involved. An exception is (Fan et al., 2019), which focus on non-factoid questions, i.e. questions start with "why," "how," and long-form answer generation, i.e. the answer is an elaborate and in-depth passage. Our work differs from ELI5 with a specific emphasis on *how-to* questions, and subtopic structures of their answers.

Question Answering Models As open domain question answering is a knowledge intensive task, most state of art models (Chen et al., 2017; Guu et al., 2020; Lewis et al., 2020b; Izacard and Grave, 2020; Asai et al., 2021) apply a "retrieve-generate" paradigm, where the retriever collects supporting paragraphs related to the question from a large external corpus, the generator then generates an answer based on the question and the supporting paragraphs. Compared to previous works which apply the "retrieve-generate" paradigm, we use the retriever not only to retrieve supporting paragraphs, but also to evaluate and select subtopics.

Planning Based Text Generation Content planning is widely used to improve diversity and coherence in various text generation tasks including story generation (Yao et al., 2019; Goldfarb-Tarrant et al., 2019), argument generation (Hua et al., 2019b), Wikipedia article generation (Hua and Wang, 2019) and abstractive summarization (Liu et al., 2015; Huang et al., 2020) etc. While most research studies resort to key words or knowledge graph entities for content planning, we use subtopics for planning our answers.

Procedural Text Our work is also related to procedural text understanding such as recipes (Tandon et al., 2020; Rajagopal et al., 2020; Du et al., 2019; Dalvi et al., 2019; Tandon et al., 2019; Chu et al., 2017). However, instead of tracking state changes in procedure text, we focus on generating subtopics to improve the coherence of answers.

Wikihow In previous researches, Wikihow data (Koupaee and Wang, 2018) was mostly used in summarization (Zhang et al., 2019; Kryscinski et al., 2019) or step reasoning (Zhang et al., 2020), The task we propose aims at different goals, i.e, decomposing a question into subtopics and generating answer based on the question and subtopics.

5 Conclusion and Future Work

We proposed a novel subtopic planning based architecture for answering *How-to* questions. Our architecture is able to generate answers with better structure, higher diversity and more consistent quality. Moreover, our subtopic selection method effectively singles out high quality subtopics with relevance and independence. Both automatic and human evaluation proved the effectiveness of our methods. We consider the two directions for future research: 1) Improving the answer's quality by applying end-to-end retrieval-generation models, e.g. (Lewis et al., 2020b). 2) Developing precise metrics to evaluate long-form and non-factoid answers.

Acknowledgement

We are grateful to the reviewers for their insightful comments. Fei Liu is supported in part by National Science Foundation grant IIS-2303678. Hong Yu is supported in part by UMass Lowell startup fund.

References

Akari Asai, Jungo Kasai, Jonathan H. Clark, Kenton Lee, Eunsol Choi, and Hannaneh Hajishirzi. 2021. XOR QA: Cross-lingual open-retrieval question answering. In *Proceedings of the North American Chapter of the Association for Computational Linguistics (NAACL)*.

Antoine Bordes, Nicolas Usunier, Alberto Garcia-Duran, Jason Weston, and Oksana Yakhnenko. 2013. Translating embeddings for modeling multi-relational data. In *Advances in neural information processing systems*, pages 2787–2795.

Danqi Chen, Adam Fisch, Jason Weston, and Antoine Bordes. 2017. Reading Wikipedia to answer open-domain questions. In *Proceedings of the 55th Annual Meeting of the Association for Computational Linguistics (Volume 1: Long Papers)*, pages 1870–1879, Vancouver, Canada. Association for Computational Linguistics.

Cuong Xuan Chu, Niket Tandon, and Gerhard Weikum. 2017. Distilling task knowledge from how-to communities. In *Proceedings of the 26th International Conference on World Wide Web*, pages 805–814.

Daniel Cohen, Liu Yang, and W Bruce Croft. 2018. Wikipassageqa: A benchmark collection for research on non-factoid answer passage retrieval. In *The 41st International ACM SIGIR Conference on Research & Development in Information Retrieval*, pages 1165–1168.

Bhavana Dalvi, Niket Tandon, Antoine Bosselut, Wen-tau Yih, and Peter Clark. 2019. Everything happens for a reason: Discovering the purpose of actions in procedural text. In *Proceedings of the 2019 Conference on Empirical Methods in Natural Language Processing and the 9th International Joint Conference on Natural Language Processing (EMNLP-IJCNLP)*, pages 4496–4505, Hong Kong, China. Association for Computational Linguistics.

Cicero Dos Santos, Luciano Barbosa, Dasha Bogdanova, and Bianca Zadrozny. 2015. Learning hybrid representations to retrieve semantically equivalent questions. In *Proceedings of the 53rd Annual Meeting of the Association for Computational Linguistics and the 7th International Joint Conference on Natural Language Processing (Volume 2: Short Papers)*, pages 694–699.

Xinya Du, Bhavana Dalvi, Niket Tandon, Antoine Bosselut, Wen-tau Yih, Peter Clark, and Claire Cardie. 2019. Be consistent! improving procedural text comprehension using label consistency. In *Proceedings of the 2019 Conference of the North American Chapter of the Association for Computational Linguistics: Human Language Technologies, Volume 1 (Long and Short Papers)*, pages 2347–2356, Minneapolis, Minnesota. Association for Computational Linguistics.

Matthew Dunn, Levent Sagun, Mike Higgins, V Ugur Guney, Volkan Cirik, and Kyunghyun Cho. 2017. Searchqa: A new q&a dataset augmented with context from a search engine. *arXiv preprint arXiv:1704.05179*.

Angela Fan, Yacine Jernite, Ethan Perez, David Grangier, Jason Weston, and Michael Auli. 2019. ELI5: Long form question answering. In *Proceedings of the 57th Annual Meeting of the Association for Computational Linguistics*, pages 3558–3567, Florence, Italy. Association for Computational Linguistics.

Seraphina Goldfarb-Tarrant, Haining Feng, and Nanyun Peng. 2019. Plan, write, and revise: an interactive system for open-domain story generation.

Kelvin Guu, Kenton Lee, Zora Tung, Panupong Pasupat, and Ming-Wei Chang. 2020. Realm: Retrieval-augmented language model pre-training. *arXiv preprint arXiv:2002.08909*.

Helia Hashemi, Mohammad Aliannejadi, Hamed Zamani, and W Bruce Croft. 2019. Antique: A non-factoid question answering benchmark. *arXiv preprint arXiv:1905.08957*.

Tianxing He, Jingzhao Zhang, Zhiming Zhou, and James Glass. 2019. Quantifying exposure bias for neural language generation. *arXiv preprint arXiv:1905.10617*.

Marti A Hearst and Jan O Pedersen. 1996. Reexamining the cluster hypothesis: scatter/gather on retrieval results. In *Proceedings of the 19th annual international ACM SIGIR conference on Research and development in information retrieval*, pages 76–84.

Ari Holtzman, Jan Buys, Li Du, Maxwell Forbes, and Yejin Choi. 2020. The curious case of neural text degeneration. In *International Conference on Learning Representations*.

Ari Holtzman, Jan Buys, Maxwell Forbes, Antoine Bosselut, David Golub, and Yejin Choi. 2018. Learning to write with cooperative discriminators. In *Proceedings of the 56th Annual Meeting of the Association for Computational Linguistics (Volume 1: Long Papers)*, pages 1638–1649, Melbourne, Australia. Association for Computational Linguistics.

Xinyu Hua, Zhe Hu, and Lu Wang. 2019a. Argument generation with retrieval, planning, and realization. In *Proceedings of the 57th Annual Meeting of the Association for Computational Linguistics*, pages 2661–2672, Florence, Italy. Association for Computational Linguistics.

Xinyu Hua, Zhe Hu, and Lu Wang. 2019b. Argument generation with retrieval, planning, and realization. In *Proceedings of the 57th Annual Meeting of the Association for Computational Linguistics*, pages 2661–2672, Florence, Italy. Association for Computational Linguistics.

Xinyu Hua and Lu Wang. 2019. Sentence-level content planning and style specification for neural text generation. In *Proceedings of the 2019 Conference on Empirical Methods in Natural Language Processing and the 9th International Joint Conference on Natural Language Processing (EMNLP-IJCNLP)*, pages 591–602, Hong Kong, China. Association for Computational Linguistics.

Luyang Huang, Lingfei Wu, and Lu Wang. 2020. Knowledge graph-augmented abstractive summarization with semantic-driven cloze reward. In *Proceedings of the 58th Annual Meeting of the Association for Computational Linguistics*, pages 5094–5107, Online. Association for Computational Linguistics.

Daphne Ippolito, Reno Kriz, João Sedoc, Maria Kustikova, and Chris Callison-Burch. 2019. Comparison of diverse decoding methods from conditional language models. In *Proceedings of the 57th Annual Meeting of the Association for Computational Linguistics*, pages 3752–3762, Florence, Italy. Association for Computational Linguistics.

Gautier Izacard and Edouard Grave. 2020. Leveraging passage retrieval with generative models for open domain question answering. *arXiv preprint arXiv:2007.01282*.

Mandar Joshi, Eunsol Choi, Daniel Weld, and Luke Zettlemoyer. 2017. TriviaQA: A large scale distantly supervised challenge dataset for reading comprehension. In *Proceedings of the 55th Annual Meeting of the Association for Computational Linguistics (Volume 1: Long Papers)*, pages 1601–1611, Vancouver, Canada. Association for Computational Linguistics.

Vladimir Karpukhin, Barlas Oguz, Sewon Min, Patrick Lewis, Ledell Wu, Sergey Edunov, Danqi Chen, and Wen-tau Yih. 2020. Dense passage retrieval for open-domain question answering. In *Proceedings of the 2020 Conference on Empirical Methods in Natural Language Processing (EMNLP)*, pages 6769–6781, Online. Association for Computational Linguistics.

Mahnaz Koupaee and William Yang Wang. 2018. Wikihow: A large scale text summarization dataset. *arXiv preprint arXiv:1810.09305*.

Wojciech Kryscinski, Nitish Shirish Keskar, Bryan McCann, Caiming Xiong, and Richard Socher. 2019. Neural text summarization: A critical evaluation. In *Proceedings of the 2019 Conference on Empirical Methods in Natural Language Processing and the 9th International Joint Conference on Natural Language Processing (EMNLP-IJCNLP)*, pages 540–551, Hong Kong, China. Association for Computational Linguistics.

Mike Lewis, Yinhan Liu, Naman Goyal, Marjan Ghazvininejad, Abdelrahman Mohamed, Omer Levy, Veselin Stoyanov, and Luke Zettlemoyer. 2020a. BART: Denoising sequence-to-sequence pre-training for natural language generation, translation, and comprehension. In *Proceedings of the 58th Annual Meeting of the Association for Computational Linguistics*, pages 7871–7880, Online. Association for Computational Linguistics.

Patrick Lewis, Ethan Perez, Aleksandara Piktus, Fabio Petroni, Vladimir Karpukhin, Naman Goyal, Heinrich Küttler, Mike Lewis, Wen-tau Yih, Tim Rocktäschel, et al. 2020b. Retrieval-augmented generation for knowledge-intensive nlp tasks. *arXiv preprint arXiv:2005.11401*.

Jiwei Li, Michel Galley, Chris Brockett, Jianfeng Gao, and Bill Dolan. 2016. A diversity-promoting objective function for neural conversation models. In *Proceedings of the 2016 Conference of the North American Chapter of the Association for Computational Linguistics: Human Language Technologies*, pages 110–119, San Diego, California. Association for Computational Linguistics.

Fei Liu, Jeffrey Flanigan, Sam Thomson, Norman Sadeh, and Noah A. Smith. 2015. Toward abstractive summarization using semantic representations. In *Proceedings of the 2015 Conference of the North American Chapter of the Association for Computational Linguistics: Human Language Technologies*, pages 1077–1086, Denver, Colorado. Association for Computational Linguistics.

Preslav Nakov, Doris Hoogeveen, Lluís Màrquez, Alessandro Moschitti, Hamdy Mubarak, Timothy Baldwin, and Karin Verspoor. 2017. SemEval-2017 task 3: Community question answering. In *Proceedings of the 11th International Workshop on Semantic Evaluation (SemEval-2017)*, pages 27–48, Vancouver, Canada. Association for Computational Linguistics.

Kyosuke Nishida, Itsumi Saito, Kosuke Nishida, Kazutoshi Shinoda, Atsushi Otsuka, Hisako Asano, and Junji Tomita. 2019. Multi-style generative reading comprehension. In *Proceedings of the 57th Annual Meeting of the Association for Computational Linguistics*, pages 2273–2284, Florence, Italy. Association for Computational Linguistics.

Dragomir R Radev, Hong Qi, Harris Wu, and Weiguo Fan. 2002. Evaluating web-based question answering systems. In *LREC*.

Dheeraj Rajagopal, Niket Tandon, Peter Clark, Bhavana Dalvi, and Eduard Hovy. 2020. What-if I ask you to explain: Explaining the effects of perturbations in procedural text. In *Findings of the Association for Computational Linguistics: EMNLP 2020*, pages 3345–3355, Online. Association for Computational Linguistics.

Pranav Rajpurkar, Jian Zhang, Konstantin Lopyrev, and Percy Liang. 2016. SQuAD: 100,000+ questions for machine comprehension of text. In *Proceedings of the 2016 Conference on Empirical Methods in Natural Language Processing*, pages 2383–2392, Austin, Texas. Association for Computational Linguistics.

Chuanqi Tan, Furu Wei, Nan Yang, Bowen Du, Weifeng Lv, and Ming Zhou. 2018. S-net: From answer extraction to answer synthesis for machine reading comprehension. In *AAAI*.

Niket Tandon, Bhavana Dalvi, Keisuke Sakaguchi, Peter Clark, and Antoine Bosselut. 2019. WIQA: A dataset for "what if..." reasoning over procedural text. In *Proceedings of the 2019 Conference on Empirical Methods in Natural Language Processing and the 9th International Joint Conference on Natural Language Processing (EMNLP-IJCNLP)*, pages 6076–6085, Hong Kong, China. Association for Computational Linguistics.

Niket Tandon, Keisuke Sakaguchi, Bhavana Dalvi, Dheeraj Rajagopal, Peter Clark, Michal Guerquin, Kyle Richardson, and Eduard Hovy. 2020. A dataset for tracking entities in open domain procedural text. In *Proceedings of the 2020 Conference on Empirical Methods in Natural Language Processing (EMNLP)*, pages 6408–6417, Online. Association for Computational Linguistics.

Ashish Vaswani, Noam Shazeer, Niki Parmar, Jakob Uszkoreit, Llion Jones, Aidan N Gomez, Łukasz Kaiser, and Illia Polosukhin. 2017. Attention is all you need. In *Advances in neural information processing systems*, pages 5998–6008.

Ho Chung Wu, Robert Wing Pong Luk, Kam Fai Wong, and Kui Lam Kwok. 2008. Interpreting tf-idf term weights as making relevance decisions. *ACM Transactions on Information Systems (TOIS)*, 26(3):1–37.

Yi Yang, Wen-tau Yih, and Christopher Meek. 2015. Wikiqa: A challenge dataset for open-domain question answering. In *Proceedings of the 2015 conference on empirical methods in natural language processing*, pages 2013–2018.

Zhilin Yang, Peng Qi, Saizheng Zhang, Yoshua Bengio, William Cohen, Ruslan Salakhutdinov, and Christopher D. Manning. 2018. HotpotQA: A dataset for diverse, explainable multi-hop question answering. In *Proceedings of the 2018 Conference on Empirical Methods in Natural Language Processing*, pages 2369–2380, Brussels, Belgium. Association for Computational Linguistics.

Lili Yao, Nanyun Peng, Ralph Weischedel, Kevin Knight, Dongyan Zhao, and Rui Yan. 2019. Plan-and-write: Towards better automatic storytelling. In *Proceedings of the AAAI Conference on Artificial Intelligence*, volume 33, pages 7378–7385.

Jingqing Zhang, Yao Zhao, Mohammad Saleh, and Peter J. Liu. 2019. Pegasus: Pre-training with extracted gap-sentences for abstractive summarization.

Li Zhang, Qing Lyu, and Chris Callison-Burch. 2020. Reasoning about goals, steps, and temporal ordering with WikiHow. In *Proceedings of the 2020 Conference on Empirical Methods in Natural Language Processing (EMNLP)*, pages 4630–4639, Online. Association for Computational Linguistics.

A Appendices

A.1 Example Subtopic Sets

We observe that some system-generated subtopic sets are flawed, but a large portion of the subtopic sets are of good quality. Some of them are close to human-written subtopics. Examples are provided in Table 9 (examples 1–6). Moreover, we come up with imaginary questions that are quite different from those observed in Wikihow (examples 5–6) and we find the model is able to produce reasonable answers for those questions.

Irrelevant subtopics generated by our model tend to have the following characteristics:

1. **A later generated subtopic in the subtopic set tends to be less relevant**: Note that we generate a set of subtopics in a seq2seq manner, with the question and supporting documents as the source sequence, and the concatenation of all subtopics as the target sequence. Due to exposure bias (He et al., 2019), subtopic generated in the later part of the sequence are more likely to be off-topic. Examples of this kind are included in Table 9 (examples 7–10). While the subtopics in the front part are all related to the question, the later generated subtopics, marked in red, tend to deviate from the question.

2. **Commonsense mistakes**: We observe that when the question is about a problem that requires commonsense, the model tends to generate unrelated or erroneous subtopics. E.g. in Table 9 example 9, the location services have nothing to do with facebook like notification.

It suggests that incorporating commonsense knowledge may improve the performance of a subtopic decomposition model.

Overlapped subtopics generated by our model tend to have the following characteristics:

- Thanks to a repetition penalty, the generated subtopics of the same subtopic set are usually different from each other. I.e., there are only very few cases where multiple subtopics of the same subtopic set are identical. However, there is no guarantee that those generated subtopics are semantically independent. E.g., in Table 9 example 11–12, the orange subtopics have semantic overlap. According to our experimental results, the vector-space based metrics could effectively identify those semantically overlapped subtopics.

A.2 Example Long-Form Answers

Table 10 shows example answers generated by **Arc-D** and **Arc-P** models, respectively. Notable findings include the following observations:

1. Subtopics make a long answer more organized. The answers generated by **Arc-P** are split into multiple paragraphs, each paragraph focuses on a subtopic. In contrast, answers generated by **Arc-D** are quite general and sometimes disordered. Additionally, answers generated by **Arc-P** are easier to read than those of **Arc-D**, as the model leverages subtopics to generate structured answers.

2. As the target sequence gets longer, the quality of the generated sequence tends to deteriorate due to exposure bias. This is demonstrated in Table 10 example 1, where the model repeatedly generates the red part in the later stage of the generation process. Instead of generating a long paragraph as the answer, **Arc-P** generates several shorter answer paragraphs, thus reducing the risk of exposure bias.

A.3 Implementation and Hyperparameters

Both *Arc-D* and *Arc-P* are based on a retrieval-composing paradigm, which consists of a retrieval module (DPR) and a composing module (BART). We discuss the model implementation details and hyperparameters below.

A.3.1 Retrieval module (DPR) key parameters and implementation details

- Batch size: 80 (which means one positive instance corresponds to 79 negative, including 1 hard negative instance);
- Max sequence length: 256;
- Training epochs: 12 (during testing, we use the model that gives the best validation loss);
- The other hyper-parameters are based on the default parameter of DPR: `https://github.com/facebookresearch/DPR`
- DPR is trained on 4 M40 GPUs;
- Given a question, we search for a similar paragraph that has high TF-IDF similarity with the question, but is not among the question's gold supporting paragraphs as a **hard negative instance**;
- DPR is pretrained on *fairseq/roberta-base*;
- When measuring *relevance* and *independence*, we choose the top $M = 500$ paragraphs whose DPR embeddings are closest to $E_X(x)$.

A.3.2 Composing module (BART) key parameters and implementation details

- BART-large pre-trained on *yjernite/bart_eli5*;
- Max number of tokens input: 1024 (for *Arc-D*), 512 (For *Arc-P*);
- Max number of tokens output: 384 (for *Arc-D*), 128 (For *Arc-P*);
- Max number of training epochs: 9 (during testing, we use the model that gives the best validation loss);
- Learning rate: 3e-5;
- The other hyper-parameters are based on the default parameters of huggingface's BART model: `https://huggingface.co/transformers/model_doc/bart.html`
- For each question, we use *top-k* sampling to generate 10 different subtopic sets.
- The BART is trained on a single M40 GPU, the average training time is up to 4-5 days.

ID		Question & Subtopics
		Fine Subtopic Sets Produced by the Model
1	**Q**	How to be glamorous?
	G	1.Caring for your body; 2. Applying makeup; 3.Dressing glamorous
	H	1.Looking glamorous; 2.Dressing glamorous; 3.Acting glamorous
2	**Q**	How to maintain a relationship?
	G	1.Communicating your needs; 2.Keeping the romance alive; 3.Avoiding conflict
	H	1.Love them for who they are; 2.Be a good listener; 3.Be nice
3	**Q**	How to lose extreme weight?
	G	1.Eating the right foods; 2.Exercising the right way; 3.Managing emotional and mental health
	H	1.Setting a weight loss goal; 2.Designing a weight loss diet; 3.Using exercise to support weight loss; 4.Staying motivated
4	**Q**	How to coach youth basketball?
	G	1.Finding players; 2.Preparing for practice; 3.Developing effective coaching skills
	H	1.Preparing yourself; 2.Meeting your players; 3.Putting your knowledge to work
5	**Q**	How to train a dragon
	G	1.Training your dragon; 2.Mastering the dragon's flight
6	**Q**	How to master Shinobi kill
	G	1.Mastering the technique; 2. Mastering the art of killing
		Flawed Subtopic Sets Produced by the Model
7	**Q**	How to fold jeans?
	G	1. Making a triangle fold; 2.Making a rectangle fold; 3.Folding a t-shirt
	H	1. Folding jeans; 2.Storing folded jeans
8	**Q**	How to coach youth basketball?
	G	1. Becoming a good coach; 2.Developing your skills; 3.Finding a job
	H	1.Preparing yourself; 2.Meeting your players; 3.Putting your knowledge to work
9	**Q**	How to turn off facebook like notifications on iphone?
	G	1. Disabling facebook like notifications; 2. Disabling location services
	H	1. disabling notifications for a single post; 2.Disabling all facebook notifications
10	**Q**	How to switch keyboard input languages in windows 8?
	G	1. Switching keyboard input language; 2. Using the task manager
	H	1. Switching through the settings charm; 2.Switching through the taskbar on the desktop; 3. Switching through keyboard shortcuts
11	**Q**	How to maintain a relationship?
	G	1. Maintaining a healthy relationship; 2. Keeping the relationship strong; 3. Avoiding toxic relationships
	H	1.Love them for who they are; 2.Be a good listener; 3.Be nice
12	**Q**	How to start a business in New York city
	G	1. Developing your business plan; 2.Creating a marketing plan; 3. ...
	H	1.Using city services to get your business started 2.Determining your market

Table 9: Examples of system-generated subtopics. **Q** refers to a question, **G** refers to a subtopic set generated by our model, **H** refers to the subtopic set provided by human editors from Wikihow. The red subtopics are unrelated to the question, the orange subtopics have semantic overlap among themselves, the blue questions are imaginative questions made-up by the authors.

ID		Question & Answers
1	Q	**How to Give Yourself Insulin?**
	Arc-D	Determine if you need insulin. Prepare the insulin. Place the syringe in your arm. Use a needle for the injection. Inject the insulin into your skin. Do not remove the needle. Check for bleeding. Remove the needle. Prepare the insulin. Place the syringe in your arm. ... (repeated generation)
	Arc-P	**1.Getting Ready to Give Yourself Insulin:** Prepare the insulin for injection. Check your bloodsugar. Know when to give yourself insulin. Find a good needle and syringe. Clean your syringe thoroughly . Decide where to give yourself insulin. **2.Administering the Insulin Injection:** Wash your hands thoroughly with soap and water. Determine the injection site. Position the needle at a 45-degree angle to the skin. Inject the insulin into the skin. Wait for the insulin to release. Remove the needle from the skin. **3.Knowing when to Avoid Insulin Injections:** Know the risks of insulin injections. Recognize the symptoms of diabetes. Watch for signs of complications. See your doctor.
2	Q	**How to Not Worry About Something?**
	Arc-D	Think about what you're worried about. Make a worry list. Put your worries into perspective. Take some time to be in the moment. Practice mindfulness. Talk to someone. Write down your worries. Do something you enjoy. Get enough sleep. Focus on the positive. Avoid rumination. Recognize when you need professional help. See a therapist. Join a support group.
	Arc-P	**1.Facing Your Worries:** Practice mindfulness. Accept uncertainty. Set realistic goals. Don't compare yourself to others. **2.Making Time for Relaxation:** Make time for exercise. Get enough sleep. Don't procrastinate.Set aside time to think about the future **3.Taking Care of Yourself:** Get enough sleep. Eat a healthy diet. Exercise regularly. Find ways to relax. Take care of your body.
3	Q	**How to Get Your Band Noticed?**
	Arc-D	Make a website. Create a Facebook page. Create a Twitter account. Create an Instagram account. Create a YouTube account. Create a blog. Play gigs. Find a manager. Contact music labels. Perform locally. Get your music out there. Write songs. Record your music. Publish your music. Distribute your music.
	Arc-P	**1.Developing Your Band's Music:** Record your songs. Make a demo tape. Put your music on YouTube. Start a blog. Get an agent. **2.Promoting Your Band Online:** Promote your band on social media sites. Create a blog. Start a YouTube account. Get listed in music publications. **3.Promoting Your Band in Person:** Play in front of friends and family. Go to local shows. Promote your music on social media. Make a scrapbook.
4	Q	**How to Buy a Racehorse?**
	Arc-D	Determine what you want in a horse. Decide how much money you can afford to spend on a horse. Consider your finances. Find a good breeder. Research the condition of the horse. Check the horse's pedigree. Assess the horse's temperament. Look at the horse's past. Ask about the horse's health. Make sure that you have enough money before you buy the horse. Buy the horse from a reputable breeder. Purchase the horse from a trustworthy seller. Do not buy a horse from a pet store.
	Arc-P	**1.Deciding to Buy a Racehorse:** Consider the horse's pedigree. Think about the horse's age. Consider the horse's breed. Consider the horse's physical condition. Consider the horse's temperament. **2.Buying a Racehorse in Person:** Decide what type of horse you want to buy. Visit several barns and showmen. Make an appointment with the salesperson. **3.Buying a Racehorse Online:** Find a horse to buy. Search for the horse online. Purchase your horse.

Table 10: Examples of system-generated answers with or without subtopics.

- We balance equation 5 and 6 using a hyper-parameter τ, specifically, the final score of a subtopic set S to a question q is calculated as

$$\text{Score}(S, q) = \tau\text{Relv}(S, q) + (1 - \tau)\text{Indp}(S)$$

We determine τ by heuristically tuning on validation set (MMR). We did so because the quality of high-quality subtopics may not be reflected by automatic coverage-based metrics. During experiment, we set $\tau = 0.3$.

A.4 Evaluation

A.4.1 Automatic Evaluation

We use the python library rouge 1.0.0 to calculate ROUGE: `https://pypi.org/project/rouge/`; METEOR: `https://www.nltk.org/_modules/nltk/translate/meteor_score.html`

A.4.2 Human Evaluation

We recruit Amazon Turks to work on two tasks: (a) **1. Answer Preference**, where we ask the Turks to rank three answers to a given question according to their preference; (b) **2. Subtopic Selection**, where we ask our judges to grade subtopic sets from three perspectives: Relevance, Independence and Overall Preference, on the scale of 1-3 points. The grading guidelines are given below:

1. **Relevance**: How close is each subtopic set related to the question; (1-point: One or more subtopic is clearly not relevant to the question; 2-points: One or more subtopics may not relate to the question so well; 3-points: All subtopics are related to the question.)

2. **Independence**: How independent is each subtopic to the other subtopics in the same subtopic set; (1-point: There is a clear meaning overlap (or repetition) between a few subtopics; 2-points: There is a weak meaning overlap between a few subtopics; 3-points: There is no meaning overlap between subtopics.)

3. **Overall Preference** :How do judges like the subtopic set. The grading scale for each perspective is from 1 to 3. (1: A bad set of subtopics for the question; 2: An acceptable but not good subtopics for the question; 3: A good subtopics for the question)

Answer preference	47%
Subtopic-Relevance	36%
Subtopic-Independence	45%
Subtopic-Overall	39%

Table 11: Inter-annotator agreement of human evaluations

We present the screenshots of our AMTurk pages in Figure 5 and 6. We measure inter-annotator agreement using Cohen's Kappa (k), the results are presented in Table 11.

A.5 Dataset

We re-purpose the WikihowSum datasetfor our task. The source code for processing the data has been included in our project repository.

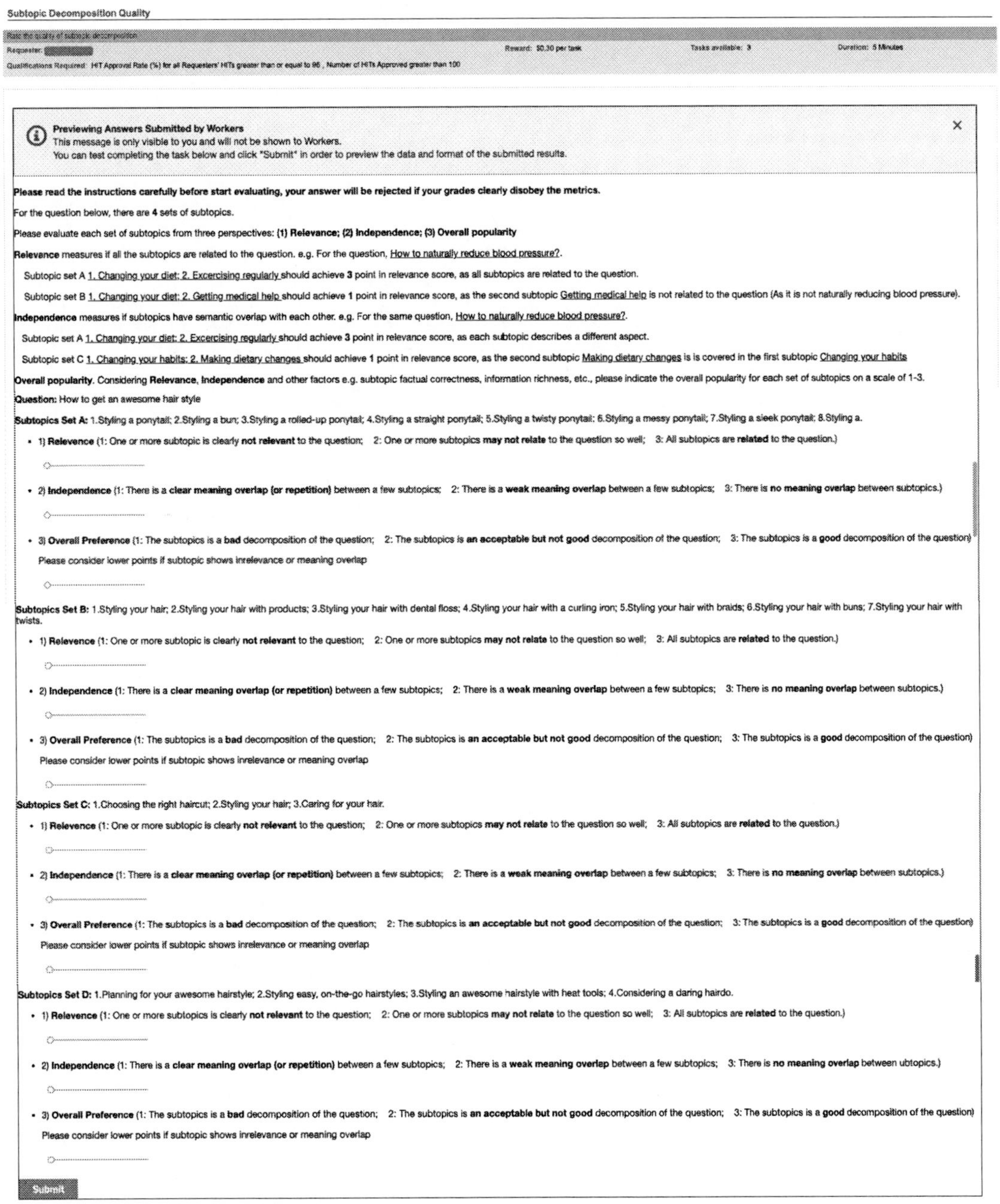

Figure 5: A screenshot of subtopic evaluation performed by mechanical turkers.

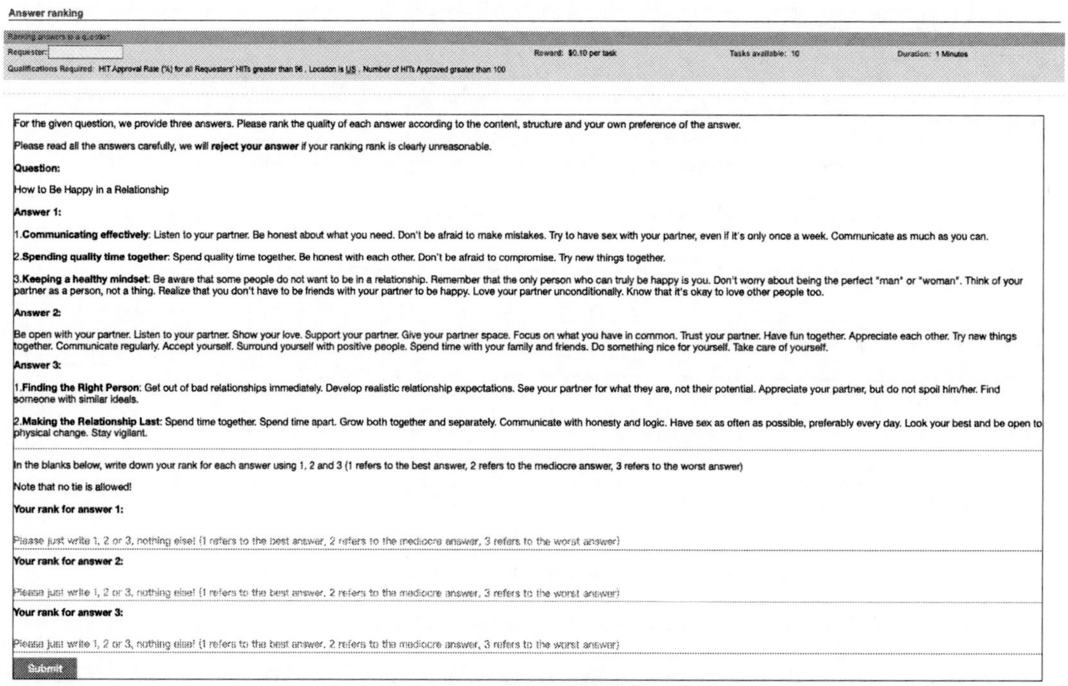

Figure 6: A screenshot of answer ranking evaluation performed by mechanical turkers.

Weakly Supervised Context-based Interview Question Generation

Samiran Pal, Kaamraan Khan, Avinash Kumar Singh, Subhasish Ghosh, Tapas Nayak, Girish Palshikar, Indrajit Bhattacharya
TCS Research, India
samiran.pal@tcs.com, kaamraankhan1@gmail.com,
{singh.avinash9, g.subhasish, nayak.tapas, gk.palshikar, b.indrajit}@tcs.com

Abstract

We explore the task of automated generation of technical interview questions from a given textbook. Such questions are different from those for reading comprehension studied in question generation literature. We curate a context-based interview questions data set for Machine Learning and Deep Learning from two popular textbooks. We first explore the possibility of using a large generative language model (GPT-3) for this task in a zero shot setting. We then evaluate the performance of smaller generative models such as BART fine-tuned on weakly supervised data obtained using GPT-3 and hand-crafted templates. We deploy an automatic question importance assignment technique to figure out suitability of a question in a technical interview. It improves the evaluation results in many dimensions. We dissect the performance of these models for this task and also scrutinize the suitability of questions generated by them for use in technical interviews.

1 Introduction

Asking good questions is crucial for assessing candidates in technical interviews. But this requires human experts with technical knowledge and experience. Therefore, the capability to automatically generate technical questions to assess knowledge and understanding for a specific subject can significantly reduce expert effort in conducting interviews and in scaling up the interview process. In this paper, we focus on automated generation of interview questions from textbook contexts.

There has a been a lot of interest in recent years on question generation (QG) (Dhole and Manning, 2020; Bang et al., 2019; Back et al., 2021), and many benchmark data sets exist (Rajpurkar et al., 2016). Dhole and Manning (2020); Mazidi and Nielsen (2014); Heilman and Smith (2010) focus on rule-based question generation, wherein Dhole and Manning (2020) transform declarative sentences into question-answer pairs using syntactic rules, universal dependencies, shallow semantic parsing and lexical resources. These generate precise questions but often fail due to their heavy reliance on manually crafted feature sets. Recent papers (Xiao et al., 2020; Zhao et al., 2018; Serban et al., 2016) use deep neural networks for QG. Serban et al. (2016) focus on generating factoid questions from knowledge bases such as Freebase. These use answers as clues to generate questions. Back et al. (2021); Cui et al. (2021); Huang et al. (2021) propose answer-agnostic QG. Back et al. (2021) predict answer-like candidates for the given passage and then generate questions from these. Huang et al. (2021); Tsai et al. (2021) use transformer-based generative models such as BART (Lewis et al., 2020) and T5 (Raffel et al., 2020). In summary, all existing models and benchmark datasets address factoid question generation for reading comprehension (RC).

Generating technical interview questions from a context is harder than generating RC questions. Such questions focus on technical concepts and their relationships and test for knowledge and understanding of these. The answers are long-form (2-5 sentences) and must be contained in the context ('What is regularization?' is not answerable from the context 'This issue can be addressed using L2 regularization'). Questions must be semantically complete ('What is the form of the optimal solution?' is an incomplete question) and of appropriate specificity ('What is machine learning' is too generic for assessing expertise in ML). Finally, questions should have a diverse mix of intent and task complexity (compared to just remembering). As a result, RC-question generation models are not appropriate for interview question generation, and RC-question generation data sets are not useful for evaluating interview question generation models.

To address this gap, we first create a dataset of textbook contexts and corresponding technical in-

Proceedings of the 2nd Workshop on Natural Language Generation, Evaluation, and Metrics (GEM), pages 43 - 53
December 7, 2022 ©2022 Association for Computational Linguistics

terview questions from two popular textbooks on Machine Learning (ML) and Deep Learning (DL). We use this for evaluation of interview question generation algorithms. Generation of large volumes of gold-standard training data for this task is difficult and expensive. So, we first evaluate pre-trained large language models (LLM) such as GPT-3 for this task in a zero-shot setting. We then explore fine-tuning a relatively smaller LM (BART) on weakly supervised training data. Wang et al. (2021) have recently explored GPT-3 for creating training data for many NLP tasks including factoid RC question generation. We explore the use of GPT-3 and template-based algorithms for silver-standard interview question generation from textbook contexts. We improve the question generation quality by developing a post-processing unit which filter out questions automatically by checking its suitability in a technical interview. We evaluate the models before and after filtering and see that it improves the performance in many evaluation dimensions.

Using detailed analysis of interview questions generated using these models, we highlight the challenges of this task, and also the key aspects that future models will need to address.

2 Technical Interview Question Dataset

There is no public dataset on technical questions from textbook contexts for evaluating our task. Available question datasets for reading comprehension such as SQuAD (Rajpurkar et al., 2016) are not ideal. So we create a gold-standard dataset by manually generating questions on Machine learning (ML) and Deep learning (DL) from two publicly available books, Bishop (2006) for ML and Goodfellow et al. (2016) for DL.

We selected 3 chapters each from the ML and DL books. We distributed these chapters to 10 annotators (internal to our organisation) with subject knowledge as well as interview experience. We consider each section in a chapter as one context, and the annotators generate all possible long-form questions from each such context. The annotators are reminded of interview question templates (Sec.3.2) but are not restricted to these. However, they are instructed to ensure answerability from context. Each chapter was first annotated independently by two annotators. Then, annotation differences, i.e., questions generated by one but not the other, are resolved via discussion. A question is added in the dataset only if both annotators are convinced after discussion, thus making the inter-annotator agreement 1 for the final dataset. We obtained 161 questions from 3 chapters of the DL book, and 187 questions from the 3 chapters of the ML book. We discuss quality aspects of the dataset in Sec.4. We will make this dataset public.

3 Question Generation Approaches

Here we describe the different question generation and post-processing technique we use in the paper.

3.1 Zero-shot Generation with GPT-3

GPT-3 (Brown et al., 2020) is a transformer-decoder based large language model (LLM) and has shown excellent performance on many NLP tasks in zero-shot settings (Wang et al., 2021; Yoo et al., 2021). We explore GPT-3 for zero-shot technical interview question generation[1]. We use its interview question generation preset, where we give a context as prompt to GPT-3 and it generates a set of interview questions from the context. At a time, we provide one context paragraph, followed by a new line and an instruction or prompt ('Give a list of questions from above passage'). We experiment with different variants of prompt that include the number of questions we want GPT to generate such as 'Generate 10 questions...'. While such prompts work, we observe that the initial set of questions does not differ if prompts are changed. But the questions in the later part of the generated set changes for different prompts. This suggests some internal ranking of the questions generated by GPT-3. So, we decide not to include the number of questions in the prompt and left this for GPT-3 to optimize. We set the temperature parameter to 0 to eliminate randomness in the generated questions, and the other parameters as default.

We ran this GPT-3 question generation process on the same chapters that were used for human question generation (Sec.2). We do a comparative analysis in Sec.4.

3.2 Generation with Fine-tuned BART

While GPT-3 is very powerful, it comes with a cost in real-world applications. As a free open-source alternative, that can be fine-tuned for our specific task, we explore BART (Lewis et al., 2020), another pre-trained language model that has been used for Question Generation (Huang et al., 2021;

[1]We use free GPT-3 APIs.

Tsai et al., 2021). Since our task is question generation, we use the BART model post-trained on SQuAD. Since SQuAD contains factoid RC questions, this need further fine-tuning for our task. For this, we create a silver-standard dataset. We take the remaining chapters of the two books (11 for ML and 17 for DL), which were not used for creating the gold-standard dataset. We use two approaches for generating silver-standard questions from these - a template-based algorithm and GPT-3.

We use an unsupervised template-based algorithm for QG given the context (Fabbri et al., 2020; Puzikov and Gurevych, 2018; Yu and Jiang, 2021). Such approaches typically have high precision while generating a smaller number of questions. We use the following templates: WHAT IS X?, WHAT ARE ADVANTAGES / DISADVANTAGES / USES OF X?, WHAT ARE THE DIFFERENCES BETWEEN X AND Y?, WHAT IS THE RELATION BETWEEN X AND Y?. We use precise regular expressions and dictionaries for each template to check applicability of a template to a sentence, and use book indices to extract concepts for X and Y. For each context, we take the union of questions generated using each template for each sentence in the context. We get 626 questions in all using this approach. More details are included in the Appendix.

We also use GPT-3 to generate silver-standard questions from the same contexts as described in Sec.3 . This gives us 3,013 questions in total.

We experiment with BART fine-tuned on template and GPT-3 questions separately, as well as together. We combine template and GPT-3 questions generated from the same context in two different ways. For a context C, let Q_t and Q_g be the sets of questions generated by the template algorithm and GPT-3. In the 'Concat' mode, we consider (C, Q_t) and (C, Q_g) as two distinct training instances (rows in the training data). In the 'Join' mode, we create a single training instance $(C, Q_t \cup Q_g)$.

3.3 Importance based Question Filtering

While analysing the generated questions we saw that many of them are trivial or obsolete. For example, 'What is a scalar?' is too basic of a question to be asked in a technical interview. Similarly 'What are the advantages of recirculation?' is also not a pressing question for a technical interview because 'recirculation' is not a very well known or popular concept in machine learning. So it does not reveal much about the expertise of a candidate by asking this question.

We assign importance scores to all the questions generated from the book and filter out questions with importance score below a threshold. We use the hierarchical Index and Table of Content (TOC) of the book for assigning the importance scores. First, we automatically create a concept list, L_c present in the book from the Index and TOC. Using this concept list, we annotate the concepts present in each question. We assign importance score for all the concepts in the question and then assign importance to the question.

We observed that concepts appear more upfront in the book are more fundamental and very often later concepts are dependent on them. So there is a strict partial order among concepts present in the book determined by prerequisites. All books are written in a way that prerequisites of a concept appear before the concept because one has to know the prerequisites to understand the current concept. With this observation, we make an assumption that concepts that appear upfront in the book or in the chapters are more fundamental, hence more important, than the concepts which appear later and dependent on them. With this assumption, we calculate two scores, namely TOC_score and Index_score for each concept to find its importance. TOC_score gives the importance score for a given concept in reference to the TOC. Each concept can appear in multiple chapters, in multiple sections within a chapter and in multiple subsections within a section. For each such occurrences, we have the associated id from the TOC. For example, 'supervised learning' can appear in multiple places in the book and suppose one occurrence has the id 4.7.2. From this id, we can infer that the above concept appears in chapter 4 (chap_id), section 7 (section_id) and subsection 2 (subsection_id). Using this information, we assign a score for a particular occurrence of the concept, c as follows.

$$
\begin{aligned}
&TOC\_occurrence\_score(c) = \\
&\quad (chap\_cnt - chap\_id) * 100 \quad + \\
&\quad (max\_sections - section\_id) * 10 \quad + \\
&\quad (max\_subsections - subsection\_id) \quad (1)
\end{aligned}
$$

Here chap_cnt, max_sections, max_subsections are total number of chapters, maximum number of sections, subsections in a chapter respectively. As it is apparent, we give highest priority to chapters, then sections in the chapter, and finally the subsections in the section. For each occurrence of a concept we calculate the score and the final TOC_score of a concept is sum of scores from all TOC_occurrence_score and normalised by the max score of all concepts.

Likewise Index_score gives a score to a concept in reference to the Index of the book. The Index is basically a forest where each concept appear once. Here we assume that a concept is more important if has more sub-concept related to it. More specifically, an important concept will have a bigger subtree under it considering the concept as root. To calculate the score, we attach a weight $w_i = d_{max} - i$ to each depth i and also count the number of different concepts in each depth i of the sub-tree, say con_cnt_i. d_{max} is the maximum depth of any tree in the Index. Then the Index_score of a concept, c is calculated as follows.

$$Index\_score(c) = \Sigma_i(con\_cnt_i * 10^{w_i})/max\_index\_score \quad (2)$$

Here max_index_score is the maximum of index scores of all concepts. So using the above formula we can have an index score for all the concepts present in the index. The final importance score of a concept is the average of the TOC score and the Index score.

Now we calculate the question importance from concept importance as follows: from the annotated concepts present in a question, we get the score for each concepts. We get the sum of concept importance as question importance and normalise the importance score by dividing each of the question score by the maximum score of all questions. Multiplying the question score by 10 makes the range of the question score as 0 to 10.

We analysed the data and found that the most of the useless questions are tagged with importance 0. Questions with importance greater than 0 is useful to variable degrees. So we only filter out all the questions with 0 importance.

Table 2 shows that filtering improves the scores in all dimensions except one: recall. Filtering will never be able to improve recall, it can at-most be equal to the manual one. Here it is decreasing because some of the good questions are being filtered out by our filtering module. But it is tightly bounded in our case. At the worst case, recall decreases by 9 points.

4 Experiments and Analysis

We present experimental evaluation and in-depth quality analysis of questions generated for test contexts by zero-shot and fine-tuned models using gold-standard technical interview questions as a reference. Detailed hyper-parameter settings are included in the Appendix. The results of our analysis before applying the importance-based question filtering are summarized in Table 1. In Table 2, we include the same analysis after doing the importance-based question filtering. We describe our findings below based on Table 1 i.e. before doing the question filtering.

4.1 Analysis of Precision

We consider a question to be a valid interview question from the context if it is (a) long-form, (b) complete, (c) of the right specificity, and (d) answerable from the context. A question is incomplete if it has unresolved co-reference or it misses some context for the question to be meaningful. We manually analyzed all the questions generated by all algorithms for the 3 test chapters of the DL book for these criteria. Performance for these individual dimensions as well as overall precision is shown in Tab.1.

Answerability from Context: For zero-shot GPT-3 questions, 35% do not have answer in context. The following are some example questions with relevant parts of the contexts: (Q:*What is the contrastive divergence training?*, C:"an autoencoder gradient provides an approximation to contrastive divergence training of RBMs"), (Q:*How can the singular value decomposition be used to invert a matrix?*, C:"the most useful feature of the SVD is that we can use it to partially generalize matrix inversion to nonsquare matrices, as we will see in the next section."). These illustrate the difficulty of ensuring answerability. BART performs similarly, in all modes but one. When fine-tuned in the 'Concat' mode, BART scores 73% and GPT-3 scores 65% (in table 1). We conjecture that this improvement in answerability over GPT-3 generated questions is due to two reasons. First, the template-based question generation conditions ensure context relevance, but GPT-3 questions are not. In the 'Concat' mode, we combine the training data from GPT-3 and template algorithms in such a way that one context have two training instances. We believe that this gives more weight to such questions which appear in both questions set and have answer in context. Second, Wang et al.

Model	Tr. Q. Src.	#Questions	% In-Context	% Complete	Prec.	Rec.	% Complex
Manual	NA	161	100	100	1.00	0.61	22
GPT	NA	**236**	65	85	0.53	**0.47**	23
BART	T	75	56	**96**	0.55	0.16	0
BART	GPT	129	63	80	0.55	0.27	34
BART	Concat(T,GPT)	95	**73**	87	**0.64**	0.23	24
BART	Join(T,GPT)	132	61	80	0.52	0.26	**37**

Table 1: Performance of zero-shot GPT-3 (GPT) and various fine-tuned versions of BART using manually curated interview questions as reference **before filtering**. Long-formness and specificity are not shown as all models score 100%. Recall is evaluated by considering all model-generated valid questions in adddition to human questions as reference. Tr. Q. Src.=Training questions source. T=template-based questions, GPT=GPT-3 generated questions.

Model	Tr. Q. Src.	#Questions	% In-Context	% Complete	Prec.	Rec.	% Complex
Manual	NA	161	100	100	1.00	0.61	22
GPT	NA	**155**	66	94	**0.8**	**0.47**	31
BART	T	53	51	96	0.49	0.1	0
BART	GPT	83	70	60	0.64	0.2	**46**
BART	Concat(T,GPT)	60	**75**	**98**	0.72	0.16	30
BART	Join(T,GPT)	79	61	90	0.57	0.17	46

Table 2: Performance of zero-shot GPT-3 (GPT) and various fine-tuned versions of BART using manually curated interview questions as reference **after filtering**.

(2021) proves that under consistency assumption, a model trained using GPT-3 labelled data has lower classification error rate than GPT-3 itself. Here, GPT-3 labelled data acts as a regularizer during training. This result shows that fine-tuning smaller LMs such as BART can achieve better performance in this dimension compared to GPT-3.

Question Completeness: 15% of all GPT-3 questions are incomplete. The following are some examples: *Q:How can the issue of scale be prevented?*, *Q:What are some of the models that this technique can be applied to?*. The percentage is slightly lower for fine-tuned BART in Concat mode (13%), but the nature of mistakes is similar.

Long-form, Specificity, Semantic correctness: We define Long-formness for a question if its answer has more than one sentence. For Specificity, we assume the contribution of the question in Interview setting for assessing the candidate's knowledge, i.e; the question shouldn't be too broad or too specific for a topic. Almost all models score $\sim$100% for long-formness and specificity level of questions. The following is an outlier example of a GPT-3 question that is too specific and simple for an ML interview: *Q:What is the multiplication of a matrix by a scalar?* However, GPT-3 does generate some questions that are semantically invalid: *Q:What is the determinant of a matrix if the determinant is 0?*, *Q:What is Shilov?* (Shilov is the name of a researcher).

Overall Precision: A question is valid if it satisfies all the listed criteria. Precision is the ratio of the number of valid questions and the number of generated questions. The precision of GPT-3 is 53%. Fine-tuned BART in 'Concat' mode has 64% precision — an 11% improvement over GPT-3.

4.2 Analysis of the Recall

Evaluating recall with respect to the human generated questions is problematic because this question set need not be exhaustive. Instead, we manually identify additional valid questions generated by each model from a context beyond those in the human generated set. We take the union of these with the human generated questions as the set of all valid questions for a context. We identify and eliminate equivalent questions when taking the union. We define recall of a model as the ratio of the number of valid generated questions and the total number of valid questions. Recall for the different models is shown in Tab.1.

Among the models, GPT-3 generates the most questions and also has the highest recall (47%). However, in general it fails to generate DEFINE, EXAMPLES OF and WHY questions. The fine-

Model	Tr. Q. Src.	#Questions	Prec.	Rec.	RougeL-Prec.	RougeL-Rec.
Manual	NA	161	–	–	–	–
GPT	NA	**236**	0.44	0.61	0.25	0.33
BART	T	75	0.69	0.34	0.35	0.14
BART	GPT	129	0.56	0.44	0.29	0.25
BART	Concat(T,GPT)	95	0.62	0.39	0.34	0.21
BART	Join(T,GPT)	132	0.55	0.44	0.27	0.25

Table 3: Automatic Evaluation of questions generated from DL book (before importance based filtering) using Mapping and RougeL based precision, recall.

Model	Tr. Q. Src.	#Questions	Prec.	Rec.	RougeL-Prec.	RougeL-Rec.
Manual	NA	187	–	–	–	–
GPT	NA	**297**	0.42	0.60	0.21	0.30
BART	T	127	0.53	0.38	0.27	0.15
BART	GPT	169	0.50	0.46	0.24	0.22
BART	Concat(T,GPT)	143	0.49	0.42	0.26	0.20
BART	Join(T,GPT)	181	0.52	0.50	0.26	0.27

Table 4: Automatic Evaluation of questions generated from ML book (before importance based filtering) using Mapping and RougeL based precision, recall.

tuned BART 'Concat' model has much lower recall (23%). Effectively, GPT-3 has higher F1 (48%) compared to BART Concat (35%).

On the other hand, GPT-3 and other models generate many questions missed by humans, so that human generated questions have a recall of only 61%. One example of GPT-3 questions missed by humans is *What is the pseudoinverse of a diagonal matrix?*. Here, the definition of *pseudoinverse* was hidden inside explanation of mathematical notation in the context. Another is *What is the difference between the singular value decomposition and the eigendecomposition?* from the context "SVD is more generally applicable. Every real matrix has a singular value decomposition, but the same is not true of the eigenvalue decomposition". The human annotator generated a *What is the Advantage of* question, but missed the *What is difference between* question. This shows the potential of model generated questions. However, GPT-3 or fine-tuned BART do not generate any questions according to a new template completely missed by humans.

4.3 Complexity and Diversity of Questions

In an interview, candidates should be asked a variety of both simple and complex questions. We define a question as complex if it contains more than 1 concept from the topic. From Table 1, we see that our BART model in 'Concat' mode, generates similar % of complex questions as GPT-3 zero-shot setting. Beyond validity, diversity and complexity of questions is also important. One simple measure of complexity is the number of concepts covered by the question. 22% of human generated questions have multiple concepts. Among the models, BART Concat as well as GPT-3 have a similar percentage. Interestingly, BART Join generates fewer questions but a higher percentage of multi-concept questions.

The 5 levels of Bloom's Taxonomy (Bloom et al., 1964) provide another definition of cognitive task complexity associated with a question (defined in A.2). Interestingly, the human generated questions are uniformly distributed across these levels. However, both GPT-3 (57%) and BART Concat (58%) have a high proportion of questions from the simplest 'Remember' level, corresponding mostly to WHAT IS questions.

4.4 Automatic Evaluation

Since manual evaluation is extensive and costly, it is not scalable for large set of data. To alleviate such scenario we also provide some automatic measure for the evaluation of generated questions from different approaches. For the given context we already have manually generated questions which can serve as gold standard so our goal is to evaluate the quality of generated questions with respect to manual questions.

Since we have multiple manual and model generated questions for each context, our first aim is to have a one to one alignment for these two sets of questions. For this, lets say there are m manual and n model generated questions for a context, then we create a $m \times n$ matrix where each cell represents the similarity score $sim_{i,j}$ between the i'th manual and j'th generated question. Here the similarity score represents the cosine similarity between the embeddings of the two questions using sentence BERT (Reimers and Gurevych, 2019). We then pass this matrix as input to Hungarian algorithm (Kuhn, 1955) which outputs one to one mapping between manual and generated questions.

Once we have pairwise questions we compute precision and recall by two different methods, namely mapping-based and RougeL-based (Lin, 2004). In the first one, for every context we filter out pairs of questions whose similarity scores are less than a threshold. Then we calculate precision per context by summing the scores of the remaining pairs and dividing it by the total number of generated questions. Likewise recall per context is obtained by dividing it by total number of manual questions. The final precision and recall is the average of all precision and recall per context.

For the second method, we filter out pairs of questions from the outputs of the Hungarian Algorithm like above using a threshold. All the unmapped questions are assumed to be mapped with an empty string. Then we calculate the RougeL precision and recall for every pair of questions. Precision per context is calculated by dividing the sum of RougeL precision by number of generated questions in the context and Recall per context is obtained by dividing sum of the RougeL recall by the number of manual questions. Final precision and recall is the average of all precision and recall per context. Just like manual evaluation, we apply the automatic evaluation on unfiltered questions. We include the automatic evaluation results for questions generated from the DL book in Table 3 whose manual evaluations are included in Table 1. We can see that both the automatic evaluation methods in Table 3 positively correlate with the manual evaluation in Table 1. Automatic mapping based precision and recall have correlation 0.43 and 0.99 respectively with the manual precision and recall. Automatic RougeL based precision and recall have correlation 0.66 and 0.94 respectively.

Seeing the above correlation, we have deployed our automatic evaluation methods on questions generated from 3 chapters of ML book for which we do not have any manual evaluation. We have given the evaluation results for ML questions in Table 4.

5 Limitations

In this work, we are trying to address what is the best way to evaluate the task of question generation for the technical interview. First limitation of this work is that we could not create a large annotated dataset as reference data as we need people with subject expertise for annotation. Due to the same reason, we were forced to train the generative models like BART on silver-standard dataset generated using GPT-3. As GPT-3 is not freely available, the amount of silver-standard data is also limited in volume. The evaluation dimensions we propose for this task involve human effort and obviously this is not scalable.

6 Ethical Impact Statement

Generating interview questions using LLMs may have some ethical concern when these questions are used in actual interviews. In this work, we propose how to evaluate such questions in multiple dimensions. People should be careful before using such questions in actual interviews.

7 Conclusion

In this paper, we explore the problem of technical question generation for interviews from textbook contexts in an weakly supervised approach. We curate a dataset for evaluation for two domains, machine learning and deep learning, using two popular books. We analyzed zero-shot question generation using GPT-3 and fine-tuning BART on silver-standard training data for the same. We also suggested a post processing filtering unit which further improves the quality of generated questions. Our manual analysis brings out the complementary strengths and weaknesses of these approaches for this task. More importantly, our detailed error analysis highlights the challenges of the task and shows a pathway to better models by identifying the major types of errors to focus on. Finally we devised automatic evaluation techniques which positively correlate with our manual evaluation.

References

Seohyun Back, Akhil Kedia, Sai Chetan Chinthakindi, Haejun Lee, and Jaegul Choo. 2021. Learning to generate questions by learning to recover answer-containing sentences. In *FINDINGS*.

Liu Bang, Zhao Mingjun, Niu Di, Lai Kunfeng, He Yancheng, Wei Haojie, and Xu Yu. 2019. Learning to generate questions by learning what not to generate. In *The World Wide Web Conference*.

Christopher M. Bishop. 2006. *Pattern Recognition and Machine Learning (Information Science and Statistics)*. Springer-Verlag, Berlin, Heidelberg.

Benjamin Samuel Bloom, Committee of College, and University Examiners. 1964. *Taxonomy of educational objectives*, volume 2. Longmans, Green New York.

Tom B. Brown, Benjamin Mann, Nick Ryder, Melanie Subbiah, Jared Kaplan, Prafulla Dhariwal, Arvind Neelakantan, Pranav Shyam, Girish Sastry, Amanda Askell, Sandhini Agarwal, Ariel Herbert-Voss, Gretchen Krueger, T. J. Henighan, Rewon Child, Aditya Ramesh, Daniel M. Ziegler, Jeff Wu, Clemens Winter, Christopher Hesse, Mark Chen, Eric Sigler, Mateusz Litwin, Scott Gray, Benjamin Chess, Jack Clark, Christopher Berner, Sam McCandlish, Alec Radford, Ilya Sutskever, and Dario Amodei. 2020. Language models are few-shot learners. In *NeurIPS*.

Shaobo Cui, Xintong Bao, Xinxing Zu, Yangyang Guo, Zhongzhou Zhao, Ji Zhang, and Haiqing Chen. 2021. Onestop qamaker: Extract question-answer pairs from text in a one-stop approach. In *ArXiv*.

Kaustubh D. Dhole and Christopher D. Manning. 2020. Syn-qg: Syntactic and shallow semantic rules for question generation. In *ACL*.

Alexander Fabbri, Patrick Ng, Zhiguo Wang, Ramesh Nallapati, and Bing Xiang. 2020. Template-based question generation from retrieved sentences for improved unsupervised question answering. In *Proceedings of the 58th Annual Meeting of the Association for Computational Linguistics*.

Ian Goodfellow, Yoshua Bengio, and Aaron Courville. 2016. *Deep Learning*. MIT Press. http://www.deeplearningbook.org.

Michael Heilman and Noah A. Smith. 2010. Good question! statistical ranking for question generation. In *ACL*.

Xinting Huang, Jianzhong Qi, Yu Sun, , and Rui Zhang. 2021. Latent reasoning for low-resource question generation. In *ACL*.

Diederik P Kingma and Jimmy Ba. 2014. Adam: A method for stochastic optimization. *arXiv preprint arXiv:1412.6980*.

Harold W Kuhn. 1955. The hungarian method for the assignment problem. *Naval research logistics quarterly*, 2(1-2):83–97.

Mike Lewis, Yinhan Liu, Naman Goyal, Marjan Ghazvininejad, Abdelrahman Mohamed, Omer Levy, Veselin Stoyanov, and Luke Zettlemoyer. 2020. Bart: Denoising sequence-to-sequence pre-training for natural language generation, translation, and com- prehension. In *In Proceedings of the 58th Annual Meeting of the Association for Computational Linguistics*.

Chin-Yew Lin. 2004. Rouge: A package for automatic evaluation of summaries. In *Text summarization branches out*, pages 74–81.

Karen Mazidi and Rodney D. Nielsen. 2014. Linguistic considerations in automatic question generation. In *ACL*.

Yevgeniy Puzikov and Iryna Gurevych. 2018. E2E NLG challenge: Neural models vs. templates. In *Proceedings of the 11th International Conference on Natural Language Generation*.

Colin Raffel, Noam Shazeer, Adam Roberts, Kather ine Lee, Sharan Narang, Michael Matena, Yanqi Zhou, Wei Li, and Peter J. Liu. 2020. Exploring the limits of transfer learning with a unified text-to-text transformer. In *Journal of Machine Learning Research, 21(140):1–67*.

Pranav Rajpurkar, Jian Zhang, Konstantin Lopyrev, and Percy Liang. 2016. Squad: 100,000+ questions for machine comprehension of text. In *EMNLP*.

Nils Reimers and Iryna Gurevych. 2019. Sentence-bert: Sentence embeddings using siamese bert-networks. *arXiv preprint arXiv:1908.10084*.

Iulian Vlad Serban, Alberto García-Durán, Caglar Gulcehre, Sungjin Ahn, Sarath Chandar, Aaron Courville, and Yoshua Bengio. 2016. Generating factoid questions with recurrent neural networks: The 30m factoid question-answer corpus. In *ACL*.

Danny C.L. Tsai, Anna Y.Q. Huang, Owen H.T. Lu, and Stephen J.H. Yang. 2021. Automatic question generation for repeated testing to learning outcome. In *ICALT*.

Shuohang Wang, Yang Liu, Yichong Xu, Chenguang Zhu, and Michael Zeng. 2021. Want to reduce labeling cost? gpt-3 can help. In *EMNLP*.

Dongling Xiao, Han Zhang, Yukun Li, Yu Sun, Hao Tian, Hua Wu, and Haifeng Wang. 2020. Ernie-gen: An enhanced multi-flow pre-training and fine-tuning framework for natural language generation. In *IJCAI*.

Kang Min Yoo, Dongju Park, Jaewook Kang, Sang-Woo Lee, and Woomyeong Park. 2021. Gpt3mix: Leveraging large-scale language models for text augmentation. In *EMNLP*.

Xiaojing Yu and Anxiao Jiang. 2021. Expanding, retrieving and infilling: Diversifying cross-domain question generation with flexible templates. In *Proceedings of the 16th Conference of the European Chapter of the Association for Computational Linguistics: Main Volume*.

Yao Zhao, Xiaochuan Ni, Yuanyuan Ding, and Qifa Ke. 2018. Paragraph-level neural question generation with maxout pointer and gated self-attention networks. In *EMNLP*.

A Appendix

A.1 Template based question generation

After going over real interview transcripts, we identify some templates for the questions and write algorithms for each of the template. We use these templates for this task. We include some of these templates and their examples in Table 5.

We run these templates on the sentences of the books to generate the context-based question. We use different algorithms for each template. Here, we describe the algorithm for 'Difference' template. Each template algorithm uses a list of concepts and a list of keywords. Let C_list={c1, c2, c3, ...} be a list of concepts present in the book. We created this list using the index and Table of content of the books. Multiple atomic concepts can combine to form a maximal concept. For ex: "convolution" and "neural network" can combine to "convolution neural network". There can be multiple maximal concept in a sentence which we store in a list denoted by Mx_c_list. Other than concepts present in the sentence we also look for template specific keywords or phrases which either give hints for attributes of a concept or relationship between two concepts. we call these phrases signals. For ex, presence of "*difference between*" in a sentence hints the possibility of distinctions between two concepts being discussed. So we can generate a 'Difference' question from this sentence. We define a function Is_signal_present(sentence,signal_list, X,Y) which will take a sentence of a book, signal lists and concepts X, Y and returns true if signal along with concepts X and Y are present in the sentence to generate a question out of it. We have shown our pseudo code in algorithm1. Here, X and Y refers to some concepts in the topic for which questions are generated. We include some examples of template generated questions from context in Table 6.

A.2 Bloom's Taxonomy

Bloom's taxonomy defined 6 categories of knowledge in terms of skills/abilities in an increasing order of cognitive load. We loosely assign different types/templates of questions with one of these Bloom's categories: (i) Remember ('What is X?') (ii) Understand ('How does SUB V X?'), (iii) apply ('What are some applications of X'), (iv) analyze ('Explain X'), (v) evaluate ('What are the differences between X and Y'), (vi) Create (We do not have any questions in this category). Here, X and Y refer to the concepts of the topic. As an example 'cross-entropy loss' is a concept in machine learning.

Algorithm 1 *Difference* template algorithm

```
for sentence in context do
  Mx_c_list = find_maximal_concept (sentence, C_list)
  for X in Mx_c_list do
    for Y in Mx_c_list do
      flag = Is_signal_present(sentence, signal_list, X,Y)
      if flag then
        Q_gen: What is the difference between X and Y?
      end if
    end for
  end for
end for
```

A.3 Question Importance Algorithm

We have described the method to calculate the question importance method in 3.3. Here we provide the pseudo-code for the same in algorithm 2.

A.4 Parameter Settings

We experiment with BART-base (Lewis et al., 2020) model post-trained on SQuAD (Rajpurkar et al., 2016). All experiments are done on 64GB CPU with 20 cores. We use a batch size of 16 and train the model for 10 epochs. The average time to train for 10 epochs is around 2 hours. We optimize the model parameters using Adam optimizer (Kingma and Ba, 2014) with a learning rate of 0.0001. Some contexts in our dataset is longer than what BART encoder can accommodate (1,024 word piece tokens). During training, we use the first 1,024 token of the context and discard the remaining part of the context. During inference, we split the longer context into multiple chunks of 1,024 tokens and run inference on each one of them. We do an union of the generated questions from all the splits.

Template	Example	#Questions
What is X?	What is EM algorithm ?	394
What are some uses of X?	What are some uses of maximum likelihood?	118
What are the advantages of X?	What are the advantages of the validation set?	66
What are the disadvantages of X?	What are disadvantages of the metropolis algorithm?	32
What are the differences between X and Y?	What are the differences between bagging and boosting?	4
What is the relation between X and Y?	What is the relation between autoencoders and latent variables?	12

Table 5: Examples of the template generated questions using some of the templates. Here, X and Y refers to some concepts in the topic for which questions are generated.

Context	Questions
An auto encoder is a neural network that is trained to attempt to copy its input to its output.Internally, it has a hidden layer h that describes a code used to represent the input. ... Recently, theoretical connections between auto encoders and latent variable models have brought auto encoders to the forefront of generative modeling.	What is an auto encoder? What is the relation between auto encoders and latent variable?
One advantage of directed graphical models is that a simple and efficient procedure called ancestral sampling can produce a sample from the joint distribution represented by the model. ... Ancestral sampling is generally very fast (assuming sampling from each conditional is easy) and convenient. One drawback to ancestral sampling is that it only applies to directed graphical models. Another drawback is that it does not support every conditional sampling operation. ...	What is ancestral sampling? What are advantages of ancestral sampling? What are disadvantages of ancestral sampling?
Unlike the deep belief network (DBN), it is an entirely undirected model. Unlike the RBM, the DBM has several layers of latent variables (RBMs have just one). ... A DBM is an energy-based model, meaning that the joint probability distribution over the model variables is parametrized by an energy function E . ... In comparison to fully connected Boltzmann machines (with every unit connected to every other unit), the DBM offers some advantages that are similar to those offered by the RBM. ...	What are some use of the dbm? What are differences between the rbm and the dbm? What is a dbm?

Table 6: Examples of generated questions from the context using corresponding template matching algorithm. We match the template algorithm at the sentence-level in the context.

Algorithm 2 Question Importance algorithm

```
concept_importance = {}
for concept in L_concept do
    toc_score = 0
    max_score = −1
    occurance_list= all_occurances(concept)
    for occurrence in occurance_list do
        toc_score += occurance_score(occurance) {from equation 1}
    end for
    toc_score = normalise(toc_score)
    score = average(toc_score, index_score) {from equation 2}
    concept_importance[concept]= score
end for
question_score.fromkeys(L_concept, 0)
for question in question_list do
    concept_list= get_concepts(question)
    for concept in concept_list do
        question_score[question]+= concept_importance[concept]
    end for
end for
max_score = find_max(question_score)
for question in question_score do
    question_score[question]= question_score[question] * 10/max_score
end for
return question_score
```

Analyzing Multi-Task Learning for Abstractive Text Summarization

Frederic Kirstein[1,2,3], Jan Philip Wahle[1], Terry Ruas[1], Bela Gipp[1]
[1]Georg-August-Universität Göttingen, Germany
[2]Mercedes-Benz Group AG, Germany
[3]kirstein@gipplab.org

Abstract

Despite the recent success of multi-task learning and pre-finetuning for natural language understanding, few works have studied the effects of task families on abstractive text summarization. Task families are a form of task grouping during the pre-finetuning stage to learn common skills, such as reading comprehension. To close this gap, we analyze the influence of multi-task learning strategies using task families for the English abstractive text summarization task. We group tasks into one of three strategies, i.e., sequential, simultaneous, and continual multi-task learning, and evaluate trained models through two downstream tasks. We find that certain combinations of task families (e.g., advanced reading comprehension and natural language inference) positively impact downstream performance. Further, we find that choice and combinations of task families influence downstream performance more than the training scheme, supporting the use of task families for abstractive text summarization. Our code is publicly available [1].

1 Introduction

Self-supervised learning has been a significant success driver for generating high-quality abstractive summaries (Devlin et al., 2019; Liu et al., 2019b; Cohen and Gokaslan, 2020; Lewis et al., 2020; Raffel et al., 2020; Radford et al., 2019). Through self-supervision, language models implicitly learn intrinsic language features (e.g., syntax) from unlabeled data that they can use to solve downstream tasks (Brown et al., 2020). However, skills necessary to perform specific tasks often can be learned from an existing set of labeled data, requiring fewer training iterations (Rajpurkar et al., 2016; See et al., 2017). For example, to perform text summarization, a helpful skill is the ability to answer questions about texts (Rajpurkar et al., 2016).

The multi-task learning paradigm and its variations aim to acquire multiple skills simultaneously to succeed on the downstream tasks, e.g., T5 (Raffel et al., 2020), and are independent of a specific training stage (Aribandi et al., 2021). While studies on the effects of multi-task learning on a large scale exist (Aghajanyan et al., 2021; Sun et al., 2020; Aribandi et al., 2021) and are evaluated on broad natural language understanding benchmarks (Wang et al., 2019), they are lacking insight on the influence on abstractive text summarization. Furthermore, multi-task learning approaches are diverse in their methods (e.g., training scheme, mixing strategy, task families), hampering their comparison.

In this work, we investigate the role of multi-task learning on English abstractive text summarization. Therefore, we organize 18 pre-selected training tasks into six higher-level, modular task families. Further, we compare three training schemes for the pre-finetuning stage and their respective mixing strategies through changes of multiple scores.

Our experiments show that families' choice significantly impacts text summarization, while different training schemes have little influence. Moreover, pairing a text summarization task family with any other helps to stabilize the overall performance when transferring to unknown data. In some cases, we also found that a text summarization task family can be substituted by other family pairs, e.g., advanced reading comprehension and classification.

To summarize our contributions:

- We study the influence of multi-task learning by training models on six task families for the English abstractive text summarization task.
- We evaluate the co-training of different task families using statistical (e.g., ROUGE) and semantic metrics (e.g., BERTScore) for 18 datasets.

[1] https://github.com/FKIRSTE/GEM_emnlp2022-TOASTS

Proceedings of the 2nd Workshop on Natural Language Generation, Evaluation, and Metrics (GEM), pages 54 - 77
December 7, 2022

- We compare the influence of three training schemes (i.e., sequential, simultaneous, continual multi-task learning) and two mixing strategies (i.e., proportional, equal).

2 Related Work

Multi-task learning and pre-finetuning. Transformers (Vaswani et al., 2017) such as BERT (Devlin et al., 2019) and GPT-3 (Brown et al., 2020) are trained using a two-step approach, the *pre-training* on large unlabeled corpora and the *finetuning* on a smaller, more specific (and usually labeled) downstream corpus. This bilateral approach allows language models to obtain general text representations once to perform many NLP downstream tasks with few gradient steps (e.g., document classification (Ostendorff et al., 2020a,b), plagiarism detection (Wahle et al., 2021, 2022b,c), media bias detection (Spinde et al., 2021, 2022)). However, pre-training is typically highly computationally expensive and requires dedicated ample infrastructure; few researchers can reproduce the pre-training of large language models. Therefore, recent works (Phang et al., 2018; Aghajanyan et al., 2021)) proposed additional training stages between pre-training and finetuning, i.e., *pre-finetuning*[2].

ERNIE 2.0 (Sun et al., 2020) proposes *continual multi-task learning*, in which tasks are trained incrementally, thereby building a queue of introduced tasks that re-appear throughout the training process, to counter catastrophic forgetting (McCloskey and Cohen, 1989; Kirkpatrick et al., 2017). MUPPET (Aghajanyan et al., 2021) and ExT5 (Aribandi et al., 2021) follow a *simultaneous* approach, drawing heterogeneous batches from multiple tasks and massively scale their training to >50 and >100 tasks respectively. MT-DNN (Liu et al., 2019a) organizes the prediction layer of a Transformer into four task families of common tasks of the GLUE benchmark (Wang et al., 2018) and learns each task *sequential* with their task order randomized. This study compares continual multi-task learning, simultaneous training, and sequential training for abstractive text summarization.

Task selection and relationship. Vu et al. (2020) conduct an empirical investigation on 33 tasks across three broad groups (i.e., text classification, question answering, and sequence labeling) to explore their inter- and intra-group training for different group sizes. Their experiments suggest that positive transfers between task groups are possible when the source dataset is small, and inter-group transfers are sensitive to group sizes. ExT5 (Aribandi et al., 2021) analyzes the correlation of task family representatives and shows, that summarization tasks (i.e., CNN/Daily Mail (See et al., 2017), XSum (Narayan et al., 2018), WikiLingua(Ladhak et al., 2020)) generally reduce performance on most other task families and that CBQA tasks (i.e., Natural Questions (Kwiatkowski et al., 2019), Trivia QA (Joshi et al., 2017), Hotpot QA (Yang et al., 2018)) are sensitive to multi-task learning. For the task relationship and transfer analysis, Aribandi et al. (2021) train on two families simultaneously and evaluate the first one. We expand the study of Aribandi et al. (2021) by adapting task families and respective representative tasks to be related to the text summarization task (Section 3.1), considering different family combinations, training approaches (Section 3.2), and tracking their performance through additional metrics for different unseen datasets (Section 4).

Multiple works leverage algorithms for the selection of training tasks, e.g., Ruder and Plank (2017) use Bayesian Optimization to learn similarity measures (i.e., Jensen-Shannon divergence (Lin, 1991) and Rényi divergence (Rényi et al., 1961)) and a Beta-Bernoulli multi-armed bandit with Thompson Sampling (Russo et al., 2018; Thompson, 1933) is used by AutoSem (Guo et al., 2019). Conversely, ExT5 (Aribandi et al., 2021) does not rely on automatic training task selection approaches as described by the preceding works and instead chooses an empirical approach to select tasks for higher-level task families. We follow the approach of Aribandi et al. (2021)'s task representative selection when choosing our tasks as the training task correlation analysis in ExT5 indicates which families could positively influence text summarization.

3 Methodology

We name our study TOASTS, a **T**ask-**O**riented **A**nalysi**S** for **T**ext **S**ummarization to investigate the effects of different task family combinations on English abstractive text summarization via a multi-task learning architecture. TOASTS groups selected pre-training tasks into task families and explores the correlation of these families, their influence on two downstream tasks, and their aggre-

[2]In this paper, we will use *intermediate training* and *pre-finetuning* interchangeably

Task Family	Task	Dataset	Source	Characteristics
Classification [CLS]	Sentiment Classification	GoEmotion (2020)	Reddit	multi-label CLS
	Sentiment Classification	IMDB (2011)	IMDB	binary CLS
	Topic Classification	AG News (2015)	ComeToMyHead	multi-class CLS
Commonsense [CMNS]	Fill-In-The-Blank	Winogrande (2021)	WSC dataset	binary options
	Question Answering	PhysicaliQA (2019)	instructables.com	binary options
	Question Answering	SocialiQA (2019)	crowdsourced	ternary options
Natural Language Inference [NLI]	Textual Entailment CLS	MNLI (2018)	SNLI corpus	multi-label CLS
	Textual Entailment CLS	ANLI (2020)	human-and-model-in-the-loop dataset	multi-label CLS
	Textual Entailment CLS	QNLI (2018)	Wikipedia	binary classification
Reading Comprehension [RC]	Binary QA	BoolQ (2019)	Google	yes/no answer
	Extractive QA	SQuAD (2016)	Wikipedia	extractive answers
	Abstractive QA	TweetQA (2019)	Twitter	abstractive answers allowed
Advanced RC [RC+]	RC + Information Retrieval	HotpotQA (2018)	Wikipedia	multi-hop question answering
	RC + Open Domain QA	Natural Questions (2019)	Google, Wikipedia	answer information seeking questions
	RC + CMNS	ReCoRD (2018)	CNN/DailyMail and Internet Archive	extractive Machine RC
Summarization [SUM]	Extractive SUM	XSum (2018)	BBC	one-sentence summary
	Abstractive SUM	WikiLingua [eng] (2020)	WikiHow	one-sentence summary
	Abstractive SUM	AESLC (2019)	E-Mail	subject line generation

Table 1: Our selection of 18 representative datasets organized by their task family. For every dataset, we list the target task, the source, and the characteristics of the data. For a complete list of tasks, please see Appendix A.

gation through three training schemes. Therefore, we use pre-finetuning, a second inexpensive pre-training stage between pre-training and fine-tuning, which was recently proposed by Muppet (Aghajanyan et al., 2021) and tested by ExT5 (Aribandi et al., 2021). Pre-finetuning has two main parts: the *task family setup* and the *training strategies*. The task family setup groups different tasks and related datasets into broader families according to their primary objective. The tasks of these families are then combined following a training strategy and evaluated into a final task. Figure 1 illustrates the components of TOASTS, which are detailed in the following sections.

3.1 Task family setup

Selection. A myriad of NLP downstream tasks (e.g., word sense disambiguation and paraphrase detection) can be considered when choosing a multi-task architecture. Without computational limits, one could explore all possible permutations of tasks and the influence of the respective tasks on downstream performance. Unfortunately, as the number of tasks grows by more than their factorial number, joint training becomes computationally prohibitive (Aribandi et al., 2021). Therefore, we organize tasks into six high-level families (Aribandi et al., 2021; Brown et al., 2020) and perform combinations on their family levels: *classification (CLS)*, *commonsense reasoning (CMNS)*, and *natural language inference (NLI)*, *reading comprehension (RC)*, *advanced reading comprehension*[3] *(RC^+)*, *summarization (SUM)*. We compose each task family of three datasets that tackle different aspects of the problem, as shown in Table 1.

The selected tasks in TOASTS should not be seen as an exhaustive list of all NLP downstream tasks; instead, they should be considered an educated selection to measure task family influence on text summarization. An extended list of planned tasks for future analyses can be found in Table 7 in Appendix A.

Task mixing. After pre-selecting representative tasks for each family, we control the percentage of data ingested from each task using a task mixing strategy. We consider two methods for processing all combinations of task families: *proportional mixing* (Sanh et al., 2019; Aribandi et al., 2021) and *equal mixing* (Raffel et al., 2020). Equal mixing picks training samples from each task with equal probability, while proportional mixing sets the probability to the proportion of each task's size. The use of proportional mixing as a default strategy is the recommended approach for various multi-task learning strategies (Sanh et al., 2019). However, continual multi-task learning (Section 3.2) requires an equal mixing strategy even though related studies have shown it to be sub-optimal (Raffel et al., 2020). While we sample either proportional or equal within task families, we draw equal between task families to balance the influence of potentially different task families. We leave to future

[3]Aribandi et al. (2021) refer to this family as Closed Book Question Answering (CBQA).

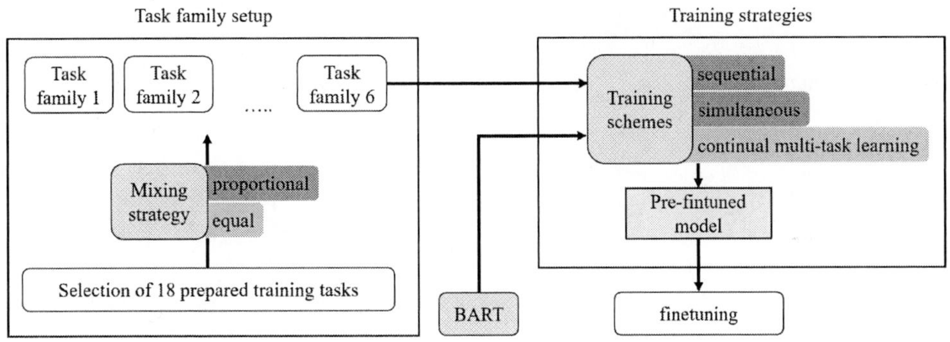

Figure 1: The central architecture of TOASTS. The intermediate training phase commences the **task family setup** (left) by organizing the pre-selected training tasks into families of similar problems and applying two (proportional, equal) intra-family mixing strategies. The **training strategies** (right) continue by processing and organizing the generated task families into batches according to one of three training schemes (sequential, simultaneous, continual multi-task learning). After pre-finetuning BART, the resulting model is finetuned and evaluated on two abstractive text summarization datasets (Reddit TIFU, arXiv). The training/mixing scheme pairings are marked by the background colors green and blue.

work the investigation of the effects of different amounts of tasks and samples per family.

3.2 Training strategies

Training Schemes. Multi-task learning during a pre-finetuning stage allows us to start from a pre-trained checkpoint, decreasing the final task's overall cost. We explore three multi-task learning training schemes for the pre-finetuning as Figure 2 shows: *sequential learning* (seq) (McCloskey and Cohen, 1989; Biesialska et al., 2020), *simultaneous learning* (sim) (Caruana, 1997; Aghajanyan et al., 2021), and *continual multi-task learning* (cMTL) (Sun et al., 2020). In the *sequential* approach, training batches are composed of a single dataset, i.e., homogeneous batches, and their processing order is sequentially randomized (Liu et al., 2019a). This approach achieves a concentrated task learning on the batch level while keeping the overall variety, therefore learning a task more thoroughly before moving to the next. For the *simultaneous* strategy, we combine all tasks into a single pool and draw randomly from it (Aghajanyan et al., 2021; Aribandi et al., 2021). This prominent approach introduces task variety on the batch level by constantly challenging the model with different approaches, forcing it to identify intrinsic commonality between the task families quickly. For *continual multi-task learning*, we adjust the concept of ERNIE 2.0 (Sun et al., 2020) to adapt it to our task family configuration. As our tasks corpus is less extensive than the training dataset used in ERNIE 2.0, we have to rejig the number of stages and training steps in TOASTS. Therefore, when including new tasks and task families, we change their total number of steps to 9k, and 27k, respectively, as Table 2 shows. One difference from ERNIE 2.0 is that once a new task is introduced to the pipeline and trained for the first time at timestep t, we move it to the end of the queue of previously trained tasks as the last one to be executed in $t+1$. Using the order in (Sun et al., 2020) as an alternative way of including and carrying new tasks, yields worse results (Table 8). Through the pre-determined task order of this approach, we can control which task families follow each other and how fundamental a task is by introducing it earlier than others.

Task	S1	S2	S3	S4	S5	...	S18
TF1.1	500	500	500	500	500	...	500
TF1.2	-	1k	500	500	500	...	500
TF1.3	-	-	1.5k	500	500	...	500
TF2.1	-	-	-	2k	500	...	500
TF2.2	-	-	-	-	2.5k	...	500
...	-	-	-	-	-	...	500
TF6.3	-	-	-	-	-	-	9k

Table 2: The number of batches during cMTL training depends on the training stage and the number of introduced tasks. S1 to S16 denote the stages when a new task TF1.1 to TF6.3 is introduced. TF1.1 indicates the first task of task family 1, TF1.2 the second task of task family 1 etc.

4 Experimental setup

Model. For all experiments, we use BART-Large (Lewis et al., 2020) to probe combinations of task families, mixing, and training strategies in

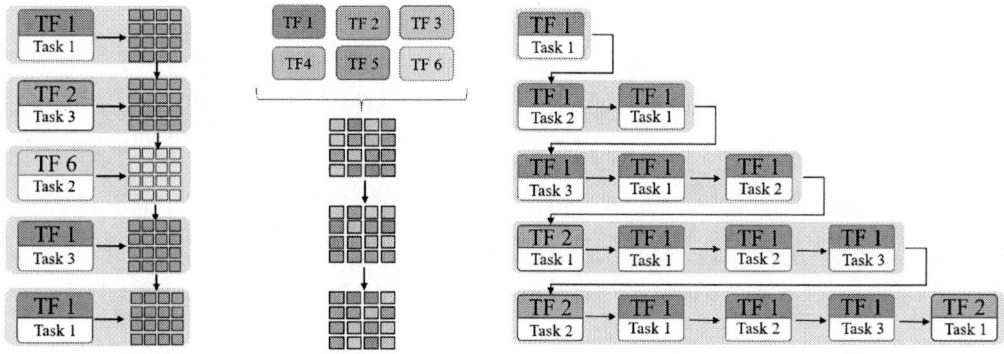

(a) Sequential learning. (b) Simultaneous learning. (c) Continual multi-task learning.

Figure 2: TOASTS's three training strategies. (a) Sequential learning (seq) draws a batch with samples from one task of a task family at a time for every training stage. The order of tasks is randomized. (b) Simultaneous learning (sim) samples from all available tasks at the same time. (c) Continual multi-task learning (cMTL) introduces a new task in each training stage, which is added to the end of the training queue.

TOASTS. BART is a two-stage denoising autoencoder that corrupts its input text and reconstructs it through a sequence-to-sequence model. We chose BART because of its ability to perform a wide range of downstream tasks, such as paraphrase detection (Wahle et al., 2022b), fake news identification (Wahle et al., 2022a), and text summarization (Lewis et al., 2020). Additionally, in our preliminary experiments, BART also performed better than other candidate models such as PEGASUS (Zhang et al., 2020) and T5 (Raffel et al., 2020) (comparison in Tables 9 and 10 in appendix B).

Tokenization. We tokenize text using the BART-Large tokenizer and augment all texts to include task-specific prompts such as `'question:'` or `'context:'`. Further, we structure the samples to follow a uniform text-to-text style which allows the model to handle multi-task learning across different task families without needing task-specific losses, loss scaling or explicit gradient accumulation on heterogeneous batches (Liu et al., 2019a; Aghajanyan et al., 2021).

Hyperparameters. We run our experiments on 8 NVIDIA A100s with a total of 320GB GPU memory. The models are trained with a total batch size of 8 for three epochs and up to 60k global steps for six task families during pre-finetuning (finetuning: 16k for Reddit TIFU, 70k for arXiv) with half-precision (fp16). The pre-finetuning takes between 17min (single task family) and 11h (all task families). The finetuning takes 2.2h for Reddit TIFU and 19.85h for arXiv. During pre-finetuning, we set the input sequence to 512 tokens and the target sequence to 128 as a compromise for training time and context. During finetuning, the sequence lengths are increased to 1024 and 512 for input and target, respectively, to capture the full context of both evaluation datasets. For other hyperparameters we refer the reader to Table 41 in Appendix D.

Evaluation. To understand each task family's influence, mixing, and training strategies, we evaluate the text summarization task using two datasets: Reddit TIFU (Kim et al., 2019) and arXiv (Cohan et al., 2018). Reddit TIFU is composed of 120K posts from online conversations, with the task of creating a tldr[4] summary from the post. The arXiv dataset consists of 250K scientific articles with the task of deriving the abstract from the full text. These datasets are commonly referred to as challenging abstractive summarization tasks (Zhang et al., 2020; He et al., 2020). In combination, they provide a balanced landscape as Reddit TIFU contains shorter examples with an average of 432 words per post and 23 per summary, relying on simpler linguistic, and arXiv longer examples with 4938 words per document and 220 per summary constructed from elaborated text.

During our experiments, we consider a combination of *count-based* and *semantic* metrics to assess the quality of produced summaries. We use BLEU (Papineni et al., 2002), ROUGE (1, 2, L) (Lin, 2004), and METEOR (Banerjee and Lavie, 2005), which favor precision, recall, and harmonic mean, respectively. Even though these traditional metrics can work well for similarly worded sum-

[4]too long; didn't read

Task Families	Reddit TIFU			arXiv		
	seq	sim	cMTL	seq	sim	cMTL
CLS	0.226	0.233	0.060	0.154	0.287	**0.286**
CMNS	0.226	0.078	0.078	0.286	0.197	0.163
NLI	0.030	0.082	0.082	0.168	0.111	0.182
RC	0.230	**<u>0.235</u>**	0.230	0.282	0.284	0.282
RC⁺	0.224	0.082	0.078	0.282	**<u>0.289</u>**	0.203
SUM	**0.231**	**<u>0.235</u>**	**0.231**	**0.288**	0.282	**0.286**
ALL	0.222	0.228	0.037	0.281	0.279	0.008
BART (baseline)	0.087†	0.087†	0.087†	0.281†	0.281†	0.281†

Table 3: Results (METEOR) for single task families and the combination of all task families for the Reddit TIFU and arXiv datasets. Values in **bold** represent the highest results for a training scheme. Underlined values are the highest results for that dataset independent from training. †Repeated result for baseline without training scheme.

maries, they are limited when wording changes, but the semantic meaning remains the same (Bhandari et al., 2020; Huang et al., 2021). To assess semantic similarity better, we also include BERTScore (Zhang et al., 2019a), a similarity measure that maximizes the cosine similarity between candidate and reference contextualized token embeddings via BERT (Devlin et al., 2019) in a greedy manner.

4.1 Experimental results and discussion

We structure our experiments into four research questions, which tackle the relevance of task families and dataset compatibility (RQ1), the effects of co-training text summarization task families with other families (RQ2), the co-training of task families excluding text summarization (RQ3), and the co-training of text summarization and two different task families (RQ4).

We pre-finetune our baseline model (BART-Large) for each experiment on specific task families (e.g., CLS, CMNS) and evaluate the resulting models into the Reddit TIFU and arXiv datasets. Tables 3 to 6 show the different task mixing and training strategies. Sequential (seq) and simultaneous (sim) training strategies use proportional mixing, while continual multi-task learning (cMTL) uses equal mixing. Because of space constraints, we report our results only for the METEOR metric, which proved to be the most sensitive to our experiments. We include a complete list of results for BertScore, BLEU, METEOR, and ROUGE (1, 2, L) in Appendices C.1 and C.2.

RQ1*: Does increasing the number of pre-finetuning datasets increase downstream task performance for text summarization?*

A. To identify if the text summarization downstream task benefits from unconstrained usage of multiple task families, we compare how each task family performs against the combination of all.

As Table 3 shows, the SUM task family consistently outperforms the combination of all families for both datasets (followed by RC), except for the sim training scheme on arXiv. The increase in performance through pre-training SUM is somehow expected, as it is the most related task family to the actual problem, i.e., abstractive text summarization. Conversely, NLI performs the worst when compared to any other task family. Pre-finetuning generally positively affects BART compared to its baseline, except for a few cases (e.g., cMTL-RC⁺, NLI). Overall, the sim training strategy greatly influenced downstream task performance.

Our results suggest that combining all task families is suboptimal for text summarization, which challenges recent observations for other NLP tasks (Aghajanyan et al., 2021; Aribandi et al., 2021). Also, increasing the number of task families requires high compute budgets. As we train each task family individually or all simultaneously, it is unclear how much influence a summarization task family (e.g., SUM) has on the others.

RQ2*: How much does the text summarization task affect other task families?*

A. As SUM is closely related to the text summarization task, and it yields the best results in RQ1, we explore how its combination with another task family affects the resulting model. Table 4 shows the results of combining SUM with other task families. Aside from a few cases (e.g., arXiv sim for SUM+RC⁺), pairing with the SUM family improves over almost every single run in Table 3 and the combination of all task families.

Task Families	Reddit TIFU			arXiv		
	seq	sim	cMTL	seq	sim	cMTL
SUM+CLS	0.230	**0.233**	0.077	**0.285**	0.285	0.283
SUM+CMNS	0.232	0.231	**0.234**	0.153	0.286	**0.288**
SUM+NLI	0.223	**0.233**	0.223	0.282	**0.287**	0.282
SUM+RC	**0.233**	0.229	**0.234**	**0.285**	0.280	0.283
SUM+RC$^+$	0.230	0.225	**0.234**	0.284	0.281	0.284
BART (baseline)	0.087†	0.087†	0.087†	0.281†	0.281†	0.281†

Table 4: Results (METEOR) for the combination of SUM and different task families for the Reddit TIFU and arXiv datasets. Values in **bold** represent the highest results for a training scheme. Underlined values are the highest results for that dataset independent of training. †Repeated result for baseline without training scheme.

While some task families' combinations obtain small benefits (seq-SUM+RC), others are greatly affected (e.g., cMTL-SUM+CMNS) for both datasets. The BART baseline performs better than the pre-finetuning in only two cases, i.e., SUM+CLS for Reddit TIFU (cMTL) and SUM+CMNS for arXiv (seq). We observe fewer outliers with low scores when pairing SUM with other task families than in RQ1. Individual training improved the performance on arXiv the most (seq and sim), while for Reddit TIFU, the combination of task families was more effective (seq and cMTL).

Low scores are also less frequent when combining task families with one exception, i.e., cMTL-SUM+CLS for Reddit TIFU. The lowest scores in RQ1 (e.g., NLI, CMNS) and RQ2 (CLS) might be related to the fact that these tasks are not contributing to the learned weights of the downstream task. As Reddit TIFU uses mostly informal language and its input sequence and summaries are short, this might justify these low scores.

The improvements in Table 4 over the BART baseline are likely to be related to the SUM family rather than a mixing strategy or training scheme. The results of individually training the SUM family (RQ1) are equal or marginally higher when combined with other task families (e.g., 0.233 for SUM+RC vs. 0.231 SUM). As the SUM family seems to substantially impact co-training multiple tasks, we are interested in evaluating the influence of families other than SUM.

RQ3*: How do non text summarization task families influence each other?*

A. We remove the SUM family and co-train all possible pairs of task families. Table 5 shows that the co-training of non text summarization task families (e.g., NLI+RC$^+$) can achieve equal or better results in comparison to single SUM training (Table 3) or its combination with other task families (Table 4) for both Reddit TIFU and arXiv. Other combinations such as CLS+RC and RC+RC$^+$ also achieve strong results.

Conversely, the combination of task families with good results individually seems to have a harmful influence on each other when paired. While CLS and CMNS have good results individually (0.226 and 0.226 for the seq strategy on Reddit TIFU), their pairing (e.g., CLS+CMNS) is strongly negative (e.g., 0.078 for the seq strategy on Reddit TIFU). As in Table 3, different training schemes seem to be a less dominant factor than task family choice during pre-finetuning. Therefore, a proper task family combination should precede architectural training options.

Our results suggest that non text summarization task families can be used to substitute for the SUM family. Specifically, all best-performing results include RC or RC$^+$ in their configuration. A possible explanation for the stark influence of RC/RC$^+$ is that their problem of understanding texts is closely related to summarizing texts. A link between reading comprehension and text summarization is also observed by psychologists in various studies (e.g., Cohen (2006); Kintsch and van Dijk (1978); Yu (2008)).

RQ4*: How are non text summarization task family pairs affected by SUM?*

A. Considering the positive effect of SUM in other families (RQ2), we investigate its influence in task family pairs (RQ3) as Table 6 shows. For this research question, we only consider Reddit TIFU as it provides a more challenging scenario (i.e., informal, short texts) and limits our computational

Task Families	Reddit TIFU			arXiv		
	seq	sim	cMTL	seq	sim	cMTL
CLS+CMNS	0.078	0.078	0.060	0.078	0.050	0.162
CLS+NLI	0.077	0.077	0.046	0.050	0.003	0.276
CLS+RC	0.231	0.231	0.230	**0.287**	0.283	0.181
CLS+RC⁺	0.229	0.229	0.082	0.284	0.288	**0.287**
CMNS+NLI	0.231	0.231	0.081	0.137	0.212	0.118
CMNS+RC	0.227	0.227	0.077	0.283	0.284	0.179
CMNS+RC⁺	0.232	0.232	**0.232**	0.279	0.280	0.082
NLI+RC	0.231	0.231	0.231	0.285	0.285	0.284
NLI+RC⁺	**0.233**	**<u>0.234</u>**	0.227	0.286	**<u>0.290</u>**	0.282
RC+RC⁺	0.228	0.228	0.228	**0.287**	0.281	0.285
BART (baseline)	0.087†	0.087†	0.087†	0.281†	0.281†	0.281†

Table 5: Results (METEOR) for the combination of all pairs of task families (except for SUM) for the Reddit TIFU and arXiv datasets. Values in **bold** represent the highest results for a training scheme. <u>Underlined</u> values are the highest results for that dataset independent of training. †Repeated result for baseline without training scheme.

Task Families	Reddit TIFU		
	seq	sim	cMTL
SUM+CLS+CMNS	0.228	0.227	0.077
SUM+CLS+NLI	0.231	0.231	0.082
SUM+CLS+RC	**0.235**	0.228	0.229
SUM+CLS+RC⁺	**0.235**	0.233	0.082
SUM+CMNS+NLI	0.230	**<u>0.236</u>**	0.229
SUM+CMNS+RC	0.234	0.232	**0.230**
SUM+CMNS+RC⁺	0.232	0.231	0.228
SUM+NLI+RC	0.229	0.231	0.228
SUM+NLI+RC⁺	0.234	0.229	0.229
SUM+RC+RC⁺	0.227	0.234	0.228
BART (baseline)	0.087†	0.087†	0.087†

Table 6: Results (METEOR) for the combination of all pairs of task families and SUM for Reddit TIFU. Values in **bold** represent the highest results for a training scheme. <u>Underline</u> values are the highest results for that dataset independent of training. †Repeated result for baseline without training scheme.

budget (family co-training is increasingly expensive when the number of task families grows).

Including SUM mitigates the adverse effects of combining CLS+CMNS (e.g., 0.228 vs. 0.078 for the seq training scheme) and CLS+NLI (e.g., 0.231 vs. 0.077 for the seq training scheme), except for the cMTL training scheme. However, the scores for CLS+RC⁺ are almost unchanged. The seq and sim training schemes still perform best (e.g., CMNS+NLI) but for different task family combinations compared to the previous research questions' results (e.g., NLI+RC⁺ in RQ3). For the best performing task families pairs in RQ3, only CLS+RC and CLS+RC⁺ are still the top results when including SUM. As in Table 4, the SUM family seems to provide stability to the results, as we see fewer fluctuations than in Table 5. We assume the stability provided by SUM would also be present in the inclusion of more task families. Further, we observe the positive influence of RC and RC⁺ when pairing three task families excluding SUM (Tables 26 to 28).

5 Conclusion & Future Work

In this work, we studied the influence of multi-task learning combinations of task families during the pre-finetuning stage for English abstractive text summarization. We trained three different training strategies, six task families composed of 18 tasks, and evaluated two downstream tasks.

Our experiments show that non text summarization task families, e.g., advanced reading comprehension, can be used as a substitute for the summarization task (RQ2) or the combination of all task families (RQ1). However, including the summarization task family in the training process positively impacts the downstream performance compared to non text summarization family combinations. Further, our analysis shows that training strategies have little influence on the overall performance compared to the task family selection.

We see this analysis as the first step to understanding training strategies and task families for text summarization. In the future, we want to investigate more tasks (both in number and diversity) per task family, training schemes, and mixing strategies. We also plan to include psychological studies comparing the similarities of textual understanding tasks as a starting point for task family preselection.

Limitations

With the organization of tasks and datasets into task families, this study highly depends on these representative tasks' domain and expressiveness. As Aribandi et al. (2021) faced similar problems, we followed their guidance to select representatives to consist of a diverse set of datasets to train and evaluate on and to partition task families as mutually exclusive as possible while being related to abstractive text summarization. However, none of the datasets are perfectly isolated and can only be used as a proxy for a larger task family.

Ethical Considerations

This study depends on existing resources and generative models; thus, it is not free of biases and possible ethical considerations. One problem is the generation of text summaries that contain non-factual information, meaning distortion, social biases such as political stances, or abusive language (Gooding, 2022). To mitigate these problems we plan to condition the generation of trained models for unsafe content or other harmful text to return an empty string.

Furthermore, TOASTS is licensed to the public under a copyright policy that allows unlimited reproduction, distribution, and hosting on any website or medium. Hence, anyone can exploit its limitations and inherited biases to propagate and amplify unintentional societal problems.

References

Armen Aghajanyan, Anchit Gupta, Akshat Shrivastava, Xilun Chen, Luke Zettlemoyer, and Sonal Gupta. 2021. Muppet: Massive multi-task representations with pre-finetuning. In *Proceedings of the 2021 Conference on Empirical Methods in Natural Language Processing*, pages 5799–5811, Online and Punta Cana, Dominican Republic. Association for Computational Linguistics.

Vamsi Aribandi, Yi Tay, Tal Schuster, Jinfeng Rao, Huaixiu Steven Zheng, Sanket Vaibhav Mehta, Honglei Zhuang, Vinh Q. Tran, Dara Bahri, Jianmo Ni, Jai Prakash Gupta, Kai Hui, Sebastian Ruder, and Donald Metzler. 2021. Ext5: Towards extreme multi-task scaling for transfer learning. *CoRR*, abs/2111.10952.

Payal Bajaj, Daniel Campos, Nick Craswell, Li Deng, Jianfeng Gao, Xiaodong Liu, Rangan Majumder, Andrew McNamara, Bhaskar Mitra, Tri Nguyen, Mir Rosenberg, Xia Song, Alina Stoica, Saurabh Tiwary, and Tong Wang. 2016. Ms marco: A human generated machine reading comprehension dataset.

Satanjeev Banerjee and Alon Lavie. 2005. METEOR: An automatic metric for MT evaluation with improved correlation with human judgments. In *Proceedings of the ACL Workshop on Intrinsic and Extrinsic Evaluation Measures for Machine Translation and/or Summarization*, pages 65–72, Ann Arbor, Michigan. Association for Computational Linguistics.

Manik Bhandari, Pranav Narayan Gour, Atabak Ashfaq, Pengfei Liu, and Graham Neubig. 2020. Re-evaluating evaluation in text summarization. In *Proceedings of the 2020 Conference on Empirical Methods in Natural Language Processing (EMNLP)*, pages 9347–9359, Online. Association for Computational Linguistics.

Magdalena Biesialska, Katarzyna Biesialska, and Marta R. Costa-jussà. 2020. Continual lifelong learning in natural language processing: A survey. In *Proceedings of the 28th International Conference on Computational Linguistics*, pages 6523–6541, Barcelona, Spain (Online). International Committee on Computational Linguistics.

Yonatan Bisk, Rowan Zellers, Ronan Le Bras, Jianfeng Gao, and Yejin Choi. 2019. Piqa: Reasoning about physical commonsense in natural language.

Daniel Borkan, Lucas Dixon, Jeffrey Sorensen, Nithum Thain, and Lucy Vasserman. 2019. Nuanced metrics for measuring unintended bias with real data for text classification. *CoRR*, abs/1903.04561.

Tom Brown, Benjamin Mann, Nick Ryder, Melanie Subbiah, Jared D Kaplan, Prafulla Dhariwal, Arvind Neelakantan, Pranav Shyam, Girish Sastry, Amanda Askell, Sandhini Agarwal, Ariel Herbert-Voss, Gretchen Krueger, Tom Henighan, Rewon Child, Aditya Ramesh, Daniel Ziegler, Jeffrey Wu, Clemens Winter, Chris Hesse, Mark Chen, Eric Sigler, Mateusz Litwin, Scott Gray, Benjamin Chess, Jack Clark, Christopher Berner, Sam McCandlish, Alec Radford, Ilya Sutskever, and Dario Amodei. 2020. Language models are few-shot learners. In *Advances in Neural Information Processing Systems*, volume 33, pages 1877–1901. Curran Associates, Inc.

Rich Caruana. 1997. Multitask learning. *Mach. Learn.*, 28(1):41–75.

Christopher Clark, Kenton Lee, Ming-Wei Chang, Tom Kwiatkowski, Michael Collins, and Kristina Toutanova. 2019. BoolQ: Exploring the surprising difficulty of natural yes/no questions. In *Proceedings of the 2019 Conference of the North American Chapter of the Association for Computational Linguistics: Human Language Technologies, Volume 1 (Long and Short Papers)*, pages 2924–2936, Minneapolis, Minnesota. Association for Computational Linguistics.

Arman Cohan, Franck Dernoncourt, Doo Soon Kim, Trung Bui, Seokhwan Kim, Walter Chang, and Nazli Goharian. 2018. A discourse-aware attention model for abstractive summarization of long documents. In *Proceedings of the 2018 Conference of the North American Chapter of the Association for Computational Linguistics: Human Language Technologies, Volume 2 (Short*

Papers), pages 615–621, New Orleans, Louisiana. Association for Computational Linguistics.

Andrew D. Cohen. 2006. The coming of age of research on test-taking strategies. *Language Assessment Quarterly*, 3(4):307–331.

Vanya Cohen and Aaron Gokaslan. 2020. Opengpt-2: Open language models and implications of generated text. *XRDS*, 27(1):26–30.

Dorottya Demszky, Dana Movshovitz-Attias, Jeongwoo Ko, Alan Cowen, Gaurav Nemade, and Sujith Ravi. 2020. GoEmotions: A dataset of fine-grained emotions. In *Proceedings of the 58th Annual Meeting of the Association for Computational Linguistics*, pages 4040–4054, Online. Association for Computational Linguistics.

Jacob Devlin, Ming-Wei Chang, Kenton Lee, and Kristina Toutanova. 2019. BERT: Pre-training of deep bidirectional transformers for language understanding. In *Proceedings of the 2019 Conference of the North American Chapter of the Association for Computational Linguistics: Human Language Technologies, Volume 1 (Long and Short Papers)*, pages 4171–4186, Minneapolis, Minnesota. Association for Computational Linguistics.

Jay DeYoung, Sarthak Jain, Nazneen Fatema Rajani, Eric Lehman, Caiming Xiong, Richard Socher, and Byron C. Wallace. Eraser: A benchmark to evaluate rationalized nlp models.

Dheeru Dua, Yizhong Wang, Pradeep Dasigi, Gabriel Stanovsky, Sameer Singh, and Matt Gardner. 2019. DROP: A reading comprehension benchmark requiring discrete reasoning over paragraphs. In *Proc. of NAACL*.

Ondřej Dušek, Jekaterina Novikova, and Verena Rieser. 2020. Evaluating the State-of-the-Art of End-to-End Natural Language Generation: The E2E NLG Challenge. *Computer Speech & Language*, 59:123–156.

Vladimir Eidelman. 2019. BillSum: A corpus for automatic summarization of US legislation. In *Proceedings of the 2nd Workshop on New Frontiers in Summarization*. Association for Computational Linguistics.

Alexander R. Fabbri, Irene Li, Tianwei She, Suyi Li, and Dragomir R. Radev. 2019. Multi-news: a large-scale multi-document summarization dataset and abstractive hierarchical model.

Sian Gooding. 2022. On the ethical considerations of text simplification. In *Ninth Workshop on Speech and Language Processing for Assistive Technologies (SLPAT-2022)*, pages 50–57, Dublin, Ireland. Association for Computational Linguistics.

Han Guo, Ramakanth Pasunuru, and Mohit Bansal. 2019. AutoSeM: Automatic task selection and mixing in multi-task learning. In *Proceedings of the 2019 Conference of the North American Chapter of the Association for Computational Linguistics: Human Language Technologies, Volume 1 (Long and Short Papers)*, pages 3520–3531, Minneapolis, Minnesota. Association for Computational Linguistics.

Junxian He, Wojciech Kryściński, Bryan McCann, Nazneen Rajani, and Caiming Xiong. 2020. Ctrlsum: Towards generic controllable text summarization.

Karl Moritz Hermann, Tomás Kociský, Edward Grefenstette, Lasse Espeholt, Will Kay, Mustafa Suleyman, and Phil Blunsom. 2015. Teaching machines to read and comprehend. In *NIPS*, pages 1693–1701.

Eduard Hovy, Laurie Gerber, Ulf Hermjakob, Chin-Yew Lin, and Deepak Ravichandran. 2001. Toward semantics-based answer pinpointing. In *Proceedings of the First International Conference on Human Language Technology Research*.

Lifu Huang, Ronan Le Bras, Chandra Bhagavatula, and Yejin Choi. 2019. Cosmos qa: Machine reading comprehension with contextual commonsense reasoning.

Yichong Huang, Xiachong Feng, Xiaocheng Feng, and Bing Qin. 2021. The factual inconsistency problem in abstractive text summarization: A survey. *arXiv preprint arXiv:2104.14839*.

Mandar Joshi, Eunsol Choi, Daniel S. Weld, and Luke Zettlemoyer. 2017. Triviaqa: A large scale distantly supervised challenge dataset for reading comprehension. In *Proceedings of the 55th Annual Meeting of the Association for Computational Linguistics*, Vancouver, Canada. Association for Computational Linguistics.

Daniel Khashabi, Snigdha Chaturvedi, Michael Roth, Shyam Upadhyay, and Dan Roth. 2018. Looking beyond the surface:a challenge set for reading comprehension over multiple sentences. In *NAACL*.

Tushar Khot, Ashish Sabharwal, and Peter Clark. 2018. Scitail: A textual entailment dataset from science question answering. In *Proceedings of the Thirty-Second AAAI Conference on Artificial Intelligence and Thirtieth Innovative Applications of Artificial Intelligence Conference and Eighth AAAI Symposium on Educational Advances in Artificial Intelligence*, AAAI'18/IAAI'18/EAAI'18. AAAI Press.

Byeongchang Kim, Hyunwoo Kim, and Gunhee Kim. 2019. Abstractive summarization of Reddit posts with multi-level memory networks. In *Proceedings of the 2019 Conference of the North American Chapter of the Association for Computational Linguistics: Human Language Technologies, Volume 1 (Long and Short Papers)*, pages 2519–2531, Minneapolis, Minnesota. Association for Computational Linguistics.

Walter Kintsch and Teun A. van Dijk. 1978. Toward a model of text comprehension and production. *Psychological Review*, 85(5):363–394.

James Kirkpatrick, Razvan Pascanu, Neil Rabinowitz, Joel Veness, Guillaume Desjardins, Andrei A Rusu, Kieran Milan, John Quan, Tiago Ramalho, Agnieszka Grabska-Barwinska, et al. 2017. Overcoming catastrophic forgetting in neural networks. *Proceedings of the national academy of sciences*, 114(13):3521–3526.

Vid Kocijan, Thomas Lukasiewicz, Ernest Davis, Gary Marcus, and Leora Morgenstern. 2020. A review of winograd schema challenge datasets and approaches.

Tom Kwiatkowski, Jennimaria Palomaki, Olivia Redfield, Michael Collins, Ankur Parikh, Chris Alberti, Danielle Epstein, Illia Polosukhin, Jacob Devlin, Kenton Lee, Kristina Toutanova, Llion Jones, Matthew Kelcey, Ming-Wei Chang, Andrew M. Dai, Jakob Uszkoreit, Quoc Le, and Slav Petrov. 2019. Natural questions: A benchmark for question answering research. *Transactions of the Association for Computational Linguistics*, 7:452–466.

Faisal Ladhak, Esin Durmus, Claire Cardie, and Kathleen McKeown. 2020. WikiLingua: A new benchmark dataset for cross-lingual abstractive summarization. In *Findings of the Association for Computational Linguistics: EMNLP 2020*, pages 4034–4048, Online. Association for Computational Linguistics.

Guokun Lai, Qizhe Xie, Hanxiao Liu, Yiming Yang, and Eduard Hovy. 2017. RACE: Large-scale ReAding comprehension dataset from examinations. In *Proceedings of the 2017 Conference on Empirical Methods in Natural Language Processing*, pages 785–794, Copenhagen, Denmark. Association for Computational Linguistics.

Mike Lewis, Yinhan Liu, Naman Goyal, Marjan Ghazvininejad, Abdelrahman Mohamed, Omer Levy, Veselin Stoyanov, and Luke Zettlemoyer. 2020. BART: Denoising Sequence-to-Sequence Pre-training for Natural Language Generation, Translation, and Comprehension. In *Proceedings of the 58th Annual Meeting of the Association for Computational Linguistics*, pages 7871–7880, Online. Association for Computational Linguistics.

Xin Li and Dan Roth. 2002. Learning question classifiers. In *COLING 2002: The 19th International Conference on Computational Linguistics*.

Bill Yuchen Lin, Wangchunshu Zhou, Ming Shen, Pei Zhou, Chandra Bhagavatula, Yejin Choi, and Xiang Ren. 2019. Commongen: A constrained text generation challenge for generative commonsense reasoning.

Chin-Yew Lin. 2004. ROUGE: A package for automatic evaluation of summaries. In *Text Summarization Branches Out*, pages 74–81, Barcelona, Spain. Association for Computational Linguistics.

J. Lin. 1991. Divergence measures based on the shannon entropy. *IEEE Transactions on Information Theory*, 37(1):145–151.

Xiaodong Liu, Pengcheng He, Weizhu Chen, and Jianfeng Gao. 2019a. Multi-task deep neural networks for natural language understanding. In *Proceedings of the 57th Annual Meeting of the Association for Computational Linguistics*, pages 4487–4496, Florence, Italy. Association for Computational Linguistics.

Yinhan Liu, Myle Ott, Naman Goyal, Jingfei Du, Mandar Joshi, Danqi Chen, Omer Levy, Mike Lewis, Luke Zettlemoyer, and Veselin Stoyanov. 2019b. Roberta: A robustly optimized bert pretraining approach.

Andrew L. Maas, Raymond E. Daly, Peter T. Pham, Dan Huang, Andrew Y. Ng, and Christopher Potts. 2011. Learning word vectors for sentiment analysis. In *Proceedings of the 49th Annual Meeting of the Association for Computational Linguistics: Human Language Technologies*, pages 142–150, Portland, Oregon, USA. Association for Computational Linguistics.

Michael McCloskey and Neal J. Cohen. 1989. Catastrophic interference in connectionist networks: The sequential learning problem. volume 24 of *Psychology of Learning and Motivation*, pages 109–165. Academic Press.

R. Thomas McCoy, Ellie Pavlick, and Tal Linzen. 2019. Right for the wrong reasons: Diagnosing syntactic heuristics in natural language inference.

Shashi Narayan, Shay B. Cohen, and Mirella Lapata. 2018. Don't give me the details, just the summary! Topic-aware convolutional neural networks for extreme summarization. In *Proceedings of the 2018 Conference on Empirical Methods in Natural Language Processing*, Brussels, Belgium.

Malte Ostendorff, Terry Ruas, Till Blume, Bela Gipp, and Georg Rehm. 2020a. Aspect-based Document Similarity for Research Papers. In *Proceedings of the 28th International Conference on Computational Linguistics*, pages 6194–6206, Barcelona, Spain (Online). International Committee on Computational Linguistics.

Malte Ostendorff, Terry Ruas, Moritz Schubotz, Georg Rehm, and Bela Gipp. 2020b. Pairwise Multi-Class Document Classification for Semantic Relations between Wikipedia Articles. In *Proceedings of the ACM/IEEE Joint Conference on Digital Libraries in 2020*, pages 127–136, Virtual Event China. ACM.

Bo Pang and Lillian Lee. 2005. Seeing stars: Exploiting class relationships for sentiment categorization with respect to rating scales. In *Proceedings of the ACL*.

Kishore Papineni, Salim Roukos, Todd Ward, and Wei-Jing Zhu. 2002. Bleu: a method for automatic evaluation of machine translation. In *Proceedings of the 40th Annual Meeting of the Association for Computational Linguistics*, pages 311–318, Philadelphia, Pennsylvania, USA. Association for Computational Linguistics.

Jason Phang, Thibault Févry, and Samuel R. Bowman. 2018. Sentence encoders on stilts: Supplementary training on intermediate labeled-data tasks. *CoRR*, abs/1811.01088.

Mohammad Taher Pilehvar and Jose Camacho-Collados. 2018. Wic: the word-in-context dataset for evaluating context-sensitive meaning representations.

Adam Poliak. 2020. A survey on recognizing textual entailment as an nlp evaluation.

Alec Radford, Jeffrey Wu, Rewon Child, David Luan, Dario Amodei, and Ilya Sutskever. 2019. Language Models are Unsupervised Multitask Learners.

Colin Raffel, Noam Shazeer, Adam Roberts, Katherine Lee, Sharan Narang, Michael Matena, Yanqi Zhou, Wei Li, and Peter J. Liu. 2020. Exploring the limits of transfer learning with a unified text-to-text transformer. *Journal of Machine Learning Research*, 21(140):1–67.

Pranav Rajpurkar, Jian Zhang, Konstantin Lopyrev, and Percy Liang. 2016. SQuAD: 100,000+ questions for machine comprehension of text. In *Proceedings of the 2016 Conference on Empirical Methods in Natural Language Processing*, pages 2383–2392, Austin, Texas. Association for Computational Linguistics.

Alfréd Rényi et al. 1961. On measures of entropy and information. In *Proceedings of the fourth Berkeley symposium on mathematical statistics and probability*, volume 1. Berkeley, California, USA.

Sebastian Ruder and Barbara Plank. 2017. Learning to select data for transfer learning with Bayesian optimization. In *Proceedings of the 2017 Conference on Empirical Methods in Natural Language Processing*, pages 372–382, Copenhagen, Denmark. Association for Computational Linguistics.

Alexander M. Rush, Sumit Chopra, and Jason Weston. 2015. A neural attention model for abstractive sentence summarization.

Daniel J. Russo, Benjamin Van Roy, Abbas Kazerouni, Ian Osband, and Zheng Wen. 2018. A tutorial on thompson sampling. *Found. Trends Mach. Learn.*, 11(1):1–96.

Amrita Saha, Vardaan Pahuja, Mitesh M. Khapra, Karthik Sankaranarayanan, and Sarath Chandar. 2018. Complex sequential question answering: Towards learning to converse over linked question answer pairs with a knowledge graph.

Keisuke Sakaguchi, Ronan Le Bras, Chandra Bhagavatula, and Yejin Choi. 2021. Winogrande: An adversarial winograd schema challenge at scale. *Commun. ACM*, 64(9):99–106.

Victor Sanh, Thomas Wolf, and Sebastian Ruder. 2019. A hierarchical multi-task approach for learning embeddings from semantic tasks. In *Proceedings of the Thirty-Third AAAI Conference on Artificial Intelligence and Thirty-First Innovative Applications of Artificial Intelligence Conference and Ninth AAAI Symposium on Educational Advances in Artificial Intelligence*, AAAI'19/IAAI'19/EAAI'19. AAAI Press.

Maarten Sap, Hannah Rashkin, Derek Chen, Ronan Le-Bras, and Yejin Choi. 2019. Socialiqa: Commonsense reasoning about social interactions.

Abigail See, Peter J. Liu, and Christopher D. Manning. 2017. Get to the point: Summarization with pointer-generator networks. In *Proceedings of the 55th Annual Meeting of the Association for Computational Linguistics (Volume 1: Long Papers)*, pages 1073–1083, Vancouver, Canada. Association for Computational Linguistics.

Richard Socher, Alex Perelygin, Jean Wu, Jason Chuang, Christopher D. Manning, Andrew Ng, and Christopher Potts. 2013. Recursive deep models for semantic compositionality over a sentiment treebank. In *Proceedings of the 2013 Conference on Empirical Methods in Natural Language Processing*, pages 1631–1642, Seattle, Washington, USA. Association for Computational Linguistics.

Timo Spinde, Jan-David Krieger, Terry Ruas, Jelena Mitrović, Franz Götz-Hahn, Akiko Aizawa, and Bela Gipp. 2022. Exploiting Transformer-Based Multitask Learning for the Detection of Media Bias in News Articles. In Malte Smits, editor, *Information for a Better World: Shaping the Global Future*, volume 13192, pages 225–235. Springer International Publishing, Cham.

Timo Spinde, Manuel Plank, Jan-David Krieger, Terry Ruas, Bela Gipp, and Akiko Aizawa. 2021. Neural Media Bias Detection Using Distant Supervision With BABE - Bias Annotations By Experts. In *Findings of the Association for Computational Linguistics: EMNLP 2021*, pages 1166–1177, Punta Cana, Dominican Republic. Association for Computational Linguistics.

Yu Sun, Shuohuan Wang, Yukun Li, Shikun Feng, Hao Tian, Hua Wu, and Haifeng Wang. 2020. Ernie 2.0: A continual pre-training framework for language understanding. *Proceedings of the AAAI Conference on Artificial Intelligence*, 34(05):8968–8975.

Alon Talmor, Jonathan Herzig, Nicholas Lourie, and Jonathan Berant. 2018. Commonsenseqa: A question answering challenge targeting commonsense knowledge.

William R Thompson. 1933. On the Likelihood that one unknown probability exceeds another in view of the evidence of two samples. *Biometrika*, 25(3-4):285–294.

James Thorne, Andreas Vlachos, Christos Christodoulopoulos, and Arpit Mittal. 2018. FEVER: a large-scale dataset for fact extraction and VERification. In *Proceedings of the 2018 Conference of the North American Chapter of the Association for Computational Linguistics: Human Language Technologies, Volume 1 (Long Papers)*, pages 809–819, New Orleans, Louisiana. Association for Computational Linguistics.

Ashish Vaswani, Noam Shazeer, Niki Parmar, Jakob Uszkoreit, Llion Jones, Aidan N Gomez, Ł ukasz Kaiser, and Illia Polosukhin. 2017. Attention is all you need. In *Advances in Neural Information Processing Systems*, volume 30. Curran Associates, Inc.

Tu Vu, Tong Wang, Tsendsuren Munkhdalai, Alessandro Sordoni, Adam Trischler, Andrew Mattarella-Micke, Subhransu Maji, and Mohit Iyyer. 2020. Exploring and predicting transferability across NLP tasks. In *Proceedings of the 2020 Conference on Empirical Methods in Natural Language Processing (EMNLP)*, pages 7882–7926, Online. Association for Computational Linguistics.

Jan Philip Wahle, Nischal Ashok, Terry Ruas, Norman Meuschke, Tirthankar Ghosal, and Bela Gipp. 2022a. Testing the Generalization of Neural Language Models for COVID-19 Misinformation Detection. In Malte Smits, editor, *Information for a Better World: Shaping the Global Future*, volume 13192, pages 381–392. Springer International Publishing, Cham.

Jan Philip Wahle, Terry Ruas, Tomáš Foltýnek, Norman

Meuschke, and Bela Gipp. 2022b. Identifying Machine-Paraphrased Plagiarism. In Malte Smits, editor, *Information for a Better World: Shaping the Global Future*, volume 13192, pages 393–413. Springer International Publishing, Cham.

Jan Philip Wahle, Terry Ruas, Frederic Kirstein, and Bela Gipp. 2022c. How large language models are transforming machine-paraphrased plagiarism. *arXiv preprint arXiv:2210.03568*.

Jan Philip Wahle, Terry Ruas, Norman Meuschke, and Bela Gipp. 2021. Incorporating Word Sense Disambiguation in Neural Language Models. *arXiv:2106.07967 [cs]*.

Alex Wang, Yada Pruksachatkun, Nikita Nangia, Amanpreet Singh, Julian Michael, Felix Hill, Omer Levy, and Samuel Bowman. 2019. Superglue: A stickier benchmark for general-purpose language understanding systems. In *Advances in Neural Information Processing Systems*, volume 32. Curran Associates, Inc.

Alex Wang, Amanpreet Singh, Julian Michael, Felix Hill, Omer Levy, and Samuel Bowman. 2018. GLUE: A multi-task benchmark and analysis platform for natural language understanding. In *Proceedings of the 2018 EMNLP Workshop BlackboxNLP: Analyzing and Interpreting Neural Networks for NLP*, pages 353–355, Brussels, Belgium. Association for Computational Linguistics.

Alex Warstadt, Amanpreet Singh, and Samuel R Bowman. 2018. Neural network acceptability judgments. *arXiv preprint arXiv:1805.12471*.

Adina Williams, Nikita Nangia, and Samuel Bowman. 2018. A broad-coverage challenge corpus for sentence understanding through inference. In *Proceedings of the 2018 Conference of the North American Chapter of the Association for Computational Linguistics: Human Language Technologies, Volume 1 (Long Papers)*, pages 1112–1122. Association for Computational Linguistics.

Adina Williams, Tristan Thrush, and Douwe Kiela. 2020. Anlizing the adversarial natural language inference dataset.

Wenhan Xiong, Jiawei Wu, Hong Wang, Vivek Kulkarni, Mo Yu, Shiyu Chang, Xiaoxiao Guo, and William Yang Wang. 2019. TWEETQA: A social media focused question answering dataset. In *Proceedings of the 57th Annual Meeting of the Association for Computational Linguistics*, pages 5020–5031, Florence, Italy. Association for Computational Linguistics.

Vikas Yadav, Steven Bethard, and Mihai Surdeanu. 2019. Quick and (not so) dirty: Unsupervised selection of justification sentences for multi-hop question answering. In *Proceedings of the 2019 Conference on Empirical Methods in Natural Language Processing and the 9th International Joint Conference on Natural Language Processing (EMNLP-IJCNLP)*. Association for Computational Linguistics.

Zhilin Yang, Peng Qi, Saizheng Zhang, Yoshua Bengio, William Cohen, Ruslan Salakhutdinov, and Christopher D. Manning. 2018. HotpotQA: A dataset for diverse, explainable multi-hop question answering. In *Proceedings of the 2018 Conference on Empirical Methods in Natural Language Processing*, pages 2369–2380, Brussels, Belgium. Association for Computational Linguistics.

Guoxing Yu. 2008. Reading to summarize in english and chinese: A tale of two languages? *Language Testing*, 25(4):521–551.

Rowan Zellers, Yonatan Bisk, Roy Schwartz, and Yejin Choi. 2018. SWAG: A large-scale adversarial dataset for grounded commonsense inference. In *Proceedings of the 2018 Conference on Empirical Methods in Natural Language Processing*, pages 93–104, Brussels, Belgium. Association for Computational Linguistics.

Rowan Zellers, Ari Holtzman, Yonatan Bisk, Ali Farhadi, and Yejin Choi. 2019. HellaSwag: Can a machine really finish your sentence? In *Proceedings of the 57th Annual Meeting of the Association for Computational Linguistics*, pages 4791–4800, Florence, Italy. Association for Computational Linguistics.

Jingqing Zhang, Yao Zhao, Mohammad Saleh, and Peter J. Liu. 2020. PEGASUS: Pre-training with Extracted Gap-sentences for Abstractive Summarization. *arXiv:1912.08777 [cs]*.

Rui Zhang and Joel Tetreault. 2019. This email could save your life: Introducing the task of email subject line generation.

Sheng Zhang, Xiaodong Liu, Jingjing Liu, Jianfeng Gao, Kevin Duh, and Benjamin Van Durme. 2018. Record: Bridging the gap between human and machine commonsense reading comprehension.

Tianyi Zhang, Varsha Kishore, Felix Wu, Kilian Q. Weinberger, and Yoav Artzi. 2019a. Bertscore: Evaluating text generation with BERT. *CoRR*, abs/1904.09675.

Xiang Zhang, Junbo Zhao, and Yann LeCun. 2015. Character-level convolutional networks for text classification.

Zhuosheng Zhang, Yuwei Wu, Hai Zhao, Zuchao Li, Shuailiang Zhang, Xi Zhou, and Xiang Zhou. 2019b. Semantics-aware bert for language understanding.

A Tasks and Families

Table 7 shows an extended version of pre-finetuning tasks in Table 1 to-be-considered in future work

B Additional Models

Tables 8 to 10 shows the results for different models and loop orders. BART performed best compared to models from related work, which is why we chose the model throughout our experiments.

C Extended Results

C.1 Extended Results on Reddit TIFU

Tables 13 to 27 show the detailed evaluation for each research question and all tested combinations of task families evaluated on the Reddit TIFU datasets. The tables are divided according to their training scheme, i.e., each table shows one of the three training schemes (sim, seq, cMTL).

C.2 Extended Results on arXiv

Tables 31 to 39 show the detailed evaluation for each research question and all tested combinations of task families evaluated on the arXiv datasets. The tables are divided according to their training scheme, i.e., each table shows one of the three training schemes (sim, seq, cMTL).

D Hyperparameters

Table 41 shows the hyperparameters used throughout the pre-finetuning and finetuning experiments.

TF	Task	Dataset	Citation
CLS	Topic Classification	AG News	(Zhang et al., 2015)
	Text Classification	Civil Comments	(Borkan et al., 2019)
	Text Classification	FEVER	(Thorne et al., 2018)
	Emotion Classification	GoEmotions	(Demszky et al., 2020)
	Sentiment Classification	IMDB	(Maas et al., 2011)
	Sentiment Classification	Rotten Tomatoes	(Pang and Lee, 2005)
	Text Classification	Trec	(Li and Roth, 2002; Hovy et al., 2001)
	classification	Word-in-Context	(Pilehvar and Camacho-Collados, 2018)
	Sentiment Classification	Yelp Polarity	(Zhang et al., 2015)
	Linguistic Acceptability	CoLA	(Warstadt et al., 2018)
	Sentiment Classification	SST-2	(Socher et al., 2013)
CMNS	Open Domain QA	AI2 Reasoning (Challenge ARC)	(Yadav et al., 2019)
	Concepts to Text Generation	CommonGen (CG)	(Lin et al., 2019)
	Sequential Question Answering	CQA	(Saha et al., 2018)
	Commonsense Inference	HellaSWAG	(Zellers et al., 2019)
	Question Answering	PhysicaliQA	(Bisk et al., 2019)
	Question Answering	SocialiQA	(Sap et al., 2019)
	Text Classification	SWAG	(Zellers et al., 2018)
	Fill-In-A-Blank	WinoGrande	(Sakaguchi et al., 2021)
	Question Answering	Winograd Scheme (Challenge)	(Kocijan et al., 2020)
	Open-Domain-QA	CommonSense QA	(Talmor et al., 2018)
NLI	Textual Entailment Classification	ANLI (Adverserial NLI)	(Williams et al., 2020)
	Natural Language Inference	HANS	(McCoy et al., 2019)
	Textual Entailment Classification	MNLI	(Williams et al., 2018)
	Textual Entailment Classification	QNLI	(Wang et al., 2018)
	Textual Entailment Classification	RTE	(Poliak, 2020)
	Textual Entailment Classification	SciTail	(Khot et al., 2018)
	Natural Language Inference	SNLI	(Zhang et al., 2019b)
	Natural Language Inference	WNLI	(Wang et al., 2018)
RC	Binary QA	BoolQ	(Clark et al., 2019)
	Multiple Choice QA	Cosmos QA	(Huang et al., 2019)
	Multi-Sentence QA	Eraser Multi RC	(DeYoung et al.; Khashabi et al., 2018)
	Extractive QA	SQUAD	(Rajpurkar et al., 2016)
	Extractive QA	TriviaQA	(Joshi et al., 2017)
	Abstractive QA	TweetQA	(Xiong et al., 2019)
	Multiple Choice QA	RACE	(Lai et al., 2017)
RC^{+}	Text2Text Generation	E2E	(Dušek et al., 2020)
	RC + Question Answering	MSMarco	(Bajaj et al., 2016)
	RC + Open Domain QA	Natural Questions	(Kwiatkowski et al., 2019)
	RC + Commonsense Reasoning	RECORD	(Zhang et al., 2018)
	RC + Information Retrieval	HotpotQA	(Yang et al., 2018)
	RC + Extractive QA	DROP	(Dua et al., 2019)
SUM	Abstractive Summarization	Aeslc	(Zhang and Tetreault, 2019)
	Extractive Summarization	Billsum	(Eidelman, 2019)
	Abstractive Summarization	CNN	(See et al., 2017; Hermann et al., 2015)
	Headline Generation	Gigaword	(Rush et al., 2015)
	Abstractive Summarization	Multinews	(Fabbri et al., 2019)
	Abstractive Summarization	WikiLingua [eng]	(Ladhak et al., 2020)
	Extractive Summarization	XSUM	(Narayan et al., 2018)

Table 7: An extended list of Table 1. This list can be used to extend TOASTS to more tasks and datasets in future work. TF stands for Task Family.

order	BERTScore	BLEU	METEOR	ROUGE-1	ROURGE-2	ROUGE-L
ascending (ours)	0.881	0.057	0.229	0.284	0.096	0.228
descending	0.861	0.003	0.082	0.095	0.012	0.085

Table 8: Results of different loop orders tested. Let t denote the current training stage, then the ascending order for the training stage t is Task_t, Task_1, Task_2, ..., Task_{t-1}. The descending order follows for the same training stage t the form Task_t, Task_{t-1}, Task_{t-2}, ..., Task_1.

model	BERTScore	BLEU	METEOR	ROUGE-1	ROUGE-2	ROUGE-L	Time
BART	**0.881**	**0.061**	**0.231**	**0.286**	**0.100**	**0.233**	0.75h
T5	**0.881**	0.052	0.218	0.282	0.090	0.229	1.15h
PEGASUS	0.876	0.058	0.215	0.264	0.094	0.216	1h

Table 9: Results of different models used. The models were finetuned on Reddit TIFU without pre-finetuning and with full precision. Values in **bold** represent the highest results for a training scheme.

model	BERTScore	BLEU	METEOR	ROUGE-1	ROUGE-2	ROUGE-L	Time
BART	**0.864**	**0.129**	**0.306**	**0.444**	**0.168**	0.267	13.5h
T5	**0.864**	0.120	0.291	0.416	0.153	**0.272**	27.5h
PEGASUS	0.858	0.122	0.291	0.414	0.148	0.253	18.5h

Table 10: Results of different models used. The models were finetuned on arXiv without pre-finetuning and with full precision. Values in **bold** represent the highest results for a training scheme.

Task Families	BERTScore	BLEU	METEOR	ROUGE-1	ROUGE-2	ROUGE-L
CLS	0.881	0.057	0.226	0.282	0.097	0.229
CMNS	0.881	0.055	0.226	0.282	0.095	0.228
NLI	0.869	0.000	0.030	0.088	0.006	0.083
RC	<u>**0.882**</u>	0.057	0.230	0.285	**0.098**	0.230
RC+	0.881	0.056	0.224	0.281	0.096	0.229
SUM	0.881	**0.061**	**0.231**	**0.287**	**0.098**	**0.231**
BART	0.858	0.003	0.087	0.105	0.011	0.090

Table 11: RQ1 results (single task family) for Reddit TIFU and the sequential strategy. Values in **bold** represent the highest results for a training scheme. <u>Underlined</u> values are the highest results for that dataset independent of training.

Task Families	BERTScore	BLEU	METEOR	ROUGE-1	ROUGE-2	ROUGE-L
CLS	0.881	0.061	0.233	0.286	0.099	0.232
CMNS	0.863	0.003	0.078	0.091	0.013	0.081
NLI	0.863	0.003	0.082	0.095	0.012	0.085
RC	0.881	0.061	**0.235**	<u>**0.290**</u>	0.100	0.232
RC+	0.863	0.003	0.082	0.095	0.012	0.085
SUM	<u>**0.882**</u>	**0.062**	**0.235**	0.288	**0.102**	**0.234**
BART	0.858	0.003	0.087	0.105	0.011	0.090

Table 12: RQ1 results (single task family) for Reddit TIFU and the simultaneous strategy. Values in **bold** represent the highest results for a training scheme. <u>Underlined</u> values are the highest results for that dataset independent of training.

Task Families	BERTScore	BLEU	METEOR	ROUGE-1	ROUGE-2	ROUGE-L
CLS	0.853	0.002	0.060	0.095	0.012	0.085
CMNS	0.863	0.003	0.078	0.091	0.013	0.081
NLI	0.863	0.003	0.082	0.095	0.012	0.085
RC	**0.881**	**0.059**	0.230	**0.287**	**0.098**	0.231
RC+	0.863	0.003	0.078	0.091	0.013	0.080
SUM	**0.881**	**0.059**	**0.231**	**0.287**	**0.098**	**0.232**
BART	0.858	0.003	0.087	0.105	0.011	0.090

Table 13: RQ1 results (single task family) for Reddit TIFU and the continual multi-task learning strategy. Values in **bold** represent the highest results for a training scheme. Underlined values are the highest results for that dataset independent of training.

Task Families	BERTScore	BLEU	METEOR	ROUGE-1	ROUGE-2	ROUGE-L
ALL	**0.880**	**0.053**	**0.222**	**0.278**	**0.092**	**0.225**
BART	0.858	0.003	0.087	0.105	0.011	0.090

Table 14: RQ1 results (all task families) for Reddit TIFU and the sequential strategy. Values in **bold** represent the highest results for a training scheme. Underlined values are the highest results for that dataset independent of training.

Task Families	BERTScore	BLEU	METEOR	ROUGE-1	ROUGE-2	ROUGE-L
ALL	**0.881**	**0.057**	**0.228**	**0.283**	**0.095**	**0.228**
BART	0.858	0.003	0.087	0.105	0.011	0.090

Table 15: RQ1 results (all task families) for Reddit TIFU and the simultaneous strategy. Values in **bold** represent the highest results for a training scheme. Underlined values are the highest results for that dataset independent of training.

Task Families	BERTScore	BLEU	METEOR	ROUGE-1	ROUGE-2	ROUGE-L
ALL	0.819	0.000	0.037	0.000	0.000	0.000
BART	0.858	0.003	0.087	0.105	0.011	0.090

Table 16: RQ1 results (all task families) for Reddit TIFU and the continual multi-task learning strategy. Values in **bold** represent the highest results for a training scheme. Underlined values are the highest results for that dataset independent of training.

Task Families	BERTScore	BLEU	METEOR	ROUGE-1	ROUGE-2	ROUGE-L
SUM + CLS	0.881	**0.061**	0.230	0.284	0.098	0.230
SUM + CMNS	0.881	0.060	0.232	0.287	0.098	0.231
SUM + NLI	0.881	0.053	0.223	0.280	0.094	0.225
SUM + RC	**0.882**	**0.061**	**0.233**	**0.288**	**0.100**	**0.235**
SUM + RC+	0.881	0.060	0.230	0.285	0.098	0.232
BART	0.858	0.003	0.087	0.105	0.011	0.090

Table 17: RQ2 results (pairing of the summarization task family with another task family) for Reddit TIFU and the sequential strategy. Values in **bold** represent the highest results for a training scheme. Underlined values are the highest results for that dataset independent of training.

Task Families	BERTScore	BLEU	METEOR	ROUGE-1	ROUGE-2	ROUGE-L
SUM + CLS	**0.881**	0.061	**0.233**	**0.287**	0.096	**0.232**
SUM + CMNS	**0.881**	0.059	0.231	0.284	0.097	0.230
SUM + NLI	**0.881**	**0.062**	**0.233**	**0.287**	**0.098**	0.231
SUM + RC	**0.881**	0.059	0.229	0.286	0.097	0.231
SUM + RC^{+}	**0.881**	0.057	0.225	0.283	0.096	0.229
BART	0.858	0.003	0.087	0.105	0.011	0.090

Table 18: RQ2 results (pairing of the summarization task family with another task family) for Reddit TIFU and the simultaneous strategy. Values in **bold** represent the highest results for a training scheme. Underlined values are the highest results for that dataset independent of training.

Task Families	BERTScore	BLEU	METEOR	ROUGE-1	ROUGE-2	ROUGE-L
SUM + CLS	0.864	0.003	0.077	0.093	0.013	0.081
SUM + CMNS	**0.881**	**0.062**	0.234	0.289	**0.100**	**0.236**
SUM + NLI	**0.881**	0.053	0.223	0.280	0.095	0.225
SUM + RC	**0.881**	**0.062**	**0.234**	**0.290**	**0.100**	0.233
SUM + RC^{+}	**0.881**	0.061	0.234	0.288	**0.100**	0.233
BART	0.858	0.003	0.087	0.105	0.011	0.090

Table 19: RQ2 results (pairing of the summarization task family with another task family) for Reddit TIFU and the continual multi-task learning strategy. Values in **bold** represent the highest results for a training scheme. Underlined values are the highest results for that dataset independent of training.

Task Families	BERTScore	BLEU	METEOR	ROUGE-1	ROUGE-2	ROUGE-L
CLS + CMNS	0.863	0.003	0.078	0.091	0.013	0.081
CLS + NLI	0.864	0.003	0.077	0.093	0.013	0.081
CLS + RC	**0.881**	0.059	0.231	0.288	0.097	0.232
CLS + RC^{+}	**0.881**	0.059	0.229	0.286	0.097	0.231
CMNS + NLI	**0.881**	0.060	0.231	0.286	0.099	0.231
CMNS + RC	**0.881**	0.059	0.227	0.282	0.096	0.228
CMNS + RC^{+}	**0.881**	**0.061**	0.232	0.287	0.097	0.231
NLI + RC^{+}	**0.881**	**0.061**	**0.233**	**0.289**	**0.100**	**0.234**
NLI + RC	**0.881**	0.058	0.231	0.286	0.097	0.231
RC + RC^{+}	**0.881**	0.058	0.228	0.284	0.096	0.230
BART	0.858	0.003	0.087	0.105	0.011	0.090

Table 20: RQ3 results (pairing of two task families excluding the text summarization family) for Reddit TIFU and the sequential strategy. Values in **bold** represent the highest results for a training scheme. Underlined values are the highest results for that dataset, independent of training.

Task Families	BERTScore	BLEU	METEOR	ROUGE-1	ROUGE-2	ROUGE-L
CLS + CMNS	0.863	0.003	0.078	0.091	0.013	0.081
CLS + NLI	0.864	0.003	0.077	0.093	0.013	0.081
CLS + RC	**0.881**	0.059	0.231	0.288	0.097	0.232
CLS + RC^{+}	**0.881**	0.059	0.229	0.286	0.097	0.231
CMNS + NLI	**0.881**	0.060	0.231	0.286	0.099	0.231
CMNS + RC	**0.881**	0.059	0.227	0.282	0.096	0.228
CMNS + RC^{+}	**0.881**	**0.061**	0.232	0.287	0.097	0.231
NLI + RC	**0.881**	0.058	0.231	0.286	0.097	0.231
NLI + RC^{+}	**0.881**	**0.061**	**0.234**	**0.289**	**0.100**	**0.234**
RC + RC^{+}	**0.881**	0.058	0.228	0.284	0.096	0.223
BART	0.858	0.003	0.087	0.105	0.011	0.090

Table 21: RQ3 results (pairing of two task families excluding the text summarization family) for Reddit TIFU and the simultaneous strategy. Values in **bold** represent the highest results for a training scheme. Underlined values are the highest results for that dataset independent of training.

Task Families	BERTScore	BLEU	METEOR	ROUGE-1	ROUGE-2	ROUGE-L
CLS + CMNS	0.853	0.002	0.060	0.095	0.012	0.085
CLS + NLI	0.869	0.000	0.046	0.056	0.007	0.055
CLS + RC	**0.881**	0.060	0.230	0.286	0.099	0.232
CLS + RC$^+$	0.863	0.003	0.082	0.095	0.012	0.085
CMNS + NLI	0.865	0.002	0.081	0.099	0.012	0.089
CMNS + RC	0.864	0.003	0.077	0.093	0.013	0.081
CMNS + RC$^+$	**0.881**	**0.062**	**0.232**	**0.287**	**0.099**	**0.233**
NLI + RC	**0.881**	0.060	0.231	0.287	0.098	0.232
NLI + RC$^+$	**0.881**	0.057	0.227	0.283	0.096	0.229
RC + RC$^+$	**0.881**	0.059	0.228	0.284	0.098	0.230
BART	0.858	0.003	0.087	0.105	0.011	0.090

Table 22: RQ3 results (pairing of two task families excluding the text summarization family) for Reddit TIFU and the continual multi-task learning strategy. Values in **bold** represent the highest results for a training scheme. Underlined values are the highest results for that dataset independent of training.

Task Families	BERTScore	BLEU	METEOR	ROUGE-1	ROUGE-2	ROUGE-L
SUM + CLS + CMNS	0.881	0.060	0.228	0.286	0.098	0.232
SUM + CLS + NLI	0.881	0.059	0.231	0.285	0.098	0.231
SUM + CLS + RC	**0.882**	0.060	**0.235**	0.288	0.099	**0.234**
SUM + CLS + RC$^+$	0.881	**0.062**	**0.235**	0.288	**0.100**	0.232
SUM + CMNS + NLI	0.881	0.059	0.230	0.284	0.096	0.229
SUM + CMNS + RC	**0.882**	0.061	0.234	0.288	0.099	0.232
SUM + CMNS + RC$^+$	0.881	**0.062**	0.232	0.287	**0.100**	0.233
SUM + NLI + RC	0.881	0.060	0.229	0.283	0.096	0.230
SUM + NLI + RC$^+$	0.881	0.061	0.234	**0.289**	0.099	**0.234**
SUM + RC + RC$^+$	**0.882**	0.058	0.227	0.284	0.099	0.232
BART	0.858	0.003	0.087	0.105	0.011	0.090

Table 23: RQ4 results (pairing of the summarization task family with two other task families) for Reddit TIFU and the sequential strategy. Values in **bold** represent the highest results for a training scheme. Underlined values are the highest results for that dataset independent of training.

Task Families	BERTScore	BLEU	METEOR	ROUGE-1	ROUGE-2	ROUGE-L
SUM + RC$^+$ + CLS	**0.881**	0.061	0.233	0.289	0.099	0.232
SUM + RC$^+$ + CMNS	**0.881**	0.061	0.231	0.286	0.099	0.232
SUM + RC$^+$ + NLI	**0.881**	0.058	0.229	0.285	0.098	0.231
SUM + RC$^+$ + RC	**0.881**	0.059	0.234	0.287	0.097	0.232
SUM + CLS + CMNS	**0.881**	0.057	0.227	0.283	0.096	0.229
SUM + CLS + NLI	**0.881**	0.060	0.231	0.284	0.099	0.229
SUM + CLS + RC	**0.881**	0.058	0.228	0.286	0.098	0.230
SUM + CMNS + NLI	**0.881**	**0.064**	**0.236**	**0.289**	**0.100**	**0.233**
SUM + CMNS + RC	**0.881**	0.061	0.232	0.288	0.099	**0.233**
SUM + NLI + RC	**0.881**	0.061	0.231	0.287	0.098	**0.233**
BART	0.858	0.003	0.087	0.105	0.011	0.090

Table 24: RQ4 results (pairing of the summarization task family with two other task families) for Reddit TIFU and the simultaneous strategy. Values in **bold** represent the highest results for a training scheme. Underlined values are the highest results for that dataset independent of training.

Task Families	BERTScore	BLEU	METEOR	ROUGE-1	ROUGE-2	ROUGE-L
SUM + CLS + CMNS	0.864	0.003	0.077	0.093	0.013	0.081
SUM + CLS + NLI	0.863	0.003	0.082	0.095	0.012	0.085
SUM + CLS + RC	**0.881**	0.058	0.229	**0.285**	0.098	0.231
SUM + CLS + RC+	0.863	0.003	0.082	0.095	0.012	0.085
SUM + CMNS + NLI	**0.881**	**0.059**	0.229	**0.285**	0.098	0.230
SUM + CMNS + RC	**0.881**	**0.059**	**0.230**	**0.285**	**0.099**	**0.232**
SUM + CMNS + RC+	**0.881**	**0.059**	0.228	0.284	0.096	0.229
SUM + NLI + RC	**0.881**	**0.059**	0.228	0.284	0.096	0.230
SUM + NLI + RC+	**0.881**	0.058	0.229	0.284	0.096	0.230
SUM + RC + RC+	**0.881**	**0.059**	0.228	**0.285**	0.097	0.230
BART	0.858	0.003	0.087	0.105	0.011	0.090

Table 25: RQ4 results (pairing of the summarization task family with two other task families) for Reddit TIFU and the contniual multi-task learning strategy. Values in **bold** represent the highest results for a training scheme. Underlined values are the highest results for that dataset independent of training.

Task Families	BERTScore	BLEU	METEOR	ROUGE-1	ROUGE-2	ROUGE-L
CLS + CMNS + NLI	0.752	0.000	0.034	0.044	0.000	0.040
CLS + CMNS + RC	**0.881**	**0.062**	**0.235**	0.287	**0.099**	0.231
CLS + CMNS + RC+	**0.881**	**0.062**	0.231	0.286	0.098	0.232
CLS + NLI + RC	**0.881**	0.059	0.233	**0.289**	**0.099**	**0.233**
CLS + NLI + RC+	**0.881**	0.059	0.232	0.286	0.097	0.231
CLS + RC + RC+	0.880	0.060	0.232	0.285	0.098	0.230
CMNS + NLI + RC	0.880	0.059	0.229	0.284	0.095	0.230
CMNS + NLI + RC+	**0.881**	0.059	0.231	0.284	0.096	0.230
CMNS + RC + RC+	**0.881**	0.058	0.232	0.285	0.097	0.230
NLI + RC + RC+	**0.881**	0.058	0.230	0.284	0.097	0.229
BART	0.858	0.003	0.087	0.105	0.011	0.090

Table 26: RQ4 results (pairing of three task families excluding the text summarization family) for Reddit TIFU and the sequential strategy. Values in **bold** represent the highest results for a training scheme. Underlined values are the highest results for that dataset independent of training.

Task Families	BERTScore	BLEU	METEOR	ROUGE-1	ROUGE-2	ROUGE-L
CLS + CMNS + NLI	0.746	0.000	0.024	0.028	0.000	0.275
CLS + CMNS + RC	**0.881**	0.060	0.232	0.287	**0.099**	**0.232**
CLS + CMNS + RC+	0.863	0.003	0.082	0.095	0.012	0.085
CLS + NLI + RC	**0.881**	0.059	0.228	0.285	0.098	0.230
CLS + NLI + RC+	**0.881**	0.057	0.225	0.283	0.097	0.231
CLS + RC + RC+	**0.881**	0.058	0.227	0.282	0.097	0.229
CMNS + NLI + RC	0.766	0.000	0.020	0.009	0.000	0.009
CMNS + NLI + RC+	**0.881**	0.058	0.230	0.283	0.097	0.229
CMNS + RC + RC+	**0.881**	**0.061**	**0.234**	**0.288**	0.097	0.231
NLI + RC + RC+	**0.881**	0.059	0.230	0.284	0.096	0.229
BART	0.858	0.003	0.087	0.105	0.011	0.090

Table 27: RQ4 results (pairing of three task families excluding the text summarization family) for Reddit TIFU and the simultaneous strategy. Values in **bold** represent the highest results for a training scheme. Underlined values are the highest results for that dataset independent of training.

Task Families	BERTScore	BLEU	METEOR	ROUGE-1	ROUGE-2	ROUGE-L
CLS + CMNS + NLI	0.751	0.000	0.017	0.000	0.000	0.000
CLS + CMNS + RC	0.753	0.000	0.009	0.015	0.000	0.015
CLS + CMNS + RC^{+}	0.861	0.002	0.064	0.057	0.012	0.054
CLS + NLI + RC	0.864	0.003	0.077	0.093	0.013	0.081
CLS + NLI + RC^{+}	0.863	0.003	0.082	0.095	0.012	0.085
CLS + RC + RC^{+}	0.747	0.000	0.025	0.020	0.000	0.020
CMNS + NLI + RC	0.867	0.004	0.105	0.125	0.012	0.101
CMNS + NLI + RC^{+}	**0.881**	0.058	0.228	0.285	0.096	0.230
CMNS + RC + RC^{+}	**0.881**	**0.060**	0.229	0.284	**0.098**	0.230
NLI + RC + RC^{+}	**0.881**	0.059	**0.231**	**0.286**	**0.098**	**0.231**
BART	0.858	0.003	0.087	0.105	0.011	0.090

Table 28: RQ4 results (pairing of three task families excluding the text summarization family) for Reddit TIFU and the continual multi-task learning strategy. Values in **bold** represent the highest results for a training scheme. Underlined values are the highest results for that dataset independent of training.

Task Families	BERTScore	BLEU	METEOR	ROUGE-1	ROUGE-2	ROUGE-L
CLS	0.820	0.018	0.154	0.248	0.048	0.163
CMNS	**0.860**	0.119	0.286	**0.432**	**0.167**	**0.249**
NLI	0.817	0.020	0.168	0.266	0.048	0.169
RC	0.859	0.117	0.282	0.427	0.165	0.247
RC^{+}	0.859	0.117	0.282	0.426	0.164	0.246
SUM	0.859	**0.121**	**0.288**	0.431	**0.167**	**0.249**
BART	0.859	0.116	0.281	0.425	0.163	0.246

Table 29: RQ1 results (single task family) for arXiv and the sequential strategy. Values in **bold** represent the highest results for a training scheme. Underlined values are the highest results for that dataset independent of training.

Task Families	BERTScore	BLEU	METEOR	ROUGE-1	ROUGE-2	ROUGE-L
CLS	**0.860**	**0.120**	0.287	0.430	**0.167**	**0.248**
CMNS	0.806	0.011	0.197	0.215	0.038	0.137
NLI	0.812	0.006	0.111	0.187	0.016	0.123
RC	0.859	0.119	0.284	0.430	0.166	**0.248**
RC^{+}	0.859	**0.120**	**0.289**	**0.431**	**0.167**	**0.248**
SUM	0.859	0.117	0.282	0.429	0.166	**0.248**
BART	0.859	0.116	0.281	0.425	0.163	0.246

Table 30: RQ1 results (single task family) for arXiv and the simultaneous strategy. Values in **bold** represent the highest results for a training scheme. Underlined values are the highest results for that dataset independent of training.

Task Families	BERTScore	BLEU	METEOR	ROUGE-1	ROUGE-2	ROUGE-L
CLS	0.859	**0.119**	**0.286**	0.429	0.166	0.248
CMNS	0.819	0.017	0.163	0.295	0.051	0.171
NLI	0.815	0.018	0.182	0.272	0.044	0.170
RC	0.859	0.117	0.282	0.426	0.164	0.246
RC^{+}	0.817	0.020	0.203	0.249	0.051	0.159
SUM	**0.860**	**0.119**	**0.286**	**0.431**	**0.167**	**0.249**
BART	0.859	0.116	0.281	0.425	0.163	0.246

Table 31: RQ1 results (single task family) for arXiv and the continual multi-task learning strategy. Values in **bold** represent the highest results for a training scheme. Underlined values are the highest results for that dataset independent of training.

Task Families	BERTScore	BLEU	METEOR	ROUGE-1	ROUGE-2	ROUGE-L
ALL	0.859	0.116	0.281	**0.427**	**0.165**	**0.248**
BART	0.859	0.116	0.281	0.425	0.163	0.246

Table 32: RQ1 results (all task families) for arXiv and the sequential strategy. Values in **bold** represent the highest results for a training scheme. Underlined values are the highest results for that dataset independent of training.

Task Families	BERTScore	BLEU	METEOR	ROUGE-1	ROUGE-2	ROUGE-L
ALL	0.859	0.115	0.279	0.425	**0.164**	0.246
BART	0.859	0.116	0.281	0.425	0.163	0.246

Table 33: RQ1 results (all task families) for arXiv and the simultaneous strategy. Values in **bold** represent the highest results for a training scheme. Underlined values are the highest results for that dataset independent of training.

Task Families	BERTScore	BLEU	METEOR	ROUGE-1	ROUGE-2	ROUGE-L
ALL	0.729	0.000	0.008	0.009	0.000	0.009
BART	0.859	0.116	0.281	0.425	0.163	0.246

Table 34: RQ1 results (all task families) for arXiv and the continual multi-task learning strategy. Values in **bold** represent the highest results for a training scheme. Underlined values are the highest results for that dataset independent of training.

Task Families	BERTScore	BLEU	METEOR	ROUGE-1	ROUGE-2	ROUGE-L
SUM + CLS	**0.860**	**0.119**	**0.285**	**0.430**	**0.167**	**0.249**
SUM + CMNS	0.811	0.016	0.153	0.254	0.046	0.164
SUM + NLI	0.859	0.117	0.282	0.427	0.165	0.247
SUM + RC	0.859	**0.119**	**0.285**	**0.430**	0.166	0.248
SUM + RC+	0.859	0.118	0.284	0.428	0.166	0.247
BART	0.859	0.116	0.281	0.425	0.163	0.246

Table 35: RQ2 results (pairing of the summarization task family with another task family) for arXiv and the sequential strategy. Values in **bold** represent the highest results for a training scheme. Underlined values are the highest results for that dataset independent of training.

Task Families	BERTScore	BLEU	METEOR	ROUGE-1	ROUGE-2	ROUGE-L
SUM + CLS	**0.860**	0.119	0.285	0.429	0.166	0.247
SUM + CMNS	**0.860**	0.119	0.286	**0.432**	**0.167**	**0.249**
SUM + NLI	0.859	**0.120**	**0.287**	0.431	**0.167**	**0.249**
SUM + RC	0.859	0.115	0.280	0.427	0.164	0.247
SUM + RC+	0.859	0.116	0.281	0.427	0.164	0.247
BART	0.859	0.116	0.281	0.425	0.163	0.246

Table 36: RQ2 results (pairing of the summarization task family with another task family) for arXiv and the simultaneous strategy. Values in **bold** represent the highest results for a training scheme. Underlined values are the highest results for that dataset independent of training.

Task Families	BERTScore	BLEU	METEOR	ROUGE-1	ROUGE-2	ROUGE-L
SUM + CLS	0.859	0.117	0.283	0.429	0.165	0.248
SUM + CMNS	**0.860**	**0.120**	**0.288**	**0.432**	**0.167**	**0.249**
SUM + NLI	0.859	0.117	0.282	0.427	0.165	0.247
SUM + RC	0.859	0.118	0.283	0.428	0.166	0.247
SUM + RC+	0.859	0.118	0.284	0.428	0.166	0.247
BART	0.859	0.116	0.281	0.425	0.163	0.246

Table 37: RQ2 results (pairing of the summarization task family with another task family) for arXiv and the continual multi-task learning strategy. Values in **bold** represent the highest results for a training scheme. Underlined values are the highest results for that dataset independent of training.

Task Families	BERTScore	BLEU	METEOR	ROUGE-1	ROUGE-2	ROUGE-L
CLS + CMNS	**0.863**	0.003	0.078	0.091	0.013	0.081
CLS + NLI	0.731	0.000	0.050	0.086	0.000	0.050
CLS + RC	0.859	0.116	**0.287**	0.427	0.165	0.247
CLS + RC$^+$	0.859	0.118	0.284	0.430	**0.167**	**0.248**
CMNS + NLI	0.821	0.010	0.137	0.261	0.045	0.176
CMNS + RC	0.860	0.117	0.283	0.429	0.165	**0.248**
CMNS + RC$^+$	0.859	0.115	0.279	0.426	0.164	0.247
NLI + RC	0.859	0.119	0.285	0.429	0.166	**0.248**
NLI + RC$^+$	0.859	**0.119**	0.286	**0.431**	**0.167**	**0.248**
RC + RC$^+$	0.859	0.116	**0.287**	0.428	0.165	**0.248**
BART	0.859	0.116	0.281	0.425	0.163	0.246

Table 38: RQ3 results (pairing of two task families excluding the text summarization family) for arXiv and the sequential strategy. Values in **bold** represent the highest results for a training scheme. Underlined values are the highest results for that dataset independent of training.

Task Families	BERTScore	BLEU	METEOR	ROUGE-1	ROUGE-2	ROUGE-L
CLS + CMNS	0.704	0.000	0.050	0.076	0.000	0.046
CLS + NLI	0.743	0.000	0.003	0.006	0.000	0.006
CLS + RC	0.859	0.118	0.283	0.428	0.165	0.247
CLS + RC$^+$	0.859	0.120	0.288	**0.432**	0.167	0.248
CMNS + NLI	0.805	0.012	0.212	0.215	0.041	0.134
CMNS + RC	0.859	0.118	0.284	0.428	0.165	0.248
CMNS + RC$^+$	0.859	0.115	0.280	0.426	0.165	0.247
NLI + RC	0.859	0.119	0.285	0.430	0.166	0.248
NLI + RC$^+$	0.859	**0.121**	**0.290**	**0.432**	**0.168**	**0.249**
RC + RC$^+$	0.859	0.116	0.281	0.426	0.164	0.247
BART	0.859	0.116	0.281	0.425	0.163	0.246

Table 39: RQ3 results (pairing of two task families excluding the text summarization family) for arXiv and the simultaneous strategy. Values in **bold** represent the highest results for a training scheme. Underlined values are the highest results for that dataset independent of training.

Task Families	BERTScore	BLEU	METEOR	ROUGE-1	ROUGE-2	ROUGE-L
CLS + CMNS	0.813	0.018	0.162	0.259	0.052	0.176
CLS + NLI	0.859	0.113	0.276	0.422	0.161	0.245
CLS + RC	0.810	0.018	0.181	0.269	0.048	0.168
CLS + RC$^+$	0.860	**0.120**	**0.287**	**0.432**	**0.167**	**0.249**
CMNS + NLI	0.806	0.009	0.118	0.181	0.016	0.117
CMNS + RC	0.812	0.019	0.179	0.282	0.041	0.157
CMNS + RC$^+$	**0.863**	0.003	0.082	0.095	0.117	0.085
NLI + RC	0.860	0.118	0.284	0.429	0.166	0.247
NLI + RC$^+$	0.859	0.117	0.282	0.426	0.164	0.246
RC + RC$^+$	0.859	0.118	0.285	0.429	0.165	0.248
BART	0.859	0.116	0.281	0.425	0.163	0.246

Table 40: RQ3 results (pairing of two task families excluding the text summarization family) for arXiv and the continual multi-task learning strategy. Values in **bold** represent the highest results for a training scheme. Underlined values are the highest results for that dataset independent of training.

Hyper parameter	**Value**
Optimizer	AdamW
Adam-betas	(0.9, 0.999)
Adam-eps	1e-8
LR	5e-05
LR Scheduler	linear decay
Dropout	0.1
Weight Decay	0
Warmup Updates	0

Table 41: Hyperparameters used throughout all pre-finetuning and finetuning experiments.

CLSE: Corpus of Linguistically Significant Entities

Aleksandr Chuklin[*, G], **Justin Zhao**[*, P], **Mihir Kale**[G]
[G] Google, [P] Predibase
{chuklin,mihirkale}@google.com, justin@predibase.com

Abstract

One of the biggest challenges of natural language generation (NLG) is the proper handling of named entities. Named entities are a common source of grammar mistakes such as wrong prepositions, wrong article handling, or incorrect entity inflection. Without factoring linguistic representation, such errors are often underrepresented when evaluating on a small set of arbitrarily picked argument values, or when translating a dataset from a linguistically simpler language, like English, to a linguistically complex language, like Russian. However, for some applications, broadly precise grammatical correctness is critical—native speakers may find entity-related grammar errors silly, jarring, or even offensive.

To enable the creation of more linguistically diverse NLG datasets, we release a Corpus of Linguistically Significant Entities (CLSE) annotated by linguist experts. The corpus includes 34 languages and covers 74 different semantic types to support various applications from airline ticketing to video games. To demonstrate one possible use of CLSE, we produce an augmented version of the Schema-Guided Dialog Dataset, SGD-CLSE. Using the CLSE's entities and a small number of human translations, we create a linguistically representative NLG evaluation benchmark in three languages: French (high-resource), Marathi (low-resource), and Russian (highly inflected language). We establish quality baselines for neural, template-based, and hybrid NLG systems and discuss the strengths and weaknesses of each approach.

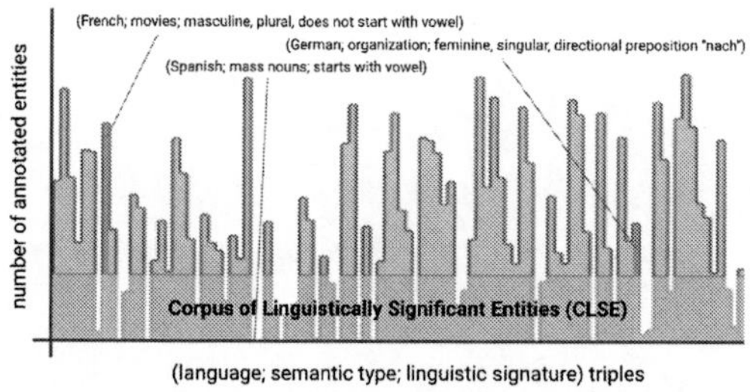

Figure 1: The corpus of linguistically significant entities (CLSE) is created by annotating a large number of entities with their linguistic properties. Entities are grouped by ($language$, $semantic\_type$, $linguistic\_signature$) triples. This results in a corpus of entities that, for a given language and semantic type, is balanced across linguistic properties. Note that some linguistic signatures have few or no annotated entities because they simply do not occur.

1 Introduction

Natural language generation (NLG) (Reiter and Dale, 2000) is an umbrella term for the problem of generating fluent, human-like text from a variety of inputs. It covers, among others, text-to-text problems such as text summarization or machine translation (Allahyari et al., 2017; Stahlberg, 2020; Malmi et al., 2022), image-to-text problems (Hossain et al., 2019), and structured data to text (Kukich, 1983; McKeown, 1985).

Unlike most natural language processing tasks, it is hard to produce reusable ground truth labeled data for NLG: there can be many different outputs that are grammatical and human-like. This is why it is important to invest in NLG resources, especially for non-English languages. The GEM benchmark (Gehrmann et al., 2021) is such an initiative for NLG evaluation. Its second version (Gehrmann et al., 2022) covers 40 tasks and 51 languages and provides an easy way for others to contribute.

In parallel to adding new NLG resources, a framework for dataset augmentation has recently been introduced by Dhole et al. (2021). The main idea is to perform transformation and slicing of the existing datasets to boost certain properties as a

[*] The first two authors contributed equally to this work.
[P] Part of this work done while at Google.

Proceedings of the 2nd Workshop on Natural Language Generation, Evaluation, and Metrics (GEM), pages 78 - 96
December 7, 2022

case	singular	plural
nominative	книга (kniga)	книги (knigi)
genitive	книги (knigi)	книг (knig)
dative	книге (knige)	книгам (knigam)
accusative	книгу (knigu)	книги (knigi)
instrumental	книгой (knigoy)	книгами (knigami)
prepositional	книге (knige)	книгах (knigakh)

Table 1: Inflections of the word "book" in Russian. Cf. "Я купил <книгу>" ("I bought a <book>"; dative case) and "Моя <книга> потерялась" ("My <book> got lost; nominative case).

way to adversarially test the generalization abilities of the benchmarked models. Our contribution is similar in spirit: the corpus of linguistically significant entities (CLSE) enables transforming existing datasets to be more balanced by linguistic phenomena covered by named entities (Figure 1).

Ensuring grammatical correctness is arguably a basic requirement for any NLG system in any language. Native speakers may find grammatical errors produced by such systems silly, jarring, or even offensive, for example if the utterance refers to an entity with the wrong tense, formality, animacy, or gender (Dinan et al., 2020). The CLSE resource we introduce here is particularly useful for stress-testing the linguistic robustness of NLG systems.

The rest of the paper is organized as follows. Section 2 introduces the CLSE corpus annotated by linguist experts. In Section 3, we discuss the problem of NLG for task-oriented dialogs and how CLSE can be applied to it. In Section 4 we show how to construct a linguistically diverse dataset for this task, a dataset we refer to as SGD-CLSE. In Section 5, we introduce three different baseline NLG systems which we evaluate on this dataset. Results are discussed in Section 6.

2 Corpus of Linguistically Significant Entities (CLSE)

The Google Knowledge Graph API[1] (Guha et al., 2016) provides access to millions of entries that describe real-world entities like people, places, and things. Each entity is a node in the graph and can be associated with any number of schema.org semantic types, such as Person, AdministrativeArea, or TouristAttraction.

We first source lexical annotations from expert linguists for a large number of entities in the knowledge graph. Lexical annotations are language-specific and pertain to broader categories of linguistic properties like Animacy,[2] Case,[3] Classifier, Countability, Definiteness, Gender, and Number. Different languages consists of different linguistic properties. For example, the concept of animacy is not used in the English language. Descriptions of each linguistic property class are included alongside the dataset release.

Linguistic annotations for an entity include those that are important to handle in a template-based language generation context. For instance in English, location entities have locative preposition annotations while people entities have gender annotations.[4] In other languages like French, *all* entities are annotated for grammatical gender, and entities with an article are marked depending on whether its article stays unchanged or gets merged with a preposition (like it would for common nouns).

We use linguists who are native speakers in their corresponding language to source linguistic annotations for popular entities. Except for the following eight low-resource languages—Bengali (bn), Gujarati (gu), Kannada (kn), Malayalam (ml), Marathi (mr), Tamil (ta), Telugu (te), and Urdu (ur)—all annotators possess at least a bachelors degree in some branch of linguistics. Linguist annotators' median age ranges from 25 to 35, and they are roughly equally split between male and female. Instead of expert linguists—or in addition to them—one may use data mining techniques (Gutman et al., 2018).

We introduce the concept of a *linguistic signature*, which is a linearized string representation of an entity's linguistic attributes for a specific language. Table 2 illustrates some examples of linguistic signatures.

The maximum hypothetical number of distinct linguistic signatures for a language is the Cartesian product of all linguistic features and values for that language. However, not all linguistic signatures are naturally occurring or relevant. For example, mass nouns[5] that start with a vowel do not occur in Spanish. Consequently we source *different* entities for different languages (and different number of

[1] developers.google.com/knowledge-graph

[2] en.wikipedia.org/wiki/Animacy

[3] See Table 1 as an illustration.

[4] Note that the gender annotations may be sometimes incomplete or inaccurate due to changed state of the world, an annotator mistake, or a lack of standard linguistic handling for gender non-binary persons in certain languages.

[5] thoughtco.com/uncountable-noun-spanish-3079280

lang	name	signature	semantic type
fr	Suisse	`number:SINGULAR,gender:FEMININE, starts_w_vowel:0`	Country
de	Champions League	`number:SINGULAR,gender:FEMININE, article:DEFINITE, locative_prep:PREP_IN, directional_prep:PREP_NACH`	Event
ru	Саратовские авиалини	`number:PLURAL,casus:NOMINATIVE, allative:PREP_K, comitative:PREP_S,topical:PREP_O, locative_prep_geo:PREP_V`	Corporation

Table 2: Examples of CLSE linguistic signatures (truncated for conciseness).

them) to ensure linguistic diversity appropriate for each language.

To obtain entities based on linguistic variation, we annotate a large number of entities for each semantic type to create a table of ($language$, $semantic\_type$, $entity\_id$, $name$, $linguistic\_signature$). We group rows in the table by ($language$, $semantic\_type$, $linguistic\_signature$) triples. The complete corpus covers 34 languages, 74 semantic types, and 222 distinct linguistic signatures.

The full Corpus of Linguistically Significant Entities is available at `clse.page.link/data`.

3 CLSE Case Study: Task-Oriented Dialogs

To demonstrate how one may use this corpus, we consider the problem of NLG for task-oriented dialog systems (Wen et al., 2015). Unlike open-domain chit-chat systems, the natural language interface of virtual assistants such as Amazon Alexa, Apple Siri, or Google Assistant is highly task-oriented. Users often interact with their virtual assistants to accomplish a specific action, like finding flights, booking restaurants, buying tickets, etc.

In a task-oriented dialogue, the conversation between the user and the assistant is tracked by a dialog manager that uses a dialog state, a summary of the entire conversation up to the current turn (see, e.g., (Pieraccini, 2021)). The dialog state consists of slots and values related to the specific intents, services, and actions in question. The assistant uses the dialog state to 1) invoke external APIs with appropriate parameter values, as specified by the user over the dialog history, and 2) generate next actions to continue the dialog, for example soliciting for more information from the user or confirming the user's intent or request (Aliannejadi et al., 2021). Finally, 3) the selected dialog actions along with structured data is used to generate a new utterance to respond back to the user (the NLG task).

	Wikidata	CLSE
Total # of arguments	20	17
Output is missing "the"	1	6
Wrong preposition "in"	0	3
Grammatical outputs	95%	47%

Table 3: Comparing CLSE and WikiData as sources of arguments for testing an NLG system.

Task-oriented NLG datasets like MultiWOZ (Budzianowski et al., 2018) and SGD (Rastogi et al., 2020) are designed to be balanced with respect to the number of turns, intent and slot usage, etc., without much focus on the *linguistic* properties of incoming parameter values. For the sake of illustration, let us consider the following simplistic NLG system. It receives a `location` argument and returns the following templated response:

```
EMNLP will be held in ${location}.
```

Without consulting a linguist or a native speaker, one can try exposing the issues of this template by substituting different argument values for `location`. The CLSE has 17 entries of type `AdministrativeArea` with unique linguistic signatures in English. Note that some signatures may only differ in ways that are inconsequential to the

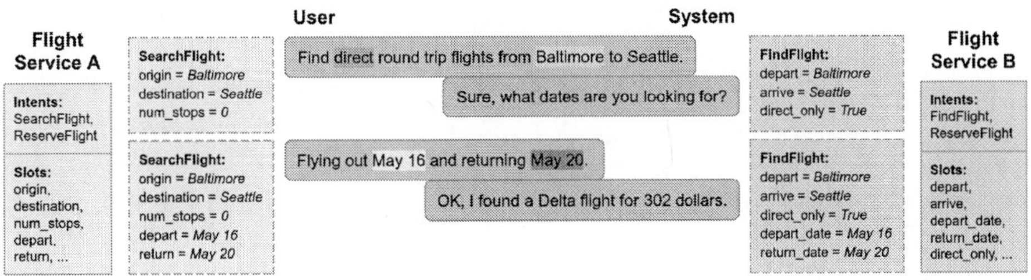

Figure 2: An example of a conversation from a schema-guided dialog (Rastogi et al., 2020). The predicted dialogue state (shown with dashed edges) for the first two user turns for an example dialogue, showing the active intent and slot assignments, with two related annotation schemas. Note that the dialogue state representation is conditioned on the schema under consideration, which is provided as input, as are the user and system utterances.

above templates, but the hope is still that they will be more diverse than a general-purpose list. For comparison, we consider a general-purpose list of 20 entities of type "administrative territorial entity" (Q56061) from Wikidata (Vrandečić and Krötzsch, 2014).[6] Table 3 summarizes the errors using entity arguments from Wikidata and the CLSE. Wikidata exposes only one potential issue: a missing determiner in front of "Bahamas." Even worse, as of 2022-09-09, our SPARQL query returns the surface form as "The Bahamas," which means that if we were to evaluate our NLG system purely based on the realized output texts, we may declare our system to have 100% fluency, while using the entities from CLSE we immediately see that the system is linguistically brittle, and there is more than 50% fluency headroom (one sentence has two mistakes).

Factual accuracy mistakes are also unforgivable when it comes to virtual assistants. Kale and Roy (2020) point out delexicalized models as a less error-prone alternative to lexicalized models. In the delexicalized setting, models are trained to produce output text with placeholders, which are filled in via a separate lexicalization step (usually naive string substitution). The semantic accuracy of delexicalized models tends to be far ahead of their lexicalized counterparts, especially in the presence of slot values not seen during training. However, delexicalization and other copy-based methods are more grammatically deficient in the presence of linguistic phenomena such as morphological inflection (changing surface form of a word depending on its function in a sentence; see, e.g., Table 1). This makes a naive delexialization approach suboptimal for highly inflected languages (Dušek and Jurčíček, 2019), a claim that we will also test below.

[6]SPARQL query: `pastebin.com/KBk17G5k`.

4 SGD-CLSE: Generating Linguistically Diverse Data Using the CLSE

We perform our experiments on the Schema-Guided Dialog dataset from DCT8 (Rastogi et al., 2020). To emulate a data-to-text setup, we pair each utterance (text) with that utterance's acts, services, and slots. An example of such a pair can be seen in Table 4. Since the scope of our experiments is to focus on linguistic robustness with regard to entities, we only look at SYSTEM utterances, and ignore all examples that don't use any entity slots. This results in 707 $(service\_name, action, slot\_names)$ triples from the SGD train set and 23 triples from the SGD test set.

Owing to the lack of noun inflections in English, we can also produce a delexicalized form of the utterance by searching for and stubbing out the argument values within. E.g., for the utterance in Table 4 we would get "`How would you like ${restaurant}, which is situated in ${city}?`". The delexicalized form gives us an English template that allows us to substitute other values for the placeholders to produce new realistic utterances, enabling data augmentation methods like the one described by Kale and Siddhant (2021).

In our case study, we assume that we already have a system that can produce English utterances—arguably a much easier task given the simplicity of English grammar—and instead focus on localization: generating fluent and grammatical output in a target language. In this setup we get the following as input: dialog state, structured data, English text, and target language. We focus on three languages: French, Russian, and Marathi. The motivation for choosing these languages is to have a widely studied high-resource language (French), a highly inflected language (Russian), and a low-

input (structured data)	**output (utterance)**
service_name: "Restaurants_1" **actions:** ["OFFER_restaurant", "OFFER_city"] **slots:** {restaurant: "Bazille", city: "San Jose"}	"How would you like Bazille, which is situated in San Jose?"

Table 4: An example of structured data input and free text output for an SGD dialog utterance.

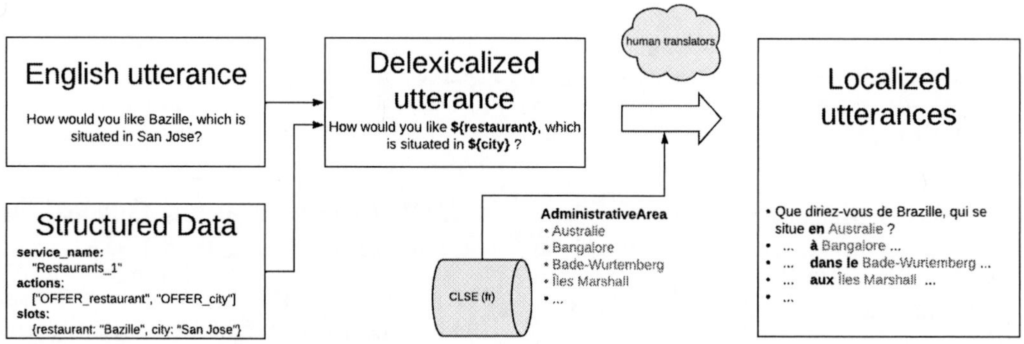

Figure 3: Algorithm for creating the SGD-CLSE dataset (example for French).

resource language (Marathi).

The process of creating the SGD-CLSE dataset, leveraging the CLSE, is as follows. 1) for every $(service\_name, action, slot\_names)$ triple, we generate argument values by randomly sampling slot values from the CLSE for a specific *target* language: French, Russian, or Marathi respectively. This requires us to establish a mapping from each entity-related slot name to a semantic type. For example, $city$ slots in the SGD schemas would be mapped to the City schema.org type in the CLSE corpus. 2) we substitute these new argument values into the English delexicalized utterances (templates) from SGD. The goal of entity re-sampling using the CLSE is to generate as linguistically diverse data as possible, for maximum linguistic coverage in the *target* language.[7] 3) Finally, we use professional translators to translate those utterances into the corresponding languages. Figure 3 illustrates the algorithm.

We use the aforementioned process with three examples per $(service, action, slot\_names)$ triple to generate language-specific linguistically diverse examples in French, Russian, and Marathi[8] on the train partition of the SGD dataset. We then use two of these examples for **train** and one for what we call "within-triple test" split (**wt-test**).[9] Unlike the SGD dev and test splits, the wt-test split has a particular focus on linguistics as opposed to generalization across dialog states: it contains states that were seen during training, but with a linguistically diverse set of slot values. In addition to train and wt-test sets, we also use a sample from the original SGD **dev** and **test** sets translated into the target languages. Table 5 has dataset statistics.

5 Experimental Setup

Below we describe our setup to evaluate different NLG models using the SGD-CLSE dataset.

5.1 Models for Comparison

- **nmt**: An out-of-the-box machine translation model with English plain text as input.

[7] It is possible that substituting new arguments could break the fluency of the example in the source language (English, in our case). However, we found that imperfect substitutions in the source language do not influence the quality of human translations, produced by the process we describe further.

[8] It is worth noting that the quality bar for the CLSE annotations was higher in Hindi compared to the other Indic languages. While it might still be more appropriate to use the Marathi section of the CLSE for other applications, we empirically found that the Hindi section yields SGD-based realizations of higher quality, while maintaining linguistic diversity. This is not entirely surprising, since the languages are close geographically (both are spoken in India) and linguistically (both are Indo-Aryan languages stemming from Sanskrit). We therefore use the CLSE's Hindi entities as a proxy for Marathi ones.

[9] In cases where we were only able to obtain two distinct examples, we use one of them for train and one for wt-test. In case of a single example, the triple is discarded completely.

lang	train	wt-test	SGD test	SGD dev
fr	451	233	277	187
ru	451	236	277	187
mr	451	234	277	187

Table 5: Number of items in different partitions of the SGD-CLSE dataset.

	French	Russian	Marathi
Accuracy	0.77 (s)	0.69 (s)	0.63 (s)
Fluency	0.43 (m)	0.51 (m)	0.35 (f)

Table 6: Kappa coefficient (Cohen, 1960) inter-rater agreement. Values 0.21–0.40 are considered fair (f), 0.41–0.60 moderate (m) and 0.61–0.80 substantial (s).

We used the `GOOGLETRANSLATE` function of Google Sheets.[10]

- **d2t**: A data-to-text model fine-tuned on the available train set, with best checkpoint picked on the dev set. We use a pretrained *mT5 xxl* model (Xue et al., 2021) as a basis for our fine-tuning.[11]

- **tmpl**: Collect translated templates (delexicalized utterances) for the train set. Slot values are plugged in verbatim without any morphological inflection. Note that for most triples we have two different translations available for train (Table 5). We only use one of them (picked at random) but also report confidence intervals based on possibly picking different translations as bases for delexicalization.[12]

- **tmpl+G**: Same as above with a grammatical error correction (GEC) model applied on top of the template output. We use *gT5 xxl* model by Rothe et al. (2021).

Figure 4 illustrates which parts of the input data are consumed by which models.

5.2 Training Details

For fine-tuning the **d2t** model we use a batch size of 64 and fine-tuned on TPU for 5'000 steps with a learning rate of 10^{-3}. We trained the models independently for each language and picked the stopping point based on the corresponding dev set. The model has 13B parameters.

[10] `support.google.com/docs/answer/3093331`; translations for the wt-test were obtained on 2022-01-28, for SGD test/dev: on 2022-02-02.

[11] Our early experiments with *mT5 base* gave substantially lower BLEU scores, suggesting that the bigger models yield stronger baselines. We use *xxl* models going forward.

[12] We use a simple bootstrap procedure: pick one of the two translations for each triple by flipping a fair coin. The process is repeated 1000 times and the 5th and 95th percentiles are reported as the confidence interval bounds.

5.3 Metrics

We use BLEU[13] (Papineni et al., 2002) and BLEURT[14] (Sellam et al., 2020) as our automatic metrics. For human evaluation, we assess fluency and factual accuracy. Table 6 summarizes agreement between raters.

Accuracy: Human raters are shown an NLG system's output in the target language as well as the English text as a reference. They are instructed to mark the NLG system output as inaccurate if any information contradicts the English reference. This effectively catches errors due to hallucinations, incorrect grounding etc. Each example is rated by three raters. We take the average of the accuracy scores (1 for accurate, 0 otherwise).

Fluency: We ask the raters how grammatical an NLG system's output sounds on a 1 to 5 Likert scale, with 5 being the highest score. Again, each example is rated by three raters. We average the scores across all the ratings to get the fluency score.

6 Results

We split this section into two. First, we look at the results on the unseen test set. These contain dialog situations, $(service\_name, action, slot\_names)$, which the systems did not see during training. We then move to the wt-test split, where we expect the gap to the human-written responses to be smaller.

6.1 Unseen Test Set

Table 7 contains the summary of the results. Naturally, the template-based approaches are not able to generalize to these situations, so they are not included in the results here.

We could verify that all NLG systems are noticeably (and significantly) behind human translations in terms of fluency. In terms of accuracy, on the other hand, the **nmt** baseline is *in*significantly below the human bar for French, suggesting that we

[13] `github.com/tuetschek/e2e-metrics`.

[14] BLEURT-20 `github.com/google-research/bleurt`.

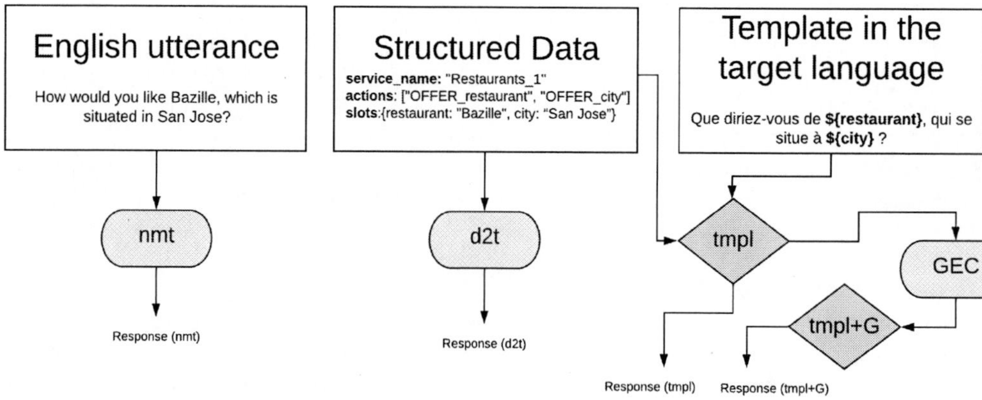

Figure 4: Input data flow for various baseline NLG systems. **GEC** and **nmt** (green) are off-the-shelf models, while **d2t** (azure) is a model fine-tuned on given data. **tmpl** and **tmpl+G** are simple pipeline algorithms (rhombus shape).

		BLEU	BLEURT	acc.	fl.
fr	d2t	0.14	0.39	0.78	4.58
	nmt	0.32	0.62	0.96▲	4.43▼
	human	-	-	0.98	4.78▲
ru	d2t	0.15	0.50	0.50	4.35
	nmt	0.16	0.57	0.79▲	3.70▼
	human	-	-	0.96▲	4.89▲
mr	d2t	0.07	0.60	0.41	3.50
	nmt	0.12	0.71	0.77▲	4.15▲
	human	-	-	0.92▲	4.71▲

Table 7: Results of the NLG models on the SGD test set (unseen triples). For human scores—accuracy (acc.) and fluency (fl.)—we also mark whether those are statistically significantly different from the *previous row* using paired t-test: ▲ or ▼ denote significant difference at $p = 0.01$, △ or ▽ — at $p = 0.05$ respectively.

do benefit from the high-resource nature of the language. Another observation is that, while the **nmt** baseline appears to outperform **d2t** on all dimensions for a low-resource Marathi, the picture is less clear for French and Russian. There we see that the **d2t** actually scores significantly *lower* than **nmt** in terms of accuracy but *higher* in terms of fluency. We believe that the accuracy gap could be lowered with more training data, which we leave for future work to investigate.

6.2 Within-Triples Test

Table 8 contains a summary of performance of different NLG systems while Table 11 in Appendix B contains example outputs. We see notable quality gains of the **d2t** or template-based approaches compared to the off-the-shelf **nmt** system.

The grammatical error correction model (**tmpl+G** baseline), appears to improve the results on top of the pure template-based **tmpl** baseline for high-resource languages. The gain is higher for Russian, a highly inflected language. No measurable effect is reported on Marathi, a low resource language, suggesting that the grammar error correction model itself may not be of sufficient quality. The fluency **tmpl+G** achieves for Russian is still significantly lower than that of **d2t**, but comes with a significantly higher accuracy (inasmuch as we can compare them given that the fluency and accuracy scores for **d2t** come from a different rater pool).

It is interesting to note that the **d2t** model appears to get higher human scores for French than the other NLG systems, but scores lower on automatic metrics. In fact, the human scores are not statistically different from that of the human baseline. Upon closer examination, however, we see that this model still frequently makes grave mistakes. One explanation for this could be that the humans have a tolerance for hallucinations or missing facts when there are many of them presented in the same utterance. This is consistent with previous findings of Freitag et al. (2021). Appendix B shows examples where the automatic metrics are right to penalize the **d2t** model for accuracy while raters completely miss it. While prior work such as (Pagnoni et al., 2021; Honovich et al., 2022)

		BLEU	BLEURT	acc.	fl.
fr	nmt	0.39	0.65	0.90	4.19
	tmpl	0.46	0.70	0.88 [0.87, 0.90]	$4.31^{\triangle}$ [4.26, 4.34]
	tmpl+G	0.47	0.71	$0.91^{\blacktriangle}$ [0.88, 0.91]	$4.48^{\blacktriangle}$ [4.43, 4.49]
	d2t	0.41	0.65	0.91	$4.64^{\blacktriangle}$
	human	-	-	0.94	4.63
ru	nmt	0.15	0.57	0.71	3.37
	d2t	0.37	0.66	0.72^{*}	$4.51^{\blacktriangle *}$
	tmpl	0.41	0.72	$0.79^{\blacktriangle}$ [0.79, 0.83]	$3.95^{\blacktriangledown}$ [3.93, 4.03]
	tmpl+G	0.44	0.74	0.79 [0.77, 0.81]	$4.21^{\blacktriangle}$ [4.17, 4.28]
	human	-	-	$0.87^{\blacktriangle}$	$4.62^{\blacktriangle}$
mr	nmt	0.15	0.69	0.72	3.73
	d2t	0.33	0.69	0.66	$4.05^{\blacktriangle}$
	tmpl	0.51	0.78	$0.83^{\blacktriangle}$ [0.80, 0.83]	$4.32^{\blacktriangle}$ [4.27, 4.34]
	tmpl+G	0.51	0.78	0.82 [0.79, 0.81]	4.29 [4.26, 4.33]
	human	-	-	$0.92^{\blacktriangle}$	$4.50^{\blacktriangle}$

Table 8: Results of the baseline NLG systems on the wt-test set (seen triples). For human scores—accuracy (acc.) and fluency (fl.)—we also mark whether those are statistically significantly different from the *previous row* using paired t-test: $^{\blacktriangle}$ or $^{\blacktriangledown}$ denote significant difference at $p = 0.01$, $^{\triangle}$ or $^{\triangledown}$ — at $p = 0.05$ respectively. The square brackets for template-based approaches denote 95% confidence intervals obtained using the bootstrap procedure described in Section 5.1.

(*) Human scores for d2t in Russian come from a different rater population and may not be directly comparable.

studies factual consistency in English, further work on evaluating factual consistency of *localization* approaches is needed.

To summarize the above results, we can conclude that there is still a gap between outputs generated by our baseline NLG systems and responses written by humans, especially for lower-resource languages like Marathi or morphologically complex languages such as Russian. Among baseline systems, the template-based **tmpl/tmpl+G** approaches, when available, clearly outperform the **d2t** model for Marathi. The results of the automatic metrics in other languages suggest the same conclusion, though human scores are not always consistent with that. We attribute this inconsistency to the fact that the **d2t** system can generate seemingly good responses that, while missing or introducing facts, manage to convince human raters of their accuracy (see Appendix B).

Even with this caveat, we can see that accuracy scores of the template-based approach (**tmpl+G**) is the same or higher than that of **nmt** or **d2t** baselines, suggesting that the factual accuracy is a fundamental weakness of neural approaches. At the same time, the template-based approaches still suffer from fluency issues, even with the grammatical error correction model applied. We hypothesize that the main reason is that the task of correcting mistakes in the template-based approach does not exactly map to the grammatical error correction task. There are types of mistakes we see here that humans rarely make: e.g., inserting determiners in front of popular city names like "London" or "Paris" or confusing dative for nominative (dative and accusative are more commonly confused by humans). This suggests that developing a dedicated grammar model for NLG may be helpful.

7 Conclusion and Discussion

Building a natural language generation system that can handle a broad diversity of entities with varying linguistic phenomena remains an open challenge. With the CLSE, any schema-informed NLG datasets can use techniques described in Sections 3 and 4 to produce better linguistically represented data, and measure metrics on that data to draw more linguistically thoughtful conclusions. The space of possible inputs that NLG systems will be expected to handle may be highly unconstrained, and designing solutions that are linguistically robust, and defensibly so, is an ambitious and worthwhile pursuit.

Our results in Section 6 establish an evaluation procedure probing NLG systems for their linguistic capabilities. We also evaluate four baselines using this procedure and conclude that none of them is at the human level yet. Improving upon these baselines can be approached from two sides: either 1) improving factual accuracy and reducing hallucinations of a purely neural data-to-text approach or 2) improving the quality of grammatical error correction applied to a template-based approach.

Beyond NLG for virtual assistants, the CLSE data may also be used for other NLG tasks. E.g., we can use it to augment machine translation datasets by swapping named entities to further probe the fluency of generated translations.

The full CLSE dataset is openly available at `clse.page.link/data`.

8 Ethical Considerations

Releasing a dataset in multiple languages, including several low-resource ones, would allow to push the state of research in non-English NLG. While it is not impossible that this dataset might be used for building ML models for malicious applications, we believe it will be widely used for public good and will be a net positive contribution to society.

Crowd-sourced annotations were collected using a proprietary crowd-sourcing platform. Workers were paid at least 50% more than the minimum hourly wage. No information about the workers will be released and worker IDs are anonymized.

9 Limitations

The dataset we release and the experiments we conduct have number of limitations. Firstly, there are other linguistically significant phenomena that arise from non-entities like verbs and numbers that the CLSE does not include. Then we only cover 34 languages—small in comparison to, say, Wikipedia or Common Crawl datasets (Conneau and Lample, 2019; Xue et al., 2021) covering 100+ languages. Moreover, the quality of annotations for low-resource languages is lower due to limited linguist resources. Not only the quality, but the quantity of annotated entities varies greatly across languages (Table 9), either due to some languages having fewer linguistic signatures, or annotator resource constraints. The experiments we conduct with SGD cover only a subset of CLSE in terms of languages and semantic types. The SGD-based dataset we used for our case study is rather small (limited by the human translation budget), and human ratings were not free of biases (e.g., humans were often more forgiving for accuracy mistakes than the automatic metrics were). Our experiments do not include an NMT model fine-tuned on the human translations—a common domain adaptation technique (Luong and Manning, 2015; Neubig and Hu, 2018; Bapna and Firat, 2019)—in favor of a direct data-to-text model. Finally, we used the *xxl* versions of the models, which require significant computational resources to train and run.

10 Acknowledgements

The authors would like to thank Ariel Gutman, Eric Malmi, Jelena Čuklina, and anonymous reviewers for their comments and suggestions on how to improve the paper. We would also like to thank Katie Vadella for her help annotating the linguistic phenomena as well as the Google Assistant Linguist Team, Google AI Ethics Team, Google Search Data Team for shaping and supporting the data release.

All content represents the opinion of the authors, which is not necessarily shared or endorsed by their respective employers.

References

Mohammad Aliannejadi, Julia Kiseleva, Aleksandr Chuklin, Jeff Dalton, and Mikhail Burtsev. 2021. Building and evaluating open-domain dialogue corpora with clarifying questions. In *EMNLP 2021*, Online and Punta Cana, Dominican Republic.

Mehdi Allahyari, Seyedamin Pouriyeh, Mehdi Assefi, Saeid Safaei, Elizabeth D Trippe, Juan B Gutierrez, and Krys Kochut. 2017. Text summarization techniques: a brief survey. *arXiv preprint arXiv:1707.02268*.

Ankur Bapna and Orhan Firat. 2019. Simple, scalable adaptation for neural machine translation. In *EMNLP-IJCNLP 2019*.

Paweł Budzianowski, Tsung-Hsien Wen, Bo-Hsiang Tseng, Iñigo Casanueva, Stefan Ultes, Osman Ramadan, and Milica Gašić. 2018. MultiWOZ - a large-scale multi-domain Wizard-of-Oz dataset for task-oriented dialogue modelling. In *EMNLP 2018*, Brussels, Belgium. Association for Computational Linguistics.

Jacob Cohen. 1960. A coefficient of agreement for nominal scales. *Educational and psychological measurement*, 20(1):37–46.

Alexis Conneau and Guillaume Lample. 2019. Cross-lingual language model pretraining. *Advances in neural information processing systems*, 32.

Kaustubh D Dhole, Varun Gangal, Sebastian Gehrmann, Aadesh Gupta, Zhenhao Li, Saad Mahamood, Abinaya Mahendiran, Simon Mille, Ashish Srivastava, Samson Tan, et al. 2021. Nl-augmenter: A framework for task-sensitive natural language augmentation. *arXiv preprint arXiv:2112.02721*.

Emily Dinan, Angela Fan, Adina Williams, Jack Urbanek, Douwe Kiela, and Jason Weston. 2020. Queens are powerful too: Mitigating gender bias in dialogue generation. In *EMNLP 2020*, Online.

Ondřej Dušek and Filip Jurčíček. 2019. Neural generation for Czech: Data and baselines. In *INLG 2019*, Tokyo, Japan.

Markus Freitag, George Foster, David Grangier, Viresh Ratnakar, Qijun Tan, and Wolfgang Macherey. 2021. Experts, errors, and context: A large-scale study of human evaluation for machine translation. *Transactions of the Association for Computational Linguistics*.

Sebastian Gehrmann, Tosin Adewumi, Karmanya Aggarwal, Pawan Sasanka Ammanamanchi, Aremu Anuoluwapo, Antoine Bosselut, Khyathi Raghavi Chandu, Miruna Clinciu, Dipanjan Das, Kaustubh D Dhole, et al. 2021. The gem benchmark: Natural language generation, its evaluation and metrics. *arXiv preprint arXiv:2102.01672*.

Sebastian Gehrmann, Abhik Bhattacharjee, Abinaya Mahendiran, Alex Wang, Alexandros Papangelis, Aman Madaan, Angelina McMillan-Major, Anna Shvets, Ashish Upadhyay, Bingsheng Yao, et al. 2022. Gemv2: Multilingual nlg benchmarking in a single line of code. *arXiv preprint arXiv:2206.11249*.

Ramanathan V Guha, Dan Brickley, and Steve Macbeth. 2016. Schema.org: evolution of structured data on the web. *Communications of the ACM*, 59(2):44–51.

Ariel Gutman, Alexandros Andre Chaaraoui, and Pascal Fleury. 2018. Crafting a lexicon of referential expressions for nlg applications. In *LREC 2018, GLOBALEX Workshop: Lexicography & WordNets*.

Or Honovich, Roee Aharoni, Jonathan Herzig, Hagai Taitelbaum, Doron Kukliansy, Vered Cohen, Thomas Scialom, Idan Szpektor, Avinatan Hassidim, and Yossi Matias. 2022. True: Re-evaluating factual consistency evaluation. In *NAACL 2022*, Seattle, Washington, USA. Association for Computational Linguistics.

MD Zakir Hossain, Ferdous Sohel, Mohd Fairuz Shiratuddin, and Hamid Laga. 2019. A comprehensive survey of deep learning for image captioning. *ACM Computing Surveys (CsUR)*, 51(6):1–36.

Mihir Kale and Scott Roy. 2020. Machine translation pre-training for data-to-text generation - a case study in czech. In *INLG 2020*, pages 91–96, Dublin, Ireland. Association for Computational Linguistics.

Mihir Kale and Aditya Siddhant. 2021. Mixout: A simple yet effective data augmentation scheme for slot-filling. In *Conversational Dialogue Systems for the Next Decade*, pages 279–288. Springer.

Karen Kukich. 1983. Design of a knowledge-based report generator. In *21st Annual Meeting of the Association for Computational Linguistics*, pages 145–150, Cambridge, Massachusetts, USA. Association for Computational Linguistics.

Minh-Thang Luong and Christopher D Manning. 2015. Stanford neural machine translation systems for spoken language domains. In *Proceedings of the 12th International Workshop on Spoken Language Translation: Evaluation Campaign*.

Eric Malmi, Yue Dong, Jonathan Mallinson, Aleksandr Chuklin, Jakub Adamek, Daniil Mirylenka, Felix Stahlberg, Sebastian Krause, Shankar Kumar, and Aliaksei Severyn. 2022. Text generation with text-editing models. *NAACL 2022*, page 1.

Kathleen R McKeown. 1985. *Text generation: using discourse strategies and focus constraints to generate natural language text*. Cambridge University Press.

Graham Neubig and Junjie Hu. 2018. Rapid adaptation of neural machine translation to new languages. In *EMNLP 2018*, pages 875–880.

Artidoro Pagnoni, Vidhisha Balachandran, and Yulia Tsvetkov. 2021. Understanding factuality in abstractive summarization with FRANK: A benchmark for factuality metrics. In *NAACL 2021*, Online. Association for Computational Linguistics.

Kishore Papineni, Salim Roukos, Todd Ward, and Wei-Jing Zhu. 2002. Bleu: a method for automatic evaluation of machine translation. In *ACL 2002*, Philadelphia, Pennsylvania, USA. Association for Computational Linguistics.

Roberto Pieraccini. 2021. *AI Assistants*. MIT Press.

Abhinav Rastogi, Xiaoxue Zang, Srinivas Sunkara, Raghav Gupta, and Pranav Khaitan. 2020. Towards scalable multi-domain conversational agents: The schema-guided dialogue dataset. In *AAAI 2020*, 05.

Ehud Reiter and Robert Dale. 2000. *Building natural language generation systems*. Cambridge university press.

Sascha Rothe, Jonathan Mallinson, Eric Malmi, Sebastian Krause, and Aliaksei Severyn. 2021. A simple recipe for multilingual grammatical error correction. In *ACL-IJCNLP 2021*, Online.

Thibault Sellam, Dipanjan Das, and Ankur Parikh. 2020. BLEURT: Learning robust metrics for text generation. In *ACL 2020*, Online. Association for Computational Linguistics.

Felix Stahlberg. 2020. Neural machine translation: A review. *Journal of Artificial Intelligence Research*, 69:343–418.

Denny Vrandečić and Markus Krötzsch. 2014. Wikidata: a free collaborative knowledgebase. *Communications of the ACM*, 57(10):78–85.

Tsung-Hsien Wen, Milica Gašić, Nikola Mrkšić, Pei-Hao Su, David Vandyke, and Steve Young. 2015. Semantically conditioned LSTM-based natural language generation for spoken dialogue systems. In *EMNLP 2015*, pages 1711–1721, Lisbon, Portugal.

Linting Xue, Noah Constant, Adam Roberts, Mihir Kale, Rami Al-Rfou, Aditya Siddhant, Aditya Barua, and Colin Raffel. 2021. mT5: A massively multilingual pre-trained text-to-text transformer. In *NAACL 2021*, Online. Association for Computational Linguistics.

A CLSE Dataset Statistics

Table 9 contains statistics of the CLSE dataset per language. We employ commonly used 2-letter language tags (ISO-639-1), except for "cmn-CN" for Chinese Mandarin written using the simplified script, "cmn-TW" for Chinese Mandarin written with traditional script, and "yue" for the Cantonese Chinese (written using traditional script). We do not use the Chinese macro-tag "zh" because it is important to distinguish the above locales for NLG purposes.

language	ar	bn	cmn-CN	cmn-TW	cs	da	de	en	es	fr	gu
# unique entities	899	721	530	529	1238	1286	2922	4076	3181	4312	798
# ling. attributes	21	6	5	6	20	23	37	32	26	26	6

language	hi	id	it	ja	jv	kn	ko	ml	mr	nl	no
# unique entities	950	705	2510	1063	55	849	885	888	924	1049	1237
# ling. attributes	18	9	41	47	2	6	9	6	6	20	23

language	pl	pt	ru	su	sv	ta	te	th	tr	ur	vi	yue
# unique entities	1606	2464	3039	29	1309	891	885	724	1262	883	612	551
# ling. attributes	30	25	31	2	19	6	6	9	10	6	8	19

Table 9: Per language statistics of the CLSE dataset. The number of annotated entities across different languages varies greatly, either due to fewer linguistic signatures applicable to a given language or annotator resource constraints.

The complete corpus covers 34 languages, 74 semantic types, and 222 distinct linguistic signatures. Table 10 contains a full list of the semantic types present in the dataset.

Semantic Type	**Description**
AdministrativeArea	A geographical region, typically under the jurisdiction of a particular government.
Airline	An organization that provides flights for passengers.
Airport	An airport.
AmusementPark	An amusement park.
Article	An article, such as a news article or piece of investigative report. Newspapers and magazines have articles of many different types and this is intended to cover them all.
BodyOfWater	A body of water, such as a sea, ocean, or lake.
Book	A book.
BookSeries	A series of books. Included books can be indicated with the hasPart property.
Brand	A brand is a name used by an organization or business person for labeling a product, product group, or similar.
Bridge	A bridge.
BroadcastChannel	A unique instance of a BroadcastService on a CableOrSatelliteService lineup.
BroadcastService	A delivery service through which content is provided via broadcast over the air or online.
BusStation	A bus station.
CableOrSatelliteService	A service which provides access to media programming like TV or radio. Access may be via cable or satellite.
Cemetery	A graveyard.
City	A city or town.
CivicStructure	A public structure, such as a town hall or concert hall.
CollegeOrUniversity	A college, university, or other third-level educational institution.
Continent	One of the continents (for example, Europe or Africa).

Table 10 – continued from previous page

Semantic Type	Description
Corporation	Organization: A business corporation.
Country	A country.
CreativeWork	The most generic kind of creative work, including books, movies, photographs, software programs, etc.
DefenceEstablishment	A defence establishment, such as an army or navy base.
Diet	A strategy of regulating the intake of food to achieve or maintain a specific health-related goal.
EducationalOrganization	An educational organization.
Event	An event happening at a certain time and location, such as a concert, lecture, or festival. Ticketing information may be added via the offers property. Repeated events may be structured as separate Event objects.
Game	The Game type represents things which are games. These are typically rule-governed recreational activities, e.g. role-playing games in which players assume the role of characters in a fictional setting.
GovernmentOrganization	A service provided by a government organization, e.g. food stamps, veterans benefits, etc.
GovernmentService	A service provided by a government organization, e.g. food stamps, veterans benefits, etc.
Hospital	A hospital.
ItemList	A list of items of any sort—for example, Top 10 Movies About Weathermen, or Top 100 Party Songs. Not to be confused with HTML lists, which are often used only for formatting.
LakeBodyOfWater	A lake (for example, Lake Pontrachain).
LandmarksOrHistoricalBuildings	An historical landmark or building.
LocalBusiness	A particular physical business or branch of an organization. Examples of LocalBusiness include a restaurant, a particular branch of a restaurant chain, a branch of a bank, a medical practice, a club, a bowling alley, etc.
LodgingBusiness	A lodging business, such as a motel, hotel, or inn.
MobileApplication	A software application designed specifically to work well on a mobile device such as a telephone.
Mountain	A mountain, like Mount Whitney or Mount Everest.
Movie	A movie.
MovieSeries	A series of movies. Included movies can be indicated with the hasPart property.
MovieTheater	A movie theater.
Museum	A museum.
MusicAlbum	A collection of music tracks.
MusicComposition	A musical composition.
MusicGroup	A musical group, such as a band, an orchestra, or a choir. Can also be a solo musician.
MusicRecording	A music recording (track), usually a single song.
MusicVenue	A music venue.
Organization	An organization such as a school, NGO, corporation, club, etc.
Periodical	A publication in any medium issued in successive parts bearing numerical or chronological designations and intended, such as a magazine, scholarly journal, or newspaper to continue indefinitely.
Person	A person (alive, dead, undead, or fictional).
Place	Entities that have a somewhat fixed, physical extension.
PlaceOfWorship	Place of worship, such as a church, synagogue, or mosque.

Table 10 – continued from previous page

Semantic Type	Description
Product	Any offered product or service. For example: a pair of shoes; a concert ticket; the rental of a car; a haircut; or an episode of a TV show streamed online.
ProductModel	A datasheet or vendor specification of a product (in the sense of a prototypical description).
RadioStation	A radio station.
Restaurant	A restaurant.
RiverBodyOfWater	A river (for example, the broad majestic Shannon).
School	A school.
SingleFamilyResidence	Residence type: Single-family home.
SoftwareApplication	A software application.
SportsOrganization	Represents the collection of all sports organizations, including sports teams, governing bodies, and sports associations.
SportsTeam	Organization: Sports team.
StadiumOrArena	A stadium.
TVSeason	Season dedicated to TV broadcast and associated online delivery.
TVSeries	CreativeWorkSeries dedicated to TV broadcast and associated online delivery.
TelevisionChannel	A unique instance of a television BroadcastService on a CableOrSatelliteService lineup.
TheaterGroup	A theater group or company, for example, the Royal Shakespeare Company or Druid Theatre.
TouristAttraction	A tourist attraction. In principle any Thing can be a TouristAttraction, from a Mountain and LandmarksOrHistoricalBuildings to a LocalBusiness. This Type can be used on its own to describe a general TouristAttraction, or be used as an additionalType to add tourist attraction properties to any other type.
VideoGame	A video game is an electronic game that involves human interaction with a user interface to generate visual feedback on a video device.
VideoGameSeries	A video game series.
VisualArtwork	A work of art that is primarily visual in character.
Volcano	A volcano, like Fuji san.
Waterfall	A waterfall, like Niagara.
WebSite	A WebSite is a set of related web pages and other items typically served from a single web domain and accessible via URLs.
Zoo	A zoo.

Table 10: List of all semantic types in the CLSE with descriptions from `schema.org`. Entities can be associated with multiple semantic types. See (Guha et al., 2016) or `schema.org` for more details about the semantic types.

B Model Output Examples

structured data	`service_name: Hotels_2 | confirm, where_to: Amsterdam | confirm, number_of_adults: 5 | confirm, check_in_date: July 24, 2019 | confirm, check_out_date: April 22, 2021`		
English	Alright. So you'd like to make a reservation for 5 in Amsterdam. You are checking in July 24, 2019 and checking out on April 22, 2021.	Alright. So you'd like to make a reservation for 5 in Amsterdam. You are checking in July 24, 2019 and checking out on April 22, 2021.	
nmt	Bien. Donc, vous aimeriez faire une réservation pour 5 à Amsterdam. Vous vérifiez le 24 juillet 2019 et vous vérifiez le 22 avril 2021.	Good. So you would like to make a reservation for 5 in Amsterdam. You **verify** on July 24, 2019 and you **verify** on April 22, 2021.	*"check in/out" mistranslated as "verify"*
d2t	Très bien. Vous arrivez le 24 juillet 2019 et partez le 22 avril 2021. C'est bien ça?	Very well. You are arriving on July 24, 2019 and departing on April 22, 2021. **Is that correct?**	*missing "for 5" and "Amsterdam", asking a question in the end*
tmpl	D'accord. Vous souhaitez faire une réservation pour 5 personne à Amsterdam. Vous arrivez le 24 juillet 2019 et partez le 22 avril 2021.	OK. You want to make a reservation for 5 **person** in Amsterdam. You arrive on July 24, 2019 and depart on April 22, 2021.	*"5 personne" is ungrammatical*
tmpl+G	D'accord. Vous souhaitez faire une réservation pour 5 personnes à Amsterdam. Vous arrivez le 24 juillet 2019 et partez le 22 avril 2021.	OK. You want to make a reservation for 5 people in Amsterdam. You arrive on July 24, 2019 and depart on April 22, 2021.	
human	D'accord. Vous souhaitez faire une réservation pour 5 personnes à Amsterdam. Vous arrivez le 24 juillet 2019 et partez le 22 avril 2021.	OK. You want to make a reservation for 5 people in Amsterdam. You arrive on July 24, 2019 and depart on April 22, 2021.	

Table 11: Example of different NLG system outputs in French.

We often see raters reporting perfect accuracy despite missed facts or new facts introduced by the model. This is understandable, as humans are not perfect and often miss things. For example, the **d2t** output in Table 11 misses multiple aspects, yet all three raters gave it a perfect accuracy score of 1. Despite high human scores, such a model would be problematic to put in front of real users, as rightfully signalled by the automatic metric(s). Therefore, one should not completely discard automatic metrics, and use them in addition to human scores to flag potential model issues. Table 12 exemplifies this: all results get perfect accuracy scores from the raters whereas BLEURT successfully catches the mismatch.

English reference	d2t model prediction	BLEURT
Satire.	Je vais lancer la lecture. C'est une satire tirée de l'album de musique techno. / [I am going to start. It's a satire taken from **the techno music** album].	0.11
Please confirm the address of destination as 2901 East Hastings Street. Also for how many person do you want to book the cab and **what type of ride** you want?	Vous allez au 2901 East Hastings Street, c'est ça? Vous serez combien? / [You're going to 2901 East Hastings Street, right? How many of you?]	0.16
Is your destination 2033 Camden Avenue # F3? Please tell me the number of seats you need, as well as your ride preference. You can say Pool, Luxury or something else.	Vous souhaitez une course luxe, unisexe au 2033 Camden Avenue # F3, pour combien de personnes? / [Would you like a luxury, **unisex** ride at 2033 Camden Avenue #F3, for how many people?]	0.18

Table 12: **d2t** model outputs with the lowest BLEURT scores in French. Mismatched facts are marked in bold. All three of them get perfect accuracy scores from all three raters. Human raters are imperfect, and for factual accuracy, there seems to be some tolerance for hallucinations or missing facts when there are many pieces of information presented in the same utterance.

C Datasheet

Datasheets for Datasets "document [the dataset] motivation, composition, collection process, recommended uses, and so on. [They] have the potential to increase transparency and accountability within the machine learning community, mitigate unwanted biases in machine learning systems, facilitate greater reproducibility of machine learning results, and help researchers and practitioners select more appropriate datasets for their chosen tasks."

Motivation

For what purpose was the dataset created? Was there a specific task in mind? Was there a specific gap that needed to be filled? Please provide a description.

CLSE was created for training, testing, and evaluating NLG systems in multiple languages, including several low-resource ones. It allows to do sampling and slicing by language, semantic type, or linguistic phenomena.

Who created this dataset (e.g., which team, research group) and on behalf of which entity (e.g., company, institution, organization)?

Google Assistant NLP Team.

Who funded the creation of the dataset? If there is an associated grant, please provide the name of the grantor and the grant name and number.

Google Assistant NLP Team.

Composition

What do the instances that comprise the dataset represent (e.g., documents, photos, people, countries)? Are there multiple types of instances (e.g., movies, users, and ratings; people and interactions between them; nodes and edges)? Please provide a description.

Entities of semantic types detailed in Appendix A.

How many instances are there in total (of each type, if appropriate)?

80'893 language entries (13'649 unique entities).

Does the dataset contain all possible instances or is it a sample (not necessarily random) of instances from a larger set? If the dataset is a sample, then what is the larger set? Is the sample representative of the larger set (e.g., geographic coverage)? If so, please describe how this representativeness was validated/verified. If it is not representative of the larger set, please describe why not (e.g., to cover a more diverse range of instances, because instances were withheld or unavailable).

The dataset represents a sample of all entities found in the Knowledge Graph. For each language and semantic type, the sample is meant to limit over-representation of entities with common linguistic attributes (see Figure 1).

What data does each instance consist of? "Raw" data (e.g., unprocessed text or images) or features? In either case, please provide a description.

See Table 2 for examples.

Is there a label or target associated with each instance? If so, please provide a description.

No.

Is any information missing from individual instances? If so, please provide a description, explaining why this information is missing (e.g., because it was unavailable). This does not include intentionally removed information, but might include, e.g., redacted text.

Certain linguistic attributes may not be annotated for some languages due to limited language support.

Are relationships between individual instances made explicit (e.g., users' movie ratings, social network links)? If so, please describe how these relationships are made explicit.

No, except for the same entity—identified by its ID—appearing for multiple languages as a separate row.

Are there recommended data splits (e.g., training, development/validation, testing)? If so, please provide a description of these splits, explaining the rationale behind them.

No.

Are there any errors, sources of noise, or redundancies in the dataset? If so, please provide a description.

Surface forms (entity names) and linguistic annotations were created by humans and therefore may be inaccurate or incomplete.

Is the dataset self-contained, or does it link to or otherwise rely on external resources (e.g., websites, tweets, other datasets)? If it links to or relies on external resources, a) are there guarantees that they will exist, and remain constant, over time; b) are there official archival versions of the complete dataset (i.e., including the external resources as they existed at the time the dataset was created); c) are there any restrictions (e.g., licenses, fees) associated with any of the external resources that might apply to a future user? Please provide descriptions of all external resources and any restrictions associated with them, as well as links or other access points, as appropriate.

The dataset is self-contained. Entity IDs refer to the Google Knowledge Graph API, but this is as an implementation detail (API stability does not affect the usefulness of the dataset).

Does the dataset contain data that might be considered confidential (e.g., data that is protected by legal privilege or by doctor-patient confidentiality, data that includes the content of individuals non-public communications)? If so, please provide a description.

No.

Does the dataset contain data that, if viewed directly, might be offensive, insulting, threatening, or might otherwise cause anxiety? If so, please describe why.

No, to the best of our knowledge.

Does the dataset relate to people? If not, you may skip the remaining questions in this section.

Some entities in the dataset are of semantic type "Person."

Does the dataset identify any subpopulations (e.g., by age, gender)? If so, please describe how these subpopulations are identified and provide a description of their respective distributions within the dataset.

No.

Is it possible to identify individuals (i.e., one or more natural persons), either directly or indirectly (i.e., in combination with other data) from the dataset? If so, please describe how.

Yes, people with a Knowledge Graph entry can be uniquely identified.

Does the dataset contain data that might be considered sensitive in any way (e.g., data that reveals racial or ethnic origins, sexual orientations, religious beliefs, political opinions or union memberships, or locations; financial or health data; biometric or genetic data; forms of government identification, such as social security numbers; criminal history)? If so, please provide a description.

No, to the best of our knowledge.

Collection Process

How was the data associated with each instance acquired? Was the data directly observable (e.g., raw text, movie ratings), reported by subjects (e.g., survey responses), or indirectly inferred/derived from other data (e.g., part-of-speech tags, model-based guesses for age or language)? If data was reported by subjects or indirectly inferred/derived from other data, was the data validated/verified? If so, please describe how.

The data was curated by linguists. See Section 2 for more details.

What mechanisms or procedures were used to collect the data (e.g., hardware apparatus or sensor, manual human curation, software program, software API)? How were these mechanisms or procedures validated?

The data was curated in spreadsheets and text files and, as a rule, reviewed by another linguist.

If the dataset is a sample from a larger set, what was the sampling strategy (e.g., deterministic, probabilistic with specific sampling probabilities)?

Exact details of the sampling procedure cannot be disclosed at the moment to preserve anonymity and to comply with internal policies of the authors' organizations.

Who was involved in the data collection process (e.g., students, crowdworkers, contractors) and how were they compensated (e.g., how much were crowdworkers paid)?

Contractors. Each contract is reviewed, approved, and executed according to the strict company policies.

Over what timeframe was the data collected? Does this timeframe match the creation timeframe of the data associated with the instances (e.g., recent crawl of old news articles)? If not, please describe the timeframe in which the data associated with the instances was created.

The bulk of linguistic data was collected over the years 2020 and 2021. Semantic type associations were retrieved from the Google Knowledge Graph API on 2022-05-18.

Were any ethical review processes conducted (e.g., by an institutional review board)? If so, please provide a description of these review processes, including the outcomes, as well as a link or other access point to any supporting documentation.

Yes. The dataset description was improved and this datasheet was created as an outcome.

Does the dataset relate to people? If not, you may skip the remaining questions in this section.

Some entities in the dataset are of semantic type "Person." These are limited to individuals (alive, dead, or fictional) who are popular enough to have a Knowledge Graph entry.

Did you collect the data from the individuals in question directly, or obtain it via third parties or other sources (e.g., websites)?

No.

Were the individuals in question notified about the data collection? If so, please describe (or show with screenshots or other information) how notice was provided, and provide a link or other access point to, or otherwise reproduce, the exact language of the notification itself.

No.

Did the individuals in question consent to the collection and use of their data? If so, please describe (or show with screenshots or other information) how consent was requested and provided, and provide a link or other access point to, or otherwise reproduce, the exact language to which the individuals consented.

N/A.

If consent was obtained, were the consenting individuals provided with a mechanism to revoke their consent in the future or for certain uses? If so, please provide a description, as well as a link or other access point to the mechanism (if appropriate).

N/A.

Has an analysis of the potential impact of the dataset and its use on data subjects (e.g., a data protection impact analysis) been conducted? If so, please provide a description of this analysis, including the outcomes, as well as a link or other access point to any supporting documentation.

N/A.

Preprocessing/cleaning/labeling

Was any preprocessing/cleaning/labeling of the data done (e.g., discretization or bucketing, tokenization, part-of-speech tagging, SIFT feature extraction, removal of instances, processing of missing values)? If so, please provide a description. If not, you may skip the remainder of the questions in this section.

No.

Was the "raw" data saved in addition to the preprocessed/cleaned/labeled data (e.g., to support unanticipated future uses)? If so, please provide a link or other access point to the "raw" data.

N/A.

Is the software used to preprocess/clean/label the instances available? If so, please provide a link or other access point.

N/A.

Uses

Has the dataset been used for any tasks already? If so, please provide a description.

Yes, for experiments in Section 5.

Is there a repository that links to any or all papers or systems that use the dataset? If so, please provide a link or other access point.

No.

What (other) tasks could the dataset be used for?

E.g., for balancing machine translation data.

Is there anything about the composition of the dataset or the way it was collected and preprocessed/cleaned/labeled that might impact future uses? For example, is there anything that a future user might need to know to avoid uses that could result in unfair treatment of individuals or groups (e.g., stereotyping, quality of service issues) or other undesirable harms (e.g., financial harms, legal risks) If so, please provide a description. Is there anything a future user could do to mitigate these undesirable harms?

The linguistic attributes are provided "as is" and may be innacurate or incomplete.

Are there tasks for which the dataset should not be used? If so, please provide a description.

The dataset should not be used to infer non-linguistic properties of entities. In particular, the linguistic attributes are not appropriate proxy data to infer a person's aliveness or gender.

Distribution

Will the dataset be distributed to third parties outside of the entity (e.g., company, institution, organization) on behalf of which the dataset was created? If so, please provide a description.

Yes.

How will the dataset will be distributed (e.g., tarball on website, API, GitHub) Does the dataset have a digital object identifier (DOI)?

As a CSV file retrievable from `https://clse.page.link/data`.

When will the dataset be distributed?
Upon acceptance of the publication.

Will the dataset be distributed under a copyright or other intellectual property (IP) license, and/or under applicable terms of use (ToU)? If so, please describe this license and/or ToU, and provide a link or other access point to, or otherwise reproduce, any relevant licensing terms or ToU, as well as any fees associated with these restrictions.
Yes, CC-BY license.

Have any third parties imposed IP-based or other restrictions on the data associated with the instances? If so, please describe these restrictions, and provide a link or other access point to, or otherwise reproduce, any relevant licensing terms, as well as any fees associated with these restrictions.
No, to the best of our knowledge.

Do any export controls or other regulatory restrictions apply to the dataset or to individual instances? If so, please describe these restrictions, and provide a link or other access point to, or otherwise reproduce, any supporting documentation.
No, to the best of our knowledge.

Maintenance

Who will be supporting/hosting/maintaining the dataset?
The authors of this publication.

How can the owner/curator/manager of the dataset be contacted (e.g., email address)?
Yes, by email or any other contact point provided at `https://clse.page.link/data`.

Is there an erratum? If so, please provide a link or other access point.
No.

Will the dataset be updated (e.g., to correct labeling errors, add new instances, delete instances)? If so, please describe how often, by whom, and how updates will be communicated to users (e.g., mailing list, GitHub)?
No updates are planned at the moment. If any is made, it will be communicated at `https://clse.page.link/data`.

If the dataset relates to people, are there applicable limits on the retention of the data associated with the instances (e.g., were individuals in question told that their data would be retained for a fixed period of time and then deleted)? If so, please describe these limits and explain how they will be enforced.
N/A.

Will older versions of the dataset continue to be supported/hosted/maintained? If so, please describe how. If not, please describe how its obsolescence will be communicated to users.
Yes.

If others want to extend/augment/build on/contribute to the dataset, is there a mechanism for them to do so? If so, please provide a description. Will these contributions be validated/verified? If so, please describe how. If not, why not? Is there a process for communicating/distributing these contributions to other users? If so, please provide a description.
Please, contact the dataset mainteners using the contact information above.

Revisiting text decomposition methods for NLI-based factuality scoring of summaries

John Glover[1] Federico Fancellu[1] Vasudevan Jagannathan[1]
Matthew R. Gormley[1,2] Thomas Schaaf[1]

[1]3M Health Information Systems
{jglover,ffancellu,juggy,tschaaf}@mmm.com

[2]Carnegie Mellon University
mgormley@cs.cmu.edu

Abstract

Scoring the factuality of a generated summary involves measuring the degree to which a target text contains factual information using the input document as support. Given the similarities in the problem formulation, previous work has shown that Natural Language Inference models can be effectively repurposed to perform this task. As these models are trained to score entailment at a sentence level, several recent studies have shown that decomposing either the input document or the summary into sentences helps with factuality scoring. But is fine-grained decomposition always a winning strategy? In this paper we systematically compare different granularities of decomposition – from document to sub-sentence level, and we show that the answer is no. Our results show that incorporating additional context can yield improvement, but that this does not necessarily apply to all datasets. We also show that small changes to previously proposed entailment-based scoring methods can result in better performance, highlighting the need for caution in model and methodology selection for downstream tasks.

1 Introduction

With improvements largely driven by recent advances in pre-trained language models (Vaswani et al., 2017; Radford et al., 2018; Lewis et al., 2020), modern abstractive summarization models are capable of producing summaries that are both fluent and coherent. However, they are still prone to various forms of "hallucination", generating statements that are not supported by the input text (Cao et al., 2018; Maynez et al., 2020). This has lead to a growing interest in being able to accurately measure the degree to which machine-generated output is non-factual (Falke et al., 2019; Kryscinski et al., 2020; Pagnoni et al., 2021; Laban et al., 2022).

In factuality scoring and other closely related tasks such as fact verification (Vlachos and Riedel, 2014; Thorne et al., 2018), the objective is to assess whether or to what degree the claims in a given text can be supported by other "evidence" texts. Given this setup, previous work has drawn a parallel with the task of Natural Language Inference (NLI), which has a similar goal of determining whether the meaning of one text can be inferred (entailed) from another (Dagan et al., 2006). As a consequence, models trained on large NLI datasets (Bowman et al., 2015; Williams et al., 2018; Nie et al., 2020) have often been successfully repurposed for the task of detecting factual inconsistencies in machine-generated summaries (Falke et al., 2019; Kryscinski et al., 2020; Maynez et al., 2020; Zhang and Bansal, 2021). It is now common that high-performance NLI models are trained on a combination of NLI and fact verification datasets (Nie et al., 2020; Schuster et al., 2021).

One way to repurpose NLI models for factuality scoring is to use the full text of the input and summary as the premise and hypothesis respectively, then take the factuality score to be a function of the model output distribution. However, NLI models are usually trained with sentence pairs as input, and can suffer performance degradation with the longer contexts that arise in summarization (Laban et al., 2022; Honovich et al., 2022). Worse yet, the majority of modern NLI models are based on architectures such as the Transformer (Vaswani et al., 2017) that use fixed-length input sizes, and it may not be possible for a full document and summary pair to fit into this context.

Another approach to NLI-based factuality scoring is grounded in the idea of first decomposing the input text into finer levels of granularity, followed by a later score aggregation step. Falke et al. (2019) proposed a scoring method based on sentence level decomposition, but concluded that the NLI models at the time were not robust enough for the task. However, recently both Schuster et al. (2022) and Laban et al. (2022) have shown that variations on this decomposition-based strategy, in combination

Proceedings of the 2nd Workshop on Natural Language Generation, Evaluation, and Metrics (GEM), pages 97 - 105
December 7, 2022 ©2022 Association for Computational Linguistics

with the improved performance of modern NLI models, can produce systems that perform well at the task of detecting factual inconsistencies in generated summaries.

In this work we revisit existing studies of NLI-based factuality scoring and perform a systematic comparison of input-summary decomposition methodologies at different levels of granularity – from document to sub-sentence level. We show that contrary to previous findings, adding more context to the premise (the source document) can sometimes outperform approaches based on a more fine-grained decomposition. We also find that small changes to the factuality scoring function can lead to a substantial increase in performance, but that model performance does not necessarily generalize across benchmarks that use different metrics (even when applied to the same underlying data). Our results highlight the need for caution and additional evaluation when selecting a model and methodology for downstream tasks.

2 Decomposition-based factuality scoring

In this work we are primarily concerned with *referenceless* factuality scoring of document summaries. To do so, we therefore require a function from an input $(document, summary)$ pair to a score value $Z \in \mathbb{R}$. NLI models typically learn a function that maps a pair of input text strings (X_{prem}, X_{hyp}), commonly referred to as the *premise* and *hypothesis*, to a probability distribution over the output classes *entailment*, *neutral*, or *contradiction*. One simple way to repurpose NLI models for factuality scoring is with $(document, summary)$ as (X_{prem}, X_{hyp}), and to take the score Z to be some function $f_Z(p_e, p_n, p_c)$ over the probability values given for entailment (p_e), neutral (p_n), or contradiction (p_c)[1]. We experiment with three decomposition-based scoring methods, described in the following sections.

2.1 SummaC

The SummaC models proposed by Laban et al. (2022) decompose the document and summary into sentences. A document is split into M sentences labelled $D_1, \ldots, D_M$, and a summary into N sentences $S_1, \ldots, S_N$. Each (D_m, S_n) combination is then passed through an NLI model, with scores computed using a function of the output probabilities. This decomposition results in an $M \times N$ score matrix for each $(document, summary)$. Laban et al. (2022) describe two model classes, which differ in how they process the score matrix to create a final factuality score for a summary:[2]

SUMMAC ZERO-SHOT (SC_{ZS}): each summary sentence is first scored by taking the maximum score value computed against any of the document sentences (max over each column in the $M \times N$ matrix). These summary sentence scores are then averaged to compute the final score.

SUMMAC CONVOLUTION (SC_{Conv}): the pair matrix is converted to a histogram by placing the score values into evenly spaced bins, then the resulting matrix is passed through a 1-D convolutional layer. We refer the reader to Laban et al. (2022) for further details.

We observe that although Laban et al. (2022) indicate that the scoring function f_Z that they use is given by $f_Z = p_e$, the default parameters in their publicly available code[3] describe $f_Z = p_e - p_c$. We compare these two variants of the score function f_Z in § 3.1.

2.2 SENTLI

Similarly to Laban et al. (2022), Schuster et al. (2022) propose a factuality scoring model that assigns a score for each summary sentence S_n according to the maximum score across all $(D_{1,\ldots,M}, S_n)$ pairs. Each (D_m, S_n) is scored using a custom NLI model based on T5 (Raffel et al., 2020) and fine-tuned on a combination of the SNLI (Bowman et al., 2015), MNLI (Williams et al., 2018), ANLI (Nie et al., 2020), FEVER (Thorne et al., 2018) and VitaminC (Schuster et al., 2021) datasets.

Final scores are either the average score for all $S_{1,\ldots,N}$ in an aggregation method referred to as "soft aggregation", or the *minimum* score across $S_{1,\ldots,N}$ in their "hard aggregation" method. In addition, Schuster et al. (2022) propose an extension to this approach called "retrieve and rerank" (SENTLI_{RR}). Here they again first score all (D_m, S_n) using an NLI model. For each S_n, the top-K D_m are selected according to both the entailment and contradiction scores p_e and p_c. The NLI

[1]We note that generally the NLI models are not well-calibrated, and so these probability values may not necessarily have semantically meaningful interpretations, but empirically they can often be used directly in this manner.

[2]These models are agnostic to the particular NLI model being used for scoring, but the best performing model in the paper uses a version of ALBERT (Lan et al., 2020) fine-tuned on a combination of MNLI and VitaminC.

[3]https://github.com/tingofurro/summac

model is then presented with the same hypothesis S_n, together with a concatenation of the top-K entailing and contradicting sentences, with the output used to create the final score that S_n. For further details we refer the reader to Schuster et al. (2022).

2.3 Summarization Content Units (SCU)

Following Nenkova and Passonneau (2004) and Shapira et al. (2019), we take decomposition a step further and segment each summary into smaller units called *Summarization Content Units* (SCUs). In its original formulation, SCUs are hand-crafted short spans of text describing a single fact contained in one or more reference summaries[4]. As our evaluation data is not manually annotated with SCUs, we follow the method in Zhang and Bansal (2021), where the authors show that SCUs can be approximated using heuristics applied to the output of a Semantic Role Labeler. However, whereas these methods apply to *reference-based* evaluation of summaries, in the absence of human reference, here we adapt them to fit the reference*less* evaluation scenario. We refer to our method of decomposition and scoring with SCUs as SCU_{ZS}, and describe the details of the method in Appendix D.

3 Experiments and evaluation

We evaluate the performance of our models on the SummaC benchmark (Laban et al., 2022), which comprises of six datasets for summary inconsistency detection: CoGenSumm (CGS) (Falke et al., 2019), XSumFaith (XSF) (Maynez et al., 2020), Polytope (PT) (Huang et al., 2020), FactCC (FCC) (Kryscinski et al., 2020), SummEval (SE) (Fabbri et al., 2021), and FRANK (FR) (Pagnoni et al., 2021). Evaluation is standardized by casting each task as binary classification, and then measuring performance using balanced accuracy. As the NLI-based factuality scoring methods all output a scalar score value, we follow Laban et al. (2022) and tune thresholds separately for all methods and all datasets on the validation set, and report results using these threshold values on the test set. Although the FRANK dataset is part of SummaC, we also perform a separate evaluation of it using the original metrics of Pearson and Spearman correlations of the model output scores with (non-binary) human scores.

To assess the benefits of decomposing text for NLI-based factuality scoring, we compare the performance of the aforementioned decomposition methods with full text scoring, where either or both the source document or the summary has not been decomposed. We also test with a context length of several sentences, computed using a simplified version of the $\text{SENTLI}_{\text{RR}}$ method that we refer to as TOPK, as follows:

- First decompose the document and summary into individual sentences $(D_{1,\ldots,M}, S_{1,\ldots,N})$, and score all combinations using an NLI model.
- For each S_n, select the top-K sentences in $D_1, \ldots, D_M$ according to p_e.
- Concatenate these top-K sentences to form a new premise string.
- Run hypothesis S_n and the new premise through the NLI model, again taking p_e as the final score for S_n.
- Compute the final factuality score as the average over the scores for each S_n.

To split text into sentences we use spaCy (Honnibal et al., 2020). We note that Laban et al. (2022) used NLTK (Bird et al., 2009) for sentence-splitting, but this fails to correctly split sentences on some examples with bad punctuation (which are common in the FRANK dataset in particular[5]). In all experiments, unless otherwise specified we use the NLI model from Schuster et al. (2021) that is fine-tuned on a combination of Vitamin-C and MNLI datasets[6], which we refer to as VITC. For fair comparison with Laban et al. (2022), we set the maximum "full document" context for the premise to be 500 tokens.

3.1 Results

Our main results are summarized in Table 1, with SummaC results at the top and FRANK results at the bottom. In general, we find that factuality scoring using $f_Z = p_e$ has superior performance to $f_Z = p_e - p_c$, for all levels of input granularity, and for all evaluation metrics. We surpass both the original SC_{ZS}/SC_{Conv} and SENTLI/$\text{SENTLI}_{\text{RR}}$ SummaC results using SC_{ZS} with this scoring function. Further performance gains are also obtained from using additional context for the premise using TOPK, and we find that including the full document

[4]Example SCUs are given in Appendix D

[5]see Appendix A for details

[6]This is the best performing NLI model in Laban et al. (2022).

	System	f_Z	PG	HG	CGS	XSF	PT	FCC	SE	FR	Overall
SummaC	SC$_{ZS}$				70.4∗	58.4∗	62.0∗	83.8∗	78.7∗	79.0∗	72.1∗
	SC$_{Conv}$				64.7∗	66.4∗	**62.7∗**	89.5∗	81.7∗	81.6∗	74.4∗
	SENTLI (soft)				79.3∗	59.3∗	52.4∗	89.5∗	77.2∗	82.1∗	73.3∗
	SENTLI$_{RR}$ (soft)				79.6∗	62.7∗	52.8∗	86.1∗	78.5∗	80.4∗	73.3∗
	SENTLI$_{RR}$ (hard)				**80.5∗**	64.2∗	55.1∗	83.3∗	79.7∗	78.4∗	73.5∗
	SC$_{ZS}$	$p_e - p_c$	sent	sent	62.5	53.8	57.6	83.9	77.1	79.2	69.0
	SC$_{ZS}$	p_e	sent	sent	76.8	65.6	57.6	**89.9**	79.7	81.3	75.1
	SC$_{ZS}$	p_e	doc	doc	59.3	**69.9**	59.9	84.7	78.7	81.2	72.3
	SC$_{ZS}$	p_e	TOPK	sent	79.7	67.3	56.9	89.4	81.8	81.4	76.1
	SC$_{ZS}$	$p_e - p_c$	doc	sent	76.3	69.0	58.2	85.4	83.3	**82.6**	75.8
	SC$_{ZS}$	p_e	doc	sent	76.2	69.8	61.7	84.6	**84.0**	82.0	**76.4**
	SCU$_{ZS}$	p_e	TOPK	SCU	72.9	65.6	57.1	80.5	82.1	81.7	73.3
	SCU$_{ZS}$	p_e	sent	SCU	71.4	63.4	55.0	77.0	80.0	81.4	71.4

	System	f_Z	PG	HG	Pearson ρ	p-val	Spearman r	p-val
FRANK	FactCC				0.20∗	0.00∗	0.30∗	0.00∗
	BertScore P Art				0.30∗	0.00∗	0.25∗	0.00∗
	SC$_{ZS}$	$p_e - p_c$	sent	sent	0.32	0.00	0.26	0.00
	SC$_{ZS}$	p_e	sent	sent	0.35	0.00	**0.36**	0.00
	SC$_{ZS}$	p_e	doc	doc	0.31	0.00	0.25	0.00
	SC$_{ZS}$	p_e	TOPK	sent	**0.37**	0.00	0.34	0.00
	SC$_{ZS}$	$p_e - p_c$	doc	sent	0.30	0.00	0.26	0.00
	SC$_{ZS}$	p_e	doc	sent	0.34	0.00	0.29	0.00
	SCU$_{ZS}$	p_e	TOPK	SCU	0.36	0.00	0.30	0.00
	SCU$_{ZS}$	p_e	sent	SCU	0.36	0.00	0.34	0.00

Table 1: Test set results for SummaC and FRANK. Results marked "∗" are taken from prior work, the rest are from our implementations. "PG" and "HG" are the premise and hypothesis levels of granularity respectively. Sentences in our implementations are split using spaCy.

context in the premise performs best of all, in contradiction to previous findings on this benchmark[7]. We see no additional performance benefit in going below the sentence level and using SCUs on these benchmarks, but the SCU decomposition does perform competitively across both benchmarks.

None of our variations achieve similar performance to the published SC$_{ZS}$ results, either performing better or worse depending on whether f_Z is p_e or $p_e - p_c$ respectively. We believe that this discrepancy is due to the fact that the published SC$_{ZS}$ results use classification thresholds that are tuned on the test set[8] rather than validation set.

On FRANK, we find that there is no single method that performs best across both correlation metrics, TOPK having the highest Pearson correlation, and the sentence level SC$_{ZS}$ the highest Spearman correlation. It is notable however that the larger premise context granularity DOC-SENT is not as strong when using the original FRANK metrics as it is on SummaC, highlighting the need to be careful when comparing methods using different metrics, even on the same underlying data.

4 Conclusion

In this work we revisited prior findings that the best way to use NLI models for factuality scoring of machine-generated summaries is to first decompose the input to sentence level, score using NLI, then aggregate the sentence level scores to produce a document-level score. Contrary to prior work, we find that there is no single optimal level of decomposition that performs best across all tasks and evaluation metrics. We showed that in general, sentence level decomposition is preferable for the summary/hypothesis side of the NLI input, but on the premise side recent models such as VITC often benefit from having longer input contexts available when scoring. We also show that for the six datasets in the SummaC benchmark, there is still considerable variation in the performance of our methods both across the individual datasets, and also within different metrics on the same dataset.

[7] In Appendix B we show that some of these findings appear to be unique to this particular choice of NLI model.

[8] Confirmed via correspondence with Laban et al. (2022).

Limitations

Although we evaluate our methods across six different datasets, all are broadly from the same narrow domain, namely English news articles. We also note that despite the methods in Section 2 being agnostic to the choice of the NLI model that is used for scoring, there can be considerable degradation in the performance of methods that use longer premise contexts with some NLI models. More details can be found in Appendix B.

References

Stephen Bird, Edward Loper, and Ewan Klein. 2009. *Natural Language Processing with Python*. O'Reilly Media Inc.

Samuel R. Bowman, Gabor Angeli, Christopher Potts, and Christopher D. Manning. 2015. A large annotated corpus for learning natural language inference. In *Proceedings of the 2015 Conference on Empirical Methods in Natural Language Processing*, pages 632–642, Lisbon, Portugal. Association for Computational Linguistics.

Ziqiang Cao, Furu Wei, Wenjie Li, and Sujian Li. 2018. Faithful to the Original: Fact-Aware Neural Abstractive Summarization. *Proceedings of the AAAI Conference on Artificial Intelligence*, 32(1).

Ido Dagan, Oren Glickman, and Bernardo Magnini. 2006. The PASCAL recognising textual entailment challenge. In *Machine learning challenges. Evaluating predictive uncertainty, visual object classification, and recognising tectual entailment*, pages 177–190, Berlin, Heidelberg. Springer Berlin Heidelberg.

Alexander R. Fabbri, Wojciech Kryściński, Bryan McCann, Caiming Xiong, Richard Socher, and Dragomir Radev. 2021. SummEval: Re-evaluating Summarization Evaluation. *Transactions of the Association for Computational Linguistics*, 9:391–409.

Tobias Falke, Leonardo F. R. Ribeiro, Prasetya Ajie Utama, Ido Dagan, and Iryna Gurevych. 2019. Ranking Generated Summaries by Correctness: An Interesting but Challenging Application for Natural Language Inference. In *Proceedings of the 57th Annual Meeting of the Association for Computational Linguistics*, pages 2214–2220, Florence, Italy. Association for Computational Linguistics.

Matthew Honnibal, Ines Montani, Sofie Van Landeghem, and Adriane Boyd. 2020. spaCy: Industrial-strength Natural Language Processing in Python.

Or Honovich, Roee Aharoni, Jonathan Herzig, Hagai Taitelbaum, Doron Kukliansy, Vered Cohen, Thomas Scialom, Idan Szpektor, Avinatan Hassidim, and Yossi Matias. 2022. TRUE: Re-evaluating Factual Consistency Evaluation. ArXiv:2204.04991 [cs].

Dandan Huang, Leyang Cui, Sen Yang, Guangsheng Bao, Kun Wang, Jun Xie, and Yue Zhang. 2020. What Have We Achieved on Text Summarization? In *Proceedings of the 2020 Conference on Empirical Methods in Natural Language Processing (EMNLP)*, pages 446–469. Association for Computational Linguistics.

Mandar Joshi, Danqi Chen, Yinhan Liu, Daniel S. Weld, Luke Zettlemoyer, and Omer Levy. 2020. SpanBERT: Improving Pre-training by Representing and Predicting Spans. *Transactions of the Association for Computational Linguistics*, 8:64–77.

Wojciech Kryscinski, Bryan McCann, Caiming Xiong, and Richard Socher. 2020. Evaluating the Factual Consistency of Abstractive Text Summarization. In *Proceedings of the 2020 Conference on Empirical Methods in Natural Language Processing (EMNLP)*, pages 9332–9346. Association for Computational Linguistics.

Philippe Laban, Tobias Schnabel, Paul N. Bennett, and Marti A. Hearst. 2022. SummaC : Re-Visiting NLI-based Models for Inconsistency Detection in Summarization. *Transactions of the Association for Computational Linguistics*, 10:163–177.

Zhenzhong Lan, Mingda Chen, Sebastian Goodman, Kevin Gimpel, Piyush Sharma, and Radu Soricut. 2020. ALBERT: A Lite BERT for Self-supervised Learning of Language Representations. In *8th International Conference on Learning Representations, ICLR 2020*, Addis Ababa, Ethiopia.

Mike Lewis, Yinhan Liu, Naman Goyal, Marjan Ghazvininejad, Abdelrahman Mohamed, Omer Levy, Veselin Stoyanov, and Luke Zettlemoyer. 2020. BART: Denoising Sequence-to-Sequence Pre-training for Natural Language Generation, Translation, and Comprehension. In *Proceedings of the 58th Annual Meeting of the Association for Computational Linguistics, ACL 2020, Online, July 5-10, 2020*, pages 7871–7880. Association for Computational Linguistics.

Yinhan Liu, Myle Ott, Naman Goyal, Jingfei Du, Mandar Joshi, Danqi Chen, Omer Levy, Mike Lewis, Luke Zettlemoyer, and Veselin Stoyanov. 2019. RoBERTa: A Robustly Optimized BERT Pretraining Approach. *arXiv:1907.11692 [cs]*. ArXiv: 1907.11692.

Joshua Maynez, Shashi Narayan, Bernd Bohnet, and Ryan McDonald. 2020. On Faithfulness and Factuality in Abstractive Summarization. In *Proceedings of the 58th Annual Meeting of the Association for Computational Linguistics*, pages 1906–1919. Association for Computational Linguistics.

Ani Nenkova and Rebecca Passonneau. 2004. Evaluating content selection in summarization: The pyramid method. In *Proceedings of the human language technology conference of the north American chapter of the association for computational linguistics:*

HLT-NAACL 2004, pages 145–152, Boston, Massachusetts, USA. Association for Computational Linguistics.

Yixin Nie, Adina Williams, Emily Dinan, Mohit Bansal, Jason Weston, and Douwe Kiela. 2020. Adversarial NLI: A New Benchmark for Natural Language Understanding. In *Proceedings of the 58th Annual Meeting of the Association for Computational Linguistics*, pages 4885–4901. Association for Computational Linguistics.

Artidoro Pagnoni, Vidhisha Balachandran, and Yulia Tsvetkov. 2021. Understanding Factuality in Abstractive Summarization with FRANK: A Benchmark for Factuality Metrics. In *Proceedings of the 2021 Conference of the North American Chapter of the Association for Computational Linguistics: Human Language Technologies*, pages 4812–4829. Association for Computational Linguistics.

Alec Radford, Karthik Narasimhan, Tim Salimans, and Ilya Sutskever. 2018. Improving Language Understanding by Generative Pre-Training. *OpenAI Technical Report.*

Colin Raffel, Noam Shazeer, Adam Roberts, Katherine Lee, Sharan Narang, Michael Matena, Yanqi Zhou, Wei Li, and Peter J. Liu. 2020. Exploring the limits of transfer learning with a unified text-to-text transformer. *Journal of Machine Learning Research*, 21(140):1–67.

Tal Schuster, Sihao Chen, Senaka Buthpitiya, Alex Fabrikant, and Donald Metzler. 2022. Stretching Sentence-pair NLI Models to Reason over Long Documents and Clusters. *arXiv:2204.07447 [cs].*

Tal Schuster, Adam Fisch, and Regina Barzilay. 2021. Get Your Vitamin C! Robust Fact Verification with Contrastive Evidence. In *Proceedings of the 2021 Conference of the North American Chapter of the Association for Computational Linguistics: Human Language Technologies*, pages 624–643. Association for Computational Linguistics.

Ori Shapira, David Gabay, Yang Gao, Hadar Ronen, Ramakanth Pasunuru, Mohit Bansal, Yael Amsterdamer, and Ido Dagan. 2019. Crowdsourcing Lightweight Pyramids for Manual Summary Evaluation. In *Proceedings of the 2019 Conference of the North*, pages 682–687, Minneapolis, Minnesota. Association for Computational Linguistics.

Peng Shi and Jimmy Lin. 2019. Simple BERT Models for Relation Extraction and Semantic Role Labeling. *arXiv:1904.05255 [cs].*

James Thorne, Andreas Vlachos, Christos Christodoulopoulos, and Arpit Mittal. 2018. FEVER: a large-scale dataset for Fact Extraction and VERification. In *Proceedings of the 2018 Conference of the North American Chapter of the Association for Computational Linguistics: Human Language Technologies, Volume 1 (Long Papers)*, pages 809–819. Association for Computational Linguistics.

Ashish Vaswani, Noam Shazeer, Niki Parmar, Jakob Uszkoreit, Llion Jones, Aidan N Gomez, Łukasz Kaiser, and Illia Polosukhin. 2017. Attention is all you need. *Advances in neural information processing systems*, 30.

Andreas Vlachos and Sebastian Riedel. 2014. Fact Checking: Task definition and dataset construction. In *Proceedings of the ACL 2014 Workshop on Language Technologies and Computational Social Science*, pages 18–22, Baltimore, MD, USA. Association for Computational Linguistics.

Adina Williams, Nikita Nangia, and Samuel R. Bowman. 2018. A Broad-Coverage Challenge Corpus for Sentence Understanding through Inference. In *Proceedings of the 2018 Conference of the North American Chapter of the Association for Computational Linguistics: Human Language Technologies, Volume 1 (Long Papers)*, pages 1112–1122. Association for Computational Linguistics.

Shiyue Zhang and Mohit Bansal. 2021. Finding a Balanced Degree of Automation for Summary Evaluation. In *Proceedings of the 2021 Conference on Empirical Methods in Natural Language Processing*, pages 6617–6632. Association for Computational Linguistics.

A Performance variations with different sentence-splitting methods

Table 2 describes how the performance of the SummaC Zero-Shot factuality scoring method varies based on whether NLTK or spaCy is used for sentence-splitting. All methods use the VITC NLI model. On SummaC, we see that using spaCy results in a slight improvement overall, whether our scoring function is $f_Z = pe$ or $f_Z = p_e - p_c$. We note that this is true for the FRANK dataset when scored using the SummaC balanced accuracy metric. However, on the FRANK dataset with the original metrics, we mostly see the opposite effect; using NLTK results in higher Pearson correlations for both scoring functions, and a higher Spearman for $f_Z = p_e - p_c$. Notably, the 0.39 Pearson correlation for $\mathrm{SC_{ZS}}$ at sentence level granularity using NLTK is the highest score that we obtain on this benchmark.

However, the results on Frank seem to be partly an artifact of inaccurate sentence-splitting by NLTK resulting in $(premise, hypotheis)$ pairs that are in fact at much larger levels of granularity than the intended sentence level, making this result

	System	f_Z	Splitter	CGS	XSF	PT	FCC	SE	FR	Overall
SummaC	SC_{ZS}	$p_e - p_c$	NLTK	61.9	53.7	56.3	83.4	78.2	78.4	68.6
	SC_{ZS}	$p_e - p_c$	spaCy	62.5	53.8	57.6	83.9	77.1	79.2	69.0
	SC_{ZS}	p_e	NLTK	75.6	65.3	60.4	89.5	80.1	79.1	75.0
	SC_{ZS}	p_e	spaCy	76.8	65.6	57.6	89.9	79.7	81.3	75.1

	System	f_Z	Splitter	Pearson ρ	p-val	Spearman r	p-val
FRANK	SC_{ZS}	$p_e - p_c$	spaCy	0.27	0.00	0.23	0.00
	SC_{ZS}	$p_e - p_c$	NLTK	0.32	0.00	0.26	0.00
	SC_{ZS}	p_e	spaCy	0.35	0.00	0.36	0.00
	SC_{ZS}	p_e	NLTK	0.39	0.00	0.34	0.00

Table 2: Performance differences on SummaC and FRANK test sets based on choice of sentence-splitting method. All methods use sentence level granularity for both premise and hypothesis. For SummaC all methods use thresholds selected using the validation set.

difficult to interpret. The following is an example of a passage of text taken verbatim from the FRANK validation set:

> Thousands attended the early morning service at Hyde Park Corner and up to 400 people took part in a parade before the wreath-laying at the Cenotaph.Anzac Day commemorates the first major battle involving Australian and New Zealand forces during World War One.A service was also held at Westminster Abbey.The national anthems of New Zealand and Australia were sung as the service ended.

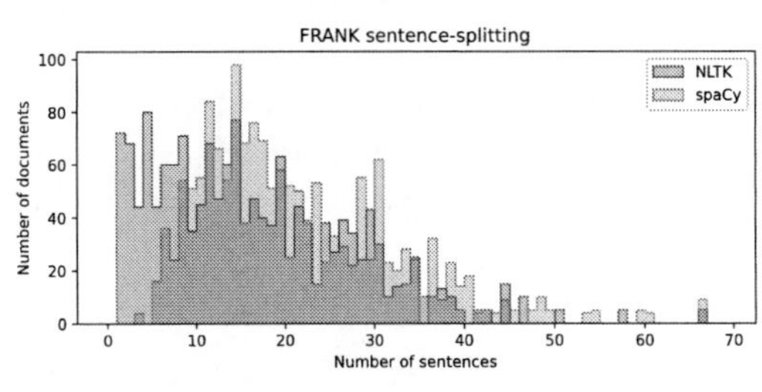

Figure 1: The number of sentences produced by NLTK and spaCy on SummaC and FRANK.

We note that in this example there is no space after the fullstops, which causes NLTK's parser to break. NLTK produces 1 sentence for this block of text, while spaCy produces 4 as we would expect. This issue is relatively frequent in the FRANK dataset. Figure 1 shows the distributions of the number of sentences produced by NLTK versus spaCy for all of the documents in both SummaC and FRANK, with statistics given in Table 4. We see that spaCy produces more sentences generally, with the difference being more pronounced on the FRANK dataset.

B Performance variations with different NLI models and levels of granularity

In Table 3 we investigate how changing the level of decomposition effects the performance of two additional NLI models. Notably with both of these models, scoring using the full document as the premise is significantly worse than either sentence level decomposition, TopK, or SCU, emphasizing that the results in Table 3 are highly dependent on the performance of the VitC NLI model. TopK and sentence level both perform reasonably well with these NLI models however, with the former being the best method to use on SummaC with RoBERTa$_{ANLI}$ and the latter the best with RoBERTa$_{MNLI}$. Again, we see no performance benefit when going to the SCU level.

C SCU examples

Two example one-line summaries, along with two extracted SCUs are shown below. Colors indicate which parts of the generated summaries the SCUs are extracted from.

> Summary$_1$: In 1998 two Libyans indicted in 1991 for the Lockerbie bombing were still in

	System	PG	HG	CGS	XSF	PT	FCC	SE	FR	Overall
SummaC	RoBERTa$_{MNLI}$	doc	sent	58.1	56.2	52.9	62.5	57.0	66.2	58.8
	RoBERTa$_{MNLI}$	TopK	sent	61.5	63.3	60.0	81.5	75.1	76.4	69.6
	RoBERTa$_{MNLI}$	sent	sent	75.2	61.3	59.2	90.7	80.1	79.5	74.3
	RoBERTa$_{MNLI}$	TopK	SCU	66.3	62.0	51.5	74.8	73.2	76.2	67.3
	RoBERTa$_{MNLI}$	sent	SCU	71.6	65.1	53.9	81.9	77.0	80.0	71.6
	RoBERTa$_{ANLI}$	doc	sent	53.5	62.9	55.8	62.3	59.6	69.5	60.6
	RoBERTa$_{ANLI}$	TopK	sent	77.3	65.4	58.4	82.4	78.4	76.9	73.2
	RoBERTa$_{ANLI}$	sent	sent	73.1	61.2	59.6	87.6	74.1	80.2	72.7
	RoBERTa$_{ANLI}$	TopK	SCU	74.5	64.3	59.2	82.1	77.8	77.9	72.6
	RoBERTa$_{ANLI}$	sent	SCU	70.8	64.4	55.8	79.8	76.7	81.0	71.4

	System	PG	HG	Pearson ρ	p-val	Spearman r	p-val
FRANK	RoBERTa$_{MNLI}$	doc	sent	0.16	0.00	0.11	0.00
	RoBERTa$_{MNLI}$	TopK	sent	0.23	0.00	0.21	0.00
	RoBERTa$_{MNLI}$	sent	sent	0.27	0.00	0.27	0.00
	RoBERTa$_{MNLI}$	TopK	SCU	0.23	0.00	0.21	0.00
	RoBERTa$_{MNLI}$	sent	SCU	0.26	0.00	0.27	0.00
	RoBERTa$_{ANLI}$	doc	sent	0.05	0.04	-0.04	0.16
	RoBERTa$_{ANLI}$	TopK	sent	0.27	0.00	0.30	0.00
	RoBERTa$_{ANLI}$	sent	sent	0.27	0.00	0.32	0.00
	RoBERTa$_{ANLI}$	TopK	SCU	0.24	0.00	0.23	0.00
	RoBERTa$_{ANLI}$	sent	SCU	0.27	0.00	0.29	0.00

Table 3: Performance differences on SummaC and FRANK test sets based on choice of NLI model and level of granularity. For SummaC all methods use thresholds selected using the validation set. Sentences are split using spaCy. RoBERTa$_{MNLI}$ is the NLI model from Liu et al. (2019), and RoBERTa$_{ANLI}$ is from Nie et al. (2020).

Libya.

Summary$_2$: Two Libyans were indicted in 1991 for blowing up a Pan Am jumbo jet over Lockerbie, Scotland in 1988.

SCUs: [two Libyans were officially accused of the Lockerbie bombing, the indictment of the two Lockerbie suspects was in 1991]

D SCU-based decomposition details

To create SCUs for a passage of text, we first split it into sentences using spaCy. We then pass each sentence through co-reference resolution (Joshi et al., 2020), and then finally we create SCUs using the method based on Semantic Role Labeling (SRL) (Shi and Lin, 2019) described in Zhang and Bansal (2021). We use the publicly available code from Zhang and Bansal (2021)[9] for both the co-reference resolution and SRL-based SCU generation.

[9] `https://github.com/ZhangShiyue/Lite2-3Pyramid`, the authors refer to their SRL-based SCUs as *Semantic Triplet Units* (STUs).

To score a $(document, summary)$ pair, we experimented with decomposing either the document, the summary, or both into SCUs. Here we describe the two variations that performed best on initial validation experiments. The first scores summary SCUs against document sentences, and the second scores summary SCUs using longer passages of text from the document as context.

D.1 sent-SCU

This method is the most similar conceptually to SC$_{ZS}$.

- First decompose the document and summary into individual sentences $(D_{1,...,M}, S_{1,...,N})$, and then further decompose each S_n into SCUs $S_{SCU_1}, \ldots, S_{SCU_J}$.
- Score all (D_m, S_{SCU_j}) combinations using an NLI model, and $f_Z = p_e$.
- The score for each S_{SCU_j} is taken to be the maximum over the $(D_1, \ldots, D_M, S_{SCU_j})$ pairs.
- For each S_n, average over the scores for $S_{SCU_1}, \ldots, S_{SCU_J}$ to calculate a score for

SummaC		
	NLTK	spaCy
Mean	20.6	22.4
Std. dev.	16.4	18.0
25th %	11.0	12.0
50th %	17.0	18.0
75th %	26.0	28.0

FRANK		
	NLTK	spaCy
Mean	16.0	20.9
Std. dev.	11.3	11.3
25th %	7.0	13.0
50th %	14.0	18.0
75th %	24.0	28.0

Table 4: Mean, standard deviation, and percentiles of the number of sentences produced by NLTK and spaCy on SummaC and FRANK.

that summary sentence, before averaging over the scores for each S_n to create the document factuality score.

D.2 TopK-SCU

This is similar to the TopK scoring method from § 3.

- First decompose the document and summary into individual sentences $(D_{1,\ldots,M}, S_{1,\ldots,N})$, and then further decompose each S_n into SCUs $S_{SCU_1}, \ldots, S_{SCU_J}$.
- Score all (D_m, S_{SCU_j}) combinations using an NLI model, and $f_Z = p_e$.
- For each S_{SCU_j}, we select the top-K sentences in $D_1, \ldots, D_M$ according to $f_Z = p_e$, and concatenate them to form a new premise string.
- Hypothesis S_{SCU_j} is re-scored using the new premise string, using $f_Z = p_e$ as the score for S_{SCU_j}.
- For each S_n we then first average over the scores for $S_{SCU_1}, \ldots, S_{SCU_J}$ to calculate a score for that summary sentence, before averaging over the scores for each S_n to create the document factuality score.

Semantic Similarity as a Window into Vector- and Graph-Based Metrics

Wai Ching Leung
Georgetown University
wl607@georgetown.edu

Shira Wein
Georgetown University
sw1158@georgetown.edu

Nathan Schneider
Georgetown University
nathan.schneider@georgetown.edu

Abstract

In this work, we use sentence similarity as a lens through which to investigate the representation of meaning in graphs vs. vectors. On semantic textual similarity data, we examine how similarity metrics based on vectors alone (SENTENCE-BERT and BERTSCORE) fare compared to metrics based on AMR graphs (SMATCH and S^{2}MATCH). Quantitative and qualitative analyses show that the AMR-based metrics can better capture meanings dependent on sentence structures, but can also be distracted by structural differences—whereas the BERT-based metrics represent finer-grained meanings of individual words, but often fail to capture the ordering effect of words within sentences and suffer from interpretability problems. These findings contribute to our understanding of each approach to semantic representation and motivate distinct use cases for graph and vector-based representations.

1 Introduction

Deriving sentence-level semantics is a nontrivial task and is fundamental to natural language understanding. Word embeddings (vectors) and graph-based formalisms are two kinds of sentence meaning representations that are widely used in NLP and NLG. One way to evaluate semantic representations is to compare their judgments on semantic similarity, often using human judgments as a reference, and there are automatic sentence similarity metrics that have been developed which make use of vector and graph-based models.

Vector-based models, such as SENTENCE-BERT (Reimers and Gurevych, 2019) and BERTSCORE (Zhang et al., 2019), rely on BERT embeddings. Though they are robust and highly efficient, they often suffer from interpretability issues and do not meet all of the expectations of a distributional semantics model (Mickus et al., 2019).

On the other hand, semantic formalisms such as Abstract Meaning Representation (AMR; Banarescu et al., 2013) are more explicit, and can be compared via graph-based similarity measures (Cai and Knight, 2013). While the explainability of these metrics is high, some studies have shown that they do not correlate with cross-lingual human-level judgments of similarity as well as embedding-based metrics (Wein and Schneider, 2022).

What is the difference between a stock and a bond?
What is the difference between a mode and a scale?

Figure 1: A sentence pair in the STS (Agirre et al., 2016) dataset which receives a human judgment of 0 (no similarity), an S^{2}MATCH similarity score of 0.75, a SENTENCE-BERT similarity score of 0.10, and a BERTSCORE score of 0.94. All three automatic metrics range from 0 to 1, where 1 indicates that the sentences are identical.

AMR-based metrics reflect the semantics of a sentence while abstracting away from syntactic features, while word-embedding based-metrics compare the tokens with contextualized embeddings. To this date, there is not a single approach that fully captures sentence meaning in a transparent fashion, so we need to investigate the strengths and weaknesses of different approaches in order to develop a better representation.

Given the importance of reflecting semantic similarity in formalisms of meaning, we hypothesize that semantic similarity is an informative way to investigate these representations. In this work, we investigate these semantic models through the lens of semantic textual similarity to investigate the differences between the various representations. These graph-based and the BERT-based approaches to automatically assessing semantic similarity have different strengths, but no work to date has thoroughly compared these metrics as a way to better understand their applicability and utility. We investigate how these metrics compare to human judgments of similarity on a semantic similarity task. Specifically, we compare and analyze the scores of two

Proceedings of the 2nd Workshop on Natural Language Generation, Evaluation, and Metrics (GEM), pages 106 - 115
December 7, 2022 ©2022 Association for Computational Linguistics

AMR-based metrics—SMATCH and S²MATCH—as well as two BERT-based metrics—BERTSCORE and SENTENCE-BERT—in relation to each other and in relation to human similarity judgments. For example, Figure 1 features a sentence pair with vastly different similarity judgments via human annotation and three of our automatic metrics.

Our primary contributions include:

- Quantitative results comparing AMR-based metrics and BERT-based metrics, with each other and with human judgments of similarity
- Analysis of points of low and high agreement between metrics
- Investigation of semantic features captured by the metrics
- Discussion of the successes and weaknesses of the performance of the metrics

Our data are publicly available.[1]

2 Background & Related Work

Abstract Meaning Representation. Graph-based semantic representations take an explicit approach to representing the meaning of the sentence by defining the roles and relations of the concepts within the sentence. AMR is a semantic representation which captures the meaning of a phrase or sentence in the form of a directed, acyclic graph (Banarescu et al., 2013). The graph's nodes and edges correspond to concepts in the sentence and the relations between the concepts, respectively. Methods for evaluating the performance of a text-to-AMR parser or computing the similarity of two AMRs include SMATCH and S²MATCH, described in §3.

Wein and Schneider (2022) introduce three methods for comparing cross-lingual pairs of AMRs and evaluate the AMR-based metrics against human judgments of sentence similarity and BERTSCORE. Cross-lingually, Wein and Schneider (2022) found that BERTSCORE was more correlated with human judgments than the AMR-based metrics.

Semantic Textual Similarity. Semantic textual similarity (STS) is the task of judging the semantic equivalence of two sentences (Agirre et al., 2016).

In the most recent SemEval Semantic Textual Similarity for monolingual data in 2016 (Agirre et al., 2016), the top performing team at that time incorporates WordNet information into word embeddings in their model (Rychalska et al., 2016). Wang et al. (2022) combine FrameNet information with SENTENCE-BERT (Reimers and Gurevych, 2019) to compute sentence similarity. WordNet and FrameNet focus on lexical information and relations between words or frames, which is distinctively different from AMR which represents lexical concepts and their relations within the *same* sentence. The state-of-the-art systems most correlated with human judgments consistently make use of Transformers, such as SMART-Roberta Large (Jiang et al., 2020), which achieves state-of-the-art 92.9 and 92.5 on Spearman's and Pearson's correlations.

Opitz and Frank (2022) introduced a similarity metric, Semantically Structured SENTENCE-BERT (S³BERT), which combines the explainability of AMR metrics with the high performance of BERT-based approaches. For the STS task, S³BERT obtains a correlation score of 83.7 on Spearman's rank correlation coefficient. S³BERT separates SENTENCE-BERT embeddings into partitions and trains the sub-embeddings on individual aspects of AMR metrics. Opitz and Frank (2022) developed S³BERT with the motivation of uncovering the semantic features that contribute to similarity ratings, and in doing so, develops hypotheses and conjectures about the reasons to combine these two methods based on their potential strengths and weaknesses. For example, AMR metrics are said to be able to capture specific aspects related to semantic similarity, such as semantic roles, but are less correlated with human judgments; the BERT-based metrics are more similar to human judgments but might lack sensitivity to word order. Relatedly, Mohebbi et al. (2022) combine semantic roles labels and dependency grammar on top of the BERT Transformer model (Devlin et al., 2019) with the aim of computing semantic textual similarity.

In order to provide a more fine-grained evaluation of existing AMR parsers, Damonte et al. (2016) compare their parser with JAMR (Flanigan et al., 2014) and CAMR (Wang et al., 2015) on various sub-tasks, such as named entity identification and semantic role labeling, and conclude that there is not a single parser that outperforms others in all sub-tasks.

While prior research efforts have focused on either combining explicit information from graph-based resources with vectors, to the best of our knowledge, there has not been a direct, fine-grained comparison between these two formalisms. In our

[1] `https://github.com/chingachleung/Vector-and-Graph-Based-Metrics`

work, we perform a comparative analysis testing the hypotheses proposed in Opitz and Frank (2022) and analyzing the distinct strengths of graph versus vector-based representations on the task of semantic similarity.

3 Sentence Similarity Metrics

In this work, we investigate the performance of and differences between four metrics of sentence-level semantics: SMATCH (Cai and Knight, 2013), S^{2}MATCH (Opitz et al., 2020), SENTENCE-BERT (Reimers and Gurevych, 2019), and BERTSCORE (Zhang et al., 2019). We select these four metrics, two AMR-based and two BERT-based, because they are popularly used to compute sentence similarity (Wang et al., 2022), and are often used for downstream NLP tasks which depend on sentence semantics, such as paraphrase detection (Issa et al., 2018) and coreference predictions (Anikina et al., 2020). Moreover, we wish to contrast the weaknesses and strengths of graph and BERT based metrics.

SMATCH: SMATCH is a widely used metric that measures whole sentence semantic structure similarity by computing the overlaps of structures between sentences that are represented in AMR graphs (Cai and Knight, 2013). Since AMR abstracts away from syntax, syntactic paraphrases are expected to be represented with the same graph. A SMATCH score of 1 indicates semantic equivalence between two sentences, and a SMATCH score of 0 indicates that two sentences are completely dissimilar. Figure 2 shows the AMR graph of two semantically identical sentences. In order to compute sentence similarity, sentences are first parsed into AMR graphs. SMATCH then aligns the graphs by finding the maximum number of triple matches (there are two types of triple matches: <var, instance, concept> and <var, relationship, var>), which is achieved by using a hill-climbing method with a smart initialization and 4 random starts to increase the probability in finding the highest number of matches (Cai and Knight, 2013).

```
(g / give-01
      :ARG0 (h / he)
      :ARG1 (m / money)
      :ARG2 (s / school)
```

Figure 2: The AMR graph for two syntactic paraphrases: *He gives the school money*, and *He gives money to the school*

S^{2}MATCH: This metric is an extension of SMATCH which incorporates word-embeddings to match synonyms or near-synonyms (Opitz et al., 2020). During graph alignment, if the cosine similarity between the word-embeddings of two nodes meets a threshold, these two nodes, even if they have a different surface form, are considered a match. As a result, the S^{2}MATCH score will go up according to the cosine similarity score. This addresses the disadvantage of SMATCH (Cai and Knight, 2013) that graded meanings are not measured. For example, <var, instance, skinny> and <var, instance, thin> are considered a match in S^{2}MATCH since "skinny" and "thin" are synonyms, but not in SMATCH since "skinny" and "thin" are two different words.

Following Reimers and Gurevych (2019), we set the S^{2}MATCH alignment threshold value to 0.5. Therefore, we only consider the similarity between nodes if their cosine similarity reaches 0.5 or higher.

In order to use SMATCH and S^{2}MATCH to compare sentence similarity, we first use an automated AMR parser (Bai et al., 2022) to convert sentence pairs into AMR graphs. The parser is a BART-based model (Lewis et al., 2020) that is trained on a self-supervised graph-to-graph method. The accuracy of the parser is 83.6% on the **AMR2.0** (LDC2017T10) dataset.

SENTENCE-BERT: SENTENCE-BERT (Reimers and Gurevych, 2019) is a BERT-based model that is pre-trained on the SNLI (Bowman et al., 2015) and the Multi-Genre NLI (Williams et al., 2017) datasets. It generates sentence embeddings using the Siamese BERT model architecture (Devlin et al., 2019). To measure sentence similarity using SENTENCE-BERT, we pass sentence pairs into this model to obtain sentence embeddings, and compute their cosine similarity.

BERTSCORE: This metric was designed with the intention to evaluate text generation quality (Zhang et al., 2019). To obtain BERTSCOREs between reference and candidate sentences, this metric first matches the tokens in the sentences using a greedy method: each token in a sentence is matched to the most similar token in the other sentence. Therefore, tokens are potentially matched more than once. After, the normalized pairwise cosine similarity between their word embeddings are computed with an optional idf-importance weight-

Metric	Pearson	Spearman
SMATCH	0.54	0.52
S^2MATCH	0.55	0.53
SENTENCE-BERT	0.80	0.81
BERTSCORE	0.67	0.66

Table 1: Pearson and Spearman's Rho correlations with gold labels for each of the four metrics.

Metric	Mean
SMATCH	0.54
S^2MATCH	0.56
SENTENCE-BERT	0.63
BERTSCORE	0.93
Gold	0.53

Table 2: Mean scores of the metrics and the gold labels

ing which can put more weight on more indicative words of sentences during computation.

4 Data & Evaluation Protocol

We use the test data from the SemEval-2016 Semantic Textual Similarity English Subtask (Agirre et al., 2016) to evaluate the metrics on their degree of alignment with human judgments. The data contains 1,189 pairs of English snippets from five sources: newswire headlines, short-answer plagiarism, machine translation post-editing, Q&A forum answers, and Q&A forum questions. All the pairs are labeled on an ordinal scale from 0 to 5, with 0 indicating the texts are completely dissimilar, and 5 indicating they are semantically equivalent. For example, the sentences *the bird is bathing in the sink* and *birdie is washing itself in the water basin* are labeled as 5, while *John went horse riding at dawn with a whole group of friends* and *Sunrise at dawn is a magnificent view to take in if you wake up early enough for it* are labeled as 0.

To measure the correlation between each metric with human judgments, we use both the Spearman's and Pearson's rank correlation statistics. SENTENCE-BERT (Reimers and Gurevych, 2019) also use the same task to evaluate their model and report 74% Spearman's Rank correlation.

Since the AMR parser (Bai et al., 2022) used in this experiment may output multiple alternative AMR graphs due to linguistic ambiguity, we only select sentences that are only parsed into a single graph to avoid impact caused by ambiguity on the correlation results. As a result, a total of 1138 sentence pairs are selected in our test set. This pre-processing step is very likely the reason why there is a discrepancy between our reported score as shown in Table 1 and the reported score from (Reimers and Gurevych, 2019).

5 Results and Analyses

In this section, we present qualitative and quantitative analyses of the performance of each of the four metrics: SMATCH, S^2MATCH, SENTENCE-BERT, and BERTSCORE. Specifically, we aim to:

- Evaluate metric quality for measuring semantic similarity, using human judgments as a reference
- Identify the challenges of incorporating embeddings into graph-based metrics
- Identify challenging and easy scenarios, by looking at what types of sentences the metrics correlate best and worst with each other
- Uncover the strengths and weaknesses of each metric, by analyzing what semantic aspects these metrics are able to capture

5.1 Semantic Metric Quality

In our experiment, we use both Pearson's and Spearman's correlation coefficients to compute correlations between the metrics and human judgments to avoid bias towards certain metrics due to our choice of correlation tests. As shown in Table 1, SENTENCE-BERT has the strongest correlation with the gold labels on both the Pearson's and Spearman's Rho. SMATCH and S^2MATCH have the lowest correlations with the the gold labels: 0.54 and 0.55 on Pearson's, and 0.52 vs. 0.53 on Spearman's respectively.

Although SENTENCE-BERT has the highest similarity with human judgments, it suffers from low interpretability. In particular, we find it hard to account for seemingly inconsistent predictions. For example, the sentence pair *What is the best way to store fresh berries?* vs. *What is the best way to cite an anonymous writer?* receives a similarity score of 0.06 from SENTENCE-BERT, but this pair *What is the best way to treat a feline ringworm?* vs. *What is the best way to clean a grater?* receives a similarity of 0.4 from the same model. Intuitively, the differences in these two sentence pairs are very similar, but they have very different similarity scores.

Besides correlation with human judgments, we also look at the mean scores of the metrics versus that of the human judgments, in order to understand the likelihood of each metric considering sentences similar or dissimilar. This will be particularly useful if the metrics are used as an off-the-shelf tool to compute similarity in downstream NLP tasks. The mean score of the test data in our experiment is 3.2 on an ordinal scale from 0 to 5, which translates to 0.53 on a 0–1 scale. We find that the graph-based metrics' scores are closest to the mean score of human judgments, whereas BERTSCORE's mean is significantly higher (see details in Table 2). The high scores produced by BERTSCORE could be misleading, especially in cases where sentences are completely dissimilar. Therefore, we also investigate how this metric scores dissimilar sentences. Out of 198 sentence pairs that are annotated as completely dissimilar by human judgments, BERTSCORE gives an average score of 0.89, remarkably higher than the average scores of S^{2}MATCH and SENTENCE-BERT for the same pairs, which are 0.36 and 0.28. For example, *Step towards* and *Not in sight* is a sentence pair rated as 0 by human judgments, but BERTSCORE gives a similarity score of 0.86. A potential cause is its greedy approach for token matching: tokens are matched with the most similar tokens from the other sentence, even if they have already been matched with other tokens. The way the sentences are constructed in the STS data also exacerbates this behavior: on average, 57% of the tokens in reference sentences also occur in their candidate sentences, which means that there are over 50% of the tokens which are considered exact matches by BERTSCORE, even if the tokens are used differently.

Based on the correlations with human judgments and the mean scores of the metrics, we conclude that SENTENCE-BERT's scores are the most indicative of semantic similarity between sentences.

5.2 Challenges of Incorporating Embeddings into AMR Metrics

Theoretically, S^{2}MATCH combines the strengths of graph-based and vector-based metrics, but its low correlation with human judgments calls into question how embeddings have been incorporated into graphs. In order to distinguish the performance of SMATCH and S^{2}MATCH, we first compare the similarity between SMATCH and S^{2}MATCH by running the Spearman's and Pearson's correlation tests on their similarity scores. We obtain 0.98 on both of the tests, which serves as a strong indicator that these metrics have extremely similar behavior. As posited in Opitz et al. (2020), S^{2}MATCH scores are the same as or higher than SMATCH scores due to the additional consideration of graded meaning. Their extremely similar correlation scores with human judgments also implies that the use of vectors in S^{2}MATCH does not improve its representations of meanings. Digging into the STS data, we observe several challenges that help explain why this metric fails to achieve the 'best of both worlds'.

Cosine similarity may not reflect semantic similarity: For the sentence pair *What type of faucet is this?* vs. *What kind of socket is this?*, the words 'kind' and 'type' have a cosine similarity score of 0.6, which is above the threshold we set. As a result, S^{2}MATCH considers these two tokens a match, and incorporates the cosine similarity score into the final similarity score. This makes the S^{2}MATCH score of this pair higher than the SMATCH score. However, we also see that the cosine similarity score of 'this' and 'kind' is 0.778, which is higher than the cosine similarity score between 'kind' and 'type'. Although 'this' and 'kind' are not matched, hence their cosine similarity score is not computed into the final similarity score, it shows that embedding similarity might not be always reliable for comparing semantic similarity, which directly impacts the performance of S^{2}MATCH.

Conversion of words into frames potentially hinders embedding comparison: During AMR parsing, words can be represented with a frame that looks different. This poses a challenge for comparison via embeddings since the embeddings of words and their frames can be different. For example, there was a pair in the test data where the synonyms 'therefore' and 'thus' were used in the same way, but given different frames, `cause-01` vs. `infer-01`. The cosine similarity between similarity between 'therefore' and 'thus' is 0.91, whereas the cosine similarity between 'infer' and 'cause' is 0.23, which is lower than the threshold we set. Since S^{2}MATCH computes similarity between frames instead of words, the synonyms 'therefore' and 'thus' could not be matched during S^{2}MATCH score computation. As a result, the S^{2}MATCH and SMATCH scores are the same for this pair.

Another scenario is when AMR 'unpacks' the lexical semantics depending on derivational morphology which may differ between synonyms, obscuring their semantic similarity. For example, the relational meaning of 'employer' in *How do I maintain a good relationship with an employer after resigning?* is expressed with the AMR frame `employ-01`. This not only causes subsequent changes in its graph structures, but also makes S^{2}MATCH

Metric	Mean
S^2MATCH	0.59 (0.23_z)
SENTENCE-BERT	0.29 (-1.42_z)
BERTSCORE	0.93 (0.11_z)

Table 3: Mean absolute scores and z-scores of the metrics on 30 most dissimilar pairs (label 0 or 1). The z-score refers to the number of standard deviations from the mean value from each metric.

less likely to match it with the word 'boss' in the sentence *How do I maintain a good relationship with my old boss after being promoted?*. (The AMR graph does not unpack the relational meaning of 'boss' in the same way because it is not signaled with a derivational suffix.) Even if `boss` and `employ-01` were matched, their cosine similarity would be artificially low because they have different parts of speech.

Given the similar behavior of SMATCH and S^2MATCH, the following subsections will focus on S^2MATCH in relation to the vector-based metrics SENTENCE-BERT and BERTSCORE. We look at examples where the metrics exhibit low (§5.3) and high (§5.4) agreement with each other, to identify challenging and easy cases, and discuss the impact of three semantic features: negation (§5.5), semantic roles (§5.7) and paraphrases (§5.6).

5.3 Low Agreement Between Metrics

In order to compare how the metrics rank semantic similarity differently, we first convert the raw scores from each metric into z-scores using standard scaling. Next, for each sentence pair, we compute the variance of the 3 metrics' z-scores. We examine the sentence pairs with high cross-metric variance and observe that most are judged by humans as dissimilar in meaning (i.e., disagreement among metrics predicts low meaning similarity).

As a means of comparing the metrics, we then investigate the reverse: how pairs with the lowest meaning similarity as judged by humans tend to fare on different metrics (see Table 3). We find that SENTENCE-BERT's judgment is similar to the gold labels, whereas S^2MATCH and BERTSCORE tend to consider them more similar than they actually are. For example, the pair in Figure 1, which receives a human judgment score of 0, is found to have the highest variance between the metrics. S^2MATCH and BERTSCORE give a similarity score of 0.75 (0.97_z) and 0.94 (0.4_z) respectively, whereas SENTENCE-BERT gives a significantly lower score, 0.1 (-2.2_z).

We believe it is challenging for BERTSCORE and S^2MATCH to overcome surface level similarity when computing semantic similarity. In contrast, because of how SENTENCE-BERT is pretrained on data, surface features might not necessarily obstruct their semantic similarity judgment.

5.4 High Agreement Between Metrics

Based on our observation of the top 30 pairs that have the lowest cross-metric variance, we find that the metrics agree strongly with human judgments as well as each other on sentences that exhibit either of these two patterns:

1. rated with high similarity by all the metrics as well as human judgments; exist great overlap of words and argument structures
2. rated with low similarity by all the metrics as well as human judgments; have little or no overlap of words or argument structures

For example, this sentence pair falls into the first pattern type, and is ranked as having the most similar judgments from all the metrics, with a gold label of 4: *Sudanese soldiers had done this Sunday six of the kidnappers in the border area between Sudan, Chad and Egypt, and had arrested two of them.* and *Sudanese soldiers had killed six of the kidnappers this Sunday in the border area between Sudan, Chad and Egypt, and had arrested two of them.*

Meanwhile, this sentence pair exhibits the second pattern, has the fourth highest cross-metric agreement score and receives a gold label of 0: *The other method is the top down approach which is a method that combines memorization and recursion* vs. *The easiest way to look at inheritance is as an '... is a kind of' relationship.*

Since all of the metrics show a similar behavior with each other as well as with human judgments on both highly similar and highly dissimilar sentences, we can conclude that sentences with semantic similarity strongly correlated with their number of mutual surface features are "easy cases", i.e represented well by all the metrics.

5.5 Negation

Ettinger (2019) finds that pre-trained BERT is unable to capture the effect on negation on meaning. By contrast, AMR explicitly encodes negation through the inclusion of a polarity role, and the remainder of the graph is structured as if the negated statement did not appear. Currently, scope of nega-

Metric	Mean
S²MATCH	0.92
SENTENCE-BERT	0.88
BERTSCORE	0.99

Table 4: Mean scores of the metrics on negated pairs.

Metric	Mean
S²MATCH	0.74
SENTENCE-BERT	0.90
BERTSCORE	0.96

Table 5: Mean scores of the metrics on paraphrases.

tion is not captured in the AMR annotation schema (Stein and Donatelli, 2021).

We find that there is a significant discrepancy between human judgments and the metrics on the evaluation of negation. For example, the pair *You should do it* vs. *You should never do it* is considered very dissimilar (with label 1 on a scale from 0 to 5) by annotators , but is rated relatively more similar by the metrics: 0.86 by S²MATCH, 0.97 by BERTSCORE and 0.45 by SENTENCE-BERT. Since there are only two negated pairs in the test data, we also randomly select 10 negated sentences from the NegDDI-DrugBank corpus (Bokharaeian et al., 2014) and the BioScope corpus (Szarvas et al., 2018), and manually construct their positive equivalents to compute their semantic similarity, in order to form a more robust analysis. For example, the positive equivalent of *These differences in gene expression have not been molecularly defined.* is *These differences in gene expression have been molecularly defined.*. As shown in Table 4, all the metrics rate the 20 pairs with high similarity. Since negation often reverses meanings of sentences, we believe it is essential to address the degree of impact of negation on meaning which both the graph-based and vector-based metrics fail to capture. We hope this result encourages more robust research in the future on determining the role of negation in semantic metrics.

5.6 Paraphrases

Compared with the BERT-based metrics, S²MATCH is found to struggle more with paraphrases, especially when there are syntactic differences. We compare their scores on 164 paraphrase pairs (with gold label 5) in the test data, and find that S²MATCH on average gives considerably lower similarity scores in comparison with the BERT-based metrics (see Table 5 for details). For example, the two sentences in Figure 3 are semantically identical, but S²MATCH scores it with 0.65, which is considerably lower than the SENTENCE-BERT and BERTSCORE scores, 0.92 and 0.97 respectively. There are multiple potential explanations for this outcome: first, S²MATCH cannot capture that 'use' and 'cash out' have the same contextual meaning because it uses static GloVe embeddings to compute similarity. Second, the arguments of 'to' are parsed into `:ARG2` and `:purpose` respectively, even they serve the same function in the sentences. In other words, the lexical and structural differences of these sentences lead to differences in their AMR graphs, resulting in a lower S²MATCH score.

Therefore, although AMR is intended to abstract away from syntax and sentences with similar meanings should have similar graph structures, we have observed that this is not always the case: sentence structure affects AMR graphs and thus affects semantic similarity for AMR-based metrics.

Sentence 1: *Should I use IRA money to pay down my student loans?*

```
(r / recommend-01
      :ARG1 (u / use-01
            :ARG0 (ii / i)
            :ARG1 (m / money
                  :source (o / organization
                        :name (n / name
                              :op1 "IRA")))
            :ARG2 (p / pay-down-05
                  :ARG0 ii
                  :ARG1 (l / loan-01
                        :ARG2 ii
                        :mod (p2 / person
                              :ARG0-of (s / study-01)))))
      :polarity (a / amr-unknown))
```

Sentence 2: *Should I cash out my IRA to pay my student loans?*

```
(r / recommend-01
      :ARG1 (c / cash-out-03
            :ARG0 (ii / i)
            :ARG1 (p / product
                  :name (n / name
                        :op1 "IRA")
                  :poss ii)
            :purpose (p2 / pay-01
                  :ARG0 ii
                  :ARG3 (l / loan-01
                        :ARG2 ii
                        :ARG3 (p3 / person
                              :ARG0-of (s / study-01)))))
      :polarity (a / amr-unknown))
```

Figure 3: AMR graphs for two paraphrases.

5.7 Semantic Roles

We observe that the AMR-based metrics are able capture semantic roles and argument structures, which might not be captured by BERT-based metrics, or even human judgment.

For example, the pair in Figure 4 has the 9th highest cross-metric variance, which has a z-score of -0.655_z from S^{2}MATCH, -3.31_z from SENTENCE-BERT and -2.67_z from BERTSCORE, and is annotated as completely dissimilar by human annotators. In other words, S^{2}MATCH considers this pair much more similar than the BERT-based metrics as well as human judgments.

Sentence 1: *Spanish bulls gore seven to death.*

```
(g / gore-01
      :ARG0 (b / bull
            :mod (c / country
                  :name (n / name
                        :op1 "Spain")))
      :ARG1 (p / person
            :quant 7)
      :ARG2 (d / die-01
            :ARG1 p))
```

Sentence 2: *Obama queries Turnbull over China port deal.*

```
(q / query-01
      :ARG0 (p / person
            :name (n / name
                  :op1 "Obama"))
      :ARG1 (p2 / person
            :name (n2 / name
                  :op1 "Turnbull"))
      :ARG2 (d / deal-01
            :ARG2 (p3 / port
                  :location (c / country
                        :name (n3 / name
                              :op1 "China")))))
```

Figure 4: AMR graphs for two sentences that have similar argument structures.

One reason that accounts for such a distinct judgment from S^{2}MATCH is that the two sentences share certain similarity in their argument structures: their main predicates have these three arguments ARG0, ARG1, ARG2. Both the ARG0s refer to an agent, and the ARG1s refer to a patient or theme.

Although we use human judgments as a reference to evaluate the performance of the metrics, this example pairs shed some lights on the dimensions of meaning: argument structures represent semantic relationship between arguments, providing a high level of meaning representation of a sentence. It is then worth asking if we should take argument structure into consideration when comparing semantic similarity, and in what use cases we should or should not.

One might argue that since this pair is completely irrelevant, it makes sense not to consider them similar at all. However, we observe that the sensitivity to argument structures of the AMR-based metrics can address drastic change of meaning due to change of semantic roles. For example, the sentence pair *(A|B) is the conditional probability of A, given B* vs. *P(B|A) is the conditional probability of B given A* has a gold label of 3, S^{2}MATCH score of 0.39, SENTENCE-BERT score of 0.99 and BERTSCORE score of 0.98. In this case, S^{2}MATCH's judgment is much more similar with human judgments than the BERT-based metrics which regard this pair as almost equivalent.

The cause for such a difference between the graph-based and the vector-based metrics is that the former identifies the argument of `give-01` changes from `B` to `A`, whereas since word order is not explicitly encoded in the computations of the vector metrics, such a change is likely to have no impact in their similarity judgments.

5.8 Summary of Findings

Among the metrics we compared, we found that SENTENCE-BERT is most similar to human judgments, but its judgment lacks interpretability because it is a pretrained model with its performance dependent on the training data.

S^{2}MATCH's design takes advantage of both graph-based and vector-based metrics, but fails to take full advantage of vectors to compare word similarity due to changes caused by AMR parsing. Therefore, we suggest concepts that S^{2}MATCH aligns could have their embeddings represented by their original words in the sentence, not the concept labels themselves, so embeddings of words instead of embeddings of their concepts are compared for cosine similarity. For example, taking advantage of a system that maps AMR concepts to tokens, 'employer' would be aligned with 'boss', not `employ-01` with `boss`.

We have also identified challenging cases where S^{2}MATCH and BERTSCORE fail to account for the inverse relationship between surface level similarity and semantic similarity, and easy scenarios when semantic similarity positively correlates with surface level similarity.

Finally, we looked at three semantic features, negation, semantic role arguments and paraphrases. We found that all the metrics do not account for the impact of negation on meaning, only the graph-based metrics are sensitive to role arguments but fail to capture semantic similarity of paraphrases.

6 Conclusion

We compared four graph- and vector-based semantic metrics via a semantic similarity task. In the task, we used human judgments as a reference and explored various scenarios to investigate the strengths and weaknesses of these metrics, both qualitatively with examples and quantitatively via correlation with human judgments. We found that graph-based metrics are highly accurate in capturing meaning variations driven by change in sentence structures, whereas vector-based metrics allow more fine-grained meanings of individual words due to contextual embeddings.

As we used automatic parsers in our experiments, the results were certainly affected by some amount of parser error. In future work, it would be interesting to see how gold AMR graphs perform in the same experiment. We also hope that our analyses can motivate more robust research on utilizing the strengths of both vector- and graph-based meaning representations, allowing more effective semantic representation at both the word and sentence levels.

Acknowledgements

Thank you to anonymous reviewers for their feedback. This work is partially supported by a Clare Boothe Luce Scholarship.

References

Eneko Agirre, Carmen Banea, Daniel Cer, Mona Diab, Aitor Gonzalez-Agirre, Rada Mihalcea, German Rigau, and Janyce Wiebe. 2016. SemEval-2016 task 1: Semantic textual similarity, monolingual and cross-lingual evaluation. In *Proceedings of the 10th International Workshop on Semantic Evaluation (SemEval-2016)*, pages 497–511, San Diego, California. Association for Computational Linguistics.

Tatiana Anikina, Alexander Koller, and Michael Roth. 2020. Predicting coreference in Abstract Meaning Representations. In *Proceedings of the Third Workshop on Computational Models of Reference, Anaphora and Coreference*, pages 33–38, Barcelona, Spain (online). Association for Computational Linguistics.

Xuefeng Bai, Yulong Chen, and Yue Zhang. 2022. Graph pre-training for AMR parsing and generation. *ArXiv*, abs/2203.07836.

Laura Banarescu, Claire Bonial, Shu Cai, Madalina Georgescu, Kira Griffitt, Ulf Hermjakob, Kevin Knight, Philipp Koehn, Martha Palmer, and Nathan Schneider. 2013. Abstract meaning representation for sembanking. In *Proceedings of the 7th Linguistic Annotation Workshop and Interoperability with Discourse*, pages 178–186, Sofia, Bulgaria. Association for Computational Linguistics.

Behrouz Bokharaeian, Alberto Diaz, Mariana Neves, and Virginia Francisco. 2014. Exploring negation annotations in the drugddi corpus. *Fourth Workshop on Building and Evaluating Resources for Health and Biomedical Text Processing (BIOTxtM 2014).*

Samuel R. Bowman, Gabor Angeli, Christopher Potts, and Christopher D. Manning. 2015. A large annotated corpus for learning natural language inference. *CoRR*, abs/1508.05326.

Shu Cai and Kevin Knight. 2013. Smatch: an evaluation metric for semantic feature structures. In *Proceedings of the 51st Annual Meeting of the Association for Computational Linguistics (Volume 2: Short Papers)*, pages 748–752, Sofia, Bulgaria. Association for Computational Linguistics.

Marco Damonte, Shay B. Cohen, and Giorgio Satta. 2016. An incremental parser for abstract meaning representation.

Jacob Devlin, Ming-Wei Chang, Kenton Lee, and Kristina Toutanova. 2019. BERT: Pre-training of deep bidirectional transformers for language understanding. In *Proceedings of the 2019 Conference of the North American Chapter of the Association for Computational Linguistics: Human Language Technologies, Volume 1 (Long and Short Papers)*, pages 4171–4186, Minneapolis, Minnesota. Association for Computational Linguistics.

Allyson Ettinger. 2019. What BERT is not: Lessons from a new suite of psycholinguistic diagnostics for language models. *CoRR*, abs/1907.13528.

Jeffrey Flanigan, Sam Thomson, Jaime Carbonell, Chris Dyer, and Noah A. Smith. 2014. A discriminative graph-based parser for the Abstract Meaning Representation. In *Proceedings of the 52nd Annual Meeting of the Association for Computational Linguistics (Volume 1: Long Papers)*, pages 1426–1436, Baltimore, Maryland. Association for Computational Linguistics.

Fuad Issa, Marco Damonte, Shay B. Cohen, Xiaohui Yan, and Yi Chang. 2018. Abstract Meaning Representation for paraphrase detection. In *Proceedings of the 2018 Conference of the North American Chapter of the Association for Computational Linguistics: Human Language Technologies, Volume 1 (Long Papers)*, pages 442–452, New Orleans, Louisiana. Association for Computational Linguistics.

Haoming Jiang, Pengcheng He, Weizhu Chen, Xiaodong Liu, Jianfeng Gao, and Tuo Zhao. 2020. SMART: Robust and efficient fine-tuning for pre-trained natural language models through principled regularized optimization. In *Proceedings of the 58th*

Annual Meeting of the Association for Computational Linguistics, pages 2177–2190, Online. Association for Computational Linguistics.

Mike Lewis, Yinhan Liu, Naman Goyal, Marjan Ghazvininejad, Abdelrahman Mohamed, Omer Levy, Veselin Stoyanov, and Luke Zettlemoyer. 2020. BART: Denoising sequence-to-sequence pretraining for natural language generation, translation, and comprehension. In *Proceedings of the 58th Annual Meeting of the Association for Computational Linguistics*, pages 7871–7880, Online. Association for Computational Linguistics.

Timothee Mickus, Denis Paperno, Mathieu Constant, and Kees Van Deemter. 2019. What do you mean, BERT? Assessing BERT as a distributional semantics model. *arXiv preprint arXiv:1911.05758*.

Majid Mohebbi, Seyed Naser Razavi, and Mohammad Ali Balafar. 2022. Computing semantic similarity of texts based on deep graph learning with ability to use semantic role label information. *Scientific Reports*, 12(1):1–11.

Juri Opitz and Anette Frank. 2022. SBERT studies meaning representations: decomposing sentence embeddings into explainable AMR meaning features. arXiv:2206.07023 [cs].

Juri Opitz, Letitia Parcalabescu, and Anette Frank. 2020. AMR similarity metrics from principles. *Transactions of the Association for Computational Linguistics*, 8:522–538.

Nils Reimers and Iryna Gurevych. 2019. Sentence-BERT: Sentence embeddings using Siamese BERT-networks. *arXiv preprint arXiv:1908.10084*.

Barbara Rychalska, Katarzyna Pakulska, Krystyna Chodorowska, Wojciech Walczak, and Piotr Andruszkiewicz. 2016. Samsung Poland NLP team at SemEval-2016 task 1: Necessity for diversity; combining recursive autoencoders, WordNet and ensemble methods to measure semantic similarity. In *Proceedings of the 10th International Workshop on Semantic Evaluation (SemEval-2016)*, pages 602–608, San Diego, California. Association for Computational Linguistics.

Katharina Stein and Lucia Donatelli. 2021. Representing implicit positive meaning of negated statements in AMR. In *Proceedings of The Joint 15th Linguistic Annotation Workshop (LAW) and 3rd Designing Meaning Representations (DMR) Workshop*, pages 23–35, Punta Cana, Dominican Republic. Association for Computational Linguistics.

Gyorgy Szarvas, Veronika Vincze, Richard Farkas, and Janos Csirik. 2018. The BioScope corpus: Annotation for negation, uncertainty and their scope in biomedical texts. *Proceedings of the Workshop on Current Trends in Biomedical Natural Language Processing*, pages 38–45.

Chuan Wang, Nianwen Xue, and Sameer Pradhan. 2015. A transition-based algorithm for amr parsing. In *Proceedings of the 2015 Conference of the North American Chapter of the Association for Computational Linguistics: Human Language Technologies*, pages 366–375, Denver, Colorado. Association for Computational Linguistics.

Tiexin Wang, Hui Shi, Wenjing Liu, and Xinhua Yan. 2022. A joint FrameNet and element focusing Sentence-BERT method of sentence similarity computation. *Expert Systems with Applications*, 200:117084.

Shira Wein and Nathan Schneider. 2022. Accounting for language effect in the evaluation of cross-lingual AMR parsers. In *Proceedings of the 29th International Conference on Computational Linguistics*, pages 3824–3834, Gyeongju, Republic of Korea. International Committee on Computational Linguistics.

Adina Williams, Nikita Nangia, and Samuel R. Bowman. 2017. A broad-coverage challenge corpus for sentence understanding through inference. *CoRR*, abs/1704.05426.

Tianyi Zhang, Varsha Kishore, Felix Wu, Kilian Q. Weinberger, and Yoav Artzi. 2019. BERTScore: Evaluating text generation with BERT. *CoRR*, abs/1904.09675.

Towards In-Context Non-Expert Evaluation of Reflection Generation for Counselling Conversations

Zixiu Wu
Philips Research & University of Cagliari
zixiu.wu@philips.com

Simone Balloccu
University of Aberdeen
s.balloccu.19@abdn.ac.uk

Rim Helaoui
Philips Research
rim.helaoui@philips.com

Diego Reforgiato Recupero and **Daniele Riboni**
University of Cagliari
{diego.reforgiato, riboni}@unica.it

Abstract

Reflection is an essential counselling strategy, where the therapist listens actively and responds with their own interpretation of the client's words. Recent work leveraged pretrained language models (PLMs) to approach reflection generation as a promising tool to aid counsellor training. However, those studies used limited dialogue context for modelling and simplistic error analysis for human evaluation. In this work, we take the first step towards addressing those limitations. First, we fine-tune PLMs on longer dialogue contexts for reflection generation. Then, we collect free-text error descriptions from non-experts about generated reflections, identify common patterns among them, and accordingly establish discrete error categories using thematic analysis. Based on this scheme, we plan for future work a mass non-expert error annotation phase for generated reflections followed by an expert-based validation phase, namely "whether a coherent and consistent response is a good reflection".

Context		
Utt.	**Role**	**Text**
u_{t-3}	**Client**	The baby was up all night and I'm exhausted.
u_{t-2}	**Therapist**	So, what you're saying is you've had a rough night?
u_{t-1}	**Client**	Yes. She was up every three hours to eat, I don't understand it.
Response (Reflection)		
u_t	**Therapist**	So, she needed to eat every three hours last night and that was really frustrating for you?

Table 1: A 3-turn context and the ground-truth reflection from an MI dialogue.

1 Introduction

Patient health can be greatly improved by changing behaviours such as smoking and alcohol consumption. As patients rarely ask for help with it, healthcare practitioners often need to encourage, counsel and advise them to make changes (Rollnick et al., 2008). An effective counselling approach for this purpose is motivational interviewing (MI, Miller and Rollnick, 2012), which aims to elicit the motivation for change from the client[1] themselves.

In particular, *reflection* — also known as *reflective listening* — is an essential conversational strategy in MI that has been shown to be related to positive counselling outcomes (Moyers et al., 2009). A good reflection conveys to the client that the therapist is listening, hearing and understanding them by reflecting back a short summary of how the therapist understands what the client has said (Rollnick et al., 2008), as shown in Table 1.

Reflection is a crucial skill for counsellors (Braillon and Taiebi, 2020), but its training is time-consuming and reliant on human supervision (Rautalinko and Lisper, 2004; Rautalinko et al., 2007). Therefore, an automatic assistant that offers reflection examples given a particular dialogue context can speed up the process while relieving the burden of supervision. Indeed, recent years have seen studies (Shen et al., 2020, 2022) on reflection generation that fine-tune pretrained language models (PLMs) to produce a reflection given some preceding utterances as the context.

Despite the progress in reflection generation, its evaluation remains a challenge. Automated metrics in language generation tasks are often not robust (Liu et al., 2016) and human evaluation is thus necessitated. Moreover, reflection requires specialised knowledge and counselling is complex and delicate. Ideally, therefore, generated reflections need evaluation by experienced therapists. However, expert annotation is time-consuming and costly (Moyers et al., 2005). Thus, human evaluation in previous work suffers from issues including

[1] A person receiving MI is not necessarily a patient, therefore we use "client" instead of "patient" in this work.

Proceedings of the 2nd Workshop on Natural Language Generation, Evaluation, and Metrics (GEM), pages 116 - 124
December 7, 2022 ©2022 Association for Computational Linguistics

simplistic evaluation scheme (e.g., good vs. bad) and small (≤ 50) number of annotated reflections.

Another significant but underexplored weakness is the lack of context. In prior work, dialogue models are given as the input context only a few (≤ 5) preceding utterances. This can be inadequate for models to produce context-aware responses and for human evaluators to provide context-informed assessment, considering that 1) therapy dialogues are relatively long — often between 10 and 120 minutes (Rubak et al., 2005) — and 2) spoken-dialogue utterances are typically short, unlike in written conversations. In particular, sufficient context is important for assessing if a generated text contains hallucination (Ishii et al., 2022), a well-known issue of neural natural language generation where the output is unfaithful/ungrounded w.r.t. the input, for example when a chatbot contradicts what it said previously during a chat with the user (Vinyals and Le, 2015).

To alleviate the time and resource requirement for human evaluation, we advocate for disentangling the human evaluation into two phases: 1) **by non-experts**[2]**:** whether a generated reflection is coherent and consistent w.r.t. its context and what the issue of an incoherent/inconsistent reflection is; 2) **by experts:** whether a coherent and consistent reflection is a good reflection that conforms to therapy guidelines. We argue that a non-expert is perfectly capable as an evaluator for the first phase, and that this setup saves time and resources as a whole, especially in the second phase. **In this work, we conduct an initial study for the non-expert annotation phase.**

We use longer contexts — 14 turns on average — to better ground reflection generation and human evaluation. We devise a non-expert annotation scheme by 1) collecting free-text error descriptions w.r.t. generated reflections from non-experts and 2) identifying common patterns in the error descriptions and summarising them into discrete categories using thematic analysis (Braun and Clarke, 2012), similar to recent work (e.g., Thomson and Reiter, 2020) adopting bottom-up designs of text error annotation schemes. Thus, we establish {**Malformed**, **Off-topic**, **Dialogue-contradicting**, **Parroting**, **On-topic but unverifiable**} as the error categories, and a generated reflection may suffer from one or more categories of error. Most of these categories require a deeper understanding of the dialogue context but the latter three have not been explicitly included in previous studies on reflection generation.

Based on these error categories, we plan for future work a mass non-expert error annotation phase for generated reflections followed by an expert-based validation phase, namely "whether a coherent and consistent response is a good reflection".

2 Related Work

2.1 Reflection Generation

PLM-based empathetic dialogue generation (EDG, e.g., Rashkin et al., 2019) has seen considerable development in recent years. Of particular interest to us is EDG in counselling, which has taken the form of reflection generation so far. In particular, Shen et al. (2020) build a reflection generator that leverages responses from similar conversations as auxiliary input, while Shen et al. (2022) utilise domain and commonsense knowledge, both studies using only 5 preceding utterances as the context. Ahmed (2022) probes few-shot reflection generation for individual patient statements instead of multi-turn dialogues. Compared to those works, ours differs in its use of long dialogue contexts (14 turns on average) for the generator to enable more context-aware reflections.

2.2 Human Evaluation of Empathetic Dialogue Generation

The standard EDG human evaluation assesses the dialogue-relevance, fluency and empathy[3] (Rashkin et al., 2019; Li et al., 2020b) of a response on a Likert scale. A/B testing has also been used to compare responses from different models (e.g., Xie and Pu, 2021; Kim et al., 2021).

For evaluating reflection generation, Shen et al. (2020, 2022) tweak the standard EDG human evaluation slightly by replacing "empathy" with "reflection-likeness" in {dialogue-relevance, fluency, empathy} to gauge if the response interprets what the client means. Those human evaluation setups are small-scale, with less than 50 sampled reflections per model. On the other hand, 369 responses generated by the patient-statement-based reflection models in Ahmed (2022) are evaluated

[2]"experts" refers to people well-versed in psychology/psychotherapy and "non-experts" refers to the opposite.

[3]Usually rephrased, e.g., "did the responses show understanding of the feelings of the person talking about their experience?" (Rashkin et al., 2019)

Label	Reflection	Question	Input	Other
Prop.	28%	28%	11%	33%

Table 2: Proportion of therapist utterances of each label in high-quality AnnoMI dialogues.

by experts in a good-vs-bad binary setup. In comparison, our human evaluation is novel in its explicit focus on long-context-based error analysis of generated reflections.

One issue not explicitly addressed in EDG human evaluation so far is hallucination, where the output is unfaithful/ungrounded w.r.t. the input. While "off-topic-ness" is roughly equivalent to "dialogue (ir)relevance", it is only one type of hallucination. Ishii et al. (2022) define a response to be "intrinsic hallucination" if it contradicts the input(e.g., Dziri et al., 2019; Li et al., 2020a) and "extrinsic hallucination" if it cannot be verified based on the input (e.g., Mielke et al., 2022; Roller et al., 2021). Therefore, a hallucinating reflection can be on-topic but contradict the context (intrinsic) or be unverifiable based on the context (extrinsic). Since reflective listening is based entirely on the context, we argue that a hallucinating reflection can cause quick client disengagement, since it is very likely unnatural in the conversation context. Therefore, we take hallucination into consideration explicitly, in contrast to prior work.

3 Modelling of Reflection Generator

3.1 Counselling Dialogue Data: AnnoMI

We utilise AnnoMI (Wu et al., 2022), a corpus of expert-annotated MI counselling sessions. AnnoMI contains both "good" (high-quality) and "bad" (low-quality) examples of MI. Aiming at generating **good** reflections, we leverage the 110 conversations (8839 utterances) of high-quality MI.

Each therapist utterance in AnnoMI is annotated by MI experts as **Reflection**, **Question**, **Input**, or **Other**. Specifically, **Reflection** is reflective listening, **Question** means an open/closed question, **Input** encompasses providing information and suggestions, etc., while **Other** is the default and mostly covers conversation facilitators like "Uh-huh". The utterances label distribution is shown in Table 2.

3.2 Model Input Format

We train similarly sized `gpt2-medium` (Radford et al., 2019, 355M parameters) and `bart-large` (Lewis et al., 2020, 406M parameters) as reflection generators. Like most open-domain dialogue models, our models generate a response (therapist reflection) based on an N-turn dialogue history (namely the context), where the last turn comes from the client. An illustrative 3-turn context and its ground-truth reflection are shown in Table 1. Pre-trained dialogue models like DialoGPT (Zhang et al., 2020) are not used because they are mostly pre-trained on written conversations with only a few turns as the context, whereas therapy dialogues are spoken and long, causing a large domain gap.

As the volume of AnnoMI reflections is relatively small, we also train the models to generate other types of therapist responses using ground-truth utterance labels as plain-text conditioning codes, inspired by recent work (e.g., Rashkin et al., 2021) of similar approaches. Specifically, we construct the input as a sequence of context utterances with interlocutor labels and utterance separators, appended by the ground-truth therapist response label. For example, the context in Table 1 would become[4]:

> "$\langle client \rangle$*The baby was up all night and I'm exhausted.*|$\langle therapist \rangle$*So, what you're saying is you've had a rough night?*|$\langle client \rangle$*Yes. She was up every three hours to eat, I don't understand it.*|$\langle therapist \rangle$~$\langle listening \rangle$"

while the ground-truth response is simply

> *"So, she needed to eat every three hours last night and that was really frustrating for you?"*

The underlying assumption is that this will enable more training data for the language modelling of therapy dialogue while better shaping the boundaries of reflections in the latent semantic space.

Thus, a training/validation/test example is simply a $\langle context, response \rangle$ pair representing the $\langle input, output \rangle$. Each context is left-truncated to the most recent 384 tokens to preserve the most recent dialogue turns[5], while each ground-truth response is right-truncated to 128 tokens.

3.3 Training Response Generator

For both GPT-2 and BART we adopt 10-fold cross validation (CV) for training, in order to obtain

[4] In practice, we use "⟨asking⟩", "⟨informing⟩", "⟨listening⟩", "⟨other⟩" as the plain-text control codes for Question, Input, Reflection and Other, respectively.

[5] 384 tokens make up N turns where N vares depending on the individual utterance lengths, but on average $N = 14$.

Model	GPT-2	BART
Perplexity	17.36	13.29

Table 3: Perplexity of each reflection generator under cross validation.

a test-time generated response for each example in the dataset (See §3.4). As noted in §3.2, we train a **generic** response generator that can produce any type (namely **Reflection**, **Question**, **Input** or **Other**) of therapist response. The examples of each fold are ensured to be from different dialogues, thus maximising mutual exclusivity between the training (8 folds), validation (1 fold) and test (1 fold) data for each of the 10 CV models. Also, the CV is stratified so that the distribution of ground-truth response types in each fold is the same.

To gauge the performance of the response generators on generating **reflections**, we evaluate them only on the test-fold examples where the ground-truth response is a reflection. Following most recent studies (Thoppilan et al., 2022, Shuster et al., 2022, *inter alia*) on response generation, we report in Table 3 the perplexity (the lower the better) of each model, which quantifies how uncertain a model is about generating the ground-truth reflections in the test data. We do not compare these numbers with other studies because 1) achieving state-of-the-art is not our focus, 2) the dataset and task are unique and have no comparable state-of-the-art, and 3) to the best of our knowledge, there is no study on the utility of perplexity as a metric for reflection generation or counselling dialogue modelling. We also experimented with paraphrasing-based data augmentation, with no significant improvement gained.

3.4 Test-Time Reflection Generation

Once the models are trained, we use them to generate alternative reflections for the context of each ground-truth reflection in AnnoMI, by conditioning the output using the $\langle listening \rangle$ code as before.

Following recent work (e.g., Santhanam et al., 2021) on hallucination in dialogue generation, we experiment with a range of decoding strategies, in order to capture a broad spectrum of potential errors in model-generated reflections. For both GPT-2 and BART, we explore

- Greedy decoding
- 5-Beam decoding, using all of the 5 decoded sequences at the final time step
- Nucleus decoding (Holtzman et al., 2019), $p \in \{0.4, 0.6, 0.8, 0.95\}$, 5 sequences sampled for each p

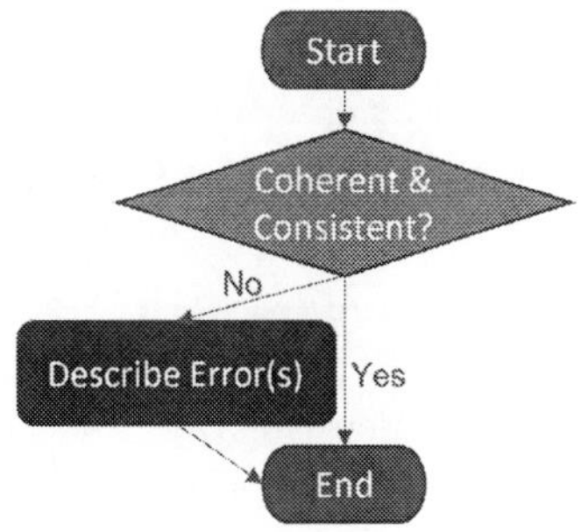

Figure 1: Annotation Flow

4 Human Annotation

As the underlying assumption of our human annotation is that incoherence/inconsistency errors can be spotted by non-experts, we survey laypeople for their own descriptions of reflection errors and then summarise those free-text descriptions into categories.

Annotation Materials We sample 3 contexts from 3 different dialogues and use their respective ground-truth and model-generated reflections for annotation. Based on the responses generated for the 3 contexts, we randomly sample a subset of 60 for human annotation.

Annotators We recruited 6 volunteers with high proficiency in English and no prior experience in NLP or psychology/psychotherapy. Each annotator worked on the same batch of 60 reflections for the aforementioned 3 contexts in total.

Annotation Procedure The procedure is illustrated in Figure 1, and the annotation interface is presented in Appendix A. The annotators are shown each $\langle context, reflection \rangle$ pair and first need to answer whether the reflection feels coherent and consistent given the context. If they choose "No", they are asked to describe the incoherence/inconsistency-causing error(s) of the reflection, otherwise they will proceed to the next example. We note that we do not define "incoherent" or "inconsistent" and instead leave it to the discretion of the annotators, in order to gather more natural insights on response errors. For the same reason, we use the word "response candidate" instead of the more complex term "reflection", and we do not mention that some response candidates came from models instead of humans.

Inter-Annotator Agreement The inter-annotator agreement (IAA) on the "Coherent & Consistent?" question is 0.37 in terms of Fleiss' kappa (Fleiss, 1971), which is in the "fair agreement" range (0.2-0.4) but close to the "moderate agreement" threshold of 0.4. We attribute the relatively low IAA to two factors: 1) We purposely did not provide a strict definition of "coherence" or "consistency" to the annotators, which led some of them to consider issues like "intimidating tone" as causes for incoherence/inconsistency, but those are actually reserved for the expert-phase, since therapy experts should be the ones to judge whether a response is appropriate in a counselling setting. 2) 6 annotators are involved in the annotation process rather than just 2 to 3 as is commonly done for human evaluation of generated reflections (Shen et al., 2020, 2022), and it is usually less likely to get higher agreement with more raters.

Established Error Categories We use thematic analysis (Braun and Clarke, 2012) to manually and systematically identify common patterns in the annotators' feedback and summarise them into the following error categories:

- **Malformed**: a response that "feels broken" because 1) it has unclear references, 2) it is incomprehensibly ungrammatical, and/or 3) its sentences are issue-free on their own but confusing when combined.
- **Dialogue-contradicting**: a response that contradicts the context, either partially or fully.
- **Parroting**: a response that repeats a certain part of the context in an unnatural way.
- **Off-topic**: a reply that has little to no relevance to the dialogue.
- **On-topic but unverifiable**: an on-topic reply that cannot be verified based on the context.

For concrete examples of the categories, see Table 4.

Other Considerations Good reflections sometimes repeat something that the client has said, for example to affirm it, but those are natural and good practices rather than unnatural repetition (**Parroting**). Also, broadly speaking, **Dialogue-contradicting**, **Off-topic** and **On-topic but unverifiable** reflections are all unfaithful and ungrounded w.r.t. the context, making them all manifestations of hallucination. Finally, we note that a small percentage ($\approx 8\%$) of error descriptions do not contain sufficient information (e.g., "Doesn't feel like a natural response") and are therefore excluded from the thematic analysis. To account for such generic feedback and also to capture potential errors that do not fit neatly into the categories above, future users of this scheme may optionally create an "Other" category.

5 Conclusion

In this work, we explored non-expert annotation of machine-generated reflections for counselling dialogues, based on the assumption that non-experts are capable of context-informed 1) judgement of whether a reflection is coherent and consistent and 2) identification of the errors in an incoherent/inconsistent reflection. We identified common patterns among the free-text error descriptions from non-experts about generated reflections and accordingly used thematic analysis to establish discrete error categories that emphasised context understanding. Based on these categories, we plan for future work A) a mass non-expert error annotation phase for generated reflections, followed by B) an expert-based validation phase, and the results from both phases will be released to the public.

Limitations

In this preliminary study, our goal is to establish error categories for annotating machine-generated reflections. While we believe the human annotation conducted in this work is sufficient for achieving the goal, its limited annotation scale precludes drawing reliable conclusions from more advanced analysis, such as 1) coherence/consistency rates of different models and decoding strategies, and 2) correlation between human judgement and existing automatic metrics that are commonly used for dialogue generation tasks. Therefore, in our next step, we plan to carry out significantly scaled-up human annotation, in order to facilitate further analysis.

Ethical Aspects

Before starting the experiment, the procedure and materials were carefully reviewed by the University of Aberdeen's Ethics Board. Our experiment proposal was accepted without major revisions. All

Utt.	Role	Text
		Context
u_{t-16}	**Therapist**	Mm. So, embraces this life of the picket fence and the, you know, the little house and having the baby in this-
u_{t-15}	**Client**	Yeah, suburbs. Yeah.
u_{t-14}	**Therapist**	So, you don't wanna be that- that- that woman that's just sort of living in this house with the baby carriage, and at the same time, that world's kind of saying it's behind you.
u_{t-13}	**Client**	Yeah, I-I guess. Like, I don't wanna- I don't wanna lose my friends because of this. And I don't wanna put pressure on them to change because they're, I mean, they're good people. They're just–
u_{t-12}	**Therapist**	You care about them.
u_{t-11}	**Client**	Yeah.
u_{t-10}	**Therapist**	It's just the scene that they're-they're still in because their life maybe hasn't taken that change that your life has made. And so now, you're here and you're not sure. You want the baby, but you're not sure about the suburbs and the picket fence thing. You're not sure–
u_{t-9}	**Client**	I don't want that.
u_{t-8}	**Therapist**	You don't want that.
u_{t-7}	**Client**	No.
u_{t-6}	**Therapist**	You want this baby.
u_{t-5}	**Client**	Yeah.
u_{t-4}	**Therapist**	And you wanna be, um, take care of your baby as the baby's growing.
u_{t-3}	**Client**	Like, I wanna- I wanna be responsible for this thing.
u_{t-2}	**Therapist**	You don't wanna let your baby down.
u_{t-1}	**Client**	No.
		Ground-Truth Response (Reflection), Coherent & Consistent
u_t	**Therapist**	And at the same time, it's hard to let go of the past, but on the other hand, you're thinking, "I don't have a choice. I've got to look this way." Is that kind of what it feels like?
		Malformed
	Therapist	You-you wanna be the one that, um–you're the one who's gonna pick up the phone, uh, uh–you wanna pick up and, uh –or call them, um –to-to-unquote-the-mother and-to tell them that your-your daughter is going to come home and she's, uh...
		Dialogue-contradicting
	Therapist	OK, so what I'm hearing you say is that taking care of a baby would be too much responsibility for you right now, so you are not ready to have a baby.
		Parroting
	Therapist	Mm-hmm. So, you don't want to let your baby down.
		Off-topic
	Therapist	So you do not wanna allow your kids to go across the street without you.
		On-topic but unverifiable
	Therapist	You've really wanted to be a mom since you were a little girl.

Table 4: Example for each error category, as established in §4.

of the recruited annotators were volunteers. Upon starting the experiment, each annotator was shown a consent form containing all the information regarding the experiment procedure. All workers had to confirm their acceptance of these conditions before proceeding. Workers were given an email contact in case of problems during the experiment. No personal data about the annotators was kept stored at the end of the experiment.

Acknowledgements

This work has been funded by the EC in the H2020 Marie Skłodowska-Curie PhilHumans project, contract no. 812882.

References

Imtihan Ahmed. 2022. *Automatic Generation and Detection of Motivational-Interviewing-Style Reflections for Smoking Cessation Therapeutic Conversations Using Transformer-based Language Models*. Ph.D. thesis, University of Toronto.

Alain Braillon and Françoise Taiebi. 2020. Practicing "reflective listening" is a mandatory prerequisite for empathy. *Patient Education and Counseling*, 103(9):1866–1867.

Virginia Braun and Victoria Clarke. 2012. *Thematic analysis.* American Psychological Association.

Nouha Dziri, Ehsan Kamalloo, Kory Mathewson, and Osmar R Zaiane. 2019. Evaluating coherence in dialogue systems using entailment. In *Proceedings of the 2019 Conference of the North American Chapter of the Association for Computational Linguistics: Human Language Technologies, Volume 1 (Long and Short Papers)*, pages 3806–3812.

Joseph L Fleiss. 1971. Measuring nominal scale agreement among many raters. *Psychological bulletin*, 76(5):378.

Ari Holtzman, Jan Buys, Li Du, Maxwell Forbes, and Yejin Choi. 2019. The curious case of neural text degeneration. In *International Conference on Learning Representations*.

Y Ishii, ANDREA Madotto, and PASCALE Fung. 2022. Survey of hallucination in natural language generation. *ACM Comput. Surv*, 1(1).

Hyunwoo Kim, Byeongchang Kim, and Gunhee Kim. 2021. Perspective-taking and pragmatics for generating empathetic responses focused on emotion causes. In *Proceedings of the 2021 Conference on Empirical Methods in Natural Language Processing*, pages 2227–2240.

Mike Lewis, Yinhan Liu, Naman Goyal, Marjan Ghazvininejad, Abdelrahman Mohamed, Omer Levy, Veselin Stoyanov, and Luke Zettlemoyer. 2020. Bart: Denoising sequence-to-sequence pre-training for natural language generation, translation, and comprehension. In *Proceedings of the 58th Annual Meeting of the Association for Computational Linguistics*, pages 7871–7880.

Margaret Li, Stephen Roller, Ilia Kulikov, Sean Welleck, Y-Lan Boureau, Kyunghyun Cho, and Jason Weston. 2020a. Don't say that! making inconsistent dialogue unlikely with unlikelihood training. In *Proceedings of the 58th Annual Meeting of the Association for Computational Linguistics*, pages 4715–4728.

Qintong Li, Hongshen Chen, Zhaochun Ren, Pengjie Ren, Zhaopeng Tu, and Zhumin Chen. 2020b. Empdg: Multi-resolution interactive empathetic dialogue generation. In *Proceedings of the 28th International Conference on Computational Linguistics*, pages 4454–4466.

Chia-Wei Liu, Ryan Lowe, Iulian Vlad Serban, Mike Noseworthy, Laurent Charlin, and Joelle Pineau. 2016. How not to evaluate your dialogue system: An empirical study of unsupervised evaluation metrics for dialogue response generation. In *Proceedings of the 2016 Conference on Empirical Methods in Natural Language Processing*, pages 2122–2132.

Sabrina J Mielke, Arthur Szlam, Emily Dinan, and Y-Lan Boureau. 2022. Reducing conversational agents' overconfidence through linguistic calibration. *Transactions of the Association for Computational Linguistics*, 10:857–872.

William R Miller and Stephen Rollnick. 2012. *Motivational interviewing: Helping people change*. Guilford press.

Theresa B Moyers, Tim Martin, Jon M Houck, Paulette J Christopher, and J Scott Tonigan. 2009. From in-session behaviors to drinking outcomes: a causal chain for motivational interviewing. *Journal of consulting and clinical psychology*, 77(6):1113.

Theresa B Moyers, Tim Martin, Jennifer K Manuel, Stacey ML Hendrickson, and William R Miller. 2005. Assessing competence in the use of motivational interviewing. *Journal of substance abuse treatment*, 28(1):19–26.

Alec Radford, Jeffrey Wu, Rewon Child, David Luan, Dario Amodei, and Ilya Sutskever. 2019. Language models are unsupervised multitask learners. *OpenAI Blog*, 1(8):9.

Hannah Rashkin, David Reitter, Gaurav Singh Tomar, and Dipanjan Das. 2021. Increasing faithfulness in knowledge-grounded dialogue with controllable features. In *Proceedings of the 59th Annual Meeting of the Association for Computational Linguistics and the 11th International Joint Conference on Natural Language Processing (Volume 1: Long Papers)*, pages 704–718.

Hannah Rashkin, Eric Michael Smith, Margaret Li, and Y-Lan Boureau. 2019. Towards empathetic open-domain conversation models: A new benchmark and dataset. In *Proceedings of the 57th Conference of the Association for Computational Linguistics, ACL 2019, Florence, Italy, July 28- August 2, 2019, Volume 1: Long Papers*, pages 5370–5381. Association for Computational Linguistics.

Erik Rautalinko and Hans-Olof Lisper. 2004. Effects of training reflective listening in a corporate setting. *Journal of Business and Psychology*, 18(3):281–299.

Erik Rautalinko, Hans-Olof Lisper, and Bo Ekehammar. 2007. Reflective listening in counseling: effects of training time and evaluator social skills. *American journal of psychotherapy*, 61(2):191–209.

Stephen Roller, Emily Dinan, Naman Goyal, Da Ju, Mary Williamson, Yinhan Liu, Jing Xu, Myle Ott, Eric Michael Smith, Y-Lan Boureau, et al. 2021. Recipes for building an open-domain chatbot. In *Proceedings of the 16th Conference of the European Chapter of the Association for Computational Linguistics: Main Volume*, pages 300–325.

Stephen Rollnick, William R Miller, and Christopher Butler. 2008. *Motivational interviewing in health care: helping patients change behavior*. Guilford Press.

Sune Rubak, Annelli Sandbæk, Torsten Lauritzen, and Bo Christensen. 2005. Motivational interviewing: a systematic review and meta-analysis. *British journal of general practice*, 55(513):305–312.

Sashank Santhanam, Behnam Hedayatnia, Spandana Gella, Aishwarya Padmakumar, Seokhwan Kim, Yang Liu, and Dilek Hakkani-Tur. 2021. Rome was built in 1776: A case study on factual correctness in knowledge-grounded response generation. *arXiv preprint arXiv:2110.05456*.

Siqi Shen, Verónica Pérez-Rosas, Charles Welch, Soujanya Poria, and Rada Mihalcea. 2022. Knowledge enhanced reflection generation for counseling dialogues. In *Proceedings of the 60th Annual Meeting of the Association for Computational Linguistics (Volume 1: Long Papers)*, pages 3096–3107.

Siqi Shen, Charles Welch, Rada Mihalcea, and Verónica Pérez-Rosas. 2020. Counseling-style reflection generation using generative pretrained transformers with augmented context. In *Proceedings of the 21th Annual Meeting of the Special Interest Group on Discourse and Dialogue*, pages 10–20.

Kurt Shuster, Jing Xu, Mojtaba Komeili, Da Ju, Eric Michael Smith, Stephen Roller, Megan Ung, Moya Chen, Kushal Arora, Joshua Lane, et al. 2022. Blenderbot 3: a deployed conversational agent that continually learns to responsibly engage. *arXiv preprint arXiv:2208.03188*.

Craig Thomson and Ehud Reiter. 2020. A gold standard methodology for evaluating accuracy in data-to-text systems. In *Proceedings of the 13th International Conference on Natural Language Generation*, pages 158–168.

Romal Thoppilan, Daniel De Freitas, Jamie Hall, Noam Shazeer, Apoorv Kulshreshtha, Heng-Tze Cheng, Alicia Jin, Taylor Bos, Leslie Baker, Yu Du, et al. 2022. Lamda: Language models for dialog applications. *arXiv preprint arXiv:2201.08239*.

Oriol Vinyals and Quoc Le. 2015. A neural conversational model. *arXiv preprint arXiv:1506.05869*.

Zixiu Wu, Simone Balloccu, Vivek Kumar, Rim Helaoui, Ehud Reiter, Diego Reforgiato Recupero, and Daniele Riboni. 2022. Anno-mi: A dataset of expert-annotated counselling dialogues. In *ICASSP 2022-2022 IEEE International Conference on Acoustics, Speech and Signal Processing (ICASSP)*, pages 6177–6181. IEEE.

Yubo Xie and Pearl Pu. 2021. Empathetic dialog generation with fine-grained intents. In *Proceedings of the 25th Conference on Computational Natural Language Learning*, pages 133–147.

Yizhe Zhang, Siqi Sun, Michel Galley, Yen-Chun Chen, Chris Brockett, Xiang Gao, Jianfeng Gao, Jingjing Liu, and Bill Dolan. 2020. DIALOGPT : Large-scale generative pre-training for conversational response generation. In *Proceedings of the 58th Annual Meeting of the Association for Computational Linguistics: System Demonstrations, ACL 2020, Online, July 5-10, 2020*, pages 270–278. Association for Computational Linguistics.

A Annotation Interface

In Figure 2, we show the annotation interface for collecting free-text error descriptions from non-experts about generated reflections.

Evaluating Response Candidates in Counselling (pt. 2/2)

* Required

Response Candidate 2/19, Partial Dialogue 3/3

Partial Dialogue

Client: Hmm. Seven?

Therapist: Seven.

Client: Wow. I knew my doctor didn't like me drinking the amount that I did but I didn't know that seven was the limit.

Therapist: Yeah, you're surprised to hear that?

Client: Yes. What-what kind of health problems?

Therapist: Well things like heart disease, cancer, liver problems, uh, stomach pains, insomnia. Unfortunately, uh, people who drink at a risky level are more likely to be diagnosed with depression and alcohol can make depression worse or harder to treat.

Client: Hmm. Well, that's not good news.

Therapist: Well, how do you think your drinking relates to the depression you've experienced?

Client: Well, to be honest, I drink sometimes when I'm feeling down and I find it more interesting and not so blur.

Therapist: Okay. And how do you feel after you drink?

Client: Well, then I feel blur again.

Therapist: So, there are some answers on this form here. Uh, less than monthly you drank more than you intended to.

Client: Yes on occasion.

Therapist: And sometimes you feel guilty after you drink.

Client: Sometimes I just don't like how much I drink. I sometimes finish a bottle in one night.

Therapist: So you're not proud of finishing a bottle?

Client: No, it's not like I get crazy or anything but I just don't like the amount that I'm drinking.

Response Candidate

Therapist: Surely, too much can go wrong if you don't manage it well.

4. Does the ***response candidate*** feel coherent and natural/consistent with respect to the ***partial dialogue***? *

○ Yes

◉ No

5. Please describe, **clearly and concisely**, the issue(s) of the ***response candidate*** that make(s) it incoherent/inconsistent/unnatural/etc *

Enter your answer

Back Next

Figure 2: Annotation Interface

WikiOmnia: filtration and evaluation of the generated QA corpus on the whole Russian Wikipedia

Dina Pisarevskaya
Independent Researcher
dinabpr@gmail.com

Tatiana Shavrina
Artificial Intelligence Research Institute (AIRI)
SberDevices
rybolos@gmail.com

Abstract

The General QA field has been developing the methodology referencing the Stanford Question answering dataset (SQuAD) as the significant benchmark. Compiling factual questions datasets requires manual annotations, limiting the training data's potential size. We present the WikiOmnia dataset, a new publicly available set of QA pairs and corresponding Russian Wikipedia article summary sections, composed with a fully automated generation and filtration pipeline. To ensure high quality of generated QA pairs, diverse manual and automated evaluation techniques were applied. The WikiOmnia pipeline is available open-source and is also tested for creating SQuAD-formatted QA on other domains, like news texts, fiction, and social media. The resulting dataset includes two parts: raw data on the whole Russian Wikipedia (7,930,873 QA pairs with paragraphs for ruGPT-3 XL and 7,991,040 QA pairs with paragraphs for ruT5-large) and cleaned data with strict automatic verification (over 160,000 QA pairs with paragraphs for ruGPT-3 XL and over 3,400,000 QA pairs with paragraphs for ruT5-large).

1 Introduction

Generative abilities of large and high-performing pre-trained language models (LMs) are widely investigated now, and special interest is aroused around generating datasets in a fully unsupervised way (Schick and Schütze, 2021). Question answering (QA) datasets can be easily adjusted to the generation pipeline formats and become a source for training generative reading comprehension systems (Brown et al., 2020; Wei et al., 2021), dialogue systems (Nehring et al., 2021), various tasks in the field of information retrieval for various languages (Shavrina et al., 2021).

In this work, we present WikiOmnia - the largest QA dataset for Russian, obtained in a fully-automated way. The dataset contains QA pairs for every article of Russian Wikipedia [1], based on the summary sections. WikiOmnia consists of 2 parts:

1. the voluminous, automatically generated part: 15,9 million triplets consisting of the original article summary, a corresponding generated question and a generated answer;
2. the filtered part: the subsample of 3,5 million triplets, fully verified with automatic means.

Apart from the data, we present a fully-automated pipeline for SQuAD-like data generation for Russian, based on *generative part* represented by the ruGPT-3 XL[2] and ruT5-large [3] models, and *filtering part* that includes Russian BERT[4] baseline and rich heuristic approach. All stated models were fine-tuned on SberQuAD (Efimov et al., 2020) that is based on the methodology of the original English SQuAD (Rajpurkar et al., 2016). The whole automated and unsupervised generation and filtration pipeline was also tested for creating SQuAD-formatted QA on other domains: news texts, customer reviews, fiction, and social media. QA datasets generated with ruGPT3XL and ruT5 will be available on HuggingFace.

After some related work overview in Section 2, QA generation and filtration details are demonstrated in Sections 3 and 4 respectively, followed by the corpus statistics in Section 5. Evaluation details are described in Sections 6 and 7.

2 Related Work

The proposed work is based upon the recent architectures in transformer language modelling - GPT-3 (Brown et al., 2020) and T5 (Raffel et al., 2019),

[1] as of March 2021

[2] https://huggingface.co/sberbank-ai/rugpt3xl

[3] https://huggingface.co/sberbank-ai/ruT5-large

[4] http://docs.deeppavlov.ai/en/master/features/models/squad.html

Proceedings of the 2nd Workshop on Natural Language Generation, Evaluation, and Metrics (GEM), pages 125 - 135
December 7, 2022 ©2022 Association for Computational Linguistics

and solves a standard SQuAD format problem, resulting in triplets *"text paragraph - question based on paragraph - answer from the paragraph"*, see the following example:

- **Original Wikipedia paragraph:**[5] Коити Масимо (яп. Масимо Ко:ити) — известный режиссёр аниме и основатель японской анимационной студии Bee Train. С момента основания студии он руководит производством почти всех её картин, а также время от времени принимает участие в работе над анимацией и музыкой. *Kōichi Mashimo is a famous anime director and the founder of the Japanese animation studio Bee Train. Since the creation of the studio, he directed almost all studio's works, and he also sometimes participates in art and sound tasks.* **Generated question (ruT5):** Кто является основателем японской анимационной студии Bee Train? **Generated answer (ruT5):** Коити Масимо **English QA translation:** *Who is the founder of the Japanese animation studio Bee Train? Kōichi Mashimo*

The following subsections of this section will break down previous work on the topic of QA datasets and their generation.

Datasets. For English, SQuAD 1.1 (Rajpurkar et al., 2016) consists of 107,785 question-answer pairs. SQuAD 2.0, combines SQuAD 1.1 questions with over 50,000 unanswerable questions (questions that cannot be answered based on the corresponding paragraph) (Rajpurkar et al., 2018). The following datasets for English were of comparable size or bigger. Trivia QA (Joshi et al., 2017) includes 95 thousand QA pairs. Natural Questions (NQ) (Kwiatkowski et al., 2019) contains questions from Google search queries and corresponding spans from Wikipedia articles as answers: 307,373 training examples, 7,830 development and 7,842 test examples. With the development of deep learning models, over 80 new datasets on QA and reading comprehension appeared in the past two years (Rogers et al., 2021). Several multilingual QA datasets contain Russian examples: MKQA (Longpre et al., 2020), TYDI QA (Clark et al., 2020), a dataset for 7 languages (Asai et al., 2020). Artetxe et al. (2020) conducted experiments on the Cross-lingual Question Answering Dataset (XQuAD) benchmark that consists of a subset from SQuAD v1.1 and its translations into 10 languages.

Wikipedia is commonly used as a relevant source for new datasets: for example, Yang et al. (2015) presented WIKIQA dataset of QA pairs. It contains 3,047 questions from Bing query logs, where each one is associated with a Wikipedia page. Manual annotation was used to check if a sentence from a page summary paragraph is the correct answer to the question. Lewis et al. (2021) automatically generated 65M QA pairs from Wikipedia paragraphs, using four steps with separate models: passage selection, possible answer extraction (with BERT), question generation (with BART), and filtering.

For Russian, SberQuAD (Efimov et al., 2020)[6] is the main resource for the QA system development and evaluation. The dataset was created following the methodology of the original English SQuAD, it contains about 50 thousand QA pairs. No bigger QA datasets for Russian were created yet, and synthetic QA generation approaches were not applied to Russian yet. Although, pre-trained language models, which are suitable for generative tasks, might help create better QA systems: ruGPT-3 models (ruGPT3XL, ruGPT3Large, ruGPT3Medium, ruGPT3Small) and ruT5 models (ruT5-base, ruT5-large) exist for Russian and can be implemented for the task.

Question-answer generation.. Classical QA pair generation pipeline lets firstly choose among text points that should be asked, then ask a question based on these points, and after that find the most likely candidate from the answer spans in text (Reddy et al., 2017; Du et al., 2017; Alberti et al., 2019; Lee et al., 2020). Joint models, for question and answer generation can be also used (Shakeri et al., 2020; Cui et al., 2021) - i.e. based on BART. Lyu et al. (2021) proposed BERT-based model which generates questions heuristically from summaries. Some filtering steps can be done after creating QA too (Alberti et al., 2019; Puri et al., 2020; Lewis et al., 2021). Shakeri et al. (2020) proposed likelihood of the generated question-answers as a measure for it.

In the recent years, pre-trained language models as unsupervised open-domain QA systems, that incorporate factual knowledge, were studied (Petroni et al., 2019; Jiang et al., 2020b,a; Kassner and

[5] https://en.wikipedia.org/wiki/K%C5%8Dichi_Mashimo

[6] https://huggingface.co/datasets/sberquad

Schütze, 2020; Bouraoui et al., 2020) and criticized (Cao et al., 2021). Other pre-trained language models were also examined for the task: Wang et al. (2021) fine-tuned BART to answer closed-book questions, and Wang et al. (2020) studied GPT-2-based models performance for constructing knowledge graphs.

To the best of our knowledge, the only approach to GPT-based QA generation and filtration was suggested in (Liu et al., 2020), who used a QA generation pipeline to generate diverse question-answer pairs from unlabeled text corpus. For question generation, GPT-2 small model, fine-tuned on SQuAD 1.1 training dataset, was used. To filter out low-quality generated data, fine-tuned BERT-based QA model utilizing the SQuAD 1.1 dataset was used: examples were kept if F1 similarity score between the answer span and the answer span predicted by BERT-based QA was above 0.9. The performance of question generation was evaluated by BLEU, ROUGE-L, METEOR metrics. However, the approach was examined only for English.

3 Implementation Details

We used the biggest freely available Russian GPT3 model: ruGPT-3 XL. The model was trained using Deepspeed and Megatron code and had sparse attention blocks. Maximal sequence length for generation was 2048 tokens. We fine-tuned the model on SberQuAD dataset with the following parameters: batch-size = 2, sequence length = 2048, learning rate = 0.000015. The model fine-tuning required 10 GPUs per worker, and it took 135,000 iterations. After that we ran parallel QA generation with the parameters: maximal length = 1048, beam search with 7 as a number of beams, all 3grams can only occur once, repetition penalty = 2.

We also fine-tuned ruT5-large model for Russian on SberQuAD dataset with such parameters: number of epochs = 5, maximal length = 512, batch size = 16, number of beams = 12.

For ruGPT-3 XL, we turned each example into a line starting with a special text beginning token (<[TEXT]>), a text, then a special question beginning token (<[QUESTION]>), a question, a special answer beginning token (<[ANSWER]>), and, finally, an answer, followed with the end-of-sequence special token. For ruT5-large, we presented each example in the same way, but special text beginning, question beginning and answer beginning tokens were in Russian. Both models were fine-tuned to generate 3 QA pairs for a text.

For QA generation we crawled all Wikipedia for the Russian language (up to March 2021) - 2,682,680 articles in general. We took only text from summary sections in every Wikipedia article. Based on page categories, we excluded disambiguation articles from the data. Then we kept Wikipedia article categories for each summary, for filtration and analysis purposes. For processing purposes, we splitted all Wikipedia data into 20 batches. Both for ruGPT-3 XL and for ruT5-large, we generated 3 QA pairs per summary. So the dataset contains summaries, QA pairs for them, and additional information, such as page title and corresponding Wikipedia categories. All QA pairs for a summary are included in one batch, and each summary appeared in the Wikipedia summaries dataset only once.

The dataset is presented in 20 batches, it lets use any 18 batches as train set, and the remaining two batches as development set and test set, if needed. Both ruGPT-3 XL and ruT5-large fine-tuning, generation, filtration and evaluation tasks were performed on 4 Tesla V100 GPU (32GB RAM) server and in Google Colab.

4 Filtration of Generated Data

Inspired by (Liu et al., 2020), we applied a set of hand-crafted heuristics to filter out generated QA pairs of poor quality in the following steps, based on manual evaluation (See Subsection 6.1.).

1. First of all, we dropped QA pairs with more than one interrogative pronoun in a question.

2. Then we applied squad_ru_rubert_infer BERT model for Russian pre-trained on SberQuad [7]. We created 'gold' answers for all generated questions with it, letting it answer the questions generated by ruGPT-3 or ruT5. After that we left strings with exact match between lemmatized generated answer and BERT model answer, with intersection of lemmas between two answers over 70%. This threshold was chosen manually based on the analysis of one data sample - batch 2 (random 50,000 examples from 90,927 summaries).

3. After that, we extracted named entities using Natasha python library for Russian.[8] We re-

[7] http://docs.deeppavlov.ai/en/master/features/models/squad.html

[8] https://github.com/natasha/natasha

moved QA pairs in which entities (of different types) in a generated question were not presented in Wikipedia summary, and/or entities (of different types) in a generated answer were not presented in summary, using string match methods.

4. Finally, we deleted duplicated QA pairs for the same summaries where Levenshtein distance similarity ratio between questions and Levenshtein distance similarity ratio between answers was more than 70%.

Several additional options were implemented and can be used too, but they were not included into the final heuristics version for this specific task after the manual analysis (See Subsection 6.1.): 1) ROUGE (Lin, 2004), METEOR (Banerjee and Lavie, 2005; Denkowski and Lavie, 2014) and BLEU (Papineni et al., 2002) metrics in the second step. For each pair among *'gold' answer - generated answer, question - generated answer, text - generated answer, text - question*, three metrics for lemmatized strings were calculated. The mean result for each pair was counted, and QA pairs where values were less than the corresponding thresholds 60%, 50%, 40%, were removed. 2) Matching persons and locations separately instead of the third step. 3) Checking if the 'gold' BERT model score is over 0.99, filtering out complicated examples. 4) Calculating if word mover's distance between generated answer and 'gold' answer is between 1.1 and 1.5, using the fastText model for Russian[9].

The overall pipeline is presented in Figure 1.

5 Corpus Statistics

We describe the main characteristics of the resulting corpus. For synthetic data, it is especially important to control their diversity and frequency of words.

Basic statistics. For ruGPT-3 and ruT5 generated data, generation and filtration results in a detailed way are presented in Tab. 1 for Wikipedia batches 1-5. We see that quality of ruT5 generated QA pairs is much better; however, both models require a filtration step for a 'clean' dataset version. In general, the raw dataset version for ruGPT-3 contained 7,930,873 examples, and filtered version had more than 160,000 examples. For ruT5, the raw dataset version consisted of 7,991,040 examples; filtered version included over 3,400,000 examples.

The most frequent words in questions and answers for all 4 setups do not differ: they are about years, names, places, numbers etc. For instant, in questions the most frequent lemmas are 'god' (*year*), 'nazyvat'sja' (*to be named*), 'rodit'sja' (*to be born*), 'skol'ko' (*how many*), 'gorod' (*town*), and in answers the most frequent lemmas are 'god' (*year*), 'rajon' (*district*), 'chelovek' (*human, person*), 'gorod' (*town*), 'rossijskij' (*Russian*).[10] Average length for ruT5 before and after filtration is about 52 characters (7 tokens) for questions and about 24 characters (4 tokens) for answers. For ruGPT-3, average length before filtration is 47 characters (7 tokens) for questions and 19 characters (3 tokens) for answers; after filtration its is slightly shorter: 46 characters (7 tokens) for questions and 12 characters (2 tokens) for answers. In SberQuAD train set, questions (64.4 characters, 8.7 tokens) and answers (25.9 characters, 3.7 tokens) are longer (Efimov et al., 2020).

Self-BLEU for questions diversity. We computed Self-BLEU as a metric of diversity for generated questions, as they are more specific for a model than answers that depend on questions. We followed (Holtzman et al., 2020) approach that is based on (Zhu et al., 2018). It yields how one sentence (a question) resembles other generated questions in the collection: for each question as a hypothesis and all other questions as references, the BLEU score is calculated. Due to computational reasons, we took random samples of 5,000 examples from raw ruGPT-3 data (batch 2), raw ruT5 data (batch 2), filtered ruGPT-3 data (including batch 2), and filtered ruT5 data (including batch 2). To compare, we measured Self-BLEU for a random sample of 5,000 questions from the original SberQuAD too. For each text, there was only one corresponding question in the data. Questions were lemmatized before calculation.

Median Self-BLEU scores are presented in Tab. 2, where lower Self-BLEU scores represent higher diversity. SberQuAD data demonstrated the highest diversity. While ruT5 generated questions imply higher diversity after filtration, for ruGPT-3 the most relevant questions that remain after filtration are less diverse.

Wh-questions ratio. We also use wh-questions

[9]araneum fasttextcbow-300-5-2018.model https://rusvectores.org/en/models/

[10]Here Russian words are given in Latin transliteration, for readability purpose.

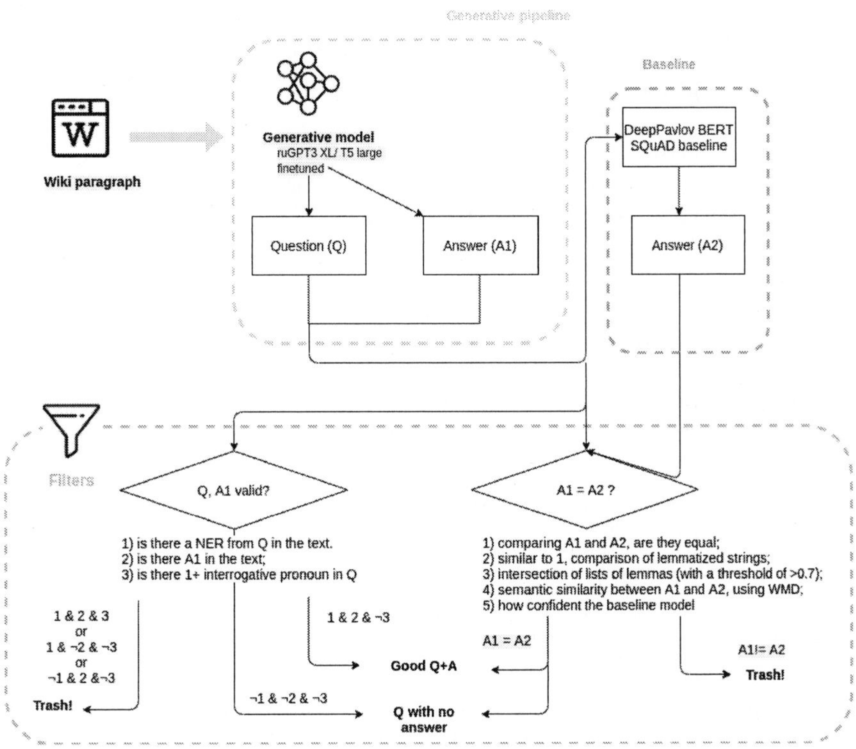

Figure 1: The full WikiOmnia pipeline for QA generation.

Batch	ruGPT-3 before filtering	filtered ruGPT-3	ruT5 before filtering	filtered ruT5
Batch1	266,332	10,079	272,397	152,884
Batch2	268,795	8,034	271,281	113,964
Batch3	276,618	6,176	275,412	124,784
Batch4	272,875	7,042	270,534	146,627
Batch5	276,107	5,536	279,363	157,535

Table 1: Number of QA pairs in ruGPT-3 and ruT5 generated batches before and after filtering: on the example of Wikipedia batches 1-5.

Data	Median Self-BLEU
Raw ruGPT-3 data (1)	0.45
Filtered ruGPT-3 data (2)	0.49
Raw ruT5 data (3)	0.40
Filtered ruT5 data (4)	0.38
SberQuAD data (5)	0.20

Table 2: Median Self-BLEU scores calculated for raw ruGPT-3 generated data (1), filtered ruGPT-3 generated data (2), raw ruT5 generated data (3), filtered ruT5 generated data (4), SberQuAD data (5).

ratio to check how diverse are the questions. We select 15 Wh-words and similar words in Russian: 'kto' (*who*), 'chto' (*what*), 'kakoj' (*which, what*), 'chej' (*whose*), 'gde' (*where*), 'kotoryj' (*what, which*), 'otkuda' (*where from*), 'skol'ko' (*how many*), 'kakovoj' (*what, by which*), 'kakov' (*what, which*), 'zachem' (*what for*), 'kogda' (*when*), 'pochemu' (*why*), 'chem' (*with what*), 'kak' (*how*).[11] On the example of 5 batches, we checked how many such questions were presented in data before and after filtration, compared with SberQuAD ratios. Tab. 3 demonstrates results for 10 Wh-words and similar words, excluding 'chej' (*whose*), 'otkuda' (*where from*), 'zachem' (*what for*), 'kotoryj' (*what, which*), 'kakovoj' (*what, 'by which'*), that were underrepresented both in 5 batches and in SberQuAD. For both ruGPT-3 and ruT5 generated questions, ratios for 'skol'ko' (*how*

[11] Here Russian words are given in Latin transliteration, for readability purpose.

Wh-word	1	2	3	4	5
kto (*who*)	0.15	0.04	0.14	0.12	0.05
chto (*what*)	0.08	0.10	0.06	0.07	0.13
kakoj (*which, what*)	0.08	0.12	0.09	0.08	0.11
gde (*where*)	0.07	0.04	0.12	0.10	0.03
skol'ko (*how many*)	0.02	0.06	0.04	0.04	0.03
kakov (*what, which*)	0.05	0.02	0.01	0.00	0.01
kogda (*when*)	0.06	0.04	0.11	0.12	0.05
pochemu (*why*)	0.00	0.00	0.00	0.00	0.01
chem (*with what*)	0.01	0.01	0.01	0.01	0.03
kak (*how*)	0.18	0.13	0.14	0.11	0.07

Table 3: Wh-questions median ratios for raw ruGPT-3 generated data (1), filtered ruGPT-3 generated data (2), raw ruT5 generated data (3), filtered ruT5 generated data (4) on the example of Wikipedia batches 1-5; Wh-questions ratio for SberQuAD data (5).

many) and 'kak' (*how*) after filtration are higher than in SberQuAD questions. Generated QA pairs of good quality more often contain a numerical answer. Questions with 'kto' (*who*), 'gde' (*where*), and 'kogda' (*when*) have higher ratios in ruT5 questions than in SberQuAD. On the contrary, more complicated questions with 'pochemu' (*why*) and 'chem' (*with what*) are less presented in generated QA pairs. It can be also noticed that ruGPT-3 generates questions with 'kakov' (*what, which*) (a short form of a wh-word) more often than ruT5. ruGPT-3 generated QA pairs with 'kto' (*who*) have rather low quality and contain information about persons not from the summaries, that's why they are strictly filtered out. On the example of 'kogda' (*when*), we see that QA pairs with dates, provided by ruT5, are more correct than such pairs from ruGPT-3. Therefore, in comparison with SberQuAD, both generated datasets remain diverse, too.

6 Performance Evaluation

6.1 Human Evaluation and Error Analysis

Human Evaluation for editing the pipeline. We took human evaluation into account for the data generated by a fully automated generative pipeline twice, conducting the intermediate and the final evaluation stages. This manual evaluation was conducted by the authors, as well as discussions about problematic points to handle disagreements. On the intermediate stage, we took multiple series of 10,000 random summaries and analysed manually the generated QA pairs for them, as well as the examples remaining after filtration with different filtration options; the same steps were reproduced for QA pairs by ruGPT-3 and ruT5. Based on this intermediate evaluation, the generation and filtration pipeline was edited: step 1 was added; step 3 was placed after step 2 (not before it); several steps were removed from the pipeline (See Section 4). After that, the final evaluation stage was conducted for the same samples with the final filtration options results: for these samples, rate of examples remaining after filtration reached about 5% for QA pairs generated by ruGPT-3 and about 30% for QA pairs generated by ruT5. During the final stage, we also checked manually, in addition, several random samples of 10,000 QA pairs for specific evaluation tasks.

Wikipedia topics before and after filtration. To estimate if filtration ratio varies for different topics, we checked the ratio of examples that remained after filtration for various Wikipedia categories groups (on the example of Batches 1-5): history events, famous persons biographies, plants, technical descriptions, geography, mathematics, sports, actors, and movies. Categories for the selected topics were grouped using heuristics rules, based on saved Wikipedia category names for each example (one example could have multiple categories).

Both ruGPT-3 and ruT5 generated QA pairs showed the best results for articles about sports, perhaps due to simple and well-structured summaries. Error analysis showed that ruGPT-3 also performed rather well on history and plants topics, but answers to the correct questions, also correct in meaning, did not match the 'gold' answers well. In addition to sports, ruT5 QA pairs for technical, history and geography articles also yielded higher quality, they did not contain additional information not from the corresponding summaries, unlike ruGPT-3. In general, for technical topics (i.e. computer science), generated QA pairs yielded worse quality before filtration than for other topics.

Example of an erroneous QA pair generation with ruT5, detected by filtering:

- **Original Wikipedia paragraph:**[12] Псатирелла водолюбивая (лат. Psathyrella piluliformis) — гриб рода Псатирелла (Psathyrella) семейства Псатирелловые (Psathyrellaceae). Съедобность гриба спорна, чаще он считается несъедобным, иногда — условно съедобным, но невысокого качества. *Psathyrella piluliformis is a species of agaric fungus in the family Psathyrellaceae. It is considered edible but of low quality, with fragile flesh and being difficult to identify.* **Generated question (ruT5):** Какова способность гриба менять окраску? **Generated answer (ruT5):** в зависимости от условий **English QA translation:** *What is the ability of a fungus to change color? Depends on conditions*

The filtered dataset may still contain two types of errors that were not detected by the filters: 1) questions about information that was not presented in a summary (0.008% for ruGPT-3, based on a random example of 10,000 QA pairs); 2) erroneous answers with numbers (if not years).

6.2 Automated Evaluation

During all evaluation experiments, we focused mostly on training QA systems using the filtered WikiOmnia part with QA pairs generated by ruT5, as it is bigger (than the part with QA pairs by ruGPT-3) and lets experiment with different sample sizes. We took random dataset parts of 50,000 examples, 100,000 examples, and 300,000 examples. For each sample size, we took 2 random samples and calculated the average score values for them.

Experiment set 1. We fine-tuned ruBERT base cased model (BERT model for Russian [13]) on each of these samples and then evaluated it on development and test parts of SberQuAD dataset. As a baseline, we fine-tuned ruBERT on the train part of SberQuAD dataset. F1 score and exact match (EM) were used as standard SQuAD evaluation metrics. For all setups, the following parameters were used for fine-tuning: 3 epochs, learning rate = 2e-5, weight decay = 0.01.

Experiment set 2. We took models above, already fine-tuned on WikiOmnia samples (100,000 examples and 300,000 examples), and fine-tuned them further on SberQuAD train part (1, 2 and 3 epochs). Results for Experiment sets 1 and 2 are presented in Tab. 4. In the second experiment set, the models fine-tuned on 100,000 or 300,000 WikiOmnia triplets and then fine-tuned on SberQuAD train part (2 epochs), perform better than models fine-tuned only on 100,000 or 300,000 WikiOmnia triplets, or the baseline model fine-tuned on SberQuAD train part (3 epochs). Fine-tuning first on WikiOmnia and then on SberQuAD yields better results than fine-tuning only on SberQuAD.[14] The WikiOmnia size lets conduct experiments with different sample sizes.

Experiment set 3. Following the Experiment set 2 results, we decided to take an 'own' development set from WikiOmnia (10,000 triplets) and to compare results on it with results on development and test parts of SberQuAD (Tab. 5). We took a random sample with 110,000 examples from WikiOmnia by ruT5. We conducted ruBERT base model fine-tuning: 5 runs for different folds where 10,000 triplets were taken as a development set for evaluation, and the remaining 100,000 triplets were used for fine-tuning, 2 epochs in each run. Results on the WikiOmnia development set, in all runs, are much better than results on SberQuAD development and test sets. Perhaps, due to the datasets specifics, SberQuAD development and test sets are suitable for models, fine-tuned on WikiOmnia, evaluation, only if they were fine-tuned on SberQuAD train as a second step.

7 Pipeline Evaluation on Other Domains

For evaluation purposes, we also tested the full pipeline on data samples of four other text genres in Russian: news stories, social media posts, product reviews, and fiction texts. Each sample has 2,000 examples taken randomly from the following datasets: 1) news from the newspaper

[12] https://en.wikipedia.org/wiki/Psathyrella_piluliformis

[13] https://huggingface.co/DeepPavlov/rubert-base-cased

[14] Models, fine-tuned on the ruGPT-3 generated WikiOmnia part, showed the same peruliarity: after fine-tuning on WikiOmnia and then on SberQuAD train, EM on the development set was 67.71, F1 score on the development set was 86.64, EM on the test set was 66.57, and F1 score on the test set was 85.88. All metrics, excepting the last one, are better than the baseline. As the filtered ruGPT-3 generated WikiOmnia part is rather small and contains only 164,253 examples, all experiments were conducted for this whole part.

Model setup	EM on dev	F1 on dev	EM on test	F1 on test
Baseline (1)	66.39	85.92	66.46	85.93
(2)	59.26	79.89	58.30	79.26
(3)	60.04	80.57	58.64	79.94
(4)	59.80	80.50	58.36	79.97
(5)	67.32	86.26	66.29	85.76
(6)	67.04	86.18	66.96	86.03
(7)	65.95	85.67	65.48	85.40

Table 4: Evaluation scores for ruBERT base model fine-tuned on: SberQuAD train (1), WikiOmnia 50,000 examples by ruT5 (2); WikiOmnia 100,000 examples by ruT5 (3); WikiOmnia 300,000 examples by ruT5 (4); WikiOmnia 100,000 examples and then SberQuAD train 1 epoch (5); WikiOmnia 100,000 examples and then SberQuAD train 2 epochs (6); WikiOmnia 100,000 examples and then SberQuAD train 3 epochs (7).

Model	EM on own dev	F1 on own dev	EM on dev	F1 on dev	EM on test	F1 on test
1 run	87.47	95.14	59.32	80.00	58.30	79.71
2 run	87.89	95.24	59.86	80.40	58.46	79.87
3 run	88.08	95.46	59.83	80.33	58.57	79.92
4 run	87.53	95.18	60.22	80.66	58.64	79.89
5 run	87.90	95.18	59.39	80.18	58.21	79.70

Table 5: Evaluation on the development set from WikiOmnia (own dev), in comparison with evaluation on SberQuAD development (dev) and test (test) sets (5 runs).

Gazeta,[15] (Gusev, 2020) with text lengths up to 3,500 characters; 2) social media texts from the Taiga corpus[16] (Shavrina and Shapovalova, 2017), with texts lengths up to 3,000 characters; 3) reviews from the dataset[17] on product reviews about clothes from an e-commerce website (Smetanin and Komarov, 2019), with text lengths over 500 characters and up to 1,007 characters, as these texts are rather short; 4) fiction texts from the collection of Russian classical literature texts[18]: fragments from texts, with text lengths up to 3,000 characters.

For every text, three QA pairs were generated. Filtration steps were the same as for QA pairs based on Wikipedia summaries. After filtration, we got the following results for ruGPT3XL: 497 pairs remained for fiction texts, and 559 pairs were left for news texts. For reviews, the pipeline performed in the best way: 1379 pairs were left. The worst performance was for social media: only 154 pairs remained. ruT5-large also yielded good performance on reviews: 1,542 pairs were left after filtration. The explanation might be that review texts as a genre usually have definite patterns and structure. The worst ruT5-large results were also for social media: only 945 pairs remained. Social media texts looked mostly like opinionated pieces where it would be hard to create QA pairs manually too.

Both pipelines, for ruGPT3 XL and ruT5-large, can be generalized comparatively well to other genres. Although ruT5-large performed generally better on all four genres, the results mostly differed on news texts: 3,204 texts remained after filtering. Other filtration techniques should be investigated, handling the remaining errors, i.e. how to check quality of numerical answers (especially by ruGPT-3), or how to check question and answer similarity to the corresponding summary, considering paraphrases. Reasons of the results of the automated evaluation on SberQuAD development and test sets should be also explored further. The dataset implementation for various and diverse tasks and its evaluation on them remains a separate point for further research.

8 Conclusions

We propose WikiOmnia, the new largest question-answering dataset for Russian: it contains QA pairs and corresponding Russian Wikipedia article summaries. It can be used to improve the quality of monolingual and multilingual information re-

[15] https://github.com/IlyaGusev/gazeta

[16] https://tatianashavrina.github.io/taiga_site/

[17] https://github.com/sismetanin/rureviews

[18] https://www.kaggle.com/d0rj3228/russian-literature

trieval systems, open domain question answering, etc. Quality of generated QA pairs in the filtered part of the dataset is ensured by diverse automated filtration techniques, manual and automated evaluation. We also present the automated generation and filtration pipeline that can be applied to various sources of text data, including expanding the applicability of QA systems to news data, fiction, reviews.

We welcome researchers in the fields of information retrieval and language technology to use both the dataset to train the models, and the pipeline to expand the capabilities and robustness of the existing QA systems. We invite the community to reproduce the work on materials of other languages, using multilingual models and existing baselines.

References

Chris Alberti, Daniel Andor, Emily Pitler, Jacob Devlin, and Michael Collins. 2019. Synthetic QA corpora generation with roundtrip consistency. In *Proceedings of the 57th Annual Meeting of the Association for Computational Linguistics*, pages 6168–6173, Florence, Italy. Association for Computational Linguistics.

Mikel Artetxe, Sebastian Ruder, and Dani Yogatama. 2020. On the cross-lingual transferability of monolingual representations. In *Proceedings of the 58th Annual Meeting of the Association for Computational Linguistics*, pages 4623–4637, Online. Association for Computational Linguistics.

Akari Asai, Jungo Kasai, Jonathan H Clark, Kenton Lee, Eunsol Choi, and Hannaneh Hajishirzi. 2020. Xor qa: Cross-lingual open-retrieval question answering. *arXiv preprint arXiv:2010.11856*.

Satanjeev Banerjee and Alon Lavie. 2005. METEOR: An automatic metric for MT evaluation with improved correlation with human judgments. In *Proceedings of the ACL Workshop on Intrinsic and Extrinsic Evaluation Measures for Machine Translation and/or Summarization*, pages 65–72, Ann Arbor, Michigan. Association for Computational Linguistics.

Zied Bouraoui, Jose Camacho-Collados, and Steven Schockaert. 2020. Inducing relational knowledge from bert. *Proceedings of the AAAI Conference on Artificial Intelligence*, 34(05):7456–7463.

Tom B Brown, Benjamin Mann, Nick Ryder, Melanie Subbiah, Jared Kaplan, Prafulla Dhariwal, Arvind Neelakantan, Pranav Shyam, Girish Sastry, Amanda Askell, et al. 2020. Language models are few-shot learners. *arXiv preprint arXiv:2005.14165*.

Boxi Cao, Hongyu Lin, Xianpei Han, Le Sun, Lingyong Yan, Meng Liao, Tong Xue, and Jin Xu. 2021. Knowledgeable or educated guess? revisiting language models as knowledge bases. In *Proceedings of the 59th Annual Meeting of the Association for Computational Linguistics and the 11th International Joint Conference on Natural Language Processing (Volume 1: Long Papers)*, pages 1860–1874, Online. Association for Computational Linguistics.

Jonathan H. Clark, Eunsol Choi, Michael Collins, Dan Garrette, Tom Kwiatkowski, Vitaly Nikolaev, and Jennimaria Palomaki. 2020. TyDi QA: A benchmark for information-seeking question answering in typologically diverse languages. *Transactions of the Association for Computational Linguistics*, 8:454–470.

Shaobo Cui, Xintong Bao, Xinxing Zu, Yangyang Guo, Zhongzhou Zhao, Ji Zhang, and Haiqing Chen. 2021. Onestop qamaker: Extract question-answer pairs from text in a one-stop approach. *CoRR*, abs/2102.12128.

Michael Denkowski and Alon Lavie. 2014. Meteor universal: Language specific translation evaluation for any target language. In *Proceedings of the Ninth Workshop on Statistical Machine Translation*, pages 376–380, Baltimore, Maryland, USA. Association for Computational Linguistics.

Xinya Du, Junru Shao, and Claire Cardie. 2017. Learning to ask: Neural question generation for reading comprehension. In *Proceedings of the 55th Annual Meeting of the Association for Computational Linguistics (Volume 1: Long Papers)*, pages 1342–1352, Vancouver, Canada. Association for Computational Linguistics.

Pavel Efimov, Andrey Chertok, Leonid Boytsov, and Pavel Braslavski. 2020. Sberquad–russian reading comprehension dataset: Description and analysis. In *International Conference of the Cross-Language Evaluation Forum for European Languages*, pages 3–15. Springer.

Ilya Gusev. 2020. Dataset for automatic summarization of russian news. In *Artificial Intelligence and Natural Language*, pages 122–134, Cham. Springer International Publishing.

Ari Holtzman, Jan Buys, Li Du, Maxwell Forbes, and Yejin Choi. 2020. The curious case of neural text degeneration. In *International Conference on Learning Representations*.

Zhengbao Jiang, Antonios Anastasopoulos, Jun Araki, Haibo Ding, and Graham Neubig. 2020a. X-FACTR: Multilingual factual knowledge retrieval from pretrained language models. In *Proceedings of the 2020 Conference on Empirical Methods in Natural Language Processing (EMNLP)*, pages 5943–5959, Online. Association for Computational Linguistics.

Zhengbao Jiang, Frank F. Xu, Jun Araki, and Graham Neubig. 2020b. How Can We Know What Language Models Know? *Transactions of the Association for Computational Linguistics*, 8:423–438.

Mandar Joshi, Eunsol Choi, Daniel S Weld, and Luke Zettlemoyer. 2017. Triviaqa: A large scale distantly supervised challenge dataset for reading comprehension. In *Proceedings of the 55th Annual Meeting of the Association for Computational Linguistics (Volume 1: Long Papers)*, pages 1601–1611.

Nora Kassner and Hinrich Schütze. 2020. BERT-kNN: Adding a kNN search component to pretrained language models for better QA. In *Findings of the Association for Computational Linguistics: EMNLP 2020*, pages 3424–3430, Online. Association for Computational Linguistics.

Tom Kwiatkowski, Jennimaria Palomaki, Olivia Redfield, Michael Collins, Ankur Parikh, Chris Alberti, Danielle Epstein, Illia Polosukhin, Jacob Devlin, Kenton Lee, et al. 2019. Natural questions: a benchmark for question answering research. *Transactions of the Association for Computational Linguistics*, 7:453–466.

Dong Bok Lee, Seanie Lee, Woo Tae Jeong, Donghwan Kim, and Sung Ju Hwang. 2020. Generating diverse and consistent QA pairs from contexts with information-maximizing hierarchical conditional VAEs. In *Proceedings of the 58th Annual Meeting of the Association for Computational Linguistics*, pages 208–224, Online. Association for Computational Linguistics.

Patrick Lewis, Yuxiang Wu, Linqing Liu, Pasquale Minervini, Heinrich Küttler, Aleksandra Piktus, Pontus Stenetorp, and Sebastian Riedel. 2021. PAQ: 65 million probably-asked questions and what you can do with them. *Transactions of the Association for Computational Linguistics*, 9:1098–1115.

Chin-Yew Lin. 2004. ROUGE: A package for automatic evaluation of summaries. In *Text Summarization Branches Out*, pages 74–81, Barcelona, Spain. Association for Computational Linguistics.

Bang Liu, Haojie Wei, Di Niu, Haolan Chen, and Yancheng He. 2020. Asking questions the human way: Scalable question-answer generation from text corpus. *CoRR*, abs/2002.00748.

Shayne Longpre, Yi Lu, and Joachim Daiber. 2020. Mkqa: A linguistically diverse benchmark for multilingual open domain question answering. *arXiv preprint arXiv:2007.15207*.

Chenyang Lyu, Lifeng Shang, Yvette Graham, Jennifer Foster, Xin Jiang, and Qun Liu. 2021. Improving unsupervised question answering via summarization-informed question generation.

Jan Nehring, Nils Feldhus, Harleen Kaur, and Akhyar Ahmed. 2021. Combining open domain question answering with a task-oriented dialog system. In *Proceedings of the 1st Workshop on Document-grounded Dialogue and Conversational Question Answering (DialDoc 2021)*, pages 38–45, Online. Association for Computational Linguistics.

Kishore Papineni, Salim Roukos, Todd Ward, and Wei-Jing Zhu. 2002. Bleu: A method for automatic evaluation of machine translation. In *Proceedings of the 40th Annual Meeting on Association for Computational Linguistics*, ACL '02, page 311–318, USA. Association for Computational Linguistics.

Fabio Petroni, Tim Rocktäschel, Sebastian Riedel, Patrick Lewis, Anton Bakhtin, Yuxiang Wu, and Alexander Miller. 2019. Language models as knowledge bases? In *Proceedings of the 2019 Conference on Empirical Methods in Natural Language Processing and the 9th International Joint Conference on Natural Language Processing (EMNLP-IJCNLP)*, pages 2463–2473, Hong Kong, China. Association for Computational Linguistics.

Raul Puri, Ryan Spring, Mohammad Shoeybi, Mostofa Patwary, and Bryan Catanzaro. 2020. Training question answering models from synthetic data. In *Proceedings of the 2020 Conference on Empirical Methods in Natural Language Processing (EMNLP)*, pages 5811–5826, Online. Association for Computational Linguistics.

Colin Raffel, Noam Shazeer, Adam Roberts, Katherine Lee, Sharan Narang, Michael Matena, Yanqi Zhou, Wei Li, and Peter J Liu. 2019. Exploring the limits of transfer learning with a unified text-to-text transformer. *arXiv preprint arXiv:1910.10683*.

Pranav Rajpurkar, Robin Jia, and Percy Liang. 2018. Know what you don't know: Unanswerable questions for SQuAD. In *Proceedings of the 56th Annual Meeting of the Association for Computational Linguistics (Volume 2: Short Papers)*, pages 784–789, Melbourne, Australia. Association for Computational Linguistics.

Pranav Rajpurkar, Jian Zhang, Konstantin Lopyrev, and Percy Liang. 2016. Squad: 100,000+ questions for machine comprehension of text.

Sathish Reddy, Dinesh Raghu, Mitesh M. Khapra, and Sachindra Joshi. 2017. Generating natural language question-answer pairs from a knowledge graph using a RNN based question generation model. In *Proceedings of the 15th Conference of the European Chapter of the Association for Computational Linguistics: Volume 1, Long Papers*, pages 376–385, Valencia, Spain. Association for Computational Linguistics.

Anna Rogers, Matt Gardner, and Isabelle Augenstein. 2021. QA dataset explosion: A taxonomy of NLP resources for question answering and reading comprehension. *CoRR*, abs/2107.12708.

Timo Schick and Hinrich Schütze. 2021. Generating datasets with pretrained language models. In *Proceedings of the 2021 Conference on Empirical Methods in Natural Language Processing*, pages 6943–6951, Online and Punta Cana, Dominican Republic. Association for Computational Linguistics.

Siamak Shakeri, Cícero Nogueira dos Santos, Henry Zhu, Patrick Ng, Feng Nan, Zhiguo Wang, Ramesh Nallapati, and Bing Xiang. 2020. End-to-end synthetic data generation for domain adaptation of question answering systems. *CoRR*, abs/2010.06028.

T. Shavrina and O. Shapovalova. 2017. To the methodology of corpus construction for machine learning: «taiga» syntax tree corpus and parser. In *proc. of "CORPORA2017", international conference*, Saint-Petersbourg.

Tatiana Shavrina, Dina Pisarevskaya, and Valentin Malykh. 2021. Building a bilingual qa-system with rugpt-3. *Lecture Notes in Computer Science*.

Sergey Smetanin and Michail Komarov. 2019. Sentiment analysis of product reviews in russian using convolutional neural networks. In *2019 IEEE 21st Conference on Business Informatics (CBI)*, volume 01, pages 482–486.

Chenguang Wang, Xiao Liu, and Dawn Song. 2020. Language models are open knowledge graphs. *CoRR*, abs/2010.11967.

Cunxiang Wang, Pai Liu, and Yue Zhang. 2021. Can generative pre-trained language models serve as knowledge bases for closed-book QA? In *Proceedings of the 59th Annual Meeting of the Association for Computational Linguistics and the 11th International Joint Conference on Natural Language Processing (Volume 1: Long Papers)*, pages 3241–3251, Online. Association for Computational Linguistics.

Jason Wei, Maarten Bosma, Vincent Y Zhao, Kelvin Guu, Adams Wei Yu, Brian Lester, Nan Du, Andrew M Dai, and Quoc V Le. 2021. Finetuned language models are zero-shot learners. *arXiv preprint arXiv:2109.01652*.

Yi Yang, Wen-tau Yih, and Christopher Meek. 2015. WikiQA: A challenge dataset for open-domain question answering. In *Proceedings of the 2015 Conference on Empirical Methods in Natural Language Processing*, pages 2013–2018, Lisbon, Portugal. Association for Computational Linguistics.

Yaoming Zhu, Sidi Lu, Lei Zheng, Jiaxian Guo, Weinan Zhang, Jun Wang, and Yong Yu. 2018. Texygen: A benchmarking platform for text generation models. *The 41st International ACM SIGIR Conference on Research & Development in Information Retrieval.*

Evaluation of Response Generation Models: Shouldn't It Be Shareable and Replicable?

Seyed Mahed Mousavi, Gabriel Roccabruna, Michela Lorandi, Simone Caldarella, Giuseppe Riccardi
Signals and Interactive Systems Lab, University of Trento, Italy
{mahed.mousavi,gabriel.roccabruna,giuseppe.riccardi}@unitn.it

Abstract

Human Evaluation (HE) of automatically generated responses is necessary for the advancement of human-machine dialogue research. Current automatic evaluation measures are poor surrogates, at best. There are no agreed-upon HE protocols and it is difficult to develop them. As a result, researchers either perform non-replicable, non-transparent and inconsistent procedures or, worse, limit themselves to automated metrics. We propose to standardize the human evaluation of response generation models by publicly sharing a detailed protocol. The proposal includes the task design, annotators recruitment, task execution, and annotation reporting. Such protocol and process can be used as-is, as-a-whole, in-part, or modified and extended by the research community. We validate the protocol by evaluating two conversationally fine-tuned state-of-the-art models (GPT-2 and T5) for the complex task of personalized response generation. We invite the community to use this protocol - or its future community amended versions - as a transparent, replicable, and comparable approach to HE of generated responses[1].

1 Introduction

Early attempts to evaluate automatic Natural Language Generation (NLG) models using human judges dates back to before the appearance of end-to-end models (Jones and Galliers, 1995; Coch, 1996; Lester and Porter, 1997). However, due to the expensive requirements such as training skilled annotators and the time-consuming nature of this evaluation, automatic metrics became the common evaluation criteria in several NLG tasks. Metrics such as BLEU (Papineni et al., 2002), METEOR (Banerjee and Lavie, 2005) and ROUGE (Lin, 2004) have been used to evaluate the model performance in machine translation and automatic summarization tasks as inexpensive and rapid evaluations. After observing the reliability of these metrics for the task they are designed for (if applied correctly), they have been used to evaluate the models in other tasks such as response generation. However, several studies have shown that currently available automatic metrics can not be good candidates for evaluating a generated response (Liu et al., 2016; Sai et al., 2022); these criteria co-relate poorly with human judgement and are inadequate since the generation is subject to trivial factors such as coherency, fluency and grammatical structure, as well as non-trivial factors such as appropriateness, engagement, and user acceptance.

Human Evaluation (HE) is still the necessary approach to evaluate the generated responses (Smith et al., 2022). With the development of crowdsourcing annotation platforms, conducting an HE task is less expensive and more feasible than early methodologies. Nonetheless, little attention has been given to the assessment of the design of HE task. Due to the lack of an agreed upon and standard protocol, HE tasks have been performed while suffering from nontransparent procedures, non-replicable and incomparable results, and unclear resource allocations.

In this work, we propose to standardize the experimental methodology for human evaluation for response generation models. We present a detailed protocol to the community for this task, in order to increase the comparability, replicability, and interpretability of such evaluations among works and domains. All the required steps and materials to conduct a HE in a transparent and extendable way (including task design, annotator recruitment, task execution, and annotation reporting) are described and shared with the community. The proposed protocol is domain-agnostic, language-independent, and open to be extended to different versions and standards. We invite the community to not only utilize this protocol but also to improve and extend it into referable and version-able standards for the

[1] Link to the protocol and materials Repository

Proceedings of the 2nd Workshop on Natural Language Generation, Evaluation, and Metrics (GEM), pages 136 - 147
December 7, 2022 ©2022 Association for Computational Linguistics

HE task. In order to validate the proposed protocol, we evaluate two conversationally fine-tuned state-of-the-art models for the Italian language, based on GPT-2 (De Mattei et al., 2020) and T5 (Sarti and Nissim, 2022), for the task of response generation in personal dialogues using knowledge grounding.

2 Literature Review

Earlier attempts to evaluate dialogue systems by human judges considered user satisfaction as the evaluation criterion (Walker et al., 1997). Despite the introduction of automatic metrics and a research direction aiming to better the metrics used for the evaluation of dialogue models (Zhang et al., 2019; Huang et al., 2020; Mehri and Eskenazi, 2020), Human Evaluation (HE) is still the gold standard for assessing the qualities of a generated response and a generative model.

While the importance of the proper evaluation of a dialogue model using human judges is well-established in the community, how to perform such evaluation is still an unsolved question (Smith et al., 2022). As an outcome, countless HE tasks have been presented and conducted in this domain, resulting in non-comparable and non-replicable results. Dialogue systems have been evaluated with different granularity (turn-level vs dialogue-level), different evaluation policies (single-model vs pairwise-model, candidate-ranking vs. winner-selection) and in different modalities (interactive vs static) (Smith et al., 2022). The ambiguities in HE tasks conducted so far have also been studied by Belz et al. (2020), where the authors focused on disentangling the characteristics of already conducted HE tasks to increase the interpretability and comparability of the evaluations and results. Further inconsistency in the evaluations includes the ambiguity in the criterion name, i.e. two criteria with the same name assess two different qualities in different works, whereas the same quality has been named with various terms among works (Howcroft et al., 2020). In addition to the aforementioned works, this naming inconsistency can also be found in the grounded generation literature (Zhang et al., 2020; Wang et al., 2020; Huang et al., 2021; Hedayatnia et al., 2020; Zhang et al., 2020) where a criterion with the same name refers to two different qualities and presents different definitions among works.

An important factor for reproducing any crowd-sourcing experiment is reporting the details related to that experiment and its settings. This issue has been studied by Ramírez et al. (2021), where the authors identify the properties that researchers have to provide to facilitate the reproducibility of any crowd-sourcing experiments. The same problem has been studied specifically for HE experiments by Howcroft et al. (2020) where the authors identify the lack of reporting crucial details, and other issues such as high levels of variation among the evaluation procedures. Howcroft et al. (2020) further stress the need for a standard and coherent experimental design and terminology for the task of HE in the community.

3 Proposed Human Evaluation Protocol

We propose to standardize the Human Evaluation (HE) experiments through a referable and replicable protocol to address the problems of non-comparability and inconsistency in the literature. Considering the complexity of designing and executing such evaluations, we unfold the task into four main steps in order to study and analyze the crucial aspects at each step. We aim to maximize the reliability and replicability of the evaluation while minimizing the task difficulty and complexity. Our proposed protocol consists of four executive steps, i.e. 1) Task Design; 2) Annotator Recruiting; 3) Task Execution; and 4) Reporting.

3.1 Step 1: Task Design

The first step is to design the evaluation task, which can be characterized by the two aspects of evaluation and annotation characteristics. Defining these characteristics clearly and transparently is paramount to achieve replicability and comparability among works and models.

3.1.1 Evaluation Characteristics

As the initial step, definition of the evaluation characteristics of the task include the evaluation granularity, quality dimensions to evaluate and their definitions, the questions to be asked to the annotators, and the annotations format.

Granularity The evaluations conducted in the literature can be categorized into two levels of granularity as dialogue-level, where the model is evaluated at the end of a complete dialogue, and turn-level, where the model is evaluated based on its output for a specific turn in the dialogue. Recent works indicate that the turn-level evaluation is more fine-grained since it captures errors such as contradictions and response repetitions (Smith et al.,

2022). Turn-level evaluation can be further categorized as absolute (single-model, or rating) or comparative (winner-selecting, or ranking). In this protocol, we evaluate the models at the turn-level; and in order to avoid biasing the annotators with the quality of other candidates which may result in an unintentional pick-the-best response, we evaluate the candidates using the absolute setting (i.e. presenting one candidate per time for each dialogue history). In this way, the performance quality of each model is evaluated independently and we can obtain a model-specific list of limitations and error signals. Furthermore, the ground truth turn is also provided as a response candidate to the annotators, representing a point of reference.

Quality Dimensions We include four criteria in this version of the protocol, based on the most common errors and qualities for an end-to-end response generation model. Nevertheless, the proposed protocol can be extended to other criteria and quality dimensions. The proposed criteria and their definitions are as follows;

- **Appropriate** whether the proposed response candidate makes sense with respect to the dialogue history; and to investigate if it is a proper continuation of the given dialogue (thus coherent).
- **Contextual** whether the proposed response candidate contains references to the dialogue context (thus not generic); and to investigate whether the response refers to non-existing or contradicting information (such as model hallucination).
- **Listening** whether the speaker of the proposed response is following the dialogue with attention (note that generic responses are also indicating that the speaker is not following the dialogue).
- **Correct** whether the response candidate is correct considering the grammar, syntax and structure of the response.

Questions One of the important details, which is usually missing in the evaluation reports in the literature, is the formulation of the questions the annotators are prompted for the quality of the responses. The questions must be designed in a clear and neutral form in order to avoid any possible bias while addressing the important factors evaluated by each criterion. We present the questions designed to evaluate the responses in each dimension in the Appendix, Section A (The protocol can be expanded to other dimensions used by adding the corresponding criteria and questions).

Decisions For each criterion, the annotators are asked to select an answer from a 3-point Likert scale modeled as positive (eg. Correct, Appropriate), negative (eg. Not Correct, Not Appropriate), and *"I don't know"*. The purpose of the third choice, *"I don't know"*, is to avoid forcing non-deterministic and error-prone judgements on one of the other two options. That is, the non-expert annotator (in some cases nor the expert annotator) may not be able to make a deterministic decision due to the residual and inevitable ambiguity of the annotation task.

Explanations In order the obtain better insights into the capabilities and limitations of the models, we ask the annotators to explain their judgement by pointing out possible errors or rightness of a response. The explanation is asked for three of the criteria (listening is excluded) and mostly when the response is negatively evaluated or the annotator is not sure ("*I don't know.*"). In order to introduce the minimum amount of cognitive workload to the task, the annotators are asked to explain their judgement for each response right after evaluating a response candidate, through predefined options to select from, and/or free text. The list of predefined explanation options to select from and the cases for which the explanation is asked is presented in Table 1.

3.1.2 Annotation Characteristics

Another principal aspect of HE experiments is the annotation characteristics. Despite the importance of this aspect and its influence on the resulting quality, little attention is given to the careful design of the HE annotation task.

We can model the annotation task as the interactions of the human (in our setting the annotator) with a task system (the evaluation). From the beginning of the task, the annotator tends to create a Mental Model of the task according to the properties and information she/he is presented to (Moray, 1998). One of the main causes of issues in such settings is the gap between the user's and the designers' mental model (Norman, 1988; Xie et al., 2017). Furthermore, studies show high levels of cognitive workload in a task reduce the humans' ability to retrieve and exploit knowledge while reducing the mental workload helps to reduce the frequency of errors (Leveson, 2016; Zenati et al., 2020; Ramírez et al., 2021). Therefore, it is necessary to carefully design the annotation task to

Quality Dimension	Annotators' Decision: Value	Annotators' Decision: Explanation Options	Quality Sub-dimension
Appropriateness	Appropriate	❑ ***"The proposed response is coherent with the dialogue context."***	*Coherence*
		❑ Add free form text explanation	-
	Not Appropriate	❑ ***"The proposed response is not coherent with the dialogue context."***	*Incoherence*
		❑ Add free form text explanation	-
	I don't know	❑ **Please Add free form text explanation (required)**	-
Contextualization	Not Contextualized	❑ ***"The response is generic or does not contain any explicit or implicit reference to what it has been said in the dialogue context."***	*Genericness*
		❑ ***"The response is not consistent with the information contained in the dialogue context."***	*Hallucination*
		❑ Add free form text explanation	-
	I don't know	❑ **Please Add free form text explanation (required)**	-
Correctness	Not Correct	❑ ***"The response contains grammatical errors."***	*Grammaticality*
		❑ ***"The response contains one or more parts that are repetitive."***	*Repetition*
		❑ Add free form text explanation	-
	I don't know	❑ **Please Add free form text explanation (required)**	-

Table 1: The explanation options provided to the annotators to support their decisions. The annotators can select predefined option(s) and/or write a free form text. Each explanation option refers to a sub-dimension which is used as interpretations for the result analysis. The sub-dimensions are not presented to the annotators.

ensure a controlled level of cognitive workload throughout the task and minimize the possibility of misunderstanding or ambiguity for the annotators by using well-explained guidelines, a simplified User Interface, and a clear annotation process.

Guidelines & Examples An important resource in crowd-sourcing annotation tasks is the guidelines, which have the objective to introduce the task to the annotator and instruct them about the process. The task guidelines and the examples must be written with a clear and simple structure in order to minimize possible ambiguities for the annotators and help them form a mental model in line with the one of the task designers. The examples should be carefully selected to point out the possible ambiguities and difficulties during the annotation and to help the workers get familiar with the task. Our task guidelines include an introduction to the task, the definition and description of each criterion and corresponding answer sets, as well as examples of various scenarios and annotations. The complete format of this version of our guidelines can be found on repository.

User Interface We designed and implemented a User Interface (UI) for the task of Human Evaluation, with the objective of an easy-to-use and intuitive platform that is extendable to other versions of the evaluation. A complete description of the UI is presented in Appendix, Section C.

Internal Pilots Internal pilots can provide reliable feedback about the difficulty/subjectivity of the task, the amount of time required to perform the task, and a threshold for the expected output quality of the task if done correctly. Internal pilots also help to detect and resolve possible ambiguity and issues in the task and its materials prior to the main task.

3.2 Step 2: Annotator Recruitment

After designing the task, we need to recruit the required number of annotators to perform the task. In most cases the annotation is done through crowd-sourcing. In that case, there are several aspects involved in the process of recruiting the crowd-workers that can affect the outcome quality including the sampling policy, the qualification, and the compensation.

Sampling In order to obtain reliable results, it is important to recruit the annotators from the correct target group. Selecting the annotators in the literature has been mostly conditioned by prerequisites such as location, language fluency, and level of education. Further, Mousavi et al. (2021) studied the impact of domain expertise in a domain-specific annotation task.

Qualification Karpinska et al. (2021) observed that when the annotators are sampled from workers in crowd-sourcing platforms, sampling conditions are not adequate as they may be fulfilled inappropriately (for instance the use of VPNs to fake a certain location). Therefore, in addition to the mentioned prerequisites, it is essential to set up a qualification task for the workers. The qualification task helps the task designers to filter out contributors with low-quality performance and helps the crowd-workers to get familiar with the main task and the UI.

Compensation Proper compensation is an important extrinsic factor that can affect the performance of crowd workers, and the time it takes for the job to be selected and worked on by the workers (Mason and Suri, 2012; Whiting et al., 2019; Ramírez et al., 2021). Therefore, it is crucial to estimate properly and fairly the time and complexity needed to complete the task and set a fair wage in order to ensure a proper compensation.

3.3 Step 3: Task Execution

The execution of the main task is subject to continuous control of the progress and quality. In this phase, the agreement level among the annotators can indicate whether the outcome quality is maintained throughout the task. Sudden drops or jumps in the agreement level can be due to unbalanced difficulty among batches, or a low-quality contributor. While the former should be addressed using stratified sampling when designing the task, Riccardi et al. (2013) observed that providing real-time feedback to the annotators helps them to recover their mistakes and improve their performance for the upcoming tasks.

3.4 Step 4: Annotation Reporting

Howcroft et al. (2020) highlights the lack of a standard for reporting the description and the results of HE experiments and points out the need for proper reporting of the evaluation details and results analysis. Furthermore, Ramírez et al. (2021) stresses the importance of reporting the crowd-sourcing experiment in a proper and standard way in order to facilitate replicability of the experiment and reproducibility of the results. In this protocol, we provide a checklist of aspects and elements that are necessary to be reported along with the final results in order to ensure a clear and transparent presentation of the protocol and possible outcomes. The characteristics of the task that should be reported are:

- Evaluation granularity (dialogue-level vs. response-level, comparative vs. absolute)
- Quality dimensions, their definitions, and corresponding questions
- Annotation format (item selection, free form text, ranking, rating, etc.)

While the details regarding the recruitment of the crowd-workers include:

- Sampling criteria, the description of qualification task and acceptance\rejection criterion
- Number of workers recruited

Besides the mentioned details, there are certain statistics related to the execution of the evaluation task and its final outcome that should be reported to increase the credibility of the results. These statistics include:

- Annotators participated in the study
- Samples annotated in the study
- Votes per each sample
- Inter-Annotator Agreement level & the metric used
- Workload allocated per annotator
- Demographic of the annotators
- Resource Utilization (time to perform the task, payment to the annotator, crowd-sourcing platform)

4 Validation of the Protocol

We validate the proposed protocol by evaluating two response generation models for the task of personal and grounded response generation. For this purpose, we fine-tuned two of the state-of-the-art Pre-trained Language Models (PLMs) for the Italian language. The first model fine-tuned is iT5 (Sarti and Nissim, 2022), which has the same architecture as T5 PLM (Raffel et al., 2020), pre-trained on a large Italian corpus. We used iT5-Base which consists of 12 layers per stack (encoder or decoder) with 220M parameters. The second model fine-tuned in this work is GePpeTto (De Mattei et al., 2020) which is a decoder-only autoregressive PLM based on GPT-2 small (Radford et al., 2019), for the Italian language. The model consists of 12 layers of decoder and byte-pair encoding, with 117M parameters.

The fine-tuning of the two models was done using the dataset of Follow-Up dialogues collected by Mousavi et al. (2021). This dataset is a collection of dyadic conversations about personal events and emotions the narrator has experienced while the listener tends to respond with personalized and helpful suggestions. The dialogues in this data set are based on a personal narrative about the same event and participant that the narrator has shared prior to the dialogue. We fine-tuned the models with and without grounding the generation on the corresponding narrative for each dialogue via the same approach used by Zhao et al. (2020). In our setting the knowledge selection module is not required since the correct narrative for each dialogue is deterministic.

iT5-Base was fine-tuned using AdaFactor optimizer (Vaswani et al., 2017) and early stopping wait counter equal to 3, with batch size and dialogue history window equal to 4. GePpeTto was fine-tuned using AdamW optimizer (Loshchilov and Hutter, 2017) and early-stopping wait counter equal to 3, with batch size and dialogue history window equal to 2. For fine-tuning the models 80% of the dataset was used, while 10% was used as the validation set for early stopping and parameter engineering and the rest of the data, unseen 10%, was used as the test set (the splits were sampled at dialogue level to ensure no history overlap among splits). The automatic evaluation of fine-tuned models is presented in Table 3.

4.1 Implementation of the HE Protocol

We implemented the proposed protocol to evaluate the performance of the two models by human crowd-workers.

Task Design We followed the Task Design step explained in subsection 3.1 closely. We then sampled 42 different dialogue histories from the fine-tuning test set (approximately 50%) for the evaluation (the length of histories varies from 2 to 4 turns) and sampled the responses of all models for each dialogue. We conducted two internal pilots using 5 dialogues with 3 internal experts (the experts were not involved in the design of the task), as well as 3 internal non-expert annotators. After each pilot, the feedback of both groups was collected and few refinements were made to the UI and the guidelines.

Using the feedback obtained from the internal pilots regarding the difficulty of the task and the amount it takes to annotate the samples, we prepared the annotation batches so that each batch consists of approximately 10 dialogue histories of 4 turns in average, with 3 response candidates (including the ground truth) to evaluate for the next turn. During the internal pilots, each batch of 5 dialogues took an average of 15 minutes for the non-expert annotators. Therefore, we set the average required time to 35 minutes and the maximum time possible to annotate a batch to 90 minutes, in order to factor in the possible lower pace of non-expert annotators.

Recruiting Crowd-worker We used Prolific crowd-sourcing platform[2], and selected the crowd-workers using the following prerequisites:

- **Location**: Italy
- **Gender Distribution**: Available to All
- **First Language**: Italian
- **Minimum Approval rate**: 95%
- **Minimum complete submissions**: 20 jobs
- **Education**: Available to all
- **Expertise**: Available to all

In addition to the sampling policy, the annotators were asked to perform a qualification task. The task consisted of evaluating the response candidates for 5 dialogues (same dialogues used in the internal pilots) in an identical setting to the main task. We considered the Inter-Annotator Agreement (IAA) of the internal non-expert annotators calculated by Fleiss' κ (Fleiss, 1971) as the threshold (0.21). In order to qualify each worker, we computed the agreement level among the internal annotators and the worker and if it was above the threshold, the worker was qualified for the main task.

Based on the workload and the estimated time required for the task, we set the wage as 4.67 pounds for 35 minutes, equal to 8 pounds per hour[3]. In this protocol, qualified crowd-workers were also paid for the qualification task.

4.2 Annotation Statistics

In total, 40 workers participated in the annotation task and 35 of them were qualified. The 42 samples to annotate were distributed in two batches of 11 and two batches of 10 samples. Each batch is annotated by 7 annotators and the annotators spent an average of 19 minutes for the qualification batch and 45 minutes for annotating the main batches. In addition to the decided compensations, one annotator was rewarded a bonus of two pounds since he/she informed us about an unexpected bug in the UI via email.

[2]Prolific: `https://www.prolific.co/`

[3]Prolific's Payment Principles mandates a fair and ethical payment to the workers with the minimum of 6 pounds (8 dollars) per hour. While deploying the study on the platform, the task owner is prompted with recommended payment level for the study, for which our payment of 8 pounds per hour was labelled as "Good".

Models	Inter Annotator Agreement Level measured by Fleiss' κ				
	Appropriateness	*Contextualization*	*Correctness*	*Listening*	IAA per Model
GePpeTto	0.27	0.14	0.64	0.15	0.32±0.10
+Knowledge	0.42	0.22	0.36	0.27	0.36±0.11
iT5-Base	0.24	0.19	0.06	0.18	0.27±0.04
+Knowledge	0.18	0.03	0.30	0.21	0.19±0.06
IAA per Dimension	0.30 ±0.10 Fair	0.15±0.05 Poor	0.41±0.20 Moderate	0.23±0.07 Fair	-

Table 2: The Inter-Annotator Agreement (IAA) level calculated by Fleiss' κ. The last row and last column represent the average IAA (and the standard deviation) per each of the criteria and each model, respectively. The low IAA on *Contextualization* indicates the high level of complexity and subjectivity in this criterion. In contrast, the moderate level of IAA is achieved over *Correctness* criterion, suggesting a lower level of subjectivity in the judgements.

Models	Automatic Evaluation		Human Evaluation			
	nll	*ppl*	Appropriateness	Contextualization	Correctness	Listening
Ground Truth	-	-	100.0%	97.62%	97.62%	97.62%
GePpeTto	2.76	15.84	66.67%	69.05%	83.33%	64.29%
+Knowledge	2.79	16.33	59.52%	57.14%	83.33%	57.14%
iT5-Base	2.05	7.79	66.67%	73.81%	100.0%	66.67%
+Knowledge	2.04	7.70	80.95%	80.95%	85.71%	76.19%

Table 3: The automatic and human evaluation outcome of the fine-tuned models. The results are obtained by majority voting. The evaluations indicate that grounding mostly improves the performance of iT5 Base, while it worsens GePpeTto's performance. Note that the perplexity can not be compared among models since the pre-training data and thus the vocabulary distributions are not identical.

During the execution of the task, we calculated the agreement between each pair of annotators using Cohen's kappa (Cohen, 1960) as well as the agreement among all annotators in the same batch using Fleiss' κ (Fleiss, 1971) metrics. We further calculated the agreement among all annotators on strong judgements, by removing items that were labelled as "I don't know." by at least one annotator. Despite little fluctuations in the agreement level, no low-quality contributions were detected and the agreement level on different batches was consistent throughout the evaluation.

Table 2 presents the average Inter Annotator Agreement (IAA) measured by Fleiss' κ. The agreement is calculated per each model and criterion in each batch (for the 7 annotators who annotated the batch) and averaged over all batches. The results indicate that *Contextualization* and *Listening* are the two criteria with the highest levels of subjectivity and complexity. In contrast, high IAA over *Correctness* suggests that it has been easier for the annotators to assess the grammatical and structural aspects of the response samples.

4.3 Evaluation Results

Table 3 presents the results of the HE based on the majority voting for each model. While the grounding generally improved the performance of iT5-Base, it worsened the performance of GePpeTto in all aspects. Nevertheless, it introduced grammatical and structural errors in iT5-Base output. Moreover, grounding did not improve GePpeTto to generate more contextualized responses. While grounded iT5-Base outputs were evaluated the highest among the models, there is still a huge gap to reach the quality of the ground truth. This matter shows the complexity of generating an appropriate and contextual response in personal dialogues.

Figure 1 represents the sub-dimension errors that the annotators selected to explain their negative votes on the response candidates. The explanation option corresponding to each error is presented in Table 1. The figure is obtained by considering all the votes of the annotators on every response sampled from the models (each response is evaluated by 7 annotators, thus 294 votes in total). Therefore, for instance, while iT5-Base achieves 100% of "*Correctness*" by majority voting, there are 7

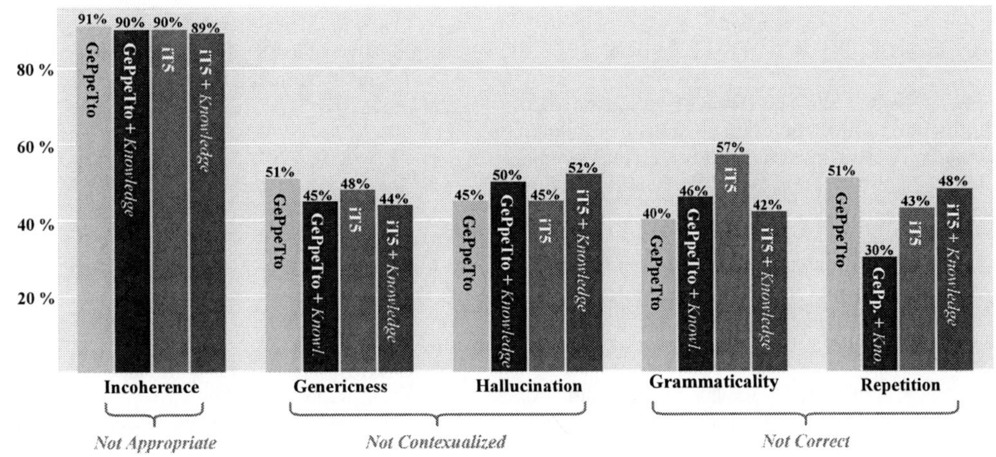

Figure 1: The sub-dimension errors selected by the annotators for the explanation of negative judgements in each criterion. Each bar represents the percentage of the times the error category (x-axis) was selected as the reason to reject the output of the corresponding model. The figure is obtained by considering all the votes (i.e. not majority voting). Note that the labels are not mutually exclusive.

cases (out of 294) where the annotators labelled it as "Not Correct"; the selected reason in 4 cases was grammatical error and in 3 cases a repetition in the response.

These results indicate that, regardless of the model, while grounding reduces the cases that a response is labelled as "*Not Contextualized*" due to being a *Generic* response, it increases the cases of *Hallucination* problem with almost the same proportion. Nevertheless, the percentage of cases where a response is labelled as "*Not Appropriate*" due to being *Incoherent* is not affected by the grounding technique and all models suffer from this error equally. Furthermore, we observe that grounding slightly increases the cases in which a response by GePpeTto is labelled as "*Not Correct*" due to errors related to *Grammaticality*, while it considerably reduces the cases of *Repetition* in such responses.

In addition to the pre-defined explanations, in a few cases the annotators also provided us with free-form explanations. Specifically, in 10% of the cases in which the model outputs were labelled as "*Not Correct*", the annotators provided us further explanations to indicate the exact grammatical error such as punctuation or subjunctive errors (Congiuntivo in Italian). In 5% of the times in which the model responses were considered "*Not Contextualized*" the annotators pointed out the exact part of the response which is mentioning a wrong event/participant, or is in contradiction to the dialogue history. Lastly, in 10% of the cases where the response candidate was evaluated as "*Not Appropriate*" the annotators provided explanations to highlight the exact segment of the response that is not right or is ambiguous.

5 Conclusion

While Human Evaluation is the necessary methodological step in the assessment of response generation models, there is a lack of a standard. This deficiency has resulted in often ambiguous, incomparable and non-replicable published experiments. In this work, we aim at addressing this problem by sharing a complete methodology for evaluating generated responses using human judges. We publish the first version of the protocol and all its materials to the community. The expectation is to engage them to utilize, extend, and complement this protocol into further versions and a transparent resource that can be publicly accessed. The ultimate goal is to engage the community to consider HE as an important topic of research. The complete protocol and supporting materials can be found in a public repository (including the guidelines, task design, the UI, and the analysis scripts).

References

Satanjeev Banerjee and Alon Lavie. 2005. Meteor: An automatic metric for mt evaluation with improved correlation with human judgments. In *Proceedings of the acl workshop on intrinsic and extrinsic evaluation measures for machine translation and/or summarization*, pages 65–72.

Anya Belz, Simon Mille, and David M. Howcroft. 2020. Disentangling the properties of human evaluation methods: A classification system to support comparability, meta-evaluation and reproducibility testing. In *INLG*.

José Coch. 1996. Evaluating and comparing three text-production techniques. In *COLING 1996 Volume 1: The 16th International Conference on Computational Linguistics*.

Jacob Cohen. 1960. A coefficient of agreement for nominal scales. *Educational and Psychological Measurement*, 20:37 – 46.

Lorenzo De Mattei, Michele Cafagna, Felice Dell'Orletta, Malvina Nissim, and Marco Guerini. 2020. Geppetto carves italian into a language model. *arXiv preprint arXiv:2004.14253*.

Joseph L Fleiss. 1971. Measuring nominal scale agreement among many raters. *Psychological bulletin*, 76(5):378.

Behnam Hedayatnia, Karthik Gopalakrishnan, Seokhwan Kim, Yang Liu, Mihail Eric, and Dilek Hakkani-Tur. 2020. Policy-driven neural response generation for knowledge-grounded dialog systems. In *Proceedings of the 13th International Conference on Natural Language Generation*, pages 412–421.

David M. Howcroft, Anya Belz, Miruna Clinciu, Dimitra Gkatzia, Sadid A. Hasan, Saad Mahamood, Simon Mille, Emiel van Miltenburg, Sashank Santhanam, and Verena Rieser. 2020. Twenty years of confusion in human evaluation: Nlg needs evaluation sheets and standardised definitions. In *INLG*.

Lishan Huang, Zheng Ye, Jinghui Qin, Liang Lin, and Xiaodan Liang. 2020. Grade: Automatic graph-enhanced coherence metric for evaluating open-domain dialogue systems. In *Proceedings of the 2020 Conference on Empirical Methods in Natural Language Processing (EMNLP)*, pages 9230–9240.

Xinxian Huang, Huang He, Siqi Bao, Fan Wang, Hua Wu, and Haifeng Wang. 2021. Plato-kag: Unsupervised knowledge-grounded conversation via joint modeling. In *Proceedings of the 3rd Workshop on Natural Language Processing for Conversational AI*, pages 143–154.

Karen Sparck Jones and Julia R Galliers. 1995. Evaluating natural language processing systems: An analysis and review.

Marzena Karpinska, Nader Akoury, and Mohit Iyyer. 2021. The perils of using mechanical turk to evaluate open-ended text generation. In *Proceedings of the 2021 Conference on Empirical Methods in Natural Language Processing*, pages 1265–1285.

James Lester and Bruce Porter. 1997. Developing and empirically evaluating robust explanation generators: The knight experiments. *Computational Linguistics*, 23(1):65–101.

Nancy G Leveson. 2016. *Engineering a safer world: Systems thinking applied to safety*. The MIT Press.

Chin-Yew Lin. 2004. Rouge: A package for automatic evaluation of summaries. In *Text summarization branches out*, pages 74–81.

Chia-Wei Liu, Ryan Lowe, Iulian Vlad Serban, Mike Noseworthy, Laurent Charlin, and Joelle Pineau. 2016. How not to evaluate your dialogue system: An empirical study of unsupervised evaluation metrics for dialogue response generation. In *Proceedings of the 2016 Conference on Empirical Methods in Natural Language Processing*, pages 2122–2132.

Ilya Loshchilov and Frank Hutter. 2017. Decoupled weight decay regularization. *arXiv preprint arXiv:1711.05101*.

Winter Mason and Siddharth Suri. 2012. Conducting behavioral research on amazon's mechanical turk. *Behavior research methods*, 44(1):1–23.

Shikib Mehri and Maxine Eskenazi. 2020. Usr: An unsupervised and reference free evaluation metric for dialog generation. In *Proceedings of the 58th Annual Meeting of the Association for Computational Linguistics*, pages 681–707.

Neville Moray. 1998. Identifying mental models of complex human–machine systems. *International Journal of Industrial Ergonomics*, 22(4-5):293–297.

Seyed Mahed Mousavi, Alessandra Cervone, Morena Danieli, and Giuseppe Riccardi. 2021. Would you like to tell me more? generating a corpus of psychotherapy dialogues. In *Proceedings of the Second Workshop on Natural Language Processing for Medical Conversations*, pages 1–9.

Donald A Norman. 1988. *The psychology of everyday things*. Basic books.

Kishore Papineni, Salim Roukos, Todd Ward, and Wei-Jing Zhu. 2002. Bleu: a method for automatic evaluation of machine translation. In *Proceedings of the 40th annual meeting of the Association for Computational Linguistics*, pages 311–318.

Alec Radford, Jeffrey Wu, Rewon Child, David Luan, Dario Amodei, Ilya Sutskever, et al. 2019. Language models are unsupervised multitask learners. *OpenAI blog*, 1(8):9.

Colin Raffel, Noam Shazeer, Adam Roberts, Katherine Lee, Sharan Narang, Michael Matena, Yanqi Zhou, Wei Li, Peter J Liu, et al. 2020. Exploring the limits of transfer learning with a unified text-to-text transformer. *J. Mach. Learn. Res.*, 21(140):1–67.

Jorge Ramírez, Burcu Sayin, Marcos Baez, Fabio Casati, Luca Cernuzzi, Boualem Benatallah, and Gianluca Demartini. 2021. On the state of reporting in crowdsourcing experiments and a checklist to aid current practices. *Proceedings of the ACM on Human-Computer Interaction*, 5(CSCW2):1–34.

Giuseppe Riccardi, Arindam Ghosh, SA Chowdhury, and Ali Orkan Bayer. 2013. Motivational feedback in crowdsourcing: a case study in speech transcription. In *INTERSPEECH*, pages 1111–1115.

Ananya B Sai, Akash Kumar Mohankumar, and Mitesh M Khapra. 2022. A survey of evaluation metrics used for nlg systems. *ACM Computing Surveys (CSUR)*, 55(2):1–39.

Gabriele Sarti and Malvina Nissim. 2022. It5: Large-scale text-to-text pretraining for italian language understanding and generation. *arXiv preprint arXiv:2203.03759*.

Eric Smith, Orion Hsu, Rebecca Qian, Stephen Roller, Y-Lan Boureau, and Jason Weston. 2022. Human evaluation of conversations is an open problem: comparing the sensitivity of various methods for evaluating dialogue agents. In *Proceedings of the 4th Workshop on NLP for Conversational AI*, pages 77–97.

Ashish Vaswani, Noam Shazeer, Niki Parmar, Jakob Uszkoreit, Llion Jones, Aidan N Gomez, Łukasz Kaiser, and Illia Polosukhin. 2017. Attention is all you need. *Advances in neural information processing systems*, 30.

Marilyn A Walker, Diane J Litman, Candace A Kamm, and Alicia Abella. 1997. Paradise: A framework for evaluating spoken dialogue agents. *arXiv preprint cmp-lg/9704004*.

Yanmeng Wang, Wenge Rong, Jianfei Zhang, Yuanxin Ouyang, and Zhang Xiong. 2020. Knowledge grounded pre-trained model for dialogue response generation. In *2020 International Joint Conference on Neural Networks (IJCNN)*, pages 1–8. IEEE.

Mark E Whiting, Grant Hugh, and Michael S Bernstein. 2019. Fair work: Crowd work minimum wage with one line of code. In *Proceedings of the AAAI Conference on Human Computation and Crowdsourcing*, volume 7, pages 197–206.

Bingjun Xie, Jia Zhou, and Huilin Wang. 2017. How influential are mental models on interaction performance? exploring the gap between users' and designers' mental models through a new quantitative method. *Advances in Human-Computer Interaction*, 2017.

Marco A Zenati, Lauren Kennedy-Metz, and Roger D Dias. 2020. Cognitive engineering to improve patient safety and outcomes in cardiothoracic surgery. In *Seminars in thoracic and cardiovascular surgery*, volume 32, pages 1–7. Elsevier.

Tianyi Zhang, Varsha Kishore, Felix Wu, Kilian Q Weinberger, and Yoav Artzi. 2019. Bertscore: Evaluating text generation with bert. *arXiv preprint arXiv:1904.09675*.

Yizhe Zhang, Siqi Sun, Michel Galley, Yen-Chun Chen, Chris Brockett, Xiang Gao, Jianfeng Gao, Jingjing Liu, and William B Dolan. 2020. Dialogpt: Large-scale generative pre-training for conversational response generation. In *Proceedings of the 58th Annual Meeting of the Association for Computational Linguistics: System Demonstrations*, pages 270–278.

Xueliang Zhao, Wei Wu, Can Xu, Chongyang Tao, Dongyan Zhao, and Rui Yan. 2020. Knowledge-grounded dialogue generation with pre-trained language models. In *Proceedings of the 2020 Conference on Empirical Methods in Natural Language Processing (EMNLP)*, pages 3377–3390, Online. Association for Computational Linguistics.

Appendix

A Questions

Dimension	Question	Answer Option	Option Definition
Appropriateness	*Is the proposed response candidate appropriate?*	Appropriate	The response makes sense and it can be the natural continuation of the shown dialogue context.
		Not Appropriate	The response does not make sense in the current dialogue context.
		I don't know	The candidate contains some elements which make sense with respect to the dialogue context, but some that do not.
Contextualization	*Does the proposed response contain references to the context of the dialogue?*	Contextualized	The candidate contains implicit or explicit references to the dialogue context.
		Not Contextualized	The candidate doesn't contain any reference to the dialogue context, or contains references that are incoherent with the dialogue context.
		I don't know	The response contains some references to the dialogue context, but contains other references that are not clear or relevant.
Listening	*In the proposed response candidate, how much do you think person A is listening to person B?*	Listening	Speaker A is listening with attention to speaker B and follows the dialogue.
		Not Listening	Speaker A seems not to pay attention to what speaker B is saying.
		I don't know	It is unclear if speaker A is listening to speaker B or not.
Correctness	*Is the proposed response grammatically correct?*	Correct	The response does not contain any type of grammatical or structural error, any repetitions, misspellings or any other types of error.
		Not Correct	The response contains some grammatical or structural errors such as, repetitions, misspelling, any other types of error.
		I don't know	It is hard to identify if the response contains errors or not.

Table 4: The questions and possible answer options presented to the annotators for the evaluation of the response candidates in this version of the protocol. The complete version of the option definitions is presented to the annotators in the guidelines.

B Model Response Evaluation

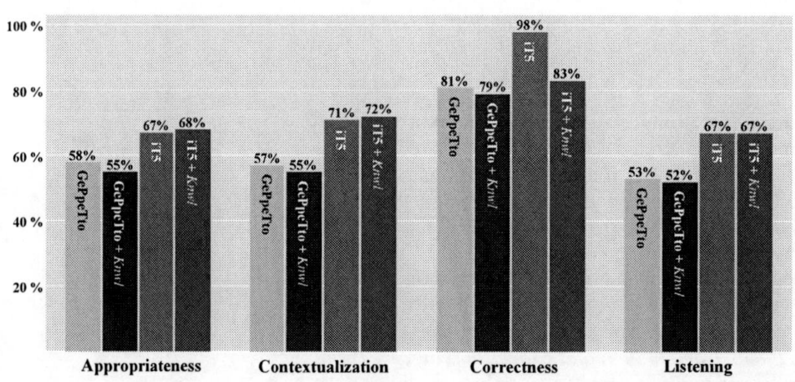

Figure 2: The human evaluation of the models in each criterion by considering all the votes (i.e. not majority voting). Each bar represents the percentage of the times the corresponding model was labelled positively by the criterion on x-axis. While Table 3 is obtained by majority voting, this figure is obtained by considering all the annotators votes on the response samples (i.e. not majority voting). iT5-Base variations outperform GePpeTto variations, regardless of the presence of grounding.

C User Interface

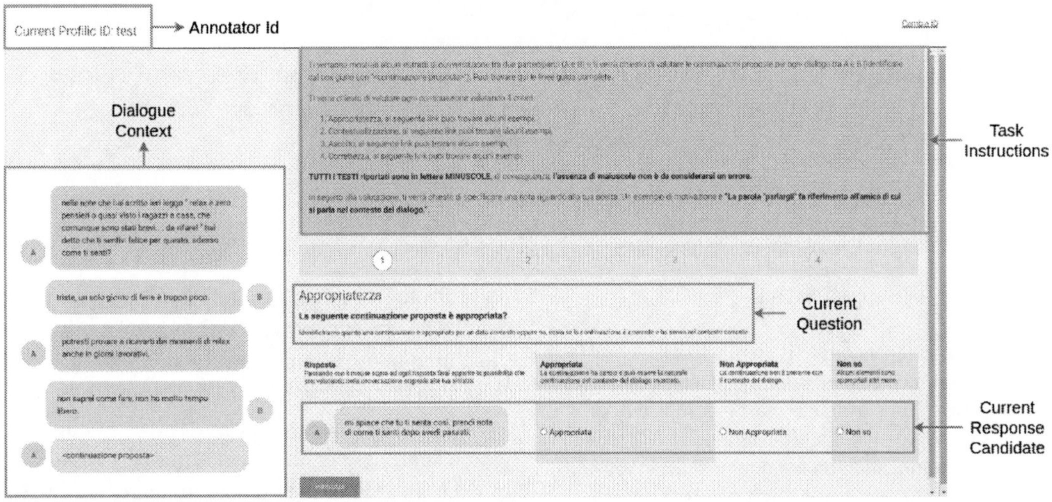

Figure 3: Throughout the task, a short version of the guidelines is always presented to the annotator with the possibility to access the complete version via hyperlinks. During the evaluation, the corresponding dialogue context is shown to the annotator on the left, while the criterion question and the proposed response candidate are presented on the right, along with the name of the dimension, the definition of the dimension, and the possible decision values and their definitions. In order to reduce the cognitive workload of the annotators, all candidates for a specific dialogue context are evaluated one by one for the same criterion after one another (i.e. the annotator evaluates all the candidates of the presented dialogue history for criterion A, and then all the same candidates regarding criterion B). In this way, the left side of the UI (dialogue history) remains unchanged so that the annotator does not have to go through the dialogue history several times, and focuses on each evaluation metric per sets of response candidate.

Enhancing and Evaluating the Grammatical Framework Approach to Logic-to-Text Generation

Eduardo Calò[*] and **Elze van der Werf**[*] and **Albert Gatt** and **Kees van Deemter**
Department of Information and Computing Sciences
Utrecht University
Utrecht, the Netherlands
{e.calo, a.gatt, c.j.vandeemter}@uu.nl elzevanderwerf@gmail.com

Abstract

Logic-to-text generation is an important yet underrepresented area of natural language generation (NLG). In particular, most previous works on this topic lack sound evaluation. We address this limitation by building and evaluating a system that generates high-quality English text given a first-order logic (FOL) formula as input. We start by analyzing the performance of Ranta (2011)'s system. Based on this analysis, we develop an extended version of the system, which we name LoLA, that performs formula simplification based on logical equivalences and syntactic transformations. We carry out an extensive evaluation of LoLA using standard automatic metrics and human evaluation. We compare the results against a baseline and Ranta (2011)'s system. The results show that LoLA outperforms the other two systems in most aspects.

https://gitlab.nl4xai.eu/eduardo.calo/LoLa

1 Introduction

Logical formalisms play a pivotal role in many areas of science. Hence, grasping the meaning of these formalisms is crucial for many scholars and researchers. However, this task is not straightforward, and sometimes even experienced logicians might have trouble deciphering a complex formula.

Natural language generation (NLG) techniques can be employed to ease this task. However, logic-to-text generation is understudied, compared to text generation from other inputs (Reiter and Dale, 2000; Gatt and Krahmer, 2018). One notable exception (see §2 for some other examples) is Ranta (2011), a rule-based system that translates between first-order logic (FOL) formulae and natural language (NL). While providing a promising starting point for logic-to-text generation, the system is not evaluated. In our work, we first address this gap via a human translation quality assessment (TQA). Based on this, we propose LoLA, a novel logic-to-text system extending Ranta (2011)'s architecture, which searches for the most suitable formula for translation among the pool of logically equivalent formulae.

We also address one of the many issues that make NLG evaluation challenging (Novikova et al., 2017; Zhou et al., 2022), namely, defining the core dimensions to evaluate (Howcroft et al., 2020), especially issues of meaning vs. grammaticality. These issues come to the fore in logic-to-text generation, where text should be faithful to the original formula, comprehensible, and fluent. These are the central requirements to look for, as text generated from logic can be extremely disfluent and incomprehensible (e.g., a literal translation from a formula), while still being faithful. Furthermore, evaluating faithfulness cannot rely on checking factual accuracy (as in, e.g., WebNLG (Gardent et al., 2017)), due to the problem of *logical form equivalence* (Shieber, 1993), which implies that every formula of FOL is equivalent with infinitely many other FOL formulae, where the question of whether two FOL formulae are logically equivalent is, in general, undecidable. This complicates the problem of finding a formula that is most suitable for being input to an NLG program.

There are also potential trade-offs between evaluation dimensions. For instance, more fluent realizations may sometimes be more ambiguous with respect to a formula, compromising faithfulness (Khan et al., 2012). To use a well-worn example, *Everyone loves someone* can be seen as a correct realization of $\forall x(Person(x) \rightarrow \exists y(Person(y) \wedge Love(x, y)))$, but the sentence is ambiguous, also allowing for the more specific interpretation that there exists someone who is loved by everyone (i.e., with the scope of the quantifiers reversed).

*These authors contributed equally to this work.

Proceedings of the 2nd Workshop on Natural Language Generation, Evaluation, and Metrics (GEM), pages 148 - 171
December 7, 2022 ©2022 Association for Computational Linguistics

In our work, we use a deterministic procedure for generating text from formulae, allowing us to hold faithfulness constant in order to address issues of comprehensibility and fluency.

Our work also addresses the question of which human evaluation task is appropriate for a given system (Gehrmann et al., 2022), proposing a novel evaluation using natural language inference (NLI; Storks et al., 2019; Poliak, 2020).

In outline, the main contributions of this paper are the following:

i) We analyze the quality of the translations of the FOL-to-text system presented in Ranta (2011) via a human translation quality assessment.
ii) We exploit the outcomes of the quality assessment to develop the improved system LoLA.
iii) We present the results of a comprehensive automatic and human evaluation of LoLA.

2 Related Work

Although receiving far less attention than other tasks, generating NL text from (logically rich) meaning representation (MR) formalisms has a relatively long tradition in NLG, with approaches ranging from rule-based (Wang, 1980; Appelt, 1987; Shieber et al., 1990) to statistical (Lu and Ng, 2011; Basile, 2015) and neural models (Wu et al., 2022).

Several MRs have been the focus of the task: logic-based (e.g., description logic (Androutsopoulos et al., 2013), FOL (Mpagouli and Hatzilygeroudis, 2007), and discourse representation structures (Liu et al., 2021; Wang et al., 2021)), graph-based (e.g., Abstract Meaning Representation (AMR; Konstas et al., 2017; Bai et al., 2022, *i.a.*)), and formal languages (e.g., SPARQL (Ngonga Ngomo et al., 2013; Ell et al., 2015)).

Some of these MR formalisms are much simpler than FOL. For example, AMR has less descriptive power (Bos, 2016), whereas datasets such as GEOQUERY (Zelle and Mooney, 1996) and ROBOCUP (Chen and Mooney, 2008), used in, e.g., Wong and Mooney (2007), omit logical operators and variable binding. For these reasons, we select FOL as our formalism, incorporating different types of formulae and defining a concept of *well-behavedness* (see §4.2) to characterize those best suited for logic-to-text translation.

Apart from Ranta (2011), closest to our work are the following approaches. Phillips (1993) considers the problem of logical form equivalence. Mpagouli and Hatzilygeroudis (2009) present a rule-based approach to generate text from FOL with some syntactic optimizations. Coppock and Baxter (2010) propose an algorithm based on dynamic semantics for a specific class of formulae. Kutlak and van Deemter (2015) use background axioms to simplify a FOL formula. Flickinger (2016) generates multiple paraphrases from an input formula. Manome et al. (2018) is one of the few logic-to-text approaches using a sequence-to-sequence framework. Kasenberg et al. (2019) generate explanations from a well-defined logical formalism in the context of human-robot dialogue.

A common thread in most of this work is the absence of (proper) evaluations. In particular, as in Ranta (2011), the proposals in Phillips (1993), Mpagouli and Hatzilygeroudis (2009), Coppock and Baxter (2010), and Kutlak and van Deemter (2015) do not include any attempt at systematic evaluations. In Flickinger (2016), there is a mention of a very preliminary inspection of the paraphrases generated, with pointers for improving the evaluation left for future work. Manome et al. (2018) make an effort to move beyond standard metrics proposing an automatic evaluation based on recognizing textual entailment and present an informal analysis of some generated sentences. However, a proper human evaluation is missing. Kasenberg et al. (2019) do not evaluate their system using automatic metrics. Yet, they perform a human evaluation based on three dimensions and statistically analyze the results. We aim to build a system that, given a logical formula, will produce *effective* texts (i.e., optimally helpful to the needs of the user) (Mayn and van Deemter, 2020), thus, carrying out proper evaluations is one of the main focuses of our work.

3 Model and Data

Ranta (2011) We consider the logic-to-text generation system presented in Ranta (2011)[1] as the starting point for our experiments. The system translates a string from one language into another in two steps: (i) the string in the source language is parsed into an abstract syntax tree (AST), and (ii) the AST is linearized into a string in the target language via language-specific concrete syntax.

The abstract syntax defines functions for several logical constructs, while concrete syntaxes are for-

[1]https://github.com/GrammaticalFramework/gf-contrib/tree/master/cade-2011

mulated to generate FOL linearizations in six NLs. In addition to this, the system performs some *core-to-extended* AST manipulations (e.g., flattening, aggregation, in-situ quantification, verb negation, and reflexivization) to improve fluency. Figure 3 in Appendix A shows a graphical visualization of Ranta (2011)'s system. The system can parse all well-formed FOL formulae without identity (Shapiro and Kouri Kissel, 2021), containing unary and binary predicates and bound variables.

Grade Grinder Corpus The Grade Grinder Corpus (GGC; Barker-Plummer et al., 2011) is a corpus of $> 4.5m$ FOL translations (correct and incorrect) of ca. 300 sentences made by $55k$ students answering exercises in Barwise et al. (2000). Each NL sentence can have multiple (logically equivalent) correct answers.

We select just the portion of answers that are marked as correct and filter the formulae that are not parsable by Ranta (2011)'s system (i.e., formulae with time stamps, mathematical operators, $3-$ and $4-$ary predicates, the identity symbol, and more than 100 characters). This yields around $5,500$ formulae.

Random Generator In GGC, formulae are understandable by humans and have corresponding sentences that are semantically and pragmatically acceptable. However, it might not be representative of the space of all possible formulae. Therefore, we additionally create a tool that generates a random FOL formula in the space of all possible formulae for a given domain lexicon.

4 Assessing Ranta (2011)

To judge the quality of Ranta (2011)'s translation system, we set up a translation quality assessment (TQA; Castilho et al., 2018; Han et al., 2021). A group of human evaluators was asked to analyze a list of English translations from FOL formulae, generated by Ranta (2011)'s system. Specifically, we were interested in receiving feedback on three dimensions: (i) **faithfulness** (i.e., whether the generated text conveys all and only the information of the input formula), (ii) **comprehensibility** (i.e., whether the generated text is clearly understandable by the evaluator), and (iii) **fluency** (i.e., whether the generated text is grammatically accurate and natural-sounding). The evaluation dimensions, especially faithfulness and comprehensibility, are not entirely independent of each other. Nonetheless, they possess their own traits that we wanted to assess separately. A problematic point is establishing faithfulness to an underlying formula in presence of an ambiguous or incomprehensible sentence. To mitigate this problem, in the NLI task introduced for the human evaluation (see §6.2), we gave participants the opportunity to signal text that is ambiguous or incomprehensible.

A total of 10 participants (master students, 4 males and 6 females, with a median age of 24.0 years, SD $= 1.2$) with sufficient knowledge of logic and proficiency in English[2] voluntarily participated in the study.

Setup Evaluators were shown batches of 25 formula-translation pairs consisting of (i) a random selection of 10 formulae extracted from the parsable portion of the GGC corpus and their Ranta (2011)'s translations, (ii) 10 randomly generated formulae and their Ranta (2011)'s translations, and (iii) 5 filler formulae with incorrect translations created manually. All participants saw the same 5 filler items. The purpose of the fillers was to verify the participants' knowledge of FOL. Were at least 2 out of 5 filler items not identified as such by a participant, their survey response would be ignored entirely in the analysis. None of the participants was omitted by this criterion. See Appendix G for details on the construction of the fillers and Table 13 for the complete list.

To ensure coverage, each participant was presented with a different batch of experimental items.[3] They were required to judge formula-translation pairs under the three dimensions mentioned above. In particular, for each pair, they had to answer a polar question on the translation's faithfulness with the original formula, and rate on a $5-$point Likert scale the translation's comprehensibility and fluency. Moreover, the evaluators were asked to perform *full post-editing* (Hu and Cadwell, 2016) on the translations. The instructions given, the questions asked, and one example batch of experimental items can be found in Appendix G.

[2]The participants involved were students of a MSc in artificial intelligence taught in English, which requires knowledge of logic (in particular, propositional logic and FOL) and proficiency in English for enrolling. Moreover, at the beginning of the questionnaire, participants were required to rate their own knowledge of FOL on a $5-$point Likert scale.

[3]Presenting different batches to each subject prevented us from computing some quantitative analyses, such as inter-annotator agreement. However, the main goal of the TQA was to perform a qualitative study of the system performance and get a more thorough overview of the quality of the translations.

4.1 TQA Results

Evaluators marked 91% of Ranta (2011)'s translations as faithful to the original formula. Most of the translations marked as unfaithful consisted of filler translations. The few non-filler translations that were marked incorrectly were ambiguous and misunderstood by the participants. Thus, we can safely assume that Ranta (2011)'s system, due to its deterministic nature, is robust enough in correctly parsing the structure of the input formula, producing faithful translations.

The average rating of the translations was 3.99 (SD $= 1.10$) for comprehensibility and 3.26 (SD $= 1.32$) for fluency. Interestingly, we found that the average faithfulness, comprehensibility, and fluency of the translations from randomly generated formulae are lower than those of the translations from the GGC formulae, as shown in Table 1. We observed a moderate positive correlation (using Pearson's r coefficient) between the comprehensibility and fluency of the (non-filler) translations ($r(198) = 0.60$, $p < .01$). Furthermore, we found a weak negative correlation between formula complexity (in number of connectives, i.e., a formula with more connectives is more complex) and comprehensibility of the corresponding translations ($r(198) = -0.18$, $p < .01$) and a weak negative correlation between formula complexity and fluency of the corresponding translations ($r(198) = -0.24$, $p < .01$). We also observed weak negative correlations between translation length (in number of words) and comprehensibility ($r(198) = -0.23$, $p < .01$), as well as between translation length and fluency ($r(198) = -0.34$, $p < .01$).

Type	#	Faithfulness	Comprehensibility		Fluency	
			μ	σ	μ	σ
GGC	100	93%	4.10	1.02	3.37	1.34
RG	100	88%	3.87	1.15	3.15	1.29

Table 1: The percentage of translations marked as faithful, and the mean (μ) and standard deviation (σ) of the comprehensibility and fluency of translations on a scale of 1 to 5, reported for corpus formulae (GGC) vs. randomly generated formulae (RG).

Post-Edits Post-edits were suggested for 51% of Ranta (2011)'s translations and are often shorter (in word count) than the original translations. The edits can be roughly divided into three categories: (i) syntactic optimizations similar to the *core-to-extended* AST manipulations introduced in Ranta (2011) (see §3), (ii) conversions based on logical equivalences, and (iii) paraphrases using a variety of linguistic constructions. Table 2, Table 3, and Table 9 respectively show some examples for each of the three categories. See Appendix D for a detailed description of these categories.

4.2 Well-Behavedness

Ranta (2011)'s system accepts as input all well-formed FOL formulae (see §3). However, the TQA results suggest that it might be practical to narrow down the definition of formulae suitable for translation to a more restricted subset. The set of well-formed formulae also includes formulae which the participants in the TQA had difficulties with or provided post-edit suggestions for, i.e., formulae with vacuous quantification (e.g., $(\forall x)Even(2)$ or $(\forall x)(\forall x)Even(x)$), formulae with double negation (e.g., $\neg\neg Even(2)$), formulae with nested implication (e.g., $(Odd(1) \to (Odd(3)) \to Odd(5))$, and formulae with 8 or more connectives. Translating literally such formulae could result in incomprehensible and disfluent sentences.

Therefore, we operationalize *well-behavedness* as 'the property that a formula should have to be structurally suitable as input for translation into NL'. Well-behavedness is achieved by applying a number of rules to avoid formulae with certain properties, such as double negation and vacuous quantification. The formal definition is present in Appendix B. Formulae that are not well-behaved will be referred to as *ill-behaved*.

5 LoLA

Based on the post-edits we received in the TQA described in §4, we developed LoLA (system for translating between **Lo**gic and **La**nguage), a new logic-to-text system that keeps Ranta (2011)'s original system as its backbone but improves it by extending its algorithm. In particular, LoLA implements the first two categories of post-edits derived from the results of the TQA, i.e., *core-to-extended* AST-like manipulations and logic-based simplification, leaving out the third one (stylistic paraphrases) for future work.

The first class of improvements extends the list of Ranta (2011)'s *core-to-extended* AST conversions with some additional optimizations. See Appendix C for details on their implementation. The second class of improvements manipulates an input FOL formula through the application of logical equivalence laws, based on Partee et al. (1993),

Optimization	Original Formula	Ranta (2011) Translation	Post-Edit
Moving the negation inward	$\neg(\exists x)FrontOf(x, a)$	*It is not the case that there is an element **x** such that **x** is in front of **a**.*	*There is no element in front of **a**.*
In-situ quantification	$(\exists x)Small(x)$	*There is an element **x** such that **x** is small.*	*Something is small.*
Predicate-sharing aggregation	$Larger(d, b) \wedge Larger(e, b) \wedge FrontOf(b, e) \wedge FrontOf(b, d)$	***d** is larger than **b**, **e** is larger than **b**, **b** is in front of **e** and **b** is in front of **d**.*	*Both **d** and **e** are larger than **b**, and **b** is in front of both **e** and **d**.*
Reflexivization	$\neg SameShape(a, a)$	***a** is not of the same shape as **a**.*	***a** does not have the same shape as itself.*

Table 2: Optimizations similar to Ranta (2011) *core-to-extended* AST manipulations suggested in the post-edits of the TQA, with the original formulae and Ranta (2011) translations.

Equivalence Law	Original Formula	Ranta (2011) Translation	Post-Edit
Double negation	$\neg\neg(Medium(a) \vee FrontOf(a, b))$	*It is not the case that it is not the case that **a** is medium or in front of **b**.*	***a** is medium or in front of **b**.*
Redundant information	$\neg SameCol(e, d) \wedge \neg SameCol(e, c) \wedge \neg SameCol(e, d)$	***e** is not in the same column as **d**, **e** is not in the same column as **c** and **e** is not in the same column as **d**.*	***e** is neither in the same column as **d**, nor in the same column as **c**.*
De Morgan's laws	$\neg(Tet(b) \vee Tet(d))$	*It is not the case that **b** is a tetrahedron or **d** is a tetrahedron.*	*Neither **b** nor **d** is a tetrahedron.*
Simplification of $\neg(\exists x)\phi$ to $(\forall x)\neg\phi$	$\neg(\exists y)SameCol(a, y)$	*It is not the case that there is an element **y** such that **a** is in the same column as **y**.*	*All **y**'s are not in the same column as **a**.*

Table 3: Optimizations based on logical equivalence laws suggested in the post-edits of the TQA, with the original formulae and Ranta (2011) translations.

with two additional laws to deal with vacuous quantification. See Table 8 for the list of laws.

The search for the optimal translation is performed as follows. A tree of possible formula manipulations is constructed, with as root node the input formula's AST, and where each node's children are manipulations of the AST that result in a different AST. This tree has a maximum depth because in many cases there are infinitely many manipulations. The maximum depth was experimentally set to 5. After the construction of the search tree, all ASTs in the tree are optimized with the full list of *core-to-extended* AST conversions and linearized, after which the shortest linearization in the tree is returned. The results of the TQA (see §4.1) show that there is a weak negative correlation ($r(198) = -0.23$) between translation length and its assessed comprehensibility but a somewhat stronger negative correlation ($r(198) = -0.34$) between translation length and its assessed fluency. Therefore, we decided to pick the length of the translation (in number of words) as the selection criterion.[4] Figure 4 in Appendix C shows an example of a search tree of formula manipulation sequences.

6 Evaluation

To assess the quality of FOL to NL translations of LoLA, we set up a thorough comparative evaluation experiment. We compared the translation quality of three different systems: (i) a BASELINE generating near-literal translations of formulae, which is Ranta (2011)'s system without its *core-to-extended* AST optimizations, (ii) Ranta (2011), and (iii) LoLA. We run standard automatic NLG metrics based on $n-$gram overlap and semantic similarity, conduct a human evaluation, and compute correlations between the results. The dimensions on which the translation quality of the systems was evaluated are **comprehensibility** and **fluency**.[5] The evaluation also partly focused on well-behaved vs. ill-behaved formulae (see §4.2), investigating how different types of formulae impact the quality of the translations.

6.1 Automatic Evaluation

For the automatic evaluation, we considered all the formulae included in the parsable portion of the GGC (see §3) with their associated ground truth NL references. Each formula was given as input to the three systems to be translated into English.[6] We then compared the realizations of the three systems with the ground truth references. We used seven automatic metrics, three of which are based on $n-$gram overlap, namely, BLEU (Papineni et al., 2002),[7] METEOR (Banerjee and Lavie, 2005), and ROUGE-L (Lin, 2004), two on ELMo embeddings (Peters et al., 2018), namely, Word Mover's Distance (WMD; Kusner et al., 2015)[8] and Sentence Mover's Similarity (SMS; Clark et al., 2019),[9] and two on BERT (Devlin et al., 2019), namely, BERTScore (Zhang et al., 2020),[10] and SBERT (Reimers and Gurevych, 2019).[11] For BERTScore, METEOR, ROUGE-L, and SacreBLEU, we used the implementations provided by Hugging Face (Wolf

[4] If there are multiple shortest linearizations, the first occurrence encountered in a depth-first traversal is chosen.

[5] In contrast to the TQA (see §4), faithfulness was not considered one of the evaluation dimensions because the results of the TQA show that the translations of Ranta (2011) are always faithful. This also holds for BASELINE (since the extended syntax constructs are inherently equivalent to their core syntax counterparts), and remains true for LoLA (since the formula simplifications are based precisely on the laws of logical equivalence).

[6] See Table 10 in Appendix E for some examples.

[7] We used the SacreBLEU (Post, 2018) implementation for improved reproducibility.

[8] `https://github.com/src-d/wmd-relax`

[9] `https://github.com/eaclark07/sms`

[10] We used the model `roberta-large_L17_no-idf`.

[11] We computed cosine similarity after obtaining sentence embeddings with the model `all-distilroberta-v1`.

et al., 2020).[12] Table 4 summarizes the results obtained.

System	$n-$gram-based Metrics			Semantics-based Metrics			
	METEOR	ROUGE-L	SacreBLEU	BERTScore	SBERT	SMS	WMD
BASELINE	46.66	31.46	9.69	88.10	72.18	6.30	1.19
Ranta (2011)	50.10	36.54	11.70	89.00	72.93	23.68	14.69
LOLA	**53.87**	**45.01**	**17.27**	**90.77**	**77.89**	**54.11**	**38.92**

Table 4: Performance of the three systems against the GGC ground truth references according to the automatic metrics. All scores are reported on the same scale to improve readability.

LOLA outperforms the other two systems on all metrics. However, in the context of logic-to-text generation, the results of metrics based on $n-$gram overlap vs. metrics based on semantic similarity should be interpreted differently. The texts that we are comparing (i.e., GGC ground truth references and texts generated by the three systems) differ considerably in their structural realization, while keeping the same underlying meaning (i.e., they are paraphrases). This is due to the fact that the GGC ground truth references explain the logical formulae, which, in turn, are given as input to the three systems that operate in deterministic ways, ensuring faithfulness of the output texts. Therefore, we expect the results of metrics based on semantic similarity to be comparable across the three systems. On the contrary, we should notice more variance with metrics based on $n-$gram overlap, since they are more reliant on the surface structure of the texts.

Nevertheless, BERTScore is the only semantics-based metric that is close to following the expected behavior. This might be an additional indication that neural language models are not capable yet to capture deep semantics of NLs, but are still biased towards morphosyntactic realizations (Bender and Koller, 2020). On the other hand, we can observe substantial variance in the results involving $n-$gram-based metrics. All these metrics favor LOLA, which apparently creates texts structurally closer to the original GGC ground truth references.

6.2 Human Evaluation

The human evaluation consisted of two tasks: (i) a natural language inference (NLI) task to assess the comprehensibility of the translations and (ii) a fluency ranking (FR) task (Bojar et al., 2014) to assess the fluency of the translations. The instructions given and the questions asked to the participants can be found in Appendix H.

Half of the formulae used in the experimental items were extracted from the GGC, while the other half were randomly generated. This resulted in a set of formulae that contained both well-behaved and ill-behaved formulae and was representative of the entire space of FOL formulae. Each formula was given as input to the three systems to be translated into English.

A total of 21 participants (researchers and students, 9 males and 12 females, with a median age of 25.0 years, SD $=$ 12.2) with sufficient knowledge of logic and proficiency in English[13] were recruited for the task.

Setup The rationale for using NLI is that it taps comprehension, allowing us to gauge the extent to which FOL translations by different systems facilitate inference. In this case, the fact that the underlying meaning is captured by a logical formula ensures that the task is highly controlled. Additionally, NLI allows checking more objectively how well participants understand text, removing the factor of subjectivity that characterizes other evaluation methods such as Likert scales.

The NLI task was framed in such a way that the three system translations (one per system) of the same formula were considered as *premises* associated with the same *hypothesis* (manually crafted) each time. An illustration of this is presented in Table 5. The third answer option *Other* was added for cases in which the premise was ambiguous or unclear for the participant.[14]

Participants were randomly assigned to one of three groups. Items for the experiment (where an item consists of a formula translation by only one of the three systems and the associated hypothesis) and participant groups were counterbalanced by rotating through a 3 (system) $\times$ 3 (participant group) Latin square (Fisher, 1925). This ensured that the experimental items were counterbalanced, so that every item was shown to approximately the same number of participants and every participant was shown the same number of items (42), while participants only saw one system translation per

[12]https://huggingface.co/evaluate-metric

[13]All participants had taken at least one course on FOL. Furthermore, at the beginning of the questionnaire, participants were asked to rate their knowledge of logic on a 4$-$point Likert scale and their proficiency in English on a 5$-$point Likert scale.

[14]In the analysis, the *Other* option was always marked incorrect because ambiguous and unclear translations are less understandable.

formula.

BASELINE	Does the hypothesis automatically follow from the premise? Premise: *"b is a cube or it is not the case that b is a cube and c is a cube."* Hypothesis: *"only c is a cube."* Yes | No | Other ______
Ranta (2011)	Does the hypothesis automatically follow from the premise? Premise: *"All these hold:* *- b is a cube or b is not a cube;* *- c is a cube."* Hypothesis: *"only c is a cube."* Yes | No | Other ______
LoLA	Does the hypothesis automatically follow from the premise? Premise: *"c is a cube."* Hypothesis: *"only c is a cube."* Yes | No | Other ______

Table 5: Example of three NLI experimental items derived from translating the formula $(Cube(b) \vee \neg Cube(b)) \wedge Cube(c)$ with the three systems.

The motivation behind using FR is that evaluating fluency in an absolute manner can be tricky. Comparing different outputs can aid evaluators to make more informed judgments. In this task, participants were asked to rank the translations of the three different systems of the same source formula according to the criterion of fluency. Ties were allowed. An illustration of this is presented in Figure 1. The FR task did not require a Latin square design because all three translations per formula were presented together in the same experimental item. Therefore, each group of participants was shown the same set of 20 FR questions.

Given the following formula and candidate translations, rank the translations from most fluent to least fluent.	
Formula:	$(Cube(b) \vee \neg Cube(b)) \wedge Cube(c)$
System 1:	*"b is a cube or it is not the case that b is a cube and c is a cube."*
System 2:	*"All these hold:* *- b is a cube or b is not a cube;* *- c is a cube."*
System 3:	*"c is a cube."*

Figure 1: An illustration of a FR question in the experiment.

NLI Results The comprehensibility of a translation was calculated as the proportion of correct answers (i.e., correctly spotted presence or absence of entailment) to its corresponding NLI question. The mean of the percentage of correct NLI answers per participant was 70.4% (SD = 8.9%) and the mean of the percentage of correct answers per question was 70.2% (SD = 28.7%). The inter-annotator agreement was very low (Krippendorff's $\alpha = 0.181$), highlighting the difficulty of this task. Two outlier NLI questions, on which the participants performed significantly worse than on other questions, with the percentage of correct answers being more than two standard deviations below the mean, were removed from the analysis.

The translations from LoLA had the highest mean of the percentage of correct answers. Figure 2 shows the distribution of the percentages of correct participant responses for the different types of formulae.[15] A two-way system $\times$ well-behavedness ANOVA revealed that there was a significant interaction between the effects of translation system and formula type on the percentage of correct answers ($F(2, 114) = 3.11, p = .048$). Simple main effects analysis showed that translations from well-behaved formulae received a significantly higher percentage of correct answers than translations from ill-behaved formulae ($F(1) = 8.87, p = .004$), and that there was a significant effect of translation system on the percentage of correct answers ($F(2) = 5.50, p = .005$).

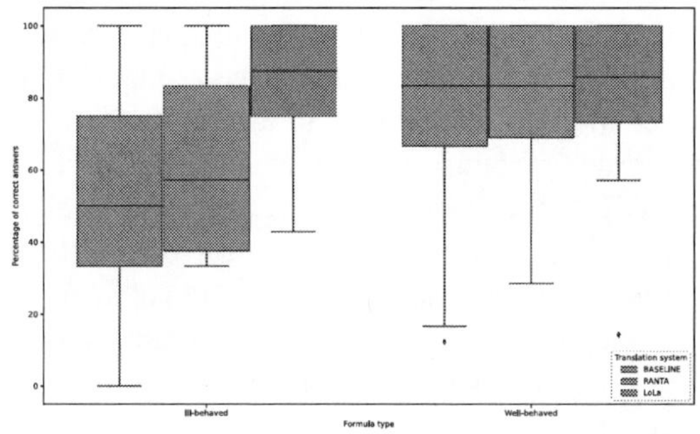

Figure 2: The distribution of the percentage of correct answers to the NLI questions (outliers excluded), grouped by formula type and translation system, as a boxplot showing the medians, lower quartiles, and upper quartiles, along with extreme values. Diamonds are outlier values.

Tukey's HSD test for multiple pairwise comparisons showed that the effect of translation system is mainly due to a difference between BASELINE and LoLA ($p = .005$, $+16.59$ under LoLA). There were no significant differences between BASELINE and Ranta (2011) ($p = .657$) and LoLA and Ranta (2011) ($p = .053$). Tukey's HSD test revealed also that the interaction effect found is mainly due to

[15]Note that this figure shows some outliers other than the ones removed from the analysis. The outliers removed from the analysis were the questions with a mean of the percentage of correct answers more than two standard deviations below the mean over all the questions, while the outliers in this figure are the outlier questions per formula type per translation system.

the extremely low percentage of correct answers for BASELINE translations from ill-behaved formulae. All three translation systems had a higher percentage of correct answers for well-behaved formulae: BASELINE ($p = .021$, $+23.75$ under BASELINE's translations from well-behaved formulae), Ranta (2011) ($p = .013$, $+24.97$ under Ranta (2011)'s translations from well-behaved formulae), and LOLA ($p = .002$, $+29.52$ under LOLA's translations from well-behaved formulae). Furthermore, LOLA's translations from ill-behaved formulae were higher than BASELINE's translations from ill-behaved formulae ($p = .002$, $+8.19$ under LOLA).

FR Results To calculate the ranking of the three systems based on the individual rankings the participants gave in each of the FR questions, we used the TRUESKILL adaptation of Sakaguchi et al. (2014).[16] TRUESKILL was run 200 times on 1260 pairwise rankings derived from the 420 collected system rankings (20 per participant; Krippendorff's $\alpha = 0.475$). The results of the clustering of systems with overlapping rank ranges are presented in Table 6. There were significant differences between the ranked fluency of the three systems, such that they were all in a different cluster. The final ranking was LOLA > Ranta (2011) > BASELINE.

#	μ	Rank Range	System
1	3.539	$1-1$	LOLA
2	-0.643	$2-2$	Ranta (2011)
3	-2.873	$3-3$	BASELINE

Table 6: The final ranking of the three systems according to TRUESKILL (significance cluster number at $p-$level $p \leq .02$ (#), the final estimate of the system's ability (μ; inferred mean), the range of ranks in which the system falls, and system name).

To test whether there was an interaction effect on ranked fluency between the type of formulae (well-behaved or ill-behaved) and translation system, TRUESKILL was run for well-behaved and ill-behaved formulae separately. For well-behaved formulae, the model was run 200 times on 693 pairwise collected rankings derived from the 231 system rankings (11 per participant). For ill-behaved formulae, the model was run 200 times on 567 pairwise collected rankings derived from the 189 system rankings (9 per participant). The results of the clustering of systems with overlapping rank ranges for well-behaved formulae vs. ill-behaved formulae are presented in Table 7. We found a difference between the fluency of translations from well-behaved formulae by Ranta (2011) vs. LOLA, in addition to a difference in fluency between the two systems for translations from ill-behaved formulae (in both cases, LOLA had a higher rank than Ranta (2011)).

Well-Behaved Formulae				Ill-Behaved Formulae			
#	μ	Rank Range	System	#	μ	Rank Range	System
1	2.256	$1-1$	LOLA	1	3.826	$1-1$	LOLA
2	0.325	$2-2$	Ranta (2011)	2	-1.423	$2-2$	Ranta (2011)
3	-2.594	$3-3$	BASELINE	3	-2.355	$3-3$	BASELINE

Table 7: The final rankings of the three systems for well-behaved formulae vs. ill-behaved formulae according to TRUESKILL (significance cluster number at $p-$level $p \leq .02$ (#), the final estimate of the system's ability (μ; inferred mean), the range of ranks in which the system falls, and system name).

6.3 Correlations between Automatic Metrics and Human Judgments

In order to have a more comprehensive picture of our experiments, we calculated correlations (using Pearson's r coefficient) between the results of the automatic evaluation and the judgments obtained during the human evaluation. We considered only the experimental items derived from the formulae extracted from the GGC used for the NLI and FR tasks, as they have ground truth NL references and thus were scored using the automatic metrics. As for the metrics, we considered BERTScore, ROUGE-L, and SBERT.

For computing the correlation on the NLI task, we calculated a normalized score on $[0, 1]$ per translation, based on the answers given by the participants, such that the closer the score is to 1, the more comprehensible the translation. Similarly, the higher the score given by the automatic metrics to the translation, the more similar (structurally or semantically) to the ground truth reference it is. We observed no correlation between human judgments and any of the metrics ($r(55) = 0.05$, $p = .737$ with BERTScore; $r(55) = -0.08$, $p = .540$ with ROUGE-L; $r(55) = 0.009$, $p = .947$ with SBERT). For reference, Figure 5 in Appendix E shows the scatterplots.

For computing the correlation on the FR task, we scored each translation based on the average ranking received in the FR task. Each translation was scored from 1 (most fluent) to 3 (least fluent) by the participants, so we obtained translations

[16] www.github.com/keisks/wmt-trueskill. See Appendix F for a high-level description of TRUESKILL.

scored on $[1,3]$. In this case, the higher the average FR score, the more the translation is likely to be disfluent. Conversely, the higher the score of the automatic metrics, the more similar to the ground truth reference the translation is. Allegedly, a more fluent translation for humans should receive a higher score from the automatic metrics, so we expect a negative correlation between the average FR scores and the metric scores. This is supported by the results, where we observe weak to moderate negative correlations ($r(25) = -0.48, p = .01$ with BERTScore; $r(25) = -0.51$, $p < .01$ with ROUGE-L; $r(25) = -0.35, p = .08$ with SBERT), statistically significant for two out of three metrics (BERTScore and ROUGE-L). Figure 6 in Appendix E shows the scatterplots representing the negative correlations.

We proceeded with a manual analysis to further inspect the misalignments between automatic scores and human judgments in the two evaluation tasks. Specifically, we wanted to study two extreme cases, namely, when a high score from the automatic metrics corresponded to poor human judgments, and vice versa. See Appendix E for a detailed report.

Our results highlight an apparent lack of appropriate metrics to automatically evaluate the task of logic-to-text generation, as the metrics that we considered measure different properties than the dimensions we are interested in assessing. Semantics-based metrics focus exclusively on computing semantic similarity between texts. Moreover, they should theoretically be solid enough to capture nuances in meaning, yet we saw that this is mostly not the case (with BERTScore being the only exception). Consequently, the nature of these metrics does not allow them to tackle the core issue of comprehensibility, i.e., whether a text is more understandable than another. Our results also suggest that these metrics are of limited use for assessing fluency. Similarly, metrics relying only on $n-$gram overlap are unsuitable for any task involving comprehension, as they simply compare surface realizations of texts. On the other hand, they might be slightly more appropriate to evaluate fluency, as overlapping tokens can be an indication of fluency.

7 Future Work

We see two main areas for further investigation. First, we will examine to what extent our approach can be scaled up to include FOL with identity by enhancing the generator, the logical equivalence laws, and crucially, the optimization operations that were applied to the sentences generated. Second, we will try to implement the list of linguistic improvements that emerged from the TQA (see Table 9) by investigating methods to programmatically exploit paraphrasing techniques (rule-based, neural, or hybrid), and adequately scoring the resulting translations.

8 Conclusion

We conducted a human TQA on the faithfulness, comprehensibility, and fluency of Ranta (2011)'s translations. We implemented part of the results to build LoLA, an enhanced version of Ranta (2011)'s FOL-to-text system, which optimizes the input formula when generating text. We evaluated LoLA against a baseline and Ranta (2011)'s original system, performing both automatic and human evaluations. Our results suggest that Ranta (2011)'s framework, once adequately enhanced with logical equivalence laws, lends itself well to generating NL translations of FOL formulae. Furthermore, the results indicate the inappropriateness of current standard automatic metrics to evaluate logic-to-text generation, as they focus on assessing different properties than the dimensions relevant for this task.

The present work on logic-to-text generation can be potentially beneficial for a variety of applications. Paraphrasing systems could profit from the constraints given by logical equivalence laws to generate faithful paraphrases. Logic teaching can benefit by incorporating LoLA in an intelligent tutoring system supporting students and educators. LoLA could also be the base for a system helping engineers comprehend the convoluted outputs of theorem provers, as literally translating those formulae might result in quite cumbersome text.

We hope that this paper will motivate researchers in the broader NLG community to focus more on the issue of generating faithful, comprehensible, and fluent text from logically rich inputs.

Limitations

At present, both Ranta (2011) and LoLA do not cover identity (=). When identity is added to FOL, the expressive power of FOL increases very significantly, allowing it to express things like "there are more/fewer than n A's", "exactly n A's are B's", and so on, often using formulae whose structure is very distant from those of normal English sentences.

The current experimental design of the NLI task does not allow us to get fine-grained insights on ambiguity (i.e., the different readings that a translation may induce), which is crucial to avoid misunderstandings about the original meaning of a formula. In particular, the choice of the *Other* option revealed that the participants did spot the existence of ambiguities in the premises, or did not detect them at all, resulting in different interpretations of the premise.

The vocabulary of entities and relations from the GGC is limited in nature, given its pedagogical origin. Enlarging and diversifying the language domain would raise complications such as dealing with logical properties of the predicates, both in isolation and compositionally, implicatures, and world knowledge. Consequently, ensuring the creation of a fair and proper evaluation, especially for the NLI task, would be significantly more challenging.

Our evaluation focused exclusively on English. However, studying this subject from the perspectives of (typologically) different languages would bring up an incredibly wide range of research questions, e.g., is the concept of well-behavedness language-independent? Do the modifications performed to Ranta (2011)'s system scale up to other languages?

Ethics Statement

In the TQA, all the participants (10 master students) agreed to voluntarily participate. In the human evaluation, we paid 14 of the 21 evaluators (researchers and students) €5 upon completion of the survey. The other 7 agreed to participate without remuneration. In both studies, all the participants gave their informed consent to participate anonymously.

Acknowledgements

We thank the anonymous reviewers for their careful reading of our manuscript and their insightful comments and suggestions.

This project has received funding from the European Union's Horizon 2020 research and innovation program under the Marie Skłodowska-Curie grant agreement No. 860621.

References

Ion Androutsopoulos, Gerasimos Lampouras, and Dimitrios Galanis. 2013. Generating Natural Language Descriptions from OWL Ontologies: the NaturalOWL System. *Journal of Artificial Intelligence Research*, 48:671–715.

Douglas E. Appelt. 1987. Bidirectional grammars and the design of natural language generation systems. In *Theoretical Issues in Natural Language Processing 3*.

Xuefeng Bai, Yulong Chen, and Yue Zhang. 2022. Graph pre-training for AMR parsing and generation. In *Proceedings of the 60th Annual Meeting of the Association for Computational Linguistics (Volume 1: Long Papers)*, pages 6001–6015, Dublin, Ireland. Association for Computational Linguistics.

Satanjeev Banerjee and Alon Lavie. 2005. METEOR: An automatic metric for MT evaluation with improved correlation with human judgments. In *Proceedings of the ACL Workshop on Intrinsic and Extrinsic Evaluation Measures for Machine Translation and/or Summarization*, pages 65–72, Ann Arbor, Michigan. Association for Computational Linguistics.

Dave Barker-Plummer, Richard Cox, and Robert Dale. 2011. Student translations of natural language into logic: the Grade Grinder Corpus release 1.0. In *Proceedings of the 4th International Conference on Educational Data Mining*, pages 51–60.

Jon Barwise. 1977. An introduction to first-order logic. In *Studies in Logic and the Foundations of Mathematics*, volume 90, pages 5–46. Elsevier.

Jon Barwise, John Etchemendy, Gerard Allwein, Dave Barker-Plummer, and Albert Liu. 2000. *Language, Proof and Logic*. CSLI publications.

Valerio Basile. 2015. *From logic to language: Natural language generation from logical forms*. Ph.D. thesis, University of Groningen.

Emily M. Bender and Alexander Koller. 2020. Climbing towards NLU: On meaning, form, and understanding in the age of data. In *Proceedings of the 58th Annual Meeting of the Association for Computational Linguistics*, pages 5185–5198, Online. Association for Computational Linguistics.

Ondřej Bojar, Christian Buck, Christian Federmann, Barry Haddow, Philipp Koehn, Johannes Leveling, Christof Monz, Pavel Pecina, Matt Post, Herve Saint-Amand, Radu Soricut, Lucia Specia, and Aleš Tamchyna. 2014. Findings of the 2014 workshop on statistical machine translation. In *Proceedings of the Ninth Workshop on Statistical Machine Translation*, pages 12–58, Baltimore, Maryland, USA. Association for Computational Linguistics.

Johan Bos. 2016. Squib: Expressive power of Abstract Meaning Representations. *Computational Linguistics*, 42(3):527–535.

Sheila Castilho, Stephen Doherty, Federico Gaspari, and Joss Moorkens. 2018. Approaches to human and machine translation quality assessment. In *Translation Quality Assessment*, pages 9–38. Springer.

David L. Chen and Raymond J. Mooney. 2008. Learning to sportscast: A test of grounded language acquisition. In *Proceedings of the 25th International Conference on Machine Learning*, ICML '08, page 128–135, New York, NY, USA. Association for Computing Machinery.

Elizabeth Clark, Asli Celikyilmaz, and Noah A. Smith. 2019. Sentence mover's similarity: Automatic evaluation for multi-sentence texts. In *Proceedings of the 57th Annual Meeting of the Association for Computational Linguistics*, pages 2748–2760, Florence, Italy. Association for Computational Linguistics.

Elizabeth Coppock and David Baxter. 2010. A translation from logic to english with dynamic semantics. In *New Frontiers in Artificial Intelligence*, pages 197–216, Berlin, Heidelberg. Springer Berlin Heidelberg.

Jacob Devlin, Ming-Wei Chang, Kenton Lee, and Kristina Toutanova. 2019. BERT: Pre-training of deep bidirectional transformers for language understanding. In *Proceedings of the 2019 Conference of the North American Chapter of the Association for Computational Linguistics: Human Language Technologies, Volume 1 (Long and Short Papers)*, pages 4171–4186, Minneapolis, Minnesota. Association for Computational Linguistics.

Basil Ell, Denny Vrandečić, and Elena Simperl. 2015. SPARTIQULATION: Verbalizing SPARQL Queries. In *The Semantic Web: ESWC 2012 Satellite Events*, Lecture Notes in Computer Science, pages 117–131, Berlin, Heidelberg. Springer.

Arpad E Elo. 1978. *The rating of chessplayers, past and present*. Arco Pub.

Ronald Aylmer Fisher. 1925. *Statistical methods for research workers*. Edinburgh, Scotland: Oliver and Loyd.

Dan Flickinger. 2016. Generating English paraphrases from logic. *From Semantics to Dialectometry*.

Claire Gardent, Anastasia Shimorina, Shashi Narayan, and Laura Perez-Beltrachini. 2017. The WebNLG challenge: Generating text from RDF data. In *Proceedings of the 10th International Conference on Natural Language Generation*, pages 124–133, Santiago de Compostela, Spain. Association for Computational Linguistics.

Albert Gatt and Emiel Krahmer. 2018. Survey of the state of the art in natural language generation: Core tasks, applications and evaluation. *Journal of Artificial Intelligence Research*, 61:65–170.

Sebastian Gehrmann, Elizabeth Clark, and Thibault Sellam. 2022. Repairing the cracked foundation: A survey of obstacles in evaluation practices for generated text.

Lifeng Han, Alan Smeaton, and Gareth Jones. 2021. Translation quality assessment: A brief survey on manual and automatic methods. In *Proceedings for the First Workshop on Modelling Translation: Translatology in the Digital Age*, pages 15–33, online. Association for Computational Linguistics.

Ralf Herbrich, Tom Minka, and Thore Graepel. 2006. Trueskill™: A bayesian skill rating system. In *Advances in Neural Information Processing Systems*, volume 19. MIT Press.

David M. Howcroft, Anya Belz, Miruna-Adriana Clinciu, Dimitra Gkatzia, Sadid A. Hasan, Saad Mahamood, Simon Mille, Emiel van Miltenburg, Sashank Santhanam, and Verena Rieser. 2020. Twenty years of confusion in human evaluation: NLG needs evaluation sheets and standardised definitions. In *Proceedings of the 13th International Conference on Natural Language Generation*, pages 169–182, Dublin, Ireland. Association for Computational Linguistics.

Ke Hu and Patrick Cadwell. 2016. A comparative study of post-editing guidelines. In *Proceedings of the 19th Annual Conference of the European Association for Machine Translation*, pages 346–353.

Daniel Kasenberg, Antonio Roque, Ravenna Thielstrom, Meia Chita-Tegmark, and Matthias Scheutz. 2019. Generating justifications for norm-related agent decisions. In *Proceedings of the 12th International Conference on Natural Language Generation*, pages 484–493, Tokyo, Japan. Association for Computational Linguistics.

Imtiaz H. Khan, Kees van Deemter, and Graeme Ritchie. 2012. Managing ambiguity in reference generation: The role of surface structure. *Topics in Cognitive Science*, 4(2):211–231.

Ioannis Konstas, Srinivasan Iyer, Mark Yatskar, Yejin Choi, and Luke Zettlemoyer. 2017. Neural AMR: Sequence-to-sequence models for parsing and generation. In *Proceedings of the 55th Annual Meeting of the Association for Computational Linguistics (Volume 1: Long Papers)*, pages 146–157, Vancouver, Canada. Association for Computational Linguistics.

Matt Kusner, Yu Sun, Nicholas Kolkin, and Kilian Weinberger. 2015. From word embeddings to document distances. In *Proceedings of the 32nd International Conference on Machine Learning*, volume 37 of *Proceedings of Machine Learning Research*, pages 957–966, Lille, France. PMLR.

Roman Kutlak and Kees van Deemter. 2015. Generating Succinct English Text from FOL Formulae. In *Procs. of First Scottish Workshop on Data-to-Text Generation*, page 3.

Chin-Yew Lin. 2004. ROUGE: A package for automatic evaluation of summaries. In *Text Summarization Branches Out*, pages 74–81, Barcelona, Spain. Association for Computational Linguistics.

Jiangming Liu, Shay B. Cohen, and Mirella Lapata. 2021. Text generation from discourse representation structures. In *Proceedings of the 2021 Conference of the North American Chapter of the Association for Computational Linguistics: Human Language Technologies*, pages 397–415, Online. Association for Computational Linguistics.

Wei Lu and Hwee Tou Ng. 2011. A probabilistic forest-to-string model for language generation from typed lambda calculus expressions. In *Proceedings of the 2011 Conference on Empirical Methods in Natural Language Processing*, pages 1611–1622, Edinburgh, Scotland, UK. Association for Computational Linguistics.

Kana Manome, Masashi Yoshikawa, Hitomi Yanaka, Pascual Martínez-Gómez, Koji Mineshima, and Daisuke Bekki. 2018. Neural sentence generation from formal semantics. In *Proceedings of the 11th International Conference on Natural Language Generation*, pages 408–414, Tilburg University, The Netherlands. Association for Computational Linguistics.

Alexandra Mayn and Kees van Deemter. 2020. Towards generating effective explanations of logical formulas: Challenges and strategies. In *2nd Workshop on Interactive Natural Language Technology for Explainable Artificial Intelligence*, pages 39–43, Dublin, Ireland. Association for Computational Linguistics.

Aikaterini Mpagouli and Ioannis Hatzilygeroudis. 2007. Converting first order logic into natural language: A first level approach. In *Current Trends in Informatics: 11th Panhellenic Conference on Informatics, PCI*, pages 517–526.

Aikaterini Mpagouli and Ioannis Hatzilygeroudis. 2009. A Knowledge-based System for Translating FOL Formulas into NL Sentences. In Iliadis, Maglogiann, Tsoumakasis, Vlahavas, and Bramer, editors, *Artificial Intelligence Applications and Innovations III*, volume 296, pages 157–163. Springer US, Boston, MA. Series Title: IFIP Advances in Information and Communication Technology.

Axel-Cyrille Ngonga Ngomo, Lorenz Bühmann, Christina Unger, Jens Lehmann, and Daniel Gerber. 2013. Sorry, i don't speak SPARQL: translating SPARQL queries into natural language. In *Proceedings of the 22nd international conference on World Wide Web - WWW '13*, pages 977–988, Rio de Janeiro, Brazil. ACM Press.

Jekaterina Novikova, Ondřej Dušek, Amanda Cercas Curry, and Verena Rieser. 2017. Why we need new evaluation metrics for NLG. In *Proceedings of the 2017 Conference on Empirical Methods in Natural Language Processing*, pages 2241–2252, Copenhagen, Denmark. Association for Computational Linguistics.

Kishore Papineni, Salim Roukos, Todd Ward, and Wei-Jing Zhu. 2002. Bleu: a method for automatic evaluation of machine translation. In *Proceedings of the 40th Annual Meeting of the Association for Computational Linguistics*, pages 311–318, Philadelphia, Pennsylvania, USA. Association for Computational Linguistics.

Barbara BH Partee, Alice G ter Meulen, and Robert Wall. 1993. *Mathematical methods in linguistics*, volume 30 of *Studies in Linguistics and Philosophy (SLAP)*. Springer Dordrecht.

Matthew E. Peters, Mark Neumann, Mohit Iyyer, Matt Gardner, Christopher Clark, Kenton Lee, and Luke Zettlemoyer. 2018. Deep contextualized word representations. In *Proceedings of the 2018 Conference of the North American Chapter of the Association for Computational Linguistics: Human Language Technologies, Volume 1 (Long Papers)*, pages 2227–2237, New Orleans, Louisiana. Association for Computational Linguistics.

John D. Phillips. 1993. Generation of text from logical formulae. *Machine Translation*, 8(4):209–235.

Adam Poliak. 2020. A survey on recognizing textual entailment as an NLP evaluation. In *Proceedings of the First Workshop on Evaluation and Comparison of NLP Systems*, pages 92–109, Online. Association for Computational Linguistics.

Matt Post. 2018. A call for clarity in reporting BLEU scores. In *Proceedings of the Third Conference on Machine Translation: Research Papers*, pages 186–191, Brussels, Belgium. Association for Computational Linguistics.

Aarne Ranta. 2011. Translating between language and logic: what is easy and what is difficult. In *Proceedings of the International Conference on Automated Deduction*, pages 5–25. Springer.

Nils Reimers and Iryna Gurevych. 2019. Sentence-BERT: Sentence embeddings using Siamese BERT-networks. In *Proceedings of the 2019 Conference on Empirical Methods in Natural Language Processing and the 9th International Joint Conference on Natural Language Processing (EMNLP-IJCNLP)*, pages 3982–3992, Hong Kong, China. Association for Computational Linguistics.

Ehud Reiter and Robert Dale. 2000. *Building Natural Language Generation Systems*. Studies in Natural Language Processing. Cambridge University Press.

Keisuke Sakaguchi, Matt Post, and Benjamin Van Durme. 2014. Efficient elicitation of annotations for human evaluation of machine translation. In *Proceedings of the Ninth Workshop on Statistical Machine Translation*, pages 1–11, Baltimore, Maryland, USA. Association for Computational Linguistics.

Stewart Shapiro and Teresa Kouri Kissel. 2021. Classical Logic. In Edward N. Zalta, editor, *The Stanford Encyclopedia of Philosophy*, Spring 2021 edition. Metaphysics Research Lab, Stanford University.

Stuart M. Shieber. 1993. The problem of logical form equivalence. *Computational Linguistics*, 19(1):179–190.

Stuart M. Shieber, Gertjan van Noord, Fernando C. N. Pereira, and Robert C. Moore. 1990. Semantic-head-driven generation. *Computational Linguistics*, 16(1):30–42.

Shane Storks, Qiaozi Gao, and Joyce Y. Chai. 2019. Recent advances in natural language inference: A survey of benchmarks, resources, and approaches.

Chunliu Wang, Rik van Noord, Arianna Bisazza, and Johan Bos. 2021. Evaluating text generation from discourse representation structures. In *Proceedings of the 1st Workshop on Natural Language Generation, Evaluation, and Metrics (GEM 2021)*, pages 73–83, Online. Association for Computational Linguistics.

Juen-tin Wang. 1980. On computational sentence generation from logical form. In *COLING 1980 Volume 1: The 8th International Conference on Computational Linguistics*.

Thomas Wolf, Lysandre Debut, Victor Sanh, Julien Chaumond, Clement Delangue, Anthony Moi, Pierric Cistac, Tim Rault, Remi Louf, Morgan Funtowicz, Joe Davison, Sam Shleifer, Patrick von Platen, Clara Ma, Yacine Jernite, Julien Plu, Canwen Xu, Teven Le Scao, Sylvain Gugger, Mariama Drame, Quentin Lhoest, and Alexander Rush. 2020. Transformers: State-of-the-art natural language processing. In *Proceedings of the 2020 Conference on Empirical Methods in Natural Language Processing: System Demonstrations*, pages 38–45, Online. Association for Computational Linguistics.

Yuk Wah Wong and Raymond Mooney. 2007. Generation by inverting a semantic parser that uses statistical machine translation. In *Human Language Technologies 2007: The Conference of the North American Chapter of the Association for Computational Linguistics; Proceedings of the Main Conference*, pages 172–179, Rochester, New York. Association for Computational Linguistics.

Yuhuai Wu, Albert Q. Jiang, Wenda Li, Markus N. Rabe, Charles Staats, Mateja Jamnik, and Christian Szegedy. 2022. Autoformalization with large language models.

John M. Zelle and Raymond J. Mooney. 1996. Learning to parse database queries using inductive logic programming. In *Proceedings of the Thirteenth National Conference on Artificial Intelligence - Volume 2*, AAAI'96, page 1050–1055. AAAI Press.

Tianyi Zhang, Varsha Kishore, Felix Wu, Kilian Q Weinberger, and Yoav Artzi. 2020. Bertscore: Evaluating text generation with bert. In *International Conference on Learning Representations*.

Kaitlyn Zhou, Su Lin Blodgett, Adam Trischler, Hal Daumé III, Kaheer Suleman, and Alexandra Olteanu. 2022. Deconstructing NLG evaluation: Evaluation practices, assumptions, and their implications. In *Proceedings of the 2022 Conference of the North American Chapter of the Association for Computational Linguistics: Human Language Technologies*, pages 314–324, Seattle, United States. Association for Computational Linguistics.

A Details on Ranta (2011)

Figure 3 shows a graphical schematization of Ranta (2011)'s translation system.

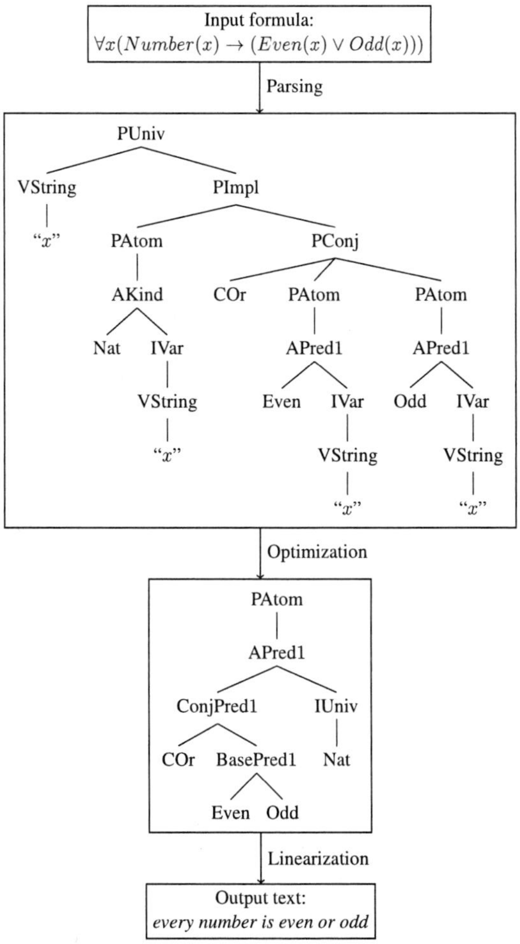

Figure 3: A model of Ranta (2011)'s translation system, with an example translation of a FOL formula into English. Each AST node is named after the syntactic function used to construct the constituent.

B Formal Definition of Well-Behavedness

The following is the formal definition of *well-behavedness*, stating all the conditions that a formula should have to be suitable for translation into NL:

1. All atomic propositions are well-behaved formulae.
2. Negation: if ϕ is a well-behaved formula and it does not contain subformulae of the form $\neg\psi$ for any formula ψ, then $\neg\phi$ is a well-behaved formula.
3. Conjunction: if ϕ and ψ are well-behaved formulae, then $(\phi \wedge \psi)$ is a well-behaved formula.
4. Disjunction: if ϕ and ψ are well-behaved formulae, then $(\phi \vee \psi)$ is a well-behaved formula.
5. Implication: if ϕ and ψ are well-behaved formulae and neither of them has any subformulae of the form $\alpha \to \beta$ for any set of formulae $\{\alpha, \beta\}$, then $(\phi \to \psi)$ is a well-behaved formula.
6. Universal quantification: if ϕ is a well-behaved formula, x is a variable, and ϕ contains at least one free occurrence of x, then $(\forall x)\phi$ is a well-behaved formula.
7. Existential quantification: if ϕ is a well-behaved formula, x is a variable, and ϕ contains at least one free occurrence of x, then $(\exists x)\phi$ is a well-behaved formula.
8. Bounded quantification: if ϕ is a proposition, x is a variable, K is a kind predicate, and ϕ contains at least one free occurrence of x, then $(\forall x : K)\phi$ and $(\exists x : K)\phi$ are well-behaved formulae.
9. Conjunction and disjunction of proposition lists: if $\phi_1, ..., \phi_n$ are propositions, then $\wedge[\phi_1, ..., \phi_n]$ and $\vee[\phi_1, ..., \phi_n]$ are propositions.
10. Nothing else is a well-behaved formula.

In addition to this definition, the well-behavedness of a formula also depends on its complexity, calculated in the number of connectives. Only if a formula contains < 8 connectives, it is considered well-behaved.

C Additional Details on LoLA

The list of *core-to-extended* AST conversions was expanded with the following optimization rules.

The rule of *existential negation* turns a negated existential quantifier into a *negative existential*, which asserts the non-existence of an element in the domain of quantification. This optimization should improve translations such as *it is not the case that there exists an element x such that [...]* to *there exists no element x such that [...]*, pushing the negation inward.

The rule of *in-situ quantification without a kind predicate* applies to the special case of *kind predicates* such as *natural number* that, according to Ranta (2011), serve to restrict the domain of quantification. This rule replaces an occurrence of a bound variable in the quantified proposition ($\forall$, $\exists$, or $\perp$) with simpler expressions (*everything*, *some-*

Propositional Logic	First-Order Logic
Idempotence	Quantifier Negation
$P \vee P \Leftrightarrow P$	$\neg(\forall x)\phi(x) \Leftrightarrow (\exists x)\neg\phi(x)$
$P \wedge P \Leftrightarrow P$	$(\forall x)\phi(x) \Leftrightarrow \neg(\exists x)\neg\phi(x)$
	$\neg(\forall x)\neg\phi(x) \Leftrightarrow (\exists x)\phi(x)$
Associativity	$(\forall x)\neg\phi(x) \Leftrightarrow \neg(\exists x)\phi(x)$
$(P \vee Q) \vee R \Leftrightarrow P \vee (Q \vee R)$	
$(P \wedge Q) \wedge R \Leftrightarrow P \wedge (Q \wedge R)$	Quantifier Distribution
	$(\forall x)(\phi(x) \wedge \psi(x)) \Leftrightarrow (\forall x)\phi(x) \wedge (\forall x)\psi(x)$
Commutativity	$(\exists x)(\phi(x) \vee \psi(x)) \Leftrightarrow (\exists x)\phi(x) \vee (\exists x)\psi(x)$
$P \vee Q \Leftrightarrow Q \vee P$	
$P \wedge Q \Leftrightarrow Q \wedge P$	Quantifier Independence
	$(\forall x)(\forall y)\phi(x, y) \Leftrightarrow (\forall y)(\forall x)\phi(x, y)$
Distributivity	$(\exists x)(\exists y)\phi(x, y) \Leftrightarrow (\exists y)(\exists x)\phi(x, y)$
$(P \vee Q) \wedge (P \vee R) \Leftrightarrow P \vee (Q \wedge R)$	
$(P \wedge Q) \vee (P \wedge R) \Leftrightarrow P \wedge (Q \vee R)$	Quantifier Movement
	$\phi \rightarrow (\forall x)\psi(x) \Leftrightarrow (\forall x)(\phi \rightarrow \psi(x))$
Identity	(if x is not free in ϕ)
$P \vee \bot \Leftrightarrow P$	$\phi \rightarrow (\exists x)\psi(x) \Leftrightarrow (\exists x)(\phi \rightarrow \psi(x))$
$P \vee \top \Leftrightarrow \top$	(if x is not free in ϕ)
$P \wedge \bot \Leftrightarrow \bot$	$(\forall x)\psi(x) \rightarrow \phi \Leftrightarrow (\exists x)(\psi(x) \rightarrow \phi)$
$P \wedge \top \Leftrightarrow P$	(if x is not free in ϕ)
	$(\exists x)\psi(x) \rightarrow \phi \Leftrightarrow (\forall x)(\psi(x) \rightarrow \phi)$
Complement	(if x is not free in ϕ)
$P \vee \neg P \Leftrightarrow \top$	
$\neg\neg P \Leftrightarrow P$ (double negation)	Vacuous Quantification
$P \wedge \neg P \Leftrightarrow \bot$	$(\forall x)\phi \Leftrightarrow \phi$ (if x is not free in ϕ)
	$(\exists x)\phi \Leftrightarrow \phi$ (if x is not free in ϕ)
De Morgan	
$\neg(P \vee Q) \Leftrightarrow \neg P \wedge \neg Q$	
$\neg(P \wedge Q) \Leftrightarrow \neg P \vee \neg Q$	
Conditional	
$P \rightarrow Q \Leftrightarrow \neg P \vee Q$	
$P \rightarrow Q \Leftrightarrow \neg Q \rightarrow \neg P$ (contraposition)	

Table 8: List of logical equivalence laws used as formula conversions in LoLA, where P, Q, or R stand for any arbitrarily chosen well-formed formula, and $\phi(x)$ or $\psi(x)$ for any formula in which x is free.

thing, or *nothing*). As an example, *for all x, x is even* would be optimized to *everything is even*.

The rules for 2*−place predicate-sharing aggregation* are of two kinds: in *subject-sharing*, different occurrences of the same predicate in a formula share the first argument; in *object-sharing*, different occurrences of the same predicate share the second argument. In these cases, the formula is flattened to merge the occurrences of the predicate. For example, $Parallel(a, b) \land Parallel(c, b)$ would be translated as *a and c are parallel to b*.

Finally, the optimization rule to perform *reflexivization* on negated predicates improves translations such as *x is not bigger than x* to *x is not bigger than itself*.

Given the optimization rules presented in this section and in §3 and the equivalence laws in Table 8, the selection of the optimal translation is performed as described in §5. Figure 4 shows an example of a search tree.

D Details on the TQA's Post-Edits

The post-edits suggested by the participants in the TQA (see §4.1) can be divided into three categories. The first category is in the spirit of Ranta (2011)'s *core-to-extended* AST manipulations. The optimizations that the evaluators suggested are: moving the negation inward if an existential quantifier is negated, in-situ quantification without a kind predicate present, two-place predicate-sharing aggregation, and reflexivization of negated predicates. Table 2 shows one example for each suggested optimization.

The second category includes conversions based on the structural manipulation of the form of the input using logical equivalence laws. This way, logically equivalent but arguably more comprehensible and fluent translations can be obtained. Examples of this are the elimination of double negation, the use of De Morgan's laws (Barwise, 1977), and the simplification of $\neg(\exists x)\phi$ to $(\forall x)\neg\phi$. Table 3 presents some examples of conversions suggested in this category.

The third category consists of linguistic and stylistic optimizations of the translations, introducing a greater variety of terms, expressions, and syntactic constructions than those employed by Ranta (2011). Examples of some linguistic constructions introduced are relative clauses, anaphoric expressions, periphrastic expressions, and the rephrasing of connectives. Table 9 presents the complete list of linguistic constructions, together with the logical constructs they can convey.

E Details on the Evaluation

Table 10 presents some outputs generated by the three systems we compared for evaluation. The table highlights the different operations to translate formulae into text used by the three systems. Note, in particular, the convoluted nature of the quasi-literal translations of BASELINE, and the techniques employed by Ranta (2011) and LoLA to improve them. Specifically, Ranta (2011) implements some common techniques in NLG (e.g., aggregation in (3)), while LoLA additionally employs logical equivalence laws (e.g., double negation in (1)) to further refine the translations.

Figure 5 presents the scatterplots showing the relationships (not statistically significant) between the average NLI score and the scores assigned by the automatic metrics to the translations (BERTScore in Figure 5a, ROUGE-L in Figure 5b, and SBERT in Figure 5c). Figure 6 presents the scatterplots showing the weak to moderate negative correlations (statistically significant for BERTScore and ROUGE-L) between the average FR ranking and the scores assigned by the automatic metrics to the translations (BERTScore in Figure 6a, ROUGE-L in Figure 6b, and SBERT in Figure 6c). Note, however, that the FR rank alone (1, 2, or 3) of a translation might not be ideal to measure its fluency. Given that ties were allowed in the FR task, it might be the case that all the translations of an input formula receive a 1. However, this might mean that the translations are all equally disfluent. Therefore, two translations of different formulae receiving a 1 cannot be viewed as equally fluent. Nonetheless, the correlations we found might be due to the fact that few FR rankings resulted in ties.

In order to shed some light on the evaluation methods, we inspected cases in which the automatic scores and the human judgments of a realization are misaligned. Table 11 and Table 12 (concerning NLI and FR, respectively) show some samples. In Table 11, a particularly interesting example is (7): the text is extremely comprehensible for humans, however, since none of the tokens of the generated text overlaps with those of the reference, the score assigned by ROUGE-L is 0. A similar thing happens in (8) but for different reasons: SBERT is unable to get the semantic similarity between the generated text and the more natural-

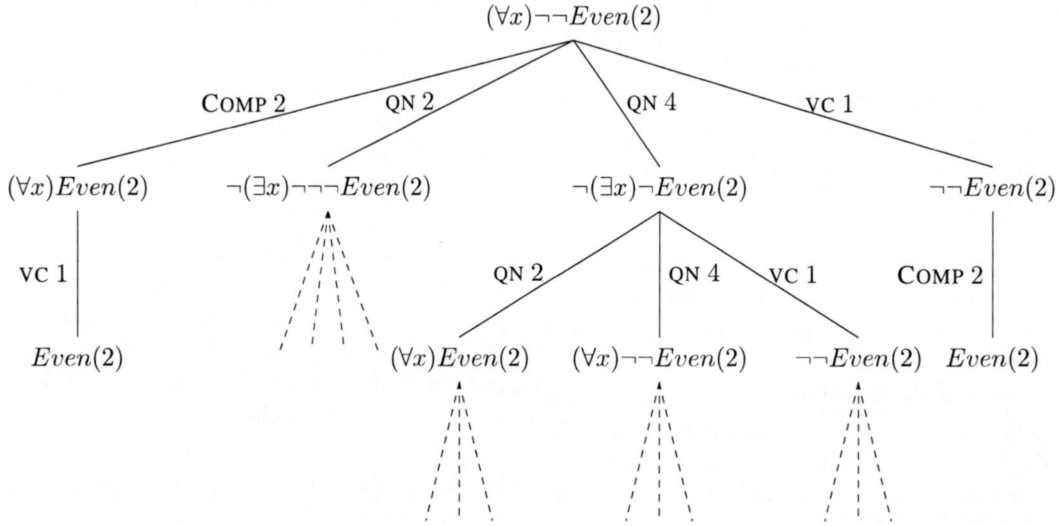

Figure 4: A part of the search tree of possible manipulations for the formula $(\forall x)\neg\neg Even(2)$, where the names of the logic laws are abbreviated (e.g., QN $1 =$ the first law of quantifier negation, see Table 8). In the system, this tree has ASTs as nodes, but for readability, the formula linearizations are displayed instead.

Linguistic Construction	Logical Construct	Example
Relative clause	Conjunction	*There exists something that is not prime.*
Adverbial clause	Conjunction	*Something is in the same row as **a**, while **a** is even.*
Adverbial clause	Implication	*Everything is small as long as it is a dodecahedron.*
		***a** is smaller than **b** if **a** is a cube.*
Correlative conjunction	Conjunction	*Both **a** is in the same row as **b** and **b** is a dodecahedron.*
Correlative conjunction	Exclusive or	*Everything is either a cube or a tetrahedron.*
Correlative conjunction	Negated disjunction	*Neither **b** nor **d** is a tetrahedron.*
Deixis	Identity	*If **b** is small, it is a tetrahedron.*
		*If **w** and **y** are tetrahedrons, they are in the same column.*
Referring expression	Identity	*If something is in front of a cube, then the cube is large.*
		*At least one of **d** and **b** is left of the other.*
Conditional mood	Implication	*If **a** had the same shape as **b**, then **c** would be in the same row as **c**.*
Modality	Implication	*If **a** is even, then there must be something that is even.*
Present participle	Implication	***a** being left of **b** implies that **b** is a dodecahedron.*
Adverbial clause	Reverse relation	***a** is to the left of **d** or the other way around.*
Modifier	Inequality	*Nothing is smaller than something else.*
Collective predicate	Distributive predication	*If **w** and **y** are tetrahedrons, they are in the same column.*

Table 9: Linguistic and stylistic constructions suggested in the post-edits of the TQA, with the logical constructs they can express or emphasize, illustrated with (slightly revised) examples.

sounding reference, thus assigning a low score to a comprehensible translation. In the opposite case (i.e., incomprehensible translations receiving high automatic scores), a noteworthy example is (9): the realization is quite convoluted (containing two negations, an implication, and the repetition of a constant), yet surprisingly, BERTScore catches the semantic similarity with the reference, even though equivalence laws are involved. Example (11) is obscure: in this case, in contrast to (8), SBERT is able to capture the semantic similarity with the reference, albeit the convoluted realization received a rather poor human judgment.

In Table 12, the realization in (12), (13), and (14) turns out to be particularly problematic. Although receiving a high score in the FR task, it is scored poorly by all the metrics, for the same reasons as above: as for ROUGE-L, the $n-$gram overlap between the realization and the reference is weak, while SBERT does not capture the semantic similarity. BERTScore is seemingly the only metric that handles semantics satisfactorily, as its score is anyhow relatively high. In the opposite case (i.e., disfluent translations receiving high automatic scores), (15) is particularly remarkable as BERTScore is capable of detecting the semantic similarity of logically equivalent constructions involving antonyms (***x*** *is smaller than* ***y*** $\equiv$ ***y*** *is larger than* ***x***). The realization in (16) is a nearly-literal translation of the original formula that is considered very disfluent by humans. Regardless, the $n-$gram overlap with the reference is prominent, so ROUGE-L gives it a relatively high score. (17) shows similar behavior to (11): SBERT surprisingly catches the semantic similarity between the realization and the reference, despite the involvement of equivalence laws.

F TRUESKILL Description

TRUESKILL was originally developed in Herbrich et al. (2006) for modeling the relative skills of players in online gaming communities, echoing Elo (1978). In higher-level terms, TRUESKILL assumes that the skill level (score) of each player (system) S_j is defined by its estimated mean performance μ_{S_j} and the uncertainty of this estimate $\sigma^2_{S_j}$. Before any match is played, μ_{S_j} is initialized to 0. These Bayesian estimates are continually updated with each match.[17] The size of the updates depends on the amount of *surprisal* and *confidence*. A player with a relatively low mean performance beating a player with a relatively high mean performance is more surprising than the opposite outcome. Thus, more surprising outcomes result in bigger updates than less surprising ones.

G TQA Questionnaire

Figure 7 presents the instruction text shown to the participants at the beginning of the survey, and Figure 8 the set of questions provided to the participants. Table 13 shows an example batch of formulae and translations used as experimental items. The filler formulae and translations present in the table were designed in such a way that the translations resembled those of Ranta (2011), they were incorrect, and their incorrectness would be easily detectable for people with a moderate amount of experience in logic.

H Human Evaluation Questionnaire

Figure 9 presents the instructions and questions shown to the participants.

[17]Note that μ_{S_j} can take negative values.

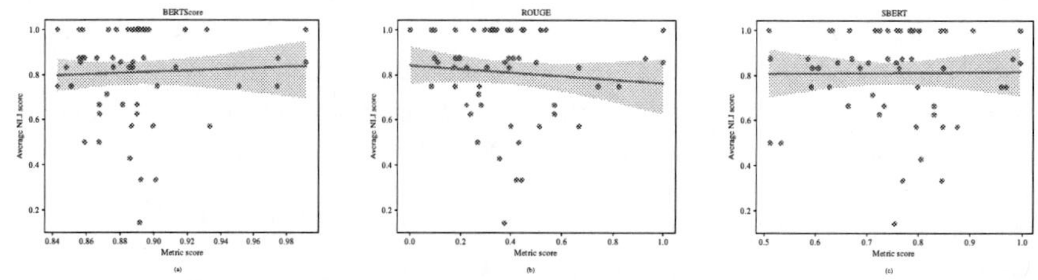

Figure 5: Scatterplots with the relationship between the average NLI score and the score assigned by the automatic metrics to the translations.

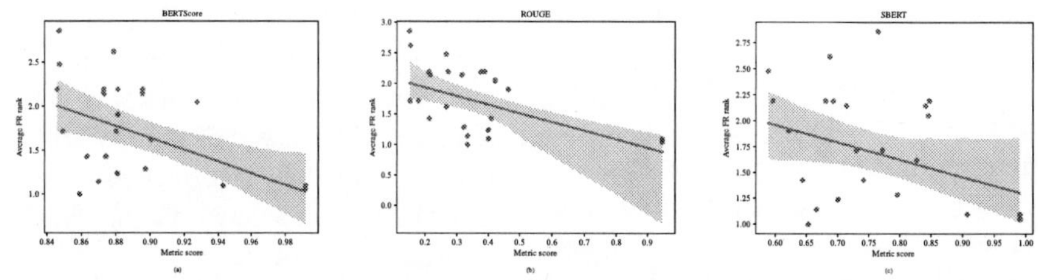

Figure 6: Scatterplots highlighting the negative correlations between the average FR rank and the score assigned by the automatic metrics to the translations.

	Formula and Reference	BASELINE	Ranta (2011)	LoLA
(1)	$\neg\neg Large(d)$ *d is large.*	*It is not the case that it is not the case that **d** is large.*	*It is not the case that **d** is not large.*	***d** is large.*
(2)	$\forall x \forall y((Cube(x) \wedge FrontOf(y,x)) \rightarrow Small(x))$ *If a cube has something in front of it, then it's small.*	*For all **x**, for all **y**, if **x** is a cube and **y** is in front of **x**, then **x** is small.*	*For all **x**, for all **y**, if **x** is a cube and **y** is in front of **x**, then **x** is small.*	*For all **y**, for all cubes **x**, **y** is not in front of **x** or **x** is small.*
(3)	$Smaller(f,a) \vee BackOf(f,a)$ ***f** is either in back of or smaller than **a**.*	***f** is smaller than **a** or **f** is in back of **a**.*	***f** is smaller than **a** or in back of **a**.*	***f** is smaller than **a** or in back of **a**.*
(4)	$\exists u(Dodec(u) \wedge \neg(Large(u) \vee Small(u)))$ *Some dodecahedron is neither large nor small.*	*There is an element **u** such that **u** is a dodecahedron and it is not the case that **u** is large or **u** is small.*	*There is a dodecahedron **u** such that it is not the case that **u** is large or small.*	*It is not the case that every dodecahedron is small or large.*
(5)	$\neg\exists w(Person(w) \wedge Pet(w))$ *People are not pets.*	*It is not the case that there is an element **w** such that **w** is a person and **w** is a pet.*	*It is not the case that some person is a pet.*	*For all persons **w**, **w** is not a pet.*

Table 10: Examples of text generated by the three systems compared in the evaluation, together with the input formula and the ground truth reference.

	Formula and Reference	Realization	System	NLI Score (↑)	Metric Score (↑)	Metric
(6)	$\forall x \neg\exists x Cube(x)$ *There are no cubes.*	*For all **x**, it is not the case that there is an element **x** such that **x** is a cube.*	Ranta (2011)	[illegible]	0.843	BERTScore
(7)	$\forall x \neg\exists x Cube(x)$ *There are no cubes.*	*Nothing is a cube.*	LoLA	[illegible]	0.000	ROUGE-L
(8)	$\exists x \exists y(Cube(x) \wedge Cube(y) \wedge Large(x) \wedge Small(y) \wedge FrontOf(x,y))$ *A large cube is in front of a small cube.*	*There is an element **x** such that there is an element **y** such that **x** is a cube and **y** is a cube and **x** is large and **y** is small and **x** is in front of **y**.*	BASELINE	[illegible]	0.509	SBERT
(9)	$\neg(Larger(b,a) \rightarrow \neg Larger(b,e))$ ***b** is larger than both **a** and **e**.*	*It is not the case that if **b** is larger than **a**, then **b** is not larger than **e**.*	Ranta (2011)	0.333	[illegible]	BERTScore
(10)	$\neg(Larger(b,a) \rightarrow \neg Larger(b,e))$ ***b** is larger than both **a** and **e**.*	*It is not the case that if **b** is larger than **a**, then **b** is not larger than **e**.*	Ranta (2011)	0.333	[illegible]	ROUGE-L
(11)	$\exists x(Larger(a,x) \wedge Cube(x)) \rightarrow \neg \exists y(Tet(y) \wedge \neg Smaller(a,y))$ *If **a** is larger than some cube then it is smaller than every tetrahedron.*	*If there is an element **x** such that **a** is larger than **x** and **x** is a cube, then it is not the case that there is a tetrahedron **y** such that **a** is not smaller than **y**.*	Ranta (2011)	0.333	[illegible]	SBERT

Table 11: Selected cases of misalignment between the normalized score retrieved from the NLI task vs. the score assigned to the realizations by some automatic metrics against the ground truth reference.

	Formula and Reference	Realization	System	FR Score (↓)	Metric Score (↑)	Metric
(12)	$\forall x((Cube(x) \wedge Small(x)) \rightarrow \exists t(Large(t) \wedge Cube(t) \wedge BackOf(x,t)))$ *Every small cube is in back of a large cube.*	*For all small cubes **x**, there is an element **t** such that **t** is large, **t** is a cube and **x** is in back of **t**.*	LoLA	[illegible]	0.859	BERTScore
(13)	$\forall x((Cube(x) \wedge Small(x)) \rightarrow \exists t(Large(t) \wedge Cube(t) \wedge BackOf(x,t)))$ *Every small cube is in back of a large cube.*	*For all small cubes **x**, there is an element **t** such that **t** is large, **t** is a cube and **x** is in back of **t**.*	LoLA	[illegible]	0.333	ROUGE-L
(14)	$\forall x((Cube(x) \wedge Small(x)) \rightarrow \exists t(Large(t) \wedge Cube(t) \wedge BackOf(x,t)))$ *Every small cube is in back of a large cube.*	*For all small cubes **x**, there is an element **t** such that **t** is large, **t** is a cube and **x** is in back of **t**.*	LoLA	[illegible]	0.653	SBERT
(15)	$Smaller(a,b) \wedge Smaller(e,b)$ ***b** is larger than both **a** and **e**.*	***a** is smaller than **b** and **e** is smaller than **b**.*	BASELINE	2.048	[illegible]	BERTScore
(16)	$\neg\exists x(LeftOf(x,a) \wedge \exists z(Smaller(x,z) \wedge LeftOf(z,b)))$ *Nothing to the left of **a** is smaller than anything to the left of **b**.*	*It is not the case that there is an element **x** such that **x** is to the left of **a** and there is an element **z** such that **x** is smaller than **z** and **z** is to the left of **b**.*	BASELINE/Ranta (2011)	1.905	[illegible]	ROUGE-L
(17)	$Large(a) \vee Large(c) \vee \neg(Tet(a) \wedge Tet(c))$ ***a** and **c** are both tetrahedra only if at least one of them is large.*	***a** is large or **c** is large or it is not the case that **a** is a tetrahedron and **c** is a tetrahedron.*	BASELINE	2.190	[illegible]	SBERT

Table 12: Selected cases of misalignment between the score (averaged) assigned to the realizations by humans in the FR task vs. the score assigned by some automatic metrics against the ground truth reference.

EVALUATING ENGLISH TRANSLATIONS FROM FIRST-ORDER LOGIC FORMULAE

Thank you very much for participating in this experiment. It will take approximately 15 to 30 minutes to fill in this survey. If at any point you would like to stop, you can close this form and your response will be deleted. If you do wish to participate, your response will be handled anonymously: The information in this study will only be used in ways that will not reveal who you are. You will not be identified in any publication from this study or in any data files shared with other researchers. Your participation in this study is confidential.

The purpose of this experiment is to evaluate the strengths and weaknesses of a system that translates first-order logic formulas into English. We will present to you, one by one, 25 formulas with their translations, such as the one below:

Formula: $\neg \exists x (\text{Cube} (x) \wedge \text{LeftOf} (b , x))$
English translation: It is not the case that b is to the left of some cube

Please answer the following questions for each of them:
1. Is the translation correct, yes or no? By a correct translation, we mean that the sentence conveys the same information as the input logical formula (there is no possible world in which the formula is true while the English translation is false, or vice versa).
2. Is the translation clear? By a clear translation, we mean that the sentence is understandable and does not have multiple readings.
3. Is the translation fluent? By a fluent translation, we mean that the sentence sounds like a natural English sentence.
4. Do you have a suggestion for a better translation? Think, for example, about how the translation can be improved given the above three criteria (correctness, clarity, and fluency). However, you can be very free in your ideas here, write whatever you like!

Your answer to question 4 is most important for us. Especially if you think the given translation is unclear and/or not fluent, write down a translation that you think is more understandable and/or sounds better. A translation should always be one or more whole sentences.

In answering all questions, please note that it is very important that you evaluate the quality of the translations and base your opinion only on the semantic content (the meaning) of the formula, not on its specific syntactic form (such as the order of the conjuncts). In other words, think about whether the translation is suitable given the formula's meaning, no matter what the formula looks like.

The survey will start off with a few personal questions and a practice example. After you have answered all of the questions for each formula and translation pair, you will be asked to give a general structured review of the strengths and weaknesses of the translation system. With which types of sentences does the system have difficulties? For which types of sentences do you believe the system performs sufficiently well? Please keep this final question in mind while evaluating the translations.

For your information, these are the interpretations of the predicates used:

Dodec (x)	x is a dodecahedron
Small (x)	x is small
Student (x)	x is a student
Medium (x)	x is medium
Cube (x)	x is a cube
Prime (x)	x is a prime
Person (x)	x is a person
Tet (x)	x is a tetrahedron
Pet (x)	x is a pet
Large (x)	x is large
Even (x)	x is even
Adjoins (x , y)	x is adjacent to y
SameCol (x , y)	x is in the same column as y
LeftOf (x , y)	x is to the left of y
RightOf (x , y)	x is to the right of y
Smaller (x , y)	x is smaller than y
FrontOf (x , y)	x is in front of y
Larger (x , y)	x is larger than y
SameRow (x , y)	x is in the same row as y
SameShape (x , y)	x is of the same shape as y
SameSize (x , y)	x is of the same size as y
BackOf (x , y)	x is in back of y

Here are two example formula-translation pairs with potential answers (but many more can be correct!) that would be helpful for us in thinking about how to improve the translation system:

Example 1

Formula: $\forall x \exists y ((\text{LeftOf} (x , y)) \wedge \neg \text{Dodec} (y))$
Translation: for all x , there is an element y such that x is to the left of y and y is not a dodecahedron

1. Is the translation correct, yes or no?
   "Yes"

2. Is the translation clear, on a scale of 1 to 5?
   "3"

3. Is the translation fluent, on a scale of 1 to 5?
   "2"

4. Do you have a suggestion for a better translation?
   "everything has something to the right of it that is not a dodecahedron"

Example 2

Formula: Pet (a) → ∃ x Adjoins (b , b)
Translation: if a is a pet , then there is an element x such that x is adjacent to b

1. Is the translation correct, yes or no?
   "No"

2. Is the translation clear, on a scale of 1 to 5?
   "3"

3. Is the translation fluent, on a scale of 1 to 5?
   "1"

4. Do you have a suggestion for a better translation?
   "if a is a pet, then b is adjacent to itself"

Now it is your turn!

Figure 7: The instruction text shown to the participants at the beginning of the TQA.

0. Informed consent
   I have read the above information and understand the purpose of the research and that data will be collected from me. I also understand that participating in this study is completely voluntary. I agree that data gathered for the study may be published or made available provided my name or other identifying information is not used.
   - O I confirm this
   - O I do not confirm this and want to withdraw from participation

1. Personal questions
   What is your gender?
   - O Male
   - O Female
   - O Prefer not to say

   How old are you?

   How would you rate your knowledge of and familiarity with first-order logic? Where 1 stands for "I have been introduced to logic but it is long ago and I am a bit rusty", and 5 stands for "I use logic on a daily basis".
   1 2 3 4 5

2. Questions for each of the formula-translation pairs in the experimental items of the batch:
   Formula: <formula>
   Translation: <translation>

   1. Is the translation correct? Correct means that the sentence conveys exactly the same information as the input logical formula.
      - O Yes
      - O No

   2. Is the translation clear? Clear means that the sentence is understandable and does not have multiple readings.
      (Very unclear) 1 2 3 4 5 (Very clear)

   3. Is the translation fluent? Fluent means that the sentence sounds as a natural English sentence.
      (Not fluent) 1 2 3 4 5 (Very fluent)

   4. Do you have a suggestion for a better translation? If so, then write it down here.

3. Final questions
   Give a general structured review of the strengths and weaknesses of the translation system. With which types of formulas does the system have difficulties? For which types of formulas do you believe the system performs sufficiently well?

   Do you have any final comments?

Figure 8: The set of questions provided to the participants in the TQA.

Item	Type	FOL Formula	English Translation
1	GGC	$\forall z((Cube(z) \land \exists uFrontOf(u, z)) \to Small(z))$	*for all z , if z is a cube and there is an element u such that u is in front of z , then z is small*
2	GGC	$\forall v((Dodec(v) \land \neg\exists wRightOf(w, v)) \to Small(v))$	*for all v , if v is a dodecahedron and it is not the case that there is an element w such that w is to the right of v , then v is small*
3	GGC	$\neg Cube(a) \to (Cube(c) \lor (\neg Cube(c) \to Cube(e)))$	*if a is not a cube , then at least one of these holds :* • *c is a cube* • *if c is not a cube , then e is a cube*
4	GGC	$\forall x(\forall y(Dodec(x) \land \neg RightOf(y, x)) \to Small(x))$	*for all x , if for all y , x is a dodecahedron and y is not to the right of x , then x is small*
5	GGC	$\neg\exists y(\neg Tet(y) \land \neg\exists xFrontOf(x, y))$	*it is not the case that there is an element y such that y is not a tetrahedron and it is not the case that there is an element x such that x is in front of y*
6	GGC	$\neg\exists x(\neg\exists yFrontOf(y, x) \land \neg Tet(x))$	*it is not the case that there is an element x such that it is not the case that there is an element y such that y is in front of x and x is not a tetrahedron*
7	GGC	$\forall x((Dodec(x) \land \neg\exists yRightOf(x, y)) \to \exists zLeftOf(x, z))$	*for all x , if x is a dodecahedron and it is not the case that there is an element y such that x is to the right of y , then there is an element z such that x is to the left of z*
8	GGC	$\forall y\forall x((Dodec(y) \land Tet(x)) \to FrontOf(x, y))$	*for all y , for all x , if y is a dodecahedron and x is a tetrahedron , then x is in front of y*
9	GGC	$\forall y\forall z((Cube(y) \land Dodec(z) \land BackOf(y, z)) \to Smaller(y, z))$	*for all y , for all z , if y is a cube , z is a dodecahedron and y is in back of z , then y is smaller than z*
10	GGC	$\neg(Cube(a) \land Cube(d)) \lor LeftOf(a, d) \lor LeftOf(d, a)$	*it is not the case that a is a cube and d is a cube , a is to the left of d or d is to the left of a*
11	RG	$Student(a) \lor (Medium(b) \lor \forall xSameSize(x, x))$	*a is a student , b is medium or for all x , x is of the same size as itself*
12	RG	$\forall x\neg(LeftOf(x, x) \to LeftOf(a, b))$	*for all x , it is not the case that if x is to the left of itself , then a is to the left of b*
13	RG	$Adjoins(a, b) \land ((SameRow(a, b) \land Person(b)) \to (Dodec(c) \land RightOf(c, a)))$	*all these hold :* • *a is adjacent to b* • *if a is in the same row as b and b is a person , then c is a dodecahedron and c is to the right of a*
14	RG	$\forall xRightOf(a, a)$	*for all x , a is to the right of itself*
15	RG	$\forall x\forall x\exists xSameSize(x, a)$	*for all x , for all x , there is an element x such that x is of the same size as a*
16	RG	$\exists x\forall x\neg Larger(x, x)$	*there is an element x such that for all x , x is not larger than x*
17	RG	$\neg(Adjoins(a, b) \to Adjoins(a, c)) \lor \neg(Student(c) \land Medium(a))$	*it is not the case that if a is adjacent to b , then a is adjacent to c or it is not the case that c is a student and a is medium*
18	RG	$Medium(a) \lor ((Small(b) \to Tet(b)) \to \neg Person(c))$	*at least one of these holds :* • *a is medium* • *if if b is small , then b is a tetrahedron , then c is not a person*
19	RG	$\forall x\exists xSameSize(x, a)$	*for all x , there is an element x such that x is of the same size as a*
20	RG	$(\exists xFrontOf(a, x) \to (Large(a) \land SameSize(a, b))) \lor Smaller(c, c)$	*at least one of these holds :* • *if there is an element x such that a is in front of x , then a is large and of the same size as b* • *c is smaller than itself*
21	Filler	$\neg\exists x(SameShape(a, b) \to SameRow(c, c))$	*it is not the case that there is an element x such that a is in the same shape as b and c is in the same row as itself*
22	Filler	$\forall x(Tet(x) \lor Prime(a)) \lor \exists x(Person(x) \to Student(a))$	*for all x , x is a tetrahedron or a is a prime or there is an element x such that a is a student*
23	Filler	$\exists x\forall yLarger(x, a) \land \forall y\neg Pet(b)$	*there is an element x such that for all y , x is larger than a and there is an element x such that for all y , b is not a pet*
24	Filler	$\exists x(((SameShape(x, a) \land Tet(x)) \to Adjoins(x, a))$	*for all x , if x is of the same shape as a, then x is adjacent to a*
25	Filler	$\exists xCube(x)(Person(a) \to Adjoins(x, a))$	*there is a cube such that a is a person or x is adjacent to a*

Table 13: One example batch of formulae and translations of the experimental items used in the TQA (GGC = formulae taken from the Grade Grinder Corpus with Ranta (2011)'s translation, RG = randomly generated formulae with Ranta (2011)'s translation, Filler = randomly generated formulae with manually crafted incorrect translation).

NATURAL LANGUAGE INFERENCE & FLUENCY RANKING

Thank you very much for participating in this experiment! In this experiment, you will be performing 2 separate tasks, which will be explained to you beforehand. It will take approximately 30 minutes to complete the tasks. If at any point you would like to stop, you can close this form and your response will be deleted. If you do want to participate, your response will be handled anonymously: The information in this study will only be used in ways that will not reveal who you are. You will not be identified in any publication from this study or in any data files shared with other researchers. Your participation in this study is confidential. If you wish to participate, please confirm your consent in the following question. For any questions about the survey, you can contact us.

0. Informed consent
   I have read the above information and understand the purpose of the research and that data will be collected from me. I also understand that participating in this study is completely voluntary. I agree that data gathered for the study may be published or made available provided my name or other identifying information is not used.
   O I confirm this
   O I do not confirm this and want to withdraw from participation

1. Personal questions
   What is your gender?
   O Male
   O Female
   O Prefer not to say

   How old are you?

   How would you rate your proficiency in English?
   1 2 3 4 5

   How would you rate your knowledge of and familiarity with first-order logic?
   1 Lower level than the ones below
   2 Level of a bachelor/master student who has followed 1 or 2 classes of logic.
   3 Level of a bachelor/master student who has followed more than 2 classes of logic.
   4 Higher level than the ones above

   From which perspective have you mainly studied logic?
   O Computational/mathematical perspective
   O Linguistic/philosophical perspective
   O Another perspective

   Did you participate in our previous experiment in March 2022? This experiment was called "Evaluating English translations from First-Order Logic formulae". The participants were asked to judge the quality of English translations from First-Order Logic formulae, and provide suggestions for better translations.
   O Yes
   O No

2. Natural Language Inference

As we explained before, you will be performing 2 separate tasks in this experiment. The first one is called Natural Language Inference task, which works as follows: In each question, you are shown two sentences, which are called the premise and the hypothesis. You will be asked to think about whether the hypothesis follows from the premise or not.

For your information, the premises and hypotheses always make claims about a domain consisting of objects called A, B, C, D, E and F. There are no other objects in this domain. Some premises and hypotheses might describe weird or impossible situations. This is because the domain is part of an extraordinary world, where it can happen that something is smaller than itself, or next to itself; where something can be smaller and larger than something else at the same time; where cubes can be even and odd; where objects are not always of the same size as itself. The only thing you have to worry about, however, is whether the hypothesis is automatically true if the premise is true, no matter how odd their interpretations.

Here are two example questions to give you an idea of what the task looks like:

Example 1. Does the hypothesis automatically follow from the premise?
Premise: It is not the case that B is to the left of some cube.
Hypothesis: There is no cube.

- O Yes
- O No
- O Other (pick this option if is unclear whether the hypothesis follows from the premise, and explain why)

In this example, the correct answer is No, because the premise only states that B is not to the left of some cube, but does not state anything about the existence of cubes in general. So it does not follow from the premise that there is no cube.

Example 2. Does the hypothesis automatically follow from the premise?
Premise: For all x, x is a cube.
Hypothesis: B is a cube.

- O Yes
- O No
- O Other (pick this option if is unclear whether the hypothesis follows from the premise, and explain why)

The premise is a translation from a first-order logic formula. It quantifies over the entire domain, stating that for all objects x in the domain, x is a cube. In other words: Everything is a cube. So the correct answer is Yes, because if everything in the domain is a cube, then B, an object in the domain, is a cube.

In answering the following questions, choose the third answer option Other if it is debatable whether the hypothesis follows from the premise (e.g., if the premise is open to multiple interpretations, or if you do not understand the premise or hypothesis). Explain there shortly what is unclear. Please do not think too long about each question. If you have much trouble understanding the premise or hypothesis, choose the Other option and move on.

(Now 42 NLI questions of the following form are shown:)

Does the hypothesis automatically follow from the premise? Pick the third answer option if it is unclear whether the hypothesis follows from the premise (e.g., if the premise is open to multiple interpretations, or if you do not understand the premise or hypothesis), and explain why.
Premise: <premise>
Hypothesis: <hypothesis>

- O Yes
- O No
- O Other

3. Fluency Ranking

The purpose of this second (and final) task, which is called Fluency Ranking task, is to evaluate the fluency of English translations from first-order logic formulas. We will present to you, one by one, 20 formulas with 3 candidate translations, like in the example below:

Formula:	$\neg \exists x (Cube (x) \land LeftOf (B , x))$
Translation 1:	There is no element x such that x is a cube and B is to the left of x.
Translation 2:	It is not the case that there is an element x such that x is a cube and B is to the left of x.
Translation 3:	For all cubes x, B is not to the left of x or x is not even.

Please rank the translations by the criterion of fluency, where rank 1 stands for the most fluent, and 3 for the least fluent translation. By a fluent translation, we mean a translation that sounds as a natural English sentence. In ranking, ties are allowed. So, for example, if you think Translation 1 is best and Translation 2 and 3 are equally bad, give Translation 1 the highest rank (1), and Translation 2 and 3 the next highest rank (2), assigning nothing to the third rank.

In ranking the translations, please note that it is very important that you evaluate the fluency of the translations based only on the form of the translations (not on their adequacy given the formula). It can happen that two candidate translations are exactly the same. Please assign them the same rank always.

For your information, these are the interpretations of the predicates used in the formulas:

Dodec (x)	x is a dodecahedron
Small (x)	x is small
Student (x)	x is a student
Medium (x)	x is medium
Cube (x)	x is a cube
Prime (x)	x is a prime
Person (x)	x is a person
Tet (x)	x is a tetrahedron
Pet (x)	x is a pet
Large (x)	x is large
Even (x)	x is even
Adjoins (x , y)	x is adjacent to y
SameCol (x , y)	x is in the same column as y
LeftOf (x , y)	x is to the left of y
RightOf (x , y)	x is to the right of y

```
Smaller ( x , y )           x is smaller than y
FrontOf ( x , y )           x is in front of y
Larger ( x , y )            x is larger than y
SameRow ( x , y )           x is in the same row as y
SameShape ( x , y )         x is of the same shape as y
SameSize ( x , y )          x is of the same size as y
BackOf ( x , y )            x is in back of y

(Now 20 FR questions of the following form are shown:)
    Given the following formula and candidate translations, rank the translations from most fluent (1) to least fluent (3). Base
    your ranking only on the criterion of fluency (how natural the sentence sounds in English). Ties are allowed.
    Formula:            <formula>
    Translation 1:      <translation 1>
    Translation 2:      <translation 2>
    Translation 3:      <translation 3>

      (Most fluent) 1  2  3 (Least fluent)
Translation 1       O  O  O
Translation 2       O  O  O
Translation 3       O  O  O

4. Final question
Do you have any final comments on the survey?
```

Figure 9: The instructions and questions shown to the participants in the human evaluation.

Controllable Text Generation *for All Ages*: Evaluating a Plug-and-Play Approach to Age-Adapted Dialogue

Lennert Jansen[†], Štěpán Lars Laichter[†], Arabella Sinclair[‡], Margot J. van der Goot[†], Raquel Fernández[†], Sandro Pezzelle[†]
[†]University of Amsterdam, [‡]University of Aberdeen
{lennertjansen95|lars.laichter}@gmail.com
arabella.sinclair@abdn.ac.uk
{m.j.vandergoot|raquel.fernandez|s.pezzelle}@uva.nl

Abstract

To be trusted and perceived as natural and coherent, conversational systems must adapt to the language of their users. While personalized dialogue is a promising direction, controlling generation for fine-grained language features remains a challenge in this approach. A recent line of research showed the effectiveness of leveraging pre-trained language models toward adapting to a text's topic or sentiment. In this study, we build on these approaches and focus on a higher-level dimension of language variation: speakers' age. We frame the task as a dialogue response generation, and test methods based on bag-of-words (BoW) and neural discriminators (Disc) to condition the output of GPT-2 and DialoGPT without altering the parameters of the language models. We show that Disc models achieve a higher degree of detectable control than BoW models based on automatic evaluation. In contrast, humans can partially detect age differences in BoW but not Disc responses. Since BoW responses are deemed better than Disc ones by humans, simple controllable methods thus appear to be a better tradeoff between adaptation and language quality. Our work confirms the challenges of adapting to higher-level dimensions of language variation. Moreover, it highlights the need to evaluate natural language generation thoroughly.

1 Introduction

Developing dialogue systems that can hold human-like conversations has been a long-standing goal in Artificial Intelligence (AI) research. This includes the ability to mimic speakers' speaking styles and language traits, which is shown to be of crucial importance for systems to be trusted and perceived as natural and coherent (Shum et al., 2018; van der Goot and Pilgrim, 2019).

Current approaches in conversational models typically aim to improve dialogues by leveraging *persona*-specific traits—a speaker's age, gender, geographic location, etc. This is achieved by training systems with either implicit (Kottur et al., 2017; Li et al., 2016) or explicit (Qian et al., 2018; Zhang et al., 2018; Zheng et al., 2019) representations of a speaker. These approaches are generally shown to produce multi-turn conversations that are deemed of better quality by humans, but they pay little attention to understanding what factors determine human judgements. Recently, See et al. (2019) showed that linguistic aspects such as specificity, relatedness, and repetition play an important role, and that explicitly controlling for them during generation increases human engagement in a conversation. However, fine-tuning these large models to control the generation turns out to be a challenging task, which is further limited by the scarcity of annotated conversational datasets.

A recent growing interest in controllable text generation has been fostered by approaches leveraging large pre-trained language models (PLMs; see Sec. 2.2). In particular, one direction is to operate at the decoding stage while leaving the underlying PLM unaltered (Dathathri et al., 2020; Li et al., 2022), which was shown to be successful in generating texts that adapt to a specific topic, length or sentiment. Though these approaches are not typically aimed at modelling conversations, they have been shown to be also suitable to generate controlled responses to dialogue utterances (Madotto et al., 2020).

Building on this line of research, in this study we explore adaptation by large PLMs to a specific, yet unexplored dimension: language variation due to speakers' **age**. The relationship between a person's age and their use of language is a thoroughly studied subject in linguistics and psychology, and various differences between younger and older speakers have been reported at the level of both content and style (see Pennebaker and Stone, 2003). While a few studies showed that speakers' age can be predicted both in discourse and dialogue (see Sec. 2.1),

Proceedings of the 2nd Workshop on Natural Language Generation, Evaluation, and Metrics (GEM), pages 172 - 188
December 7, 2022

no work to date has explored whether, and to what extent, age-related detectable features can be leveraged by controllable text generation models.

In this study, we explore this issue for the first time. Though previous work showed that some degree of adaptation can be achieved to a text's sentiment or topic, we argue that age-related traits are different since they involve subtle, fine-grained features lying at a more abstract level compared to other language dimensions. Therefore, we hypothesize that this task is more challenging and possibly requires complex adaptation strategies.

Following the approach by Madotto et al. (2020), we experiment with dialogue data and frame the controlled generation problem as the task of generating a response to a dialogue utterance. We opt for this setup since it allows us to genuinely investigate language adaptation while leaving aside the extra challenges of modelling full, multi-turn dialogues. Though generally short, single dialogue utterances are shown to contain a fair amount of age-related language signal (Jansen et al., 2021).

We employ the Plug-and-Play Language Model (PPLM) method by Dathathri et al. (2020) and condition the generation of two large PLMs, GPT-2 (Radford et al., 2019) and DialoGPT (Zhang et al., 2020a), by means of various age-specific attribute models. With this approach, generation is steered leaving the underlying PLM unaltered. We test two attribute models based on bag-of-words (BoW) methods or more complex neural discriminators, and perform extensive evaluation of the generated outputs.

Through automatic evaluation, we show that (1) some degree of detectable age adaptation is achieved by all tested models, with (2) discriminator methods outperforming simpler BoW strategies. At the same time, (3) BoW models turn out to produce more fluent and less repetitive responses compared to the more complex models. These results are partially disconfirmed when moving to human evaluation. Indeed, (1) humans can detect age-related differences in the generated language only to a very limited extent, and (2) this is restricted to responses by BoW but not discriminator models. As for the quality of the generated language, (3) outputs by BoW are deemed more fluent and human-like compared to discriminator ones, though this does not systematically correspond to a perceived *better* output. Based on these results, BoW-based controllable strategies appear to be a better tradeoff between adaptation and language quality compared to more complex methods.

Overall, our results confirm the challenges of adapting to higher-level dimensions of language variation, such as those due to speakers' age. Moreover, we highlight the need of complementing automatic analyses with fine-grained human evaluation. Data and code to reproduce our experiments can be found here: `https://github.com/lennertjansen/pplm-age-adapt-dialogue`.

2 Related Work

2.1 Language and Age

A wealth of studies in linguistics and psychology showed that age plays a role in affecting both the content and style of the speaker's language (for further references and discussion, see Pennebaker and Stone, 2003). These findings motivated NLP research aimed at predicting the age of a speaker based on their language. By training a feature-based classifier on a corpus of age-annotated blog posts, Schler et al. (2006) found that speakers' age is best predicted by a combination of content and style features. A similar pattern of results was reported by Nguyen et al. (2011), who extended the investigation to phone conversations and online posts, and by Nguyen et al. (2013), who focused on tweets. Rao et al. (2010) further showed the advantage of including sociolinguistic features when dealing with tweets, with Rosenthal and McKeown (2011) showing that including features of a speaker's online behavior is beneficial when experimenting with blog posts. Recently, Jansen et al. (2021) went beyond feature-based approaches and showed that BERT (Devlin et al., 2019) outperforms other methods when fine-tuned on a dataset of dialogue utterances. Again, both stylistic and lexical cues were reported to be relevant for distinguishing between age groups.

Overall, these studies revealed that the language by younger and older speakers can be detected, among other aspects, by the use of slang and neologisms, pronouns, affect words, capitalizations, alphabetical lengthening, acronyms and verb tenses. Surprisingly, little attention has been paid to model age-related differences in language generation. One exception is represented by research on personalized conversational models, where age is typically considered as one of the speaker-specific traits (Li et al., 2016; Zheng et al., 2019). In these approaches, however, age adaptation is neither explicitly enforced nor directly measured. We tackle this problem by leveraging recent methods from controllable text generation.

2.2 Controllable Text Generation

Broadly speaking, controllable text generation (CTG) refers to the problem of generating texts that meet certain controllable constraints, which are usually task-specific (for an overview, see Prabhumoye et al., 2020; Zhang et al., 2022). In the context of storytelling, for example, endowing a story with a plot and an ending is a CTG problem, as is the control of topic, sentiment or style in a discourse or dialogue response. The latter line of research, aimed at enforcing attribute-based generation, is particularly relevant to our work. Focusing on discourse data such as reviews or news, various studies demonstrated the effectiveness of RNN language models (Ficler and Goldberg, 2017), VAEs (Hu et al., 2017; Wang et al., 2019; Xu et al., 2020), and GANs (Wang and Wan, 2018) in controlling for attributes such as sentiment, theme, style or, more rarely, age (Lample et al., 2019). As for dialogue, early approaches showed the effectiveness of SEQ2SEQ models in capturing speaking style and background information of specific speakers (Li et al., 2016). However, all these approaches heavily rely on large-scale datasets, which is a challenge for supervised and cross-domain text generation tasks (Zhang et al., 2022).

To alleviate this limitation, approaches that leverage large pre-trained language models (PLMs) such as GPT (Radford et al., 2019), GPT-3 (Brown et al., 2020), T5 (Raffel et al., 2020) or DialoGPT (Zhang et al., 2020a) were recently proposed. Some of them model CTG by fine-tuning the PLM parameters (Lin et al., 2021); others by changing the PLM architecture or training a large conditional model from scratch (Keskar et al., 2019; Zhang et al., 2020b; Wang et al., 2021; He, 2021; Zeng and Nie, 2021). While these methods have generally proven effective in controlling for the desired attribute in a dialogue, discourse, and even image captioning setting, they are often computationally expensive to train and involve fine-tuning or modifying the PLM for each desired attribute. To avoid these issues, a few approaches have proposed to operate at the decoding stage by steering the PLM outputs while leaving its parameters unaltered (Dathathri et al., 2020; Khalifa et al., 2020; Krause et al., 2021; Liu et al., 2021; Yang and Klein, 2021; Li et al., 2022).

One of the most successful and popular methods is the Plug-and-Play Language Model (PPLM; Dathathri et al., 2020). Using a previously trained attribute-based classifier (with 100,000 times fewer parameters than the PLM) to guide text generation by the PLM, this approach was shown to achieve a good degree of CTG for topic and sentiment in a discourse setting while being very inexpensive to train. Motivated by this, Madotto et al. (2020) extended the approach to model dialogue response generation and demonstrated its portability to the conversational domain, where a high degree of control for sentiment and topic was achieved while ensuring fluency. In this work, we build on Madotto et al. (2020) and make a step forward by controlling a more abstract, higher-level dimension compared to sentiment or topic: language variation due to speakers' age.

3 Problem Formulation

In general terms, the problem we tackle is the following: given a dialogue utterance (*prompt*), we generate a dialogue response (*output*).

3.1 Non-Adaptive Setting

In the non-adaptive setting, we tackle the task as a plain text generation problem. Given a prompt, a Transformer-based pre-trained language model $p(\mathbf{x})$ generates an output **x** by sampling from the distribution of words that are assigned the highest likelihood of following the prompt. This can be seen as sampling from a conditional distribution, $p(\mathbf{x}|\texttt{prompt})$.

3.2 Age-Adaptive Setting

In the age-adaptive setting, the task is an instance of controllable text generation (CTG). Given a prompt, we seek to generate an output that is controlled for age, i.e., that resembles a response by a *younger/older* speaker. This can be seen as a subproblem of vanilla text generation: the conditioning factor for the generated text is further constrained to also include some predefined attribute, a (in our case, age). CTG is then analogous to sampling from the conditional distribution, $p(\mathbf{x}|\texttt{prompt}, a)$.

PPLM To control generation, we use the PPLM method (Dathathri et al., 2020). PPLM builds on a text classifier or attribute model, $p(a|x)$, that represents the degree of adherence of text x to a certain attribute a, e.g., age. Since the attribute model,

$p(a|x)$, is used to control the generation by a pre-trained Transformer-based language model, $p(x)$, PPLM can be seen as modeling the conditional distribution of generated text x given a, i.e., $p(x|a)$.

In simple terms, the attribute model perturbs the activation space of the underlying language model by making it more likely to generate text that aligns with the predefined attribute. This is achieved by leaving the parameters of the underlying language model unaltered. More formally, PPLM perturbs the generated output one token at a time in the direction of the sum of two gradients: (1) by maximizing the loglikelihood of a under the conditional attribute model $p(a|x)$ (to enforce control); (2) by ensuring high loglikelihood of the generated text under the unaltered language model $p(x)$ (to enforce fluency). The gradient updates only affect the activation space, i.e., the original model parameters are preserved. Sampling is done by following gradients in the latent representation space by approximately implementing the Metropolis-adjusted Langevin sampler (Roberts and Tweedie, 1996) deployed in Nguyen et al. (2017).[1]

4 Method

In our experimental pipeline, we condition the generation of two large pre-trained language models by means of two age-specific attribute models. In particular, we generate responses to a number of dialogue utterances used to prompt text generation. We then evaluate the extent to which the generated responses contain age-related features that can be detected by automatic metrics.

4.1 Data

To train/initialize our attribute models, we use the data introduced by Jansen et al. (2021). This data comes from the spoken partition of the British National Corpus (BNC; Love et al., 2017) and includes dialogue utterances by users from either of two age groups: a *younger* group (age: 19-29) and an *older* group (age: 50 or more). In total, the data consists of 172,303 utterances, i.e., 138,662 *younger* utterances and 33,641 *older* ones. In addition to the full dataset, Jansen et al. (2021) also use a partition of it which is balanced per age group and includes 67,282 total utterances. This is the split of the data they employ to train their *younger/older* classifiers (Sec. 4.5). As described in Sec. 4.3, we use both the full and balanced version of the data.

[1]See Dathathri et al. (2020) for further details.

younger-specific words	older-specific words
um, sh*t, cool, f*cking, friends, literally, weekend, amazing, friend, ha, huh, hate, fun, blah, uni, massive, Friday, parents, mate, hell, annoying, wait, ridiculous, crazy, horrible	may, mother, perhaps, huge, business, although, certainly, email, along, often, possibly, wonderful, dear, supposed, otherwise, asked, gosh, bits, almost, particularly, decided, finished, across, near, flat

Table 1: Some of the younger- (age 19-29) and older-specific (age 50+) words used by the BoW method.

4.2 Pre-Trained Language Models

We experiment with two large pre-trained language models: GPT-2 (Radford et al., 2019) and DialoGPT (Zhang et al., 2020a). We generate responses using these two models both in a non-adaptive (Sec. 3.1) and age-adaptive setting (Sec. 3.2). In the age-adaptive setting, the models are conditioned by an attribute model. Similarly to Dathathri et al. (2020), we experiment with two attribute models.

4.3 Age-Controlled Language Models

Below, we describe the attribute models used in our study. For both models, we experiment with the same hyperparameters, reported in Appendix A.

BoW-based attribute model This method relies on lists of words that are representative of each age group's language. We automatically extract them from the full version of the dataset via a frequency-based approach. In particular, for each age group, we (i) order all unique words by frequency; (ii) keep the most frequent words—the ones that make up for at least 85% of the cumulative occurrences; (iii) remove words that are in both age groups; (iv) keep, for each group, only the words that account for at least 85% of the respective cumulative occurrences.[2] Our final lists include 56 younger- and 92 older-specific words. A few examples can be found in Table 1. The BoW-based attribute model gives the log of the sum of likelihoods of each word in the list. Given a bag-of-word $\{w_1, ..., w_k\}$ that represents a given age group a, and the output distribution of the language model p_{t+1}, the attribute model's log-likelihood is:

$$\log p(a|x) = \log \left(\sum_{i}^{k} p_{t+1}[w_i] \right) \quad (1)$$

[2]The 85-th percentile cutoff points are used to yield wordlists of similar lengths as those by Dathathri et al. (2020).

Ascending $\nabla \log p(a|x)$ increases the likelihood of generating words that are either in the BoW or not in the BoW, but semantically related.

Neural discriminator attribute model We randomly split the balanced version of the dataset into a training (90%) and test (10%) set and train a neural classifier to distinguish between dialogue utterances from the two age groups. The classifier receives the representation of the sentence from the last layer of a frozen pre-trained language model and performs the binary task via a single linear layer. The size of both the input and linear layer is equal to the size of the LM's output layer. The discriminator is trained using Adam (Kingma and Ba, 2015) with a learning rate of $1 \cdot 10^{-4}$ and default values for all other parameters from PyTorch's implementation of Adam, with a maximum sequence length of 512 tokens, for 20 epochs, and a batch size of 64. The discriminator parameters that are used in the age-adaptive setting come from the epoch with the highest test accuracy (67.4% accuracy for GPT-2, 67.6% for DialoGPT).

4.4 Prompts

In both the non-adaptive and age-adaptive settings, we prompt the models with handcrafted dialogue utterances. This allows us to devise dialogue utterances that are neither younger- nor older-sounding,[3] so as to genuinely explore age adaptation of the tested methods while minimizing bias effects. We experiment with the following 5 prompts: (i) *Good weather we're having*; (ii) *Can we talk?*; (iii) *Hi, how's it going?*; (iv) *Hey*; (v) *Hello, tell me about your latest holiday*.[4] For each prompt, we let models generate 6 outputs of a given token length. Since we experiment with 9 output lengths (6, 12, 24, 30, 36, 42, 48, 54, and 60 tokens), each model is evaluated over a total of 270 dialogue responses, i.e., 5 prompts $\times$ 9 lenghts $\times$ 6 outputs. [5]

4.5 Evaluation

We evaluate model outputs along two dimensions: age adaptation and quality of generated language.

[3]We verify this by feeding the prompts to the best-performing BERT-based younger/older classifier by Jansen et al. (2021). We consider them *neutral* if the classifier assigns a probability of 0.6 or lower to both age groups.

[4]For comparison, we have also experimented with prompts that are classified as either younger- or older-sounding. Results are in Appendix C.

[5]An exhaustive exploration of the effect of various prompts and output lengths is beyond the scope of this study. We leave it for future work.

Age adaptation To quantify age adaptation, we leverage the best-predictive younger/older classifier by Jansen et al. (2021). This model adds a dropout layer and a linear layer on top of BERT embeddings (Devlin et al., 2019), which are fine-tuned on the age classification task. In particular, we use the weights of the best-performing run of their model (achieving 73% accuracy) and report accuracy in predicting the expected age, i.e., the one which the model has been adapted to. Note that we do not use this classifier as an attribute model to condition generation for 2 main reasons: (1) BERT and *GPT models differ on several levels, which would make the implementation technically challenging; (3) using BERT as an attribute model would go against the overall goal of PPLM, which is to use tiny models to condition large models.

Language quality Following standard practice in NLG, we take perplexity of an external LM as a proxy for fluency of the generated language: the lower the perplexity, the higher the fluency of the generated output. Perplexity (ppl) is expressed as:

$$\text{ppl}(\mathbf{x}) = \exp\left\{-\frac{1}{t}\sum_{i}^{t} \ln p_\theta(x_i|x_{<i})\right\} \quad (2)$$

where $\mathbf{x}$ represents a sequence of tokens, t is sequence length, x_i is the i-th token, and θ denotes the LM's parameters. Following Dathathri et al. (2020), we obtain perplexity scores by GPT-1 (Radford et al., 2018).

Furthermore, we evaluate the degree of text diversity by considering the normalized number of distinct unigrams (Dist-1), bigrams (Dist-2), and trigrams (Dist-3) in the generated output. The higher the score, the less repetitive the language is.

5 Results

Age adaptation Tables 2a and 2b report the results by the younger-adapted and older-adapted models, respectively. As can be seen, discriminator-based models (Disc) achieve a higher degree of age control as detected by automatic means compared to bag-of-words (BoW). This is particularly the case for the older setting, where both GPT2-based and DialoGPT-based Disc models outperform their BoW counterparts by more than 30 accuracy points, with BoW models being far below chance level. As for the younger setting, BoW models perform comparably better by slightly underperforming (DialoGPT) or outperforming (GPT2) their Disc coun-

Model	ppl ↓ better	Dist-1 ↑ better	Dist-2 ↑ better	Dist-3 ↑ better	Acc. ↑ better
GPT-2 (G)	**27.50** (6.58)	0.87 (0.09)	**0.94** (0.04)	**0.90** (0.06)	-
G-BoW	27.91 (7.18)	0.87 (0.10)	0.93 (0.05)	**0.90** (0.06)	70.4%
G-Discrim	32.09 (18.98)	0.77 (0.20)	0.86 (0.13)	0.84 (0.15)	67.8%
DialoGPT (D)	37.52 (12.06)	0.86 (0.13)	0.90 (0.08)	0.85 (0.10)	-
D-BoW	38.53 (12.64)	0.87 (0.12)	0.90 (0.08)	0.86 (0.10)	83.0%
D-Discrim	42.01 (16.94)	**0.90** (0.12)	0.86 (0.14)	0.77 (0.22)	**85.9%**

(a) Younger-adapted models

Model	ppl ↓ better	Dist-1 ↑ better	Dist-2 ↑ better	Dist-3 ↑ better	Acc. ↑ better
GPT-2 (G)	**27.50** (6.58)	**0.87** (0.09)	**0.94** (0.04)	**0.90** (0.06)	-
G-BoW	27.58 (7.07)	0.86 (0.10)	0.93 (0.04)	**0.90** (0.06)	43.0%
G-Discrim	47.15 (47.56)	0.73 (0.24)	0.75 (0.28)	0.75 (0.27)	**74.3%**
DialoGPT (D)	37.52 (12.06)	0.86 (0.13)	0.90 (0.08)	0.85 (0.10)	-
D-BoW	37.85 (11.17)	**0.87 (0.12)**	0.90 (0.08)	0.86 (0.09)	21.5%
D-Discrim	41.17 (20.72)	**0.87 (0.12)**	0.89 (0.13)	0.83 (0.16)	56.7%

(b) Older-adapted models

Table 2: Results of age-controlled dialogue generation. Format: *average metric (standard error)*. **ppl** is perplexity wrt GPT-1. **Dist-n** (for $n = 1, 2, 3$) is the number of distinct n-grams normalized by text length. **Acc.** stands for accuracy of the younger/older classifier. Values in **bold** are the best in the column; the second-best are underlined.

terparts. Overall, these results show that Disc models are more effective than simple BoW ones to control for age-related language features, with this advantage being particularly evident in the older setting.

Striking differences in performance can be observed between GPT2- and DialoGPT-based models. While the latter clearly outperform the former in the younger setting (+13-18 acc. points), an opposite pattern is observed in the older setting, with GPT2-based models gaining 18-22 points over their DialoGPT-based counterparts. This divergent pattern is interesting, and could be due to a younger-language bias of DialoGPT (fine-tuned on Reddit threads, where the majority of users are in the age range 20-29), which would limit adaptation toward the older group.[6] On average, BoW models are more effective in GPT-2 than DialoGPT (56.7 vs 52.3), while Disc results are on par (71.1 vs 71.3).

Taken together, these results show that the PPLM approach is effective in controlling for age-related language features that can be detected by a trained classifier, and that adaptation is stronger when using a neural discriminator attribute model.

Language quality Moving to measures of language quality, we observe that the base GPT-2 is either the best or the second-best with respect to both perplexity and number of distinct n-grams. As for age-adapted models, BoW ones are generally shown to outperform Disc models. GPT2-based BoW models, in particular, appear to be the best overall age-adapted models: they compare to GPT-2 in terms of both fluency and diversity, which confirms that conditioning generation through wordlists does not negatively impact on the quality of the generated language. In contrast, Disc models perform comparably worse on these metrics, which suggests a much bigger impact.

Since automatic metrics are known to have their own limitations (see, e.g., the case of perplexity in capturing language fluency; Mir et al., 2019), in the next section we complement the results by the automatic metrics via extensive human analysis.

[6]This is supported by the mean probabilities assigned by the BERT-based classifier to the younger class on DialoGPT and GPT-2 outputs: 0.76 for DialoGPT, 0.62 for GPT-2.

6 Analysis

We run 3 crowdsourcing studies with human participants aimed at (1) exploring whether age differences detected by a classifier correspond to human intuitions on age-related language features; (2) assessing the quality of each model's generated language; (3) testing which age-adapted model produces the best outputs. Based on their overall better age control and language quality, we choose to focus on GPT2-based models: GPT2 (hence, *base*), BoW-younger, BoW-older, Disc-younger, and Disc-older. Data collection is performed on Appen (`appen.com`). Participants are paid 0.08$ per judgement (which corresponds to around 10$/hour considering a conservative rate of 2 judgements/minute). In total, the full data collection costed around 2.5K$. The instructions given to the participants in the three studies we describe below are available in Appendix D. Participants were restricted to be from English-speaking countries and we used test-questions for quality control: only participants who correctly answered at least 70% of test-questions were considered trustworthy.

6.1 Are Age-Related Differences Detectable?

We aim at testing whether the age-adapted outputs by a model (e.g., BoW-younger) are perceived as sounding more like their target age group (*younger*) than those by both its counterpart (BoW-older) and the base model. Therefore, we set up three comparisons of outputs by BoW and Disc models, respectively: younger vs older, younger vs base, and older vs base. In particular, we experiment with 300 outputs per model,which sums up to 900 unique outputs within BoW and 900 within Disc models. Outputs from various models are paired based on the same prompt and if they have similar length.[7] We ask 5 participants to judge which of the two outputs in a given comparison pair sounds younger/older than the other. In total, we collect 9K judgements by 467 different participants. Table 3 shows some examples.

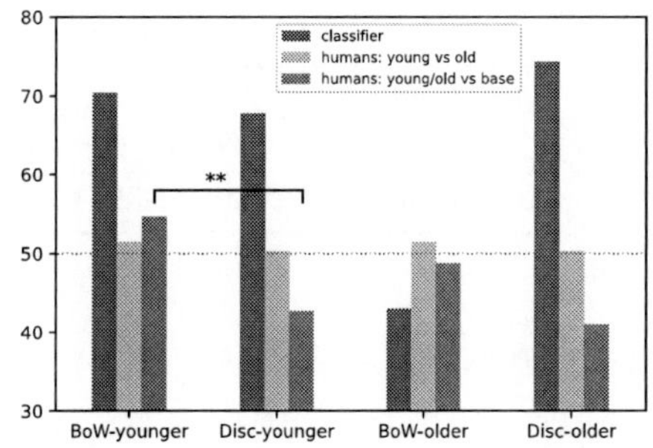

Figure 1: Accuracy by humans and the classifier in detecting age-adapted outputs. The dotted red line indicates chance level; ** stands for statistical significance at $p < 0.01$. Best viewed in color.

Results We consider the assessment for a pair as correct if at least 3 out of 5 participants converge on the target age group; otherwise, we deem it wrong. In Figure 1, we report the results of this analysis. As can be seen, human 'accuracy' lags well behind the accuracy by the classifier in 3 models out of 4. This is not the case only for BoW-older, where the classifier's accuracy is below chance level. One striking observation is that, overall, the degree of age control detected by humans is very limited, and indeed never significantly outperforming chance level (50%) for $p < 0.05$.[8] This suggests that what makes an output sound as younger or older for a text classifier is not something that is clearly detectable by humans. This could be due to the different type of language features that human speakers and the models leverage when making this assessment. For example, a classifier could exploit regularities on topics or domains that are present in the training data, while human participants solely rely on information from their language competence.[9]

At the same time, some age-related features appear to be present in the outputs by BoW-younger, where human accuracy in detecting younger from base outputs reaches 55% – though this comparison is not significantly different from chance according to conventional statistical criteria.[10] Moreover, we find that the difference between BoW-younger (M = 0.55, SD = 0.5) and Disc-younger (M = 0.43, SD = 0.5) is statistically significant via an unpaired t-test, t(587) = 2.9, $p = .003$. In contrast, no adaptation at all is detected by humans in the outputs by Disc models.

These results indicate that the adaptation to age brought by a PPLM approach can be detected by human speakers only to a limited extent. At the same time, BoW models are generally better than Disc ones, and this difference is statistically significant

[7]See Appendix E for more details on data preprocessing.

[8]We test this by means of a one-sample t-test.

[9]What are the cues that guide this assessment is in itself an interesting question, which deserves further investigation.

[10]One-sample t-test between BoW-younger (M = 0.55, SD = 0.5) and chance (M = 0.5), t(288) = 1.6, one-tailed $p = .056$

model	age group	output
BoW	younger	*We have the best weather in the world. I*
BoW	older	*The weather is good and I think you're all going to love it. I'm happy to announce that I have a new home*
Disc	younger	*This is great. It gives us more fun than ever before, and we can enjoy a great coffee. Happy birthday guys. ...*
Disc	older	*The sun was setting when we were getting up with a huge rain and we got stuck in on one one of the three*

Table 3: One example generated for the prompt *'Good weather we're having.'* by each age-adapted model for which at least 4 / 5 participants agreed the response sounds like language from the target age group, both against the other age model and the base model. Some outputs are truncated due to the fixed-length criterion used.

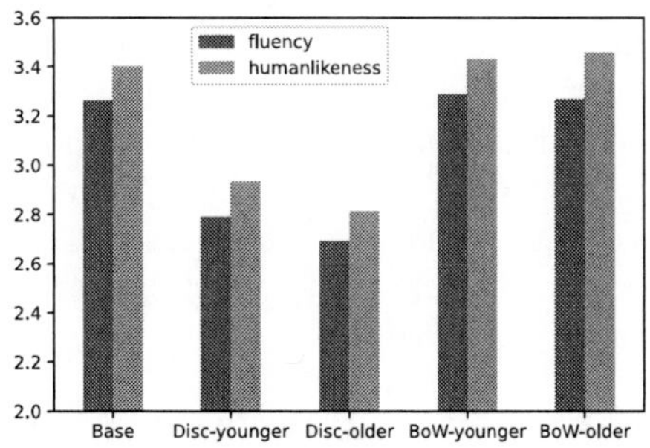

Figure 2: Human judgements on a scale from 1 to 5 on fluency and human-likeness of outputs by the base and the age-adapted models. Best viewed in color.

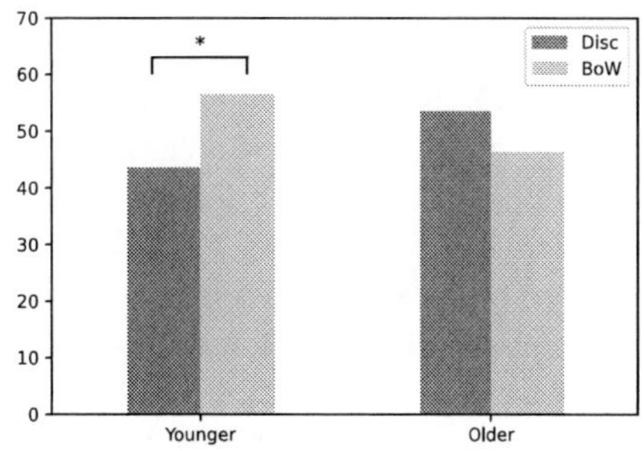

Figure 3: Percentage of human participants who judged an output by a model to be better than an output by another model. Best viewed in color.

for the younger age group. Here, people appear to be better than chance in detecting age-related differences, though this is only a trend without statistical significance (possibly due to sample size).

6.2 Is the Generated Language Good?

We test whether, and to what extent, the language generated by the 4 age-adapted models and the base model, that we use as a control, is deemed good by humans. We consider all the outputs generated by the 5 models, i.e., 1.5K outputs in total. We then ask 5 participants to judge, on a 5-point scale, the degree of *fluency* and *human-likeness* of the output. We define fluent language as having few repetitions and a good flow; human-like as being likely to be produced by a human speaker. We collect a total of 15K judgements, i.e., 7.5K per property, by 278 unique participants.

Results We compute the average score obtained by an output for a property, and then average over all the samples. Results are reported in Figure 2. As can be seen, while BoW models are on par with the base model with respect to both properties, Disc models are assigned much lower values. That is, the outputs by Disc models are deemed much less fluent and less human-like than those by BoW models and the base model. One interesting observation is that judgements of human-likeness are systematically higher than fluency, and this holds for all models. This reveals that the two properties capture different and possibly complementary aspects (a text can be human-like though not perfectly fluent), which highlights the need of using multiple metrics to assess the quality of NLG systems.

Taken together, these results suggest that the perturbations operated by Disc models on the decoding of the LM are heavier than those by BoW models, and that Disc models achieve a level of control that is more detectable by automatic classifiers at the cost of being less fluent and less human-like. It is worth noting that this pattern closely mirrors the perplexity and Dist-n scores reported in Tables 2, where Disc models are shown to be systematically behind GPT2 and BoW-based models.

6.3 Which Models Produce Better Outputs?

We focus on the two younger-adapted and older-adapted models and test which of the two produces an overall better output according to humans. We pair each output by a model with an output by the other model for the same target age group: i.e., BoW-younger vs Disc-younger and BoW-older vs

Disc-older. We end up with 300 pairs per age group, i.e., 600 pairs in total. We then ask 5 participants to judge which of the two outputs in the pair is *overall better*. In total, we collect 3K judgements by 230 distinct participants.

Results For each pair, we take the output with the majority of votes (3 or more). We then compute the proportion of cases in the data where the output by BoW/Disc was chosen. Results are reported in Figure 3. For the younger group, BoW-based outputs (M = 0.56, SD = 0.5) are deemed better than those by Disc (M = 0.44, SD = 0.5), and this difference is statistically significant as per a paired t-test, t(293) = 2.2, p = .026. Surprisingly given the results of the previous analysis (where BoW neatly outperforms Disc in terms of fluency and human-likeness), an opposite pattern is observed for the older group, though the difference between BoW and Disc is not significant (p = .222). We hypothesize that this dissociation could be due to the different types of evaluation (rating vs. binary choice), which deserves further investigation.

7 Conclusion

We focused on age-related language variation and tested whether current approaches to controllable text generation can capture it in a dialogue response. We showed that models achieve substantial adaptation based on automatic metrics, while age-related differences can be detected only to a limited extent by humans. At the same time, simple controllable methods based on BoW appear to be a good trade-off between control and quality. From a broader perspective, our case-study on age adaptation reveals that controlling for subtle, fine-grained language features remains an open challenge. Moreover, we show that human evaluation is crucial to assess the degree of achieved control since it provides different insights compared to automatic metrics (Li et al., 2018; Sudhakar et al., 2019).

Limitations

On the need for age adaptation This work starts from the assumption that users of language technologies, such as dialogue systems or chatbots, would appreciate an age-adaptive system, i.e., would perceive age-adaptation as positive. This is motivated by evidence from psychology and sociolinguistics showing that age-driven linguistic variation is typically in play. Nevertheless, this assumption remains to be validated by means of user studies.

On the impact of prompts While we experiment with both age-neutral and age-adapted prompts, texts are generated based on a limited number of prompts. Further attention should be paid to investigating the impact of prompts (and prompt features) on the resulting outputs.

On the experimental setting While we formulate the problem as dialogue response generation, dialogue features are not exploited. A simple step in this direction could be to experiment with other ways of prompting the model, e.g., by providing a signal of which dialogue participant is speaking (A, B) and whether there is a turn transition between prompt and generated response.

On the use of other CTG methods We experiment with only one CTG method, namely PPLM. In future work, we plan to address this limitation by extending our investigation to other approaches.

Ethics Statement

Broader impact As for most technologies, ours can have a positive impact on society, e.g., by promoting the development of more inclusive systems that speak the language of their users, independently of their age; or, by informing work on debiasing language models, that appear to be biased toward the language of younger groups of users. On the other hand, we acknowledge and are aware of possible harmful or undesirable uses of this technology, e.g., toward amplifying biases or explicitly/implicitly discriminating people based on their age (Rosales and Fernández-Ardèvol, 2020; Stypińska, 2021; Noble, 2018). We advocate for a responsible, rigorous use of the methodology and materials described in this study.

Privacy and discrimination Age is personal data or privately identifying information according to the EU or US defintion, respectively. As such, it is a protected class in US and various other anti-discrimination regulations. In the present sttudy, we experiment with anonymous textual data aggregated at the level of two macro age classes: younger vs older speakers. For a given utterance, we only consider the age range of the speaker who uttered it, 19-29 vs 50+. No info regarding speaker identity (ID, previous dialogues, etc.) or their demographics (gender, location, social status, etc.) is ever considered. We argue this is a valuable way to limit as much as possible any privacy and discrimination risks. We thank the anonymous ethics reviewer for providing valuable input on this and for pointing to the studies cited in the paragraph above.

Human evaluation We ensure human participants taking part in our human evaluation are paid properly according to the standards of our institution's country/countries. To avoid any harm, we carefully remove any offensive or inappropriate language from the samples. Participants were given the opportunity to report any problem when participating in the evaluation. No issues were reported.

Pretrained language models There are serious risks associated with the development and use of large PLMs (Bender et al., 2021), which we leverage in this research. Such risks include the environmental impact of the computational resources required for training and the encoding and possible amplification of biases present in the massive amounts of un-curated data the models learn from. The PPLM approach we explore in the present work provides an alternative to re-training or finetuning the model and in this sense it does not incur further environmental cost. Nevertheless, the approach does rely on a large PLM, with all the lack of transparency regarding the pre-training data that this involves. Our attribute models are trained on the BNC, a carefully curated and documented dataset. Yet, we acknowledge that the lack of control over the PLM pre-training data is likely to occasionally lead to undesirable outputs.

Acknowledgements

We would like to thank the four anonymous GEM reviewers for their valuable feedback and the participants of our crowdsourcing experiments. The work received funding from the University of Amsterdam's Research Priority Area Human(e) AI and from the European Research Council (ERC) under the European Union's Horizon 2020 research and innovation programme (grant agreement No. 819455).

References

Emily M Bender, Timnit Gebru, Angelina McMillan-Major, and Shmargaret Shmitchell. 2021. On the dangers of stochastic parrots: Can language models be too big? In *Proceedings of the 2021 ACM Conference on Fairness, Accountability, and Transparency*, pages 610–623.

Tom Brown, Benjamin Mann, Nick Ryder, Melanie Subbiah, Jared D Kaplan, Prafulla Dhariwal, Arvind Neelakantan, Pranav Shyam, Girish Sastry, Amanda Askell, Sandhini Agarwal, Ariel Herbert-Voss, Gretchen Krueger, Tom Henighan, Rewon Child, Aditya Ramesh, Daniel Ziegler, Jeffrey Wu, Clemens Winter, Chris Hesse, Mark Chen, Eric Sigler, Mateusz Litwin, Scott Gray, Benjamin Chess, Jack Clark, Christopher Berner, Sam McCandlish, Alec Radford, Ilya Sutskever, and Dario Amodei. 2020. Language models are few-shot learners. In *Advances in Neural Information Processing Systems*, volume 33, pages 1877–1901. Curran Associates, Inc.

Sumanth Dathathri, Andrea Madotto, Janice Lan, Jane Hung, Eric Frank, Piero Molino, Jason Yosinski, and Rosanne Liu. 2020. Plug and play language models: A simple approach to controlled text generation. In *International Conference on Learning Representations*.

Jacob Devlin, Ming-Wei Chang, Kenton Lee, and Kristina Toutanova. 2019. BERT: Pre-training of deep bidirectional transformers for language understanding. In *Proceedings of the 2019 Conference of the North American Chapter of the Association for Computational Linguistics: Human Language Technologies, Volume 1 (Long and Short Papers)*, pages 4171–4186, Minneapolis, Minnesota. Association for Computational Linguistics.

Jessica Ficler and Yoav Goldberg. 2017. Controlling linguistic style aspects in neural language generation. In *Proceedings of the Workshop on Stylistic Variation*, pages 94–104, Copenhagen, Denmark. Association for Computational Linguistics.

Xingwei He. 2021. Parallel refinements for lexically constrained text generation with bart. In *Proceedings of the 2021 Conference on Empirical Methods in Natural Language Processing*, pages 8653–8666.

Zhiting Hu, Zichao Yang, Xiaodan Liang, Ruslan Salakhutdinov, and Eric P Xing. 2017. Toward controlled generation of text. In *International conference on machine learning*, pages 1587–1596. PMLR.

Lennert Jansen, Arabella Sinclair, Margot J van der Goot, Raquel Fernández, and Sandro Pezzelle. 2021. Detecting age-related linguistic patterns in dialogue: Toward adaptive conversational systems. In *CLiC-it*.

Nitish Shirish Keskar, Bryan McCann, Lav Varshney, Caiming Xiong, and Richard Socher. 2019. CTRL - A Conditional Transformer Language Model for Controllable Generation. *arXiv preprint arXiv:1909.05858*.

Muhammad Khalifa, Hady Elsahar, and Marc Dymetman. 2020. A distributional approach to controlled text generation. In *International Conference on Learning Representations*.

Diederik P. Kingma and Jimmy Ba. 2015. Adam: A method for stochastic optimization. In *ICLR (Poster)*.

Satwik Kottur, Xiaoyu Wang, and Vitor Carvalho. 2017. Exploring personalized neural conversational models. In *Proceedings of the Twenty-Sixth International Joint Conference on Artificial Intelligence, IJCAI-17*, pages 3728–3734.

Ben Krause, Akhilesh Deepak Gotmare, Bryan McCann, Nitish Shirish Keskar, Shafiq Joty, Richard Socher, and Nazneen Fatema Rajani. 2021. Gedi: Generative discriminator guided sequence generation. In *Findings of the Association for Computational Linguistics: EMNLP 2021*, pages 4929–4952.

Guillaume Lample, Sandeep Subramanian, Eric Michael Smith, Ludovic Denoyer, Marc'Aurelio Ranzato, and Y-Lan Boureau. 2019. Multiple-attribute text rewriting. In *7th International Conference on Learning Representations, ICLR 2019, New Orleans, LA, USA, May 6-9, 2019*. OpenReview.net.

Jiwei Li, Michel Galley, Chris Brockett, Georgios Spithourakis, Jianfeng Gao, and Bill Dolan. 2016. A persona-based neural conversation model. In *Proceedings of the 54th Annual Meeting of the Association for Computational Linguistics (Volume 1: Long Papers)*, pages 994–1003, Berlin, Germany. Association for Computational Linguistics.

Juncen Li, Robin Jia, He He, and Percy Liang. 2018. Delete, retrieve, generate: a simple approach to sentiment and style transfer. In *Proceedings of the 2018 Conference of the North American Chapter of the Association for Computational Linguistics: Human Language Technologies, Volume 1 (Long Papers)*, pages 1865–1874, New Orleans, Louisiana. Association for Computational Linguistics.

Xiang Lisa Li, John Thickstun, Ishaan Gulrajani, Percy Liang, and Tatsunori B Hashimoto. 2022. Diffusion-LM improves controllable text generation. *arXiv preprint arXiv:2205.14217*.

Zhaojiang Lin, Andrea Madotto, Yejin Bang, and Pascale Fung. 2021. The adapter-bot: All-in-one controllable conversational model. In *Proceedings of the AAAI Conference on Artificial Intelligence*, volume 35, pages 16081–16083.

Alisa Liu, Maarten Sap, Ximing Lu, Swabha Swayamdipta, Chandra Bhagavatula, Noah A Smith, and Yejin Choi. 2021. Dexperts: Decoding-time controlled text generation with experts and anti-experts. In *Proceedings of the 59th Annual Meeting of the Association for Computational Linguistics and the 11th International Joint Conference on Natural Language Processing (Volume 1: Long Papers)*, pages 6691–6706.

R Love, C Dembry, A Hardie, V Brezina, and T McEnery. 2017. The spoken bnc2014: designing and building a spoken corpus of everyday conversations. *In International Journal of Corpus Linguistics*, 22(3):319–344.

Andrea Madotto, Etsuko Ishii, Zhaojiang Lin, Sumanth Dathathri, and Pascale Fung. 2020. Plug-and-play conversational models. In *Findings of the Association for Computational Linguistics: EMNLP 2020*, pages 2422–2433, Online. Association for Computational Linguistics.

Remi Mir, Bjarke Felbo, Nick Obradovich, and Iyad Rahwan. 2019. Evaluating style transfer for text. In *Proceedings of the 2019 Conference of the North American Chapter of the Association for Computational Linguistics: Human Language Technologies, Volume 1 (Long and Short Papers)*, pages 495–504.

Anh Nguyen, Jeff Clune, Yoshua Bengio, Alexey Dosovitskiy, and Jason Yosinski. 2017. Plug & play generative networks: Conditional iterative generation of images in latent space. In *Proceedings of the IEEE conference on computer vision and pattern recognition*, pages 4467–4477.

Dong Nguyen, Rilana Gravel, Dolf Trieschnigg, and Theo Meder. 2013. "how old do you think i am?" a study of language and age in twitter. In *Proceedings of the International AAAI Conference on Web and Social Media*, volume 7.

Dong Nguyen, Noah A. Smith, and Carolyn P. Rosé. 2011. Author age prediction from text using linear regression. In *Proceedings of the 5th ACL-HLT Workshop on Language Technology for Cultural Heritage, Social Sciences, and Humanities*, pages 115–123, Portland, OR, USA. Association for Computational Linguistics.

Safiya Umoja Noble. 2018. Algorithms of oppression. In *Algorithms of Oppression*. New York University Press.

James W Pennebaker and Lori D Stone. 2003. Words of wisdom: Language use over the life span. *Journal of Personality and Social Psychology*, 85(2):291–301.

Shrimai Prabhumoye, Alan W Black, and Ruslan Salakhutdinov. 2020. Exploring controllable text generation techniques. In *Proceedings of the 28th International Conference on Computational Linguistics*, pages 1–14, Barcelona, Spain (Online). International Committee on Computational Linguistics.

Qiao Qian, Minlie Huang, Haizhou Zhao, Jingfang Xu, and Xiaoyan Zhu. 2018. Assigning personality/profile to a chatting machine for coherent conversation generation. In *Proceedings of the Twenty-Seventh International Joint Conference on Artificial*

Intelligence, IJCAI-18, pages 4279–4285. International Joint Conferences on Artificial Intelligence Organization.

Alec Radford, Karthik Narasimhan, Tim Salimans, and Ilya Sutskever. 2018. Improving language understanding by generative pre-training.

Alec Radford, Jeffrey Wu, Rewon Child, David Luan, Dario Amodei, and Ilya Sutskever. 2019. Language models are unsupervised multitask learners. *OpenAI blog*, 1(8):9.

Colin Raffel, Noam Shazeer, Adam Roberts, Katherine Lee, Sharan Narang, Michael Matena, Yanqi Zhou, Wei Li, and Peter J Liu. 2020. Exploring the limits of transfer learning with a unified text-to-text transformer. *Journal of Machine Learning Research*, 21:1–67.

Delip Rao, David Yarowsky, Abhishek Shreevats, and Manaswi Gupta. 2010. Classifying latent user attributes in twitter. In *Proceedings of the 2nd international workshop on Search and mining user-generated contents*, pages 37–44.

Gareth O Roberts and Richard L Tweedie. 1996. Exponential convergence of Langevin distributions and their discrete approximations. *Bernoulli*, pages 341–363.

Andrea Rosales and Mireia Fernández-Ardèvol. 2020. Ageism in the era of digital platforms. *Convergence*, 26(5-6):1074–1087.

Sara Rosenthal and Kathleen McKeown. 2011. Age prediction in blogs: A study of style, content, and online behavior in pre-and post-social media generations. In *Proceedings of the 49th annual meeting of the association for computational linguistics: human language technologies*, pages 763–772.

Jonathan Schler, Moshe Koppel, Shlomo Argamon, and James W Pennebaker. 2006. Effects of age and gender on blogging. In *AAAI spring symposium: Computational approaches to analyzing weblogs*, volume 6, pages 199–205.

Abigail See, Stephen Roller, Douwe Kiela, and Jason Weston. 2019. What makes a good conversation? how controllable attributes affect human judgments. In *Proceedings of the 2019 Conference of the North American Chapter of the Association for Computational Linguistics: Human Language Technologies, Volume 1 (Long and Short Papers)*, pages 1702–1723.

Heung-Yeung Shum, Xiao-dong He, and Di Li. 2018. From Eliza to XiaoIce: Challenges and opportunities with social chatbots. *Frontiers of Information Technology & Electronic Engineering*, 19(1):10–26.

Justyna Stypińska. 2021. Ageism in AI: new forms of age discrimination in the era of algorithms and artificial intelligence. In *CAIP 2021: Proceedings of the 1st International Conference on AI for People: Towards Sustainable AI, CAIP 2021, 20-24 November 2021, Bologna, Italy*, page 39. European Alliance for Innovation.

Akhilesh Sudhakar, Bhargav Upadhyay, and Arjun Maheswaran. 2019. "transforming" delete, retrieve, generate approach for controlled text style transfer. In *Proceedings of the 2019 Conference on Empirical Methods in Natural Language Processing and the 9th International Joint Conference on Natural Language Processing (EMNLP-IJCNLP)*, pages 3269–3279.

Margot J van der Goot and Tyler Pilgrim. 2019. Exploring age differences in motivations for and acceptance of chatbot communication in a customer service context. In *International Workshop on Chatbot Research and Design*, pages 173–186. Springer.

Ke Wang and Xiaojun Wan. 2018. SentiGAN: Generating sentimental texts via mixture adversarial networks. In *Proceedings of the 27th International Joint Conference on Artificial Intelligence*, pages 4446–4452.

Wenlin Wang, Zhe Gan, Hongteng Xu, Ruiyi Zhang, Guoyin Wang, Dinghan Shen, Changyou Chen, and Lawrence Carin. 2019. Topic-guided variational auto-encoder for text generation. In *Proceedings of the 2019 Conference of the North American Chapter of the Association for Computational Linguistics: Human Language Technologies, Volume 1 (Long and Short Papers)*, pages 166–177.

Yufei Wang, Ian Wood, Stephen Wan, Mark Dras, and Mark Johnson. 2021. Mention flags (MF): Constraining transformer-based text generators. In *Proceedings of the 59th Annual Meeting of the Association for Computational Linguistics and the 11th International Joint Conference on Natural Language Processing (Volume 1: Long Papers)*, pages 103–113, Online. Association for Computational Linguistics.

Peng Xu, Jackie Chi Kit Cheung, and Yanshuai Cao. 2020. On variational learning of controllable representations for text without supervision. In *International Conference on Machine Learning*, pages 10534–10543. PMLR.

Kevin Yang and Dan Klein. 2021. Fudge: Controlled text generation with future discriminators. In *Proceedings of the 2021 Conference of the North American Chapter of the Association for Computational Linguistics: Human Language Technologies*, pages 3511–3535.

Yan Zeng and Jian-Yun Nie. 2021. A simple and efficient multi-task learning approach for conditioned dialogue generation. In *Proceedings of the 2021 Conference of the North American Chapter of the Association for Computational Linguistics: Human Language Technologies*, pages 4927–4939.

Han Zhang, Haolin Song, Shaoyu Li, Ming Zhou, and Dawei Song. 2022. A survey of controllable text generation using transformer-based pre-trained language models. *ArXiv*, abs/2201.05337.

Saizheng Zhang, Emily Dinan, Jack Urbanek, Arthur Szlam, Douwe Kiela, and Jason Weston. 2018. Personalizing dialogue agents: I have a dog, do you have pets too? In *Proceedings of the 56th Annual Meeting of the Association for Computational Linguistics (Volume 1: Long Papers)*, pages 2204–2213, Melbourne, Australia. Association for Computational Linguistics.

Yizhe Zhang, Siqi Sun, Michel Galley, Yen-Chun Chen, Chris Brockett, Xiang Gao, Jianfeng Gao, Jingjing Liu, and Bill Dolan. 2020a. DIALOGPT : Large-scale generative pre-training for conversational response generation. In *Proceedings of the 58th Annual Meeting of the Association for Computational Linguistics: System Demonstrations*, pages 270–278, Online. Association for Computational Linguistics.

Yizhe Zhang, Guoyin Wang, Chunyuan Li, Zhe Gan, Chris Brockett, and William B Dolan. 2020b. POINTER: Constrained progressive text generation via insertion-based generative pre-training. In *Proceedings of the 2020 Conference on Empirical Methods in Natural Language Processing (EMNLP)*, pages 8649–8670.

Yinhe Zheng, Guanyi Chen, Minlie Huang, Song Liu, and Xuan Zhu. 2019. Personalized dialogue generation with diversified traits. *arXiv preprint arXiv:1901.09672*.

Appendices

A PPLM Hyperparameters

Table 4 reports the hyperparameters used for both the BoW and Disc models. Please refer to Dathathri et al. (2020) for further details on the hyperparameters. For comparison, the set of hyperparameters used in the paper by Dathathri et al. (2020) is given in their Table S18.

B Examples of Generated Outputs

In Table 5, we report a few more outputs generated by GPT2-based models.

C Results with Younger / Older Prompts

For comparison, we also experiment with prompts that are automatically classified as either younger- or older-sounding. Younger-sounding prompts: *What are your plans this week?; What do you wanna eat?; Do you have any hobbies?; Can I add you on Facebook?; When did you go? Awesome! I actually haven't been there.* Older-sounding prompts: *Tell me about your family.; Good afternoon.; I had a splendid weekend.; Hello, how are you?; Hello, tell me about yourself.* the results of the models using these prompts are reported in Tables 6 and 7.

D Instructions to Participants

The instructions given to the participants in the human evaluation studies can be found in Figures 4, 5 and 6.

E Preprocessing for Human Evaluation

The generated samples were checked for the presence of inappropriate language using a list of over 1300 English words that can potentially be offensive, available at `https://www.cs.cmu.edu/~biglou/resources/bad-words.txt`. The samples that contained terms in this list were manually scanned and those that were deemed actual instances of offensive language use were discarded. Altogether, 39 offensive samples were removed (BoW-younder: 3; BoW-older: 1; Disc-younger: 35). To counter the fact that some adapted models had fewer samples, some of the samples were reused with different pairings to arrive at 300 samples per model.

Outputs from different models being compared in the human evaluation always involve the same

method type	attribute	hyperparameters
BoW / Disc	younger / older	m = 3, λ_{kl} = 0.01, α = 0.02, γ = 1.5, γ_{gm} = 0.9, r = 10, τ = 1.0

Table 4: Hyperparameters used in our experiments. Please refer to Dathathri et al. (2020) for further details. An important hyperparameter is m, i.e., the number of perturbation steps/iterations.

model	age	prompt	output
BoW	Y	Can we talk?	*Yes, I can. And I hope you will join me in this discussion.*
BoW	O	Can we talk?	*What about the world? What is reality? Can we make it? Are we really all*
BoW	Y	Hey.	*My name is Alex. I am a programmer by trade. I've spent the past 3 years working,...*
BoW	O	Hey.	*I'm just getting my new laptop and I noticed that my wallpaper was getting a weird,...*
Disc	Y	Hey.	*I I I love my parents*
Disc	O	Hi, how is it going?	*The summer of 2015 has begun and it seems that I'm finally going home to Spain,...*
Disc	Y	Hello, tell me about your latest holiday.	*Do you wish you were you will be happy with it?You can use this technique,...*
Disc	O	Hey.	*ITheItIfThatYouWeAndItThatItIfItYouItItThereItItInThisItIfYouItYouThereIfThatYouItIt,...*

Table 5: A few more examples of outputs generated by GPT2-based models. **Y** stands for younger, **O** for older.

Model	ppl. ↓ better	Dist-1 ↑ better	Dist-2 ↑ better	Dist-3 ↑ better	$\bar{P}_Y$ ↑ better	Acc. ↑ better
GPT2 (G)	**28.05** (±6.12)	0.85 (±0.13)	0.91 (±0.08)	0.88 (±0.08)	0.80 (±0.33)	-
G-BoW	28.81 (±7.09)	0.86 (±0.12)	**0.92** (±0.08)	**0.89** (±0.08)	0.82 (±0.32)	83.3%
G-Disc	39.32 (±37.49)	0.84 (±0.21)	0.61 (±0.40)	0.57 (±0.40)	0.70 (±0.40)	70.7%
DialoGPT (D)	36.69 (±9.11)	0.87 (±0.10)	0.91 (±0.06)	0.87 (±0.08)	**0.90** (±0.24)	-
D-BoW	37.35 (±8.60)	0.88 (±0.10)	0.91 (±0.06)	0.87 (±0.08)	0.90 (±0.26)	**90.0%**
D-Disc	39.22 (±14.96)	**0.89** (±0.12)	0.86 (±0.19)	0.79 (±0.23)	0.89 (±0.25)	91.1%

Table 6: Results of age-controlled dialogue generation: **younger**-targeted models, conditioned on **younger prompts**. Format: *average metric (standard error)*. **ppl.** is perplexity w.r.t. GPT-1. **Dist-n** (for $n = 1, 2, 3$) is the number of distinct n-grams normalized by text length, as a measure of diversity. $\bar{P}_Y$ is the sample's average probability to contain features learned to be younger by BERT-based classifier. **Acc.** is BERT-based classifier's accuracy when classifying the row's samples. Values in **bold** are the best in the column.

Model	ppl. ↓ better	Dist-1 ↑ better	Dist-2 ↑ better	Dist-3 ↑ better	$\bar{P}_O$ ↑ better	Acc. ↑ better
GPT2 (G)	29.34 (±10.30)	**0.86** (±0.09)	**0.94** (±0.04)	**0.90** (±0.06)	0.40 (±0.43)	-
G-BoW	**28.81** (±10.10)	**0.86** (±0.10)	0.93 (±0.05)	**0.90** (±0.06)	0.41 (±0.43)	41.1%
G-Disc	95.21 (±174.42)	0.65 (±0.27)	0.78 (±0.18)	0.78 (±0.18)	**0.90** (±0.25)	**90.3%**
DialoGPT (D)	38.18 (±12.03)	**0.86** (±0.12)	0.90 (±0.08)	0.86 (±0.09)	0.28 (±0.38)	-
D-BoW	37.80 (±11.74)	**0.86** (±0.12)	0.90 (±0.07)	0.87 (±0.08)	0.28 (±0.39)	29.3%
D-Disc	40.08 (±16.77)	0.85 (±0.14)	0.88 (±0.10)	0.83 (±0.14)	0.61 (±0.42)	61.1%

Table 7: Results of age-controlled dialogue generation: **older**-targeted models, conditioned on **older prompts**. Format: *average metric (standard error)*. **ppl.** is perplexity w.r.t. GPT-1. **Dist-n** (for $n = 1, 2, 3$) is the number of distinct n-grams normalized by text length, as a measure of diversity. $\bar{P}_Y$ is the sample's average probability to contain features learned to be younger by BERT-based classifier. **Acc.** is BERT-based classifier's accuracy when classifying the row's samples. Values in **bold** are the best in the column.

prompt. In addition, we make sure that the length of the generated outputs being compared is similar. We do this by always picking two relevant samples from the same length class.

Judging Language Produced By An Artificial Intelligence (A)

Overview

This job will require you to evaluate the outputs of different AI models that generate language.

We are interested in understanding how good the language generated by these systems is and in testing whether the generated language sounds like it is written by speakers belonging to **younger** or **older** age groups.

You will be asked to evaluate short pieces of text automatically generated by two AI models and compare them in this respect.

Your evaluation will help us to better understand the performance of different language generation models. In the future, this can help make technologies, such as virtual assistants and chatbots, more accessible to all people regardless of their age.

Instructions

You will see two short pieces of text generated by two AI models and you will be asked to compare them and decide which text is better or which text could have been produced by a **younger** or an **older** speaker.

Note: some of the texts may look unfinished or cut-off and this should **not** be taken into account in your assessment.

You will also be asked about your age, because this can have an effect on your evaluation. You only need to enter your age once per job.

Example 1:

Question: ***Which one of the two outputs sounds like a text that could be written by a younger speaker?***

1) Can you tell what is being done to fix the water repair at the Water Treatment Plants. This is a couple months before a year and the first water damage is not visible to be noticed. The damage to some parts of the water treatment plants. In the winter this is a water plant at
2) A lot of fun, good vibes. I love the music and dancing. It's a great night out. Great atmosphere. Lots of energy.Good vibes. Great vibes! The crowd was great, there was a lot of energy and a lot

Reasonable response: It would be reasonable to select the second text as produced by a younger speaker. The text includes some stylistic traits and expressions, such as "good vibes" or "lot of fun", that are likely to be used by younger speakers.

Figure 4: Participant guidelines for the crowdsourcing study reported in Section 6.1.

Judging Language Produced By An Artificial Intelligence (R)

Overview

This job will require you to evaluate the outputs of different AI models that generate language.

We are interested in understanding how good the language generated by these models is with respect to **fluency** and **human likeness**.

You will be asked to evaluate short pieces of text automatically generated by an AI model and to rate them on a scale from 1 to 5.

Your evaluation will help us to better understand the performance of different language generation models. In the future, this can help make technologies, such as virtual assistants and chatbots, more accessible.

Instructions

You will see a short piece of text generated by an AI model and you will be asked some questions about it that will require you to rate the text on a scale from 1 to 5.

Note: some of the texts may look unfinished or cut-off and this should **not** be taken into account in your assessment.

Example:

Text: *This is the most important question you have ever you you have presented me this you, so*

Question: ***Does it flow well? (fluency)***

Reasonable judgement: Here, giving 3 or 4 is reasonable since most of the text is fluent, that is, it is a sequence of fairly well-connected words with few repetitions. At the same time, a 1 or 2 would not be appropriate, since it is fluent to some reasonable degree.

Question: ***Could it have been produced by a human? (human-likeness)***

Reasonable judgement: Here, giving a 2 or 3 would be reasonable since the text is less likely to come from a human due to repetitions and unclear meaning. At the same time, a 1 would not be appropriate since it is still possible that it was produced by a human.

Figure 5: Participant guidelines for the crowdsourcing study reported in Section 6.2.

Judging Language Produced By An Artificial Intelligence (C)

Overview

This job will require you to evaluate the outputs of different AI models that generate language.

We are interested in understanding how good the language generated by these models is.

You will be asked to evaluate the overall goodness of short pieces of text automatically generated by two AI models.

Your evaluation will help us to better understand the performance of different language generation models. In the future, this can help make technologies, such as virtual assistants and chatbots, more accessible.

Instructions

You will see two short piece of text generated by two AI models and you will be asked to compare them.

Note: some of the texts may look unfinished or cut-off and this should **not** be taken into account in your assessment.

Example:

Question: *Which one of the two outputs is better overall?*

1) *Can we talk?ClWe,.w,,,k?,?k.k?WwW??.!?!w(?!!??!?)!WwW*
2) *This holiday, we celebrate the season by giving gifts*

Reasonable response: Although the second option constitutes an incomplete sentence, it would be reasonable to pick the second option as the better output, given that the first option contains a random string of characters.

Figure 6: Participant guidelines for the crowdsourcing study reported in Section 6.3.

Template-based Recruitment Email Generation for Job Recommendation

Qiuchi Li and **Christina Lioma**
Department of Computer Science
University of Copenhagen
{qiuchi.li, c.lioma}@di.ku.dk

Abstract

Text generation has long been a popular research topic in NLP. However, the task of generating recruitment emails from recruiters to candidates in the job recommendation scenario has received little attention by the research community. This work aims at defining the topic of automatic email generation for job recommendation, identifying the challenges, and providing a baseline template-based solution for Danish jobs. Evaluation by human experts shows that our method is effective. We wrap up by discussing the future research directions for better solving this task.

1 Introduction and Prior Work

Recruitment email generation is a crucial step in the overall job recruitment process. When recruiters find suitable candidates for a job, they need to write emails to contact the candidates, explaining why they are fit for the job and inviting them to apply. The job market produces a huge number of job postings on a daily basis, which results in a significant amount of human labor required to write recruitment emails. The recruiters are in urgent need of an automatic approach to compose these emails, to reduce their efforts and increase productivity.

The core challenges facing the task are two-fold: **persuasiveness** and **personalization**. First, the emails should contain sufficient reasons to convince the candidate that their qualifications match the requirements of the position, and illustrate that the position meets the candidate's expectations. Second, personalized emails should let the job seekers feel that the recruiters pay special attention to them and in turn motivate them to apply. In an interview of recruiters of varying recruitment experience, recruiters believe that proper personalization on the recruitment emails could boost candidate positive response rate, and admit that the current emails, largely composed based on fixed templates, are not personalized and persuasive enough (Bogers and Kaya, 2021).

Recruitment email generation can be seen as a task-oriented text generation problem. One needs to extract information from the input job description and candidate profile, and generate the recruitment email accordingly. A large body of research on emails focuses on the analysis side, typically automatic detection of phishing emails by extracting features (Basnet et al., 2008; Verma and El Aassal, 2017; Yu et al., 2009). In the realm of email synthesis, email subject line generation (Xue et al., 2020; Zhang and Tetreault, 2019) has been studied. For generation of the main email body, attempts have been made on fake email generation for malicious purposes (Das and Verma, 2019; Baki et al., 2017) based on a two-step pipeline (Chen and Rudnicky, 2014a,b) for email synthesis. As far as we know, generating recruitment emails in job recruitment is an unexplored task in literature, despite its practical significance and challenging nature.

We therefore formally formulate the task of recruitment email generation and provide a baseline template-based system for it by extending Chen and Rudnicky (2014a)'s approach. In particular, we randomly generate an email from a library of different pre-defined components, and fill the motivational sentence with certain slots by combining matched skills and occupations extracted from the job and candidate in question. We conduct a user study to evaluate the quality of the generated text and examine if it can save recruiters' time in writing emails. The results show that recruiters under test are overall satisfied with the generated emails, and the time spent on writing emails for each candidate is significantly reduced.

The rest of the paper is organized as follows. We define the problem formally in Section 2. We run a pilot study to examine the simple end-to-end neural generation algorithm in Section 3 and elicit the need for a fine-grained synthesizing approach. Our

Proceedings of the 2nd Workshop on Natural Language Generation, Evaluation, and Metrics (GEM), pages 189 - 197
December 7, 2022 ©2022 Association for Computational Linguistics

template-based approach is described in Section 4, and the user evaluation is reported and discussed in Section 5. We conclude and point out future directions in Section 6.

2 Task Definition and Notations

Recruitment email generation calls for generating an email based on an input the job and a candidate . It requires us to extract the matched information from different job and candidate fields, and convert it to natural language expressions in the email. Typically, a job posting contains its title, company name and a textual description. A candidate profile has a headline, a list of keywords, a list of preferred job titles, the candidate's work experience and educational experience, and the candidate's resume text.

The data we work with comes from Jobindex[1], one of Scandinavia's largest job portals and recruitment agencies. In the Jobindex system, the above-mentioned fields are the main source of information for jobs and candidates. The majority of the jobs and candidate profiles are in Danish. Please refer to Fig. 1 for an example of a pair of job and candidate, and the real recruitment email written by a human recruiter. The personal information has been removed from the example and all texts are translated to English.

3 Pilot Study: end-to-end neural generation

The most intuitive way to handle the recruitment email generation task is to generate the whole email in a fully end-to-end fashion by concatenating the job and company text. We conduct a pilot study to examine whether this setting works in practice.

Model. We build a Transformer encoder-decoder, the state-of-the-art architecture for natural language generation, to support a sequence-to-sequence generation of recruitment email. The job and candidate texts are fed to the encoder side, and the recruitment email is generated in a token-by-token auto-regressive manner. The Transformer structure enables us to load the weights of the pre-trained Danish language model, Danish-BERT [2]. Rothe et al. (2020) conducted a comprehensive comparison of different strategies to use the pre-trained BERT weights for sequence-to-sequence generation, and found that the *bert2bert* setting can yield robust performance across different text generation tasks. Therefore, we follow this setting and initialize the weights for both encoder and decoder with the Danish-BERT checkpoint. Please refer to Rothe et al. (2020) for further details. We claim that this model may not be the state-of-the-art for Danish text generation, since Danish GPT is publicly available [3]. However, it is a strong-performing model due to its Transformer architecture, and its generated text is representative of the state-of-the-art neural generation models.

Data Preprocessing. We focus on generating Danish emails from Danish jobs and candidate profiles. We mine (job, candidate, email) triplets from the Jobindex database. We filter out samples with non-Danish text, too short job descriptions and empty job titles. A total number of 317566 samples are obtained. Due to the limitation on input length by the model, we concatenate the summary of job description and the headline, job titles, education experience and work experience of candidate. Different fields are split by the periods. For recruitment emails, we only take their main bodies. We replace specific job title and company name with special tokens "[job]" and "[cpy]" respectively.

Training and Evaluation. Our Transformer encoder-decoder has 12 layers and 12 attention heads and a maximum length of 512 tokens on both encoder and decoder sides. The embedding dimension and hidden dimension are set to 768 and 3072, respectively. We split all samples into training, validation and test set at a 7:2:1 ratio. We perform mini-batch learning to train the model with a batch size of 32. The average cross-entropy loss over all tokens at the decoder side is used as the loss function. We train the model on the training set for a maximum number of 5 epochs with Adam optimizer, and stop training when the validation loss stops dropping.

We use bilingual evaluation understudy (BLEU) as the quantitative metric for the generated message. The BLEU scores are calculated for individual translated segments, by comparing them with a set of good quality reference translations. The average scores over the whole test corpus are computed as an estimation of the overall quality.

Result. We obtained a BLEU score of 23.2 on test samples for the generated texts, which is far from the SOTA neural text generation system for Danish (32.5 - 33.8) (Fan and Gardent, 2020). This

[1] https://www.jobindex.dk/

[2] https://huggingface.co/Maltehb/danish-bert-botxo

[3] https://huggingface.co/flax-community/dansk-gpt-wiki

Figure 1: Example of a real recruitment email for the given job and candidate pair. The texts are translated from Danish to English.

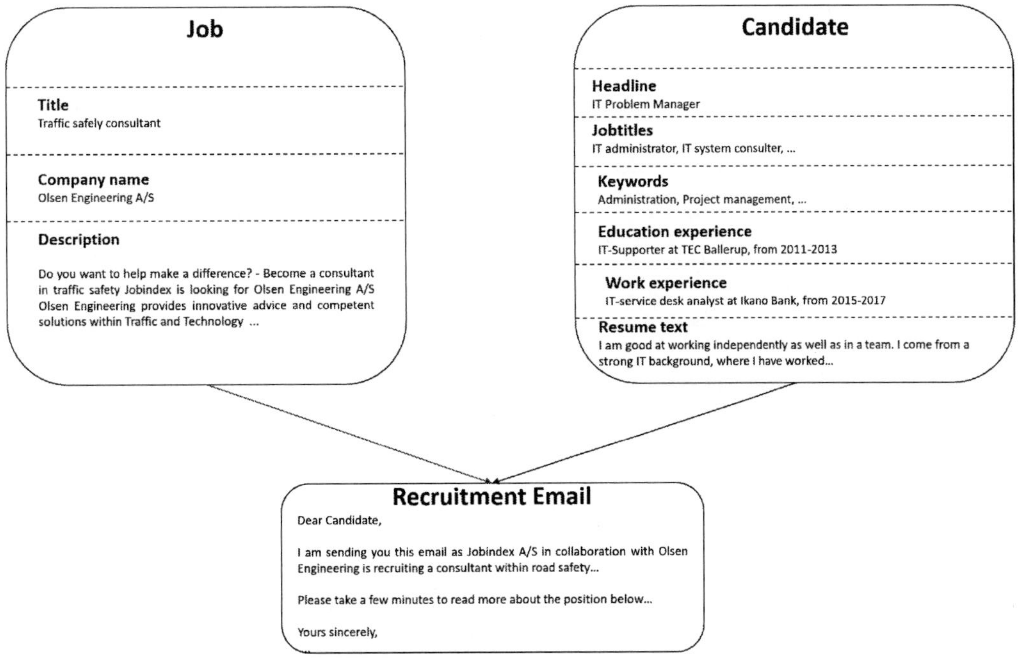

reveals that the generated emails have a limited overall quality.

Additionally, manual inspection shows that the auto-generated emails have low extent of personalization and persuasiveness. The generated motivational sentences usually do not contain specific reasons of match and are prone to grammatical errors. See Fig. 2 for concrete examples. We posit that it is because the motivational sentences are usually located in the middle of email body, embedded in texts primarily generated from templates. Also, over 80% of the motivational sentences are devoid of case-specific information such as the matched skills or occupations. Therefore, an end-to-end generation system is capable of learning these recurring template-based texts quite well, but poor at learning case-specific motivational sentences.

4 Proposed Methodology

The evaluation result of end-to-end neural generation indicates the need for a finer-grained generation system. Instead of generating the email as a whole, a special module should be developed to generate case-specific information, such as the motivational sentence, from the input job and candidate texts. We are inspired by the two-step email synthesis (Chen and Rudnicky, 2014a) to generate recruitment emails: email structure generation and slot filling. Specifically, we randomly generate an email template from a pre-constructed library of email components. The slots of the template indicate case-specific fields, and are then filled by extracting information from the matched job and candidate. The overall process of the system is shown in Fig. 3.

Potentially, our approach is superior to end-to-end generation in three aspects: 1) recruiters follow a similar process to write emails in a real-case scenario, so the generated emails are more likely to be accepted by and benefit recruiters; 2) the algorithm has a better control of the generated content, and ensures a certain extent of grammatical correctness and readability; 3) by explicitly composing case-specific information, the algorithm enhances personalization and persuasiveness of the generated recruitment emails.

In the following text, we introduce the implementation details of our template-based generation system.

4.1 Template Parsing

Template data cleaning. We get a total number of 553 raw templates from Jobindex system. We remove the non-Danish templates and templates for

Figure 2: Examples of generated emails by the end-to-end neural model. The generated motivational sentences are translated in English and colored in red.

Recruitment Emails Generated by End-to-end Neural Model

- jeg har fundet din profil i cv - index og sender dig denne mail, fordi [cpy] har bedt jobindex opfordre relevante kandidater til at søge denne stilling som [job]. you can you have a relevant background of a a a an an exciting new for you... du kan læse hele annoncen pa http : / / www. jobindex. dk / annoncer.
- jeg skriver til dig, fordi [cpy] a / s har bedt jobindex opfordre fagligt relevante kandidater fra vores cv database til at søge deres ledige stilling som [job]... da det af dit cv fremgar, that, among other things, you have relevant relevant relevant background, sa maske kunne være en spændende ny mulighed for dig. sa haber, at du har lyst til at læse stillingsopslaget og ikke mindst, at du ogsa finder det interessant og far lyst til at søge det. du kan læse jobannoncen nedenfor, og hvis du ønsker yderligere oplysninger om stillingen eller rekrutteringsprocessen, kan du kontakte [cpy] direkte.
- jeg skriver til dig, fordi [cpy] a / s har bedt jobindex opfordre fagligt relevante kandidater fra vores cv database til at søge deres ledige stilling som [job].... du kan du blandt andet har erfaring med dit cv. jeg tænker, at you, among other things, have relevant experience within you. du kan læse jobannoncen nedenfor, og se, om jobbet matcher dine ønsker. hvis du har spørgsmal til jobbet eller vil sende en ansøgning, sa kontakt [cpy] direkte. hjælp os med fremover at matche dig med de rigtige job ved at klikke " jeg er interesseret " eller " jeg er ikke interesseret " nedenfor. hav en god dag.

other purposes from the collection, and the remaining ones are classified into company-specific and general templates. Company-specific templates are provided by some companies to the recruiters with the request that these templates are strictly used when generating recruitment emails for these specific companies. General templates are used for all other cases. Eventually, 270 general templates and 81 specific templates remain in the database.

Manual annotation. We define a list of email components (or fields) according to their functions based on manual inspection. They are mainly categorized into **functional**, **case-specific** and **auto-fill** fields. Functional fields are indicative of email structure, and do not entail case-specific information. Case-specific fields contain information specific to the matched pair of job and candidate, such as the job title, company name, motivational sentences expressing why the candidate is fit for the job, and so on. Some case-specific fields are automatically filled by the Jobindex system, and they are referred to as auto-fill fields instead. A total number of 54 email components are defined.

For each template in the database, we manually annotate the text by inserting HTML tags before and after a certain text segment to indicate its function in the email.

Parsing. We parse the annotated templates to construct the email component library, essentially a dictionary of (component_name, content list) pairs. The annotated templates are each parsed in a recursive fashion by an HTML parser. Starting from the root element of the whole template, the parser performs the same operations for each element: identify its child elements, process each the child element, append the processed child element content to the dictionary, and replace the child element with the marker "**[% f %]**". As such, the parser navigates all HTML tags in the template and adds their contents to the corresponding component content list. In the text content of each component, its child components are all masked with "**[% f %]**" tags as desired. The output of the algorithm is the top-level structure of the email templates, which are stored in the dictionary as values of "**skeleton_follower**" and "**skeleton_non_follower**" for followers and for non-followers, respectively. Followers are candidates who follow a company in their profile, and non-followers are candidates who do not follow a company. After parsing all templates, we obtain a list of contents for each pre-defined email component. Examples of extracted email components are shown in Fig. 4. It is worth noting that nested structures universally appear among functional components, i.e. the textual content of one component may contain other components.

4.2 Baseline Template-based Email Generation Algorithm

We build an email generation system based on the constructed email component library. The algorithm randomly generates a template from the constructed library, based on whether the database contains the company name and whether the candidate is a follower of the company. Then,

Figure 3: Diagram of the email generation system. The final generated messages are the main body of a real recruitment email, translated to English for this example.

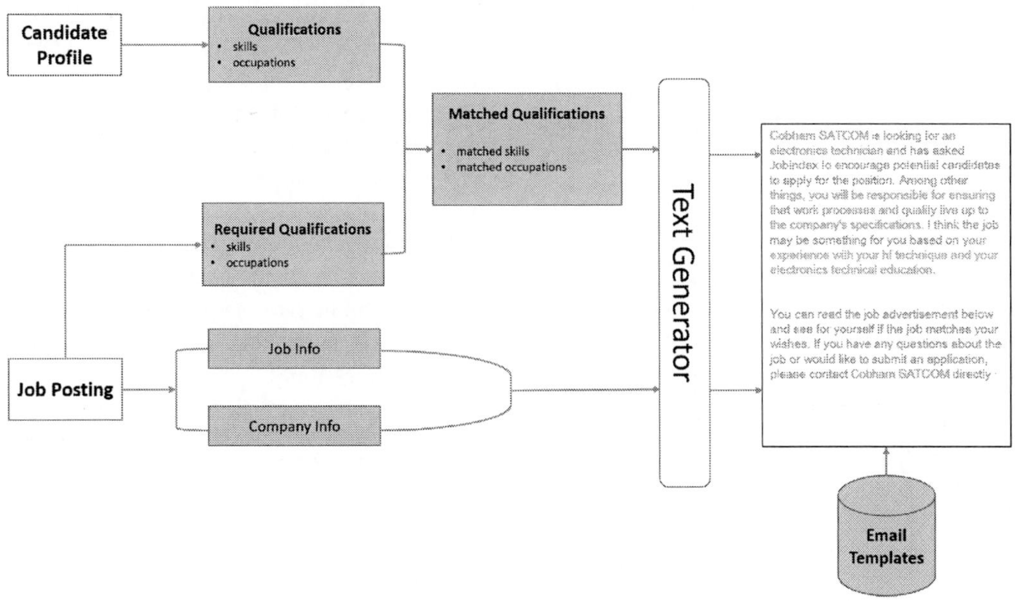

Figure 4: The HTML tag, description and example of email components, extracted from the template database.

HTML Tag	Description	Example in the library	Type
general_statement	Statement that a position is available for a company	[% humanjob.company.name %] har bedt [% sender.companyname %] at opfordre mulige kandidater fra vores CV-database til at søge denne ledige stilling.	Functional
motivational_sentence	To express interest to the candidate	du blandt andet har [% matched_education %] relevant uddannelsesbaggrund, erfaring med [% matched_experience %]	Functional
ask_to_contact	To ask the candidate to contact the company for more information	Du kan læse annoncen nedenfor, og hvis du ønsker yderligere oplysninger om stillingen eller rekrutteringsprocessen, kan du kontakte [% humanjob.company.name %] direkte.	Functional
job_responsibility	What a candidate is supposed to do in the job position		Case-specific
matched_experience	Candidate's work experience that matches the job request		Case-specific
humanjob.company.name	Company name of the job		Auto-fill
humanjob.title	Job title		Auto-fill

we extract the matched skills and occupations from the input job and candidate, and convert them to a coherent expression for the motivational sentence explaining why the candidate fits the job.

Random template generation. Two issues should be accounted for when generating a proper template for a matched (job, candidate) pair. First, some companies prefer writing recruitment emails based on company-specific templates, so the system should always use a company template where possible. Second, followers should be contacted with slightly different emails to stress that the candidate follows the company.

The algorithm works as follows. First, we search for templates with the company name of the job posting. If company-specific templates can be found, then we randomly choose a template from the matched company templates. If it returns an empty list, then we randomly generate a template from the email component library. We start with a randomly selected follower skeleton or a non-follower skeleton according to whether the company is in the candidate's following list. Then, we navigate through all unfilled slots in an iterative fashion. For each slot, we randomly pick a text content from all its respective candidates in the library. Since the text expression may contain other unfilled slots, this process goes in an iterative fashion until no functional component tags appear in the templates.

To this end, we have obtained a template for the recruitment email. An example can be seen in Fig. 5.

Figure 5: A randomly generated template for non-followers.

Kære følger af [% humanjob.company.name %]

Jeg kontakter dig, da [% humanjob.company.name %] lige nu søger en [% humanjob.title %], og derfor har de bedt [% sender.companyname %] om at opfordre mulige kandidater fra vores CV-database til at søge stillingen.

Jeg kan se, at du har relevant erhvervserfaring med [% matched_experience %]. Jeg kontakter dig fordi du følger [% humanjob.company.name %] på [% sender.companyname %], og jeg tænker at du vil finde stillingen interessant.

Hvis du har spørgsmål til jobbet, så kontakt [% sender.name %] på [% sender.telephone %].

For fremover at finde de match, som er mest relevante for dig, kan du hjælpe os ved at klikke "Jeg er interesseret" eller "Jeg er ikke interesseret" nedenfor.

Med venlig hilsen

[% sender.signature %]

Template filling. We compose the motivational sentence based on the matched qualifications of the candidate, including skills and occupations. For this purpose, we construct a dictionary of skills and occupations from the ESCO (European Skills, Competences, Qualifications and Occupations) database[4]. ESCO has a 4-level category annotation for skills and occupations in different languages. We include both skills and occupations as dictionary keys in English and Danish. We also add the list of IT-related skills from Microsoft Skills library[5] into the dictionary. A total number of 129474 skills and 46060 occupations are collected.

Based on the dictionary, we extract skills and occupations from the matched pair of job and candidate texts and obtain their intersections. We first use a built-in name entity recognition (NER) algorithm in the spaCy[6] package to identify text spans that may contain skills and occupations, and check whether each is a skill or an occupation. The matched skills and occupations are obtained by taking the set intersections. We further split the language skills from the matched skills set.

Simple rules are then applied to convert the matched skills, occupations and language skills to a coherent expression as explanations of why the candidate fits the job. The skills and occupations are respectively concatenated with the "{ }, { } og { }" pattern, and conjunctive expressions are added to combine the expressions for skill and occupation match. It is further appended by the language skill match expression, if non-Danish skills are detected in both the job and candidate. The whole expression is inserted to the motivation sentence template with modifications of the pre-slot expressions to ensure coherence. When multiple slots appear in a motivational sentence template, they are inserted with matched skills and matched occupations, respectively. As a back-up, a general text expression will be randomly chosen from a list of contents in case of no matched qualifications.

Please see Fig. 6 for a visual illustration of how the matched qualifications are converted to a motivational expression.

Figure 6: An example of composed motivational sentence from matched skills, occupations and language skills.

Matched skills	statistik
Matched occupations	embedsmand
Matched language skills	engelsk
Motivational sentence template	du har erfaring som [% matched_experience %]
Motivational sentence	du har erfaring som (embedsmand, og med erfaring inden for statistik, især dine sprogkundskaber af engelsk)

Text post-processing. We automatically post-process the generated email in the final step. Specifically, if multiple punctuations appear in a row, we keep only the last punctuation. We also make sure the first letter of a sentence is upper-cased. Finally, we correct the spacing errors between words in a sentence, between sentences, and between paragraphs. This gives the final output message produced by the template-based recruitment email generation algorithm.

5 Evaluation

We conduct an offline evaluation with real expert recruiters to evaluate the performance of the template-based email generation algorithm. The quantitative measures for natural language generation are not employed, since the template-based approach may produce significantly different structures from the real recruitment emails and still be reasonably good. Indeed, it remains an open question to design quantitative measures for evaluating the generated recruitment emails, as the judgments on the persuasiveness or personalization of the email vary from person to person.

We randomly sample a collection of truly matched (job, candidate) pairs from the Jobindex database. They are randomly assigned to each of a group of 10 recruiters. The pairs are randomly split

[4]https://esco.ec.europa.eu/

[5]https://learn.microsoft.com/en-us/

[6]https://spacy.io/

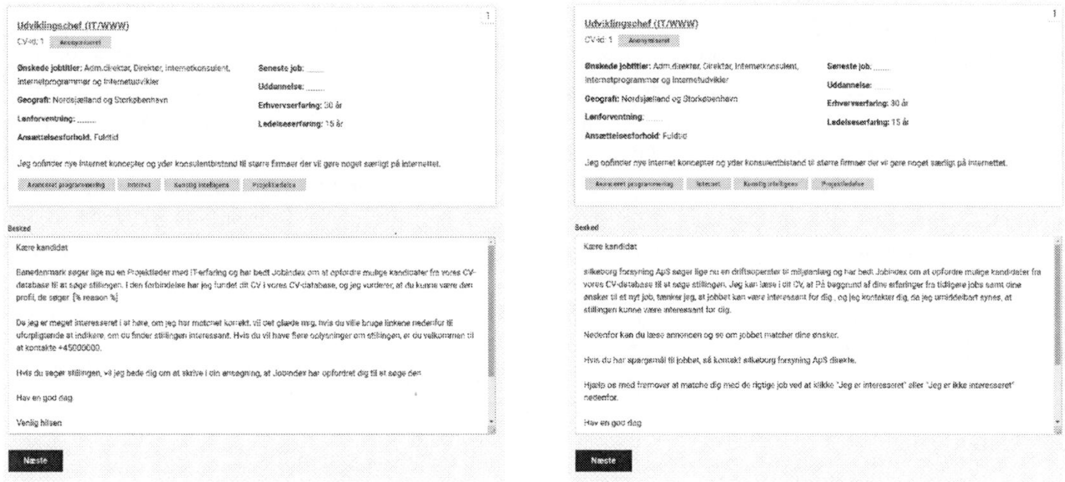

(a) Unhelped case.

(b) Helped case.

Figure 7: Screenshots of the interface in (a) "unhelped" and (b) "helped" case.

into 5 sessions of 10 pairs each. Each recruiter is randomly assigned with "helped" tasks (with generated texts) and "unhelped" tasks (with generated templates). Each task is "helped" for half of the recruiters and "unhelped" for the other half. The interface contained pairs of matched job postings and candidate profiles, and an interface is provided to the recruiter with either pre-generated template ("unhelped") or the email ("helped"). For the email, the inserted case-specific information is wrapped by brackets "{ }". A checkbox is also presented to the recruiters for providing a 4-level judgment on the quality of the email or template (4 = Perfect, 3 = Minor Revision, 2 = Major Revision, 1 = Useless). The judgment is on language quality for templates and on both language quality and information correctness for emails. The recruiters are asked to click a button before and after writing the recruitment email, so that the difference between the recorded time stamps are the time spent on it. The screenshots of the interface are shown in Fig. 7.

Result on text quality. We have collected the results of 224 helped tasks (with generated emails by our algorithm) and 241 unhelped tasks (with our generated templates by our algorithm). The recruiters' annotations on the quality of the generated texts are shown in Fig. 8. In terms of average ratings, we obtained a value of 2.53 for generated emails and 2.46 for generated templates for the evaluation of the new template-based system. Over 50% of the generated texts (53.58% for emails and 51.03% for templates) are satisfactory, requiring minor or no edits. It is interesting to see that more recruiters are satisfied with the generated texts than the templates. This implies that the generated motivational sentence is exceptionally helpful for recruiters. In the same time, there is still room for the text quality to improve, and neural method for generating case-specific information is a feasible direction.

Figure 8: Bar plots of annotations for the offline-evaluation in Apr 2022. The red bars are the recruiters' judgments on the quality of generated templates, and blue bars are the recruiters on the quality of generated messages.

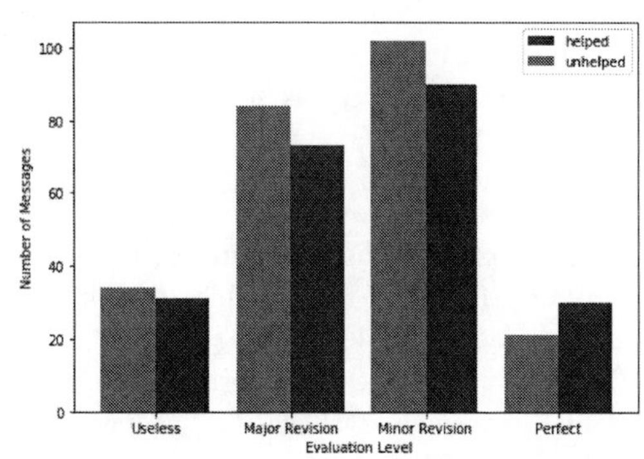

Result on time cost. We computed the average time a recruiter spent on writing the message in the unhelped and helped case, respectively. The time difference between the two scenarios is the reduction of recruiters' time by our template-based automatic text generation system. As a consequence, recruiters spent an average of 178.99s on each matched pair in the helped case, and an average of 235.63s on each matched pair in the unhelped case. On average, a recruiter spends 56.64s shorter on writing an email with automatically generated messages than merely on top of the provided templates. In order to remove the discrepancy across individual recruiters, we zero-averaged the time for each recruiter and recalculated the time difference. A closer but still remarkable gap between the times (51.31s) is observed. It shows that this simple template-based system can significantly save recruiters time on writing recruitment emails.

6 Conclusion

We have proposed recruitment email generation for job recruitment, a novel task in text generation. We demonstrate its challenge and significance in the pilot study and a user study of our template-based approach. The challenge mainly resides in constructing case-specific components of the email from the input job and candidate to enhance personalization and persuasiveness. Quite often, the reasons of a good match are semantically non-explicit and cannot be extracted by common word or phrase matching. At the same time, we have observed that a simple approach can remarkably benefit recruiters by saving around 1/4 of their time.

Future work could contribute to this task in the following aspects:

- End-to-end neural generation of motivational sentences. Rather than the simple rule-based algorithm for composing the motivational sentences, we may learn a neural generation system from the real emails in a data-driven manner.

- Robust intrinsic evaluation metrics. The n-gram matching-based metrics, such as BLEU or ROUGE, are not suitable for this task. Beyond the real-user evaluation, it remains an open challenge to propose robust metrics that objectively evaluate the generated text, in terms of both language quality and task-related aspects.

- Deep representations of job and candidate to better extract reasons of match. Deep neural models should be constructed to perform deep understanding of jobs and candidates in order to support extraction of below-the-surface matched qualifications.

- Generating explanation of recommendations. Currently, the email generation is a separate process from job recommendation. It would be interesting to view recruitment emails instead as explanations of the recommendation systems, and propose recommendation models that supports interpretations of the recommendations. The authentic explanations of recommendation will be then be incorporated in the recruitment email.

Acknowledgements

This research was supported by the Innovation Fund Denmark, grant no. 0175-000005B.

References

Shahryar Baki, Rakesh Verma, Arjun Mukherjee, and Omprakash Gnawali. 2017. Scaling and effectiveness of email masquerade attacks: Exploiting natural language generation. In *Proceedings of the 2017 ACM on Asia Conference on Computer and Communications Security*, ASIA CCS '17, page 469–482, New York, NY, USA. Association for Computing Machinery.

Ram Basnet, Srinivas Mukkamala, and Andrew H. Sung. 2008. *Detection of Phishing Attacks: A Machine Learning Approach*, pages 373–383. Springer Berlin Heidelberg, Berlin, Heidelberg.

Toine Bogers and Mesut Kaya. 2021. An Exploration of the Information Seeking Behavior of Recruiters. In *Proceedings of the RecSys in HR 2021 workshop*, pages 11–18.

Yun-Nung Chen and Alexander Rudnicky. 2014a. Two-stage stochastic email synthesizer. In *Proceedings of the 8th International Natural Language Generation Conference (INLG)*, pages 99–102, Philadelphia, Pennsylvania, U.S.A. Association for Computational Linguistics.

Yun-Nung Chen and Alexander Rudnicky. 2014b. Two-stage stochastic natural language generation for email synthesis by modeling sender style and topic structure. In *Proceedings of the 8th International Natural Language Generation Conference (INLG)*, pages 152–156, Philadelphia, Pennsylvania, U.S.A. Association for Computational Linguistics.

Avisha Das and Rakesh M. Verma. 2019. Automated email generation for targeted attacks using natural language. *CoRR*, abs/1908.06893.

Angela Fan and Claire Gardent. 2020. Multilingual AMR-to-text generation. In *Proceedings of the 2020 Conference on Empirical Methods in Natural Language Processing (EMNLP)*, pages 2889–2901, Online. Association for Computational Linguistics.

Sascha Rothe, Shashi Narayan, and Aliaksei Severyn. 2020. Leveraging pre-trained checkpoints for sequence generation tasks. *Transactions of the Association for Computational Linguistics*, 8:264–280.

Rakesh Verma and Ayman El Aassal. 2017. Comprehensive method for detecting phishing emailsusing correlation-based analysis and user participation. CODASPY '17, page 155–157, New York, NY, USA. Association for Computing Machinery.

Mingfeng Xue, Hang Zhang, and Jiancheng Lv. 2020. Key factors of email subject generation. In *Neural Information Processing*, pages 668–675, Cham. Springer International Publishing.

Weider D. Yu, Shruti Nargundkar, and Nagapriya Tiruthani. 2009. Phishcatch - a phishing detection tool. In *Proceedings of the 2009 33rd Annual IEEE International Computer Software and Applications Conference - Volume 02*, COMPSAC '09, page 451–456, USA. IEEE Computer Society.

Rui Zhang and Joel R. Tetreault. 2019. This email could save your life: Introducing the task of email subject line generation. *CoRR*, abs/1906.03497.

Are Abstractive Summarization Models truly 'Abstractive'? An Empirical Study to Compare the two Forms of Summarization

Vinayshekhar Bannihatti Kumar
AWS AI Labs
vinayshk@amazon.com

Rashmi Gangadharaiah
AWS AI Labs
rgangad@amazon.com

Abstract

Automatic Text Summarization has seen a large paradigm shift from extractive methods to abstractive (or generation-based) methods in the last few years. This can be attributed to the availability of large autoregressive language models (Lewis et al., 2019; Zhang et al., 2019a) that have been shown to outperform extractive methods. In this work, we revisit extractive methods and study their performance against state of the art(SOTA) abstractive models. Through extensive studies, we notice that abstractive methods are not yet completely *abstractive* in their generated summaries. In addition to this finding, we propose an evaluation metric that could benefit the summarization research community to measure the degree of *abstractiveness* of a summary in comparison to their extractive counterparts. To confirm the generalizability of our findings, we conduct experiments on two summarization datasets using five powerful techniques in extractive and abstractive summarization and study their levels of abstraction.

1 Introduction

The amount of data on the internet has been growing exponentially creating excessive information for users to consume. Automatic text summarization alleviates this issue of information overload by producing shorter and concise summaries that capture the *essence* of the long source text. Automatic text summarization can be broadly classified into kinds- Extractive summarization and Abstractive summarization. Extractive summarization identifies important excerpts from the source document to produce summaries. These excerpts are composed of sentences and phrases which the model deems most appropriate for summarizing the source document. With the advent of sophisticated language models trained on large amounts of data, most of the recent work in summarization has drifted towards abstractive summarization. Summarization tasks have now become one of the benchmarks to beat with many of the SOTA generation models. In abstractive summarization, natural language generation techniques are employed to generate a summary.

Humans write concise summaries by introducing novel words and only using information from the source text that they deem absolutely necessary. Since abstractive summarization models generate words which are not necessarily present in the source text as is, the expectation is that the summaries generated would be truly *abstractive* and hence closer to human generated summaries. In theory, abstractive summarization models should outperform extractive methods as they have the ability to generate free form text like humans. In practice, however, we find that the abstractive summaries of SOTA models today are closer to extractive summaries than to the human generated summaries against which they are compared. Table 1 shows a generated summary by BART that has many overlapping snippets with the context. These observations have previously been unnoticed largely due to the evaluation methods that have been employed. As performing human evaluations is expensive, automatic metrics like BLEU (Papineni et al., 2002) and ROUGE (Papineni et al., 2002) have been used widely to measure the amount of overlap between generated summaries and reference summaries. As a result, these evaluation methods were not geared towards measuring *abstractiveness* of summaries. To better differentiate summaries generated by abstractive summarization models from their extractive counterparts, we also propose an evaluation metric called AbsExtScore.

In order to analyze the extent of these issues in abstractive summarization models, we chose three SOTA abstractive summarization models trained on CNN DailyMail (See et al., 2017) and the X-Sum (Narayan et al., 2018) datasets (Section 3). We also chose two SOTA extractive summarization

Proceedings of the 2nd Workshop on Natural Language Generation, Evaluation, and Metrics (GEM), pages 198 - 206
December 7, 2022 ©2022 Association for Computational Linguistics

Context	Abstractive Summary	Ground Truth
...prince george's first year - which boosted the economy by £247m...that a little girl could bring in £150m for the british economy...a princess would be able to set trends throughout her life...which will be great for the people who designed her clothes or those who can make quick knock-off copies	prince george's first year boosted the economy by £247m. a little girl could bring in £150m for the british economy. a princess would be able to set trends throughout her life. this will be great for the people who designed her clothes or those who can make quick knock-off copies.	as kate and william prepare to welcome their second child , there 's no doubt that the royal couple 's favoured childrenswear brands are hoping to cash in on the arrival .indeed , if prince george 's first year - which boosted the economy by 247m - is anything to go by , anything that the second-born touches will turn to gold and copycat designs will bring a welcome boost to the high street .the baby could generate a billion pounds over its lifetime .

Table 1: Example of Context, Ground truth and Abstractive Summary from CNN/DM dataset.

models trained on the same datasets (Section 4). We make the following observations and contributions:

- We observe that abstractive summarization models are not introducing enough novelty words and more simply copying over the words from the source text (Section 5).
- We observe that there is a large overlap between the extractive and abstractive summaries which questions the *abstractiveness* of the summaries generated by abstractive summarization models.
- To measure the quality of summaries in terms of *abstractiveness*, we propose an evaluation metric called AbsExtScore (Section 5.3). We also show that there is a correlation between human judgements and this evaluation metric by conducting a human subject study on a sample of summaries.

2 Related Work

Both extractive and abstractive summarization techniques have been well studied in the Natural Language Processing (NLP) community. Earlier work in extractive summarization relied on clues such as position of sentences and frequency of words while extracting most important snippets for summaries (Khan and Salim, 2014; Baxendale, 1958). More recently, neural network-based extractive summarization have gained more popularity (Alami et al., 2019; Xu and Durrett, 2019; Chen et al., 2018; Mohsen et al., 2020; Anand and Wagh, 2019; Zhong et al., 2020; Liu et al., 2019).

There has also been significant work in abstractive summarization (Genest and Lapalme, 2012; Barzilay et al., 1999; Tanaka et al., 2009). Most of the recent approaches use encoder-decoder architectures to generate summaries (Lee et al., 2020; Yao et al., 2020; Iwasaki et al., 2019; Zhang et al., 2019a; Raffel et al., 2019a; Lewis et al., 2019). These methods produce summaries using words that are not present in the source text and hence these methods have gained more popularity over the last few years. Transformer models with self-supervised training (Devlin et al., 2018; Radford et al., 2018; Raffel et al., 2019a; Yang et al., 2019; Clark et al., 2020; Liu et al., 2019) have shown to perform well on language learning when fine-tuned on various NLP tasks. More recently, BART(Lewis et al., 2019), PEGASUS (Zhang et al., 2019a) and T5 (Raffel et al., 2019b) have shown state-of-the-art performance in abstractive summarization, so we analyze the generated summaries of these models in comparison with SOTA methods in extractive summarization (Zhong et al., 2020; Liu et al., 2019). Previous work on measuring the abstractiveness and extractiveness in summaries has been restricted to measuring diversity of n-grams (Scialom et al., 2020; Grusky et al., 2018) but we move to a more semantic based metric to measure these aspects of a summary.

3 Datasets

We use two standard summarization benchmarks:
CNN-Dailymail (2017) : a corpus of news articles and human generated summaries. We use the entire test set of size 11, 490.
X-Sum (2018) : corpus of news articles and the task is to predict the first sentence given the remaining article content. We again use the entire test set of 11, 334 samples from this dataset.

4 Models

We study BART (Lewis et al., 2019), PEGASUS and T-5 (Raffel et al., 2019c) for abstractive summarization. For extractive summarization we use, BertSumExt (Liu, 2019) and MatchSum (Zhong et al., 2020). We use the versions fine-tuned on the datasets described in Section 3 for experiments. These models are in the top 10 on the leaderboard at the time of writing this paper [1]. These approaches are described below:
BART: An encoder decoder model that uses a bidirectional encoder and an autoregressive model as its decoder. The model is trained using de-noising objective.
PEGASUS: Encoder decoder model that is pre-trained to encourage abstractive summarization.

[1]https://paperswithcode.com/dataset/cnn-daily-mail-1

	CNN			XSum		
	$\text{Mean}_{[std]}$	BLEU-1	BLEU-2	$\text{Mean}_{[std]}$	BLEU-1	BLEU-2
ground truth	$0.751_{[0.098]}$	0.833	0.605	$0.519_{[0.158]}$	0.572	0.279
bart	$0.942_{[0.053]}$	0.955	0.903	$0.608_{[0.169]}$	0.661	0.383
pegasus	$0.889_{[0.063]}$	0.913	0.833	$0.584_{[0.174]}$	0.641	0.371
t5	$0.932_{[0.081]}$	0.937	0.849	$0.685_{[0.187]}$	0.726	0.446

Table 2: We measure the overlap between the source article and summaries by different models. Both the overlap metric defined in Section 5.1 and the BLEU metric without brevity penalty are shown in the tables. For the overlap metric we show both the mean(μ) and sigma(σ).

The model is trained to predict masked out sentences in the source text.

T-5: Text-based language problems are handled in a unified Text to Text framework to obtain significant improvements on several benchmark tasks.

BertSumExt: Model learns to pick the top 3 sentences that seem most relevant from the source text using Bert and inter-sentence transformer layers.

MatchSum: Model uses semantic matching between the document and the candidate summaries to pick the summary that is closest to the document. They achieve this using a margin-based triplet loss.

5 Experiments and Results

The summarization community has looked at using text overlap metrics like, BLEU or METEOR. The widely used text overlap metric for summarization is ROUGE-L that measures the overlap of words using Longest Common Subsequence between the generated summary and the ground truth. While these metrics attempt to compare the ground truth with the generated sentences, they certainly do not measure the *abstractive* component that one expects from abstractive summarization models. We describe experiments that show the model is merely copying words from the source text and not introducing novel words present in the ground truth. In order to allow future models to measure this abstractiveness we introduce a metric called *AbsExtScore* that will allow us to measure the abstractive prowess of these summarization models.

5.1 Source Text and Summary Overlap

We measure the percentage overlap of the words between the summary and the article for both the ground truth and the generated summaries, $overlap\_metric(J) = (S \cap T)/|T|$, S represents the set of source words and T represents the set of target words in the summary (be it ground truth or model generated). We also use the conventional BLEU metric to measure overlap between the source article and the target. However, we set the brevity penalty (BP) to 1 in order to reduce the penalty owing to the long sentences in the source article.

We see that the ground truth summaries have a much lower overlap with the article indicating that humans write a more abstractive version of the summary when compared to how a model performs abstractive summarization (Table 2). All the results are statistically significant using t-test. We see that there is at least 15% less overlap between the ground truth and generated summaries from any model on the CNN dataset and 8% less overlap on the XSum dataset. We also see that the overlap with BLEU is $10 - 15$ points higher for the generated summaries than the ground truth showing that the models are copying several words from the source text without actually introducing novel words.

5.2 Overlap between Abstractive and Extractive Summaries

We wanted to understand if the overlap between the abstractive summary and the ground truth was larger than the abstractive summary and the extractive summary. To investigate this, we measure the overlap between the summaries produced by 3 abstractive models and the summaries produced by 2 extractive models on 2 different datasets using Equation 1. However, in Table 3 we see that all the 3 abstractive models overlap more with the extractive summaries than the actual ground truth.

5.3 AbsExtScore

Abstractive summaries have to be closer to the ground truth in semantic space when compared to the extractive summary for any given source text. We use this as the foundational principle for our AbsExtScore which measures these distances in the semantic space. We project all the three summaries (abstractive, extractive and ground truth) into semantic space using the Siamese Distil Bert model (Reimers and Gurevych, 2019) trained on Bing queries. We use this model as it allows us to adapt well to different domains of source texts. Owing to the contrastive loss that this model was

	CNN			XSum		
	MatchSum	BertSumExt	Ground Truth	MatchSum	BertSumExt	Ground Truth
BART	$0.534_{[0.157]}$	$0.528_{[0.159]}$	$0.348_{[0.129]}$	$0.324_{[0.132]}$	$0.419_{[0.177]}$	$0.419_{[0.183]}$
PEGASUS	$0.547_{[0.157]}$	$0.532_{[0.16]}$	$0.381_{[0.142]}$	$0.309_{[0.134]}$	$0.411_{[0.18]}$	$0.447_{[0.194]}$
T5	$0.706_{[0.22]}$	$0.657_{[0.239]}$	$0.498_{[0.227]}$	$0.375_{[0.166]}$	$0.466_{[0.204]}$	$0.368_{[0.181]}$

Table 3: Overlap between the abstractive and extractive summaries. We see that the abstractive summaries overlap more with their extractive counterpart than with the ground truth.

	CNN						**XSum**					
	Eucledian Distance			**Cosine Similarity**			**Eucledian Distance**			**Cosine Similarity**		
	BART	**PEGASUS**	**T5**	**BART**	**PEGASUS**	**T5**	**BART**	**PEGASUS**	**T5**	**BART**	**PEGASUS**	**T5**
MatchSum	**0.72**	**0.663**	**0.615**	**0.724**	**0.668**	**0.629**	0.13	0.103	0.25	0.14	0.108	0.277
BertSumExt	**0.714**	**0.654**	**0.643**	**0.713**	**0.656**	**0.646**	**0.472**	0.405	**0.683**	**0.4661**	0.398	**0.674**

Table 4: AbsExtScore between different Abstractive and Extractive Summarization models. On CNN/DM we observe that both the Euclidean distance and cosine similarity favors the extractive summary over the ground truth for all scenarios. While on the XSum dataset it favors the ground truth in $3/6$ scenarios. We conducted a proportions z test and all results are statistically significant.

trained on, the model should be capable of capturing the difference in semantics of the three summaries. We define the score as below:

$$AbsExtScore = \frac{\sum_{n=1}^{N} argmin(d(e_{abs}, e_{gt}), d(e_{abs}, e_{ext}))}{N} \quad (1)$$

Here N is the total number of samples present in the test set. e_{abs}, e_{gt} and e_{ext} refers to embeddings obtained by using the MS Marco Distil Bert model (Reimers and Gurevych, 2019). d refers to the L2 distance between the two vectors. We also experimented with the use of a cosine similarity function. In this case we take $argmax$ as we want the vectors to be close to each other. We want the *AbsExtScore* to be close to 0 so that the abstractive vectors are closer to the ground truth vectors and not the extractive vectors. However, from Table 4 we see that in only $3/12$ different scenarios is the score less than 0.40, showing that the abstractive models overlap quite significantly with the extractive summaries in semantic space. We observe the same correlation with both the cosine similarity and Euclidean distance measures (L2 distance). Our metric is different from semantic measure metrics like BERTScore (Zhang et al., 2019b) and BARTScore (Yuan et al., 2021) as our metric captures both semantic similarity and 'abstractiveness' measures. We are not proposing a metric that measures the overlap between generated sentence and ground truth. We are only trying to introduce another dimensionality of measurement that helps answer the degree of abstractiveness of the model at a corpus level.

5.3.1 Human Subject study

To understand if there is a correlation between the automated metric proposed above and human judgement, we conducted a pilot human evaluation by randomly sampling 50 data points from the test set of CNN/DM. We presented the abstractive summary of this data point and asked the annotator to judge if it was closer to the ground truth over its extractive counterpart. We picked the BART abstractive model and MatchSum extractive model for this study. We got 3 annotations per datapoint (150 total). We said that *"An example of close resemblance includes but not limited to having similar phrases or having matching words."* to provide a judgement baseline to the annotators. We ran this study on Amazon Mechanical Turk. We removed a few annotations which were done in under 15 seconds (random annotations) . This reduced our total annotations to 62. Out of the 62 annotations, 41 said that the abstractive summaries are closer to extractive summary while 21 felt that it was closer to ground truth. We conducted a proportion z test to find that this result is statistically significant (p-value=0.007). Humans thought the abstractive summaries are close to extractive summaries 66% of the time while our metric gave a score of 72%. Agreement between humans and our metric was 76%.

6 Conclusion and Future Work

A central tenet of abstractive models is to abstract relevant information from source text. We find that the abstractive models merely copy words from source text and are failing to insert novelty words. We show that the abstractive summaries are closer to the extractive summaries than they are to ground truth. We use models built for semantic understanding to introduce a new metric called *AbsExtScore* which the summarization community can adopt to understand the level of abstraction introduced by their proposed abstractive models in comparison to their extractive counterparts. We conducted a human subject study to show the correlation between the automated metric and human judgements.

Acknowledgement

We thank the anonymous reviewers for their valuable suggestions.

References

Nabil Alami, Mohammed Meknassi, and Noureddine Ennahnahi. 2019. Enhancing unsupervised neural networks based text summarization with word embedding and ensemble learning. *Expert Syst. Appl.*, 123:195–211.

Deepa Anand and Rupali Sunil Wagh. 2019. Effective deep learning approaches for summarization of legal texts. *Journal of King Saud University - Computer and Information Sciences*.

Regina Barzilay, Kathleen R. McKeown, and Michael Elhadad. 1999. Information fusion in the context of multi-document summarization. In *Proceedings of the 37th Annual Meeting of the Association for Computational Linguistics*, pages 550–557, College Park, Maryland, USA. Association for Computational Linguistics.

P. B. Baxendale. 1958. Machine-made index for technical literature—an experiment. *IBM Journal of Research and Development*, 2(4):354–361.

Kuan-Yu Chen, Shih-Hung Liu, Berlin Chen, and Hsin-Min Wang. 2018. An information distillation framework for extractive summarization. *IEEE/ACM Transactions on Audio, Speech, and Language Processing*, 26(1):161–170.

Kevin Clark, Minh-Thang Luong, Quoc V. Le, and Christopher D. Manning. 2020. ELECTRA: pre-training text encoders as discriminators rather than generators. *CoRR*, abs/2003.10555.

Jacob Devlin, Ming-Wei Chang, Kenton Lee, and Kristina Toutanova. 2018. Bert: Pre-training of deep bidirectional transformers for language understanding. *arXiv preprint arXiv:1810.04805*.

Pierre-Etienne Genest and Guy Lapalme. 2012. Fully abstractive approach to guided summarization. In *Proceedings of the 50th Annual Meeting of the Association for Computational Linguistics (Volume 2: Short Papers)*, pages 354–358, Jeju Island, Korea. Association for Computational Linguistics.

Max Grusky, Mor Naaman, and Yoav Artzi. 2018. Newsroom: A dataset of 1.3 million summaries with diverse extractive strategies. *arXiv preprint arXiv:1804.11283*.

Yuuki Iwasaki, Akihiro Yamashita, Yoko Konno, and Katsushi Matsubayashi. 2019. Japanese abstractive text summarization using bert. In *2019 International Conference on Technologies and Applications of Artificial Intelligence (TAAI)*, pages 1–5.

Atif Khan and Naomie Salim. 2014. A review on abstractive summarization methods. *Journal of theoretical and applied information technology*, 59:64–72.

Hyunsoo Lee, YunSeok Choi, and Jee-Hyong Lee. 2020. *Attention History-Based Attention for Abstractive Text Summarization*, page 1075–1081. Association for Computing Machinery, New York, NY, USA.

Mike Lewis, Yinhan Liu, Naman Goyal, Marjan Ghazvininejad, Abdelrahman Mohamed, Omer Levy, Veselin Stoyanov, and Luke Zettlemoyer. 2019. BART: denoising sequence-to-sequence pre-training for natural language generation, translation, and comprehension. *CoRR*, abs/1910.13461.

Yang Liu. 2019. Fine-tune bert for extractive summarization. *arXiv preprint arXiv:1903.10318*.

Yinhan Liu, Myle Ott, Naman Goyal, Jingfei Du, Mandar Joshi, Danqi Chen, Omer Levy, Mike Lewis, Luke Zettlemoyer, and Veselin Stoyanov. 2019. Roberta: A robustly optimized BERT pretraining approach. *CoRR*, abs/1907.11692.

Farida Mohsen, Jiayang Wang, and Kamal Al-Sabahi. 2020. A hierarchical self-attentive neural extractive summarizer via reinforcement learning (hsasrl). *Applied Intelligence*, 50(9):2633–2646.

Shashi Narayan, Shay B Cohen, and Mirella Lapata. 2018. Don't give me the details, just the summary! topic-aware convolutional neural networks for extreme summarization. *arXiv preprint arXiv:1808.08745*.

Kishore Papineni, Salim Roukos, Todd Ward, and Wei-Jing Zhu. 2002. Bleu: a method for automatic evaluation of machine translation. In *Proceedings of the 40th annual meeting of the Association for Computational Linguistics*, pages 311–318.

Alec Radford, Jeffrey Wu, Rewon Child, David Luan, Dario Amodei, and Ilya Sutskever. 2018. Language models are unsupervised multitask learners.

Colin Raffel, Noam Shazeer, Adam Roberts, Katherine Lee, Sharan Narang, Michael Matena, Yanqi Zhou, Wei Li, and Peter J. Liu. 2019a. Exploring the limits of transfer learning with a unified text-to-text transformer. *CoRR*, abs/1910.10683.

Colin Raffel, Noam Shazeer, Adam Roberts, Katherine Lee, Sharan Narang, Michael Matena, Yanqi Zhou, Wei Li, and Peter J. Liu. 2019b. Exploring the limits of transfer learning with a unified text-to-text transformer.

Colin Raffel, Noam Shazeer, Adam Roberts, Katherine Lee, Sharan Narang, Michael Matena, Yanqi Zhou, Wei Li, and Peter J Liu. 2019c. Exploring the limits of transfer learning with a unified text-to-text transformer. *arXiv preprint arXiv:1910.10683*.

Nils Reimers and Iryna Gurevych. 2019. Sentence-bert: Sentence embeddings using siamese bert-networks. *arXiv preprint arXiv:1908.10084*.

Thomas Scialom, Paul-Alexis Dray, Sylvain Lamprier, Benjamin Piwowarski, and Jacopo Staiano. 2020. Mlsum: The multilingual summarization corpus. *arXiv preprint arXiv:2004.14900*.

Abigail See, Peter J Liu, and Christopher D Manning. 2017. Get to the point: Summarization with pointer-generator networks. *arXiv preprint arXiv:1704.04368*.

Hideki Tanaka, Akinori Kinoshita, Takeshi Kobayakawa, Tadashi Kumano, and Naoto Kato. 2009. Syntax-driven sentence revision for broadcast news summarization. In *Proceedings of the 2009 Workshop on Language Generation and Summarisation*, UCNLG+Sum '09, page 39–47, USA. Association for Computational Linguistics.

Jiacheng Xu and Greg Durrett. 2019. Neural extractive text summarization with syntactic compression.

Zhilin Yang, Zihang Dai, Yiming Yang, Jaime Carbonell, Ruslan Salakhutdinov, and Quoc V. Le. 2019. Xlnet: Generalized autoregressive pretraining for language understanding.

Kaichun Yao, Libo Zhang, Dawei Du, Tiejian Luo, Lili Tao, and Yanjun Wu. 2020. Dual encoding for abstractive text summarization. *IEEE Transactions on Cybernetics*, 50(3):985–996.

Weizhe Yuan, Graham Neubig, and Pengfei Liu. 2021. Bartscore: Evaluating generated text as text generation. *Advances in Neural Information Processing Systems*, 34:27263–27277.

Jingqing Zhang, Yao Zhao, Mohammad Saleh, and Peter J. Liu. 2019a. PEGASUS: pre-training with extracted gap-sentences for abstractive summarization. *CoRR*, abs/1912.08777.

Tianyi Zhang, Varsha Kishore, Felix Wu, Kilian Q Weinberger, and Yoav Artzi. 2019b. Bertscore: Evaluating text generation with bert. *arXiv preprint arXiv:1904.09675*.

Ming Zhong, Pengfei Liu, Yiran Chen, Danqing Wang, Xipeng Qiu, and Xuanjing Huang. 2020. Extractive summarization as text matching. *arXiv preprint arXiv:2004.08795*.

A Appendices

A.1 Overlap of Abstractive models with Source Text

A.1.1 CNN/DM Dataset

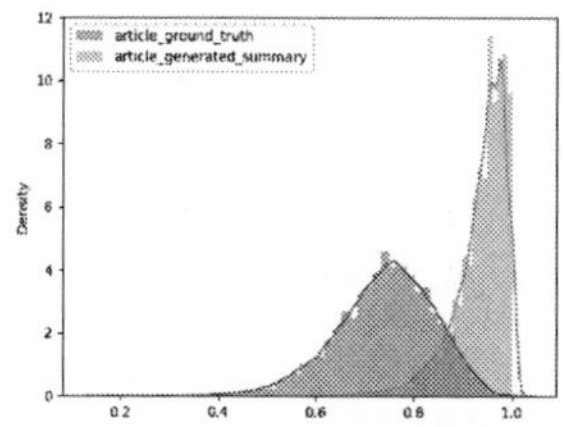

(a) Bart

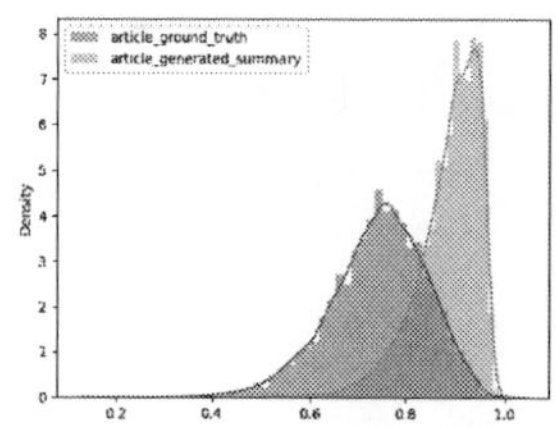

(b) Pegasus

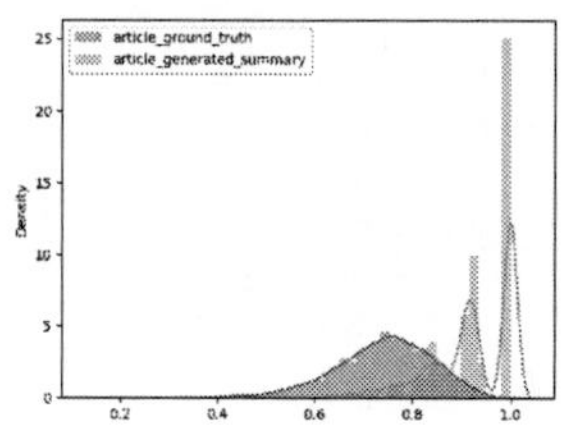

(c) T5

A.1.2 XSum Dataset

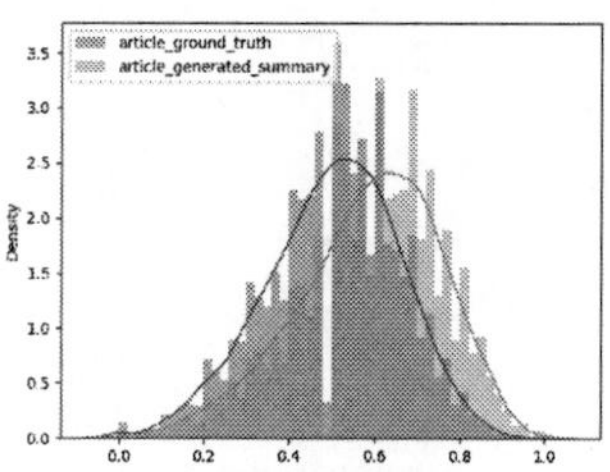

(a) Bart

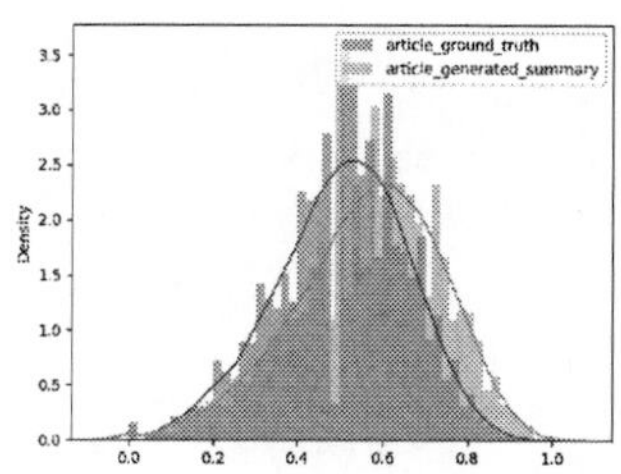

(b) Pegasus

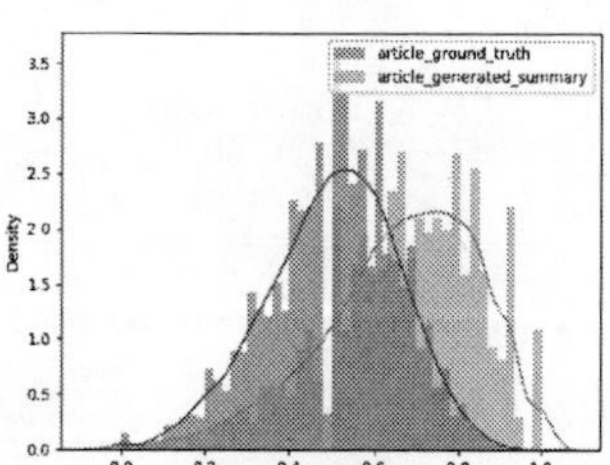

(c) T5

A.2 Overlap of Abstractive models with Extractive Models.

A.2.1 CNN/DM Dataset

BertSumExt

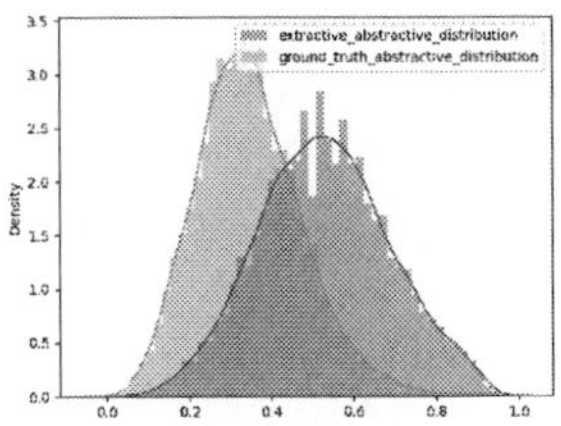

(a) Bart

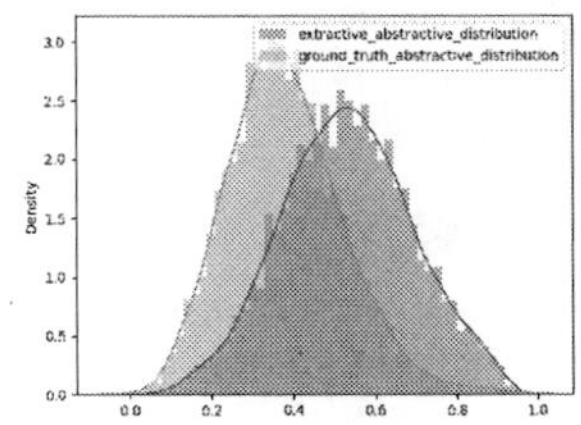

(b) Pegasus

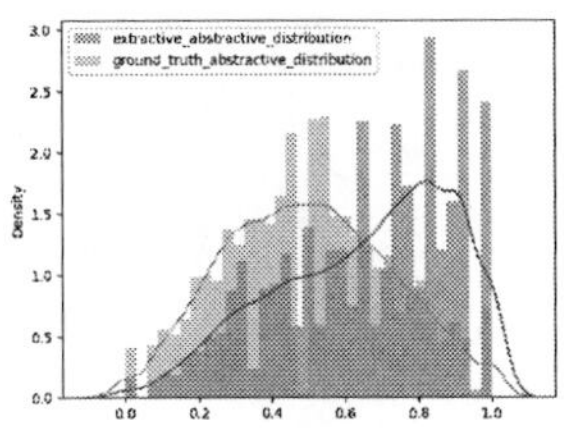

(c) T5

MatchSum

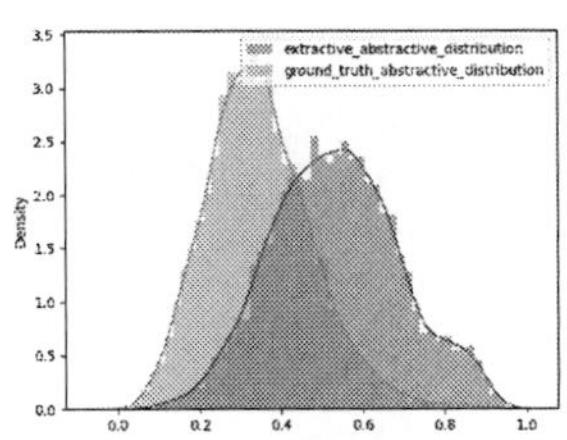

(a) Bart

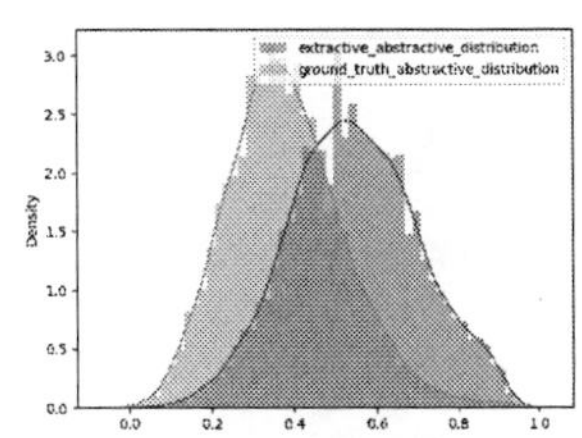

(b) Pegasus

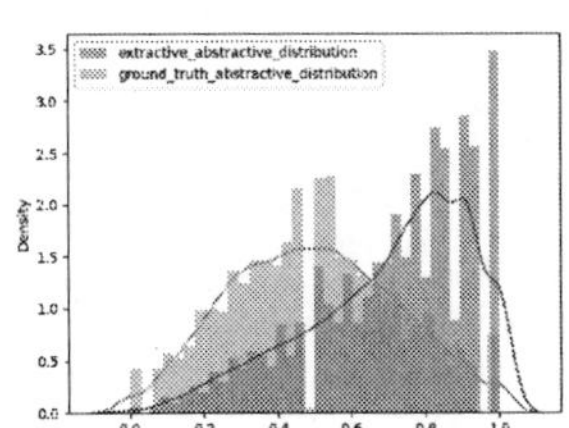

(c) T5

A.2.2 XSum Dataset

BertSumExt

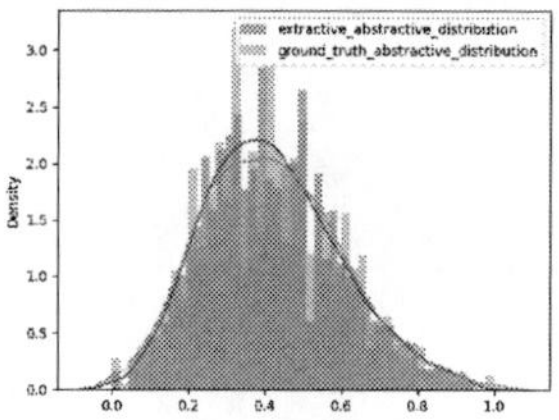

(a) Bart

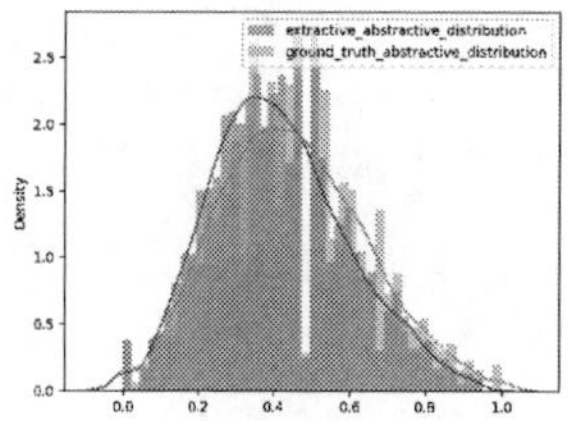

(b) Pegasus

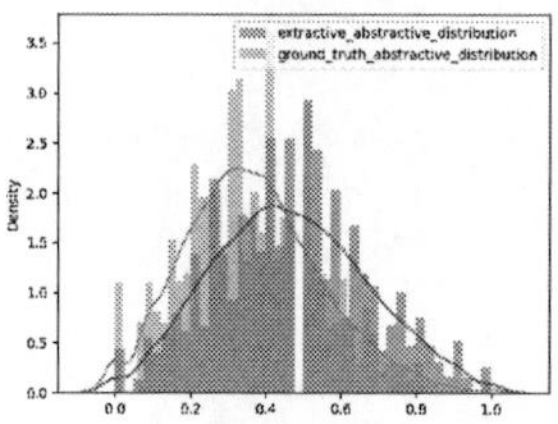

(c) T5

MatchSum

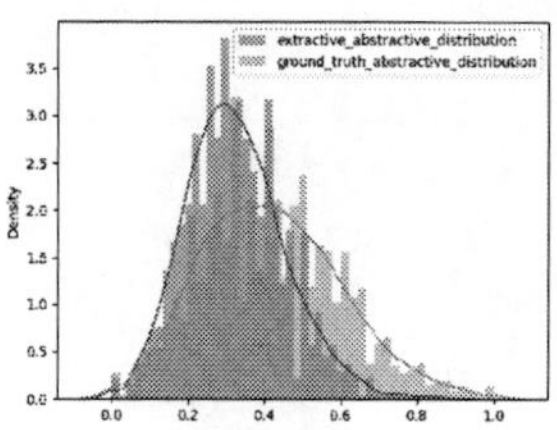

(a) Bart

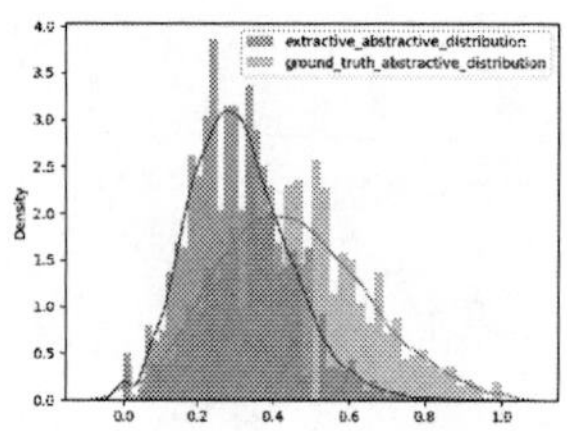

(b) Pegasus

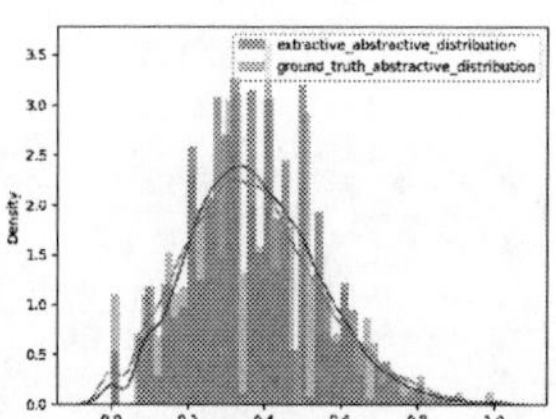

(c) T5

Transfer learning for multilingual vacancy text generation

Anna Lőrincz
University of Amsterdam
anna@lorincz.org

David Graus
Randstad Groep Nederland
david.graus@randstadgroep.nl

Dor Lavi
Meta
dorlavi@meta.com

João L. M. Pereira
University of Amsterdam
INESC-ID and IST, Universidade de Lisboa
j.p.pereira@uva.nl

Abstract

Writing job vacancies can be a repetitive and expensive task for humans. This research focuses on automatically generating parts of vacancy texts, i.e., the benefits section, given structured job attributes as input using mT5, the multilingual version of the state-of-the-art T5 transformer model. While transformers are accurate at generating coherent text, they can struggle with correctly including structured (input) data in the generated text. Including this input data correctly is crucial for vacancy text generation; otherwise, job seekers may be misled. To evaluate how the model includes the different types of structured input, we propose a novel domain-specific metric: 'input generation accuracy'. Our metric aims to address the shortcomings of Relation Generation, a commonly used evaluation metric for data-to-text generation that relies on string matching, as our task includes evaluating generated texts based on binary and categorical inputs. Using our novel evaluation method, we measure how well the input is included in the generated text separately for different types of inputs (binary, categorical, numeric), offering another contribution to the field. In addition, we evaluate how accurately the mT5 model generates texts in the requested languages. Our experiments show that mT5 is highly accurate at generating texts in the correct (requested) languages, and at handling seen categorical and binary inputs correctly. However, mT5 performed worse when generating text from unseen city names or working with numeric inputs.

1 Introduction

Integrating Natural Language Processing (NLP) solutions to improve the human workforce offers great opportunities for process automation (Devarajan, 2018). Such process automation can be to automate the writing of parts of the vacancies using the given structured data. This research was carried out with Randstad Netherlands, a Dutch HR services company that provides vacancies in Dutch and English.

Natural Language Generation (NLG) is the subfield of NLP focusing on automatic text writing. Text generation tasks can be categorized depending on the input into text-to-text generation (e.g., text translation) and data-to-text generation (e.g., the generation of Wikipedia biographies). Generating vacancy text falls under the data-to-text generation category, since particular job-specific information (for example: `MINSALARY = 2500, MAXSALARY = 2700, SALARYTYPE = 'per month'`) is provided as input and a coherent sentence that combines the given information must be generated as the output (for example *'You will receive between 2500 and 2700 euros on a monthly bases'*). Early data-to-text generation approaches used hand-engineered templates (Kukich, 1983; McKeown, 1992; McRoy et al., 2000) to generate texts. These templates can be intuitively explained as a series of written text elements, with certain segments serving as the template's 'backbone' and the remaining segments being filled up with information from the structured data (Wang and Cardie, 2013). From the previous example: *'You will receive between 2500 and 2700 euros on a monthly bases'* the following template can be created *'You will receive between <MINSALARY> and <MAXSALARY> euros on a monthly bases'*. Such simple (template-based) method was used as the baseline for this research. While this solution is computationally cheap, fast and the inputs will be correctly included, a lot of manual effort is required to create the templates and the generated texts will be very repetitive.

Transformer models are a type of neural network architecture that use transfer learning. Transfer learning is the technique where these models are initially trained (pre-trained) on a large unlabeled text dataset and some supervised tasks. The 'knowledge' learned through pre-training is then reused on the new task, making transformer methods cur-

Proceedings of the 2nd Workshop on Natural Language Generation, Evaluation, and Metrics (GEM), pages 207 - 222
December 7, 2022 ©2022 Association for Computational Linguistics

rently the most effective solution for text generation (Devlin et al., 2019). While there is no transformer model available that was pre-trained on data-to-text generation tasks, recent research in (Kale and Rastogi, 2020) showed that transformer models - that were pre-trained on text-to-text generations tasks - outperform traditional (non-transformer) neural network solutions for data-to-text generation task after fine-tuning. Based on this finding and the fact that our dataset is multilingual, we used the multilingual version of T5, mT5 (Xue et al., 2021). In contrast to the template-based method, transformers can provide a wide range of text variation. However, when generating text, transformers pick the next word with some randomness, thus they are less accurate at including the input correctly.

This paper investigates how the benefit sections of vacancies (namely: *salary, hours, contract and location*) can be generated using mT5. Our contribution is three-fold. On one hand, we use mT5 in a new domain, with a relatively small and proprietary dataset - that contains many noise and incorrect samples - in a multilingual setting. On the other hand, we confirm the importance of domain specific evaluation metrics in data-to-text generation, by analyzing - with the metrics developed by us - how accurate mT5 is in terms of including the input correctly in the generated text. We also investigate how creating more training data (through translation and generating synthetic samples) can improve this accuracy. Focusing on including the input correctly is particularly important in this domain, where incorrect wages, or stating hourly salaries instead of monthly can be misleading to candidates.

This paper focuses on answering the following research question:

RQ1 To what extent can the state-of-the-art multilingual text-to-text generation transformer, mT5 (Xue et al., 2021) be used to generate the benefit sections of vacancies in a multilinguistic environment?

To answer this research question we aim to answer the following sub-questions:

RQ1.1 How accurate is mT5 in terms of generating the text in the correct language for the benefit sections of vacancies?

RQ1.2 When using new domain specific metrics to measure the input generation accuracy, how does mT5 perform, in terms of including different types of inputs (numerical, binary, categorical) in the generated text?

RQ1.3 How can creating extra training data by translating the training samples automatically and generating synthetic training data increase the accuracy of the model regarding language and input generation?

2 Related Work

The current state-of-the art solutions in text generation are transformer models that rely on transfer learning, where a model is initially pre-trained on a large dataset, before being fine-tuned on a downstream task (for example text summarization). Pre-training on a large, unlabelled dataset is important for transformer models, because during this pre-training the model learns the basics of language. T5 transformer was proposed with a new dataset by Google Raffel et al. (2020). This so called Colossal Clean Crawled Corpus (C4)[*] is a thoroughly cleaned massive text dataset, scraped from many websites for pre-training the model. The model is classified as text-to-text, since both the input and output are always text strings. To define which task (for example text summarization) the model should perform, a task-specific prefix was appended to the input during the pre-training. This prefix is simply a short synopsis of the task that is subsequently used throughout fine-tuning to teach the model a new task. This same prefix is then used to specify what task to perform when employing the model. Such a prefix may be 'Translate English to German:' (for machine translation) or 'Summarize' (for text summarization) (Raffel et al., 2020). Thanks to this task-specific prefix and the large pre-training dataset, the model is adaptable enough to be fine-tuned on different downstream tasks with the same loss function and hyperparameters.

2.1 Transformer-based data-to-text generation application domains

All relevant transformer based data-to-text research have been conducted in three domains (sport game summaries, open and closed domain Wikipedia). The researches in the Wikipedia domain use ToTTo (Parikh et al., 2020) and WebNLG [†] (Gardent et al., 2017; Zhou and Lampouras, 2020; Castro Ferreira et al., 2020) datasets with training sizes of 120K

[*]https://www.tensorflow.org/datasets/catalog/c4

[†]https://webnlg-challenge.loria.fr/challenge_2020

and 25.3K. The best performing model for the ToTTo dataset is a simple fine-tuned T5 model (Kale and Rastogi, 2020). For the WebNLG domain the best one is T5 with some adjustment to control the generation by including conditional, input-dependent information in the prefixes (Clive et al., 2021). This domain has received more attention than the others for multilingual data-to-text generation (Moussallem et al., 2020). Agarwal et al. (2020) found that by fine-tuning the model in two languages via machine translation (on the WebNLG dataset), a bilingual T5 model can outperform two separate monolingual T5 models. We use an equivalent strategy for enhancing the multilingual model by automatically translating the training samples.

The last domain - sport game summaries - uses the RotoWire dataset (Wiseman et al., 2017) with 4.9K training samples to generate NBA basketball game summaries from the structured game scores. An intriguing transformer-based approach (Gong et al., 2019) demonstrated how producing syntactic training data by replacing the scores with new, synthetic values improves performance. We use the same concept in this paper.

Recently, Qin et al. (2022) proposed a neural approach to generate the requirements section of the job description. This research however is not a data-to-text generation study, because it focuses on generating the requirements for jobs (such as the required skills), based on the fluent text of the tasks section of the job descriptions. Our research concentrates on a different task within the domain by generating the benefit section of the vacancies. We use a transformer model and a data-to-text approach on a bilingual dataset, which is highly unbalanced (having about 95% of the samples in Dutch) and diverse regarding the data types (numeric, categorical, binary), which sets the research apart from previous work.

2.2 Existing evaluation methods

Typical quality of text generation metrics are Bilingual Evaluation Understudy (BLEU) score (Papineni et al., 2002), Recall-Oriented Understudy for Gisting Evaluation (ROUGE) score (Lin, 2004) and Metric for Evaluation of Translation with Explicit ORdering (METEOR) score (Lavie and Agarwal, 2007). ROUGE measures the recall by concentrating on how many n-grams of the reference (human written text) appeared in the generated text, whereas BLEU measures precision of the appearing n-grams by measuring on how much of the output text appeared in the reference (Lin, 2004). METEOR was proposed for machine translation to improve the alignment with human judgement. The metric computes the explicit word-to-word match between the output and the reference, however it has many properties that are missing from the previous metrics. METEOR performs stemming (using the Porter Stemmer) and also takes synonyms into consideration (Lavie and Agarwal, 2007). The traditional quality of text evaluation methods however, fail to evaluate the generated text in terms of their fidelity to the input data (Wiseman et al., 2017). To solve this issue Relation Generation (RG) metric was proposed in (Wiseman et al., 2017). The metric measures how well the system includes the input, however it assumes that the entities can be detected in the generated text using string matching (Dhingra et al., 2019). This is not the case for our task, because while some entities can be detected: like the `location` (the city name), numbers are more problematic due to the monetary units. For example, in the Netherlands the decimal point is indicated by a comma instead of a period. Lastly, measuring the binary variable (`hidesalary`) is not in any way detectable by string matching only. Therefore, we propose new rule based domain specific measures, which we describe in subsection 3.6.

3 Methodology

3.1 Dataset

The internal dataset of Randstad Netherlands was used for the research which contains both structured vacancy data (e.g., salary amount), which we use as input for text generation, and the corresponding human written vacancy texts (`targettext`), i.e., the desired output of the text generation. We focused on the following four benefit sections: *salary, location, hours and contract.* Figure 1 shows an example for each of these benefit sections, using a vacancy for a Customer Service Representative published on Randstad Netherlands' website[‡]. Table 1 shows the 11 different input fields and how each benefit section uses different ones (except the language, which is used for every section). Four data types are present in the dataset: integer (`min/maxhours`) and non-integer (`min/maxsalary`) numericals, categoricals

[‡] https://www.randstad.com/find-a-job/

(location, contracttype, salarytype) and binary (hidesalary, fixhour, fixsalary).

Figure 1: The figure illustrates the layout of the benefit section on the website of Randstad Netherlands.

3.2 Template-based method

When designed properly, template-based models always perform perfect in terms of including the inputs and using the correct language. We implemented a template-based method to compare the performance of mT5 and to provide an alternative solution to the transformer approach for this domain. The pipeline of this method starts by creating a template of every targettext from the training data, by replacing the numeric and the location input values in the text with a token corresponding to the feature name. (For example from the sample '€2800 - €3000 gross per month' we create a template as ' €<MINSALARY> - €<MAXSALARY> gross per month'.) Next, we choose a set of templates for each combination of categorical data by selecting the top five most common templates for each combination from the training data. These previous steps are performed only once, whereas the next step, the text generation, is performed every time a new benefit section needs to be generated with the method. As part of this text generation step, for each sample a template is picked from the correct combination and then, this picked template is filled with the correct values by replacing the feature tags with their values. The steps are the same for every section and every combination of categories has five templates. Appendix A contains an example for the template-based method.

3.3 mT5 model

We used hugging face's PyTorch implementation[§] with the default tokenizer and default loss (cross-entropy loss) to fine-tune the base version of the mT5 model. For optimizer we used Adafactor with the recommended setting by Shazeer and Stern (2018). Similar to the task-specific prefix, the input for the mT5 model is provided in a text format. For data-to-text generation, the input is typically provided by first including the feature name and then the feature value. Because transformer models are extremely sensitive to how the input is given (Lester et al., 2021), we experimented for each section with three distinct input formats during the fine-tuning of the model. The only difference between the inputs is how the feature name is represented in the input. For each section the 'FEATURENAME' token was changed to the feature name which we want to include and the 'value' token was replaced by the value of the feature. For each of our three formats, listed below, we present an example from the location benefit section, where our only feature is the location and the value of the feature is 'Amsterdam'.

- **input A:** <FEATURENAME> value
  example: *<LOCATION> Amsterdam*
- **input B:** FEATURENAME = value
  example: *LOCATION = Amsterdam*
- **input C:** <FEATURENAME> value </FEATURENAME>
  example: *<LOCATION> Amsterdam </LOCATION>*

For English text generation we used the prefix 'Generate in English' and for Dutch 'Generate in Dutch'. We specified the prefix and the input in English.

We fine-tuned the original dataset using each input format and choose the best performing one based on the input generation accuracy score (the newly developed metrics explained in subsection 3.6). When fine-tuning the models on the translated and the synthetic dataset we used the same input and prefix as on the original dataset. Our hyperparameter tuning consisted of finding the number of epochs that had the highest input generation accuracy. For the generation, we set the sampling parameter to True. Allowing sampling means that the next word is randomly picked from the conditional probability distribution, thus the model is more diverse and does not generate the same sentence for the same input, unless the random seed is identical. This is important, because otherwise all samples with the same input would have the same generated text, making the outputs very repetitive (for example every job that has 40 working hours, which is quite common). For the text generation, we also set the 'top_p' parameter to 1 to ensure that only the tokens whose combined probability adds

[§]https://huggingface.co/docs/transformers/model_doc/mt5

Relevant benefit section	Feature	Description	Data type	Occurring values
All	`language`	Language of the vacancy text	categorical (string)	{English, Dutch}
Salary	`hidesalary`	Whether salary amount should be mentioned	binary	{True, False}
	`minsalary`	Lower limit of salary amount in euro	numeric (float)	9.63 - 41.0 for hourly, 250 - 4500 for monthly
	`maxsalary`	Upper limit of salary amount in euro	numeric (float)	9.7 - 45.0 for hourly, 250 - 6000 for monthly
	`fixsalary`	Whether `minsalary` and `maxsalary` are equal	binary	{True, False}
	`salarytype`	Frequency of payment	categorical (string)	{Monthly, Hourly}
Hours	`minhour`	Minimum working hours per week	numeric (int)	2 - 55
	`maxhour`	Maximum working hours per week	numeric (int)	2 - 55
	`fixhour`	Whether `minhour` and `maxhour` are equal	binary	{True, False}
Contract	`contracttype`	Type of offered contract	categorical (string)	{Temporary, Temporary with a possibility of fixed, Fixed}
Location	`location`	City name of work location	categorical (string)	-

Table 1: Overview of the features in the dataset

up to 100% are kept for generation. Additionally, we set 'top_k' parameter to 10 to make sure to only choose from the ten most probable tokens.

3.4 Generating extra training data

We applied two methods to generate extra training data. One for producing additional examples in each language (inspired by Agarwal et al. (2020)) by translating all English training samples to Dutch and all Dutch training samples to English using the Googletrans library[¶]. Then, we repeated the pre-processing steps, removed the duplicated samples and appended this new training set to our original training set, approximately doubling our training set and obtaining a balanced dataset in terms of language. We refer to this training set as the translated training set. For the second method (similarly to Gong et al. (2019)), we generated synthetic data for the sections with the numeric inputs (salary and hours). We guaranteed that the range between the lower and higher values (lower and higher bounds) were not exceeded (for working hours and monthly and hourly salary amount separately). After randomly selecting the new numbers, we replaced the original numeric values in the `targettext` to create the new synthetic training samples. We rounded every value to two decimals and ensured using the correct monetary unit for the salary section. For the hours section, we only picked from integer numbers, following the nature of the training data. We created such synthetic training samples by replacing values three times on every training sample from the translated dataset. After creating the synthetic data we performed the pre-processing steps and removed any duplicates, thus we received an approximately three times larger, balanced - regarding the language - dataset that included some randomness and covered more numeric values than our previous training sets. We then added this training set to our translated dataset, which we refer to as synthetic training data in the rest of the paper.

[¶] `https://pypi.org/project/googletrans/`

3.5 Experimental setup

We split the data for each benefit section into training, validation and test sets with a 60-20-20% ratio. Table 9 in Appendix C contains the sample sizes for each benefit sections. The details about how the random seed was set for different parts of the workflow in order to ensure reproducibility and fair comparison between models can be found in Appendix D.

3.6 Evaluation metrics

3.6.1 Text Quality

To measure the quality of text, we use the BLEU-1, BLEU-2, ROUGE-1, ROUGE-2 and METEOR scores (previously explained in section 2). We only use the BLEU and ROUGE scores up to two n-grams because our sections are rather short (5.5 to 7 words on average). Additionally, we record the size of vocabulary by automatically counting the number of unique words in the generated texts after removing all numeric values, and excluding the city name for the location section. This way we ensure that including a wrong input does not change the size of vocabulary.

3.6.2 Language accuracy

A main goal of this study is to determine, whether the mT5 model is reliable in terms of generating text in the requested language. Thus, we compare the requested language to the language of the generated text. We used the Lingua library[1] for language detection, as this library is suitable for detecting language of short sentences specifically. To determine the language accuracy we calculate the percentage for each language where the detected language matches the intended one.

3.6.3 Input generation accuracy

For the newly developed 'input generation accuracy' metrics, we calculate the number of correct samples divided by the number of all samples. The correct samples are identified with predefined rules with string matching. For the location section a sample is considered correct if the city name is correctly included. For the contract section, we use a collection of terms to classify the created text into one of three potential categories (Temporary, Temporary with a possibility of fixed, Fixed). For the hours and salary sections we extract the numbers from the generated text and compare them to the input numbers. If there is any difference between the two set of numbers we treat the sample incorrect. Furthermore we check whether each number is only included once. This is especially crucial for the fix salaries otherwise for example the following text would be considered correct: *'You will work between 40 and 40 hours'*. For the salary section, we also check whether the monetary unit is set properly (the decimal is separated with a comma) and the rounding is correct (all integers are rounded to whole numbers and non-integers to two decimals). Additionally, we use string matching to assess the categorical `salarytype` input generation accuracy. First, we lowercase the generated text and then for example if the salary type is 'per month', we consider the sample correct if the generated text contains 'month' but not 'hour'. As a result, records are not only penalized if they include the wrong salary type, but also if they do not contain the correct one. Finally, we measure the binary input generation accuracy (for `hidesalary`) by detecting whether any numeric values appear in the generated text.

4 Results

Table 2 shows the results for each section. It shows the input format *(Input)*, epoch size *(Epoch)*, quality of text scores *(METEOR, BLEU-1, BLEU-2, ROUGE-1, ROUGE-2)*, language accuracy scores *(English, Dutch)*, input generation accuracy *(for categorical, numerical and binary inputs)*, and vocabulary size in words.

4.1 Location

Rows 1-3 in Table 2 show the results obtained for the location benefit section. The best performing input format for mT5 (based on input generation accuracy) was *'FEATURE = value'* (input B). A perfect language accuracy was already achieved on the original dataset (row 2). By fine-tuning the model on the translated dataset, we were able to increase the input generation accuracy to 84.87% (row 3). mT5 fine-tuned on this translated data (row 3) reached similar results regarding the METEOR score and slightly outperformed the template-based method (row 1) in terms of BLEU-2 and ROUGE-2 score. Additionally, the size of vocabulary was more than twice (315-339) for the generated text when compared to the template-based method (129).

4.2 Contract

As mentioned in section 3, we used the English prefix value of the input when fine-tuning the models. However, in the case of the contract section the English language accuracy remained zero even after using the translated dataset for fine-tuning (row 6 on Table 2). Then we fine-tuned the model using a translated version of the prefix and the input. For example for an English sample the prefix was given as *'Generate in English'* and the input format was *'CONTRACTTYPE = fix'*, while for a Dutch sample the prefix was specified as *'Genereren in het Nederlands'* and the input was translated to Dutch and given as *'CONTRACTTYPE = vast'*. As shown on row 7, with the translated prefix and input, the model was able to achieve high language accuracy for English (92.31%) and a high input generation accuracy (96.44%) too. Adding the translated data (row 8), however was found unnecessary as it resulted in a decrease in the categorical input generation accuracy (to 74.19%). Overall, the transformer model achieved similar results to the template-based method (row 4) regarding the language and the input accuracy, while under performing in terms of the quality of text scores. Furthermore, the used vocabulary by the transformer had a 3.5 times larger size (170-263) than the template-based method (77).

[1] https://pypi.org/project/lingua/

	Benefit section	Model	Training data	Input	Epochs	METEOR	BLEU-1	BLEU-2	ROUGE-1	ROUGE-2	English lang. acc.	Dutch lang. acc.	Binary input gen. acc.	Categorical input gen. acc.	Numeric input gen. acc.	Size of voc.
1	Location	Template-based	Original	-	-	19.95	**30.24**	11.84	**37.67**	10.62	**100.00**	**100.00**	NA	**100.00**	NA	129
2	Location	mT5	Original	B	40	**20.88**	28.35	**13.53**	34.43	**13.09**	**100.00**	**100.00**	NA	76.97	NA	315
3	Location	mT5	Translated	B	50	20.33	27.77	13.40	32.36	11.87	**100.00**	**100.00**	NA	84.87	NA	**339**
4	Contract	Template-based	Original	-	-	**37.16**	**36.88**	**25.93**	**56.03**	**30.63**	**100.00**	**100.00**	NA	**100.00**	NA	77
5	Contract	mT5	Original	C	15	25.43	26.42	14.43	34.81	15.12	0.00	99.54	NA	78.42	NA	219
6	Contract	mT5	Trans.	C	20	25.09	26.55	14.10	34.02	14.33	0.00	99.77	NA	66.63	NA	170
7	Contract	mT5	Original	B (tran.)	15	29.10	29.42	16.51	39.14	16.88	92.31	98.97	NA	96.44	NA	**263**
8	Contract	mT5	Translated	B (tran.)	15	26.71	27.37	15.02	34.85	15.28	92.31	99.77	NA	74.19	NA	224
9	Hours	Template-based	Original	-	-	**46.38**	**42.11**	**35.34**	**80.16**	**63.92**	**100.00**	**100.00**	NA	NA	**100.00**	51
10	Hours	mT5	Original	B	15	35.82	35.16	25.90	61.18	40.91	15.38	99.50	NA	NA	83.17	137
11	Hours	mT5	Translated	B	30	40.22	37.92	29.01	60.06	41.30	92.31	**100.00**	NA	NA	77.51	**184**
12	Hours	mT5	Synthetic	B	50	42.62	39.83	31.69	63.38	45.28	**100.00**	99.83	NA	NA	98.06	163
13	Salary	Template-based	Original	-	-	**30.45**	**32.03**	**22.34**	**60.80**	**38.09**	**100.00**	**100.00**	**100.00**	**100.00**	**100.00**	112
14	Salary	mT5	Original	A	30	28.27	31.16	20.53	46.82	28.10	96.88	99.85	89.71	99.06	85.31	528
15	Salary	mT5	Translated	A	40	29.20	31.67	20.56	48.22	28.57	96.88	99.93	99.21	97.44	84.23	585
16	Salary	mT5	Synthetic	A	40	27.70	29.74	18.70	46.32	25.89	**100.00**	99.93	99.93	97.44	68.06	**607**

Table 2: The results for each benefit section. NA refers to 'Not Applicable

4.3 Hours

For the experiments on the hours section, the best performing input format was B; *'FEATURE=value'*. The results show that by using the translated dataset, the model reaches a significantly higher language accuracy, with English language accuracy improving from 15.38% to 92.31% (row 11 on Table 2). However, by using the translated training set for fine-tuning, and having two samples for the same number, the model's input accuracy decreased to 77.51% (row 11). By using the synthetic training data for fine-tuning, thus adding more randomness, the input accuracy increased to 98.06% and approached the template-based method, while keeping a high language accuracy (row 12). Moreover, the experiments show that the transformers use about 3 times more words (137-184) than the template-based method (51).

4.4 Salary

For the salary section the best performing input format was input A. Row 13-16 on Table 2 illustrates that a high language accuracy (>96.88%) is achieved by the transformer regardless of the training data. While the categorical input generation accuracy was not significantly affected by the training data (decrease of 1.62%), the binary input accuracy improved (by 9.5%) with added translated data (row 15). In contrast, when fine-tuning on more training data, numeric input accuracy dropped, in particular with synthetic data (by 16.17%, row 16). Lastly, the vocabulary size is around 2.5 times higher for transformers (528-607) compared to the template-based method (127).

5 Analysis and discussion

5.1 Language accuracy

Table 2 shows how fine-tuning the model on different training data affected the language accuracy for each benefit section. The Dutch language accuracy was high (between 98.97% and 100%) for each benefit section regardless of the training data. In terms of English language accuracy, the location and salary sections performed well (with a language accuracy between 96.9% and 100%) regardless of the training data. While the extra training data was beneficial for the hours section (and lead to an accuracy of 92.3% from 15.4%), it was ineffective for the contract section, keeping the English language accuracy at zero. Meanwhile, by translating the input and the prefix, a good level of English language accuracy (92.31%) was obtained for the contract section too. While intuition suggests that language accuracy may be affected by the volume of training samples - as Dutch samples account for approximately 95% of each section - this idea cannot be supported, because both the contract and hours sections have approximately 3-4 times more training data (and approximately 2.5-3.5 times more English samples in the training data), than the location section, which was still able to reach a perfect English language accuracy with such a small training set as 454 samples (from which 20 were English).

5.2 Input generation accuracy

Appendix F contains three correct and three incorrect examples for each type of input generation (categorical, binary and numeric) and each benefit section.

Location The categorical input in the location benefit is unique because the input can only be generated in one single way (mentioning the city name can not be done differently). Row 2 on Table 2 shows that when fine-tuned on the original training data, the model achieved an input accuracy of 76.96%. Using the translated training data for fine-tuning, significantly increased this score and resulted in an accuracy of 84.87%. However, this is still a long way from the rule-based approach. Previous work (Kale and Rastogi, 2020) pointed out that data-to-text generation algorithms perform worse on test samples that have an unseen input. This decrease was major, around 23.2% (with an accuracy of 60%) for a neural-based model, but only 2% (with an accuracy of 90%) for T5 transformer, when applied in the closed Wikipedia domain (Kale and Rastogi, 2020). Our test set had five cities that were unseen; not present in the training data. The input accuracy for the 9 samples, which used one of these unseen cities, was 44.44%. Whereas the input accuracy for the samples with the seen input was 96.06%. In case of some samples with unseen inputs, the model generated text with a new city name. For example, when the input was *'Zwaag'* the model generated the following sentence *'Pal gelegen achter her centraal station Zwaaijdijk'*, naming a non-existing city. The samples with unseen inputs in our dataset are very specific, small Dutch city names, that were allegedly not part of the corpus mT5 was trained on, which could explain why transfer learning had a major impact when using the closed domain Wikipedia dataset (WebNLG) in the related work (Kale and Rastogi, 2020), but not in our domain.

Contract and salary We see a high accuracy for categorical input generation (96.44% and 99.06%) at the contract and salary sections, using only the original training data. Fine-tuning on extra training data had no significant impact on salary, however adding translated training data caused a drop in categorical input accuracy by 25.25% for the contract section.

Binary input generation The salary section of Table 2 reveals that fine-tuning the model on the translated dataset significantly improves binary input generation accuracy (from 89.71% to 99.21%). This accuracy nears perfection, which demonstrates the transformer can learn domain knowledge by learning to hide the salary amount. Some of the correctly generated text for hidden salaries were: *'Based on experience', 'A good salary and excellent reimbursement overtime'*.

Numeric input accuracy The hours section of Table 2 illustrate that fine-tuning on the translated training set resulted in some decrease (5.66%, from 83.17% to 77.51%) for the hours benefit section regarding the numeric input generation accuracy. This is not surprising given that by translating, all covered numbers in the training samples were covered roughly twice as much. However, by using the synthetic dataset for training the distribution of the samples in the training set was very even (because randomly choosing the values during the method of creating the synthetic data) and the model reached a 98.06% input generation accuracy. Compared to prior work (Gong et al., 2019) where including synthetic data lead to an accuracy increase of 2.6%, in our case accuracy increased by 14.89%. However, this strategy of fine-tuning on synthetic data did not work for the salary section. The accuracy of numeric input generation actually decreased significantly (from 85.31% to 68.06%). This might be explained by the nature of the data, because the hours section only includes integer numbers and covers a very limited range of numbers (between 2 and 55 in the training data). On the other hand the salary section contains monthly and hourly salaries too. Monthly salary are integers with a wide range (the range in the training data is: 250 - 6000) while the hourly wages are rounded to two decimals and cover the range (in the training data) between 9.63 - 45.00. A possible explanation might be that the original dataset focuses on certain numbers. The proportion of the unique numbers (for both minimum and maximum and hourly and monthly salaries) was between 20.5% and 36.05%. There are some patterns in the data, which were not matched when adding synthetic data. For example, next to understandably common decimal values for hourly salaries (0, 50, 99) other values (e.g., 48, 97, 29 or 8) are common too. This could be caused by collective labor agreements, minimum wage, yearly salary increases, or inflation correction.

5.3 Limitations

One limitation of our work is the unbalanced nature of the original dataset in terms of language. While this provides a unique opportunity and challenge, it also leads to having only very few (between 2-64) English samples for some sections. These small sample sizes may make our findings less reliable regarding the English language accuracy. A second limitation concerns our focus on the benefit sections of vacancies. These sections are rather general and typically do not vary between jobs as much as other vacancy sections (e.g., the task section), which might make our finding less generalizable. However, due to absence of structured input we were unable to study other vacancy sections.

6 Conclusion

Although the amount and the imbalanced nature of the dataset (in terms of language) prevent us from drawing definite conclusions, our analysis reveals several insights into the behavior of the mT5 model, which we use to answer our three sub-questions.

RQ1.1 First, we focus on finding how accurately mT5 generates text in the correct language. Overall, we found that with the right parameter tuning, prefix, and input, mT5 performs very well in generating text in the correct language.

RQ1.2 To find how accurate mT5 is at including different types of inputs (numerical, binary, categorical) correctly in the generated text, we used our own new, domain-specific metrics in the generated text. We conclude that while mT5 is highly accurate at generating from binary inputs, and seen categorical inputs, it struggles with unseen categorical and numeric inputs.

RQ1.3 Finally, we explore how fine-tuning mT5 on translated and synthetic data affects the language and input generation accuracy. We found that fine-tuning mT5 on additional training data (translated and synthetic) can lead to major improvements, however the rate of which strongly depends on the nature of the task and the distribution of numeric samples in the dataset.

In conclusion, we evaluated how accurately mT5 includes inputs in the generated text with custom metrics developed by us, on a novel task in the job description domain. We applied transfer learning on a new and unique dataset in terms of volume and language balance. While our findings are mostly in line with earlier studies, we demonstrate that language accuracy, input generation accuracy, and the effectiveness of extra training data are highly dependent on the nature of data and task. Overall, even though the model may not be as accurate as a template-based approach, it can be employed under human supervision to generate benefit sections of vacancies, and will yield more diverse outputs. Additionally, when using the model, the users can rely on custom evaluation metrics developed by us.

Promising future work directions include using more languages and other sections of vacancy texts. For example, while the requirements section of the vacancies currently do not have structured input data available; these inputs may be extracted automatically using a skill extraction model, such as LinkedIn's Job2Skills model (Shi et al., 2020). Extending the study to novel sections of the vacancy could give a great opportunity to observe how transformers work with categorical input with a wider range of values than our `salarytype` and `contracttype`, while still being more general than the `location` input. Another intriguing step is to investigate how automatically generated text affects the accessibility of job descriptions. Finally, evaluating the models with the recruiters would be a logical next step too.

References

Oshin Agarwal, Mihir Kale, Heming Ge, Siamak Shakeri, and Rami Al-Rfou. 2020. Machine translation aided bilingual data-to-text generation and semantic parsing. In *Proceedings of the 3rd International Workshop on Natural Language Generation from the Semantic Web (WebNLG+)*, pages 125–130, Dublin, Ireland (Virtual). Association for Computational Linguistics.

Thiago Castro Ferreira, Claire Gardent, Nikolai Ilinykh, Chris van der Lee, Simon Mille, Diego Moussallem, and Anastasia Shimorina. 2020. The 2020 bilingual, bi-directional WebNLG+ shared task: Overview and evaluation results (WebNLG+ 2020). In *Proceedings of the 3rd International Workshop on Natural Language Generation from the Semantic Web (WebNLG+)*, pages 55–76, Dublin, Ireland (Virtual). Association for Computational Linguistics.

Jordan Clive, Kris Cao, and Marek Rei. 2021. Control prefixes for text generation. *arXiv preprint arXiv:2110.08329*.

Yuvaraja Devarajan. 2018. A study of robotic process automation use cases today for tomorrow's business. *International Journal of Computer Techniques*, 5(6):12–18.

Jacob Devlin, Ming-Wei Chang, Kenton Lee, and Kristina Toutanova. 2019. BERT: Pre-training of deep bidirectional transformers for language understanding. In *Proceedings of the 2019 Conference of the North American Chapter of the Association for Computational Linguistics: Human Language Technologies, Volume 1 (Long and Short Papers)*, pages 4171–4186, Minneapolis, Minnesota. Association for Computational Linguistics.

Bhuwan Dhingra, Manaal Faruqui, Ankur Parikh, Ming-Wei Chang, Dipanjan Das, and William Cohen. 2019. Handling divergent reference texts when evaluating table-to-text generation. In *Proceedings of the 57th Annual Meeting of the Association for Computational Linguistics*, pages 4884–4895, Florence, Italy. Association for Computational Linguistics.

Claire Gardent, Anastasia Shimorina, Shashi Narayan, and Laura Perez-Beltrachini. 2017. Creating training corpora for nlg micro-planning. In *55th annual meeting of the Association for Computational Linguistics (ACL)*.

Li Gong, Josep Crego, and Jean Senellart. 2019. Enhanced transformer model for data-to-text generation. In *Proceedings of the 3rd Workshop on Neural Generation and Translation*, pages 148–156, Hong Kong. Association for Computational Linguistics.

Mihir Kale and Abhinav Rastogi. 2020. Text-to-text pre-training for data-to-text tasks. In *Proceedings of the 13th International Conference on Natural Language Generation*, pages 97–102, Dublin, Ireland. Association for Computational Linguistics.

Karen Kukich. 1983. Design of a knowledge-based report generator. In *Proceedings of the 21st Annual Meeting on Association for Computational Linguistics*, ACL '83, page 145–150, USA. Association for Computational Linguistics.

Alon Lavie and Abhaya Agarwal. 2007. Meteor: An automatic metric for mt evaluation with high levels of correlation with human judgments. In *Proceedings of the second workshop on statistical machine translation*, pages 228–231.

Brian Lester, Rami Al-Rfou, and Noah Constant. 2021. The power of scale for parameter-efficient prompt tuning. *arXiv preprint arXiv:2104.08691*.

Chin-Yew Lin. 2004. Rouge: A package for automatic evaluation of summaries. In *Text summarization branches out*, pages 74–81.

Kathleen McKeown. 1992. *Text generation*. Cambridge University Press.

Susan W McRoy, Songsak Channarukul, and Syed S Ali. 2000. Yag: A template-based generator for real-time systems. In *INLG'2000 Proceedings of the First International Conference on Natural Language Generation*, pages 264–267.

Diego Moussallem, Dwaraknath Gnaneshwar, Thiago Castro Ferreira, and Axel-Cyrille Ngonga Ngomo. 2020. Nabu – multilingual graph-based neural rdf verbalizer. In *The Semantic Web – ISWC 2020*, pages 420–437, Cham. Springer International Publishing.

Kishore Papineni, Salim Roukos, Todd Ward, and Wei-Jing Zhu. 2002. Bleu: a method for automatic evaluation of machine translation. In *Proceedings of the 40th annual meeting of the Association for Computational Linguistics*, pages 311–318.

Ankur Parikh, Xuezhi Wang, Sebastian Gehrmann, Manaal Faruqui, Bhuwan Dhingra, Diyi Yang, and Dipanjan Das. 2020. ToTTo: A controlled table-to-text generation dataset. In *Proceedings of the 2020 Conference on Empirical Methods in Natural Language Processing (EMNLP)*, pages 1173–1186, Online. Association for Computational Linguistics.

Chuan Qin, Kaichun Yao, Hengshu Zhu, Tong Xu, Dazhong Shen, Enhong Chen, and Hui Xiong. 2022. Towards automatic job description generation with capability-aware neural networks. *IEEE Transactions on Knowledge and Data Engineering*.

Colin Raffel, Noam Shazeer, Adam Roberts, Katherine Lee, Sharan Narang, Michael Matena, Yanqi Zhou, Wei Li, and Peter J. Liu. 2020. Exploring the limits of transfer learning with a unified text-to-text transformer. *Journal of Machine Learning Research*, 21(140):1–67.

Noam Shazeer and Mitchell Stern. 2018. Adafactor: Adaptive learning rates with sublinear memory cost. In *International Conference on Machine Learning*, pages 4596–4604. PMLR.

Baoxu Shi, Jaewon Yang, Feng Guo, and Qi He. 2020. Salience and market-aware skill extraction for job targeting. In *Proceedings of the 26th ACM SIGKDD International Conference on Knowledge Discovery & Data Mining*, pages 2871–2879.

Lu Wang and Claire Cardie. 2013. Domain-independent abstract generation for focused meeting summarization. In *Proceedings of the 51st Annual Meeting of the Association for Computational Linguistics (Volume 1: Long Papers)*, pages 1395–1405.

Sam Wiseman, Stuart Shieber, and Alexander Rush. 2017. Challenges in data-to-document generation. In *Proceedings of the 2017 Conference on Empirical Methods in Natural Language Processing*, pages 2253–2263, Copenhagen, Denmark. Association for Computational Linguistics.

Linting Xue, Noah Constant, Adam Roberts, Mihir Kale, Rami Al-Rfou, Aditya Siddhant, Aditya Barua, and Colin Raffel. 2021. mT5: A massively multilingual pre-trained text-to-text transformer. In *Proceedings of the 2021 Conference of the North American Chapter of the Association for Computational Linguistics: Human Language Technologies*, pages 483–498, Online. Association for Computational Linguistics.

Giulio Zhou and Gerasimos Lampouras. 2020. WebNLG challenge 2020: Language agnostic delexicalisation for multilingual RDF-to-text generation. In *Proceedings of the 3rd International Workshop on Natural Language Generation from the Semantic Web (WebNLG+)*, pages 186–191, Dublin, Ireland (Virtual). Association for Computational Linguistics.

Appendix A Template-based method

This appendix helps to understand the template-based method described in subsection 3.2. It contains the pipeline for the template-based method with an example (Figure 2) as well as the combinations for the templates.

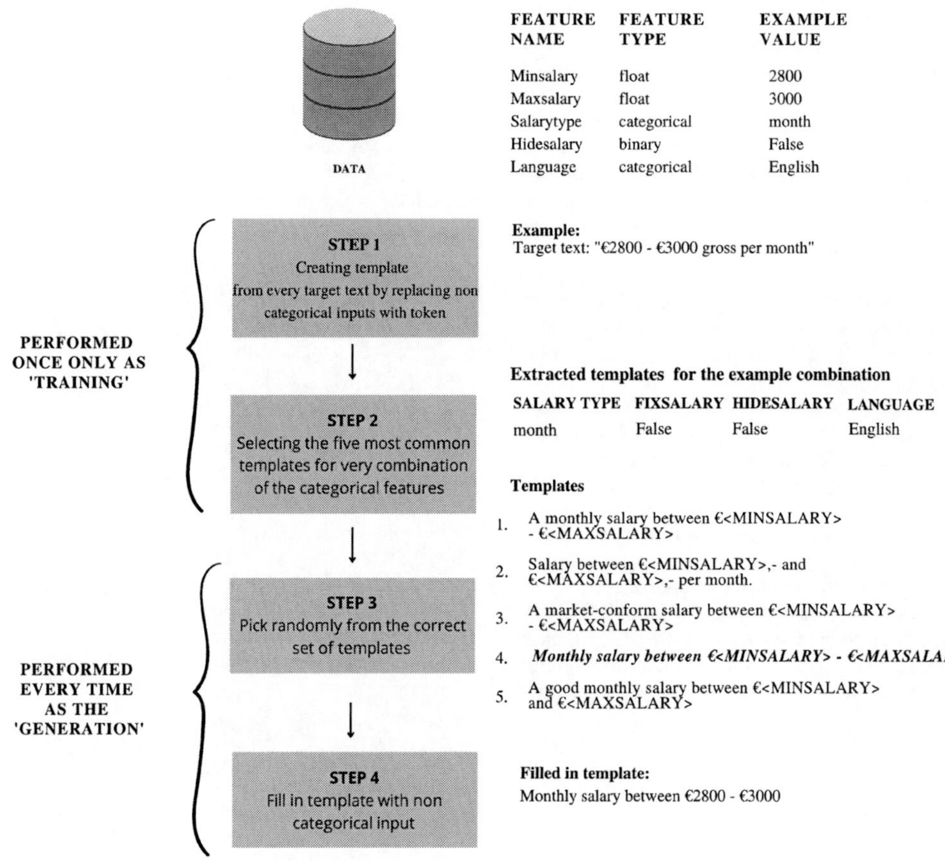

Figure 2: The pipeline of the template-based method with an example for the salary benefit section. In the first step the values of all non categorical features get replaced by the feature name resulting in a template for every training sample. Next, for all combination the five most common template gets extracted. In the third step, one of the chosen template gets randomly picked which then is filled in by replacing the non categorical feature names with their values in step 4.

A.1 Template combinations

This Section contains the combination of templates for each benefit section. Table 3 shows that the location section only had two different types of templates, the contract and the hours benefit sections had six (show on Table 4 and Table 5), while the salary benefit section had ten different types (shown on Table 6).

Combination	Language
1	English
2	Dutch

Table 3: There are 2 combinations for the location section, each combination contains 5 templates.

Combination	Language	Fix hour	Full time
1.	English	False	False
2.	English	True	False
3.	English	True	True
4.	Dutch	False	False
5.	Dutch	True	False
6.	Dutch	True	True

Table 4: There are 6 combinations for the hours section, each combination contains 5 templates.

Combination	**Language**	**Contract type**
1	English	Temporary
2	English	Temporary with a possibility to fixed
3	English	Fixed
4	Dutch	Temporary
5	Dutch	Temporary with a possibility to fixed
6	Dutch	Fixed

Table 5: There are 6 combinations for the contract section, each combination contains 5 templates.

Combination	**Language**	**Hidesalary**	**Fixsalary**	**Salary type**
1.	English	True	-	-
2.	Dutch	True	-	-
3.	English	False	True	Hourly
4.	English	False	True	Monthly
5.	Dutch	False	True	Hourly
6.	Dutch	False	True	Monthly
7.	English	False	False	Hourly
8.	English	False	False	Monthly
9.	Dutch	False	False	Hourly
10.	Dutch	False	False	Monthly

Table 6: There are 10 combinations for the salary section, each combination contains 5 templates.

Appendix B mT5 model

For optimizer we used the Adafactor optimizer, with the default parameters suggested by Shazeer and Stern (2018). Table 7 shows the values of the parameters.

Parameter	**Parameter name**	**Set value**
ϵ_1	regularization constants for square gradient	10^{-30}
ϵ_2	parameter scale	10^{-3}
d	threshold of root mean square of final gradient update	1
$\hat{\beta}_{2t}$	decay rate	$1 - t^{-0.8}$
α	external learning rate	10^{-3}

Table 7: The hyperparameter settings for the Adafactor optimezer based on Shazeer and Stern (2018)

Appendix C Details of dataset, pre- and postprocessing steps

First, we fixed the monetary units and the `hidesalary` binary field for the salary benefit section. Then, we excluded samples that were not correct based on the language and at including the input (for which we used our own input accuracy metrics explained in subsection 3.6).
In Table 8, we show the set of words for each benefit section that were removed before running the language detection on the generated text.

Section	Words removed for language detection
Location	`location` from input
Contract	words : contract, direct, per, week, of, permanent
Hours	-
Salary	per, week

Table 8: Words removed for each section before running the language detection on the generated text

In Table 9, we show the size of training, validation and test set for each benefit sections.

Benefits section	Size of training set	Size of validaiton set	Size of test set
Location	454	152	152
Contract	2696	899	899
Hours	1854	618	618
Salary	4197	1399	1399

Table 9: Size of training, validation and test set for each benefit section

In Table 10, we show the number of English and Dutch samples for each benefit section in the training, validation and test set.

Section	Samples in training set			Samples in validation set			Samples in test set		
	All	Dutch	English	All	Dutch	English	All	Dutc	English
Location	454	434	20	152	148	4	152	150	2
Contract	2696	2626	70	899	881	18	899	873	26
Hours	1854	1807	47	618	608	10	618	605	13
Salary	4197	4061	136	1399	1353	46	1399	1335	64

Table 10: The number of samples for each section in the training, validation and test set. The sample size is further braked down regarding the language.

Appendix D Random seed

The random seed was set to 1 for the splitting the dataset into training, validation and test set. The validation set was used for hyperparameter tuning and deciding which input format to use. Additionally, because both the template-based method and the transformer method has some randomness we assigned a random integer number between 1 and 9999 to every sample in the validation and the test set, which we then used as the random seed for generating the text, for the template-based method and the mT5 models. This way we ensured reproducibility and fair comparison between models. Additionally, we set the random seed for the transformer models to be 1 before fine-tuning the models.

Appendix E Rule-based classifier for the contract type evaluation

The following algorithm contains the rule-based classifier that was used to detect the contract type in the generated text for the contract benefit section.

Algorithm 1 Contract type classifier

```
words = set of lower case words of generated text
if any words in {'prospect', 'possibility' , 'opportunity' , 'chance', 'kans', 'mogelijkheid' , 'uitzicht' ,
'view', 'option'} then
    return Temporary with a possibility to fixed
else if any words in { 'temporary', 'tijdelijk' } then
    return Temporary
else if any words in {'permanent', 'direct', 'directly', 'long', 'vast', 'dienstverband', 'jaarcontract'}
then
    return Fixed
end if
```

Appendix F Examples

The following tables contain 3 correct and 3 incorrect examples for each type of input (categorical, binary, numeric) for each section. The Dutch samples have been translated by the authors to English for a better understanding of the examples.

F.1 Examples of categorical input generation

Examples of correct samples from test set		Examples of incorrect samples from test set	
Input	**Output**	**Input**	**Output**
LOCATION = Veghel	Super mooi bekend bedrijf in Veghel (Translated: Super nice well-known company in Veghel)	LOCATION = RIJEN	Werken in de omgeving van Rijk (Translated: Work in the area of Rijk)
LOCATION = Schiphol	Werken in de dynamische omgeving Schiphol (Translated: Work in the dynamic environment of Schiphol)	LOCATION = Zwaag	Pal gelegen achter het centraal station Zwaaijdijk! (Translated: Located right behind Zwaaijdijk central station!)
LOCATION = Amstelveen	Werken op een mooie locatie in Amstelveen (Translated: Work at a beautiful location in Amstelveen)	LOCATION = Oud Gastel	Een baan in de Hoeksche Waard: Oud-Beijerland (Translated: A job in the Hoeksche Waard: Oud-Beijerland)

Table 11: Correct and incorrect examples of the categorical location generation from the test set

Examples of correct samples from test set		Examples of incorrect samples from test set	
Input	**Output**	**Input**	**Output**
<CONTRACTTYPE>temporary with a view to permanent	The chance of permanent contract	<CONTRACTTYPE>temporary with a view to permanent	Fulltime with our client
<CONTRACTTYPE>temporary with a view to permanent	Opportunity to get a permanent contract	<CONTRACTTYPE>fix	Een temporary baan (Translated: A temporary job)
<CONTRACTTYPE>vast	Direct op contract bij het bedrijf (Translated: Direct contract with the company)	<CONTRACTTYPE>fix	The possibility to get a permanent contract

Table 12: Correct and incorrect examples of the categorical contract generation from the test set

Examples of correct samples from test set		Examples of incorrect samples from test set	
Input	**Output**	**Input**	**Output**
<FIXSALARY>2100.0 <SALARYTYPE>per month	A salary of € 2100 gross per month.	<FIXSALARY>10.0 <SALARYTYPE>per hour	Salaris €10. (Translated: Salary €10.)
<MINSALARY>2600.0 <MAXSALARY>3000.0 <SALARYTYPE>per month	Salary between € 2600 and € 3000 gross per month.	<MINSALARY>11.0 <MAXSALARY>12.0 <SALARYTYPE>per hour	Salaris tussen de €11,- en €12 (Translated: Salary between €11 and €12.)
<FIXSALARY>14.0 <SALARYTYPE>per hour	Good hourly rate of € 14 gross per hour.	<FIXSALARY>11.5 <SALARYTYPE>per hour	Salaris Bespreekbaar, per week betaald! (Translated: Salary Negotiable, paid per week!)

Table 13: Correct and incorrect examples of the categorical salary generation from the test set

F.2 Examples of binary input generation

Examples of correct samples from test set		Examples of incorrect samples from test set	
Input	**Output**	**Input**	**Output**
<HIDESALARY>TRUE	Based on experience	<HIDESALARY>TRUE	Een salaris van €11,- bruto per uur! (Translated: A salary of €11 gross per hour!)
<HIDESALARY>TRUE	A good salary and excellent reimbursement overtime	<HIDESALARY>TRUE	Een salaris van €11,49 per uur (Translated: A salary of €11.49 per hour)
<HIDESALARY>TRUE	A good salary in accordance with the collective labor agreement	<HIDESALARY>TRUE	Een loon van € 16,- per uur (Translated: A wage of €16 per hour)

Table 14: Correct and incorrect examples of the binary salary generation from the test set

F.3 Examples of numeric input generation

Examples of correct samples from test set		Examples of incorrect samples from test set	
input	**output**	**inpug**	**output**
FIXHOUR = 32	Work week of 32 hours	FIXHOUR = 32	De mogelijkheid om 32 ur tot 32 uur te werken (Translated: Possibility to work from 32 to 32 hours)
MINHOUR = 24| MAXHOUR = 40	24 to 40 hours, choose how many hours you work	MINHOUR = 10| MAXHOUR = 15	11-15 uur, vraag naar het rooster. (Translated: 11-15 hours, ask for the schedule.
MINHOUR = 32| MAXHOUR = 40	A working week from 32 to 40 hours (your preference)	FIXHOUR = 38	Een werkweek tussen de 38 en 38 uur. (Translated: A work week between 38 and 38 hours.)

Table 15: Correct and incorrect examples of the numeric hours generation from the test set

	Examples of correct samples from test set		Examples of incorrect samples from test set	
	Input	**Output**	**Input**	**Output**
Montlhy	<FIXSALARY>500.0 <SALARYTYPE>per month	max. 500 euro gross per month	<MINSALARY>2400.0 <MAXSALARY>3100.0 <SALARYTYPE>per month	Salaris tussen de €2400 en €.- €3300 per maand (Translated: Salary between €2400 and €.- €3300 per month)
	<FIXSALARY>500.0 <SALARYTYPE>per month	Stage starting salary of €500 per month	<FIXSALARY>2200.0 <SALARYTYPE>per month	Goed salaris van rond de €2200 en €2200 per maand! (Translated: Good salary of around €2200 and €2200 per month!)
	MINSALARY>3000.0 <MAXSALARY>3500.0 <SALARYTYPE>per month	Salary between €3000 and €3500 per month	<MINSALARY>2771.0 <MAXSALARY>3934.0 <SALARYTYPE>per month	Salaris tussen de €2110 en €3738 bruto per maand (Translated: Salary between €2110 and €3738 gross per month)
Hourly	FIXSALARY>11.0 <SALARYTYPE>per hour	11 euros per hour and shifts allowances	<FIXSALARY>11.67 <SALARYTYPE>per hour	Een salaris van €11,62 bruto per uur (Translated: A salary of €11.62 gross per hour)
	<MINSALARY>14.27 <MAXSALARY>17.68 <SALARYTYPE>per hour	Salaris tussen de €14,27 en €17,68 per uur (Translated: Salary between €14.27 and €17.68 per hour)	<MINSALARY>12.42 <MAXSALARY>18.47 <SALARYTYPE>per hour	€12,42 - €18,57 per uur op basis van ervaring (Translated: €12.42 - €18.57 per hour based on experience)
	<FIXSALARY>11.5 <SALARYTYPE>per hour	Een lekker salaris van €11,50 per uur (Translated: A nice salary of €11.50 per hour)	<FIXSALARY>11.27 <SALARYTYPE>per hour	Uurloon van €12,27 (Translated: Hourly wage of €12.27)

Table 16: Correct and incorrect examples of the numeric salary generation from the test set

Plug-and-Play Recipe Generation with Content Planning

Yinhong Liu[♠] **Yixuan Su**[♠] **Ehsan Shareghi**[♡♠] **Nigel Collier**[♠]
[♠]Language Technology Lab, University of Cambridge
[♡]Department of Data Science and AI, Monash University
{yl535,ys484,nhc30}@cam.ac.uk
ehsan.shareghi@monash.edu

Abstract

Recent pre-trained language models have shown promising capabilities in generating fluent and realistic natural language text. However, generating multi-sentence text with global content planning has been a long-existing research question. Current approaches for controlled text generation can hardly address this issue, as they usually condition on *single* known control attributes. In this study, we propose a low-cost yet effective framework which explicitly models the global content plan of the generated text. Specifically, it optimizes the joint distribution of the natural language sequence and the global content plan in a *plug-and-play* manner. We conduct extensive experiments on the well-established Recipe1M+ benchmark. Both automatic and human evaluations verify that our model achieves the state-of-the-art performance on the task of recipe generation.[1]

1 Introduction

Recent progress in large-scale language model pre-training has facilitated significant improvement in generating increasingly realistic natural language text. Although this has been achieved on the surface-level fluency, it has been pointed that generating multi-sentence text with global constraints, or long-term planning is still far from being solved. Typical examples of such task include story continuation with logical coherency (Nye et al., 2021; Sinha et al., 2019), and recipe generation with step-by-step planning (Marin et al., 2019).

As suggested by LeCun (2022), the aforementioned issues cannot be ameliorated by simply increasing the size of model parameters or the scale of pre-training data. Adding to this, current approaches for controlled text generation cannot directly tackle those issues either. For example, CTRL (Keskar et al., 2019), which trains a class-conditional language model, and PPLM (Dathathri et al., 2019), which re-ranks the language model predictions by an attribute model. They usually share a common setup of optimizing conditional distributions $P(\boldsymbol{y}|a)$, where $\boldsymbol{y}$ is the text sequence and a is the desired single control attribute. Examples of control attribute include sentiment (Ghosh et al., 2017), topic (Tang et al., 2019) and formality (Wang et al., 2019). However, content planning requires controlling with consideration of global context, which is more sophisticated than the single control attributes. Therefore, we identify the research gap for the current controlled text generation models to generate multi-sentence text with long-term content planning.

Motivated by previous research in cognitive science (Evans, 2003), Nye et al. (2021) pointed out that the reasoning of a neural-based model should consist of two systems, i.e. the *system 1* makes intuitive and associative responses, and the *system 2* makes deliberative and logical decisions. With greatly increased capabilities, large language models have become sufficiently competent to act as the system 1. However, we argue that, to address the aforementioned research gap, it is vital to empower the language models with the ability to make logical decisions, i.e. predict content plans.

In contrast to the existing methods that optimize the conditional distributions, we propose a novel framework which explicitly models the content plan $\boldsymbol{c}$ and optimizes the joint distribution $P(\boldsymbol{y}, \boldsymbol{c})$ in a *plug-and-play* manner. Figure 1 depicts an overview of our approach. Specifically, our proposed framework consists of (i) a content planner which predicts the global content plan of the output text; and (ii) a sequence generator, based on pre-trained language models, that generates the output following the content plan. The predicted content plan steers the generation of the sequence generator through a lightweight and plug-and-play style plan

[1]Our code and other related resources are publicly available at `https://github.com/williamLyh/RecipeWithPlans`.

Proceedings of the 2nd Workshop on Natural Language Generation, Evaluation, and Metrics (GEM), pages 223 - 234
December 7, 2022 ©2022 Association for Computational Linguistics

classifier. It worth emphasizing that the sequence generator does not need to be trained with plan-specific data, which means adapting our framework to other Natural Language Generation (NLG) tasks is cheap and efficient.

We comprehensively evaluate our approach on the recipe generation task using the widely-used Recipe1M+ benchmark (Marin et al., 2019). The experimental results demonstrate that our approach significantly outperforms previous state-of-the-art (SOTA) as judged by both automatic and human evaluations. In particular, the results show that the recipes generated by our model are more accurate and highly controllable.

In summary, we conclude our contributions as two-fold: Firstly, we identify the current research gap and propose a novel framework that generates text with content plans in a plug-and-play manner. Secondly, we conduct extensive experiments to show that our framework achieves SOTA performance on the widely-used Recipe1M+ benchmark.

2 Background and Related Works

2.1 Controlled Text Generation

Controlled Text Generation (CTG) refers to tasks of generating natural text conditioned on given controlled attributes. CTG approaches that leverage transformer-based Pre-trained Language Model (PLM) could be classified into three categories according to their required computation resources (Zhang et al., 2022). We provide a brief overview of these three categories.

Retraining. These methods usually modify the original architecture of PLMs and retrain them for a specific downstream task. For example, CTRL, proposed by Keskar et al. (2019), is a representative that trains a language model with task-specific control codes for each type of text corpus. Another work is POINTER, proposed by Zhang et al. (2020), which stacks the architecture of insertion-based transformer (Chan et al., 2019) in a hierarchical manner to enforce hard lexical constrains during text generation. This type of methods could control the generated text effectively, but may negatively affect generalization of the PLM. They also usually have high computational footprint, and large-scale task-specific annotated data.

Fine-tuning. These methods require partial or full fine-tuning of a PLM for each individual target attribute. For example, Bostrom et al. (2021) proposed ParaPattern which fine-tunes BART-based models (Lewis et al., 2020a) to generate text via applying different logical operations to premise inputs. Ribeiro et al. (2021) fine-tunes PLMs to control the generation from different types of graphical data. The prefix-tuning, proposed by Li and Liang (2021), only optimizes a task-specific vector (prefix), while freezing the rest of PLM, to control the domain of generation. Fine-tuning PLMs based on a small amount of labelled data for the specific downstream task has achieved competitive performance. However, fine-tuning based methods usually steer the PLM from the side of input, which means it could be hard to enforce hard constrains on the outputs directly.

Post-processing. These methods usually do not require task-specific data to fine-tune the PLM, but require decoding algorithms to re-rank the generated text in a post-processing manner. As a representative work, PPLM, proposed by Dathathri et al. (2019), uses gradients from an attribute discriminant model to steer the text generation. FUDGE, proposed by Yang and Klein (2021), weights the decoding probabilities with an attribute predictor which takes partial sequence as input. Su et al. (2022b); Su and Collier (2022) proposed Contrastive Search decoding, which encourages diversity by penalizing repetitive tokens. Lu et al. (2021) proposed NeuroLogic Decoding, which enforces the generation to satisfy a set of pre-defined hard lexical constrains. MAGIC, proposed by Su et al. (2022a), applies an image relevance discriminator to guide the generation process with visual information. This type of methods are usually computationally cheap and flexible, because they have a separate guiding module. The increasing number of parameters of the PLM would not affect the complexities of the methods. Our approach falls into this category of methods.

2.2 Generation with Plan

From the perspective of CTG tasks, attributes to control during generation include sentiment, topic, style, formality, story structure, content plan, among others. For example, Ghosh et al. (2017) proposed Affect-LM, which extend an LSTM language model by conditioning on pre-defined affect categories and strength. Fu et al. (2018) investigated the task of learning paper-news title style transfer from non-parallel data. Li et al. (2020)

proposed the framework of SongNet which studies rigid format control to generate poems or songs that obey pre-defined rhyming schemes.

Previous works in controlling the generation with content planning are mainly focusing on the task of data-to-text generation and always taking *schema selection* and *ordering* as content plans.[2] For example, Moryossef et al. (2019) separates planning from neural text realization and takes the most probable traversal of RDF graph trees as content plan. Zhao et al. (2020) employs a GCN encoder to order the nodes of input RDF data as content plan. Su et al. (2021) proposed Plan-then-Generate, which treats orders of tabular schema as plans and then plans are encoded along with linearized data as inputs to a generative model. However, those methods require graphical or tabular input data and can only model content planning based on the data schema, which limits their domain of application. Yao et al. (2019) proposed a hierarchical generation framework that first plans a keyword storyline and then generate a story based on the storyline. However, the generated keywords do not capture any global relation between each other.

2.3 Recipe Generation

Recipe generation refers to the task of generating recipe instructions from food images or textual ingredients and food title. Because recipes have the natural step-by-step sequence flow, sentence-level content planning is desired in order to generate high quality recipes.

Previous works tackled this issue in many directions. Chandu et al. (2019) treated this problem as a Visual Story Telling task and built a dataset containing images and text for each intermediate step. The recipe instructions are generated from the sequential images. Kiddon et al. (2016) models global coherence of the recipes by maintaing an ingredient checklist dynamically. During generation, a language model is encouraged to refer to the checklist item. Bosselut et al. (2018) tracks ingredient entity with a recurrent memory module and explicitly models actions as a set of per-defined state transforming operations. The recipes are then interpreted as structured collections of ingredient entities executed upon by cooking actions. (Majumder et al., 2019) investigated the task of personalized recipe generation. The user's previously consumed recipes are encoded and attended by recipe name and ingredients to generate complete instructions. However, they require complicated input data format, and sophisticated planning templates.

Recipe1M+, introduced by Marin et al. (2019), is an extension of Recipe1M (Salvador et al., 2017) and contains over 1M textual recipes and ingredients and 13M corresponding food images. The dataset has been used for versatile tasks, such as image-recipe retrieval (Chen et al., 2017), multi-modal embedding learning (Min et al., 2017), and recipe generation (Salvador et al., 2019). The RecipeGPT, proposed by H. Lee et al. (2020), fine-tuned a GPT-2 as a backbone generation model, taking only recipe titles and ingredients as input and recipe instructions as output. The NeuroLogic Decoding (Lu et al., 2021) takes the same setup, while enforcing hard lexical constrains on the occurrence of the ingredients. We follow the setup of these works and only consider the textual components of the Recipe1M+.

To the best of our knowledge, for the task of CTG with content planning, there has been no previous attempt neither on dataset with more flexible format such as recipe, nor with a plug-and-play post-process method.

3 Methodology

3.1 Overview

Figure 1 depicts our proposed framework. Given the recipe title and ingredients, the content planner (§3.2) first predicts the most probable content plan. The predicted content plan then guides the generation of the sequence generator (§3.3) via a lightweight and plug-and-play operation. Below, we elaborate the details of the proposed approach.

3.2 Content Planner

A carefully designed plan schema is vital for systems that require sophisticated controls. By examining recipe instructions, we observe the fact that they share a common structure of sequence of step-by-step stages and there are natural patterns behind those stage sequences. Therefore, we treat a content plan as a sequence of stages, where some stages could be of the same type. Specifically, we define 7 types of instruction stage based on the processing step of the food, including:

- **Pre-processing** means the preparations of ingredients or cooker.

[2] Schema selection and ordering depend on input data structure, e.g. selecting and re-ordering the cells of tabular data or the nodes of graphical data.

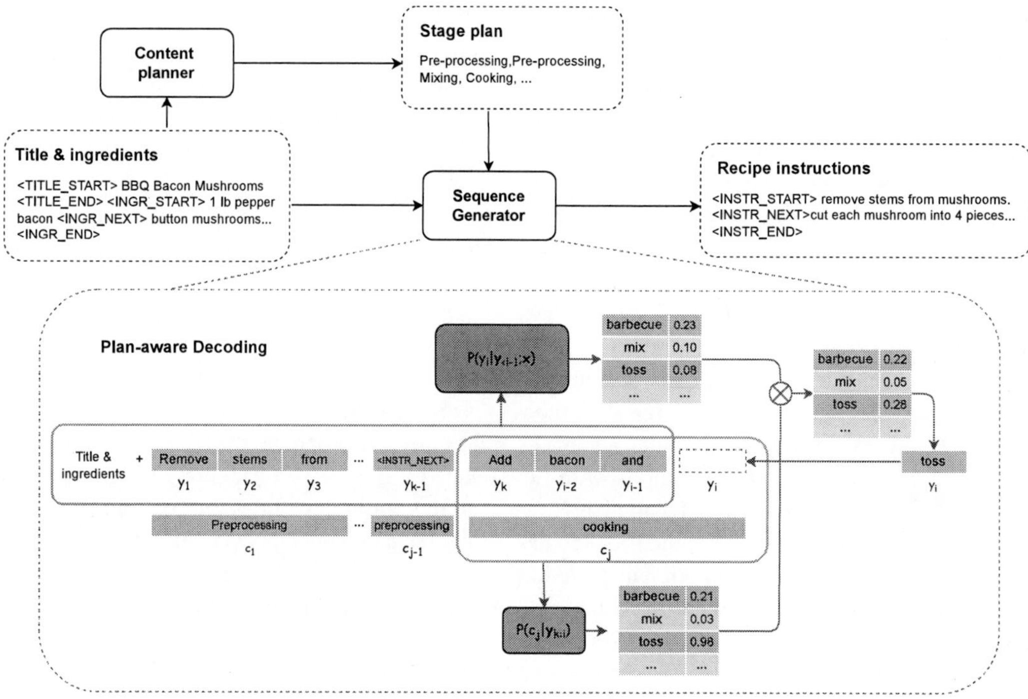

Figure 1: Model overview. The upper half demonstrates our framework. Firstly, the title and ingredients are used to predict the stage plan by the content planner module. Then, the sequence generator module, guided by the stage plan, generates the recipe instructions. The bottom half illustrates one step of the plan-aware decoding. In the given example, the current stage is 'cooking'. The language model (blue) outputs unconditional probabilities based on all previous context and inputs. The stage classifier (red) computes the probabilities of the current partial sentences belonging to the current stage 'cooking'.

- **Mixing** includes actions of combining one or more ingredients together.
- **Transferring** is for the actions of moving or transferring food or intermediate food to a specific place.
- **Cooking** represents the actual cooking actions, which could vary drastically across different recipes.
- **Post-processing** usually refers to the following up actions after the 'cooking' stage, such as 'cooling down', 'garnish'.
- **Final** refers to the last few actions before serving the food or the serving action itself.
- **General** includes the rest of actions which cannot be classified into the above categories.

As recipe instructions are usually sentences led by action verbs, an assumption is made that the stage types of the instructions are decided by their main action verbs. For each type of stage, we assign a set of exclusive stage-specific action verbs, as shown in Table 1. For example, the 'cooking' stage includes actions such as 'fry', 'bake', 'boil', etc. Then, we built a rule-based system that automatically tags recipe instructions with stage labels according to the pre-defined verb sets. We tag the instructions from train set of Recipe1M+, which contains around 710K recipes, with the stage labels and refer to them as *silver labels*. [3] By this way, we can obtain the content plan of a recipe, i.e. the

Stage Types	Keywords
Pre-processing	Peel, beat, rinse, prepare ...
Mixing	Mix, add, combine, blend ...
Transferring	Move, put, pour, place ...
Cooking	Fry, bake, cook, boil, grill ...
Post-processing	Cool, shake, garnish, cover ...
Final	Serve, yield, wrap, enjoy ...
General	Uncovered or ambiguous verbs

Table 1: Seven stage types and example keywords for each stage type.

[3] In Appendix A.3, we elaborate more implementation details of the rule-based stage tagging system. In §4.2, we evaluate the quality of the silver labels with human annotations on an evaluation subset.

sequence of the stage labels.

After acquiring the content plan $\boldsymbol{c} = \{c_1, c_2, ..., c_{|\boldsymbol{c}|}\}$ using our rule-based system, the distribution of $\boldsymbol{c}$ is then modelled by the content planner as $P(\boldsymbol{c}|\boldsymbol{x})$, where $\boldsymbol{x}$ is the given recipe title as well as ingredients, and c_j belongs to one of the seven stage types shown in Table 1. Specifically, given the recipe title and ingredients, we use a Seq2seq model, i.e. BART (Lewis et al., 2020b), to model the content plan as

$$P(\boldsymbol{c}|\boldsymbol{x}) = \prod_{j=1}^{|\boldsymbol{c}|} p_{\theta_c}(c_j|\boldsymbol{c}_{<j}; \boldsymbol{x}), \tag{1}$$

where θ_c is the parameters of the content planner. The main assumption of our modelling choice is that the content plan, i.e. cooking procedure, could be mostly determined once the target food and ingredients are known.

3.3 Plan-Aware Decoding

Given the recipe title and ingredients $\boldsymbol{x}$, and the content plan $\boldsymbol{c}$, we formulate the conditional distribution of recipe $\boldsymbol{y}$ by following the Bayes rule as

$$\begin{aligned} P(\boldsymbol{y}|\boldsymbol{x}, \boldsymbol{c}) &= \prod_{i=1}^{|\boldsymbol{y}|} p(y_i|\boldsymbol{y}_{<i}; \boldsymbol{x}, \boldsymbol{c}) \\ &\propto \prod_{i=1}^{|\boldsymbol{y}|} p_{\theta_g}(y_i|\boldsymbol{y}_{<i}; \boldsymbol{x}) \cdot p_{\theta_f}(c_j|\boldsymbol{y}_{k:i}), \end{aligned} \tag{2}$$

where c_j refers to the stage that the current partial sequence $\boldsymbol{y}_{k:i}$ belongs to. The θ_f is an *off-the-shelf* stage classifier which predicts the probability distribution over 7 stage classes by taking the partial sequence $\boldsymbol{y}_{k:i}$ as input. It should be noted that we assume the probability of the current stage label should *only* depend on the partial sequence that belongs to the current stage.

During inference, based on Equation 2, the selection of the output token $\hat{y}_i$ at step i follows

$$\hat{y}_i = \underset{y_i \in V_S}{\operatorname{argmax}}\, p_{\theta_g}(y_i|\boldsymbol{y}_{<i}; \boldsymbol{x})^{(1-\alpha)} \cdot p_{\theta_f}(c_j|\boldsymbol{y}_{k:i})^{\alpha}, \tag{3}$$

where α is a hyper-parameter that regulates the importance of two terms. V_S is the set of top-S predictions from the sequence generator's probability $p_{\theta_g}(\cdot|\boldsymbol{y}_{<i}; \boldsymbol{x})$ and S is set as 5 by default. We use the sequence generator's predictions on subset V_S to approximate the predictions over the total vocabulary. With this approximation, the stage classifier only needs to be applied upon S candidates, therefore assuring the computational efficiency.

In this work, we fine-tune a GPT-2 model (Radford et al.) on the training set of the Recipe1M+ benchmark to make it the sequence generator. To acquire the stage classifier, we fine-tune a lightweight DistilBERT (Sanh et al., 2019) on the partial recipe instructions with the silver stage labels that we obtain as described in §3.2.

Intuitively, our approach can be deemed as utilizing the stage classifier as a re-ranking step on the top S candidates predicted by the sequence generator. Figure 1 illustrates an example, in which the sequence generator first predicts probabilities across all the vocabulary and the word 'barbeque' has the highest likelihood. Then, the stage classifier re-ranks the predictions based on the current stage label 'cooking' and assigns the highest probability to 'toss'.

We note that using a partial sequence stage classifier to guide the decoding shares a similar idea with the previous study, i.e. FUDGE (Yang and Klein, 2021). However, in contrast to FUDGE, our approach works on discriminating 7-class planning stages rather than only supporting binary attributes. In addition, to ensure the structural fluency of the generated recipe, we also control the generation from the perspective of global content planning, rather than focusing on one single control attribute.

3.4 Advantages and Limitations

In this section, we discuss the theoretical advantages and limitations of our proposed approach.

We highlight the advantages that: (i) We control the generation process in the plug-and-play manner, without the need of fine-tuning the language model, i.e. sequence generator module, with plan-specific data. In other words, given an off-the-shelf stage classifier and content planner, our framework is training-free. (ii) The stage classifier and content planner are both lightweight models compared to the sequence generator and can be fine-tuned with non-parallel data. (iii) Because the content plan schema is designed by humans, our framework can effectively inject human knowledge of the constrain patterns explicitly into the generation process.

We also point out the limitations of our framework: (i) The overall performance of our model depends on the manually designed plan schema, which cannot be perfect, as it is based on heuristic experience. There are many cases where the stage of the instructions could be ambiguous. For example, in a real recipe, it is possible for 'slice the steak' to be both type of 'pre-processing' or 'post-processing'. It is hard for humans to decide whether 'add salt and pepper' is a special case of 'seasoning', which belongs to the stage 'pre-processing' or 'mixing'. Another example is 'pour milk and mix well', which contains two verbs from two stages. (ii) As pointed out by Zhang et al. (2022), guided re-ranking algorithm, as a method of controlled text generation based on post-processing, suffers the problem of relatively low control strength, compared with the methods based on fine-tuning or retraining.

4 Experiments

In this section, we evaluate our method from three aspects: (i) The performance of planner module; (ii) the performance of the stage classifier; and (iii) the performance of the recipe generation. The implementation details on these three parts are explained in §4.1, §4.2, and §4.3, respectively. In Appendix A.5, we provide examples that compare the generated results from our model and the baselines.

We pre-processed the Recipe1M+ dataset by firstly filtering out instructions that contain less than 3 words, e.g. 'combine all', as they are usually trivial. We also truncate recipes with too many instructions at the length of 15, because recipes with too many instructions usually include irrelevant information due to data scraping errors. By this way, about 9% of the original Recipe1M+ are filtered out and the resulting dataset are used in our experiments.

4.1 Planner Evaluation

As described in §3.2, the content planner predicts the sequence of stage plans from the given recipe title and ingredients. We took the sequences of the silver stage labels as reference plans and finetuned a seq2seq model, i.e. BART base version (Lewis et al., 2020b). The silver labels are generated through the automatic tagging system described in §3.2. We evaluate the content planner module on the test set of the Recipe 1M+.

Table 2 presents the evaluation results on the content planner, where the exact match rate is the

Metrics	Planner
Uni-gram	69.4
Bi-gram	42.3
Tri-gram	16.9
Exact match	39.0

Table 2: Planner module evaluation results. Match rate accuracy (in percentage) for uni-gram, bi-gram, tri-gram and exact match, between predicted and reference plans

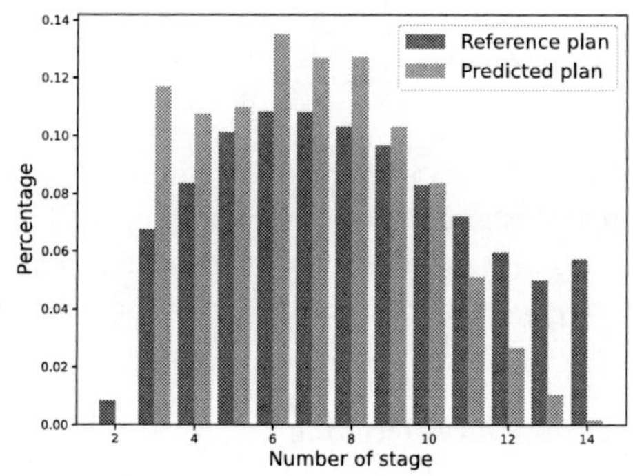

Figure 2: Histograms of the length of the predicted and the corresponding reference plans.

percentage of matched stages in their exact positions of the reference plan. From the results, we see that our planner module achieves 39% accuracy. Additional to this, because we are comparing two plan sequences, n-gram match rates are also important indicators to measure how good underlying patterns are learnt. We show that for uni-gram and bi-gram we achieved relatively high match rates at 69.4% and 42.3%, respectively; For tri-gram, we got 16.9% accuracy. This performance drop shows that our planner can learn the patterns between two successive instructions to an acceptable level, but the patterns among three successive instructions become hard to predict.

To further illustrate the performance of the content planner module, we also compare the distribution of lengths of the predicted and reference stage plans. As shown in Figure 2, their histograms show similar bell-shape and the percentage of their mismatching is around 29.1%, which we consider as acceptably low. The main source of this, we believe, is due to the heavy tail of the distribution at length of 15. As explained in Appendix A.1, this is caused by the truncation of recipe instructions during the pre-processing steps.

Model	Accuracy
Stage classifier	56.3
Silver label	62.7

Table 3: Stage classifier evaluation results. The accuracy (in percentage) of the predictions of our stage classifier and automatically tagged silver stage labels, compared with manually labeled gold annotations.

4.2 Stage Classifier Evaluation

As described in §3.3, the stage classifier predicts the stage label for the given full or partial recipe instruction. In our experiments, we implement the stage classifier by fine-tuning a DistilBERT with partial instructions along with the corresponding silver stage labels. The partial instructions can be obtained by truncating the instructions from the training set of the Recipe1M+ at random positions. The size of the resulting partial instructions training set is around 4.9M. Below, we evaluate the performance of our stage classifier.

We construct a evaluation set by randomly sampling 300 examples from the recipes instructions in the test set of Recipe1M+. Then, we ask three human annotators proficient in English to annotate the instructions with stage labels following our provided guidelines. The human annotations are referred as *gold labels*. In Table 3, we evaluate the stage classifier and the rule-based tagging system with the gold labelled evaluation set. The stage classifier achieves accuracy of 56.3%, while its upper bound, the silver labels, has accuracy of 62%. We consider this is an acceptable performance, because this is a 7-class classification problem and there is subjective understanding of the imperfect plan schema, as explained in §3.4.

4.3 Recipe Generation

In this section, we evaluate our plan-aware decoding method with both automatic and human evaluations, and compare the performance with two strong baseline methods. The sequence generator of our model is a base version of GPT-2, finetuned on the training set of the Recipe1M+ dataset. We pre-processed the recipe data with special separation tokens, as shown in the example in Figure 1, and more details are provided in Appendix A.1. Both our sequence generator as well as the compared baselines are fine-tuned on the same processed data.

4.3.1 Baselines

RecipeGPT, proposed by H. Lee et al. (2020), finetuned a base version of GPT-2 with the training set of the Recipe1M+ dataset. During generation, it employs two types of decoding methods, top-k sampling and beam search. We re-implement the RecipeGPT as a representative of finetune-based methods and set the sampling candidate number and the beam size as 5.

NeuroLogic decoding, proposed by Lu et al. (2021), is a post-processing method which can be applied to different generative models. It tries to search for optimal output sequences that satisfy a set of pre-defined lexical constrains. The constrains enforce certain words to appear or not appear in the generated sequences. In this work, we choose the base version of GPT-2 as the underlying generative model and set the constrains such that all ingredients from the inputs should appear in the generated sequences. The beam size is set as 5.

4.3.2 Metrics

Automatic Metrics. We use two widely-used metrics to assess the surface-level accuracy of the generated result, including BLEU (Papineni et al., 2002) and ROUGE-L (Lin and Hovy, 2002). To measure the controlling ability of different models, we measure the plan match rate, which is the average percentage of the stage plan of the generated recipes that agree with the input stage plan. The stage plans of the generated recipes are also labelled by the rule-based stage tagging system described in §3.2. In Table 4, we refer the plan match rate as Plan Match.

We also explicitly measures the average percentage of coverage of the given ingredients and the percentage of hallucinated ingredients. In Table 4, we refer to them as coverage and extra, respectively. . The details of how they are calculated are provided in Appendix A.2

Human evaluations. To make a similar comparison, we follow the same human evaluation setup as previous studies such as FUDGE and PPLM (Yang and Klein, 2021; Dathathri et al., 2019). Specifically, we run A/B test style human evaluations to compare our model with the two baselines on the aspects of fluency and quality in a manner of one-to-one pairwise comparison. For each comparison, the two compared models both generate recipes based on 100 randomly selected recipe title and ingredients. The evaluators were asked to rate the fluency, in Likert scale from 1 to 5, and the quality

Model	BLEU↑	ROUGE-L↑	Plan Match↑	Coverage↑	Extra↓
RecipeGPT, top-k	11.5	34.8	26.0	59.0	24.0
RecipeGPT, beam	12.2	37.1	24.0	63.1	21.9
NeuroLogic	11.8	38.2	21.8	**67.1**	22.5
Our model	**13.9**	**39.1**	**40.6**	65.4	**20.7**
Our model, oracle	14.3	40.6	39.2	65.8	22.0

Table 4: Experimental results for our models and the baselines. *Oracle* version of our model represents the plan-aware decoding is guided by the reference plan. All models are evaluated on the same evaluation subset. ↑ means the higher the better, and ↓ means the lower the better.

Method	Fluency	Quality
RecipeGPT, beam	4.07	0.68
Our model	**4.34**	**0.88**
NeuroLogic	3.87	0.59
Our model	**4.27**	**0.85**
Our model, oracle	**4.31**	**0.81**
Our model	4.28	0.76

Table 5: Human evaluations on the generated recipes. A/B test style pairwise comparisons.

of the generated recipes. For the quality, the evaluators need to decide which recipe can reproduce the food described by the given title (recipe A, recipe B, neither or both). In Table 5, we report quality as the percentage of the recipes that are labelled as able to reproduce the food. The details of the human evaluators are described in Appendix A.4.

4.3.3 Results

We create an evaluation subset by randomly sampling 4000 examples from the test set of the Recipe1M+. All experiments are conducted on this same subset. Table 4 presents the results of different methods averaged over 5 runs with different random seeds.

Apart from the the aforementioned baselines, we also evaluate the oracle version of our model, which takes the reference stage plans as the guidance. The experimental results show that our model outperforms all compared baselines on all metrics except for the ingredient coverage. The differences are statistically significant for BLEU, ROUGE-L and Plan Match as judged by Sign Test with $p < 0.01$. For the percentage of hallucination ingredients, the difference is weakly significant ($p < 0.1$). The performance gains of our model on BLEU and ROUGE-L suggests that it can produce recipes with better surface-level similarities by injecting the knowledge of content plans. On the metric of ingredient coverage, NeuroLogic decoding achieves the best results as it explicitly priorities the hard constrain of occurrence of the ingredients over surface-level fluency. It is worth noting that our models, including the oracle version, generally achieve significantly higher plan match rate than all the compared baselines. This verifies that our model can effectively control the generation process of the recipe by following the given content plans.

For the human evaluation, our model is compared with the RecipeGPT and NeuroLogic baselines in pair and outperforms them on both fluency and recipe quality. In addition, we observe that, with the help of the stage plan, our model can produce much less repeated, irrelevant or redundant instructions. Furthermore, by explicitly conditioning on stage plans, the recipes generated by our model are considered of better quality, which means they are easier for human readers to follow successfully.[4] Lastly, the oracle version of our model achieves further improved performances, suggesting that better stage plans can effectively provide human readers with better reading experience and more helpful guidance.

5 Conclusion

In this work, we first identify the research gap of the current controlled text generation models to generate text with sentence-level content planning. Then we propose a framework that optimizes the joint distribution of the natural language sequence and the content plans in a lightweight as well as plug-and-play manner. Extensive automatic and human evaluations demonstrate that our model achieves a new state of the art on the recipe generation task and outperforms previous studies by significant margins. Lastly, we show that our model can generate recipes that are more accurate and controllable by following the guidance of explicit content plans.

[4] In Appendix A.5, we provide detailed examples to compare the generated results from different methods.

References

Antoine Bosselut, Omer Levy, Ari Holtzman, Corin Ennis, Dieter Fox, and Yejin Choi. 2018. Simulating action dynamics with neural process networks. In *International Conference on Learning Representations*.

Kaj Bostrom, Xinyu Zhao, Swarat Chaudhuri, and Greg Durrett. 2021. Flexible generation of natural language deductions. In *Proceedings of the 2021 Conference on Empirical Methods in Natural Language Processing*, pages 6266–6278.

William Chan, Nikita Kitaev, Kelvin Guu, Mitchell Stern, and Jakob Uszkoreit. 2019. Kermit: Generative insertion-based modeling for sequences. *arXiv preprint arXiv:1906.01604*.

Khyathi Chandu, Eric Nyberg, and Alan W Black. 2019. Storyboarding of recipes: Grounded contextual generation. In *Proceedings of the 57th Annual Meeting of the Association for Computational Linguistics*, pages 6040–6046, Florence, Italy. Association for Computational Linguistics.

Jing-jing Chen, Chong-Wah Ngo, and Tat-Seng Chua. 2017. Cross-modal recipe retrieval with rich food attributes. In *Proceedings of the 25th ACM international conference on Multimedia*, pages 1771–1779.

Sumanth Dathathri, Andrea Madotto, Janice Lan, Jane Hung, Eric Frank, Piero Molino, Jason Yosinski, and Rosanne Liu. 2019. Plug and play language models: A simple approach to controlled text generation. In *International Conference on Learning Representations*.

Jonathan St BT Evans. 2003. In two minds: dual-process accounts of reasoning. *Trends in cognitive sciences*, 7(10):454–459.

Zhenxin Fu, Xiaoye Tan, Nanyun Peng, Dongyan Zhao, and Rui Yan. 2018. Style transfer in text: Exploration and evaluation. In *Proceedings of the AAAI Conference on Artificial Intelligence*, volume 32.

Sayan Ghosh, Mathieu Chollet, Eugene Laksana, Louis-Philippe Morency, and Stefan Scherer. 2017. Affect-lm: A neural language model for customizable affective text generation. In *Proceedings of the 55th Annual Meeting of the Association for Computational Linguistics (Volume 1: Long Papers)*, pages 634–642.

Helena H. Lee, Ke Shu, Palakorn Achananuparp, Philips Kokoh Prasetyo, Yue Liu, Ee-Peng Lim, and Lav R Varshney. 2020. Recipegpt: Generative pre-training based cooking recipe generation and evaluation system. In *Companion Proceedings of the Web Conference 2020*, pages 181–184.

Matthew Honnibal and Ines Montani. 2017. spaCy 2: Natural language understanding with Bloom embeddings, convolutional neural networks and incremental parsing. To appear.

Nitish Shirish Keskar, Bryan McCann, Lav R Varshney, Caiming Xiong, and Richard Socher. 2019. Ctrl: A conditional transformer language model for controllable generation. *arXiv preprint arXiv:1909.05858*.

Chloé Kiddon, Luke Zettlemoyer, and Yejin Choi. 2016. Globally coherent text generation with neural checklist models. In *Proceedings of the 2016 Conference on Empirical Methods in Natural Language Processing*, pages 329–339, Austin, Texas. Association for Computational Linguistics.

Yann LeCun. 2022. A path towards autonomous machine intelligence version 0.9. 2, 2022-06-27.

Mike Lewis, Yinhan Liu, Naman Goyal, Marjan Ghazvininejad, Abdelrahman Mohamed, Omer Levy, Veselin Stoyanov, and Luke Zettlemoyer. 2020a. BART: Denoising sequence-to-sequence pre-training for natural language generation, translation, and comprehension. In *Proceedings of the 58th Annual Meeting of the Association for Computational Linguistics*, pages 7871–7880, Online. Association for Computational Linguistics.

Mike Lewis, Yinhan Liu, Naman Goyal, Marjan Ghazvininejad, Abdelrahman Mohamed, Omer Levy, Veselin Stoyanov, and Luke Zettlemoyer. 2020b. Bart: Denoising sequence-to-sequence pre-training for natural language generation, translation, and comprehension. In *Proceedings of the 58th Annual Meeting of the Association for Computational Linguistics*, pages 7871–7880.

Piji Li, Haisong Zhang, Xiaojiang Liu, and Shuming Shi. 2020. Rigid formats controlled text generation. In *Proceedings of the 58th annual meeting of the association for computational linguistics*, pages 742–751.

Xiang Lisa Li and Percy Liang. 2021. Prefix-tuning: Optimizing continuous prompts for generation. In *Proceedings of the 59th Annual Meeting of the Association for Computational Linguistics and the 11th International Joint Conference on Natural Language Processing (Volume 1: Long Papers)*, pages 4582–4597.

Chin-Yew Lin and Eduard Hovy. 2002. Manual and automatic evaluation of summaries. In *Proceedings of the ACL-02 Workshop on Automatic Summarization*, pages 45–51.

Ximing Lu, Peter West, Rowan Zellers, Ronan Le Bras, Chandra Bhagavatula, and Yejin Choi. 2021. Neurologic decoding:(un) supervised neural text generation with predicate logic constraints. In *Proceedings of the 2021 Conference of the North American Chapter of the Association for Computational Linguistics: Human Language Technologies*, pages 4288–4299.

Bodhisattwa Prasad Majumder, Shuyang Li, Jianmo Ni, and Julian McAuley. 2019. Generating personalized recipes from historical user preferences. In *Proceedings of the 2019 Conference on Empirical*

Methods in Natural Language Processing and the 9th International Joint Conference on Natural Language Processing (EMNLP-IJCNLP), pages 5976–5982.

Javier Marin, Aritro Biswas, Ferda Ofli, Nicholas Hynes, Amaia Salvador, Yusuf Aytar, Ingmar Weber, and Antonio Torralba. 2019. Recipe1m+: A dataset for learning cross-modal embeddings for cooking recipes and food images. *IEEE transactions on pattern analysis and machine intelligence*, 43(1):187–203.

Weiqing Min, Shuqiang Jiang, Shuhui Wang, Jitao Sang, and Shuhuan Mei. 2017. A delicious recipe analysis framework for exploring multi-modal recipes with various attributes. In *Proceedings of the 25th ACM international conference on Multimedia*, pages 402–410.

Amit Moryossef, Yoav Goldberg, and Ido Dagan. 2019. Step-by-step: Separating planning from realization in neural data-to-text generation. In *Proceedings of the 2019 Conference of the North American Chapter of the Association for Computational Linguistics: Human Language Technologies, Volume 1 (Long and Short Papers)*, pages 2267–2277, Minneapolis, Minnesota. Association for Computational Linguistics.

Maxwell Nye, Michael Tessler, Josh Tenenbaum, and Brenden M Lake. 2021. Improving coherence and consistency in neural sequence models with dual-system, neuro-symbolic reasoning. *Advances in Neural Information Processing Systems*, 34:25192–25204.

Kishore Papineni, Salim Roukos, Todd Ward, and Wei-Jing Zhu. 2002. Bleu: a method for automatic evaluation of machine translation. In *Proceedings of the 40th annual meeting of the Association for Computational Linguistics*, pages 311–318.

Alec Radford, Jeffrey Wu, Rewon Child, David Luan, Dario Amodei, Ilya Sutskever, et al. Language models are unsupervised multitask learners.

Leonardo FR Ribeiro, Martin Schmitt, Hinrich Schütze, and Iryna Gurevych. 2021. Investigating pretrained language models for graph-to-text generation. In *Proceedings of the 3rd Workshop on Natural Language Processing for Conversational AI*, pages 211–227.

Amaia Salvador, Michal Drozdzal, Xavier Giro-i Nieto, and Adriana Romero. 2019. Inverse cooking: Recipe generation from food images. In *Proceedings of the IEEE/CVF Conference on Computer Vision and Pattern Recognition (CVPR)*.

Amaia Salvador, Nicholas Hynes, Yusuf Aytar, Javier Marin, Ferda Ofli, Ingmar Weber, and Antonio Torralba. 2017. Learning cross-modal embeddings for cooking recipes and food images. In *Proceedings of the IEEE Conference on Computer Vision and Pattern Recognition (CVPR)*.

Victor Sanh, Lysandre Debut, Julien Chaumond, and Thomas Wolf. 2019. Distilbert, a distilled version of bert: smaller, faster, cheaper and lighter. *arXiv preprint arXiv:1910.01108*.

Koustuv Sinha, Shagun Sodhani, Jin Dong, Joelle Pineau, and William L Hamilton. 2019. Clutrr: A diagnostic benchmark for inductive reasoning from text. In *Proceedings of the 2019 Conference on Empirical Methods in Natural Language Processing and the 9th International Joint Conference on Natural Language Processing (EMNLP-IJCNLP)*, pages 4506–4515.

Yixuan Su and Nigel Collier. 2022. Contrastive search is what you need for neural text generation. *arXiv preprint arXiv:2210.14140*.

Yixuan Su, Tian Lan, Yahui Liu, Fangyu Liu, Dani Yogatama, Yan Wang, Lingpeng Kong, and Nigel Collier. 2022a. Language models can see: Plugging visual controls in text generation. *arXiv preprint arXiv:2205.02655*.

Yixuan Su, Tian Lan, Yan Wang, Dani Yogatama, Lingpeng Kong, and Nigel Collier. 2022b. A contrastive framework for neural text generation. *arXiv preprint arXiv:2202.06417*.

Yixuan Su, David Vandyke, Sihui Wang, Yimai Fang, and Nigel Collier. 2021. Plan-then-generate: Controlled data-to-text generation via planning. In *Findings of the Association for Computational Linguistics: EMNLP 2021*, pages 895–909.

Hongyin Tang, Miao Li, and Beihong Jin. 2019. A topic augmented text generation model: Joint learning of semantics and structural features. In *Proceedings of the 2019 Conference on Empirical Methods in Natural Language Processing and the 9th International Joint Conference on Natural Language Processing (EMNLP-IJCNLP)*, pages 5090–5099.

Wenlin Wang, Zhe Gan, Hongteng Xu, Ruiyi Zhang, Guoyin Wang, Dinghan Shen, Changyou Chen, and Lawrence Carin. 2019. Topic-guided variational auto-encoder for text generation. In *Proceedings of the 2019 Conference of the North American Chapter of the Association for Computational Linguistics: Human Language Technologies, Volume 1 (Long and Short Papers)*, pages 166–177.

Kevin Yang and Dan Klein. 2021. Fudge: Controlled text generation with future discriminators. In *Proceedings of the 2021 Conference of the North American Chapter of the Association for Computational Linguistics: Human Language Technologies*, pages 3511–3535.

Lili Yao, Nanyun Peng, Ralph Weischedel, Kevin Knight, Dongyan Zhao, and Rui Yan. 2019. Plan-and-write: Towards better automatic storytelling. In *Proceedings of the AAAI Conference on Artificial Intelligence*, volume 33, pages 7378–7385.

Hanqing Zhang, Haolin Song, Shaoyu Li, Ming Zhou, and Dawei Song. 2022. A survey of controllable text generation using transformer-based pre-trained language models. *arXiv preprint arXiv:2201.05337*.

Yizhe Zhang, Guoyin Wang, Chunyuan Li, Zhe Gan, Chris Brockett, and William B Dolan. 2020. Pointer: Constrained progressive text generation via insertion-based generative pre-training. In *Proceedings of the 2020 Conference on Empirical Methods in Natural Language Processing (EMNLP)*, pages 8649–8670.

Chao Zhao, Marilyn Walker, and Snigdha Chaturvedi. 2020. Bridging the structural gap between encoding and decoding for data-to-text generation. In *Proceedings of the 58th Annual Meeting of the Association for Computational Linguistics*, pages 2481–2491, Online. Association for Computational Linguistics.

A Appendix

A.1 Details of preprocessing

We then further processed the recipes by adding special separation tokens, as shown in the example in Figure 1. The separation tokens include $< TITLE\_START >$ and $< TITLE\_END >$ to wrap the recipe title, $< INGR\_START >$, $< INGR\_END >$ and $< INGR\_NEXT >$ to wrap and split the recipe ingredients. Similarly, $< INSTR\_START >$, $< INSTR\_END >$ and $< INSTR\_NEXT >$ are used to wrap and split the recipe instructions. There is no leaking of the stage label information from the separation tokens.

A.2 Details of metrics computing

To identify the ingredients in the generated recipes, we first create a list of total input ingredients in the Recipe1M+ dataset and then identify the ingredients in the recipes by string match. The hallucination percentage is the number of hallucinated ingredients over the total number of ingredients in the input. Ingredients that are not included in the input, but included in the total ingredient list, are considered as hallucinated. It is worth noting that because of the limitations of string match, which cannot deal with plural, quantifier, synonym and etc, the coverage and hallucination percentages are not perfect. Therefore, they are better interpreted as rough indicators and used to compare between models parallelly.

A.3 Rule-based stage label tagging system

In this section, we elaborate how we implement the rule-based tagging system. To process on instruction, firstly we use the tokenizer from Python package Spacy (Honnibal and Montani, 2017) to identify all the verbs by checking the Part-Of-Speech (POS) tag of each token. Then we remove the verbs that are in the clauses by identifying punctuation and conjunction words. If, by this point, there are more than one verbs left, we always keep the first verb as the main verb and tag the instruction base on this verb. We tag the stage label by looking up which stage type the main verb belongs to, as shown in the example keywords in Table 1.

A.4 Details of Human evaluators

For the tasks of human annotator in Section 4.2 and evaluation in Section 4.3.2, we ask three voluntary university students whose first language are English to conduct each task. They are paid with rate of 10 GBP per hour, which is above the minimum hourly wage in UK.

A.5 Case study: Recipe Generation Example

In Table 6, we show generation examples of three recipes. Instructions labeled in red show undesired characteristics.

In the first example, the 'Eggs Barbados', the recipes generated by baselines, RecipeGPT and NeuroLogic, both have the instruction 'Preheat oven to 350 degrees f.'. We consider this instruction is irrelevant because the oven is never used in the rest of the recipes.

In the second example, the 'Our Favourite Wheat Bread', the recipe generated by RecipeGPT shows undesired repetitive patterns on the instructions 'Punch down and let rise again.'.

In the third example, the 'Pomegranate Ice Tea', the recipe generated by RecipeGPT is inaccurate by 'Serve immediately', because it lacks the step of 'Pour over ice' or 'add ice'.

Recipe Title	Ingredients	Model	Generated Results
Eggs Barbados	1 bunch green onions; 1 package cream cheese; 1 tablespoon butter; 12 whole eggs; 1 tablespoon milk; salt and pepper to taste	RecipeGPT	Preheat oven to 350 degrees f. Slice the green onions in half lengthwise. Slice the cream cheese in half lengthwise. Melt the butter in a large skillet over medium heat. Add the green onions and saute until tender. Add the cream cheese, eggs, milk and salt and pepper to taste. Cook until the eggs are set. Serve immediately.
		NeuroLogic	Preheat oven to 350 degrees f. Slice the green onions and the cream cheese in half lengthwise. Melt the butter in the pan over medium heat. Add the green onions and saute until tender. Add the cream cheese, eggs, milk and salt and pepper to taste. Cook until the eggs are completely cooked.
		Ours	Slice the green onions into 1/4 inch slices. Melt the butter in a frying pan. Add the chopped onions and saute until they are soft. Add the cream cheese and mix well. In a separate bowl, beat the eggs and milk. Add the eggs to the cream cheese mixture and mix well. Add the green onions and salt and pepper to taste. Drop by spoonfuls onto a greased baking sheet. Bake at 350 degrees for 20 minutes.
		Reference	Chop your green onions and break up the cream cheese into little chunks. Melt the butter in your frying pan on medium-low heat. While the butter melts, beat the eggs with the milk until combined. Add your salt and pepper. pour the egg mixture into the pan. Dont stir up the eggs too much, just occasionally scrape the bottom to mix up the cooked egg with the runny stuff. Once the eggs are mostly cooked but still look a little wet, turn off the heat. You dont want overcooked eggs, theyre rubbery and icky! As soon as you turn off the heat, mix the cream cheese chunks and chopped green onions into the eggs. Let it sit for just a few seconds, so that the heat of the pan melts the cream cheese.
Our Favourite Wheat Bread	1 tablespoon dry yeast; 2 cups warm water; 14 cup soft butter; 18 cup molasses; 14 cup honey; 1 teaspoon salt; 3 cups whole wheat flour; 2 cups white flour.	RecipeGPT	Dissolve yeast in warm water. Add butter, molasses, honey, and salt. Mix well. Add whole wheat flour and white flour. Knead until smooth and elastic. Cover and let rise in a warm place for 1 hour. Punch down and let rise again. Punch down again and let rise again. Punch down again and let rise again. Punch down again and let rise again. Punch down again and let rise again. Punch down again and let rise again. Punch down again and let rise again. Punch down again and let rise again
		NeuroLogic	Dissolve yeast in warm water. Add water, butter, molasses, honey, and salt. Mix well. Add whole wheat flour and white flour. Mix well. Knead until smooth and elastic. Cover and let rise in a warm place for 1 hour. Bake for 1 hour.
		Ours	Dissolve yeast in warm water. Add butter, molasses, honey, and salt. Add whole wheat flour and white flour. Mix until smooth. Cover and allow to rise in a warm place until doubled in size. Punch down and let rise again. Pre-heat oven to 350 degrees. Grease a loaf pan. Pour in batter. Bake for 1 hour.
		Reference	Dissolve yeast in warm water. Combine butter, molasses, honey, and salt. Add yeast mixture. Gradually add flour. Turn onto floured surface and knead until smooth. Place in greased bowl and let rise until double. Let dough rest a few minutes. Shape into 2 loaves. Place in greased bread pans. Let rise about 1 hour. Bake at 375 for 35-40 minutes.
Pomegranate Iced Tea	2 ounces freshly squeezed pomegranate juice or 2 ounces store-bought pomegranate juice; 5 ounces tea; 1 ounce simple syrup; lemon wedge.	RecipeGPT	Combine the pomegranate juice, tea, simple syrup, and lemon wedge in a pitcher. Serve immediately.
		NeuroLogic	Combine the pomegranate juice, tea, simple syrup, and lemon wedge in a pitcher. Add ice and stir well.
		Ours	Combine the pomegranate juice, tea, simple syrup and lemon wedge in a pitcher. Add ice and stir well. Pour into a chilled glass and garnish with a lemon wedge.
		Reference	Prepare tea and cool. Mix the rest of the ingredients. Pour over ice in an iced tea glass. Garnish with lemon wedge.

Table 6: Case Study. Generation examples of 3 recipes by our model and baselines. Instructions labeled in red are considered problematic.

Towards Attribute-Entangled Controllable Text Generation: A Pilot Study of Blessing Generation

Shulin Huang[1*], **Shirong Ma**[1*], **Yinghui Li**[1], **Yangning Li**[1], **Shiyang Lin**[2], **Hai-Tao Zheng**[1,3†] and **Ying Shen**[2†]

[1]Tsinghua Shenzhen International Graduate School, Tsinghua University

[2]School of Intelligent Systems Engineering, Sun-Yat Sen University

[3]Peng Cheng Laboratory

{sl-huang21, masr21}@mails.tsinghua.edu.cn

Abstract

Controllable Text Generation (CTG) has obtained great success due to its fine-grained generation ability obtained by focusing on multiple attributes. However, most existing CTG researches overlook *how to utilize the attribute entanglement to enhance the diversity of the controlled generated texts*. Facing this dilemma, we focus on a novel CTG scenario, i.e., **blessing generation** which is challenging because high-quality blessing texts require CTG models to comprehensively consider the entanglement between multiple attributes (e.g., objects and occasions). To promote the research on blessing generation, we present EBleT, a large-scale **E**ntangled **Ble**ssing **T**ext dataset containing 293K English sentences annotated with multiple attributes. Furthermore, we propose novel evaluation metrics to measure the quality of the blessing texts generated by the baseline models we designed. Our study opens a new research direction for controllable text generation and enables the development of attribute-entangled CTG models. Our dataset and source codes are available at https://github.com/huangshulin123/Blessing-Generation.

1 Introduction

Controllable Text Generation (CTG) aims to automatically generate the text under the restrictions of given conditions (Prabhumoye et al., 2020; Dong et al., 2021; Sun et al., 2022). As the mainstream, controlling multiple attributes enriches the information contained by generation and matches the demand of application scenarios, such as generating Chinese poetry (Yi et al., 2020), restaurant reviews (Chen et al., 2021), and product descriptions (Xu et al., 2019).

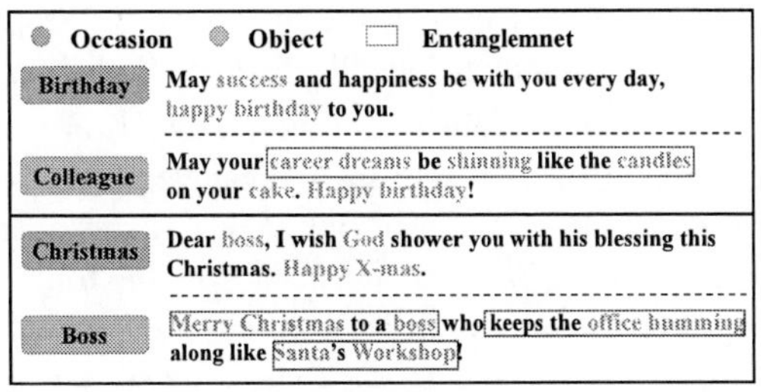

Figure 1: Two groups of blessing examples. Each group contains blessing messages without (top) and with (bottom) the attribute entanglement. **Representative elements** of occasion/object attributes are marked.

Take the Chinese poetry generation task as an example, one beautiful poetry sentence should contain multiple attributes and reflect the entanglement (or mixture) of them through reasonable connection, e.g., in the sentence "胡马南来路已荒(The enemy's warhorses march to the south, through destroyed roads)", "胡马(enemy's warhorses)" is a representative element of the military career, "南来(march to the south)" and "荒(destroyed)" represent the attribute of troubled times. This poetry sentence vividly depicts a picture of War in troubled times through the entanglement of attributes in just seven characters. Yi et al. (2020) also claim that considering the entanglement among attributes can effectively enhance the quality and diversity of generated poetry. Therefore, we believe that *better CTG models must focus on the effect of attribute entanglement, i.e., enhancing the reflection of multiple attributes through the use of various representative elements in the generated text.*

For Chinese CTG, with poetry generation as a typical scenario, researchers have conducted in-depth research on attribute entanglement, but in the English CTG field, the research on attribute entanglement has not been explored. Therefore, to promote research on attribute-entangled CTG in the English community, in this paper we focus on **blessing generation**, a new CTG task that plays

* indicates equal contribution.

† Corresponding author: Hai-Tao Zheng and Ying Shen. (E-mail: zheng.haitao@sz.tsinghua.edu.cn, sheny76@mail.sysu.edu.cn)

Proceedings of the 2nd Workshop on Natural Language Generation, Evaluation, and Metrics (GEM), pages 235 - 247
December 7, 2022 ©2022 Association for Computational Linguistics

a key role in social scenarios. The automatically generated blessings will greatly promote interpersonal communication and enrich people's daily life. More crucially, the blessing generation task is challenging due to its high requirement for entanglement between attributes, such as objects and occasions. As shown in Figure 1, "Santa's Workshop" connects the occasion (Christmas) and object (Boss) into one phrase, making the blessing wonderful. A more vivid blessing embodies these two attributes in an intertwined manner, such as "keeps the office humming along like Santa's Workshop".

Facing the vacant of blessing generation, we construct EBleT, a large-scale **E**ntangled **Ble**ssing **T**ext dataset annotated with multiple attributes. Particularly, the EBleT is constructed with the following two features: (1) EBleT contains 23 occasions and 34 objects annotated on 293,403 blessing texts from 12 blessing websites. (2) As 92% of the blessing texts are personalized for the corresponding attributes, EBleT has at least 82% data containing the entanglement between attributes.

Additionally, the common generation evaluation metrics cannot reflect the characteristics of blessings clearly. To evaluate the generated blessings more comprehensively, we propose novel metrics to automatically calculate the degree of attribute entanglement and the quality of blessings. Our experiments demonstrate that mainstream CTG methods struggle to contain the entanglement. Moreover, existing methods can not balance the fluency, diversity, and entanglement between attributes. These results indicate that the blessing generation task we focus on is challenging and could serve as a useful benchmark for CTG research.

2 Task Definition

The blessing generation task aims to obtain a generation model $\mathcal{G}(x_1, x_2; \theta)$ parameterized by θ. Given the input attributes containing an object $x_1 \in X_1$ and an occasion $x_2 \in X_2$, the model $\mathcal{G}$ should output a blessing text y sent to x_1 for x_2, where $y = \{y_1, y_2, ..., y_n\}$ is a sequence containing n words, and $x_i (i = 1, 2)$ is a word or a phrase belonging to a collection of objects or occasions. The generated text y should reflect not only the language style of blessing, but also effective entanglement between both attributes. Additionally, the evaluation metrics for the language style of blessing and entanglement are described in Section 4.

3 EBleT Dataset

3.1 Dataset Construction

Data Collection We search blessing-related keywords (e.g., "send blessing", "send wish") via Google Search and obtain 12 blessing websites. We check the licences of those websites to ensure that data from these websites can be legally employed for our non-profit academic research. The occasions and objects are labeled by page headings and subheadings from these websites. Therefore, we obtain the headings and subheadings, as well as corresponding lists of blessing texts. The occasions and objects are extracted from the headings and subheadings. We totally collect about 1 million texts from the web as the raw corpus.

Data Cleaning After acquiring the original corpus, we remove completely duplicate sentences, delete all non-English text, and remove the sentences that do not reflect corresponding occasion/object attributes. Additionally, we observe that too long or too short sentences are mostly noise. Therefore, to further clean the dataset, we keep only sentences in the range of 10 to 200 words in length.

Human Evaluation To manually evaluate the quality of EBleT, we randomly select 20 data samples from each "object-occasion" pair except for the pairs related to the "General" object and finally obtain 5,520 data samples. Then we employ 3 college students who are English native speakers as annotators to manually assess the personalization and entanglement scores of these samples. As the annotation payment, we provide them 5 dollars for every 100 sentences they judged. Besides, to ensure the reliability of their scores, we carefully explain the concept of personalization and entanglement to them before the start of annotation. Specifically, **a blessing can be called personalized if the annotator can easily know its labeled occasion/object. Moreover, a blessing can be called entangled if it cleverly blends the characteristics of the labeled occasion/object, rather than combining the two so rigidly that it can be substituted for any other occasions or objects.** After being familiar with the concepts of personalization and entanglement, our annotators are asked to judge the sampled data and give the score (0 - common, 1 - personalized, 2 - both personalized and entangled). We take the majority vote as the annotation result for a data sample. The Fleiss' kappa (Fleiss, 1971) of the annotations is 0.837, which indicates the annotation results of our annotators can be regarded as "almost perfect agreement" (Landis and Koch, 1977). The results of human evaluation will be presented and analyzed in the "Dataset Quality" of Section 3.2.

3.2 Dataset Analysis

Dataset Statistics Table 1 describes statistics of EBleT. Compared with previous annotated CTG datasets, e.g., ROCStories (Mostafazadeh et al., 2016) with 50K stories, GYAFC (Rao and Tetreault, 2018) with 53K sentences and ToTTo (Parikh et al., 2020) with 121K tables, our EBleT containing 293K blessing texts with corresponding occasion and object labels can be regarded as a sufficiently large-scale dataset. Moreover, our dataset consists of up to 276 pairs crossed by 23 categories of occasions and 34 categories of objects, which is challenging for models to learn the characteristics of each category of occasions and objects and to entangle them. More details and examples of EBleT are shown in Appendix A.1.

Property	Value
Dataset Size	293,403
Average Length	43.06
# Occasions	23
# Objects	34
# Occasion-object Pairs	276

Table 1: Dataset statistics of EBleT.

Dataset Quality Table 2 shows human evaluation results of EBleT. It indicates that about 92% of the blessing texts are personalized for the corresponding attributes, and about 82% data reflect the entanglement between attributes, which demonstrates the quality of EBleT.

		#Sample	#Per.	#Ent.
Occasion	Christmas	480	445	397
	Halloween	160	144	134
Object	Teacher	200	181	164
	Boss	140	126	118
	Total	5,060	4,676	4,170

Table 2: Partial human evaluation results of EBleT. #Sample, #Per. and #Ent. denote the total number of sampled sentences, the number of personalized sentences and the number of entangled sentences respectively. The full list is presented in Table 7.

Dataset Visualization After removing the stopwords and the words related to specific occasions and objects, we plot the word cloud of EBleT as shown in Figure 2. We find out that some words (e.g., "wish", "love", and "happiness") appear frequently. This phenomenon not only meets our common sense, i.e., blessing texts usually express wishes for each other, but also provides a class of words that need to be focused on for the development of future blessing generation models.

Figure 2: The word cloud visualization of EBleT.

4 Evaluation Metrics

4.1 Blessing Score

To measure the quality of blessings, Blessing Score should reflect the extent to which a sentence fits the language style of the blessing. By counting word frequency, we observe that some words, e.g., "happy", "merry", and "heart", frequently appear in blessing texts rather than in other texts. We obtain the 50 most frequently occurring words and remove the stopwords. These words are utilized to construct the bag-of-words of the blessing B.

For a sentence to be evaluated, to avoid the influence of irrelevant words, we use KeyBERT (Grootendorst, 2020) to extract 10 keywords to form a keyword list K as a representative of the sentence. All words in B and K are converted to word embeddings by Word2Vec (Mikolov et al., 2013) model $E(.)$. For each keyword, we calculate its maximum similarity to all words in B, and then average the maximum similarity of all keywords to obtain the Blessing Score (BLE). It is formulated as follows:

$$\text{BLE} = \frac{1}{|K|} \sum_{w \in K} \max_{b \in B} \frac{E(w) \cdot E(b)}{\|E(w)\| \cdot \|E(b)\|}. \quad (1)$$

4.2 Entanglement Score

To evaluate the degree of attribute entanglement, we assume that a blessing sentence with higher Entanglement Score should satisfy that the elements

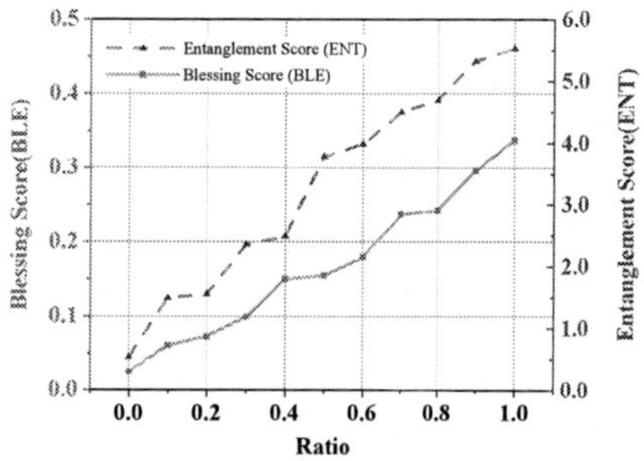

Figure 3: The correlation between human annotations and automatic metrics. The horizontal axis represents the proportion of the set that is manually annotated as blessing or entanglement.

related to the occasions and objects appear simultaneously in more clauses. Further, occasion-related and object-related elements should alternate more times in one more entangled blessing sentence.

We construct two bags-of-words B_1, B_2 to represent the occasion-related and object-related elements respectively. Specifically, the bags-of-words contain words directly related to the corresponding occasions and objects, which are listed in Table 8 and Table 9 of the Appendix.

For the Entanglement Score, we calculate whether words related to the two attributes occur simultaneously within each clause by cosine similarity, and add a bonus term O[1] for the cases where related words occur alternately multiple times. Formally, for each sentence S to be evaluated, we split S into m clauses $S = \{s_1, s_2, ..., s_m\}$ and each clause s_i consists of n words $s_i = \{w_{i1}, w_{i2}, ..., w_{in}\}$. The Entanglement Score (ENT) for S is calculated as follows:

$$\text{ENT} = \sum_{s_i \in S} I((\exists\, w_{ij}, w_{ik} \in s_i)\; C(w_{ij}, w_{ik})) + O, \quad (2)$$

$$C(w_1, w_2) = \text{sim}(w_1, B_1) > t \wedge \text{sim}(w_2, B_2) > t, \quad (3)$$

$$\text{sim}(w, B) = \max_{b \in B} \frac{E(w) \cdot E(b)}{\|E(w)\| \cdot \|E(b)\|}, \quad (4)$$

where $I(c)$ is the indicator function, which has a value of 1 when the condition c is satisfied, t is a predetermined threshold.

4.3 Metric Verification

To verify the effectiveness of our proposed blessing and entanglement score, we conduct consistency analyses between automatic scores and human annotations. We extract 11 subsets and each of them has 100 pieces of data. Meanwhile, we make the proportion of blessings or entanglement (annotated by humans) in each set different, which is from 0.0 to 1.0. The average blessing score and entanglement score for the 11 subsets are calculated by our metrics. The results presented in Figure 3 demonstrate that our proposed metrics are highly consistent with the results of manual annotation.

5 Experiments

5.1 Experiment Setup

We set up experiments to evaluate the performance of existing models to generate entangled blessing texts. The full dataset is divided into a training set, a validation set and a test set in the ratio of 9:0.5:0.5 by stratified sampling.

To measure the consistency of generated outputs and reference blessing texts, we utilize BLEU (Papineni et al., 2002) and WMD (Kusner et al., 2015). WMD is a method to calculate the minimum embedded word distance required for a document to transfer to another one. In addition, we use Perplexity and Distinct-n(n=1,2,3) (Li et al., 2016) to evaluate the fluency and diversity of generated outputs. Specifically, GPT-Neo (Gao et al., 2020) is employed as the language model to obtain the perplexity. Furthermore, we use Blessing Score and Entanglement Score mentioned in Section 4 to evaluate the quality of blessings.

We evaluate two widely used generation models on EBleT for our proposed task:

GPT-2 (Radford et al., 2019) is a Transformer-based decoder-only model (Liu et al., 2022) which achieves stable and excellent generation performance. For this task, we design a prompt: "Send this blessing to *<object>* for *<occasion>*", where *<object>* and *<occasion>* represent the object and occasion attributes, respectively. The prompt is utilized for the prefix input of GPT-2 model. Diverse Beam Search (Vijayakumar et al., 2016) is employed as the decoding method during the generation process to ensure diversity of generated blessings.

T5 (Raffel et al., 2020) is a model of the encoder-decoder framework which is commonly used for text-to-text generation tasks. The prompt mentioned above is utilized for the input of encoder side of T5 model.

Additionally, we consider applying CVAE (Sohn et al., 2015) for generation and using the latent variables to represent the entanglement of the two input

[1] The specific implementation of our designed bonus is presented in the source code of the supplementary material.

	BLEU↑	ROUGE-L↑	WMD↓	PPL↓	DIST-1↑	DIST-2↑	DIST-3↑	BLE↑	ENT↑
Common	-	-	-	-	0.609	0.953	0.998	0.022	-
GPT-2	0.225	0.382	1.018	20.12	0.176	0.327	0.405	0.308	3.52
T5	**0.247**	**0.393**	**1.015**	**13.47**	0.140	0.274	0.358	**0.334**	3.23
GPT-2 + CVAE	0.137	0.340	1.058	28.84	**0.409**	**0.788**	**0.907**	0.223	3.63
GPT-2 + Adv.	0.147	0.349	1.050	28.32	0.397	0.778	0.903	0.226	**3.78**
Reference	-	-	-	-	0.455	0.830	0.928	-	4.54

Table 3: Performance of different models on EBleT. **Common** represents the news texts collected from British Broadcasting Corporation which is used to make the comparison with blessings. "↑" represents higher is better for this metric and "↓" represents lower is better.

attributes. Following the previous work (Fang et al., 2021), we employ pretrained GPT-2 as the backbone of CVAE to obtain higher quality generated results. Furthermore, we employ adversarial training (Adv.) (Yi et al., 2020) instead of minimizing KL divergence in CVAE to allow the model to learn more complex entangled representations.

5.2 Experiment Results

The results of Table 3 demonstrate that: (1) Models trained on EBleT can generate fluent blessing texts. The language style of generated texts is generally consistent with that of the blessing texts in the dataset. (2) The diversity and Entanglement Score of texts generated by GPT-2 and T5 are actually low. Meanwhile, employing CVAE or adversarial training architecture based on GPT-2 can effectively improve these two metrics but slightly reduce the quality of blessing. Additionally, the architecture of adversarial training outperforms CVAE in the entanglement and the quality of blessing, suggesting that the adversarial training architecture is more appropriate for entangling the attributes into generation. (3) There exists a gap of diversity and Entanglement Score between generated texts and references. It indicates that EBleT is a challenging benchmark for exploring the entanglement of attributes in CTG. Future work on this task should consider all the metrics of fluency, diversity, quality of blessings, and entanglement to generate blessings that are more in line with human expression.

6 Related Work

Controllable text generation (CTG) usually takes the controlled element and source text (which can be missing) as the input. Based on the input, the generation model produces the target text satisfying controlled elements. According to the core of CTG, i.e., the diversified controlled elements, we can divide CTG into the following two categories:

Attribute Control: Ghosh et al. (2017) add the sentiment information into the generator to control the sentiment of the generated sentences. Luo et al. (2019) explore a framework including sentiment analysis and sentiment generator to control the fine-grained sentiment of generation. Chen et al. (2021) introduce a mutual learning framework to generate emotionally controllable comments. In addition, Wang et al. (2019) control the style of the generated text to present a specific style of writing. Zhang et al. (2018) build a generation system to generate conversations with the specific persona.

Content Control: Cao et al. (2015) control the topic of generation, exploring the latent semantics of vocabularies and texts to get the distribution of the topic. Keskar et al. (2019) add different controlling code to realize topic control. Koncel-Kedziorski et al. (2016) use the generator to edit the articles written by humans, changing the theme without changing the original story. Additionally, Zheng et al. (2020) build LSTML and LSTMR to make sure the entities appear in the generated summary. Xu et al. (2020) incorporate keywords into each sentence of the story over the generation process. Kikuchi et al. (2016); Duan et al. (2020) introduce the methods for controlling the output sequence length.

However, existing research work on controlled generation doesn't include the work related to blessing and neglects the entanglement among attributes. Blessings can be used in many aspects of life, such as e-cards, advertisements, and so on. Thus we introduce a new task - blessing generation and propose the corresponding dataset EBleT.

7 Conclusion

To explore the entanglement between attributes, we present EBleT, a blessing dataset that presents a new controllable generation task. We propose novel metrics to automatically measure attribute entanglement and the quality of blessings. We also provide several baselines and conduct experiments for blessing generation. Experimental results demonstrate that EBleT could serve as a useful benchmark for attribute entanglement in CTG.

Limitations

In this paper, we conduct experiments on EBleT employing some representative mainstream models. Since our work is only a pilot study of attributed-entangled CTG, we do not conduct experiments on more controllable generation models. Because of the challenge of EBleT, we suggest that more complex models can be implemented for improving the performance of blessing generation.

Ethical Considerations

In this paper, to facilitate the study of attribute-entangled CTG, we propose the blessing generation task which needs to pay attention to the attribute entanglement to obtain vivid blessings. We believe that the blessing generation task embodies humanistic care, and the various generated blessing texts can not only enrich people's daily life, but also promote interpersonal relationships. We also present EBleT, a large-scale annotated blessing dataset. All the corpora used in EBleT come from freely available resources on public websites and do not involve any sensitive or illegal data. Additionally, we design new automatic evaluation metrics to measure the quality of blessings. We think that our designed metrics are instructive for future research on the CTG tasks. After all, in the current CTG field, how to conduct an effective evaluation is also an important and yet unsolved problem.

Acknowledgement

This research is supported by National Natural Science Foundation of China (Grant No.62276154 and 62011540405), Beijing Academy of Artificial Intelligence (BAAI), the Natural Science Foundation of Guangdong Province (Grant No. 2021A1515012640), Basic Research Fund of Shenzhen City (Grant No. JCYJ20210324120012033 and JSGG20210802154402007), and Overseas Cooperation Research Fund of Tsinghua Shenzhen International Graduate School (Grant No. HW2021008).

References

Ziqiang Cao, Sujian Li, Yang Liu, Wenjie Li, and Heng Ji. 2015. A novel neural topic model and its supervised extension. In *Proceedings of the AAAI Conference on Artificial Intelligence*, volume 29.

Huimin Chen, Yankai Lin, Fanchao Qi, Jinyi Hu, Peng Li, Jie Zhou, and Maosong Sun. 2021. Aspect-level sentiment-controllable review generation with mutual learning framework. In *Proceedings of the AAAI Conference on Artificial Intelligence*, volume 35, pages 12639–12647.

Chenhe Dong, Yinghui Li, Haifan Gong, Miaoxin Chen, Junxin Li, Ying Shen, and Min Yang. 2021. A survey of natural language generation. *CoRR*, abs/2112.11739.

Yuguang Duan, Canwen Xu, Jiaxin Pei, Jialong Han, and Chenliang Li. 2020. Pre-train and plug-in: Flexible conditional text generation with variational autoencoders. In *Proceedings of the 58th Annual Meeting of the Association for Computational Linguistics*, pages 253–262.

Le Fang, Tao Zeng, Chaochun Liu, Liefeng Bo, Wen Dong, and Changyou Chen. 2021. Transformer-based conditional variational autoencoder for controllable story generation. *arXiv e-prints*, pages arXiv–2101.

Joseph L Fleiss. 1971. Measuring nominal scale agreement among many raters. *Psychological bulletin*, 76(5):378.

Leo Gao, Stella Biderman, Sid Black, Laurence Golding, Travis Hoppe, Charles Foster, Jason Phang, Horace He, Anish Thite, Noa Nabeshima, et al. 2020. The pile: An 800gb dataset of diverse text for language modeling. *arXiv preprint arXiv:2101.00027*.

Sayan Ghosh, Mathieu Chollet, Eugene Laksana, Louis-Philippe Morency, and Stefan Scherer. 2017. Affect-lm: A neural language model for customizable affective text generation. In *Proceedings of the 55th Annual Meeting of the Association for Computational Linguistics (Volume 1: Long Papers)*, pages 634–642.

Maarten Grootendorst. 2020. Keybert: Minimal keyword extraction with bert.

Nitish Shirish Keskar, Bryan McCann, Lav R Varshney, Caiming Xiong, and Richard Socher. 2019. Ctrl: A conditional transformer language model for controllable generation.

Yuta Kikuchi, Graham Neubig, Ryohei Sasano, Hiroya Takamura, and Manabu Okumura. 2016. Controlling output length in neural encoder-decoders. In *Proceedings of the 2016 Conference on Empirical Methods in Natural Language Processing*, pages 1328–1338.

Rik Koncel-Kedziorski, Ioannis Konstas, Luke Zettlemoyer, and Hannaneh Hajishirzi. 2016. A theme-rewriting approach for generating algebra word problems. In *Proceedings of the 2016 Conference on Empirical Methods in Natural Language Processing*, pages 1617–1628.

Matt Kusner, Yu Sun, Nicholas Kolkin, and Kilian Weinberger. 2015. From word embeddings to document distances. In *International conference on machine learning*, pages 957–966. PMLR.

J Richard Landis and Gary G Koch. 1977. The measurement of observer agreement for categorical data. *biometrics*, pages 159–174.

Jiwei Li, Michel Galley, Chris Brockett, Jianfeng Gao, and William B Dolan. 2016. A diversity-promoting objective function for neural conversation models. In *Proceedings of the 2016 Conference of the North American Chapter of the Association for Computational Linguistics: Human Language Technologies*, pages 110–119.

Ruiyang Liu, Yinghui Li, Linmi Tao, Dun Liang, and Hai-Tao Zheng. 2022. Are we ready for a new paradigm shift? a survey on visual deep mlp. *Patterns*, 3(7):100520.

Fuli Luo, Damai Dai, Pengcheng Yang, Tianyu Liu, Baobao Chang, Zhifang Sui, and Xu Sun. 2019. Learning to control the fine-grained sentiment for story ending generation. In *Proceedings of the 57th Annual Meeting of the Association for Computational Linguistics*, pages 6020–6026.

Tomás Mikolov, Ilya Sutskever, Kai Chen, Gregory S. Corrado, and Jeffrey Dean. 2013. Distributed representations of words and phrases and their compositionality. In *Advances in Neural Information Processing Systems 26: 27th Annual Conference on Neural Information Processing Systems 2013. Proceedings of a meeting held December 5-8, 2013, Lake Tahoe, Nevada, United States*, pages 3111–3119.

Nasrin Mostafazadeh, Nathanael Chambers, Xiaodong He, Devi Parikh, Dhruv Batra, Lucy Vanderwende, Pushmeet Kohli, and James Allen. 2016. A corpus and cloze evaluation for deeper understanding of commonsense stories. In *Proceedings of the 2016 Conference of the North American Chapter of the Association for Computational Linguistics: Human Language Technologies*, pages 839–849, San Diego, California. Association for Computational Linguistics.

Kishore Papineni, Salim Roukos, Todd Ward, and Wei-Jing Zhu. 2002. Bleu: a method for automatic evaluation of machine translation. In *Proceedings of the 40th annual meeting of the Association for Computational Linguistics*, pages 311–318.

Ankur Parikh, Xuezhi Wang, Sebastian Gehrmann, Manaal Faruqui, Bhuwan Dhingra, Diyi Yang, and Dipanjan Das. 2020. ToTTo: A controlled table-to-text generation dataset. In *Proceedings of the 2020 Conference on Empirical Methods in Natural Language Processing (EMNLP)*, pages 1173–1186, Online. Association for Computational Linguistics.

Shrimai Prabhumoye, Alan W Black, and Ruslan Salakhutdinov. 2020. Exploring controllable text generation techniques. In *Proceedings of the 28th International Conference on Computational Linguistics*, pages 1–14, Barcelona, Spain (Online). International Committee on Computational Linguistics.

Alec Radford, Jeffrey Wu, Rewon Child, David Luan, Dario Amodei, Ilya Sutskever, et al. 2019. Language models are unsupervised multitask learners. *OpenAI blog*, 1(8):9.

Colin Raffel, Noam Shazeer, Adam Roberts, Katherine Lee, Sharan Narang, Michael Matena, Yanqi Zhou, Wei Li, and Peter J Liu. 2020. Exploring the limits of transfer learning with a unified text-to-text transformer. *Journal of Machine Learning Research*, 21:1–67.

Sudha Rao and Joel Tetreault. 2018. Dear sir or madam, may I introduce the GYAFC dataset: Corpus, benchmarks and metrics for formality style transfer. In *Proceedings of the 2018 Conference of the North American Chapter of the Association for Computational Linguistics: Human Language Technologies, Volume 1 (Long Papers)*, pages 129–140, New Orleans, Louisiana. Association for Computational Linguistics.

Kihyuk Sohn, Honglak Lee, and Xinchen Yan. 2015. Learning structured output representation using deep conditional generative models. In *Advances in Neural Information Processing Systems 28: Annual Conference on Neural Information Processing Systems 2015, December 7-12, 2015, Montreal, Quebec, Canada*, pages 3483–3491.

Rongyi Sun, Borun Chen, Qingyu Zhou, Yinghui Li, Yunbo Cao, and Hai-Tao Zheng. 2022. A non-hierarchical attention network with modality dropout for textual response generation in multimodal dialogue systems. In *ICASSP 2022-2022 IEEE International Conference on Acoustics, Speech and Signal Processing (ICASSP)*, pages 6582–6586. IEEE.

Ashwin K. Vijayakumar, Michael Cogswell, Ramprasaath R. Selvaraju, Qing Sun, Stefan Lee, David J. Crandall, and Dhruv Batra. 2016. Diverse beam search: Decoding diverse solutions from neural sequence models. *CoRR*, abs/1610.02424.

Yunli Wang, Yu Wu, Lili Mou, Zhoujun Li, and Wenhan Chao. 2019. Harnessing pre-trained neural networks with rules for formality style transfer. In *Proceedings of the 2019 Conference on Empirical Methods in Natural Language Processing and the 9th International Joint Conference on Natural Language Processing (EMNLP-IJCNLP)*, pages 3573–3578.

Peng Xu, Mostofa Patwary, Mohammad Shoeybi, Raul Puri, Pascale Fung, Animashree Anandkumar, and Bryan Catanzaro. 2020. Megatron-cntrl: Controllable story generation with external knowledge using large-scale language models. In *Proceedings of the 2020 Conference on Empirical Methods in Natural Language Processing (EMNLP)*, pages 2831–2845.

Shilin Xu, Zhimin He, Junjian Su, Liangsheng Zhong, Yue Xu, Huimin Gu, and Yubing Huang. 2019. A shopping guide text generation system based on deep neural network. In *2019 International Conference on Wavelet Analysis and Pattern Recognition (ICWAPR)*, pages 1–5.

Xiaoyuan Yi, Ruoyu Li, Cheng Yang, Wenhao Li, and Maosong Sun. 2020. Mixpoet: Diverse poetry generation via learning controllable mixed latent space. In *Proceedings of the AAAI conference on artificial intelligence*, volume 34, pages 9450–9457.

Saizheng Zhang, Emily Dinan, Jack Urbanek, Arthur Szlam, Douwe Kiela, and Jason Weston. 2018. Personalizing dialogue agents: I have a dog, do you have pets too? In *Proceedings of the 56th Annual Meeting of the Association for Computational Linguistics (Volume 1: Long Papers)*, pages 2204–2213.

Changmeng Zheng, Yi Cai, Guanjie Zhang, and Qing Li. 2020. Controllable abstractive sentence summarization with guiding entities. In *Proceedings of the 28th International Conference on Computational Linguistics*, pages 5668–5678.

A Appendix

A.1 Dataset Details

The size of each object/occasion category is shown in Table 4 and Table 5 respectively. It is worth noting that the "General" category refers to the case where the sending object of corresponding blessing is not acquired during the data collection process. In addition, there is mutual inclusion between some objects in our dataset. We consider this phenomenon is reasonable, e.g., we may write only one blessing message for elders, and send it to others, such as parents, uncles, and teachers, with a little modification.

Some examples of EBleT are shown in Table 6 which contain the blessings and the corresponding attributes (i.e., occasions and objects).

Object	Size	Object	Size
General	102,284	Customer	4,220
Friend	48,058	Parent	3,791
Lover	20,314	Newlywed	3,210
Teacher	14,092	Senior	2,785
Girlfriend	9,323	Daughter	2,614
Dad	8,871	Son	2,610
Kid	8,373	Employee	2,272
Wife	7,584	Grandma	427
Husband	7,478	Cousin	403
Boyfriend	6,603	Niece	319
Student	6,600	Granddaughter	238
Boss	5,592	Aunt	215
Sister	5,208	Grandson	210
Colleague	4,896	Nephew	160
Brother	4,884	Grandpa	155
Classmate	4,770	Uncle	135
Mom	4,602	Grandparent	107

Table 4: The data size of each object category.

Occasion	Size	Occasion	Size
New Year	55,162	Farewell	9,046
Birthday	36,329	Valentine's Day	8,727
Christmas	27,713	Halloween	6,050
Wedding	21,039	Mother's Day	4,132
Good Morning	18,197	Exam	3,659
Thanksgiving	15,245	Happy Weekend	3,506
Graduation	15,234	Good Afternoon	2,284
Father's Day	14,344	Fool's Day	2,074
Teacher's Day	12,321	Easter	1,999
Good Night	11,667	Housewarming	1,810
Children's Day	11,067	Women's Day	1,239
Anniversary	10,559		

Table 5: The data size of each occasion category.

[Anniversary] [Aunt] Happy Anniversary to the people I look up to whenever I am in doubt. Dear uncle and aunty, you guys are surely made for each other. Have a great year ahead.

[Anniversary] [Parents] You are the parents that all kids hope to have, you are the couple that all lovers hope to be and you both are the pillars of support that every family wishes it had. Happy anniversary to the best parents ever.

[Birthday] [Daughter] This day is truly a special day for us because this is the day when we first had a glimpse on our angel. Have a lovely birthday our dear daughter!

[Birthday] [Colleague] Ignite one candle, happiness will last forever. We work together for around one-third in a day, and it's more than we spend time with our family, and It means we are colleagues. Happy birthday, dear colleague!

[Children's Day] [Kid] My child, I bless you on this special day. You will never grow up, I wish you a happy Children's Day!

[Children's Day] [Student] We may be your teachers but we also have a lot more things to learn from you, especially how to laugh with all your hearts. Happy children's day!

[Christmas] [Boss] Merry Christmas to a boss who keeps the office humming along like Santa's Workshop!

[Christmas] [Wife] Precious wife, my heart hangs on your every breath, like lights hanging on a Christmas tree. Merry Christmas my dear love!

[Easter] [Boyfriend] One the beautiful Easter day, my boyfriend, let the prayers and fasting for Lord Jesus bring much love and happiness in our lives. I pray to the Lord to make our relationship fruitful and prosperous. Have a happy Easter.

[Easter] [Teacher] Dear teacher, you are my inspiration and I am happy to be under your guidance. It's such a hopeful time of year, I hope your heart gets filled with love, baskets with candies and Easter eggs this Easter.

[Thanksgiving] [Boss] It has always been a pleasure working with you because it has been great learning. Thanking you for playing a leading role in my happiness at work. Warm greetings on Thanksgiving!

[Thanksgiving] [Wife] Today, I want to say thanks so much for accepting to spend the rest of your life with me. Thanks so much for being my heart beat. I love you, dear wife. Happy Thanksgiving day!

Table 6: The examples of EBleT. The words related to the attribute **Occasion** and **Object** are highlighted(e.g. Happy Anniversary).

Object	#Sample	#Per.	#Ent.	Occasion	#Sample	#Per.	#Ent.
Aunt	80	73	66	Anniversary	260	239	214
Boss	140	126	118	Birthday	520	479	436
Boyfriend	240	223	197	Children's Day	120	112	104
Brother	220	199	180	Christmas	480	445	397
Classmate	220	206	183	Easter	100	92	81
Colleague	200	187	162	Exam	200	185	163
Cousin	60	55	48	Farewell	220	205	186
Customer	100	90	83	Father's Day	120	112	99
Dad	140	128	115	Fool's Day	40	38	35
Daughter	200	188	168	Good Afternoon	120	113	100
Employee	120	112	97	Good Morning	340	310	279
Friend	440	405	361	Good Night	260	239	213
Girlfriend	300	278	248	Graduation	300	285	243
Granddaughter	60	55	52	Halloween	160	144	134
Grandma	40	38	33	Happy Weekend	60	56	48
Grandpa	20	18	16	Housewarming	60	53	50
Grandparent	20	17	14	Mother's Day	140	131	114
Grandson	40	37	31	New Year	440	404	368
Husband	260	237	211	Teacher's Day	80	76	63
Kid	180	168	145	Thanksgiving	320	300	260
Lover	340	319	282	Valentine's Day	300	274	245
Mom	200	188	165	Wedding	320	289	262
Nephew	20	19	17	Women's Day	100	95	76
Newlywed	20	18	16				
Niece	60	56	51				
Parent	160	147	133				
Senior	80	73	69				
Sister	240	216	195				
Son	200	189	166				
Student	160	149	130				
Teacher	200	181	164				
Uncle	40	37	33				
Wife	260	244	221				

Table 7: Complete human evaluation results of EBleT. #Sample, #Per. and #Ent. denote the total number of sampled sentences, the number of personalized sentences and the number of entangled sentences respectively.

Object/Occasion	Related Words
Colleague	colleague, work, workplace, office, workshop, companion, workmate, coworker, mate, associate, helper, partner, hard, company, career, wealth, business
Boss	boss, work, workplace, office, workshop, chairman, chief, head, sir, supervisor, leader, charge, administrator, management, leadership, dictator, rule, thank, success, company, full, career, team, support, help, guidance, money, business, mentor, job, employees, create, development, professional, encouragement, achievements
Girlfriend	girlfriend, queen, love, addicted, kiss, sweetheart, mate, bestie, date, babe, baby, partner, forever, heart, beautiful, dear, sweet, forever, together, give, long, dreams, warm, sun, care, thank, future, moment, wind, bright, gift, remember, lovely, honey, promise, cherish, promise, shining, flower
Aunt	aunt, uncle, aunty, dear, sweet, family
Boyfriend	boyfriend, love, addicted, kiss, sweetheart, mate, bestie, date, babe, baby, partner, heart, forever, darling, honey, promise, charming, precious, hugs, accompany
Brother	brother, dear, forever, sister, sweet, heart, luck, joy, proud, engagement, health, family, harmony, thanks, handsome, follow, childhood, room
Classmate	classmate, friend, together, forever, long, sincere, graduation, cherish, youth, road, think, school, everyone, memory, success, grow, accompany
Cousin	cousin, grow, hand, family, forever
Customer	new, customer, work, health, joy, friendship, money, client, gifts
Dad	father, dad, love, thank, hard, warm, care, healthy, forever, family, dear, work, rain, give, young, strong, back, child, grow, son, daughter, support, parents, longevity, gratitude, kindness, umbrella, gentle, teaching, understand, journey, lamp, encouragement, illuminating, handsome, stalwart
Daughter	daughter, dear, sweet, baby, family, princess, enjoy, gift, lovely, parents, born, th
Employee	work, employee, thank, luck, future, success, career, dedication, together, forever, colleagues, team, success, appreciate, office
Friend	happiness, friend, forever, dear, joy, friendship, warm, work, smile, care, sun, miss, sincerely, reunion, help, grow, accompany, kind, cherish, sunshine, gratitude, drink, successful, buddy, embrace, invite, lonely
Granddaughter	granddaughter, dear, candies, sweet, grandpa, grandma, favorite, happy, trick, toy, beautiful
Grandma	grandma, health, longevity, dear, old, thank, grandmother, joy, beautiful, sweet, kind
Grandpa	grandpa, healthy, longevity, heart, smile, dear, old, thank, grandfather, joy, beautiful, sweet, kind, grandson, embrace
Grandparents	grandparents, healthy, longevity, heart, smile, dear, old, thank, joy, beautiful, sweet, kind, grandson, embrace
Grandson	grandson, cute, dear, candies, sweet, grandpa, grandma, favorite, happy, trick, toy, handsome, magic
Husband	love, husband, dear, heart, life, always, thank, only, father, special, sweet, everything, marriage, wife, honey, baby, children, grateful, family, kind, wedding, marriage, cherish, met, deep, promise, moments, engagement
Kid	children, kid, happy, childhood, childlike, innocence, child, little, heart, face, fun, growth, dreams, laugh, play, enjoy, haha, colorful, free, fly, lively
Lover	love, heart, life, dear, sweet, forever, dreams, together, sweetheart, thank, wife, husband, honey, moment, light, warm, babe, cherish, promise, sure, met, shining, angels, partner, hug, breath, important
Mom	mom, mother, love, thank, health, hard, forever, son, woman, daughter, grateful, parents, kindness
Nephew	nephew, success, future, dear, life, proud, achieve, niece, adult
Newlywed	newlywed, love, together, wedding, life, marriage, beautiful, new, congratulations, hundred, harmony, wife, pair, bridegroom, moment, phoenix, candles
Niece	success, future, dear, life, proud, achieve, niece, adult, hard, beauty
Parent	mom, parent, care, mother, family, father, life, thank, grateful, forever, children, warm, dear
Senior	health, senior, old, long, longevity, thank, care, wealth, give, sir
Sister	sister, dear, beautiful, heart, brother, old, little, gift, proud, family

Table 8: Bag-of-words related to objects and occasions.

Object/Occasion	Related Words
Son	son, dear, sweet, baby, family, prince, enjoy, follow, handsome, gift, pride, lovely, parents, born, th
Student	student, children, future, childhood, friends, innocence, childlike, smile, classmates, knowledge, grow, road, college, proud, career, study, wisdom, university, achieve, examination
Teacher	teacher, hard, students, full, knowledge, care, light, podium, gratitude, chalk, soul, sun, wisdom, thank, kindness, forward, tree, dreams, education, support, learning, accompany, class, illuminating, wings, guidance, watering
Uncle	uncle, old, aunt, dear, sweet, family
Wife	wife, love, life, beautiful, heart, dear, mother, woman, everything, family, darling, warm, sweetheart, moment, thanks, dream, children, married, accompany, sunshine, given, deserve, help
Christmas	Christmas, Xmas, merry, santa, card, tree, eve, stocking, humming, peace, claus, warm, night, gift, bell, snow, cold, deer, candlelight, chimney, elk, sled, shining, jesus
Thanksgiving	thanksgiving, thank, grateful, gratitude, care, give, warm, smile, kindness, bright, cherish
Graduation	graduation, congratulation, graduate, determination, dedication, achievement, life, future, success, proud, work, teacher, school, classmates, dreams, youth, journey, forward, college, leave, knowledge, continue, grow, study, society, examination
Anniversary	wedding, love, increase, darling, marriage, th, year, couple, life, together, best, believe, more, wonderful, always, heart, wife, husband, long, future, relationship, sweet
Birthday	birthday, happy, years, health, long, forever, special, gift, dreams
Children's Day	children, childhood, always, sweet, play, innocent, smile, june, forever, face, young, grow
Easter	easter, god, christ, lord, resurrection, new, eggs, spring, pray, basket, renewal, prosperity, bunny, rejoice, risen, holy
Exam	exam, success, luck, god, pray, comes, write, believe, sure, result, grades, final, proud, study, lord, pass, wisdom, efforts, questions, victory, preparation, excellent, paper, deserve, confidence
Farewell	farewell, life, goodbye, thank, friend, future, miss, luck, again, back, remember, memories, leaving, cherish, years
Father's Day	father, dad, love, thank, mountain, sea, deep, strong, support, son, shoulders, strength, light, parents, tired, accompany, busy, gentle, umbrella, teachings, given, heavy
Fool's Day	fool, april, happy, stupid, look, phone, money, really, smile, read, haha
Good Afternoon	afternoon, day, enjoy, everything, sunshine, lunch, midday, relaxing, breath
Good Morning	morning, face, new, smile, sun, start, light, mood, yesterday, embrace
Good Night	night, sleep, goodnight, dreams, tomorrow, sweet, stars, pray, today, bed, moon, close, asleep, sound, amen
Halloween	halloween, ghost, fun, pumpkin, afraid, lantern, candy, mask, witches, broom, moon, children, vampires, monster
Happy Weekend	weekend, work, fun, relax, saturday, busy, enjoy, rest, tired, sleep
Housewarming	new, house, housewarming, move, congratulations, come, neighbors, firecrackers, welcome
Mother's Day	mother, love, thank, children, women, daughter, son, giving, grow, sea, raising, sunshine, breeze, embrace
New Year	new, spring, coming, eve, change, warm, year, red, together, fireworks, welcome, forward, bright, prosperity, winter, busy, snow, cold, bloom, approaching, continue
Teacher's Day	teacher, thank, work, students, knowledge, full, flowers, light, chalk, podium, sun, warm, candle, dedication, school, september, growth, tree, garden, respect, illuminate, education, children, classroom, guidance, ignited
Valentine's Day	valentine, love, heart, dear, darling, together, sweet, promise, honey, share, romantic, handsome, beautiful, kiss, important, partner, babe
Wedding	love, wedding, life, forever, marriage, congratulations, sweet, future, bride, harmony, wife, always, year, fate, home, share, moment
Women's Day	women, beautiful, special, strength, wife, work, power, inspiration, proud, deserve, queen

Table 9: Bag-of-words related to objects and occasions.

Unsupervised Token-level Hallucination Detection from Summary Generation By-products

Andreas Marfurt
Idiap Research Institute, Switzerland
EPFL, Switzerland
andreas.marfurt@idiap.ch

James Henderson
Idiap Research Institute, Switzerland
james.henderson@idiap.ch

Abstract

Hallucinations in abstractive summarization are model generations that are unfaithful to the source document. Current methods for detecting hallucinations operate mostly on noun phrases and named entities, and restrict themselves to the XSum dataset, which is known to have hallucinations in 3 out of 4 training examples (Maynez et al., 2020). We instead consider the CNN/DailyMail dataset where the summarization model has not seen abnormally many hallucinations during training. We automatically detect candidate hallucinations at the token level, irrespective of its part of speech. Our detection comes essentially *for free*, as we only use information the model already produces during generation of the summary. This enables practitioners to jointly generate a summary and identify possible hallucinations, with minimal overhead. We repurpose an existing factuality dataset and create our own token-level annotations. The evaluation on these two datasets shows that our model achieves better precision-recall tradeoffs than its competitors, which additionally require a model forward pass.

1 Introduction

Large pretrained Transformers (Vaswani et al., 2017; Devlin et al., 2019) have considerably advanced the state of the art in abstractive summarization (Liu and Lapata, 2019; Lewis et al., 2020; Zhang et al., 2020). However, model hallucinations – where the information in the generated summary is not faithful to the source document – are a prominent remaining failure mode of these models.

A lot of recent work has addressed this problem, predominantly on the XSum dataset (Narayan et al., 2018). XSum is an outlier, however, in that over 75% of its reference summaries contain hallucinations (Maynez et al., 2020). Models trained (or finetuned) on this dataset are consequently prone to hallucinate themselves when summarizing an article. Additionaly, current work focuses on detecting hallucinations for noun phrases and named entities (Wang et al., 2020; Durmus et al., 2020; Scialom et al., 2021), sometimes with the addition of dates and numbers (Narayan et al., 2021). Recent work has shown, however, that summarization models also make mistakes in other parts of speech, such as predicates (Pagnoni et al., 2021).

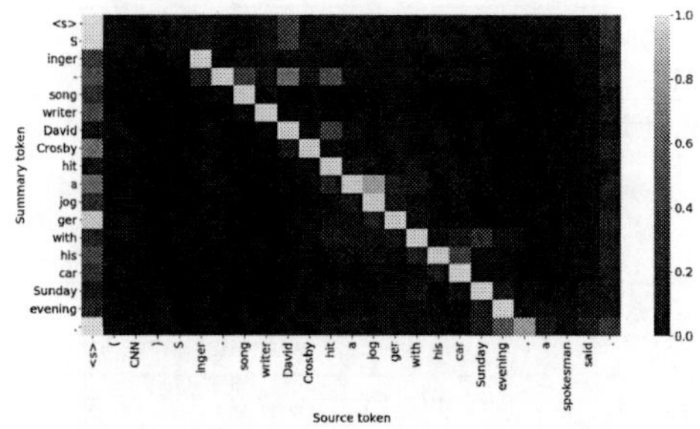

Figure 1: BART cross-attentions align copied segments of the summary with the respective segments in the source. Attention weights are normalized by row. Only the first summary and source sentences are shown.

In this paper, we aim to expand the current line of research to a different dataset, and to remove the restriction to entities. We use the diagonal cross-attention patterns present in Transformer-based abstractive summarization models (see Figure 1) to align the summary with the source document. We detect hallucinations in an unsupervised fashion for segments of aligned and unaligned tokens by computing statistics from the encoder's self-attentions and the decoder's next-word probabilities. These by-products arise when generating a summary with any Transformer model. In this paper, we use BART (Lewis et al., 2020). We evaluate our approach on two datasets.[1] We repurpose the factuality dataset FRANK (Pagnoni et al., 2021), but only 0.4% of tokens turn out to be hallucinations. Therefore, we additionally create our own dataset

[1] Our data and code are available at https://github.com/idiap/hallucination-detection.

Proceedings of the 2nd Workshop on Natural Language Generation, Evaluation, and Metrics (GEM), pages 248 - 261
December 7, 2022 ©2022 Association for Computational Linguistics

called TLHD-CNNDM, which contains token-level annotations on examples heuristically selected to have a higher chance of containing a hallucination. Indeed 14.2% of tokens in TLHD-CNNDM are hallucinations. Our method demonstrates good results compared to its competitors, while at the same time requiring negligible additional computation. At the same time, hallucination detection proves to be a difficult task, in particular on intrinsic hallucinations (defined in Section 3), where all models struggle to detect any hallucinations.

2 Related Work

Several different methods have been proposed to detect hallucinations. Specialized decoding strategies are used to nudge the model to stay closer to the source vocabulary (Aralikatte et al., 2021) or its entities (Narayan et al., 2021). Multiple studies use automatic question generation and answering models to ask questions about entities in the generated summary, and try to answer them from the source document (Wang et al., 2020; Durmus et al., 2020; Scialom et al., 2021). If the question cannot be answered from the source document, the entity is considered a hallucination. Filippova (2020) determine the degree of hallucination from the differences in probabilities assigned by a conditional and an unconditional language model. In the related area of factuality detection, Cao et al. (2022) use the same idea to identify hallucinated but factual summaries. Entailment-based classifiers are used to evaluate a summary's factuality at the level of text or dependency arcs (Falke et al., 2019; Goyal and Durrett, 2020). It is also common to create synthetic data for a classifier by corrupting the input, for hallucinations (Zhou et al., 2021) as well as factuality (Cao et al., 2020; Kryściński et al., 2020). However, the error distributions obtained synthetically can differ from those of models (Goyal and Durrett, 2021). More types of factuality errors are identified in Pagnoni et al. (2021) with a detailed human annotation, finding discourse and semantic frame errors. These detection methods can be used to identify mistakes or rerank multiple outputs (e.g. Ladhak et al., 2022).

3 Hallucination Detection

Definition. We adopt the definition from Maynez et al. (2020), and define *intrinsic hallucinations* as combinations of information from the source document that cannot be inferred from it, and *extrinsic hallucinations* as information that is not present in the source document. Paraphrases and information that can be directly inferred from the source document, however, do not constitute hallucinations. Furthermore, whether some information is a hallucination is an orthogonal problem to whether that information is factually correct, a question we do not consider in this paper.

3.1 Unsupervised Hallucination Detection

In the process of generating a summary, a Transformer-based abstractive summarization model creates a number of by-products, such as decoder next-token generation probabilities, encoder and decoder self-attentions, and decoder to encoder cross-attentions, for each layer and attention head of the model. These can be easily accessed from e.g. the HuggingFace transformers library (Wolf et al., 2020).

Motivation. It is debated whether model attentions can be used to explain model decisions (Jain and Wallace, 2019; Wiegreffe and Pinter, 2019) and how much a Transformer encoder's output representation still represents the token at its position in the input (Brunner et al., 2020). Nevertheless, we posit that the diagonal attention patterns observed in Figure 1, together with the fact that the source and target tokens match for the entire segment, is a strong enough signal to claim that a summarization model copied this segment from the source.

Additionally, we conjecture that the faithfulness of a summary to the source document is not inherently a question that spans multiple sentences, in contrast to a summary's factuality (Pagnoni et al., 2021). As a consequence, we detect hallucinations at the token level by processing summary sentences in isolation.

Initial alignment. From the observations above, we start by aligning summary and source positions based on cross-attentions. In BART cross-attentions, the maximum cross-attention weight is often put on the beginning-of-sequence token in the source. If the token is a preposition, a high attention weight is also put on its preceding and succeeding tokens. We therefore accept a target-source alignment of target token t_i iff it matches a source token in its top-4 cross-attention weights. This constitutes our initial alignment.

Context voting. In a second step, we expand the initial alignment with a position-based voting algo-

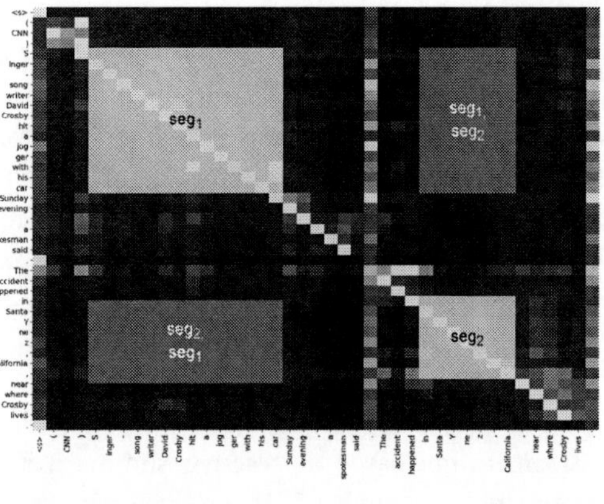

Figure 2: BART encoder self-attentions relate the aligned segments seg_1 and seg_2 of the source document (grey boxes) by their interactions (blue boxes). Only the first two source sentences are shown.

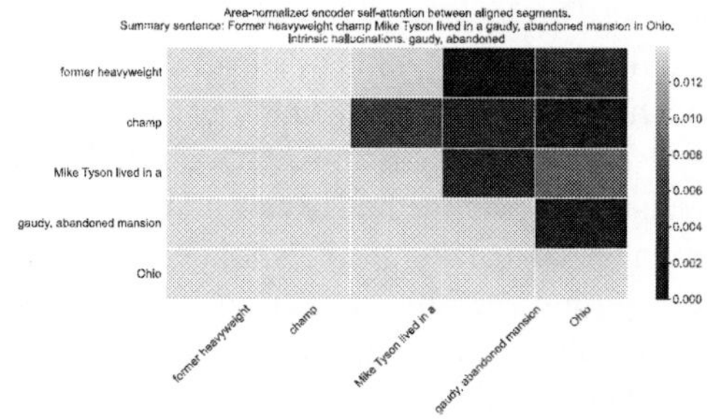

Figure 3: Association strength α between aligned segments. The intrinsic hallucinations in the fourth segment show the least interaction with other segments. Full example in Appendix B.

rithm. For each target token t_i, its context tokens $t_{i-l}, \ldots, t_{i-1}, t_{i+1}, \ldots, t_{i+l}$ in a window of size l[2] around t_i vote on the expected source position of t_i given their own alignment and an assumed diagonal attention pattern. If a token is not aligned to the source, it does not vote. We accept a vote when at least half the neighboring tokens agree. We perform voting for a maximum of 10 rounds, and we stop early when it has converged, which often happens after 2 rounds.

After these two alignment stages, we have a set of aligned segments, with a token-level correspondence between summary and source, and a set of unaligned tokens. We now look to detect intrinsic hallucinations in the former set, and extrinsic ones in the latter.

Classifying aligned tokens. Aligned tokens appear in the source document, and consequently do not constitute extrinsic hallucinations. To assign a probability of them being intrinsic hallucinations, we compare characteristics of their aligned source segments. Maynez et al. (2020) speculate that intrinsic hallucinations are potentially a failure of document modeling. We add that the encoder may also have performed well at document modeling, but the communication to the decoder through the representational bottleneck may have failed. In the latter case, we should be able to read the association of two source segments from the strength of the encoder's self-attentions between the two segments. We determine the association strength α of two aligned segments seg_1 and seg_2 by the area-normalized sum of encoder self-attention weights (enc_{ij} and enc_{ji}) between the two segments:

$$\alpha(\text{seg}_1, \text{seg}_2) = \frac{\sum_{i \in \text{seg}_1, j \in \text{seg}_2} \text{enc}_{ij} + \text{enc}_{ji}}{2 * |\text{seg}_1| * |\text{seg}_2|} \quad (1)$$

where i and j are the source indices of segments seg_1 and seg_2, and $|.|$ is the cardinality. Figure 2 visualizes the areas whose attention weights are summed with blue boxes. The score for a segment is the mean α to all other segments in its summary sentence. The higher the score, the higher our confidence in the two segments being semantically close, and therefore not intrinsic hallucinations. As an example, Figure 3 shows that the fourth segment has the smallest association strength to the other segments. Indeed, this is an intrinsic hallucination. It talks about the present state of the mansion, while the predicate concerns the past.

Classifying unaligned tokens. While unaligned tokens can still appear in the source document and result in an intrinsic hallucination, the prevalent error mode for this set of tokens are extrinsic hallucinations. We found that generated summaries sometimes contain sentences entirely unrelated to the article, most likely an artefact of data collection. Our first score β_{align} is the fraction of the summary sentence tokens that are aligned.

For unaligned tokens in mostly-aligned sentences, we conjecture that generations by a strong language model fit in well (both syntactically and semantically) with the source document and the summary written so far, and thus should be expected by the model. In the opposite case, unexpected generations lead to a higher amount of surprisal. The expected surprisal of a language model can be quantified with the entropy of its next-word

[2] We choose $l = 3$ as our window size.

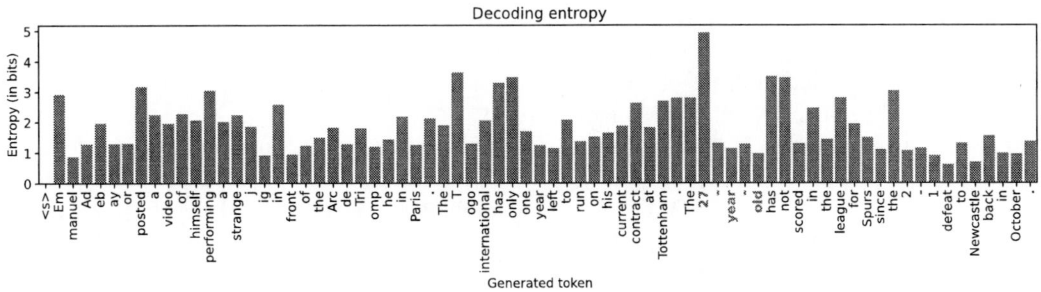

Figure 4: Summary containing an extrinsic hallucination (tokens in bold red). The decoding entropy of the first hallucinated token is high, those of the subsequent tokens are low. We determine the hallucination score (Eq. 2) of the entire segment (Definition in Eq. 3) from its first token.

decoding probabilities (Meister et al., 2020). Figure 4 shows the decoding entropy of an example summary. We thus propose a second score β_{entropy} as the inverse smoothed decoding entropy:

$$\beta_{\text{entropy}}(t_i) = \frac{1}{H(t_i)+1} \tag{2}$$

with $H(t_i)$ the entropy of the next-word probability distribution of target token t_i.

Only the generation of the first token of an unexpected segment is surprising (as seen in Figure 4), and subsequent completions of the segment have high probability and low entropy. We therefore split a span of unaligned tokens into segments based on the decoding entropy. The construction is as follows: As long as the decoding entropy of the next token t_i decreases the mean decoding entropy of the current segment seg, it is added. Otherwise a new segment is started.

$$\text{seg}' := \begin{cases} \text{seg} \cup t_i & \text{if } H(t_i) < \frac{\sum_{t_j \in \text{seg}} H(t_j)}{|\text{seg}|}, \\ t_i & \text{otherwise.} \end{cases} \tag{3}$$

Converting scores to probabilities. All our faithfulness scores are nonnegative, and upper bounded by 1. A higher score means less chance of hallucination. We therefore convert each faithfulness score s to a hallucination probability p by scaling and inverting it.

$$p = 1 - \frac{s - s_{\text{min}}}{s_{\text{max}} - s_{\text{min}}} \tag{4}$$

where s_{min} and s_{max} are the minimum and maximum scores across the entire dataset. In an offline evaluation setting, one can compute all scores on a dataset first, and then get s_{min} and s_{max}. For the online setting, these values have to be set. On our two datasets, we observe that the minimum and maximum values do not change much, so we expect the current values to transfer to new datasets. They are $[0, 0.02]$ for α, $[0.08, 0.71]$ for β_{entropy}, and β_{align} is already in the correct range.

BART-GBP. As we will see in the ablation study in the results in Section 5, the association strength α decreases the performance of our detection method. Our final model, *BART-GBP* (BART generation by-products), therefore only uses the β_{align} and β_{entropy} scores.

4 Experiments

We study CNN/DailyMail (Hermann et al., 2015), a summarization dataset known to be highly extractive (Grusky et al., 2018) and therefore less likely to contain a lot of hallucinations.

4.1 Datasets

Finding an existing dataset to evaluate our method is difficult, since we need access to the model's attentions and decoding probabilities alongside the outputs.

FRANK. We repurpose FRANK, a factuality metric evaluation dataset (Pagnoni et al., 2021). It consists of 250 summaries from the CNN/DailyMail test set, obtained from SummEval (Fabbri et al., 2021). FRANK introduces a typology of factual errors, which we convert to hallucination annotations by using examples of predicate, entity and circumstance errors as candidates for intrinsic hallucinations, and out-of-article errors as candidates for extrinsic hallucinations. Our publically available model version produces slightly different outputs from theirs, so we manually correct labels where the outputs differ. Our adapted dataset contains 57 hallucinated words (31 intrinsic, 26 extrinsic) which corresponds to 0.4% of the 15,700 total words. At the sentence level, 3.5% contain at least one hallucinated word (31/897), while at the summary level it is 9.2% (23/250).

TLHD-CNNDM. Since the number of hallucinations in FRANK is low, we additionally collect human annotations ourselves. We produce BART model outputs for the CNN/DailyMail test set (excluding the FRANK examples) by using the standard HuggingFace implementation with the default parameters. To arrive at an interesting dataset, we first rank summary sentences by two criteria: 1) the number of non-contiguous alignments to the source document found by lexical overlap, and 2) the number of words that do not appear in the source document. Both criteria are length-normalized. We pick the top 75 examples from both lists, arriving at 150 summary sentences. We then perform a human annotation as detailed in Appendix C. Our dataset contains 299 hallucinated words out of a total 2,100 (14.2%). Of those hallucinations, 51 are intrinsic, and 248 are extrinsic. Of the 150 sentences, 78 contain at least one hallucination (52%). The annotator agreement with the majority class (following Durmus et al., 2020) is 94.6%, and 73.9% and 86.3% for intrinsic and extrinsic hallucinations, respectively. We name our dataset *TLHD-CNNDM* (token-level hallucination detection for CNN/DailyMail).

4.2 Model Details

For generating our summaries, attentions and decoding probabilities, we use the BART-large model finetuned on CNN/DailyMail (`'facebook/bart-large-cnn'`) from the HuggingFace transformers library[3], with its default parameters. In generation with beam search, multiple beams are active at each generation step, but only one beam is eventually selected. We extract the attention and decoding probabilities of this beam with our own code. When inspecting cross-attentions, we found layers 10 and 11 (out of 12) to show the cleanest diagonal patterns (as presented in Figure 1). Other layers either have less focused attention, or they look at the previous token (mostly lower layers), the beginning-of-sequence token, or periods. We average the attentions from layers 10 and 11. We select the same layers for the encoder self-attentions.

4.3 Baselines

As baselines, we use four classes of models: lexical overlap, an entity-focused question-generation-answering model, a dependency entailment-based model, and a token-level classification model trained on synthetic data.

Lexical-n. This baseline lexically aligns the summary and the source document. It greedily adds the longest matching span, down to a span length of n. This baseline classifies all unaligned tokens as (presumably extrinsic) hallucinations. For aligned tokens, our most successful heuristic determines the hallucination probability for each aligned span as the fraction of aligned tokens that have an alignment in the same source sentence as the current span:

$$1-\frac{|\text{tokens aligned to same source sentence}|}{|\text{all aligned tokens}|}. \quad (5)$$

FEQA. FEQA (Durmus et al., 2020) generates questions about the summary's entities, then tries to answer them from the source document. It then computes the token-level F1 score between the summary's text and the predicted text span from the source. Unmatched answers indicate hallucinations. We compute word-level probabilities by averaging the F1 scores of all spans the word is part of.

DAE. Dependency arc entailment (DAE) (Goyal and Durrett, 2020, 2021) decides from its dependency arcs whether the generated summary sentence is entailed by the source document. While DAE is technically a factuality detection method, we conjecture that hallucinations in the summary should not be entailed by the source document either. In footnote 6 of Goyal and Durrett (2021), the authors propose that a word is non-factual if any of its arcs is non-factual. We therefore compute word hallucination probabilities as the maximum probability of non-factuality of its dependency arcs. We use their model variant trained with entity-based synthetic data on CNN/DailyMail.

Fairseq. With the help of synthetic training data, where factual tokens have been automatically replaced with hallucinations, pretrained language models can be finetuned to directly predict a hallucination label for each input token

[3]https://github.com/huggingface/transformers

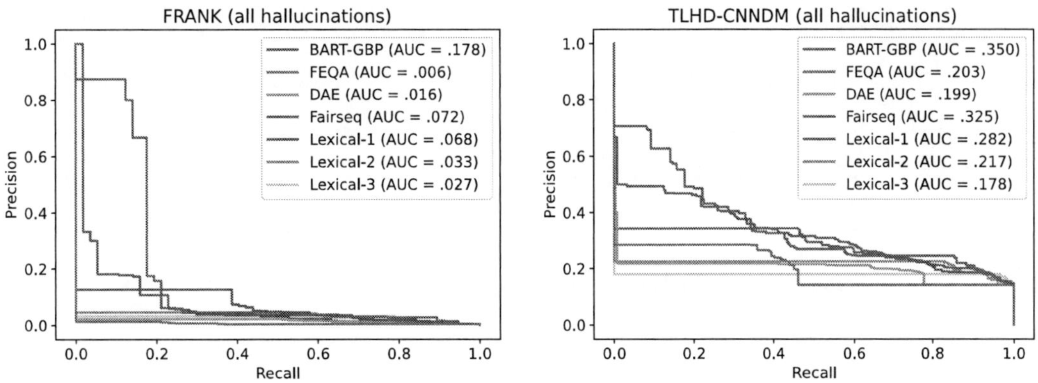

(a) FRANK

(b) TLHD-CNNDM

Figure 5: Precision-recall curves for all hallucinations in the FRANK and TLHD-CNNDM datasets.

Method	Best F1	PR AUC	ROC AUC
	FRANK		
FEQA*	0.0245	0.0062	0.3327
DAE*	0.0419	0.0157	0.7164
Fairseq w/o ref*	0.1651	0.0723	0.8129
Fairseq w/ ref*	0.0682	0.0232	0.7017
Lexical-1	0.1913	0.0677	0.8788
Lexical-2	0.0854	0.0335	0.8058
Lexical-3	0.0610	0.0268	0.7672
BART-GBP	**0.2778**	**0.1777**	**0.8934**
	TLHD-CNNDM		
FEQA*	0.3156	0.2031	0.3899
DAE*	0.3167	0.1988	0.5803
Fairseq w/o ref*	**0.3957**	0.3255	**0.7375**
Fairseq w/ ref*	0.2672	0.1714	0.5521
Lexical-1	0.3937	0.2819	0.6846
Lexical-2	0.3535	0.2166	0.4802
Lexical-3	0.3025	0.1785	0.2599
BART-GBP	0.3806	**0.3502**	0.7332

Table 1: Best F1 score on the precision-recall curve, area under precision-recall curve, and area under the ROC curve. Methods marked with * require an additional model forward pass, which increases runtime and resource use.

(Zhou et al., 2021). We use the model finetuned on XSum and evaluate how it transfers to the CNN/DailyMail dataset. Since we compare to our unsupervised method, we leave retraining the model on CNN/DailyMail to future work. We evaluate both model settings, with and without access to the reference summary. We call this method *Fairseq* based on its Github repository name.

5 Results

We use precision-recall curves to evaluate the hallucination detection methods. Precision-recall is the preferred metric when finding the instances of the positive class (hallucinations) has exceptionally high value compared to the instances of the negative class. Appendix A also shows ROC curves.

Main result. Our main result is shown in Table 1, which considers performance when classifying hallucinations of both intrinsic and extrinsic type. We present the best F1 score on the precision-recall curve, the area under the precision-recall curve, and the area under the ROC curve. Additionally, we show whether the method requires an additional model forward pass, which incurs a longer runtime and higher resource costs, by marking the respective methods (with *). BART-GBP performs best on the FRANK dataset, and has the largest AUC for precision-recall on the TLHD-CNNDM dataset. For the other metrics, it is close behind the highest score, all while being completely unsupervised. Fairseq without access to the reference summary performs well on TLHD-CNNDM, but worse on FRANK. The setting without access to the reference summary does better across all datasets and metrics, and is therefore reported from now on.

The precision-recall plots in Figure 5 give further details on the main result. BART-GBP manages to get high precision for the data points where it is most certain, something other methods struggle with. At higher levels of recall, the difficulty of the task leads to lower precision scores across all methods. The FRANK dataset, where only 0.4% of tokens are hallucinations, is very challenging (see Figure 5a). With 14.2% of positive labels, TLHD-CNNDM is less extreme, but still proves to be difficult for all methods, as seen in Figure 5b.

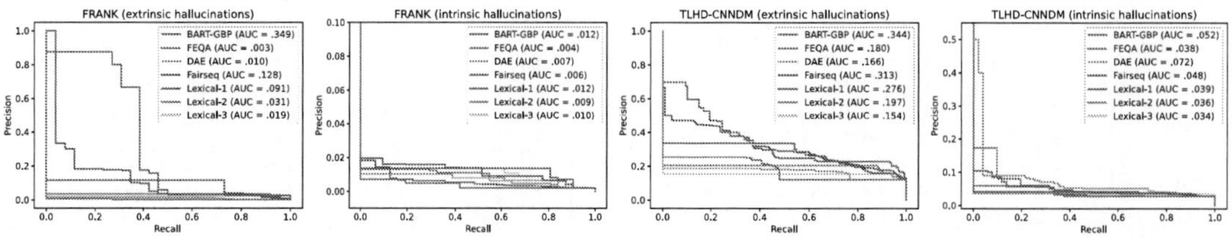

(a) Extrinsic hallucinations (b) Intrinsic hallucinations (c) Extrinsic hallucinations (d) Intrinsic hallucinations

Figure 6: Precision-recall curves for the label subsets of extrinsic and intrinsic hallucinations in the FRANK (6a, 6b) and TLHD-CNNDM (6c, 6d) datasets.

Extrinsic hallucinations. Figures 6a and 6c show the models' performance on the label subset of extrinsinc hallucinations. To evaluate on this subset, we remove data points that are gold intrinsic hallucinations in order to not unfairly penalize models for detecting those, and vice versa for evaluation of intrinsic hallucinations. Apart from BART-GBP and Fairseq, the Lexical-1 baseline manages to find some hallucinations. However, it does not provide a fine-grained trade-off between precision and recall, in contrast to BART-GBP.

Intrinsic hallucinations. As we can see from Figures 6b and 6d, finding intrinsic hallucinations proves to be very difficult for all methods. We therefore zoom in both graphs on the y-axis. BART-GBP performs well relative to the baselines. Notably for the TLHD-CNNDM dataset, DAE manages to find some hallucinations at some of its highest probability selections, but quickly diminishes at higher recall.

In summary, BART-GBP gets consistent and very competitive results in both datasets and on all label subsets, even while being an unsupervised method. The ROC curves in Figures 8 and 9 in Appendix A further confirm this finding.

Ablation study. We are interested to see how each of our designed scores contributes to finding hallucinations. In Table 2, we show an ablation study with the area under the precision-recall curve as the performance metric. We see that of all individual scores, β_{align} performs best. Combining it with β_{entropy} (by taking the maximum of both probabilities for each token) further improves results on the TLHD-CNNDM dataset, but not on FRANK. α performs barely above a baseline that would classify all data points as hallucinations. This came as a surprise to us, as we expected α to perform better from the motivation in Section 3.1. Adding α to the β scores decreases performance drastically.

Scores	FRANK	TLHD-CNNDM
α	0.0051	0.1440
β_{align}	**0.1993**	0.3260
β_{entropy}	0.0685	0.3198
β_{align}, β_{entropy}	0.1777	**0.3502**
α, β_{align}, β_{entropy}	0.0390	0.1687

Table 2: Ablation study for different combinations of scores. Metric is area under precision-recall curve. BART-GBP is the combination of β_{align} and β_{entropy}.

This comes from the fact that our scores are not calibrated, so the distribution of each score will be different. As a result, when taking the max of multiple scores, one of them may dominate. When we plot a histogram of our scores' values, we see that this is the case for α, leading to such a performance deterioration in the case of combining all three scores. Since α on its own does not score well, we do not further calibrate our scores.

Maximum possible hallucination recall. We motivated our approach by arguing that token-level methods are superior to entity-based question-generation-answering systems (like FEQA) or dependency arc entailment-based DAE. These methods may miss some hallucinated tokens as they only compute hallucination probabilities for a subset of all tokens. To verify how many these are, we analyze the recall each method achieves when it classifies all tokens that it considers as positives.

The results are shown in Table 3. The disadvantage for FEQA and DAE is substantial. FEQA classifies less than half of the tokens labeled as hallucinations in the FRANK and TLHD-CNNDM dataset. DAE is limited to a recall of around 80%, as it cannot detect tokens that are not part of one of the dependency arcs considered for entailment.

Method	Maximum possible recall
FRANK	
FEQA	38.60%
DAE	80.70%
Fairseq	100.00%
Lexical-n	100.00%
BART-GBP	100.00%
TLHD-CNNDM	
FEQA	46.15%
DAE	77.93%
Fairseq	100.00%
Lexical-n	100.00%
BART-GBP	100.00%

Table 3: Maximum possible recall of FEQA (entity-based), DAE (dependency arc entailment), and the token-level methods Fairseq, Lexical-n and BART-GBP.

Score	All	Extrinsic	Intrinsic
FRANK			
Aligned (α)	50.88%	11.54%	83.87%
Unaligned (β_{entropy})	52.63%	96.15%	16.13%
Both (β_{align})	100.00%	100.00%	100.00%
TLHD-CNNDM			
Aligned (α)	19.06%	11.29%	56.86%
Unaligned (β_{entropy})	81.27%	88.71%	45.10%
Both (β_{align})	100.00%	100.00%	100.00%

Table 4: Maximum possible recall of aligned and unaligned token scores wrt. all, extrinsic, or intrinsic hallucinations.

Maximum recall of (un)aligned tokens. Aligning the summary with the source document forms the basis of our method. How many hallucinations are part of aligned spans, and how many are unaligned? We perform this analysis in Table 4. We can see that extrinsic hallucinations are mostly part of unaligned spans, which are scored by β_{entropy}. Intrinsic hallucinations in the FRANK dataset are mostly part of aligned spans, scored by α. In the TLHD-CNNDM dataset, however, intrinsic hallucinations are only part of aligned spans around half of the time.

Note that aligned and unaligned scores can add up to slightly more than 100%. This occurs when some BPE tokens of the same word are aligned and others are not (e.g. when a name appears together with a possessive *'s*).

6 Conclusion

We have presented BART-GBP, a method to detect hallucinations from the by-products of summary generation of a BART abstractive summarization model, trained and evaluated on CNN/DailyMail. We first aligned the segments of the summary and source document using cross-attentions, and then used encoder self-attentions and decoding probabilities to detect intrinsic and extrinsic hallucinations, respectively. This happens with minimal computational overhead, compared to prior work that uses external models that require an additional model forward pass. Our evaluations show that this is a difficult task, and especially intrinsic hallucination detection needs to be addressed by future work. We hope to contribute to this endeavor with our method and our token-level annotated dataset, TLHD-CNNDM.

Limitations

The results in this paper are limited by several factors. Firstly, the definition of what constitutes a hallucination is neither set in stone, nor a mathematical construct, and therefore open to interpretation. We experienced this first-hand from the feedback of our annotators. This makes the task of teaching a model to identify hallucinations all the more difficult, and the gap to optimal performance in the results (for all methods) makes this visible.

Another limitation is given by the model under study. We already mentioned in Section 3.1 that the interpretability of attention patterns is a debated topic in the research community. A model trained to faithfully *explain* its decisions would be even better suited to perform this kind of analysis.

Transfer to other models. While we do not assume that our method transfers easily to some attention-based RNN architectures, we saw indications that it could transfer to other Transformer-based summarization models. In initial experiments, we have used BERTSUMABS (Liu and Lapata, 2019), which shows very similar cross-attention patterns (see Figure 7). There are some small differences, however. BERTSUMABS puts its maximum attention weight to the copied word more often, but still shows a lot of attention to CLS/SEP tokens in the source and BOS/EOS tokens in the summary. Additionally, the tokenization is different which can have an impact on the alignment stage. In BART, for example, the same word can

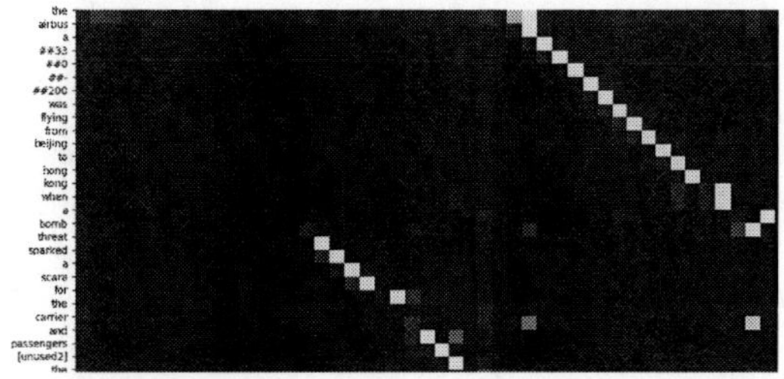

Figure 7: BERTSUMABS cross-attention patterns are very similar to those of BART, both Transformer-based summarization models.

be tokenized in different ways when it is preceeded by the BOS token, a whitespace, or punctuation. This sometimes prevented our method from aligning the same word due to unmatched tokens.

Transfer to other datasets. We do not expect these results to transfer to datasets that have a large percentage of hallucinations, i.e. XSum. We are not aware of other datasets with those same hallucination characteristics. However, we expect that other summarization datasets could benefit from our method, especially those that are similarly extractive as CNN/DailyMail. The scoring range to convert scores into probabilities may have to be recomputed.

Prevalence of sports topics in hallucinations. The prevalence of sports topics in CNN/DailyMail hallucinations hints at divergence issues between the source and reference (Wiseman et al., 2017; Dhingra et al., 2019; Kryscinski et al., 2019) for these topics: True additional information (such as standings) is added by the author/editor. It is interesting to note that while models trained on XSum learn to hallucinate consistently, CNN/DM models learn to hallucinate on sports topics. While removing hallucinations from the training data could address hallucinations, this seems infeasible, and detecting hallucinated model outputs is a more practical approach.

Ethical Considerations

By using a large pretrained language model, this study inherits the issues that come with these models, i.e. reproduction of biased or offensive content that appeared in the pretraining corpus, which includes documents on the web. Unexpected and unwanted model behavior should be reduced. Detecting hallucinations is one of the methods to do so, which can prevent misrepresentation of the text to be summarized by the model, and avoid distributing potentially misleading and in the worst case harmful content. On the other hand, a danger in using an imperfect model to detect hallucinations can be to create a false sense of security and lower the vigilance of people tasked with checking model outputs.

In this study, we also conducted a human evaluation. The privacy of our annotators is respected by labeling each example's answers with annotator_0, annotator_1 and annotator_2, respectively. Their answers consist exclusively of an extracted text span from the summary sentence in question. No personal information was collected. With regard to the presented content in the evaluation, the articles are part of the publically available CNN/DailyMail test set, and supposedly do not contain offensive content. The generated summaries were checked manually. We did not hear any negative feedback from our annotators in this or any other regard.

Acknowledgments

This work was supported as a part of the grant Automated interpretation of political and economic policy documents: Machine learning using semantic and syntactic information, funded by the Swiss National Science Foundation (grant number CRSII5_180320). We would also like to thank our family, friends and colleagues who graciously volunteered to annotate the TLHD-CNNDM dataset.

References

Rahul Aralikatte, Shashi Narayan, Joshua Maynez, Sascha Rothe, and Ryan McDonald. 2021. Focus attention: Promoting faithfulness and diversity in summarization. In *Proceedings of the 59th Annual Meeting of the Association for Computational Linguistics and the 11th International Joint Conference on Natural Language Processing (Volume 1: Long Papers)*, pages 6078–6095.

Gino Brunner, Yang Liu, Damian Pascual Ortiz, Oliver Richter, Massimiliano Ciaramita, and Roger Wattenhofer. 2020. On identifiability in transformers. In *International Conference on Learning Representations*.

Meng Cao, Yue Dong, and Jackie Chi Kit Cheung. 2022. Hallucinated but factual! inspecting the factuality of hallucinations in abstractive summarization. In *Proceedings of the 60th Annual Meeting of the Association for Computational Linguistics (Volume 1: Long Papers)*, pages 3340–3354.

Meng Cao, Yue Dong, Jiapeng Wu, and Jackie Chi Kit Cheung. 2020. Factual error correction for abstractive summarization models. In *Proceedings of the 2020 Conference on Empirical Methods in Natural Language Processing (EMNLP)*, pages 6251–6258.

Jacob Devlin, Ming-Wei Chang, Kenton Lee, and Kristina Toutanova. 2019. Bert: Pre-training of deep bidirectional transformers for language understanding. In *Proceedings of NAACL-HLT 2019*, pages 4171–4186.

Bhuwan Dhingra, Manaal Faruqui, Ankur Parikh, Ming-Wei Chang, Dipanjan Das, and William Cohen. 2019. Handling divergent reference texts when evaluating table-to-text generation. In *Proceedings of the 57th Annual Meeting of the Association for Computational Linguistics*, pages 4884–4895, Florence, Italy. Association for Computational Linguistics.

Esin Durmus, He He, and Mona Diab. 2020. Feqa: A question answering evaluation framework for faithfulness assessment in abstractive summarization. In *Proceedings of the 58th Annual Meeting of the Association for Computational Linguistics*, pages 5055–5070.

Alexander R. Fabbri, Wojciech Kryściński, Bryan McCann, Caiming Xiong, Richard Socher, and Dragomir Radev. 2021. SummEval: Re-evaluating summarization evaluation. *Transactions of the Association for Computational Linguistics*, 9:391–409.

Tobias Falke, Leonardo FR Ribeiro, Prasetya Ajie Utama, Ido Dagan, and Iryna Gurevych. 2019. Ranking generated summaries by correctness: An interesting but challenging application for natural language inference. In *Proceedings of the 57th Annual Meeting of the Association for Computational Linguistics*, pages 2214–2220.

Katja Filippova. 2020. Controlled hallucinations: Learning to generate faithfully from noisy data. In *Findings of the Association for Computational Linguistics: EMNLP 2020*, pages 864–870.

Tanya Goyal and Greg Durrett. 2020. Evaluating factuality in generation with dependency-level entailment. In *Findings of the Association for Computational Linguistics: EMNLP 2020*, pages 3592–3603.

Tanya Goyal and Greg Durrett. 2021. Annotating and modeling fine-grained factuality in summarization. In *Proceedings of the 2021 Conference of the North American Chapter of the Association for Computational Linguistics: Human Language Technologies*, pages 1449–1462.

Max Grusky, Mor Naaman, and Yoav Artzi. 2018. Newsroom: A dataset of 1.3 million summaries with diverse extractive strategies. In *Proceedings of the 2018 Conference of the North American Chapter of the Association for Computational Linguistics: Human Language Technologies, Volume 1 (Long Papers)*, pages 708–719, New Orleans, Louisiana. Association for Computational Linguistics.

Karl Moritz Hermann, Tomas Kocisky, Edward Grefenstette, Lasse Espeholt, Will Kay, Mustafa Suleyman, and Phil Blunsom. 2015. Teaching machines to read and comprehend. In *Advances in Neural Information Processing Systems*, pages 1693–1701.

Sarthak Jain and Byron C. Wallace. 2019. Attention is not Explanation. In *Proceedings of the 2019 Conference of the North American Chapter of the Association for Computational Linguistics: Human Language Technologies, Volume 1 (Long and Short Papers)*, pages 3543–3556, Minneapolis, Minnesota. Association for Computational Linguistics.

Wojciech Kryscinski, Nitish Shirish Keskar, Bryan McCann, Caiming Xiong, and Richard Socher. 2019. Neural text summarization: A critical evaluation. In *Proceedings of the 2019 Conference on Empirical Methods in Natural Language Processing and the 9th International Joint Conference on Natural Language Processing (EMNLP-IJCNLP)*, pages 540–551, Hong Kong, China. Association for Computational Linguistics.

Wojciech Kryściński, Bryan McCann, Caiming Xiong, and Richard Socher. 2020. Evaluating the factual consistency of abstractive text summarization. In *Proceedings of the 2020 Conference on Empirical Methods in Natural Language Processing (EMNLP)*, pages 9332–9346.

Faisal Ladhak, Esin Durmus, He He, Claire Cardie, and Kathleen Mckeown. 2022. Faithful or extractive? on mitigating the faithfulness-abstractiveness trade-off in abstractive summarization. In *Proceedings of the 60th Annual Meeting of the Association for Computational Linguistics (Volume 1: Long Papers)*, pages 1410–1421.

Mike Lewis, Yinhan Liu, Naman Goyal, Marjan Ghazvininejad, Abdelrahman Mohamed, Omer Levy, Veselin Stoyanov, and Luke Zettlemoyer. 2020. Bart: Denoising sequence-to-sequence pre-training for natural language generation, translation, and comprehension. In *Proceedings of the 58th Annual Meeting of the Association for Computational Linguistics*, pages 7871–7880.

Yang Liu and Mirella Lapata. 2019. Text summarization with pretrained encoders. In *Proceedings of the 2019 Conference on Empirical Methods in Natural Language Processing*.

Joshua Maynez, Shashi Narayan, Bernd Bohnet, and Ryan McDonald. 2020. On faithfulness and factuality in abstractive summarization. In *Proceedings of the 58th Annual Meeting of the Association for Computational Linguistics*, pages 1906–1919.

Clara Meister, Ryan Cotterell, and Tim Vieira. 2020. If beam search is the answer, what was the question? In *Proceedings of the 2020 Conference on Empirical Methods in Natural Language Processing (EMNLP)*, pages 2173–2185, Online. Association for Computational Linguistics.

Shashi Narayan, Shay B Cohen, and Mirella Lapata. 2018. Don't give me the details, just the summary! topic-aware convolutional neural networks for extreme summarization. In *Proceedings of the 2018 Conference on Empirical Methods in Natural Language Processing*, pages 1797–1807.

Shashi Narayan, Yao Zhao, Joshua Maynez, Gonçalo Simões, Vitaly Nikolaev, and Ryan McDonald. 2021. Planning with learned entity prompts for abstractive summarization. *Transactions of the Association for Computational Linguistics*, 9:1475–1492.

Artidoro Pagnoni, Vidhisha Balachandran, and Yulia Tsvetkov. 2021. Understanding factuality in abstractive summarization with frank: A benchmark for factuality metrics. In *Proceedings of the 2021 Conference of the North American Chapter of the Association for Computational Linguistics: Human Language Technologies*, pages 4812–4829.

Thomas Scialom, Paul-Alexis Dray, Sylvain Lamprier, Benjamin Piwowarski, Jacopo Staiano, Alex Wang, and Patrick Gallinari. 2021. Questeval: Summarization asks for fact-based evaluation. In *Proceedings of the 2021 Conference on Empirical Methods in Natural Language Processing*, pages 6594–6604.

Ashish Vaswani, Noam Shazeer, Niki Parmar, Jakob Uszkoreit, Llion Jones, Aidan N Gomez, Łukasz Kaiser, and Illia Polosukhin. 2017. Attention is all you need. In *Advances in neural information processing systems*, pages 5998–6008.

Alex Wang, Kyunghyun Cho, and Mike Lewis. 2020. Asking and answering questions to evaluate the factual consistency of summaries. In *Proceedings of the 58th Annual Meeting of the Association for Computational Linguistics*, pages 5008–5020.

Sarah Wiegreffe and Yuval Pinter. 2019. Attention is not not explanation. In *Proceedings of the 2019 Conference on Empirical Methods in Natural Language Processing and the 9th International Joint Conference on Natural Language Processing (EMNLP-IJCNLP)*, pages 11–20, Hong Kong, China. Association for Computational Linguistics.

Sam Wiseman, Stuart Shieber, and Alexander Rush. 2017. Challenges in data-to-document generation. In *Proceedings of the 2017 Conference on Empirical Methods in Natural Language Processing*, pages 2253–2263, Copenhagen, Denmark. Association for Computational Linguistics.

Thomas Wolf, Lysandre Debut, Victor Sanh, Julien Chaumond, Clement Delangue, Anthony Moi, Pierric Cistac, Tim Rault, Remi Louf, Morgan Funtowicz, Joe Davison, Sam Shleifer, Patrick von Platen, Clara Ma, Yacine Jernite, Julien Plu, Canwen Xu, Teven Le Scao, Sylvain Gugger, Mariama Drame, Quentin Lhoest, and Alexander Rush. 2020. Transformers: State-of-the-art natural language processing. In *Proceedings of the 2020 Conference on Empirical Methods in Natural Language Processing: System Demonstrations*, pages 38–45, Online. Association for Computational Linguistics.

Jingqing Zhang, Yao Zhao, Mohammed Saleh, and Peter J. Liu. 2020. PEGASUS: Pre-training with extracted gap-sentences for abstractive summarization. In *Proceedings of the 37th International Conference on Machine Learning*.

Chunting Zhou, Graham Neubig, Jiatao Gu, Mona Diab, Francisco Guzmán, Luke Zettlemoyer, and Marjan Ghazvininejad. 2021. Detecting hallucinated content in conditional neural sequence generation. In *Findings of the Association for Computational Linguistics: ACL-IJCNLP 2021*, pages 1393–1404, Online. Association for Computational Linguistics.

A ROC Results

Figures 8 and 9 show the ROC curves on the FRANK and TLHD-CNNDM datasets. There is a large label imbalance in both datasets, with the positive class only making up 0.4% of FRANK's labels, and 14.2% of those in the TLHD-CNNDM dataset. This has to be considered when looking at these figures.

BART-GBP performs best on both datasets and label subsets, except for intrinsic hallucinations in the TLHD-CNNDM dataset in Figure 9c, where DAE and Lexical-1 perform better.

One thing that is easily visible from the ROC curves is the fraction of positive labels that can be discovered by a detection method. When a curve flattens out, it is no longer able to find more hallucinations without labeling all tokens as positive. This further highlights the strengths of the token-level methods BART-GBP and Lexical-n.

B Hallucination Examples

We present two examples of hallucinations, one of intrinsic hallucination from the FRANK dataset, and one of extrinsic hallucination from the TLHD-CNNDM dataset. In the former example, Mike Tyson's mansion is now in a gaudy, abandoned state, but was not while he still lived in it. In the latter example, the name of the stadium (Old Trafford) is never mentioned in the article, so it is an extrinsic hallucination. As an aside, factuality cannot be determined, since the article only talks about a "meeting" of the two teams and does not mention the home team.

Intrinsic hallucination from FRANK.
Article: (CNN)A trip to a former heavyweight champ's gaudy, abandoned mansion. The tallest

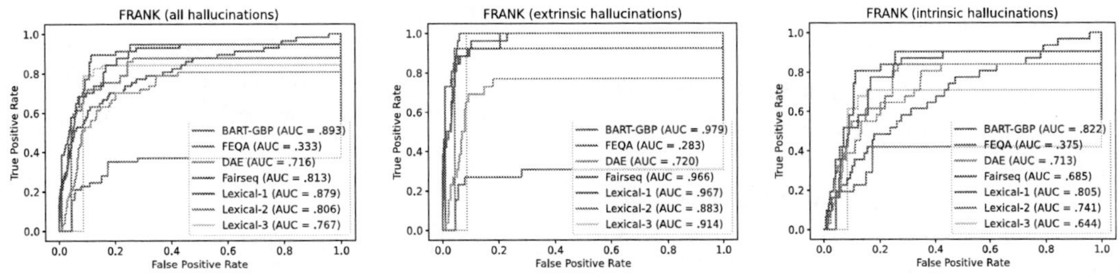

(a) All hallucinations (b) Extrinsic hallucinations (c) Intrinsic hallucinations

Figure 8: ROC curves for hallucinations in the FRANK dataset.

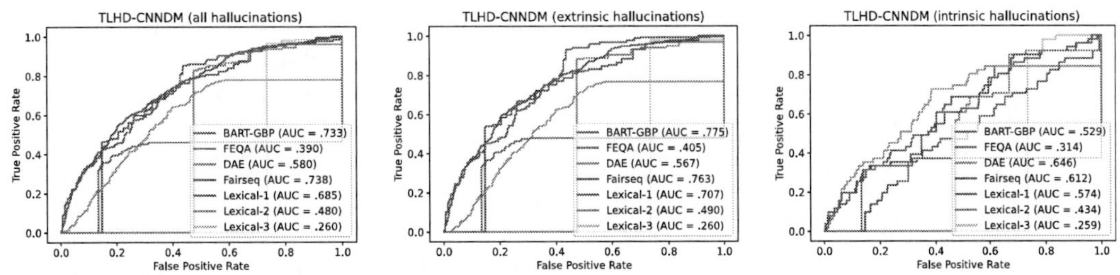

(a) All hallucinations (b) Extrinsic hallucinations (c) Intrinsic hallucinations

Figure 9: ROC curves for hallucinations in the TLHD-CNNDM dataset.

and fastest "giga-coaster" in the world. A dramatic interview with a famed spiritual leader – and the tearful reaction by one of his former students. These are some of the best videos of the week: In the 1980s and '90s – before he moved to Vegas and started keeping tigers as pets – former heavyweight boxer Mike Tyson lived in a Southington, Ohio, mansion. The home featured an indoor swimming pool, a marble-and-gold Jacuzzi (with mirrored ceiling, naturally) and an entertainment room large enough for small concerts. Tyson sold the house in 1999; it's due to become, of all things, a church. The video can be seen at the top of this story. Not a fan of roller coasters? You may want to skip the next video – but for the rest of us, the thrill of watching is the next best thing to being there. The Fury 325 can be found at Carowinds amusement part in Charlotte, North Carolina. Watch the video: In a CNN exclusive, Alisyn Camerota looked into allegations that Bikram yoga creator Bikram Choudhury sexually assaulted six former students. "He's a person who's based a lot of truths on a lot of lies," said Sarah Baughn, who alleges that Choudhury sexually assaulted her. Watch the video: CNN's Karl Penhaul spoke to a shepherd who witnessed the final seconds of Germanwings Flight 9525, which crashed in the French Alps last week. "I saw the plane heading down along the valley and I said, 'My God, it's going to hit the mountain,' " Jean Varrieras told Penhaul. "I ducked my head. ... Then after that, I saw the smoke." Watch the video: Magician and comedian Penn Jillette was part of a panel speaking to CNN's Don Lemon about the controversial Indiana religious freedom law. Jillette, an avowed atheist and libertarian, noted "we are not talking about forcing people to engage in gay sex, or even endorse gay sex." His provocative opening led to an energetic back-and-forth with the Alliance Defending Freedom's Kristen Waggoner and the ACLU's Rita Sklar. Watch the video: A professor of physics at a British university asked 100 people to create a composite with facial features they thought were beautiful – and then asked another 100 to rate their attractiveness. You'll never guess what celebrities best fit the model. Watch the video:

BART summary: Former heavyweight champ Mike Tyson lived in a gaudy, abandoned mansion in Ohio. CNN's Karl Penhaul spoke to a shepherd who witnessed the final seconds of Germanwings Flight 9525. Penn Jillette was part of a panel speaking to CNN's Don Lemon about the controversial Indiana religious freedom law.

Intrinsic hallucinations: gaudy, abandoned

Extrinsic hallucination from TLHD-CNNDM.
Article: Gareth Barry has advised his Everton team-mate Ross Barkley against moving to Manchester City at this young stage of his career. Barry speaks from experience having spent four seasons at the Etihad before arriving on Merseyside and the veteran midfielder believes it is still too early for the 21-year-old to decide on his future. Ahead of the Toffees meeting with Manchester United on Sunday, Barry told the Mirror: 'Personally, I think he's still too young to make that move. Ross Barkley's rise to stardom has seen him repeatedly linked with Premier League champions Man City . Everton team-mate Gareth Barry has advised the youngster not to leave Goodison too soon . 'He's still learning the game. He's got the right manager here to push him to the next level. 'As soon as he reaches that next level, then there's another decision to be made. At the moment, I think it's too early.' And asked if considered the Premier League champions to be a graveyard for young talent, Barry added: 'I think so, yeah.' Barkley has overcome his early season struggles to play an influential role in Everton's recent revival and Barry believes the youngster he mentors daily can achieve anything he wants in the game. The 21-year-old signs autographs for fans after coming through a difficult start to the season . Veteran midfielder Barry spent four seasons at City before being found surplus to requirements . 'I sit next to him in the changing room at the training ground. I speak to Ross quite often,' said Barry. 'You feel sorry for him sometimes because the expectation is getting thrown on to his shoulders – people are expecting of him, week in, week out, goals and assists. 'That hasn't happened, but at the same time he's still improving as a player and growing in maturity. 'His ability and his strengths are there for everyone to see, he can go on and be a top top player.'
BART summary: Ross Barkley has been linked with a move to Manchester City. Everton team-mate Gareth Barry believes it is too early for the 21-year-old to leave Goodison Park. Barry spent four seasons at the Etihad before arriving on Merseyside. Everton face Manchester United at Old Trafford on Sunday.
Extrinsic hallucinations: at Old Trafford

C Human Annotation Details

Our human annotation was performed with 3 sets of 3 annotators, each annotating 50 examples. The full instructions are given below, together with an example of how the human annotation task looks.

Hallucination detection

This study evaluates hallucinations in automatic summarization models. A hallucination is information that is not directly supported by the article that the model has to summarize.
Main question: Can the summary sentence in question be inferred directly from the article?
There are two types of hallucinations: intrinsic and extrinsic hallucinations. They are defined as follows (from Maynez et al., 2020):
Intrinsic hallucination: Combination of information from the article that does not follow from it
Extrinsic hallucination: Information not present in the article
Not a hallucination: Paraphrases, or information directly inferred from the article
Importantly, this is not a question of whether the summary is true or false, just whether it faithfully represents the information in the article.

The goal in this study is to annotate a summary sentence with intrinsic and extrinsic hallucinations, by copying the words that cannot be inferred from reading the article. Here's an example (the part in red is the annotation that you will do [your annotations can stay black]):
Example annotation
Article: Manchester City was defeated by Crystal Palace 2-1 at the Etihad Stadium on Sunday. Glenn Murray and Jason Puncheon scored the goals for Palace, while Yaya Toure was the only scorer for City. City's best striker Sergio Aguero was left on the bench for yet another game. The result is especially shocking when comparing the squad's total transfer fees: £40m pounds for Crystal Palace vs. £500m for Manchester City.
Full summary: Crystal Palace beat Manchester City 2-1 on Saturday. Yaya Toure was left on the bench, and Crystal Palace have spent £40m on transfer fees so far this season.
Sentence in question: Yaya Toure was left on the bench, and Crystal Palace have spent £40m on transfer fees so far this season.
Intrinsic hallucinations: Yaya Toure
Extrinsic hallucinations: so far this season
Explanation: It was Sergio Aguero that was left

on the bench, not Yaya Toure (since he scored a goal, we know that he was playing). We're looking for a hallucination that is as small as possible, that's why we didn't mark "Yaya Toure was left on the bench", or "was left on the bench". For the extrinsic hallucination, there is no mentioning that the spending was for this season only. There is also a mistake in the first sentence of the summary (Saturday vs. Sunday in the article), but this is not the sentence in question, so we ignore it.

Notes

- If there are no hallucinations, leave the line blank.
- If there are multiple hallucinations in the sentence, separate them with a comma.
- Sometimes a sentence is not complete, or there are multiple sentences in one, but a period is missing to separate them. Just treat the "sentence in question" as if it were a single sentence. (These are artifacts of sentence splitting/the training data, which we do not evaluate here.)
- The examples below have a visual help: Text overlaps of more than two words between the sentence and the article are written in **bold** and numbered at the end, like this: [1]. This is just a help for you to find information faster, and does not mean the model copied the parts from there. Example: **Article: This year's harvest was**[1] especially rich **on apples.**[2] **Sentence: This year's harvest was**[1] high **on apples.**[2]
- Hint: Read the sentence in question first, and then look for the relevant information in the article.

A Corpus and Evaluation for Predicting Semi-Structured Human Annotations

Andreas Marfurt[1,2,*], **Ashley Thornton**[3], **David Sylvan**[3], **Lonneke van der Plas**[1,4], and **James Henderson**[1]

[1]Idiap Research Institute, Switzerland
[2]EPFL, Switzerland
[3]Graduate Institute of International and Development Studies, Switzerland
[4]University of Malta, Malta

Abstract

A wide variety of tasks have been framed as text-to-text tasks to allow processing by sequence-to-sequence models. We propose a new task of generating a semi-structured interpretation of a source document. The interpretation is semi-structured in that it contains mandatory and optional fields with free-text information. This structure is surfaced by human annotations, which we standardize and convert to text format. We then propose an evaluation technique that is generally applicable to any such semi-structured annotation, called equivalence classes evaluation. The evaluation technique is efficient and scalable; it creates a large number of evaluation instances from a comparably cheap clustering of the free-text information by domain experts. For our task, we release a dataset about the monetary policy of the Federal Reserve. On this corpus, our evaluation shows larger differences between pretrained models than standard text generation metrics.

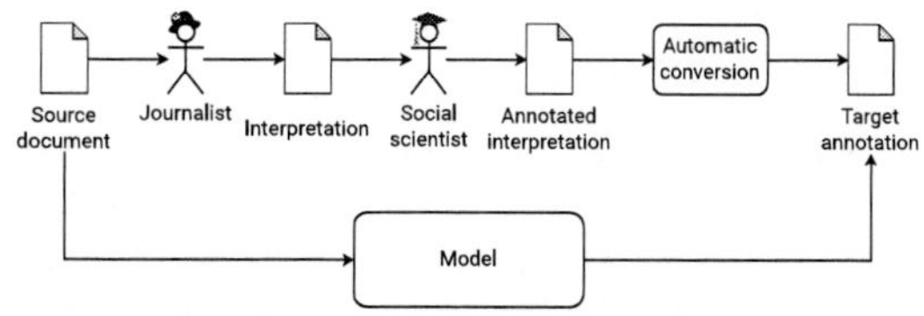

Figure 1: Our proposed interpretation task. A journalist creates an interpretation of a source document. A social scientist extracts and categorizes the relevant parts of the interpretation by means of annotation, which is converted into text-only format. The model learns the interpretation process by directly predicting the target annotation from the source document.

1 Introduction

General-purpose sequence-to-sequence models have achieved impressive results on conditional text generation (Radford et al., 2019; Brown et al., 2020), machine translation (Liu et al., 2020; Xue et al., 2021), and text summarization (Lewis et al., 2020; Zhang et al., 2020a). This has lead to their application to ever more tasks; as long as the task can be formalized in a text-to-text format, it can be processed by these models (Raffel et al., 2020).

We apply sequence-to-sequence models in a different setting: documents interpreting other documents. This phenomenon is pervasive in our daily lives, be it a critic reviewing a play or book, a website presenting highlights of a travel guide, or, as in this paper, a journalist writing an article about an organization's press release.

For social scientists, these reviews or articles present an interesting subject of study; they surface the author's interpretation of the original source document. With the tool of human annotations, domain experts can extract the core constituents and surface implicit information in these various interpretations to make them comparable.

In this paper, we train models to learn this interpretation process (see Figure 1).[1] We describe how human annotations can be standardized and converted into a text-only format to serve as semi-structured targets in this interpretation prediction task. We introduce the *FOMC* dataset, a corpus about the monetary policy of the Federal Reserve, the central bank of the United States of America. The dataset contains source documents of greatly varying length, containing policy announcements such as press releases or speeches. The target interpretations are short, and consist of selected sentences taken from New York Times articles, which are then annotated by domain experts. We also devise a scalable evaluation technique for semi-structured outputs, which we call *equivalence classes evaluation.* Domain experts cluster highlighted text spans from the human annotations into equivalence classes, signifying their semantic inter-

*Correspondence to andreas.marfurt@idiap.ch.

[1]Our data, code and finetuned models are available at https://github.com/idiap/semi-structured-annotations.

Proceedings of the 2nd Workshop on Natural Language Generation, Evaluation, and Metrics (GEM), pages 262 - 275
December 7, 2022 ©2022 Association for Computational Linguistics

changeability. A generative model is then probed with a prefix and either a true continuation from the data or a wrong continuation from a different equivalence class. If the model learned the process of interpretation well, it will give higher probability to the true continuation. From a single clustering, we can automatically generate a large number of evaluation instances by sampling negative text spans. We train Transformer (Vaswani et al., 2017) sequence-to-sequence models with varying levels of pretraining on the FOMC dataset, and find that BART (Lewis et al., 2020) performs well on our equivalence classes evaluation and standard text generation evaluation metrics.

Our contributions are: 1) We introduce a new dataset on document interpretation, with semi-structured annotations and documents on the monetary policy of the Federal Reserve. 2) We introduce a method to convert these annotations into text format and apply generative text models. 3) We devise a scalable technique to evaluate models on the task of generating semi-structured outputs, by efficiently utilizing domain experts' grouping of text spans into equivalence classes. 4) We perform an evaluation with our technique, and showcase its flexibility with an in-depth error analysis.

2 Semi-Structured Human Annotations

We consider a setting where a long text is interpreted in a few sentences. The interpretation may select an aspect of the source text to focus on, and it may be opinionated. Each sentence is annotated by domain experts to surface and structure the important information.

2.1 Standardizing Human Annotations

We aim to standardize the human annotations into a general but flexible semi-structured format which should make it possible for NLP models to process them. In order to do so, we first have to define the possible annotation operations.

Our annotations are created from two operations: 1) marking spans with a label in order to categorize them, and 2) optionally commenting on a marked span to give context, paraphrase or make implicit information explicit.

2.2 Converting Annotations to Text

We convert annotations into a text-only format by inserting category-specific start and end tokens for each marked span. Overlapping or fully contained spans are allowed. We include the comments by adding them in parentheses (imitating a similar use in natural language) at the end of the respective marked span and before the category end token. An example annotation transformed to text format is shown in Figure 2.

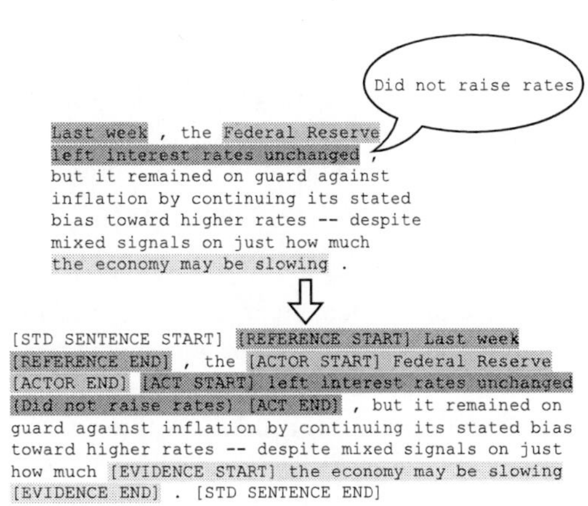

Figure 2: Example of the automatic conversion of an annotated interpretation into text format.

2.3 The Interpretation Task

We propose the task of generating the interpretations, including the human annotations, from the source documents. This task can be formalized as a sequence-to-sequence generation task, with pairs of a single source document x_i and one or more target annotations y_{ij} in text format, with $1 \leq j \leq m_i$. The multiple target annotations are equivalent to multiple references in traditional text generation tasks, i.e. they are all equally valid solutions to the task. In total, there are n source documents and $m = \sum_{i=1}^{n} m_i$ targets.

The targets y_{ij} contain marked spans of categories c from a predefined set of categories C. Some categories occur in every target, and some are optional, as illustrated in the paragraph *Annotation Categories* below.

2.4 The FOMC Dataset

We now present our dataset constructed according to the guidelines above. The source documents and targets were selected and annotated by domain experts. They are on the topic of the monetary policy of the Federal Open Market Committee (FOMC) of the Federal Reserve, the central bank of the United States of America, in the years from 1967 to 2018. The source documents are policy announcements of the FOMC such as press releases, speeches, testimonies, Q&A sessions, or meeting minutes. The targets are sentences from news articles of the New York Times which conform to the requirements (see *Annotation Categories* below). An example is shown in Appendix D.

Data collection. Domain experts[2] searched the New York Times archives for articles on the monetary policy of the Federal Reserve. Candidate articles were searched for sentences that contain all mandatory categories described below. If a sentence is found, it is annotated by highlighting the categories and adding comments. All annotations are validated by a senior domain expert[3]. Sentences from the same article referencing the same source document are collected in a single target annotation. If multiple articles reference the same source document, one target annotation is created per article.

Annotation Categories. A selected sentence is called a *standardized sentence* in the corpus terminology. The mandatory and optional categories, as well as their purpose, are listed below:

- **Standardized sentence:** Mandatory. Marks the start and end of a target sentence.
- **Act:** Mandatory. Most often contains a comment. Marks an action (or non-action) on monetary policy. Example: "left interest rates unchanged (Did not raise rates)".
- **Actor:** Mandatory. Marks the entity performing the act. By design, this is exclusively the Federal Reserve or FOMC. Example: "Fed".
- **Reference:** Mandatory. Provides a link to the source document, which can be opaque in the article, e.g. saying that something happened yesterday. That source is systematically tracked down by the domain experts. Example: "yesterday's meeting".
- **Attribution:** Optional. Marks the individual advocating for the Federal Reserve to perform a certain action. Example: "Greenspan".
- **Motive:** Optional. Can appear multiple times. States the goal of an act. Example: "to fight inflation".

[2]PhD students in economics and political science at the Graduate Institute

[3]Ashley Thornton and David Sylvan

	Train	Valid	Test
Source documents	1342	167	169
Target annotations	3246	364	380
Mean targets/source	2.42	2.18	2.25
Max targets/source	36	17	16

Table 1: Number of examples in each split in the FOMC dataset.

Count	Source documents	Targets
(Std) Sentences	262.6 ($\pm$ 688.6)	1.6
Words	6054.1 ($\pm$ 12639.4)	123.6
Start/end tokens	-	18.2
Total tokens	6054.1 ($\pm$ 12639.4)	141.8

Table 2: Mean length of source documents and target annotations in the FOMC dataset.

- **Evidence:** Optional. Can appear multiple times. States an observation, e.g. about the current economic state, that served as an incentive for the act. Example: "high oil prices".
- **Scope:** Optional. Marks the temporal scope of an act. Example: "by the end of the year".

Dataset statistics. We now show dataset statistics. First, the number of examples in each split (80%/10%/10% for train/validation/test) is presented in Table 1. Second, the number of tokens in source and target texts is shown in Table 2.

Filtering source documents. As is evident from Table 2, the source documents are generally very long. In contrast, the maximum number of input tokens that state-of-the-art models are pretrained on, lies between 512 in BERT (Devlin et al., 2019) and 1024 in BART (Lewis et al., 2020). This limitation is due to the quadratic complexity of self-attention in the Transformer architecture (Vaswani et al., 2017) and its resulting strain on computational resources.

As a consequence, there are two ways to define the prediction task for the FOMC dataset. The first one is to condition on the full text document, but devise models capable of handling very long inputs, such as adding a filtering module (used below) or using appropriate architectures such as the Longformer (Beltagy et al., 2020). The second option is to condition on a specific filtering of the source documents which reduces them to a length that can be processed by the chosen model. Alongside the data, we provide a script that allows for selecting sentences from the source document,

```
Evaluation: Act type
Category: Act
Equivalence class 1:
  - left interest rates
    unchanged (Did not
    raise rates)
Equivalence class 2:
  - decided to raise interest
    rates (Did raise rates)
  - voted to raise rates (Did
    raise rates)
Equivalence class 3:
  - lowered interest rates a
    quarter point (Cut rates)
```

Figure 3: Definition of an evaluation with its equivalence classes.

while satisfying the length restriction for a given tokenizer from the HuggingFace transformers library (Wolf et al., 2020). The selection logic can be set to either pick sentences from the top of the source document (*Lead* strategy), or to use an oracle that greedily picks sentences that maximize the length-normalized ROUGE-2 recall gain (*Oracle* strategy).

3 Equivalence Classes Evaluation

To evaluate a model on predicting the marked spans of individual annotation categories, we propose the *equivalence classes evaluation* as an efficient way of generating evaluation instances from domain experts' knowledge.

3.1 Definition

An evaluation selects a category c that it wants to evaluate, which in turn consists of 2 or more equivalence classes. The members of an equivalence class are marked spans of category c in the dataset. Members of the same equivalence class are semantically interchangeable in the target annotation, with respect to the objective of the evaluation. The members of all equivalence classes must be syntactically interchangeable, such that replacing one for the other still results in a grammatically correct sentence. An example is given in Figure 3.

3.2 Creating Evaluation Instances

Evaluation instances are then created by searching target annotations in the validation/test set for a member of an equivalence class. If one is found, an evaluation instance is created consisting of 1) the prefix y_{prefix} up until the selected span, 2) the selected span $a^{(\text{pos})}$ as the true (positive) continuation, and 3) a randomly selected span $a^{(\text{neg})}$ from a different equivalence class as the false (negative) continuation. $a^{(\text{neg})}$ is chosen by uniformly sampling a negative equivalence class, and then uniformly sampling one of its members. An example is shown in Figure 4, where $a^{(\text{pos})}$ is in equivalence class 1 of the example evaluation in Figure 3, and $a^{(\text{neg})}$ has been sampled as the first member of equivalence class 2. Any other member of equivalence classes 2 or 3 could have been chosen as well.

y_{prefix}	`[REFERENCE START] Last week [REFERENCE END] , the [ACTOR START] Federal Reserve [ACTOR END] [ACT START]`
$a^{(\text{pos})}$	`left interest rates unchanged (Did not raise rates)`
$a^{(\text{neg})}$	`decided to raise interest rates (Did raise rates)`

Figure 4: Equivalence classes evaluation instance with prefix y_{prefix}, a positive continuation $a^{(\text{pos})}$ and a negative continuation $a^{(\text{neg})}$.

For a single match of a positive span in the evaluation set, one can create a large number of evaluation instances by sampling negative continuations without replacement.

Optionally, the positive span $a^{(\text{pos})}$ can be replaced by a different member of the same equivalence class (for equivalence classes with more than one member). This can help mitigating lexical inaccuracies that can arise from replacing a span with another, which otherwise only exist for $a^{(\text{neg})}$.

Relation to Pattern-Exploiting Training. In Schick and Schütze (2021a), Pattern-Exploiting Training (PET) is introduced. The concept of verbalizers is similar to equivalence classes. In their work, verbalizers are manually predefined single tokens that represent a class label.[4] Our equivalence classes consist of expert-selected multi-word spans from the data, that each represent the concept of their equivalence class. Equivalence classes are multi-faceted: They determine both a semantic concept and a grammatical structure, and are always defined with respect to a certain aspect under evaluation.

3.3 Model Evaluation

To evaluate the generative model, we obtain the probability p_θ it assigns to $a^{(\text{pos})}$ and $a^{(\text{neg})}$ by getting its next-token probabilities given the prefix y_{prefix}. We apply teacher-forcing and obtain the

[4]In their follow-up work, they extend verbalizers to multiple tokens (Schick and Schütze, 2021b).

probabilities autoregressively, extending the prefix with the previous token at each turn. The probability of the entire span is computed as

$$p_\theta(a) = \prod_{i=1}^{l} p_\theta(a_i | y_{\text{prefix}}, a_{<i}) \quad (1)$$

where $a \in \{a^{(\text{pos})}, a^{(\text{neg})}\}$, and l is the length of a. The model solves an instance correctly if $p_\theta(a^{(\text{pos})}) > p_\theta(a^{(\text{neg})})$.

If the lengths of $a^{(\text{pos})}$ and $a^{(\text{neg})}$ are substantially different, the value of p_θ could be determined more by the difference in length than in semantics. We avoid this during sampling of $a^{(\text{neg})}$ by restricting the maximum difference in number of words between $a^{(\text{neg})}$ and $a^{(\text{pos})}$ to 2.

3.4 In-Depth Analysis

The equivalence classes evaluation also allows for an in-depth error analysis. First, we can test specific properties for a category, such as how well the model handles negation in acts. Second, we can break down an evaluation's score by combinations of equivalence classes, and identify the hardest combinations for the model. We show examples of such analyses in Section 5.3.

Data augmentation. As an added benefit, equivalence classes give rise to a simple training data augmentation method. We create additional training examples from equivalence classes by exchanging the ground-truth highlighted span with a different one from the same equivalence class. We postpone testing the efficacy of this data augmentation method to future work.

4 Experiments

In our experiments, we use the FOMC dataset described in Section 2.4.

4.1 Equivalence Classes

The equivalence classes for our evaluations were proposed by one of the authors[5] and validated by the same senior domain experts as for the FOMC dataset described in Section 2.4. We create an evaluation for each of the following 5 categories: act, attribution, motive, evidence, and scope. We add one evaluation for the act comments, without the act itself. Furthermore, we create additional in-depth evaluation examples for modal verbs and negation, which our domain experts are especially interested in. We create separate evaluations for modal verbs in positive (e.g. *should*) and in negative formulation (e.g. *might not*), to avoid confounding with the effect of negation. These 3 evaluations (positive modal verbs, negative modal verbs, negation) are created for acts without comments, act comments, and acts concatenated with comments.

One evaluation instance is created for each example in the evaluation set that contains any member of the evaluation's equivalence classes. If the evaluation instances n have not reached 100 yet, $\lfloor \frac{100}{n} \rfloor$ negative spans $a^{(\text{neg})}$ are sampled per instance, such that the total number is close to 100. If more than 100 matches are found, all of them are included in the evaluation with one randomly sampled negative span. We do not replace positive spans. This procedure generates 1974 total evaluation instances from the validation set, and 2104 from the test set. The general evaluations of the 5 categories plus the act comments (excluding in-depth evaluations) contain 818 evaluation instances from the validation set, and 886 from the test set. The smallest category (motive) has 74 and the largest (act labels) has 336 test evaluation instances.

4.2 Standard Text Generation Metrics

Since our task is a sequence-to-sequence task, we also report standard text generation metrics. If not mentioned otherwise, we compute the following metrics for generated annotations without special tokens (category start and end tokens).

ROUGE. ROUGE (Lin, 2004) is a textual overlap metric which is widely used in text summarization, a task with strong connections to ours. As is common in summarization, we report ROUGE-1/2/L as the unigram and bigram overlap, and the longest common subsequence, respectively. We compute ROUGE with and without special tokens, as we want to see both how well the model generates the annotations as well as the original article.

BERTScore. We use BERTScore (Zhang et al., 2020b) as a semantic similarity metric between the generated and reference target annotations. We do not use idf-importance weighting, and we use baseline rescaling.[6] If multiple target annotations are present, the maximum similarity is reported, as proposed by the authors.

[5] Andreas Marfurt

[6] Evaluation hash: `roberta-large_L17_no-idf_version=0.3.11(hug_trans=4.6.1)-rescaled`

Distinct bigrams. We report the distinct bigrams in the generated target annotations. This metric checks if the model produces overly generic and repetitive outputs. A higher number of distinct bigrams corresponds to higher lexical diversity in the output and is desirable.

Novel bigrams. Novel bigrams measure the percent of bigrams in a generated annotation that do not appear in the filtered source document that serves as input text. This metric measures the extractiveness of the model, i.e. its tendency to copy text from the input.

4.2.1 Annotation Category Metrics

We add annotation category-specific metrics to the text generation metrics. These metrics are designed to detect if any category or the target format are ignored by the model.

Category counts. We report the mean and standard deviation of each annotation category's occurrence over the generated target annotations.

Categories correctly closed. This evaluation measures the percent of annotation spans that are correctly encompassed by a category start and end token. This evaluation shows whether the decoder correctly learned to generate in the target format.

4.3 Filtering Source Documents

As detailed in Section 2.4, the source documents are much longer than current Transformer models with quadratic self-attention complexity can process. However, we conjecture that only very specific parts of these documents are needed to generate the comparably very short target annotations (see Table 2). On top of mentioned filtering strategies, we train a filtering model. For this purpose, we finetune a BERT model (Devlin et al., 2019) for sequence classification.[7] We split long inputs at sentence boundaries into chunks of at most 512 tokens, and then predict whether to keep the sentences in the current chunk.

We train the model with a cross-entropy loss between the predictions and the oracle selection described in Section 2.4. We train with a batch size of 5 for 10 epochs, but stop early when the F1 score on the validation set no longer improves. We use the same learning rate schedule as for the generative models described below, with a maximum learning rate of 1e-3. During inference, we select the sentences with the highest logits until we reach the token limit. The selected sentences are concatenated in the order in which they appear in the source document. We name this filtering model *FilterBERT*.

4.4 Generative Models

For our generative models, we rely on the Transformer architecture (Vaswani et al., 2017), and compare finetuning differently pretrained models.

Transformer. We use a randomly initialized Transformer encoder-decoder to test the effect of skipping pretraining. Our implementation of the Transformer is the same as the BERT model below.

BERT. We finetune a pretrained BERT encoder (Devlin et al., 2019) and train a randomly initialized Transformer decoder, as proposed in Liu and Lapata (2019). Unless otherwise mentioned, we use the base model size.

BART. We finetune the BART model (Lewis et al., 2020) as a proponent of a jointly pretrained encoder and decoder.

Training details. Training steps and learning rate hyperparameters were selected on the validation set with a grid search with exponential step sizes. We train our models for a maximum of 10 (Transformer/BERT) or 20 (BART) epochs, which corresponds to 8000 or 16000 steps with a batch size of 4, respectively. We stop training early if the validation loss does not improve any further. We set the maximum learning rate to 1e-4 for randomly initialized parameters, and 1e-5 for pretrained ones. Exceptionally for BART, we use a learning rate of 1e-6 for the tied input/output embeddings. We warm up the learning rate for a tenth of the total epochs, with a linear increase from 1/100-th of the maximum learning rate, and then a linear decay back down to the starting point. We use the Adam optimizer (Kingma and Ba, 2015).

Generation details. For our evaluation of text generation metrics (see Section 4.2), we generate text with beam search. We use 5 beams, a minimum generation length of 50 tokens and a maximum of 500, no length penalty, and no n-gram blocking (Paulus et al., 2018).

[7] We use the standard implementation in the HuggingFace transformers library (Wolf et al., 2020).

Model	Act	Act comments	Attribution	Motive	Evidence	Scope	Mean
Transformer	93.18%	93.45%	94.79%	66.22%	43.68%	50.00%	73.55%
BERT	97.73%	94.64%	97.16%	66.22%	45.98%	54.44%	76.03%
BART	98.86%	96.13%	97.16%	71.62%	81.61%	80.00%	87.56%

Table 3: Accuracy of main equivalence classes evaluations.

Model	ROUGE-1	ROUGE-2	ROUGE-L	BERTScore	Distinct bigrams	Novel bigrams
References	-	-	-	-	9961	82.68%
Transformer	31.89	10.27	25.06	0.72	214	87.61%
BERT	41.09	18.31	31.63	19.00	965	82.75%
BART	42.73	20.64	33.08	26.78	3011	73.62%

Table 4: Text generation evaluation results. ROUGE is computed on targets including special tokens.

5 Results

5.1 Equivalence Classes Evaluation

Our main results for the general equivalence classes evaluations on the 5 categories plus act comments are shown in Table 3. The BART model with a jointly pretrained encoder and decoder substantially outperforms the Transformer and BERT models. The act, act comments and attribution evaluations are solved nearly perfectly, but the others are harder. For the evidence evaluation, Transformer and BERT perform substantially below the random baseline, which would achieve 50% in expectation. We analyze the case of the evidence evaluation further in Section 5.3.

5.2 Text Generation Metrics

We show the results of text generation metrics in Table 4. Again, BART outperforms the other models. The low scores in BERTScore and distinct bigrams (excluding special tokens) indicate that the Transformer fails to generate diverse and topical target annotation sentences. However, the comparably high ROUGE scores (including special tokens) show that it learns to generate the target format well, which is also supported by the last column of Table 5. BART generates the most diverse and topical target annotations, and is also the most extractive method, showing that it makes use of the input document.

In Table 5 in the appendix, we show the mean and standard deviation of each category's annotation counts for our three models. BERT produces outputs that stay closest to the number of category annotations of the reference target annotations. BART under-generates all categories, which can be partially explained by it not having learned to open and close category spans reliably. The combination of not having seen the format during pretraining and a lower decoder learning rate, which was helpful for the other tasks, explains why BART performs worse than the models with randomly initialized Transformer decoders.

5.3 In-Depth Analysis

Table 6 in the appendix shows a selection of equivalence classes evaluations where equivalence classes were built for a specific purpose. In our evaluations, these measure performance on act modal verbs (e.g. *raised rates* vs. *might raise rates*) and act negation, both aspects that are of high importance to our domain experts. We can see that negation is handled well by all models, and that modals are substantially harder for acts, but not for act comments (where the act is part of the prefix). Acts with comments (last column) do not necessarily make the task easier than acts without comments (second column).

We also perform a qualitative in-depth analysis of the evidence evaluation for the BART model. To that effect, we count the percentage of evaluation instances the model gets wrong for each pair of equivalence classes, which is shown in the confusion matrix in Figure 5. The number in each square corresponds to the number of mistakes in the evaluation. Some of the mistakes occur for the following pairs of equivalence classes, where $a^{(\text{pos})}$ is taken from the first, and $a^{(\text{neg})}$ from the second:

- deflation – low/declining inflation
- cooling housing market – tightening credit market (full example in Appendix E)
- high unemployment – high oil prices
- high unemployment – weak economic activity

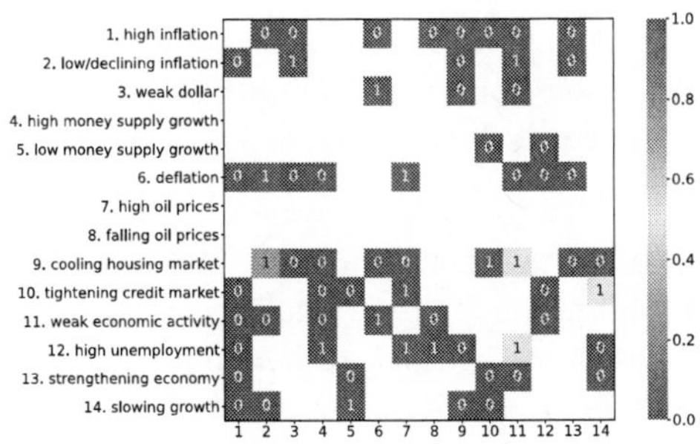

Figure 5: Confusion matrix of BART's accuracy on pairs of evidence equivalence classes. The equivalence class for $a^{(\text{pos})}$ is on the y-axis, the one for $a^{(\text{neg})}$ on the x-axis. Each cell contains the number of mistakes the model makes for that combination. Empty cells do not have a corresponding pair in the evaluation.

- slowing growth – low money supply growth

The mentioned combinations of economic processes are correlated or even co-occurring, making it difficult for the model to distinguish the positive from the negative span. In these cases of close semantic similarity, the model may fall back to ranking candidate text spans higher based on e.g. their frequency in the training data, where inflation is one of the dominant subjects. For other combinations, such as weak dollar – deflation, the model just makes mistakes.

5.4 Ablation Study

We perform ablation studies with respect to model size, filtering strategy and source document input length. The tables with the results have been moved to Appendix C.

Model sizes. In the results shown so far, BART has outperformed the Transformer and BERT. However, those models operate with 247 million parameters (size of BERT-base), while BART has 406 million. In Table 7, we see that increasing BERT's parameters to the size of BERT-large only provides small to no benefits. BART still outperforms BERT-large, even with almost half of the parameters, due to – as we believe – the beneficial initialization from joint encoder-decoder pretraining. This is especially valuable on the FOMC dataset, which has comparably few training instances.

Filtering strategies. In Section 4.3, we introduced the FilterBERT model for identifying and selecting salient sentences from long source documents. As stated in Section 2.4, together with the dataset, we make available a script for filtering source documents with either the Lead or the Oracle strategy. The former selects sentences from the top of the source document, the latter selects those that most increase the length-normalized ROUGE-2 recall with the target annotations. In Table 8, we see that Oracle filtering generally performs best on generation metrics, but not on equivalence classes. The FilterBERT model outperforms the Lead strategy for BART but not for generation metrics on BERT. In general, the differences between the generative models are much larger than between the filtering strategies.

Source document input length. Finally, since BART has the ability to process inputs of up to 1024 tokens in length, we evaluate how that compares to the input length of 512 tokens that we have used so far. The results in Table 9 show that for the Lead filtering strategy, longer inputs benefit all metrics except ROUGE-2. With Oracle filtering, ROUGE-2 and distinct bigram evaluations perform slightly worse with longer inputs, while the rest improve. In summary, the additional input sentences only make a small difference for BART.

6 Related Work

To the best of our knowledge, our setting, task, and evaluation have not been studied in prior work.

Evaluation. The closest approach to our equivalence classes evaluation is the concept of verbalizers in Pattern-Exploiting Training (PET) (Schick and Schütze, 2021a,b), the relation to which we already discussed in Section 3.2. The biggest difference to our approach is that PET's verbalizers are limited to a small, bounded set of predefined single tokens or few-token spans, while our equivalence classes are unbounded, and their members are collected from the data without restrictions on length or content.

Other work has also tried to make human annotations more efficient, e.g. for importance judgements of sentences in multi-domain summarization (Jha et al., 2020), or multi-task information extraction (Bikaun et al., 2022). AnnIE builds fact synsets to speed up open information extraction (Friedrich et al., 2022).

Aspect-oriented summarization. Interpretations may focus on certain aspects in the source documents, making them somewhat similar to aspect-oriented summarization. AspectNews

(Ahuja et al., 2022) and SPACE (Angelidis et al., 2021) are two recent datasets with accompanying models.

News summarization. Since our interpretations are excerpts of New York Times articles, news summarization is relevant to our work as well. This is a very active field of research, with multiple large-scale datasets (e.g. CNN/DM (Hermann et al., 2015; Nallapati et al., 2016), XSum (Narayan et al., 2018), among others). A lot of methods have been tried on these datasets. BART (Lewis et al., 2020) and PEGASUS (Zhang et al., 2020a) have shown some of the best results for fine-tuned models.

7 Conclusion

We have devised a method to convert semi-structured human annotations into text format. We then introduced a task of predicting annotated interpretations of source documents that can be tackled with sequence-to-sequence models. We presented a human-annotated corpus about the monetary policy of the Federal Reserve. Our equivalence classes evaluation is an efficient technique to create a large number of targeted evaluation instances from a comparably cheap clustering by domain experts. We use this technique to evaluate state-of-the-art generative models on our task, and find that it shows larger differences between pretrained models than standard text generation metrics. In further in-depth analyses, the equivalence classes evaluation tests the models for specific properties, such as how they handle negation, and detects why models struggle to correctly rank alternative text spans of certain human annotation categories.

Limitations

In the following we discuss some limitations of our paper.

Subjectivity of the annotation process. Even though annotation protocols can be standardized and outputs aggregated over multiple annotators, the process of annotation remains subjective. In our interpretation task, social scientists extract and categorize information, providing additional context where necessary, and all annotations are validated by a senior domain expert. The models trained on the data will focus on the aspects that the annotators deemed important. This is not inherently a bad thing. Human annotation is a flexible tool that a different set of annotators could use to highlight other aspects of the data. Note that this is a separate consideration from reproducibility of our results, which we enable by open-sourcing our data, code and models.

Application to other domains. We have yet to establish transferability of our allowed set of annotations and task setup to other domains. While we expect our procedure to be general enough to work in different areas, this paper only uses a single corpus about macroeconomics. The reason for the limitation to one corpus is the high cost of finding relevant interpretation documents, performing the extraction and annotation, and standardizing the resulting annotations.

Equivalence classes creation. While the creation of equivalence classes is less expensive than directly creating evaluation examples, it still requires manual effort by domain experts, which is an expensive resource. This could be alleviated with an automatic method to obtain equivalence classes. In theory, the identification of candidate members of equivalence classes should be facilitated by the category annotations. The two member properties of 1) semantic interchangeability within equivalence classes and 2) syntactic interchangeability across equivalence classes could potentially be judged by a strong language model.

Syntactic structure of equivalence class members. Syntactic interchangeability is a requirement on equivalence class members within one equivalence classes evaluation. This limits us to one syntactic construction per evaluation. We select the most common one in each category to obtain a large enough number of evaluation instances. As a consequence, the model will not be tested on different syntactic structures. Unfortunately, testing all possible syntactic constructions suffers from 1) a data sparsity problem, where not enough examples of the same construction occur in the data, and 2) a large increase in manual effort required to construct one evaluation per syntactic structure.

Ethical Considerations

Since this work uses pretrained language models, it inherits the problems of those models with respect to reproducing biased or offensive content present in the pretraining data. We finetune our models on the FOMC dataset, which consists of policy announcements of the FOMC and news article sentences of the New York Times. Both of these sources can be considered trustworthy and careful with respect to the language that they use, in contrast to general text on the web that was present in BART's pretraining data. The topic of our dataset is the monetary policy of the Fed. Non-topical content was filtered in the data collection stage. All included news article sentences (which form the targets of our finetuning) were carefully selected and annotated. We therefore expect not to have introduced additional ethical issues with our dataset or finetuning. It should be noted that the dataset dates from 1967 to 2018, so it spans different historical contexts.

The annotations were performed by researchers of the Graduate Institute in their capacity as PhD students, postdocs and professors.

Acknowledgments

This work was supported as a part of the grant Automated interpretation of political and economic policy documents: Machine learning using semantic and syntactic information, funded by the Swiss National Science Foundation (grant number CRSII5_180320), and led by the co-PIs James Henderson, Jean-Louis Arcand and David Sylvan. We would also like to thank Maria Kamran, Alessandra Romani, Julia Greene, Clarisse Labbé, Shekhar Hari Kumar, Claire Ransom, Daniele Rinaldo, Eugenia Zena and Raphael Leduc for their invaluable data collection and annotation efforts.

References

Ojas Ahuja, Jiacheng Xu, Akshay Gupta, Kevin Horecka, and Greg Durrett. 2022. ASPECTNEWS: Aspect-oriented summarization of news documents. In *Proceedings of the 60th Annual Meeting of the Association for Computational Linguistics (Volume 1: Long Papers)*, pages 6494–6506, Dublin, Ireland. Association for Computational Linguistics.

Stefanos Angelidis, Reinald Kim Amplayo, Yoshihiko Suhara, Xiaolan Wang, and Mirella Lapata. 2021. Extractive opinion summarization in quantized transformer spaces. *Transactions of the Association for Computational Linguistics*, 9:277–293.

Iz Beltagy, Matthew E. Peters, and Arman Cohan. 2020. Longformer: The long-document transformer. *arXiv:2004.05150*.

Tyler Bikaun, Michael Stewart, and Wei Liu. 2022. QuickGraph: A rapid annotation tool for knowledge graph extraction from technical text. In *Proceedings of the 60th Annual Meeting of the Association for Computational Linguistics: System Demonstrations*, pages 270–278, Dublin, Ireland. Association for Computational Linguistics.

Tom Brown, Benjamin Mann, Nick Ryder, Melanie Subbiah, Jared D Kaplan, Prafulla Dhariwal, Arvind Neelakantan, Pranav Shyam, Girish Sastry, Amanda Askell, et al. 2020. Language models are few-shot learners. *Advances in neural information processing systems*, 33:1877–1901.

Jacob Devlin, Ming-Wei Chang, Kenton Lee, and Kristina Toutanova. 2019. Bert: Pre-training of deep bidirectional transformers for language understanding. In *Proceedings of NAACL-HLT 2019*, pages 4171–4186.

Niklas Friedrich, Kiril Gashteovski, Mingying Yu, Bhushan Kotnis, Carolin Lawrence, Mathias Niepert, and Goran Glavaš. 2022. AnnIE: An annotation platform for constructing complete open information extraction benchmark. In *Proceedings of the 60th Annual Meeting of the Association for Computational Linguistics: System Demonstrations*, pages 44–60, Dublin, Ireland. Association for Computational Linguistics.

Karl Moritz Hermann, Tomas Kocisky, Edward Grefenstette, Lasse Espeholt, Will Kay, Mustafa Suleyman, and Phil Blunsom. 2015. Teaching machines to read and comprehend. In *Advances in Neural Information Processing Systems*, pages 1693–1701.

Rahul Jha, Keping Bi, Yang Li, Mahdi Pakdaman, Asli Celikyilmaz, Ivan Zhiboedov, and Kieran McDonald. 2020. Artemis: A novel annotation methodology for indicative single document summarization. In *Proceedings of the First Workshop on Evaluation and Comparison of NLP Systems*, pages 69–78, Online. Association for Computational Linguistics.

Diederik P Kingma and Jimmy Ba. 2015. Adam: A method for stochastic optimization. In *International Conference on Learning Representations*.

Mike Lewis, Yinhan Liu, Naman Goyal, Marjan Ghazvininejad, Abdelrahman Mohamed, Omer Levy, Veselin Stoyanov, and Luke Zettlemoyer. 2020. Bart: Denoising sequence-to-sequence pre-training for natural language generation, translation, and comprehension. In *Proceedings of the 58th Annual Meeting of the Association for Computational Linguistics*, pages 7871–7880.

Chin-Yew Lin. 2004. ROUGE: A package for automatic evaluation of summaries. In *Text Summarization Branches Out*, pages 74–81. Association for Computational Linguistics.

Yang Liu and Mirella Lapata. 2019. Text summarization with pretrained encoders. In *Proceedings of the 2019 Conference on Empirical Methods in Natural Language Processing*.

Yinhan Liu, Jiatao Gu, Naman Goyal, Xian Li, Sergey Edunov, Marjan Ghazvininejad, Mike Lewis, and Luke Zettlemoyer. 2020. Multilingual denoising pre-training for neural machine translation. *Transactions of the Association for Computational Linguistics*, 8:726–742.

Ramesh Nallapati, Bowen Zhou, Cicero dos Santos, Caglar Gulcehre, and Bing Xiang. 2016. Abstractive text summarization using sequence-to-sequence rnns and beyond. In *Proceedings of The 20th SIGNLL Conference on Computational Natural Language Learning*, pages 280–290.

Shashi Narayan, Shay B Cohen, and Mirella Lapata. 2018. Don't give me the details, just the summary! topic-aware convolutional neural networks for extreme summarization. In *Proceedings of the 2018 Conference on Empirical Methods in Natural Language Processing*, pages 1797–1807.

Romain Paulus, Caiming Xiong, and Richard Socher. 2018. A deep reinforced model for abstractive summarization. In *International Conference on Learning Representations*.

Alec Radford, Jeffrey Wu, Rewon Child, David Luan, Dario Amodei, and Ilya Sutskever. 2019. Language models are unsupervised multitask learners. *https://openai.com/blog/better-language-models*.

Colin Raffel, Noam Shazeer, Adam Roberts, Katherine Lee, Sharan Narang, Michael Matena, Yanqi Zhou, Wei Li, and Peter J Liu. 2020. Exploring the limits of transfer learning with a unified text-to-text transformer. *Journal of Machine Learning Research*, 21:1–67.

Timo Schick and Hinrich Schütze. 2021a. Exploiting cloze-questions for few-shot text classification and natural language inference. In *Proceedings of the 16th Conference of the European Chapter of the Association for Computational Linguistics: Main Volume*, pages 255–269, Online. Association for Computational Linguistics.

Timo Schick and Hinrich Schütze. 2021b. It's not just size that matters: Small language models are also few-shot learners. In *Proceedings of the 2021 Conference of the North American Chapter of the Association for Computational Linguistics: Human Language Technologies*, pages 2339–2352, Online. Association for Computational Linguistics.

Ashish Vaswani, Noam Shazeer, Niki Parmar, Jakob Uszkoreit, Llion Jones, Aidan N Gomez, Łukasz Kaiser, and Illia Polosukhin. 2017. Attention is all you need. In *Advances in neural information processing systems*, pages 5998–6008.

Thomas Wolf, Lysandre Debut, Victor Sanh, Julien Chaumond, Clement Delangue, Anthony Moi, Pierric Cistac, Tim Rault, Remi Louf, Morgan Funtowicz, Joe Davison, Sam Shleifer, Patrick von Platen, Clara Ma, Yacine Jernite, Julien Plu, Canwen Xu, Teven Le Scao, Sylvain Gugger, Mariama Drame, Quentin Lhoest, and Alexander Rush. 2020. Transformers: State-of-the-art natural language processing. In *Proceedings of the 2020 Conference on Empirical Methods in Natural Language Processing: System Demonstrations*, pages 38–45, Online. Association for Computational Linguistics.

Linting Xue, Noah Constant, Adam Roberts, Mihir Kale, Rami Al-Rfou, Aditya Siddhant, Aditya Barua, and Colin Raffel. 2021. mT5: A massively multilingual pre-trained text-to-text transformer. In *Proceedings of the 2021 Conference of the North American Chapter of the Association for Computational Linguistics: Human Language Technologies*, pages 483–498, Online. Association for Computational Linguistics.

Jingqing Zhang, Yao Zhao, Mohammed Saleh, and Peter J. Liu. 2020a. PEGASUS: Pre-training with extracted gap-sentences for abstractive summarization. In *Proceedings of the 37th International Conference on Machine Learning*.

Tianyi Zhang, Varsha Kishore, Felix Wu, Kilian Q. Weinberger, and Yoav Artzi. 2020b. BERTScore: Evaluating text generation with bert. In *International Conference on Learning Representations*.

A Category Counts

The mean and standard deviation of category counts, for the references as well as the model generations, are listed in Table 5.

B In-Depth Results

Selected results of the in-depth analysis are shown in Table 6.

C Ablation Results

We present the results of our ablation study on model sizes in Table 7, on filtering strategies in Table 8, and on source document input lengths in Table 9.

D Full FOMC Example

We present the first example from the FOMC test set. We show the source document filtered with FilterBERT, the target annotation and BART's prediction. At the end, we show the generation scores for this example.

Filtered source document: FEDERAL RESERVE press release For Use at 4:30 p.m. August 22, 1986 The Federal Reserve Board and the Federal Open Market Committee today released the attached record of policy actions taken by the Federal Open Market Committee at its meeting on July 8-9, 1986. Such records for each meeting of the Committee are made available a few days after the next regularly scheduled meeting and are published in the Federal Reserve Bulletin and the Board's Annual Report. The summary descriptions of economic and financial conditions they contain are based solely on the information that was available to the Committee at the time of the meeting. Attachment RECORD OF POLICY ACTIONS OF THE FEDERAL OPEN MARKET COMMITTEE Meeting Held on July 8-9, 1986 Domestic policy directive The information reviewed at this meeting indicates that economic activity has expanded at a relatively slow pace recently. The intermeeting range for the federal funds rate was reduced to 5 to 9 percent. Other interest rates rose early in the period but then retreated amid signs of weakness in the economies of the United States and some of its major trading partners, renewing expectations of a discount rate cut in the near future. Since the May meeting short-term market rates had declined 10 to 40 basis points on balance. In their discussion of policy implementation for the weeks immediately ahead, Committee members took account of the likelihood that the discount rate would be reduced within a few days after the meeting. Against the background of sluggish expansion in economic activity and a subdued rate of inflation, most of the members believed that some easing was desirable and they indicated a preference for implementing the easing, at least initially, through a lower discount rate rather than through open market operations. In one view, a cut in the discount rate might need to be accompanied by some increase in the degree of pressure on reserve positions, pending evaluation of further economic and financial developments. The reduction was viewed as a technical adjustment that would provide a more symmetrical range around a lower federal funds rate that could be expected to emerge following the anticipated reduction in the discount 7/8-9/86 - 18 rate. Most short-term interest rates have declined on balance since the May 20 meeting of the Committee. In the implementation of policy for the immediate future, the Committee seeks to decrease somewhat the existing degree of pressure on reserve positions, taking account of the possibility of a change in the discount rate.

Target annotation: [STD SENTENCE START] Policymakers at the [ACTOR START] Federal Reserve [ACTOR END] [ACT START] decided at their July meeting to loosen credit conditions (Loosened monetary policy) [ACT END] [MOTIVE START] in an effort to stimulate the sluggish economy [MOTIVE END], according to [REFERENCE START] minutes [REFERENCE END] of the meeting released today. [STD SENTENCE END] [STD SENTENCE START] Members of the [ACTOR START] Federal Open Market Committee (Fed / FOMC) [ACTOR END] [REFERENCE START] voted [REFERENCE END] 10 to 1 to follow a strategy that would push interest rates lower, [ACT START] despite [ATTRIBUTION START] objections from one member (Should not loosen monetary policy) [ACT END] (One member of the FOMC) [ATTRIBUTION END] that [EVIDENCE START] such a course might threaten renewed inflation later [EVIDENCE END]. [STD SENTENCE END] [STD SENTENCE START] Thomas C. [ATTRIBUTION START] Melzer [ATTRIBUTION END], president of the St. Louis [ACTOR START] Federal Reserve Bank [ACTOR END], [ACT START] cast the single dissenting vote (Should not loosen money supply) [ACT END]. The minutes said Mr. Melzer [REFERENCE START] expressed concern [REFERENCE END] that [EVIDENCE START] looser Fed controls could initiate renewed inflation [EVIDENCE END] and [EVIDENCE START] weaken the dollar on foreign exchange markets [EVIDENCE END]. [STD SENTENCE END]

BART prediction: [STD SENTENCE START] The [ACTOR START] Federal Reserve's Open Market Committee (Fed) [ACTOR END] [ACT START] voted unanimously at its July 8-9 meeting to ease monetary policy further (Might cut rates, in future) [ACT END], according to [REFERENCE START] minutes [REFERENCE END] of the session released today. [STD SENTENCE END]

ROUGE-1/2/L (including category markers): 31.68/17.00/28.71
ROUGE-1/2/L (excluding category markers): 30.38/15.38/27.85
BERTScore: 27.29
Novel bigrams: 84.38%
Closed correctly: 100.00%

E Equivalence Classes Evaluation Example

We present an evaluation instance from the equivalence classes evaluation for the evidence category. BART got this example wrong, i.e. judged the negative continuation $a^{(\text{neg})}$ as more likely than the positive $a^{(\text{pos})}$ (appears in Figure 5, positive class 9, negative class 10).

$y_{\textbf{prefix}}$**:** [STD SENTENCE START] Ben S. [ATTRIBUTION START] Bernanke [ATTRIBUTION END] , the chairman of the [ACTOR START] Federal Reserve [ACTOR END] Board, [REFERENCE START] declared [REFERENCE END] on Friday that the central bank [ACT START] "stands ready to take additional actions as needed" (Might cut rates, in future) [ACT END] [MOTIVE START] to prevent the chaos in mortgage markets from derailing the broader economy [MOTIVE END] . Mr. Bernanke avoided any specific promise to lower the central bank's benchmark federal funds rate at its next policy meeting on Sept. 18. But he acknowledged [EVIDENCE START]
$a^{(\textbf{pos})}$**:** the dangers posed by the twin storms in housing and mortgage lending
$a^{(\textbf{neg})}$**:** credit was becoming harder to get for both consumers and businesses

Model	Std sent	Act	Actor	Reference	Attribution	Motive	Evidence	Scope	Closed correctly
References	1.60 (± 0.93)	1.60 (± 0.93)	1.60 (± 0.93)	1.60 (± 0.93)	0.87 (± 1.18)	0.39 (± 0.72)	1.22 (± 1.41)	0.21 (± 0.45)	100.00%
Transformer	2.69 (± 0.62)	2.69 (± 0.62)	2.69 (± 0.62)	2.60 (± 0.64)	0.02 (± 0.22)	0.08 (± 0.31)	0.05 (± 0.22)	0.01 (± 0.11)	100.00%
BERT	1.63 (± 0.75)	1.63 (± 0.75)	1.63 (± 0.75)	1.63 (± 0.77)	0.73 (± 0.73)	0.43 (± 0.62)	0.07 (± 0.26)	0.14 (± 0.38)	99.97%
BART	1.55 (± 0.70)	0.79 (± 0.71)	1.22 (± 0.84)	1.37 (± 0.68)	0.29 (± 0.55)	0.02 (± 0.17)	0.13 (± 0.44)	0.05 (± 0.21)	69.44%

Table 5: Mean and standard deviation of category counts.

Model	Act negation	Act modals (pos)	Act comment modals (pos)	Act with comment modals (pos)
Transformer	89.58%	70.65%	93.81%	68.13%
BERT	93.75%	70.65%	93.81%	69.23%
BART	95.83%	89.13%	97.94%	80.22%

Table 6: Accuracy on selected in-depth equivalence classes evaluations.

Model	Parameters	EQ mean	ROUGE			BERTScore	Distinct bigrams
			R-1	R-2	R-L		
Transformer	247M	73.55%	31.89	10.27	25.06	0.72	214
BERT-base	247M	76.03%	41.09	18.31	31.63	19.00	965
BERT-large	771M	75.76%	41.26	17.91	31.39	19.30	1232
BART	406M	87.56%	42.73	20.64	33.08	26.78	3011

Table 7: Selected evaluation metrics for different model sizes.

Model	Filter model	EQ mean	ROUGE			BERTScore	Distinct bigrams
			R-1	R-2	R-L		
BERT	FilterBERT	76.03%	41.09	18.31	31.63	19.00	965
BERT	Lead	75.51%	41.27	18.74	31.44	19.59	1012
BERT	Oracle	75.15%	41.38	18.54	32.05	19.96	1010
BART	FilterBERT	87.56%	42.73	20.64	33.08	26.78	3011
BART	Lead	86.90%	41.56	19.79	32.09	25.15	1976
BART	Oracle	87.16%	44.04	21.84	33.87	26.98	3528

Table 8: Selected evaluation metrics for different filtering strategies.

Model	Filter model	Input tokens	EQ mean	ROUGE			BERTScore	Distinct bigrams
				R-1	R-2	R-L		
BART	Lead	512	86.90%	41.56	19.79	32.09	25.15	1976
BART	Lead	1024	87.12%	42.39	19.64	32.20	25.44	2421
BART	Oracle	512	87.16%	44.04	21.84	33.87	26.98	3528
BART	Oracle	1024	89.15%	44.81	21.36	34.77	27.79	3296

Table 9: Selected evaluation metrics for different source document input lengths.

T5QL: Taming language models for SQL generation

Samuel Arcadinho, David Aparício, Hugo Veiga, António Alegria
Outsystems
{samuel.arcadinho, david.aparicio, hugo.veiga, antonio.alegria}@outsystems.com

Abstract

Automatic SQL generation has been an active research area, aiming at streamlining the access to databases by writing natural language with the given intent instead of writing SQL. Current state-of-the-art (SOTA) methods for semantic parsing depend on large language models (LLMs) to achieve high predictive accuracy on benchmark datasets. This reduces their applicability, since LLMs require expensive GPUs. Furthermore, SOTA methods are ungrounded and thus not guaranteed to always generate valid SQL. Here we propose T5QL, a new SQL generation method that improves the performance in benchmark datasets when using smaller LMs, namely T5-Base, by $\approx$ 13pp when compared against SOTA methods. Additionally, T5QL is guaranteed to always output valid SQL using a context-free grammar to constrain SQL generation. Finally, we show that dividing semantic parsing in two tasks, candidate SQLs generation and candidate re-ranking, is a promising research avenue that can reduce the need for large LMs.

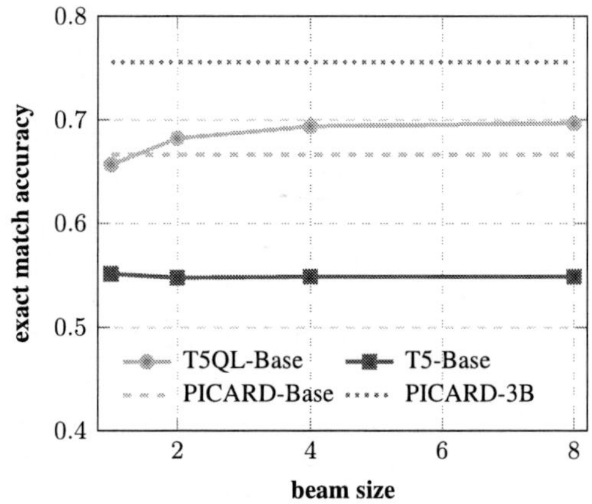

Figure 1: Exact-match accuracy of the highest scoring prediction as a function of beam size on the Spider development set. Our method, T5QL, significantly improves upon T5-Base and is superior to PICARD-Base. PICARD-3B remains the SOTA for very large LMs, i.e., PICARD-3B uses T5-3B which is $\approx 13x$ larger than T5-Base. Results for PICARD-Base and PICARD-3B are straight (dashed) lines since Scholak et al. (2021) only report results in the setting using database content for a single point, namely beam search with 4 beams.

1 Introduction

Automated code generation has long been considered one of the fundamental tasks in computer science (Pnueli and Rosner, 1989). Recently, deep learning (DL) methods for code generation have been proposed which overcome the lack of flexibility of more traditional approaches (Le et al., 2020). Some DL approaches can act as code completion tools (Svyatkovskiy et al., 2020; Chen et al., 2021) while others can use natural language (NL) as input to generate code (Yin and Neubig, 2017), i.e., semantic parsing (Kamath and Das, 2018). The latter methods are particularly helpful for developers that are not proficient in all programming languages that are part of their development pipeline. For example, a developer might be familiar with the controller language (e.g., Python) but unfamiliar with the database access language (e.g., SQL).

Generating SQL from NL is challenging because the NL query might be ambiguous (e.g., columns from different tables can have the same name). Futhermore, obtaining labelled pairs of NL queries to SQL is hard, time-consuming, and requires labellers that are proficient in SQL. In recent years, benchmark datasets have been used by developers to evaluate their methods, namely Spider (Raffel et al., 2019) and CoSQL (Yu et al., 2019).

PICARD (Scholak et al., 2021) is the current SOTA method, i.e., the highest ranked method on Spider. It is built on top of T5 (Raffel et al., 2019), a general purpose LLM. As proven by Merrill et al. (2021), LLMs are ungrounded and thus can generate any token at any given step, which may result in invalid SQL; thus, to improve upon T5, PICARD

Proceedings of the 2nd Workshop on Natural Language Generation, Evaluation, and Metrics (GEM), pages 276 - 286
December 7, 2022 ©2022 Association for Computational Linguistics

prunes the search tree in order to avoid generating invalid SQL. However, since PICARD fully prunes branches during beam search, it is not guaranteed to always generate an answer. Another major issue with PICARD is that it needs a very large LM to achieve good performance: PICARD gets $\approx 75.5\%$ exact match (EM) accuracy in Spider's development set when using T5-3B, but only $\approx 66.6\%$ when using the smaller T5-Base.

Here, we propose T5QL, a novel SQL generation method that achieves 69.3% EM on Spider development set using T5-Base instead of the $\approx$13x larger T5-3B. T5QL uses constrained decoding to ensure that it always generates valid SQL, and it always generates an answer. Our main contributions are:

1. Narrow the gap between large and small LMs (Figure 1). With beam size equal to 4 and using T5-Base, T5QL achieves 69.3% EM accuracy on Spider, versus 66.6% obtained by PICARD. PICARD with T5-3B is still SOTA (75.5%) but it requires much larger GPUs, which are expensive and thus not available for regular practitioners.

2. Propose a constrained decoding method that always generates valid SQL, except for infrequent model hallucinations. In Appendix A.1 we show one such case.

3. Propose a novel ranker model for SQL generation. This model re-ranks the generator model's predictions after beam search, boosting EM on Spider for larger beam sizes (e.g., 8 beams) from 67.9% to 69.6%.

The remainder of the paper is organized as follows. Section 2 presents SOTA for SQL generation. Section 3 describes T5QL's main components, namely constrained decoding and the ranker. Section 4 shows our results. Finally, Section 5 concludes our work.

2 State-of-the-art

Automated program generation has long been one of the major goals of computer science. Various program synthesis tools have been proposed that generate SQL from code fragments (Cheung et al., 2012) or pairs of input-output examples (Orvalho et al., 2020). However, code fragments might not be readily available if the developer does not write code or does not want to, and creating enough input-output examples for the program synthesis tool to be effective might be cumbersome. Other tools generate SQL from NL which is more developer-friendly (Yaghmazadeh et al., 2017).

The complexity of generating SQL from NL varies with the length and complexity of the SQL query and the size of the database schema. Thus, in order to properly evaluate and compare methods' performance, multiple benchmark datasets have been proposed, namely Spider (Raffel et al., 2019), Spider-SSP (Shaw et al., 2021), and CoSQL (Yu et al., 2019). We describe these benchmarks in detail in Section 4.2 and discuss how they relate to our research questions (enumerated at the start of Section 4).

The current SOTA for SQL generation (i.e., the methods that achieve the highest performance on benchmark datasets) comprises DL methods. DL methods for code generation avoid the complexity of traditional program synthesis and, thus, are generally faster during generation (Parisotto et al., 2016; Hayati et al., 2018; Sun et al., 2019).

RatSQL's authors argue that predicting SQL directly from NL is hard and can be made easier by instead predicting an intermediate representation (IR) that is more similar to NL than SQL is (Wang et al., 2019; Gan et al., 2021). With this insight, they obtained SOTA results on Spider. However, their IR is not capable of representing all SQLs and, thus, for some queries the correct SQL is not obtainable, leading to a loss of EM accuracy. Other approaches were built on top of RatSQL with good results (Zhao et al., 2021; Shi et al., 2020; Yu et al., 2020). One of the major disadvantages of these methods is that, since they use custom architectures, they cannot leverage pre-trained LLMs in their decoding step. Being able to leverage LLMs is beneficial since they can be used for multiple tasks. For example, Xie et al. (2022) unifies structured knowledge grounding tasks into a text-to-text format and are thus able to train the same model for different tasks.

To the best of our knowledge, Shaw et al. (2021) were the first to propose a method that uses an LLM, namely T5, and evaluate it on Spider. They concluded that their method had good predictive capabilities, but sometimes generated syntactically incorrect SQL and had lower precision in out-of-distribution examples. Since T5 is ungrounded, it cannot be guaranteed to always generate valid SQL; the same is true for other LLMs (Merrill et al., 2021). In order to address the issue, Xiao et al.

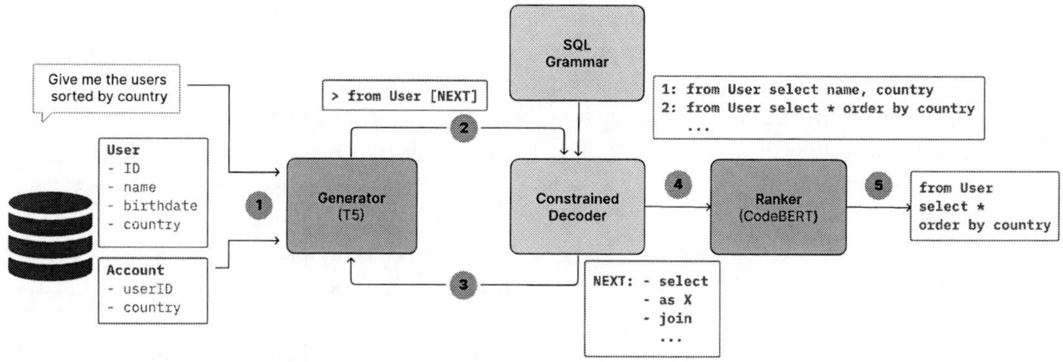

Figure 2: T5QL model architecture. T5QL receives as input an NL query and a database schema (step 1). Then, the generator model, T5, consults the constrained decoder to know which tokens are valid (step 2) and predicts the next token (step 3). This step is done iteratively. The generation is done using beam search, thus producing a set of k candidates which are given as input to the ranker model (step 4). Finally, the ranker model ranks all candidates and a final prediction is outputted by T5QL (step 5).

(2016) propose a method that constrains the output generation based on grammatical rules. They also compare a model trained with constraints and verify that using the constraints only during inference improves the model.

Targeting code generation specifically, Scholak et al. (2021) propose PICARD, a method that constrains the model generation by removing wrong outputs during beam search. By doing so, PICARD is the current SOTA in the Spider benchmark. However, they report that PICARD did not generate any SQL for 2% of the queries. Poesia et al. (2022) improve LLM performance in the few-shot setting by introducing two components, one that selects the examples to be given to the model and another that constrains the generation of syntactically correct SQL. However, fine-tuned models (e.g., PICARD) still perform better in the general task than their model, which was trained in the few-shot setting.

In this work, we use one model to generate candidates, a *generator*, and another to re-rank them, a *ranker*. This choice is motivated by recent work (Chen et al., 2021) where the authors show that a re-ranking method boosted performance for code generation. Regarding semantic parsing more concretely, Ye et al. (2022) use a ranker model to select candidates, and then a fine-tuned model generates the final output; their model shows good generalization capabilities and outperforms previous methods for question answering on knowledge graphs. More recently, Krishna et al. (2022) argue that when current LLMs are given a prefix prompt they can often generate text that is incoherent with the prefix. They propose a ranker model that scores the generator's candidates for an input prefix and obtain results that outperform earlier models in both automatic and human evaluation.

3 Method

We start this section by presenting an overview of our method and its architecture (Figure 2). Then, we focus on each of its main components, namely constrained decoding and the ranker. Finally, we discuss the scoring function and evaluation metrics.

3.1 Overview

Our method outputs the corresponding SQL query for a given NL query and a database schema. The database schema comprises a list of tables and their respective columns. Figure 2 shows a simple NL query, "Give me the users sorted by country", and a toy database schema with only two tables, `User` and `Account`. The generator, T5, receives the NL and the database schema as input and, starting with an empty string, it iteratively predicts the next token. However, unlike regular T5, the next token prediction is limited by the constrained decoder to only consider tokens that form a valid SQL query up to that point. For example, if the current query is `"from User"`, the next valid tokens include `"select"`, `"as X"`, and `"join"`, but do not include `"from"` or `"User"`. We discuss why we invert the *from* and the *select* statements in Section 3.2. We use beam search to generate multiple candidate queries, which are given as input to the ranker model.

3.2 Constrained decoding

We use constrained decoding to limit which tokens are considered by the generator to make the next token prediction. In order to enforce valid tokens, we build a context-free grammar (CFG) of SQL statements. Our constrained decoding method, described in Algorithm 1, is similar to the one proposed by Poesia et al. (2022): for each decoding step, given the current generation P, T5QL finds the maximum parsable prefix P^*, this means that all SQL tokens in the prefix P^* have valid syntax (lines 2–5). Then, using the lookahead feature of the parser, T5QL tokenizes all possible suffixes for P^* and adds them to trie T (lines 6–10). Finally, T5QL computes possible generation tokens by searching the possibles suffixes for P in T (lines 11–12).

Algorithm 1 Constrained decoding

```
1:  procedure NEXTTOKEN(P, T)       ▷ P is the current SQL generation and T the current trie
2:      P* ← FINDPARSABLEPREFIX(P)
3:      S ← GETPARSERSTATE(P*)
4:      N ← PARSERNEXTTOKENS(S)
5:      N* ← FILTERWRONGTOKENS(S, N)
6:      for n in N* do
7:          C ← P* + n
8:          C^T ← SENTENCETOKENIZER(C)
9:          T ← ADDTOTRIE(T, C^T)
10:     end for
11:     P^T ← SENTENCETOKENIZER(P)
12:     returnGETCHILDREN(T, P^T)
13: end procedure
```

We note that, while our grammar is context free, our constrained decoding method uses context to make decisions: FILTERWRONGTOKENS (line 5 of Algorithm 1) constrains the SQL generation by only allowing the generation of columns that are defined in the *from* statement and by mapping table aliases to the original tables. We should point out that, while this is currently not performed by our method, we could extend constrained decoding to enforce more rules, such as only allowing tables to be joined using valid foreign keys or limiting the *where* statement to only have conditions that have the proper return type given the column types (e.g., if a column "`X`" is of type *string*, "`X > 10`" is not a valid generation).

Next, we focus on the grammar. For brevity, we only show higher-level statements below; the entire grammar is shown in our Codalab page[1]. Statements inside square brackets indicate that they are optional (e.g., a SQL query can have an empty *where* statement).

```
⟨sql⟩    ⊨ ⟨expr⟩
⟨expr⟩   ⊨ ⟨query⟩ |
           ⟨expr⟩ union ⟨expr⟩ |
           ⟨expr⟩ intersect ⟨expr⟩ |
           ⟨expr⟩ except ⟨expr⟩
⟨query⟩  ⊨ from ⟨from-expr⟩
           select ⟨select-expr⟩
           [where ⟨where-expr⟩]
           [group by ⟨groupby-expr⟩]
           [having ⟨having-expr⟩]
           [order by ⟨orderby-expr⟩]
           [limit ⟨limit-expr⟩]
```

Our grammar only supports SQL *select* statements since our focus are queries that retrieve data from a database. These *select* statements can be a single query or contain subqueries joined by *unions*, *intersects*, and *excepts*. We note that the *from* and the *select* statements are inverted. This is done because, besides restricting T5 to only generate syntactically correct SQL, we also restrict it to only generate SQL with valid table names (i.e., tables that exist in the database schema) and valid column names (i.e., columns that exist in the database schema for the given table). To restrict the generation to only valid columns, it is helpful to first know the valid tables, which are obtained in the *from* statement. Thus, T5QL first parses the *from* statement and stores the selected tables; then, when the *select* statement is parsed, T5QL already knows what columns are valid since they had to appear in the selected tables (e.g., from the example from Figure 2, if the current query is "`from User select`", then "`user.ID`" and "`user.name`" are valid token predictions while "`account.country`" and "`account.userId`" are not).

For a given query and database schema pair, we augment the grammar shown previously with two extra rules specifying the valid tables and the valid columns. For the example from Figure 2, we would add the following production rules:

[1]https://worksheets.codalab.org/worksheets/0x0049b642db90440e9eaf9cf6a850b4c9

$$
\begin{aligned}
\langle\text{table-name}\rangle &\models \texttt{user} \mid \texttt{account} \\
\langle\text{column-name}\rangle &\models \texttt{user.id} \mid \texttt{user.name} \mid \\
&\quad \texttt{user.birthdate} \mid \\
&\quad \texttt{user.name} \mid \\
&\quad \texttt{user.country} \mid \\
&\quad \texttt{account.userId} \mid \\
&\quad \texttt{account.country}
\end{aligned}
$$

When a table has an an alias, we add one expression for the alias and another for the original table table (e.g., for a column "`alias1.columnA`", we add two expressions to the ⟨column-name⟩ rule: "`alias1.columnA`" and "`tableX.columnA`", assuming that `alias1` corresponds to `tableX`).

The grammar is given as input to the Lark parser[2]. We use Lark since it is one of the fastest parsers for Python, and it includes a look-ahead feature that we require.

3.3 Ranker

We use beam search to generate a set of k candidate queries and employ a ranker model to choose the best option among the k candidates. We hypothesize that splitting the task of SQL generation into two tasks, (1) SQL candidates generation and (2) SQL candidate ranking, boosts the performance of the complete task since each model is only focused on a simpler task.

We use a trained generator model to generate the dataset to train the ranker model. The T5 model described in Section 3.2 samples 16 SQL queries for each input (NL query and database schema pair) in the training dataset using beam search. From the 16 generated SQLs we sample the 12 with lowest tree edit distance (TED) (discussed in Section 3.5) to guarantee that we select hard negative examples. If the generator model does not predict the correct SQL in any of the 12 SQLs samples, we discard the one with the highest TED and add the correct SQL as one of the samples. Using the same sampling strategy (i.e., based on TED), we sample an additional two SQLs from the training dataset pertaining to the same database as the input, for a total of 14 SQLs for each input.

For the ranker model, we fine-tune CodeBERT (Feng et al., 2020) in a cross encoder setting. The ranker is given pairs of NL and SQL and predicts the probability of the pairs being correct, i.e., the SQL corresponding to the NL. We also append the terminals found in the NL using the method proposed by Lin et al. (2020) to the final NL (e.g., for the NL "People from 'France'", the NL is transformed into "People from 'France' | France").

3.4 Scoring Function

Similarly to Yee et al. (2019), we compute the final prediction score for a given input by combining the generator's probability score with the ranker's probability score using the linear combination shown in Equation 1, where t is the length of the SQL, and λ is a tunable weight. In order to compare the generator's probability $p(y|x)$ with the ranker's probability $p(x, y)$, we scale the generator's probability by t.

$$\frac{1}{t}\log p(y|x) + \lambda \log p(x, y) \tag{1}$$

3.5 Evaluation metrics

The most commonly used evaluation metrics for SQL comparison are EM and execution match (EX). EM checks if two SQLs are syntactically equivalent, while EX checks if running two SQLs yields the same output. While desirable, EX is more computationally expensive than EM since it requires running the SQL statements, which might not even be possible if we do not have access to the database content. When measuring the method's performance, it is also relevant to highlight if it also predicts terminal values or not; T5QL generates the full SQL query, including terminal values.

Since EM is binary, its value might not be very informative for the user nor the model. Partial matches sub-divide the comparison to only portions of the SQL statement, such as the *from* clause or the *where* clause. Thus, one SQL prediction might be wrong in multiple parts of the query, and this more granular information can be useful to improve the model. However, these measures are still coarse; thus, we use the TED in some experiments (namely in the ranker) when we want more information on the difference (or distance) between two SQLs.

In order to compute the TED between two SQL statements, we transform each SQL statement into a tree and use APTED[3] to compute the TED between two trees. Due to SQL's semantics, we first normalize the SQL to a canonical representation

[2] https://github.com/lark-parser/lark

[3] https://github.com/DatabaseGroup/apted

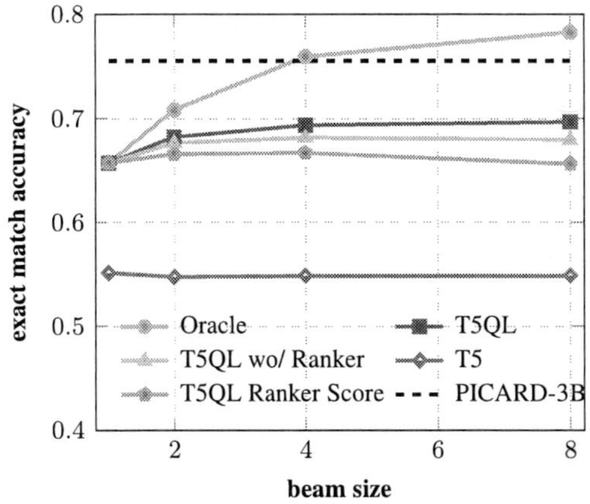

Figure 3: EM accuracy in Spider's development set by beam size. All methods use T5-Base as their LM except for PICARD-3B which uses T5-3B. The performance of PICARD-3B is shown as a straight line since the authors only report results on the development set using database content for a single point (beam search with 4 beams). The Oracle plot shows the performance ceiling for T5QL, i.e., the performance of T5QL using a perfect ranker that always outputs the correct SQL if the generator offers it as one of the candidates after beam search.

(e.g., sort the list of tables in the *select* alphabetically, transform *left joins* into *right joins*). Then modify APTED to guarantee that the TED is meaningful (e.g., the cost of removing a terminal and column name should be the same).

4 Experiments

We start by describing the experimental setup in Section 4.1. Then, we detail each dataset and the relevant evaluation metrics in Section 4.2. Then, each subsequent section (Section 4.3–4.6) tries to answer each of the following research questions:

Q1. Does constrained decoding improve the generator's performance?

Q2. Does T5QL have compositional generalization capabilities?

Q3. Does T5QL generalize to the conversational setting?

Q4. Instead of using a very large generator, can we improve performance using a ranker?

4.1 Experimental setup

For our experiments we use a G4DN Extra Large AWS machine, which has an NVIDIA T4 Tensor Core GPU installed and 4 CPU-cores. We make our code available in our public Codalab page[45].

4.2 Datasets

We evaluate T5QL on three benchmark datasets: Spider (Raffel et al., 2019), Spider-SSP (Shaw et al., 2021), and CoSQL (Yu et al., 2019).

Spider comprises 10,181 NL and database schemas pairs, on 200 different database schemas. Evaluation on Spider consists of two main leaderboards: EX with terminal values and EM without terminal values. At the time of writing, PICARD is the current SOTA method on both leaderboards.

Spider-SSP is a different splitting of the Spider dataset, with the aim of testing compositional generation instead of cross-database generalization, i.e., in the original Spider data split, a database schema seen in train is not seen in eval or test. Splits in the Spider-SSP dataset are made in three different fashions: random split, a split based on source length, and a split based on Target Maximum Compound Divergence (TMCD). The goal here is to evaluate if the model can have good performance on queries that it has not seen in training.

While Spider consists of a single NL and domain model pair mapped into a single SQL query, CoSQL consists of a conversational dataset with multiple iterations of NL plus data model being mapped to a SQL query. The goal of CoSQL is to simulate a user progressively exploring a data model. CoSQL contains 4,298 interactions and $\approx 12,000$ questions, on the same 200 data models used in Spider. Evaluation is done using EM without terminal values and reported using two different metrics: question match (QM) and interaction match (IM). QM evaluates if all SQLs are correctly predicted, while IM evaluates if the questions for the same interaction are correctly predicted.

4.3 Q1. Constrained decoding

LMs are unconstrained and thus can generate any token at any given time. For SQL generation, LMs may generate SQL that are syntactically incorrect, which impact their performance.

Here, we compare the performance of an unconstrained LM against T5QL without the ranker component. Both methods use the same LM, namely T5-Base, and are trained using the same training

[4]https://worksheets.codalab.org/worksheets/0x0049b642db90440e9eaf9cf6a850b4c9

[5]We will make the code available in github after the blind review process is finalized.

configuration; the only difference is that T5QL uses constrained decoding as described in Section 3.2. Both methods serialize the database schema as a string and append it to the source sequence similarly to Suhr et al. (2020). Similarly to Scholak et al. (2021), we train both methods for a maximum of 512 training epochs with mini batch size of 5, 205 gradient accumulation steps, with a learning rate of $1e^{-4}$, and an adafactor optimizer with epsilon set as $1e^{-6}$. We evaluate the models using beam search with 1, 2, 4, and 8 beams. Contrary to Scholak et al. (2021), we report results for a batch size of 1025 instead of 2048 since it lead to better results in our case.

Figure 3 shows the performance of several methods and those results are discussed in this subsection and in the next ones. All methods use T5-Base as its LLM, except for PICARD which is the current SOTA and uses T5-3B, a much larger LM.

From Figure 3, we observe that T5 achieves $\approx 55.1\%$ EM accuracy using one beam, and its performance does not improve with the beam size. Our method, T5QL, without the ranker component (i.e., T5QL wo/ Ranker in Figure 3) achieves $\approx 65.7\%$ EM accuracy using one beam, a gain of $\approx$ 10.6pp, which is a relative gain of $\approx 19.2\%$. Using 2 and 4 beams, we improve T5QL's performance to $\approx 67.6\%$ and $\approx 68\%$, a gain of ≈ 1.9pp and ≈ 2.3pp, respectively, when compared against T5QL using only one beam. We observe a loss of performance when using 8 beams. These results highlight the advantage of using constrained decoding for SQL generation: by using a CFG to guarantee that the LM always generates valid SQL, we improve the model's performance.

4.4 Q2. Compositional generalization

Compositional generalization of LLMs has attracted attention in recent years. Shaw et al. (2021) propose Spider-SSP, a dataset that can be used to measure the compositional generalization of SQL generation methods. In this section we use Spider-SSP to evaluate if constraint decoding increases the compositional generalization capabilities of T5QL.

Shaw et al. (2021) already reported that T5-Base model struggles in most splitting strategies, particularly when using length-based split and TMCD split; we reproduce those results in Table 1 in rows T5-Base and T5-3B. We note that, in their experiments, the predicted SQL follows the convention of predicting first the *select* statement and then the *from* statement. As discussed in Section 3.2, T5QL first predicts the *from* statement and then the *select* statement. Thus, we evaluate two different models: T5-Base, which is similar to the model evaluated by Shaw et al. (2021), and T5QL-Base wo/ CD which is T5QL without the constrained decoding component (and without the ranker). We compare these models against T5QL-Base and T5-3B; the latter also predicts the *select* statement first.

We observe that T5QL-Base wo/ CD obtains significantly higher EM than T5-Base, namely for the TMCD split where there is a gain of 22pp, which is a 52% relative gain. These results highlight that predicting the tables before predicting the columns seems to help the model. This result corroborates the results obtained by Lin et al. (2020), which use a representation similar to ours. We also verify that T5QL-Base slightly, but consistently, improves upon the results obtained by T5QL-Base wo/ CD for all splitting strategies, namely in TMCD where there is a gain of 2pp. Finally, we conclude that our strategy narrows the performance gap between the performance of methods using small LMs (i.e., T5-Base) and very large LMs (i.e., T5-3B) by comparing the performance of T5QL-Base against T5-3B.

4.5 Q3. Generalize to conversational setting

Often users might want to explore their data without having to write SQL. Thus, a conversational setting where user's iteratively ask questions to an AI is particularly interesting. Yu et al. (2019) propose a dataset comprised of multiple question-SQL pairs, each consisting of several user interactions. They evaluate SQL generation methods using QM and IM. In this section we use CoSQL to evaluate if constrained decoding increases the performance of T5SQL in the conversational setting.

We observe gains of $\approx 7.9\%$ and $\approx 5.5\%$ in QM

	Spider-SSP			
Model	Rand.	Templ.	Len.	TMCD
T5-Base	76.5	45.3	42.5	42.3
T5QL-Base wo/ CD	84.7	58.3	50.6	64.4
T5QL-Base	85.7	61.1	54.4	65.9
T5-3B	85.6	64.8	56.7	69.6

Table 1: EM accuracy in the Spider-SSP dataset using different splitting strategies. T5QL-Base wo/ CD (i.e., without constrained decoding) and T5QL-Base adopt the strategy of predicting SQL with the *from* statement before the *select* statement, while T5-Base and T5-3B do the opposite, which is the default.

Model	CoSQL	
	QM	IM
T5QL-Base wo/ CD	42.8	14.8
T5QL-Base	50.7	20.3
PICARD - 3B	56.9	24.2

Table 2: QM and IM in the CoSQL development set.

and IM, respectively, when we add constrained decoding to T5QL-Base. We observe that PICARD-3B is still SOTA for the task, but the gap is significantly narrower. This is further evidence that constrained decoding can improve the performance of LMs in multiple SQL generation tasks.

4.6 Q4. Ranker

Current SOTA methods, such as PICARD, use beam search to find the best candidate and output it as the final prediction. Here we test whether we can boost predictive performance by, instead of using the beam-selected best candidate as the final prediction, having a ranker that finds the best candidate among the list of candidate predictions found by the generator.

Our first step to validate this hypothesis is to run beam search for multiple beam sizes k, namely 1, 2, 4, and 8, and measure the accuracy@k. In our setting, the accuracy@k can be regarded as an *oracle* ranker than can always find the correct candidate if it is present in the list of candidate generations. From Figure 3 we observe that this *oracle* could achieve 78.2% EM accuracy with 8 beams, surpassing the performance of PICARD-3B but using T5-Base instead of T5-3B, which is highly desirable due to T5-3B's expensive nature in terms of GPU costs. Thus, our goal here is to build a ranker model that can boost the performance of T5QL without the ranker (T5QL wo/ Ranker in Figure 3) and approximate it to the *oracle*'s performance.

We note that the ranker model should be of a comparable size to the generator, i.e., fit in the same GPU. Otherwise, the advantage of using a small LM as the generator is lost since we assume that the practitioner has hardware that can fit the larger ranker, which might not be true. Here we use T5-Base as the generator and CodeBERT as the ranker, which are of comparable size.

To train the ranker model, we first create a dataset following the steps described in Section 3.5. Then, we fine-tune a CodeBERT model for 50,000 training steps, using a batch size of 32 and 1 gradient accumulation step, with a $1e^{-3}$ learning rate and an AdamW optimizer with weight decay of $1e^{-2}$ and a linear schedule with warmup of 1% of the steps. We use Equation 1 to score the generated SQL; we conduct hyperparameter tuning for λ and conclude that $\lambda = 2e^{-2}$ performs best.

We analyze if combining the generator's score with the ranker's score is superior to using each of the score's individually. From Figure 3 we conclude that combining the ranker model's score with the generator model's score (i.e., the T5QL plot) improves the best EM from 67.9% to 69.3% when compared against T5QL without the ranker score. Furthermore, we also observe that using only the ranker score (i.e., the T5QL Ranker Score plot) leads to a drop in performance even when compared against T5QL wo/ Ranker. This effect is more noticeable for larger beam sizes, which indicates that the ranker model struggles to differentiate the correct SQL from the wrong SQL.

From these experiments, we conclude that the ranker boosts the performance of the generator. However, the ranker's score needs to be combined with the generator's score to guarantee that the ranker's score does not completely dominate the generator's predictions. We should also note that there is a very large gap between our ranker and the oracle, which leaves room for future research to improve the ranker model. We believe that this a promising line of research that can further narrow the gap between the performance between small LMs and large LMs.

Finally, we run T5SQL on Spider's test set and obtain 66.8% EX and 65.9% EM. These results rank among the top-10 best models in terms of EX, and as the 22nd best in terms of EM[6], whilst using small models. Small models have the advantage of being less computationally expensive and allowing more easily for the use of ensemble methods.

5 Conclusion

Here we put forward T5QL, a new method for SQL generation with SOTA performance on benchmark datasets when using small LMs. T5QL uses constrained decoding to improve predictive performance and also to guarantee that the generated SQL is always valid. Futhermore, we complement the generator model with a ranker model that is capable of choosing the best candidate SQL from a pool of a few candidates.

[6] https://yale-lily.github.io/spider

References

Mark Chen, Jerry Tworek, Heewoo Jun, Qiming Yuan, Henrique Ponde de Oliveira Pinto, Jared Kaplan, Harri Edwards, Yuri Burda, Nicholas Joseph, Greg Brockman, et al. 2021. Evaluating large language models trained on code. *arXiv preprint arXiv:2107.03374*.

Alvin Cheung, Armando Solar-Lezama, and Samuel Madden. 2012. Inferring sql queries using program synthesis. *arXiv preprint arXiv:1208.2013*.

Zhangyin Feng, Daya Guo, Duyu Tang, Nan Duan, Xiaocheng Feng, Ming Gong, Linjun Shou, Bing Qin, Ting Liu, Daxin Jiang, and Ming Zhou. 2020. CodeBERT: A Pre-Trained Model for Programming and Natural Languages. *arXiv e-prints*, page arXiv:2002.08155.

Yujian Gan, Xinyun Chen, Jinxia Xie, Matthew Purver, John R Woodward, John Drake, and Qiaofu Zhang. 2021. Natural sql: Making sql easier to infer from natural language specifications. *arXiv preprint arXiv:2109.05153*.

Shirley Anugrah Hayati, Raphael Olivier, Pravalika Avvaru, Pengcheng Yin, Anthony Tomasic, and Graham Neubig. 2018. Retrieval-based neural code generation. *arXiv preprint arXiv:1808.10025*.

Aishwarya Kamath and Rajarshi Das. 2018. A survey on semantic parsing. *arXiv preprint arXiv:1812.00978*.

Kalpesh Krishna, Yapei Chang, John Wieting, and Mohit Iyyer. 2022. Rankgen: Improving text generation with large ranking models. *arXiv preprint arXiv:2205.09726*.

Triet HM Le, Hao Chen, and Muhammad Ali Babar. 2020. Deep learning for source code modeling and generation: Models, applications, and challenges. *ACM Computing Surveys (CSUR)*, 53(3):1–38.

Xi Victoria Lin, Richard Socher, and Caiming Xiong. 2020. Bridging textual and tabular data for cross-domain text-to-sql semantic parsing. *arXiv preprint arXiv:2012.12627*.

William Merrill, Yoav Goldberg, Roy Schwartz, and Noah A Smith. 2021. Provable limitations of acquiring meaning from ungrounded form: What will future language models understand? *Transactions of the Association for Computational Linguistics*, 9:1047–1060.

Pedro Orvalho, Miguel Terra-Neves, Miguel Ventura, Ruben Martins, and Vasco Manquinho. 2020. Squares: a sql synthesizer using query reverse engineering. *Proceedings of the VLDB Endowment*, 13(12):2853–2856.

Emilio Parisotto, Abdel-rahman Mohamed, Rishabh Singh, Lihong Li, Dengyong Zhou, and Pushmeet Kohli. 2016. Neuro-symbolic program synthesis. *arXiv preprint arXiv:1611.01855*.

Amir Pnueli and Roni Rosner. 1989. On the synthesis of a reactive module. In *Proceedings of the 16th ACM SIGPLAN-SIGACT symposium on Principles of programming languages*, pages 179–190.

Gabriel Poesia, Oleksandr Polozov, Vu Le, Ashish Tiwari, Gustavo Soares, Christopher Meek, and Sumit Gulwani. 2022. Synchromesh: Reliable code generation from pre-trained language models. *arXiv preprint arXiv:2201.11227*.

Colin Raffel, Noam Shazeer, Adam Roberts, Katherine Lee, Sharan Narang, Michael Matena, Yanqi Zhou, Wei Li, and Peter J Liu. 2019. Exploring the limits of transfer learning with a unified text-to-text transformer. *arXiv preprint arXiv:1910.10683*.

Torsten Scholak, Nathan Schucher, and Dzmitry Bahdanau. 2021. Picard: Parsing incrementally for constrained auto-regressive decoding from language models. *arXiv preprint arXiv:2109.05093*.

Peter Shaw, Ming-Wei Chang, Panupong Pasupat, and Kristina Toutanova. 2021. Compositional generalization and natural language variation: Can a semantic parsing approach handle both? *ArXiv*, abs/2010.12725.

Peng Shi, Patrick Ng, Zhiguo Wang, Henghui Zhu, Alexander Hanbo Li, Jun Wang, Cicero Nogueira dos Santos, and Bing Xiang. 2020. Learning Contextual Representations for Semantic Parsing with Generation-Augmented Pre-Training. *arXiv e-prints*, page arXiv:2012.10309.

Alane Laughlin Suhr, Kenton Lee, Ming-Wei Chang, and Pete Shaw. 2020. Exploring unexplored generalization challenges for cross-database semantic parsing.

Zeyu Sun, Qihao Zhu, Lili Mou, Yingfei Xiong, Ge Li, and Lu Zhang. 2019. A grammar-based structural cnn decoder for code generation. In *Proceedings of the AAAI conference on artificial intelligence*, volume 33, pages 7055–7062.

Alexey Svyatkovskiy, Shao Kun Deng, Shengyu Fu, and Neel Sundaresan. 2020. Intellicode compose: Code generation using transformer. In *Proceedings of the 28th ACM Joint Meeting on European Software Engineering Conference and Symposium on the Foundations of Software Engineering*, pages 1433–1443.

Bailin Wang, Richard Shin, Xiaodong Liu, Oleksandr Polozov, and Matthew Richardson. 2019. Rat-sql: Relation-aware schema encoding and linking for text-to-sql parsers. *arXiv preprint arXiv:1911.04942*.

Chunyang Xiao, Marc Dymetman, and Claire Gardent. 2016. Sequence-based structured prediction for semantic parsing. In *Proceedings of the 54th Annual Meeting of the Association for Computational Linguistics (Volume 1: Long Papers)*, pages 1341–1350, Berlin, Germany. Association for Computational Linguistics.

Tianbao Xie, Chen Henry Wu, Peng Shi, Ruiqi Zhong, Torsten Scholak, Michihiro Yasunaga, Chien-Sheng Wu, Ming Zhong, Pengcheng Yin, Sida I. Wang, Victor Zhong, Bailin Wang, Chengzu Li, Connor Boyle, Ansong Ni, Ziyu Yao, Dragomir R. Radev, Caiming Xiong, Lingpeng Kong, Rui Zhang, Noah A. Smith, Luke Zettlemoyer, and Tao Yu. 2022. Unifiedskg: Unifying and multi-tasking structured knowledge grounding with text-to-text language models. *CoRR*, abs/2201.05966.

Navid Yaghmazadeh, Yuepeng Wang, Isil Dillig, and Thomas Dillig. 2017. Type-and content-driven synthesis of sql queries from natural language. *arXiv preprint arXiv:1702.01168*.

Xi Ye, Semih Yavuz, Kazuma Hashimoto, Yingbo Zhou, and Caiming Xiong. 2022. Rng-kbqa: Generation augmented iterative ranking for knowledge base question answering. In *ACL*.

Kyra Yee, Yann Dauphin, and Michael Auli. 2019. Simple and effective noisy channel modeling for neural machine translation. In *Proceedings of the 2019 Conference on Empirical Methods in Natural Language Processing and the 9th International Joint Conference on Natural Language Processing (EMNLP-IJCNLP)*, pages 5696–5701, Hong Kong, China. Association for Computational Linguistics.

Pengcheng Yin and Graham Neubig. 2017. A syntactic neural model for general-purpose code generation. *arXiv preprint arXiv:1704.01696*.

Tao Yu, Chien-Sheng Wu, Xi Victoria Lin, Bailin Wang, Yi Chern Tan, Xinyi Yang, Dragomir Radev, Richard Socher, and Caiming Xiong. 2020. Grappa: grammar-augmented pre-training for table semantic parsing. *arXiv preprint arXiv:2009.13845*.

Tao Yu, Rui Zhang, He Yang Er, Suyi Li, Eric Xue, Bo Pang, Xi Victoria Lin, Yi Chern Tan, Tianze Shi, Zihan Li, et al. 2019. Cosql: A conversational text-to-sql challenge towards cross-domain natural language interfaces to databases. *arXiv preprint arXiv:1909.05378*.

Liang Zhao, Hexin Cao, and Yunsong Zhao. 2021. GP: Context-free Grammar Pre-training for Text-to-SQL Parsers. *arXiv e-prints*, page arXiv:2101.09901.

A SQL generation analysis

In this section we analyse in detail the predictions generated by T5QL. In Appendix A.1 we measure how often T5QL outputs valid SQLs and give an example of one invalid SQL. In Appendix A.2 we show an example of how constraining column name generation can boost performance.

A.1 Valid SQL generation

First, we check if T5QL using constrained decoding can still generate unparsable SQL. We obtain T5QL-Base's predictions in Spider's development set for beam sizes of 1, 2, 4 and 8. We observe that:

- T5QL never generates an unparsable SQL for the top-1 beam when the beam size > 1.
- Invalid SQL is generated when the LM (i.e., T5) enters a loop, as can be seen in Listing 1. Since the SQL length is limited, T5QL outputs the incomplete (and invalid) SQL. The loop, even if abnormal, is valid SQL syntax, e.g, an average of averages.
- For larger beam sizes (e.g, 8) we saw that the aforementioned model hallucinations are mainly present in the lower scored beams.

Listing 1: Invalid SQL generated by T5QL. For space concerns we abbreviate the generated SQL.

```
from stadium select name, capacity
    order by avg( avg( avg( avg(
    avg( avg( avg( avg( avg( avg(
    avg( avg( avg( avg( avg( avg(
    avg( avg( avg( avg( max( avg(
    min( min( min( min( min( max(
    max( max( max( max( max( max(
    max( max( max( max( max( max(
    max( max( max( max( max( max(
    max( max( max( max( ...
```

Next, we analyse whether model size reduces the number of invalid SQL generated by T5QL. We obtain the predictions in Spider's development set using T5QL-Base and T5QL-Large with and without constrained decoding. We report results of the four methods using 4 beams.

We observe that increasing the size of the model also increases the ability of the model to generate parsable SQL: T5QL-Base wo/ CD generates $\approx 20\%$ invalid SQLs, while T5QL-Large wo/ CD generates only $\approx 5\%$ invalid SQLs (Figure 4). Notice, however, that 5% is still a substantial amount of invalid SQLs. On the other hand, when using constrained decoding, T5QL always produces valid

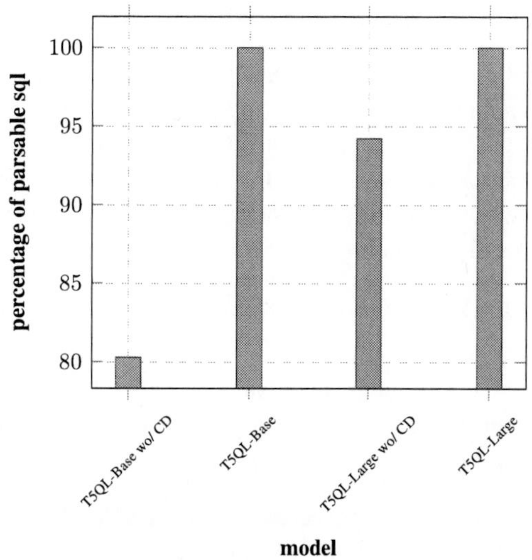

Figure 4: Percentage of parsable SQL, in the Spider's development set, in each model configuration. All methods use beam search with 4 beams and we report results for the first beam.

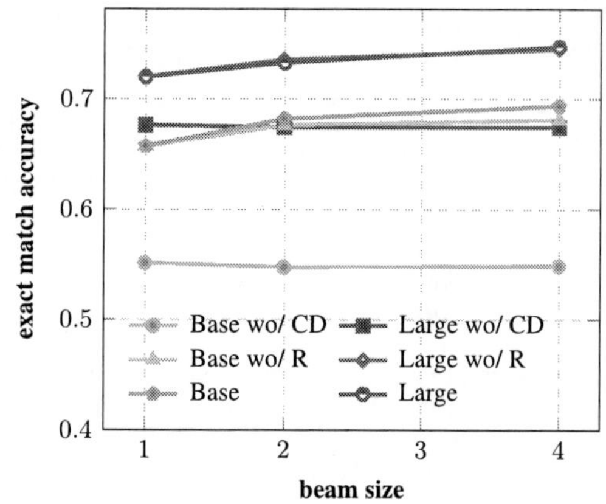

Figure 5: Comparison of EM accuracy in Spider's development between different model configurations. The "Base" model refers to T5QL-Base with constraint decoding and reranking; models "wo/ CD" are the models without constraint decoding nor reranking, whereas models "wo/ R" are the models without reranking.

SQLs when considering only the top-1 beam of beam search with 4 beams; this is true for both T5QL-Base and T5QL-Large.

A.2 Enforce existing table and column names

Finally, we analyse what is the impact of constraining the table and column names during SQL generation. When T5QL does not constrain column and table names, it can generate examples such as the one in Listing 2 where "song_id" is a column name that does not exist in the schema. When constraining column and table names, T5QL always generates existing column and table names, and, in this case, predicts the correct SQL (Listing 3).

Listing 2: Invalid SQL generated by T5QL wo/ CD. In this case the T5QL generated an non-existing column.

```
from singer as t1 join
    singer_in_concert as t2 on
    t1.song_id = t2.song_id
    select t1.name, count( * )
    group by t1.song_id
```

Listing 3: Valid and correct SQL generated by T5QL with CD for the same example as Listing 2.

```
from singer as t1 join
    singer_in_concert as t2 on
    t1.singer_id = t2.singer_id
     select t1.name, count( * )
     group by t1.singer_id
```

B Larger models

Experiments shown for our proposed method, T5QL, used T5-Base as the generator LM. We make this choice since our focus is to show that small LMs can have good performance even when compared against very large LMs. Nevertheless, evaluating if the proposed techniques, namely constrained decoding and reranking, scale to larger LMs is an interesting research question. Thus, we evaluate whether constrained decoding and reranking improve the performance of T5SQL-Large.

From Figure 5 we observe that the performance of T5QL-Base (i.e., Base) is superior to T5-Large (i.e., Large wo/CD) for 2–4 beams. When we add the constrained decoding component to T5-Large (i.e., Large wo/ R), the performance is significantly superior. This results highlights the importance of adding constrained decoding for SQL generation. However, we do not observe gains of adding the reranker model to T5-Large (i.e., Large), which we observed in T5-Base. This might indicate, as we pointed out in Section 3.3, that finding better reranking strategies is an interesting research path.

We do not include results for T5QL-3B since our main goal in this work is to increase performance using multiple smaller components and domain-aware techniques (e.g., constrained decoding) instead of relying on very large models. Furthermore, computing results for T5-3B is very costly in terms of money and time.

Human perceiving behavior modeling in evaluation of code generation models

Sergey Kovalchuk, Vadim Lomshakov, Artem Aliev
Huawei
{sergey.kovalchuk,vadim.lomshakov,artem.aliev}@huawei.com

Abstract

In this study, we evaluated a series of code generation models based on CodeGen and GPTNeo to compare the metric-based performance and human evaluation. For a deeper analysis of human perceiving within the evaluation procedure, we implemented a 5-level Likert scale assessment of the model output using a perceiving model based on the Theory of Planned Behavior (TPB). Through this analysis, we demonstrated an extension of model assessment as well as a deeper understanding of the quality and applicability of generated code for answering practical questions. The approach was evaluated with several model settings in order to assess diversity in the quality and style of answer. With the TPB-based model, we showed a different level of perceiving of the model result, namely, personal understanding, agreement level, and readiness to use the particular code. With this analysis, we investigate a series of issues in code generation, namely, natural language generation (NLG) problems observed in the context of programming and question-answering with code.

1 Introduction

Recent advances in natural language generation (NLG) support rapid growth in potential areas of application. One of the significant successes of NLG is the possible generation of code in various settings (Lu et al., 2021; Zhong et al., 2022): the translation of explicit specification into code, fixing errors, suggesting short snippets, etc. The common practice in NLG problems is the usage of known metrics (BertScore, BLEU, etc.) to evaluate models. Moreover, specific metrics dedicated to code generation evaluation were developed, such as CodeBLEU (Ren et al., 2020), RUBY (Tran et al., 2019), and others. Still, recent studies (Evtikhiev et al., 2022) show that the direct application of metrics often leads to issues in code generation evaluation.

With this in mind, investigated the applicability of human evaluation widely spread in NLG problems (De Mattei et al., 2021; Hämäläinen & Alnajjar, 2021) to assess an alternative approach to code evaluation and a deeper understanding of human perceiving of code generation (and NLG output in general). The study poses two research questions. First, how is human perceiving reflected by the text- or code-oriented NLP metrics? Second, what is the structure of human perceiving in the human evaluation procedure in the question-answering scenario? Here we consider perceiving as an act of becoming subjectively aware and conscious of the observed information.

The structure of the paper is as follows. The next section describes the datasets used in the study. The following section presets the details of code generation models' selection and preparation. Section 4 describes human evaluation solutions and procedures. Section 5 discusses the study results and evaluation results. Finally, Sections 6 and 7 provide a discussion and concluding remarks respectively.

2 Dataset

Within the study, we focused on question answering (QA) with a generation of short snippets as answers to real-world problems such as questions asked in Stack Overflow [1] (SO). For consistency, we added the following restrictions to the questions and answers considered within the study, taking SO as a reference for the analysis.

[1] https://stackoverflow.com/

Proceedings of the 2nd Workshop on Natural Language Generation, Evaluation, and Metrics (GEM), pages 287 - 294
December 7, 2022 ©2022 Association for Computational Linguistics

- We considered "conceptual" and "API usage" questions according to the taxonomy presented in (Beyer et al., 2020).
- We selected the questions that mainly contain a short textual description without explicit code presented.
- Contrarily, we use answers with explicit code snippets giving the solution to the proposed problem.
- To further specify the scope of the study, we only considered one programming language, Python, as it is one of the most popular ones.

To prepare an appropriate dataset we followed two steps. First, we used the publicly available dataset CoNaLa[2] (Yin et al., 2018) with explicitly identified train (2379 entries) and test parts (500 entries). The dataset originates from SO and contains explicit short questions and reference code snippets.

Alternatively, we prepared our own dataset from the original data on SO questions available on Stack Exchange[3]. To follow our requirements, we selected questions with the tag "python". For reference, we selected answers that earned maximum scores according to the SO data. To filter questions on presence or absence of code, we search the text for <pre><code> in HTML data. After that, we selected questions with no explicit code paired with answers with a single code snippet. Finally, we used regular expressions following (Beyer et al., 2020) to select "conceptual" and "API usage" classes of questions. Furthermore, we performed cleaning of the code (e.g. removing decorations inserted by software (">>>", "In [1]:", etc.), comments, and checked the parsing status using Tree-sitter[4]. After these steps, we obtained a dataset containing 42292 entries (pairs of questions and answers). Out of them, we selected 1000 entries as a test dataset. The test dataset was built using questions from 2021 and beyond to lower possible data leaking as we are using models trained on publicly available data.

3 Code generation models

3.1 Model selection

To select models for our study, we evaluated those which are publicly available, computationally inexpensive, and applicable on our data with finetuning. First, we selected GPT-Neo(-J)[5] (Black, Sid et al., 2021, p.), which shows high performance compared to Codex (Xu et al., 2022). Second, we chose CodeGen-mono-2B by Salesforce (Nijkamp et al., 2022), which was trained not only on the Pile dataset but also separately on the code from BigQuery and BigPython. CodeGen-mono-2B shows good results on HumanEval, which was similar to the Codex model of the same size (Chen et al., 2021). Additionally, we picked CoPilot by Microsoft as an industrial SOTA reference solution, which is also based on Codex (Chen et al., 2021).

3.2 Finetuning

Finetuning was performed for the selected models on training datasets from both CoNaLa (further denoted as FT:C) and SO (further denoted as FT:SO). We used Transformers and DeepSpeed libraries with common hyperparameters (optimizer = AdamW, Adam betas = (0.9, 0.999), Adam epsilon = 1e-08, weight decay = 0.0, learning rate = 5e-06, learning rate decay = linear, batch size(#samples) = 40, fp16). Moreover, we performed experiments with various code wrapping for prompt preparation. A query wrapped as a multiline comment to the generated code was selected as a well-performing baseline. Additionally, we performed a series of experiments in prompt engineering and selected the best performing solution for further experiments (denoted as FT:C+).

4 Human evaluation

4.1 User interface implementation

For performing the human evaluation, a user interface (UI) was developed as a web application using the Dash[6] framework (see Figure 1). The UI enables the collection of feedback information in two ways.

First (***HF1*** - human feedback 1), the UI shows a pair of answers generated for the same question by different models. The pairwise comparison of two answers was collected from the user by asking them to select the best answer with a 3 or 5 (depending on configuration) levels Likert scale

[2] https://conala-corpus.github.io/

[3] https://stackexchange.com/

[4] https://tree-sitter.github.io/

[5] https://github.com/EleutherAI/gpt-neo

[6] https://dash.plotly.com/

from -2 (the left answer is the best) to +2 (the right answer is the best). This feedback is collected for further research purposes to improve model performance with human-centered prediction models (currently considered as future research plans following the works (Nakano et al., 2022; Stiennon et al., 2020)).

Second (***HF2***), the user was asked to assess both answers (code snippets) with three scores using a 5-level Likert scale (from -2 to +2) by estimating:

- The general consistency of the code (whether the code is readable/understandable). The scale is considered to reflect how well the user ***understands*** the answer.
- The correctness of the answer with respect to the proposed question. The scale is considered to reflect the user's ***agreement*** with the answer.
- The usability of the provided answer. The scale is considered to reflect the user's expected ***intention to use***.

These scales analyze human behavior aspects by assessing the information perceiving in alignment with a model based on the theory of planned behavior (TPB) (Ajzen, 1991), widely used to quantify human behavior as reflected by attitude, subjective norms, and perceived control affecting target intention to use a considered technology. In our case, we consider "agreement" as the first criterion, reflecting the general user's attitude, "understand" as the second one, reflecting correspondence to subjective norms and perceived control, and "use" as a final target criterion, the obtained intention to use the solution.

The human feedback is collected for each pair of answers storing the scores provided by the user and his/her provided name. After each evaluation round (ended by clicking the "Submit" button), the interface is updated with a new pair of answers for further analysis.

For evaluation purposes, the original and finetuned models were applied to test sets in the selected datasets (CoNaLa and SO) forming a collection of alternative answers to 1500 questions. Applying the selected models and filtering empty answers, we obtained 10013 answers of different origin and quality. On each round, a random sample of two different answers was presented to the user. With this approach, a subset of 1364 questions was selected, supported with two or more answers by different models.

4.2 Human perceiving assessment

Within the presented study, we focused on the internal structure of answer perceiving during human evaluation. Thus, we performed a deeper analysis of HF2 to understand the connections between different features. For this purpose, we consider three main groups of features.

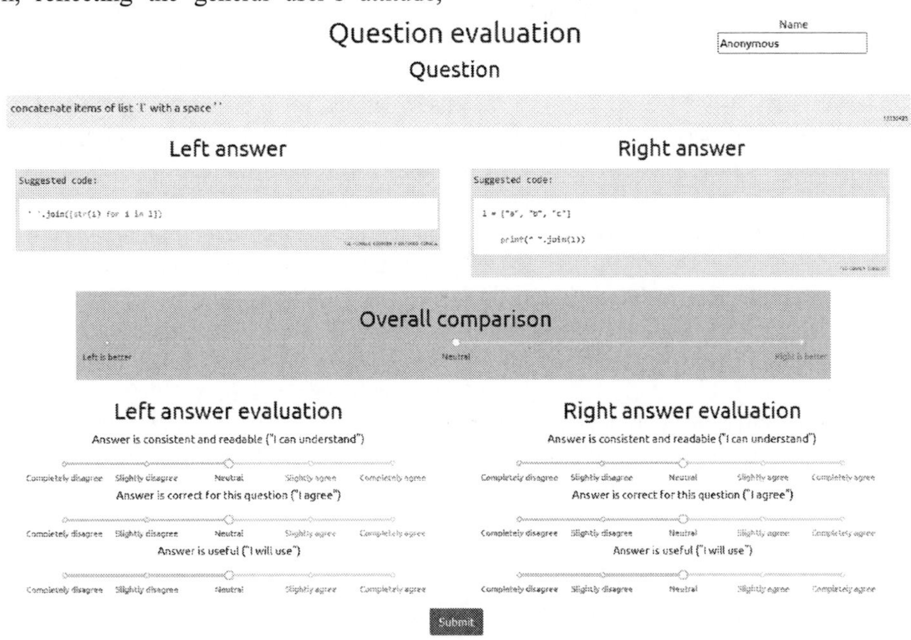

Figure 1. User interface for human evaluation

	BertScore		Rouge		CodeBLEU		Ruby		SacreBLEU	
Model	**mean**	**std**	**mean**	**std**	**mean**	**std**	**mean**	**std**	**mean**	**std**
Dataset: CoNaLa										
CodeGen	0.8068	0.1827	0.3142	0.2638	0.2821	0.2379	0.2791	0.2363	0.1196	0.1493
CodeGen *FT:C*	0.9017	0.1132	0.5532	0.2976	0.4848	0.2861	0.5392	0.3151	0.2142	0.1759
CodeGen *FT:SO*	0.8326	0.0379	0.1707	0.1316	0.0918	0.1095	0.1014	0.1348	0.0522	0.0658
CodeGen *FT:C+*	**0.9235**	0.0511	**0.6070**	0.2763	**0.5802**	0.2519	**0.6246**	0.2845	**0.2571**	0.1952
GPT-Neo	0.7370	0.1688	0.0503	0.0688	0.0785	0.0670	0.1460	0.1190	0.0111	0.0151
GPT-Neo *FT:C*	0.8366	0.1518	0.2926	0.2648	0.2298	0.2401	0.2619	0.2759	0.0900	0.1096
GPT-Neo *FT:SO*	0.8251	0.0380	0.1453	0.1122	0.0749	0.0858	0.0909	0.1192	0.0400	0.0455
CoPilot	0.8520	0.0398	0.3668	0.2075	0.2815	0.1554	0.2812	0.1899	0.1179	0.1162
Dataset: SO										
CodeGen	0.7434	0.1838	0.0790	0.0951	0.1687	0.1549	0.0974	0.1025	0.0176	0.0331
CodeGen *FT:C*	**0.8178**	0.0923	**0.1473**	0.1447	**0.3311**	0.2488	**0.1615**	0.1935	**0.0396**	0.0572
CodeGen *FT:SO*	0.8099	0.0825	0.1298	0.1188	0.1729	0.1773	0.0933	0.1062	0.0327	0.0452
GPT-Neo	0.7543	0.1286	0.0511	0.0577	0.1411	0.1074	0.0991	0.1101	0.0093	0.0123
GPT-Neo *FT:C*	0.7912	0.1488	0.1193	0.1265	0.2986	0.2295	0.1433	0.1606	0.0292	0.0419
GPT-Neo *FT:SO*	0.8003	0.1126	0.1156	0.1109	0.1574	0.1675	0.0953	0.1069	0.0275	0.0378

Table 1. Metric-based evaluation

FG1 (feature group 1) includes the common metrics used for the NLG task. The selection of metrics includes general purpose metrics (BertScore, Rouge, SacreBLEU) and metrics specific to code generation problems (CodeBLEU, Ruby). The metrics were evaluated for each model applied for test datasets.

FG2 includes votes collected from the users along three selected scores, namely, subjective consistency (understanding), subjective correctness (agreement), and subjective intention (use).

FG3 includes simple test features (linguistic features), namely, question and answer length, average lines number in answer, and average lines number in question.

To answer the proposed research questions, we analyzed the interconnection between the features in the three groups by assessing the pairwise mutual information (MI) between features. As we focused mainly on perceiving structure and interconnection, the main analysis and interpretation were applied to a) internal MI between features in FG2; b) MI between features in FG2 and features in other groups.

5 Results

5.1 Metric-based evaluation

Weused a common train-eval-test split for evaluation. In the case of the CoNaLa dataset, the test dataset was pre-selected by the authors. In the case of the SO dataset, we composed the test dataset as random samples of 1000 answers dated 2021 and beyond, while the answers dated 2020 and earlier were used for training. In both cases, we split the training dataset into train and validation parts as 9:1 randomly.

Table 1 shows the main evaluation results according to the selected NLP metrics. In the case of the CoNaLa dataset, the best results were obtained by CodeGen FT:C+, followed by CoPilot. In the case of the SO dataset, the best performance was achieved with CodeGen FT:C.

5.2 Human evaluation

With the implemented UI and judgment collection procedure, the human evaluation was performed in a semi-open way by exposing the UI with a pre-defined collection of answers to independent groups of users of different backgrouds, but having a basic understanding of coding and the principles of software engineering. The user set includes MSc/PhD students and researchers in computer science and related areas, as well as professional software developers. The diversity in experience of the users enables further deeper analysis of the nature of human perceiving , along with the possible assessment of experience influence.

During a week-long evaluation period, the collection of votes for 614 answers in the HF2 part was collected from 43 different users. Within the analysis, we exclude the original models and only consider finetuned models. The average scores for FG2 with the selected pairs model/dataset are presented in Table 2.

We observe the highest perceiving in CoPilot and finetuned CodeGen. The CoNaLa dataset shows slightly lower Understand scores compared to the SO dataset. At the same time, the SO dataset shows negative Agree and Use scores reflecting wrong (but consistent) answers generated by the model. A more interesting observation is the diversity in scores exhibited by the best CodeGen and CoPilot in the CoNaLa dataset: CoPilot shows slightly higher Understand and Agree scores, while the Use score is much higher for CodeGen.

Model	N	Under-stand	Agree	Use
Dataset: CoNaLa				
CodeGen *FT:C*	58	0.5345	0.3966	0.4310
CodeGen *FT:SO*	68	0.0882	-0.1471	-0.1912
CodeGen *FT:C+*	56	0.8571	0.4464	**0.4286**
GPT-Neo *FT:C*	62	0.0000	-0.4677	-0.5323
GPT-Neo *FT:SO*	55	-0.0364	-0.6364	-0.8364
CoPilot	39	**0.8974**	**0.4872**	0.2308
Dataset: SO				
CodeGen *FT:C*	25	**0.9200**	**-0.3200**	**-0.2000**
CodeGen *FT:SO*	13	0.0769	-0.6154	-0.4615
GPT-Neo	21	-0.9048	-1.8095	-1.8095
GPT-Neo *FT:C*	21	0.2381	-0.5238	-0.4286
GPT-Neo *FT:SO*	16	-0.6250	-1.1875	-1.1250

Table 2. Human perceiving evaluation

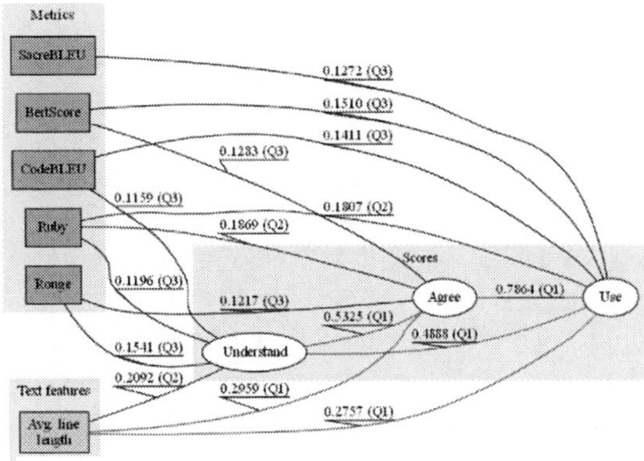

Figure 2. Mutual information and feature connection

For the analysis of MI, we divided the selection of the connections between features (FG2-FG2, FG2-FG1, FG2-FG3) into four groups according to the quartiles of the MI distribution (the division levels correspond to MI of 0.1144, 0.1621, 0.2683 for thresholds between Q4-Q3, Q3-Q2, Q2-Q1 respectively). We dropped Q4 (lowest MI) connections as insignificant and considered the others for further analysis. Figure 2 shows the selection of features connected with the labels denoting MI level and the quartile to which the value belongs. Also, the quartiles are shown in color (Q1 – red, Q2 – blue, Q3 – black).

As expected, the internal connections of perceiving features have high MI. The highest interconnection is observed between Agree and Use scores. Additionally, they are highly correlated ($cor = 0.8981$). A simple linear regression model was estimated as $U = 0.8389A + 0.0764C + 0.0134$ ($R^2 = 0.8098$) where U is for intention to use, A is for agreement, C is for understanding (internal consistency). Thus, we expect that the intention to use is highly defined by the agreement to the answer. On the other hand, the dependency between understanding and agreement can also be observed, but is rather lower: $A = 0.6687C + 0.0376$ (with $R^2 = 0.4358$).

We see that the connection of most of the NLP metrics is rather low (Q3), except for the Ruby metric showing a more significant (Q2) influence on the agreement and the intention to use. This can be interpreted as a good evaluation of code quality. The remaining features are mostly low and have interconnection with different perceiving scores. In general, the MI for interconnection with the intention to use is slightly higher.

The analysis shows that basic linguistic features (FG3) mainly have low interconnection with perceiving votes (FG2) as the connections were assessed with low MI (Q4) with one exception for average line length having high (Q1 or Q2) impact on the perceiving features. Further analysis shows that there are weak results where a model failed to generate a structured answer and produce long (mainly erroneous) lines of code.

6 Discussion

The study focused on code generation problems. For this purpose, we used modern NLG models (CodeGen, GPT) and performed fine-tuning to obtain a higher quality of the results according to the common pipeline. The results we obtained with the CodeGen model look promising and produce high-quality results comparable to the industrial solutions (CoPilot). Still, we consider the further improvement of the code generation QA model as one of our future research directions.

The main goal of the study is the investigation of the human perceiving structure in the NLG problem. The area of human evaluation is widely studied in different NLG settings including general assessment of natural language generation, as well as distinguishing model-generated from human-generated answer. The common goal of most studies in the area is model improvement with collected evaluation feedback. Still, the question of how we can evaluate human feedback and which level of trust can be given to it is still open. This problem becomes more challenging if the evaluation is performed in a complex domain where a human annotator needs to be a domain expert. In that case, the human feedback collection could be more expensive and can provide more diversity in judgments. With this in mind, we considered a problem of NLG in programming QA and code generation, with programmers as experts evaluating high-level correspondence of the answer to a proposed question. Within the study, we focused on the general structure of human perceiving divided into three main parts: whether the human understands the model output; whether he/she considers it as correct; whether he/she is ready to use it in practice. This structure of human perceiving was considered previously in the expert-based evaluation of decision support systems (Kovalchuk et al., 2022) and showed good results in understanding human intentions in perceiving AI-based prediction in such complex domains as medicine.

Within the study, we analyzed internal interconnection between human perceiving features in code generation and discovered that although the agreement and intention to use are highly correlated, the understanding (subjective correctness) and agreement show lower interconnections. This could be interpreted as a sign of existing issues in generated code properly recognized by a human, i.e., the answer generated by the model "looks like code" but doesn't resolve the question properly. On the other hand, the high interconnection between agreement and intention to use could be treated as promising results for code generation problems: if the code answers the question, it is good enough to be used.

An interesting result obtained in the analysis of external interconnection of perceiving score is a rather weak MI of connections to the common NLP metrics. The only metric showing medium interconnection is Ruby, intentionally developed for code evaluation with semantic comparison (Tran et al., 2019). We consider this result as a sign of the rather weak applicability of common NLP metrics to complex NLG problems.

One of the questions raised during the evaluation is whether we can compare the syntactic correctness of the code to the subjective correctness (understanding) of the code. During the evaluation, we see several examples of code that was syntactically incorrect but may have been evaluated as useful (e.g. containing the correct line of code followed by an ill-formatted line). We believe that continuous Likert-scale-based evaluation may help to improve the model training/finetuning in further studies with human evaluation. Still, we consider this issue as one of the directions for the future development of the proposed approach.

It is worth mentioning that CodeGen FT:SO shows lower performance compared to CodeGen FT:C even on the SO dataset. We suppose that a possible reason for such behavior is the fact that the CoNaLa dataset was manually curated and contains only one-line code answers. At the same time, the SO dataset was not filtered in that way and contains answers of diverse length, structure, and quality. A further investigation of this issue is one of the directions for further research.

The presented results can be used in two ways. First, to improve models by training with a deeper understanding of human perceiving structure. For example, the mentioned values could be considered as a sequential filter where the next step can be considered only by the answer passed from the previous one. In this way, the perceiving may be considered as a reward for the model in the generation of the answer.

Second, the understanding of human perceiving may improve human-computer interaction in AI-based applications. For instance, the separate prediction of human perceiving features may provide important information depending on the interaction scenario. In particular, the Agree score may be more influential in code automatically generated by explicit specification, while the Use score may be more important in direct human-centered QA (e.g., in a form of an intelligent IDE assistant).

7 Conclusion and future work

The current study shows early results in the research of human perceiving understanding within the context of NLG human evaluation. Being aimed at a deeper understanding of the internal structure of human perceiving and interconnection with common metrics, the study shows that perceiving structure may be decomposed into a complex value with implicit interconnection directing from model-generated structure evaluation to subjective intention to use. The proposed structure of human perceiving may be further used for collecting judgments in complex domains where direct application of common NLP metrics gives rather weak results and where a high semantic diversity in the possible answer may be observed.

We consider the further development of the proposed study in the following directions. First, we would like to continue collecting human feedback in order to advance the development of the perceiving model. Additionally, we would like to extend the research to analyze the personal characteristics of the human (in our case, it may be a personal experience, relevance to the question, etc.). Second, we would like to investigate the possible application of the decomposed human perceiving value to model training/finetuning. Third, we are interested in the extension of the model with technical characteristics of generated code (e.g. checking for syntactic errors, test-based evaluation). Finally, we are planning to investigate the influence of the context on human perceiving including the dependencies from the application scenario.

Acknowledgements

We thank all the users involved into the evaluation procedure presented in this study for their effort in assessment of the generated answers. We are also grateful to the anonymous GEM reviewers for their valuable comments and suggestions.

References

Ajzen, I. (1991). The theory of planned behavior. *Organizational Behavior and Human Decision Processes*, *50*(2), 179–211. https://doi.org/10.1016/0749-5978(91)90020-T

Beyer, S., Macho, C., Di Penta, M., & Pinzger, M. (2020). What kind of questions do developers ask on Stack Overflow? A comparison of automated approaches to classify posts into question categories. *Empirical Software Engineering*, *25*(3), 2258–2301. https://doi.org/10.1007/s10664-019-09758-x

Black, Sid, Leo, Gao, Wang, Phil, Leahy, Connor, & Biderman, Stella. (2021). *GPT-Neo: Large Scale Autoregressive Language Modeling with Mesh-Tensorflow* (1.0). Zenodo. https://doi.org/10.5281/ZENODO.5297715

Chen, M., Tworek, J., Jun, H., Yuan, Q., Pinto, H. P. de O., Kaplan, J., Edwards, H., Burda, Y., Joseph, N., Brockman, G., Ray, A., Puri, R., Krueger, G., Petrov, M., Khlaaf, H., Sastry, G., Mishkin, P., Chan, B., Gray, S., … Zaremba, W. (2021). *Evaluating Large Language Models Trained on Code* (arXiv:2107.03374). arXiv. http://arxiv.org/abs/2107.03374

De Mattei, L., Lai, H., Dell'Orletta, F., & Nissim, M. (2021). Human Perception in Natural Language Generation. *Proceedings of the 1st Workshop on Natural Language Generation, Evaluation, and Metrics (GEM 2021)*, 15–23. https://doi.org/10.18653/v1/2021.gem-1.2

Evtikhiev, M., Bogomolov, E., Sokolov, Y., & Bryksin, T. (2022). *Out of the BLEU: How should we assess quality of the Code Generation models?* (arXiv:2208.03133). arXiv. http://arxiv.org/abs/2208.03133

Hämäläinen, M., & Alnajjar, K. (2021). Human Evaluation of Creative NLG Systems: An Interdisciplinary Survey on Recent Papers. *Proceedings of the 1st Workshop on Natural Language Generation, Evaluation, and Metrics*

(GEM 2021), 84–95. https://doi.org/10.18653/v1/2021.gem-1.9

Kovalchuk, S. V., Kopanitsa, G. D., Derevitskii, I. V., Matveev, G. A., & Savitskaya, D. A. (2022). Three-stage intelligent support of clinical decision making for higher trust, validity, and explainability. *Journal of Biomedical Informatics*, *127*, 104013. https://doi.org/10.1016/j.jbi.2022.104013

Lu, S., Guo, D., Ren, S., Huang, J., Svyatkovskiy, A., Blanco, A., Clement, C., Drain, D., Jiang, D., Tang, D., Li, G., Zhou, L., Shou, L., Zhou, L., Tufano, M., Gong, M., Zhou, M., Duan, N., Sundaresan, N., … Liu, S. (2021). *CodeXGLUE: A Machine Learning Benchmark Dataset for Code Understanding and Generation* (arXiv:2102.04664). arXiv. http://arxiv.org/abs/2102.04664

Nakano, R., Hilton, J., Balaji, S., Wu, J., Ouyang, L., Kim, C., Hesse, C., Jain, S., Kosaraju, V., Saunders, W., Jiang, X., Cobbe, K., Eloundou, T., Krueger, G., Button, K., Knight, M., Chess, B., & Schulman, J. (2022). *WebGPT: Browser-assisted question-answering with human feedback* (arXiv:2112.09332). arXiv. http://arxiv.org/abs/2112.09332

Nijkamp, E., Pang, B., Hayashi, H., Tu, L., Wang, H., Zhou, Y., Savarese, S., & Xiong, C. (2022). *A Conversational Paradigm for Program Synthesis* (arXiv:2203.13474). arXiv. http://arxiv.org/abs/2203.13474

Ren, S., Guo, D., Lu, S., Zhou, L., Liu, S., Tang, D., Sundaresan, N., Zhou, M., Blanco, A., & Ma, S. (2020). *CodeBLEU: A Method for Automatic Evaluation of Code Synthesis* (arXiv:2009.10297). arXiv. http://arxiv.org/abs/2009.10297

Stiennon, N., Ouyang, L., Wu, J., Ziegler, D., Lowe, R., Voss, C., Radford, A., Amodei, D., & Christiano, P. F. (2020). Learning to summarize with human feedback. In H. Larochelle, M. Ranzato, R. Hadsell, M. F. Balcan, & H. Lin (Eds.), *Advances in Neural Information Processing Systems* (Vol. 33, pp. 3008–3021). Curran Associates, Inc. https://proceedings.neurips.cc/paper/2020/file/1f89885d556929e98d3ef9b86448f951-Paper.pdf

Tran, N., Tran, H., Nguyen, S., Nguyen, H., & Nguyen, T. (2019). Does BLEU Score Work for Code Migration? *2019 IEEE/ACM 27th International Conference on Program Comprehension (ICPC)*, 165–176. https://doi.org/10.1109/ICPC.2019.00034

Xu, F. F., Alon, U., Neubig, G., & Hellendoorn, V. J. (2022). *A Systematic Evaluation of Large Language Models of Code* (arXiv:2202.13169). arXiv. http://arxiv.org/abs/2202.13169

Yin, P., Deng, B., Chen, E., Vasilescu, B., & Neubig, G. (2018). Learning to mine aligned code and natural language pairs from stack overflow. *Proceedings of the 15th International Conference on Mining Software Repositories*, 476–486. https://doi.org/10.1145/3196398.3196408

Zhong, M., Liu, G., Li, H., Kuang, J., Zeng, J., & Wang, M. (2022). *CodeGen-Test: An Automatic Code Generation Model Integrating Program Test Information* (arXiv:2202.07612). arXiv. http://arxiv.org/abs/2202.07612

Nearest Neighbor Language Models for Stylistic Controllable Generation

Severino Trotta † and **Lucie Flek** †‡ and **Charles Welch** †‡
† Conversational AI and Social Analytics (CAISA) Lab
Department of Mathematics and Computer Science, University of Marburg
‡ The Hessian Center for Artificial Intelligence (Hessian.AI)
severino.trotta@gmail.com,{lucie.flek,welchc}@uni-marburg.de

Abstract

Recent language modeling performance has been greatly improved by the use of external memory. This memory encodes the context so that similar contexts can be recalled during decoding. This similarity depends on how the model learns to encode context, which can be altered to include other attributes, such as style. We construct and evaluate an architecture for this purpose, using corpora annotated for politeness, formality, and toxicity. Through extensive experiments and human evaluation we demonstrate the potential of our method to generate text while controlling style. We find that style-specific datastores improve generation performance, though results vary greatly across styles, and the effect of pretraining data and specific styles should be explored in future work.

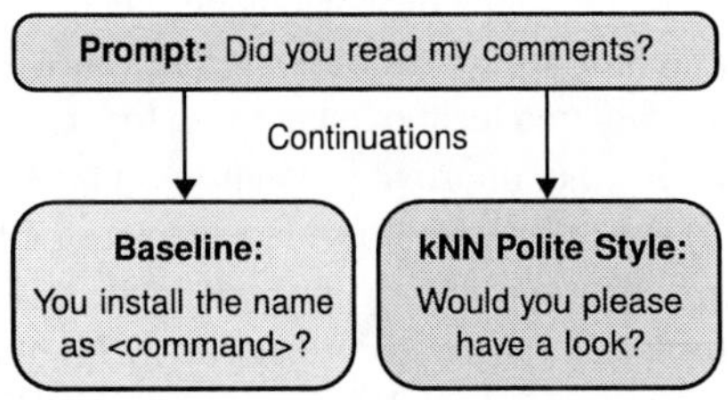

Figure 1: Example prompt continuations of the baseline kNN language model and our model, which continues generation in a specified style (e.g. polite). This example is based on a real example from our human evaluation but shortened for brevity and clarity. Full examples are provided in Appendix A.

1 Introduction

Language models with external memory, like Khandelwal et al. (2020b)'s recent k-nearest neigbour language model (kNN-LM), have demonstrated impressive predictive performance. Great reductions in perplexity are achieved through storing the encoding of contexts from the training data. A sequence of tokens is encoded by the model and stored as a key, which is paired with a value representing the next token in the sequence. During decoding, similar contexts are recalled based on their key similarity, and values are interpolated with the base language model's predictions.

In this work, we augment the encoding with stylistic attributes, such that the keys are more heavily influenced by the style of the encoded text. By explicitly encoding the style, the similarity is more strongly affected by the stylistic attributes than previous models. When decoding, we can then provide a style (e.g. polite or formal) and the most similar contexts are both relevant in content and more likely to conform to the provided style. The example in Figure 1 shows a prompt and two continuations, one with the baseline kNN language model and one with our model given a polite style value as input, signaling that it should continue the prompt in a polite style.

Through our architecture implementation, we show that we not only improve language modeling performance over previous models, but that we can control generation to produce text of a particular style. We provide human evaluation of our stylistic outputs and an analysis of the performance of our approach and modeling decisions that affect how style attributes are represented in memory. To the best of our knowledge, this is the first work to modify a language model's external memory in order to control generated style.

2 Related Work

Recent approaches to controllable generation have included fine-tuning large models, such as Keskar et al. (2019), who condition on 50 control codes during training, which represent different styles, topics, and languages. Other approaches avoid retraining by modifying the predictions only at decoding time. The FUDGE model predicts for a sequence, the likelihood that possible generation steps will result in a sequence that satisfies

Proceedings of the 2nd Workshop on Natural Language Generation, Evaluation, and Metrics (GEM), pages 295 - 305
December 7, 2022

a given constraint (Yang and Klein, 2021). The DExperts model alters the probability distribution of a language model (LM) based on the predictions of other LMs that are fine-tuned on specific desired or undesired attributes (Liu et al., 2021). Dathathri et al. (2020) and others similarly modify gradients directly during prediction.

Khandelwal et al.'s k-nearest neigbour language model is based on the groundwork laid by previous work that augmented language models with a cache memory of recent observations. Grave et al. (2017b) captured local context of up to a few thousands tokens to improve predictions. Grave et al. (2017a) expanded upon this idea by storing all past hidden activations in a memory. Khandelwal et al. then replaced the recurrent network with a transformer to better model long-term dependencies. Aspects of kNN-LMs have been improved upon, in terms of performance, efficiency, and additional functionality.

Even though kNN-LMs achieve state-of-the-art predictive performance, the retrieval operation is very computationally expensive. He et al. (2021) and Alon et al. (2022) explored techniques to improve inference speed, such as compressing embeddings, or training an additional model to dynamically disable retrieval for predictions where the datastore is unlikely to improve the result. Wu et al. (2022) implemented a similar model and focused on improving scalability. Yogatama et al. (2021) extended the model with a gating mechanism that learns to combine short and long term memory with local context. Xu et al. (2021) improved performance by leveraging structural locality features such as topic clusters in text or project hierarchies in source code repositories. Khandelwal et al. (2020b) also extended their model for use in machine translation (Khandelwal et al., 2020a), which has also received efficiency improvements (Meng et al., 2021; Wang et al., 2021).

3 Methodology

The main goal of our work is to expand kNN-LM functionality and we build off of Khandelwal et al. (2020b), which we will refer to as the baseline architecture. We modified this architecture to accept additional style attributes as input, and concatenate these to the input text encoding. This has the effect of modifying the embedding space such that it encodes both semantic and stylistic properties (see Appendix B). We will refer to this as the style architecture.

After the input style and context are encoded, they are stored in the datastore. We experimented with separating datastores based on the distribution of style values in the dataset. For this part we take subsets with specific style values (e.g. only toxic or only polite) from the datasets and construct datastores containing only data from those subsets. We refer to this as *separate datastores*. Datastores containing examples of different style are referred to as *mixed datastores*.

4 Datasets

We use 4 datasets, 3 of which contain style attributes. Unless stated otherwise, we use the default splits provided by the original work.

Wikitext-103 Wikitext-103 (WT103) is a collection of *Good* and *Featured* Wikipedia articles (Merity et al., 2017). It is provided in a tokenized form, with case, punctuation and numbers, totalling 103 B tokens. For better compatibility with our tokenization of other datasets we modified WT103's tokenization by replacing all occurrences of `*n 't` (e.g. in "can't") with `* n't`.

Politeness The Stanford Politeness Corpus (SPC) consists of 11k utterances from StackExchange and Wikipedia Talk pages, annotated with politeness scores, which we use as style attributes (Danescu-Niculescu-Mizil et al., 2013). We created an 85-7.5-7.5 split for training, validation, and test.

Formality Grammarly's Yahoo! Answers Formality Corpus (GYAFC) is the largest available corpus for formality style transfer, containing about 110K formal/informal sentence pairs (Rao and Tetreault, 2018). It is divided into the domains *Entertainment & Music* and *Family & Relationships*, which makes it suitable for training and evaluation with in/out-of-domain data. We do not use the parallel nature of the corpus, but assign each sentence a style attribute (-1 for informal- and 1 for formal sentences) and re-split the training subset to obtain an 80-10-10 train/validation/test split.

Toxicity For toxicity we use the Jigsaw Unintended Bias in Toxicity Classification dataset, which contains comments from the Civil Comments platform annotated with several binary toxicity labels representing types of toxicity (e.g. insult, identity attack, sexually explicit) (Borkan et al.,

2019). We use only the *toxic* label as a style attribute. We further use the Real Toxicity Prompts dataset for human evaluation (Gehman et al., 2020). This dataset contains the beginning of sentences and has been used to test if models can continue generation without toxicity.

4.1 Preprocessing

We largely follow Merity et al. (2017)'s preprocessing of WT103 for all data. Additionally, we perform the following replacements:

what	replacement
inline/block code	`<code>`
usernames	`<person>`
hyperlinks	`[title](url)` $\mapsto$ title
URLs	`<url>`

Unlike Merity et al. (2017) we use `spaCy.io` for normalization and tokenization, but perform the same tokenization of infix punctuation and symbols. This serves to differentiate number separator punctuation from word punctuation, and hyphens from minus signs or ranges.

5 Experiments

In preliminary experiments we examined the effect of float precision on model performance. Using WT103 and the setup of Khandelwal et al. (2020b) we found that using half precision halves inference time without hurting perplexity, and reduces inference time for the kNN-LM with a negligible 0.25 increase in perplexity. In the following sections we use half-precision to speed up the experimentation process.

In the main experiments we first examine the impact on perplexity when incorporating style values into the model. Then we compare our method to the baseline through human evaluation.

5.1 Language Modeling with Style Attributes

We train the style model, S, using the modified architecture, and baseline model, B, which uses the original architecture. To achieve high predictive performance on text, we first train both on WT103.

For each dataset we then fine-tune a copy of S and B on the dataset. Using these fine-tuned models we generate and evaluate a datastore for each a model, using the dataset the respective model was fine-tuned on.

We additionally build and evaluate a datastore on domain and style subsets, to test our model's performance on out-of-domain data and across subsets with specific style. The subsets are listed in Table 3 in the Appendix.

5.2 Setup & parameters

Unless stated otherwise, we use the default parameters used by the `transformer_lm_wiki103` architecture and Khandelwal et al. (2020b).

Vocabulary To avoid a high number of OoV tokens, we chose to use a shared vocabulary from the union of all datasets. Tokens occurring less than 3 times were mapped to <unk>. The resulting vocabulary has a size of 375k tokens. Since Merity et al. (2017) have shown that a large vocabulary with adaptive input representation can outperform a smaller BPE vocabulary, we chose the former over the latter – although this choice has its own limitations (see limitations section).

Training During pretraining on WT103, we use random style values normally distributed around the median, set patience to 5 epochs, and the style embedding dimension to 96. During fine-tuning we use Adam instead of the NAG optimizer and set patience to 10 epochs.

Datastore We use half-precision vectors in the datastore. Since the context embedding dimension (1,120) must be divisible by the number of FAISS index subquantizers, we use 70 instead of 64. For smaller subsets of data we use 2,048 cluster centroids, rather than the default 4,096.

5.3 Fine-tuning Results

The results of fine-tuning for each style attribute are shown in Table 1. We find that simply encoding the style value improves model performance on all datasets, including the original WT103, though this is likely due to the small increase in the number of parameters. Fine-tuning predictably lowers perplexity on the style datasets and slightly increases the WT103 perplexity as the model shifts away from the corpus it was originally trained on. The best performance is on formality, followed by politeness, which we expect to more closely resemble WT103. The addition of the style input allows for much greater improvement on politeness as compared to toxicity which shows near equal performance without it. We also provide perplexity for the kNN-LM in Appendix C.

Dataset	Baseline PT	Baseline FT	Style PT	Style FT
Politeness	218	126	164	78
Formality	161	77	148	60
Toxicity	212	125	186	93
WT103	31	35-64	29	32-59

Table 1: Perplexity before (using the pretrained model; PT) and after fine-tuning (FT). All models were evaluated on the FT dataset and on WT103. The value ranges in the WT103 row indicate the performance range of the FT models on the WT103 dataset.

		Fluency (%)	Style (%)
Datastore	Mixed	45.8	48.2
	Specific	54.2	51.8
Model type	LM	47.7	50.7
	kNN-LM	52.3	49.3
Architecture	Baseline	48.8	47.3
	Style	51.2	52.7

Table 2: Human evaluation preferences for model pairs. Column-wise percentage pairs sum to 100.0.

5.4 Human Evaluation

We aimed to answer three questions; (1) do the style-specific datastores outperform the mixed datastore, (2) does the kNN-LM outperform the LM, and (3) does the style architecture outperform the baseline? To address these questions we asked a group of 11 students to annotate model outputs.

Generating Output We follow the idea of Gehman et al. (2020) and generate outputs by supplying prompts of different styles to the models. We use both non-toxic (toxicity $= 0$) and neutral ($0 <$ toxicity < 0.5) and created prompts from the formality and politeness datasets by cutting off the second half of randomly sampled sentences. The prompts are then used as input to the models, which generate continuations to the prompts. All combinations of models and inputs are detailed in Table 4 in the Appendix. For all kNN-LM outputs we use $\lambda = 0.8$ as interpolation parameter.

Survey Setup We asked annotators to select which of a pair of prompt continuations was more fluent and which more closely followed one of the given styles. The pair combinations are based on the three comparisons listed at the beginning of this section, but are fully listed in Tables 5-7 in the Appendix and result in a total of 440 survey questions. The questions were presented to annotators in random subsets of 20 % of the full set. Each output pair was rated by 2-4 people.

Results The results in Table 2 show which model is preferred, in percentage of annotators, in terms of fluency and style for each pair. We find that when comparing mixed and specific datastores, the specific datastores are preferred for style and even more strongly for fluency. While the kNN-LM is preferred over the LM in fluency, the style preference is more evenly split. When comparing the style architecture to the baseline, we find that the ours is preferred, with style more strongly preferred to fluency.

These results are an aggregation over the styles, however the performance on specific styles reveals more varied results. The specific datastores give more style control for politeness than for other styles and for some combinations of the prompt style and target style, the mixed datastore was preferred. We see that when we want to generate non-toxic, polite, or formal text; those that more closely resemble the pretraining data style, the preference leans more toward the mixed datastore.

When comparing the LM to the kNN-LM, we found that the LM style was often preferred when provided an informal, non-toxic, or impolite prompt, regardless of the target style. We also found that the fluency of the LM is preferred when generating polite or impolite text. Lastly, the style architecture is not always preferred over the baseline either. The baseline shows stronger fluency for toxic and impolite prompts. The style architecture has the best style control when generating formal, toxic, and impolite text. Overall, there appears to be a trade-off between style-control and fluency. The full breakdown by prompt and input type is shown in Figures 4-6 in the appendix.

6 Conclusion

We examined the use of kNN language models for controllable stylistic generation using politeness, formality, and toxicity as target styles. Our findings show that simply encoding style in the architecture improved perplexity of the language model. A human evaluation further showed that specific datastores for target styles outperform the standard mixed datastore, and that our model generally outperformed the baseline kNN model in terms of fluency and style control, though results on specific styles varied. Future work is needed to fully understand the effect of pretraining and benefits of the model variants for specific styles and should also consider comparisons to other controllable generation models, such as Keskar et al. (2019).

Our code is available on Github at `https://github.com/d8xa/style-knnlm`.

Limitations

Vocabulary Choice We chose a shared vocabulary to reuse the same baseline model for fine-tuning on multiple datasets. Since less frequent tokens are assigned less parameters by the adaptive input representation, this could lead to under-representation of rare, style-specific tokens in general, and worse fine-tuning results for smaller datasets or datasets with many rare tokens. The same problem applies for single-dataset vocabularies as well, when rare tokens are more prevalent for a particular style. Byte-pair encoding would avoid these problems, but make comparability to the vanilla kNN-LM more difficult.

Sequence Length The original kNN-LM was trained with sequences of up to 3,072 tokens in length, which helps model long-term dependencies in the WT103 dataset. Since all of our datasets with style attributes contain much shorter sequences, single-dataset training with shorter input sizes might be better suited and achieve better performance than pre-training on WT103 and fine-tuning on the style dataset.

Comparability with Khandelwal et al. (2020b) When training our style architecture, we had to choose between a combined embedding dimension of $C + S_{\text{emb}} = 1{,}024$ (token- and style embedding dimensions C and S_{emb}), or to use $C = 1{,}024$. In any case the resulting language model would have a different number of parameters than in the original kNN-LM . We chose to use $C = 1{,}024$ and $S_{\text{emb}} = 96$. FAISS requires the vector dimension to be divisible by the number of subquantizers. Since our combined embedding dimension is different from 1,024, we had to choose 70 instead of 64 subquantizers.

Another difference is the choice of vocabulary. The WT103-only vocabulary would make results more comparable, but also lead to a high number of `UNK` tokens for the style datasets, and therefore reduce performance greatly.

Token to Style Embedding Dimension Ratio To limit the scope of this work we did not perform an analysis on the ratio between token- and style embedding dimension. Other ratios might achieve better fluency or style control.

Choice of Interpolation Parameter For our human evaluation we put $\lambda = 0.8$ weight on kNN-LM probabilities. A lower λ, more close to the vanilla kNN-LM, might achieve better fluency.

Ethics Statement

Work on controllable generation allows models to generate text in styles such as those presented here, which include polite/impolite, formal/informal, and toxic/non-toxic. There may be applications where each style is appropriate or desirable, but some styles of text such as impolite and toxic, may be undesired or even harmful. Application of our models should involve careful consideration of desired styles and the context in which they are deployed.

Acknowledgements

This work has been supported by the Alexander von Humboldt Foundation, and by Hessian.AI. Any opinions, findings, conclusions, or recommendations in this material are those of the authors and do not necessarily reflect the views of the Alexander von Humboldt Foundation, or Hessian.AI.

References

Uri Alon, Frank F. Xu, Junxian He, Sudipta Sengupta, Dan Roth, and Graham Neubig. 2022. Neuro-symbolic language modeling with automaton-augmented retrieval. *CoRR*, abs/2201.12431.

Daniel Borkan, Lucas Dixon, Jeffrey Sorensen, Nithum Thain, and Lucy Vasserman. 2019. Nuanced metrics for measuring unintended bias with real data for text classification. *CoRR*, abs/1903.04561.

Cristian Danescu-Niculescu-Mizil, Moritz Sudhof, Dan Jurafsky, Jure Leskovec, and Christopher Potts. 2013. A computational approach to politeness with application to social factors. In *Proceedings of the 51st Annual Meeting of the Association for Computational Linguistics (Volume 1: Long Papers)*, Sofia, Bulgaria.

Sumanth Dathathri, Andrea Madotto, Janice Lan, Jane Hung, Eric Frank, Piero Molino, Jason Yosinski, and Rosanne Liu. 2020. Plug and play language models: A simple approach to controlled text generation. In *8th International Conference on Learning Representations, ICLR 2020, Addis Ababa, Ethiopia, April 26-30, 2020.*

Samuel Gehman, Suchin Gururangan, Maarten Sap, Yejin Choi, and Noah A. Smith. 2020. RealToxicityPrompts: Evaluating neural toxic degeneration in language models. In *Findings of the Association for Computational Linguistics: EMNLP 2020*, Online.

Edouard Grave, Moustapha Cissé, and Armand Joulin. 2017a. Unbounded cache model for online language modeling with open vocabulary. In *Advances in Neural Information Processing Systems 30: Annual Conference on Neural Information Processing Systems 2017, December 4-9, 2017, Long Beach, CA, USA*.

Edouard Grave, Armand Joulin, and Nicolas Usunier. 2017b. Improving neural language models with a continuous cache. In *5th International Conference on Learning Representations, ICLR 2017, Toulon, France, April 24-26, 2017, Conference Track Proceedings*.

Junxian He, Graham Neubig, and Taylor Berg-Kirkpatrick. 2021. Efficient nearest neighbor language models. *CoRR*, abs/2109.04212.

Nitish Shirish Keskar, Bryan McCann, Lav R Varshney, Caiming Xiong, and Richard Socher. 2019. CTRL: A conditional transformer language model for controllable generation. *arXiv preprint arXiv:1909.05858*.

Urvashi Khandelwal, Angela Fan, Dan Jurafsky, Luke Zettlemoyer, and Mike Lewis. 2020a. Nearest neighbor machine translation. *CoRR*, abs/2010.00710.

Urvashi Khandelwal, Omer Levy, Dan Jurafsky, Luke Zettlemoyer, and Mike Lewis. 2020b. Generalization through memorization: Nearest neighbor language models. In *8th International Conference on Learning Representations, ICLR 2020, Addis Ababa, Ethiopia, April 26-30, 2020*.

Alisa Liu, Maarten Sap, Ximing Lu, Swabha Swayamdipta, Chandra Bhagavatula, Noah A. Smith, and Yejin Choi. 2021. DExperts: Decoding-time controlled text generation with experts and anti-experts. In *Proceedings of the 59th Annual Meeting of the Association for Computational Linguistics and the 11th International Joint Conference on Natural Language Processing (Volume 1: Long Papers)*, Online.

Yuxian Meng, Xiaoya Li, Xiayu Zheng, Fei Wu, Xiaofei Sun, Tianwei Zhang, and Jiwei Li. 2021. Fast nearest neighbor machine translation. *CoRR*, abs/2105.14528.

Stephen Merity, Caiming Xiong, James Bradbury, and Richard Socher. 2017. Pointer sentinel mixture models. In *5th International Conference on Learning Representations, ICLR 2017, Toulon, France, April 24-26, 2017, Conference Track Proceedings*.

Sudha Rao and Joel R. Tetreault. 2018. Dear sir or madam, may i introduce the GYAFC corpus: Corpus, benchmarks and metrics for formality style transfer. *CoRR*, abs/1803.06535.

Shuhe Wang, Jiwei Li, Yuxian Meng, Rongbin Ouyang, Guoyin Wang, Xiaoya Li, Tianwei Zhang, and Shi Zong. 2021. Faster nearest neighbor machine translation. *CoRR*, abs/2112.08152.

Yuhuai Wu, Markus N Rabe, DeLesley Hutchins, and Christian Szegedy. 2022. Memorizing transformers. In *10th International Conference on Learning Representations, ICLR 2022*.

Frank F. Xu, Junxian He, Graham Neubig, and Vincent J. Hellendoorn. 2021. Capturing structural locality in non-parametric language models. *CoRR*, abs/2110.02870.

Kevin Yang and Dan Klein. 2021. FUDGE: Controlled text generation with future discriminators. In *Proceedings of the 2021 Conference of the North American Chapter of the Association for Computational Linguistics: Human Language Technologies*, Online.

Dani Yogatama, Cyprien de Masson d'Autume, and Lingpeng Kong. 2021. Adaptive semiparametric language models. *Transactions of the Association for Computational Linguistics*, 9.

A Generation Examples

Here we include three examples of generation comparing the baseline LM to the kNN-LM where human annotators found our model to be both more fluent and more closely aligned with the desired target style.

B Modified Architecture

Our architecture, modified from Khandelwal et al. (2020b), is shown in Figure 2. The left side of the figure shows the original model and the right shows our modification which incorporates style attributes.

C Fine-tuning Experiment

The fine-tuning experiments in the main paper summarize the performance of our models pretrained on WT103 and fine-tuned on one of the style datasets each. Here we also include the performance on other subsets of the finetuning dataset, such as different toxicity levels for the toxicity data, and domain subsets for the politeness and formality data. A full list of subsets is given in Table 3.

D Human Evaluation

For the human evaluation task, we generated sentences for different combinations of the model architecture, target style, and prompt style. The high-level summary of combinations is presented in Table 4. For the three test conditions in §5.4, we have

Target Style: Polite	
Prompt:	<person>: Yes. Did you read my comments?
Baseline:	Also, you install the name as <unk> (") <url>??
Our Model:	Vote under the changed circumstances? Would you please have a look?
Target Style: Formal	
Prompt:	ok let me answer u
Baseline:	'm not in pain, and I say ... graham understand your problem
Our Model:	are alike. You should wait a little longer to enter your full name and play your live show.
Target Style: Formal	
Prompt:	THis is one way to keep it out of your system ...
Baseline:	sings u love bio <unk>
Our Model:	with the following words coming out of Gardisil ... Peter Pan, or just those are some favorite books that I am able to mail.

listed the model and style combinations that we tested in Tables 5-7. Finally, the full breakdown of the human evaluation for fluency and style preferences are shown in Figures 4-6. The heatmaps show the tendency of annotator choices, where tendency is the mean model choice per question (-1 and 1 encode the choices), aggregated across all questions in the survey and normalized to -100 and 100.

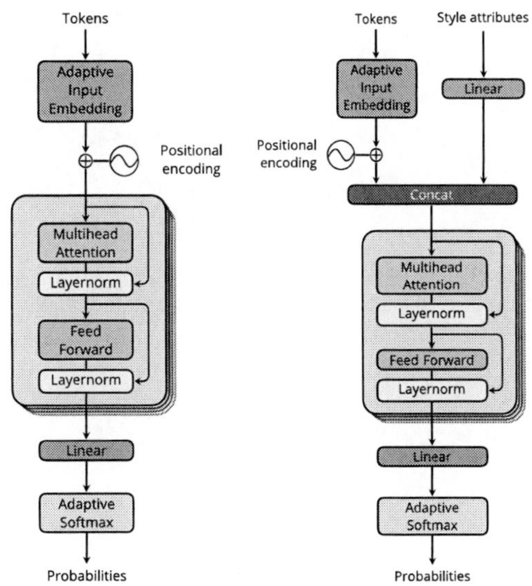

Figure 2: Changes made to the LM architecture (left: unmodified, right: our version).

dataset	subset	size		comment
		samples (%)	samples	
WT103	all	100	1.8 M	
Formality	all	100	214 k	
	formal	49.8	106.7 k	
	informal	50.2	107.3 k	
	family & relationships	49.7	106.3 k	
	entertainment & music	50.3	107.7 k	
Toxicity	all		1.4 M	Only used for evaluation; due to imbalance not suited for training or Datastores (DSes).
	non-toxic	75.6	1 M	Toxicity score = 0 .
	non-toxic-sample	11.8	159.8 k	Sample from *non-toxic*.
	toxic-gte-0.5	11.8	159.8 k	Toxicity score $\geq$ 0.5.
	toxic-gte-0.8	2.5	34.1 k	Toxicity score $\geq$ 0.8.
	toxic-gte-0.9	0.8	10.2 k	Toxicity score $\geq$ 0.9.
	all-sample	23.5	319.6 k	Combination of *toxic-gte-0.5* and *non-toxic-sample*.
Politeness	all	100	11.1 k	
	neutral	30.3	3.4 k	Center 30 % of politeness scores.
	polite	36.9	4.1 k	Upper 36.9 % of politeness scores.
	impolite	32.8	3.6 k	Lower 32.8 % of politeness scores.
	stackexchange	60.8	6.8 k	
	wikipedia	39.2	4.4 k	

Table 3: List of dataset subsets. Note: Proportions of subsets within splits are subject to variations due to random sampling. Not all subsets are presented in the results of the main paper. Some subsets are only shown in Figure 3.

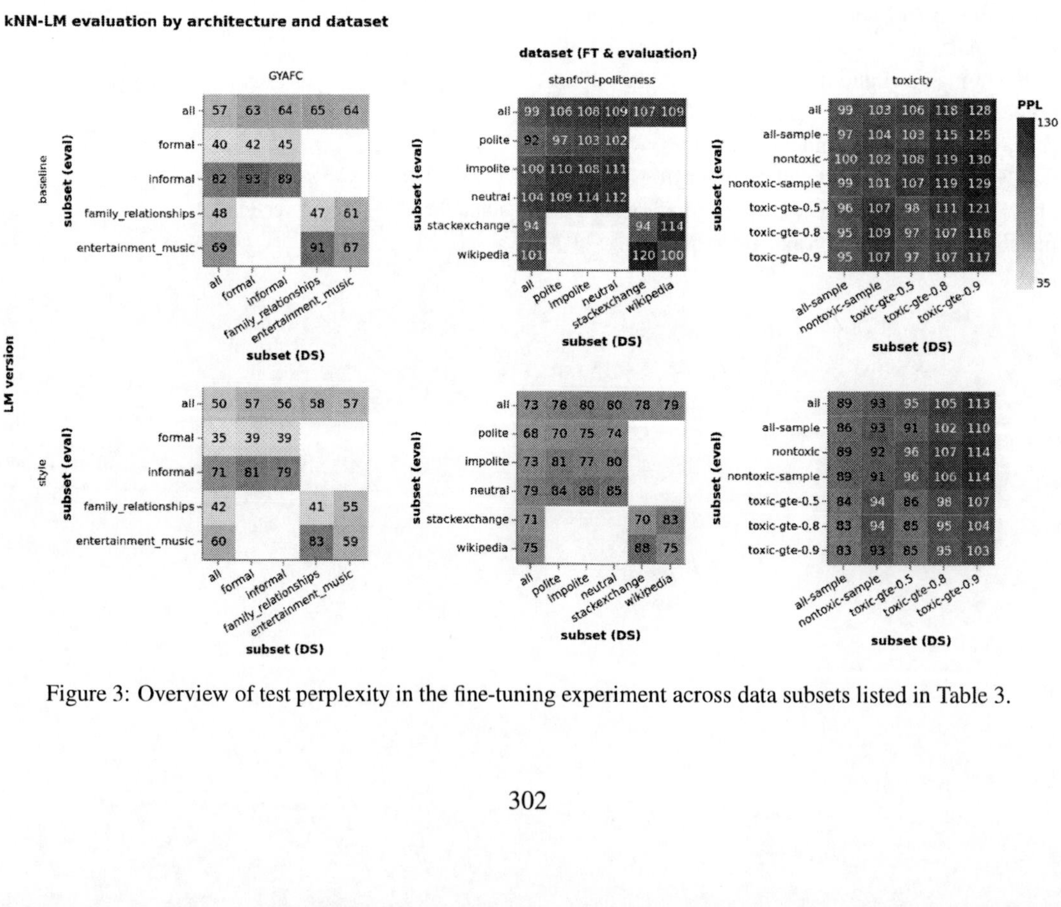

Figure 3: Overview of test perplexity in the fine-tuning experiment across data subsets listed in Table 3.

dataset	source style	target style	LM	datastore styles
Formality	formal	formal	style	none, formal, mixed
		informal	style	none, informal, mixed
		n.a.	baseline	none, informal, formal
	informal	formal	style	none, formal, mixed
		informal	style	none, informal, mixed
		n.a.	baseline	none, formal, informal
Toxicity	neutral	n.a.	baseline	none, non-toxic, toxic, mixed
		non-toxic	style	none, non-toxic, mixed
		toxic	style	none, toxic, mixed
	non-toxic	n.a.	baseline	none, non-toxic, toxic, mixed
		non-toxic	style	non-toxic, none, mixed
		toxic	style	none, toxic, mixed
Politeness	impolite	impolite	style	none, impolite, mixed
		n.a.	baseline	none, polite, impolite, mixed
		polite	style	none, polite, mixed
	polite	impolite	style	none, impolite, mixed
		n.a.	baseline	none, polite, impolite, mixed
		polite	style	none, polite, mixed

Table 4: Combinations of models and inputs used for generating the outputs for human evaluation. *n.a.* in the *target style* column refers to the baseline LM architecture, since it has no style input.

dataset	source style	target style	specific datastore style
Formality	formal	formal	formal
		informal	informal
	informal	formal	formal
		informal	informal
Toxicity	neutral	non-toxic	non-toxic
		toxic	toxic
	non-toxic	non-toxic	non-toxic
		toxic	toxic
Politeness	impolite	impolite	impolite
		polite	polite
	polite	impolite	impolite
		polite	polite

Table 5: Model combinations for the human evaluation to address whether the style-specific datastores outperform the mixed datastores.

dataset	source style	target style	datastore style
Formality	formal	formal	formal
		informal	informal
	informal	formal	formal
		informal	informal
Toxicity	neutral	non-toxic	non-toxic
		toxic	toxic
	non-toxic	non-toxic	non-toxic
		toxic	toxic
Politeness	impolite	impolite	impolite
		polite	polite
	polite	impolite	impolite
		polite	polite

Table 6: Model combinations for the human evaluation to address whether the kNN-LM outperforms the baseline LM. Both models being compared use the style architecture.

dataset	source style	datastore	target style
Formality	formal	formal	formal
		informal	informal
	informal	formal	formal
		informal	informal
Toxicity	neutral	mixed	non-toxic, toxic
		non-toxic	non-toxic
		toxic	toxic
	non-toxic	mixed	non-toxic, toxic
		non-toxic	non-toxic
		toxic	toxic
Politeness	impolite	impolite	impolite
		mixed	impolite, polite
		polite	polite
	polite	impolite	impolite
		mixed	impolite, polite
		polite	polite

Table 7: Model combinations for human evaluation to address whether the style architecture outperforms the baseline kNN-LM.

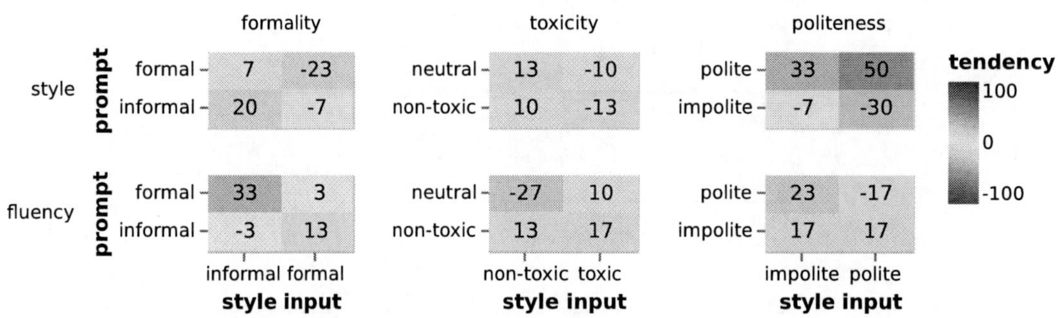

Figure 4: Survey results: Comparison of kNN-LM with mixed DS and style-specific DS. A tendency < 0 corresponds to the mixed DS being preferred by annotators.

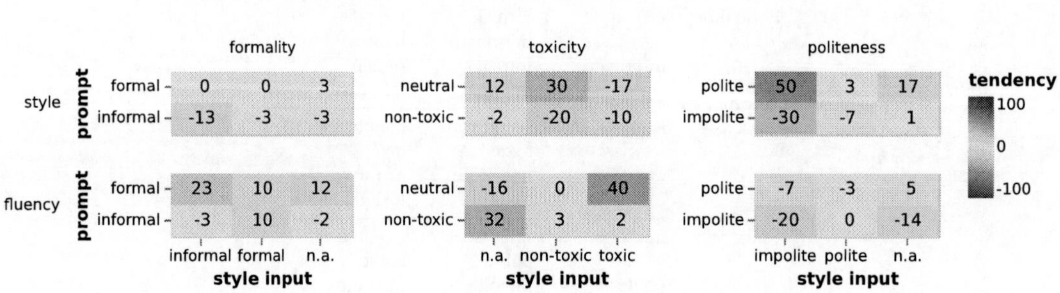

Figure 5: Survey results: Comparison of LM to kNN-LM for both architectures. A tendency < 0 corresponds to the LM being preferred by annotators.

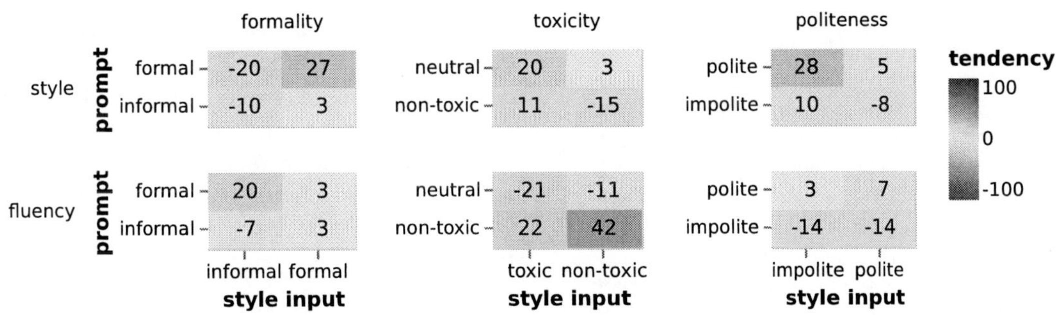

Figure 6: Survey results: Comparison of kNN-LM with baseline architecture vs. style architecture. Style input on the x-axis refers only to the style LM, since the baseline LM has no style input. A tendency < 0 corresponds to the the baseline architecture being preferred by annotators.

Reporting Scores and Agreement for Error Annotation Tasks

Maja Popović and **Anya Belz**
ADAPT Centre, School of Computing
Dublin City University, Ireland
name.surname@adaptcentre.ie

Abstract

The work reported in this paper examines different ways of aggregating scores for error annotation in MT outputs: raw error counts, error counts normalised over total number of words ('word percentage'), and error counts normalised over total number of errors ('error percentage'). We use each of these three scores to calculate inter-annotator agreement in the form of Krippendorff's α and Pearson's r and compare the obtained numbers, overall and separately for different types of errors. While each score has its advantages depending on the goal of the evaluation, we argue that the best way of estimating inter-annotator agreement using such numbers are raw counts. If the annotation process ensures that the total number of words cannot differ among the annotators (for example, due to adding omission symbols), normalising over number of words will lead to the same conclusions. In contrast, total number of errors is subjective because different annotators often perceive different numbers of errors in the same text, therefore normalising over this number can be associated with lower agreement.

1 Introduction

Manual error annotation is an increasingly investigated component of assessing the quality of automatically translated or otherwise generated text (Federico et al., 2014; Costa et al., 2015; Caseli and Inácio, 2020; Thomson and Reiter, 2020). Error annotation can be construed as a word-span labelling task, and a variety of different error labelling schemes have been proposed (Vilar et al., 2006; Lommel et al., 2014b; He et al., 2021; Belkebir and Habash, 2021; Al Sharou and Specia, 2022). If annotators are instructed to assign a predefined error type to given word-spans, the task is called error classification (Vilar et al., 2006; Costa et al., 2015; Lommel et al., 2014b). If annotators are asked only to mark the erroneous word-spans without assigning any particular error type, the task is called error marking (Kreutzer et al., 2020; Popović and Belz, 2021). Both for classification and marking, approaches differ in how they report the results from error annotation, i.e. how they convert the word-span labels obtained in the annotation process to aggregated, quantified results on the basis of which conclusions can be drawn. It is currently unclear how the choice of aggregation method affects conclusions, e.g. when comparing systems, or assessing inter-annotator agreement and reproducibility.

This paper aims to investigate three widely used ways of aggregating error scores, namely (i) raw error counts, (ii) error counts normalised by total number of words (referred to in this paper as 'word percentage'), and (iii) error counts normalised by total number of errors (referred to as 'error percentage'). We carried out our experiments on a publicly available data set consisting of annotated machine translated outputs which was also used in previous work (Popović, 2021).

2 Related Work

In an early paper reporting an approach to systematic error classification in MT outputs, Vilar et al. (2006) analyse several MT systems for two language pairs in order to obtain details about their weakest points. The results are reported as error percentages (in the above sense) for each defined error type in order to see which error types are predominant in each of the MT systems. Since in this work different annotators evaluated different texts, it was not possible to report inter-annotator agreement in any manner.

Lommel et al. (2014a) specifically address IAA for error classification in MT using the MQM[1] error scheme. IAA was calculated using both pairwise matching/accuracy between assigned labels on the word level as well as Cohen's κ coefficient on the

[1] https://themqm.org/

Proceedings of the 2nd Workshop on Natural Language Generation, Evaluation, and Metrics (GEM), pages 306 - 315
December 7, 2022 ©2022 Association for Computational Linguistics

word level. Although the work did not aim to evaluate MT systems, some overall results are reported: raw error counts as well as what might be called 'sentence percentage' – error counts normalised by the total number of sentences. It should be noted that the error counts did not take into account the number of words in the error span, but each span is counted as one error no matter how many words the span comprises. Lommel et al. also investigated sentence-level agreement, which led to much better agreement since evaluators often identified the same error types in a sentence although on different spans. These differences in spans are mentioned as the main reason for low κ coefficients, apart from annotators' personal preferences.

Another work which deals with IAA (Castilho, 2020) for error classification compares (a) IAA when evaluators see only isolated sentences, with (b) IAA when evaluators see larger portions of text in context (paragraphs, "documents"). Since the goal was not analysis of MT systems, a simple scheme involving four error types was used. The tool used for error annotation allowed only marking on the sentence level, so that Cohen's κ is also calculated on the sentence level. In addition, Pearson's r calculated on error counts and percentage of matched error types are reported as well. Since the focus of the work was fully on IAA, no error scores were reported.

Klubička et al. (2018) use the MQM error scheme for error classification to compare phrase-based and neural based systems for translating into Croatian. They mention that there is no standard in reporting numerical results for error classification and discuss two possibilities: (1) counting only error spans (without taking the word span into account), (2) counting number of words in error spans and normalising this word count over the sentence length (what we call word percentage). They argue that although raw error counts provide useful information, they do not enable drawing statistically meaningful conclusions about the results. They further argue that different MT systems may generate different sentence lengths which would make comparison of raw error counts unfair. Therefore, they decide to report the word percentage. As for IAA, Cohen's κ on the sentence level was calculated and compared across different error types. They obtained higher agreement coefficients than (Lommel et al., 2014c) and commented that the reason is calculating κ on sentence-level instead of word-level.

Kreutzer et al. (2020) perform error marking (annotation without classification into types) for use in a loss function in order to improve an MT system. Therefore, no scores were reported, and IAA was reported as Krippendorff's α calculated on raw error counts. The same approach, error marking and α calculated on error counts, was used by Popović and Belz (2021), together with the percentage of label matches (F-score). The error annotation results were reported in the form of word percentages.

Freitag et al. (2021) apply the MQM error scheme on large amounts of texts for two language pairs. They use raw span counts weighted with the error severity so that each minor error span is counted as 1 and each major error span as 5. A restriction of a maximum of five errors per segment is applied, and evaluators are instructed to choose the five most severe errors. As for IAA, for each rater Freitag et al. report the score and the ratio over the average score of all raters. They also report pairwise agreement, and discuss that there is no obvious best way to compute it, especially since they take into account error severity. The chosen approach groups the scores of each rater into numeric intervals, and then compares these intervals. The authors report average, minimum, and maximum pairwise annotator agreements, but do not specify how exactly these agreements were calculated.

A previous investigation (Popović, 2021) also concentrated on IAA, with the focus on pairwise word level matches for different error types, and reported overall Krippendorff's α calculated on error counts. The work reported in this paper was carried out on part of the same corpus, but with the following differences: (i) we introduce Krippendorff's α and Pearson's r calculated on three types of numerical scores, and (ii) we compare all IAA coefficients (including word overlap) and analyse the differences in depth. Also, we choose a subset of the corpus for which we have annotations by four evaluators as a result of an earlier reproduction study (Popović and Belz, 2021), in order to have more variation.

3 Annotated Data Set

Our experiments were carried out on a subset of the publicly available annotated QRev data set.[2] The full set consists of English user reviews about

[2] https://github.com/m-popovic/QRev-annotations

QRev data set	
language pair	en→hr
domain	user reviews
# of MT systems	3
# of unique segments	1217
total # of annotators	14
# of annotators per segment	4
quality criterion	Adequacy, Comprehension

Table 1: Descriptive statistics for the data set used in our analyses.

IMDb movies and Amazon products translated into Croatian and Serbian by five different MT systems for each language pair. Each text was annotated by two different evaluators. In the sub-set we used[3] (Popović and Belz, 2021), we had additional annotations obtained in a reproduction study (Popović and Belz, 2021); therefore in this subset each text was annotated by four different evaluators. The sub-set consists of Croatian MT outputs generated by three systems (Amazon Translate, Microsoft Bing and Google Translate). In total, 14 different evaluators, computational linguistics students and researchers as well as translation students fluent in the source language and native speakers of the target language, participated in the annotation of this sub-set. Some descriptive statistics for the data sub-set we used are shown in Table 1.

The annotation of MT outputs was carried out in two stages. In the first stage, a group of annotators provided error marks (*Major*, *Minor* and *None* for correct words) according to two quality criteria: Adequacy and Comprehension. For both quality aspects, the evaluators were asked to concentrate on problematic parts of the text and to highlight them. For Adequacy, they were instructed to highlight parts which entirely or partially change the meaning of the source text. For Comprehension, they were asked to mark parts which are impossible or hard to understand. They were also asked to add omission tags "XX" whenever necessary.

Since it was an error marking task, i.e. not guided by any predefined error scheme, only by the quality criteria, the evaluators had more freedom in annotating errors than in error classification tasks. Therefore, this annotation represents a descriptive type of evaluation (Rottger et al., 2022) which allows and encourages subjectivity.

The annotators were also asked to distinguish between major and minor errors, however we did not use this distinction in the experiments reported here. This could be an interesting direction for future work.

Error types were assigned in the second stage by the first author of this paper, a computational linguistics researcher with expertise in translation, who analysed the marked errors and assigned error type labels according to their cause and/or origin. The error types were not predefined by any particular error typology, but defined on the fly, while looking at the annotated text. For some words, multiple error types were identified. Some of these error types have small word spans (1–2 words) while others can involve a larger number of words, even the entire sentence. Since the evaluation protocol in the first stage allowed free annotation, evaluators often perceived the same issue but marked different words. This freedom also allowed evaluators to express their individual stylistic preferences. Moreover, it led to evaluators often marking up many consecutive words even in cases where only some of the words were actually part of an error. In some of these cases, the second-stage annotator was unable to identify an error type; to indicate this, such cases were tagged as *None*.

4 Aggregated Error Scores

We investigated the following aggregated scores:

1. **error count** $C(err\_type)$
    - number of words marked as an error type
    - ranges from 0 to total number of words in the text
2. **word percentage** $\frac{C(err\_type)}{C(all\_words)} \cdot 100$
    - number of words marked as an error type divided by the total number of words in the text
    - ranges from 0 to 100
3. **error percentage** $\frac{C(err\_type)}{C(all\_errors)} \cdot 100$
    - number of words marked as an error type divided by the total number of errors in the text
    - ranges from 0 to 100

[3] https://github.com/m-popovic/QRev-annotations/tree/master/reproduction_second-round_hr

5 Inter-Annotator Agreement

We estimated inter-annotator agreement in the following three ways:

1. **word overlap** (Popović, 2021)
   - number of words marked as errors by all annotators divided by number of all words perceived as errors by any annotator
   - ranges between 0 and 100, higher value indicating higher agreement
   - not based on aggregated error scores, only on actual words annotated as errors
2. **Krippendorff's α** (Krippendorff, 2004)
   - compares numerical scores obtained by different annotators
   - ranges between -1 and 1
   - 0 indicates no agreement, and common practice is to consider $\alpha \geq 0.667$ as acceptable and $\alpha \geq 0.8$ as strong agreement (Krippendorff, 2004)
3. **Pearson's r**
   - compares numerical scores obtained by different annotators
   - ranges between -1 and 1
   - absolute values from 0.8 to 1 are commonly considered as strong correlation, between 0.6 and 0.8 as high correlation, between 0.4 and 0.6 as moderate, between 0.2 and 0.4 as fair, and between 0 and 0.2 as weak (0 meaning no correlation at all)

Since Krippendorff's α and Pearson's r are measures computed on numerical values, we compared their values as obtained when using the three different types of aggregated scores above (raw counts, word percentage and error percentage). We additionally compared these values with word overlap values as used in previous work and calculated in a different way, independently of numerical scores.

Word overlap as well as Pearson's r are calculated on all pairs of annotators (e1-e2, e1-e3, e1-e4, e2-e3, e2-e4, e3-e4).

6 Results

As a first step, we calculated IAA measures for all error types combined, taking into account only whether a word is tagged as an error or not, independently of the error type. We compared IAA measures for all aggregation methods except calculating coefficients on error percentage (count of a particular error type normalised over the total number of errors) because without distinguishing error types it would simply be 100% and therefore does not make sense.

After observed certain tendencies in this first step, we calculated all values for each individual error type and analysed all observations in depth.

6.1 Overall results

Table 2 shows error levels as perceived by each of the four annotators in the two versions, raw count and word percentage, together with the corresponding agreement measures. As already mentioned, word overlap is not based on the quantity of errors but on actual tagged words.

First, it can be seen that agreement between annotators is higher in all cases when assessing Adequacy than Comprehension, which confirms results from previous work (Popović, 2021) where however only word overlap was reported. It should be noted that word overlap is slightly different in the present context, because it was calculated on a different subset, but the tendency is the same.

As for comparing different IAA measures, it can be noted that both coefficients, α and r, are lower for word percentage than for raw count, in all cases. Manual inspection revealed that the reason lies in variations of sentence length between annotators caused by different numbers of omission tags and/or differences in tokenisation affected by annotations.

Two examples are shown in Table 3, the sentence in the top half of the table illustrates the effect of omission tags and the sentence in the bottom half the effect of altering tokenisation through annotation. In the first sentence, all four annotators marked two errors, so the agreement on the raw error counts is perfect. However, since the fourth annotator perceived one omission error while the other three did not, this sentence became longer than others due to the added omission tag, and the word percentage became smaller. If omission tags were excluded from sentence length, word percentages for segments with omissions could become overly high and difficult to interpret.

In the second sentence in Table 3, three annotators marked two errors and one did not mark any.

		amount of errors				coefficients		
		ev1	ev2	ev3	ev4	$\alpha\uparrow$	$r\uparrow$	*overlap* $\uparrow$
Adequacy	counts	3282	3377	3910	4310	*.705*	*.714*	*59.6*
	word %	20.3	20.9	24.0	26.5	*.567*	*.579*	
Comprehension	counts	3380	3684	4336	5487	*.659*	*.687*	*57.4*
	word %	20.9	22.8	26.6	33.5	*.496*	*.523*	

Table 2: Results for all error types combined: error count and word percentage (count normalised by total number of words) for each of four annotators together with coefficients of agreement: word overlap, Krippendorff's α and Pearson's r.

original	annotated MT output	# errors	# words	word%
Usually a fan but not impressed	Obično ventilator|AMBIGUITY , ali neimpresioniran|NON_EXISTING	2	5	40.0
	Obično ventilator|AMBIGUITY , ali neimpresioniran|NON_EXISTING	2	5	40.0
	Obično ventilator|AMBIGUITY , ali neimpresioniran|NON_EXISTING	2	5	40.0
	Obično ventilator|AMBIGUITY , ali **XX|OMISSION** neimpresioniran	2	**6**	**33.3**
Wayne's World is hardly a plot driven film.	Wayneov|NE svijet|NE teško da je film pokrenut **zapletom.**	2	8	25.0
	Wayneov|NE svijet|NE teško da je film pokrenut **zapletom.**	2	8	25.0
	Wayneov svijet teško da je film pokrenut|NOUN_PHRASE **zapletom|NOUN_PHRASE .**	2	**9**	**22.2**
	Wayneov svijet teško da je film pokrenut **zapletom.**	0	8	0.0

Table 3: Examples of two sentences resulting in different lengths after annotation by inserting omission mark (above) and separating punctuation mark (below). This leads to different word percentages for same error counts.

However, the first three annotators marked different errors, one of them involved a word next to a punctuation mark. Therefore, the annotator separated the word from the punctuation mark increasing the total number of words and decreasing the word percentage.

6.2 Different error types

The next step in our experiment was to investigate the effects on different error types. Here, we want to compare the numerically based coefficients α and r when calculated on counts vs. word percentage separately for each error type. In addition, we want to investigate the error percentage (count of a particular error type normalised over total number of errors, see Section 4).

6.2.1 Aggregated error scores

The list of error types together with their quantification in the three forms (raw count, word percentage and error percentage) can be seen in Table 4, sorted by the frequency in the analysed corpus. It can be noted that the conclusions about their distribution will be exactly the same for each of the three numerical scores. For example, ambiguity is one of the predominant types according to raw count, word percentage as well as error percentage.

The question is now what happens with agreement coefficients for each of the error types when we use each of the three different numerical scores? Will word percentage be associated with lower agreement for each error type? What will happen when using error percentage?

6.2.2 Agreement measures for different error types

Tables 5 and 6 present all agreement measures, word overlap and both number-based coefficients α and r, calculated on three types of scores: count, word percentage and error percentage. The error types are ordered from lowest to highest word overlap.

It can be noted that there is very low agreement for the tag *None*, which could be expected since, as explained in Section 3, these error marks are related to evaluators' stylistic preferences as well as different perceptions of the word span.

As the results for rare error types are likely to be less reliable we also mark the frequency of each type in the first columns of Tables 5 and 6: '++'

(a) Adequacy

Adequacy issue type	count	word%	err%
REPHRASING	3197	4.93	21.49
AMBIGUITY	1841	2.84	12.37
NOUN PHRASE	1006	1.55	6.76
MISTRANSLATION	651	1.00	4.38
VERB FORM	618	0.95	4.15
NAMED ENTITY	561	0.86	3.77
CASE	529	0.82	3.56
GENDER	424	0.65	2.85
UNTRANSLATED	387	0.60	2.60
PRONOUN	338	0.52	2.27
NEGATION	333	0.51	2.24
OMISSION	288	0.44	1.94
ORDER	266	0.41	1.79
-ING	245	0.38	1.65
NON-EXISTING	216	0.33	1.45
SOURCE ERROR	207	0.32	1.39
PREPOSITION	189	0.29	1.27
POS AMBIGUITY	161	0.25	1.08
ADDITION	102	0.16	0.69
PASSIVE	101	0.16	0.68
NUMBER	84	0.13	0.56
CONJUNCTION	73	0.11	0.49
REPETITION	33	0.05	0.22
SR	18	0.03	0.12
HALLUCINATION	15	0.02	0.10
None	3755	5.79	25.24

(b) Comprehension

Comprehension issue type	count	word%	err%
REPHRASING	3368	5.18	19.94
AMBIGUITY	1670	2.57	9.89
NOUN PHRASE	992	1.53	5.87
NAMED ENTITY	594	0.91	3.52
VERB FORM	567	0.87	3.36
MISTRANSLATION	553	0.85	3.27
CASE	539	0.83	3.19
GENDER	428	0.66	2.53
UNTRANSLATED	412	0.63	2.44
NEGATION	344	0.53	2.04
PRONOUN	322	0.50	1.91
ORDER	283	0.44	1.68
OMISSION	261	0.40	1.55
-ING	244	0.38	1.44
NON-EXISTING	219	0.34	1.30
SOURCE ERROR	212	0.33	1.26
PREPOSITION	179	0.28	1.06
POS AMBIGUITY	133	0.20	0.79
ADDITION	109	0.17	0.65
PASSIVE	100	0.15	0.59
CONJUNCTION	79	0.12	0.47
NUMBER	71	0.11	0.42
REPETITION	34	0.05	0.20
SR	20	0.03	0.12
HALLUCINATION	7	0.01	0.04
None	5904	9.08	34.96

Table 4: Error levels for different Adequacy and Comprehension error types annotated by all evaluators, in the form of counts, word percentages and error percentages.

denotes error types accounting for more than 5% of all errors, '+' denotes error types accounting for 2–5%, '−' for 1–2%, and '−−' for less than 1%.

It can further be noted that for the majority of error types, the coefficients calculated on error counts indicate the same level of agreement as the word overlap. For several error types, however, the overlap is smaller (conjunction, negation, rephrasing), but this could be expected: these error types have long word spans, so annotators often perceive the same number of errors but mark different words.

As for comparing numerically based coefficients calculated on the three scores, bold values indicate that the agreement is lower than the agreement calculated on raw counts, while underlined values indicate higher agreement than counts. Overall, for a number of error types, using error percentage results in lower agreement than using word percentage or raw counts. For some types, word percentage is lower, too, as observed in the overall values in Table 2. For a few types, however, word percentage results in higher agreement. These are the Adequacy-related omission and verb form errors as well as the Comprehension-related noun-phrase and source errors. For the Comprehension-related conjunction error, the highest agreement is obtained when using error percentage.

In order to understand these observations, we further analysed all error types where conclusions about IAA differ for different numerical scores.

7 Analysis of Differing Agreement Levels

Decreased agreement when using error percentage. For a large number of error types, calculating Krippendorff's α and Pearson's r on error percentage results in much lower agreement compared to using raw counts or word percentage. In order to explain this phenomenon, further analysis was carried out on these error types, and a systematic pattern was found: the total number of errors marked by different annotators often varies notably so that identical error counts become very different error percentages.

Table 7 illustrates the phenomenon on two sentences. In the first sentence (top half of the table), two annotators perceived one mistranslation. However, for the first annotator, this was the only error in the sentence, while the other spotted a problem with the verb form. Therefore, the total number of errors for the first annotator is one and for the second one is two, resulting in double the error percentage of mistranslations for the first annotator.

A issue type	word overlap	$\alpha \uparrow$ count	$\alpha \uparrow$ word %	$\alpha \uparrow$ error %	$r \uparrow$ count	$r \uparrow$ word %	$r \uparrow$ error %
OMISSION^{-}	26.6	.236	.645	.275	.238	.650	.275
CONJUNCTION^{-}	53.0	.700	.767	.703	.706	.767	.860
ORDER^{-}	58.1	.554	.558	.500	.577	.599	.500
NEGATION^{+}	59.0	.713	.744	.778	.714	.744	.783
NAMED ENTITY^{+}	66.9	.748	.617	.647	.748	.619	.647
PREPOSITION^{-}	66.0	.689	**.649**	**.503**	.691	.649	**.583**
PRONOUN^{+}	66.5	.667	**.562**	**.454**	.667	**.562**	**.454**
REPHRASING^{++}	68.4	.772	.757	.747	.776	.762	.748
REPETITION^{--}	68.8	.879	.919	.841	.905	.933	.844
SR^{--}	70.4	.703	.698	**.580**	.703	.699	**.581**
NOUN PHRASE^{++}	70.8	.797	.757	.749	.798	.762	.749
GENDER^{+}	72.8	.758	**.523**	**.580**	.758	**.543**	**.584**
CASE^{+}	74.8	.800	**.763**	**.703**	.800	**.766**	**.707**
AMBIGUITY^{++}	75.2	.791	.744	**.596**	.794	.745	**.596**
POS AMBIGUITY^{-}	75.4	.889	**.799**	**.752**	.890	.813	**.752**
NUMBER^{--}	76.2	.771	.767	**.517**	.772	.773	**.519**
ADDITION^{--}	76.5	.742	.736	**.491**	.743	.741	**.496**
VERB FORM^{+}	76.6	.764	.825	**.650**	.764	.825	**.653**
PASSIVE^{--}	77.2	.829	**.754**	**.672**	.831	**.774**	**.690**
MISTRANSLATION^{+}	85.0	.941	.885	**.709**	.941	.885	**.718**
UNTRANSLATED^{+}	87.3	.961	.939	**.768**	.964	.939	**.771**
-ING^{-}	88.1	.899	**.751**	**.707**	.900	**.751**	**.707**
SOURCE ERROR^{-}	88.6	.884	.879	**.702**	.885	.879	**.704**
NON-EXISTING^{-}	90.7	.943	.933	**.786**	.943	.933	**.791**
HALLUCINATION^{--}	93.3	.982	.982	.997	.983	.983	.998
None	21.5	.233	.125	.131	.245	.138	.141

Table 5: Agreement coefficients for Adequacy error types ('++' denotes error types accounting for more than 5% of all errors, '+' denotes error types accounting for 2–5%, '−' for 1–2%, and '−−' for less than 1%) : word overlap together with α and r calculated on counts, word percentages and error percentages. Bold values indicate lower agreement than counts, underline values indicate higher agreement than counts.

In the second sentence (lower half of the table), all four annotators perceived one ambiguity error, but due to differences in perception of other error types (in this case presence and span of negation errors) the total number of errors, and therefore the error percentage, are different.

This finding indicates that, regardless of which score is considered best for reporting the results of the analysis, error percentage is not suitable for calculating agreement coefficients.

Increased agreement when using word percentage. For some error types, coefficients calculated on word percentage are associated with higher agreement than those calculated on raw counts and error percentage. One of these error types is Adequacy-related omission, which at first might look contradictory to the findings in the overall scores, where they contribute to decreased agreement by changing sentence length. However, increasing sentence length has another effect, namely 'smoothing' the number of omissions. An example can be in Table 8: one annotator did not perceive any omission, two perceived one omission, while one perceived two. The resulting sentence lengths are therefore different, and the increase of the sentence length is larger in the sentence with more omissions. Therefore, the difference between the amounts of omissions are smaller for word percentage than for count: while one evaluator tagged twice as many omissions than the other (2:1), the difference between word percentages is only 1.6 (40:25).

Besides omission, such tendencies can be seen in a few other error types (verb form error for Adequacy, noun phrase and source errors for Comprehension). However, the analysis revealed that in those cases, there are no reasons related to the nature of the error type itself (as is the case for omissions). The only reason is that these error types often occur in sentences where lengths are different due to tokenisation changes and/or omission annotations, as mentioned in Section 6.1.

Other differences in agreement. As previously mentioned, we carried out a more in-depth analysis of a few other kinds of differences in agreement related to certain error types.

C issue type	word overlap	$\alpha\uparrow$ count	$\alpha\uparrow$ word %	$\alpha\uparrow$ error %	$r\uparrow$ count	$r\uparrow$ word %	$r\uparrow$ error %
OMISSION^{-}	17.9	.160	.116	.092	.161	.119	.094
HALLUCINATION^{--}	28.6	.320	.320	.331	.374	.374	.362
CONJUNCTION^{--}	50.6	.712	.718	.843	.712	.718	.847
PRONOUN^{-}	58.4	.581	.404	**.320**	.590	.496	**.322**
ORDER^{-}	59.3	.552	.534	.516	.575	.553	.520
NEGATION^{+}	63.2	.758	.712	.838	.760	.713	.838
NAMED ENTITY^{+}	64.3	.684	**.600**	**.569**	.690	.604	**.570**
PREPOSITION^{-}	68.2	.694	.764	**.582**	.702	.764	**.583**
REPETITION^{--}	69.8	.879	.828	**.731**	.918	.875	**.777**
SR^{--}	70.0	.699	.719	**.634**	.702	.719	.658
GENDER^{+}	71.5	.727	**.609**	**.533**	.728	.617	**.533**
NOUN PHRASE^{++}	71.9	.791	.809	.737	.796	.812	.737
REPHRASING^{++}	72.0	.787	.748	.791	.794	.754	.791
VERB FORM^{+}	73.1	.776	.743	**.627**	.777	.745	**.627**
POS AMBIGUITY^{--}	73.7	.827	**.226**	.719	.827	**.261**	**.720**
AMBIGUITY^{++}	74.4	.783	.734	**.586**	.789	.744	**.589**
CASE^{+}	76.9	.784	.746	**.685**	.785	.748	**.690**
NUMBER^{--}	78.9	.789	.776	**.465**	.791	.777	**.466**
PASSIVE^{--}	79.3	.854	.866	.837	.858	.873	.837
SOURCE ERROR^{-}	81.4	.787	.833	.708	.793	.837	.711
MISTRANSLATION^{+}	82.2	.918	.850	**.646**	.921	.854	**.647**
ADDITION^{--}	83.2	.842	.796	**.607**	.797	.731	**.575**
-ING^{-}	85.8	.888	.824	**.700**	.893	.825	**.700**
UNTRANSLATED^{+}	87.7	.933	.870	**.775**	.934	.871	**.775**
NON-EXISTING^{-}	89.8	.920	.938	**.722**	.920	.938	**.725**
None	29.1	.317	.190	.212	.355	.218	.235

Table 6: Agreement coefficients for Comprehension error types ('++' denotes error types accounting for more than 5% of all errors, '+' denotes error types accounting for 2–5%, '−' for 1–2%, and '−−' for less than 1%): word overlap together with α and r calculated on counts, word percentages and error percentages. Bold values indicate lower agreement than counts, underline values indicate higher agreement than counts.

original	annotated MT output	# mistrans.	# errors	error%
Don't waste your money.	Nemoj|VERB trošiti novac.	0	1	0.00
	Nemoj trošiti|MISTRANSLATION novac.	1	1	100.0
	Nemoj trošiti novac.	0	0	0.00
	Nemoj|VERB trošiti|MISTRANSLATION novac.	1	2	50.0

original	annotated MT output	# ambiguity	# errors	error%
Sadly, I can't review them as they were both non-responsive.	Nažalost, ne mogu ih pregledati|AMBIGUITY jer oboje nisu reagirali	1	1	100
	Nažalost, ne mogu ih pregledati|AMBIGUITY jer oboje|NEGATION nisu|NEGATION reagirali	1	3	33.3
	Nažalost, ne mogu ih pregledati|AMBIGUITY jer oboje nisu|NEGATION reagirali|NEGATION	1	3	33.3
	Nažalost, ne mogu ih pregledati|AMBIGUITY jer oboje nisu reagirali|NEGATION	1	2	50.0

Table 7: Examples of sentences with identical error counts for a particular error type (mistranslation at the top and ambiguity below) but different total number of errors perceived by different annotators. This leads to different error percentages for same error counts.

One phenomenon is that both word percentage and error percentage decrease the agreement for certain error types including gender, case (Adequacy), named entity (Comprehension), etc. We have also observed cases where word percentage notably decreases agreement while error percentage does not, e.g. for POS ambiguity (Comprehension); in fact, conjunction error percentage even increases agreement (Comprehension).

Nevertheless, these differences in agreement are not related to error type, but rather to the circumstances in which the majority of errors occur (variations in sentence length and total number of errors). Moreover, many of the error types are relatively rare, which makes these effects even stronger. For example, conjunction errors are very rare, and al-

original	annotated MT output	# omissions	# words	word%
...from other of the genre, ...	... od ostalih žanra, ...	0	3	0.0
	... od ostalih XX|OMISSION XX|OMISSION žanra, ...	2	5	40.0
	... od ostalih XX|OMISSION žanra, ...	1	4	25.0
	... od ostalih XX|OMISSION žanra, ...	1	4	25.0

Table 8: Examples illustrating reduction in differences in omission error levels.

most all of them are marked by annotators which assign a higher total number of errors, too, so that error percentage is 'smoother' than raw error count.

It should also be noted that while the results reported here indicate that error percentage is often associated with misleadingly *low* agreement, it is theoretically possible to find misleadingly *high* agreement (for example, if one annotator marks twice as many errors in total than another, but the proportions of error types are exactly the same, the agreement on error percentages will be perfect).

8 Conclusions

This paper examined different ways of aggregating scores for error annotation in automatically generated text, more specifically MT outputs: we compared raw error counts, error counts normalised over total number of words (word percentage), and error counts normalised over total number of errors (error percentage), and the associated difference in inter-annotator agreement measures calculated on the different aggregated scores. While reporting each type of aggregated score as the evaluation result has its advantages depending on the goal of the evaluation, our experiments indicate that the overall best way to estimate inter-annotator agreement using such scores are raw counts. If the annotation process ensures that the total number of words cannot differ among the annotators (for example, due to adding omission symbols or separating punctuation marks), word percentage will lead to the same conclusions.

In contrast, error percentage can be associated with misleading agreements for a number of error types, chiefly because the total number of errors is subjective as different annotators often perceive different numbers of errors in the same text. Therefore, normalising one subjective number (error count for a particular type) by another subjective number (total number of errors) can notably influence the agreement.

Limitations

The work was carried out only on one language pair, for one translation direction. The identification of the error types in the second stage was carried out by a single annotator.

Ethics Statement

This statement follows the structure of the ARR responsible research checklist. We discuss limitations of the work presented in this paper in the previous section. No new data or computational resources were created, no computational experiments were run, no human annotation or evaluations were carried out for this paper. The work computes and analyses scores obtained from a previously annotated corpus. Results are of potential use in improving comparability and reliability in quantified error reporting.

Acknowledgements

The ADAPT SFI Centre for Digital Media Technology which is funded by Science Foundation Ireland through the SFI Research Centres Programme and is co-funded under the European Regional Development Fund (ERDF) through Grant 13/RC/2106.

References

Khetam Al Sharou and Lucia Specia. 2022. A taxonomy and study of critical errors in machine translation. In *Proceedings of the 23rd Annual Conference of the European Association for Machine Translation*, pages 171–179.

Riadh Belkebir and Nizar Habash. 2021. Automatic error type annotation for arabic. In *Proceedings of the 25th Conference on Computational Natural Language Learning*, pages 596–606.

Helena Caseli and Marcio Inácio. 2020. Nmt and pbsmt error analyses in english to brazilian portuguese automatic translations. In *Proceedings of the 12th Language Resources and Evaluation Conference*, pages 3623–3629.

Sheila Castilho. 2020. On the same page? comparing inter-annotator agreement in sentence and document level human machine translation evaluation.

In *Proceedings of the Fifth Conference on Machine Translation (WMT 20)*, pages 1150–1159, Online.

Ângela Costa, Wang Ling, Tiago Luís, Rui Correia, and Luísa Coheur. 2015. A linguistically motivated taxonomy for machine translation error analysis. *Machine Translation*, 29(2):127–161.

Marcello Federico, Matteo Negri, Luisa Bentivogli, and Marco Turchi. 2014. Assessing the impact of translation errors on machine translation quality with mixed-effects models. In *Proceedings of the 2014 Conference on Empirical Methods in Natural Language Processing (EMNLP)*, pages 1643–1653.

Markus Freitag, George Foster, David Grangier, Viresh Ratnakar, Qijun Tan, and Wolfgang Macherey. 2021. Experts, errors, and context: A large-scale study of human evaluation for machine translation. *Transactions of the Association for Computational Linguistics*, 9:1460–1474.

Jie He, Bo Peng, Yi Liao, Qun Liu, and Deyi Xiong. 2021. Tgea: An error-annotated dataset and benchmark tasks for textgeneration from pretrained language models. In *Proceedings of the 59th Annual Meeting of the Association for Computational Linguistics and the 11th International Joint Conference on Natural Language Processing (Volume 1: Long Papers)*, pages 6012–6025.

Filip Klubička, Antonio Toral, and Víctor M. Sánchez-Cartagena. 2018. Quantitative Fine-grained Human Evaluation of Machine Translation Systems: A Case Study on English to Croatian. *Machine Translation*, 32(3):195–215.

Julia Kreutzer, Nathaniel Berger, and Stefan Riezler. 2020. Correct Me If You Can: Learning from Error Corrections and Markings. *Proceedings of the 22nd Annual Conference of the European Association for Machine Translation (EAMT 2020)*.

Klaus Krippendorff. 2004. *Content Analysis, an Introduction to Its Methodology*. Sage Publications.

Arle Lommel, Maja Popović, and Aljoscha Burchardt. 2014a. Assessing inter-annotator agreement for translation error annotation. In *Proceedings of the 9th International Conference on Language Resources and Evaluation (LREC 14)*, Reykjavik, Iceland.

Arle Lommel, Hans Uszkoreit, and Aljoscha Burchardt. 2014b. Multidimensional Quality Metrics (MQM): A Framework for Declaring and Describing Translation Quality Metrics. *Tradumatica*.

Arle Lommel, Hans Uszkoreit, and Aljoscha Burchardt. 2014c. Multidimensional quality metrics (mqm): A framework for declaring and describing translation quality metrics. *Revista Tradumàtica: tecnologies de la traducció*, (12):455–463.

Maja Popović. 2021. Agree to Disagree: Analysis of Inter-Annotator Disagreements in Human Evaluation of Machine Translation Output. In *Proceedings of the 25th Conference on Computational Natural Language Learning (CoNLL 2021)*, Punta Cana, Dominican Republic.

Maja Popović and Anya Belz. 2021. A reproduction study of an annotation-based human evaluation of MT outputs. In *Proceedings of the 14th International Conference on Natural Language Generation (INLG 2021)*, Aberdeen, Scotland, UK.

Paul Rottger, Bertie Vidgen, Dirk Hovy, and Janet Pierrehumbert. 2022. Two Contrasting Data Annotation Paradigms for Subjective NLP Tasks. In *Proceedings of the 2022 Conference of the North American Chapter of the Association for Computational Linguistics: Human Language Technologies (NAACL 2022)*, pages 175–190, Seattle, United States.

Craig Thomson and Ehud Reiter. 2020. A gold standard methodology for evaluating accuracy in data-to-text systems. In *Proceedings of the 13th International Conference on Natural Language Generation (INLG 2020)*, pages 158–168, Dublin, Ireland.

David Vilar, Jia Xu, Luis Fernando D'Haro, and Hermann Ney. 2006. Error analysis of statistical machine translation output. In *Proceedings of the Fifth International Conference on Language Resources and Evaluation (LREC'06)*, Genoa, Italy. European Language Resources Association (ELRA).

Answerability: A custom metric for evaluating chatbot performance

Pranav Gupta* **Anand A. Rajasekar*†** **Amisha Patel**

Mandar Kulkarni **Alexander Sunell** **Kyung Hyuk Kim** **Ganapathy Krishnan**

Anusua Trivedi†

Flipkart US R&D Center, Redmond, USA 98052

Abstract

Most commercial conversational AI products in domains spanning e-commerce, health care, finance, and education involve a hierarchy of NLP models that perform a variety of tasks such as classification, entity recognition, question-answering, sentiment detection, semantic text similarity, and so on. Despite our understanding of each of the constituent models, we often do not have a clear view as to how these models affect the overall platform metrics. To bridge this gap, we define a metric known as *answerability*, which penalizes not only irrelevant or incorrect chatbot responses but also unhelpful responses that do not serve the chatbot's purpose despite being correct or relevant. Additionally, we describe a formula-based mathematical framework to relate individual model metrics to the answerability metric. We also describe a modeling approach for predicting a chatbot's answerability to a user question and its corresponding chatbot response.

1 Introduction

Conversational AI has been making great strides in the past few years. Several commercial chatbots powered by NLP have been deployed for diverse sectors, ranging from banking to health care (Adewumi et al., 2022). While end-to-end chatbots based on a single neural network architecture have been proposed (Komeili et al., 2021; Adiwardana et al., 2020), most commercial organizations still deploy a hierarchy of machine learning models working together in unison to come up with an answer to a user's question, rather than relying on the output of a single end-to-end neural network, for instance, the popular Rasa NLU framework used by several industrial organizations (Bocklisch et al., 2017). In such a case, it is important to have a single unified metric that defines the effectiveness of a conversational AI product, such as a chatbot. Moreover, one needs to have a framework that links individual model metrics to the overall chatbot effectiveness metric. This way, we can understand the "weak links" in the entire chatbot workflow, i.e., models whose relative improvement can have the maximum effect on the global chatbot effectiveness metric. This is crucial for a commercial organization, where business impact needs to be routinely demonstrated, requiring teams to prioritize which models they are going to focus on improving.

Moreover, by incorporating other business-motivated factors such as helpfulness into the overall chatbot effectiveness metric, we are ensuring that we are optimizing not just for peak performance from each of the constituent machine learning models inside a chatbot, but also for the ability of the chatbot to serve the organization's business goals. For example, if an e-commerce website does not sell women's Reebok shoes of size 10, its chatbot might answer "correctly" to a user who asked if those shoes are available, by responding "No we do not have women's Reebok shoes of size 10." However, this answer is not "helpful," that is, a user shown this answer will not be tempted to search for other products on the website. A helpful answer could not only acknowledge the lack of Reebok shoes of the required size, but could also suggest other similar shoes of size 10 from a similar brand, say Skechers or Nike, so that an originally unhelpful answer could potentially become helpful. In this case, the answer is not only correct but also helpful, just like how a salesperson in a brick-and-

*Both authors contributed equally to this work

† {anand.ar,anusua.trivedi}@flipkart.com

Proceedings of the 2nd Workshop on Natural Language Generation, Evaluation, and Metrics (GEM), pages 316 - 325
December 7, 2022 ©2022 Association for Computational Linguistics

mortar store would be when they are asked about the availability of a certain product. Similar examples apply to other use-cases of conversational AI such as banking, governance, and health care. By emphasizing such business-relevant expectations from a task-oriented chatbot, we are encouraging it to provide a more relatable experience to the user, just like a human agent or salesperson.

This paper seeks to make 2 contributions: the first is to define a stringent global effectiveness metric for a task-oriented chatbot called "answerability," which penalizes not only incorrect or irrelevant responses but also unhelpful responses. Our metric is quite general in its definition and can be utilized in any chatbot application. Our second contribution is to describe a framework to relate the answerability metric to individual model metrics, along with a modeling approach for predicting the answerability for an individual user query-chatbot response pair. We shall focus on the concrete example of a pre-purchase e-commerce chatbot that answers user questions about products sold on an e-commerce marketplace to illustrate our ideas where necessary. This example is ideal and instructive for the concepts explained in this paper, given the variety of NLP models it encompasses, such as multi-class text classification, span detection-based question answering, and semantic text similarity-based retrieval of user-generated content such as user-generated frequently asked questions (FAQs) and user reviews for the product.

2 Related Work

We review the existing literature for chatbot evaluation metrics below.

2.1 Metrics for evaluating chatbot performance

While several metrics for evaluating chatbots have been suggested, (Abd-Alrazaq et al., 2020; Shawar and Atwell, 2007) we did not find any mathematical frameworks that relate chatbot effectiveness metrics to individual model performances. Typically metrics have been based on response generation (Cameron et al., 2019), usability (Abdullah et al., 2018), response understanding (Yokotani et al., 2018), and global aesthetics (Wargnier et al., 2018).

Other metrics proposed for chatbots such as perplexity, sensibleness and specificity average (SSA) (Adiwardana et al., 2020), and percentage of per-turn engaging responses (Xu et al., 2022) focus on how closely the bot-user conversation resembles a human conversation over multiple turns. While these metrics are crucial for a general, open-domain chatbot, most business applications measure the success of their conversational AI products based on not only the coherence within the chatbot responses but also the effectiveness of the chatbot in helping the user's specific needs. Metrics intended for open-domain chatbots may not always be appropriate for a business use case. General-purpose NLG metrics such as ROUGE (Lin, 2004) and BLEU (Papineni et al., 2001), despite having the benefit of being automated, do not work for cases where there could be multiple responses that are equally effective.

2.2 Typical model hierarchies in a chatbot

Popular chatbot frameworks such as Daniel et al. (2020); Bocklisch et al. (2017), and winning chatbots in competitions such as the Alexa Prize competition (Serban et al., 2017), demonstrate that superior chatbot designs comprise a collection of several models, each geared towards a specific kind of conversation. For instance, Serban et al. (2017) consists of 22 response models, thus making it crucial for a team of engineers to have clear visibility into how sensitive the overall chatbot metrics are to the metrics of each of the constituent models. As new use cases emerge and a chatbot grows in complexity, having a quantitative view of the contribution of each model to the overall chatbot performance is crucial.

Most open-source chatbot designs begin with an intent recognition layer that decides the category of the user query before directing it to an appropriate downstream model,(Adamopoulou and Moussiades, 2020; Lokman and Ameedeen, 2018) whereas downstream models could include question-answering and/or other information retrieval models.(Kulkarni et al., 2019)

3 Description of the chatbot architecture

As described in Fig. 1, the chatbot consists of an intent classification model, which detects the overall intent of the user query. If the intent is not a product-specific intent (e.g., stock availability, introductory greeting, etc.), then we answer using standard templates that do not involve any predictive model. On the other hand, if the intent is a product-specific intent, then we invoke a binary classifier that predicts whether the query is factual or subjective.

Factual queries, such as "what is the battery capacity of this phone?", "does this phone support 5G?" are sent first to a question-answering model based on unstructured data such as product description text or structured data such as key-value specification pairs, e.g., "battery capacity: 5000 mAh", and "camera resolution: 48 megapixel".

Subjective queries, such as "is the camera good?," "can I play PUBG on this phone without lag?" are sent first to a semantic text similarity model that retrieves the most similar user FAQ or user reviews from the product webpage that can potentially answer this subjective user query.

We define the chatbot answerability metric as follows: for a given response by the chatbot to a user's question, we assign it a score between -1 and +1 based on the criteria described in Table 1.

Note that the weights assigned to each answer category in Table 1 could be modified as per product objectives. One example in an e-commerce setting could be to assign a weight proportional to the probability of conversion, i.e., the user buys the product they are consulting the chatbot about. The *answerability* of the chatbot is then defined as the mean of answerability scores over the entire dataset of chatbot responses.

We describe two kinds of modeling approaches in this paper:

- Section 5 describes a mathematical model for connecting individual model metrics to answerability.
- Section 6 describes a multi-class classification approach where we train a model to classify a query-response pair between one of the answerability classes.

4 Data

For the modeling described in this paper, we sampled actual user-chatbot conversations from the production logs of the pre-purchase chatbot and asked an in-house team of labelers, based in India and familiar with the English-Hindi code-mixed vocabulary used by the users of the pre-purchase chatbot, to label each chatbot response with one of the 7 labels described in Table 1. Labelers were provided with explicit examples of correct and incorrect labels in a detailed labeling guideline document, so that they label user query-bot response pairs consistently. Chatbot responses that did not fall into any of these 7 categories were not considered. Every data point was labeled by two labelers. Whenever there was a disagreement between the labels, the tie was broken by a third labeler. Labelers used Taskmonk, a data labeling platform specific to e-commerce applications[1]. User queries are either in English or code-mixed English-Hindi, written using the Roman script. Examples from labelled dataset are listed below:

1) Product: ABC mobile phone
User question: Auto call recording available
Bot response: (from FAQs) Here is what I found- Q: All call Auto call recording hogi kya[2] A: yes
Label: Excellent Relevance, Helpful Answer

2) Product: XYZ mobile phone
User question: earphone support this phone
Bot response: (from the product description) Here's what you'll get in the box: 1 Handset, 1 Battery, 1 Charger.
Label: Poor Relevance, Unhelpful Answer

In the first example, the chatbot returned a relevant user FAQ, whereas in the next example, the chatbot responded with information that was not relevant to the question asked by the user.

5 Modeling for predicting the answerability from individual model metrics

5.1 Framework to link answerability to individual model metrics

Now that we have defined the answerability metric, let us formulate our framework for linking individual model metrics to the answerability metric defined in Section 3. For the purposes of this paper, we shall use a simplified version of the chatbot to describe our approach and results. This chatbot is used for answering pre-purchase customer questions related to products listed on the e-commerce platform. The components of the chatbot cover the major categories of models typically used in chatbot architectures, hence it is an ideal example for illustrating our answerability framework.

[1]https://taskmonk.ai/about-us.html

[2]This code-mixed utterance translates to: "Will all calls be automatically recorded?"

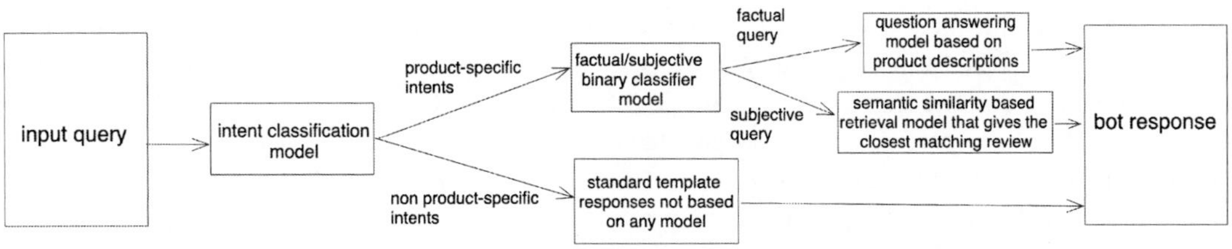

Figure 1: Schematic of a simplified version of the e-commerce chatbot used for the purposes of this paper.

Type of response	Answerability score	Symbol
• Poor Relevance	-1	S_p
• No Answer • Transfer to a Human Agent	0	S_n
• Excellent Relevance, Unhelpful Answer • Fair Relevance, Unhelpful Answer	0.5	$S_{r,\ uh}$
• Excellent Relevance, Helpful Answer • Fair Relevance, Helpful Answer	1	$S_{r,\ h}$

Table 1: Criteria for answerability scores based on the relevance and helpfulness of the chatbot responses

5.2 Intent classification model

Let $S = \{\text{ps}, \text{non-ps}_1, \text{non-ps}_2, \dots\}$ denote the list of chatbot intents, where "ps" indicates the "product-specific" intent, and "non-ps$_1$", "non-ps$_2$", etc. indicate the non-product specific intents for which there is no predictive model to be run downstream. For a text classification model, if the predicted label is correct, then the answerability will be the true answerability associated with that class of intent. Otherwise, we assume that the answerability will be 0.

Therefore, the contribution of intent $i \in S$ to the answerability is given as $f_i A_i P_i$, where f_i denotes the fraction of queries with the predicted intent label being i, A_i denotes the answerability associated with queries with intent label i, and P_i denotes the probability of correctly predicting a query with a predicted intent label i (precision).

Thus, the overall chatbot answerability A is given as:

$$\begin{aligned} A &= \sum_{i \in S} f_i A_i P_i \\ &= f_{ps} P_{ps} A_{ps} + A_{non-ps}, \end{aligned} \tag{1}$$

where

$$A_{non-ps} = \sum_{i=1,2,\dots} f_{non-ps,i} P_{non-ps,i} A_{non-ps,i}. \tag{2}$$

Note that $\sum_{i \in S} f_i = 1$ here. When the intent i is ps (product-specific), we can expand the answerability in terms of downstream model metrics from the semantic text similarity, factual-subjective classifier, and question-answering models. However, when the intent is not the product-specific (ps) intent, there is no dependence of the answerability of that specific intent on any of the model metrics. Therefore, we can substitute the answerabilities of those intents, namely $\{A_{non-ps,i}\}$, with a constant, average answerability value A_{non-ps}, calculated from labeled data corresponding to the appropriate non-product specific intents, such as stock availability, offers and discounts, etc.

5.3 Factual/subjective classifier

Just like the intent classification model, the factual-subjective binary classifier, which is invoked for product-specific queries, contributes to the chatbot answerability in the following way:

$$\begin{aligned} A_{ps} = &\ f_{factual}\ P_{factual}\ A_{factual} \\ &+ f_{subjective}\ P_{subjective}\ A_{subjective}. \end{aligned} \tag{3}$$

, where $P_{factual}$ and $P_{subjective}$ denote the precisions of the factual and subjective classes of the factual/subjective binary classifier, and $f_{factual}$ and $f_{subjective}$ denote the fraction of queries recognized as product-specific (ps) by the intent model.

5.4 Question-answering model

The question-answering models based on product features are called when the above-mentioned factual-subjective classifier predicts the user query to the chatbot as factual. Thus, $A_{factual}$ mentioned in Eqn. 3 can be further expanded in terms of the metrics of the question-answering model. While answering from product specifications, the ground truth could be either null or non-null, depending on whether the answer to the question asked is actually available in the product specifications. Furthermore, for null or non-null ground truth, we could have either null or non-null predictions from the question-answering model. The question-answering model metrics we use are described in Table 2. We also assume that the 2 models for question-answering from unstructured product description text and structured key-value specification pairs have the same model metrics, thus effectively reducing the 2 models into a single question-answering model.

Combining Tables 2 and 1, we can derive the following formula for $A_{factual}$:

$$\begin{aligned} A_{factual} = & S_{r,\,h} \times C_{QnA} \times \rho \times f_{H,QnA} \\ & + S_{r,\,uh} \times C_{QnA} \times \rho \times (1 - f_{H,QnA}) \\ & + S_p \times (1 - C_{QnA}) \times \rho \\ & + S_p \times \text{FPR}_{null} \times (1 - \rho) \end{aligned} \tag{4}$$

Here $S_{r,\,h}$, $S_{r,\,uh}$, and S_p denote the answerability scores for relevant and helpful, relevant but unhelpful, and poor relevance answers respectively, as described in Table 1. Terms in Eqn. 4 with coefficients $S_{r,\,h}$, $S_{r,\,uh}$, and S_p denote the contributions of relevant and helpful, relevant but unhelpful, and poorly relevant answers respectively to $A_{factual}$. We exclude terms with S_n (no answer/agent transfer cases) from these equations for simplification purposes, because $S_n = 0$ according to Table 1.

Note that in case the question-answering model cannot answer a question, there is a fallback to semantic search-based retrieval models. However, in this formula, we ignore this in order to simplify our description.

5.5 Semantic-text similarity based retrieval models

Among the queries detected as subjective by the factual/subjective classifier, some queries are answered by a retrieval model that searches for the most relevant user review, whereas others are answered by a retrieval model that searches for the most relevant user FAQ. While there is a fallback on the question-answering model in case the retrieval models are unable to answer the user question, we chose to ignore it in order to simplify our modeling.

We now expand $A_{subjective}$ as

$$\begin{aligned} A_{subjective} = & f_{FAQ}\, A_{FAQ} \\ & + f_{Reviews}\, A_{Reviews}, \end{aligned} \tag{5}$$

where A_{FAQ} and $A_{Reviews}$ are the answerabilities of the FAQ and Reviews models, and f_{FAQ} and $f_{Reviews}$ denote the fraction of user queries that were detected as subjective answered by FAQ and reviews retrieval models respectively. For the case of retrieval models, we use model metrics as described in Table 3.

We further expand $A_{Reviews}$ and A_{FAQ} in terms of the model metrics described in Table 3 as follows:

$$\begin{aligned} A_{Reviews} = & S_{r,\,h} \times P_{Reviews} \times C_{Reviews} \times f_{H,Reviews} \\ & + S_{r,\,uh} \times P_{Reviews} \times C_{Reviews} \times (1 - f_{H,Reviews}) \\ & + S_p \times (1 - P_{Reviews}) \times C_{Reviews} \end{aligned} \tag{6}$$

Similarly,

$$\begin{aligned} A_{FAQ} = & S_{r,\,h} \times P_{FAQ} \times C_{FAQ} \times f_{H,FAQ} \\ & + S_{r,\,uh} \times P_{FAQ} \times C_{FAQ} \times (1 - f_{H,FAQ}) \\ & + S_p \times (1 - P_{FAQ}) \times C_{FAQ}. \end{aligned} \tag{7}$$

5.6 Overall expression for the chatbot answerability A

By combining Eqns. 1, 3, 4, 5, 6, and 7, we get the expression for the overall chatbot answerability A. The approach we describe does not require any additional model training and can act as a simple, first-principles baseline for expressing A as a function of the individual model metrics.

For a chatbot that is different from the pre-purchase e-commerce chatbot we describe here, we need to modify the expressions Eqns. 1, 3, 4, 5, 6, and 7 according to its specific architecture. For example, if a chatbot does not have access to user-generated content such as reviews or FAQs, we could ignore the terms A_{FAQ} and $A_{Reviews}$. However, in most multi-model chatbot architectures, we should be able to derive similar expressions for an answerability-like metric.

By differentiating the overall expression for A with respect to each of the model metrics, we get the *sensitivity* of A to the product metric. For example, $\frac{\partial A}{\partial P_{FAQ}}$ tells us the sensitivity of A to P_{FAQ}. By using our mathematical model, we could know

Metric	Symbol	Description
Coverage	C_{QnA}	fraction of non-null ground truth cases the model answered correctly
Answer rate	ρ	fraction of queries for which answer is available in product descriptions
Helpful fraction	$f_{H,QnA}$	fraction of answers that were helpful to the user
Null false positive rate	FPR_{null}	fraction of false positives within null ground truth cases

Table 2: Question-answering model metrics

Metric	Symbol	Description
Coverage of the FAQ retrieval model	C_{FAQ}	fraction of queries for which the FAQ retrieval model gave a non-null answer
Coverage of the reviews retrieval model	$C_{Reviews}$	fraction of queries for which the reviews retrieval model gave a non-null answer
Precision of the FAQ retrieval model	P_{FAQ}	fraction of non-null answers from the FAQ retrieval model which have excellent or fair relevance
Precision of the reviews retrieval model	$P_{Reviews}$	fraction of non-null answers from the reviews retrieval model which have excellent or fair relevance
Helpful fraction of the FAQ retrieval model	$f_{H,FAQ}$	fraction of helpful answers from the FAQ retrieval model
Helpful fraction of the reviews retrieval model	$f_{H,Reviews}$	fraction of helpful answers from the reviews retrieval model

Table 3: FAQ and reviews retrieval model metrics used for the answerability calculation

which metric from Tables 2 and 3 has the highest sensitivity of A, and based on this we could prioritize model improvements focused on that metric. This can be of immense help for complicated chatbot architectures where it is hard to accurately predict which model metric has the potential to have the maximum positive impact on the bottom-line business metric, such as answerability. Moreover, our framework could be used as a way to estimate the expected business impact before an improved model is launched into production.

To illustrate this, let us take the example of the answerability calculated by combining Eqns. 1, 3, 4, 5, 6, and 7, for the mobile phone product category. Let us hold all the other metrics to be constant, and change only the answer rate, ρ, and the precision of the subjective class of the factual/subjective binary classifier, $P_{subjective}$. According to the model, the overall answerability A increases from 0.3256 to 0.3324 when $P_{subjective}$ goes up by 0.1, from 0.8 to 0.9, whereas A increases from 0.3256 to 0.3467 when ρ goes up by 0.1, from 0.5 to 0.6. This means that ρ could be a better metric to invest in than $P_{subjective}$, given that it has a higher positive impact on A. However, in some cases, a normalized sensitivity, for example, $\frac{P_{FAQ}}{A}\frac{\partial A}{\partial P_{FAQ}}$, might be a more appropriate measure.

5.7 Limitations of this approach

Our approach makes the following assumptions, which could result in an inaccurate prediction of the chatbot answerability:

- We assume that if the intent is wrongly predicted or the factual/subjective classifier misclassifies the user query, the answerability is going to be 0, which is not necessarily true.
- We assume fractions such as f_{ps}, $f_{subjective}$, and $f_{H,QnA}$ to be constant and not a function of model metrics. In reality, as model metrics change, these fractions will change too.
- We ignore the possibility that the chatbot has a fallback to reviews/FAQ models when the question-answering model cannot answer, and vice-versa.

A query-wise answerability score prediction model that predicts an answerability score for a user query-bot response pair can help address these limitations.

The overall answerability A is then defined as the average of the model predictions of answerability scores over the test dataset. However, a query-wise answerability prediction model relates an individual query-response pair to the answerability score, rather than connecting the model metrics to the overall chatbot answerability as in Section 5. Thus, the formula-based approach described in this section should be used in cases where we wish to get a rough estimate of how much a particular metric improvement is expected to increase the chatbot answerability, or know the sensitivity of a business-motivated metric such as A to the product metrics. Whereas the per-query approach should be used when the goal is to get an accurate prediction of the overall answerability A.

6 Per-query predictive model for the chatbot answerability A

Apart from helping us understand the relative importance of each constituent model used in a chatbot, the answerability labels described in Table 1 can also be used for training a model to predict the relevance and helpfulness of chatbot response, which in turn can be used to compute the answerability directly. Also, detecting whether a chatbot response is helpful or not can be used to modify our planned response so that an originally unhelpful response could potentially become helpful. For example, if the model predicts that an answer is not helpful, then we could provide recommendations of similar products, or alter the conversational design in a way that helps the user. Moreover, as described in Section 5.7, such a per-query modeling approach does not suffer from the limitations of the formula-based approach described in Section 5.

6.1 Approach

We propose to model helpful/unhelpful answer prediction as a multi-class classification task at the query level by using the question and its corresponding response from the chatbot as the input. We chose an in-house Large Language Model (LLM) based on the BERT architecture (Devlin et al., 2019) pre-trained on an approximately 50 GB in-house training corpus consisting of product descriptions, catalog attributes, reviews, QnA pairs, and addresses as our pre-trained model. The maximum sequence length while training is limited to 192 based on the distribution of the number of tokens. This model has 12 Encoder layers with an embedding size of 768. This model is trained on 3 A100 GPUs for 14 days with a batch size of 420 for 1M steps. This model gains significantly lower perplexity on in-domain test sets, especially for code-mixed data and noisy search queries. We fine-tune this pre-trained model on the dataset described in Table 4.

Let a^i be the response given by the chatbot for question q^i. The question q^i and the response a^i are concatenated, tokenized and passed to an embedding layer. The word embeddings along with their positional signals are passed to a transformer encoder, whose head predicts the output probabilities.

$$\begin{aligned} w^i &= \text{tokenizer}([q^i; a^i]) \\ \hat{y}^i &= \text{BertClassifier}(w^i) \end{aligned} \tag{8}$$

"; " denote the appropriate concatenation of input sentences as required by the pre-trained model, i.e, the [SEP] token. The classification task is trained to minimize the cross entropy loss,

$$L_{nsp} = -\frac{1}{N_1}\sum_{i=1}^{N_1} y^i log\hat{y}^i \tag{9}$$

where y^i is the ground truth label indicating the answer class and N_1 refers to the number of data points in the dataset.

6.2 Dataset

We train the multi-class answer classification model using our in-house dataset consisting of answered queries from mobile phone and fashion product categories on the e-commerce platform (see Section 4). We remove queries falling under "No Answer" groups since they are unhelpful by default. We group the remaining responses into 3 classes based on their corresponding labels. The statistics of the dataset are presented in Table 4.

6.3 Results

We use Term Frequency - Inverse Document Frequency (TF-IDF) scores to vectorize user queries and chatbot responses before feeding them as input to one-vs-all Logistic Regression (LR). This method was used as the baseline for this task. We also experimented with the publicly available BERT model (*bert-base-cased*) for the dataset. Table 5 shows the comparison results. Our in-domain BERT-based classification method outperforms the simple baseline (TF-IDF + LR) by a significant

<table>
<tr><td></td><td></td><td>Train dataset</td><td>Test dataset</td></tr>
<tr><td>Class 1 - Poor Relevance Unhelpful</td><td>Poor relevance</td><td>2652</td><td>278</td></tr>
<tr><td rowspan="3">Class 2 - Excellent/Fair Relevance Unhelpful</td><td>Fair relevance</td><td>428</td><td>44</td></tr>
<tr><td>Excellent relevance</td><td>4661</td><td>479</td></tr>
<tr><td>Total datapoints</td><td>5089</td><td>523</td></tr>
<tr><td rowspan="3">Class 3 - Excellent/Fair Relevance Helpful</td><td>Fair relevance</td><td>1387</td><td>156</td></tr>
<tr><td>Excellent relevance</td><td>10197</td><td>1043</td></tr>
<tr><td>Total datapoints</td><td>11584</td><td>1199</td></tr>
</table>

Table 4: Helpful/Unhelpful answers dataset

Model	Precision	Recall	F1-score
TF-IDF + LR	0.745	0.754	0.737
open-domain BERT	0.794	0.799	0.795
in-domain BERT	0.824	0.826	0.825

Table 5: Comparison of different models. Note that the precision, recall, and F1 scores indicate the weighted precision, recall, and F1 scores respectively.

Source	Mobile	Fashion
Ground Truth	0.546	0.637
BERT classifier	0.559	0.662
Mathematical formulation (Section 5)	0.326	0.308

Table 6: Comparing the overall chatbot answerability A for the BERT-based classifier and the mathematical formulation from Section 5. The columns "Mobile" and "Fashion" indicate mobile phone and fashion product categories on the e-commerce platform respectively.

margin. It also achieves an improvement of **3.77%** on weighted F1 score over the public BERT model. The above result underlines the effectiveness of in-domain pre-training of BERT. The detailed classification report of our model is presented in Figure 2.

6.4 Computing Answerability

We use the trained model to compute the product-specific answerability A_{ps} on the test dataset using model predictions. We choose to focus on A_{ps} rather than the overall chatbot answerability A to simplify our description, and also because A_{ps} includes all the models present in the chatbot architecture described in Section 3 except the intent classification model. This is because the dataset consist of queries where the intent has been identified as product specification related. In order to compare the approaches described in Sections 5 and 6, we also compute an estimate of A_{ps} using the mathematical formulation in Section 5 and compare the scores with the ground truth A_{ps} from the human-annotated test dataset. The results are tabulated in Table 6. We observe that the BERT classifier is able to match the ground truth answerability scores closely.

For the mathematical formulation described in Section 5, the predicted answerability underestimates the ground truth answerability. This could be due to distribution shifts between the evaluation datasets used for calculating the model metrics versus the test dataset used in Table 6, along with the assumptions made by the mathematical model listed in Section 5.7. Given that the test dataset used here ignores cases where the chatbot gave a null response or transferred to a human agent, we normalized the answerability appropriately by a normalizing factor. Also, for all calculations with the mathematical formulation, the fractions in Eqns. 3, 4, 5, 6, and 7 such as $f_{subjective}$ and $f_{H,QnA}$ were calculated from the test dataset. To simplify our description further through binary formulation, we derived binary labels from the test dataset where answerability score for helpful and unhelpful is set as 1 and 0 respectively. We then compute the answerability scores as per the mathematical model described in Section 5, by choosing $S_{r,\,uh} = S_p = 0$ and $S_{r,\,h} = 1$ in Table 1. For this case, we get answerability scores of 0.469 and 0.442 for mobile phone and fashion product categories respectively. These scores are closer to the respective ground truth answerability scores of 0.599 and 0.6 calculated for this binary formulation of the answerability metric. This suggests that the mathematical formulation of Section 5 shows better agreement with the ground truth answerability scores when we assume answerability to take a binary value of either 0 or 1.

7 Conclusion

In this paper, we introduce answerability as a global chatbot effectiveness metric and show how it can be used to guide model development decisions for a

	precision	recall	f1-score	support
Excellent/Fair Relevance - Helpful Answer	0.875	0.881	0.878	1199
Excellent/Fair Relevance - Unhelpful Answer	0.788	0.811	0.799	523
Poor Relevance - Unhelpful Answer	0.675	0.619	0.645	278
accuracy			0.826	2000
macro avg	0.779	0.770	0.774	2000
weighted avg	0.824	0.826	0.825	2000

Figure 2: Classification report of the in-domain BERT classifier

conversational AI product such as the pre-purchase chatbot, by relating answerability to all the metrics of all the models that are a part of the chatbot. Our framework is general and can be easily extended to chatbot metrics other than answerability depending on the domain of application, be it in finance, governance, or health care, as long as there is a concept of helpfulness associated with the chatbot's responses. For example, a health care chatbot helping patients understand their medical symptoms and pointing them to an appropriate health care provider needs to not only provide accurate information but also guide patients in the correct direction when such information is not available. The answerability metric will directly apply to such a case, and help guide the development of individual models within the chatbot's architecture in a way that maximizes patient satisfaction.

Future work could involve the joint training of all the models within a chatbot with a differentiable version of the answerability objective. Further iterations of the formula-based modeling approach described in Section 5 could involve the inclusion of other upstream models such as spell checking, automated speech recognition, and machine translation, which are used to interpret voice/multilingual user input before the input is sent to the intent classification model in the chatbot. We hope that the answerability metric and the modeling methods described in this paper will help guide product development and model prioritization in conversational AI products in the academic, government and industrial domains.

8 Limitations and Ethical Impact

The answerability metric could inspire other business-oriented metrics and also drive the development of task-oriented chatbots across various domains such as e-commerce, health care, and governance. These use cases could have various social implications: dialog systems such as customer support bots could bring in benefits such as cost savings, convenience, and the availability of 24-hour assistance, while decreasing the number of job opportunities for human service agents and salespersons. Language models underlying such dialog systems could reinforce social biases and impact the environment negatively (Bender et al., 2021; Schramowski et al., 2022). Moreover, any widely used metric or benchmark carries the inherent risk of biasing the research in a certain direction.

References

Alaa Abd-Alrazaq, Zeineb Safi, Mohannad Alajlani, Jim Warren, Mowafa Househ, Kerstin Denecke, et al. 2020. Technical metrics used to evaluate health care chatbots: scoping review. *Journal of medical Internet research*, 22(6):e18301.

Abu S Abdullah, Stephan Gaehde, and Tim Bickmore. 2018. A tablet based embodied conversational agent to promote smoking cessation among veterans: A feasibility study. *Journal of Epidemiology and Global Health*, 8:225–230.

Eleni Adamopoulou and Lefteris Moussiades. 2020. An overview of chatbot technology. In *Artificial Intelligence Applications and Innovations*, pages 373–383, Cham. Springer International Publishing.

Tosin Adewumi, Foteini Liwicki, and Marcus Liwicki. 2022. State-of-the-art in open-domain conversational ai: A survey. *Information*, 13(6).

Daniel Adiwardana, Minh-Thang Luong, David R. So, Jamie Hall, Noah Fiedel, Romal Thoppilan, Zi Yang, Apoorv Kulshreshtha, Gaurav Nemade, Yifeng Lu, and Quoc V. Le. 2020. Towards a human-like open-domain chatbot.

Emily M. Bender, Timnit Gebru, Angelina McMillan-Major, and Shmargaret Shmitchell. 2021. On the dangers of stochastic parrots: Can language models be too big? In *Proceedings of the 2021 ACM Conference on Fairness, Accountability, and Transparency*, FAccT '21, page 610–623, New York, NY, USA. Association for Computing Machinery.

Tom Bocklisch, Joey Faulkner, Nick Pawlowski, and Alan Nichol. 2017. Rasa: Open source language understanding and dialogue management.

Gillian Cameron, David Cameron, Gavin Megaw, Raymond Bond, Maurice Mulvenna, Siobhan O'Neill, Cherie Armour, and Michael McTear. 2019. Assessing the usability of a chatbot for mental health care. In *Internet Science*, pages 121–132, Cham. Springer International Publishing.

Gwendal Daniel, Jordi Cabot, Laurent Deruelle, and Mustapha Derras. 2020. Xatkit: A multimodal low-code chatbot development framework. *IEEE Access*, 8:15332–15346.

Jacob Devlin, Ming-Wei Chang, Kenton Lee, and Kristina Toutanova. 2019. BERT: Pre-training of deep bidirectional transformers for language understanding. In *Proceedings of the 2019 Conference of the North American Chapter of the Association for Computational Linguistics: Human Language Technologies, Volume 1 (Long and Short Papers)*, pages 4171–4186, Minneapolis, Minnesota. Association for Computational Linguistics.

Mojtaba Komeili, Kurt Shuster, and Jason Weston. 2021. Internet-augmented dialogue generation. *CoRR*, abs/2107.07566.

Ashish Kulkarni, Kartik Mehta, Shweta Garg, Vidit Bansal, Nikhil Rasiwasia, and Srinivasan Sengamedu. 2019. Productqna: Answering user questions on e-commerce product pages. In *Companion Proceedings of The 2019 World Wide Web Conference*, WWW '19, page 354–360, New York, NY, USA. Association for Computing Machinery.

Chin-Yew Lin. 2004. ROUGE: A package for automatic evaluation of summaries. In *Text Summarization Branches Out*, pages 74–81, Barcelona, Spain. Association for Computational Linguistics.

Abbas Saliimi Lokman and Mohamed Ariff Ameedeen. 2018. Modern chatbot systems: A technical review. In *Proceedings of the future technologies conference*, pages 1012–1023. Springer.

Kishore Papineni, Salim Roukos, Todd Ward, and Wei-Jing Zhu. 2001. BLEU. In *Proceedings of the 40th Annual Meeting on Association for Computational Linguistics*. Association for Computational Linguistics.

Patrick Schramowski, Cigdem Turan, Nico Andersen, Constantin A. Rothkopf, and Kristian Kersting. 2022. Large pre-trained language models contain human-like biases of what is right and wrong to do. *Nature Machine Intelligence*, 4(3):258–268.

Iulian V. Serban, Chinnadhurai Sankar, Mathieu Germain, Saizheng Zhang, Zhouhan Lin, Sandeep Subramanian, Taesup Kim, Michael Pieper, Sarath Chandar, Nan Rosemary Ke, Sai Rajeshwar, Alexandre de Brebisson, Jose M. R. Sotelo, Dendi Suhubdy, Vincent Michalski, Alexandre Nguyen, Joelle Pineau, and Yoshua Bengio. 2017. A deep reinforcement learning chatbot.

Bayan Abu Shawar and Eric Atwell. 2007. Different measurement metrics to evaluate a chatbot system. In *Proceedings of the workshop on bridging the gap: Academic and industrial research in dialog technologies*, pages 89–96.

Pierre Wargnier, Samuel Benveniste, Pierre Jouvelot, and Anne-Sophie Rigaud. 2018. Usability assessment of interaction management support in LOUISE, an ECA-based user interface for elders with cognitive impairment. *Technol. Disabil.*, 30(3):105–126.

Jing Xu, Arthur Szlam, and Jason Weston. 2022. Beyond goldfish memory: Long-term open-domain conversation. In *Proceedings of the 60th Annual Meeting of the Association for Computational Linguistics (Volume 1: Long Papers)*. Association for Computational Linguistics.

Kenji Yokotani, Gen Takagi, and Kobun Wakashima. 2018. Advantages of virtual agents over clinical psychologists during comprehensive mental health interviews using a mixed methods design. *Computers in Human Behavior*, 85:135–145.

Improved Evaluation of Automatic Source Code Summarisation

Jesse Phillips and **David Bowes** and **Mahmoud El-Haj** and **Tracy Hall**
School of Computing and Communications
Lancaster University, UK
{j.m.phillips, d.h.bowes, m.el-haj, tracy.hall}@lancaster.ac.uk

Abstract

Source code summarisation is a vital tool for the understanding and maintenance of source code as summarisations can be used to explain code in simple terms. However, source code with missing, incorrect, or outdated summaries is a common occurrence in production code. Automatic source code summarisation seeks to solve these issues by generating up-to-date summaries of source code methods. Recent work in automatically generating source code summaries uses neural networks for generating summaries; commonly Sequence-to-Sequence or Transformer models, pretrained on method-summary pairs. The most common method of evaluating the quality of these summaries is comparing the machine-generated summaries against human-written summaries. Summaries can be evaluated using n-gram-based translation metrics such as BLEU, METEOR, or ROUGE-L. However, these metrics alone can be unreliable and new Natural Language Generation metrics based on large pretrained language models provide an alternative. In this paper, we propose a method of improving the evaluation of a model by improving the preprocessing of the data used to train it, as well as proposing evaluating the model with a metric based off a language model, pretrained on a Natural Language (English) alongside traditional metrics. Our evaluation suggests our model has been improved by cleaning and preprocessing the data used in model training. The addition of a pretrained language model metric alongside traditional metrics shows that both produce results which can be used to evaluate neural source code summarisation.

1 Introduction

Research producing models for neural source code summarisation frequently uses metrics designed for translation and Natural Language Generation (NLG) tasks, such as BLEU (Papineni et al., 2002), METEOR (Banerjee and Lavie, 2005), (Denkowski and Lavie, 2014), and ROUGE-L (Lin, 2004). These metrics are oriented to tasks such as translation and summarisation. Mahmud et al. (2021) used these metrics and a shared dataset to compare state-of-the-art models for neural source code summarisation. These metrics are based on n-gram matching, which compares the lexical similarity of texts, but lacks a comparison of the meaning of the texts - the semantic similarity. A lack of semantic comparison means that machine-generated texts which share sequences of n-grams with reference texts score well regardless of their ability to convey a similar meaning; whereas texts which convey a similar meaning but don't share many sequences of n-grams with reference texts score poorly. For summarisation tasks, the ability to replicate the semantics of a text where the generated language may be abstractive is more significant than the ability to generate as many n-grams matching those in a human-written summary as possible because the purpose of a summary is to provide the reader with an overview of the meaning of a larger text (or in this case, a source code method).

NLG metrics based on Large Language Models (LLM) aim to improve the reliability of evaluation scores by capturing semantics through reliance on contextual embeddings. However, these metrics require large amounts of computational resources - making them expensive to run in comparison to traditional n-gram matching metrics. New efforts in making these LLM-based metrics more accessible attempt to reduce the number of parameters compared to previous LLM-based models whilst retaining similar accuracy. This allows for faster calculation of LLM-based metrics. One such new effort is the *FrugalScore* metric (Kamal Eddine et al., 2022) for evaluating NLG tasks. FrugalScore uses previous LLM-based metrics to train a miniature language model which learns on the internal mapping of the expensive metric. It is this model which is used for generating scores for pairs of sequences of text.

Proceedings of the 2nd Workshop on Natural Language Generation, Evaluation, and Metrics (GEM), pages 326 - 335
December 7, 2022

In this paper, our aim is to train a state-of-the-art neural network model (we use the NeuralCodeSum model (Ahmad et al., 2020)) designed for source code summarisation, using a dataset of source code - summary pairs as described in Section 2. The dataset we use is a modified version of the Funcom dataset (LeClair and McMillan, 2019). We selected this dataset to allow us to compare our model to previous research (Mahmud et al., 2021) which trains NeuralCodeSum on the same dataset and evaluates the results using traditional n-gram matching metrics. We then evaluate our trained model using the FrugalScore metric (Kamal Eddine et al., 2022) to show the ability of such a metric to evaluate neural source code summarisation.

1.1 Research Questions

RQ1.1 What does a comparison of commonly used metrics show about our model following our data cleaning?

We train our model and evaluate it using a series of n-gram-based NLG metrics. We can then use these results to compare to previous research.

RQ1.2 How does the model trained on our dataset compare against previous experiments on the same model?

We compare our results to previous research training NeuralCodeSum models. Comparing our model to Mahmud et al.'s (2021) model will show the effect of our improved pretraining of training data on improving the evaluation of the model.

RQ2 How do the results of traditional metrics compare to those of FrugalScore?

We present an alternative method of evaluating neural source code summarisation, by using a metric based on a language model - FrugalScore (Kamal Eddine et al., 2022). We show the difference between traditional and LLM-based metrics and the ability to use both for a more complete evaluation of source code summarisation.

2 Dataset

The data we used comes from the filtered version of the Funcom dataset (LeClair and McMillan, 2019). Funcom was proposed in the paper "Recommendations for Datasets for Source Code Summarization" as a dataset of Java methods with associated English Javadoc comments including summaries. There are three versions of the Funcom dataset: raw, filtered, and tokenised. The filtered dataset is chosen over the raw dataset as it removes automatically generated code and code without English summaries. We chose the filtered dataset over the tokenised dataset for the purposes of this experiment to give us greater control over the data preprocessing; the tokenised dataset implements their own removal of special characters, tokenisation, splitting of camel case, and lowercasing. These are all steps which we perform, but intend to control.

Mahmud et al. (2021) set out a method for preprocessing the Funcom dataset for use with NeuralCodeSum, alongside other neural networks for neural source code summarisation. However, this method does not require code to be compilable, and the script provided by the authors for replicating the experiment contains a flaw as described below (also, see Listing 1 and Appendix A).

In attempting to remove comments, Mahmud et al.'s (2021) method strips all lines containing the string "//". Whilst this is the identifier for an inline comment in Java, the same string may be used elsewhere. For example: "//" occurs numerous times in our dataset as part of a URL.

Listing 1: Mahmud et al.'s (2021) method for removing comments: pseudocode

```
function remove_comments(method)
{
    create an array (of strings)
    for each line of text in a
        method:
    {
        if the line does not
            contain "//"
             add the line to the
                array
    }
    combine the contents of the
        array into a new method
    return the new method
}
```

We created a new method for preprocessing the filtered version of the Funcom dataset (LeClair and McMillan, 2019), based on that followed by Mahmud et al. (2021), with some changes to fix these issues. The first of these changes is parsing the Java code used to ensure that only compilable code is included in the experiment. We did this using JavaParser (van Bruggen et al., 2020). The use of only

Figure 1: Dataset Preprocessing

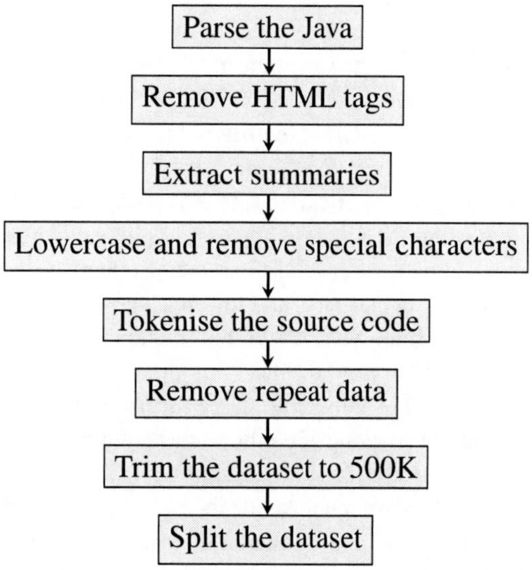

compilable code focuses the model on "production" code. Following the principle that we can disregard code which cannot be used in a real-world system to allow the model to focus solely on code used in production. We then used JavaParser to remove inline code comments written by the developers without the risk of damaging the code itself. Removal of natural language code comments from the code removes bias due to encountering potentially incorrect summaries written by the developers. Our method of using JavaParser to remove only strings the Java compiler would recognise as code comments ensures that potentially useful data within the Java source code which contains the string "//" does not get removed. For example:

```
// Example A:
public void play() {
    // If no sound file is there
        nothing can be played.
    ...

// Example B:
location = linkUrl.toString().
    replaceFirst("file:/", "file
    ://");
```

Example A would have the string "// If no sound file is there nothing can be played." removed, but Example B would not be affected.

As Figure 1 shows, the dataset is first parsed by JavaParser, and method-comment pairs where the methods cannot be interpreted are removed from the data. During this parsing phase, comments within the methods are stripped from the methods to remove noise as described above.

HTML data is then removed from the comments, as remnants of HTML tags in the comments used for training may influence the predictions and skew the results of the experiment. This is because after removing special characters, leftover text from the HTML tags could be present in the training data, and the model would - therefore - attempt to replicate that pattern in evaluation.

Following this, we extract the section of each comment in a method-comment pair most likely to represent a basic summary. For example, from:

```
/**
 * Returns the pushes lowerbound
     of this board position.
 *
 * @return the pushes lowerbound
*/
```

we extract the string "Returns the pushes lowerbound of this board position.". This is done by extracting the first line of non-whitespace (that is: not composed entirely of space and/or tab characters) text with more than 8 characters. As the comments in the method-comment pairs are extracted from method-level Javadoc, the first line of meaningful text in our dataset is usually a method summary.

These summaries are lowercased and special characters (characters which are not alphanumeric, full-stops, or apostrophes) are removed from them, in order to ensure each method has a plain natural language summary with minimal noise which could interfere with the neural network model. Much like with the removal of HTML tags, these special characters which may not add to the natural language summary of the method would be replicated by the model, potentially worsening results.

The source code methods are then tokenised. As part of our tokenisation, camel case phrases are split into individual words, punctuation is spaced out from words, and the text is then lowercased. This maintains the structure of the source code (including any structural information), whilst removing information which may be misleading. For example, one camel case word may contain a string of words which provide useful information to the model when tokenised.

Repeat data is then removed to prevent any bias on the final results. In our initial testing, we found our model scored highly on all metrics, but when we generated a histogram of the results, we discovered that this was due to an incredibly high number of perfect matches, rather than a single right-skewed peak. By comparing our test data to our training data, we discovered multiple copies of the same method in the dataset, which were present in both testing and evaluation data. Removing these repeats allows us to reduce this effect.

The size of the dataset is then reduced in order to decrease the time and compute power needed to run this experiment. The first 500,000 valid method-comment pairs are used as the data for this experiment. Selecting only the first 500,000 pairs is a technique used by Mahmud et al. (2021), which means that our results are still comparable. However, this means there is potential to improve the model further in future by training it on a larger dataset.

We further split our dataset into training, validation, and evaluation (80% / 10% / 10%) datasets. We chose this split as that is the same split chosen by both Ahmad et al. (2020) and Mahmud et al. (2021) for training and evaluating their NeuralCodeSum models. The data is split with a randomised mixture of code from multiple projects in each dataset to prevent the artificial inflation of results due to any one dataset having a majority of code from a single project within the larger dataset, which may cause artificial inflation of performance due to data snooping in our evaluation which wouldn't reflect real conditions (as suggested by both LeClair and McMillan (2019), and Mahmud et al. (2021)).

3 Research Methodology

We began by building our dataset, as described in the Section 2. We used the Funcom dataset (LeClair and McMillan, 2019), as this will allow us to compare our results to Mahmud et al.'s (2021) evaluation of NeuralCodeSum, and added our own preprocessing steps in order to improve our model. The model was trained and evaluated on a machine using an `Intel i9-12900KF` CPU, 128GB DDR4 RAM, and an `Nvidia GeForce RTX 3090` GPU, using the official implementation of NeuralCodeSum, `PyTorch 1.3`, and `Python 3.6`. The result data from the evaluation process is collected in JSON format. The code used to process the dataset is available at github.com/phillijm/JavaDatasetCleaner.

3.1 Methodology for RQ1.1

In testing our model using metrics, we selected the metrics previously used for research on NeuralCodeSum, Ahmad et al. (2020) and Mahmud et al. (2021) both used Smoothed BLEU-4 (Papineni et al., 2002), METEOR (Banerjee and Lavie, 2005), and ROUGE-L (Lin, 2004) for the evaluation of their NeuralCodeSum models. In using these metrics, we can compare our results to previous research more accurately. We also calculated BLEU-1-4. By analysing the difference between these, we can identify some strengths and weaknesses of our model. The smoothing technique used for Smoothed BLEU-4 was Lin and Och's (2004) technique. METEOR was measured using the official Java implementation of METEOR 1.5 (Denkowski and Lavie, 2014). ROUGE-L was measured using the Google Research python implementation of the metric (Liu, 2022).

3.2 Methodology for RQ1.2

To establish whether our model has improved based on our improvements to the preprocessing of training data, we compare our results from RQ1.1 to those of Mahmud et al. (2021) in Table 2. Mahmud et al. (2021) also trained a NeuralCodeSum Model on the Funcom dataset, but with a simpler approach to preprocessing. We hypothesise our model should outperform Mahmud et al.'s (2021) model in evaluation against the same metrics: Smoothed BLEU-4 (Papineni et al., 2002), METEOR (Banerjee and Lavie, 2005), and ROUGE-L (Lin, 2004), due to the improvements made in preprocessing the dataset used to train the model, as detailed in the Dataset Section, where we train the model on only compilable code, with the training summaries heavily sanitised.

3.3 Methodology for RQ2

Once this baseline comparison of our model against Mahmud et al.'s (2021) model has been established, we evaluate our model against the FrugalScore (Kamal Eddine et al., 2022) metric, in order to compare FrugalScore against traditional n-gram-based metrics for a neural source code summarisation task. Our aim in evaluating the model against FrugalScore is to see a FrugalScore value which is comparable with traditional metrics and be able to compare the distribution of FrugalScore to traditional metrics on a histogram. This will suggest that the results produced by the model are able to be measured reliably using FrugalScore as a metric.

4 Result Analysis

Table 1: Comparison of n-gram based metrics against FrugalScore, measuring summaries generated by our NeuralCodeSum Model.

Metric	Score
BLEU-1	37.70
BLEU-2	27.03
BLEU-3	19.94
BLEU-4	14.67
Smoothed BLEU-4	29.17
METEOR	19.93
ROUGE-L	45.82
FrugalScore	65.76

In answer to RQ1.1: how our model compares against commonly used metrics; as seen in Table 1, our model scores well with lower n-gram BLEU metrics, but that decreases with higher numbers of n-grams. Lin and Och (2004) suggest that a drop in BLEU from lower to higher orders of n-grams could correlate a high degree of adequacy (the generated summary is still understandable), but a lower degree of fluency in the language generated. A lack of fluency in the text generated by our model would also explain the lower METEOR score. Banerjee and Lavie (2005) suggest that whilst higher order n-gram BLEU scores can be used as an indirect measure of grammatical well-formedness, METEOR directly measures this. If the model were trained on a larger dataset, we expect this would be improved.

Comparing our results to previous experiments (RQ1.2), Table 2 shows an improvement in both Smoothed BLEU-4 and ROUGE-L scores when compared to Mahmud et al. (2021). These metrics suggest that our model has been improved in its ability to generate source code summaries by the improvements in Figure 1 in the preprocessing of the dataset used, with an improvement in Smoothed BLEU-4 of 7.67 and an improvement in ROUGE-L of 12.11.

We compared the performance of our model to previous experiments using the Smoothed BLEU-4, ROUGE-L, and METEOR metrics - as these metrics were presented by both Ahmad et al. (2020) and Mahmud et al. (2021). A possible future work would be to test these models against a wider range of n-gram-based metrics and LLM-based metrics.

In answer to RQ2: when comparing traditional n-gram-based natural language generation metrics to FrugalScore (Kamal Eddine et al., 2022) for the task of neural source code summarisation, our model scored an average FrugalScore value of 65.76, as shown in Table 1. The distribution of these can be seen in Figure 2, and more clearly in Figures 3-6 in Appendix B. The distribution of FrugalScore is a bimodal distribution, with both peaks to the right of the graph, and most results between 40 and 80. These second peak represents where FrugalScore measures the machine-generated summary as being identical or near-identical to the original human-written summary, which could potentially show some degree of overfitting in the model.

It is notable that - when compared to traditional metrics - FrugalScore gives far fewer "bad" results (for example, 31.308% of Smoothed BLEU-4 results were above 30, compared to 99.998% of FrugalScore results). FrugalScore also gives fewer "perfect" or "near-perfect" results than traditional metrics (for example, 6.571% of Smoothed BLEU-4 results were above 99, compared to 4.215% of FrugalScore results). The difference between these results suggests that FrugalScore gives more credit to summaries which other metrics rank poorly and less credit to summaries which other metrics rank highly, with higher median and mean values. This should be taken into account when directly comparing FrugalScore to traditional metrics.

Our results show that - on average - FrugalScore ranks summaries more highly than traditional metrics. This is likely either due to the ability of LLM-based metrics to take the semantics of a sentence into account, where n-gram-based metrics do not, or due to a possible overestimation of results. To determine this would require further human evaluation, as mentioned in the Limitations Section.

5 Related Work

5.1 Neural Source Code Summarisation Using Transformer Models

The Transformer model was initially proposed by Vaswani (Vaswani et al., 2017) and initially tested on the WMT 2014 English-to-German translation task. CodeBERT (Feng et al., 2020) and NeuralCodeSum (Ahmad et al., 2020) both use the Transformer architecture to form a model for neural source code summarisation, with NeuralCodeSum being a simple Transformer model, and CodeBERT being a larger bidirectional model, built on BERT (Devlin et al., 2019) and RoBERTa (Liu et al.,

Table 2: Comparison of metrics against those reported by previous papers.

Model	Smoothed BLEU-4	METEOR	ROUGE-L
Ahmad et al. (2020)*	44.58	26.43	54.76
Mahmud et al. (2021)	21.50	**27.78**	33.71
Our Model	**29.17**	19.93	**45.82**

* Ahmad et al.'s (2020) original experiment used a different dataset for training, so there is little relevance in directly comparing results.

Figure 2: Frequency Distribution of Metrics

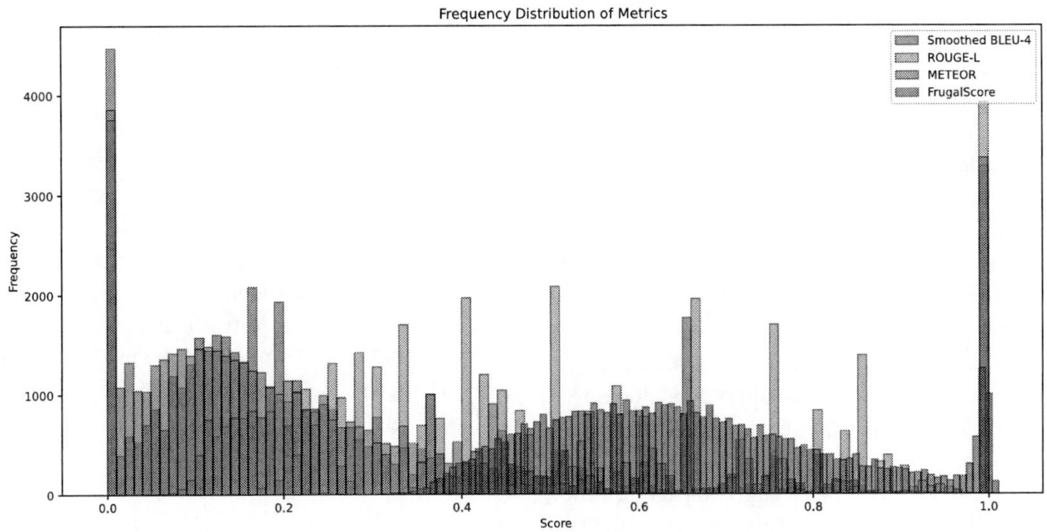

2019).

Mahmud et al. (Mahmud et al., 2021) compare both of these models, as well as the Code2Seq (Alon et al., 2019) model when trained on the Funcom dataset (LeClair and McMillan, 2019).

5.2 Metrics for Evaluating Automatic Natural Language Generation Systems

Whilst there are many metrics for evaluating natural language generation tasks BLEU (Papineni et al., 2002) has become a common metric, with other metrics, such as ROUGE (Lin, 2004) and METEOR (Banerjee and Lavie, 2005) designed to be used alongside it, addressing potential flaws in BLEU itself. METEOR has been updated multiple times, with the current version being METEOR 1.5 (Denkowski and Lavie, 2014). Other metrics, such as ORANGE (Lin and Och, 2004) also suggest techniques which can be used to improve BLEU, such as the application of smoothing techniques.

Recent work in using language models as metrics to evaluate natural language generation tasks have presented a potential leap forwards in our ability to automatically evaluate such models. BERTScore (Zhang et al., 2020) is one such metric, as is MoverScore (Zhao et al., 2019). These metrics use large language models which require vast amounts of compute power, and may lead to ethical concerns due to the impact of training large language models on the environment. FrugalScore (Kamal Eddine et al., 2022) aims to go some way to solving this dilemma by reducing the environmental impact of the metric, whilst maintaining accuracy.

6 Conclusion

In testing a NeuralCodeSum model trained on a dataset of source code which has been parsed and had developer comments accurately removed, with accurate tokenisation of both source code and summaries, we have demonstrated the effect of ensuring a higher quality of training data has on improving the quality of a model - with our model outperforming that of Mahmud et al. (2021). In evaluating our model with FrugalScore alongside traditional metrics, we have shown how the two can be used alongside each other to provide an improved method of evaluating a model for neural source code summarisation.

Limitations

The first limitation to our research is that we have only tested the summarisation of Java source code in English. Whilst this research was limited in this aspect, it opens the possibility for future research, not only in the evaluation of neural source code summarisation, but also cross-language summarisation in general.

In this study, we used FrugalScore as a metric using a language model. Other metrics, such as BERTScore (Zhang et al., 2020) could be applied to compare language model-based metrics for this task, but this would require a far larger amount of GPU resources, as FrugalScore is designed as a lightweight metric. For this reason, we chose to use FrugalScore instead of other LLM-based metrics. Generating FrugalScore for our outputs took over 2 days and 18 hours using the HuggingFace implementation of the metric. Using more robust large language models also has a larger impact on ethics as the effect on the environment of these large language models would be greater. The use of further LLM-based metrics (potentially on smaller samples of data to reduce environmental impact and processing time) in an effort to show how these metrics compare to both n-gram-based metrics and human evaluation of neural source code summarisation is possible future work to expand upon this research.

The use of FrugalScore showed the possibility for the use of LLM-based metrics in analysing neural source code summarisation. The difference in distribution between FrugalScore and traditional metrics suggests that further analysis is needed to compare FrugalScore and traditional metrics with human evaluation. Only then can we determine whether FrugalScore better aligns with human evaluation or overestimates the quality of summaries.

This study also focused on the NeuralCodeSum model (Ahmad et al., 2020), as one example of a cutting edge model. However, other models, such as Code2Seq (Alon et al., 2019), or CodeBERT (Feng et al., 2020) have the potential to yield different results, something which could be explored in future.

The use of NeuralCodeSum also limited us in that to build the official implementation of the model required us to use old versions of Python (`Python 3.6`) and PyTorch (`PyTorch 1.3`), which are now deprecated. As time passes, the use of deprecated systems will produce an increased limitation on the reproducibility of our results.

Ethics Statement

The primary ethical considerations of our research are twofold: the environmental impact of our research, and the use of a large dataset of code we have not generated.

The dataset comes from LeClair and McMillan (2019) and consists of methods and Javadoc comments from publicly available Java source code.

Whilst in our research, we have taken precautions to limit our environmental impact (the selection of FrugalScore as a language model-based metric due to its lower environmental impact compared to BERTScore or MoverScore, and the selection of NeuralCodeSum as our test model, rather than a larger model with more parameters, such as CodeBERT), any research involving the training and evaluation of neural networks will have an environmental impact.

References

Wasi Ahmad, Saikat Chakraborty, Baishakhi Ray, and Kai-Wei Chang. 2020. A transformer-based approach for source code summarization. In *Proceedings of the 58th Annual Meeting of the Association for Computational Linguistics*, pages 4998–5007, Online. Association for Computational Linguistics.

Uri Alon, Shaked Brody, Omer Levy, and Eran Yahav. 2019. code2seq: Generating sequences from structured representations of code. In *International Conference on Learning Representations*.

Satanjeev Banerjee and Alon Lavie. 2005. METEOR: An automatic metric for MT evaluation with improved correlation with human judgments. In *Proceedings of the ACL Workshop on Intrinsic and Extrinsic Evaluation Measures for Machine Translation and/or Summarization*, pages 65–72, Ann Arbor, Michigan. Association for Computational Linguistics.

Michael Denkowski and Alon Lavie. 2014. Meteor universal: Language specific translation evaluation for any target language. In *Proceedings of the Ninth Workshop on Statistical Machine Translation*, pages 376–380, Baltimore, Maryland, USA. Association for Computational Linguistics.

Jacob Devlin, Ming-Wei Chang, Kenton Lee, and Kristina Toutanova. 2019. BERT: Pre-training of deep bidirectional transformers for language understanding. In *Proceedings of the 2019 Conference of the North American Chapter of the Association for Computational Linguistics: Human Language Technologies, Volume 1 (Long and Short Papers)*, pages 4171–4186, Minneapolis, Minnesota. Association for Computational Linguistics.

Zhangyin Feng, Daya Guo, Duyu Tang, Nan Duan, Xiaocheng Feng, Ming Gong, Linjun Shou, Bing Qin, Ting Liu, Daxin Jiang, and Ming Zhou. 2020. CodeBERT: A pre-trained model for programming and natural languages. In *Findings of the Association for Computational Linguistics: EMNLP 2020*, pages 1536–1547, Online. Association for Computational Linguistics.

Moussa Kamal Eddine, Guokan Shang, Antoine Tixier, and Michalis Vazirgiannis. 2022. FrugalScore: Learning cheaper, lighter and faster evaluation metrics for automatic text generation. In *Proceedings of the 60th Annual Meeting of the Association for Computational Linguistics (Volume 1: Long Papers)*, pages 1305–1318, Dublin, Ireland. Association for Computational Linguistics.

Alexander LeClair and Collin McMillan. 2019. Recommendations for datasets for source code summarization. In *Proceedings of the 2019 Conference of the North American Chapter of the Association for Computational Linguistics: Human Language Technologies, Volume 1 (Long and Short Papers)*, pages 3931–3937, Minneapolis, Minnesota. Association for Computational Linguistics.

Chin-Yew Lin. 2004. ROUGE: A package for automatic evaluation of summaries. In *Text Summarization Branches Out*, pages 74–81, Barcelona, Spain. Association for Computational Linguistics.

Chin-Yew Lin and Franz Josef Och. 2004. ORANGE: a method for evaluating automatic evaluation metrics for machine translation. In *COLING 2004: Proceedings of the 20th International Conference on Computational Linguistics*, pages 501–507, Geneva, Switzerland. COLING.

Peter Liu. 2022. rouge-score 0.1.2.

Yinhan Liu, Myle Ott, Naman Goyal, Jingfei Du, Mandar Joshi, Danqi Chen, Omer Levy, Mike Lewis, Luke Zettlemoyer, and Veselin Stoyanov. 2019. Roberta: A robustly optimized bert pretraining approach.

Junayed Mahmud, Fahim Faisal, Raihan Islam Arnob, Antonios Anastasopoulos, and Kevin Moran. 2021. Code to comment translation: A comparative study on model effectiveness & errors. In *Proceedings of the 1st Workshop on Natural Language Processing for Programming (NLP4Prog 2021)*, pages 1–16, Online. Association for Computational Linguistics.

Kishore Papineni, Salim Roukos, Todd Ward, and Wei-Jing Zhu. 2002. Bleu: a method for automatic evaluation of machine translation. In *Proceedings of the 40th Annual Meeting of the Association for Computational Linguistics*, pages 311–318, Philadelphia, Pennsylvania, USA. Association for Computational Linguistics.

Danny van Bruggen, Federico Tomassetti, Roger Howell, Malte Langkabel, Nicholas Smith, Artur Bosch, Malte Skoruppa, Cruz Maximilien, ThLeu, Panayiotis, Sebastian Kirsch, Simon, Johann Beleites, Wim Tibackx, jean pierre L, André Rouél, edefazio, Daan Schipper, Mathiponds, Why you want to know, Ryan Beckett, ptitjes, kotari4u, Marvin Wyrich, Ricardo Morais, Maarten Coene, bresai, Implex1v, and Bernhard Haumacher. 2020. javaparser/javaparser: Release javaparser- parent-3.16.1.

Ashish Vaswani, Noam Shazeer, Niki Parmar, Jakob Uszkoreit, Llion Jones, Aidan N Gomez, Ł ukasz Kaiser, and Illia Polosukhin. 2017. Attention is all you need. In *Advances in Neural Information Processing Systems*, volume 30. Curran Associates, Inc.

Tianyi Zhang, Varsha Kishore, Felix Wu, Kilian Q. Weinberger, and Yoav Artzi. 2020. Bertscore: Evaluating text generation with bert. In *International Conference on Learning Representations*.

Wei Zhao, Maxime Peyrard, Fei Liu, Yang Gao, Christian M. Meyer, and Steffen Eger. 2019. MoverScore: Text generation evaluating with contextualized embeddings and earth mover distance. In *Proceedings of the 2019 Conference on Empirical Methods in Natural Language Processing and the 9th International Joint Conference on Natural Language Processing (EMNLP-IJCNLP)*, pages 563–578, Hong Kong, China. Association for Computational Linguistics.

A Appendix A

Listing 2: Mahmud et al.'s (2021) method for removing comments: official python implementation

```
def remove_comments_inside_mthd(
    mthd: str) -> str:
    lines = mthd.split("\n")
    eachLine = []
    for line in lines:
        if "//" in line:
            continue
        else:
            eachLine.append(line)

    return "\n".join(eachLine)
```

B Appendix B

Below, we have provided histograms showing 1-to-1 comparisons of the frequency distribution of the FrugalScore metric against BLEU-1, Smoothed BLEU-4, METEOR, and ROUGE-L.

Figure 3: Frequency Distribution of BLEU-1 vs FrugalScore

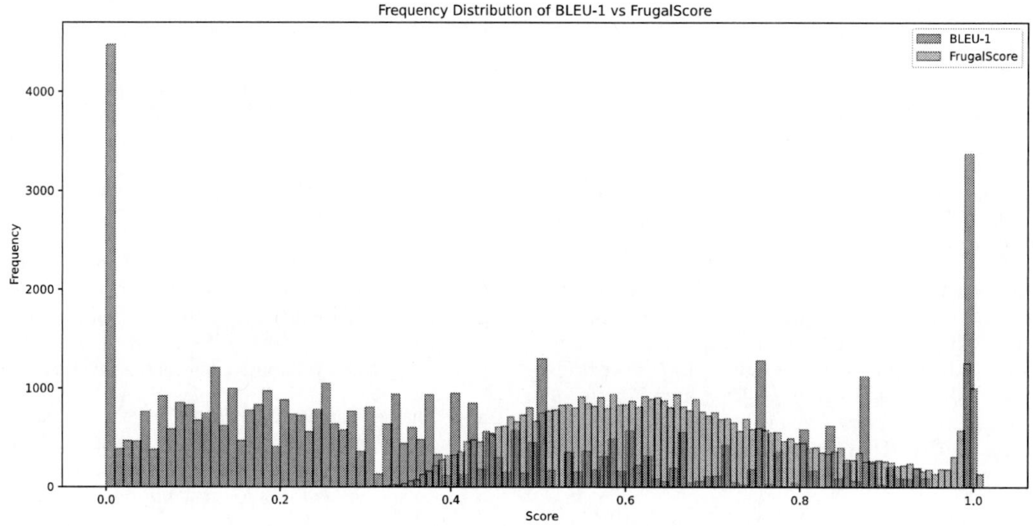

Figure 4: Frequency Distribution of Smoothed BLEU-4 vs FrugalScore

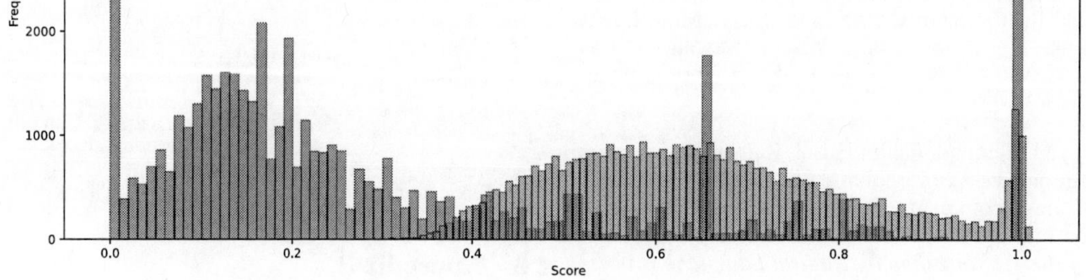

Figure 5: Frequency Distribution of METEOR vs FrugalScore

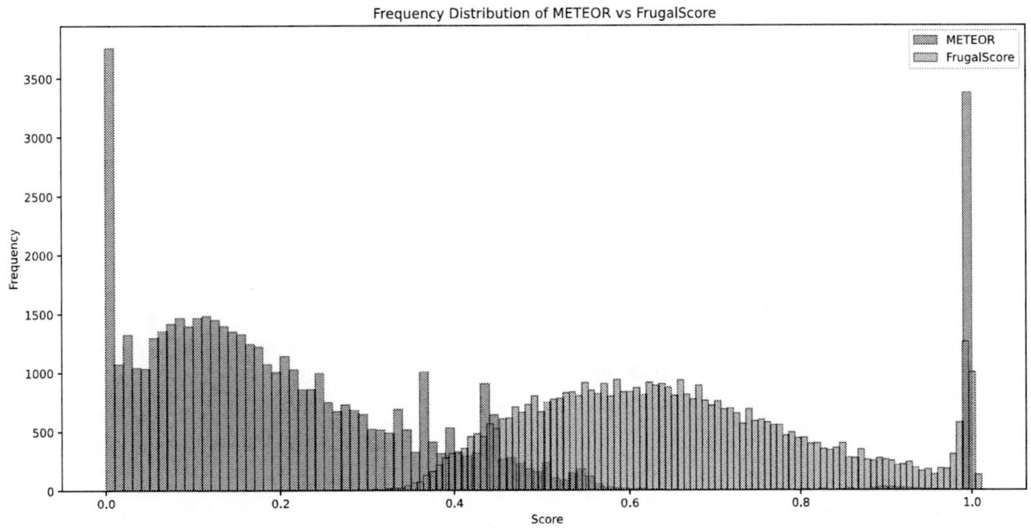

Figure 6: Frequency Distribution of ROUGE-L vs FrugalScore

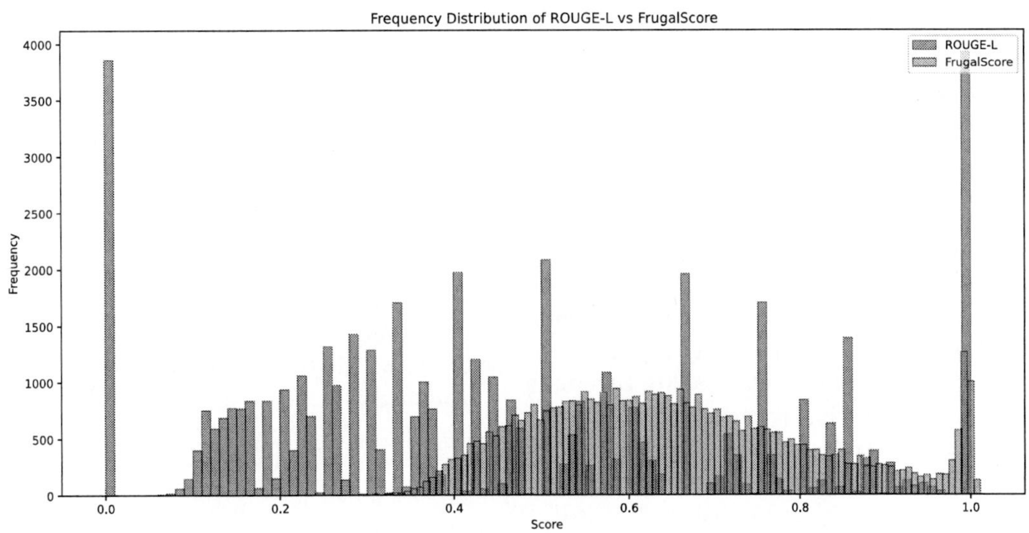

Most NLG is Low-Resource: here's what we can do about it

David M. Howcroft and **Dimitra Gkatzia**
School of Computing
Edinburgh Napier University
Edinburgh, Scotland, United Kingdom
{d.howcroft,d.gkatzia}@napier.ac.uk

Abstract

Many domains and tasks in natural language generation (NLG) are inherently 'low-resource', where training data, tools and linguistic analyses are scarce. This poses a particular challenge to researchers and system developers in the era of machine-learning-driven NLG. In this position paper, we initially present the challenges researchers & developers often encounter when dealing with low-resource settings in NLG. We then argue that it is unsustainable to collect large aligned datasets or build large language models from scratch for every possible domain due to cost, labour, and time constraints, so researching and developing methods and resources for low-resource settings is vital. We then discuss current approaches to low-resource NLG, followed by proposed solutions and promising avenues for future work in NLG for low-resource settings.

Language			Domain			Illustrative examples of
C	A	T	C	A	T	task or data availability
-	-	-	-	-	-	most languages, any domain
-	-	-	-	+	-	domains with linguistic analyses
-	+	-	-	-	-	well-studied minority languages
-	+	+	-	-	-	lg.s not very present online that are well-studied and have, e.g., parsers, etc, *but few* domain-specific resources
-	+	+	+	+	+	lg.s not very present online that are well-studied & have parsers, etc, *and* substantial domain-specific resources
+	+	+	-	-	-	novel NLG domains in English
+	+	+	-	+	-	domains with lots of analysis in a high-resource language but little specialised data or tooling (e.g. political rhetoric)
+	+	+	+	+	+	Restaurant reviews, weather forecasts, and sports reporting in English

Table 1: Dimensions of resource availability at the language & domain level, sketching variation with respect to C(orpora), A(nalysis), & T(ool) availability. Plus/minus indicate relatively more/less availability, respectively. Examples demonstrate the logical possibilities associated with different combinations of language and domain resource availability.

1 Introduction

Natural Language Generation (NLG) is the process of generating text from structured or unstructured data and has recently received renewed attention due to the emergence of large pre-trained language models (e.g. Brown et al., 2020) that promise to generate output that is more natural, variable, and adaptable to new domains as compared to rule-based approaches. However, the development of robust, *controllable*, and usable NLG systems depends heavily on the availability of large, high-quality, labelled datasets that are appropriate for the task at hand (Fan and Gardent, 2020). Unfortunately, for most domains such data is unavailable, probably with the exception of weather, restaurant, and sports domains. Even in the aforementioned domains, data is fairly small compared to low-resource tasks & languages in other areas, such as in machine translation.

In this paper, we focus on *controllable* NLG tasks that can be framed as data-to-text generation tasks, rather than language prediction models. We center our discussion around the *low-resource* nature of controllable NLG, that is, on the limitations to the creation of new NLG systems due to a lack of **corpora**, **analyses**, or **tools** for a target domain or language (illustrated in Table 1). Here, we define as *corpora* paired input representations and texts which serve as reference outputs. *Analyses* are linguistic analyses relevant to a domain of application, including but not limited to grammars of a target language or conversation analyses of a target domain. *Tools* can then be automated means of analysing linguistic data (e.g. parsers, part-of-speech taggers, etc.), secondary resources based on primary data (e.g. word embeddings), or software libraries for different NLG (sub)tasks.

This position paper contributes:

- a discussion of the availability of NLG resources in terms of Corpora, Analyses, & Tools for different languages and domains and the challenges this presents;

Proceedings of the 2nd Workshop on Natural Language Generation, Evaluation, and Metrics (GEM), pages 336 - 350
December 7, 2022

- a high-level overview of mitigation strategies for addressing low resource availability; and
- a call to focus future work on particularly promising directions which we highlight.

2 Corpora for NLG

Corpora are essential to the development of both data-driven and knowledge-driven NLG systems. We focus here on NLG corpora for generating full utterances of at least one complete sentence which include input *meaning representations* (MRs, ranging from raw sensor data to morphologically specified syntax trees)[1] and corresponding texts, in situations where existing resources are limited. Currently, the most studied language for NLG is English (cf. Fan and Gardent, 2020) with few data-to-text corpora available for other languages. The domains with the most data-to-text corpora available are restaurant descriptions, weather forecasts, and sports reporting[2]. Corpora for the widely studied restaurant domain range in size from 400 utterances (Mairesse et al., 2010) to 50k utterances (Dušek et al., 2020), some being based on hand-crafted systems while the majority are crowdsourced. We now highlight prominent strategies for building NLG corpora; however, even with a simple MR format (e.g. CUED slot value pairs (Young, 2007)), collecting high-quality parallel MR-text corpora is expensive so most such datasets remain small.

'Found' NLG Corpora Sometimes data-to-text corpora can be adapted from existing sources of semantic and textual data. For instance, Belz and Kow (2010) assembled a parallel corpus of sets of facts (from hobbyists) and corresponding texts (from Wikipedia) about British hills. Similarly, the WikiBio dataset (Lebret et al., 2016) pairs the first sentence of each article in the WikiProject Biography dataset with the facts reported in that article's 'infobox'. GenWiki extends these approaches even further, aiming to provide an automatically aligned corpus of texts from Wikipedia paired with graphs from DBPedia identified based on overlapping entities for more than one million texts (Jin et al., 2020). Apart from Wikipedia, researchers have collected datasets from other online resources that contain both data (in metadata) and (somewhat) aligned text (e.g. Liang et al., 2009; Barzilay and Lapata, 2005). Note that these approaches rely on the fact that others, such as domain experts, have already chosen to create a semantic or tabular representation of important details; therefore, this method of building new datasets is not generalisable.

Creating meaning annotations Some research has annotated existing data-to-text corpora with discourse structures, such as Balakrishnan et al. (2019)—who semi-automatically added discourse structures to the E2E Challenge corpus—and Stevens-Guille et al. (2020)—who leveraged the rule-based Methodius system (Isard, 2016) to create a discourse-annotated corpus. Based on the automatically derived Methodius Corpus, Maskharashvili et al. (2021) observe that "discourse relations are enormously helpful when the dataset for the domain is limited", highlighting the importance of fine-grained MRs in low-resource domains.

Other work has sought to address the issue of content selection for corpus creation, independent of the actual text to be associated with each MR (see also Gkatzia, 2016). For example, Perez-Beltrachini et al. (2016) leverage DBPedia to construct trees of semantic triples based on their frequency and relationship to one another in a large ontology, with the goal of selecting content which forms a natural unit that can be later associated with a human-written text.

Eliciting texts for given meanings Early datasets typically relied on domain experts or NLG researchers directly, but most recent work uses crowdsourcing to quickly collect texts from a variety of speakers (e.g. Mairesse et al., 2010; Wen et al., 2015, 2016; Juraska et al., 2019). Where early work tended to use prompts similar to a set of slot-value pairs, later work observed that such prompts encouraged the use of particular words & phrases—thus reducing textual diversity—and found that using images (Novikova et al., 2016) or full sentences (Howcroft et al., 2017) as prompts resulted in better quality. Recent work has incorporated quality estimates and text suggestions to fill gaps in datasets (Chang et al., 2020). While these methods can quickly provide varied data, it remains

[1] While we would like to see more emphasis on representations based on semantic, linguistic, or logical representations of meaning and discourse structure, such as Montagovian semantics, HLDS (Kruijff, 2001), DRS (Kamp and Reyle, 1993), etc., common data-to-text MRs more commonly resemble tabular data, taking the form of slot-value pairs plus an optional dialogue act annotation or RDF triples. For simplicity, we refer to the input to a data-to-text NLG system as an MR, regardless of the degree to which the encoding is developed as a representation of *meaning* per se.

[2] https://aclweb.org/aclwiki/Data_sets_for_NLG

impractical to create large, targeted datasets for all domains, and most languages do not even have these small datasets available.

3 Analyses & Tools

While the primary data for NLG are parallel corpora, a variety of other resources can facilitate development. Language models (LMs) can approximate fluency measures and can be used to produce texts using sampling (Brown et al., 2020). Linguistic analyses provide insight into what makes a text well-formed and assist in the design of rule-based systems and architectures for ML-based approaches. Finally, tools & resources such as parsers, part-of-speech taggers, semantic role labellers, ontologies, morphological analysers, and word embeddings can help to decompose NLG subtasks and make the problem more approachable.

3.1 (Large) Language Models

Statistical language models have been used since the late 1990s to help rank potential NLG outputs (Langkilde and Knight, 1998; Knight and Hatzivassiloglou, 1995). With the rise of large pre-trained language models (e.g. BERT, GPT: Devlin, 2018; Brown et al., 2020), there has been renewed interest in sampling-based approaches to generation, where an LM trained exclusively on text (i.e. without parallel MRs) generates a continuation for an initial string. While the challenge of making sampling-based NLG more *controlled* is an active area of research[3], these tools continue to be helpful to rank texts with likelihood as a fluency approximation.

Unfortunately, good language models require large collections of text in the target language in order to perform well and only very limited digitized data is available for most languages. For example, Joshi et al. (2020) found that only seven languages (of the world's approximately 7000 languages) qualify as truly high-resource[4]. One major factor in corpus availability is the cost of technology relative to typical incomes in countries where a language is spoken (Ahia et al., 2021). Given the high cost of collecting & annotating data, this observation is not surprising. Recent approaches to text generation have emphasised the use of large-pretrained LMs (see Section 3.1) and task-specific fine-tuning in order to transfer general language statistics to a particular task. Consider for instance GPT3 (Brown et al., 2020), trained on 45TB of text data in English. Training such a model for any language requires an amount of data and compute power unavailable in most regions, meaning that such models can typically be used only for low-resource domains in high-resource languages.

Candidate languages include the roughly 100 languages covered by mBERT (Devlin, 2018) and mT5 (Xue et al., 2021). More often, though, available language models for lower resource languages are often based on legal, journalistic, or governmental language rather than everyday language, resulting in a genre mismatch making them poor off-the-shelf models for many applications. For those cases where appropriate LMs do exist, Section 4.2 covers their usefulness in transfer learning.

3.2 Analysis

With enough data, we can hope that a powerful ML architecture might detect the patterns necessary to produce good texts. However, when corpora are not large enough for this, descriptive and automated linguistic analyses can help. Researchers can use linguistic documentation to develop their system, consulting formal grammars & lexica to understand the kinds of constructions possible in a target language. Researchers & developers can also partner with speakers of their target language to ensure that the system serves community needs while working together to understand the language they are generating (Hirmer et al., 2021).

Generally speaking, it is easiest to leverage these linguistic resources when developing a rule-based NLG system, where observations can be encoded explicitly. For example, three grammars of Rapanui have been published in English in the past 110 years (Churchill, 1912; Du Feu, 2012; Kieviet, 2017), giving insight into word order, morphology, and agreement phenomena.[5] Such features can then be input in grammar engineering tools like the Lingo matrix grammar construction toolkit[6] (Bender et al., 2002, 2010), to provide a starting point for building a rule-based NLG system.

Both rule-based and end-to-end ML approaches benefit from tools for automated linguistic analy-

[3]e.g. https://ctrlgenworkshop.github.io/

[4]English, Spanish, German, Japanese, French, Arabic, Mandarin

[5]We use Rapanui as an example of a very low-resource language which, nevertheless, has been the subject of multiple grammars published as monographs. For more information, see the cited grammars or https://en.wikipedia.org/wiki/Rapa_Nui_language.

[6]https://matrix.ling.washington.edu

sis, such as lemmatisers, part-of-speech taggers, parsers, and semantic role labellers. To learn to map input MRs to output texts, a system or developer must recognise useful generalisations and abstractions. For example, part-of-speech tags and constituency parses provide information about the order in which words of a given class should appear, while dependency parses and semantic role labels can relate individual words to each other. Similarly, normalization diminishes the impact of noise, lemmatization helps associate word 'stems' with meanings, morphological analysers/realisers help with word forms, parsers help get words in the right order, semantic role labellers & natural language understanding systems help associate chunks of form & meaning directly.

All of these individual analyses together help decompose the task. Although data-to-text systems have used modular architectures for decades (Reiter, 2007), there is now a shift towards end-to-end architectures. However, we argue here that modular architectures are important for low-resource settings, as they might require less training data than end-to-end. This is an important promising direction, therefore we discuss pipelines and problem structuring further in Section 4.5.

3.3 NLG Libraries

Similarly to general NLP tools, NLG-specific tooling shows variable availability. While SimpleNLG has been adapted to at least eight other languages[7] (English: Gatt and Reiter, 2009), this library still requires significant effort to develop supporting components. Other available tools for developing NLG systems include FUF/SURGE[8] (Elhadad and Robin, 1997, 1996) for surface realisation and OpenCCG[9] (White, 2006) for generation from hybrid logic dependency semantics, which can be used to represent meaning at deeper and shallower levels alike, using combinatory categorial grammar (Steedman and Baldridge, 2006). For a recent survey of surface realisation systems for low-resource languages, see (Mahlaza and Keet, 2022).

A number of neural NLG models are also publicly available, such as Wen et al.'s (2015) SC-LSTM[10] and Dusek & Jurcicek's (2016) TGen[11]. While TGen has been widely used as a baseline for end-to-end NLG tasks, these systems generally represent the outcome of a particular research project rather than being intended to be used as a platform for developing future NLG systems.

4 Mitigation strategies

So far we have discussed the corpora, analyses, & tools that are often missing in low-resource settings. We now turn to mitigation strategies for dealing with this lack of resources, namely data augmentation, transfer learning, meta-learning, feedback-based learning, and rule-based methods. Table 2 gives an overview of the requirements for and outcomes of using these different mitigation strategies.

4.1 Data Augmentation

Data augmentation (DA) describes a family of approaches that aim to increase the number of training examples automatically, without manual data collection. Despite their popularity and demonstrated efficiency in other areas such as computer vision (Shorten and Khoshgoftaar, 2019) and NLP (Dhole et al., 2021), this area is still relatively under-explored in NLG, partly due to unique challenges. This section reviews existing approaches to DA for text generation; for DA approaches to NLP in general we refer the reader to the survey by Feng et al. (2021).

DA methods promise to enrich current datasets, potentially increasing the linguistic diversity of the dataset (e.g., by enhancing stylistic traits as proposed by Oraby et al. (2018)). In order to train NLG models, we require text that is not only grammatically correct but also semantically correct, coherent, and appropriate for the task at hand (cf. Dušek et al., 2019, on semantic noise). Therefore, straightforward approaches used in computer vision, such as cropping and rotation are not appropriate, though adaptations of these techniques can help with simpler NLP tasks like part of speech tagging for low-resource languages (Şahin and Steedman, 2018). More elaborate approaches such as back-translation & paraphrasing have been used in other areas of NLP, such as MT, and are also promising for NLG. Here, however, we only review methods specifically developed and applied in **NLG settings**.

There are two predominant DA methods used in NLG: (1) generation of new examples with pretrained LMs; and (2) generation of new examples

[7] https://github.com/simplenlg/simplenlg

[8] https://www.cs.bgu.ac.il/~elhadad/install-fuf.html

[9] https://github.com/OpenCCG/openccg

[10] https://github.com/shawnwun/RNNLG

[11] https://github.com/UFAL-DSG/tgen

Mitigation Strategy	Requirements	Outcome
Data Augmentation	labelled data, rules	additional labelled data
Pre-training/Fine-tuning	existing LM or high-resource data, low-resource data	knowledge transfer to new domain
Zero-shot	existing LM	adapting to new scenarios with no labelled data
Few-shot	existing LM, few training examples	adapting to new scenarios with few labelled data
Prompt-based	existing LM, prompts	adapting to new scenarios with few or no labelled data
Meta-learning	high-resource data, low-resource dataset	weight initialisation for better training
Feedback-based	small domain dataset	better learning through interaction
Multi-task	multiple auxiliary tasks	learning more general representations, multiple tasks

Table 2: Summary of mitigation strategies for low-resource NLG, their requirements, and their outcomes.

with statistical or rule-based NLG systems.

An example of the former DA methods is Chang et al. (2021a)'s approach to generating new samples for NLG using a pretrained LM, by firstly creating an unannotated dataset with unlabeled MR instances by randomly selecting MRs from a pre-existing expert-annotated dataset and populating them with existing values. This dataset is then automatically annotated with noisy text labels generated by a pre-trained model, fine-tuned on joint MR and text conditioned on samples from the augmented MR set.

Examples of the latter include employing rule-based systems to generate new examples for developing or evaluating other NLG methods. For instance, Belz (2008) created an automatically generated version of SUMTIME meteo (Sripada et al., 2008), an expert annotated data-to-text dataset in the weather domain, which has been used to explore statistical NLG (Angeli et al., 2010, inter alia). Similarly, Oraby et al. (2018) utilised a statistical natural language generator to create a corpus of stylistic texts used to train seq2seq neural NLG models. Other apporaches have proposed utilising distant supervision can also be used to create new NLG corpora. For example, Agarwal et al. (2021) use distant supervision to verbalize knowledge graph subgraphs centered on entities, producing a large secondary dataset, a subset of which they were able to clean to a sufficiently high quality for fine-tuning their models.

4.2 Transfer Learning

Transfer learning uses the knowledge gained from a previous task (in a high-resource setting) to improve model performance for a related task in a lower-resource setting (Torrey and Shavlik, 2009). Typically, a model is trained with data from one or more high-resource domains/languages and then the model's weights are used to initialise the model to be trained in the low-resource setting through a process called *fine-tuning*. Similarly, *few-shot* and *zero-shot* approaches aim to develop general language models which are applied to new tasks with limited intervention (Zhao and Eskenazi, 2018).

Pre-training & Fine-tuning Transfer learning via *fine-tuning* typically requires the adaptation of a large pre-trained language model by updating and storing all of the parameters, resulting in a new language model for every task. One of the earliest works in this setting involved training a model from scratch in a related domain and then fine-tuning it in a new domain (Dethlefs, 2017). Kale and Roy (2020) propose transferring knowledge from a NMT model trained on English-Czech, which is then fine tuned for a data-to-text task in Czech. Pasricha et al. (2020) proposed a transfer learning approach which actually utilises one of the large language models (see Section 3.1) which is fine-tuned in the target task. In this setting, the data used for fine tuning is pre-pended with tags describing the part of speech as well as the type of the entity and are included in the vocabulary. Ribeiro et al. (2021) also show that pre-trained language models perform well in graph-based MR to text generation, even when the input is reduced to bags of nodes and edge labels. Most works in this area generate text in English. However, fine-tuning large models also works in other languages. For instance, Naous et al. (2021) propose fine-tuning AraBERT (Antoun et al., 2020) for empathetic NLG in Arabic.

Although fine-tuning requires significantly less computational power and time as compared to training models from scratch, it can still pose a considerable deployment challenge as the magnitude of pre-trained models continues to increase from millions to billions of parameters. As such, other data- and compute-efficient transfer learning approaches have been explored that try to minimize the number of parameters that are fine-tuned. Such methods include prompt-based, few- and zero-shot learning approaches which are discussed next.

Prompt-based, Few- and Zero-shot learning To alleviate the need to update all parameters of a pre-trained model, researchers have explored prompt-based methods that keep the parameters of a model frozen and instead use *prompts* as part of the input (Liu et al., 2021) to perform downstream tasks without further training. Although no training is required, prompt-based methods require: 1) a prompting function that converts the input into some specific form; 2) template prompts, which can be created manually or automatically; 3) corresponding filled & answer prompts; and 4) answers. In many cases, prompt methods do not require any further training and providing the aforementioned prompting elements is enough for a model to perform *zero-shot* learning (as in Dou and Peng, 2022). In other settings, though, prompting can be used for further training/fine-tuning a model, when at least a small amount of data is available. For instance, Li and Liang (2021) proposed an approach to NLG that keeps pre-trained LM parameters fixed, while employing a task-specific prefix vector, which is tuned for the task at hand. Clive et al. (2021) extend this approach for controlled text generation. Prompt-learning is a very recent paradigm, so we expect to see more work in this promising area.

Similarly to prompting, zero- and few-shot learning aim to achieve learning with minimal training/new data instances. Transfer learning aims to 'learn' transferable features that can be used in downstream tasks. In few-shot learning, there might be only a few examples to learn from (or zero in zero-shot). Ma et al. (2019) proposed decomposing table-to-text generation into content selection and surface realisation, so that each subtask can be trained with a smaller dataset than it would be needed for the end-to-end task. Chen et al. (2020) also proposed pre-training a model from scratch, although their paradigm employed distant supervision before fine-tuning the model to specific tasks. Finally, Chang et al. (2021b) focused on improving few-shot NLG by prioritising informative training instances to fine-tune the model.

4.3 Meta-learning

Meta learning can be thought of as the machine learning process of 'learning how to learn' (Mi et al., 2019a). Meta-learning approaches are split into *metric-learning* (Koch et al., 2015), *model-based* (Andrychowicz et al., 2016), and *optimisation-based* approaches (Finn et al., 2017). Most of recent meta-learning approaches to NLG follow an optimisation approach, the Model-Agnostic Meta-Learning (MAML) algorithm, originally proposed by Finn et al. (2017). MAML aims to make models achieve good generalisation performance by adapting quickly to a new task during training in low-resource settings, despite a low quantity of training data, by learning a better initialization of model parameters that facilitates fast adaptation to new low-resource scenarios. Mi et al. (2019b) explored different adaptation settings based on domain similarity and showed that 'nearer' domains can adapt better through a meta-learning setting, outperforming other optimisation methods such as multi-task learning. Meta-learning has also shown promising results in MT. Gu et al. (2018) compared MAML to transfer learning (Zoph et al., 2016) and showed that meta-learning leads to further improvements, despite training data for the low-resource language being limited to a significantly smaller dataset. As the corpus size of the low-resource language decreases, transfer learning approaches suffer significantly more than meta-learning approaches, demonstrating the effectiveness of MAML for low-resource languages. However, as corpus size increases, the differences between the two approaches are much less significant. Exploring the trade-off between data size and learning paradigm (meta-learning versus transfer learning) is a promising direction for this line of work.

4.4 Feedback-based Learning

Low-resource settings have always been a bottleneck for NLG. Earlier work in this area employed reinforcement learning (RL) in dialogue systems for NLG (Rieser and Lemon, 2011; Dethlefs and Cuayáhuitl, 2011) to overcome the issue of limited data, whereas more recent approaches showed that RL can help train better NLG systems (Panagiaris et al., 2021). Low-resource settings can manifest themselves also in domains where large collections of unlabelled data are available without parallel inputs. For instance, in MT one might have access to large monolingual datasets in both source and target languages but not an aligned one. In this case, feedback-based methods can help, such as the dual-learning setup from Kim et al. (2019), presented as a two-agent communication game. In this setting, the first agent only understands language A, and the second agent only understand language B. The two agents communicate through translation models and provide feedback on whether the translated message they received is a natural sentence in their own language. They then use this feedback to improve their individual models.

Similarly, Shen et al. (2019) propose treating language production as a game between speakers and listeners, where listeners must be able to reconstruct the intended meaning. Their models are trained to predict and avoid confusing outputs based on either reconstruction or distraction pragmatics (this is however not low-resource). Tran and Nguyen (2018) propose an adversarial training procedure for domain adaptation with two critics, which guide the generator to generate outputs similar to the sentences in the target domain, when limited amount of target domain data exist.

4.5 Task structure & rule-based approaches

While 'fully end-to-end' machine learning models are always enticing, careful thought about how to structure the task(s) can lead to significant improvements in outcomes. For example, in *multitask learning* a single model is trained on multiple tasks, allowing feedback from learning to perform well on one task to influence the others. Even without jointly learning to solve multiple tasks, decomposing generation into a sequence of stages in a pipeline can improve performance by simplifying what the model needs to learn.

Multi-task learning To our knowledge, there is no related work in multi-task learning for low-resource data-to-text generation. The closest work in this area jointly learns a semantically conditioned and unconditioned LMs for generation across multiple datasets (Zhu et al., 2019). For text-to-text generation, Magooda et al. (2021) showed that abstractive summarisation can benefit from being learnt in a multi-task framework, especially when combined with paraphrase learning. In addition to their target task, they train their model to perform extractive summarisation, concept & paraphrase detection, and language modelling. In a larger resource setting, Agarwal et al. (2020) adapt T5 (Raffel et al., 2020) to data-to-text generation for English and Russian while jointly learning text-to-data semantic parsing for both languages.

Pipelines & Problem Structuring Where in multitask learning the focus is on training a single neural network to perform multiple tasks, pipeline

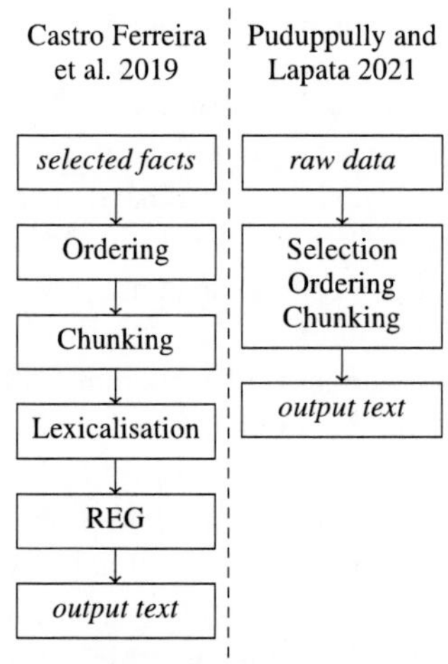

Figure 1: Two neural pipelines: Castro Ferreira et al. (2019) use four stages to produce a text based on chosen facts; Puduppully and Lapata (2021) use two stages to select & group facts and realise the text.

models use separate stages for each subproblem and do not require a single unified neural network (cf. Figure 1). This allows for specialisation, where solutions to subproblems can be refined independently. For example, a surface realisation module could be trained on multiple domains regardless of the handling required at the level of document or sentence planning. Of course, modularity comes with the risk of error propagation, as errors in an early component can break later ones.

Recent work has explored various decompositions of data-to-text generation based on the conventional NLG pipeline. For example, Howcroft et al. (2018) proposed a model to learn sentence planning rules for use with an off-the-shelf surface realiser while Moryossef et al. (2019) reversed this focus, using rule-based planning to handle content ordering & chunking and training a surface realiser.

Figure 1 sketches two fully neural NLG pipelines as examples. Castro Ferreira et al. (2019) decomposed generation into content ordering, content chunking, lexicalisation, referring expression generation (REG), & textual realisation and trained a neural model for each subtask, finding that pipelines improve text quality. Both Perez-Beltrachini and Lapata (2018) and Puduppully and Lapata (2021) created higher level pipelines which perform content selection (with the latter also performing content ordering and sentence chunking) before generating a text. Other work has used latent variable models to learn ordering and chunking constraints instead of focusing on explicit pipelines (Shen et al., 2020; Xu et al., 2021).

These models generally preserve the 'fluency' expected of modern neural network LMs and improve semantic fidelity. This is especially encouraging for low resource NLG where the relative pay-off for adding intermediate annotations to train pipeline models is likely to be higher. Such approaches are further enhanced by 'delexicalisation', e.g. replacing certain values with placeholders (Shimorina and Gardent, 2019) to limit spurious variation and facilitate training.

For low-resource domains in better resourced languages, useful resources for AMR-to-text generation[12] and UD-to-text[13] generation (Mille et al., 2018, 2019, 2020) could be used for the final stage of generation, simplifying system development and allowing researchers to focus on developing components for document and sentence planning.

Complementary to these efforts are a number of new corpora (van der Lee et al., 2020) and extensions of existing corpora (Castro Ferreira et al., 2020, 2021) with annotations for intermediate representations in an NLG pipeline.

5 Discussion & Promising directions

So far, we have highlighted the ways in which NLG is influenced by the availability of data, analyses, and tools at both the language and the domain level and described a number of trainable approaches which aim to learn an NLG system given different resource limitations. It is clear that it is neither sustainable to collect large aligned datasets for every domain nor use general purpose language models off-the-shelf for *controlled* NLG, so researching and developing approaches for low-resource settings that distill the strengths of pre-trained language models while focusing on controllable approaches is vital. Here we outline some promising directions in this area.

Data Augmentation Although it is clear that controllable NLG approaches could benefit from as large corpora as possible, data augmentation is still under-explored for NLG. Approaches developed for other NLP tasks could be explored here whereas others will not be applicable for structured prediction problems. The potential future directions can be split into three main categories: (a) Data augmentation through paraphrasing where a slot is replaced with another slot randomly: e.g. 'cheapest' is replaced with 'most expensive'; (b) using pre-trained models to distill knowledge; (c) back-translation to create resources in different languages.

Prompt-based Learning Prompt-based learning is a fairly novel direction for NLP (including NLG) in general and our understanding is quite limited to a few experimental works. Work on this area can highlight limitations of current pre-trained models and lead to potential improvements as well as can reveal situations where large models are safe (and might not need to be controllable) to use. Prompt-based approaches might also call for novel evaluation metrics in order to better understand the influence of prompts on the generated outputs.

Feedback-based approaches Although there has been a lot of discussion in AI in general about machines learning through feedback as humans can, research focused on increasing a NLG system's capabilities have been limited to game-based settings or simulation (as in the case of Reinforcement Learning). More research in this area, might be useful to endow models with new capabilities as in the frameworks proposed by Gkatzia and Belvedere (2021) and Wang et al. (2016).

Multitask learning & pipelines Very few of the combinatorial possibilities for neural NLG pipelines have been explored to date, so it remains unclear which tasks are best solved in sequence versus jointly. One especially promising direction is to approach such pipelines in a multitask setting: when annotated data exists for subtasks, the model can receive feedback for individual tasks during training while passing along the penultimate layers of the network to each subsequent task, thus allowing later tasks in the pipeline to influence the hidden representations learnt in earlier tasks.

When to use meta-learning and when to use transfer-learning? There is some evidence from MT that transferring models between related languages increases performance Zoph et al. (2016). On the other hand, data size matters (Kocmi and Bojar, 2018). Previous work has also shown that once you start increasing the amount of data in the target domain, transfer learning achieves better results. However, it is unclear where the 'sweet spot' lies, and more research in this area is required.

[12] https://nert-nlp.github.io/AMR-Bibliography/

[13] Universal Dependencies (de Marneffe et al., 2021)

Evaluation in low-resource NLG In addition to the specific challenges and mitigation strategies for system development above, evaluation has its own challenges in the low-resource setting and is a promising direction for future work in itself. For instance, having less validation and test data reduces the applicability of automated, reference-based evaluations, necessitating alternative evaluation strategies such as an emphasis on error analysis (van Miltenburg et al., 2021) or standardised human evaluations (Howcroft et al., 2020). Methods for maximising the efficiency of input from domain and language experts will also be necessary for human evaluations when access to these persons is more limited than usual.

6 Conclusion

In this paper we have highlighted ways in which NLG is often low-resource in data, analyses, or tools with respect to either the target language or domain. The number of corpora for data-to-text generation remain limited, but there are a number of strategies for adding meaning annotations to existing texts, or vice versa, and crowdsourcing new data sets. Large language models are also not always available: they are typically only available for relatively high-resource languages. Linguistic analyses and automated analysis tools are more widely available and can help decompose the generation task to make it easier to develop systems in low-resource settings. Fortunately there are a variety of mitigation strategies available, including methods for data augmentation, transfer learning, meta- and feedback-based-learning, and different ways of structuring the task.

This makes for an interesting set of challenges and an exciting set of opportunities to improve the state-of-the-art for natural language generation in low resource settings. Our own current work is beginning to explore some of these promising directions, including multi-task learning, pipeline approaches to NLG, and transfer learning from related languages and general purpose LLMs. However, there is much work to be done, and we hope the community embraces these challenges.

Ethics Statement

One goal of our paper is explicitly to encourage further research in low-resource settings for natural language generation. While we have argued that many 'typical' NLG settings can be thought of as relatively low-resource compared to other areas of NLP, it is worth noting that some topics (e.g., legal, medical) are especially sensitive and that working with low-resource languages in particular introduces challenges in privacy (for an extensive discussion on this topic see (Hirmer et al., 2021)). For work such as developing mental health support chatbots or developing systems for minoritised language communities, we especially encourage our fellow researchers to engage with their local ethics boards and adopt a participatory approach to data collection and system design to ensure that their efforts work in collaboration with the affected communities.

Limitations

While this position paper includes an overview of the current literature, a systematic survey (e.g. following PRISMA, Moher et al., 2009) of all work in low-resource NLG is beyond the scope of the paper: the relative novelty of the topic makes it difficult to determine appropriate selection criteria for a systematic survey on this topic. Usually a systematic survey would include papers based on keyword searches in academic databases, but almost no papers explicitly focus on natural language generation in low-resource settings, making it difficult to identify phrases which reliably indicate all and only the relevant works. This limits the coverage of the current paper, though we believe this limitation is a reasonable trade-off when highlighting an area requiring more attention in future work.

Acknowledgements

The research is supported under the EPSRC projects NLG for low-resource domains (EP/T024917/1) and CiViL (EP/T014598/1).

References

Oshin Agarwal, Heming Ge, Siamak Shakeri, and Rami Al-Rfou. 2021. Knowledge graph based synthetic corpus generation for knowledge-enhanced language model pre-training. In *Proceedings of the 2021 Conference of the North American Chapter of the Association for Computational Linguistics: Human Language Technologies*, pages 3554–3565, Online. Association for Computational Linguistics.

Oshin Agarwal, Mihir Kale, Heming Ge, Siamak Shakeri, and Rami Al-Rfou. 2020. Machine translation aided bilingual data-to-text generation and semantic parsing. In *Proceedings of the 3rd International*

Workshop on Natural Language Generation from the Semantic Web (WebNLG+), pages 125–130, Dublin, Ireland (Virtual). Association for Computational Linguistics.

Orevaoghene Ahia, Julia Kreutzer, and Sara Hooker. 2021. The low-resource double bind: An empirical study of pruning for low-resource machine translation. In *Findings of the Association for Computational Linguistics: EMNLP 2021*, pages 3316–3333, Punta Cana, Dominican Republic. Association for Computational Linguistics.

Marcin Andrychowicz, Misha Denil, Sergio Gómez Colmenarejo, Matthew W. Hoffman, David Pfau, Tom Schaul, Brendan Shillingford, and Nando de Freitas. 2016. Learning to learn by gradient descent by gradient descent. In *Proceedings of the 30th International Conference on Neural Information Processing Systems*, NeurIPS'16, page 3988–3996, Red Hook, NY, USA. Curran Associates Inc.

Gabor Angeli, Percy Liang, and Dan Klein. 2010. A simple domain-independent probabilistic approach to generation. In *Proceedings of the 2010 Conference on Empirical Methods in Natural Language Processing*, pages 502–512, Cambridge, MA. Association for Computational Linguistics.

Wissam Antoun, Fady Baly, and Hazem Hajj. 2020. AraBERT: Transformer-based model for Arabic language understanding. In *Proceedings of the 4th Workshop on Open-Source Arabic Corpora and Processing Tools, with a Shared Task on Offensive Language Detection*, pages 9–15, Marseille, France. European Language Resource Association.

Anusha Balakrishnan, Jinfeng Rao, Kartikeya Upasani, Michael White, and Rajen Subba. 2019. Constrained decoding for neural NLG from compositional representations in task-oriented dialogue. In *Proceedings of the 57th Annual Meeting of the Association for Computational Linguistics*, pages 831–844, Florence, Italy. Association for Computational Linguistics.

Regina Barzilay and Mirella Lapata. 2005. Collective content selection for concept-to-text generation. In *Proceedings of Human Language Technology Conference and Conference on Empirical Methods in Natural Language Processing*, pages 331–338, Vancouver, British Columbia, Canada. Association for Computational Linguistics.

Anja Belz. 2008. Automatic generation of weather forecast texts using comprehensive probabilistic generation-space models. *Natural Language Engineering*, 14(4):431–455.

Anja Belz and Eric Kow. 2010. Extracting parallel fragments from comparable corpora for data-to-text generation. In *Proceedings of the 6th International Natural Language Generation Conference*. Association for Computational Linguistics.

Emily M. Bender, Scott Drellishak, Antske Fokkens, Laurie Poulson, and Safiyyah Saleem. 2010. Grammar Customization. *Research on Language and Computation*, 8(1):23–72.

Emily M. Bender, Dan Flickinger, and Stephan Oepen. 2002. The grammar matrix: An open-source starter-kit for the rapid development of cross-linguistically consistent broad-coverage precision grammars. In *COLING-02: Grammar Engineering and Evaluation*.

Tom Brown, Benjamin Mann, Nick Ryder, Melanie Subbiah, Jared D Kaplan, Prafulla Dhariwal, Arvind Neelakantan, Pranav Shyam, Girish Sastry, Amanda Askell, Sandhini Agarwal, Ariel Herbert-Voss, Gretchen Krueger, Tom Henighan, Rewon Child, Aditya Ramesh, Daniel Ziegler, Jeffrey Wu, Clemens Winter, Chris Hesse, Mark Chen, Eric Sigler, Mateusz Litwin, Scott Gray, Benjamin Chess, Jack Clark, Christopher Berner, Sam McCandlish, Alec Radford, Ilya Sutskever, and Dario Amodei. 2020. Language models are few-shot learners. In *Advances in Neural Information Processing Systems*, volume 33, pages 1877–1901. Curran Associates, Inc.

Thiago Castro Ferreira, Claire Gardent, Nikolai Ilinykh, Chris van der Lee, Simon Mille, Diego Moussallem, and Anastasia Shimorina. 2020. The 2020 bilingual, bi-directional WebNLG+ shared task: Overview and evaluation results (WebNLG+ 2020). In *Proceedings of the 3rd International Workshop on Natural Language Generation from the Semantic Web (WebNLG+)*, pages 55–76, Dublin, Ireland (Virtual). Association for Computational Linguistics.

Thiago Castro Ferreira, Chris van der Lee, Emiel van Miltenburg, and Emiel Krahmer. 2019. Neural data-to-text generation: A comparison between pipeline and end-to-end architectures. In *Proceedings of the 2019 Conference on Empirical Methods in Natural Language Processing and the 9th International Joint Conference on Natural Language Processing (EMNLP-IJCNLP)*, pages 552–562, Hong Kong, China. Association for Computational Linguistics.

Thiago Castro Ferreira, Helena Vaz, Brian Davis, and Adriana Pagano. 2021. Enriching the E2E dataset. In *Proceedings of the 14th International Conference on Natural Language Generation*, pages 177–183, Aberdeen, Scotland, UK. Association for Computational Linguistics.

Ernie Chang, Jeriah Caplinger, Alex Marin, Xiaoyu Shen, and Vera Demberg. 2020. DART: A lightweight quality-suggestive data-to-text annotation tool. In *Proceedings of the 28th International Conference on Computational Linguistics: System Demonstrations*, pages 12–17, Barcelona, Spain (Online). International Committee on Computational Linguistics (ICCL).

Ernie Chang, Vera Demberg, and Alex Marin. 2021a. Jointly improving language understanding and generation with quality-weighted weak supervision of automatic labeling. In *Proceedings of the 16th Conference of the European Chapter of the Association for Computational Linguistics: Main Volume*, pages 818–829, Online. Association for Computational Linguistics.

Ernie Chang, Xiaoyu Shen, Hui-Syuan Yeh, and Vera Demberg. 2021b. On training instance selection for few-shot neural text generation. In *Proceedings of the 59th Annual Meeting of the Association for Computational Linguistics and the 11th International Joint Conference on Natural Language Processing (Volume 2: Short Papers)*, pages 8–13, Online. Association for Computational Linguistics.

Zhiyu Chen, Harini Eavani, Wenhu Chen, Yinyin Liu, and William Yang Wang. 2020. Few-shot NLG with pre-trained language model. In *Proceedings of the 58th Annual Meeting of the Association for Computational Linguistics*, pages 183–190, Online. Association for Computational Linguistics.

William Churchill. 1912. *Easter Island: The Rapanui Speech and the Peopling of Southeast Polynesia*. Carnegie Institution, Washington.

Jordan Clive, Kris Cao, and Marek Rei. 2021. Control prefixes for text generation. *CoRR*, abs/2110.08329.

Marie-Catherine de Marneffe, Christopher D. Manning, Joakim Nivre, and Daniel Zeman. 2021. Universal Dependencies. *Computational Linguistics*, 47(2):255–308.

Nina Dethlefs. 2017. Domain transfer for deep natural language generation from abstract meaning representations. *IEEE Computational Intelligence Magazine*, 12(3):18–28.

Nina Dethlefs and Heriberto Cuayáhuitl. 2011. Hierarchical reinforcement learning and hidden Markov models for task-oriented natural language generation. In *Proceedings of the 49th Annual Meeting of the Association for Computational Linguistics: Human Language Technologies*, pages 654–659, Portland, Oregon, USA. Association for Computational Linguistics.

Jacob Devlin. 2018. Multilingual BERT README.

Kaustubh D. Dhole, Varun Gangal, Sebastian Gehrmann, Aadesh Gupta, Zhenhao Li, Saad Mahamood, Abinaya Mahendiran, Simon Mille, Ashish Srivastava, Samson Tan, Tongshuang Wu, Jascha Sohl-Dickstein, Jinho D. Choi, Eduard H. Hovy, Ondrej Dusek, Sebastian Ruder, Sajant Anand, Nagender Aneja, Rabin Banjade, Lisa Barthe, Hanna Behnke, Ian Berlot-Attwell, Connor Boyle, Caroline Brun, Marco Antonio Sobrevilla Cabezudo, Samuel Cahyawijaya, Emile Chapuis, Wanxiang Che, Mukund Choudhary, Christian Clauss, Pierre Colombo, Filip Cornell, Gautier Dagan, Mayukh Das, Tanay Dixit, Thomas Dopierre, Paul-Alexis Dray, Suchitra Dubey, Tatiana Ekeinhor, Marco Di Giovanni, Rishabh Gupta, Rishabh Gupta, Louanes Hamla, Sang Han, Fabrice Harel-Canada, Antoine Honore, Ishan Jindal, Przemyslaw K. Joniak, Denis Kleyko, Venelin Kovatchev, and et al. 2021. Nl-augmenter: A framework for task-sensitive natural language augmentation. *CoRR*, abs/2112.02721.

Zi-Yi Dou and Nanyun Peng. 2022. Zero-shot commonsense question answering with cloze translation and consistency optimization. In *The Thirty-Sixth AAAI Conference on Artificial Intelligence (AAAI)*.

Veronica. Du Feu. 2012. *Rapanui: A Descriptive Grammar.* Taylor and Francis, Hoboken.

Ondřej Dušek, David M. Howcroft, and Verena Rieser. 2019. Semantic noise matters for neural natural language generation. In *Proceedings of the 12th International Conference on Natural Language Generation*, pages 421–426, Tokyo, Japan. Association for Computational Linguistics.

Ondřej Dušek and Filip Jurčíček. 2016. Sequence-to-sequence generation for spoken dialogue via deep syntax trees and strings. In *Proceedings of the 54th Annual Meeting of the Association for Computational Linguistics (Volume 2: Short Papers)*, pages 45–51, Berlin, Germany. Association for Computational Linguistics.

Ondřej Dušek, Jekaterina Novikova, and Verena Rieser. 2020. Evaluating the State-of-the-Art of End-to-End Natural Language Generation: The E2E NLG Challenge. *Computer Speech & Language*, 59:123–156.

Michael Elhadad and Jacques Robin. 1996. An overview of SURGE: a reusable comprehensive syntactic realization component. In *Eighth International Natural Language Generation Workshop (Posters and Demonstrations)*.

Michael Elhadad and Jacques Robin. 1997. Surge: A comprehensive plug-in syntactic realisation component for text generation.

Angela Fan and Claire Gardent. 2020. Multilingual AMR-to-text generation. In *Proceedings of the 2020 Conference on Empirical Methods in Natural Language Processing (EMNLP)*, pages 2889–2901, Online. Association for Computational Linguistics.

Steven Y. Feng, Varun Gangal, Jason Wei, Sarath Chandar, Soroush Vosoughi, Teruko Mitamura, and Eduard Hovy. 2021. A survey of data augmentation approaches for NLP. In *Findings of the Association for Computational Linguistics: ACL-IJCNLP 2021*, pages 968–988, Online. Association for Computational Linguistics.

Chelsea Finn, Pieter Abbeel, and Sergey Levine. 2017. Model-agnostic meta-learning for fast adaptation of deep networks. *CoRR*, abs/1703.03400.

Albert Gatt and Ehud Reiter. 2009. SimpleNLG: A realisation engine for practical applications. In *Proceedings of the 12th European Workshop on Natural Language Generation (ENLG 2009)*, pages 90–93,

Athens, Greece. Association for Computational Linguistics.

Dimitra Gkatzia. 2016. Content selection in data-to-text systems: A survey. *CoRR*, abs/1610.08375.

Dimitra Gkatzia and Francesco Belvedere. 2021. *"What's This?" Comparing Active Learning Strategies for Concept Acquisition in HRI*, page 205–209. Association for Computing Machinery, New York, NY, USA.

Jiatao Gu, Yong Wang, Yun Chen, Victor O. K. Li, and Kyunghyun Cho. 2018. Meta-learning for low-resource neural machine translation. In *Proceedings of the 2018 Conference on Empirical Methods in Natural Language Processing*, pages 3622–3631, Brussels, Belgium. Association for Computational Linguistics.

Stephanie Hirmer, Alycia Leonard, Josephine Tumwesige, and Costanza Conforti. 2021. Building representative corpora from illiterate communities: A reviewof challenges and mitigation strategies for developing countries. In *Proceedings of the 16th Conference of the European Chapter of the Association for Computational Linguistics: Main Volume*, pages 2176–2189, Online. Association for Computational Linguistics.

David M. Howcroft, Anya Belz, Miruna-Adriana Clinciu, Dimitra Gkatzia, Sadid A. Hasan, Saad Mahamood, Simon Mille, Emiel van Miltenburg, Sashank Santhanam, and Verena Rieser. 2020. Twenty years of confusion in human evaluation: NLG needs evaluation sheets and standardised definitions. In *Proceedings of the 13th International Conference on Natural Language Generation*, pages 169–182, Dublin, Ireland. Association for Computational Linguistics.

David M. Howcroft, Dietrich Klakow, and Vera Demberg. 2017. The Extended SPaRKy Restaurant Corpus: Designing a Corpus with Variable Information Density. In *Proc. of Interspeech 2017*, pages 3757–3761, Stockholm, Sweden. ISCA.

David M. Howcroft, Dietrich Klakow, and Vera Demberg. 2018. Toward Bayesian synchronous tree substitution grammars for sentence planning. In *Proceedings of the 11th International Conference on Natural Language Generation*, pages 391–396, Tilburg University, The Netherlands. Association for Computational Linguistics.

Amy Isard. 2016. The methodius corpus of rhetorical discourse structures and generated texts. In *Proceedings of the Tenth International Conference on Language Resources and Evaluation (LREC'16)*, pages 1732–1736, Portorož, Slovenia. European Language Resources Association (ELRA).

Zhijing Jin, Qipeng Guo, Xipeng Qiu, and Zheng Zhang. 2020. GenWiki: A dataset of 1.3 million content-sharing text and graphs for unsupervised graph-to-text generation. In *Proceedings of the 28th International Conference on Computational Linguistics*, pages 2398–2409, Barcelona, Spain (Online). International Committee on Computational Linguistics.

Pratik Joshi, Sebastin Santy, Amar Budhiraja, Kalika Bali, and Monojit Choudhury. 2020. The state and fate of linguistic diversity and inclusion in the NLP world. In *Proceedings of the 58th Annual Meeting of the Association for Computational Linguistics*, pages 6282–6293, Online. Association for Computational Linguistics.

Juraj Juraska, Kevin Bowden, and Marilyn Walker. 2019. ViGGO: A video game corpus for data-to-text generation in open-domain conversation. In *Proceedings of the 12th International Conference on Natural Language Generation*, pages 164–172, Tokyo, Japan. Association for Computational Linguistics.

Mihir Kale and Scott Roy. 2020. Machine translation pre-training for data-to-text generation - a case study in Czech. In *Proceedings of the 13th International Conference on Natural Language Generation*, pages 91–96, Dublin, Ireland. Association for Computational Linguistics.

Hans Kamp and Uwe Reyle. 1993. *From Discourse to Logic: Introduction to Modeltheoretic Semantics of Natural Language, Formal Logic and Discourse Representation Theory*. Studies in Linguistics and Philosophy. Springer Netherlands.

Paulus Kieviet. 2017. *A Grammar Of Rapa Nui*. Zenodo.

Young Jin Kim, Marcin Junczys-Dowmunt, Hany Hassan, Alham Fikri Aji, Kenneth Heafield, Roman Grundkiewicz, and Nikolay Bogoychev. 2019. From Research to Production and Back: Ludicrously Fast Neural Machine Translation. In *Proceedings of the 3rd Workshop on Neural Generation and Translation*, pages 280–288, Hong Kong. Association for Computational Linguistics.

Kevin Knight and Vasileios Hatzivassiloglou. 1995. Two-level, many-paths generation. In *33rd Annual Meeting of the Association for Computational Linguistics*, pages 252–260, Cambridge, Massachusetts, USA. Association for Computational Linguistics.

Gregory Koch, Richard Zemel, and Ruslan Salakhutdinov. 2015. Siamese neural networks for one-shot image recognition.

Tom Kocmi and Ondřej Bojar. 2018. Trivial transfer learning for low-resource neural machine translation. In *Proceedings of the Third Conference on Machine Translation: Research Papers*, pages 244–252, Brussels, Belgium. Association for Computational Linguistics.

Geert-Jan M. Kruijff. 2001. *A Categorial-Modal Logical Architecture of Informativity*. Ph.D. thesis, Charles University, Prague, Czech Republic.

Irene Langkilde and Kevin Knight. 1998. Generation that exploits corpus-based statistical knowledge. In *36th Annual Meeting of the Association for Computational Linguistics and 17th International Conference on Computational Linguistics, Volume 1*, pages 704–710, Montreal, Quebec, Canada. Association for Computational Linguistics.

Rémi Lebret, David Grangier, and Michael Auli. 2016. Neural Text Generation from Structured Data with Application to the Biography Domain. In *Proceedings of the 2016 Conference on Empirical Methods in Natural Language Processing*, pages 1203–1213, Austin, Texas. Association for Computational Linguistics.

Xiang Lisa Li and Percy Liang. 2021. Prefix-tuning: Optimizing continuous prompts for generation. In *Proceedings of the 59th Annual Meeting of the Association for Computational Linguistics and the 11th International Joint Conference on Natural Language Processing (Volume 1: Long Papers)*, pages 4582–4597, Online. Association for Computational Linguistics.

Percy Liang, Michael Jordan, and Dan Klein. 2009. Learning semantic correspondences with less supervision. In *Proceedings of the Joint Conference of the 47th Annual Meeting of the ACL and the 4th International Joint Conference on Natural Language Processing of the AFNLP*, pages 91–99, Suntec, Singapore. Association for Computational Linguistics.

Pengfei Liu, Weizhe Yuan, Jinlan Fu, Zhengbao Jiang, Hiroaki Hayashi, and Graham Neubig. 2021. Pretrain, prompt, and predict: A systematic survey of prompting methods in natural language processing. *CoRR*, abs/2107.13586.

Shuming Ma, Pengcheng Yang, Tianyu Liu, Peng Li, Jie Zhou, and Xu Sun. 2019. Key fact as pivot: A two-stage model for low resource table-to-text generation. In *Proceedings of the 57th Annual Meeting of the Association for Computational Linguistics*, pages 2047–2057, Florence, Italy. Association for Computational Linguistics.

Ahmed Magooda, Diane Litman, and Mohamed Elaraby. 2021. Exploring multitask learning for low-resource abstractive summarization. In *Findings of the Association for Computational Linguistics: EMNLP 2021*, pages 1652–1661, Punta Cana, Dominican Republic. Association for Computational Linguistics.

Zola Mahlaza and C. Maria Keet. 2022. Surface realisation architecture for low-resourced african languages. *ACM Trans. Asian Low-Resour. Lang. Inf. Process.* Just Accepted.

François Mairesse, Milica Gašić, Filip Jurčíček, Simon Keizer, Blaise Thomson, Kai Yu, and Steve Young. 2010. Phrase-based statistical language generation using graphical models and active learning. In *Proceedings of the 48th Annual Meeting of the Association for Computational Linguistics*, pages 1552–1561, Uppsala, Sweden. Association for Computational Linguistics.

Aleksandre Maskharashvili, Symon Stevens-Guille, Xintong Li, and Michael White. 2021. Neural methodius revisited: Do discourse relations help with pre-trained models too? In *Proceedings of the 14th International Conference on Natural Language Generation*, pages 12–23, Aberdeen, Scotland, UK. Association for Computational Linguistics.

Fei Mi, Minlie Huang, Jiyong Zhang, and Boi Faltings. 2019a. Meta-learning for low-resource natural language generation in task-oriented dialogue systems. In *Proceedings of the Twenty-Eighth International Joint Conference on Artificial Intelligence, IJCAI-19*, pages 3151–3157. International Joint Conferences on Artificial Intelligence Organization.

Fei Mi, Minlie Huang, Jiyong Zhang, and Boi Faltings. 2019b. Meta-learning for low-resource natural language generation in task-oriented dialogue systems. In *Proceedings of the 28th International Joint Conference on Artificial Intelligence*, IJCAI'19, page 3151–3157. AAAI Press.

Simon Mille, Anja Belz, Bernd Bohnet, Yvette Graham, Emily Pitler, and Leo Wanner. 2018. The First Multilingual Surface Realisation Shared Task (SR'18): Overview and Evaluation Results. In *Proceedings of the First Workshop on Multilingual Surface Realisation*, pages 1–12, Melbourne, Australia. Association for Computational Linguistics.

Simon Mille, Anja Belz, Bernd Bohnet, Yvette Graham, and Leo Wanner. 2019. The Second Multilingual Surface Realisation Shared Task (SR'19): Overview and Evaluation Results. In *Proceedings of the 2nd Workshop on Multilingual Surface Realisation (MSR 2019)*, pages 1–17, Hong Kong, China. Association for Computational Linguistics.

Simon Mille, Anya Belz, Bernd Bohnet, Thiago Castro Ferreira, Yvette Graham, and Leo Wanner. 2020. The third multilingual surface realisation shared task (SR'20): Overview and evaluation results. In *Proceedings of the Third Workshop on Multilingual Surface Realisation*, pages 1–20, Barcelona, Spain (Online). Association for Computational Linguistics.

D. Moher, A. Liberati, J. Tetzlaff, D. G Altman, and for the PRISMA Group. 2009. Preferred reporting items for systematic reviews and meta-analyses: The PRISMA statement. *BMJ*, 339(jul21 1):b2535–b2535.

Amit Moryossef, Yoav Goldberg, and Ido Dagan. 2019. Step-by-step: Separating planning from realization in neural data-to-text generation. In *Proceedings of the 2019 Conference of the North American Chapter of the Association for Computational Linguistics: Human Language Technologies, Volume 1 (Long and Short Papers)*, pages 2267–2277, Minneapolis, Minnesota. Association for Computational Linguistics.

Tarek Naous, Wissam Antoun, Reem Mahmoud, and Hazem Hajj. 2021. Empathetic BERT2BERT conversational model: Learning Arabic language generation with little data. In *Proceedings of the Sixth Arabic Natural Language Processing Workshop*, pages 164–172, Kyiv, Ukraine (Virtual). Association for Computational Linguistics.

Jekaterina Novikova, Oliver Lemon, and Verena Rieser. 2016. Crowd-sourcing NLG data: Pictures elicit better data. In *Proceedings of the 9th International Natural Language Generation conference*, pages 265–273, Edinburgh, UK. Association for Computational Linguistics.

Shereen Oraby, Lena Reed, Shubhangi Tandon, Sharath T.S., Stephanie Lukin, and Marilyn Walker. 2018. Controlling personality-based stylistic variation with neural natural language generators. In *Proceedings of the 19th Annual SIGdial Meeting on Discourse and Dialogue*, pages 180–190, Melbourne, Australia. Association for Computational Linguistics.

Nikolaos Panagiaris, Emma Hart, and Dimitra Gkatzia. 2021. Generating unambiguous and diverse referring expressions. *Computer Speech Language*, 68:101184.

Nivranshu Pasricha, Mihael Arcan, and Paul Buitelaar. 2020. NUIG-DSI at the WebNLG+ challenge: Leveraging transfer learning for RDF-to-text generation. In *Proceedings of the 3rd International Workshop on Natural Language Generation from the Semantic Web (WebNLG+)*, pages 137–143, Dublin, Ireland (Virtual). Association for Computational Linguistics.

Laura Perez-Beltrachini and Mirella Lapata. 2018. Bootstrapping generators from noisy data. In *Proceedings of the 2018 Conference of the North American Chapter of the Association for Computational Linguistics: Human Language Technologies, Volume 1 (Long Papers)*, pages 1516–1527, New Orleans, Louisiana. Association for Computational Linguistics.

Laura Perez-Beltrachini, Rania Sayed, and Claire Gardent. 2016. Building RDF content for data-to-text generation. In *Proceedings of COLING 2016, the 26th International Conference on Computational Linguistics: Technical Papers*, pages 1493–1502, Osaka, Japan. The COLING 2016 Organizing Committee.

Ratish Puduppully and Mirella Lapata. 2021. Data-to-text generation with macro planning. *Transactions of the Association for Computational Linguistics*, 9:510–527.

Colin Raffel, Noam Shazeer, Adam Roberts, Katherine Lee, Sharan Narang, Michael Matena, Yanqi Zhou, Wei Li, and Peter J. Liu. 2020. Exploring the limits of transfer learning with a unified text-to-text transformer. *Journal of Machine Learning Research*, 21(140):1–67.

Ehud Reiter. 2007. An architecture for data-to-text systems. In *Proceedings of the Eleventh European Workshop on Natural Language Generation (ENLG 07)*, pages 97–104, Saarbrücken, Germany. DFKI GmbH.

Leonardo F. R. Ribeiro, Martin Schmitt, Hinrich Schütze, and Iryna Gurevych. 2021. Investigating pretrained language models for graph-to-text generation. In *Proceedings of the 3rd Workshop on Natural Language Processing for Conversational AI*, pages 211–227, Online. Association for Computational Linguistics.

V. Rieser and O. Lemon. 2011. *Reinforcement learning for adaptive dialogue systems: a data-driven methodology for dialogue management and natural language generation.* Theory and Applications of Natural Language Processing. Springer.

Gözde Gül Şahin and Mark Steedman. 2018. Data augmentation via dependency tree morphing for low-resource languages. In *Proceedings of the 2018 Conference on Empirical Methods in Natural Language Processing*, pages 5004–5009, Brussels, Belgium. Association for Computational Linguistics.

Sheng Shen, Daniel Fried, Jacob Andreas, and Dan Klein. 2019. Pragmatically informative text generation. In *Proceedings of the 2019 Conference of the North American Chapter of the Association for Computational Linguistics: Human Language Technologies, Volume 1 (Long and Short Papers)*, pages 4060–4067, Minneapolis, Minnesota. Association for Computational Linguistics.

Xiaoyu Shen, Ernie Chang, Hui Su, Cheng Niu, and Dietrich Klakow. 2020. Neural data-to-text generation via jointly learning the segmentation and correspondence. In *Proceedings of the 58th Annual Meeting of the Association for Computational Linguistics*, pages 7155–7165, Online. Association for Computational Linguistics.

Anastasia Shimorina and Claire Gardent. 2019. Surface realisation using full delexicalisation. In *Proceedings of the 2019 Conference on Empirical Methods in Natural Language Processing and the 9th International Joint Conference on Natural Language Processing (EMNLP-IJCNLP)*, pages 3086–3096, Hong Kong, China. Association for Computational Linguistics.

Connor Shorten and Taghi M. Khoshgoftaar. 2019. A survey on image data augmentation for deep learning. *J. Big Data*, 6:60.

Somayajulu Gowri Sripada, Jin Yu, Ian P. Davy, and Wni Oceanroutes. 2008. Sumtime-meteo: Parallel corpus of naturally occurring forecast texts and weather data.

M. Steedman and J. Baldridge. 2006. Combinatory categorial grammar. In Keith Brown, editor, *Encyclopedia of Language Linguistics (Second Edition)*, second edition edition, pages 610–621. Elsevier, Oxford.

Symon Stevens-Guille, Aleksandre Maskharashvili, Amy Isard, Xintong Li, and Michael White. 2020. Neural NLG for methodius: From RST meaning representations to texts. In *Proceedings of the 13th International Conference on Natural Language Generation*, pages 306–315, Dublin, Ireland. Association for Computational Linguistics.

Lisa A. Torrey and Jude W. Shavlik. 2009. Transfer learning. In *Handbook of Research on Machine Learning Applications*.

Van-Khanh Tran and Le-Minh Nguyen. 2018. Adversarial domain adaptation for variational neural language generation in dialogue systems. In *Proceedings of the 27th International Conference on Computational Linguistics*, pages 1205–1217, Santa Fe, New Mexico, USA. Association for Computational Linguistics.

Chris van der Lee, Chris Emmery, Sander Wubben, and Emiel Krahmer. 2020. The CACAPO dataset: A multilingual, multi-domain dataset for neural pipeline and end-to-end data-to-text generation. In *Proceedings of the 13th International Conference on Natural Language Generation*, pages 68–79, Dublin, Ireland. Association for Computational Linguistics.

Emiel van Miltenburg, Miruna Clinciu, Ondřej Dušek, Dimitra Gkatzia, Stephanie Inglis, Leo Leppänen, Saad Mahamood, Emma Manning, Stephanie Schoch, Craig Thomson, and Luou Wen. 2021. Underreporting of errors in NLG output, and what to do about it. In *Proceedings of the 14th International Conference on Natural Language Generation*, pages 140–153, Aberdeen, Scotland, UK. Association for Computational Linguistics.

Sida I. Wang, Percy Liang, and Christopher D. Manning. 2016. Learning language games through interaction. In *Proceedings of the 54th Annual Meeting of the Association for Computational Linguistics (Volume 1: Long Papers)*, pages 2368–2378, Berlin, Germany. Association for Computational Linguistics.

Tsung-Hsien Wen, Milica Gašić, Nikola Mrkšić, Lina M. Rojas-Barahona, Pei-Hao Su, David Vandyke, and Steve Young. 2016. Multi-domain neural network language generation for spoken dialogue systems. In *Proceedings of the 2016 Conference of the North American Chapter of the Association for Computational Linguistics: Human Language Technologies*, pages 120–129, San Diego, California. Association for Computational Linguistics.

Tsung-Hsien Wen, Milica Gašić, Nikola Mrkšić, Pei-Hao Su, David Vandyke, and Steve Young. 2015. Semantically conditioned LSTM-based natural language generation for spoken dialogue systems. In *Proceedings of the 2015 Conference on Empirical Methods in Natural Language Processing*, pages 1711–1721, Lisbon, Portugal. Association for Computational Linguistics.

Michael White. 2006. CCG chart realization from disjunctive inputs. In *Proceedings of the Fourth International Natural Language Generation Conference*, pages 12–19, Sydney, Australia. Association for Computational Linguistics.

Xinnuo Xu, Ondřej Dušek, Verena Rieser, and Ioannis Konstas. 2021. AggGen: Ordering and aggregating while generating. In *Proceedings of the 59th Annual Meeting of the Association for Computational Linguistics and the 11th International Joint Conference on Natural Language Processing (Volume 1: Long Papers)*, pages 1419–1434, Online. Association for Computational Linguistics.

Linting Xue, Noah Constant, Adam Roberts, Mihir Kale, Rami Al-Rfou, Aditya Siddhant, Aditya Barua, and Colin Raffel. 2021. mT5: A Massively Multilingual Pre-trained Text-to-Text Transformer. In *Proceedings of the 2021 Conference of the North American Chapter of the Association for Computational Linguistics: Human Language Technologies*, pages 483–498, Online. Association for Computational Linguistics.

Steve Young. 2007. CUED standard dialogue acts. *Report, Cambridge University Engineering Department, 14th October*, 2007.

Tiancheng Zhao and Maxine Eskenazi. 2018. Zero-shot dialog generation with cross-domain latent actions. In *Proceedings of the 19th Annual SIGdial Meeting on Discourse and Dialogue*, pages 1–10, Melbourne, Australia. Association for Computational Linguistics.

Chenguang Zhu, Michael Zeng, and Xuedong Huang. 2019. Multi-task learning for natural language generation in task-oriented dialogue. In *Proceedings of the 2019 Conference on Empirical Methods in Natural Language Processing and the 9th International Joint Conference on Natural Language Processing (EMNLP-IJCNLP)*, pages 1261–1266, Hong Kong, China. Association for Computational Linguistics.

Barret Zoph, Deniz Yuret, Jonathan May, and Kevin Knight. 2016. Transfer learning for low-resource neural machine translation. In *Proceedings of the 2016 Conference on Empirical Methods in Natural Language Processing*, pages 1568–1575, Austin, Texas. Association for Computational Linguistics.

GiCCS: A German in-Context Conversational Similarity Benchmark

Shima Asaadi* and **Zahra Kolagar*** and **Alina Liebel**
Fraunhofer IIS
{shima.asaadi,zahra.kolagar,alina.liebel}@iis.fraunhofer.de

Alessandra Zarcone
Hochschule Augsburg
alessandra.zarcone@hs-augsburg.de

Abstract

The Semantic textual similarity (STS) task is commonly used to evaluate the semantic representations that language models (LMs) learn from texts, under the assumption that good-quality representations will yield accurate similarity estimates. When it comes to estimating the similarity of two utterances in a dialogue, however, the conversational context plays a particularly important role. We argue for the need of benchmarks specifically created using conversational data in order to evaluate conversational LMs in the STS task. We introduce GiCCS, a first conversational STS evaluation benchmark for German. We collected the similarity annotations for GiCCS using best-worst scaling and presenting the target items in context, in order to obtain highly-reliable context-dependent similarity scores. We present benchmarking experiments for evaluating LMs on capturing the similarity of utterances. Results suggest that pretraining LMs on conversational data and providing conversational context can be useful for capturing similarity of utterances in dialogues. GiCCS is publicly available to encourage benchmarking of conversational LMs.

1 Introduction

The Semantic Textual Similarity (STS) framework is typically used for the extrinsic evaluation of NLP models (Agirre et al., 2012), and in particular for language models (LMs): if a model can successfully estimate the similarity between sentences, it's a good sign that it has learned good-quality semantically meaningful representations. In natural language generation, STS can provide a useful alternative to word overlap measures to analyse system output similarity (Dušek et al., 2020; Novikova et al., 2016). STS has been used both for training (Reimers and Gurevych, 2019; Vulic et al., 2021) and for evaluating LMs (Yang et al., 2018).

To the best of our knowledge, the majority of STS benchmarks have been created from written language resources using non-conversational data, and are mainly in English. Conversational data, however, has some peculiarities which make it potentially challenging for the STS task: (1) questions and requests are frequent, (2) whether two sentences are semantically similar may depend on pragmatic factors triggered by the conversational context. For example, it may be challenging for human annotators to assess that *Could you turn it up a bit?* and *I'd like the AC to be colder* advance the conversation in a similar way, without (1) sufficient conversational context and (2) an operative definition of what it means for a question and a declarative sentence to be semantically similar. Moreover, STS datasets are typically annotated on a rating scale, which may lead to inconsistencies in annotation, scale region bias, and fixed granularity issues (Kiritchenko and Mohammad, 2017).

In this paper, we introduce GiCCS, the first German in-Context Conversational benchmark for evaluating LMs on the STS task. GiCCS is a multi-domain dataset containing 300 items, each consisting of a domain name, a multi-turn German dialogue context (i.e., dialogue history) where the last utterance is paired with a target utterance, and a semantic similarity score between the paired utterances. GiCCS contains data from German dialogue resources as opposed to machine-translated data (e.g. the GLUE benchmark for STS; Wang et al. 2018). The similarity scores were crowdsourced using the Best-Worst Scaling (BWS) annotation technique (Louviere et al., 2015), as it was shown to address the limitations of the rating scales technique (Kiritchenko and Mohammad, 2017; Asaadi et al., 2019). The dialogue history (the previous 3

*These authors contributed equally to this work.

Proceedings of the 2nd Workshop on Natural Language Generation, Evaluation, and Metrics (GEM), pages 351 - 362

or 5 turns) was presented to the crowd-workers during crowdsourcing for better similarity judgements based on the conversational context.

Adopting BWS in order to overcome the limitations of rating scales led to a high inter-annotator agreement with an overall Krippendorff's α of 0.74. Furthermore, we present a reliability study of the similarity scores obtained from the BWS annotations and based on the conversational context.

Lastly, we present benchmarking experiments to evaluate different LMs on the STS task using GiCCS. Experiments show that pre-training LMs on conversational data is beneficial for capturing conversational representations in downstream tasks and conversational applications, such as dialogue systems. GiCCS has a wide range of further applications, such as the evaluation of dialogue generation models, answer selection and ranking systems, and question answering based on dialogue history.

2 Background and Related Work

2.1 Semantic Textual Similarity

Agirre et al. (2012) introduced a large-scale STS benchmark, consisting of pairs of sentences and similarity scores on a $0-5$ ordinal scale (from semantically unrelated to equivalent). Similar benchmarks have been introduced and extended to multiple languages (Agirre et al. 2013; 2014; 2015; 2016; Cer et al. 2017). Sentences in these benchmarks have been collected from news headlines, video and image descriptions, glosses, machine translation evaluation data, tweet news and comments, questions and answers from Q&A forums, and Wikipedia sentences. Annotations are crowdsourced in the form of similarity judgements on a rating scale. The STS benchmark (Cer et al., 2017) included in the GLUE benchmark (Wang et al., 2018) has been translated to German using machine translation systems.[1]

Generally, the STS task evaluates how well a model has learned the semantic space and how semantically meaningful the representations created by the model are. It is widely used for evaluating autoregressive and autoencoding language models. Autoregressive LMs, such as GPT models (Radford et al., 2018), can be tested on producing similar text given a context and autoencoding LMs are tested on creating semantically similar representations for similar texts. Typically, STS is an approach for evaluating conversational LMs, which are in turn employed in the natural language understanding (NLU) components of task-oriented dialogue systems (Yang et al., 2018; Henderson et al., 2019b, 2020; Casanueva et al., 2020; Vulic et al., 2021; Henderson and Vulić, 2021).

To the best of our knowledge, the majority of the benchmarks have been mainly created from written language resources. This results in a sub-optimal benchmark for the evaluation of conversational language models in dialogue systems.

2.2 Conversational Datasets

In order to train, fine-tune or evaluate conversational models for task-oriented dialogue systems, it is crucial to have datasets which are representative of the interaction in task-oriented dialogue. Henderson et al. (2019a) introduce a repository of three large and diverse datasets (Reddit, OpenSubtitles, AmazonQA) for conversational tasks and LM training, each consisting of context–response pairs. Among these, the OpenSubtitles data contains other languages, including German. Prior to this work, Wang et al. (2013) present a dataset of over 12K labeled post–response pairs from the microblog domain. Moreover, Yang et al. (2018) extracted pairs of input–response from a multi-turn open-domain dialogue data, collected by Al-Rfou et al. (2016) from Reddit. Given pairs of related utterances, conversational LMs can be evaluated on capturing the similarity of pairs of utterances by generating semantically similar representations.

There are a few German conversational datasets which are available for research purposes. Among those, the BAS SmartKom corpus is a multi-modal corpus, released in two versions (Schiel et al., 2002; Schiel and Türk, 2006).[2] The data has been recorded in a Wizard-of-Oz setting and is labeled with emotions, gestures, domains, noises, etc., and therefore, it has a wide range of applications including task-oriented dialogue systems. Frommherz and Zarcone (2021) published 113 German dialogues, called CROWDSS[3], collected using the Wizard-of-Oz framework. Data is labeled with dialogue acts and covers one domain. Therefore, it can be used for a variety of NLP tasks. These datasets cannot be directly used as a German STS benchmark. In this paper, we use the audio transcriptions of BAS SmartKom and the dialogues in CROWS-

[1]https://github.com/t-systems-on-site-services-gmbh/german-STSbenchmark

[2]https://www.phonetik.uni-muenchen.de/Bas/BasSmartKomPubliceng.html

[3]https://fordatis.fraunhofer.de/handle/fordatis/198

DSS as our main resources for collecting multi-turn German dialogues in our STS benchmark.

2.3 Conversational Fine-Tuning of LMs

Conversational learning tasks have been introduced to adapt pretrained LMs to conversational models in dialogue systems (Yang et al., 2018; Henderson et al., 2019b, 2020; Casanueva et al., 2020; Vulic et al., 2021; Henderson and Vulić, 2021). The core idea in these tasks is to transform the pretraining or target task into a language understanding task, such as a pairwise STS task and a semantic relatedness task. For this purpose, pairs of queries and responses are created from conversational data and models are trained to score pair items. For instance, Yang et al. (2018), Henderson et al. (2019b) and Henderson et al. (2020) propose a pretraining response selection task (Wang et al., 2013; Al-Rfou et al., 2016; Yang et al., 2018) for learning conversational representations of dialogues. Vulic et al. (2021) introduce CONVFIT, which is a two-stage conversational fine-tuning approach. Similar to previous approaches, first, pretrained LMs are transformed into conversational encoders using the response ranking task. Then, the target intent classification task is treated as a semantic similarity task by pairing utterances in the same intent class as positive pairs and in different classes as negative pairs. Fine-tuning is therefore performed via the STS task. A very recent generative language model, PaLM (Chowdhery et al., 2022), is pretrained on conversations, which is useful in conversational applications and dialogue systems. This model has shown state-of-the-art performance on numerous language understanding tasks.

3 The GiCCS Benchmark

3.1 Data Collection

Creating natural and diverse conversations is a major challenge in the development of task-oriented dialogue systems. It requires manual effort to create such data by crowdsourcing or collecting them from available resources. In this benchmark, we leverage two crowdsourced conversational datasets for German, CROWDSS[4] (Frommherz and Zarcone, 2021) and BAS SmartKom corpora (Schiel et al., 2002; Schiel and Türk, 2006). Both datasets have been collected via the Wizard-of-Oz approach (Budzianowski et al., 2018) to simulate human-machine interaction and contain commonly-used scenarios and domains in dialogue systems.

The CROWDSS dataset contains 113 multi-turn dialogues in the restaurant booking domain and is labeled with dialogue acts. We selected 24 unique dialogues from the dataset starting with the machine's first turn. We randomly split the collected dialogues into two groups of size 12. Keeping all turns would have resulted in a long dialogue history. Moreover, in some cases, the dialogue flow changes from the initial intent after a few turns, which is undesired in our benchmark. Therefore, for the first group, we kept the first three turns of 12 dialogues and for the second group, we kept the first five turns of the 12 dialogues. In a few cases, we corrected some misspelled words or modified the utterances to be more concise. We further extracted transcribed multi-turn dialogues from the BAS SmartKom corpus along with their domain labels for six out of eight domains: cinema, fax, navigation, phone, tourist, and tv.[5] From these, we selected 6 unique multi-turn dialogues for each domain, resulting in 36 unique dialogues in total. Half of the dialogues contained three turns and the second half contained five turns. In some dialogues, we shortened long utterances with multiple sentences by removing irrelevant and unnecessary information from the dialogue, resulting in more focused dialogues.

After the dialogue collection process, we paired the last turn of each dialogue with a set of five hand-written utterances, which were produced by native speakers of German language for this purpose. We chose to hand-write the paired utterances, as pairing randomly-selected sentences with the last turn of each dialogue would have resulted in most sentences being unrelated, which is sub-optimal for benchmarking the models. We thus made sure that the five utterances in the set had different relevancy scores, ranging from unrelated to maximally similar. Following Cer et al. (2017), paired utterances had to satisfy the following criteria to cover the whole range of similarity scores: one paraphrase of the last turn, one sentence that differs in some unimportant details, one sentence that differs in important details, one sentence that shares some details with the last turn but it is not necessarily on the same topic, and one completely unrelated sentence. These similarity judgements on the utter-

[4]https://fordatis.fraunhofer.de/handle/fordatis/198

[5]We extracted data from SK-Home, SK-Public, and SK-Mobil corpora in the following link: http://hdl.handle.net/11022/1009-0000-0001-231F-6.

ances, based on above-mentioned criteria with the main purpose of improving the diversity of the similarity scores, were not used in the main annotation task.

In the end, we obtained 60 dialogues, each paired with five sentences, which resulted in 300 items for the similarity score annotation.

3.2 Data Annotation

Best-Worst Scaling (BWS) (Cohen, 2003; Louviere et al., 2015) is an annotation technique that addresses the limitations of rating scale techniques by employing comparative annotations. In BWS, annotators are presented with n items (n-tuple) at a time and asked which item is the *best*, i.e., highest in terms of the property of interest (for example, *most similar* in our study), and which is the *worst*, e.g., *least similar* in our study. Annotations are then aggregated to obtain real-valued scores of association between the items and the property (Orme, 2009). It has been practically shown that for N items to be annotated, $1.5N$ to $2N$ tuples are sufficient to obtain reliable scores (Louviere et al., 2015; Kiritchenko and Mohammad, 2016). Tuples have to be unique and the items in tuples are distinct. Moreover, each item occurs in approximately the same number of tuples.

In this work, we used BWS to obtain the similarity annotations in GiCCS. We created tuples for each dialogue as follows: From $N = 5$ paired utterances in each dialogue, we generated $2N = 10$ distinct 3-tuples, where each tuple is a random set of three paired utterances. The order of the terms in the 3-tuples is not important, and (following BWS) each term appears in six tuples. We obtained 600 distinct 3-tuples to be annotated.

We set up the annotation task on the crowdsourcing platform Amazon Mechanical Turk (AMT). As requirements for selecting crowd-workers on AMT, we set the approval rate to greater than 98% and the location to Germany. We provided a detailed annotation instruction with examples and asked the annotators to only participate in this study if they were fluent in German. The annotators were presented with two dialogues at a time (one 3-turn dialogue and one 5-turn dialogue), each followed by a 3-tuple for the best- and worst-questions (*which sentence is the most similar to the last utterance in the dialogue? which is the least similar?*). See Appendix A.1 for details on the annotation instructions and a sample of the task presented to the workers. We also included an optional comment section for workers. We collected five different annotations for each 3-tuple.

Dataset	Dialogue turns	α	BW question	Strong agreement
BAS SmartKom	3-turn	0.87	best	99
			worst	100
	5-turn	0.80	best	98
			worst	100
CROWDSS	3-turn	0.63	best	90
			worst	94
	5-turn	0.67	best	95
			worst	97

Table 1: Krippendorff's α and percentage of strong-agreement cases for both source datasets.

3.3 Inter-Annotator Agreement

We computed inter-annotator agreement by considering cases where two annotators provided the same answer to the best- and worst-questions as cases of agreement and cases where two annotators provided different answers to the best- and worst-questions as cases of disagreement. The annotation yielded an acceptable inter-annotator agreement with an overall Krippendorff's α of 0.74 (Artstein and Poesio, 2008). Moreover, Table 1 shows the Krippendorff's α in each source dataset. As can be seen, the overall agreement in BAS SmartKom is higher than CROWDSS.

To provide a better overview of agreements, Table 1 also shows the percentage of items in each portion of the source dataset that had a *strong agreement*. We define strong agreement as cases where at least four out of five annotators selected the same answer in the best and worst questions. Percentages of strong agreement cases are high for both source datasets, which speaks for the validity of the best-worst scaling task. On the other hand, we assume that the slightly lower percentages obtained from the CROWDSS dataset might stem from the fact that CROWDSS has a higher lexical diversity and contains only one domain. This may result in a more difficult comparison between best and worst pairs for the annotators during the annotation process. Results are also in agreement with the lower inter-annotator agreement (α) for the CROWDSS dataset.

3.4 Dataset Preparation

Annotation Aggregation. After the completion of the annotation task, we calculated the final semantic similarity scores for dialogue–utterance pairs from the BWS responses using a simple counting method (Orme, 2009). For each pair, the semantic similarity score is the proportion of times the utterance was chosen as the best minus the proportion of times the utterance was chosen as the worst in the annotation task. This results in similarity scores ranging from -1 to 1, which we normalized to the interval $[0, 1]$. Finally, GiCCS includes 300 items, each containing a domain label, a multi-turn dialogue context, a comparison utterance, and a similarity score between the comparison utterance and the last utterance in the dialogue.

Managing Domain Labels Since the domain of some dialogues didn't perfectly match the dialogues' context (e.g., phone domain in the BAS SmartKom corpora), we have relabeled some of the dialogues from the original labels to obtain a consistent domain labeling; also specified in 3.1. The final dataset includes the following domains: *find_restaurant*, *find_tvProgram*, *find_cinema*, *find_hotel*, *find_touristAttraction*, *find_navigation*.

3.5 The Dataset

Table 2 presents descriptive statistics about GiCCS. We report the average turn length per domain, number of tokens per domain, and the unique count of the lemmatized forms of the words. Tokens were obtained by splitting text based on the whitespaces. To obtain lemmas, i.e., the base form of words that are present in a dictionary, we used the German SpaCy model de_core_news_sm version 3.3.0 (Honnibal et al., 2020).[6]

In order to compare lexical richness between dialogues in each domain, we show root type-token ratio (RTTR) as well as the measure of textual lexical diversity (MTLD; McCarthy and Jarvis 2010) computed with the threshold of 0.72 using the LexicalRichness library (Shen, 2022)[7], as MTLD is more robust to changes in text length. High RTTR and MTLD in both 3-turn and 5-turn dialogues indicate the lexical diversity of GiCCS. In particular, both measures are high in the find_restaurant domain suggesting that this domain may be more complex and challenging for the annotators. This is reflected by lower agreement scores for CROWDSS compared to BAS SmartKom (see Table 1) as most dialogues in the find_restaurant domain are from the CROWDSS dataset.

[6]https://github.com/explosion/spacy-models/releases/tag/de_core_news_sm-3.3.0

[7]https://github.com/LSYS/LexicalRichness

4 Score Reliability Study

We now provide an analysis of the similarity scores obtained with the BWS and of their reliability.

4.1 Score Distribution

Figure 1 shows the distribution of the obtained similarity scores. As expected, the final scores cover a wide range of similarity in the interval $[0, 1]$, which is useful for evaluating LMs on fine-grained scoring and their ability on detecting the nuances in semantics.

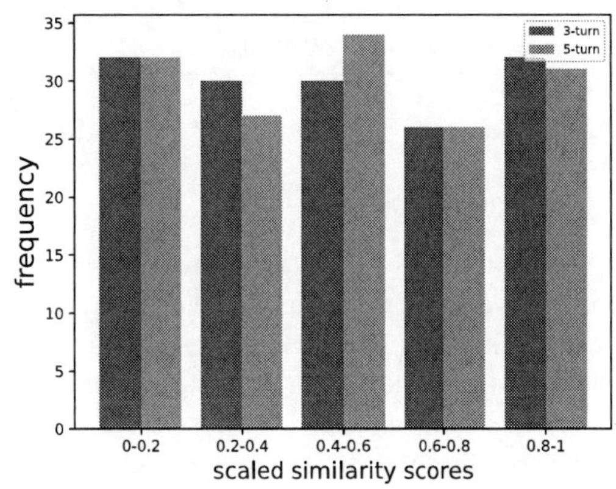

Figure 1: Distribution of the final similarity scores in the interval $[0, 1]$.

A common issue in the rating scales technique is the scale region bias, i.e., annotators have a bias towards a portion of the scale, for instance, towards the middle of the scale. The distribution of the scores in our dataset exhibits that the scale region bias issue was avoided using the BWS technique.

4.2 Split-Half Reliability

Another approach to measure the reliability of the annotations is to assess the reproducibility of the final scores. To measure this, we compute split-half reliability (SHR; Cronbach 1951). To compute SHR, we split the five annotations per tuple to two halves of odd vs. even number of annotations randomly. The first half (group A) includes two annotators, while the second half (group B) includes three annotators. Then, similarity scores of paired utterances are computed based on BWS responses in each half. Finally, the Spearman correlation between the scores obtained by these halves is calculated as an estimate of the annotation reliability.

Dialogue turns	Domain	RTTR	MTLD	Tokens	Lemma	Average turn length
3-turn	find_restaurant	3.04	46.22	377	21	10.47
	find_cinema	1.43	20.34	128	39	10.66
	find_hotel	1.53	15.90	77	35	8.55
	find_navigation	1.48	21.31	82	33	9.11
	find_touristAttraction	1.78	29.60	114	30	12.66
	find_tvProgram	1.81	30.06	165	28	11.00
5-turn	find_restaurant	3.01	36.91	739	47	11.36
	find_cinema	2.08	25.06	297	66	11.88
	find_hotel	1.53	17.56	106	76	7.06
	find_navigation	1.62	21.80	122	27	8.13
	find_touristAttraction	1.76	21.96	132	82	13.20
	find_tvProgram	2.50	32.03	247	51	12.35

Table 2: Descriptive statistics of GiCCS (RTTR = root type-token ratio; MTLD = measure of textual lexical diversity).

We repeat the SHR computation three times and report the average correlations over the repeated runs as shown in Table 3. A high Spearman correlation in both datasets shows that the obtained similarity scores are highly reliable. These results correspond to the percentage of strong agreement cases in Table 1. Slightly lower scores in CROWDSS are due to the fact that the utterances from CROWDSS are less varied in terms of domain diversity and an agreement on the best and worst questions is more challenging for the annotators.

Dataset	Dialogue turns	Spearman
BAS SmartKom	3-turn	0.975
	5-turn	0.970
CROWDSS	3-turn	0.953
	5-turn	0.946

Table 3: Average split-half reliability scores in each source dataset.

4.3 Score Reliability Assessment with Expert Annotation

We conduct an expert evaluation to ensure the final scores per paired utterances match expert expectations. We presented the final dataset to a trained linguist, excluding the final scores, and asked whether the last turn of the dialogue and the paired utterance showed either higher or lower than 0.5 similarity. After assessing the results of the expert evaluation, only two instances out of 300 items didn't match the evaluation (see Table 4). These are interesting cases showing what it means for two utterances in a conversational context to be similar or not: besides a higher or lower degree of lexical overlap, the degree of overlap in the intent behind the utterances - only partial in one case but full in the other - is what motivates the expert score.

5 Experiments

5.1 Evaluating Language Models on GiCCS

We conduct experiments on using GiCCS to evaluate autoencoding and autoregressive multilingual LMs, respectively. More specifically, we consider two types of evaluation tasks for these models. The first task, called **pairwise STS**, is about predicting the similarity score for pairs of utterances, which is a real-valued score between 0 and 1. This task is used for examining autoencoding LMs, such as BERT-based models (Devlin et al., 2019), on creating meaningful conversational representations for utterances. The latter, called **multiple-choice STS**, is about selecting the most similar utterance in a multiple-choice question task. In this task, we evaluate autoregressive models, such as GPT models (Radford et al., 2018, 2019), by considering the dialogue history.

We focus on unsupervised STS, i.e., we evaluate the performance of LMs without training or fine-

Last turn of the dialogue	Paired sentence	Calculated score	Expert evaluation
Die Innenstadt. *Downtown.*	Das Restaurant kann auf dem Land oder in der Stadt sein. *The restaurant may be in the country or downtown.*	0.65	< 0.5
Wie weit ist das? *How far is it?*	Wo befindet sich das Restaurant? *Where is the restaurant located?*	0.35	> 0.5

Table 4: Cases where the expert evaluation does not match the calculated score.

Model	Pearson r	Spearman ρ
STransformers		
distiluse-base-multilingual-cased-v2	0.859	0.855
paraphrase-xlm-r-multilingual-v1	0.849	0.845
paraphrase-multilingual-MiniLM-L12-v2	0.842	0.842
paraphrase-multilingual-mpnet-base-v2	0.830	0.829
distilbert-multilingual-nli-stsb-quora-ranking	0.794	0.814
Encoder		
deepset/gbert-large	0.666	0.680
deepset/gbert-large-sts	0.622	0.679

Table 5: Pearson and Spearman correlation results on all pairs in GiCCS.

tuning them on our data. All studied models are downloaded from the Hugging Face Model Hub.[8]

5.1.1 Pairwise STS Evaluation Task

We examine the following LMs: 1) Multilingual Sentence-Transformers (STransformers) (Reimers and Gurevych, 2019), which are fine-tuned on Natural Language Inference (NLI) and STS tasks, and 2) German encoder-based LMs (Chan et al., 2020). STransformers have been partly trained on spoken text from the English MultiNLI corpus (Williams et al., 2018) and extended to multilingual models using various datasets including conversational data (Reimers and Gurevych, 2020). We conducted experiments on five selected STransformer models, three of them have been trained on paraphrases from conversational data, such as quora and Stackexchange[9]. Selected models can be found in Table 5. German encoder models have been pre-trained partly on conversational corpora such as movie subtitles and one model was further fine-tuned on the German STS benchmark[10] (Cer et al., 2017).

In each model, the utterance embedding is computed from the mean aggregation of its token embeddings. Then, the similarity score is obtained by computing the cosine between the embeddings of utterances in each pair. Following Cer et al. (2017) and Reimers and Gurevych (2019), we measure the performance of the models using the Spearman rank r and Pearson ρ correlations of predicted and gold scores. Table 5 shows the performance results of different models on all dialogues.

As can be seen in Table 5, STransformers outperform pre-trained encoder models. In general, since sentence transformers are finetuned on NLI and STS containing spoken data and are trained to specifically encode sentences, they can better capture the semantic similarity of utterances on sentence level compared to pretrained models. Results of the two encoder models indicate that finetuning LMs on STS, which is a typical task for evaluating language understanding through semantic similarity, may not be always sufficient for improving the model performance on conversations.

5.1.2 Multiple-Choice STS Evaluation Task

To examine autoregressive models, we follow the prompting approach in GPT-3 (Brown et al., 2020) and construct a prompt template for the multiple-choice question task. For this purpose, each multi-turn dialogue (containing the target utterance) is followed by a question and five possible answers. The question is to *select the most similar utterance to the last turn in the dialogue*, and the possible answers are the five utterances paired with the target

[8]https://huggingface.co/models

[9]Please refer to the following link for more information on the training data: https://www.sbert.net

[10]https://github.com/t-systems-on-site-services-gmbh/german-STSbenchmark

Dialog:
Äußerung 1: Ich habe den Nachmittag in Heidelberg frei, möchte einen Bekannten treffen.
Informationen brauche ich über Sehenswürdigkeiten der Stadt. Kann ich bitte einen Plan haben?
Äußerung 2: Die Sehenswürdigkeiten von Heidelberg. Wenn du möchtest, kann ich auch einen Vorschlag machen.
Äußerung 3: Ich möchte gerne Museen, Kloster und Gebäude auch natürlich sehen. Aber zunächst Museen.

Frage: Wählen Sie die Äußerung, die der letzten Äußerung im Dialog am ähnlichsten ist.
Auswahl:
A. Ich habe vor, heute Reiten zu gehen.
B. Ich möchte gern zuerst Klöster sehen.
C. Ich würde gerne Kloster, Museen und Gebäude selbstverständlich auch sehen, aber zuerst Museen.
D. Ich würde gerne das Sportzentrum besuchen.
E. Ich würde gerne die Gebäude sehen, aber ich bin offen für andere Optionen, wie Klöster oder Museen.
Antwort:

Figure 2: A prompt example for the multiple-Choice STS evaluation task.

Model	**3-turn Dialogue**		**5-turn Dialogue**	
	w/ context	**w/o context**	**w/ context**	**w/o context**
mGPT (Shliazhko et al., 2022)	0.133 ± 0.063	0.166 ± 0.069	0.100 ± 0.055	0.067 ± 0.046

Table 6: Zero-shot accuracy results on multiple-choice STS task for 3- and 5-turn dialogues.

sentence in GiCCS, among which the most similar utterance is the correct answer. Figure 2 shows a prompt example in our task. The model takes a multi-turn dialogue followed by the question as the input context. Then, it computes the likelihood of generating each answer sentence, and the sentence with the highest likelihood is selected as the correct answer. Since the STS task is reformulated as a multiple-choice question with only one correct answer, we compute the accuracy of predicting correct answers for all questions. We report the results in the zero-shot setting.

Table 6 shows the evaluation results of a multilingual autoregressive model, mGPT (Shliazhko et al., 2022). We assume that the low performance is due to the fact that the model is mainly trained on written language data and is not focused on conversational training. Providing the dialogue history as the context for 5-turn dialogues resulted in a slightly higher performance compared to an evaluation without the dialogue history. This is not the case for 3-turn dialogues. We speculate that shorter dialogue history can be confusing for the model and increasing the history helps in capturing the context. Moreover, the task setup influences the model performance. Therefore, the prompt can be adapted to condition the LMs on the given task to obtain a better performance.

6 Conclusion

We introduce GiCCS, a first German conversational STS benchmark for evaluating language models on semantic similarity. Each item in the benchmark consists of a domain name, a multi-turn dialogue history, a target utterance paired with the last utterance in the dialogue, and a similarity score between the paired utterances. We leveraged two German dialogue resources, BAS SmartKom and CROWDSS, to collect our data as opposed to machine-translated data. Annotations were crowdsourced using the best-worst scaling technique, which shows a high inter-annotator agreement with an overall Krippendorff's α of 0.74 and reliable annotations with an average split-half reliability score of 0.973 for BAS SmartKom and 0.949 for CROWDSS. Moreover, the dialogue history was presented to the crowdworkers for better similarity judgements based on the conversational context. Final similarity scores cover a wide range of similarities between 0 and 1 introducing a challenge for language models to identify the nuances in semantics of different utterances. Moreover, as the last utterance of each dialogue is paired with five different utterances each with its similarity score, GiCCS can be used for evaluating ranking systems.

Results of evaluating LMs on the STS task using GiCCS shows that pre-training LMs on conversational data brings benefits for the LMs on meaningful representations of conversations.

Overall, GiCCS is a useful resource for evaluating conversational models on capturing similarity in conversational data. Moreover, due to the lack of enough resources for evaluating conversational models in non-English languages, we hope that the annotation procedure described in this work will foster an interest in creating more reliable and high-quality resources similar to GiCCS.

7 Ethical Considerations and Licenses

The crowd-workers on Amazon Mechanical Turk remain anonymous on AMT to adhere to the ethical standards in the community. They were voluntarily recruited, they provided their written informed consent to participate in the study and were allowed to opt out at any point in time .

To create GiCCS, two German dialogue resources, BAS SmartKom and CROWDSS, were used. In the BAS SmartKom resource, texts were partly derived from the BAS SmartKom corpora (corpus PID: 11022/1009-0000-0001-231F-6; Schiel and Türk 2006)[11] and we have received the permission of the copyright holders of the BAS SmartKom corpora to publish the derived text data in our benchmark. CROWDSS corpora is licensed under Attribution 4.0 International (CC BY 4.0). GiCCS is released upon publication of this paper and licensed under CC BY-NC-ND 3.0.[12]

Acknowledgements

This work is supported by the German Federal Ministry for Economic Affairs and Energy (BMWi) through the SPEAKER project (FKZ 01MK19011). This research project was started while Alessandra Zarcone was affiliated with the Fraunhofer IIS. We thank Florian Schiel and the copyright holders of the BAS SmartKom corpora for providing access and permission to publish the derived text data. We thank Sabrina Stehwien and the anonymous reviewers for their constructive feedback.

References

Eneko Agirre, Carmen Banea, Claire Cardie, Daniel Cer, Mona Diab, Aitor Gonzalez-Agirre, Weiwei Guo, Iñigo Lopez-Gazpio, Montse Maritxalar, Rada Mihalcea, German Rigau, Larraitz Uria, and Janyce Wiebe. 2015. SemEval-2015 task 2: Semantic textual similarity, English, Spanish and pilot on interpretability. In *Proceedings of the 9th International Workshop on Semantic Evaluation (SemEval 2015)*, pages 252–263, Denver, Colorado. Association for Computational Linguistics.

Eneko Agirre, Carmen Banea, Claire Cardie, Daniel Cer, Mona Diab, Aitor Gonzalez-Agirre, Weiwei Guo, Rada Mihalcea, German Rigau, and Janyce Wiebe. 2014. SemEval-2014 task 10: Multilingual semantic textual similarity. In *Proceedings of the 8th International Workshop on Semantic Evaluation (SemEval 2014)*, pages 81–91, Dublin, Ireland. Association for Computational Linguistics.

Eneko Agirre, Carmen Banea, Daniel Cer, Mona Diab, Aitor Gonzalez-Agirre, Rada Mihalcea, German Rigau, and Janyce Wiebe. 2016. SemEval-2016 task 1: Semantic textual similarity, monolingual and cross-lingual evaluation. In *Proceedings of the 10th International Workshop on Semantic Evaluation (SemEval-2016)*, pages 497–511, San Diego, California. Association for Computational Linguistics.

Eneko Agirre, Daniel Cer, Mona Diab, and Aitor Gonzalez-Agirre. 2012. SemEval-2012 task 6: A pilot on semantic textual similarity. In **SEM 2012: The First Joint Conference on Lexical and Computational Semantics – Volume 1: Proceedings of the main conference and the shared task, and Volume 2: Proceedings of the Sixth International Workshop on Semantic Evaluation (SemEval 2012)*, pages 385–393, Montréal, Canada. Association for Computational Linguistics.

Eneko Agirre, Daniel Cer, Mona Diab, Aitor Gonzalez-Agirre, and Weiwei Guo. 2013. *SEM 2013 shared task: Semantic textual similarity. In *Second Joint Conference on Lexical and Computational Semantics (*SEM), Volume 1: Proceedings of the Main Conference and the Shared Task: Semantic Textual Similarity*, pages 32–43, Atlanta, Georgia, USA. Association for Computational Linguistics.

Rami Al-Rfou, Marc Pickett, Javier Snaider, Yun-Hsuan Sung, Brian Strope, and Ray Kurzweil. 2016. Conversational contextual cues: The case of personalization and history for response ranking. *CoRR*, abs/1606.00372.

Ron Artstein and Massimo Poesio. 2008. Survey article: Inter-coder agreement for computational linguistics. *Computational Linguistics*, 34(4):555–596.

Shima Asaadi, Saif Mohammad, and Svetlana Kiritchenko. 2019. Big BiRD: A large, fine-grained, bigram relatedness dataset for examining semantic composition. In *Proceedings of the 2019 Conference of the North American Chapter of the Association for Computational Linguistics: Human Language Technologies, Volume 1 (Long and Short Papers)*, pages 505–516, Minneapolis, Minnesota. Association for Computational Linguistics.

[11] http://hdl.handle.net/11022/1009-0000-0001-231F-6

[12] https://doi.org/10.5281/zenodo.7266256

Tom Brown, Benjamin Mann, Nick Ryder, Melanie Subbiah, Jared D Kaplan, Prafulla Dhariwal, Arvind Neelakantan, Pranav Shyam, Girish Sastry, Amanda Askell, Sandhini Agarwal, Ariel Herbert-Voss, Gretchen Krueger, Tom Henighan, Rewon Child, Aditya Ramesh, Daniel Ziegler, Jeffrey Wu, Clemens Winter, Chris Hesse, Mark Chen, Eric Sigler, Mateusz Litwin, Scott Gray, Benjamin Chess, Jack Clark, Christopher Berner, Sam McCandlish, Alec Radford, Ilya Sutskever, and Dario Amodei. 2020. Language models are few-shot learners. In *Advances in Neural Information Processing Systems*, volume 33, pages 1877–1901. Curran Associates, Inc.

Paweł Budzianowski, Tsung-Hsien Wen, Bo-Hsiang Tseng, Iñigo Casanueva, Stefan Ultes, Osman Ramadan, and Milica Gašić. 2018. MultiWOZ - a large-scale multi-domain Wizard-of-Oz dataset for task-oriented dialogue modelling. In *Proceedings of the 2018 Conference on Empirical Methods in Natural Language Processing*, pages 5016–5026, Brussels, Belgium. Association for Computational Linguistics.

Iñigo Casanueva, Tadas Temčinas, Daniela Gerz, Matthew Henderson, and Ivan Vulić. 2020. Efficient intent detection with dual sentence encoders. In *Proceedings of the 2nd Workshop on Natural Language Processing for Conversational AI*, pages 38–45, Online. Association for Computational Linguistics.

Daniel Cer, Mona Diab, Eneko Agirre, Iñigo Lopez-Gazpio, and Lucia Specia. 2017. SemEval-2017 task 1: Semantic textual similarity multilingual and crosslingual focused evaluation. In *Proceedings of the 11th International Workshop on Semantic Evaluation (SemEval-2017)*, pages 1–14, Vancouver, Canada. Association for Computational Linguistics.

Branden Chan, Stefan Schweter, and Timo Möller. 2020. German's next language model. In *Proceedings of the 28th International Conference on Computational Linguistics*, pages 6788–6796, Barcelona, Spain (Online). International Committee on Computational Linguistics.

Aakanksha Chowdhery, Sharan Narang, Jacob Devlin, Maarten Bosma, Gaurav Mishra, Adam Roberts, Paul Barham, Hyung Won Chung, Charles Sutton, Sebastian Gehrmann, Parker Schuh, Kensen Shi, Sasha Tsvyashchenko, Joshua Maynez, Abhishek Rao, Parker Barnes, Yi Tay, Noam Shazeer, Vinodkumar Prabhakaran, Emily Reif, Nan Du, Ben Hutchinson, Reiner Pope, James Bradbury, Jacob Austin, Michael Isard, Guy Gur-Ari, Pengcheng Yin, Toju Duke, Anselm Levskaya, Sanjay Ghemawat, Sunipa Dev, Henryk Michalewski, Xavier Garcia, Vedant Misra, Kevin Robinson, Liam Fedus, Denny Zhou, Daphne Ippolito, David Luan, Hyeontaek Lim, Barret Zoph, Alexander Spiridonov, Ryan Sepassi, David Dohan, Shivani Agrawal, Mark Omernick, Andrew M. Dai, Thanumalayan Sankaranarayana Pillai, Marie Pellat, Aitor Lewkowycz, Erica Moreira, Rewon Child, Oleksandr Polozov, Katherine Lee, Zongwei Zhou, Xuezhi Wang, Brennan Saeta, Mark Diaz, Orhan Firat, Michele Catasta, Jason Wei, Kathy Meier-Hellstern, Douglas Eck, Jeff Dean, Slav Petrov, and Noah Fiedel. 2022. Palm: Scaling language modeling with pathways.

Steven H. Cohen. 2003. Maximum difference scaling: Improved measures of importance and preference for segmentation.

Lee J. Cronbach. 1951. Coefficient alpha and the internal structure of tests. *Psychometrika*, 16:297–334.

Jacob Devlin, Ming-Wei Chang, Kenton Lee, and Kristina Toutanova. 2019. BERT: Pre-training of deep bidirectional transformers for language understanding. In *Proceedings of the 2019 Conference of the North American Chapter of the Association for Computational Linguistics: Human Language Technologies, Volume 1 (Long and Short Papers)*, pages 4171–4186, Minneapolis, Minnesota. Association for Computational Linguistics.

Ondřej Dušek, Jekaterina Novikova, and Verena Rieser. 2020. Evaluating the state-of-the-art of end-to-end natural language generation: The e2e nlg challenge. *Computer Speech & Language*, 59:123–156.

Yannick Frommherz and Alessandra Zarcone. 2021. Crowdsourcing ecologically-valid dialogue data for german. *Frontiers in Computer Science*, 3.

Matthew Henderson, Paweł Budzianowski, Iñigo Casanueva, Sam Coope, Daniela Gerz, Girish Kumar, Nikola Mrkšić, Georgios Spithourakis, Pei-Hao Su, Ivan Vulić, and Tsung-Hsien Wen. 2019a. A repository of conversational datasets. In *Proceedings of the First Workshop on NLP for Conversational AI*, pages 1–10, Florence, Italy. Association for Computational Linguistics.

Matthew Henderson, Iñigo Casanueva, Nikola Mrkšić, Pei-Hao Su, Tsung-Hsien Wen, and Ivan Vulić. 2020. ConveRT: Efficient and accurate conversational representations from transformers. In *Findings of the Association for Computational Linguistics: EMNLP 2020*, pages 2161–2174, Online. Association for Computational Linguistics.

Matthew Henderson and Ivan Vulić. 2021. ConVEx: Data-efficient and few-shot slot labeling. In *Proceedings of the 2021 Conference of the North American Chapter of the Association for Computational Linguistics: Human Language Technologies*, pages 3375–3389, Online. Association for Computational Linguistics.

Matthew Henderson, Ivan Vulić, Daniela Gerz, Iñigo Casanueva, Paweł Budzianowski, Sam Coope, Georgios Spithourakis, Tsung-Hsien Wen, Nikola Mrkšić, and Pei-Hao Su. 2019b. Training neural response selection for task-oriented dialogue systems. In *Proceedings of the 57th Annual Meeting of the Association for Computational Linguistics*, pages 5392–5404, Florence, Italy. Association for Computational Linguistics.

Matthew Honnibal, Ines Montani, Sofie Van Landeghem, and Adriane Boyd. 2020. spaCy: Industrial-strength Natural Language Processing in Python.

Svetlana Kiritchenko and Saif Mohammad. 2017. Best-worst scaling more reliable than rating scales: A case study on sentiment intensity annotation. In *Proceedings of the 55th Annual Meeting of the Association for Computational Linguistics (Volume 2: Short Papers)*, pages 465–470, Vancouver, Canada. Association for Computational Linguistics.

Svetlana Kiritchenko and Saif M. Mohammad. 2016. Capturing reliable fine-grained sentiment associations by crowdsourcing and best–worst scaling. In *Proceedings of the 2016 Conference of the North American Chapter of the Association for Computational Linguistics: Human Language Technologies*, pages 811–817, San Diego, California. Association for Computational Linguistics.

Jordan J Louviere, Terry N Flynn, and Anthony Alfred John Marley. 2015. *Best-worst scaling: Theory, methods and applications*. Cambridge University Press.

Philip M McCarthy and Scott Jarvis. 2010. Mtld, vocd-d, and hd-d: A validation study of sophisticated approaches to lexical diversity assessment. *Behavior research methods*, 42(2):381–392.

Jekaterina Novikova, Oliver Lemon, and Verena Rieser. 2016. Crowd-sourcing nlg data: Pictures elicit better data. In *Proceedings of the 9th International Natural Language Generation conference*, pages 265–273.

Bryan K. Orme. 2009. Maxdiff analysis : Simple counting , individual-level logit , and hb.

Alec Radford, Karthik Narasimhan, Tim Salimans, Ilya Sutskever, et al. 2018. Improving language understanding by generative pre-training. OpenAI.

Alec Radford, Jeffrey Wu, Rewon Child, David Luan, Dario Amodei, Ilya Sutskever, et al. 2019. Language models are unsupervised multitask learners. *OpenAI blog*, 1(8):9.

Nils Reimers and Iryna Gurevych. 2019. Sentence-BERT: Sentence embeddings using Siamese BERT-networks. In *Proceedings of the 2019 Conference on Empirical Methods in Natural Language Processing and the 9th International Joint Conference on Natural Language Processing (EMNLP-IJCNLP)*, pages 3982–3992, Hong Kong, China. Association for Computational Linguistics.

Nils Reimers and Iryna Gurevych. 2020. Making monolingual sentence embeddings multilingual using knowledge distillation. In *Proceedings of the 2020 Conference on Empirical Methods in Natural Language Processing (EMNLP)*, pages 4512–4525, Online. Association for Computational Linguistics.

Florian Schiel, Silke Steininger, and Ulrich Türk. 2002. The SmartKom multimodal corpus at BAS. In *Proceedings of the Third International Conference on Language Resources and Evaluation (LREC'02)*, Las Palmas, Canary Islands - Spain. European Language Resources Association (ELRA).

Florian Schiel and Ulli Türk. 2006. *Wizard-of-Oz Recordings*, pages 541–570. Springer Berlin Heidelberg, Berlin, Heidelberg.

Lucas Shen. 2022. LexicalRichness: A small module to compute textual lexical richness.

Oleh Shliazhko, Alena Fenogenova, Maria Tikhonova, Vladislav Mikhailov, Anastasia Kozlova, and Tatiana Shavrina. 2022. mgpt: Few-shot learners go multilingual.

Ivan Vulic, Pei-Hao Su, Sam Coope, Daniela Gerz, Pawel Budzianowski, Iñigo Casanueva, Nikola Mrksic, and Tsung-Hsien Wen. 2021. Convfit: Conversational fine-tuning of pretrained language models. *CoRR*, abs/2109.10126.

Alex Wang, Amanpreet Singh, Julian Michael, Felix Hill, Omer Levy, and Samuel Bowman. 2018. GLUE: A multi-task benchmark and analysis platform for natural language understanding. In *Proceedings of the 2018 EMNLP Workshop BlackboxNLP: Analyzing and Interpreting Neural Networks for NLP*, pages 353–355, Brussels, Belgium. Association for Computational Linguistics.

Hao Wang, Zhengdong Lu, Hang Li, and Enhong Chen. 2013. A dataset for research on short-text conversations. In *Proceedings of the 2013 Conference on Empirical Methods in Natural Language Processing*, pages 935–945, Seattle, Washington, USA. Association for Computational Linguistics.

Adina Williams, Nikita Nangia, and Samuel Bowman. 2018. A broad-coverage challenge corpus for sentence understanding through inference. In *Proceedings of the 2018 Conference of the North American Chapter of the Association for Computational Linguistics: Human Language Technologies, Volume 1 (Long Papers)*, pages 1112–1122, New Orleans, Louisiana. Association for Computational Linguistics.

Yinfei Yang, Steve Yuan, Daniel Cer, Sheng-yi Kong, Noah Constant, Petr Pilar, Heming Ge, Yun-Hsuan Sung, Brian Strope, and Ray Kurzweil. 2018. Learning semantic textual similarity from conversations. In *Proceedings of The Third Workshop on Representation Learning for NLP*, pages 164–174, Melbourne, Australia. Association for Computational Linguistics.

A Appendix

A.1 Annotation Instruction

By accepting the task, the workers are directed to an interface where they are presented with a brief as well as a detailed instruction in German on how to accomplish the task. The detailed instruction contains a description of what the workers will observe in the actual HITS along with one example. In the example, a dialogue history followed by two questions are posed similar to what appears in the actual experiment. The first question expects the participants to choose an utterance from three given options that is most similar to the last utterance of the dialogue. Then, they are asked to choose an utterance that is least similar to the last utterance of the dialogue. In the instruction section, the right answers are already selected. A sample of a dialogue and the two questions are presented in Figure 3.

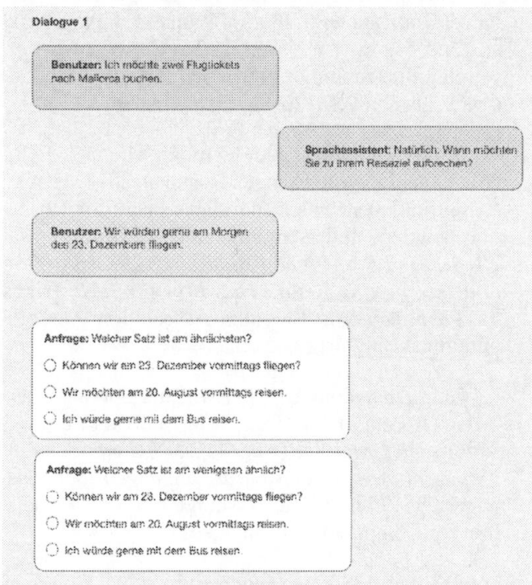

Figure 3: A sample of the annotation task presented on Amazon Mechanical Turk.

CONTROL PREFIXES for Parameter-Efficient Text Generation

Jordan Clive[1], **Kris Cao**[2], **Marek Rei**[1,3]
[1]Department of Computing, Imperial College London, United Kingdom
[2]DeepMind, London, United Kingdom
[3]ALTA Institute, University of Cambridge, United Kingdom
jordan.clive19@imperial.ac.uk, kriscao@deepmind.com, marek.rei@imperial.ac.uk

Abstract

Prefix-tuning is a parameter-efficient and powerful technique for adapting a pre-trained language model to a downstream application. However, it uses the same dataset-level tuned set of parameters for all examples in the dataset. We extend the framework with a dynamic method, CONTROL PREFIXES, which allows for the effective inclusion of input-dependent information, thereby demonstrating how prefix-tuning can be used for controlled text generation tasks. The method incorporates attribute-level learnable representations into different layers of a pre-trained Transformer, enabling the generated text to be guided in a particular direction. We provide a systematic evaluation of the technique and apply it to five datasets from the GEM benchmark for natural language generation (NLG). Using only 0.1–2% additional trainable parameters, we show CONTROL PREFIXES can even outperform full fine-tuning methods, and present state-of-the-art results on several data-to-text datasets, including WebNLG. We also examine the common case where input-dependent information is unavailable at test time and show CONTROL PREFIXES can excel in this setting also.

1 Introduction

Approaches in text generation have been dominated by adapting pre-trained language models (PLM) to various downstream tasks. As the scale of PLMs continue to climb, the cost of updating *all* the PLM parameters per task, and resultant overhead of entirely new parameter-sets per task becomes impractical. Furthermore, full fine-tuning has been shown to result in catastrophic forgetting where knowledge learnt from the pre-training task is lost and natural language understanding overwritten (Peters et al., 2019).

Recent work has demonstrated that it is possible to train these models by optimizing a negligible fraction (0.01-2%) of additional parameters while leaving the base PLM parameters unchanged (Houlsby et al., 2019; Lester et al., 2021). Such parameter-efficient transfer learning (PETL) can achieve performance comparable to fine-tuning. Prefix-tuning (Li and Liang, 2021), which trains a prefix of additional key-value pairs at each layer, and adapters (Rebuffi et al., 2017) are the two current most popular PETL methods. Another alternative is in-context learning (ICL) (Brown et al., 2020; Schick and Schütze, 2020), which supplies hand-written prompts and requires no gradient-based training. ICL has however shown to result in poor performance as the number of fine-tuning examples increases beyond a handful (Lester et al., 2021). We therefore believe that PETL methods provide a more promising direction for study.

A weakness of most PETL methods is that the same additional parameters are used for all examples within a single task. As yet, there has been little research exploring PETL methods that incorporate input-dependent parameters (Liu et al., 2021a) for finer-grained control. Our work closes this gap by introducing a novel framework which extends prefix-tuning and demonstrates the utility of controlling parameter-efficient learning for data-to-text tasks. The method uses multiple modular *control prefixes*, trained simultaneously, which can change alongside the input according to the guidance signal. These dynamic prefixes operate together with the static prefix parameters and allow for finer-grained control over the frozen PLM. The chosen attributes can provide additional context about the input, for example, the sub-domain of a data-to-text triple, or specify some aspect of the desired output, such as the target length for text simplification.

Controlled text generation aims to guide generation towards the desired attributes, by incorporating various types of guidance (e.g. highlighted phrases (Grangier and Auli, 2018)). Previous work has focused on directly updating all the existing model's

Proceedings of the 2nd Workshop on Natural Language Generation, Evaluation, and Metrics (GEM), pages 363 - 382
December 7, 2022 ©2022 Association for Computational Linguistics

parameters (Keskar et al., 2019) or using a discriminator to guide generation (Dathathri et al., 2020). Other methods aim to generate text with specific target qualities, independent of overall task performance (Yu et al., 2021). In contrast, our proposed method is designed for maximizing downstream task performance through controlled text generation, while also doing it in a way that is parameter-efficient and compatible with PETL.

The resulting parameter-efficient architecture outperforms previous approaches, many of them based on full fine-tuning, when evaluated on the WebNLG (Gardent et al., 2017), WebNLG+ 2020 (Castro Ferreira et al., 2020), DART (Radev et al., 2020) and E2E Clean (Dušek et al., 2019) data-to-text datasets using the official evaluation scripts. We also show that although these modular prefixes are formed from shared reparameterizations and operate at every layer, they provide a level of interpretability, as similar control prefix representations are learned by the model for semantically similar attribute labels. This fact allows us to employ a zero-shot technique to deal with the more common case in controlled generation, where attribute-level information is absent at inference time. In addition, we show the superiority of the architecture to an alternative architecture of introducing identical guidance signal into prefix-tuning. In total, we evaluate CONTROL PREFIXES on five popular datasets from the GEM benchmark (Gehrmann et al., 2021, 2022) for natural language generation and demonstrate the technique is easily extendable to new tasks.[1]

2 CONTROL PREFIXES

2.1 Background

To evaluate our architecture, we focus on the data-to-text generation task, where structured data (such as database fields or tuples from a knowledge graph) is transformed into natural language. The objective is to model the conditional probability $P(Y|X)$ with X representing the structured input and Y representing the tokenized output sequence. As is done for current state-of-the-art (SOTA) systems (Ribeiro et al., 2020; Radev et al., 2020), we linearize the structured table or graph input into a tokenized sequence. For example, with the WebNLG dataset, X is the linearized graph and Y is a lexicalization of this graph—descriptive text expressing all and only the information in the input. However, the data also contains additional information we can exploit: WebNLG is clustered semantically into 15 different subdomains, and we can use the subdomain of each example as an explicit input-dependent attribute for our model.

In this work, we experiment with T5-large (Raffel et al., 2020) and $\text{BART}_{\text{LARGE}}$ (Lewis et al., 2020) as the underlying pre-trained LMs with parameters ϕ. As we consider *fixed LM* methods, these parameters ϕ are always kept frozen. Both are Transformer encoder-decoder where decoding proceeds auto-regressively. They have been pre-trained with the denoising objective, so they are good candidates for the data-to-text task. They have also been employed by top performers in public challenges such as the WebNLG+ 2020 Challenge (Castro Ferreira et al., 2020).

2.2 Intuition

Using a frozen PLM that captures broad natural language understanding provides the model with a parameter-efficient starting point that already has capacity for linguistic fluency. Combining these frozen parameters with a trainable task representation for data-to-text allows the model to learn how to use the LM to lexicalize graphs. Moreover, introducing attribute-level parameters, such as the subdomain of the data-to-text input, allows us to guide the generation further into a required direction relevant to all inputs associated with that domain.

The general task-specific parameters can themselves adapt to the modular *control prefixes*, which change according to the guidance signal for each input X. CONTROL PREFIXES can therefore leverage input-level information while being a parameter-efficient tuning method.[2] For this work, we only consider discrete labels as attributes for the guidance signal.

2.3 Description

A prefix (Li and Liang, 2021) is a set of additional learned key-value pairs at every layer. Our model uses a general task prefix P_θ ("task-specific parameters") and also trains a set of control prefixes C_θ that change depending on the input ("attribute-level parameters"). This requires attribute-level information or guidance G, to indicate which control prefixes to be used while processing a given

[1]We open-source CONTROL PREFIXES at https://github.com/jordiclive/ControlPrefixes.

[2]We use the term parameter-efficient to denote methods that update <2% of a base LM's parameters.

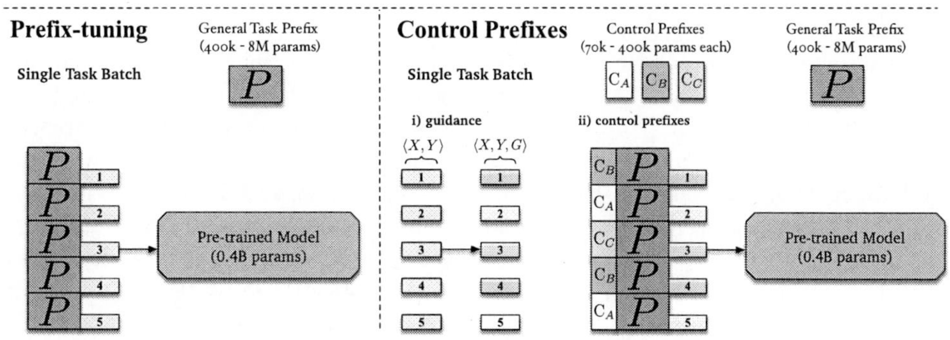

Figure 1: Prefix-tuning and CONTROL PREFIXES in the single-task setup for a PLM such as $\text{BART}_{\text{LARGE}}$. The same single-task batch (examples 1,2,3,4 and 5) is considered for both setups. Left: Prefix-tuning has one general prefix P for all examples. Right: CONTROL PREFIXES utilizes additional attribute information at the input-level, G, in **i)**. This conditional information is used in **ii)** to dictate which control prefix (C_A, C_B, C_C) to use for a particular example in a batch. This takes advantage of prefix-tuning's capacity to include different prefixes in one forward pass.

input X.[3] Let us consider the parallel corpus $\mathcal{Z} = \{\langle X^j, Y^j, G^j\rangle\}_{j=1,..,N}$, where G^j indicates all the conditional attribute-level information for the sample j. The goal is to optimize through gradient descent the final inference parameters, θ, whilst the underlying ϕ parameters of the pre-trained LM remain frozen:

$$\theta^* = \arg\max_{\theta} \sum_{j=1}^{N} \log\, p\left(Y^j \mid X^j, G^j; P_\theta, C_\theta, \phi\right). \tag{1}$$

Encoder-decoder We use d to represent the hidden state dimension and L the number of layers. We use (E, Dc, Ds) to denote the three classes of attention present in each layer: self-attention in the encoder (E), decoder cross-attention (Dc) and decoder self-attention (Ds). For an attention computation in the l-th layer, the query, key and value matrices are denoted $Q_l \in \mathbb{R}^{N\times d}$, and K_l, $V_l \in \mathbb{R}^{M\times d}$, where N is the number of tokens in the series relating to queries, and M is the number of tokens in the series relating to keys and values.

General Prefix For each attention class (E, Dc, Ds), a distinct prefix of key-value pairs is learnt, $P = \{P_1, \ldots, P_L\}$, where $P_l \in \mathbb{R}^{\rho\times 2d}$ $\forall l \in \{1, \ldots, L\}$. $P \in \mathbb{R}^{\rho\times 2dL}$ and ρ is the prompt length, i.e. the number of additional key-value pairs in each attention computation. In prefix-tuning[4], for an attention computation in the l-th layer, K_l and V_l are augmented to become

$$K'_l = [P_{l,K}; K_l]\ , V'_l = [P_{l,V}; V_l] \tag{2}$$

where $K'_l, V'_l \in \mathbb{R}^{(\rho+M)\times d}$. The overall general prefix, parameterized by θ, is $P_\theta = \{P^E, P^{Dc}, P^{Dm}\}$, where $P_\theta \in \mathbb{R}^{\rho\times 6dL}$.

Control Prefixes In addition to the general prefixes, we introduce control prefixes that change depending on the input attribute value. Let us consider one attribute, for example the domain of the input table (e.g. sports team, athlete etc.) with R possible values: $C_\theta = \{C_{\theta,1}, \ldots, C_{\theta,R}\}$, where $C_{\theta,r} \in \mathbb{R}^{\rho_c\times 6dL}$, $\forall r \in \{1 \ldots . R\}$. $C_{\theta,r}$ represents the control prefix learnt for the r-th attribute label and the parameter ρ_c denotes the control prompt length for this particular attribute.[5] Let $\mathcal{A}$ be a function which returns the corresponding control prefix for the attribute label indicated by G. Using CONTROL PREFIXES, the attention keys K_l and values V_l are augmented to become:

$$\begin{aligned} K''_l &= [\mathcal{A}(G)_{l,K}; P_{l,K}; K_l]\,, \\ V''_l &= [\mathcal{A}(G)_{l,V}; P_{l,V}; V_l] \end{aligned} \tag{3}$$

where $K''_l, V''_l \in \mathbb{R}^{(\rho_c+\rho+M)\times d}$.

Shared Re-parameterization Li and Liang (2021) found that prefix optimization is stabilized by increasing the number of trainable parameters. This is achieved by introducing a feed-forward network to re-parameterize the prefix. Rather than one network, we use three distinct two-layered large

[3] We discuss cases where G is not present in §5.2.

[4] There has been confusion in recent work concerning different forms of prefix-tuning (Li and Liang, 2021). For details and observations of the benefits conferred by key-value pair prefix-tuning, see Appendix C.

[5] The method can be generalized to multiple attributes, each with control prefixes of different length.

feed-forward neural networks for each attention class, applied row-wise. For each attention class (E, Dc, Ds), P = MLP($\tilde{P}$) where $\tilde{P} \in \mathbb{R}^{\rho \times d}$ is smaller than the matrix $P \in \mathbb{R}^{\rho \times 2dL}$, and each MLP has an intermediate dimension k which we set to 800. Once training is complete, the output of the MLP can be saved as the new prefix and the MLP parameters themselves can be discarded.

As described for the general prefix, P_θ, each control prefix, $C_{\theta,r}$, comprises three constituents for each attention class: $C_{\theta,r} = \{C_r^E, C_r^{Dc}, C_r^{Ds}\}$. The re-parameterization of $C_{\theta,r}$ occurs in the same manner as P_θ, sharing the same MLP^E, MLP^{Dc} and MLP^{Ds}. We found that using shared re-parameterization matrices provided performance improvements and led to more stable learning, while also significantly reducing the total number of parameters.

3 Experimental Setup

3.1 Datasets, Guidance and Metrics

Following Li and Liang (2021), we evaluate on the data-to-text datasets DART (Radev et al., 2020) and WebNLG (Gardent et al., 2017). In addition, we report results on E2E Clean (Dušek et al., 2019)[6], a dataset focused on the restaurant domain. The structured knowledge input in these datasets is in the form of a graph or table and can be linearized for sequence-to-sequence learning.

WebNLG contains graphs from DBPedia (Auer et al., 2007) and the dataset is clustered semantically into different categories. The test set is divided into two partitions: "Seen", which contains 10 DBpedia categories present in the training set, and "Unseen", which covers 5 categories never seen during training.[7] These categories, such as *Airport* or *Food* are used as a guidance attributes for CONTROL PREFIXES (indicated by A_1 in Table 1); our approach for the unseen categories is discussed in §5.2. The intuition of the category providing useful information is supported by studies showing a clear disparity in the performance of different model types between different categories (Moryossef et al., 2019; Castro Ferreira et al., 2020). By providing the category explicitly, the model is able to adjust its generation depending on the required target domain.

[6]The same version as in GEM (Gehrmann et al., 2021).

[7]All the training category labels are visible in Appendix D, where we visualize control prefixes, corresponding to each training category.

DART is an open-domain, multi-source corpus, with six sources: internal and external human annotation of both Wikipedia tables and WikiSQL, as well as the two existing datasets WebNLG and E2E Clean. Radev et al. (2020) showed fine-tuning T5-large on the WebNLG dataset with only the human annotated portion of DART achieves SOTA performance, whilst using the whole DART dataset is not as effective. Nevertheless, this inspired the idea of using the six DART sub-dataset sources as a controllable attribute, represented by A_2 in Table 1. This strategy was inspired by previous work which incorporates auxiliary scaffold tasks in multitask learning to improve span-labeling and text classification (Swayamdipta et al., 2018; Cohan et al., 2019; Cachola et al., 2020). For E2E Clean, which is itself a part of DART, our CONTROL PREFIXES model is trained on the additional components of the DART dataset with the explicit data source labels as guidance to act as scaffold framework.

CONTROL PREFIXES incorporates the attribute knowledge into a parameter-efficient architecture, giving it greater control over the generation process and allowing us to guide the output in a required direction. This provides a way of incorporating information about the data that would otherwise be left unused (such as the source domain of the input), or directing the generated output based on user preferences (for example by specifying the length of a simplified text).

We ensured that the attribute values used at inference time are permitted by all the shared task organizers corresponding to each dataset. In section §5.2 we also investigate settings where the attribute values are previously unseen or unavailable during inference. Also, note that additional training data is permitted by the organizers of the E2E Clean and WebNLG datasets. For example, the SOTA for WebNLG is a T5-large model fine-tuned on WebNLG and the human annotated portion of DART (Radev et al., 2020).

3.2 Metrics and Evaluation using GEM

We use the official evaluation scripts and report BLEU (Papineni et al., 2002), METEOR (Lavie and Agarwal, 2007), and TER (Snover et al., 2006) metrics[8]. In support of thorough NLG evaluation, we also report lexical similarity and diversity char-

[8]Additional evaluation script metrics, including machine-learned are found in Appendix A

acterization metrics, including machine-learned metrics, from the GEM (Gehrmann et al., 2021) evaluation suite in Appendix Tables 8,9.

Although we use data-to-text and text simplification datasets to demonstrate the technique is effective, it can be applied to any generation task cast as a sequence-to-sequence problem which similarly benefit form parameter-efficient control.

3.3 Training Details

We implement prefix-tuning and CONTROL PREFIXES for T5-large rather than GPT-2, as T5-large provides a stronger baseline and enables comparison with SOTA systems.[9] For the data-to-text datasets, we follow Ribeiro et al. (2020) and linearize the triples that form the input graph, prepending the special tokens <H>, <R>, and <T> before the subject, predicate, and object of an individual triple. The embeddings relating to these special tokens are the only embeddings we train, as our work is focused on fixed LM methods. We also prepend "translate Graph to English: " to every input (Raffel et al., 2020). We provide full training and hyperparameter details in Appendix E.

4 Data-to-Text Results

We indicate the guidance signal(s) used by each CONTROL PREFIXES model with A_1 for the WebNLG subdomain category and A_2 for the DART sub-dataset source.

Results in Table 1 show that for DART, both CONTROL PREFIXES (A_2) and prefix-tuning attain higher performance than the current SOTA, which is T5-large fined-tuned (Radev et al., 2020), by 1.29 and 0.54 BLEU points respectively. Note the results in the main body of the GEM paper (Gehrmann et al., 2021) are reported on the validation set rather than the test set as is done here.

The SOTA for WebNLG is a T5-large model fine-tuned on WebNLG and the human annotated portion of DART (Radev et al., 2020). Compared to this model, CONTROL PREFIXES achieves a 0.83 higher BLEU overall, and 1.33 on the Seen categories. Notably, CONTROL PREFIXES (A_1) outperforms CONTROL PREFIXES (A_1,A_2) on the Seen component of the dataset, but does not generalize as well to the unseen categories, indicating the benefit of using both controllable attributes. The prefix-tuning model with additional DART data, like the SOTA, is trained on only the human annotated portion and yields a minor performance increase of 0.05 BLEU compared to prefix-tuning solely trained on WebNLG. We believe this indicates that for fine-tuning, training on a complementary type of additional data allows the PLM to maintain more NLU by not over-fitting a narrow distribution, leading to better LM generalization. In contrast, for prefix-tuning, much of this gain has already been realized by retaining the original frozen parameters.

The SOTA (Harkous et al., 2020) for E2E Clean consists of a fine-tuned GPT-2 with a semantic fidelity classifier trained on additional generated data. CONTROL PREFIXES (A_2), which can leverage the heterogeneous DART datasets, outperforms this model in terms of the BLEU score. We also report results on the less popular WebNLG+ 2020 (Castro Ferreira et al., 2020) dataset (GEM), the second official WebNLG competition, in Appendix D.

5 Zero-shot Learning

5.1 Visualizing Control Prefixes

We experiment with visualizing the optimized control prefixes, in order to investigate what patterns they have learned. For this, we train a model for the task of text simplification, using the relative text compression rate as an attribute for the control prefix (additional details of this experiment in §7). Fig. 2 displays t-SNE (Maaten and Hinton, 2008) visualizations of the learned control prefix parameters in the decoder self-attention. A clear monotonic pattern emerges, showing that control prefixes for similar compression rate values are close to each other in the representation space. This property can be useful for investigating different attributes or inferring representations for unseen attribute values. In Appendix F we present additional graphs for control prefixes in the encoder and the cross-attention of the model.

5.2 Unseen WebNLG Categories

The control prefix parameters are optimized during training for each attribute value. However, in some settings we may need to handle attribute values that were not present in the training data and therefore have no matching control prefixes available. For example, the category attributes in the WebNLG *Unseen* subset are all novel and were not repre-

[9] $BART_{LARGE}$ exhibits inferior performance to T5-large on data-to-text; for example, 9.7 BLEU points lower on WebNLG Unseen (Ribeiro et al., 2020).

	$\phi\%$	DART			$\phi\%$	WebNLG			$\phi\%$	E2E Clean	
		BLEU	METEOR	TER ↓		S	U	A		BLEU	METEOR
T5-large fine-tuned	100	50.66	40	43	100	64.89	54.01	59.95	100	41.83	38.1
SOTA	100	50.66	40	43	100	65.82	56.01	61.44	100	43.6	39
Prefix-tuning	1.0	51.20	40.62	43.13	1.0	66.95	55.39	61.73	1.0	43.66	39.0
CONTROL PREFIXES (A_1)	-	-	-	-	1.4	**67.32**	55.38	61.94	-	-	-
+Data: DART											
Prefix-tuning	1.0	51.20	40.62	43.13	1.0	67.05	55.37	61.78	1.0	43.04	38.7
CONTROL PREFIXES (A_2)	1.1	**51.95**	**41.07**	**42.75**	1.0	66.99	55.56	61.83	1.0	**44.15**	**39.2**
CONTROL PREFIXES (A_1,A_2)	-	-	-	-	1.4	67.15	**56.41**	**62.27**	-	-	-

Table 1: Data-to-text test set results reported on the respective official evaluation scripts. $\phi\%$ denotes the trainable parameters as a % of the fixed-LM parameters required at inference time. T5-large fine-tuned results for WebNLG are from Ribeiro et al. (2020) and for DART are from Radev et al. (2020). Several of the baseline results were only reported to the significant figures shown. A_1 signifies models trained with control prefixes for the *WebNLG category* attribute, and A_2 with control prefixes for the DART *sub-dataset source* attribute. For WebNLG, S, U and A refer to BLEU scores for the *Seen*, *Unseen* and *All* portions of the dataset. The DART results are reported on the official evaluation script for v1.1.1, the same version as the official leaderboard. A CONTROL PREFIXES model attains state-of-the-art results for each dataset.

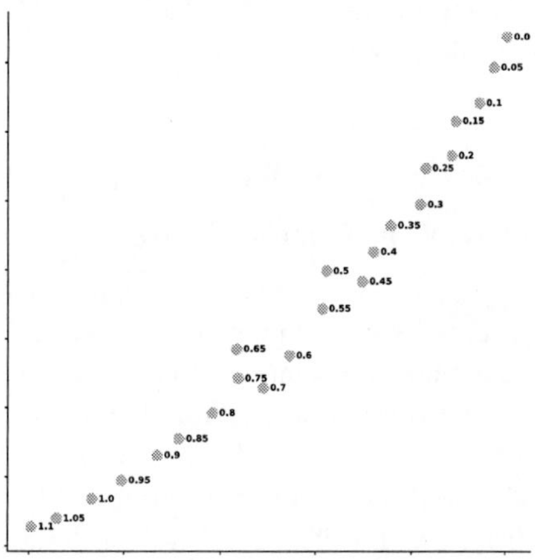

Figure 2: t-SNE visualizations for the decoder self-attention constituent of the simplification model's length compression control prefixes. Each circle represents a control prefix corresponding to each length ratio (bins of fixed width 0.05, from 0 to 1.1).

	OOV	Zero-shot
WebNLG	56.35	**56.41**
WebNLG+ 2020	50.02	**50.39**

Table 2: A comparison of the BLEU performance on the *Unseen* portions for WebNLG test sets, with i) a single OOV Control Prefix used for all samples from unseen categories, or ii) the zero-shot transfer approach outlined, utilizing the available textual labels.

sented in the training set. While no suitable control prefixes exist for these categories, they each have a textual label available in the dataset. Experiments in Fig. 2 also established that similar attribute labels learn similar parameter values in their control prefixes. This gives us some prior on the properties of the unseen categories, which we show is enough to perform zero-shot transfer with control prefixes.

We first map the textual label of each WebNLG category to a Glove embedding(Pennington et al., 2014).[10] Then for each *Unseen* category, we find the *Seen* category with the highest cosine similarity in the embedding space, and use its learned control prefix to also represet the corresponding *Unseen* category. For example, the control prefix for the seen category *SportsTeam* is used for examples relating to the unseen category *Athlete*.[11]

Table 2 shows results for the zero-shot transfer method on both WebNLG datasets. For comparison, we also report results using a single out-of-vocabulary (OOV) control prefix for all unseen categories. This OOV control prefix is trained by randomly selecting 2% of the categories in each training batch and replacing them with a general OOV category. These results indicate that zero-shot transfer based on word embeddings and textual labels provides an advantage over learning a single OOV representation.

[10]Glove Common Crawl (840B tokens, 2.2M vocab, cased, 300d vectors).

[11]Appendix I displays model output for WebNLG along with the zero-shot procedure.

	ϕ%	ASSET		TurkCorpus	
		SARI	FKGL ↓	SARI	FKGL ↓
Gold Reference	-	44.87	6.49	40.04	8.77
$\text{BART}_{\text{LARGE}}$ with ACCESS†	100	43.63	6.25	42.62	6.98
$\text{BART}_{\text{LARGE}}$ fine-tuned	100	39.91*	7.73*	39.55*	7.73*
Prefix-tuning	1.8	40.12	7.28	39.06	**7.28**
CONTROL PREFIXES	1.8	**43.58**	**5.97**	**42.32**	7.74

Table 3: Simplification results on ASSET and TurkCorpus test sets. †This model is from Martin et al. (2020), where the authors fine-tuned $\text{BART}_{\text{LARGE}}$ model alongside control tokens for the four attributes. The CONTROL PREFIXES model is trained with control prefixes for these same four attributes. Prefix-tuning and CONTROL PREFIXES use $\text{BART}_{\text{LARGE}}$ as the fixed LM. The * denotes baseline results calculated in this study—the model outputs of Martin et al. (2020) are publicly available. The $\text{BART}_{\text{LARGE}}$ with ACCESS and CONTROL PREFIXES model are the average test set results over 5 random seeds. We bold the best results of parameter-efficient models in the results tables, while fully fine-tuned models and human performance are reported for reference.

6 Token-level control

For comparison, we also investigated a simpler architecture: prefix-tuning combined with control tokens (Keskar et al., 2019). In this setting, the model receives the same guidance signals as CONTROL PREFIXES, but instead uses trainable control tokens for representing the attribute values. The main model is kept frozen, while the general prefix is optimized along with embeddings for the control tokens, allowing us to benchmark against a different parameter-efficient architecture. Note, we chose to compare against a prefix-tuning based architecture as the fully fine-tuned models lag behind prefix-tuning in Table 1.

The results for this experiment are included in Appendix G. We found that CONTROL PREFIXES consistently outperformed control tokens on all three data-to-text datasets. This indicates that CONTROL PREFIXES is a superior parameter-efficient framework for leveraging additional information, whilst maintaining the *fixed-LM* property. Control tokens lack the shared re-parameterization of static and dynamic parameters. They are only able to inject information at the embedding level, making them less expressive than the CONTROL PREFIXES method.

CONTROL PREFIXES fundamentally depends on the strength of the guidance signal. This is reflected in the constraint of attribute information being available with the dataset. However, we show that CONTROL PREFIXES is a powerful general method which can utilize this signal to achieve a consistent improvement across an array of tasks.

7 Applicability to other tasks

Finally, we investigate the application of CONTROL PREFIXES to generation tasks beyond the data-to-text setting. For these experiments, we integrate the method with a sequence-to-sequence model trained for text simplification on the WikiLarge (Zhang and Lapata, 2017) dataset. Following Martin et al. (2020), the model uses four simplification-specific attributes as control prefixes: the length compression ratio, replace-only Levenshtein similarity, aggregated word frequency ratio and dependency tree depth ratio. [12]

In Table 3 we report SARI (Xu et al., 2016) and FKGL (Kincaid et al., 1975) metrics.[13] For comparison, we report results for $\text{BART}_{\text{LARGE}}$ with ACCESS (Martin et al., 2020), which is a fully fine-tuned model that also integrates the same four attributes but uses control tokens instead. The results show that CONTROL PREFIXES is able to outperform the fully fine-tuned BART on the task of simplification, even though it optimizes only 1.8% of the parameters. When compared to $\text{BART}_{\text{LARGE}}$ with ACCESS, the results for CONTROL PREFIXES are competitive while still being substantially more parameter-efficient. Note this model has the benefit of full fine-tuning and we are already at maximum performance for the datasets as assessed by these metrics. This is indicated by the *Gold Reference* scores, which evaluates against other human annotators.

[12]Refer to Martin et al. (2020) for full attribute details.

[13]We use the FKGL and the latest version of SARI implemented in EASSE (Alva-Manchego et al., 2019) which is also used by Martin et al. (2020).

8 Related Work

Controlled generation aims to incorporate various types of guidance beyond the input text into the generation model (Kikuchi et al., 2016). Johnson et al. (2016) trained a translation model with control tokens to encode each language, and Keskar et al. (2019) pre-trained a 1.63B parameter model, alongside conditional control tokens demonstrating these learnt to govern stylistic aspects. In addition to having the benefit of updating all model parameters, these methods only act at the embedding level.

Alternatives exist, such as using a plug-and-play mechanism to perturb the LM hidden states towards a target attribute (Dathathri et al., 2020). Strategies such as these are computationally intensive, resulting in a slow generation speed and the shift in conditional probability has been shown to increase text degeneration (Holtzman et al., 2020; Gehman et al., 2020). GSum (Dou et al., 2020) is an example of work that has explored using learned guidance prediction models at test time. However, both the prompt and LM parameters are tuned.

There has been little work using controlled generation in the data-to-text domain. Su et al. (2021) were able control both the intra-text sentence and inter-sentence structure of generated output. This architecture exhibits inferior performance to our method on the mutual evaluation dataset WebNLG. Additionally, CONTROL PREFIXES uses fewer additional parameters and can incorporate multi-attribute control with prefixes of varying sizes.

Several successive works (Logeswaran et al., 2020; Liu et al., 2021b; Lester et al., 2021) employ prompt tuning, where unlike the discrete text prompts in ICL, trainable soft embeddings are prepended to the input. Again the technique acts only at the embedding level, thus limiting any control that can be exerted from data-point guidance. This shortcoming also exists with ICL and multi-task prompting (Sanh et al., 2021; Qin and Eisner, 2021). Prefix-tuning is more expressive and, along with Vedd et al. (2021), serves as inspiration for this work. However, prefix-tuning trains each prefix separately and no relationship between prefixes is modelled. The parameters are static with no mechanism to incorporate guidance.

There have been few works exploring input-dependent parameters trained alongside static prompt parameters (Liu et al., 2021a). Perhaps most similar to our work is Yu et al. (2021), who use an attribute alignment function to encode tokens of attributes. Unlike our work, there are no dedicated task parameters and the method aims to generate text with specific target attributes, independent of task performance. With CONTROL PREFIXES, the intention is to also maximize task-specific performance, which is why we maintain a large static component to specify the task itself, which is directly learnt simultaneously with the dynamic parameters in a shared framework.

9 Conclusion

We have proposed CONTROL PREFIXES, a general framework for integrating attribute-level information into pre-trained language models. In addition to the general prefix for the overall task, special prefixes are optimized for each attribute value and incorporated into different levels of the Transformer. This allows for finer-grained control over generated text, either by providing additional context about each input example or by allowing the user to specify some aspect of the desired output. The main language model parameters are kept frozen while only the multiple prefixes are optimized for a particular task, providing a very parameter-efficient method.

Our experiments show that CONTROL PREFIXES outperforms all existing methods for several data-to-text tasks including WebNLG and DART. This is in spite of learning less than 2% of the base LM's parameters and using signal from attribute level information that is available for the tasks. CONTROL PREFIXES also achieves higher results when compared to an alternative prefix-tuning architecture that makes use of the same attribute-level information, showing that the proposed framework is better able to integrate the additional signals with the rest of the model.

We also saw that the method can still be applied when suitable prefixes do not exist for a particular attribute value, by constructing the required prefix based on semantic similarity. Experiments on text simplification also verified that CONTROL PREFIXES can be applied on other tasks and datasets beyond the data-to-text setting.

In future work, additional guiding attributes can be investigated for text generation, such as the desired formality and sentiment. In addition, this method can be integrated with a wider range of model architectures, beyond text generation applications, that require parameter-efficient methods of control.

10 Limitations & Ethical Impact

Evaluating NLG is notoriously challenging (Celikyilmaz et al., 2020). For example, Freitag et al. (2020) and Mathur et al. (2020) find that when comparing two high-quality systems, differences according to a metric may also reflect how the references are written or flaws in the metric itself. To combat this, in addition to using the official task evaluation scripts, we report an array of GEM Gehrmann et al. (2021) metrics that represent lexical similarity and semantic equivalence in Table 8. We are also conscious that NLG models intrinsically trade off diversity and quality. We therefore report diversity and system characterization results in Table 9.

The technique described requires data-point information in the form of discrete categorical variables. Future work would look to investigate how best to integrate continuous information. In addition, as highlighted throughout CONTROL PREFIXES fundamentally depends on the strength of the guidance signal. The success of the zero-shot procedure depends on how well the semantic category labels are written for the unseen categories.

The technique is also limited by the predictive capabilities of the base frozen language model. One benefit, however, is that optimizer states for the base language model do not need to be stored during training, making training more computationally efficient.

We acknowledge that biases pose a huge problem in the Machine Learning and NLP community. We conducted experiments with BART and T5. Both models are trained on large amounts of textual data such as news, books, and web text, which may contain any kinds of biases. Although our research is conducted under the purview of parameter efficient NLP methods, we still used up to 6 V100-SXM2-16GB GPUs. There is a responsibility for the considerable CO2 emissions in the NLP community and for developing more resource-efficient training and inference methods.

References

Fernando Alva-Manchego, Louis Martin, Carolina Scarton, and Lucia Specia. 2019. Easse: Easier automatic sentence simplification evaluation. *arXiv preprint arXiv:1908.04567*.

Sören Auer, Christian Bizer, Georgi Kobilarov, Jens Lehmann, Richard Cyganiak, and Zachary Ives. 2007. Dbpedia: A nucleus for a web of open data. In *The Semantic Web*, pages 722–735, Berlin, Heidelberg. Springer Berlin Heidelberg.

Tom B. Brown, Benjamin Mann, Nick Ryder, Melanie Subbiah, Jared Kaplan, Prafulla Dhariwal, Arvind Neelakantan, Pranav Shyam, Girish Sastry, Amanda Askell, Sandhini Agarwal, Ariel Herbert-Voss, Gretchen Krueger, Tom Henighan, Rewon Child, Aditya Ramesh, Daniel M. Ziegler, Jeffrey Wu, Clemens Winter, Christopher Hesse, Mark Chen, Eric Sigler, Mateusz Litwin, Scott Gray, Benjamin Chess, Jack Clark, Christopher Berner, Sam McCandlish, Alec Radford, Ilya Sutskever, and Dario Amodei. 2020. Language models are few-shot learners. *CoRR*, abs/2005.14165.

Isabel Cachola, Kyle Lo, Arman Cohan, and Daniel S. Weld. 2020. TLDR: extreme summarization of scientific documents. *CoRR*, abs/2004.15011.

Thiago Castro Ferreira, Claire Gardent, Nikolai Ilinykh, Chris van der Lee, Simon Mille, Diego Moussallem, and Anastasia Shimorina. 2020. The 2020 bilingual, bi-directional WebNLG+ shared task: Overview and evaluation results (WebNLG+ 2020). In *Proceedings of the 3rd International Workshop on Natural Language Generation from the Semantic Web (WebNLG+)*, pages 55–76, Dublin, Ireland (Virtual). Association for Computational Linguistics.

Asli Celikyilmaz, Elizabeth Clark, and Jianfeng Gao. 2020. Evaluation of text generation: A survey. *CoRR*, abs/2006.14799.

Arman Cohan, Waleed Ammar, Madeleine van Zuylen, and Field Cady. 2019. Structural scaffolds for citation intent classification in scientific publications. *CoRR*, abs/1904.01608.

Sumanth Dathathri, Andrea Madotto, Janice Lan, Jane Hung, Eric Frank, Piero Molino, Jason Yosinski, and Rosanne Liu. 2020. Plug and play language models: A simple approach to controlled text generation. In *International Conference on Learning Representations*.

Zi-Yi Dou, Pengfei Liu, Hiroaki Hayashi, Zhengbao Jiang, and Graham Neubig. 2020. Gsum: A general framework for guided neural abstractive summarization. *CoRR*, abs/2010.08014.

Ondřej Dušek, David M. Howcroft, and Verena Rieser. 2019. Semantic noise matters for neural natural language generation. In *Proc. of the 12th International Conference on Natural Language Generation*, pages 421–426, Tokyo, Japan. Association for Computational Linguistics.

Markus Freitag, David Grangier, and Isaac Caswell. 2020. BLEU might be guilty but references are not innocent. *CoRR*, abs/2004.06063.

Claire Gardent, Anastasia Shimorina, Shashi Narayan, and Laura Perez-Beltrachini. 2017. The WebNLG challenge: Generating text from RDF data. In *Proceedings of the 10th International Conference on*

Natural Language Generation, pages 124–133, Santiago de Compostela, Spain. Association for Computational Linguistics.

Samuel Gehman, Suchin Gururangan, Maarten Sap, Yejin Choi, and Noah A. Smith. 2020. RealToxicityPrompts: Evaluating neural toxic degeneration in language models. In *Findings of the Association for Computational Linguistics: EMNLP 2020*, pages 3356–3369, Online. Association for Computational Linguistics.

Sebastian Gehrmann, Tosin P. Adewumi, Karmanya Aggarwal, Pawan Sasanka Ammanamanchi, Aremu Anuoluwapo, Antoine Bosselut, Khyathi Raghavi Chandu, Miruna-Adriana Clinciu, Dipanjan Das, Kaustubh D. Dhole, Wanyu Du, Esin Durmus, Ondrej Dusek, Chris Emezue, Varun Gangal, Cristina Garbacea, Tatsunori Hashimoto, Yufang Hou, Yacine Jernite, Harsh Jhamtani, Yangfeng Ji, Shailza Jolly, Dhruv Kumar, Faisal Ladhak, Aman Madaan, Mounica Maddela, Khyati Mahajan, Saad Mahamood, Bodhisattwa Prasad Majumder, Pedro Henrique Martins, Angelina McMillan-Major, Simon Mille, Emiel van Miltenburg, Moin Nadeem, Shashi Narayan, Vitaly Nikolaev, Rubungo Andre Niyongabo, Salomey Osei, Ankur P. Parikh, Laura Perez-Beltrachini, Niranjan Ramesh Rao, Vikas Raunak, Juan Diego Rodriguez, Sashank Santhanam, João Sedoc, Thibault Sellam, Samira Shaikh, Anastasia Shimorina, Marco Antonio Sobrevilla Cabezudo, Hendrik Strobelt, Nishant Subramani, Wei Xu, Diyi Yang, Akhila Yerukola, and Jiawei Zhou. 2021. The GEM benchmark: Natural language generation, its evaluation and metrics. *CoRR*, abs/2102.01672.

Sebastian Gehrmann, Abhik Bhattacharjee, Abinaya Mahendiran, Alex Wang, Alexandros Papangelis, Aman Madaan, Angelina McMillan-Major, Anna Shvets, Ashish Upadhyay, Bingsheng Yao, Bryan Wilie, Chandra Bhagavatula, Chaobin You, Craig Thomson, Cristina Garbacea, Dakuo Wang, Daniel Deutsch, Deyi Xiong, Di Jin, Dimitra Gkatzia, Dragomir Radev, Elizabeth Clark, Esin Durmus, Faisal Ladhak, Filip Ginter, Genta Indra Winata, Hendrik Strobelt, Hiroaki Hayashi, Jekaterina Novikova, Jenna Kanerva, Jenny Chim, Jiawei Zhou, Jordan Clive, Joshua Maynez, João Sedoc, Juraj Juraska, Kaustubh Dhole, Khyathi Raghavi Chandu, Laura Perez-Beltrachini, Leonardo F. R. Ribeiro, Lewis Tunstall, Li Zhang, Mahima Pushkarna, Mathias Creutz, Michael White, Mihir Sanjay Kale, Moussa Kamal Eddine, Nico Daheim, Nishant Subramani, Ondrej Dusek, Paul Pu Liang, Pawan Sasanka Ammanamanchi, Qi Zhu, Ratish Puduppully, Reno Kriz, Rifat Shahriyar, Ronald Cardenas, Saad Mahamood, Salomey Osei, Samuel Cahyawijaya, Sanja Štajner, Sebastien Montella, Shailza, Shailza Jolly, Simon Mille, Tahmid Hasan, Tianhao Shen, Tosin Adewumi, Vikas Raunak, Vipul Raheja, Vitaly Nikolaev, Vivian Tsai, Yacine Jernite, Ying Xu, Yisi Sang, Yixin Liu, and Yufang Hou. 2022. Gemv2: Multilingual nlg benchmarking in a single line of code.

David Grangier and Michael Auli. 2018. QuickEdit: Editing text & translations by crossing words out. In *Proceedings of the 2018 Conference of the North American Chapter of the Association for Computational Linguistics: Human Language Technologies, Volume 1 (Long Papers)*, pages 272–282, New Orleans, Louisiana. Association for Computational Linguistics.

Hamza Harkous, Isabel Groves, and Amir Saffari. 2020. Have your text and use it too! end-to-end neural data-to-text generation with semantic fidelity. *CoRR*, abs/2004.06577.

Ari Holtzman, Jan Buys, Maxwell Forbes, and Yejin Choi. 2020. The curious case of neural text degeneration. *CoRR*, abs/1904.09751.

Neil Houlsby, Andrei Giurgiu, Stanislaw Jastrzebski, Bruna Morrone, Quentin De Laroussilhe, Andrea Gesmundo, Mona Attariyan, and Sylvain Gelly. 2019. Parameter-efficient transfer learning for NLP. In *Proceedings of the 36th International Conference on Machine Learning*, volume 97 of *Proceedings of Machine Learning Research*, pages 2790–2799, Long Beach, California, USA. PMLR.

Edward J. Hu, Yelong Shen, Phillip Wallis, Zeyuan Allen-Zhu, Yuanzhi Li, Shean Wang, and Weizhu Chen. 2021. Lora: Low-rank adaptation of large language models. *CoRR*, abs/2106.09685.

Melvin Johnson, Mike Schuster, Quoc V. Le, Maxim Krikun, Yonghui Wu, Zhifeng Chen, Nikhil Thorat, Fernanda B. Viégas, Martin Wattenberg, Greg Corrado, Macduff Hughes, and Jeffrey Dean. 2016. Google's multilingual neural machine translation system: Enabling zero-shot translation. *CoRR*, abs/1611.04558.

Wendell Johnson. 1944. Studies in language behavior: A program of research. *Psychological Monographs*, 56(2):1–15.

N. Keskar, B. McCann, L. R. Varshney, Caiming Xiong, and R. Socher. 2019. Ctrl: A conditional transformer language model for controllable generation. *ArXiv*, abs/1909.05858.

Yuta Kikuchi, Graham Neubig, Ryohei Sasano, Hiroya Takamura, and Manabu Okumura. 2016. Controlling output length in neural encoder-decoders. In *Proceedings of the 2016 Conference on Empirical Methods in Natural Language Processing*, pages 1328–1338, Austin, Texas. Association for Computational Linguistics.

J. Peter Kincaid, Robert P Fishburne Jr., Richard L. Rogers, and Brad S. Chissom. 1975. Derivation of new readability formulas (automated readability index, fog count and flesch reading ease formula) for navy enlisted personnel.

Alon Lavie and Abhaya Agarwal. 2007. METEOR: An automatic metric for MT evaluation with high levels of correlation with human judgments. In *Proceedings of the Second Workshop on Statistical Machine Translation*, pages 228–231, Prague, Czech Republic. Association for Computational Linguistics.

Brian Lester, Rami Al-Rfou, and Noah Constant. 2021. The power of scale for parameter-efficient prompt tuning. *CoRR*, abs/2104.08691.

Mike Lewis, Yinhan Liu, Naman Goyal, Marjan Ghazvininejad, Abdelrahman Mohamed, Omer Levy, Veselin Stoyanov, and Luke Zettlemoyer. 2020. BART: Denoising sequence-to-sequence pre-training for natural language generation, translation, and comprehension. In *Proceedings of the 58th Annual Meeting of the Association for Computational Linguistics*, pages 7871–7880, Online. Association for Computational Linguistics.

Jiwei Li, Michel Galley, Chris Brockett, Jianfeng Gao, and Bill Dolan. 2016. A diversity-promoting objective function for neural conversation models. In *Proceedings of the 2016 Conference of the North American Chapter of the Association for Computational Linguistics: Human Language Technologies*, pages 110–119, San Diego, California. Association for Computational Linguistics.

Xiang Lisa Li and Percy Liang. 2021. Prefix-tuning: Optimizing continuous prompts for generation.

Pengfei Liu, Weizhe Yuan, Jinlan Fu, Zhengbao Jiang, Hiroaki Hayashi, and Graham Neubig. 2021a. Pre-train, prompt, and predict: A systematic survey of prompting methods in natural language processing.

Xiao Liu, Yanan Zheng, Zhengxiao Du, Ming Ding, Yujie Qian, Zhilin Yang, and Jie Tang. 2021b. GPT understands, too. *CoRR*, abs/2103.10385.

Lajanugen Logeswaran, Ann Lee, Myle Ott, Honglak Lee, Marc'Aurelio Ranzato, and Arthur Szlam. 2020. Few-shot sequence learning with transformers. *CoRR*, abs/2012.09543.

Ilya Loshchilov and Frank Hutter. 2017. Fixing weight decay regularization in adam. *CoRR*, abs/1711.05101.

L. V. D. Maaten and Geoffrey E. Hinton. 2008. Visualizing data using t-sne. *Journal of Machine Learning Research*, 9:2579–2605.

Louis Martin, Angela Fan, Éric de la Clergerie, Antoine Bordes, and Benoît Sagot. 2020. Multilingual unsupervised sentence simplification. *CoRR*, abs/2005.00352.

Nitika Mathur, Timothy Baldwin, and Trevor Cohn. 2020. Tangled up in BLEU: Reevaluating the evaluation of automatic machine translation evaluation metrics. In *Proceedings of the 58th Annual Meeting of the Association for Computational Linguistics*, pages 4984–4997, Online. Association for Computational Linguistics.

Amit Moryossef, Ido Dagan, and Yoav Goldberg. 2019. Improving quality and efficiency in plan-based neural data-to-text generation.

Kishore Papineni, Salim Roukos, Todd Ward, and Wei-Jing Zhu. 2002. Bleu: A method for automatic evaluation of machine translation. In *Proceedings of the 40th Annual Meeting on Association for Computational Linguistics*, ACL '02, page 311–318, USA. Association for Computational Linguistics.

Nivranshu Pasricha, Mihael Arcan, and Paul Buitelaar. 2020. NUIG-DSI at the WebNLG+ challenge: Leveraging transfer learning for RDF-to-text generation. In *Proceedings of the 3rd International Workshop on Natural Language Generation from the Semantic Web (WebNLG+)*, pages 137–143, Dublin, Ireland (Virtual). Association for Computational Linguistics.

Jeffrey Pennington, Richard Socher, and Christopher Manning. 2014. GloVe: Global vectors for word representation. In *Proceedings of the 2014 Conference on Empirical Methods in Natural Language Processing (EMNLP)*, pages 1532–1543, Doha, Qatar. Association for Computational Linguistics.

Matthew E. Peters, Sebastian Ruder, and Noah A. Smith. 2019. To tune or not to tune? adapting pretrained representations to diverse tasks. In *Proceedings of the 4th Workshop on Representation Learning for NLP (RepL4NLP-2019)*, pages 7–14, Florence, Italy. Association for Computational Linguistics.

Guanghui Qin and Jason Eisner. 2021. Learning how to ask: Querying lms with mixtures of soft prompts. *CoRR*, abs/2104.06599.

Dragomir R. Radev, Rui Zhang, Amrit Rau, Abhinand Sivaprasad, Chiachun Hsieh, Nazneen Fatema Rajani, Xiangru Tang, Aadit Vyas, Neha Verma, Pranav Krishna, Yangxiaokang Liu, Nadia Irwanto, Jessica Pan, Faiaz Rahman, Ahmad Zaidi, Murori Mutuma, Yasin Tarabar, Ankit Gupta, Tao Yu, Yi Chern Tan, Xi Victoria Lin, Caiming Xiong, and Richard Socher. 2020. DART: open-domain structured data record to text generation. *CoRR*, abs/2007.02871.

Colin Raffel, Noam Shazeer, Adam Roberts, Katherine Lee, Sharan Narang, Michael Matena, Yanqi Zhou, Wei Li, and Peter J. Liu. 2020. Exploring the limits of transfer learning with a unified text-to-text transformer. *Journal of Machine Learning Research*, 21(140):1–67.

Sylvestre-Alvise Rebuffi, Hakan Bilen, and Andrea Vedaldi. 2017. Learning multiple visual domains with residual adapters. In *Advances in Neural Information Processing Systems*, volume 30, pages 506–516. Curran Associates, Inc.

Leonardo F. R. Ribeiro, Martin Schmitt, Hinrich Schütze, and Iryna Gurevych. 2020. Investigating pretrained language models for graph-to-text generation. *arXiv*.

Victor Sanh, Albert Webson, Colin Raffel, Stephen H. Bach, Lintang Sutawika, Zaid Alyafeai, Antoine Chaffin, Arnaud Stiegler, Teven Le Scao, Arun Raja, Manan Dey, M. Saiful Bari, Canwen Xu, Urmish Thakker, Shanya Sharma, Eliza Szczechla, Taewoon Kim, Gunjan Chhablani, Nihal V. Nayak, Debajyoti Datta, Jonathan Chang, Mike Tian-Jian Jiang, Han Wang, Matteo Manica, Sheng Shen, Zheng Xin Yong, Harshit Pandey, Rachel Bawden, Thomas Wang, Trishala Neeraj, Jos Rozen, Abheesht Sharma, Andrea Santilli, Thibault Févry, Jason Alan Fries, Ryan Teehan, Stella Biderman, Leo Gao, Tali Bers, Thomas Wolf, and Alexander M. Rush. 2021. Multitask prompted training enables zero-shot task generalization. *CoRR*, abs/2110.08207.

Timo Schick and Hinrich Schütze. 2020. It's not just size that matters: Small language models are also few-shot learners. *CoRR*, abs/2009.07118.

Noam Shazeer and Mitchell Stern. 2018. Adafactor: Adaptive learning rates with sublinear memory cost. *CoRR*, abs/1804.04235.

Matthew Snover, Bonnie Dorr, Richard Schwartz, Linnea Micciulla, and Ralph Weischedel. 2006. A study of translation error rate with targeted human annotation. In *In Proceedings of the Association for Machine Transaltion in the Americas (AMTA 2006*.

Yixuan Su, David Vandyke, Sihui Wang, Yimai Fang, and Nigel Collier. 2021. Plan-then-generate: Controlled data-to-text generation via planning. *CoRR*, abs/2108.13740.

Swabha Swayamdipta, Sam Thomson, Kenton Lee, Luke Zettlemoyer, Chris Dyer, and Noah A. Smith. 2018. Syntactic scaffolds for semantic structures. In *EMNLP*.

Nihir Vedd, Zixu Wang, Marek Rei, Yishu Miao, and Lucia Specia. 2021. Guiding visual question generation.

Thomas Wolf, Lysandre Debut, Victor Sanh, Julien Chaumond, Clement Delangue, Anthony Moi, Pierric Cistac, Tim Rault, Rémi Louf, Morgan Funtowicz, Joe Davison, Sam Shleifer, Patrick von Platen, Clara Ma, Yacine Jernite, Julien Plu, Canwen Xu, Teven Le Scao, Sylvain Gugger, Mariama Drame, Quentin Lhoest, and Alexander M. Rush. 2020. Transformers: State-of-the-art natural language processing. In *Proceedings of the 2020 Conference on Empirical Methods in Natural Language Processing: System Demonstrations*, pages 38–45, Online. Association for Computational Linguistics.

Wei Xu, Courtney Napoles, Ellie Pavlick, Quanze Chen, and Chris Callison-Burch. 2016. Optimizing statistical machine translation for text simplification. *Transactions of the Association for Computational Linguistics*, 4:401–415.

Dian Yu, Kenji Sagae, and Zhou Yu. 2021. Attribute alignment: Controlling text generation from pre-trained language models. *CoRR*, abs/2103.11070.

Xingxing Zhang and Mirella Lapata. 2017. Sentence simplification with deep reinforcement learning. *arXiv preprint arXiv:1703.10931*.

A Additional Results

Additional results using the official evaluation scripts for the data-to-text datasets are reported in Tables 4,5,6 to supplement the results in Table 1.

B GEM Automatic Evaluation

Supporting results using the GEM package for model evaluation (`https://github.com/GEM-benchmark/GEM-metrics`) are provided in Tables 8,9.

C Prefix-tuning

We make two previously unremarked upon observations of the benefits conferred by using the key-value pair prefix-tuning described in §2.3 compared to prefix-tuning involving augmenting the activations directly (Hu et al., 2021) or prompt-embedding tuning of prompt length ρ. i) The form discussed does not restrict the input length of the base LM. ii) The time complexity at inference time is reduced; for example, if we take a multi-head self-attention computation ($M = N$), the time complexity at inference time is $\mathcal{O}((N + \rho)Nd + Nd^2)$ rather than the greater $\mathcal{O}((N + \rho)^2 d + (N + \rho)d^2)$.

D WebNLG+ 2020 Results

WebNLG+ 2020 is not a component of DART—it was used for the second official WebNLG competition (Castro Ferreira et al., 2020). There are 16 training categories (the 15 categories from WebNLG, but with new examples), alongside 3 unseen categories. Table 7 displays WebNLG+ 2020 results using the same model architectures as used for WebNLG. A similar pattern is revealed, in that CONTROL PREFIXES outperforms prefix-tuning with CONTROL PREFIXES (A_1,A_2) as the top-performing model. This illustrates again the benefit of using both controllable attributes.

In the WebNLG and WebNLG+ 2020 training sets, for the same tripleset, multiple distinct lexicalizations exist. In our experiments, the examples sharing identical tripleset inputs have the same triple order after linearization. This is to aid in comparison with current systems for WebNLG, DART and E2E Clean. Permuting the triples for these examples will introduce a source of randomness for result comparison.

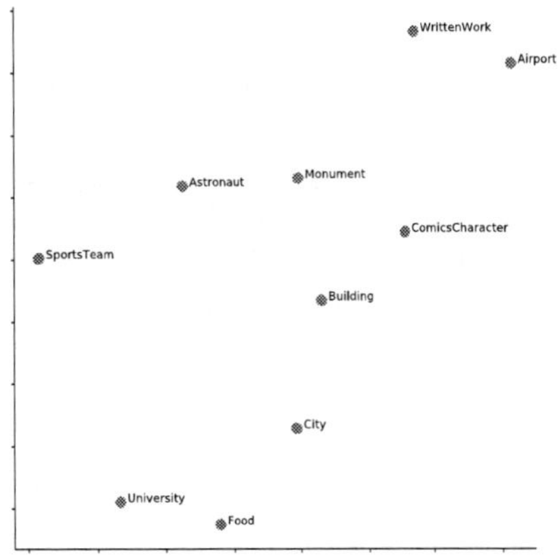

(a) WebNLG

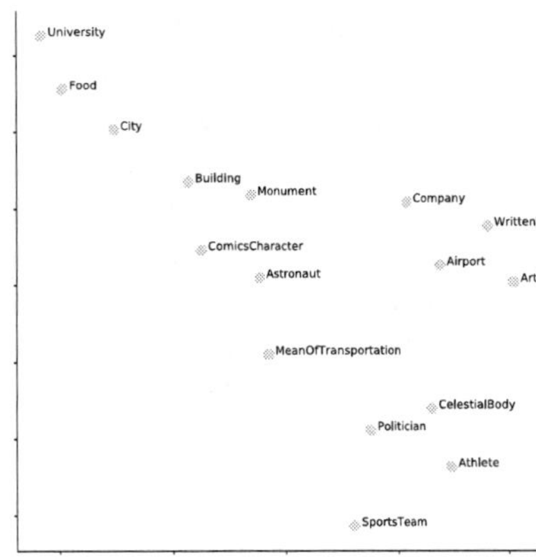

(b) WebNLG+ 2020

Figure 3: t-SNE visualizations for the encoder constituent of control prefixes representing WebNLG categories seen during training. Each circle represents a category seen during training for the CONTROL PREFIXES ($A1$) model. All 15 categories are seen categories in WebNLG+ 2020, along with the category *Company*. WebNLG+ 2020 has 3 additional unseen categories to those shown.

E Additional Training Details

All implementations in this study are built on top of the Transformers library (Wolf et al., 2020). As T5 has relative position biases, we set these in all layers pertaining to offsets where the key is part of a prefix to zero. For $\text{BART}_{\text{LARGE}}$ we adapt the original implementation (Li and Liang, 2021). Table 11 displays the hyperparameters used when training the models reported in this paper.

The general prompt length and each control prompt length are architecture-specific parameters that we choose based on performance on the validation set. We use gradient accumulation across batches to maintain an effective batch size above 64, a linear learning rate scheduler for all models and beam-search decoding. AdamW (Loshchilov and Hutter, 2017) and AdaFactor (Shazeer and Stern, 2018) were used for optimization. We chose the checkpoint with the highest validation score using BLEU for data-to-text and SARI for simplification. For all tasks, we train our models on single Tesla V100-SXM2-16GB machines, with mixed precision for $\text{BART}_{\text{LARGE}}$ based models (fp16) and full precision for T5-large based models (fp32).

The CONTROL PREFIXES models with the DART *sub-dataset source* attribute (A_2) use DART as additional data and were trained in two stages: i) on DART, ii) solely on the downstream dataset. The WebNLG prefix-tuning model with DART data shown in Table 11 uses only the human annotated portion of DART. The prefix-tuning models using all of the DART data for WebNLG and E2E Clean were similarly trained in two stages, with identical hyperparameters to CONTROL PREFIXES models using A_2. Training prefix-tuning on all of DART for WebNLG yielded lower performance than with only the human-annotated DART portion as additional data, so was not reported in Table 1.

Decoding specific parameters were not tuned—we instead mirrored what the top-performing fine-tuned based system used for the particular LM and dataset. For example, a beam width of 5 as in Ribeiro et al. (2020) for T5-large on all data-to-text datasets.

F Simplification Length Control

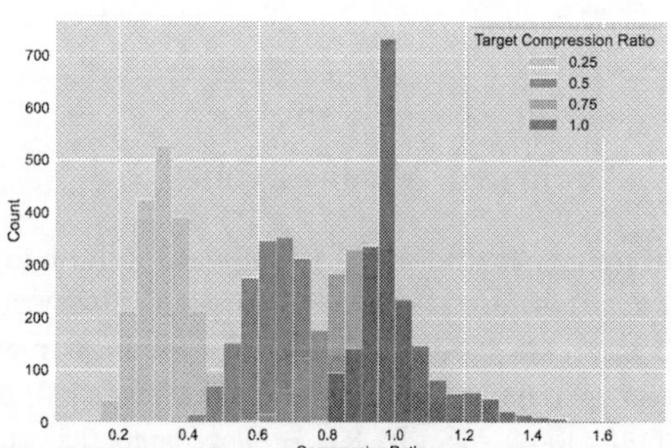

Figure 4: Histogram illustrating the influence of different target length ratios on the actual length compression ratio output distribution for the simplification CONTROL PREFIXES model on the TurkCorpus validation set.

Fig. 4 depicts the length compression ratio output distribution on the validation set for CONTROL PREFIXES, where a length control prefix of a specific attribute value (0.25,0.5,0.75,1.0) is specified. This clearly demonstrates CONTROL PREFIXES is capable of controlling the target length with respect to the input. Table 12 displays example output generations with each of the 0.25,0.5,0.75,1.0 values specified.

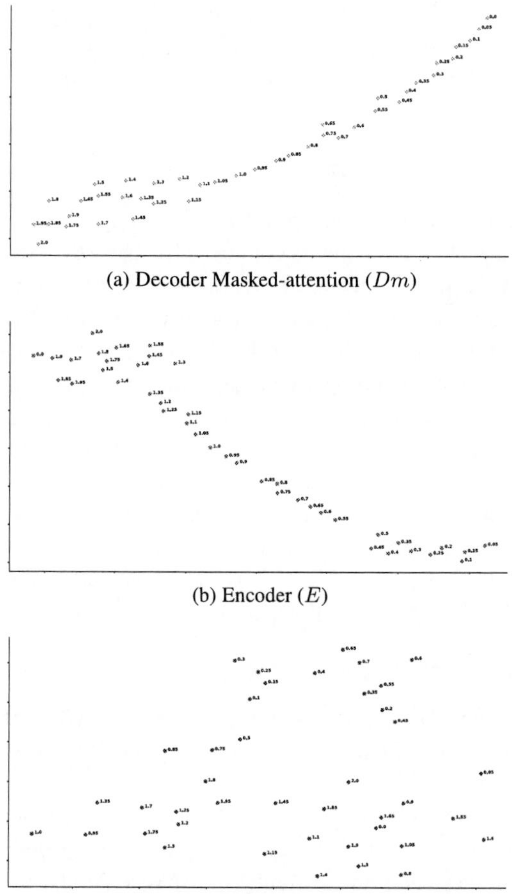

(a) Decoder Masked-attention (Dm)

(b) Encoder (E)

(c) Decoder Cross-attention (Dc)

Figure 5: t-SNE visualizations for constituents of the length compression control prefixes learnt as part of the simplification CONTROL PREFIXES model. Each diagram depicts representations of control prefixes corresponding to each length value (41 bins of fixed width 0.05, from 0 to 2) for a particular attention mechanism. The dimension represented on the x-axis is stretched from a 1:1 to 2:1 aspect ratio for labelling clarity.

Fig. 5 is supplementary to §5.1, showing all constituents of the length compression control prefixes for all attribute values. In the WikiLarge training data, there are far fewer training samples where the simplified output is much longer than the complex, original input in WikiLarge. This explains why the representations are not as interpretable for values greater than 1.2.

G Prefix-tuning + Control Tokens

We propose another architecture 'prefix-tuning + control tokens', where all of the original LM parameters, ϕ, still remain fixed, including the embedding matrix. Control has to be exerted through the few control embeddings and prefix-tuning's ability to steer the frozen ϕ parameters through $< 2\%$ additional parameters. We use this method to inform the model of the same discrete guidance information as in CONTROL PREFIXES, but with control tokens instead of control prefixes.[14] This alternative method is less expressive than CONTROL PREFIXES, in much the same way as prefix-tuning is more expressive than prompt-embedding tuning. Prefix-tuning + control tokens also does not benefit from the shared re-parameterizations (§2.3) that we argue allow for more effective demarcation of control of the fixed LM in each attention class subspace.

Table 10 reveals that CONTROL PREFIXES outperforms prefix-tuning + control tokens on the data-to-text datasets, while the results are both comparable to the *Gold References* on simplification datasets. This indicates that CONTROL PREFIXES is better able to integrate and leverage guidance signal at the input-level, whilst maintaining the *fixed-LM* property, than prefix-tuning + control tokens.

H Varying Prompt Length

Our research is not solely focused on parameter efficiency, but also on the effectiveness of adapting an already parameter efficient, fixed-LM method (adding <2% additional parameters). The only way to add parameters with prefix-tuning is to increase the prompt length. XSum is the only dataset considered where performance does not plateau when increasing prompt length[15], therefore we ensure CONTROL PREFIXES does not have more parameters than prefix-tuning to ensure a fair comparison. Fig. 6 illustrates how performance saturation is observed—after a certain prompt length performance plateaus. Different datasets require varying prompt lengths to attain near maximum performance in a parameter search for prompt length. For the data-to-text datasets, near maximum performance (>99% of the maximum validation score in the search) is reached with a prompt length of 1 or 2.

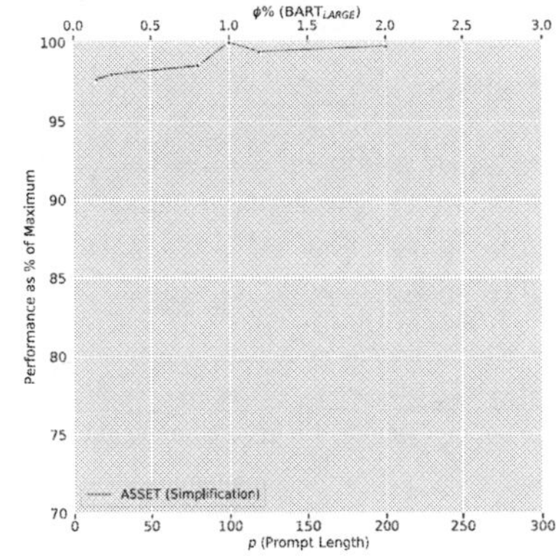

(a) BART$_{\text{LARGE}}$

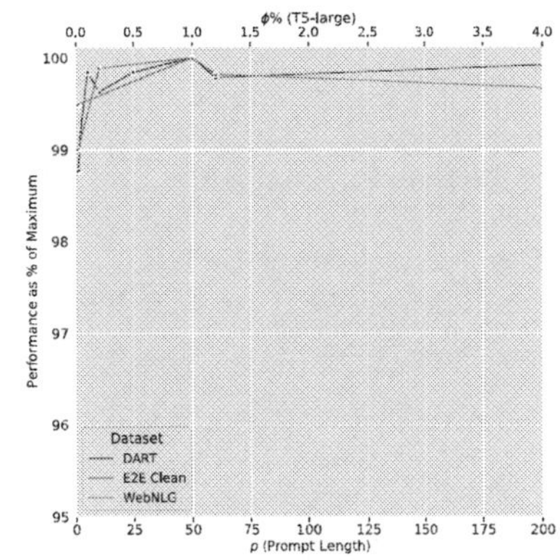

(b) T5-large

Figure 6: Prefix-tuning results of a model parameter search on several datasets for the optimal prompt length per dataset. These results are for the metric monitored per task on the respective validation sets indicated in the legend. $\phi\%$ denotes the % of additional parameters to the number of fixed-LM parameters required at inference time. The y-axis is a relative measure: the validation set performance as a % of the maximum attained in the parameter search.

I Qualitative Examples

For data-to-text, Table 14 displays example CONTROL PREFIXES output for WebNLG input belonging to unseen categories, along with the zero-shot procedure. Table 14 depicts example CONTROL PREFIXES (A_1,A_2) output alongside prefix-tuning model output for WebNLG+ 2020 input. For simplification, Table 13 compares the fixed-LM guided generations of CONTROL PREFIXES to the fine-tuned BART$_{\text{LARGE}}$ with ACCESS (Martin et al., 2020).

[14] Only the embeddings pertaining to the controllable attributes and the prefix are trained.

[15] We do not observe performance degradation, such as described by Hu et al. (2021), when utilizing different forms of prefix-tuning. This is shown in H.

	$\phi\%$	BLEU	METEOR	TER ↓	BERTScore(F1)
T5-large fine-tuned*	100	50.66	40	43	0.95
Prefix-tuning	1.0	51.20	40.62	43.13	0.95
CONTROL PREFIXES (A_1)	1.1	**51.95**	**41.07**	**42.75**	0.95

Table 4: Detailed results on the DART test set to complement Table 1. T5-large fine-tuned is the current SOTA (Radev et al., 2020). We report results on the official evaluation script for v1.1.1, the same version as the official leaderboard, available here: `https://github.com/Yale-LILY/dart`. *Results for this model were only reported to the significant figures shown. $\phi\%$ denotes the % of additional parameters to the number of fixed-LM parameters required at inference time.

	$\phi\%$	BLEU			METEOR			TER ↓		
		S	U	A	S	U	A	S	U	A
T5-large	100	64.89	54.01	59.95	46	43	44	34	41	37
SOTA	100	65.82	56.01	61.44	46	43	45	32	38	35
Prefix-tuning	1.0	66.95	55.39	61.73	46.73	42.71	44.87	31.34	39.01	34.86
CONTROL PREFIXES (A_1)	1.4	**67.32**	55.38	61.94	46.78	42.77	44.92	30.96	39.01	34.65
+Data: DART										
Prefix-tuning	1.0	67.05	55.37	61.78	46.69	42.82	44.90	31.36	38.79	34.77
CONTROL PREFIXES (A_2)	1.0	66.99	55.56	61.83	46.67	42.87	44.91	31.37	38.53	34.65
CONTROL PREFIXES (A_1,A_2)	1.4	67.15	**56.41**	<u>62.27</u>	46.64	43.18	45.03	31.08	38.78	34.61

Table 5: Detailed results on the WebNLG test set to complement Table 1. S, U and A refer to the *Seen*, *Unseen* and *All* portions of the WebNLG dataset. Several of the baseline results were only reported to the significant figures shown.

	$\phi\%$	BLEU	NIST	METEOR	R-L	CIDEr
T5-large	100	41.83	6.41	0.381	56.0	1.97
SOTA	100	43.6	-	0.39	**57.5**	2.0
Prefix-tuning	1.0	43.66	6.51	0.390	57.2	2.04
+Data: DART						
Prefix-tuning	1.0	43.04	6.46	0.387	56.8	1.99
CONTROL PREFIXES (A_2)	1.0	**44.15**	**6.51**	**0.392**	57.3	**2.04**

Table 6: Detailed results on the E2E Clean test set to complement Table 1. The SOTA baseline result was only reported to the significant figures shown.

	$\phi\%$	BLEU	METEOR	chrF++	TER ↓	BLEURT
T5-large*†	100	51.74	0.403	0.669	0.417	0.61
Prefix-tuning	1.0	54.74	0.417	0.693	0.399	0.62
CONTROL PREFIXES (A_1)	1.6	54.97	0.417	0.693	0.398	0.62
+Data: DART						
CONTROL PREFIXES (A_2)	1.0	54.92	0.418	0.695	0.397	0.62
CONTROL PREFIXES (A_1,A_2)	1.6	**55.41**	**0.419**	**0.698**	**0.392**	**0.63**

Table 7: **WebNLG+ 2020.** The overall WebNLG+ 2020 test set results using the official evaluation script. *As the model outputs are publicly available, we are able to run evaluation to achieve the same precision. †Results from Pasricha et al. (2020), who before fine-tuning on the WebNLG+ data, further pre-train T5-large using a Mask Language Modelling objective (with 15% of the tokens masked) on the WebNLG corpus and a corpus of DBpedia. A_1 signifies models trained with control prefixes for the *WebNLG category* attribute, and A_2 with control prefixes for the DART *sub-dataset source* attribute.

Dataset	Model	Metrics (Lexical Similarity and Semantic Equivalence)						
		METEOR	ROUGE-1	ROUGE-2	ROUGE-L	BLEU	BERTScore	BLEURT
DART	Prefix-tuning	0.405	76.7	53.0	61.7	50.2	0.95	0.32
	CONTROL PREFIXES (A_2)	0.410	77.3	53.7	62.4	51.1	0.96	0.33
E2E Clean	Prefix-tuning	0.385	74.5	48.3	55.8	43.7	0.95	0.23
	CONTROL PREFIXES (A_2)	0.387	74.4	48.4	55.9	44.1	0.95	0.23
WebNLG 2017	Prefix-tuning	0.443	81.1	59.6	67.8	60.3	0.96	0.43
	Prefix-tuning + DART	0.443	81.2	59.8	67.8	60.4	0.96	0.43
	CONTROL PREFIXES (A_1)	0.443	81.3	59.9	67.9	60.5	0.96	0.43
	CONTROL PREFIXES (A_2)	0.443	81.3	59.8	68.1	60.5	0.96	0.43
	CONTROL PREFIXES (A_1,A_2)	0.444	81.4	60.0	68.0	60.8	0.96	0.43
WebNLG+ 2020	Prefix-tuning	0.417	79.6	56.2	64.8	56.2	0.96	0.32
	CONTROL PREFIXES (A_1)	0.417	79.5	56.3	65.1	56.3	0.96	0.32
	CONTROL PREFIXES (A_2)	0.418	79.6	56.5	65.3	56.4	0.96	0.33
	CONTROL PREFIXES (A_1,A_2)	0.419	80.0	56.9	65.4	56.8	0.96	0.34

Table 8: The set of additional lexical similarity and semantic equivalence results on the official Data-to-text test sets. These metrics are proposed by Gehrmann et al. (2021) and calculated using the GEM evaluation suite. The hash for BERTScore used is `roberta-large_L17_no-idf_version=0.3.8(hug_trans=3.0.1)` and for BLEURT the version is BLEURT-base-128.

Dataset	Model	Metrics (Diversity and System Characterization)								
		MSTTR	Distinct_1	Distinct_2	H_1	H_2	Unique_1	Unique_2	$\|\mathcal{V}\|$	Output Len.
DART	Prefix-tuning	0.45	0.04	0.13	8.1	10.97	1.5k	5.2k	4.8k	21.2
	CONTROL PREFIXES (A_2)	0.45	0.04	0.13	8.11	10.98	1.5k	5.3k	4.8k	21.5
E2E Clean	Prefix-tuning	0.32	0.003	0.01	5.70	7.28	6	57	130	24.8
	CONTROL PREFIXES (A_2)	0.32	0.003	0.01	5.71	7.29	8	73	140	25.3
WebNLG 2017	Prefix-tuning	0.52	0.09	0.26	8.57	11.88	973	4.6k	3.4k	21.1
	Prefix-tuning + DART	0.52	0.09	0.26	8.57	11.87	968	4.6k	3.4k	21.1
	CONTROL PREFIXES (A_1)	0.52	0.09	0.26	8.57	11.89	997	4.7k	3.4k	21.2
	CONTROL PREFIXES (A_2)	0.52	0.09	0.26	8.57	11.88	965	4.6k	3.4k	21.1
	CONTROL PREFIXES (A_1,A_2)	0.52	0.08	0.25	8.52	11.81	962	4.4k	3.4k	21.3
WebNLG+ 2020	Prefix-tuning	0.66	0.04	0.13	8.05	10.94	327	1.8k	1.6k	23.0
	CONTROL PREFIXES (A_1)	0.66	0.04	0.13	8.05	10.92	326	1.8k	1.6k	23.0
	CONTROL PREFIXES (A_2)	0.66	0.04	0.13	8.04	10.92	326	1.8k	1.6k	23.1
	CONTROL PREFIXES (A_1,A_2)	0.66	0.04	0.13	8.05	10.9	300	1.7k	1.5k	23.0

Table 9: The set of additional diversity and system characterization results on the official Data-to-text test sets. These metrics are proposed by Gehrmann et al. (2021) and calculated using the GEM evaluation suite. These include the Shannon Entropy over unigrams and bigrams (H_1, H_2), the mean segmented type token ratio over segment lengths of 100 (MSTTR, Johnson (1944)), the ratio of distinct n-grams over the total number of n-grams ($\text{Distinct}_{1,2}$), and the count of n-grams that only appear once across the entire test output ($\text{Unique}_{1,2}$, Li et al. (2016)), as well as the vocabulary size over the output ($|\mathcal{V}|$) and the mean output length of a system.

	DART	WebNLG	E2E Clean	ASSET		TurkCorpus	
		BLEU		SARI	QuestEval	SARI	QuestEval
Prefix-tuning + Control Tokens	51.72	61.89	43.57	43.64	0.63	42.36	0.66
CONTROL PREFIXES	51.95	62.27	44.15	43.58	0.64	42.32	0.66

Table 10: **Prefix-tuning + Control Tokens.** Comparison of our best CONTROL PREFIXES model for each dataset with prefix-tuning + control tokens for the same attributes. The guided simplification models are the average test set results over 5 random seeds.

Model	Stage	L-rate	Opt	Warmup-steps	Epochs	Batch Size	Effective Batch	Beam Width	LN-α	Min Target	Max Target	No Repeat Trigram
DART (T5-large)												
Prefix-tuning	-	7e-5	Ada	2000	40	6	96	5	1	0	384	No
CONTROL PREFIXES (A_1)	-	7e-5	Ada	2000	40	6	96	5	1	0	384	No
E2E Clean (T5-large)												
Prefix-tuning	-	8e-5	Ada	2000	50	6	96	5	1	0	384	No
CONTROL PREFIXES (A_2)	1	7e-5	Ada	2000	30	6	96	5	1	0	384	No
	2	5e-5	Ada	2000	50	6	96	5	1	0	384	No
WebNLG (T5-large)												
Prefix-tuning	-	7e-5	Ada	2000	30	6	96	5	1	0	384	No
CONTROL PREFIXES (A_1)	-	7e-5	Ada	2000	40	6	96	5	1	0	384	No
+Data: DART												
Prefix-tuning	-	7e-5	Ada	2000	40	6	96	5	1	0	384	No
CONTROL PREFIXES (A_2)	1	7e-5	Ada	2000	30	6	96	5	1	0	384	No
	2	3e-5	Ada	2000	30	6	96	5	1	0	384	No
CONTROL PREFIXES (A_1, A_2)	1	7e-5	Ada	2000	30	6	96	5	1	0	384	No
	2	3e-5	Ada	2000	30	6	96	5	1	0	384	No
ASSET & TurkCorpus (BART$_{LARGE}$)												
Prefix-tuning	-	5e-5	AdamW	2000	30	8	64	6	0.8	3	100	✓
CONTROL PREFIXES)	-	4e-5	Ada	5000	30	8	64	6	1	3	100	✓

Table 11: **Hyperparameters.** Detailed hyperparameter reporting for the models in this work. If the training procedure is multi-stage, each stage is indicated. L-rate is the learning rate, all learning follows a linear learning rate scheduler; Opt refers to the optimizer, Ada (Adafactor) or AdamW; Effective Batch = Batch size x # of gradient accumulation batches; LN-α refers to the α in length normalization during beam search.

ASSET Corpus	
	Source: The West Coast blues is a type of blues music characterized by jazz and jump blues influences, strong piano-dominated sounds and jazzy guitar solos, which originated from Texas blues players relocated to California in the 1940s.
Gold Reference†	The West Coast blues has jazz and jump blues influences. It also has piano-dominated sounds and jazzy guitar solos, which originated from Texas blues players who moved to California in the 1940s.
CONTROL PREFIXES ($A_{1:4}$) Length Control: 0.25	West Coast blues is a type of blues music from the United States.
CONTROL PREFIXES ($A_{1:4}$) Length Control: 0.5	The West Coast blues is a type of blues music made from Texas blues players who moved to California in the 1940s. It has jazz and jump blues influences.
CONTROL PREFIXES ($A_{1:4}$) Length Control: 0.75	The West Coast blues is a type of blues music that originated in Texas in the 1940s. It is characterized by jazz and jump blues influences, strong piano-dominated sounds and jazzy guitar solos.
CONTROL PREFIXES ($A_{1:4}$) Length Control: 1.0	The West Coast blues is a type of blues music characterized by jazz and jump blues influences, strong piano-dominated sounds and jazzy guitar solos, which originated from Texas blues players who moved to California in the 1940s.

Table 12: **Controlled text simplification**: a qualitative example from the ASSET Corpus validation set, with our corresponding CONTROL PREFIXES model outputs. Only the control prefix for the length control ratio is varied, depicted in red. †Note, this is one random gold reference out of 10.

ASSET Corpus	
	Source: The Great Dark Spot is thought to represent a hole in the methane cloud deck of Neptune.
Gold Reference†	The Great Dark Spot represents a hole in the methane cloud of Neptune.
CONTROL PREFIXES	It is thought that the Great Dark Spot is a hole in Neptune's methane cloud deck.
$\text{BART}_{\text{LARGE}}$ with ACCESS	The Great Dark Spot looks like a hole in the methane cloud deck of Neptune.
	Source: Fives is a British sport believed to derive from the same origins as many racquet sports.
Gold Reference†	Fives is a British sport developed from the same origins as many racquet sports.
CONTROL PREFIXES	Fives is a British sport. It is believed to have its origins in racquet sports.
$\text{BART}_{\text{LARGE}}$ with ACCESS	Fives is a British sport. It is thought to come from the same as many racquet sports.
	Source: Nevertheless, Tagore emulated numerous styles, including craftwork from northern New Ireland, Haida carvings from the west coast of Canada (British Columbia), and woodcuts by Max Pechstein.
Gold Reference†	Tagore copied many styles. These included craftwork from northern New Ireland, Haida carvings from western Canada and woodcuts by Max Pechstein.
CONTROL PREFIXES	Tagore emulated many different styles of art, including Haida carvings from the west coast of Canada (British Columbia), and woodcuts by Max Pechstein.
$\text{BART}_{\text{LARGE}}$ with ACCESS	Tagore copied many styles. He copied craftwork from northern New Ireland, Haida carvings from the west coast of Canada (British Columbia), and woodcuts by Max Pechstein.

Table 13: ***Fixed-LM* vs fine-tuned controlled text simplification**. CONTROL PREFIXES and $\text{BART}_{\text{LARGE}}$ with ACCESS (Martin et al., 2020) generated simplifications chosen from the ASSET Corpus test set. †Note, this is one random gold reference out of 10 for each example. The examples shown for CONTROL PREFIXES and $\text{BART}_{\text{LARGE}}$ with ACCESS are also randomly selected from one of the five model outputs.

WebNLG	
Unseen Category: *Athlete* Zero-shot -> SportsTeam	**Source:** <H> FC Torpedo Moscow <R> season <T> 2014-15 Russian Premier League <H> Aleksandr Chumakov <R> club <T> FC Torpedo Moscow <H> FC Torpedo Moscow <R> manager <T> Valery Petrakov <H> FC Torpedo Moscow <R> chairman <T> Aleksandr Tukmanov
Gold	Valery Petrakov is the manager of FC Torpedo Moscow and its chairman is Aleksandr Tukmanov. Aleksandr Chumakov plays for the club which spent the 2014-15 season in the Russian Premier League.
Prefix-tuning	Aleksandr Tukmanov and Valery Petrakov are the managers of FC Torpedo Moscow. The club played in the Russian Premier League in 2014-15 and their chairman is Aleksandr Tukmanov.
CONTROL PREFIXES (A_1)	Aleksandr Chumakov plays for FC Torpedo Moscow which is managed by Valery Petrakov. The club's chairman is Aleksandr Tukmanov and they played in the Russian Premier League in the 2014-15 season.
Unseen Category: *MeanOfTransportation* Zero-shot -> Airport	**Source:** <H> Costa Crociere <R> location <T> Genoa <H> Costa Crociere <R> parent Company <T> Carnival Corporation & plc <H> AIDAstella <R> operator <T> AIDA Cruises <H> AIDAstella <R> builder <T> Meyer Werft <H> AIDAstella <R> owner <T> Costa Crociere
Gold	Carnival Corporation & plc is the parent company of Costa Crociere in Genoa, who own the AIDAstella. AIDAstella was built by Meyer Werft and is operated by AIDA Cruises.
Prefix-tuning	Costa Crociere is located in Genoa and is owned by Carnival Corporation & plc. AIDAstella is operated by AIDA Cruises and was built by Meyer Werft.
CONTROL PREFIXES (A_1)	Costa Crociere is located in Genoa and is owned by AIDA Cruises. AIDAstella was built by Meyer Werft and is operated by AIDA Cruises. The parent company of Costa Crociere is Carnival Corporation & plc.

Table 14: **WebNLG example generations:** sources are shown in their linearized form, as fed to the T5-large based models, with prefix-tuning output and one of the gold references shown for comparison with CONTROL PREFIXES output. Triplesets are from WebNLG unseen categories and the zero-shot procedure is depicted using the textual category labels. As an example, for the unseen category *Athlete*, the closest Glove embedding belonging to a *seen* category label in embedding space is SportsTeam. Therefore the trained control prefix relating to *SportsTeam* is used for this example at inference time.

WebNLG+ 2020	
WebNLG MeanOfTransportation (Seen with Unseen Entities)	**Source:** <H> Pontiac Rageous <R> production Start Year <T> 1997 <H> Pontiac Rageous <R> assembly <T> Michigan <H> Pontiac Rageous <R> assembly <T> Detroit <H> Pontiac Rageous <R> production End Year <T> 1997 <H> Pontiac Rageous <R> body Style <T> Coupe <H> Pontiac Rageous <R> manufacturer <T> Pontiac
Gold	The Pontiac Rageous was a car with a coupe body style manufactured by Pontiac. Assembled in both Michigan and Detroit, it went into production in 1997, ending in the same year.
Prefix-tuning	The Pontiac Rageous is a coupe manufactured by Pontiac. It is assembled in Detroit, Michigan and began production in 1997.
CONTROL PREFIXES (A_1,A_2)	The Pontiac Rageous is manufactured by Pontiac in Detroit, Michigan. Its production began in 1997 and ended in 1997. The Pontiac Rageous has a coupe body style.
WebNLG (Unseen) Unseen Category: MusicalWork Zero-shot -> Artist	**Source:** <H> Bootleg Series Volume 1: The Quine Tapes <R> genre <T> Rock music <H> Bootleg Series Volume 1: The Quine Tapes <R> preceded By <T> Squeeze The Velvet Underground album <H> Bootleg Series Volume 1: The Quine Tapes <R> record Label <T> Polydor Records <H> Bootleg Series Volume 1: The Quine Tapes <R> recorded In <T> San Francisco
Gold	The Velvet Underground Squeeze album was succeeded by the rock album Bootleg Series Volume 1: The Quine Tapes, recorded under record label Polydor Records in San Francisco.
Prefix-tuning	The record label of Bootleg Series Volume 1: The Quine Tapes is Polydor Records. It was recorded in San Francisco and was preceded by Squeeze The Velvet Underground. Its genre is rock music.
CONTROL PREFIXES (A_1,A_2)	Squeeze The Velvet Underground was preceded by Bootleg Series Volume 1: The Quine Tapes, which was recorded in San Francisco and released by Polydor Records. The genre of the album is rock music.

Table 15: **WebNLG+ 2020 generations:** sources are shown in their linearized form as fed to the T5-large based models. The DART sub-dataset Source control prefix is highlighted, along with the final Category control prefix. The zero-shot procedure is depicted for the Unseen Category *MusicalWork*. The closest embedding belonging to a Seen category in embedding space is Artist.

A Survey of Error Annotation Schemes for Human and Machine Generated Text

Rudali Huidrom and **Anya Belz**
ADAPT Research Centre, Dublin City University
{rudali.huidrom,anya.belz}@adaptcentre.ie

Abstract

While automatically computing numerical scores remains the dominant paradigm in NLP system evaluation, error annotation and analysis is receiving increasing attention, with several error annotation schemes recently proposed for automatically generated text. However, there is little agreement about what error annotation schemes should look like, how many different types of errors should be distinguished and at what level of granularity. In this paper, our aim is to map out work on annotating errors in human and machine generated text, with a particular focus on error taxonomies. We describe our paper selection process, and survey the error annotation schemes reported in the papers, drawing out similarities and differences between them. Finally, we characterise the issues that would make it difficult to move from the current situation to a standardised error taxonomy for annotating errors in automatically generated text.

1 Introduction

Error analysis and reporting is commonly encouraged in the natural language processing (NLP) field to aid in understanding system weaknesses, most recently those that are exhibited by state-of-the-art neural systems (van Miltenburg et al., 2021), which have led to renewed calls in NLP for error analysis and building error taxonomies (Costa et al., 2015; Rivera-Trigueros, 2021).

With the advancement of neural networks and growing interest beyond pipeline-based approaches, semantic errors are increasingly observed in generation scenarios. In data-to-text generation, for example, about 40% of the E2E Generation Challenge system outputs contained erroneously omitted or added semantic content (Dušek et al., 2020). Ideally, the data-to-text systems that we develop produce outputs that convey all and only the input content (not omitting or arbitrarily adding any content) (Dušek et al., 2019; Harkous et al., 2020), so it is important to identify and understand what kinds of semantic errors occur and for what reasons, for which error annotation and subsequent analysis provides a basis. However, there is currently little agreement on how the annotation part of this should be done.

In this paper, we present a survey of different error annotation schemes, with a particular focus on error taxonomies, that have been proposed in NLP. Our paper selection process yielded a set of 22 papers reporting error type annotations and error taxonomies from the ACL Anthology. The scope of this paper is limited to error annotation schemes that include semantic errors (as well as, possibly, other types of errors, e.g. syntactic and commonsense errors).

The paper is organised as follows: Section 2 describes the paper selection and filtering process. Section 3 provides summaries of the research presented in each paper. Section 4 presents a comparative survey of the papers in terms of shared properties, Section 5 discusses our findings, and Section 6 concludes with a summary and future directions.

2 Paper Selection and Filtering

To select papers for our survey, we searched the ACL Anthology[1] with the query terms "error taxonomy" and "NLP," and "error type annotation" and "NLP" which yielded 84 results. After removing non-paper results and duplicates,[2] we were left with 27 papers. We manually examined the remaining papers keeping only those that actually reported an error taxonomy or error annotation scheme including semantic errors, which left 18 papers. We added four relevant papers from the related work

[1] https://aclanthology.org

[2] Search results included 39 author profiles, and 18 paper duplicates, where papers are repeated in two places, e.g. when the same paper is found both individually and as a part of proceedings in the search.

Proceedings of the 2nd Workshop on Natural Language Generation, Evaluation, and Metrics (GEM), pages 383 - 398
December 7, 2022 ©2022 Association for Computational Linguistics

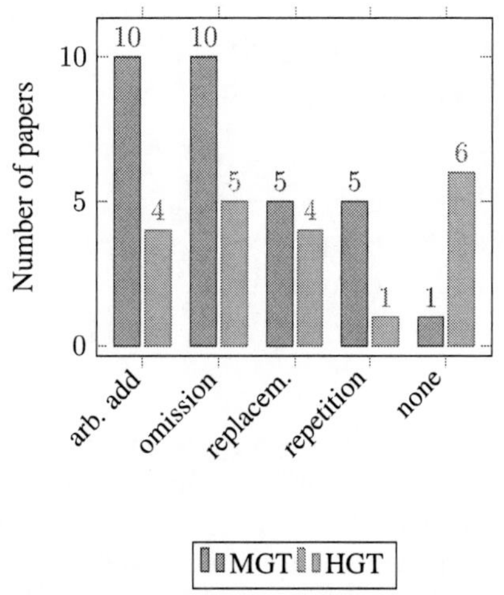

Figure 1: Number of papers reporting semantic errors in the taxonomies.

sections of three of the 18 papers. Our survey reviews the resulting 22 papers.

3 Paper Summaries

In this section, we provide high-level summaries of each of the 22 papers in our survey.

Costa et al. (2015) propose a linguistically motivated taxonomy for machine translation (MT) errors, classifying MT errors for English to European Portuguese translation. At the top level, the taxonomy is divided into five categories: orthography, lexis, grammar, semantic and discourse. It has five levels and 25 leaf nodes. The taxonomy is shown in full in Figure 3, alongside examples extracted from the paper, in Appendix A.

Extend earlier work (Specia et al., 2021), Al Sharou and Specia (2022) propose a an error annotation scheme with seven categories of critical errors, i.e. those with potential negative impact on users where the meaning of the target text deviates drastically from the source text. The work distinguishes three ways in which meaning can deviate from the source sentence: mistranslation, hallucination and deletion. A few examples extracted from the paper are in Appendix A.

Caseli and Inácio (2020) report an error analysis for neural machine translation (NMT) system outputs for Brazilian Portuguese in which errors by the NMT system are compared with those by a PBSMT system trained on the same corpus. The paper adopts the error taxonomy from Martins and Caseli (2015) which divides errors at the top level into four broad categories: syntactic errors, lexical errors, errors involving n-grams and reordering. The taxonomy has three levels and 12 leaf nodes. The taxonomy can be found in Appendix A.

Federico et al. (2014) propose a statistical framework for analysing the impact of different error types based on the results from MT evaluation metrics and human perceptions with linear mixed effects models. Experiments are carried out for English as the source and other languages that are distant from English as the target. This paper uses a set of four general error classes: (i) reordering errors (ii) lexicon errors, (iii) missing words and (iv) morphology errors.

He et al. (2021) report an error-annotated dataset called TGEA which has comprehensive annotations for texts generated with pretrained language models. It is also intended as a benchmark dataset for automatic diagnostic tasks such as error detection, error classification etc. The error taxonomy covers 25 error types in a 3-level hierarchy reflecting linguistic knowledge as shown in Figure 4 in the Appendix.

Belkebir and Habash (2021) report an automatic error type annotation system called ARETA for Modern Standard Arabic. ARETA aims to annotate and evaluate the quality of system outputs. First, it performs word alignment of the source and the target sentence. Second, the alignment is fed to the automatic error type annotation where the system tries to extract the error type. The ARETA taxonomy is based on the Arabic Learner Corpus (ALC) error tagset (Alfaifi and Atwell, 2015) with extended merge and split classes. The latter includes 29 error tags for Arabic of which 26 are used for ARETA. The ARETA taxonomy has three levels and 26 leaf nodes. The taxonomy can be found in Figure 5 in Appendix A.

Huang et al. (2020) introduce PolyTope which quantifies primary sources of errors for 10 representative models for text summarisation. While this is not an error taxonomy paper, it reports primary sources of errors with 8 'fluency' and 'accuracy' type metrics. For PolyTope, (i) Accuracy-related issues are defined as the summarisation not matching or accurately reflecting the source text, whereas (ii) Fluency-related issues are defined as problems with the linguistic qualities of the text. Level of severity is additionally marked as minor, major or critical. The paper uses the CNN/DM Dataset (in its non-anonymous version) for experiments. The taxonomy has three levels and eight leaf nodes, as

Error Types	Definition(s)
Hallucination[a] (*h*)	An example definition in the context of NLP is "generated content that is nonsensical or unfaithful to the source content." This is a widely accepted term (Ji et al., 2022) to refer to content in the output that does not have corresponding content in the input. The term comes from the field of psychology where e.g. (Blom, 2010) defines hallucination as "a percept, experienced by waking individual, in the absence of an appropriate stimulus from extracorporeal world." Some other terms used for errors very similar to hallucination are *addition, insertion, extra words, unnecessary information.*
Omission (*o*)	Used so commonly in MT that a definition is not usually given, this term refers to content in the input that should be rendered in the output not having corresponding content in the output (Weng et al., 2020) Some alternative terms in use are *deletion, absent word/n-gram, missing context/information.*
Replacement (*re*)	We use this term to refer to a range of error phenomena (given a variety of names in the literature) where some content in the output is clearly intended to convey some part of the input, but does so incorrectly (Subramaniam et al., 2009; Gouws et al., 2011; Han and Baldwin, 2011; Al Sharou and Specia, 2022). We can also look at replacement errors from the perspective of a combination of omission and addition, in the special case where what is added is the incorrect version of what is omitted. Some alternative terms also in use are *substitution, mistranslation, transposition.*
Repetition (*r*)	An example definition is "occurrence of the same words several times or syntactically similar units unintentionally or on purpose" (Al Sharou et al., 2021). Some alternative terms in use are *duplication, redundancy.*

Figure 2: Definitions of high-level semantic error types found in the literature (Col 1: semantic error types; Col 2: definitions).

[a]We generally prefer the term 'arbitrary content addition' but use the original term used in the literature to avoid confusion.

showin in Figure 6.

Di et al. (2019) report a detailed analysis of errors from four morphological inflection systems for Tibetan, using datasets developed by Cotterell et al. (2018), and the error taxonomy reported by Gorman et al. (2019) for target errors and prediction errors with a more detailed analysis on (i) errors due to words that violate lexicographic or morphophonetic constraints of the language, and (ii) allomorphy errors. This latter taxonomy has three levels and three leaf nodes, and can be found in Appendix A.

Mahmud et al. (2021) report a qualitative investigation of errors made by neural models fro which they create a taxonomy which consists of seven top level categories each with multiple lower level subcategories as shown in Figure 7 in the Appendix. Altogether there are three levels and 31 leaf nodes.

Costa et al. (2012) report a corpus of about 6,000 questions manually translated into Portuguese. They provide translation guidelines which discuss two types of problems: semantic level issues and structure level issues. In addition, they report an error taxonomy with four broad error categories and carry out an error analysis. The taxonomy has three levels and nine leaf nodes, and can be found in Appendix A.

Macklovitch (1991) introduces an error taxonomy to help with post-editing operations. The error taxonomy distinguishes three broad categories at the top level: (i) Morphology, (ii) Source language analysis and (iii) Transfer and Generation. Altogether there are three levels and 19 leaf nodes. Figure 9 shows the taxonomy extracted from the paper.

Lin et al. (2022) address automatic translation error correction (TEC) where the goal is to produce an improved translation by correcting errors found in a translation. The paper proposes a pretraining approach for TEC and also introduces a human-in-the-loop user study where it was found that higher quality translations were achieved when corrections are assisted by the TEC model. The taxonomy used has three levels and five leaf nodes. It can be found in Appendix B.

van der Goot et al. (2018) describe an error taxonomy for lexical normalisation replacements. The work makes a clear distinction between intentional and unintentional anomalies, and the taxonomy has four levels and 14 leaf nodes.

Ng et al. (2014) provide an error annotation scheme for grammar error types. The paper's goal is to evaluate algorithms and systems for automatically detecting and correcting grammatical errors present in English essays written by second language learners of English. The error annotation scheme has a set of 28 categories of grammatical error corrections as a part of the CoNLL-2014 shared task. The authors report that it is often acceptable to have multiple and different corrections in grammatical error correction. The dataset used for training is the NUCLE corpus, the NUS corpus for Learner English (Dahlmeier et al., 2013), and the test data is collected as written essays from 25

NUS students who are non-native speakers of English where each student was asked to write two essays. Figure 12 in Appendix B shows the error categories from the paper.

Dickinson and Herring (2008) report a computer-aided language learning (ICALL) system for beginner-level learners of Russian. The goal of the system is to provide exercises supporting basic grammar learning with contextualisation for morphological errors. Considering the nature of the learner's language, an error taxonomy with four broad categories for Russian verbal morphology is reported. It has three levels and nine leaf nodes. More details of the taxonomy can be found in Appendix B.

Dickinson (2010) reports work on generating linguistically informed morphological errors for Russian. An error taxonomy is reported that helps in the error generation process. It has four levels and 10 leaf nodes, and can be found at Figure 13 in Appendix B.

Nagata et al. (2018) explore the influence of spelling errors on lexical variation measures like Type-Token Ratio (TTR) and Yule's K for learner English. The error annotation scheme reported presents two ways of spelling error correction: (i) it identifies 13 errors in the corpora. (ii) it classifies them into three groups: corrected, not corrected and not counted. The scheme has 13 error types. Figure 14 in Appendix B shows the list of errors from the paper.

Gayo et al. (2016) propose the COPLE2 corpus which is a new learner corpus for Portuguese. Three different linguistic error types are defined for error tagging: orthographic, grammatical and lexical. The first error type covers spelling errors, with errors here restricted to word form and punctuation marks. The second error type is for when the student has produced an ungrammatical utterance, thus going beyond individual words and considering syntactic structures. The third error type covers lexical/semantic errors. The work is mainly concerned with errors that affects meaning. These error types help in visualising the same text progressing through corrections at different stages, from the version closest to original (orthographic corrections) to the most modified one (orthographical, grammatical and lexical corrections). Note that the sub-error types provided for this paper are unclear, and are not counted in tables below.

Barbagli et al. (2016) present a collection of essays called CItA corpus written by Italian L1 learners (Corpus Italiano di Apprendenti L1) from the first and second years of lower secondary school. In addition, they report a three-level error annotation scheme for errors made by L1 Italian learners: (i) macro-class of error (grammatical, othrographic and lexical); (ii) class of error (verb, prepositions, monosyllables); and (iii) type of modification (misuse of verb with respect to verbal tense). There are therefore four levels in the underlying taxonomy, and a total of 21 leaf nodes. Figure 15 in Appendix B shows the taxonomy from the paper.

Himoro and Pareja-Lora (2020) propose a spelling error taxonomy for Zamboanga Chabacano (ZC) formalised as an ontology and an adaptive spell checking approach using character-based statistical MT. First, an iterative process is applied to samples of the CWZCC corpus for categorising different spelling errors. Second, the errors are classified to create an error taxonomy. It is observed that spelling errors get more complex as one goes deeper down the tree. The taxonomy has eight levels and 14 leaf nodes. and is shown in Figure 16 in Appendix B.

Caines et al. (2020) introduce a corpus of one-to-one online chatroom conversations from lessons between teachers and learners of English which is known as the Teacher-Student Chatroom Corpus (TSCC). A set of 24 error types is determined on the basis of the grammatical error correction of texts in the corpus. The set is shown in Figure 17 in Appendix B.

Korre et al. (2021) introduce ERRANT which is a toolkit that annotates texts and offers error typing with detailed feedback for L2 learners of Greek. Annotation is based on a rule-based error type framework that distinguishes (i) error description (Unnecessary, Replacement and Missing), and (ii) error type. The latter disinguishes 16 error types.

4 Properties of Error Annotation Schemes

In order to be able to compare different error annotation schemes and draw conclusions about their similarities and differences, we labeled each scheme in terms of (i) whether it was designed for machine or human generated text; (ii) whether it contained error types related to semantic accuracy, fluency or both; (iii) NLP system task; (iv) purpose of the annotation that was carried out; and (v) details of how many error labels and how many hierarchical levels there are in the scheme. We describe the first two in Section 4.1 below, the third and fourth in Section 4.3, and the last in Section 4.2.

The results of labelling the 22 annotation schemes with these labels are presented in Section 4.4.

4.1 Text type and error type

We categorise each paper in terms of the (i) *text type*, and (2) *error type* addressed. Regarding the former, we group the error annotation schemes in our survey into those developed for machine-generated text (MGT) and those developed for human-generated text (HGT), according to the following definitions:

- **Machine generated texts (MGT)** i.e. synthetic texts generated by a system or a model based on pre-defined rules or algorithms, including MT, text summarisation, story generation etc. Errors like mistranslation, omission or arbitrary content addition, etc. are observed frequently in annotation schemes for this text type. Figure 7 in the Appendix provides examples of typical errors.
- **Human generated texts (HGT)** include reference texts for evaluating systems, and training corpora for various downstream NLP tasks. The nature of the text depends on its intended purpose and oftentimes, they are used for evaluation of the models we build. Compared to MGT, HGTs are less prone to semantic errors. However, it cannot be generalised that all human generated texts are of good quality, and semantic errors do occur. Figure 16 in the Appendix provides examples of errors in human-generated texts.

We further categorise error annotation schemes in terms of the broad error type(s) addressed. Here we use 'accuracy' and 'fluency' as shorthand for content type errors as per Figure 2, and non-content type errors, respectively. These two terms are used frequently in the MT literature, e.g. in the Multidimensional Quality Metrics (MQM) framework (Lommel et al., 2014) where they are defined as follows:

- **Accuracy**: Errors where the target sentence does not correspond to the source text due to omission, distortion or addition to the text. Error types include mistranslation, over-translation, under-translation, untranslated, omission, and addition.
- **Fluency**: Errors related to grammar and style. Examples include errors relating to spelling, punctuation, grammatical rules, inconsistent style, unidiomatic style etc.

4.2 Structure of annotation scheme

We also categorised error annotation schemes in terms of two structural properties:

1. The **number of different error types** included in an annotation scheme, for which we use a standardised definition as the number of nodes in the tree including the root;
2. The **depth of the hierarchical structure** underlying the scheme. If there is no underlying hierarchical structure, then depth=1. Depth = levels - 1, where levels are the number of nodes in the longest path from root to the leaf nodes.

4.3 NLP task and annotation scheme purpose

We distinguish the following **NLP System Tasks**, abbreviated as indicated in square brackets in tables below: Machine Translation [MT], Text Summarisation [TS], Textual Summarisation of source code [TS(SC)], Type-level Universal Morphological Reinflection Task [MI], Automatic Translation Error Correction [EC(T)], Text Normalisation [TN], Grammar Error Correction [EC(G)], Morphological Error Detection and Classification [MDC], Error Generation [EG], None (Corpus Linguistics) [N(CL)], Dialogue [D], Error Type Classification [ETC] and Spelling Error Correction [EC(S)].

NLP System Task also includes the following automatic forms of error annotation: Automatic Error Annotation for Dataset Creation [EA(D)], Automatic Error Annotation of System outputs for evaluation [EA(S)], Automatic Corpus Error annotation/analysis [CE]. The NLP System Task is defined for what the error annotation scheme is used for in its respective papers.

Inspired by Machine Translation (MT) research which takes a very structured approach to error analysis (Stymne and Ahrenberg, 2012; Koponen, 2010), error classification (Vilar et al., 2006; Popović and Burchardt, 2011; Popović, 2021), and building error taxonomies (Costa et al., 2015; Al Sharou and Specia, 2022), we also categorise

Sl.no	Work	Type	NLP Task	Accuracy	Fluency	# Error types	Depth	Purpose
1.	Costa et al. (2015)	MGT	MT	✓	✓	36	4	EAn+EA+EC
2.	Al Sharou and Specia (2022)	MGT	MT	✓		8	1	EAn+E(S)
3.	Caseli and Inácio (2020)	MGT	MT	✓	✓	17	2	EAn+EA+E(S)
4.	Federico et al. (2014)	MGT	MT	✓	✓	5	1	EAn+EA
5.	He et al. (2021)	MGT	EA(D)	✓		32	2	EAn+EA+E(S)
6.	Belkebir and Habash (2021)	MGT	EA(S)		✓	34	2	EAn+EA
7.	Huang et al. (2020)	MGT	TS	✓	✓	11	2	EAn+E(S)
8.	Di et al. (2019)	MGT	MI		✓	5	2	EAn+EA+E(S)
9.	Mahmud et al. (2021)	MGT	TS(SC)	✓		39	2	EAn+E(S)
10.	Costa et al. (2012)	MGT	CE	✓	✓	11	2	EAn+EA+E(C)
11.	Macklovitch (1991)	MGT	MT	✓	✓	23	2	EAn+E(S)
12.	Lin et al. (2022)	HGT	EC(T)		✓	7	2	EAn+E(C)+E(S)
13.	van der Goot et al. (2018)	HGT	TN		✓	20	3	EAn+E(S)
14.	Ng et al. (2014)	HGT	EC(G)		✓	29	1	EAn+E(S)
15.	Dickinson and Herring (2008)	HGT	MDC		✓	11	2	ED+EA
16.	Dickinson (2010)	HGT	EG		✓	14	3	EAn+E(C)
17.	Nagata et al. (2018)	HGT	EC(S)	✓	✓	14	1	EAn+E(C)+EC
18.	Gayo et al. (2016)	HGT	CE	✓	✓	4	1	EAn+E(C)
19.	Barbagli et al. (2016)	HGT	N(CL)	✓	✓	35	3	EAn+E(C)
20.	Himoro and Pareja-Lora (2020)	HGT	EC(S)		✓	39	7	EAn+E(C)+EC
21.	Caines et al. (2020)	HGT	D		✓	25	1	EAn+E(C)
22.	Korre et al. (2021)	HGT	ETC		✓	17	1	EAn+E(C)+EC

Table 1: Overview table of properties of the error annotations schemes surveyed (for explanation of abbreviations see Table 3 and in text).

our error annotation schemes in terms of the **Purpose for which an error annotation scheme was created** as follows: Error Classification is EC, Error Annotation is EAn, Evaluation for systems is E(S), Evaluation for corpus errors is E(C), Error Detection is ED and Error Analysis is EA. The purpose is defined for what the error annotation scheme that was created is used as in its respective papers.

4.4 Labelled annotation schemes

Table 1 shows each of the 22 surveyed papers alongside their individual labels. Columns 3 and 4 indicate text type and NLP Task, Columns 5 and 6 whether Accuracy or Fluency is addressed, and the last three columns show number of different Error Types, Depth, and Purpose for which the scheme was created, respectively, all as defined in the preceding section.

As can be seen, there is an even distribution of papers over text type addressed (HGT vs. MGT). Moreover, none of the 11 papers addressing HGT address only accuracy errors, most address only fluency (8 out of 11), and just three address both accuracy and fluency errors. For the 11 MGT papers, we have a fair mix of different types of errors i.e., three address only accuracy errors, two only fluency errors, and six address both. Determining the number of error types and the depth of the hierarchy (if any) has been a challenge due to lack of clarity within the papers. For example, Gayo et al. (2016) do not mention the error sub-types in the taxonomy clearly which makes counting them difficult. This means we have provided an estimate in some cases.

All 22 papers have a combination of purposes for which the scheme was created (last column).

5 Discussion

5.1 Trends Observed

Table 2 presents the overall trend in different types of semantic errors included in error annotation schemes over the years in our surveyed papers. We mark as 1 if we encounter any one of the semantic error types from Figure 2 in a paper (each paper can have more than one semantic error type). For example, we have a count of 4 for arbitrary content addition errors from 2020 which means four papers

Semantic Error	1991	2008	2010	2012	2014	2015	2016	2018	2019	2020	2021	2022	TOTAL
Arbitrary content addition (*h*)	1			1	1	1	1	1		4	4	1	15
Omission (*o*)	1			1	1	1		1		4	4	1	14
Replacement (*re*)	1				1					4	2	2	10
Repetition (*r*)						1	1			2	2	1	7
TOTAL	**3**			**2**	**3**	**3**	**2**	**2**		**14**	**12**	**5**	**46**

Table 2: Number of taxonomies that incorporated each of the four high-level semantic error types from Figure 2, shown per publication year in our set of 22 papers.

Purpose	(Paper)[Sem. Error]	MGT	HGT
Error Analysis & Error Annotation (EA+EAn)	(4,6)[*h,o,re*]	✓	
Error Detection & Error Analysis (ED+EA)	(15)[*n*]		✓
Evaluation of systems & Error Annotation (E(S)+EAn)	(2,7,9,11,13)[*h,o*],(2,11)[*re*], (7,9)[*r*],(14)[*n*]	✓	✓
Error Annotation & Error Analysis & Error Classification (EAn+EA+EC)	(1)[*h,o,r*]	✓	
Evaluation of corpus errors & Error Annotation (E(C)+EAn)	(19,21)[*o*],(21)[*h,re*], (16,18)[*n*]		✓
Error Annotation & Error Analysis & Evaluation of systems (EAn+EA+E(S))	(3,5)[*h,o,r*],(3)[*re*],(8)[*n*]	✓	
Error Annotation & Error Analysis & Evaluation of corpus errors (EAn+EA+E(C))	(10)[*h,o*]	✓	
Error Annotation & Evaluation of corpus errors & Evaluation of systems (EAn+E(C)+E(S))	(12)[*re*]		✓
Error Annotation & Evaluation of corpus errors & Error Classification (EAn+E(C)+EC)	(20,22)[*h,o,re*], (17)[*n*]		✓

Table 3: For each (combination of) purpose(s) in the 22 surveyed papers, the taxonomies to which it applies (round brackets), and the semantic error types covered by each of those taxonomies [square brackets]. We also show text type to which each (combination of) purpose(s) applies.

address such errors in the year 2020. The paper IDs are taken from Table 1.

Four out of the five papers in our survey published more than ten years ago (2012 and earlier) are categorised as HGT (except the paper by Macklovitch (1991) which is categorised as MGT), and do not report any semantic errors in their error annotation scheme. In addition, another paper, by Di et al. (2019), grouped under MGT, also does not report any semantic errors. We observe a total of 46 semantic error types reported in the papers from our survey.

Table 3 shows in the first column, all the combinations of purposes for which an error annotation scheme was created that we encountered in our 22 surveyed papers. The second column shows paper number (e.g. "(15)"), type of semantic errors addressed in each paper (e.g. "[*h, o, r*]") or none ("[*n*]"). The last two columns show text type (HGT vs. MGT).

We observe that papers where text type is MGT typically address one or more semantic errors (10 out of 11 papers), except for the paper by Di et al. (2019) whose purpose is error analysis and evaluation of systems. Half of the papers labelled HGT do not address any semantic errors. The other half of the papers with error annotation and evaluation of corpus or error classification as purpose in HGT addresses semantic errors. The statistics of how many papers address each of the high-level semantic error types in the MGT and HGT groups can easily be seen in Figure 1.

Table 2 shows the high-level semantic error types reported in each year in our survey. It is interesting to observe that addressing semantic errors has become increasingly frequent in very recent years.[3] One reason is likely to be the shift from controlled pipeline approaches to end-to-end neural approaches for many NLP tasks.

[3] Note that we performed the ACL Anthology search in August, so we may be missing some papers from 2022.

5.2 Observations

In this section, we discuss the issues we observed in labelling the error annotation schemes and taxonomies in our survey. We summarise these observations from the perspective of semantic errors as follows:

1. **Lack of standardisation across schemes** (e.g., definition, examples) is observed which hampers deriving a standardised framework for semantic errors. We found that 11 out of 22 papers (50%) mention only the name of an error type or its sub-type without defining them at all. It is highly observed in the HGT group, with eight out of 22 papers. In some cases it is difficult to categorise schemes/taxonomies in terms of the *high-level error type(s)* from Figure 2.
2. **Differing and/or incompatible error names and definitions:** In our survey, we encountered only two papers (Dickinson and Herring, 2008; Dickinson, 2010) with mutually compatible error type definitions and these are by the same first author. For the remaining papers, either the error definitions means the same but the error term is different, or vice versa.
3. **Borderline error types** that cannot clearly be assigned either to semantic accuracy or to fluency. Categorising the error annotation schemes for which this is the case in the survey as accuracy and/or fluency errors is sometimes difficult due to the (lack of) provided definitions, examples, etc. We found 12 out of 22 papers (which is more than 50%) to be difficult to categorise which corresponds to three out of 11 papers for the MGT group, and 9 out of 11 papers for HGT. This difficulty implies an unclear boundary between accuracy and fluency types of errors.

Further interesting observations can be drawn from Table 1 and Table 3 concerning the relationship between semantic errors on the one hand, and text types (MGT, HGT) and broad errors types (accuracy and fluency), on the other. Nine out of 11 papers in the MGT group address either accuracy error types only (3/9), or accuracy error types together with fluency error types (6/9). Arbitrary content addition (currently more commonly known as hallucination) and omission are the most common semantic errors reported and we see them in all nine papers under the MGT group. Repetition (in combination with other semantic errors) is the next frequently reported semantic error and we see it in five out of nine papers under the MGT group. Meanwhile, three papers in the HGT group address both accuracy and fluency error types with only one paper out of the three addressing omission.

Part of the motivation for conducting this survey was to use it as a starting point in creating our own semantic error taxonomy for annotating errors in output text in data-to-text generation. Our original aim was to base our taxonomy on common error types found in the literature, but, as we have seen in this paper, there is little agreement between existing error taxonomies beyond a distinction at the highest level between accuracy and fluency type errors, and accuracy further dividing into (a) arbitrarily content addition (currently more commonly known as hallucination), (b) omission, (c) replacement, and (d) repetition. Our next step will be to take this as a starting point and add lower taxonomy levels as required for data-to-text generation, while trying to incorporate as much common ground from the literature as possible. Another consideration will be that we wish to use the resulting error taxonomy both in performing manual error analysis, and for providing the categories in automatic error detection.

6 Conclusion

We conducted a structured survey of work on error type annotation schemes (with a focus on error taxonomies), as reported in papers from the ACL Anthology. We observed a number of issues while analysing the papers in our survey which we characterised in terms of (1) lack of standardisation, (2) differing/incompatible error names and definitions across different papers, and (3) borderline error types which resist being classified as either fluency or accuracy related. We found that the latter is mostly observed in error annotation for human-generated text rather than machine-generated. We conducted our study from the perspective of semantic error annotation, as we plan to build on it in future work on developing an error taxonomy of semantic error types for data-to-text generation.

References

Khetam Al Sharou, Zhenhao Li, and Lucia Specia. 2021. Towards a better understanding of noise in natural language processing. In *Proceedings of the International Conference on Recent Advances in Natural Language Processing (RANLP 2021)*, pages 53–62.

Khetam Al Sharou and Lucia Specia. 2022. A taxonomy and study of critical errors in machine translation. In *Proceedings of the 23rd Annual Conference of the European Association for Machine Translation*, pages 171–179.

AYG Alfaifi and ES Atwell. 2015. Computer-aided error annotation: a new tool for annotating arabic error.

Alessia Barbagli, Pietro Lucisano, Felice Dell'Orletta, Simonetta Montemagni, and Giulia Venturi. 2016. Cita: An l1 italian learners corpus to study the development of writing competence. In *Proceedings of the Tenth International Conference on Language Resources and Evaluation (LREC'16)*, pages 88–95.

Riadh Belkebir and Nizar Habash. 2021. Automatic error type annotation for arabic. In *Proceedings of the 25th Conference on Computational Natural Language Learning*, pages 596–606.

Jan Dirk Blom. 2010. *A dictionary of hallucinations*. Springer.

Andrew Caines, Helen Yannakoudakis, Helena Edmondson, Helen Allen, Pascual Pérez-Paredes, Bill Byrne, and Paula Buttery. 2020. The teacher-student chatroom corpus. In *Proceedings of the 9th Workshop on NLP for Computer Assisted Language Learning*, pages 10–20.

Helena Caseli and Marcio Inácio. 2020. Nmt and pbsmt error analyses in english to brazilian portuguese automatic translations. In *Proceedings of the 12th Language Resources and Evaluation Conference*, pages 3623–3629.

Ângela Costa, Wang Ling, Tiago Luís, Rui Correia, and Luísa Coheur. 2015. A linguistically motivated taxonomy for machine translation error analysis. *Machine Translation*, 29(2):127–161.

Ângela Costa, Tiago Luís, Joana Ribeiro, Ana Cristina Mendes, and Luísa Coheur. 2012. An english-portuguese parallel corpus of questions: translation guidelines and application in smt. In *Proceedings of the Eighth International Conference on Language Resources and Evaluation (LREC'12)*, pages 2172–2176.

Ryan Cotterell, Christo Kirov, John Sylak-Glassman, Géraldine Walther, Ekaterina Vylomova, Arya D. McCarthy, Katharina Kann, Sabrina J. Mielke, Garrett Nicolai, Miikka Silfverberg, David Yarowsky, Jason Eisner, and Mans Hulden. 2018. The CoNLL–SIGMORPHON 2018 shared task: Universal morphological reinflection. In *Proceedings of the CoNLL–SIGMORPHON 2018 Shared Task: Universal Morphological Reinflection*, pages 1–27, Brussels. Association for Computational Linguistics.

Daniel Dahlmeier, Hwee Tou Ng, and Siew Mei Wu. 2013. Building a large annotated corpus of learner english: The nus corpus of learner english. In *Proceedings of the eighth workshop on innovative use of NLP for building educational applications*, pages 22–31.

Qianji Di, Ekaterina Vylomova, and Timothy Baldwin. 2019. Modelling tibetan verbal morphology. In *Proceedings of the The 17th Annual Workshop of the Australasian Language Technology Association*, pages 35–40.

Markus Dickinson. 2010. Generating learner-like morphological errors in russian. In *Proceedings of the 23rd International Conference on Computational Linguistics (Coling 2010)*, pages 259–267.

Markus Dickinson and Joshua Herring. 2008. Developing online icall resources for russian. In *Proceedings of the Third Workshop on Innovative Use of NLP for Building Educational Applications*, pages 1–9.

Ondřej Dušek, David M. Howcroft, and Verena Rieser. 2019. Semantic noise matters for neural natural language generation. In *Proceedings of the 12th International Conference on Natural Language Generation*, pages 421–426, Tokyo, Japan. Association for Computational Linguistics.

Ondřej Dušek, Jekaterina Novikova, and Verena Rieser. 2020. Evaluating the state-of-the-art of end-to-end natural language generation: The e2e nlg challenge. *Computer Speech & Language*, 59:123–156.

Marcello Federico, Matteo Negri, Luisa Bentivogli, and Marco Turchi. 2014. Assessing the impact of translation errors on machine translation quality with mixed-effects models. In *Proceedings of the 2014 Conference on Empirical Methods in Natural Language Processing (EMNLP)*, pages 1643–1653.

Iria Del Río Gayo, Sandra Antunes, Amália Mendes, and Maarten Janssen. 2016. Towards error annotation in a learner corpus of portuguese. In *Proceedings of the joint workshop on NLP for Computer Assisted Language Learning and NLP for Language Acquisition*, pages 8–17.

Kyle Gorman, Arya D. McCarthy, Ryan Cotterell, Ekaterina Vylomova, Miikka Silfverberg, and Magdalena Markowska. 2019. Weird inflects but OK: Making sense of morphological generation errors. In *Proceedings of the 23rd Conference on Computational Natural Language Learning (CoNLL)*, pages 140–151, Hong Kong, China. Association for Computational Linguistics.

Stephan Gouws, Dirk Hovy, and Donald Metzler. 2011. Unsupervised mining of lexical variants from noisy text. In *Proceedings of the First workshop on Unsupervised Learning in NLP*, pages 82–90.

Bo Han and Timothy Baldwin. 2011. Lexical normalisation of short text messages: Makn sens a# twitter. In *Proceedings of the 49th annual meeting of the association for computational linguistics: Human language technologies*, pages 368–378.

Hamza Harkous, Isabel Groves, and Amir Saffari. 2020. Have your text and use it too! end-to-end neural data-to-text generation with semantic fidelity. In *Proceedings of the 28th International Conference on Computational Linguistics*, pages 2410–2424, Barcelona, Spain (Online). International Committee on Computational Linguistics.

Jie He, Bo Peng, Yi Liao, Qun Liu, and Deyi Xiong. 2021. Tgea: An error-annotated dataset and benchmark tasks for textgeneration from pretrained language models. In *Proceedings of the 59th Annual Meeting of the Association for Computational Linguistics and the 11th International Joint Conference on Natural Language Processing (Volume 1: Long Papers)*, pages 6012–6025.

Marcelo Yuji Himoro and Antonio Pareja-Lora. 2020. Towards a spell checker for Zamboanga Chavacano orthography. In *Proceedings of the 12th Language Resources and Evaluation Conference*, pages 2685–2697, Marseille, France. European Language Resources Association.

Dandan Huang, Leyang Cui, Sen Yang, Guangsheng Bao, Kun Wang, Jun Xie, and Yue Zhang. 2020. What have we achieved on text summarization? *arXiv preprint arXiv:2010.04529*.

Ziwei Ji, Nayeon Lee, Rita Frieske, Tiezheng Yu, Dan Su, Yan Xu, Etsuko Ishii, Yejin Bang, Andrea Madotto, and Pascale Fung. 2022. Survey of hallucination in natural language generation. *arXiv preprint arXiv:2202.03629*.

Maarit Koponen. 2010. Assessing machine translation quality with error analysis. In *Electronic proceeding of the KaTu symposium on translation and interpreting studies*.

Katerina Korre, Marita Chatzipanagiotou, and John Pavlopoulos. 2021. Elerrant: Automatic grammatical error type classification for greek. In *Proceedings of the International Conference on Recent Advances in Natural Language Processing (RANLP 2021)*, pages 708–717.

Jessy Lin, Geza Kovacs, Aditya Shastry, Joern Wuebker, and John DeNero. 2022. Automatic correction of human translations. In *Proceedings of the 2022 Conference of the North American Chapter of the Association for Computational Linguistics: Human Language Technologies*, pages 494–507.

Arle Lommel, Hans Uszkoreit, and Aljoscha Burchardt. 2014. Multidimensional quality metrics (mqm): A framework for declaring and describing translation quality metrics. *Revista Tradumàtica: tecnologies de la traducció*, (12):455–463.

Elliott Macklovitch. 1991. Evaluating commercial mt systems. In *Evaluators' Forum on MT systems, organized by ISSCO at Ste. Croix, Switzerland*.

Junayed Mahmud, Fahim Faisal, Raihan Islam Arnob, Antonios Anastasopoulos, and Kevin Moran. 2021. Code to comment translation: A comparative study on model effectiveness & errors. In *Proceedings of the 1st Workshop on Natural Language Processing for Programming (NLP4Prog 2021)*, pages 1–16.

Débora Beatriz de Jesus Martins and Helena de Medeiros Caseli. 2015. Automatic machine translation error identification. *Machine Translation*, 29(1):1–24.

Ryo Nagata, Taisei Sato, and Hiroya Takamura. 2018. Exploring the influence of spelling errors on lexical variation measures. In *Proceedings of the 27th International Conference on Computational Linguistics*, pages 2391–2398.

Hwee Tou Ng, Siew Mei Wu, Ted Briscoe, Christian Hadiwinoto, Raymond Hendy Susanto, and Christopher Bryant. 2014. The conll-2014 shared task on grammatical error correction. In *Proceedings of the Eighteenth Conference on Computational Natural Language Learning: Shared Task*, pages 1–14.

Maja Popović. 2021. On nature and causes of observed mt errors. In *Proceedings of the 18th Biennial Machine Translation Summit (Volume 1: Research Track)*, pages 163–175.

Maja Popović and Aljoscha Burchardt. 2011. From human to automatic error classification for machine translation output. In *Proceedings of the 15th Annual conference of the European Association for Machine Translation*.

Irene Rivera-Trigueros. 2021. Machine translation systems and quality assessment: a systematic review. *Language Resources and Evaluation*, pages 1–27.

Lucia Specia, Frédéric Blain, Marina Fomicheva, Chrysoula Zerva, Zhenhao Li, Vishrav Chaudhary, and André FT Martins. 2021. Findings of the wmt 2021 shared task on quality estimation. In *Proceedings of the Sixth Conference on Machine Translation*, pages 684–725.

Sara Stymne and Lars Ahrenberg. 2012. On the practice of error analysis for machine translation evaluation. In *Proceedings of the Eighth International Conference on Language Resources and Evaluation (LREC'12)*, pages 1785–1790.

L Venkata Subramaniam, Shourya Roy, Tanveer A Faruquie, and Sumit Negi. 2009. A survey of types of text noise and techniques to handle noisy text. In *Proceedings of The Third Workshop on Analytics for Noisy Unstructured Text Data*, pages 115–122.

Rob van der Goot, Rik van Noord, and Gertjan van Noord. 2018. A taxonomy for in-depth evaluation of normalization for user generated content. In *Proceedings of the Eleventh International Conference on Language Resources and Evaluation (LREC 2018)*.

Emiel van Miltenburg, Miruna Clinciu, Ondřej Dušek, Dimitra Gkatzia, Stephanie Inglis, Leo Leppänen, Saad Mahamood, Emma Manning, Stephanie Schoch, Craig Thomson, and Luou Wen. 2021. Underreporting of errors in NLG output, and what to do about it. In *Proceedings of the 14th International Conference on Natural Language Generation*, pages 140–153, Aberdeen, Scotland, UK. Association for Computational Linguistics.

David Vilar, Jia Xu, Luis Fernando d'Haro, and Hermann Ney. 2006. Error analysis of statistical machine translation output. In *Proceedings of the fifth international conference on language resources and evaluation (LREC'06)*.

Rongxiang Weng, Heng Yu, Xiangpeng Wei, and Weihua Luo. 2020. Towards enhancing faithfulness for neural machine translation. In *Proceedings of the 2020 Conference on Empirical Methods in Natural Language Processing (EMNLP)*, pages 2675–2684.

A Appendix: Error Annotation Schemes for Machine Generated Text (MGT)

In this section, we present entire taxonomies and examples of individual errors for error annotation schemes developed for HGT and extracted from the 22 surveyed papers briefly summarised in Section 3.

Costa et al. (2015) present the taxonomy found in Figure 3. Below are some error examples extracted from the paper:

Example 1: Spelling error in Orthography level

Example: Spelling error

EN: Basilica of the Martyrs

EP: Basílica dos *Mátires

Correct translation: Basílica dos Mártires

Example 2: Omission error (content word) in Lexis level

Example: Omission error (content word)

EN: In his inaugural address, Barack Obama

EP: No seu * inaugural, Barack Obama

Correct translation: No seu discurso inaugural, Barack Obama

Example 3: Addition error (content word) in Lexis level

Example: Addition error (content word)

EN: This time I'm not going to miss

EP: Desta vez *correr não vou perder

Correct translation: Desta vez não vou perder

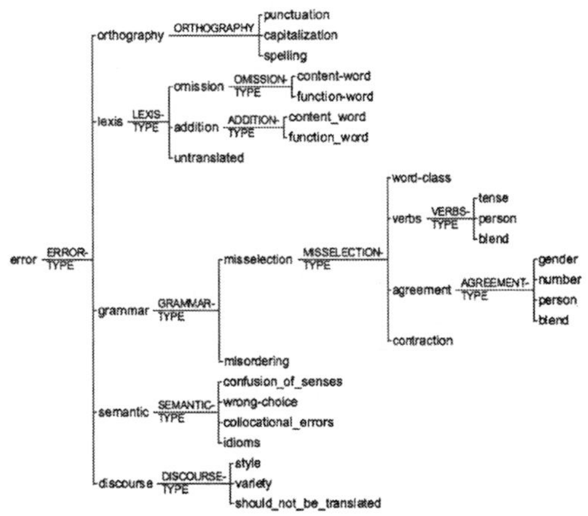

Figure 3: Figure of taxonomy extracted from (Costa et al., 2015).

Al Sharou and Specia (2022) define seven main categories as mentioned in Section 3. Here are some error examples extracted from the paper:

Example 1: Deviation in toxicity (TOX)

ST: Your killing the fucking planet.

MT-ed text: May the damn planet kill you.

Translation into Arabic by Systran

Example 2: Deviation in health/safety risks (SAF)

ST: I Know two teenagers that suffer from gerd it is a big problem for these people!

MT-ed text: I Know two teenagers that suffer from root disease it is a big problem for these people!

Translation into Chinese by GT.

Example 3: Deviation in named entities (NAM)

ST: Your fucking ass doesn't know shit about it AT ALL.Rocky.

MT-ed text: Your fucking ass doesn't know shit about it AT ALL.rock.

Translation into Italian by Bing

Caseli and Inácio (2020) presents a taxonomy found below:

1. Syntactic errors
   - Number agreement
   - Gender agreement
   - Verb inflection
   - PoS

   litem Lexical errors

   - Extra word
   - Absent word
   - Not translated word
   - Incorrectly translated word
2. N-gram
   - Absent n-gram
   - Not translated n-gram
   - Incorrectly translated n-gram
3. Reordering
   - Order

He et al. (2021) present a taxonomy found in Figure 4.

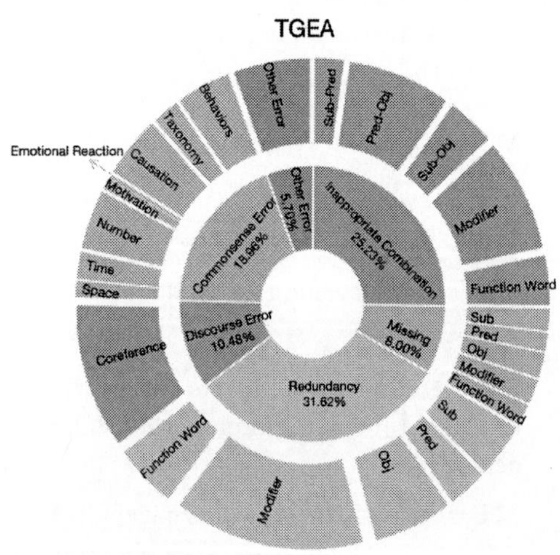

Figure 4: Figure extracted from (He et al., 2021) of level-1 and level-2 error types in TGEA which is an error annotated dataset.

Belkebir and Habash (2021) present a taxonomy found in Table Figure 5.

Huang et al. (2020) show PolyTope with each error types on a three-coordinates for syntactic and semantic roles which is found in Figure 6 and some examples extracted from the paper are found below.

Class	Err Tag	Description	Arabic Example	Transliteration
Orthography	OA	Confusion in Alif, Ya and Alif-Maqsura	علي ← على	çly → çlý
	OC	Wrong order of word characters	تبرينا ← تربينا	tbrynA → trbynA
	OD	Additional character(s)	يعدوم ← يدوم	yçdwm → ydwm
	OG	Lengthening short vowels	نقيمو ← نقيم	nqymw → nqym
	OH	Hamza errors	اكثر ← أكثر	Akθr → Âkθr
	OM	Missing character(s)	سالين ← سائلين	sAlyn → sAŷlyn
	ON	Confusion between Nun and Tanwin	ثوبن ← ثوبٌ	θwbn → θwbũ
	OR	Replacement in word character(s)	مصلنا ← وصلنا	mSlnA → wSlnA
	OS	Shortening long vowels	اوقت ← أوقات	Âwqt → ÂwqAt
	OT	Confusion in Ha, Ta and Ta-Marbuta	مشاركه ← مشاركة	mšArkh → mšArkħ
	OW	Confusion in Alif Fariqa	وكانو ← وكانوا	wkAnw→ wkAnwA
	OO	*Other orthographic errors*	-	-
Morphology	MI	Word inflection	معروف ← عارف	mçrwf → çArf
	MT	Verb tense	تفرحني ← أفرحتني	tfrHny → ÂfrHtny
	MO	*Other morphological errors*	-	-
Syntax	XC	Case	رائع ← رائعاً	rAŷç → rAŷçAã
	XF	Definiteness	السن ← سن	Alsn → sn
	XG	Gender	الغربي ← الغربية	Alγrby → Alγrbyħ
	XM	Missing word	Null ← على	*Null* → çlý
	XN	Number	فكرتي ← أفكاري	fkrty → ÂfkAry
	XT	Unnecessary word	على ← Null	çlý → *Null*
	XO	*Other syntactic errors*	-	-
Semantics	SF	Conjunction error	سبحان ← فسبحان	sbHAn → fsbHAn
	SW	Word selection error	من ← عن	mn → çn
	SO	*Other semantic errors*	-	-
Punctuation	PC	Punctuation confusion	المتوسط. ← المتوسط،	AlmtwsT. → AlmtwsT,
	PM	Missing punctuation	العظيم ← العظيم،	AlçĎym → AlçĎym,
	PT	Unnecessary punctuation	العام، ← العام	AlçAm, → AlçAm
	PO	*Other errors in punctuation*	-	-
Merge	MG	Words are merged	ذهبتالبارحة ← ذهبت البارحة	ðhbtAlbArHħ → ðhbt AlbArHħ
Split	SP	Words are split	الما حدثات ← المحادثات	AlmHA dθAt → AlmHAdθAt

Figure 5: Figure of ARETA which is an error annotation system extracted from (Belkebir and Habash, 2021).

Example 1: Inaccuracy Intrinsic

> "Pittsburgh Union Station is 10 kilometers from Exhibition Center and 3 kilometers from the University of Pittsburgh" in the source but "Pittsburgh Union Station is 3 kilometers from Exhibition Center" in the output.

Example 2: Inaccuracy Extrinsic

> it is described as "Pittsburgh Union Station, also known as Pittsburgh South Station" in the output but "Pittsburgh South Station" is neither mentioned in the source text nor exists in the real world.

Example 3: Positive-Negative Aspect

> "push a button" summarized as "don't push a button", "non-slip" summarized as "slip". This category applies only to actions and modifiers and refers to omitted or added negative particles.

Di et al. (2019) presents an error taxonomy found below.

1. Target errors: Target word errors are 'due to errors in the Wiktionary source data and incorrect extraction of paradigm tables.'
2. Prediction errors

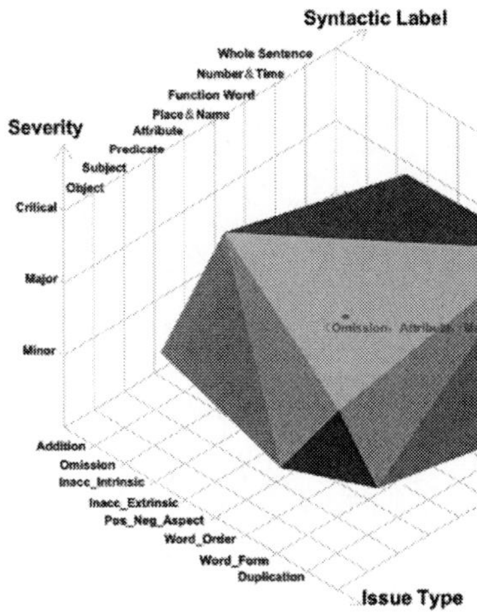

Figure 6: Figure of PolyTope with each error types on a three-coordinates for syntactic and semantic roles extracted from (Huang et al., 2020).

- nonce-word errors: Nonce word errors are 'due to illegal words, i.e. situations when the string generated by a system does not exist in Tibetan.'
- allomorphy errors: Allomorphy errors are considered for verb inflection and diacritics for Tibetan language.

Mahmud et al. (2021) present a taxonomy found in Figure 7.

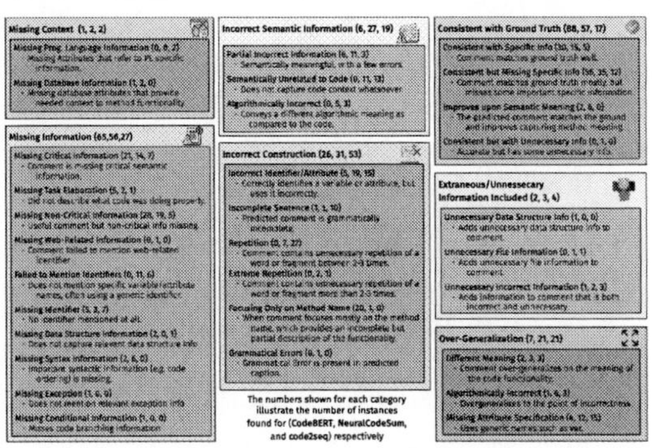

Figure 7: Figure of taxonomy of errors between the generated summaries and ground truth extracted from (Mahmud et al., 2021).

Costa et al. (2012) present a taxonomy and examples below:

The error taxonomy is as follows:

1. Missing words (when one or more words are missing in the translation)
    - Missing word fillers
    - Missing content words
2. Word order (when reordering model is unable to produce a reordering of the sentence)
3. Incorrect words (when a translation engine is unable to produce a correct translation of a word or expression)
    - Lexical choice
    - Disambiguation
    - Incorrect form
    - Extra words
    - Idiomatic Expressions
4. Unknown words (when the translation engine could not find the translation in the target language and keeps the words or expressions in the source language).

Example extracted from the paper in Figure 8:

Original: *Who was the first American to walk in space?*
Translation: *Quem foi o primeiro a andar* ***americano*** *no espaço?*
Correct Translation: *Quem foi o primeiro* ***americano*** *a andar no espaço?*

Figure 8: Examples of word order error extracted from (Costa et al., 2012)

Macklovitch (1991) presents an error tabulation for its taxonomy in Figure 9.

B Appendix: Error Annotation Schemes for Human Generated Text (HGT)

In this section, we present entire taxonomies and examples of individual errors for error annotation schemes developed for HGT and extracted from the 22 surveyed papers briefly summarised in Section 3.

Lin et al. (2022) present a taxonomy based on error correction and each edit belongs to one of the three types listed below. Figure 10 show error types and examples extracted from the paper.

The error taxonomy in Lin et al. (2022) is

1. Monolingual edits (identifiable from the target side of the text)
    - typos (spelling, punctuation, spacing and orthographic issues)
    - grammar

I.	Morphology, graphology & layout
I.1.	Number, inflection & agreement
I.2	Upper/lower case
I.3	Hyphens, slashes & quotes
I.4	Layout; underlining
I.5	References; place names
I.6	Unknown words/symbols
II.	Analysis
II.1	Categorial homography
II.2	'-ing forms
II.3	'-ed forms & passives
II.4	Coordinate structures
II.5	Stacked nominals
II.6	Anaphora & ellipsis
II.7	Articles
II.8	Gibberish
III.	Transfer and generation
III.1	Incorrect/incomplete TL equiv.
III.2	Polysemy
III.3	Restructuring
III.4	Inappropriate/incorrect form generated
III.5	Stylistic changes

Figure 9: Figure of taxonomy extracted from (Macklovitch, 1991)

- fluency

2. Bilingual edits (mismatch between source and target text) Eg, under-translation, mistranslation.
3. Preferential edits (based on the preference of the customer) Eg, terminology, style preference.

van der Goot et al. (2018) present a taxonomy; below are a few examples of errors.

Example 1: Typographical error

spiritel→spirit, complaingl→complaining, throwgl→throw

Example 2: Repetition

sooool→so, weiiiiirdl→weird

Example 3: Unknown

Error Type	Example Text
Monolingual: typos	s: Do your feet roll inwards when running? t: Kippen deine Füße beim Laufen nach innen? t': Kippen deine Füße beim Laufen nach innen?
Monolingual: grammar	s: Own tough winter runs in the ... t: Bei harten Winterläufe sorgt der ... t': Bei harten Winterläufen sorgt der ...
Monolingual: fluency	s: The traffic emerges from the VPN server and ... t: Der Verkehr wird vom VPN-Server ausgegeben und ... t': Der Datenverkehr wird vom VPN-Server ausgegeben und ...
Bilingual	s: Quad Core XEON E3-1501M, 2.9GHz t: Quad Core XEON 2,9 GHz t': Quad Core XEON E3-1501M, 2,9 GHz
Preferential	s: VersaMax I / O auxiliary spring clamp style t: VersaMax Zusatz-E / A Federklemmenart t': VersaMax Zusatz-E / A Federklemmenbauform

Figure 10: Figure of error taxonomy for ACED corpus with examples extracted from (Lin et al., 2022).

Category	Examples
1. Typographical error	spirite↦spirit, complaing↦complaining, throwg↦throw
2. Missing apostrophe	im↦i'm, yall↦y'all, microsofts↦microsoft's
3. Spelling error	favourite↦favorite, dieing↦dying, theirselves↦themselves
4. Split	pre order↦preorder, screen shot↦screenshot
5. Merge	alot↦a lot, nomore↦no more, appstore↦app store
6. Phrasal abbreviation	lol↦laughing out loud, pmsl↦pissing myself laughing
7. Repetition	soooo↦so, weiiiiird↦weird
8. Shortening vowels	pls↦please, wrked↦worked, rmx↦remix
9. Shortening end	gon↦gonna, congrats↦congratulations, g↦girl
10. Shortening other	cause↦because, smth↦something, tl↦timeline,
11. Phonetic transformation	hackd↦hacked, gentille↦gentle, rizky↦risky
12. Regular transformation	foolin↦fooling, wateva↦whatever, droppin↦dropping
13. Slang	cuz↦because, fina↦going to, plz↦please
14. Unknown	skepta↦sunglasses, putos↦photos

Figure 11: Figure of taxonomy extracted from (van der Goot et al., 2018).

skeptal→sunglasses, putosl→photos

Ng et al. (2014) present an error annotation scheme and a few examples below.

Figure 12 includes extracted error categories and its examples from the paper. Here are some examples extracted from the paper:

Example 1: Verb tense (Vt)

Medical technology during that time [is → was] not advanced enough to cure him.

Example 2: Word form (Wform)

The sense of [guilty → guilt] can be more than expected.

Example 3: Unclear meaning (Um)

Genetic disease has a close relationship with the born gene. (i.e., no correction possible without further clarification.)

Dickinson and Herring (2008) presents a taxonomy for Russian verbal morphology:

1. Inappropriate verb stem
    - Always inappropriate

Type	Description	Example
Vt	Verb tense	Medical technology during that time [**is** → was] not advanced enough to cure him.
Vm	Verb modal	Although the problem [**would** → may] not be serious, people [**would** → might] still be afraid.
V0	Missing verb	However, there are also a great number of people [**who** → who are] against this technology.
Vform	Verb form	A study in 2010 [**shown** → showed] that patients recover faster when surrounded by family members.
SVA	Subject-verb agreement	The benefits of disclosing genetic risk information [**outweighs** → outweigh] the costs.
ArtOrDet	Article or determiner	It is obvions to see that [**internet** → the internet] saves people time and also connects people globally.
Nn	Noun number	A carrier may consider not having any [**child** → children] after getting married.
Npos	Noun possessive	Someone should tell the [**carriers** → carrier's] relatives about the genetic problem.
Pform	Pronoun form	A couple should run a few tests to see if [**their** → they] have any genetic diseases beforehand.
Pref	Pronoun reference	It is everyone's duty to ensure that [**he or she** → they] undergo regular health checks.
Prep	Preposition	This essay will [**discuss about** → discuss] whether a carrier should tell his relatives or not.
Wci	Wrong collocation/idiom	Early examination is [**healthy** → advisable] and will cast away unwanted doubts.
Wa	Acronyms	After [**WOWII** → World War II], the population of China decreased rapidly.
Wform	Word form	The sense of [**guilty** → guilt] can be more than expected.
Wtone	Tone (formal/informal)	[**It's** → It is] our family and relatives that bring us up.
Srun	Run-on sentences, comma splices	The issue is highly [**debatable, a** → debatable. A] genetic risk could come from either side of the family.
Smod	Dangling modifiers	[**Undeniable,** → It is undeniable that] it becomes addictive when we spend more time socializing virtually.
Spar	Parallelism	We must pay attention to this information and [**assisting** → assist] those who are at risk.
Sfrag	Sentence fragment	**However, from the ethical point of view.**
Ssub	Subordinate clause	This is an issue [**needs** → that needs] to be addressed.
WOinc	Incorrect word order	[**Someone having what kind of disease** → What kind of disease someone has] is a matter of their own privacy.
WOadv	Incorrect adjective/ adverb order	In conclusion, [**personally I** → I personally] feel that it is important to tell one's family members.
Trans	Linking words/phrases	It is sometimes hard to find [**out** → out if] one has this disease.
Mec	Spelling, punctuation, capitalization, etc.	This knowledge [**maybe relavant** → may be relevant] to them.
Rloc−	Redundancy	It is up to the [**patient's own choice** → patient] to disclose information.
Cit	Citation	Poor citation practice.
Others	Other errors	An error that does not fit into any other category but can still be corrected.
Um	Unclear meaning	Genetic disease has a close relationship with the **born gene**. (i.e., no correction possible without further clarification.)

Figure 12: Figure of taxonomy extracted from (Ng et al., 2014).

    • Inappropriate for this context

2. Inappropriate verb affix
    • Always inappropriate
    • Always inappropriate for verbs
    • Inappropriate for this verb
3. Inappropriate combination of stem and affix
4. Well-formed word in inappropriate context
    • Inappropriate agreement features
    • Inappropriate verb form (tense, perfective/imperfective, etc.)

Dickinson (2010) present an error taxonomy in Figure 13.
Nagata et al. (2018) present a spelling error annotation scheme in Figure 14.
Barbagli et al. (2016) present error annotations and examples in Figure 15.
Himoro and Pareja-Lora (2020) present an error taxonomy and examples in Figure 16.

1. Abbreviation (ABR) in Intentional errors are due to omission of letters or use of homophones letters and/or numbers to replace syllables. Example, kme->kame.
2. Omission (OMS) in unintentional errors are due to deletion of letter from a word without an explanation. Example, Chaacano -> Chavacano.

0. Correct: The word is well-formed.
1. Stem errors:
    (a) Stem spelling error
    (b) Semantic error
2. Suffix errors:
    (a) Suffix spelling error
    (b) Lexicon error:
        i. Derivation error: The wrong POS is used (e.g., a noun as a verb).
        ii. Inherency error: The ending is for a different subclass (e.g., inanimate as an animate noun).
    (c) Paradigm error: The ending is from the wrong paradigm.
3. Formation errors: The stem does not follow appropriate spelling/sound change rules.
4. Syntactic errors: The form is correct, but used in an in appropriate syntactic context (e.g., nominative case in a dative context)

• Lexicon incompleteness: The form may be possible, but is not attested.

Figure 13: Figure of taxonomy extracted from (Dickinson, 2010)

Error code	Explanation	Treatment
SP	Spelling that does not exist in English. e.g., I am a *sistem* engineer.	✓
PC	Inappropriate plural form conjugation. e.g., I didn't do *anythings*.	✓
OC	Over-regularized morphology. e.g., I *gived* her her hat.	✓
GC	Conjugation error other than the above two. e.g., I am *driveing*.	✓
NM	Spelling error in names. e.g., I went to *Desneyland*.	✓
RE	Real word spelling error (i.e., context sensitive error). e.g., *Their* is a house.	×
RO	Romanized Japanese. e.g., I ate an *omusubi*.	-
SR	Romanized Japanese that has no equivalent English expression. e.g., I went to *Hukuoka*. or that becomes proper English if transliterated. e.g., I ate *susi*.(susi → sushi).	-
CW	Coined word that is not used in English. e.g., I want to be a *nailist*.	-
FW	Foreign words other than Japanese. e.g., I have an *Arbeit*.	-
AL	Non-American (e.g. British English) spelling. e.g., It's my *favourite*.	-
AB	Improper abbreviation that is not used in English. e.g., I went to *USJ*.	-
O	Other than the above.	-

Figure 14: Figure of spelling error and corresponding treatment extracted from (Nagata et al., 2018).

Caines et al. (2020) present the error types determined by grammatical error correction of texts in TSCC in Figure 17.
Korre et al. (2021) present an error annotation scheme in Figure 18.

Class of Error	Type of Modification	Example
Verbs	Use of tense	[...] dopo aver fatto le squadre <M t="11" c="abbiamo">avevamo</M> subito iniziato a giocare
	Use of mood	[...] il pensiero che mi tormentava di più era che tra poco si <M t="12" c="sarebbe fatto">faceva</M> il campo scuola.
	Subject-Verb agreement	[...] la mia famiglia ed io <M t="13" c="stavamo">stavo</M> al mare a Torvajanica
Prepositions	Erroneous use	<M t="14" c="in">a</M> Romania sono andata <M t="14" c="in">a</M> agosto
Pronouns	Erroneous use	Proteggere i più deboli è molto coraggioso da parte di chi <M t="16" c="li">lo</M> protegge
	Redundancy	Alla nostra maestra <M t="18" c="canc">gli</M> piaceva tanto la storia
	Erroneous use of relative pronoun	La scienza non so perché mi fa pensare a un fenomeno costruito su un'altura <M t="19" c="per cui">che</M> ci vuole molto ingegno.
Articles	Erroneous use	<M t="111" c="gli">i</M> dei, sapendo che qualcuno aveva preso senza merito il sacro vaso della Giustizia, si rattristarono molto, [...]
Use of *h*	Omission	<M t="23" c="ho">o</M> visto uno spettacolo bellissimo con i raggi laser
Lexicon	Erroneous use	C'era molta ombra nel giardino e io mi ci <M t="31" c="addormentavo">addormivo</M> sempre.

Figure 15: Figure of error annotations and examples extracted from (Barbagli et al., 2016)

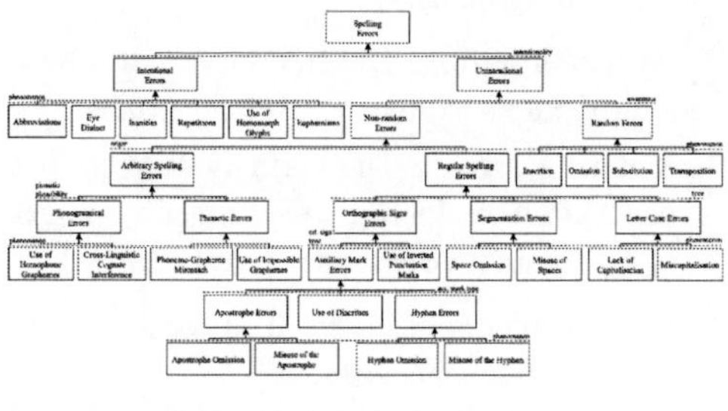

Figure 16: Figure of spelling error taxonomy for ZC extracted from (Himoro and Pareja-Lora, 2020)

Edit type	Missing Replacement Unnecessary
Error type	Adjective Adjective:form Adverb Conjunction Contraction Determiner Morphology Noun Noun:inflection Noun:number Noun:possessive Orthography Other Particle Preposition Pronoun Punctuation Spelling Verb Verb:form Verb:inflection Verb:subj-verb-agr Verb:tense Word order

Figure 17: Figure of the error types determined by grammatical error correction of texts in TSCC extracted from (Caines et al., 2020)

Error Type	Meaning	Description	Example
AD:FORM	Adverb Form	Errors concerning the form an adverb.	καλός → καλώς
ADJ:FORM*	Adjective Form	Errors concerning the form of an adjective	καλός → καλύτερος
NOUN:FORM	Noun Form	Errors concerning the number,the case or the suffix of a noun.	του νους → του νου
PRON:FORM	Pronoun Form	Errors concerning the number, the case or the suffix of a pronoun.	κάποια → κάποιας
VERB:FORM	Verb Form	Errors concerning the disposition, the voice, the inflection, the tense,the number or the person of a verb.	(εσείς) πηγαίνεται → (εσείς) πηγαίνετε
CONJ	Conjunction	Errors concerning conjunctions.	και → αλλά
PREP	Preposition	Errors concerning prepositions.	από → σε
DET*	Determiner	Errors concerning articles or determiners.	το → του τον → έναν
SPELL	Spelling	Spelling errors.	ευχέρια → ευχέρεια
FN	Final -ν/nu	Final -ν/nu addition or removal.	την → τη / μη → μην
PUNCT	Punctuation	Errors concerning the punctuation.	. → ;
OTHER	Other Errors	An error that does not fit into any other category but can still be corrected.	χαμία → για κανένα
ACC	Accentuation	Accentuation addition or removal.	καθηκοντα → καθήκοντα
UNK	Unknown error type	An error that can be detected but not corrected.	usually long error spans
WO	Words Order	Error in words order.	όταν φεύγω έρθεις → όταν έρθεις φεύγω
ORTH*	Orthography	Spacing Errors	γιασένα → για σένα
PART:FORM	Participle Form	Errors concerning the number,the case or the person of a participle.	(πήγε) τρεχόμενος → (πήγε) τρέχοντας
VERB:SVA	Subject Verb Agreement	The subject and the verb to be in person agreement.	(εγώ θα) φύγει → (εγώ θα) φύγω

Figure 18: Figure of ELERRANT and human error type annotation guide extracted from (Korre et al., 2021). The error types with (*) do not exist for human annotation scheme and the last two error types do not exist in the ELERRANT annotation scheme.

What's in a (dataset's) name? The case of BigPatent

Silvia Casola
Università degli Studi di Padua
Fondazione Bruno Kessler, Trento
scasola@fbk.eu

Alberto Lavelli
Fondazione Bruno Kessler, Trento
lavelli@fbk.eu

Horacio Saggion
Universitat Pompeu Fabra, Barcelona
horacio.saggion@upf.edu

Abstract

Sharing datasets and benchmarks has been crucial for rapidly improving Natural Language Processing models and systems. Documenting datasets' characteristics (and any modification introduced over time) is equally important to avoid confusion and make comparisons reliable.

Here, we describe the case of BigPatent, a dataset for patent summarization that exists in at least two rather different versions under the same name. While previous literature has not clearly distinguished among versions, their differences not only lay on a surface level but also modify the dataset's core nature and, thus, the complexity of the summarization task.

While this paper describes a specific case, we aim to shed light on new challenges that might emerge in resource sharing and advocate for comprehensive documentation of datasets and models.

1 Introduction

Sharing models and datasets is essential for Natural Language Processing (NLP). With the rise of transfer learning in the last few years, releasing large pre-trained models has become standard practice. Consequently, several libraries have provided APIs to access and work with those models efficiently. Datasets have followed a similar trend: they are often shared by their authors and stored in hubs that expose APIs. Two notable examples of this trend are the TensorFlow Datasets collection[1] and the Hugging Face dataset library[2] (Lhoest et al., 2021). These libraries allow accessing published data, often with just a few lines of code. They drastically ease the experimentation loop, and allow users to download, experiment with, and probe existing resources. There is, however, another side to the coin: the dataset documentation is sometimes insufficient, which might lead to inconsistencies when performing experiments and comparing results to previous work.

This paper analyzes a somewhat extreme case: the BigPatent dataset (Sharma et al., 2019). BigPatent is a dataset for patent summarization, first published in 2019. Patents have many peculiar characteristics that might be challenging for standard NLP systems: they span multiple pages, have very long sentences, contain a mix of legal and technical vocabulary, and are built out of noun phrases instead of clauses, with a long lexical chain (Casola and Lavelli, 2022). Thus, the dataset has also become popular as a general benchmark for summarization.

We show that the two popular TensorFlow and Hugging Face dataset hubs expose different versions of BigPatent. These differences are not only superficial (e.g., casing, tokenization) but regard the very content of the source documents.

We first briefly describe this difference and its impact on the dataset features (Section 2); then, we examine previous work and show it hardly ever clarifies the version of the dataset used in experiments (Section 3); finally, we show how the difference substantially impacts models' performance (Section 4).

While strongly advocating for resource sharing and infrastructure that make them easier to use, we hope that the discussion of this extreme case can shed light on the importance of careful resource documentation.

2 The BigPatent dataset

BigPatent is a dataset for the automatic summarization of patent documents.

Patents award inventors the exclusive right to use, make, and sell their inventions for a specific time and geographical area. Patents are structured legal documents containing several sections. The De-

[1] https://www.tensorflow.org/datasets (Last accessed: September 2022)

[2] https://huggingface.co/docs/datasets/ (Last accessed: September 2022)

Proceedings of the 2nd Workshop on Natural Language Generation, Evaluation, and Metrics (GEM), pages 399 - 404
December 7, 2022 ©2022 Association for Computational Linguistics

scription section reports the technical characteristics of the invention and its preferred embodiments so that a person skilled in the art can understand and reproduce it. The Description can be further divided into subsections (e.g., Background, Field of the Invention, Summary of the invention, Detailed Description, Description of the Drawings, etc.). The patent document also contains a human-written Abstract. It is thus somewhat natural to construct a summarization dataset using the Descriptions (or part of them) as the source texts and the Abstracts as the gold-standard summaries.

The dataset is not only interesting for a niche of patent mining researchers: in fact, patent documents show several interesting linguistic characteristics worth investigating (e.g., long sentences, unusual vocabulary, specific syntactic structure). Moreover, since many popular large-scale summarization datasets are in the news domain (Nallapati et al., 2016; Narayan et al., 2018; Fabbri et al., 2019), gathering data from different sources opens new challenges for NLP systems. For example, patent documents are very long, and their Abstract is not very extractive with respect to the Detailed Description, as the original dataset shows (Sharma et al., 2019).

In its original version, published by BigPatent's authors and accessible on GitHub[3], only part of the Description (typically the Detailed Description) is included in the input document, and the source does not contain any of the other subsections. The published dataset is also cased and tokenized. The Hugging Face dataset library exposes this version of the dataset (described in the related paper)[4].

With the advent of sequence-to-sequence transformer models for summarization (e.g., BART (Lewis et al., 2020) or Pegasus (Zhang et al., 2020))), however, using a strongly preprocessed dataset is not ideal. It is common practice to process the raw text with a model-specific tokenizer. This is likely why the TensorFlow Datasets collection contains a different version of the dataset that is cased and untokenized, with limited preprocessing over the original raw text[5].

However, a deeper look at the data reveals another difference: the TensorFlow source documents contain a superset of the text contained in the original version. All subsections in the patent Description are included. Thus, the input not only contains the Detailed Description but often also the Background, the Field of the invention, etc., and, interestingly, a Summary of the invention[6,7]. Table 1 shows the first tokens of the input of some entries in the corpus.

In the following, we compute some statistics on the two dataset versions (we call the original version $BigPatent_{Original}$ and the subsequent modified cased version $BigPatent_{New}$) and their different characteristics.

The dataset is divided into several subsets, following the Cooperative Patent Classification (CPC) codes. Due to the large dataset size (over 1.3 million examples), we restrict our analysis to its G (Physics) subset: it includes patents of information systems devices and processes, for which the authors of this paper might be considered skilled in the art. However, our considerations are general.

2.1 Dataset characteristics

Table 2 reports some statistics[8] over BigPatent/G. Note that the dataset split is identical in the two versions (i.e., the train, validation, and test splits contain the same documents). While the summaries characteristics are very similar between the original and the new version (we attribute the difference to errors in the tokenization, since $BigPatent_{Original}$ is pre-tokenized, while $BigPatent_{New}$ is not), $BigPatent_{New}$ clearly contains more text than the original version (38% more tokens, on average, in the training set), and more sentences (68% more, on average, in the training set). The compression ratio (i.e., the ratio between the number of tokens in the source and the number of tokens in the Abstract) is also higher in $BigPatent_{New}$.

To get a closer look at the datasets' abstractiveness, we compute their coverage and density, following Grusky et al. (2018).
Given a document $D = \langle d_1, d_2, \ldots, d_n \rangle$ where d_i is a token of D and a summary $S = \langle s_1, s_2, \ldots, s_m \rangle$, with $m \leq n$, where s_j is a token in the summary, $F(D, S)$ is the set of their shared

[3]https://evasharma.github.io/bigpatent/
(Last accessed: September 2022)
[4]https://huggingface.co/datasets/big_patent
(Last accessed: September 2022)
[5]https://www.tensorflow.org/datasets/catalog/big_patent
(Last accessed: September 2022)

[6]We will refer to this summary included in the document (input) as Summary of the Invention and to the dataset gold-standard as Abstract or gold standard.

[7]Note that this difference is not explicitly discussed on the dataset page.

[8]we use NLTK for sentence and word tokenization.

publication_number	$Description_{Original}$	$Description_{New}$
US-2007088503-A1	referring now to fig1 and 2 , a service technician visiting a customer service location is provided with a technician input device 2 for receiving and transmitting information related to a disruption or interruption of service at the service location . the input device 2 can be a wireless pc , for example , a laptop , a personal digital assistant (pda), a wireless pager or any other device suitable for receiving and transmitting data associated with providing service at the customer service location . [+2858 tokens]	This is a continuation of application Ser. No. 10/445,861 filed May 27, 2003, which is a continuation of application Ser. No. 10/032,853 filed Oct. 25, 2001 and now U.S. Pat. No. 6,772,064. The present methods and systems generally relate to processing and transmitting information to facilitate providing service in a telecommunications network. [+986 tokens] Referring now to FIG1 and 2 , a service technician visiting a customer service location is provided with a technician input device 2 for receiving and transmitting information related to a disruption or interruption of service at the service location. [+2427 tokens]
US-2011144953-A1	in the following , the invention is described in more detail referring to the attached figures by means of exemplary embodiments , wherein same reference signs refer to same components . fig1 schematically shows the system for compensating electromagnetic interfering fields . an object 2 to be protected against effects of the interfering field 1 is permeated by the interfering field 1 . here , the interfering field 1 is assumed to be a gradient field . the amplitude of the interfering field 1 is measured by two real magnetic field sensors 3 , and 4 . the first real sensor 3 provides an output signal right arrow over (s) 1 =[x 1 (t), y 1 (t), z 1 (t)], and the second real sensor 4 provides an output signal right arrow over (s) 2 =[x 2 (t), y 2 (t), z 2 (t)]. [+1855 tokens]	This application claims benefit under 35 U.S.C. (a) of German Patent Application No. 10 2009 024 826.9-32, filed Jun. 13, 2009, the entire contents of which are incorporated herein by reference.The invention relates generally to a system for compensating electromagnetic interfering fields, and in particular to a system for magnetic field compensation having two sensors and a digital processor. [+16010 tokens] In the following, the invention is described in more detail referring to the attached figures by means of exemplary embodiments, wherein same reference signs refer to same components.FIG1 schematically shows the system for compensating electromagnetic interfering fields. [+1427 tokens]
US-4830479-A	referring now to fig1 of the drawings , there is depicted a ray 12 entering the paper plane perpendicularly along an axis z orthogonal to axes x and y . ray 12 is deflected into the paper plane by a mirror 16 which is located at the origin and is oriented upwardly at a forty five degree angle from the paper plane . mirror 16 rotates with an angular velocity ω around axis z which is in line with the arriving ray 12 . [+1579 tokens]	The invention described herein may be manufactured and used by or for the Government for governmental purposes without the payment of any royalty thereon.At radio frequencies, superheterodyne receivers typically have sensitivities that are orders of magnitude higher than those of direct detection receivers. [+1044 tokens] Referring now to FIG1 of the drawings, there is depicted a ray 12 entering the paper plane perpendicularly along an axis Z orthogonal to axes X and Y. Ray 12 is deflected into the paper plane by a mirror 16 which is located at the origin and is oriented upwardly at a forty five degree angle from the paper plane. [+1380 tokens]

Table 1: Some examples from the two versions of the dataset. We report the first tokens from the input in the original version, and the first tokens in the new version of the dataset. Note that the new version might contain many paragraphs before the content of the original input.

		$BigPatent_{Original}$	$BigPatent_{New}$
# docs (train, val, test)		258,935	258,935
		14,385	14,385
		14,386	14,386
Summary	# tokens (avg)	123.9	121
		123.7	120.9
		124.1	121.2
	# sents (avg)	3.7	3.6
		3.6	3.6
		3.7	3.7
	sent len (avg)	44.3	43.4
		44.2	43.3
		44.5	43.7
Source	# tokens (avg)	3,959.2	5,488.3
		3,953.3	5,517.5
		3,976.8	5,501.9
	# sents (avg)	105.6	177.6
		105.5	178.4
		106.3	178.3
	sent length (avg)	42.6	31.8
		42.6	31.8
		42.5	31.8
compression ratio		36.1	51.2
		36.0	51.5
		35.8	50.9

Table 2: Length statistics on the two BigPatent versions. The number of tokens, sentences, tokens per sentence, and the compression ratio are computed per document and then averaged. The compression ratio is the ratio between the number of tokens in the source and the number of tokens in the Abstract.

fragments (shared sequences of tokens). The extractive fragment coverage measures the proportion of tokens in the summary belonging to an extractive fragment and qualitatively describes how much a summary vocabulary is derivative of a text.

	$BigPatent_{Original}$	$BigPatent_{New}$
Coverage (avg)	0.87	0.95
Density (avg)	2.40	20.8

Table 3: The extractive fragment coverage and the density for the two versions of the dataset. Measures are computed per document and then averaged.

$$Coverage(D, S) = \frac{1}{|S|} \sum_{f \in F(D,S)} |f|$$

where $|S|$ is the number of tokens in the summary. The density also takes into account the length of the extractive fragments: the higher the density, the more a summary can be described as a series of extractions.

$$Density(D, S) = \frac{1}{|S|} \sum_{f \in F(D,S)} |f|^2$$

Table 3 shows the measures computed for the two versions of the dataset, while Table 4 shows their percentage of novel n-grams. Note that both datasets have relatively high coverage (the increase in $BigPatent_{New}$ might be partially motivated by the increased length of the source). However, the extractive density is an order of magnitude higher in $BigPatent_{New}$, suggesting that the reference summaries are significantly more extractive than the original version.

$BigPatent_{New}$ also has a lower number of novel n-grams in the summary (and the difference with $BigPatent_{Original}$ stays high even when accounting for the length of the source). We attribute this difference to the presence of sections such as the Summary of the invention, the Background, and the Field of the invention in the input; these sections already abstract the core features of the claimed invention.

To investigate how similar the Abstract is to each subsection in $BigPatent_{New}$, we compute their ROUGE scores (Lin, 2004) with the summary[9]. We report both ROUGE f1 and recall since we want to quantify how much "information in the Abstract" each section contains. $BigPatent_{New}$ does not include the name of the patent subsections (an uppercase short header in the raw text). In fact, short sentences (including subsection names) are removed during the preprocessing. To divide the text into subsections, we regenerate the dataset using the original TensorFlow script and remove the portion of the code that gets rid of short sentences. We use a regular expression to divide the text into subsections and extract their headers. Since the headers do not have normalized names (e.g., the Background's header might be indicated as "Background", "Background of the invention", etc.), we use a simple key-based method to classify them into 9 groups. Note that not all patents include all subsection types. Table 5 reports the obtained ROUGE score, the subsection average length, and the percentage of patents that include each subsection type. Note that the Summary of the invention (in 94% of the inputs in $BigPatent_{New}$) has the highest scores; compared to the Detailed Description, the Summary of the Invention has a higher ROUGE-recall even though it is much shorter.

In a nutshell, our analysis shows that the additional text in $BigPatent_{New}$ decreases the need for an abstractive model for the task. The additional Description subsections – in some cases, already a summary of the rest of the patent – contain the most information in the patent Abstract.

[9]All ROUGE scores are computed using the Hugging Face version of the metric, with stemming.

	$BigPatent_{Original}$	$BigPatent_{New}$
Novel 1-grams (avg)	10.9%	4.21%
Novel 2-grams (avg)	46.9%	23.46%
Novel 3-grams (avg)	74.0%	42.25%
Novel 4-grams (avg)	87.1%	53.58%

Table 4: Percentage of new n-grams in the summary in the two datasets. All percentages are computed per document and then averaged.

3 How to compare to the previous literature?

While the two versions of the dataset have different characteristics, the vast majority of previous literature using BigPatent does not explicitly mention the version used.

Zhang et al. (2020) mention they "updated the BIGPATENT dataset to preserve casing, some format cleanings are also changed"; this operation might have led to the creation of the new dataset version now exposed by TensorFlow (whose differences with the original version are, however, not limited to casing and minor format cleaning). Some previous work (He et al., 2020) noticed a substantial performance gap between models trained with the original version and Pegasus and speculated this difference might be due to the different preprocessing (and, we add, possibly to the additional content); these findings are compatible with our experiments in the next section.

In the vast majority of cases, the reported statistics are directly taken from the original publication and not recomputed; in a few cases, the values computed (e.g., in terms of document lengths) are compatible with the use of the cased version (e.g., in Guo et al. (2022)).

BigPatent is widely used when testing systems, often as an example of a dataset with a very long source. The dataset was cited 115 times, according to Google Scholar[10]. Since the used dataset version is unknown, and authors are unaware of the two different versions, it is impossible to understand if comparing results to previous work is fair. Since the Tensorflow version was updated on the 31st Jan 2020[11], papers published after that date could potentially use the new version of the dataset, with likely better results. In fact, a simple BART model results in a very different performance on the two versions of the dataset, as shown in the next section.

[10]Checked on 27/10/2022

[11]See this github commit: a708d506748870237eafa2bbb659dc64cd7cf04a

	ROUGE-1		ROUGE-2		ROUGE-L		#Tokens	%
	R	f1	R	f1	R	f1		patents
SUMMARY	84.68	35.97	60.76	25.97	69.07	29.36	744.56	93.79%
FIELD	23.62	28.66	10.17	11.92	16.14	19.44	73.73	38.27%
BACKGROUND	66.04	24.45	25.38	8.60	41.42	14.70	710.04	94.85%
DRAWINGS	38.96	28.36	10.35	7.39	24.52	17.55	243.43	97.6%
EMBODIMENTS	81.39	8.58	42.44	4.14	59.21	5.92	3168.25	53.07%
REFERENCES	10.82	11.40	1.48	1.35	07.38	7.94	92.10	28.18%
RELATED ART	52.47	20.33	18.48	6.36	32.13	12.04	644.27	4.12%
OBJECTIVE	44.35	32.31	16.05	10.93	27.49	19.58	256.95	2.09%
DESCRIPTION	84.39	8.27	4.10	4.08	61.90	5.78	3404.91	55.23%

Table 5: The ROUGE score (recall (R), f1) between the different subsections of the patents and the patent Abstract. The subsections are obtained from the $BigPatent_{New}$ raw data. The scores are computed per document and normalized by the number of documents that contain each subsection. The average length of each subsection and the percentage of patents that contain the subsection are also reported.

4 Experiments

To understand if the version of the dataset impacts models' performance, we fine-tuned a pre-trained BART (Lewis et al., 2020) base model on the two versions of the dataset. We train using the Hugging Face library with early stopping on the evaluation loss (patience: 5) and the following hyperparameters: max source length: 1000; max target length: 150; number of beams: 5; eval steps: 10k; max steps: 500M. We leave all other parameters to their default values. Table 6 reports the results. Note how results on $BigPatent_{New}$ are more than 11 points of ROUGE-L over $BigPatent_{Original}$.

To corroborate the idea that the Summary of the invention in the input improves the performance on $BigPatent_{New}$, we trained a model using, as input, only the text in the Summary of the Invention subsection. In the few cases in which the patent did not include the Summary subsection, we used the Detailed Description or the Description of the embodiments. As described in Section 2, we resorted to the raw data to extract the text in the Summary of the Invention subsection. This setting further improves the performance, with an increase of almost 16 and almost 5 points of ROUGE-L with respect to the original and the new version; note, however, that since $BigPatent_{New}$ does not contain the subsection headers, it is not directly possible to train models using the Summary of the Invention only as input.

5 Conclusions

We have discussed the case of BigPatent, a dataset that exists in two very different versions. We have shown that the updated version of the dataset lacks some of the original characteristics (e.g., the high level of abstraction in the reference summaries and their high percentage of novel n-grams) and leads to much higher results with a simple transformer.

To our best knowledge, this difference is not reported elsewhere, either in published research or in the dataset's online documentation. In fact, previous work tends to ignore the difference between the original and the new version, making it virtually impossible to understand experimental results, reproduce, and compare them.

We believe BigPatent is an extreme case in which the lack of clear documentation has led to confusion – with two datasets so distant in their characteristics that they might be considered two different ones, used interchangeably. We always advise reporting the dataset version and characteristics when using BigPatent (and being aware of the possible problems with the comparison with previous work).

We hope that the analysis of this case underlines the importance of clearly documenting datasets' characteristics and any possible modifications introduced over time.

Limitations and ethical impact statement

The dataset we analyzed is public and derives from public patent data. We are not aware of any ethical concerns related to the dataset.

In this paper, we have only analyzed a subset of the dataset, but our considerations are general. We have done so for computational concerns, including trying to limit the requirement for energy resources.

	$BigPatent_{Original}$			$BigPatent_{New}$		
	ROUGE-1	ROUGE-2	ROUGE-L	ROUGE-1	ROUGE-2	ROUGE-L
Lead-3	29.54	7.95	18.15	23.15	7.27	15.42
Summary Lead-3	-	-	-	48.11	30.16	36.66
BART-base	42.25	15.99	27.58	50.18	29.46	38.64
BART-base (Summary)	-	-	-	55.16	34.85	43.56

Table 6: Results (test set) on the two dataset versions for a BART-base model. The Lead-3 baseline considers the first three sentences of the input text as a proxy for the generated summary. Summary Lead-3 uses the first 3 sentences of the Summary of the invention (obtained from the Summary of the invention as described in Section 2.1). We also trained a BART model that only uses the Summary of the Invention as input. The split is identical, i.e., the train, validation, and test splits contain the same documents in both versions.

References

Silvia Casola and Alberto Lavelli. 2022. Summarization, simplification, and generation: The case of patents. *Expert Systems with Applications*, 205:117627.

Alexander Fabbri, Irene Li, Tianwei She, Suyi Li, and Dragomir Radev. 2019. Multi-news: A large-scale multi-document summarization dataset and abstractive hierarchical model. In *Proceedings of the 57th Annual Meeting of the Association for Computational Linguistics*, pages 1074–1084, Florence, Italy. Association for Computational Linguistics.

Max Grusky, Mor Naaman, and Yoav Artzi. 2018. Newsroom: A dataset of 1.3 million summaries with diverse extractive strategies. In *Proceedings of the 2018 Conference of the North American Chapter of the Association for Computational Linguistics: Human Language Technologies, Volume 1 (Long Papers)*, pages 708–719, New Orleans, Louisiana. Association for Computational Linguistics.

Mandy Guo, Joshua Ainslie, David Uthus, Santiago Ontanon, Jianmo Ni, Yun-Hsuan Sung, and Yinfei Yang. 2022. LongT5: Efficient text-to-text transformer for long sequences. In *Findings of the Association for Computational Linguistics: NAACL 2022*, pages 724–736, Seattle, United States. Association for Computational Linguistics.

Junxian He, Wojciech Kryscinski, Bryan McCann, Nazneen Rajani, and Caiming Xiong. 2020. Ctrlsum: Towards generic controllable text summarization. *ArXiv*, abs/2012.04281.

Mike Lewis, Yinhan Liu, Naman Goyal, Marjan Ghazvininejad, Abdelrahman Mohamed, Omer Levy, Veselin Stoyanov, and Luke Zettlemoyer. 2020. BART: Denoising sequence-to-sequence pre-training for natural language generation, translation, and comprehension. In *Proceedings of the 58th Annual Meeting of the Association for Computational Linguistics*, pages 7871–7880, Online. Association for Computational Linguistics.

Quentin Lhoest, Albert Villanova del Moral, Yacine Jernite, Abhishek Thakur, Patrick von Platen, Suraj Patil, Julien Chaumond, Mariama Drame, Julien Plu, Lewis Tunstall, Joe Davison, Mario Šaško, Gunjan Chhablani, Bhavitvya Malik, Simon Brandeis, Teven Le Scao, Victor Sanh, Canwen Xu, Nicolas Patry, Angelina McMillan-Major, Philipp Schmid, Sylvain Gugger, Clément Delangue, Théo Matussière, Lysandre Debut, Stas Bekman, Pierric Cistac, Thibault Goehringer, Victor Mustar, François Lagunas, Alexander Rush, and Thomas Wolf. 2021. Datasets: A community library for natural language processing. In *Proceedings of the 2021 Conference on Empirical Methods in Natural Language Processing: System Demonstrations*, pages 175–184, Online and Punta Cana, Dominican Republic. Association for Computational Linguistics.

Chin-Yew Lin. 2004. ROUGE: A package for automatic evaluation of summaries. In *Proceedings of the workshop on Text Summarization Branches Out*, pages 74–81, Barcelona, Spain. Association for Computational Linguistics.

Ramesh Nallapati, Bowen Zhou, Cicero dos Santos, Çağlar Gulçehre, and Bing Xiang. 2016. Abstractive text summarization using sequence-to-sequence RNNs and beyond. In *Proceedings of The 20th SIGNLL Conference on Computational Natural Language Learning*, pages 280–290, Berlin, Germany. Association for Computational Linguistics.

Shashi Narayan, Shay B. Cohen, and Mirella Lapata. 2018. Don't give me the details, just the summary! topic-aware convolutional neural networks for extreme summarization. In *Proceedings of the 2018 Conference on Empirical Methods in Natural Language Processing*, pages 1797–1807, Brussels, Belgium. Association for Computational Linguistics.

Eva Sharma, Chen Li, and Lu Wang. 2019. BIGPATENT: A large-scale dataset for abstractive and coherent summarization. In *Proceedings of the 57th Annual Meeting of the Association for Computational Linguistics*, pages 2204–2213, Florence, Italy. Association for Computational Linguistics.

Jingqing Zhang, Yao Zhao, Mohammad Saleh, and Peter J. Liu. 2020. Pegasus: Pre-training with extracted gap-sentences for abstractive summarization. In *Proceedings of the 37th International Conference on Machine Learning*, ICML'20. JMLR.org.

Measuring the Measuring Tools: An Automatic Evaluation of Semantic Metrics for Text Corpora

George Kour*, **Samuel Ackerman***
Orna Raz, Eitan Farchi, Boaz Carmeli, Ateret Anaby-Tavor
IBM Research AI
{gkour, samuel.ackerman}@ibm.com
{ornar, farchi, boazc, atereta}@il.ibm.com

Abstract

The ability to compare the semantic similarity between text corpora is important in a variety of natural language processing applications. However, standard methods for evaluating these metrics have yet to be established. We propose a set of automatic and interpretable measures for assessing the characteristics of corpus-level semantic similarity metrics, allowing sensible comparison of their behavior. We demonstrate the effectiveness of our evaluation measures in capturing fundamental characteristics by evaluating them on a collection of classical and state-of-the-art metrics. Our measures revealed that recently-developed metrics are becoming better in identifying semantic distributional mismatch while classical metrics are more sensitive to perturbations in the surface text levels.

1 Introduction

While there has been a long-standing interest in developing semantic similarity metrics[1] (Rayson and Garside, 2000), measuring how close two text corpora are remains an open problem (Pillutla et al., 2021). Specifically, the recent advances in generative language models have led to an increased interest in the study of content similarity between human and generated language, as a mean for comparing the quality of generative models (Mille et al., 2021; Gehrmann et al., 2022).

The goal of a text corpus' dissimilarity or distance metric is to provide a broad representation of distance across specific linguistic aspects, such as lexical, morphological, syntactic, and semantic (Kilgarriff, 2001). Such metrics are essential for measuring how well corpus-based linguistic analysis generalizes from one data-set to another. This work focuses on semantic similarity metrics.

While one can reasonably measure the semantic distance between two individual sentences (e.g., by calculating the cosine distance between the sentence embeddings), measuring the dissimilarity between two text corpora remains a challenge (Naeem et al., 2020). Corpus-level metrics seek to assess semantic similarity at the group level. for instance, assessing generated text fidelity, diversity, and coverage compared to the reference corpus (Sajjadi et al., 2018). Thus, one common approach for measuring the semantic dissimilarity between two corpora is to compare the densities of their sentences in the embedding space (Pillutla et al., 2021).

However, there are no standard automatic procedures for evaluating the precision and robustness of such similarity metrics. The semi-manual standard approach is to correlate the results of these metrics for human judgement. However, leveraging manual human judgements to construct numeric metrics has significant weaknesses. As we explain in Section 2, human judgements are expensive to obtain, are difficult to aggregate consistently from individual text instances into a corpus-level metric, and can be subjective and non-robust.

To mitigate the dependence on human judgement, controllable synthetic distributions have been used in recent work to evaluate the metric quality (Naeem et al., 2020). For instance, this was done by calculating the distance of synthetic high dimensional samples generated by sampling from Gaussian or mixture-of-Gaussian distributions representing the reference P and target Q data, and then calculating the distance measure by shifting away the two distributions. In this paper, we adopt a middle ground between validating the metric against human judgement on real data and evaluating the metric with synthetic distributions by building "controllable-distance real data corpora" (Section 3). By precisely controlling the content of test corpora, we devised a unified evaluation of desired metric characteristics on real data. This tech-

* denotes equal contribution.

[1]In the context of this paper, a metric is a measure of difference (distance) in the general sense, and may not necessarily satisfy the properties of a metric in mathematical terms.

Proceedings of the 2nd Workshop on Natural Language Generation, Evaluation, and Metrics (GEM), pages 405 - 416
December 7, 2022 ©2022 Association for Computational Linguistics

nique allows aggregation of many small-difference judgements that should correspond to what a human would logically decide, to evaluate the distance metric overall in terms of desirable properties. The middle ground thus attempts to reflect human logical judgement in an inexpensive way, while avoiding some of the weaknesses described, such as lack of consistency.

To summarize, our contributions are as follows. First, we present a text similarity evaluation measures that allows researchers to compare the robustness of their newly proposed metrics against existing metrics using the same standards. Second, we evaluate classical and state-of-the-art similarity metrics and show that our benchmark performs well in capturing their known properties. Finally, we provide a pip-installable Python package to compute an extensive set of text dissimilarity metrics, using a unified and simple API[2].

2 Literature Review

The most widely-used method to compute the quality of text similarity metrics investigates the correlation between the scores given by the metric and human judgements. However, human judgement, even on the sentence level, has several shortcomings, mainly that it is expensive and can be inconsistent and subjective (Popescu-Belis, 2003; Lin and Och, 2004; Graham et al., 2017). Also, superficial aspects of the sentences, such as text length or syllables per sentence, may influence human judgements of the semantic similarity (Novikova et al., 2017). Furthermore, though humans may be able judge the relative similarity of a pair of *sentences*, they are usually limited in their ability to make large-scale assessments of a similar type when comparing two *corpora* (i.e., two distributions of sentences) consistently and reliably.

In an attempt to standardize metric evaluation, several competitions and standard datasets containing compared data and human assessment were created for specific tasks, such as translation (Guo et al., 2018; Mathur et al., 2020). However, there is currently a lack of benchmarks against which to assess the semantic similarity between corpora.

Text similarity metrics can be thought of as belonging to several broad and overlapping classes (see e.g., Wang and Dong 2020), which partially depend on the form of the text representation (e.g., token-based or vector embedding). Here, we investigate metrics from three of these classes, comparing corpora based on these aspects: *lexicographical* (statistical properties of words and tokens), *distribution* (densities of sentences represented in the embedding space), and *discriminatability* (ability to classify sentences as belonging to one corpus or the other). The metrics we use are summarized in Table 1.

Lexicographical Statistics These methods have been developed to compare various distributional properties of target text Q with respect to the reference samples P, based on some statistic measures $T(P)$ and $T(Q)$, operating on the surface text level, e.g., sentence, words, word-parts, tokens, etc. Such commonly-used measures include resemblance in vocabulary distribution (Kilgarriff, 2001), likelihood of repetition (Pillutla et al., 2021), and n-gram matching (Papineni et al., 2002). However, these metrics tend to be overly sensitive or easily misled by adversarial samples or text peculiarities. In general, χ^2-based metrics calculate distance between observed and expected frequencies of categorical variables. The metric in (Kilgarriff, 2001), denoted here as **CHI**, calculates E, the average (between P and Q) frequencies of the n most common tokens in the combined vocabulary of P and Q, then sums the χ^2 statistics comparing each of P and Q to the expected E, across tokens. Here, for both CHI and ZIPF, below, we use the top $n = 5000$ tokens.

In contrast, the **ZIPF** metric (Holtzman et al., 2019) compares the use of vocabulary using Zipf's law, which suggests that the frequency of a given word in human text is inversely-proportional to its frequency rank. The Zipfian coefficient is fitted on a given corpus and the further it is from 1, the more the observed corpus differs from the 'ideal' theoretical distribution (Holtzman et al., 2019). We can thus use $|z_P - z_Q|$ as a distance metric between corpora P and Q.

Distributional Metrics These metrics are based on quantifying the distributional relationship between the reference and target corpora in the embedded vector space, thereby capturing semantics beyond superficial token-level statistics. Here P and Q denote the reference and target corpora in the embedding space. Given samples from these, we can use the sample density estimates $\hat{P}$ and $\hat{Q}$ to approximate the true unknown corpus population distributions P and Q.

[2]https://github.com/IBM/comparing-corpora

Type	Metric	Measures
Lexicographical	CHI (χ^2) (Kilgarriff, 2001)	Word/Token count comparison.
Statistics	ZIPF (Holtzman et al., 2019)	Unigram rank-frequency statistics.
	FID (Heusel et al., 2017)	Wasserstein distance between densities.
Distributional	PR (Sajjadi et al., 2018)	Assessing distributional precision & recall.
	DC (Naeem et al., 2020)	Estimating manifolds density and coverage.
	MAUVE (Pillutla et al., 2021)	Quality & diversity via divergence frontiers.
Discriminative	CLASSIFIER (2016)	Classifiability between reference and target.
	IRPR (Zhao et al., 2017)	Average distance between closest samples pairs.

Table 1: Summary of investigated text similarity metrics.

The Fréchet Inception Distance (**FID**, Heusel et al. 2017) is computed by fitting a continuous multivariate Gaussian to the P and Q, and then calculating the Wasserstein-2 distance between them. However, FID is sensitive to both the addition of spurious modes as well as to mode dropping (Lucic et al., 2018). Also, while FID is able to detect distributional distances in the high-dimensional space, it cannot shed light upon the nature of this distance.

Due to these weaknesses of FID, we additionally consider a metric denoted **PR** proposed in computer vision (Sajjadi et al., 2018; Kynkäänniemi et al., 2019), which is inspired by the notion of precision and recall in machine Learning. Intuitively, the precision captures the average resemblance of the individual target samples to the reference set (i.e., fidelity), while the recall measures how well the target samples "cover" the full variability of the reference samples (i.e., diversity). To obtain a single distance value using the method in (Kynkäänniemi et al., 2019), we calculate the $F1$ measure based on the returned precision and recall, denoted here by PR.

Naeem et al. (2020) proposed an improved estimation of these precision and recall notions (called, density and coverage) by mitigating the overestimation of manifolds caused by outliers and underestimating the similarity when the target and reference are taken from the same distribution. Similarly to PR, we calculate the $F1$ to obtain a similarity value using this method, denoted as **DC**[3].

MAUVE (Pillutla et al., 2021) is a recently-developed metric that estimates the gap between human and generated text by computing the area under the information divergence frontiers in a quantized embedding space using the KL-divergence[4].

Discriminatability Metrics Similar to the distributional metrics, discriminative metrics calculate the distance using the embedding of the individual sentences in the two corpora. However, they do not aim to specifically capture the overlap between the distribution induced by the compared corpora. Rather, they calculate the relationship in classification terms, i.e., to what extent can sentences in one corpus be distinguished from the sentences in the other corpus, using a discriminative model.

CLASSIFIER: Following (Lopez-Paz and Oquab, 2016), we measure the similarity between corpora using a binary classifier. We used SVM (Cortes and Vapnik, 1995) trained on samples of both source corpora to predict corpus membership in a test set of unseen samples. A higher test accuracy indicates higher inter-corpora distance.

While CLASSIFIER is a model-based metric that uses the entire corpus distribution, **IRPR** (information-retrieval precision and recall) is an example of an instance- (individual sentence) based corpus distance metric. Inspired by Zhao et al. (2017), we calculate the dissimilarity between corpora as follows. For each embedded sentence in corpus A, we find its closest neighbor in B by cosine distance. The average of these distances is then computed to find the "precision" value. The same procedure in reverse, from B to A, gives the "recall" value. We calculate the $F1$ score of the recall and precision to obtain a single value. Note that the CLASSIFIER metric is used to represent model-based discriminative approaches, while IRPR is used to represent instance-based discriminative methods.

The values calculated by CHI, IRPR, PR, DC and Mauve capture the similarity rather than the distance between two corpora (for all metrics $v \in [0, 1]$). To make these metrics represent distances, we take $1 - v$.

Our model selection was based on considering the

[3]To calculate both PR and DC, we employed the implementation provided in the *prdc* Python package.

[4]We used the *mauve-text* Python package for calculating MAUVE as well as ZIPF.

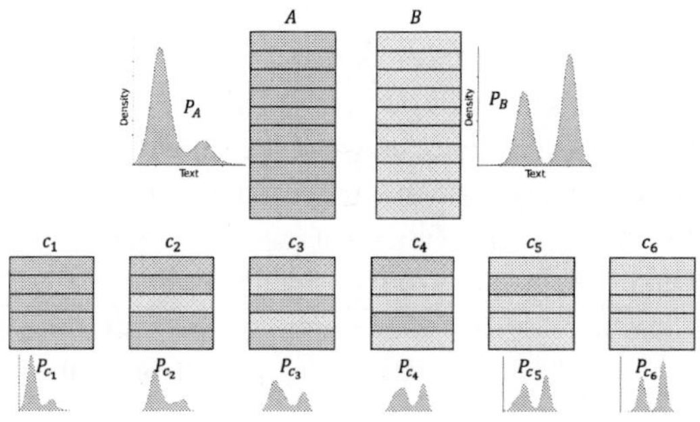

Figure 1: Construction of a $k = 6$ known similarity corpora (KSC) collection from source corpora A and B. The corpus c_i is constructed by drawing $n\left(\frac{k-i}{k-1}\right)$ and $n\left(\frac{i-1}{k-1}\right)$ samples from A and B, respectively. The adjacent densities illustrate the text distributions in the semantic space of the source and the KSC corpora.

trade-off between embedding quality and calculation time. The code as well as the scripts to reproduce the experiments are available online.[5]

3 Known Similarity Corpora

Most of the metric quality measures we propose are primarily based on the notion of *known-similarity corpora* (KSC) introduced by Kilgarriff (2001). The KSC set is created by mixing samples from two different source corpora A and B in gradually-changing proportions. The KSC set, denoted $KSC(A, B)$, consists of k corpora $\{c_1, c_2, \ldots, c_k\}$, each of size $n \geq k - 1$, where corpus c_i, $i = 1, \ldots, k$ is constructed by sampling $n\left(\frac{k-i}{k-1}\right)$ observations from A, and the remaining $n\left(\frac{i-1}{k-1}\right)$ from B (see Figure 1). The sampling resolution gradation between corpora is a fixed $\frac{1}{k-1}$.

We now introduce some notation on the KSC set, which are used to define the measures in Section 4. Let $[k] = \{1, 2, \ldots, k\}$. For given source corpora A and B, for each $\ell \in [k-1]$ we define the **ℓ-distant corpora set** as follows:

$$KSC_\ell(A, B) = \{(c_i, c_j) \colon i, j \in [k],\ j - i = \ell\} \tag{1}$$

Let $d(a, b)$ denote the distance from corpus a to b, according to metric d. Let $D_\ell(A, B, d)$— D_ℓ for short—be the set of values of distance d for corpora pairs in $KSC_\ell(A, B)$;

$$D_\ell(A, B, d) = \{d(c_i, c_j) \colon (c_i, c_j) \in KSC_\ell(A, B)\} \tag{2}$$

To pool results across ℓ, we further define:

$$D(A, B, d) = \{D_\ell(A, B, d) \colon \ell \in [k-1]\} \tag{3}$$

[5]https://github.com/IBM/meme

Name	Size	Description
atis	4978	Utterances to a flight booking system.
yahoo	20000	Yahoo non-factoid questions in 21 categories.
clinc150	22500	Utterances in 10 domains classified into 150 classes.
banking77	10000	Online banking queries.

Table 2: Datasets used as source corpora in our benchmark. Although some of the datasets are partitioned annotated with labels, in our experiments, if not mentioned otherwise, we ignored those labels.

Some of the metrics d have a pre-defined range (e.g., CHI, MAUVE, DC, PR only return values in the range [0,1]) while others have no preset scale or operation range. Therefore, to allow sensible comparison of distance metrics with different operation ranges and across source corpora, we obtain z-scores by normalizing the metric values, pooled across all $D_\ell(A, B, d)$. In the following analysis, if not specified otherwise, D_ℓ will always be the normalized rather than raw distances.

Datasets Selection The measures described in Section 4 are applicable to any pair of textual datasets with differently-distributed textual content, allowing the corpora in the KSC set to be distinguishable. To ensure that each pair of source corpora were in fact different enough, in the following experiments we use pairs of human text corpora from different domains, rather than pairing a human corpus with a machine-generated version of itself. For our experiments we selected four public datasets (ATIS, Hemphill et al. 1990; yahoo[6]; banking77, Casanueva et al. 2020; clinc150, Larson et al. 2019) containing short user utterances from different domains summarized in Table 2.

4 Metric Robustness Measures

We now describe our measurements of desirable properties for distance metrics, given the normalized D_ℓ on the KSC sets. In the three following measures (Monotonicity, Separability, and Linearity), we aim to capture three attributes of well-behaved metrics that can be understood by considering the top line scatter plots of Figure 2; these show the relation between the D_ℓ sets and ℓ. In these scatterplots, a high angle of the regression line, low vertical variability around it, and linearity

[6]https://ciir.cs.umass.edu/downloads/nfL6/

are all desirable properties for the distance metric, and are captured in these measures.

4.1 Metric Monotonicity

A well-behaved distance metric d should have a natural monotonic relationship with the separation levels ℓ of the KSC. We use Spearman's rank correlation between ℓ and D_ℓ, which we denote $\rho(d)$, to assess the monotonicity. Spearman's correlation is defined as the Pearson correlation between the order ranks of two variables, and measures the strength of their monotonic, rather than linear, association. As can be seen in Table 3, MAUVE and CHI achieve the best monotonicity results, followed by DC and FID.

4.2 Metric Separability

It is desirable that (1) for a given ℓ, D_ℓ has low variability, and (2) for different $\ell_2 > \ell_1$, the samples D_{ℓ_1} and D_{ℓ_2} are distinguishable (e.g., by a two-sample difference test), particularly as $\ell_2 - \ell_1$ grows. Here, we measure how grouping by ℓ explains the variability in D_ℓ across ℓ. We perform a one-way fixed-effects analysis of variance (ANOVA) with ℓ as the unordered categorical treatment and D_ℓ as the numeric response. Often, an F-test is performed; if its p-value is low, it means a significant amount of the variance in the response (D_ℓ) can be explained by the treatment (ℓ). Since the F-test for any reasonable d metric should be significant, we instead use the similar ω^2 effect-size metric (Hays, 1963), which is bounded by ± 1, to better assess them. It is defined as

$$\omega^2 = \frac{SS_{\text{treatment}} - df_{\text{treatment}} \times MS_{\text{residual}}}{SS_{\text{total}} + MS_{\text{residual}}} \quad (4)$$

where SS and MS are the sum and mean sums of squares, and df is the degrees of freedom, on a dataset of size n (here, $n = |D(A, B, d)|$). In the following we denote this measure as $\mathcal{W}(d)$.

4.3 Metric Linearity

Here we examine to what extent linear changes in the corpus content (ℓ) are manifested in linear changes in the distance function. To do so, we calculate the coefficient of determination (R^2), where higher values indicate stronger linearity. This measure is denoted by $\mathcal{L}(d)$. Looking at the results in Table 3, we see that MAUVE achieves the best results followed by DC and FID. It appears that this measure is more affected by the source corpora and by the resolution than other metrics.

4.4 Metric Time Efficiency

The time complexity of the metric is commonly perceived as less important, thus seldom reported (Sai et al., 2022). This aspect is becoming ever more important, especially due to the growing interest in time-consuming divergence frontier methods (Djolonga et al., 2020). Such metrics perform multiple measurements to estimate the area under the curve (similar to precision-recall curves for binary classification), with tune-able but increasing resolution. We measure the time performance of the metric $\mathcal{T}(d)$ in terms of 100 similarity measurements operations per second ($[100op/sec]$) on a standard CPU machine[7]. Note that the measurements reported in Table 3 do not include the sentences' embedding time. Predictably, methods that operate on the token level and avoid complex density estimation tend to achieve the best time performance. Among the distributional metrics, MAUVE achieves the best results, followed by FID. PR and DC produce similar results since both are based on similar manifold calculations.

4.5 Metric Accuracy

The assessment measures described earlier in Section 4 use the observed values of the metric distances (or similarities) between the KSC corpora; however, the actual values of the distance may not be known. Nevertheless, we still have some partial information about the ordering of these values, which we will use to define an accuracy measure.

4.5.1 Comparing paired corpora distances

Even though we do not have the true distance between any two corpora in the KSC set, we can still assume that certain pairwise distances are larger than others. For instance, it should be true that, say, $d(c_2, c_3) \leq (c_1, c_4)$ in expectation (across repeated random sampling). This is because the proportions of observations from A in c_2 and c_3 are more similar than the respective proportions between c_1 and c_4. Moreover, the interval of the first pair is 'contained'[8] in the second, and thus the first pair should have smaller distance. Thus, In general, whenever the interval of one corpus pair contains ($\subset$) the interval of another, we expect the contained pair to have a smaller distance.

[7]CPU: 2.3 GHz 8-Core Intel Core i9. Memory: 64 GB DDR4 (2667 MHz)

[8](c_i, c_j) contains (c_q, c_r), i.e., $(q, r) \subset (i, j)$, if $i \leq q$ and $r \leq j$ and $i < r$.

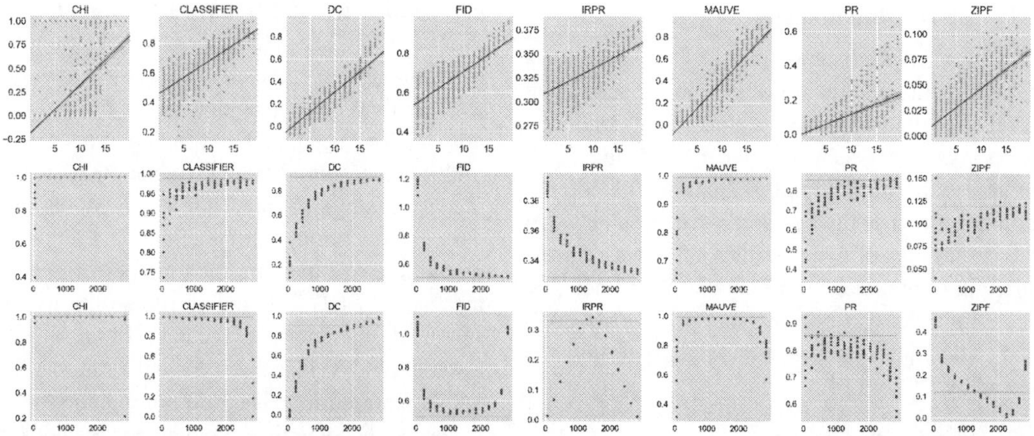

Figure 2: Top: Distance values (non-normalized) of corpora pairs in D_ℓ versus ℓ. ($n = 100, k = 12, |J| = 6053$), pooled across 5 repetitions of KSC samples. Blue line indicates regression and confidence interval at 95%. Middle: Distance values calculated on increasing s size corpora a_s and b_s sampled from sources A and B, correspondingly. Bottom: Distance between imbalanced corpora a_s and $b_{\bar{s}}$ where $|b_{\bar{s}}| = N - s$ and $N = 2900$. The x-axis represents $s \in \{50, 250, 450, \ldots, 2850\}$ ($repetitions = 10$). In middle and bottom figures, green horizontal line indicates the asymptotic distance $d(A, B)$. In all figures A=clinc150 and B=banking77.

	$\mathcal{A}(d)$		$\mathcal{A}^w(d)$		$\mathcal{T}(d)$		$\rho(d)$		$\mathcal{W}(d)$		$\mathcal{L}(d)$		$\mathcal{S}(d)$	$\mathcal{I}(d)$
k	7	12	7	12	7	12	7	12	7	12	7	12		
CHI	.945	.852	.913	.774	**4.68**	**3.29**	.875	.866	.684	.702	.810	.767	**.989**	**.994**
CLS.	.789	.701	.731	.618	1.26	1.10	.704	.735	.544	.562	.767	.767	.972	.918
DC	.958	.863	.936	.805	.031	.031	.913	**.892**	**.908**	**.879**	**.946**	**.919**	.832	.808
FID	.949	.810	.923	.753	.067	.066	.764	.695	.563	.537	.81	.759	.821	.877
IRPR	.832	.710	.784	.638	4.39	2.35	.571	.543	.258	.275	.645	.598	.949	.856
MUV.	**.976**	**.888**	**.963**	**.828**	.079	.071	**.938**	**.906**	.883	**.885**	**.947**	**.926**	**.977**	.943
PR	.820	.688	.767	.608	.031	.031	.649	.592	.577	.566	.716	.667	.909	.934
ZIPF	.886	.726	.851	.657	4.65	2.668	.751	.633	.514	.413	.785	.667	.852	.913
CHI	.953	.935	.936	.891	**5.58**	**3.33**	**.960**	**.962**	.835	**.900**	.83	.858	**1.00**	**1.00**
CLS.	.931	.827	.902	.751	1.29	1.21	.843	.836	.671	.702	.847	.847	**.993**	**.989**
DC	.773	.601	.702	.552	.031	.031	.707	.615	.763	.717	.825	.759	**.988**	**.986**
FID	.967	.904	.947	.848	.071	.067	.793	.754	.634	.636	.845	.816	.922	.898
IRPR	.697	.587	.642	.570	3.91	2.69	.382	.264	-.02	-.001	.433	.341	.951	.834
MUV.	**.999**	**.977**	**.998**	**.961**	.084	.067	.936	.943	**.856**	**.904**	**.932**	**.950**	**.999**	**.994**
PR	.722	.467	.666	.446	.031	.030	.459	.240	.488	.394	.658	.523	.890	.899
ZIPF	.854	.783	.817	.736	4.77	3.02	.660	.635	.309	.352	.687	.661	.735	.904

Table 3: Summary of metrics evaluation scoring on two pairs of source datasets in low ($k = 7$) and high ($k = 12$) resolution KSC ($n = 100$). Best results with differences below .015 are marked in bold. $\mathcal{T}(d)$ units are $[100op/sec]$. MUV. stands for MAUVE and CLS. for CLASSIFIER. In the top table, A=clinc150 and B=banking77. In the bottom table A=atis and B=yahoo. The average results of 5 repetitions are reported for all measures except size and imbalance robustness, in which the number of repetitions is 10. More statistical details are provided in Figure 6 in the Appendix.

Given two pairs, (c_i, c_j) and (c_q, c_r), of paired corpora, we can only reliably predict which of $d(c_i, c_j)$ or $d(c_q, c_r)$ is larger in expectation (a decision we call a 'judgement') if the interval of one pair contains the other's. The set J contains all and only such judgements:

$$J = \{((c_q, c_r), (c_i, c_j)) : (q, r) \subset (i, j)\} \quad (5)$$

The judgement $d(c_q, c_r) \leq d(c_i, c_j)$ is correct when the second interval contains the first. This gives the most probabilistically-logical partial order on the similarities between corpora in a KSC collection, that can be obtained without knowledge of the true pairwise d-distances between corpora[9]. Figure 3 shows a tree representation of KSC-set pair containment relations, from which the set of judgements J can be extracted.

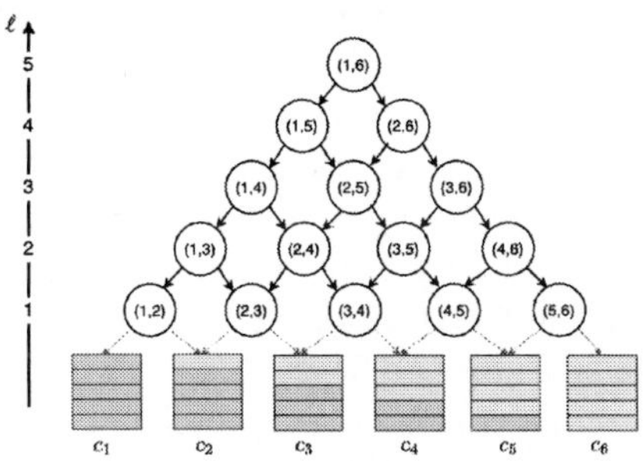

Figure 3: A tree representation of the judgements performed on the KSC collection given a metric $d(\cdot,\cdot)$, for calculating the accuracy ($\mathcal{A}$, Section 4.5) measures. The leafs are the KSC collection and the inner nodes (circles) represent the corpora tuples (c_i, c_j). The set J contains all judgements such that each node (i, j) is judged against all descended nodes. Namely, if there is a path from node a to node b, there is a judgement between the two nodes, and the judgement is correct if $d(b) \leq d(a)$. The size of the judgements set can be expressed as: $|J| = \sum_{i=1}^{k}(k-i)\left(\frac{i(i-1)}{2} - 1\right)$. For instance, $|J| = 339$ if $k = 7$, and 6053 if $k = 12$.

4.5.2 Accuracy

The metric accuracy is defined as the rate of correct judgements, formally:

$$\mathcal{A}(d) = \frac{1}{|J|} \sum_{j \in J} \mathbb{1}(d(c_q, c_r) \leq d(c_i, c_j)) \quad (6)$$

where $j = ((c_q, c_r), (c_i, c_j))$ is a judgement in J and $\mathbb{1}(\cdot)$ is the indicator function. Further, we propose a weighted version of the accuracy metric that assigns more weight to harder judgements. We define the hardness of judgement j as $w(j) = \frac{1}{\ell_2 - \ell_1}$ where $\ell_2 = j - i$ and $\ell_1 = r - q$, and $\ell_2 > \ell_1$ by definition of J. Formally,

$$\mathcal{A}^w(d) = C \sum_{j \in J} w(j) \cdot \mathbb{1}(d(c_q, c_r) \leq d(c_i, c_j))) \quad (7)$$

where $C = \left(|J| \cdot \sum_{j \in J} w(j)\right)^{-1}$. While $\mathcal{A}$ and $\mathcal{A}^w$ are correlated, as one may expect, $\mathcal{A}^w$ typically returns lower values (see Table 3).

In our implementation, the set of samples in each c_i is disjoint, namely, $c_i \cap c_j = \emptyset, \forall c_i, c_j \in KSC(A, B)$. This was done to prevent perfect judgements by naively counting the number of common instances (e.g., by defining $d(c_i, c_j) = |c_i \Delta c_j|$ where Δ denotes the symmetric difference). MAUVE, followed closely by FID, CHI and DC, achieves the highest accuracy results across resolutions and source corpora.

4.6 Size Robustness

We are also interested in capturing the sensitivity of a metric to sample sizes. To accomplish this, we need to quantify the convergence pace of $d(a_s, b_s)$ to the asymptotic distance $d(A, B)$, where a_s, b_s are samples from corpora A, B of increasing size s. Specifically, in our experiments $s \in S = \{50, 250, 450, \ldots, 2850\}$. The middle plot in Figure 2 shows convergence patterns of the different metrics to the asymptotic distance. The asymptotic distance is estimated by the mean of repeated (10) calculations of the distance on samples of size 3000 each from A, B, rather than on the full corpora. To quantify the metric size robustness, (S), we calculate the mean absolute error, $|d(a_s, b_s) - d(A, B)|$, for all $s \in S$, normalized by the asymptotic distance:

$$\mathcal{S}(d) = 1 - \sum_{s \in S} \frac{|d(a_s, b_s) - d(A, B)|}{d(A, B)} \quad (8)$$

Similar to previous measures, the normalization is performed to omit the influence of metric scale and operation ranges.

While our results demonstrate (Figure 2) that most of the metrics examined require around 1000 samples to closely estimate the asymptotic distance between the source corpora, their measured accuracy ($\mathcal{A}$(d) and $\mathcal{A}^w(d)$) is still fairly high even on

[9]For instance, say we compare pairwise distances between (c_1, c_6) and (c_5, c_7). Even though the second interval length $(7 - 5 = 2)$ is smaller than the first $(6 - 1 = 5)$, because it is not contained in the first, we cannot necessarily say that $d(c_5, c_7) \leq d(c_1, c_6)$ since inter-corpus distance may not be proportional to the interval length.

small corpora within the KSC, and can capture relative differences in corpus content.

4.7 Imbalance Robustness

Similarity metrics are frequently used to compare datasets with unequal sample size. Especially when comparing real and generated corpora, the size of a generated corpus is usually much larger than the real corpus. The imbalance robustness measure quantifies the effect of corpora size imbalance on the metric's performance (see Figure 2, bottom).

Unsurprisingly, asymmetric metrics such as PR and DC are most affected by size imbalance. While PR, DC, and MAUVE were all originally designed to measure the disparity between human and generated data (and thus asymmetric in the reference$P$ and target Q), it seems that MAUVE overcomes the sensitivity to datasets of very unequal sizes. Interestingly, imbalance causs some metrics (CLASSIFIER and MAUVE) to underestimate the distance, while others (FID) overestimate it. When we compare the convergence patterns of PR and DC, both are similarly asymmetric, maintaining $d(P,Q)$. When we increase the reference size, PR diverges from the true asymptotic distance, while DC converges to it. The Imbalance Robustness score $\mathcal{I}(d)$ is calculated similarly to the size robustness score, only that $|b_s| = N - |a_s|$.

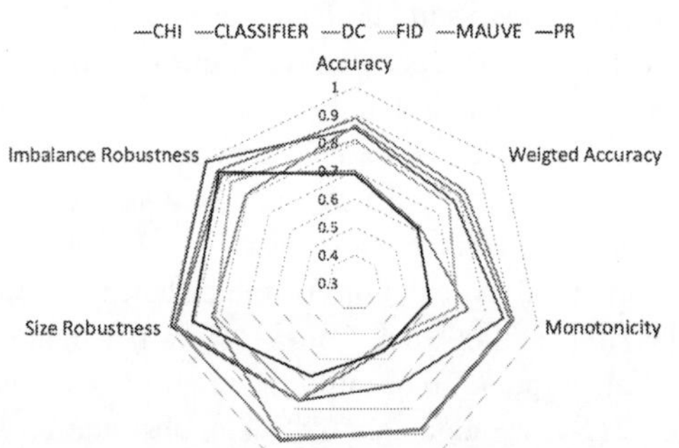

Figure 4: Leading metrics characterization radar chart. Mean results from Table 3 for A=clinc150, B=booking77 and for k = 12, excluding time efficiency to maintain scale.

KSC Parameters As shown in Section 4.6, most metrics require at least n = 1000 samples to capture the true distance between two source domain corpora; however, our experiments use n = 100. This is because our measures are relative, i.e., we do not aim to calculate the true asymptotic distance between two domains, but to measure the metrics' robustness in detecting small changes in the compared corpora. Furthermore, if n is large, k must also be large to ensure the k corpora in the KSC set have small enough absolute consecutive differences.

Note that small consecutive differences in KSC corpora are needed so that the measures in Section 4 will have a high enough resolution and large enough sample size of D_ℓ to properly differentiate the metric properties. In particular, this ensures the judgements (Section 4.5.1) used in the accuracy measures ($\mathcal{A}$ and $\mathcal{A}^w$) are not too 'easy' to make correctly, in which case they would be less useful as a tool. For instance, a metric with 100% accuracy makes all correct judgements, e.g., that $d(c_2,c_3) \leq d(c_1,c_4)$. If $k = 5$, the gap (in expectation) between the pair distances compared is large, so the judgement is easy, and thus all metrics may have full accuracy. When k increases, the absolute consecutive differences in corpora fall, and thus the difficulty of the judgement increases. Some metrics will fail to make the judgement correctly (in a given random KSC), decreasing their accuracy; this allows us to better differentiate between the more and less accurate metrics. However, setting k too high results in a computationally prohibitive number $|J|$ of judgements. Therefore, we opted to use the smaller n that are still sufficient to capture the quality and robustness of the investigated metrics.

5 Increasingly Fine-tuned Corpora

Here, we qualitatively investigate the metrics' ability to discriminate between generated and human text using the following procedure: We generated a sequence of equal-size synthetic corpora $IFC = (g_1, g_2, \ldots, g_n)$ by sampling from a gradually fine-tuned language model on a specific source corpus A. Namely, in each iteration, a fine-tuning step is performed by training the language model on a single epoch containing 1000 sentences randomly drawn from A, followed by a generation process to synthesize a corpus g_i containing around 1000 sentences. The name IFC, or "Increasingly Fine-tuned Corpora", was chosen to parallel the name KSC ("Known Similarity Corpora").

For each generated corpus g_i, we estimated the distance from A, i..e, $d_i = d(A, g_i)$, $\forall i \in [n]$. While the true distance between those synthetic corpora and A are unknown, an effective metric should

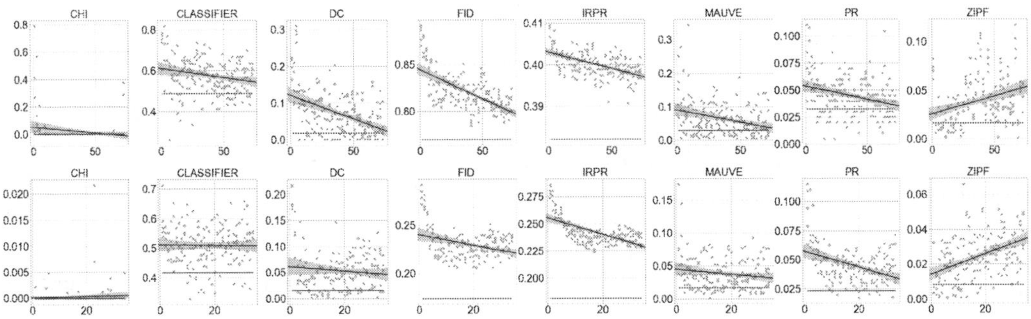

Figure 5: Similarity between reference corpus and iteratively fine-tuned corpora g_i samples. Orange dots show the similarity between samples of generated text in iteration i and the source dataset. The blue line indicates regression and confidence interval at 95%. The green horizontal line specifies the mean estimation of the distance between two random samples of the original corpus. The top figure shows iterative generation on unlabeled news headlines dataset. The bottom shows the iterative conditional generation using LAMBADA (Anaby-Tavor et al.) trained on banking77 dataset.

capture the decreasing distance between A and g_i with increasing i, namely $d_1 < d_2 < \cdots < d_n$. Due to our results, which show low imbalance robustness of some metrics, we maintained the same-size corpora when calculating corpora distance.

The results presented in Figure 5 show the gap between human and generated text captured by each metric in each iteration. To calculate the average self-distance of the reference corpus (A), we take the mean distance between two randomly sampled sub-corpora r_1 and r_2 from A, i.e. $d(A, A) = \mathbb{E}_{r_1,r_2 \sim A}[d(r_1, r_2)]$).

In our experiments we used two datasets, the banking77 dataset, mentioned above and the news dataset[10], representing different domains of text corpora. The IFC set for the banking77 dataset was generated in an iterative two-step procedure similar to the one described in LAMBADA (Anaby-Tavor et al.). This procedure first generates sentences conditioned on the label, then filters out sentences that are out-of-domain or incorrectly labeled. However, the IFC set for the news dataset was generated by finetuning the pre-trained GPT-2 medium model (Radford et al., 2019).

The results in Figure 5 show that CHI is less effective than the other metrics in capturing the gradual nature of the IFC. Also, they show that FID and IRPR are sensitive in discriminating between the original and generated corpora, even after many fine-tuning iterations. Interestingly, the ZIPF distance increases with the iteration. This indicates that the generated text, despite becoming semantically closer to the original with the increasing iterations, becomes less 'natural' in that the token frequencies deviate from that of human text and the reference corpus. This can be explained, at least in part, by the TTR measure. TTR is a standard word diversity measure, calculated by dividing the number of unique words in a text by the total word count. A high TTR indicates significant lexical variation. Indeed, in the IFC of banking77, g_1's TTR is 0.295 which is closer to the original dataset's TTR of 0.299 than g_{40}'s TTR of 0.322.

6 Conclusions

In this work, we propose a principled set of automatic measures for evaluating the quality of text dissimilarity metrics. By testing various metrics using our measures, we show that they do a good job of capturing their known characteristics, hence increasing our confidence in these measures; also, overall, recent metrics exhibit more favorable traits than their predecessors. The radar chart in Figure 4 shows that our measure scores correlate well with the compared distributional metrics recency $MAUVE > DC > PR \sim FID$ as well as their known relative strengths.

7 Limitations

Although one of the main motivations for comparing corpora is to measure the semantic gap between human and generated short text, we used pairs of human text corpora from different domains to maintain controllably-distinct corpora in the KSC set. Despite this, future efforts to develop human and machine-generated benchmark pairs (Mille et al., 2021) will allow for future work to quantitatively

[10] HuffPost (www.huffpost.com) news headlines collected from 2012 to 2018 containing around 200k headlines.(www.kaggle.com/rmisra/news-category-dataset (https://www.huffpost.com)

measure the characteristics of semantic metrics on pairs of human and generated corpora using the approach devised in this paper.

Also, for more straightforward comparisons, we used only a single sentence-embedding model. However, as other studies (e.g., GPT-2 (Radford et al., 2019) in Pillutla et al. (2021) and Bert (Devlin et al., 2018) in Lo (2019)) have shown, the quality of a corpus distance metric can be affected by the embedding choice. In future extensions of our work, we plan to allow for multiple embeddings to obtain a more refined evaluation of the metrics.

An important limitation of this work is that it considers only English corpora of short text samples. We examined only a limited set of metrics and datasets, both of which we intend to extend.

In addition, we note that while our experiments calculate all KSC-based measures using a single KSC collection (same n and k values), it could be favourable to use different n and k for different measures. For instance, the time performance is calculated using a single size small dataset $n = 100$. In future work, the time scalability of metrics can be more closely investigated by comparing their time performance on increasing corpora sizes.

As indicated in Section 4, creating KSC collections with large k creates an excessive number of judgements (e.g., for $k > 15$, $|J| > 50000$), thus limiting the scalability of our method to smaller k and thus smaller n, if high resolution is required. This would preclude comparing the robustness of metrics that require large samples. We intend to rectify this in future work by creating representative smaller judgement sets by carefully sampling from the complete set.

As mentioned in Section 2, some of the investigated metrics were adapted to return a single value summarizing the distance between two corpora (e.g., averaging the precision and recall by the $F1$ score). Further work is required to build measures that can compare metrics returning multiple values.

References

Ateret Anaby-Tavor, Boaz Carmeli, Esther Goldbraich, Amir Kantor, George Kour, Segev Shlomov, Naama Tepper, and Naama Zwerdling. Do not have enough data? deep learning to the rescue! In *Proceedings of the AAAI Conference on Artificial Intelligence*, volume 34.

Iñigo Casanueva, Tadas Temcinas, Daniela Gerz, Matthew Henderson, and Ivan Vulic. 2020. Efficient intent detection with dual sentence encoders. *CoRR*, abs/2003.04807. https://huggingface.co/datasets/banking77.

Corinna Cortes and Vladimir Vapnik. 1995. Support-vector networks. *Machine learning*, 20(3):273–297.

Jacob Devlin, Ming-Wei Chang, Kenton Lee, and Kristina Toutanova. 2018. Bert: Pre-training of deep bidirectional transformers for language understanding. *arXiv preprint arXiv:1810.04805*.

Josip Djolonga, Mario Lucic, Marco Cuturi, Olivier Bachem, Olivier Bousquet, and Sylvain Gelly. 2020. Precision-recall curves using information divergence frontiers. In *International Conference on Artificial Intelligence and Statistics*, pages 2550–2559. PMLR.

Sebastian Gehrmann, Abhik Bhattacharjee, Abinaya Mahendiran, Alex Wang, Alexandros Papangelis, Aman Madaan, Angelina McMillan-Major, Anna Shvets, Ashish Upadhyay, Bingsheng Yao, et al. 2022. Gemv2: Multilingual nlg benchmarking in a single line of code. *arXiv preprint arXiv:2206.11249*.

Yvette Graham, Timothy Baldwin, Alistair Moffat, and Justin Zobel. 2017. Can machine translation systems be evaluated by the crowd alone. *Natural Language Engineering*, 23(1):3–30.

Yinuo Guo, Chong Ruan, and Junfeng Hu. 2018. Meteor++: Incorporating copy knowledge into machine translation evaluation. In *Proceedings of the Third Conference on Machine Translation: Shared Task Papers*, pages 740–745.

William L. Hays. 1963. *Statistics for psychologists*. Holt, Rinehart, & Winston.

Charles T. Hemphill, John J. Godfrey, and George R. Doddington. 1990. The ATIS spoken language systems pilot corpus. In *Proceedings of a Workshop Held at Hidden Valley, Pennsylvania, June 24-27, 1990*. https://www.kaggle.com/datasets/hassanamin/atis-airlinetravelinformationsystem.

Martin Heusel, Hubert Ramsauer, Thomas Unterthiner, Bernhard Nessler, and Sepp Hochreiter. 2017. Gans trained by a two time-scale update rule converge to a local nash equilibrium. *Advances in neural information processing systems*, 30.

Ari Holtzman, Jan Buys, Li Du, Maxwell Forbes, and Yejin Choi. 2019. The curious case of neural text degeneration. *arXiv preprint arXiv:1904.09751*.

Adam Kilgarriff. 2001. Comparing corpora. *International journal of corpus linguistics*, 6(1):97–133.

Tuomas Kynkäänniemi, Tero Karras, Samuli Laine, Jaakko Lehtinen, and Timo Aila. 2019. Improved precision and recall metric for assessing generative models. *Advances in Neural Information Processing Systems*, 32.

Stefan Larson, Anish Mahendran, Joseph J Peper, Christopher Clarke, Andrew Lee, Parker Hill, Jonathan K Kummerfeld, Kevin Leach, Michael A Laurenzano, Lingjia Tang, et al. 2019. An evaluation dataset for intent classification and out-of-scope prediction. *arXiv preprint arXiv:1909.02027*.

Chin-Yew Lin and Franz Josef Och. 2004. Orange: a method for evaluating automatic evaluation metrics for machine translation. In *COLING 2004: Proceedings of the 20th International Conference on Computational Linguistics*, pages 501–507.

Chi-kiu Lo. 2019. Yisi-a unified semantic mt quality evaluation and estimation metric for languages with different levels of available resources. In *Proceedings of the Fourth Conference on Machine Translation (Volume 2: Shared Task Papers, Day 1)*, pages 507–513.

David Lopez-Paz and Maxime Oquab. 2016. Revisiting classifier two-sample tests. *arXiv preprint arXiv:1610.06545*.

Mario Lucic, Karol Kurach, Marcin Michalski, Sylvain Gelly, and Olivier Bousquet. 2018. Are gans created equal? a large-scale study. *Advances in neural information processing systems*, 31.

Nitika Mathur, Johnny Wei, Markus Freitag, Qingsong Ma, and Ondřej Bojar. 2020. Results of the wmt20 metrics shared task. In *Proceedings of the Fifth Conference on Machine Translation*, pages 688–725.

Simon Mille, Kaustubh D Dhole, Saad Mahamood, Laura Perez-Beltrachini, Varun Gangal, Mihir Kale, Emiel van Miltenburg, and Sebastian Gehrmann. 2021. Automatic construction of evaluation suites for natural language generation datasets. *arXiv preprint arXiv:2106.09069*.

Muhammad Ferjad Naeem, Seong Joon Oh, Youngjung Uh, Yunjey Choi, and Jaejun Yoo. 2020. Reliable fidelity and diversity metrics for generative models. In *International Conference on Machine Learning*, pages 7176–7185. PMLR.

Jekaterina Novikova, Ondřej Dušek, Amanda Cercas Curry, and Verena Rieser. 2017. Why we need new evaluation metrics for nlg. *arXiv preprint arXiv:1707.06875*.

Kishore Papineni, Salim Roukos, Todd Ward, and Wei-Jing Zhu. 2002. Bleu: a method for automatic evaluation of machine translation. In *Proceedings of the 40th annual meeting of the Association for Computational Linguistics*, pages 311–318.

Krishna Pillutla, Swabha Swayamdipta, Rowan Zellers, John Thickstun, Sean Welleck, Yejin Choi, and Zaid Harchaoui. 2021. Mauve: Measuring the gap between neural text and human text using divergence frontiers. *Advances in Neural Information Processing Systems*, 34.

Andrei Popescu-Belis. 2003. An experiment in comparative evaluation: humans vs. computers. In *Proceedings of Machine Translation Summit IX: Papers*.

Alec Radford, Jeffrey Wu, Rewon Child, David Luan, Dario Amodei, Ilya Sutskever, et al. 2019. Language models are unsupervised multitask learners. *OpenAI blog*, 1(8):9.

Paul Rayson and Roger Garside. 2000. Comparing corpora using frequency profiling. In *The workshop on comparing corpora*, pages 1–6.

Ananya B Sai, Akash Kumar Mohankumar, and Mitesh M Khapra. 2022. A survey of evaluation metrics used for nlg systems. *ACM Computing Surveys (CSUR)*, 55(2):1–39.

Mehdi SM Sajjadi, Olivier Bachem, Mario Lucic, Olivier Bousquet, and Sylvain Gelly. 2018. Assessing generative models via precision and recall. *Advances in neural information processing systems*, 31.

Jiapeng Wang and Yihong Dong. 2020. Measurement of text similarity: a survey. *Information*, 11(9):421.

Tiancheng Zhao, Ran Zhao, and Maxine Eskenazi. 2017. Learning discourse-level diversity for neural dialog models using conditional variational autoencoders. *arXiv preprint arXiv:1703.10960*.

A Appendix

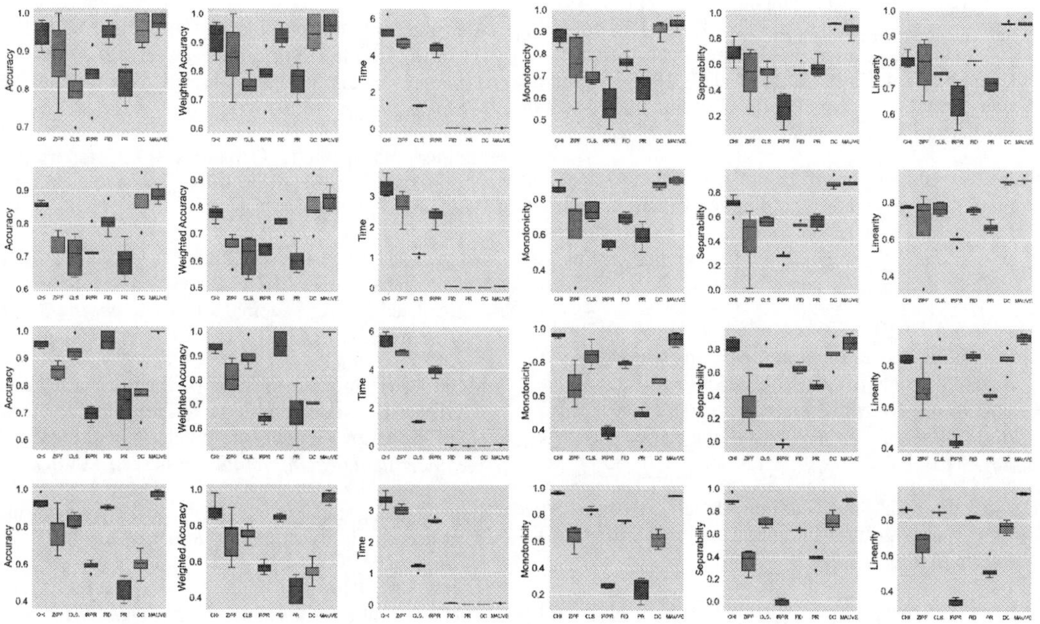

Figure 6: Distributional information of the results shown in Table 3. The top two figures showing the results for (A=clinc150 B=banking77), for k = 7 and k = 12, respectively. The bottom two figures are for (A=yahoo B=atis), for k = 7 and k = 12, respectively. Colored boxes depict the interquartile (25th to 75th) range. The mean is indicated by a horizontal line. All data points within 1.5 of the corresponding limits of the interquartile range are depicted by whiskers. Data points outside this range are plotted individually. CLS. indicates the CLASSIFIER metric.

Multilingual Social Media Text Generation and Evaluation with Few-Shot Prompting

Mack Blackburn
Leidos
mack.blackburn@leidos.com

Lizzie Yates
Leidos

Ning Yu
Leidos

Abstract

This work adapts large language models to generate multilingual social media text that meets several objectives simultaneously: topic relevance, author style consistency, and reply validity. Leveraging existing online information behavior simulators, which currently only forecast activities but not content, our approach comprised of generalizable prompt formation and efficient evaluation to produce a believable, personalized, and responsive synthetic social network. According to some preliminary experiments, our multi-objective prompt formation and automatic evaluation/selection methods are able to yield a significant number of high-quality synthetic texts according to both standardized and trained metrics.

1 Introduction

Our work on generation of synthetic social media text is motivated by existing technologies to simulate and forecast behavioral phenomena and information spread on social media platforms as part of the DARPA SocialSim program (Murić et al., 2020). While these simulators can forecast social media activity such as who will post on which topic or who will reply to whom at what time, they do not produce any text values for simulated activities. Our work fills this gap with text generation and provides a complete picture of simulated social network landscape. Novel methods for text generation are frequently explored; however our task involves the unusual aspect of generating convincing social media posts and replies in multiple languages for simulated online dialogue without human involvement and targets specific topics, author styles, and responses. In order to achieve these multiple objectives, traditional approaches like transfer learning (Raffel and Liu, 2020) make separate calls to large languages models; we leverage few-shot prompting to reduce such computing expensive calls and developed efficient automated evaluation metrics for synthetic text selection.

We employ commonly used text generation metrics (Sai et al., 2020) including BLEU scores and find that they only capture some aspects of what makes a text high-quality in our context. In general, most existing evaluation methods for synthetic text have limitations of some kind (Huang and Huang, 2020). Some synthetic texts can achieve metrics higher than real ground-truth text according to these standard metrics. Some newer metrics are too computational expensive and not suitable for supporting large scale text evaluation and selection. Therefore, we implemented three generalizable and runtime-efficient evaluation methods to measure generated text for their topic and author relevance as well as reply flow within a network, and also evaluated against more standard metrics.

Our social media text generation approach is efficient, language agnostic and generalizable, and can be used at scale to mimic social media networks with millions of simulated activities. The resulting synthetic information networks can support media analysts' training exercises, or provide large-scale datasets for AI/ML modeling studying online information behavior.

2 Related Work

There has been a significant amount of work on the use of prompts to generate desired types of text using language models such as GPT-NEO (Black et al., 2021). Multi-prompt learning incorporates multiple prompts, either answered or unanswered, into the text generation model prompting paradigm (Brown et al., 2020). Prompt augmentation uses multiple answered prompts (Liu et al., 2021). Our dataset

Proceedings of the 2nd Workshop on Natural Language Generation, Evaluation, and Metrics (GEM), pages 417 - 427
December 7, 2022 ©2022 Association for Computational Linguistics

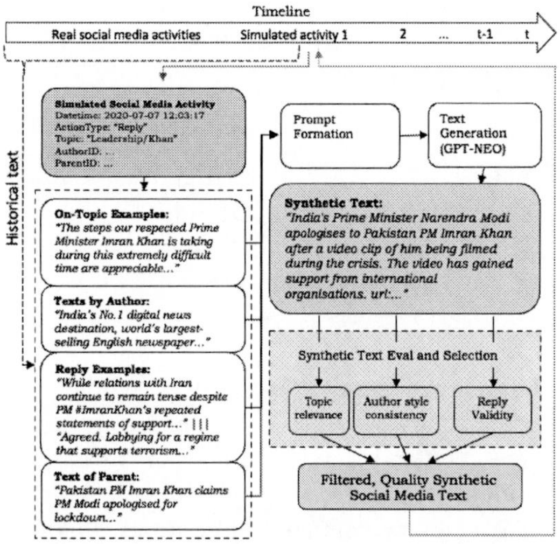

Figure 1: Text Generation and Evaluation Pipeline. In chronological order, each simulated activity is fed into this pipeline and the output is an enriched social media activity with generated text. Historical real and generated text are sampled for prompt formation.

contains many real world examples matching the multi-objective goals and many statement-reply pairs, so few-shot learning and prompt augmentation are good fits for our use case. While we are able to collect large volumes of social media text, manual annotation of text with specific labels is much more intensive, and few-shot learning allows us to utilize a smaller manually-annotated set.

3 Approach

,

3.1 Text Generation from Simulated Social Media Activities

Figure 1 depicts the high level pipeline. In chronological order, this pipeline sequentially generates and selects text for each simulated online activity. For any given simulated activity, the pipeline follows 4 steps:

1. Create a prompt that includes examples of real world historical texts (i.e., ground-truth) by the same author, followed by ground-truth texts on the same topic. Example texts were selected randomly. When the simulated activity is intended to be a reply, the prompt also includes examples of ground-truth statement-reply pairs, followed by the text of the parent text that the activity is meant to be responding to.
2. Feed formed prompts into a language model which returns generated text. We selected GPT-NEO because it has the best performance for text generation upon open sourced language models at the time when we were working on this project.
3. Evaluate and select generated text based on both standard and task-specific metrics to measure the three objectives: Topic relevance, authorship verification, and sentence-pair classification models (see 5).
4. Fill the simulated activities with generated text and move onto next simulated event on the timeline.

This pipeline for synthetic text evaluation and selection operates at scale and for multi-lingual/styled generation as well.

3.2 Prompt Formation

Single objective Few-Shot Prompts To generate text that is on-topic, in the style of a particular author, or responding to a particular statement, we use prompts that incorporate multiple examples of real-world text with these desired attributes. Specifically, on-topic prompts are selected from historical tweets based on their manual topic annotation described in section 5.2.3; user-focused prompts consist of real tweets by the same user with Twitter user's bio where available; Reply-focused prompts are more complicated and consist of examples of statement-response pairs as reference:

> *"The following is a list of tweet and response pairs:*
> *{{gold statement 1}} ||| {{gold response 1}}*
> *===*
> *{{gold statement 2}} ||| {{gold response 2}}*
> *===*
> *{{gold statement 3}} ||| ..."*

The parent tweet will also be incorporated into the prompt for generation of a reply. Because we are generating text for large-scale simulations of social media, a simulated reply can be corresponding to either a real tweet or a simulated tweet. In the latter, we look

Language Code	Count
en	2,065,581
ur	504,485
hi	196,362
la	44,959
sw	21,410
ms	20,993
zh	17,722
id	15,853
mr	14,500
xh	12,292

Table 1: Count of each of the top ten languages as detected by the langid library

up the specific synthetic text for the parent tweet. Because of this, text generation occurs sequentially in the chronological order of the simulated activities.

Multi-Objective Few-Shot Prompts In addition to evaluations of text generated with a single objective, we also generate and evaluate texts with two objectives or three objectives at once in the case of synthetic replies. Multi-objective prompts are formatted by concatenating multiple single-objective prompts.

4 Dataset

4.1 Social Media Collection

For the DARPA SocialSim program, we collected online discussions relevant to the China-Pakistan Economic Corridor (CPEC) from multiple social media platforms. The primary platforms by data volume are Twitter and YouTube, and we will focus on Twitter for the rest of the paper. Due to the nature of the event, we create a list of keywords in English, Hindi, Urdu, Chinese and several other regional languages to query tweets and replies or YouTube video titles and description. Some keyword examples are: "china pakistan economic corridor", "cpec", "ਇਕ ਬੈਲਟ ਇਕ ਰੋਡ", and "ایک بیلٹ ون روڈ". The counts of each of the top ten languages in the dataset as detected by the langid python library (Lui and Baldwin, 2012) are shown in table 1. The top three languages by volume are English, Urdu, and Hindi.

Annotation From the collected social media data covering almost 5 million Tweets and YouTube comments, we selected roughly 5,000 of the most-interacted with texts to pass to three in-house manual annotators, who annotated for 21 distinct topic labels with a cross-label average Cohen's Kappa inter-annotator agreement of 0.78. Detailed annotation procedure can be found in (Blackburn et al.). As examples of topic labels, the label "benefits/development/jobs" refers to discussion of jobs brought by the CPEC program, and the label "controversies/china/border" refers to discussion of border disputes in the China-India-Pakistan region. The set of annotated texts were used to train a supervised text classifier (F1 score of 0.73 across all 21 topics). While the manually-annotated examples have been leveraged to provide few-shot prompt examples for text generation, the classifier was used to evaluate the topic relevance of generated text, see 5.2.3.

4.2 Simulated Social Media Activities

We use simulated social media activities generated by SocialCube (Tarek Abdelzaher, 2020) as a template for the time, author, and topic of synthetic social media activities, and fill in the text value with synthetic texts that fit the desired attributes. SocialCube takes real world social media activity and news event data in the training phase, and returns social media activity simulation for the following testing phase. We used one of the simulation results that contains 1,037,782 simulated activities for a total span of 27 days. After removing retweets that do not require unique text, 149,829 activities left require synthetic text values (e.g. new tweets and replies).

5 Evaluation and Metrics

Ground Truth In our tests, the ground truth used for evaluation contains real social media texts with specific attributes. There are three groups of ground truth: one group of texts manually annotated with topic labels (the test set of the manual annotation process in section 5.2.3), a group of texts by specific authors (the test set of the data used to train the authorship verification model in section 5.2.1), and a group of valid and invalid statement-response pairs (the test set of the dataset in section5.2.2).

5.1 Standardized Metrics

Median Sentence BLEU Sentence BLEU calculated with the sacrebleu library (Post, 2018) for generated message, treating the ground truth texts with the same class (i.e., topic or author/user) as reference. Median is calculated over distribution of scores. We choose median because mean can be effected by outliers, and we are concerned with the quantity of texts with high scores rather than overall average. (Papineni et al., 2002)

Self-BLEU Sentence BLEU calculated with the sacrebleu library for generated message, treating all texts with the same class and generation method as reference. Median is calculated over distribution of scores.(Zhu et al., 2018)

GEM Metrics Library We also run evaluation with multiple metrics from the GEM metrics library trying to covering different aspects of generated text: descriptive, diversity,lexical and semantic measurements. Some examples include BLEURT, Distinct-1 (the ratio of distinct unigrams over the total number of unigrams), Entropy-1 (the Shannon Entropy over unigrams), and text length metrics (Gehrmann et al., 2021).

5.2 Trained Metrics

Since none of the standardized metrics for text generation directly measure the three objectives of our use case, we also develop three specific evaluation methods respectively leveraging the ground truth data.

5.2.1 Authorship Verification for Author Style

Using ground-truth social media data, we identify all users with over 20 unique text-valued posts, and store those users' posts into train and test sets with the ratio 0.7 to 0.3. From the stored posts, we construct 50,000 training and 10,000 test pairs, where pairs of texts by the same user are in the "1" class and pairs of texts by two separate users are in the "0" class. We then finetune the distiluse-base-multilingual-cased language model on the pairs using contrastive loss with cosine for 5 epochs (Sanh et al., 2019). Training of the model uses the SentenceTransformers library with default parameters (Reimers and Gurevych, 2019). When using cosine similarity of the embeddings of the fine-tuned model as an indicator for authorship on the test set, we find a ROC-AUC of 0.94. The ROC-AUC of 0.94 is an evaluation of how well the cosine similarity metric distinguishes between texts by different authors in the test set.

We apply the author fine-tuned language model to each generated text, and measure the cosine similarity of the vector of each text to the centroid of the vectors for the ground truth texts by the intended author. The cosine similarity is used as an indicator of the degree to which the synthetic text matches the style of the intended author.

5.2.2 Statement-Response Pair Classification for Reply Detection

Data Preparation We train a sentence pair classifier to determine whether a response replies coherently to an original sentence. We begin by extracting around 350,000 real tweet-response pairs from our curated Twitter dataset. Roughly 15 percent of the data is set aside as holdout data, while the rest is processed for training. The training data is halved, with the first half being true pairs and receiving a label of 1. The second half of the training data is then halved again, and either shuffled row wise or column wise, providing "untrue" or 0-labeled tweet-response pairs while still maintaining contextual relevance. The pairs is then concatenated, shuffled, and set aside for training and evaluation.

Classification For the sentence-pair classification task, we utilize the Simple Transformers library (Rajapakse, 2020). Our final configuration is set up for a maximum sequence length of 512 to be trained over 2 epochs with an Adam optimizer and learning rate of 4e-5. Our trained model is evaluated on our evaluation dataset and returns a F1 score of .81, accuracy of .79, AUROC of .84 and AUPRC of .77. We test several model types including BERT (Devlin et al., 2018), RoBERTa (Liu et al., 2019), distilbert (Sanh et al., 2019) and xlnet (Yang et al., 2019). BERT, and specifically bert-based-multilingual-cased, provides the strongest results for our use case.

Model	Precision	self-BLEU	Mean Topic Similarity	median BLEU
Ground Truth	0.91	38.83	0.64	38.83
gpt-neo-1.3B	0.35	67.03	0.55	43.07
gpt-neo-125M	0.33	57.59	0.46	39.18

Table 2: Topic-Relevance Evaluation Metrics, Across all Languages

5.2.3 Topic Classification Precision

We train a supervised topic classifier using the manually-annotated set described in section 4.1. Given a piece of generated text, if this classifier actually labels it with the intended topic, we assume the generated text is relevant to the intended label.

Topic Relevance In addition to the classifier precision metric, we also use the "distiluse-base-multilingual-cased" language model, which is appropriate for our multilingual dataset, and is specifically well-suited to measure semantic similarity with cosine (Cer et al., 2018). Vectors are extracted for each generated text and each ground-truth text. Ground-truth texts are grouped by topic class and an average vector for each class is computed. For each generated text, the cosine similarity of its vector to the ground-truth vector of the same class is measured. Cosine similarities are averaged across texts.

6 Evaluation and Discussion

6.1 Single-Objective Text Generation Evaluation

Topic Relevance Table 2 shows topic-relevance metrics for GPT-NEO 125M and 1.3B compared to the same metrics for real ground truth texts. For the ground truth, self-BLEU is the same as median BLEU, because median BLEU always uses the ground truth as references for computation. For some metrics such as BLEU there is an acceptable range rather than strictly "higher is better". The lower precision score of GPT-generated text compared to ground truth may show that generating text exactly on an exact topic is still a challenge.

Author Style As shown in table 3, GPT-NEO 1.3B with prompts incorporating the text of a user's self-reported social media bio and example texts by the user generated synthetic texts most similar to real ground truth texts by the same authors, according to our metric.

Method	Mean Author Similarity±Std Dev.
Ground Truth	0.93±0.08
GPT-NEO-1.3B + User Bio	0.86±0.14
GPT-NEO-125M	0.85±0.14
GPT-NEO-125M + User Bio	0.84±0.11
GPT-NEO-1.3B	0.82±0.13
Inverse Ground Truth	0.64±0.20

Table 3: Author Style Evaluation. "Mean author similarity" shows the mean of the cosine similarities between texts and the centroid of the vectors for the user's ground-truth texts. "Inverse Ground Truth" shows this metric computed on ground truth texts compared to texts by different authors, across all languages.

Synthetic Reply Evaluation Based on our evaluation shown in table 4, generating realistic synthetic replies is possible, but a significant portion of the synthetic texts generated may not be properly coherent or satisfactory replies.

Model	Mean Reply Score±Std Dev.
Ground Truth	0.89±0.31
GPT-NEO-125M	0.47±0.50
GPT-NEO-1.3B	0.41±0.49
Inverse Ground Truth	0.33±0.46

Table 4: Reply Evaluation. "Mean reply score" shows the averaged predictions of the reply classifier model. Ranged 0-1 where 0 is 0% valid replies and 1 is 100%. "Inverse Ground Truth" shows this metric computed on non-reply ground truth text pairs. Computed across all languages.

6.2 Multi-Objective Prompting Evaluation

As shown in table 5, the mean scores of most metrics degrade on the multi-objective task as compared to the single-objective tasks. However, we are still able to use our evaluation

Metric	GPT-NEO-1.3B	GPT-NEO-125M
Mean Topic Similarity ±Std Dev.	0.33±0.24	0.29±0.21
Mean Reply Score ±Std Dev.	0.37±0.48	0.39±0.49
Mean Author Similarity ±Std Dev.	0.76±0.14	0.76±0.18

Table 5: Evaluation of Texts from Multi-Objective Prompt, Across all Languages.

metrics as a filter to separate higher quality texts from lower quality ones, and still generate a relatively large number of high-quality synthetic texts, as described in section 6.3. Texts with a topic relevance score above 0.6, a user similarity score above 0.7, and a reply validity score above 0.6 are marked, and stored for use as text values of the simulated social media activities.

GEM Metrics Evaluation We use several metrics from the GEM metrics repository (Gehrmann et al., 2021) to measure the generated text from more perspectives. Some results are shown in table 6. Looking at some of the descriptive metrics, mean text length for GT and language models are similar. This is not surprising given the character limit for tweets. However, the range of generated tweet length varies much more than ground truth: as short as 1 and as long as 60+. Text length limit information can be introduced in the future to avoid generating text longer than allowed. Not included in the result table, the vocabulary size of ground truth, for topic or user relevance, is always much smaller than generated text. This suggests that machine generated text may contain terms that are not used often for social media. Conducting domain adaptation on the pre-trained language model to make it more relevant to social media data may help reduce this difference. Looking at some of the diversity metrics, the Distinct-1 metrics indicates ground truth text is much more diverse than generated text. This could due to the high creativity of language expression in social media. When it comes to semantic metrics, even ground truth tweets achieve pretty low BLUERT score. Generated text is worse, with bigger GTP-neo model performs slightly better. BLUERT is calculated for a small set of evaluation set due to its high computing demand, and we will look at this again when calculate it against the complete evaluation set.

Multi-Lingual Evaluation Because our dataset is multilingual, we also report the GEM metrics across the top 5 languages in our dataset: English, Farsi, Hindi, Urdu, and Chinese in table 7. Additional multilingual metrics are reported in appendices A, B, and C. English has the best performance in terms of BLEURT, followed by Hindi and Chinese. This could due to lack of real world data in our collection for other languages to create good prompts or the lack of explicit multilingual capabilities of GPT-NEO. All other evaluations reported in this paper are computed on texts regardless of language, including English and others.

6.3 Scalability and Runtime

We use a single-GPU instance on AWS (16vCPUs, 1 GPU, 64GB Memory) for generation and evaluation. The single-GPU machine was able to generate 29,150 synthetic texts per hour in total using GPT-NEO 125M, but after evaluation and selection of higher-quality texts, that number comes to 5,658 high-quality synthetic texts per hour.

7 Limitation

Due to the shortage of time and computing resource, we didn't finish running some of the heavy metrics such as NUBIA(Kane et al., 2020) for measuring faithfulness and BERTScore(Zhang* et al., 2020) for better semantic measurement. We also didn't measure the entire pipeline, e.g., comparing generated text and real text in the same simulation time frame and measuring the impact of generated and filtered text in simulation. We will address some of these limitations in our next steps. We will also try to evaluate the filtering step with manual review of filtered texts, and by testing the impact of synthetic texts on social media simulations.

8 Conclusions and Future Work

We show that it is feasible to generate and evaluate synthetic social media texts which not only focus on a desired topic, but also mimic an author style and properly respond to

Model	Mean Topic BLEURT	Mean User BLEURT	Distinct-1	Entropy-1	Mean Text Length
gpt-neo-1.3B	0.15±0.08	0.15±0.1	0.61±0.11	6.62±0.48	23.38±19.48
gpt-neo-125M	0.15±0.08	0.15±0.09	0.59±0.13	6.32±0.63	23.51±19.62
GT	0.21±0.06	0.25±0.09	0.85±0.12	4.59±0.85	27.03±1.39

Table 6: Selected GEM Metrics Across all Languages

Model	Lang	Mean Topic BLEURT	Mean User BLEURT	Distinct-1	Entropy-1	Mean Text Length
gpt-neo-1.3B	**en**	0.17	0.18	0.58	6.72	286.86
	fa	0.06	0.05	0.7	6.54	192.87
	hi	0.1	0.11	0.7	6.45	176.78
	ur	0.07	0.06	0.74	6.4	151.74
	zh	0.13	0.11	0.67	6.22	171.28
gpt-neo-125M	**en**	0.17	0.17	0.55	6.39	261.49
	fa	0.07	0.06	0.73	6.22	148.14
	hi	0.11	0.11	0.68	6.16	159.2
	ur	0.08	0.08	0.75	6.24	144.86
	zh	0.13	0.11	0.63	6.07	176
GT	**en**	0.22	0.27	0.85	4.61	38.86
	fa	0.04	0.17	1	4	16
	hi	0.18	0.17	0.75	5.45	65
	ur	0.12	0.13	0.85	4.79	44.91
	zh	0.12	0.09	0.86	4.92	37

Table 7: GEM Metrics by Language

existing text. We accomplish this with multi-objective few-shot prompting and automated evaluation metrics for multiple aspects of text quality. While it is clear that even in best-case scenarios language models like GPT can generate a percentage of text that does not match the given objectives, we believe that a filtering step including multiple evaluation metrics is a good approach to overcoming this limitation. Future plans include the application of domain-adaptive pre-training and platform business rules to improve relevance to social media genre, continuous/soft prompting instead of discrete/hard prompting to further improve the quality of generated text, real world events prompting similar to reply prompting, and multimedia data generation. Other work in this domain could involve testing other, potentially smaller language models, or assessing the threat posed by adversarial or malicious information campaigns that utilize text generation methods, and how best to detect them.

Acknowledgements

We also thank Graham Horwood for his suggestions on evaluation methods and Mark Williams for initial input for the project. We thank our anonymous reviewers for their valuable feedback. This material is based upon work supported by the Defense Advanced Research Projects Agency (DARPA) and the Army Research Office (ARO) under Contract No. W911NF-17-C-0095. The content of the information in this document does not necessarily reflect the position or the policy of the U.S. Government, and no official endorsement should be inferred..

References

Sid Black, Leo Gao, Phil Wang, Connor Leahy, and Stella Biderman. 2021. GPT-Neo: Large Scale Autoregressive Language Modeling with Mesh-Tensorflow.

Mack Blackburn, Ning Yu, John Berrie, Brian Gordon, David Longfellow, William Tirrell, and Mark Williams. Corpus development for studying online disinformation campaign: a narrative+ stance approach. In Proceedings for the First International Workshop on Social Threats in Online Conversations: Understanding and Management, pages 41–47.

Tom Brown, Benjamin Mann, Nick Ryder, Melanie Subbiah, Jared D Kaplan, Prafulla Dhariwal, Arvind Neelakantan, Pranav Shyam, Girish Sastry, Amanda Askell, et al. 2020. Language models are few-shot learners. Advances in neural information processing systems, 33:1877–1901.

Daniel Cer, Yinfei Yang, Sheng-yi Kong, Nan Hua, Nicole Limtiaco, Rhomni St John, Noah Constant, Mario Guajardo-Cespedes, Steve Yuan, Chris Tar, et al. 2018. Universal sentence encoder. arXiv preprint arXiv:1803.11175.

Jacob Devlin, Ming-Wei Chang, Kenton Lee, and Kristina Toutanova. 2018. BERT: pre-training of deep bidirectional transformers for language understanding. CoRR, abs/1810.04805.

Sebastian Gehrmann, Tosin P. Adewumi, Karmanya Aggarwal, Pawan Sasanka Ammanamanchi, Aremu Anuoluwapo, Antoine Bosselut, Khyathi Raghavi Chandu, Miruna Clinciu, Dipanjan Das, Kaustubh D. Dhole, Wanyu Du, Esin Durmus, Ondrej Dusek, Chris C. Emezue, Varun Gangal, Cristina Garbacea, Tatsunori B. Hashimoto, Yufang Hou, Yacine Jernite, Harsh Jhamtani, Yangfeng Ji, Shailza Jolly, Mihir Kale, Dhruv Kumar, Faisal Ladhak, Aman Madaan, Mounica Maddela, Khyati Mahajan, Saad Mahamood, Bodhisattwa Prasad Majumder, Pedro Henrique Martins, Angelina McMillan-Major, Simon Mille, Emiel van Miltenburg, Moin Nadeem, Shashi Narayan, Vitaly Nikolaev, Rubungo Andre Niyongabo, Salomey Osei, Ankur P. Parikh, Laura Perez-Beltrachini, Niranjan Rao, Vikas Raunak, Juan Diego Rodriguez, Sashank Santhanam, João Sedoc, Thibault Sellam, Samira Shaikh, Anastasia Shimorina, Marco Antonio Sobrevilla Cabezudo, Hendrik Strobelt, Nishant Subramani, Wei Xu, Diyi Yang, Akhila Yerukola, and Jiawei Zhou. 2021. The gem benchmark: Natural language generation, its evaluation and metrics. ArXiv, abs/2102.01672.

Dazhen Wan Zhihong Shao Pei Ke Jian Guan Yilin Niu Xiaoyan Zhu Huang, Fei and Minlie Huang. 2020. Cotk: An open-source toolkit for fast development and fair evaluation of text generation. arXiv:2002.00583.

Hassan Kane, Muhammed Yusuf Kocyigit, Ali Abdalla, Pelkins Ajanoh, and Mohamed Coulibali. 2020. NUBIA: NeUral based interchangeability assessor for text generation. In Proceedings of the 1st Workshop on Evaluating NLG Evaluation, pages 28–37, Online (Dublin, Ireland). Association for Computational Linguistics.

Pengfei Liu, Weizhe Yuan, Jinlan Fu, Zhengbao Jiang, Hiroaki Hayashi, and Graham Neubig. 2021. Pre-train, prompt, and predict: A systematic survey of prompting methods in natural language processing. arXiv preprint arXiv:2107.13586.

Yinhan Liu, Myle Ott, Naman Goyal, Jingfei Du, Mandar Joshi, Danqi Chen, Omer Levy, Mike Lewis, Luke Zettlemoyer, and Veselin Stoyanov. 2019. Roberta: A robustly optimized BERT pretraining approach. CoRR, abs/1907.11692.

Marco Lui and Timothy Baldwin. 2012. Langid.py: An off-the-shelf language identification tool. In Proceedings of the ACL 2012 System Demonstrations, ACL '12, page 25–30, USA. Association for Computational Linguistics.

Goran Murić, Alexey Tregubov, Jim Blythe, Andrés Abeliuk, Divya Choudhary, Kristina Lerman, and Emilio Ferrara. 2020. Massive cross-platform simulations of online social networks. In Proceedings of the 19th International Conference on Autonomous Agents and MultiAgent Systems, pages 895–903.

Kishore Papineni, Salim Roukos, Todd Ward, and Wei-Jing Zhu. 2002. Bleu: a method for automatic evaluation of machine translation. In Proceedings of the 40th annual meeting of the Association for Computational Linguistics, pages 311–318.

Matt Post. 2018. A call for clarity in reporting BLEU scores. In Proceedings of the Third Conference on Machine Translation: Research Papers, pages 186–191, Belgium, Brussels. Association for Computational Linguistics.

Noam Shazeer Adam Roberts Katherine Lee Sharan Narang Michael Matena Yanqi Zhou Wei Li Raffel, Colin and Peter J. Liu. 2020. Exploring the limits of transfer learning with a unified text-to-text transformer. Journal of Machine Learning Research 21 (2020) 1-67.

Thilina Rajapakse. 2020. Simple transformers. `https://github.com/ThilinaRajapakse/simpletransformers`.

Nils Reimers and Iryna Gurevych. 2019. Sentence-bert: Sentence embeddings using siamese bert-networks. In Proceedings of the 2019 Conference on Empirical Methods in Natural Language Processing. Association for Computational Linguistics.

Ananya B Sai, Akash Kumar Mohankumar, and Mitesh M Khapra. 2020. A survey of evaluation metrics used for nlg systems. arXiv preprint arXiv:2008.12009.

Victor Sanh, Lysandre Debut, Julien Chaumond, and Thomas Wolf. 2019. Distilbert, a distilled version of bert: smaller, faster, cheaper and lighter. ArXiv, abs/1910.01108.

Yifan Hao Andong Jing Dongxin Liu Shengzhong Liu Hoang Hai Nguyen David M. Nicol Huajie Shao Tianshi Wang Shuochao Yao Yu Zhang Omar Malik Stephen Dipple James Flamino Fred Buchanan Sam Cohen Gyorgy Korniss Boleslaw K. Szymanski Tarek Abdelzaher, Jiawei Han. 2020. Multiscale online media simulation with socialcube. Computational and Mathematical Organization Theory.

Zhilin Yang, Zihang Dai, Yiming Yang, Jaime G. Carbonell, Ruslan Salakhutdinov, and Quoc V. Le. 2019. Xlnet: Generalized autoregressive pretraining for language understanding. CoRR, abs/1906.08237.

Tianyi Zhang*, Varsha Kishore*, Felix Wu*, Kilian Q. Weinberger, and Yoav Artzi. 2020. Bertscore: Evaluating text generation with bert. In International Conference on Learning Representations.

Yaoming Zhu, Sidi Lu, Lei Zheng, Jiaxian Guo, Weinan Zhang, Jun Wang, and Yong Yu. 2018. Texygen: A benchmarking platform for text generation models. In The 41st International ACM SIGIR Conference on Research & Development in Information Retrieval, pages 1097–1100.

A Appendix: Authorship Verification Scores by Language

Chart 2 shows the average of the score used for authorship verification on GT positive (real texts by the same user), GT negative (real texts by different users) and synthetic texts, of various languages.

B Reply Validity Scores by Language

Chart 3 shows the average of the score used for reply validity on GT positive (real statement-reply pairs), GT negative (mismatched real texts that are not statement-reply pairs) and synthetic replies, of various languages.

C Statement-Reply Language Counts

Chart 4 shows the count of tweet-reply pairs by language of original tweet and reply. The high count on the diagonal means that tweets in one language are frequently replied to with replies in the same language.

D Synthetic Text Examples on Topic

Synthetic text with intended topic "controversies/china/border" (India-China border disputes) with Topic BLEURT score 0.38:
"The Tension continues between India and Beijing A #ChinaComesModiRuns official tweet says that Beijing is the only government in the world that is trying to bully India into giving way to China's agenda. @Modi ran a tweet saying that China will not be allowed to gain a better foothold in the Indian Ocean. @Modi ran a tweet saying that China will not be allowed to gain a better foothold in the Indian Ocean."

Synthetic text with intended topic "benefits/development/energy" (energy development projects in Pakistan) with Topic BLEURT score 0.27:
"by @Carr-Ebrahim @JaxyIvan 2069 @Manssazh 2069 This project is to provide for power generation facility from PJM. It will provide thermal power system from PJM. The project will be the first industrial power plant in the world to be operated by either one

Model	Language	Cosine Sim GT User Centroid	Std Dev. Cosine Sim	Relevant Text Count
The method used to generate the text	*Language code*	*Average cosine similarity of generated text to the centroid of the user's text in a GT eval set*	*Standard Dev. of the cosine similarities*	*Number of texts used in evaluation*
GT Positive	ta	0.98	0.01	40
GT Positive	de	0.96	0.05	142
GT Positive	es	0.96	0.04	108
GT Positive	bn	0.95	0.07	48
GT Positive	ja	0.95	0.06	132
GT Positive	hi	0.95	0.06	4878
GT Positive	pnb	0.94	0.05	55
EleutherAI/gpt-neo-125M	hi	0.94	0.03	62
GT Positive	fa	0.94	0.06	76
GT Positive	ur	0.93	0.07	4258
GT Positive	en	0.92	0.08	30555
GT Positive	zh	0.90	0.08	373
EleutherAI/gpt-neo-125M	ur	0.89	0.10	121
EleutherAI/gpt-neo-1.3B	en	0.84	0.13	985
EleutherAI/gpt-neo-125M	ta	0.84	0.04	63
EleutherAI/gpt-neo-125M	en	0.83	0.13	1042
EleutherAI/gpt-neo-125M	fa	0.83	0.13	71
EleutherAI/gpt-neo-125M	zh	0.83	0.14	49
GT Negative	es	0.81	0.14	108
EleutherAI/gpt-neo-1.3B	ur	0.81	0.09	69
GT Negative	de	0.80	0.17	142
EleutherAI/gpt-neo-1.3B	zh	0.75	0.18	51
GT Negative	fa	0.70	0.19	76
GT Negative	en	0.67	0.20	30555
GT Negative	pnb	0.66	0.22	55
GT Negative	ta	0.63	0.16	40
GT Negative	zh	0.63	0.18	373
GT Negative	ja	0.62	0.23	132
GT Negative	bn	0.62	0.12	48
GT Negative	ur	0.59	0.22	4258
GT Negative	hi	0.53	0.19	4878

Figure 2: Authorship Verification Scores by Language

Model	Language	NSP Classifier Output Mean	Std Dev NSP Classifier Output	NSP Classifier Prediction Mean	Std Dev NSP Classifier Prediction	Relevant Text Count
Method used to generate the text	*Language code*	*Average of row output of the NSP classifier for the statement-reply pairs. Higher is better.*	*Standard dev. of the NSP classifier outputs*	*Average of the prediction of the NSP classifier for the statement-reply pairs. Range 0-1. Higher is better*	*Standard dev. of the NSP classifier predictions*	*Number of texts used in the evaluation*
GT_positive	ur	0.37	0.53	0.91	0.28	645
GT_positive	hi	0.34	0.53	0.93	0.26	151
GT_positive	en	0.33	0.54	0.89	0.31	1674
EleutherAI/gpt-neo-1.3B	hi	(0.41)	1.32	0.66	0.47	136
EleutherAI/gpt-neo-125M	hi	(0.64)	1.40	0.56	0.50	48
EleutherAI/gpt-neo-1.3B	kn	(0.99)	1.18	0.31	0.47	65
EleutherAI/gpt-neo-125M	ur	(1.05)	1.32	0.37	0.48	628
EleutherAI/gpt-neo-1.3B	ur	(1.16)	1.29	0.32	0.47	1435
EleutherAI/gpt-neo-125M	en	(1.18)	1.22	0.32	0.47	1193
EleutherAI/gpt-neo-125M	fa	(1.23)	1.22	0.27	0.44	395
EleutherAI/gpt-neo-1.3B	en	(1.26)	1.24	0.31	0.46	973
EleutherAI/gpt-neo-1.3B	fa	(1.26)	1.10	0.24	0.43	142
EleutherAI/gpt-neo-125M	pnb	(1.27)	1.25	0.29	0.45	77
EleutherAI/gpt-neo-1.3B	ta	(1.32)	1.18	0.23	0.42	53
GT_negative	hi	(1.42)	1.56	0.37	0.48	160
EleutherAI/gpt-neo-1.3B	ar	(1.43)	1.10	0.18	0.38	68
EleutherAI/gpt-neo-1.3B	pnb	(1.43)	1.18	0.21	0.41	56
GT_negative	en	(1.50)	1.51	0.32	0.47	1566
GT_negative	ur	(1.60)	1.58	0.34	0.47	718

Figure 3: Reply Validity Scores by Language

		Real Tweet Language													
		ar	en	es	fa	gu	hi	ja	kn	mr	pnb	ru	ta	te	ur	zh
Synthetic Reply Language	ar	1	83	0	0	0	2	0	0	1	0	0	0	0	3	2
	en	1	2025	1	0	0	137	0	0	4	1	1	1	1	210	4
	es	0	23	0	0	0	1	0	0	0	0	0	0	0	3	0
	fa	1	410	1	2	0	18	0	0	0	3	0	1	0	101	1
	gu	0	25	0	0	2	5	0	0	0	0	0	0	0	0	0
	hi	0	89	0	0	0	115	0	0	4	0	0	0	0	7	1
	ja	0	19	0	0	0	1	1	0	0	0	0	0	0	3	0
	kn	0	55	0	0	0	5	0	7	2	0	0	0	0	3	0
	mr	0	7	0	0	0	1	0	0	3	0	0	0	0	0	0
	pnb	0	108	0	0	0	2	0	0	0	2	0	0	0	32	0
	ru	0	32	0	0	0	3	0	0	0	0	0	0	0	3	0
	ta	0	61	0	0	0	13	0	0	0	0	0	12	0	4	0
	te	0	23	0	0	0	1	0	0	0	0	0	1	3	0	1
	ur	1	1455	2	3	0	65	1	0	1	6	0	0	0	719	0
	zh	0	40	0	0	0	3	0	0	0	0	0	0	0	1	4

Figure 4: Statement-Reply Language Counts

company. #Pakistan#Polarity #UK-Indian Union of Petroleum, Air and Chem"

E Synthetic Text Examples in a User Style

Real user bio:
"News. Views. Analysis. Conversations. India's No.1 digital news destination, world's largest-selling English newspaper - A Times Internet Limited Product"
Real tweet from user:
"Pakistan PM Imran Khan claims PM Modi apologised for lockdown, Pak media corrects him url: https://t.co/m4vAITPOTGhdHATzA-Kxalg "

Synthetic tweets:
1. *"India's Prime Minister Narendra Modi apologises to Pakistan PM Imran Khan after a video clip of him being filmed during the crisis. The video has gained support from international organisations url: https://t..."*
2. *"The Government of Pakistan has made efforts, I am pleased to say, to ensure that the Indian government did not see the rise of Pakistans internal tensions," Foreign Minister Shah Mehmood Qureshi tells the New York Times. "The two nations have a very good relationship." He also claims Pakistan has never asked for India's "aid and support" Read: https://t.co/eMhXC7Lr1mDnT3fJL"*

Assessing Inter-metric Correlation for Multi-document Summarization Evaluation

Michael Ridenour, Ameeta Agrawal, Olubusayo Olabisi
Portland State University
{mride2,ameeta,oolabisi}@pdx.edu

Abstract

Recent advances in automatic text summarization have contemporaneously been accompanied by a great deal of new metrics of automatic evaluation. This in turn has inspired recent work to re-assess these evaluation metrics to see how well they correlate with each other as well as with human evaluation, mostly focusing on single-document summarization (SDS) paradigm. Although many of these metrics are typically also used for evaluating multi-document summarization (MDS) tasks, so far, little attention has been paid to studying them under such a distinct scenario. To address this gap, we present a systematic analysis of the inter-metric correlations for MDS tasks, while comparing and contrasting the results with SDS models. Using datasets from a wide range of domains (news, peer reviews, tweets, dialogues), we thus study a unified set of metrics under both the task setups. Our empirical analysis suggests that while most reference-based metrics show fairly similar trends across both multi- and single-document summarization, there is a notable lack of correlation between reference-free metrics in multi-document summarization tasks.

1 Introduction

Summarization systems, which aim to preserve salient information from the source text in a more concise form, are being applied to an increasingly diverse range of domains, such as summarizing news articles, messenger-style text conversations, tweets, and so on (Nallapati et al., 2016; Nguyen et al., 2018; Gliwa et al., 2019). Evaluating the performance of these systems is still challenging, and since human evaluation is expensive to obtain, automatic evaluation metrics continue to provide an effective way of evaluating summary quality.

Since no single metric can comprehensively measure every aspect of a summary, it is becoming increasingly common to report system performance in terms of multiple metrics (Fabbri et al., 2021b). As such, it becomes desirable to find a small set of metrics that each reflect different aspects of system performance without redundantly repeating information. Conversely, if a metric is highly correlated with another metric but outperforms it when compared with human evaluation, then that performance difference is more significant (Graham, 2015; Bhandari et al., 2020; Pagnoni et al., 2021). However, in order to do this, one must first understand how these different metrics correlate with each other.

Previous work has focused on studying these metrics under the single-document summarization (SDS) setup, especially news (Bhandari et al., 2020; Fabbri et al., 2021b). However, it is well known that news summarization datasets contain a strong sentence position bias where the most salient information tends to be at the beginning of the article (Nenkova, 2005), which has been shown to have a strong impact on the behavior and performance of some summarization systems (Kryscinski et al., 2019), but does not hold in other domains (Kedzie et al., 2018). Evaluation metrics have also been re-evaluated in the context of scientific articles (Cohan and Goharian, 2016), and more recently, dialogues (Gao and Wan, 2022), both using single documents as input.

In contrast to SDS, multi-document summarization (MDS) is the task of generating a summary from several related documents (Li et al., 2020; Pasunuru et al., 2021; Xiao et al., 2022). Understanding how these metrics estimate MDS tasks, however, remains unexplored. This is notable because many reference-free metrics in particular rely on the source document to evaluate the summary, and when the source consists of stylistically diverse multiple documents, we postulate that it makes the task especially challenging for reference-free metrics. It is unclear whether the automatic evaluation metrics will correlate with each other in the same

Proceedings of the 2nd Workshop on Natural Language Generation, Evaluation, and Metrics (GEM), pages 428 - 438
December 7, 2022 ©2022 Association for Computational Linguistics

way in MDS as they do in SDS tasks. To address these gaps, we present a systematic study on assessing the inter-metric correlations between evaluation metrics for multi-document summarization. Our findings suggest a striking lack of correlation between the reference-free metrics under the MDS paradigm.

Our contributions include the following: (1) We conduct a comprehensive set of experiments for multi-document summarization using several summarization models and datasets from different domains and evaluate them over a *unified set of 16 metrics*; (2) We contextualize our results by drawing comparable insights under the single-document summarization paradigm. (3) Lastly, we summarize our key takeaways and discuss some potential implications of our findings.

2 Related Work

Conventionally, automatic metrics for evaluating summarization systems are mostly reference-based which require human-written reference summaries against which system-summaries can be compared (Lin, 2004; Banerjee and Lavie, 2005). However, since human annotation remains expensive to obtain, automatic evaluation metrics that rely on the source document(s) rather than human-generated reference summaries are becoming increasingly popular (Vasilyev et al., 2020; Scialom et al., 2021).

In parallel to this, researchers have re-assessed how effective these different types of evaluation metrics are, with almost all prior work focused on the single-document framework. Cohan and Goharian (2016) find that ROUGE is not effective at evaluating the performance of summarization systems in the domain of scientific articles. More recently, Bhandari et al. (2020) collect human pyramid-score evaluations (Nenkova and Passonneau, 2004) of sets of 100 summaries generated from 25 top-scoring summarization systems on the CNN/DailyMail dataset (Hermann et al., 2015; Nallapati et al., 2016). They then assess how well 8 different automatic evaluation metrics correlate with the human annotations using the William's test (Williams, 1959), and they also see how well these metrics perform on the shared tasks from the Text Analysis Conferences (TAC). Their analysis finds that most of the metrics fail to generalize well to all the datasets they tested, and that different metrics perform well on different datasets: MoverScore (Zhao et al., 2019) is found to correlate well with human evaluation on TAC-2008, Jensen-Shannon divergence on TAC-2009, and ROUGE-2 on CNN/DM. Similarly, Fabbri et al. (2021b) collect human Likert ratings of 16 systems summarizing 100 documents from CNN/DailyMail, and then use this to assess 14 evaluation metrics. They also find that reference-free metrics are loosely correlated with other metrics. The most recent work is by Gao and Wan (2022) that assesses 18 metrics on 14 systems, generating summaries from the SAMSum dataset (Gliwa et al., 2019) which comprises of messenger-style text conversations.

Type	Dataset	Domain	#Docs/Input
MDS	Multi-News	news	~2.75
	PeerSum v2	peer reviews	~7.75
	TSix	tweets	~35.7
SDS	CNN/DM	news	1
	SAMSum	dialogues	1

Table 1: Statistics of summarization datasets

We also collect system summaries and evaluate them with automatic metrics in our work, except we focus on the correlation between metrics, rather than comparing with human evaluation which is infamously difficult (Gehrmann et al., 2022). While prior work has focused on SDS, our analysis considers both MDS and SDS frameworks, a first such study to our knowledge, across datasets from four different domains.

3 Experimental Setup

3.1 Data

For our experiments, we use three MDS datasets: Multi-News dataset from the news domain (Fabbri et al., 2019), PeerSum which involves summarizing peer reviews of scientific publications (Li et al., 2022), and TSix dataset from the tweets domain (Nguyen et al., 2018). While the first two contain abstractive summaries, the third one contains extractive summaries. Some sample instances from the datasets are included in Appendix A.

As comparison, we also include two abstractive SDS datasets: CNN/DM from the news domain (Hermann et al., 2015), and SAMSum which involves summarizing chat dialogues (Gliwa et al., 2019). Table 1 presents statistics of the five summarization datasets.

3.2 Metrics

In reference-based evaluation, the system-generated summaries are compared to human-written reference summaries, while in unsupervised reference-free evaluation, the system summaries are evaluated using the input source document(s) without relying on human annotations. In this work, we consider a total of 16 widely reported evaluation metrics, 8 each from the reference-based (RB) and reference-free (RF) categories of metrics, which we further group as follows:

1. (RB) Metrics that measure n-gram overlap between the system summary and reference summary: **BLEU**[1] (Papineni et al., 2002), **ROUGE**[2] (Lin, 2004), **METEOR** (Banerjee and Lavie, 2005).

2. (RB) Metrics that use static word embeddings to compare the system and reference summaries: **Embedding Average** (Landauer and Dumais, 1997), **Greedy Matching** (Rus and Lintean, 2012), **Vector Extrema** (Forgues et al., 2014).

3. (RB) Metrics that use contextual representations to compare the system and reference summaries: **MoverScore**[3] (Zhao et al., 2019), **BERTScore**[4] (Zhang* et al., 2020).

4. (RF) Metrics that directly compare the system summary and source document: **Jensen-Shannon divergence**[5] (Lin et al., 2006), **BLANC**[6] (Vasilyev et al., 2020), **SUPERT**[7] (Gao et al., 2020), and **ESTIME**[8] (Vasilyev and Bohannon, 2021).

5. (RF) Metrics that use question-answering to compare the system summary and source document: **SummaQA** (Scialom et al., 2019), **QuestEval**[9] (Scialom et al., 2021).

6. (RF) Metrics that use text generation to measure the conditional probability of generating the summary given the source document, or vice versa: **BARTScore**[10] (Yuan et al., 2021), **Information Difference** (Egan et al., 2021).

3.3 Models

For generating *extractive* summaries, we use **Lead**, **LexPageRank** (Erkan and Radev, 2004), **TextRank** (Mihalcea and Tarau, 2004), **Cluster-CMRW** (Wan and Yang, 2008), **BERT-Ext** and **Longformer-Ext** (Miller, 2019). For generating *abstractive* summaries, we use **BART** (Lewis et al., 2019), **T5** (Raffel et al., 2019), **LED (Longformer Encoder-Decoder)** (Beltagy et al., 2020), and **Pegasus** (Zhang et al., 2020).

In our experiments on the Multi-News dataset (Fabbri et al., 2019), we use a combination of extractive and abstractive models because both types of models were used in the original paper. For comparable results, for the CNN/DM (Hermann et al., 2015) and SAMSum (Gliwa et al., 2019) datasets, we use the model outputs from the SummEval (Fabbri et al., 2021b) and DialSummEval (Gao and Wan, 2022) collections of system summaries, respectively, rather than generating summaries from scratch. Detailed descriptions of these models and the system outputs are included in Appendix B.

3.4 Correlation Analysis

With each dataset we collect system summaries for a set of 100 randomly selected samples from the test set, following recent work on measuring correlations between metrics (Bhandari et al., 2020; Fabbri et al., 2021b; Gao and Wan, 2022). For each sample d_i, $i \in \{1...N\}$ in a dataset $\mathcal{D}$ we generate J summaries from J models, and we denote each summary as s_{ij}, $j \in \{1...J\}$. We use Pearson's r to compute the system-level correlation between two metrics m_1 and m_2 as follows:

$$r^{sys}_{m_1 m_2} = r([\frac{1}{N}\sum_{i=1}^{N} m_1(s_{i1}), ..., \frac{1}{N}\sum_{i=1}^{N} m_1(s_{iJ})], [\frac{1}{N}\sum_{i=1}^{N} m_2(s_{i1}), ..., \frac{1}{N}\sum_{i=1}^{N} m_2(s_{iJ})]).$$

[1] `https://github.com/Maluuba/nlg-eval` is used for BLEU, METEOR, and the word embedding-based metrics

[2] `https://github.com/Diego999/py-rouge`

[3] `https://github.com/AIPHES/emnlp19-moverscore`

[4] `https://github.com/Tiiiger/bert_score`

[5] `github.com/UKPLab/coling2016-genetic-swarm-MDS`

[6] BLANC-tune, which uses the summary to first fine-tune the model

[7] `https://github.com/Yale-LILY/SummEval` is used for SUPERT and SummaQA

[8] `https://github.com/PrimerAI/blanc` is used for ESTIME, BLANC, and Information Difference

[9] `https://github.com/ThomasScialom/QuestEval`

[10] `https://github.com/neulab/BARTScore` is used for BARTScore (source -> hypothesis)

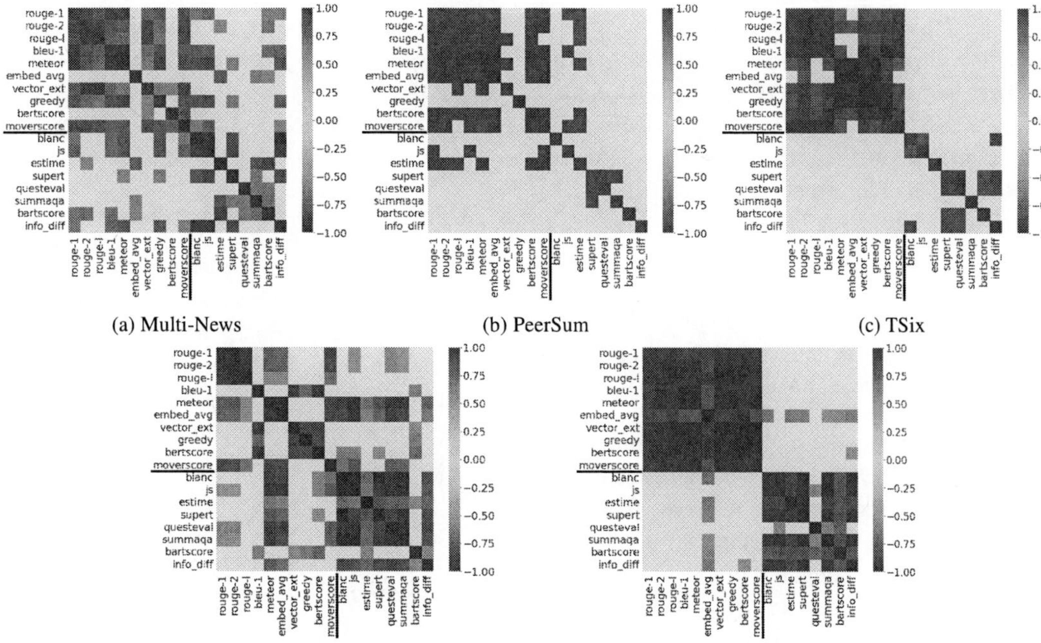

(a) Multi-News (b) PeerSum (c) TSix

(d) CNN/DM (e) SAMSum

Figure 1: Pearson's r correlation between metrics on the system level for the MDS datasets in the top row – (a) Multi-News, (b) PeerSum, and (c) TSix, followed by the SDS datasets in the bottom row – (d) CNN/DM, and (e) SAMSum. Note that only statistically significant correlations are displayed ($p \leq 0.05$), and reference-based and reference-free metrics are delineated by a line.

4 Results and Analysis

In this section, we discuss the results of two main experiments where we investigate the inter-metric correlations across two types of summarization (multi-document and single-document) over four different domains (peer reviews, tweets, news, and dialogues). In each experiment we calculate the Pearson's r correlations between metrics and report statistically significant values ($p \leq 0.05$).

4.1 Multi-document summarization

Figures 1a, 1b, and 1c present the results of correlation analysis on the Multi-News, PeerSum, and TSix multi-document summarization datasets. Across all three datasets the reference-based metrics correlate positively with each other, whereas correlations within the reference-free metrics are noticeably fragmented, with PeerSum exhibiting the most fragmentation. This is likely due to the higher diversity in the source documents that is intrinsic to these MDS tasks, especially in PeerSum where roughly 9% of ICLR paper reviews have a rating difference ≥ 5 (Li et al., 2022). This makes it harder to compare the source documents to the summary in a consistent manner. Moreover, between the two broad categories of metrics, reference-based and reference-free, no consistent correlation can be observed.

4.2 Single-document summarization

Figures 1d and 1e present the results of evaluating single-document summarization datasets (CNN/DM and SAMSum, respectively) on the same set of metrics as used in the previous section for a comparable discussion. In contrast to the observations made on the MDS datasets, here we see a strong positive correlation within almost all reference-free metrics, on both the datasets. Futhermore, it is easy to see, especially on SAMSum dataset, that reference-based and reference-free metrics are highly correlated to each other within their respective groups, but there is little positive correlation between groups (we see some statistically significant anti-correlation), confirming the results found in Gao and Wan (2022). On CNN/DM, although the results appear to be a bit more mixed, clusters of high correlation within fine-grained categories of evaluation metrics are clearly observed – metrics based on static or contextual representations (Vector Extrema, Greedy

Matching, BERTScore), metrics that use question-answering or other means to compare the system summary and source document (QuestEval, SummaQA, BLANC, Jensen-Shannon, ESTIME, SUPERT), and the metrics that use text generation (BARTScore and Information Difference) are all strongly correlated.

4.3 Discussion

In comparing all the results of Figure 1, several observations are made, thus allowing us to put forward some recommendations.

- **Reference-based vs. Reference-free metrics**. First, given almost no agreement between reference-based and reference-free metrics, it appears that these families of metrics measure distinct qualities of a summary, suggesting the need for reporting some metrics from each category, regardless of the summarization framework or dataset domain.

- **Domain-based observations**. Most noticeably, both the datasets from the news domain, whether MDS (Multi-News) or SDS (CNN/DM), exhibit similar and arguably more fragmented heatmaps. This is in sharp contrast to the results from the other three domains (peer reviews, tweets, and dialogues), all of which show similar trends. This indicates that conclusions drawn for these evaluation metrics under one domain may not hold true for another. Thus it is important to consider the differences in domain while introducing and re-assessing evaluation metrics.

- **Similarities between MDS and SDS analysis**. Across both paradigms of MDS and SDS, the reference-based metrics tend to behave similarly, i.e., correlate significantly positively with each other (with CNN/DM being somewhat of an exception).

- **Differences between MDS and SDS analysis**. In SDS tasks, in general reference-free metrics tend to show high correlation with each other suggesting that reporting a small subset of them might be adequate. However, rather interestingly, *in the case of MDS datasets, the reference-free metrics indicate little to no correlation*. We hypothesize that this is likely due to the unique construction of multiple source documents being so diverse.

The striking differences between the behavior of reference-free metrics under SDS and MDS paradigms, therefore, motivate the need for further investigation into how reference-free metrics are applied to MDS tasks.

5 Conclusions and Future Work

We conduct an in-depth assessment of the correlations between numerous evaluation metrics, including those that use reference summaries and those that do not, in the context of multi-document summarization tasks. As a further investigation, we also evaluate single-document summarization datasets on the same set of metrics. Our results indicate that evaluation metrics behave noticeably differently when studied under MDS and SDS paradigms, which makes metrics for MDS an interesting avenue of research to be explored further. Moreover, measuring how these metrics correlate with different dimensions of human evaluation on MDS might be beneficial.

Limitations

As has been recently pointed out in Deutsch et al. (2022), using system outputs on the full test set rather than just 100 samples can make these results much more robust by giving a lower-variance estimate of the inter-metric correlations.

References

Satanjeev Banerjee and Alon Lavie. 2005. METEOR: An automatic metric for MT evaluation with improved correlation with human judgments. In *Proceedings of the ACL Workshop on Intrinsic and Extrinsic Evaluation Measures for Machine Translation and/or Summarization*, pages 65–72, Ann Arbor, Michigan. Association for Computational Linguistics.

Iz Beltagy, Matthew E Peters, and Arman Cohan. 2020. Longformer: The long-document transformer. *arXiv preprint arXiv:2004.05150*.

Manik Bhandari, Pranav Narayan Gour, Atabak Ashfaq, Pengfei Liu, and Graham Neubig. 2020. Re-evaluating evaluation in text summarization. In *Proceedings of the 2020 Conference on Empirical Methods in Natural Language Processing (EMNLP)*, pages 9347–9359, Online. Association for Computational Linguistics.

Jiaao Chen and Diyi Yang. 2020. Multi-view sequence-to-sequence models with conversational structure for abstractive dialogue summarization. In *Proceedings of the 2020 Conference on Empirical Methods in*

Natural Language Processing (EMNLP), pages 4106–4118, Online. Association for Computational Linguistics.

Jiaao Chen and Diyi Yang. 2021. Structure-aware abstractive conversation summarization via discourse and action graphs. In *Proceedings of the 2021 Conference of the North American Chapter of the Association for Computational Linguistics: Human Language Technologies*, pages 1380–1391, Online. Association for Computational Linguistics.

Yen-Chun Chen and Mohit Bansal. 2018. Fast abstractive summarization with reinforce-selected sentence rewriting. In *Proceedings of the 56th Annual Meeting of the Association for Computational Linguistics (Volume 1: Long Papers)*, pages 675–686, Melbourne, Australia. Association for Computational Linguistics.

Yulong Chen, Yang Liu, Liang Chen, and Yue Zhang. 2021. DialogSum: A real-life scenario dialogue summarization dataset. In *Findings of the Association for Computational Linguistics: ACL-IJCNLP 2021*, pages 5062–5074, Online. Association for Computational Linguistics.

Arman Cohan and Nazli Goharian. 2016. Revisiting summarization evaluation for scientific articles. *arXiv preprint arXiv:1604.00400*.

Daniel Deutsch, Rotem Dror, and Dan Roth. 2022. Re-examining system-level correlations of automatic summarization evaluation metrics.

Jacob Devlin, Ming-Wei Chang, Kenton Lee, and Kristina Toutanova. 2018. Bert: Pre-training of deep bidirectional transformers for language understanding. *arXiv preprint arXiv:1810.04805*.

Li Dong, Nan Yang, Wenhui Wang, Furu Wei, Xiaodong Liu, Yu Wang, Jianfeng Gao, Ming Zhou, and Hsiao-Wuen Hon. 2019. Unified language model pre-training for natural language understanding and generation.

Yue Dong, Yikang Shen, Eric Crawford, Herke van Hoof, and Jackie Chi Kit Cheung. 2018. BanditSum: Extractive summarization as a contextual bandit. In *Proceedings of the 2018 Conference on Empirical Methods in Natural Language Processing*, pages 3739–3748, Brussels, Belgium. Association for Computational Linguistics.

Nicholas Egan, Oleg V. Vasilyev, and John Bohannon. 2021. Play the shannon game with language models: A human-free approach to summary evaluation. *ArXiv*, abs/2103.10918.

Güneş Erkan and Dragomir R. Radev. 2004. LexPageRank: Prestige in multi-document text summarization. In *Proceedings of the 2004 Conference on Empirical Methods in Natural Language Processing*, pages 365–371, Barcelona, Spain. Association for Computational Linguistics.

Alexander Fabbri, Irene Li, Tianwei She, Suyi Li, and Dragomir Radev. 2019. Multi-news: A large-scale multi-document summarization dataset and abstractive hierarchical model. In *Proceedings of the 57th Annual Meeting of the Association for Computational Linguistics*, pages 1074–1084, Florence, Italy. Association for Computational Linguistics.

Alexander Fabbri, Faiaz Rahman, Imad Rizvi, Borui Wang, Haoran Li, Yashar Mehdad, and Dragomir Radev. 2021a. ConvoSumm: Conversation summarization benchmark and improved abstractive summarization with argument mining. In *Proceedings of the 59th Annual Meeting of the Association for Computational Linguistics and the 11th International Joint Conference on Natural Language Processing (Volume 1: Long Papers)*, pages 6866–6880, Online. Association for Computational Linguistics.

Alexander R. Fabbri, Wojciech Kryściński, Bryan McCann, Caiming Xiong, Richard Socher, and Dragomir Radev. 2021b. SummEval: Re-evaluating summarization evaluation. *Transactions of the Association for Computational Linguistics*, 9:391–409.

Xiachong Feng, Xiaocheng Feng, Libo Qin, Bing Qin, and Ting Liu. 2021. Language model as an annotator: Exploring DialoGPT for dialogue summarization. In *Proceedings of the 59th Annual Meeting of the Association for Computational Linguistics and the 11th International Joint Conference on Natural Language Processing (Volume 1: Long Papers)*, pages 1479–1491, Online. Association for Computational Linguistics.

Gabriel Forgues, Joelle Pineau, Jean-Marie Larchevêque, and Réal Tremblay. 2014. Bootstrapping dialog systems with word embeddings. In *Nips, modern machine learning and natural language processing workshop*, volume 2.

Mingqi Gao and Xiaojun Wan. 2022. DialSummEval: Revisiting summarization evaluation for dialogues. In *Proceedings of the 2022 Conference of the North American Chapter of the Association for Computational Linguistics: Human Language Technologies*, pages 5693–5709, Seattle, United States. Association for Computational Linguistics.

Yang Gao, Wei Zhao, and Steffen Eger. 2020. SUPERT: Towards new frontiers in unsupervised evaluation metrics for multi-document summarization. In *Proceedings of the 58th Annual Meeting of the Association for Computational Linguistics*, pages 1347–1354, Online. Association for Computational Linguistics.

Sebastian Gehrmann, Elizabeth Clark, and Thibault Sellam. 2022. Repairing the cracked foundation: A survey of obstacles in evaluation practices for generated text. *arXiv preprint arXiv:2202.06935*.

Sebastian Gehrmann, Yuntian Deng, and Alexander Rush. 2018. Bottom-up abstractive summarization. In *Proceedings of the 2018 Conference on Empirical Methods in Natural Language Processing*, pages

4098–4109, Brussels, Belgium. Association for Computational Linguistics.

Bogdan Gliwa, Iwona Mochol, Maciej Biesek, and Aleksander Wawer. 2019. SAMSum corpus: A human-annotated dialogue dataset for abstractive summarization. In *Proceedings of the 2nd Workshop on New Frontiers in Summarization*, pages 70–79, Hong Kong, China. Association for Computational Linguistics.

Yvette Graham. 2015. Re-evaluating automatic summarization with BLEU and 192 shades of ROUGE. In *Proceedings of the 2015 Conference on Empirical Methods in Natural Language Processing*, pages 128–137, Lisbon, Portugal. Association for Computational Linguistics.

Han Guo, Ramakanth Pasunuru, and Mohit Bansal. 2018. Soft layer-specific multi-task summarization with entailment and question generation. In *Proceedings of the 56th Annual Meeting of the Association for Computational Linguistics (Volume 1: Long Papers)*, pages 687–697, Melbourne, Australia. Association for Computational Linguistics.

Karl Moritz Hermann, Tomas Kocisky, Edward Grefenstette, Lasse Espeholt, Will Kay, Mustafa Suleyman, and Phil Blunsom. 2015. Teaching machines to read and comprehend. In *Advances in Neural Information Processing Systems*, volume 28. Curran Associates, Inc.

Wan-Ting Hsu, Chieh-Kai Lin, Ming-Ying Lee, Kerui Min, Jing Tang, and Min Sun. 2018. A unified model for extractive and abstractive summarization using inconsistency loss. In *Proceedings of the 56th Annual Meeting of the Association for Computational Linguistics (Volume 1: Long Papers)*, pages 132–141, Melbourne, Australia. Association for Computational Linguistics.

Chris Kedzie, Kathleen McKeown, and Hal Daumé III. 2018. Content selection in deep learning models of summarization. In *Proceedings of the 2018 Conference on Empirical Methods in Natural Language Processing*, pages 1818–1828, Brussels, Belgium. Association for Computational Linguistics.

Wojciech Kryscinski, Nitish Shirish Keskar, Bryan McCann, Caiming Xiong, and Richard Socher. 2019. Neural text summarization: A critical evaluation. In *Proceedings of the 2019 Conference on Empirical Methods in Natural Language Processing and the 9th International Joint Conference on Natural Language Processing (EMNLP-IJCNLP)*, pages 540–551, Hong Kong, China. Association for Computational Linguistics.

Wojciech Kryściński, Romain Paulus, Caiming Xiong, and Richard Socher. 2018. Improving abstraction in text summarization. In *Proceedings of the 2018 Conference on Empirical Methods in Natural Language Processing*, pages 1808–1817, Brussels, Belgium. Association for Computational Linguistics.

Thomas K. Landauer and Susan T. Dumais. 1997. A solution to plato's problem: The latent semantic analysis theory of acquisition, induction, and representation of knowledge. *Psychological Review*, 104:211–240.

Mike Lewis, Yinhan Liu, Naman Goyal, Marjan Ghazvininejad, Abdelrahman Mohamed, Omer Levy, Ves Stoyanov, and Luke Zettlemoyer. 2019. Bart: Denoising sequence-to-sequence pre-training for natural language generation, translation, and comprehension. *arXiv preprint arXiv:1910.13461*.

Miao Li, Jianzhong Qi, and Jey Han Lau. 2022. Peersum: A peer review dataset for abstractive multi-document summarization.

Wei Li, Xinyan Xiao, Jiachen Liu, Hua Wu, Haifeng Wang, and Junping Du. 2020. Leveraging graph to improve abstractive multi-document summarization. *arXiv preprint arXiv:2005.10043*.

Chin-Yew Lin. 2004. ROUGE: A package for automatic evaluation of summaries. In *Text Summarization Branches Out*, pages 74–81, Barcelona, Spain. Association for Computational Linguistics.

Chin-Yew Lin, Guihong Cao, Jianfeng Gao, and Jian-Yun Nie. 2006. An information-theoretic approach to automatic evaluation of summaries. In *Proceedings of the Human Language Technology Conference of the NAACL, Main Conference*, pages 463–470, New York City, USA. Association for Computational Linguistics.

Rada Mihalcea and Paul Tarau. 2004. Textrank: Bringing order into text. In *Proceedings of the 2004 conference on empirical methods in natural language processing*, pages 404–411.

Derek Miller. 2019. Leveraging bert for extractive text summarization on lectures. *arXiv preprint arXiv:1906.04165*.

Ramesh Nallapati, Bowen Zhou, Cicero dos Santos, Çağlar Gulçehre, and Bing Xiang. 2016. Abstractive text summarization using sequence-to-sequence RNNs and beyond. In *Proceedings of The 20th SIGNLL Conference on Computational Natural Language Learning*, pages 280–290, Berlin, Germany. Association for Computational Linguistics.

Ani Nenkova. 2005. Automatic text summarization of newswire: Lessons learned from the document understanding conference. In *AAAI*.

Ani Nenkova and Rebecca Passonneau. 2004. Evaluating content selection in summarization: The pyramid method. In *Proceedings of the Human Language Technology Conference of the North American Chapter of the Association for Computational Linguistics: HLT-NAACL 2004*, pages 145–152, Boston, Massachusetts, USA. Association for Computational Linguistics.

Minh-Tien Nguyen, Dac Viet Lai, Huy-Tien Nguyen, and Le-Minh Nguyen. 2018. TSix: A human-involved-creation dataset for tweet summarization. In *Proceedings of the Eleventh International Conference on Language Resources and Evaluation (LREC 2018)*, Miyazaki, Japan. European Language Resources Association (ELRA).

Artidoro Pagnoni, Vidhisha Balachandran, and Yulia Tsvetkov. 2021. Understanding factuality in abstractive summarization with FRANK: A benchmark for factuality metrics. In *Proceedings of the 2021 Conference of the North American Chapter of the Association for Computational Linguistics: Human Language Technologies*, pages 4812–4829, Online. Association for Computational Linguistics.

Kishore Papineni, Salim Roukos, Todd Ward, and Wei-Jing Zhu. 2002. Bleu: A method for automatic evaluation of machine translation. In *Proceedings of the 40th Annual Meeting on Association for Computational Linguistics*, ACL '02, page 311–318, USA. Association for Computational Linguistics.

Ramakanth Pasunuru and Mohit Bansal. 2019. Continual and multi-task architecture search. In *Proceedings of the 57th Annual Meeting of the Association for Computational Linguistics*, pages 1911–1922, Florence, Italy. Association for Computational Linguistics.

Ramakanth Pasunuru, Mengwen Liu, Mohit Bansal, Sujith Ravi, and Markus Dreyer. 2021. Efficiently summarizing text and graph encodings of multi-document clusters. In *Proceedings of the 2021 Conference of the North American Chapter of the Association for Computational Linguistics: Human Language Technologies*, pages 4768–4779.

Alec Radford, Jeff Wu, Rewon Child, David Luan, Dario Amodei, and Ilya Sutskever. 2019. Language models are unsupervised multitask learners.

Colin Raffel, Noam Shazeer, Adam Roberts, Katherine Lee, Sharan Narang, Michael Matena, Yanqi Zhou, Wei Li, and Peter J Liu. 2019. Exploring the limits of transfer learning with a unified text-to-text transformer. *arXiv preprint arXiv:1910.10683*.

Vasile Rus and Mihai Lintean. 2012. An optimal assessment of natural language student input using word-to-word similarity metrics. In *Proceedings of the 11th International Conference on Intelligent Tutoring Systems*, ITS'12, page 675–676, Berlin, Heidelberg. Springer-Verlag.

Thomas Scialom, Paul-Alexis Dray, Sylvain Lamprier, Benjamin Piwowarski, Jacopo Staiano, Alex Wang, and Patrick Gallinari. 2021. QuestEval: Summarization asks for fact-based evaluation. In *Proceedings of the 2021 Conference on Empirical Methods in Natural Language Processing*, pages 6594–6604, Online and Punta Cana, Dominican Republic. Association for Computational Linguistics.

Thomas Scialom, Sylvain Lamprier, Benjamin Piwowarski, and Jacopo Staiano. 2019. Answers unite! unsupervised metrics for reinforced summarization models. In *Proceedings of the 2019 Conference on Empirical Methods in Natural Language Processing and the 9th International Joint Conference on Natural Language Processing (EMNLP-IJCNLP)*, pages 3246–3256, Hong Kong, China. Association for Computational Linguistics.

Abigail See, Peter J. Liu, and Christopher D. Manning. 2017. Get to the point: Summarization with pointer-generator networks. In *Proceedings of the 55th Annual Meeting of the Association for Computational Linguistics (Volume 1: Long Papers)*, pages 1073–1083, Vancouver, Canada. Association for Computational Linguistics.

Oleg Vasilyev and John Bohannon. 2021. ESTIME: Estimation of summary-to-text inconsistency by mismatched embeddings. In *Proceedings of the 2nd Workshop on Evaluation and Comparison of NLP Systems*, pages 94–103, Punta Cana, Dominican Republic. Association for Computational Linguistics.

Oleg Vasilyev, Vedant Dharnidharka, and John Bohannon. 2020. Fill in the BLANC: Human-free quality estimation of document summaries. In *Proceedings of the First Workshop on Evaluation and Comparison of NLP Systems*, pages 11–20, Online. Association for Computational Linguistics.

Ashish Vaswani, Noam Shazeer, Niki Parmar, Jakob Uszkoreit, Llion Jones, Aidan N Gomez, Ł ukasz Kaiser, and Illia Polosukhin. 2017. Attention is all you need. In *Advances in Neural Information Processing Systems*, volume 30. Curran Associates, Inc.

Xiaojun Wan and Jianwu Yang. 2008. Multi-document summarization using cluster-based link analysis. In *Proceedings of the 31st Annual International ACM SIGIR Conference on Research and Development in Information Retrieval*, SIGIR '08, page 299–306, New York, NY, USA. Association for Computing Machinery.

Evan James Williams. 1959. *Regression Analysis*. Wiley, New York.

Thomas Wolf, Lysandre Debut, Victor Sanh, Julien Chaumond, Clement Delangue, Anthony Moi, Pierric Cistac, Tim Rault, Rémi Louf, Morgan Funtowicz, et al. 2019. Huggingface's transformers: State-of-the-art natural language processing. *arXiv preprint arXiv:1910.03771*.

Chien-Sheng Wu, Linqing Liu, Wenhao Liu, Pontus Stenetorp, and Caiming Xiong. 2021. Controllable abstractive dialogue summarization with sketch supervision. In *Findings of the Association for Computational Linguistics: ACL-IJCNLP 2021*, pages 5108–5122, Online. Association for Computational Linguistics.

Yuxiang Wu and Baotian Hu. 2018. Learning to extract coherent summary via deep reinforcement learning. In *AAAI*.

Wen Xiao, Iz Beltagy, Giuseppe Carenini, and Arman Cohan. 2022. PRIMERA: Pyramid-based masked sentence pre-training for multi-document summarization. In *Proceedings of the 60th Annual Meeting of the Association for Computational Linguistics (Volume 1: Long Papers)*, pages 5245–5263, Dublin, Ireland. Association for Computational Linguistics.

Weizhe Yuan, Graham Neubig, and Pengfei Liu. 2021. Bartscore: Evaluating generated text as text generation. In *Advances in Neural Information Processing Systems*, volume 34, pages 27263–27277. Curran Associates, Inc.

Jingqing Zhang, Yao Zhao, Mohammad Saleh, and Peter Liu. 2020. Pegasus: Pre-training with extracted gap-sentences for abstractive summarization. In *International Conference on Machine Learning*, pages 11328–11339. PMLR.

Tianyi Zhang*, Varsha Kishore*, Felix Wu*, Kilian Q. Weinberger, and Yoav Artzi. 2020. Bertscore: Evaluating text generation with bert. In *International Conference on Learning Representations*.

Wei Zhao, Maxime Peyrard, Fei Liu, Yang Gao, Christian M. Meyer, and Steffen Eger. 2019. MoverScore: Text generation evaluating with contextualized embeddings and earth mover distance. In *Proceedings of the 2019 Conference on Empirical Methods in Natural Language Processing and the 9th International Joint Conference on Natural Language Processing (EMNLP-IJCNLP)*, pages 563–578, Hong Kong, China. Association for Computational Linguistics.

Qingyu Zhou, Nan Yang, Furu Wei, Shaohan Huang, Ming Zhou, and Tiejun Zhao. 2018. Neural document summarization by jointly learning to score and select sentences. In *Proceedings of the 56th Annual Meeting of the Association for Computational Linguistics (Volume 1: Long Papers)*, pages 654–663, Melbourne, Australia. Association for Computational Linguistics.

A Dataset Samples

Table 2 presents a sample instance of input documents and corresponding reference summary from the Multi-News dataset, Table 3 presents a sample from the PeerSum dataset, and Table 4 presents a sample from the TSix dataset. Reference-free metrics used the full source documents (no truncation) for evaluation.

B Model Details

B.1 Multi-News dataset

We generate summaries with BART (Lewis et al., 2019), T5 (Raffel et al., 2019), LED (Beltagy et al., 2020), Pegasus (Zhang et al., 2020), and Longformer (Beltagy et al., 2020). Additionally, we used the system outputs provided by (Fabbri et al., 2019), which includes LexPageRank (Erkan and Radev, 2004), TextRank (Mihalcea and Tarau, 2004), MMR (Fabbri et al., 2019), Transformer (Vaswani et al., 2017), PG-BRNN (See et al., 2017), and Hi-MAP (Fabbri et al., 2019). [11]

B.2 PeerSum dataset

For generating *abstractive* summaries, we use four neural-based abstractive summarization systems. We concatenate the input documents. All pre-trained model checkpoints accessed from the Huggingface library (Wolf et al., 2019) were further fine-tuned on PeerSum dataset (Li et al., 2022), except for Pegasus. The systems include BART (Lewis et al., 2019) which combines a bidirectional encoder with an auto-regressive decoder, T5 (Raffel et al., 2019) which is an encoder-decoder model trained using teacher forcing, LED (Longformer Encoder-Decoder) (Beltagy et al., 2020) which is a variant of the Longformer model with both encoder and decoder transformer stacks, also scaling linearly with the input, and Pegasus (Zhang et al., 2020) which is a sequence-to-sequence model with gap-sentences generation as a pretraining objective. The system outputs we use in our experiments were generated from 100 samples from the test set. Reviews, comments, and replies were used to generate the summaries.

B.3 TSix dataset

For generating *extractive* summaries, we use systems representing a mixture of traditional methods and state-of-the-art neural-based architectures.

[11] `https://github.com/Alex-Fabbri/Multi-News`

Our models consist of Lead[12] which extracts the first n-tweets, LexPageRank (Erkan and Radev, 2004) and TextRank[13] (Mihalcea and Tarau, 2004) which are unsupervised graph-based ranking methods, ClusterCMRW (Wan and Yang, 2008), BERT-Ext (Miller, 2019), an extractive summarization model[14] built on top of BERT (Devlin et al., 2018) which uses K-means clustering to select sentences closest to the centroid as the summaries, and similarly, Longformer-Ext which uses embeddings from the pretrained Longformer model (Beltagy et al., 2020). The 100 system outputs we use in our experiments are roughly 15 tweets long on average and were generated from samples that have between 50-100 tweets as input.

B.4 CNN/DM dataset

For the CNN/DM dataset (Hermann et al., 2015), we used the system outputs provided by (Fabbri et al., 2021b). This consists of 16 models, each with 100 outputs.[15]

Models: LEAD-3, NEUSUM (Zhou et al., 2018), BanditSum (Dong et al., 2018), RNES (Wu and Hu, 2018), Pointer-generator (See et al., 2017), Fast-abs-rl (Chen and Bansal, 2018), Bottom-Up (Gehrmann et al., 2018), Improve-abs (Kryściński et al., 2018), Unified-ext-abs (Hsu et al., 2018), ROUGESal (Pasunuru and Bansal, 2019), Multi-task (Ent+QG) (Guo et al., 2018), T5 (Raffel et al., 2019), GPT-2 (zero-shot) (Radford et al., 2019), BART (Lewis et al., 2019), Pegasus (C4) and Pegasus (dynamic mix) (Zhang et al., 2020).

B.5 SAMSum dataset

For the SAMSum dataset (Gliwa et al., 2019), we used system outputs provided by (Gao and Wan, 2022). This consists of 14 models, each with 100 outputs.[16] The dataset includes the human-written reference and two extractive models in the system outputs; excluding these increases correlation between reference-free and reference-based metrics but does not significantly change correlations within those groups.

Models: LEAD-3, LONGEST-3, Pointer-generator (See et al., 2017), Transformer (Vaswani et al., 2017), BART (Lewis et al., 2019), Pegasus (Zhang et al., 2020), UniLM (Dong et al., 2019), CODS (Wu et al., 2021), ConvoSumm (Fabbri et al., 2021a), MV-BART (Chen and Yang, 2020), PLM-BART (Feng et al., 2021), Ctrl-DiaSumm (Chen et al., 2021), S-BART (Chen and Yang, 2021).

---

[12] `https://github.com/PKULCWM/PKUSUMSUM` is used for Lead, LexPageRank, and ClusterCMRW

[13] `https://github.com/RaRe-Technologies/gensim`

[14] `https://pypi.org/project/bert-extractive-summarizer/`

[15] `https://github.com/Yale-LILY/SummEval`

[16] `https://github.com/kite99520/DialSummEval`

Input Documents (News Articles)
d_1: after a year in which liberals scored impressive, high-profile supreme court victories, conservatives could be in line for wins on some of this term's most contentious issues, as the justices consider cases that could gut public sector labor unions and roll back affirmative action at state universities. however, as the court's new term kicks off monday, uncertainty surrounds several other politically potent cases that could wind up on the court's agenda ...
d_2: the new term's biggest rulings will land in june, as the 2016 presidential campaign enters its final stretch, and they will help shape the political debate. "constitutional law and politics are certainly not the same thing, but they are interrelated, never more so than in a presidential election year that will likely determine who gets to appoint the next justice or two or three, " said vikram d. amar, dean of the university of illinois college of law...
d_3: the death penalty is shaping up to be a big issue for the supreme court as it begins a new term monday, with at least six capital-punishment cases on the docket and a recent wave of executions keeping the justices up late to field last-minute appeals. in the weeks ahead , the court is set to hear arguments over the constitutionality of capital sentences in florida, georgia, kansas and pennsylvania...
Reference Summary
the supreme court is facing a docket of high-profile political cases that will test whether recent liberal victories were more fluke or firm conviction, the new york times reports. the court — which is divided 5-4 for conservatives, but saw justice roberts vote liberal on obamacare and same-sex marriage — will look at cases including unions, affirmative action, and possibly abortion...

Table 2: Example instance from Multi-News dataset

Input Documents (Reviews)
$d_1(review)$: This paper proposes a method to train neural networks with low precision. However, it is not clear if this work obtains significant improvements over previous works. Note that: 1) Working with 16bit, one can train neural networks with little to no reduction in performance. For example, on ImageNet with AlexNet one gets 45.11% top-1 error if we don't do anything else, and 42.34% (similar to the 32-bit result) if we additionally adjust the loss scale...
$d_2(reply)$: We sincerely appreciate the reviewer for the comments, which indeed helps us to improve the quality of this paper. In our revised manuscript, we keep the last layer in full precision for ImageNet task (both BNN and DoReFa keep the first and the last layer in full precision). Our results have been improved from 53.5/28.6 with 28CC to 51.7/28.0 with 2888 bits setting. Results of other patterns are updated in Table4... ... ...
$d_5(review)$: The authors propose WAGE, which discretized weights, activations, gradients, and errors at both training and testing time. By quantization and shifting, SGD training without momentum, and removing the softmax at output layer as well, the model managed to remove all cumbersome computations from every aspect of the model, thus eliminating the need for a floating point unit completely. Moreover, by keeping up to 8-bit accuracy, the model performs even better than previously proposed models. I am eager to see a hardware realization for this method because of its promising results...
Reference Summary (Meta-Review)
High quality paper, appreciated by reviewers, likely to be of substantial interest to the community. It's worth an oral to facilitate a group discussion.

Table 3: Example instance from PeerSum dataset

Input Documents (Tweets)
d_1: Tech company Nanoco says #Brexit could limit supply of talent. d_2: #Pound closes at another 30 year low. Down to $1.21, fallen 7% in 10 days since #TheresaMay's "hard #Brexit" speech. #GBP.... d_3: I hope this radio host has a lot of mics, because he keeps dropping them. #brexit. d_4: Today's guest article: Gerald Stubbs laments #Britain losing 40 years of progress because of #Brexit. Please share: htt.... d_5: Perhaps we should be pleased and encouraged to see that they're worried and anxious enough about derailment of #Brexit to resor.... d_6: How to save what is left of #Greece? Here's one hint: #Brexit.. d_7: Jacob Rees Mogg's 'Ladybird Constitution'. via #Brexit #jacobreesmogg. .... d_{62}: . 'Leaked Treasury papers show UK Government #brexit chaos will damage Scottish economy'. d_{63}: GBPUSD Rallying on Back of Potential Brexit Turn Around. d_{64}: Brexit 'will stunt national living wage growth by 10p an hour'. d_{65}: UK Prime Minister May backs down on parliament vote over her Brexit terms — South China Morning Post.
Reference Summary
Prof Patrick Minford:: EU and trade #EU #brexit #referendum #voteleave 9.. Good Ganeha you think you have an understanding how dim #Brexit vote leave people are... And then you see new evidence..... Now Dutch wants own EU vote & Czechs say they might leave #EU #brexit #referendum #voteleave 4.. Pound Soars as Hard Brexit Fears Recede, US Dollar Aims Higher DailyFX on #GBPUSD.. UK Prime Minister May backs down on parliament vote over her Brexit terms: Prime Minister Theresa May has acc.... IEA cuts oil demand forecast for 2017 #healthinnovations #pharma #banking #stocks #Brexit #oil..... Leave EU and we'll make your lives a misery: Juncker's warning to Britain #EU #brexit #referendum #voteleave 3.. Still would be less crazy than hard Brexit........

Table 4: Example instance from TSix dataset

Factual Error Correction for Abstractive Summaries Using Entity Retrieval

Hwanhee Lee[1], **Cheoneum Park**[2], **Seunghyun Yoon**[3],
Trung Bui[3], **Franck Dernoncourt**[3], **Juae Kim**[2] and **Kyomin Jung**[1]
[1]Automation and Systems Research Institute, Seoul National University
[2]42dot, Hyundai Motor Group, [3]Adobe Research
{wanted1007,kjung}@snu.ac.kr, {parkce3, jju75474}@gmail.com
{syoon, bui, franck.dernoncourt}@adobe.com

Abstract

Despite the recent advancements in abstractive summarization systems leveraged from large-scale datasets and pre-trained language models, the factual correctness of the summary is still insufficient. One line of trials to mitigate this problem is to include a post-editing process that can detect and correct factual errors in the summary. In building such a system, it is strongly required that 1) the process has a high success rate and interpretability and 2) it has a fast running time. Previous approaches focus on the regeneration of the summary, resulting in low interpretability and high computing resources. In this paper, we propose an efficient factual error correction system RFEC based on entity retrieval. RFEC first retrieves the evidence sentences from the original document by comparing the sentences with the target summary to reduce the length of the text to analyze. Next, RFEC detects entity-level errors in the summaries using the evidence sentences and substitutes the wrong entities with the accurate entities from the evidence sentences. Experimental results show that our proposed error correction system shows more competitive performance than baseline methods in correcting factual errors with a much faster speed.[1]

1 Introduction

Text summarization is a task that aims to generate a short version of the text that contains the important information for the given source article. With the advances of neural text summarization systems, abstractive summarization systems (Nallapati et al., 2017) that generate novel sentences rather than extracting the snippets in the source are widely used (Lin and Ng, 2019). However, factual inconsistency between the original text and the summary is frequently observed in the abstractive summarization system (Cao et al., 2018; Zhao et al., 2020; Maynez et al., 2020). As in the example of Figure 1,

Article: *Singer-songwriter **David Crosby** hit a jogger with his car Sunday evening, a spokesman said.* The accident happened in Santa Ynez, California, near where Crosby lives. Crosby was driving at approximately 50 mph when he struck the jogger. The posted speed limit was 55. The jogger suffered multiple fractures, and was airlifted to a hospital in Santa Barbara, Clotworthy said.,...

System Summary with Factual Error: *Don Clotworthy hit a jogger with his car Sunday evening.* The jogger suffered multiple fractures and was airlifted to a hospital.

After Correction: ***David Crosby** hit a jogger with his car Sunday evening.* The jogger suffered multiple fractures and was airlifted to a hospital.

Figure 1: An example of generated summary with factual errors and the correct summary after minor modification.

many of these errors in the summaries occur at the entry-level such as person name and number. But these types of errors are sometimes trivial and can often be easily solved through simple modification like changing the wrong entities, as shown in Figure 1. For this reason, previous works (Cao et al., 2020; Zhu et al., 2021; Thorne and Vlachos, 2021) have introduced post-editing systems to alleviate these factual errors in the summary. However, all of those works adopt the seq2seq model, which requires a similar cost to the original abstractive summarization systems, as a post-editing. Therefore, using such systems based on seq2seq doubles the inference time for performing post-editing, resulting in significant inefficiency. In addition, seq2seq based post-editing model can be affected by the model's own bias to the input summary.

To overcome this issue and develop an efficient factual corrector for summarization systems, we propose a different approach, RFEC(**R**etrieval-based **F**actual **E**rror **C**orrector) that efficiently corrects the factual errors with a much faster running time compared to seq2seq model. RFEC first retrieves the evidence sentences for the given summary for correcting and detecting errors. By doing so, we shorten the input length of the model to obtain computational efficiency. Then, RFEC examines all of the entities to determine whether each

[1]https://github.com/hwanheelee1993/RFEC

Proceedings of the 2nd Workshop on Natural Language Generation, Evaluation, and Metrics (GEM), pages 439 - 444
December 7, 2022 ©2022 Association for Computational Linguistics

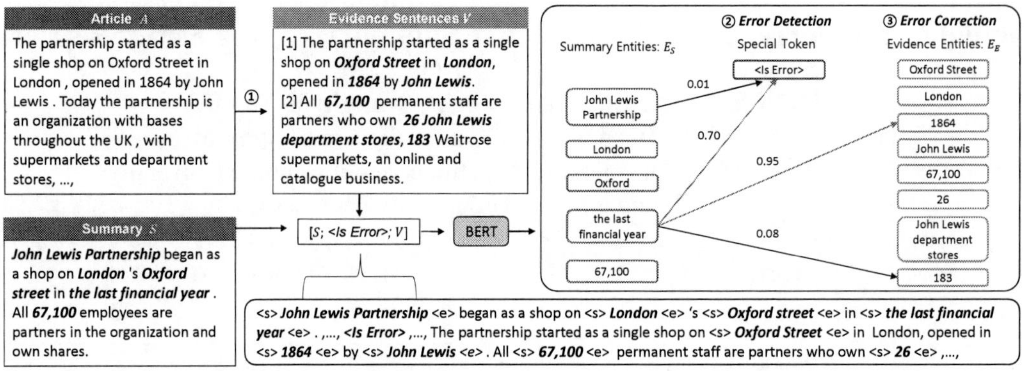

Figure 2: Overall flow of our proposed RFEC. Given a summary S and an article A, we first retrieve evidence sentences V. Using S and V, we compute BERT embeddings for entities in summary E_S and evidence sentence V. If the erroneous score computed using a special token *<Is Error>* is above threshold, we regard those entity as an error and substitute it with one of the entities in the evidence sentences that obtains highest score.

entity has a factual error. If any entities have a factual error, RFEC substitutes these wrong entities with the correct entity by choosing them among the entities in the source article. Through these steps, we do not create a whole sentence as in the seq2seq model, but decide whether to fix and correct it through the retrieval, resulting in higher computational efficiency. Experiments on both synthetic and real-world benchmark datasets demonstrate that our model shows competitive performance with the baseline model with much faster running time. Also, as shown in Figure 2, RFEC has a natural form of interpretability through the visualization of the erroneous score and the scores of each candidate entity for correcting the wrong entities.

2 Related Work

With the advancement of pre-training language models such as BERT (Devlin et al., 2019) and BART (Lewis et al., 2020), abstractive summarization systems have adopted these models to use the rich information inherent in parameters. While these models improved the performance, the generated summaries are still often factually inconsistent with the source article. (Pagnoni et al., 2021).

To solve the factual inconsistency in abstractive summarization systems, FASUM (Zhu et al., 2021) adopted graph attention network (Veličković et al., 2018) for generating the correction summary. Chen et al. (2021) studied contrast candidate generation and selection by ranking approach as a model-agnostic post-processing technique to correct the extrinsic hallucinations.

Another line of mitigating factual errors is to develop a post-editing system to fix the errors. Cao et al. (2020) presented a post-editing corrector module using a BART-based auto-regressive model. The study generated a corrupted summary to train the correction system by substituting the key information, such as an entity or a number, to construct a training dataset. Thorne and Vlachos (2021) also develop a seq2seq based error correction system in the claim of FEVER dataset (Thorne et al., 2018) by correcting the words after masking some words. Different from seq2seq based previous works, we develop a faster retrieval based factual error correction system that does not generate the whole summary, only corrects the entity-level errors by substituting them with one of the entities in the article.

3 Method

3.1 Problem Formulation

For a given summary S and an article A, we aim to develop a fast retrieval-based factual error correction system that can fix the possible factual errors in S. Since factual errors frequently appear in entity-level (Goyal and Durrett, 2021), we develop a system that is specialized in correcting entity-level errors. Specifically, we define this problem as two steps, entity-level error detection and entity-level error correction as shown in Figure 2. For given n_s entities $E_S = \{es_1, es_2, ..., es_{n_s}\}$ in a summary S, we first classify whether each entity is factually consistent with the article A. If any entity e_{S_i} is factually inconsistent, the system substitutes it with one of the n_a entities in the article $E_A = \{ea_1, ea_2, ..., ea_{n_a}\}$.

3.2 Training Dataset Construction

To train a factual error correction system, we need a triple composed of an input summary S_1 that may have factual errors, an article A and a target summary S_2 that is a modified version of S_1 without factual errors. However, it is difficult to obtain S_1 that has the errors with the position annotated and the right ground truth correction of such errors. Hence we construct a synthetic training dataset by editing the reference summaries following previous works (Cao et al., 2020; Zhu et al., 2021; Kryscinski et al., 2020). We corrupt reference summaries in CNN/DM dataset (Nallapati et al., 2016) by randomly changing one of the entities with the same type of other entities in the dataset to make a corrupted summary. Finally, we construct a triple (S_1, A, S_2). Meanwhile, in the real-world dataset, a significant number of summaries are factually consistent, so we only make errors for 50% of the summaries and set $S_1 = S_2$ for the rest of the summaries in the dataset.

3.3 Evidence Sentence Retrieval

Generally, a summary does not treat all of the contents in the article but only contains some important parts of the article. Hence, in most cases, checking for errors within the summary and correcting them does not require the entire article, and using the part related to the summary is sufficient, as shown in Figure 2. Inspired by this observation, we extract some of the sentences in the article according to the similarity with the summary to increase the efficiency of the system by shortening the input length. We use ROUGE-L (Lin, 2004) score as a similarity measure to extract top-2 evidence sentences for each sentence in the summary. Then, we remove the duplicate sentences and sort them according to the order in which they appear in the article, and combine them to form $V = \{V_1, V_2, ..., V_M\}$, a set of evidence sentences for detecting and correcting errors in the summary S.

3.4 Entity Retrieval Based Factual Error Correction

Computing Embedding Using summary S and the evidence sentences V, we first extract entities E_S and E_V respectively with SpaCy[2]. And we insert special tokens <s> and <e>, before and after each extracted entity. Then we also insert an additional token <*Is Error*>, which is later used for checking the factual consistency between S and V and concatenate them to make an input for the BERT (Devlin et al., 2019). Using BERT, we obtain the contextualized embedding of each entity in S and V as follows:

$$H=[h_1,h_2,...,h_l]=BERT([S;<IsError>;V]), \quad (1)$$

where l is the maximum sequence length of the input.

And we get the embedding of start token <s> for each entity as the entity embeddings $HE_V = \{h_{ev_1}, h_{ev_2}, ..., h_{ev_{n_v}}\}$ and $HE_S = \{h_{es_1}, h_{es_2}, ..., h_{es_{n_s}}\}$ for V and S respectively. We also get h_{er}, an embedding of <*Is Error*>.

Error Detection Using the computed embeddings, we compute the erroneous score for all of the entities in summary using h_{er} as follows.

$$\hat{s}_{er_i}=P(Err|es_i)=\sigma(h_{es_i}^{\intercal} W_{dt} h_{er}+b_{dt}), \quad (2)$$

where $i = 1, 2, 3, ..., n_s$. The W_{dt} and b_{dt} are model parameters.

Error Correction For the entities that are factual errors, we compute the correction score between the entities and all of the entities in the evidence sentences similar to error detection as follows.

$$\hat{s}_{cr_{ij}}=P(Cor|es_i,ev_j)=\sigma(h_{es_i}^{\intercal} W_{cr} h_{ev_j}+b_{cr}), \quad (3)$$

where $i = 1, 2, 3, ..., n_{s_{er}}$, $j = 1, 2, 3, ..., n_v$. $n_{s_{er}}$ is the number of errors in the summary. The W_{cr} and b_{cr} are model parameters.

Training Objective We train the model using binary cross entropy loss for both detection and correction through multi-task learning as follows.

$$L_{dt}=-\frac{\sum_{i=1}^{n_s}(s_{er_i}\log(\hat{s}_{er_i})-(1-s_{er_i})\log(1-\hat{s}_{er_i}))}{n_s} \quad (4)$$

$$L_{cr}=-\frac{\sum_{i=1}^{n_s}\sum_{j=1}^{n_v}(s_{cr_{ij}}\log(\hat{s}_{cr_{ij}})-(1-s_{cr_{ij}})\log(1-\hat{s}_{cr_{ij}}))}{n_s \cdot n_v} \quad (5)$$

$$L=L_{dt}+L_{cr}, \quad (6)$$

where $s_{er_i} \in \{0, 1\}$ and $s_{cr_{ij}} \in \{0, 1\}$, which are the ground truth labels for detection and correction.

[2]https://spacy.io/api/entityrecognizer

Inference For the inference stage, we do not have the label as to whether each entity is an error. Therefore, we calculate the two results sequentially, error detection and error correction, using the same BERT embeddings. For each entity, if an erroneous score is above thr_{dt}, then we let that entity be an error as shown in Figure 2. And then, we search the candidate of correction among the evidence entities HE_V, and substitute it with the entity that gets the maximum score as in Figure 2. We conduct correction only when the maximum score is higher than thr_{cr} to prevent unnatural correction caused by failure to find the appropriate entity within the candidate.

4 Experiments

To evaluate the performance of the proposed error correction system, we measure the success rate of correction for the systems by comparing the correction results with the ground-truth summaries or conducting a human evaluation for the corrected summaries as follows.

4.1 Benchmark Datasets

We evaluate our proposed factual error correction method on one synthetic testset and one real-world testset, based on CNN/DM. For the synthetic testset, we use the same method in Section 3.2 to make separate 3k samples using the test split of CNN/DM. For this dataset, we measure the success rate of the correction by comparing the corrected summary from the model with the ground truth summary. In addition to this synthetic data, we also use the FactCC-Test set (Kryscinski et al., 2020) that has labels on the 503 system-generated summaries whether they are factually consistent or not, as in (Cao et al., 2020). There are 62 inconsistent summaries, and 441 consistent summaries in this dataset. Different from the synthetic testset, FactCC-Test dataset does not provide the ground truth correction for the inconsistent summaries. Hence, we manually conduct a blind test to check the factual consistency of each summary after the correction for all of the systems as in the example of Figure 3.

4.2 Implementation Details

For our experiments, we use *bert-base-cased*[3] for RFEC. We train the model for five epochs with a learning rate of 3e-5. For baseline seq2seq model, we use *bart-base*[4] following the settings in the previous work (Cao et al., 2020) and train the model using the same dataset to correct the errors in the input summary. We search the hyperparmeters through the correction accuracy in the validation set among the five epochs. We set batch size of 32 for RFEC and 64 for BART models. We set both thr_{det} and thr_{cor} for 0.5 using the validation set. For maximum sequence length, we set 1024 for BART, 256 for BART with evidence selection, 256 for RFEC, and 512 for RFEC without evidence sentence selection. We measure the running time, including the preprocessing time of each method using a single A5000 GPU and Intel(R) Xeon(R) Silver 4210R CPU (2.40 GHz). We make the best effort to set the maximum batch size for each method using the same environment for a fair comparison.

4.3 Performance Comparison

Synthetic Dataset We present the results for the 3k synthetic testset in Table 1. We measure the correction accuracy by checking whether the corrected summary is same as the ground-truth summary for this dataset. We observe that the performance of BART is slightly better than RFEC, but our proposed retrieval-based model has a higher efficiency from the eight times faster running time. Also, we find that using only evidence sentences shows slightly less performance, but has advantages in computing speed for both systems. Especially for RFEC, it does not take much time to calculate the model output, but it costs relatively much time on preprocessing mostly on named entity recognition. And reducing the input length through the sentence selection also reduces the running time with a slight decrease in performance as shown in Table 1.

Method	Sample/min	Accuracy
Seq2seq - BART	933	90.93
- sentence selection	629	**92.20**
RFEC	**4024**	91.06
- sentence selection	1810	91.15

Table 1: Factual error correction results on test split of synthetic Test Dataset with the average running time.

FactCC-Test Dataset We present the results for the FactCC-Test dataset through the changes in factual consistency after the correction in Table 2. Compared to the results in the synthetic dataset, both seq2seq and RFEC do not correct many errors,

[3]https://huggingface.co/bert-base-cased

[4]https://huggingface.co/facebook/bart-base

only 9 and 7 for the best settings in both systems among 62 errors. As in the synthetic dataset, our proposed method shows almost the same results with less running time compared to the seq2seq method. Also, we can observe that using the correction model also creates a significant number of new errors (i.e. consistent->inconsistent) especially for the seq2seq model without sentence selection.

Method	Inconsistent(62)		Consistent(441)	
	Changed	Edited	Changed	Edited
Seq2seq - BART	8	15	**2**	14
- sentence selection	**9**	23	7	78
RFEC	7	9	**2**	23
- sentence selection	6	8	3	31

Table 2: Factual error correction results on FactCC-Testset. Each column represents how many corrections each system has performed for the sample of each label, and how many labels have changed from the correction.

4.4 Qualitative Analysis

We present the representative success and failure cases of our proposed retrieval-based factual error correction system with the top-3 retrieved entities for the errors in Figure 3. For the first example, RFEC successfully corrects the error *Valerie Braham* by substituting it with *Philippe Braham* which gets a higher correction score among the entities in the evidence sentences. Also, as the object to be corrected is a person's name, we can observe that other correction candidates are also names. On the other hand, for the second example, although RFEC detects the error *Raymond*, but does not find the correction candidates whose correction score is above thr_{cr}. For this example, *Raymond* should be changed to *the front bench*, but the named entity recognition model fails to capture it and leads to missing it from the correction candidate.

Example 1) - Success

Evidence Sentences: Her husband, Philippe Braham, was one of 17 people killed in January's terror attacks in Paris. One month after the terror attacks in Paris, a gunman attacked a synagogue in Copenhagen, Denmark, killing Dan Uzan, who was working as a security guard for a bat mitzvah party.

Input Summary:
Valerie Braham was one of 17 people killed in January 's terror attacks in Paris

Corrected Summary: Philippe Braham was one of 17 people killed in January's terror attacks in Paris.

Top3 Correction Candidates for Valerie Braham:
Philippe Braham, Dan Uzan, bat mitzvah

Example 2) - Failure

Evidence Sentences: Sawyer Sweeten grew up before the eyes of millions as a child star on the endearing family sitcom " Everybody Loves Raymond." Sweeten , best known for his role Geoffrey Barone , was visiting family in Texas, entertainment industry magazine Hollywood Reporter reported, where he is believed to have shot himself on the front porch.

Input Summary:
He is believed to have shot himself on Raymond

Corrected Summary: He is believed to have shot himself on Raymond.

Top3 Correction Candidates for Raymond:
Everybody Loves Raymond, Geoffrey Barone, Sawyer Sweeten

Figure 3: Case study on our proposed factual error correction system. The entities in the evidence sentences are highlighted. The blue color on each entity in each input summary represents the *erroneous score*, and the darker the color, the higher the *erroneous score*.

5 Conclusion

In this paper, we proposed an efficient factual error correction system RFEC based on two retrieval steps. RFEC first retrieves evidence sentences based on textual similarities between the summary and the article for detecting and correcting factual errors. Then, if there is an entity that is a cause of factual errors, RFEC substitutes it with one of the entities in the evidence sentences as a retrieval-based approach. Experiments on two benchmark datasets demonstrate that our proposed method shows competitive results compared to strong baseline seq2seq with a much faster inference speed.

Acknowledgement

K. Jung is with Dept. of Electrical and Computer Engineering, Seoul National University, Seoul, Korea. This work was supported by AIRS Company in Hyundai Motor and Kia through HMC/KIA-SNU AI Consortium Fund.

References

Meng Cao, Yue Dong, Jiapeng Wu, and Jackie Chi Kit Cheung. 2020. Factual error correction for abstractive summarization models. In Proceedings of the 2020 Conference on Empirical Methods in Natural Language Processing (EMNLP), pages 6251–6258.

Ziqiang Cao, Furu Wei, Wenjie Li, and Sujian Li. 2018. Faithful to the original: Fact aware neural abstractive summarization. In Proceedings of the AAAI Conference on Artificial Intelligence, volume 32.

Sihao Chen, Fan Zhang, Kazoo Sone, and Dan Roth. 2021. Improving faithfulness in abstractive summarization with contrast candidate generation and selection. In Proceedings of the 2021 Conference of the North American Chapter of the Association for Computational Linguistics: Human Language Technologies, pages 5935–5941, Online. Association for Computational Linguistics.

Jacob Devlin, Ming-Wei Chang, Kenton Lee, and Kristina Toutanova. 2019. BERT: Pre-training of deep bidirectional transformers for language understanding. In Proceedings of the 2019 Conference of the North American Chapter of the Association for Computational Linguistics: Human Language Technologies, Volume 1 (Long and Short Papers), pages 4171–4186, Minneapolis, Minnesota. Association for Computational Linguistics.

Tanya Goyal and Greg Durrett. 2021. Annotating and modeling fine-grained factuality in summarization. In Proceedings of the 2021 Conference of the North American Chapter of the Association for Computational Linguistics: Human Language Technologies, pages 1449–1462.

Wojciech Kryscinski, Bryan McCann, Caiming Xiong, and Richard Socher. 2020. Evaluating the factual consistency of abstractive text summarization. In Proceedings of the 2020 Conference on Empirical Methods in Natural Language Processing (EMNLP), pages 9332–9346, Online. Association for Computational Linguistics.

Mike Lewis, Yinhan Liu, Naman Goyal, Marjan Ghazvininejad, Abdelrahman Mohamed, Omer Levy, Veselin Stoyanov, and Luke Zettlemoyer. 2020. Bart: Denoising sequence-to-sequence pre-training for natural language generation, translation, and comprehension. In Proceedings of the 58th Annual Meeting of the Association for Computational Linguistics, pages 7871–7880.

Chin-Yew Lin. 2004. ROUGE: A package for automatic evaluation of summaries. In Text Summarization Branches Out, pages 74–81, Barcelona, Spain. Association for Computational Linguistics.

Hui Lin and Vincent Ng. 2019. Abstractive summarization: A survey of the state of the art. In Proceedings of the AAAI Conference on Artificial Intelligence, volume 33, pages 9815–9822.

Joshua Maynez, Shashi Narayan, Bernd Bohnet, and Ryan McDonald. 2020. On faithfulness and factuality in abstractive summarization. In Proceedings of the 58th Annual Meeting of the Association for Computational Linguistics, pages 1906–1919.

Ramesh Nallapati, Feifei Zhai, and Bowen Zhou. 2017. Summarunner: A recurrent neural network based sequence model for extractive summarization of documents. In Thirty-First AAAI Conference on Artificial Intelligence.

Ramesh Nallapati, Bowen Zhou, Cicero dos Santos, Çağlar Gulçehre, and Bing Xiang. 2016. Abstractive text summarization using sequence-to-sequence RNNs and beyond. In Proceedings of The 20th SIGNLL Conference on Computational Natural Language Learning, pages 280–290, Berlin, Germany. Association for Computational Linguistics.

Artidoro Pagnoni, Vidhisha Balachandran, and Yulia Tsvetkov. 2021. Understanding factuality in abstractive summarization with frank: A benchmark for factuality metrics. In Proceedings of the 2021 Conference of the North American Chapter of the Association for Computational Linguistics: Human Language Technologies, pages 4812–4829.

James Thorne and Andreas Vlachos. 2021. Evidence-based factual error correction. In Proceedings of the 59th Annual Meeting of the Association for Computational Linguistics and the 11th International Joint Conference on Natural Language Processing (Volume 1: Long Papers), pages 3298–3309.

James Thorne, Andreas Vlachos, Christos Christodoulopoulos, and Arpit Mittal. 2018. Fever: a large-scale dataset for fact extraction and verification. In Proceedings of the 2018 Conference of the North American Chapter of the Association for Computational Linguistics: Human Language Technologies, Volume 1 (Long Papers), pages 809–819.

Petar Veličković, Guillem Cucurull, Arantxa Casanova, Adriana Romero, Pietro Liò, and Yoshua Bengio. 2018. Graph attention networks. In International Conference on Learning Representations.

Zheng Zhao, Shay B. Cohen, and Bonnie Webber. 2020. Reducing quantity hallucinations in abstractive summarization. In Findings of the Association for Computational Linguistics: EMNLP 2020, pages 2237–2249, Online. Association for Computational Linguistics.

Chenguang Zhu, William Hinthorn, Ruochen Xu, Qingkai Zeng, Michael Zeng, Xuedong Huang, and Meng Jiang. 2021. Enhancing factual consistency of abstractive summarization. In Proceedings of the 2021 Conference of the North American Chapter of the Association for Computational Linguistics: Human Language Technologies, pages 718–733.

Coherent Long Text Generation by Contrastive Soft Prompt

Guandan Chen†
{chenguandan1}@163.com

Jiashu Pu†, Yadong Xi and Rongsheng Zhang*
Fuxi AI Lab, NetEase Inc., Hangzhou, China
{pujiashu,xiyadong,zhangrongsheng}@corp.netease.com

Abstract

Improving the coherence of long text generation is an important but challenging task. Existing models still struggle to generate a logical and coherent sentence sequence. It is difficult for a model to plan long text generation and avoid generating incoherent texts from a high-level semantic perspective. We conjecture that this is due to two factors: (1) current training methods mainly rely on maximum likelihood estimation computed from token-level probability prediction; (2) the role of incoherent texts has been largely under-explored, thus the noised generated texts with errors are out-of-distribution for the model. To address these issues, in this paper, we propose a Contrastive Soft Prompt (**CSP**) model for improving the coherence of long text generation. It learns text representations in the hidden space for better planning long text generation. To this end, it jointly learns to generate a text representation close to representations of coherent texts and away from incoherent ones, and then generates long text taking this representation as the soft prompt. We conduct experiments on two public story generation datasets, and experimental results show that our method can generate more coherent stories than the state-of-the-art model.

Input (Leading Sentence):
FEMALE baked a cake for her boyfriend's birthday.
Output 1:
She put the cake in the oven. When the cake was done, **she frosted it. Then she frosted it.** She forgot to put sugar in it.
Output 2:
She spent the morning preparing the cake and putting it in the oven. She left the oven on too long. When she came back the cake was ruined. FEMALE was very sad she 'd **wasted her birthday**.

Table 1: Some stories written by text generation models (The name is replaced with "FEMALE".). The generated stories suffer from incoherence issues (in **bold**), i.e. repeating "*frosted it*", "*for her boyfriend 's birthday*" but "*wasted her birthday*".

1 Introduction

Generating coherent long text plays a key role in many applications, e.g. news report generation (Leppänen et al., 2017), story generation (Guan et al., 2021), text adventure games (Hausknecht et al., 2020). Taking story generation as an example, it requires the model to generate a reasonable story for a given prompt or a given leading context.

In recent years, pre-trained language models (Lewis et al., 2020; Radford et al., 2019) have demonstrated their scalability to large-capability and datasets, becoming a de-facto standard for text generation tasks. These state-of-the-art models already closely resemble humans in the generation of short sentences (Pu et al., 2022). However, as table 1 shows, even with a pre-trained language model, it is still difficult to generate a coherent long text, which indicates that generating a coherent and logical long text is a challenging task. It is observed that pre-trained language models are capable of generating related keywords and achieving good intra-sentence coherence, but still struggle to generate coherent long texts, suffering from generating repetitive plots (Xi et al., 2021), unrelated events, or conflicting logic (Holtzman et al., 2019), e.g. "*for her boyfriend's birthday*" but "*wasted her birthday*" in table 1. We conjecture that above mentioned issues are mainly caused by two reasons. Firstly, current training methods mainly rely on maximum likelihood estimation which is computed from token-level probability prediction. It hinders the model from understanding and planning the generation in the entire text perspective. Secondly, the role of negative samples has been largely under-explored, especially hard negative samples. Thus, the noised generated texts with errors are out-of-distribution for the model.

To alleviate the above issues, in this paper, we

[†]Equal Contribution. [*]Corresponding Author.

Proceedings of the 2nd Workshop on Natural Language Generation, Evaluation, and Metrics (GEM), pages 445 - 455
December 7, 2022 ©2022 Association for Computational Linguistics

propose **CSP**, a **C**ontrastive **S**oft **P**rompt based text generation model. It learns long text representations in a hidden space, and the model can plan long text generation and distinguish coherent long text and incoherent texts in this hidden space. To this end, we design losses to jointly learn long text representations as well as the ability to plan text generation and distinguish coherent and incoherent texts from the hidden space, specifically, (1) contrastive loss for distinguishing positive samples which are human written texts and negative samples which are generated by applying perturbations to positive ones; (2) contrastive loss for distinguishing different texts; (3) the generation loss for surface realization in text taking representations in hidden space as the soft prompt (Lester et al., 2021). These losses are designed to help the model to learn text representations useful for planning coherent long-text generation. In addition, by taking the generated representations as the soft prompt for text generation, we adopt a language model to learn text representations, and the generated representations serve as extra information for the language model to condition on (Lester et al., 2021). **Our contributions are twofold**. **First**, we propose a novel generation model named CSP for improving the coherence of long text generation. CSP learns high-level representations for long text in hidden space, and jointly learns to plan text generation and distinguish between coherent and incoherent texts utilizing the high-level representations. **Secondly**, we conduct extensive experiments on two-story generation tasks. Experimental results demonstrate that our method can generate more coherent stories than the state-of-the-art model.

2 Method

Our task aims at generating a multi-sentence text $Y = (y_1, y_2, ..., y_m)$, given a text input $X = (x_1, x_2, ..., x_n)$. Figure 1 shows the structure of our proposed model. Our proposed model consists of three parts, prompt generator, prompt posterior generator, and text generator. The prompt generator aims at generating a soft prompt that represents the hidden representation of the text to be generated. The prompt posterior generator is used to help train the prompt generator, which provides the hidden representations of positive and negative samples so that the prompt generator is trained to generate soft prompts close to positive samples and away from negative ones. The text generator generates the text using the soft prompt and the input.

2.1 Prompt Generator

Soft prompt serves as extra information for the language model to condition on (Lester et al., 2021). The prompt generator aims at generating a soft prompt which is used by the text generator for generation. To improve the coherence of long text generation, the model learns to generate soft prompts close to the representations of coherent texts and away from incoherent texts in hidden space, which is introduced in the following subsections.

The prompt generator takes the concatenation of X and a special token sequence $P = ([P_1], [P_2], ..., [P_k])$ as the input, and outputs a soft prompt $S = s_1, s_2, ..., s_k$, where P represents the placeholders for generating the soft prompt, $S \in R^{k \times d}$ is the soft prompt, k is the length of soft prompt, d is the hidden dimension. The prompt generator can be any sequence-to-sequence model, e.g. a Transformer model (Vaswani et al., 2017). In our experiment, we use GPT-2 (Radford et al., 2019) as the backbone for the prompt generator. Specifically, let X' be the concatenation of X and P, and we denote the GPT-2 as a function f. We take the hidden states of GPT-2 as the output, which is a sequence with length $n + k$, we use the subsequence of the output sequence corresponding to P as the soft prompt, i.e.

$$\begin{aligned} X' &= X \parallel P \\ Y' &= f(X') \\ S &= Y'_{n+1:n+k} \end{aligned} \tag{1}$$

where $\parallel$ is the concatenation operation, and $Y'_{n+1:n+k}$ represents the sub-sequence from $n + 1$ to $n + k$ elements, i.e. the hidden states of f corresponding to P.

2.2 Posterior Prompt Generator

In analogy to the prompt generator, the posterior prompt generator is also a seq2seq model. Its input is the concatenation of three parts, (1) the input X; (2) the output Y or a negative sample Y_-, and we will introduce the construction of negative examples in the following subsection; (3) a special token sequence $Q = ([Q_1], [Q_2], ..., [Q_k])$. The posterior prompt is computed from

$$\begin{aligned} X''_+ &= X \parallel Y \parallel Q \\ Y''_+ &= f(X''_+) \\ S_+ &= Y''_{n+m+1:n+m+k} \end{aligned} \tag{2}$$

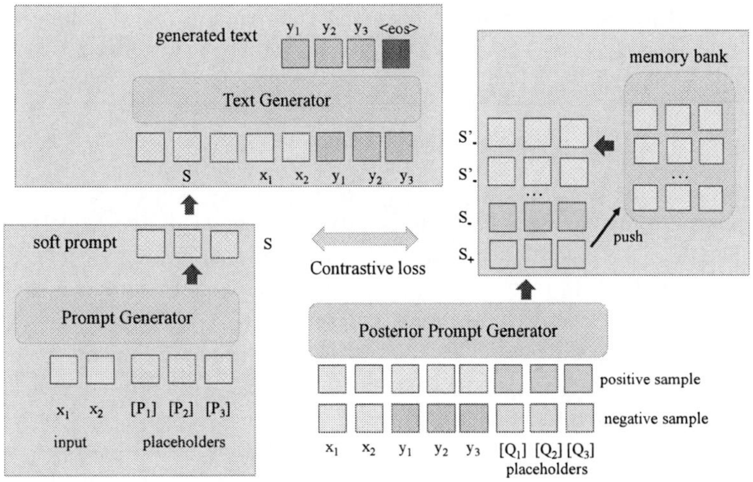

Figure 1: The structure of our proposed model. Prompt generator aims at generating a soft prompt closed to coherent texts and away from incoherent texts in the hidden space. Posterior prompt generator encodes positive and negative samples into representations in the hidden space, and helps to train prompt generator. Memory bank stores the text representations produced in previous training steps, and also help to train prompt generator. Note that the posterior prompt generator and memory bank are only used during training and can be dropped during inference. The prompt generator and posterior prompt generator share most of parameters except for embeddings of $[P_1]$, $[P_2]$, ...,$[P_k]$, and $[Q_1]$, $[Q_2]$, ...,$[Q_k]$. Text generator aims at generating text given the soft prompt and the input in auto-regressive manner. The special token <eos> represents the end of the text.

where $Y''_{n+m+1:n+m+k}$ is the hidden states of f corresponding to Q, S_+ represents the posterior soft prompt for a sample in the training dataset. The posterior soft prompt for a negative sample S_- can be generated similarly. Both S_+ and S_- will be used to train the prompt generator, which will be introduced in the subsection of contrastive loss.

2.3 Negative Sample Generation

We construct negative samples to cover unfavored incoherent texts. To enable the model to learn to distinguish both intra-sentence and inter-sentence errors, we construct negative samples from both the N-gram level and sentence level. To construct negative samples, we randomly apply the following perturbations to texts:

Repetition. In recent studies, it is observed that many NLG models produce repeated text contents, particularly with maximum-likelihood-based decoding strategies (Holtzman et al., 2019). Thus we generate negative samples by randomly repeating N-grams or sentences, aiming at telling the model to not repeat content when generating texts.

Deletion. We randomly delete sentences or N-grams from the original text, to let the model distinguish a coherent text and an incoherent text with missing content.

Insertion. We randomly insert sentences or N-grams into the random positions of the original text. In this way, the model learns to distinguish negative samples with extra text contents.

Substitution. We randomly substitute sentences or N-grams with a random sentence or N-gram in the training corpus.

Reorder. We randomly shuffle the order of the sentences in a text. This will produce stories with wrong temporal order or wrong causality.

2.4 Contrastive Loss

Given the soft prompt S and positive posterior soft prompt S_+ and negative posterior soft prompt S_-, we design the contrastive loss to let S be closed to the positive posterior soft prompt and away from negative ones, to avoid generating incoherent texts. We also adopt extra negative samples from a memory bank inspired by previous contrastive learning methods (Wu et al., 2018; He et al., 2020). We sample extra negative samples S'_- from a memory bank B. After each training step, S and S_+ are stored in the memory bank B. We map S, S_+, S_-, and S'_- to a hidden space, e.g. for S, we have

$$v = W_{proj}pool(S) \tag{3}$$

Dataset	#Input tokens	#Output tokens	#Train sample	#Val sample	#Test sample
ROCStories	14.5	56.3	88344	4908	4909
WritingPrompts	30.0	185.7	26758	2000	2000

Table 2: Statistics of the datasets.

where pool [2] represents a function which average the matrix with dimension $k \times d$ into a vector with dimension d. We use a W_{proj} to map the origin $pool(S)$ into a hidden space. Similarly, we map S_+, S_-, S'_- to v_+, v_-, v'_- respectively.

In this paper, infoNCE (Oord et al., 2018) is considered as the contrastive loss function:

$$L_c = -\log \frac{exp(\frac{v \cdot v_+}{\tau})}{\sum_{v_-} exp(\frac{v \cdot v_-}{\tau}) + \sum_{v'_-} exp(\frac{v \cdot v'_-}{\tau})} \quad (4)$$

where τ is a temperature hyperparameter.

2.5 Text Generator

Given a soft prompt S and the input X, the text generator aims at generating a text Y. We also use GPT-2 as the backbone of the text generator. Following GPT-2, we learn the text generation in an auto-regressive manner. It is learned from cross-entropy loss, i.e.

$$\begin{aligned} Z &= f(S \parallel X \parallel Y) \\ H &= Z_{k+n+1:k+n+m} \\ P(y_t|y<t, X) &= softmax(H_t W + b) \\ L_{ce} &= -\sum_{t=1}^{m} logP(y_t|y<t, X) \end{aligned} \quad (5)$$

where Z is the hidden states of the text generator, and H is the hidden states corresponding to the output, W and b are trainable parameters.

We also introduce a text reconstruction loss similar to autoencoder, i.e.

$$\begin{aligned} Z^{ae} &= f(S_+ \parallel X \parallel Y) \\ H^{ae} &= Z^{ae}_{k+n+1:k+n+m} \\ P^{ae}(y_t|y<t, X) &= softmax(H^{ae}_t W + b) \\ L_{ae} &= -\sum_{t=1}^{m} logP^{ae}(y_t|y<t, X) \end{aligned} \quad (6)$$

[2]We also tried to flatten operation in our experiments, it has similar performance with pool operation while flatten represents a function which reshapes the matrix with dimension $k \times d$ into a vector.

By optimizing L_{ae}, the model tries to learn a hidden representation for a whole text, and the text content can be reconstructed from this hidden representation.

The loss function for our model combines L_c, L_{ce}, and L_{ae}, i.e.

$$L = \lambda_c L_c + \lambda_{ce} L_{ce} + \lambda_{ae} L_{ae} \quad (7)$$

where λ_c, λ_{ce} and λ_{ae} are hyper-parameters.

3 Experiments

3.1 Dataset

We evaluate our model on two publicly available story generation datasets, named ROCStories (Mostafazadeh et al., 2016) and WritingPrompts (Fan et al., 2018). We use the same preprocessing method as the previous work (Guan et al., 2020, 2021), i.e. all the names are replaced with special placeholders for better generalization. For ROCStories, we use the first sentence as the input and expect the model to generate the remaining content of the story. For WritingPrompts, the input is the writing prompt, and the model is expected to generate a story according to the writing prompt. We use the same filter strategy and validation and test split as the previous work (Guan et al., 2021). Table 2 shows the statistics of these two datasets.

3.2 Baselines

We compare our method with several baselines, including fine-tuning pre-trained language models, the previous state-of-the-art method, and variants of our method.

BART (Lewis et al., 2020): It is fine-tuned on the ROCStories and WritingPrompts datasets based on the publicly available BART model checkpoint.

GPT-2 (Radford et al., 2019): It is fine-tuned on the ROCStories and WritingPrompts datasets based on the pre-trained GPT-2 model.

HINT (Guan et al., 2021): It is the previous state-of-the-art method on ROCStories and WritingPrompts datasets, which continue the pretraining of BART on book corpus with two additional objectives, i.e. inter-sentence semantic similarity and

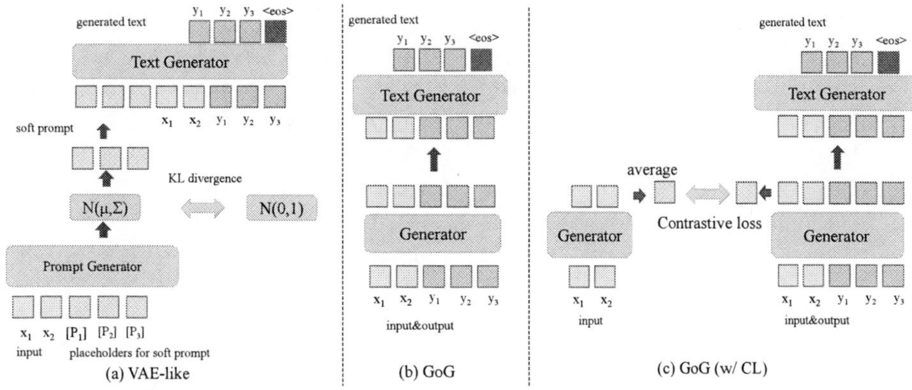

Figure 2: The structures of some baseline methods, including VAE-like, GOG, and GOG (w/ CL).

distinguishing between normal and randomly shuffled sentence orders.

VAE-like: Similar to VAE (Kingma and Welling, 2013), it uses Gaussian distribution as the prior probability distribution for the soft prompt S. Compared to our method, it replaces the contrastive loss with the ELBO loss function. The left of figure 2 shows the structure of VAE-like.

GoG: It stacks two GPT-2 models, and is fine-tuned on ROCStories and WritingPrompts datasets. The middle of figure 2 shows the structure of GoG.

GoG (w/ CL): It also stacks two GPT-2 models, and is fine-tuned on the downstream datasets with language modeling objective and contrastive loss. Compared to our method, the hidden representations used to compute contrastive loss are the linear mapping of the average of hidden representations. The right of figure 2 shows the structure of GoG (w/ CL).

CSP (w/o CL): It is a variant of our model, which removes the contrastive loss L_c.

CSP (w/o AE): It is a variant of our model, which removes the reconstruction loss L_{ae}.

CSP (w/ PT): It has the same structure and loss function as our method, but based on model parameters which are continue pre-trained on book corpus. We use the same loss as our model during continue pretraining.

3.3 Automatic Evaluation

Evaluation Metrics We adopt several commonly used metrics to evaluate the performance, including (1) **UNION**: It is a learnable metric proposed by Guan and Huang (2020), which adopts a classifier trained from human-written texts and negative samples constructed by applying perturbations to human-written texts. The UNION score is the average classifier score of texts and measures the coherence and context-relatedness of the generated texts. (2) **Orderness**: It is also a learnable metric. It relies on a classifier trained to distinguish human-written texts and randomly shuffled sentences. This metric reflects the degree to which texts are in reasonable sentence order. Both UNION and Orderness are trained on the training sets of ROCStories or WritingPrompts. (3) **Perplexity (PPL)**: It measures how well a probability model predicts the ground-truth samples. (4) **BLEU (B-n)**: It reflects the n-gram overlap ratio between generated texts and ground-truth texts (Papineni et al., 2002). (5) **Lexical Repetition (LR-n)**: It is the percentage of generated texts which repeat 4-gram at least n times (Shao et al., 2019a). (6) **Distinct-4 (D-4)**: It is the ratio of distinct 4-grams in all 4 grams in the texts.

Results on ROCStories. As shown in the table 3, our proposed method outperforms all the baselines on 6 out of 7 metrics on the ROCStories dataset. As for the structure and coherence of generated texts, our model achieves the best UNION and Orderness metrics. Our model has higher PPL compared to GPT-2, and it is because the contrastive loss L_c provides a regularization, and the model may allocate more probability to diverse texts. This conjecture can be supported by diversity-related metrics. Our model will generate more diverse texts and thus has higher distinct and lower lexical repetition. Although our model improves diversity, it still has better BLEU than baselines, indicating that our model is inclined to generate diverse but reasonable n-grams. With continued pretraining on book corpus, our model improves UNION and distinct metrics further and decreases repetition metrics. As both HINT and CSP (w/PT)

Models	UNION↑	orderness↑	PPL↓	B-1↑	B-2↑	LR-2↓	D-4↑
BART	0.684	0.906	10.72	0.293	0.131	0.312	0.651
GPT-2	0.767	0.935	**8.72**	0.315	0.143	0.239	0.695
HINT	0.772	0.920	9.20	0.331	0.154	0.263	0.678
VAE-like	0.805	0.938	9.16	0.316	0.143	0.231	0.693
GoG	0.828	0.946	9.32	0.318	0.146	0.197	0.710
GoG (w/ CL)	0.838	0.945	9.30	0.322	0.148	0.200	0.706
CSP	0.853	**0.952**	12.18	0.332	**0.158**	0.186	0.747
CSP (w/o CL)	0.837	0.945	9.31	0.315	0.144	0.202	0.714
CSP (w/o AE)	0.848	0.949	12.64	0.327	0.149	0.172	0.757
CSP (w/ PT)	**0.863**	0.950	11.72	**0.333**	0.151	**0.160**	**0.772**

Table 3: Automatic evaluation results on the ROCStories dataset.

Models	UNION↑	orderness↑	PPL↓	B-1↑	B-2↑	LR-5↓	D-4↑
BART	0.302	0.909	32.02	0.219	0.079	0.381	0.409
GPT-2	0.325	0.769	**27.11**	0.209	0.075	0.558	0.418
HINT	0.353	0.909	30.71	0.221	0.083	0.323	0.445
VAE-like	0.387	0.935	27.98	0.242	0.090	0.384	0.463
GoG	0.394	0.926	28.71	0.245	0.091	0.326	0.483
GoG (w/ CL)	0.393	0.924	28.99	0.244	0.092	0.361	0.460
CSP	0.520	0.936	32.01	0.255	0.097	0.230	0.555
CSP (w/o CL)	0.382	0.929	27.76	0.245	0.091	0.385	0.454
CSP (w/o AE)	0.449	0.932	33.26	0.246	0.092	0.274	0.537
CSP (w/ PT)	**0.711**	**0.940**	32.08	**0.278**	**0.102**	**0.154**	**0.682**

Table 4: Automatic evaluation results on the WritingPrompts dataset.

use book corpus, the comparison of these two models further shows the effectiveness of our model.

Results on WritingPrompts. Table 4 shows the results on the WritingPrompts dataset. Texts in the WitingPrompts dataset are longer than texts in ROCStories, and most baseline methods tend to repeat texts, with low distinct and high repetition metrics. However, our model can alleviate this issue evidenced by lexical repetition and distinct metrics. Our model can increase the distinct metric up to nearly 10 percents. In addition, the improvement of UNION is much more significant than on ROCStories, with about 50% relative improvement compared to HINT, although HINT also adopts specially designed loss for improving coherence. Our model also achieves 1 point BLEU improvement compared to best baseline method. With continue pretraining on book corpus, our model can further improve coherence and diversity, specifically, improve UNION from 0.520 to 0.711 and B-1 from 0.255 to 0.278, and also significantly improve distinct and decreases repetition metrics.

The comparison of GOG and CSP shows that our model structure for computing text representation is more effective than simply averaging hidden states. Furthermore, the experimental results of CSP (w/o CL) and CSP (w/o AE) show that the contrastive loss and reconstruction loss can improve the performance of our model.

3.4 Manual Evaluation

For manual evaluation, we conduct a pair-wise comparison on two aspects, namely *fluency* and *coherence*, following recent studies (Guan et al., 2021; Xu et al., 2020). The metric *fluency* measures linguistic quality while *coherence* focuses on logicality, e.g. causality and temporal relationship. We randomly sample 100 generated texts from the test set of ROCStories and invite three annotators (they are all volunteers) to give a preference concerning fluency and coherence respectively (win, lose or tie). As table 5 shows, our model outperforms all the baselines on both *fluency* and *coherence* aspects. We use Fleiss's kappa (Fleiss, 1971) to measure the inter-annotator agreements, most of the results are moderate ($0.4 \leq \kappa \leq 0.6$) or substantial ($0.6 \leq \kappa \leq 0.8$). However, our model still generates some incoherent texts and is judged to

Models	Fluency				Coherence			
	Win	Lose	Tie	κ	Win	Lose	Tie	κ
CSP vs. GPT-2	27	3	70	0.75	58	5	37	0.76
CSP vs. HINT	22	7	71	0.72	57	4	39	0.61
CSP vs. VAE-like	15	4	81	0.69	62	10	28	0.59
CSP vs. GOG	20	5	75	0.66	57	9	34	0.55
CSP vs. GOG (w/ CL)	35	3	62	0.84	52	6	42	0.79
CSP vs. CSP (w/o CL)	14	2	84	0.64	62	6	32	0.60

Table 5: Manual evaluation results on the ROCStories dataset. κ is the Fleiss' kappa (Fleiss, 1971), measuring the inter-annotator agreement (most of them are moderate or substantial).

Noise type	UNION↑	orderness↑	PPL↓	B-1↑	B-2↑	LR-2↓	D-4↑
N-gram	0.853	0.951	**11.40**	0.324	0.149	0.185	0.747
Sentence	**0.869**	0.951	11.43	0.320	0.147	**0.166**	**0.749**
N-gram+Sentence	0.853	**0.952**	12.18	**0.332**	**0.158**	0.186	0.747

Table 6: Effectiveness of different types of noise on the ROCStories dataset.

"lose" compared to baselines.

3.5 Effectiveness of different negative samples

Table 6 shows the effectiveness of different types of noise on the ROCStories dataset. Using negative samples constructed from sentence noise is more effective than N-gram noise in lexical repetition and UNION metrics, and achieves similar PPL, BLEU, distinct and Orderness metrics. Combining N-gram and sentence noise will achieve about 1 point BLEU improvement.

3.6 Influence of different memory bank sizes

Table 7 shows the performances of our models with different memory bank sizes. When the memory bank size is 0, the model only needs to distinguish between human-written texts and negative samples constructed by applying N-gram noise and sentence noise, which has better PPL and distinct metrics. We also observed that without a memory bank, the soft prompts mainly lie in two areas, one for positive samples and the other for negative samples. By adding a memory bank, the model learns better text representation that could encode the differences between different texts, and achieves better UNION and BLEU metrics. However, PPL increases when we use a memory bank, and we conjecture that it is mainly because the model allocates more probability to some other reasonable stories.

3.7 Case Study

We present a case in table 8 to demonstrate that CSP can generate texts with better coherence than the previous SOTA model HINT.

4 Related Work

Long Text Generation Many recent long text generation studies try to tackle the incoherence problem by designing model structures, training methods and incorporating extra knowledge. Li et al. (2015) propose a hierarchical RNN model to learn the sentence-level representation. Fan et al. (2018) propose a hierarchical CNN model, and they also adopt a gated multi-scale self-attention mechanism to capture long-range context information. These two methods focus on modeling both word-level and sentence-level representations aiming at capturing long-range dependency. Another line of work adopts plan-then-generate methods (Yao et al., 2019; Shao et al., 2019b; Tan et al., 2021; Goldfarb-Tarrant et al., 2020). They first generate a high-level plan, and then generate the whole text according to the plan. The main problem of these works is that the models are biased to the plans extracted from human-written texts during training and lack of exposure to generated plans (Tan et al., 2021). There are also some works that try to incorporate knowledge base into text generation models (Guan et al., 2020; Xu et al., 2020) to improve the ability to generate commonsense stories. However, these methods mainly focus on commonsense stories, and may not be effective for generating other types of stories. Guan et al. (2021) propose the HINT model, which is the previous state-of-the-art method. HINT adopts two extra losses for training, i.e. inter-sentence seman-

Memory bank size	UNION↑	orderness↑	PPL↓	B-1↑	B-2↑	LR-2↓	D-4↑
0	0.832	0.948	**9.21**	0.322	0.147	**0.164**	**0.760**
600	0.851	0.948	11.15	0.319	0.146	0.183	0.735
65536	**0.853**	**0.952**	12.18	**0.332**	**0.158**	0.186	0.747

Table 7: Influence of different memory bank sizes on the ROCStories dataset.

Input (Leading Sentence):
MALE had a roommate.
Output of HINT:
MALE was **a hard worker and a great student**. MALE knew MALE was very **smart and smart**. MALE challenged MALE to **a game of basketball**. MALE beat MALE by a landslide.
Output of CSP:
he was very messy. MALE's roommate's mom said he needed to be more organized. MALE's roommate agreed to do so. MALE's roommate was much more organized.

Table 8: Generated stories by the previous SOTA model HINT and our model CSP (Names are replaced with "MALE"). In this case, CSP generates a more coherent text than HINT (incoherent issues are in **bold**).

tic similarity and discrimination between normal and random shuffled sentence orders. Compared to HINT, our method focuses on learning a better representation in a hidden space for better planning long text generation.

Contrastive Learning In recent years, contrastive learning has made great advances in computer vision (Tian et al., 2020; He et al., 2020; Chen et al., 2020; Misra and Maaten, 2020), natural language processing tasks (Wang et al., 2021a; Pan et al., 2021; Zhang et al., 2021a; Gao et al., 2021; Kim et al., 2021), as well as multi-modal tasks (Radford et al., 2021; Wang et al., 2021b). In the NLP domain, contrastive learning is adopted for sentence representation (Zhang et al., 2021a; Gao et al., 2021; Kim et al., 2021). Pan et al. (2021) use contrastive learning to learn a universal cross-language representation for better multilingual translation performance. Inspired by these works, we adopt contrastive learning to learn a better text representation, aiming at helping the model to plan long text generation from a high level and avoid generating incoherent texts.

Prompt Tuning Recently, some works have shown the effectiveness of prompt tuning in zero-shot and few-shot tasks (Brown et al., 2020; Gao et al., 2020). By designing or automatically searching templates and demonstrations, prompt tuning provides effective techniques for fine-tuning language models using only a few examples. Furthermore, the soft prompt is proposed as a parameter-efficient finetuning method (Li and Liang, 2021; Liu et al., 2021; Lester et al., 2021; Zhang et al., 2021b), i.e. the parameters of the pretrained language model remain fixed, and we add only a few trainable parameters as a prefix to the input sequence. Our work is inspired by recent soft prompt works, however, these works mainly focus on parameter-efficient finetuning, while our work aims at improving the coherence of long text generation. We jointly learn high level text representations in hidden space and take the representation as the soft prompt for better long text generation.

Learning from Negative Examples Welleck et al. (2019) have tried to avoid the model generating repetitive, dull text by unlikelihood training. Li et al. (2019) use unlikelihood training to generate text consistent with persona information. Unlikelihood loss is computed from tokens, and our method mainly focuses on high level representations in hidden space. Another line of studies on employing negative examples is adversarial learning (Yu et al., 2017; Li et al., 2017), which plays a minimax game between a generative model and a discriminative model to generate texts that can not be distinguished from human-written texts. We anticipate that unlikelihood training and adversarial training are largely complementary to our method.

5 Conclusion

In this paper, we propose a contrastive soft prompt method for improving the coherence of long text generation. It learns long text representations in the hidden space for better planning long text generation. To this end, it jointly learns to generate a text representation close to representations of coherent texts and away from incoherent ones and generates long text taking this representation as the soft prompt. We conduct experiments on two public story generation datasets, and experimental results show that our method can generate more coherent stories than the state-of-the-art model.

References

Tom B Brown, Benjamin Mann, Nick Ryder, Melanie Subbiah, Jared Kaplan, Prafulla Dhariwal, Arvind Neelakantan, Pranav Shyam, Girish Sastry, Amanda Askell, et al. 2020. Language models are few-shot learners. *arXiv preprint arXiv:2005.14165*.

Ting Chen, Simon Kornblith, Mohammad Norouzi, and Geoffrey Hinton. 2020. A simple framework for contrastive learning of visual representations. In *International conference on machine learning*, pages 1597–1607. PMLR.

Angela Fan, Mike Lewis, and Yann Dauphin. 2018. Hierarchical neural story generation. *arXiv preprint arXiv:1805.04833*.

Joseph L Fleiss. 1971. Measuring nominal scale agreement among many raters. *Psychological bulletin*, 76(5):378.

Tianyu Gao, Adam Fisch, and Danqi Chen. 2020. Making pre-trained language models better few-shot learners. *arXiv preprint arXiv:2012.15723*.

Tianyu Gao, Xingcheng Yao, and Danqi Chen. 2021. Simcse: Simple contrastive learning of sentence embeddings. *arXiv preprint arXiv:2104.08821*.

Seraphina Goldfarb-Tarrant, Tuhin Chakrabarty, Ralph Weischedel, and Nanyun Peng. 2020. Content planning for neural story generation with aristotelian rescoring. *arXiv preprint arXiv:2009.09870*.

Jian Guan, Fei Huang, Zhihao Zhao, Xiaoyan Zhu, and Minlie Huang. 2020. A knowledge-enhanced pretraining model for commonsense story generation. *Transactions of the Association for Computational Linguistics*, 8:93–108.

Jian Guan and Minlie Huang. 2020. Union: An unreferenced metric for evaluating open-ended story generation. In *Proceedings of the 2020 Conference on Empirical Methods in Natural Language Processing (EMNLP)*, pages 9157–9166.

Jian Guan, Xiaoxi Mao, Changjie Fan, Zitao Liu, Wenbiao Ding, and Minlie Huang. 2021. Long text generation by modeling sentence-level and discourse-level coherence. *In Proceedings of the 59th Annual Meeting of the Association for Computational Linguistics*.

Matthew Hausknecht, Prithviraj Ammanabrolu, Marc-Alexandre Côté, and Xingdi Yuan. 2020. Interactive fiction games: A colossal adventure. In *Proceedings of the AAAI Conference on Artificial Intelligence*, volume 34, pages 7903–7910.

Kaiming He, Haoqi Fan, Yuxin Wu, Saining Xie, and Ross Girshick. 2020. Momentum contrast for unsupervised visual representation learning. In *Proceedings of the IEEE/CVF Conference on Computer Vision and Pattern Recognition*, pages 9729–9738.

Ari Holtzman, Jan Buys, Li Du, Maxwell Forbes, and Yejin Choi. 2019. The curious case of neural text degeneration. *arXiv preprint arXiv:1904.09751*.

Taeuk Kim, Kang Min Yoo, and Sang-goo Lee. 2021. Self-guided contrastive learning for bert sentence representations. *arXiv preprint arXiv:2106.07345*.

Diederik P Kingma and Max Welling. 2013. Auto-encoding variational bayes. *arXiv preprint arXiv:1312.6114*.

Leo Leppänen, Myriam Munezero, Mark Granroth-Wilding, and Hannu Toivonen. 2017. Data-driven news generation for automated journalism. In *Proceedings of the 10th International Conference on Natural Language Generation*, pages 188–197.

Brian Lester, Rami Al-Rfou, and Noah Constant. 2021. The power of scale for parameter-efficient prompt tuning. *arXiv preprint arXiv:2104.08691*.

Mike Lewis, Yinhan Liu, Naman Goyal, Marjan Ghazvininejad, Abdelrahman Mohamed, Omer Levy, Veselin Stoyanov, and Luke Zettlemoyer. 2020. Bart: Denoising sequence-to-sequence pre-training for natural language generation, translation, and comprehension. In *Proceedings of the 58th Annual Meeting of the Association for Computational Linguistics*, pages 7871–7880.

Jiwei Li, Minh-Thang Luong, and Dan Jurafsky. 2015. A hierarchical neural autoencoder for paragraphs and documents. *arXiv preprint arXiv:1506.01057*.

Jiwei Li, Will Monroe, Tianlin Shi, Sébastien Jean, Alan Ritter, and Dan Jurafsky. 2017. Adversarial learning for neural dialogue generation. *arXiv preprint arXiv:1701.06547*.

Margaret Li, Stephen Roller, Ilia Kulikov, Sean Welleck, Y-Lan Boureau, Kyunghyun Cho, and Jason Weston. 2019. Don't say that! making inconsistent dialogue unlikely with unlikelihood training. *arXiv preprint arXiv:1911.03860*.

Xiang Lisa Li and Percy Liang. 2021. Prefix-tuning: Optimizing continuous prompts for generation. *arXiv preprint arXiv:2101.00190*.

Xiao Liu, Kaixuan Ji, Yicheng Fu, Zhengxiao Du, Zhilin Yang, and Jie Tang. 2021. P-tuning v2: Prompt tuning can be comparable to fine-tuning universally across scales and tasks. *arXiv preprint arXiv:2110.07602*.

Ishan Misra and Laurens van der Maaten. 2020. Self-supervised learning of pretext-invariant representations. In *Proceedings of the IEEE/CVF Conference on Computer Vision and Pattern Recognition*, pages 6707–6717.

Nasrin Mostafazadeh, Nathanael Chambers, Xiaodong He, Devi Parikh, Dhruv Batra, Lucy Vanderwende, Pushmeet Kohli, and James Allen. 2016. A corpus and cloze evaluation for deeper understanding of commonsense stories. In *Proceedings of the 2016 Conference of the North American Chapter of the Association for Computational Linguistics: Human Language Technologies*, pages 839–849.

Aaron van den Oord, Yazhe Li, and Oriol Vinyals. 2018. Representation learning with contrastive predictive coding. *arXiv preprint arXiv:1807.03748*.

Xiao Pan, Mingxuan Wang, Liwei Wu, and Lei Li. 2021. Contrastive learning for many-to-many multilingual neural machine translation. *arXiv preprint arXiv:2105.09501*.

Kishore Papineni, Salim Roukos, Todd Ward, and Wei-Jing Zhu. 2002. Bleu: a method for automatic evaluation of machine translation. In *Proceedings of the 40th annual meeting of the Association for Computational Linguistics*, pages 311–318.

Jiashu Pu, Ziyi Huang, Yadong Xi, Guandan Chen, Weijie Chen, and Rongsheng Zhang. 2022. Unraveling the mystery of artifacts in machine generated text. In *Proceedings of the Language Resources and Evaluation Conference*, pages 6889–6898, Marseille, France. European Language Resources Association.

Alec Radford, Jong Wook Kim, Chris Hallacy, Aditya Ramesh, Gabriel Goh, Sandhini Agarwal, Girish Sastry, Amanda Askell, Pamela Mishkin, Jack Clark, et al. 2021. Learning transferable visual models from natural language supervision. *arXiv preprint arXiv:2103.00020*.

Alec Radford, Jeffrey Wu, Rewon Child, David Luan, Dario Amodei, Ilya Sutskever, et al. 2019. Language models are unsupervised multitask learners. *OpenAI blog*, 1(8):9.

Zhihong Shao, Minlie Huang, Jiangtao Wen, Wenfei Xu, and Xiaoyan Zhu. 2019a. Long and diverse text generation with planning-based hierarchical variational model. *arXiv preprint arXiv:1908.06605*.

Zhihong Shao, Minlie Huang, Jiangtao Wen, Wenfei Xu, and Xiaoyan Zhu. 2019b. Long and diverse text generation with planning-based hierarchical variational model. *arXiv preprint arXiv:1908.06605*.

Bowen Tan, Zichao Yang, Maruan Al-Shedivat, Eric Xing, and Zhiting Hu. 2021. Progressive generation of long text with pretrained language models. In *Proceedings of the 2021 Conference of the North American Chapter of the Association for Computational Linguistics: Human Language Technologies*, pages 4313–4324.

Yonglong Tian, Dilip Krishnan, and Phillip Isola. 2020. Contrastive multiview coding. In *Computer Vision–ECCV 2020: 16th European Conference, Glasgow, UK, August 23–28, 2020, Proceedings, Part XI 16*, pages 776–794. Springer.

Ashish Vaswani, Noam Shazeer, Niki Parmar, Jakob Uszkoreit, Llion Jones, Aidan N Gomez, Łukasz Kaiser, and Illia Polosukhin. 2017. Attention is all you need. In *Advances in neural information processing systems*, pages 5998–6008.

Dong Wang, Ning Ding, Piji Li, and Hai-Tao Zheng. 2021a. Cline: Contrastive learning with semantic negative examples for natural language understanding. *arXiv preprint arXiv:2107.00440*.

Mengmeng Wang, Jiazheng Xing, and Yong Liu. 2021b. Actionclip: A new paradigm for video action recognition. *arXiv preprint arXiv:2109.08472*.

Sean Welleck, Ilia Kulikov, Stephen Roller, Emily Dinan, Kyunghyun Cho, and Jason Weston. 2019. Neural text generation with unlikelihood training. *arXiv preprint arXiv:1908.04319*.

Zhirong Wu, Yuanjun Xiong, Stella X Yu, and Dahua Lin. 2018. Unsupervised feature learning via non-parametric instance discrimination. In *Proceedings of the IEEE conference on computer vision and pattern recognition*, pages 3733–3742.

Yadong Xi, Jiashu Pu, and Xiaoxi Mao. 2021. Taming repetition in dialogue generation. *arXiv preprint arXiv:2112.08657*.

Peng Xu, Mostofa Patwary, Mohammad Shoeybi, Raul Puri, Pascale Fung, Anima Anandkumar, and Bryan Catanzaro. 2020. Megatron-cntrl: Controllable story generation with external knowledge using large-scale language models. *arXiv preprint arXiv:2010.00840*.

Lili Yao, Nanyun Peng, Ralph Weischedel, Kevin Knight, Dongyan Zhao, and Rui Yan. 2019. Plan-and-write: Towards better automatic storytelling. In *Proceedings of the AAAI Conference on Artificial Intelligence*, volume 33, pages 7378–7385.

Lantao Yu, Weinan Zhang, Jun Wang, and Yong Yu. 2017. Seqgan: Sequence generative adversarial nets with policy gradient. In *Proceedings of the AAAI conference on artificial intelligence*, volume 31.

Dejiao Zhang, Shang-Wen Li, Wei Xiao, Henghui Zhu, Ramesh Nallapati, Andrew O Arnold, and Bing Xiang. 2021a. Pairwise supervised contrastive learning of sentence representations. *arXiv preprint arXiv:2109.05424*.

Ningyu Zhang, Luoqiu Li, Xiang Chen, Shumin Deng, Zhen Bi, Chuanqi Tan, Fei Huang, and Huajun Chen. 2021b. Differentiable prompt makes pre-trained language models better few-shot learners. *arXiv preprint arXiv:2108.13161*.

A Appendix

A.1 Details of experiments

The model structure of the prompt generator, posterior prompt generator, and text generator are the same with GPT-2, and the parameter weights are initialized with a pre-trained GPT-2 checkpoint. The soft prompt length is 20 in our experiment.

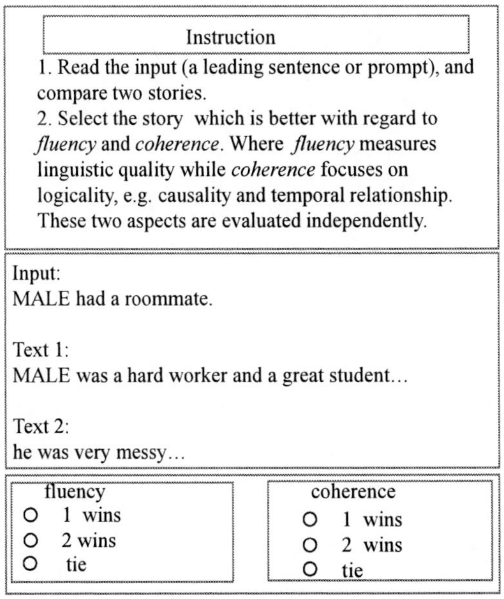

Figure 3: Manual annotation instruction.

The memory bank size is 65536. We set $\lambda_c = 1.0$, $\lambda_{ce} = 0.1$ and $\lambda_{ae} = 0.1$. We finetune the model on ROCStories and WritingPrompts for 22000 steps respectively. We use adam optimizer, and the learning rate is set to $5\text{e}{-5}$, no weight decay, and the batch size is 16. During generation, we use nucleus sampling with p=0.9, and the softmax temperature is 0.7. Our model contains 234 million parameters. We run our experiments on one GeForce RTX 3090, and it takes about 34 and 39 hours for training models on ROCStories and WritingPrompts datasets respectively.

A.2 Annotation Instruction

Figure 3 shows the annotation instruction. we conduct pair-wise comparison on two aspects, namely *fluency* and *coherence*. The metric *fluency* measures linguistic quality while *coherence* focuses on logicality, e.g. causality and temporal relationship. We randomly sample 100 generated texts from the test set of ROCStories and invite three annotators (they are all volunteers) to give a preference about fluency and coherence respectively (win, lose or tie). The comparison pair of texts are presented in random order.

Error Analysis of ToTTo Table-to-Text Neural NLG Models

Barkavi Sundararajan and **Somayajulu Sripada** and **Ehud Reiter**
Department of Computing Science, University of Aberdeen
{b.sundararajan.21, yaji.sripada, e.reiter}@abdn.ac.uk

Abstract

We report error analysis of outputs from four Table-to-Text generation models fine-tuned on ToTTo, an open-domain English language dataset. We carried out a manual error annotation of a subset of outputs (a total of 3,016 sentences) belonging to the topic of *Politics* generated by these four models. Our error annotation focused on eight categories of errors. The error analysis shows that more than 46% of sentences from each of the four models have been error-free. It uncovered some of the specific classes of errors; for example, *WORD* errors (mostly verbs and prepositions) are the dominant errors in all four models and are the most complex ones among other errors. *NAME* (mostly nouns) and *NUMBER* errors are slightly higher in two of the GeM benchmark models, whereas *DATE_DIMENSION* and *OTHER* categories of errors are more common in our Table-to-Text model. This in-depth error analysis is currently guiding us in improving our Table-to-Text model.

1 Introduction

End-to-end neural Table-to-Text models produce outputs that suffer from hallucination (output texts contain parts that are not supported by input data). This may be because these models learn the noise from complex examples during the training process and produce more errors than rule-based systems (Rebuffel et al., 2021). The automatic metrics such as BLEU and ROUGE do not uncover common classes of errors and are therefore less helpful to improve the models (Gehrmann et al., 2021a). The accuracy evaluation shared task by Thomson and Reiter (2021) using the gold standard methodology proposed by Thomson and Reiter (2020) was successful in identifying errors that are difficult to detect using automatic metrics (Gehrmann et al., 2022).

In this paper, we performed a detailed error analysis, adopting the Thomson and Reiter (2020) methodology on four Table-to-Text model outputs (trained on the ToTTo dataset) to identify and group the errors these models make in the output text. We created one of these Table-to-Text models by fine-tuning a t5-base Text-to-Text model with the ToTTo dataset using BLEU as a validation metric with the standard cross-entropy objective function, and we will be applying error corrections to this model in our future work. The other three model outputs came from GEM benchmark Table-to-Text models fine-tuned from t5-small, t5-base, and t5-large Text-to-Text models (Gehrmann et al., 2021a). Previous research studies for error analysis predominantly focused on Machine Translation (MT) systems using a simple framework by (Stymne and Ahrenberg, 2012) and extensively using Multidimensional Quality Metrics (MQM) framework by Freitag et al. (2021), and on other NLG tasks (Cai et al., 2020; Thomson and Reiter, 2020). Other annotation methods have been used to check for errors in the ToTTo dataset. Yin and Wan (2022) use a method based on MQM, assigning multiple labels to individual sentences. We take a different approach, annotating at the more granular level of token spans, i.e., words or phrases.

2 Table-to-Text

Table-to-Text generation is an important and challenging task in Natural Language Generation (NLG), which focuses on producing a factual, meaningful, and fluent output from structured tabular data. Most domains (viz. journalism, medical diagnosis, sports broadcasting and weather reports) are data-rich, and the information required for critical decision-making in these domains comes from the dataset, which is better represented as textual narratives than represented in structures such as indexes, tables and key-value pairs (Rebuffel et al., 2019).

Proceedings of the 2nd Workshop on Natural Language Generation, Evaluation, and Metrics (GEM), pages 456 - 470
December 7, 2022 ©2022 Association for Computational Linguistics

Input Table data from ToTTo (includes metadata such as Title, Highlighted cells in yellow and their headers):		
Page Title: List of ambassadors of the United States to Germany		
Section Title: Heads of the U.S. Embassy at Bonn (1955–1999)		
Name and Title	**Presentation of Credentials**	**Termination of Mission**
James B. Conant, Ambassador	May 14, 1955	February 19, 1957
David K. E. Bruce, Ambassador	April 17, 1957	October 29, 1959
Walter C. Dowling, Ambassador	December 3, 1959	April 21, 1963
George C. McGhee, Ambassador	May 18, 1963	May 21, 1968

Input Source/Linearized representation of the above Input Table data in Text format:

<page_title> List of ambassadors of the United States to Germany </page_title> <section_title> Heads of the U.S. Embassy at Bonn (1955–1999) </section_title> <table> <cell> David K. E. Bruce, Ambassador <col_header> Name and Title </col_header> </cell> <cell> April 17, 1957 <col_header> Presentation of Credentials </col_header> </cell> <cell> October 29, 1959 <col_header> Termination of Mission </col_header> </cell> </table>

Output/Reference Text faithful to the above Input Table data in Text format:

David K. E. Bruce served as the United States Ambassador to Germany from April 17, 1957 to October 29, 1959.

Table 1: Input Table sample from ToTTo (Parikh et al., 2020), Linearized representation of the Input Table data and Reference Text

2.1 ToTTo

Table 1 shows an example from a controlled Table-to-Text generation dataset (ToTTo) (Parikh et al., 2020) where a subset of the cells from the Wikipedia tables are taken as Input and paired with a relevant sentence description from the same Wikipedia page. This dataset was created using crowdsourcing to mark relevant cells from the table (shown in yellow) along with their corresponding row and column headers as inputs (removing the need for the content selection sub-task followed in the rule-based NLG systems).

As part of the Input Table data in Table 1, Page Title, Section Title and Section Text (if available) are called metadata. The ToTTo Table-to-Text task is to fine-tune neural NLG models to auto-generate output texts that describe the highlighted table cells along with their metadata faithfully and are similar (similarity measured using both automatic metrics as well as human judgement) to the reference text(s), example, the Reference Text in Table 1. Training Table-to-Text models with the more controlled ToTTo training dataset is expected to generate high-quality outputs (Parikh et al., 2020) because it focuses on addressing a simplified task instead of end-to-end Table-to-Text.

The ToTTo dataset covers a diverse distribution of topics such as Sports, Politics, Entertainment, Literature, Performing Arts, Broadcasting and so on. This dataset helps to understand how the generations differ for each domain and accordingly identify any pattern of errors made by the models. This level of insight would be helpful to improve our Table-to-Text model.

The ToTTo dataset has three splits based on the 83,141 unique Wikipedia tables: i. **Train** with 120,761 samples, ii. **Validation** with 7,700 samples and iii. **Test** with 7,700 samples[1].

The validation and test split samples are further categorised into overlap and non-overlap. Overlap split refers to the data (i.e. set of header values) already seen in training samples. Non-overlap split refers to the set of header values not seen in the training split and increases the generalization challenge (Parikh et al., 2020). In the validation split, we have 3784 overlap and 3916 non-overlap samples as further discussed in section 4.1[2].

2.2 Linearized Representation of the Input Table data

The relevant contents from the Input Table data as mentioned in section 2.1 are converted to the linearized representation i.e., metadata and highlighted texts with headers as mentioned in Table 1 for each of the training samples. The Reference Text is already 'in the text' format. The pre-trained transformer model we used takes the source-reference (input-output) pairs in a Text-to-Text format. Hence, the preprocessed Input Table data in Text format (linearized representation) and

[1]Since the output of each sample in ToTTo generates only one sentence as output, we used the term *sentence(s)* and *sample(s)* interchangeably in this paper.

[2]The test split reference outputs are not open-source and not considered in our error analysis.

its corresponding Reference Text, as shown in Table 1 for one sample, has been applied for all the training samples (120,761).

3 Table-To-Text Models included in our Error Analysis

3.1 Our Model

The Text-to-Text Transfer Transformer (T5) model pre-trained on Colossal Clean Crawled Corpus (C4) (Raffel et al., 2019) is taken to fine-tune our model with the ToTTo dataset. The T5 model is said to outperform GPT-2 and BERT models and is robust to handle out-of-domain inputs (Kale and Rastogi, 2020). The linearized representation of the Input Table data and its Reference Text pair, as shown in Table 1 and elaborated in section 2.2, are used for fine-tuning our Table-to-Text task.

The **M1: BLEU** model is a Table-to-Text model created by us by fine-tuning t5-base Text-to-Text models (220 million parameters) with the ToTTo dataset using BLEU as validation metric with the standard cross entropy objective function. The input or the encoder's maximum length of our model is 512 tokens to align with the limit of the pre-trained models. It is fine-tuned with a constant learning rate of 0.0001 and a beam size of 10 to generate the target text with at most 128 tokens (i.e., the decoder's maximum length). The batch size used for this M1: BLEU model is 2 and trained on a commodity server with GeForce RTX 2080 Ti with 11G memory using Single-precision Floating-point format (FP32). It took approximately seven days to train this model for 180,800 training steps.

3.2 GeM Benchmark Models

The error analysis also uses outputs from three GeM benchmark (Gehrmann et al., 2021a) Table-to-Text models that are fine-tuned from t5-small (GM2), t5-base (GM3) and t5-large (GM4) Text-to-Text models. These three variants of pre-trained t5 models come in different sizes. **GM2: t5-small** is pre-trained with 60 million parameters, **GM3: t5-base** is pre-trained with 220 million parameters and **GM4: t5-large** is pre-trained with 770 million parameters. Other specific fine-tuning or configuration details of these three benchmark models are unknown. In contrast, since we know these fine-tuning and configuration details for our model as described in section 3.1, the error analysis reported in this paper could be exploited to improve our model in future.

4 Evaluation and Results

4.1 Metric Based Evaluation

The best practice for evaluation choices (Gehrmann et al., 2021b) is to use a combination of metrics from at least two different categories. Hence, the scores of four Table-to-Text model outputs are computed using different types of metrics such as BLEURT (Sellam et al., 2020) and BERTScore (Zhang* et al., 2020) for **semantic** measure, BLEU (Papineni et al., 2002), ROUGE-2 (Ganesan, 2015) and METEOR (Banerjee and Lavie, 2005) for **lexical** measure and PARENT metric (Dhingra et al., 2019) that is relevant for **Table-to-Text** systems.

Table 9 and Table 11 in Appendix A shows the metric scores for the overall validation set of ToTTo (7,700 samples). The overall scores imply that GM3: t5-base (benchmark model) has the best scores for BLEU, BLEURT, ROUGE2, BERTScore and METEOR. Whereas our model M1: BLEU has the best score for PARENT (overall).

Table 10 and Table 12 in Appendix B shows the metric scores for the Politics domain (754 out of the 7,700 samples) in the validation set. The best scores slightly differ for this domain, where GM3: t5-base (benchmark model) scored well only for the overlap samples of BLEU, ROUGE2, BERTScore and METEOR. Whereas GM4: t5-large (benchmark model) has a better score for the non-overlap (challenging samples) for BLEU, BLEURT, BERTScore and METEOR. Our model M1: BLEU scored well for PARENT (both in overall and non-overlap samples).

These scores do not provide complete guidance on the actual performance of the neural models and cannot measure factual accuracy. To verify the performance of the system, we carried out a manual error analysis by focusing on eight categories of errors for the *Politics* domain (because this topic covers only 4% of the ToTTo data which is easier to error annotate) as detailed in section 4.2.

4.2 Human Evaluation

Performing a human evaluation in Amazon Mechanical Turk through crowdsourcing is expensive and is also time-consuming to screen with a qualification task before the actual experiment. Thomson and Reiter (2020) proposed a gold standard methodology for evaluating similar Table-To-Text tasks. We adapted this gold standard evaluation technique for the ToTTo dataset. The annotation procedure is discussed in section 4.2.1, and some examples are detailed in section 4.3 and Appendix C.

4.2.1 Error Categories for Annotation

Below are the eight categories of errors we used for annotating *Politics* domain outputs in ToTTo.

- WORD[W]: when incorrect words such as verbs, prepositions, adjectives and adverbs are found in the output.
- NAME[N]: when names of the Party, Leader, place (Electorate), Ambassador etc., are wrong (mostly nouns).
- **DATE_DIMENSION[D]**: when the Date and/or Month and/or Year are wrong.
- **NUMBER[U]**: when the number of seats and/or the number of votes and/or % of votes are incorrect.
- OTHER[O]: It includes mistakes in any of the below sub-categories.
  - GRAMMATICAL: when simple grammatical mistakes are identified in the output text. For example, missing articles such as 'a', 'the', and 'an', and the linking verb used for singular pronouns such as 'is' and 'was'. Any other verb mistakes belong to the WORD error. Other complex grammatical mistakes are not considered.
  - PUNCTUATION: when punctuation symbols are placed at inappropriate places, an apostrophe is missed for the Name of the Leader or Place.
  - GARBAGE: when the table data has the Politics party name in the abbreviation, it tries to produce garbage output.
  - Unclear: when the information is unclear.
- **CONTEXT[C]**: when the people will misunderstand a sentence i.e., the generated sentence is misleading, given the input data.
- NOT-CHECKABLE[X]: when the output has details that are not available in the Input Table data (i.e., relevant contents such as metadata, highlighted cells and their headers). The information may be right, but it requires checking other online resources to validate.
- NON-ENGLISH[NE]: when the Unicode characters in non-English names are either replaced with special characters or when these Unicode characters are omitted.

Our annotation scheme differs from Thomson and Reiter (2020) in terms of how the Date, Month and Year are handled. We introduced **DATE_DIMENSION[D]** category for ToTTo as the specific *Politics* domain had Date, Month and Year errors. There are also more NON-ENGLISH[NE] errors in the Unicode characters for the NAMES of a leader, place and/or party.

4.2.2 Other points for annotation

A single distinct token (i.e., word) is marked by highlighting that specific span of text for WORD, NAME, DATE_DIMENSION, NUMBER, OTHER (except GARBAGE sub-category) and NON-ENGLISH errors. For CONTEXT, OTHER-GARBAGE and NOT-CHECKABLE category of errors, it is difficult to reliably identify distinct tokens and therefore a group of tokens or relevant span of text can be marked as shown in the example annotations in Table 20, Table 21 and table 22 in Appendix C.

4.3 Results

Following the annotation guidelines defined in section 4.2.1, Table 2 and Table 3 provide the results of the manual error analysis made. Table 2 shows the overview of the error analysis identified in all four Table-to-Text models for a subset of 754 samples (Politics domain).

- **'NO ERROR'**: Around 46% of the samples out of this subset is error-free in all four models.
- **'OMISSIONS'**: Around 29% to 32% of the samples had omissions. However, these samples are not further analysed in the Table 3 (Individual Error Annotation count) due to the difficulty in objectively annotating omissions. We will independently study *Omissions* category of annotations in our future work. If a particular sample has both omission and error, the preference is given to the error alone, and its corresponding error count is included only in the *Errors Annotated* category in Table 2.
- **'META-DATA ISSUES'**: Around 6% of the samples required changes to the input records (Table metadata, cells and header) i.e., few

Category	M1: BLEU		GM2: t5-small		GM3: t5-base		GM4: t5-large	
	Count	%	Count	%	Count	%	Count	%
NO ERROR	346	46	355	47	371	49	387	51
OMISSIONS	244	32	218	29	240	32	232	31
META-DATA ISSUES*	46	6	43	6	40	5	37	5
ERRORS ANNOTATED	118	16	138	18	103	14	98	13
TOTAL COUNT	754		754		754		754	

Table 2: Sample/Sentence Count: Error Analysis of the model outputs for Politics domain of ToTTo. This table has the count of the samples with errors. Meta-data issues* are either i. when the right cells from table are not passed to the Input Data, or ii. when irrelevant cells (not highlighted in yellow) are passed as Input Data for few complex table structure.

Category	M1: BLEU	GM2: t5-small	GM3: t5-base	GM4: t5-large
WORD	63	74	49	47
NAME	14	23	24	10
DATE_DIMENSION	12	15	9	0
NUMBER	10	7	12	10
OTHER	10	11	6	6
CONTEXT	8	10	3	5
NOT-CHECKABLE	2	3	2	3
NON-ENGLISH	20	19	19	22
TOTAL ERROR COUNT	139	162	124	103

Table 3: Individual Error Annotation Count based on the *Errors Annotated* category taken from table 2. This table has the count of individual errors annotated from the samples. Hence, the total error count is higher in this table than table 2 (since each sample/sentence can contain multiple errors).

samples did not have the exact cell highlighted in the Table (compared to the Reference sentence), and few other samples had irrelevant cells passed in the Input. These samples are excluded from the Table 3 error annotations.

- **'ERRORS ANNOTATED'**: The error annotations in all four models ranged between 13% and 18%. This category is the main focus of this paper and is restricted to the eight categories of errors as presented in the Table 3.

Table 3 error analysis uncovered eight common classes of errors in all four models, which is elaborated further in each subsection along with examples [3].

4.3.1 WORD^{W} errors

This error is the dominant one committed by all four models. Our model had more WORD errors than two GeM Benchmark models (GM3: t5-base and GM4: t5-large). They belong to the below sub-groups.

- Most of them are VERB errors such as '*defeated*' versus '*succeeded*', '*won*' versus '*lost*', '*elected*' versus '*contested*', '*appointed*' versus '*nominated*' and so on.
- Some of them include errors in prepositions such as '*from*', '*with*', '*by*', '*to*', '*until*' and so on.
- Few errors are specific to the Politics related words. For example, '*swing*' that has a positive or negative percentage versus '*normal percentage of votes*'.

In Table 4, all four models made the WORD error. The word 'longest-lived' is the main error where the sentence semantic requires access to other data to compute the right word i.e., longest-lived or shortest-lived. The input header only has the term 'longevity' and could be the reason for all models to generalise it as longest-lived. 'Sanj Sanetomi' is a NON-ENGLISH error that is uniform in

[3]For better readability, the reference sentence and correct prediction sentence that have the right token without any errors are either marked with the superscript R (example, right-token^{R}) or in green colour (example, right-token) in the example annotations (i.e., in section 4.3 and Appendix C).

(a) **Input**: Table with Title, Highlighted cells and their headers

Page Title: List of Japanese prime ministers by longevity
Section Title: Longevity of Japanese prime ministers

No	Prime Minister	Total time in Office	Date of Death	Lifespan
3	Sanetomi Sanjō	60 days	28 Feb 1891	53 years, 352 days

(b) **Output**: Prediction with Error Annotations and Reference

M1: BLEU prediction: Sanj Sanetomi[NE] was the longest-lived[W] prime minister in Japan at 53 years, 352 days.

Reference: The shortest-lived[R] Prime Minister was Sanetomi Sanjō, who died at the age of 53 years and 352 days.

Table 4: WORD error made by all models

(a) **Input**: Table with Title, Highlighted cells and their headers

Page Title: Members of the Australian House of Representatives
Section Title: None

Member	Party	Electorate	State	Term in Office
Hon Les Johnson	Labor	Hughes	NSW	1955-1966, 1969-1984
Robert Tickner	Labor	Hughes	NSW	1984-1996

(b) **Output**: Prediction with Error Annotations and Reference

GM3: t5-base prediction: Hughes Labor MHA[N] Les Johnson served until 1984 and Robert Tickner served from 1984 to 1996.

Reference: The Labor member for Hughes (NSW), Les Johnson in 1984 was replaced by Labor candidate Robert Tickner as Member of the Australian House of Representatives[R].

Table 5: NAME error made by our model and two benchmark models

(a) **Input**: Table with Title, Highlighted cells and their headers

Page Title:1901 Bulgarian parliamentary election
Section Title: Results

Party	Votes	%	Seats	±
People's Party	66,910	22.8	29	+27
People's Liberal Party	65,680	22.4	24	+5
Progressive Liberal Party	58,860	20.1	40	+32
Total	344,787	100	164	-5

(b) **Output**: Prediction with Error Annotations and Reference

GM3: t5-base prediction: The result was a victory for the Progressive Liberal Party, which won 58,860[U] of the 164 seats.

Reference: Despite receiving the third highest number of votes, the Progressive Liberal Party emerged as the largest party in the 1901 Bulgarian parliamentary election with 40[R] of the 164 seats.

Table 6: NUMBER error made by all models

(a) **Input**: Table with Title, Highlighted cells and their headers

Page Title: 67th United States Congress
Section Title: Senate

Senator	Reason for Vacancy	Successor	Date of Successor's Installation
Philander C. Knox (R)	Died October 12, 1921. Successor was appointed.	William E. Crow (R)	October 24, 1921
William E. Crow (R)	Died August 2, 1922. Successor was appointed and subsequently elected.	David A. Reed (R)	August 8, 1922

(b) **Output**: Prediction with Error Annotations and Reference

M1: BLEU prediction: Philander C. Knox (R) served as senator until October 12, 1921 which was later served by William E. Crow, Jr. from October 24, 1922[D] to August 2, 1923[D] and later succeeded by David A. Reed, R, from August 8, 1932[D].

Reference: Philander C. Knox (R) served until October 12, 1921 and William E. Crow (R) served from October 24, 1921[R] until August 2, 1922[R], after whom David A. Reed (R) served from August 8, 1922[R].

Table 7: DATE_DIMENSION error made by our model

all four models because of the tokenization used in t5-base transformers. One solution could be to use a multilingual tokenizer in our future work.

In Table 14, all models except GM4: t5-large could not predict the right WORD 'lost to' or the 'right leader name' for the verb *'defeated'*. One of the reasons the GeM t5-large model predicted the right WORD could be from the huge parameters it learned during pre-training. Being certain about the configuration details of our Table-to-Text model (M1: BLEU), it does not have any arithmetic reasoning abilities to predict the right verb *'defeated'* or *'lost to'* based on the number of votes.

In Table 13, the more obvious reason for WORD errors *'from'* and *'to'* is because the input table had both years (1987 and 1992) in a single field. One reason for this error is that the table does not comply with the First Normal Form (1NF) in relational databases (one of the common patterns identified in our analysis). Another reason is that the table does not have access to the additional insight semantic of 're-elected' as mentioned in the Reference.

4.3.2 NAME^{N} and NUMBER^{U} errors

These two errors are slightly higher in the Benchmark models (GM3 and GM4) than in the model (M1: BLEU).

NAME in the prediction got jumbled/swapped when two or more names are present in the Input Table data as shown in Table 15 in Appendix C. The Table 5 shows NAME hallucinations, where the GeM benchmark models (GM2: t5-small and GM3: t5-base) and our model (M1: BLEU) hallucinated the NAME '*MHA i.e., Member of the House of Assembly*' instead of the right NAME '*Member of the Australian House of Representatives*'.

NUMBER is a common error made by all models, where *'number (or %) of seats'* versus *'number (or %) of votes'* got swapped in the prediction as shown in Table 6. For other cases, the Table 16 and Table 17 show NUMBER hallucinations, where the two GeM benchmark models tried to hallucinate and compute the incorrect margin of votes even when the input table data did not explicitly pass this value.

4.3.3 DATE_DIMENSION^{D} errors

DATE_DIMENSION errors are more common in our model. As shown in Table 7, our model had the year hallucinated even when the right values (i.e., date dimension fields) are passed to the input data. GeM Benchmark models did not face this error except for few complex samples. Even when it had multiple date-dimension fields as shown in Table 18 in Appendix C, the GeM models predicted the year correctly but they committed a different error category (NAME error) in this example. The date-dimension errors will be the first class of errors we intend to address when we improve our model.

4.3.4 OTHER^{O} errors

This error is slightly higher in our model and GM2: t5small model. A few of the miscellaneous errors we encountered in all four models are missing apostrophe (*'s*), missing article ('the', 'a') and other spans of text that does not imply any meaning, for example, ***'GSSSDULSVDHSS'*** as shown in Table 20 in Appendix C. Table 21, Table 22 and Table 19 in Appendix C present the error annotations for the remaining three errors (CONTEXT, NOT-CHECKABLE and NON-ENGLISH).

4.4 Agreement between annotators

One of the authors (the first annotator) annotated 754 predicted outputs for four systems (i.e., 3,016 sentences). In addition, the second annotator annotated predicted outputs for a random 10% of the Politics domain of ToTTo by following the defined guidelines.

The second annotator was given a word document with the screenshot of the Input Table data with highlighted cells as shown in Table 1 excluding the Linearized representation of the input and Reference Text (to focus the attention of the Annotator 2 on the underlying table to annotate errors rather than being guided by the Reference Text). We provided four model outputs for each Input Table data. The second annotator annotated 80 predicted outputs (i.e., 320 sentences for four models), and it took approximately 5 hours to complete this experiment. The annotator marked each error with the corresponding category and provided remarks/corrections where ever possible.

The confusion matrix for the annotations made between the first annotator (A1) and second annotator (A2), along with Cohen's Kappa coefficient (K value), is presented in Table 8. The NUMBER, DATE_DIMENSION, CONTEXT, and NON-ENGLISH categories have a complete agreement. We have a high agreement for both the WORD (the most dominant error) and the NAME errors. NOT-CHECKABLE errors tend to be subjective and have a weak agreement. The average

Category	Both agree: error	Both agree: no error	A1-error	A2-error	K value
WORD	25	245	7	6	0.77
NAME	7	245	0	4	0.77
DATE_DIMENSION	4	245	0	0	1
NUMBER	8	245	0	0	1
OTHER	2	245	0	0	1
CONTEXT	3	245	0	1	0.80
NOT-CHECKABLE	2	245	0	4	0.49
NON-ENGLISH	7	245	0	0	1
TOTAL COUNT AND AVERAGE K VALUE	**58**	**245**	**7**	**15**	**0.79**

Table 8: Cohen's Kappa coefficient (K value): Confusion Matrix for the agreement between two annotators

Cohen's Kappa coefficient (K value) is 0.79, indicating a high agreement between two annotators.

5 Related Work

In the field of Machine Translation, error analysis has been carried out for a long time (Stymne and Ahrenberg, 2012). More recently, the Multidimensional Quality Metrics (MQM) framework based on a hierarchy of errors was applied to carry out error analysis of WMT data (Freitag et al., 2021). This analysis identified error types (error classes) responsible for the difference in output quality between human and machine-generated translations.

Within the NLG context, Cai et al. (2020) performed error analysis for the Topic-to-Essay NLG task and proposed a human annotation framework for evaluating sub-sentence grammar, sentence logic, repetition, semantic coherence and contextual consistency. Their experiment results show that the neural models produced relatively high semantic errors compared to the grammatical and repetition errors.

Within the Table-to-Text context, Thomson and Reiter (2020) designed a gold-standard error analysis methodology with a taxonomy of simple errors for the annotators to evaluate the factual accuracy of Table-to-Text NLG models. They apply this methodology to system-generated basketball summaries from the Rotowire dataset (Wiseman et al., 2017). Thomson and Reiter (2021) described a shared task where different evaluation techniques for basketball summaries from the Rotowire dataset were submitted and their results show that metric-based techniques struggled to detect factual errors.

van Miltenburg et al. (2021) suggested expanding Wiseman et al. (2017) taxonomy to include other taxonomies such as the SCARECROW annotation schema (Dou et al., 2021) and image captioning specific taxonomy by van Miltenburg and Elliott (2017), making the resulting expanded taxonomy aligned to the quality criteria recommended by Belz et al. (2020). van Miltenburg et al. (2021) emphasised avoiding complex terms such as 'hallucinations' and 'omissions' for error categories because these are process-level (system) rather than product-level (output) descriptions of the errors. Analysing the errors using process-level descriptions cannot be reliable. We, therefore, adhered to the simple category of errors based on product-level (output) descriptions in our error analysis.

6 Conclusion

We fine-tuned our neural Table-to-Text model (M1: BLEU) with the known configuration details and compared its outputs with the GeM benchmark model outputs. This analysis provided additional insights of error classes (such as incorrect VERB predictions for WORD errors, NAME and NUMBER swap when two or more of these details are in the Input Table, hallucinations for NUMBER and DATE_DIMENSION), which is not possible to determine from evaluation metric scores. Our analysis shows that these four Transformer based models can perform textual reasoning to some extent but lack a deeper level reasoning capabilities (for example, mathematical reasoning and for more complex table structure when multiple inputs are present). This level of insights from the manual error analysis will provide opportunities to overcome this reasoning capabilities in our model in the future work.

Limitations

This error analysis is focused only on the Politics domain of the ToTTo dataset. It needs to be expanded to other domains such as Sports, Arts, Entertainment and others from the ToTTo dataset. This is the first stage of our error analysis and is restricted to the eight common classes (categories) of errors. Omission-related errors need to be better developed with different severity levels, and meta-data issues have to be corrected.

Ethics Statement

This work seeks to perform error analysis for our model and three benchmark models from GeM, which are trained using the open-source ToTTo dataset. The ground-truth generation remains the same as the original dataset, and we did not introduce any further social bias to this dataset. The three benchmark model outputs are open-source and downloaded from GeM (`https://gem-benchmark.com/resources`). We did not modify any of these three model outputs while annotating errors in our experiment. We sought consent from our second annotator (Craig Thomson), who was provided with the necessary guidelines before performing the error annotations.

Acknowledgements

We thank Craig Thomson for helping with the annotations in this work. We also thank the three anonymous reviewers and the NLG (CLAN) reading group at the University of Aberdeen for their valuable feedback.

References

Satanjeev Banerjee and Alon Lavie. 2005. METEOR: An automatic metric for MT evaluation with improved correlation with human judgments. In *Proceedings of the ACL Workshop on Intrinsic and Extrinsic Evaluation Measures for Machine Translation and/or Summarization*, pages 65–72, Ann Arbor, Michigan. Association for Computational Linguistics.

Anya Belz, Simon Mille, and David M. Howcroft. 2020. Disentangling the properties of human evaluation methods: A classification system to support comparability, meta-evaluation and reproducibility testing. In *Proceedings of the 13th International Conference on Natural Language Generation*, pages 183–194, Dublin, Ireland. Association for Computational Linguistics.

Ping Cai, Xingyuan Chen, Hongjun Wang, and Peng Jin. 2020. The errors analysis of natural language generation — a case study of topic-to-essay generation. In *2020 16th International Conference on Computational Intelligence and Security (CIS)*, pages 86–89.

Bhuwan Dhingra, Manaal Faruqui, Ankur Parikh, Ming-Wei Chang, Dipanjan Das, and William W. Cohen. 2019. Handling divergent reference texts when evaluating table-to-text generation.

Yao Dou, Maxwell Forbes, Rik Koncel-Kedziorski, Noah A. Smith, and Yejin Choi. 2021. Is gpt-3 text indistinguishable from human text? scarecrow: A framework for scrutinizing machine text.

Markus Freitag, George Foster, David Grangier, Viresh Ratnakar, Qijun Tan, and Wolfgang Macherey. 2021. Experts, errors, and context: A large-scale study of human evaluation for machine translation. *Transactions of the Association for Computational Linguistics*, 9:1460–1474.

Kavita Ganesan. 2015. Rouge 2.0: Updated and improved measures for evaluation of summarization tasks.

Sebastian Gehrmann, Tosin Adewumi, Karmanya Aggarwal, Pawan Sasanka Ammanamanchi, Anuoluwapo Aremu, Antoine Bosselut, Khyathi Raghavi Chandu, Miruna-Adriana Clinciu, Dipanjan Das, Kaustubh Dhole, Wanyu Du, Esin Durmus, Ondřej Dušek, Chris Chinenye Emezue, Varun Gangal, Cristina Garbacea, Tatsunori Hashimoto, Yufang Hou, Yacine Jernite, Harsh Jhamtani, Yangfeng Ji, Shailza Jolly, Mihir Kale, Dhruv Kumar, Faisal Ladhak, Aman Madaan, Mounica Maddela, Khyati Mahajan, Saad Mahamood, Bodhisattwa Prasad Majumder, Pedro Henrique Martins, Angelina McMillan-Major, Simon Mille, Emiel van Miltenburg, Moin Nadeem, Shashi Narayan, Vitaly Nikolaev, Andre Niyongabo Rubungo, Salomey Osei, Ankur Parikh, Laura Perez-Beltrachini, Niranjan Ramesh Rao, Vikas Raunak, Juan Diego Rodriguez, Sashank Santhanam, João Sedoc, Thibault Sellam, Samira Shaikh, Anastasia Shimorina, Marco Antonio Sobrevilla Cabezudo, Hendrik Strobelt, Nishant Subramani, Wei Xu, Diyi Yang, Akhila Yerukola, and Jiawei Zhou. 2021a. The GEM benchmark: Natural language generation, its evaluation and metrics. In *Proceedings of the 1st Workshop on Natural Language Generation, Evaluation, and Metrics (GEM 2021)*, pages 96–120, Online. Association for Computational Linguistics.

Sebastian Gehrmann, Elizabeth Clark, and Thibault Sellam. 2021b. A case for better evaluation standards in nlg.

Sebastian Gehrmann, Elizabeth Clark, and Thibault Sellam. 2022. Repairing the cracked foundation: A survey of obstacles in evaluation practices for generated text.

Mihir Kale and Abhinav Rastogi. 2020. Text-to-text pre-training for data-to-text tasks. In *Proceedings of the 13th International Conference on Natural Language Generation*, pages 97–102, Dublin, Ireland. Association for Computational Linguistics.

Kishore Papineni, Salim Roukos, Todd Ward, and Wei-Jing Zhu. 2002. Bleu: a method for automatic evaluation of machine translation. In *Proceedings of the 40th Annual Meeting of the Association for Computational Linguistics*, pages 311–318, Philadelphia, Pennsylvania, USA. Association for Computational Linguistics.

Ankur Parikh, Xuezhi Wang, Sebastian Gehrmann, Manaal Faruqui, Bhuwan Dhingra, Diyi Yang, and Dipanjan Das. 2020. ToTTo: A controlled table-to-text generation dataset. In *Proceedings of the 2020 Conference on Empirical Methods in Natural Language Processing (EMNLP)*, pages 1173–1186, Online. Association for Computational Linguistics.

Colin Raffel, Noam Shazeer, Adam Roberts, Katherine Lee, Sharan Narang, Michael Matena, Yanqi Zhou, Wei Li, and Peter J. Liu. 2019. Exploring the limits of transfer learning with a unified text-to-text transformer.

Clément Rebuffel, Marco Roberti, Laure Soulier, Geoffrey Scoutheeten, Rossella Cancelliere, and Patrick Gallinari. 2021. Controlling hallucinations at word level in data-to-text generation.

Clément Rebuffel, Laure Soulier, Geoffrey Scoutheeten, and Patrick Gallinari. 2019. A hierarchical model for data-to-text generation.

Thibault Sellam, Dipanjan Das, and Ankur Parikh. 2020. BLEURT: Learning robust metrics for text generation. In *Proceedings of the 58th Annual Meeting of the Association for Computational Linguistics*, pages 7881–7892, Online. Association for Computational Linguistics.

Sara Stymne and Lars Ahrenberg. 2012. On the practice of error analysis for machine translation evaluation. In *Proceedings of the Eighth International Conference on Language Resources and Evaluation (LREC'12)*, pages 1785–1790, Istanbul, Turkey. European Language Resources Association (ELRA).

Craig Thomson and Ehud Reiter. 2020. A gold standard methodology for evaluating accuracy in data-to-text systems. In *Proceedings of the 13th International Conference on Natural Language Generation*, pages 158–168, Dublin, Ireland. Association for Computational Linguistics.

Craig Thomson and Ehud Reiter. 2021. Generation challenges: Results of the accuracy evaluation shared task. In *Proceedings of the 14th International Conference on Natural Language Generation*, pages 240–248, Aberdeen, Scotland, UK. Association for Computational Linguistics.

Emiel van Miltenburg, Miruna Clinciu, Ondřej Dušek, Dimitra Gkatzia, Stephanie Inglis, Leo Leppänen, Saad Mahamood, Emma Manning, Stephanie Schoch, Craig Thomson, and Luou Wen. 2021. Underreporting of errors in NLG output, and what to do about it. In *Proceedings of the 14th International Conference on Natural Language Generation*, pages 140–153, Aberdeen, Scotland, UK. Association for Computational Linguistics.

Emiel van Miltenburg and Desmond Elliott. 2017. Room for improvement in automatic image description: an error analysis.

Sam Wiseman, Stuart Shieber, and Alexander Rush. 2017. Challenges in data-to-document generation. In *Proceedings of the 2017 Conference on Empirical Methods in Natural Language Processing*, pages 2253–2263, Copenhagen, Denmark. Association for Computational Linguistics.

Xunjian Yin and Xiaojun Wan. 2022. How do Seq2Seq models perform on end-to-end data-to-text generation? In *Proceedings of the 60th Annual Meeting of the Association for Computational Linguistics (Volume 1: Long Papers)*, pages 7701–7710, Dublin, Ireland. Association for Computational Linguistics.

Tianyi Zhang*, Varsha Kishore*, Felix Wu*, Kilian Q. Weinberger, and Yoav Artzi. 2020. Bertscore: Evaluating text generation with bert. In *International Conference on Learning Representations*.

Appendices

A Standard Metrics Evaluation for ToTTo

The standard metrics computed for the ToTTo dataset are BLEU, PARENT and BLEURT. Table 9 is computed for the overall validation dataset and Table 10 is specifically computed for the Politics domain of ToTTo.

B Additional Metric Evaluation for ToTTo

We computed three additional metrics (BERTScore, METEOR and ROUGE2) in Table 11 and Table 12. BERTScore is taken from the official repository (Zhang* et al., 2020), METEOR and ROUGE2 metrics are taken from `https://huggingface.co/datasets` library. Best performing metric scores are in bold.

C Example Annotations

Example annotations for different types of error categories are annotated in this section, as per the guidelines defined in section 4.2.1 for the Politics domain of the ToTTo dataset.

Model	Overall			Overlap			Non-Overlap		
	BLEU	PARENT	BLEURT	BLEU	PARENT	BLEURT	BLEU	PARENT	BLEURT
M1: BLEU	45.9	**56.49**	0.1539	53.2	**61.04**	0.2705	38.4	52.10	0.0412
GM2: t5-small	43.7	54.46	0.1203	51.0	58.43	0.2376	36.6	50.63	0.0070
GM3: t5-base	**46.2**	56.20	**0.1651**	**54.0**	60.33	**0.2773**	**38.7**	**52.20**	**0.0566**
GM4: t5-large	44.7	55.28	0.1434	52.5	59.73	0.2591	37.2	50.97	0.0316

Table 9: Standard Metric Evaluation for the overall ToTTo Validation dataset

Model	Overall			Overlap			Non-Overlap		
	BLEU	PARENT	BLEURT	BLEU	PARENT	BLEURT	BLEU	PARENT	BLEURT
M1: BLEU	49.5	**59.67**	0.1370	55.0	**63.12**	0.2130	41.7	**55.08**	0.0362
GM2: t5-small	48.0	57.80	0.1530	53.0	60.77	0.2372	41.0	53.17	0.0413
GM3: t5-base	**49.9**	57.80	0.1518	**55.9**	61.16	0.2334	41.3	53.33	0.0435
GM4: t5-large	49.6	57.39	**0.1635**	54.6	60.94	**0.2416**	**42.7**	52.67	**0.0598**

Table 10: Standard Metric Evaluation for Politics Domain of ToTTo Validation dataset

Model	Overall			Overlap			Non-Overlap		
	BERT-Score	METEOR	ROUGE2	BERT-Score	METEOR	ROUGE2	BERT-Score	METEOR	ROUGE2
M1: BLEU	0.9330	0.6145	0.4713	**0.9418**	0.6697	0.5398	0.9246	0.5611	0.405
GM2: t5-small	0.9295	0.5972	0.4562	0.938	0.6488	0.5187	0.9212	0.5474	0.3956
GM3: t5-base	**0.9332**	**0.6189**	**0.4767**	0.9415	**0.6707**	**0.5433**	**0.9252**	**0.5688**	**0.4123**
GM4: t5-large	0.9318	0.6151	0.4674	0.9404	0.6689	0.5359	0.9234	0.5631	0.4012

Table 11: Additional Metric Evaluation for the overall ToTTo Validation dataset

Model	Overall			Overlap			Non-Overlap		
	BERT-Score	METEOR	ROUGE2	BERT-Score	METEOR	ROUGE2	BERT-Score	METEOR	ROUGE2
M1: BLEU	0.9364	0.6295	0.4841	0.9434	0.6672	0.5269	0.9280	0.5793	0.4272
GM2: t5-small	0.9361	0.6162	0.4669	0.9428	0.648	0.5055	0.9272	0.5739	0.4168
GM3: t5-base	**0.9372**	**0.6304**	**0.4858**	**0.9445**	**0.6704**	**0.5298**	0.9275	0.5774	**0.4276**
GM4: t5-large	0.9369	0.6293	0.4758	0.9435	0.6650	0.5135	**0.9283**	**0.5820**	0.4267

Table 12: Additional Metric Evaluation for Politics Domain of ToTTo Validation dataset

(a) **Input**: Table with Title, Highlighted cells and their headers

Page Title: List of heads of state of Trinidad and Tobago

Section Title: President of Trinidad and Tobago

No	President (Birth - Death)	Took Office	Left Office	Elected
2	Noor Hassanali (1918 - 2006)	20 March 1987	17 March 1997	1987, 1992

(b) **Output**: Prediction with Error Annotations and Reference

GM3: t5-base prediction: Noor Hassanali (1918 – 2006) was the President of Trinidad and Tobago from[W] 1987 to[W] 1992.

Possible correction: from[W] - in ; to[W] - and in

Reference: Noor Hassanali was re-elected[R] as the president in 1992.

Table 13: WORD error made by all four models

(a) **Input**: Table with Title, Highlighted cells and their headers

Page Title: Dan Maffei
Section Title: Electoral history

Party	Candidate	Votes	%	±
Republican	Ann Marie Buerkle	104,374	50.2	+ 8.0
Democratic	Dan Maffei	103,807	49.8	-4.7
Majority		567	0.4	-10.4
Turnout		208,181	100	+23.4

(b) **Output**: Predictions with Error Annotations and Reference

M1: BLEU prediction: Maffei defeated[W] Republican Ann Marie Buerkle by a margin of 567 votes or[W] 208,181 votes.

GM3: t5-base prediction: Maffei defeated[W] Republican Ann Marie Buerkle by a margin of 567 votes, a difference[W] of 208,181 votes.

GM4: t5-large prediction: Maffei lost to[R] Republican Ann Marie Buerkle by a 567-vote margin with 103,807 votes out of[R] 208,181 votes cast[R].

Reference: Republican Ann Marie Buerkle defeated Maffei with a 567-vote majority of over 200,000 ballots cast.

Table 14: WORD error made by all models except GM4: t5-large

(a) **Input**: Table with Title, Highlighted cells and their headers

Page Title: Canterbury, New Zealand
Section Title: None

Members of Parliament for Canterbury

Electorate	Established	MP	Party
Rangitata	2008	Andrew Falloon	National
Selwyn	2008	Amy Adams	National
Waitaki	2008	Jacqui Dean	National

(b) **Output**: Predictions with Error Annotations and Reference

M1: BLEU prediction: The National MPs for Canterbury are Amy Adams for Selwyn and Jacqui Dean for Waitaki and Rangitata[N].

GM2: t5-small prediction: The National Party has represented Rangitata, Selwyn, Amy Adams[N], Waitaki and Jacqui Dean[N].

GM4: t5-large prediction: National's Amy Adams of Selwyn[R] and Jacqui Dean of Waitaki[R] were the MPs for Canterbury.

Reference: Rangitata and Selwyn are held by National MP's where Selwyn is represented by Amy Adams[R] while Waitaki is represented by Jacqui Dean[R].

Table 15: NAME error made by all models except GM4: t5-large

(a) **Input**: Table with Title, Highlighted cells and their headers

Page Title: 2010 Wellington City mayoral election
Section Title: Result

2010 Wellington City mayoral election

Candidate	Count-1	Count-2	Count-3	Count-4	Count-5
Celia Wade-Brown	18,560	18,675	19,002	21,422	24,881
Kerry Prendergast (incumbent)	21,809	21,863	22,021	22,899	24,705
Jack Yan	5,817	5,924	6,144	7,426	0 (No count)

(b) **Output**: Predictions with Error Annotations and Reference

GM3: t5-base prediction: Wade-Brown won the 2010 Wellington City mayoral election by a margin of 1,354[U] votes.

GM4: t5-large prediction: Wade-Brown was elected mayor with 24,705[U] votes over a third of a second[O].

M1: BLEU prediction: Wade-Brown received 24,881 votes out of[W] 24,705 in the 2010 Wellington City mayoral election.

Reference: Celia Wade-Brown won the 2010 Wellington City mayoral election in the final round of the vote count by 24,881 to 24,705[R].

Table 16: NUMBER error made by two benchmark models and WORD error made by other two models

(a) **Input**: Table with Title, Highlighted cells and their headers

Page Title: 2016 United States presidential election in Michigan
Section Title: Results
2016 United States presidential election in Michigan

Party	Candidate	Running mate	Votes	%	Electoral votes
Republican	Donald Trump	Mike Pence	2,279,543	47.50%	16
Democratic	Hillary Clinton	Tim Kaine	2,268,839	47.27%	0

(b) **Output**: Predictions with Error Annotations and Reference

GM4: t5-large prediction: Trump won the state of Michigan with 47.50% of the vote to Clinton's 47.27%, a margin of 17.13%[U].

GM3: t5-base prediction: Donald Trump won the 2016 United States presidential election in Michigan with 47.50% of the vote to Hillary Clinton's 47.27%, a margin of 2.94%[U].

M1: BLEU: In the 2016 United States presidential election in Michigan, Trump took 47.50 percent of the vote over Hillary Clinton's 47.27%[R].

Reference: The 2016 United States presidential election in Michigan was won by Donald Trump with 47.50% of the total votes over Hillary Clinton's 47.27%[R].

Table 17: NUMBER error made by two benchmark models

(a) **Input**: Table with Title, Highlighted cells and their headers

Page Title: Ashoknagar (Vidhan Sabha constituency)
Section Title: Members of Legislative Assembly

Election Year	Constituency	Name of M.L.A.	Party Affiliation
1967	Ashoknagar	Sadhan Kumar Sen	Communist Party of India
1969		Sadhan Kumar Sen	Communist Party of India
1971		Nani Kar	Communist Party of India (Marxist)
1972		Keshab Chandra Bhattacharya	Independent

(b) **Output**: Predictions with Error Annotations and Reference

M1:BLEU prediction: Sadhan Kumar Sen of CPI won the seat in 1967, 1969, 1971[D], and Keshab Chandra Bhattacharya of Independent won in 1972.

GM4: t5-large and GM3: t5-base predictions: Ashoknagar was represented by Sadhan Kumar Sen of CPI(M)[N] in 1967 and 1969, Nani Kar of CPI(M) in 1971, and Keshab Chandra Bhattacharya of Independent in 1972.

Reference: Keshab Chandra Bhattacharya of Independent, won in 1972, Nani Kar of CPI(M) won in 1971[R], and Sadhan Kumar Sen of CPI[R] won in 1969 and 1967.

Table 18: DATE_DIMENSION error made by our model
NAME errors made by other two benchmark models

(a) **Input**: Table with Title, Highlighted cells and their headers

Page Title: List of political parties in Norway
Section Title: Parties currently in Parliament

Name	Ideology	Position	Leader	Affiliation International
Miljøpartiet de Grønne Green Party	Green politics	Centre-left	Rasmus Hansson, Une Aina Bastholm	Global Greens

(b) **Output**: Predictions with Error Annotations and Reference

M1: BLEU prediction: The Miljpartiet de Grnne[NE] Green Party is a political party in Norway.

GM3: t5-base and GM4: t5-large predictions: The Milj ?? partiet de Gr ?? nne[NE] Green Party is a political party in Norway.

Reference: The Green Party **Miljøpartiet De Grønne** is a green political party in Norway.

Table 19: NON-ENGLISH error made by all models

(a) **Input**: Table with Title, Highlighted cells and their headers

Page Title: Liberal Democratic Party (Serbia)
Section Title: Parliamentary elections

Year	Popular vote	% of popular vote	# of seats	Seat change	Coalitions
2007	214,262	5.31%	6 / 250	6	With GSS-SDU-LSV-DHSS

(b) **Output**: Predictions with Error Annotations and Reference

M1: BLEU prediction: In the 2007 parliamentary election, the Liberal Democratic Party (Serbia) with GSSS-DULSVDHSS[O] won[W] 5.31% of the vote.

GM3: t5-base and GM4: t5-large predictions: In the 2007 parliamentary elections, the Liberal Democratic Party won[W] 5.31% of the vote.

Reference: The LDP's first electoral performance was during the 2007 Serbian parliamentary election, where the LDP ran in a coalition together with the Civic Alliance of Serbia, the Social Democratic Union and the League of Social Democrats of Vojvodina[R] which collectively received[R] 5.31% of the popular vote.

Table 20: OTHER and WORD errors made by our model; WORD error made by benchmark models

(a) **Input**: Table with Title, Highlighted cells and their headers

Page Title: List of Governors of Guam
Section Title: Elected governors (1971 - present)
Democratic (4) Republican (5)

Governor	Served	Party	Elected	Previous Office	Lieutenant Governor
Joseph F. Ada (1943–)	January 3, 1987 – January 2, 1995	Republican	1986 1990	Lieutenant Governor of Guam	Frank F. Blas

(b) **Output**: Predictions with Error Annotations and Reference

GM3: t5-base and GM4: t5-large predictions: Joseph F. Ada served as Governor of Guam from 1987 to 1995 and as Lieutenant Governor from 1986 to 1990 under Governor Frank F. Blas[C].

Reference: Blas served as the Lieutenant Governor of Guam[R] from 1987 until 1995 for two consecutive terms under Governor Joseph Franklin Ada[R].

Table 21: CONTEXT error made by all models

Complex sample: Joseph F. Ada got elected for two consecutive terms, in 1986 and 1990. Frank F. Blas was Lieutenant Governor during the same period. All the models struggled to predict the factual output. As the Input Table for this complex sample has multiple names, multiple date-dimension fields and does not comply with the First Normal Form (1NF), the predicted outputs are misleading.

(a) **Input**: Table with Title, Highlighted cells and their headers

Page Title: 1998 United States Senate elections
Section Title: Elections leading to the next Congress
Democratic (4) Republican (5)

State	Incumbent			
	Senator	Party	Results	Candidates
Georgia	Paul Coverdel	Republican	Incumbent re-elected.	Paul Coverdell (Republican) 52.3% Michael Coles (Democratic) 45.3% Bertil Armin Loftman (Libertarian) 2.5%

(b) **Output**: Predictions with Error Annotations and Reference

M1: BLEU prediction: Incumbent Republican Paul Coverdell won re-election to a second term[X] in Georgia.

GM3: t5-base prediction: Incumbent Republican Paul Coverdell won re-election to a second term[X] over Democrat Michael Coles.

Reference: In Georgia, Incumbent Republican Senator Paul Coverdell defeated Michael Coles in the 1998 United States Senate elections[R].

Table 22: NOT-CHECKABLE error made by our model and GM3: t5-base model

Improving Dialogue Act Recognition with Augmented Data

Khyati Mahajan[1]*, Soham Parikh[2], Quaizar Vohra[2], Mitul Tiwari[2], and Samira Shaikh[1]

[1]UNC Charlotte
[2]ServiceNow, Inc.
{kmahaja2,samirashaikh}@uncc.edu
{soham.parikh,quaizar.vohra,mitul.tiwari}@servicenow.com

Abstract

We present our work on augmenting dialogue act recognition capabilities utilizing synthetically generated data. Our work is motivated by the limitations of current dialogue act datasets, and the need to adapt for new domains as well as ambiguity in utterances written by humans. We list our observations and findings towards how synthetically generated data can contribute meaningfully towards more robust dialogue act recognition models extending to new domains. Our major finding shows that synthetic data, which is linguistically varied, can be very useful towards this goal and increase the performance from $0.39, 0.16$ to $0.85, 0.88$ for AFFIRM and NEGATE dialogue acts respectively.

1 Introduction

Virtual assistants have been deployed towards helping users perform various tasks, such as setting up a credit card. Behind the scenes, most dialogue systems powering these virtual assistants are built of various components which facilitate Natural Language Understanding (NLU). One such critical component is dialogue state tracking (DST), which helps systems recognize the current state and intent of the user in the conversation. DST often consists of three main sub-components - intent classification, slot filling and dialogue act recognition (DAR). Dialogue acts describe how the dialogue state should be modified from a system perspective, whereas the intents and slots help identify the user's intent in an utterance. These sub-components are usually built separately for industrial applications, since DAR could be generalizable, while intents and slots vary with the intended task or service.

Since DST can be subjective, large-scale industrial applications need to rise to many challenges, including supporting heterogeneous services and APIs. The Schema-Guided Dialogue (SGD) State Tracking task at the Eighth Dialogue System Technology Challenge (DSTC8) (Rastogi et al., 2020) introduced a dataset which could help handle these challenges, towards being able to handle multiple services and APIs while not requiring the collection of new data or retraining models. The SGD dataset includes various dialogue acts as well as intents, one of the first to allow multiple APIs with overlapping functionality in each domain.

Out of the 3 sub-components for DST, we observe that training models separately towards dialogue act recognition allows better internal utilization, since dialogue acts are similar across virtual assistant tasks and customers, whereas intent recognition and slot filling can vary across customers as well as customer specific tasks. Keeping this in mind, we focus our research towards developing robust, generalizable DAR models.

Since SGD is one of the most dialogue act-rich datasets, we explore its applications towards training dialogue act recognition models for confidential internal data. However, during our experiments, we observe that the performance drops significantly (from 0.98 to 0.39 F1 for 'AFFIRM'). Digging deeper, we observe that the form of responses for certain dialogue acts could be improved with adding variations. For example, majority of 'AFFIRM' utterances include or start with the word 'yes'. We conduct more experiments for 'AFFIRM' and 'NEGATE', and present our observations further details in Section 5.

We study the limitations of the dialogue act recognition models trained on SGD and tested on confidential internal data. We focus our study on understanding the performance for AFFIRM and NEGATE, and looking for the existence of similar patterns in existing data which could lead to overfitting. To bolster the generalizability of the model to new domains, we explore and implement data augmentation strategies which help add more variety to the form of the utterances in the dataset.

*Work conducted during an internship at ServiceNow, Inc.

Proceedings of the 2nd Workshop on Natural Language Generation, Evaluation, and Metrics (GEM), pages 471 - 479
December 7, 2022 ©2022 Association for Computational Linguistics

We present all our findings in this paper, focusing mainly on our data augmentation techniques which utilize synthetic text generation methods. Overall, our main contributions thus focus around the following studies:

1. We observe shortcomings of the variation of forms in the utterances within the Schema Guided Dialogue (SGD) dataset.
2. We study the limitations of dialogue act recognition models trained on SGD and their poor generalization on internal data (generated by linguists).
3. We present synthetic data generation techniques employed towards overcoming the aforementioned shortcomings, built with OpenAI's GPT-3 (Brown et al., 2020). We also showcase their effectiveness towards better generalization for new domains with the aforementioned dialogue act models.

2 Related Work

Dialogue state tracking, and consequently dialogue act recognition, are integral components of task-oriented dialogue systems. Recent research often focuses on utilizing neural methods towards approaching these tasks (Balaraman et al., 2021; Jacqmin et al., 2022), and both surveys find that generalizability in dialogue state tracking is understudied. They both also present various strategies towards data augmentation, including but not limited to training on resource-rich domains and applying to unseen domains (similar to SGD), using weak supervision to identify slots, reformulating dialogue state tracking as dialogue summarization to leverage external annotated data, using reinforcement learning towards generating relevant data, and prompting generative models to address unseen domains. Many of the aforementioned methods focus on the intent slot values, and not the dialogue acts. Since our work focuses mainly on dialogue act recognition, we include relevant work towards this task in this section.

2.1 Dialogue Act Recognition

Research in dialogue act modeling and recognition (DAR) has employed both statistical methods such as Bayesian classification (Grau et al., 2004), Conditional Random Fields (CRFs) (Stolcke et al., 2000), Hidden Markov Models (HMMs) (Boyer et al., 2010), and Support Vector Machines (SVMs) (Tavafi et al., 2013). Recent studies utilize neural methods such as LSTMs (Kumar et al., 2018) and structured attention network (Chen et al., 2018) with a CRF classification layer. Since most research utilizes different corpora and dialogue acts, it is difficult to compare performance across literature. However, recent research has moved further into utilizing neural methods, showing their viability of adapting to a wide range of dialogue acts as well as corpora, such as seq2seq models with attention (Colombo et al., 2020; Raheja and Tetreault, 2019).

Most recent research utilizes contextual models towards DAR (Ahmadvand et al., 2019; Saha et al., 2019), moving further towards utilizing neural methods. More recently, Noble and Maraev (2021) experiment with BERT towards DAR, and find that while pre-trained models like BERT perform well, the performance is much better with fine-tuning.

Learning from these studies as well as drawing takeaways from the Dialogue State Tracking Challenge 8 (DSTC 8) (Rastogi et al., 2020), we implement a BERT-based model in our DAR, which is also fine-tuned on the training dataset. We also keep in mind the class imbalances involved since DAR is a multi-class classification task, and describe our experiments and results in Section 5.

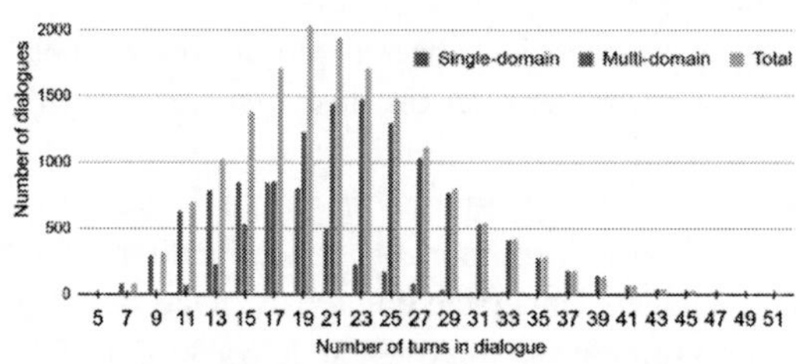

(a) Histogram of lengths of training set dialogues

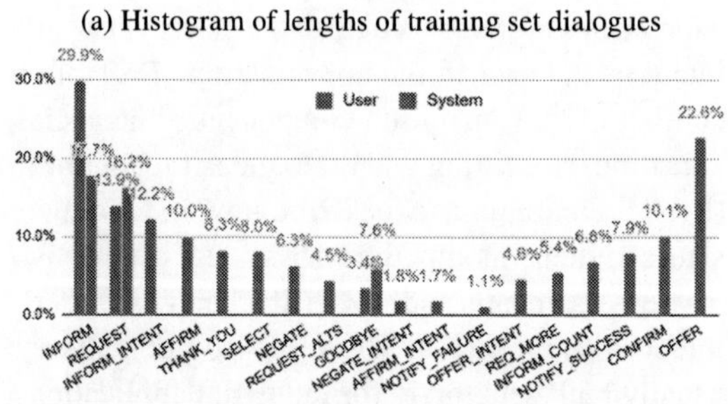

(b) Distribution of dialogue acts in training set

Figure 1: Statistics for SGD (Rastogi et al., 2020)

2.2 Synthetic Data Generation

We utilize synthetic data generation to boost the capabilities of our DAR model. We follow this method since it has been shown in the past to augment the performance of NLP classification in varied applications (Whitfield, 2021; Bartolo et al., 2021; Bonifacio et al., 2022), and since it can also help boost the performance on our private, confidential data towards better DAR. Towards this goal, we look at various strategies for data generation.

Apart from learning from the OpenAI Completions guidelines, we also draw from findings of recent work on synthetic data generation (Reynolds and McDonell, 2021). We choose to work with GPT-3 mainly since it is the current state-of-the-art for off-the-shelf text generation, and we aim to generate synthetic data with varied linguistic forms which GPT3 is highly suitable for. Thus, GPT-3 provides us a method to generate relevant and robust synthetic data without the need to fine-tune a text generation model.

We refer to current literature for further guidelines and useful strategies. There exist various paradigms which intend to help with text generation based on the generations goals, such as utilizing Reinforcement Learning (RL) techniques or Q-learning (Guo et al., 2021), and AutoPrompt (Shin et al., 2020) which uses a gradient-based search. However, these lack the interpretability which applies to our goal, and secondly they require a specified goal towards which to tune the generations. Thus we focus more on manual experimentation which could provide us with clearer takeaways for future, more subjective generations (presented in Section 4.3).

	SGD	Internal data	Test set
# of dialogues	16142	161	296
# of utterances	164982	1980	1629
# of AFFIRM	25054	1375	808
# of NEGATE	16715	605	821

Table 1: Details for each dialogue act in each dataset used for training the dialogue act recognition model. The test set is hand written by linguists.

3 Datasets

This section details the datasets we utilize in our experiments, and provides aggregate details for each without revealing private and protected information for confidential internal data. For the purposes of our research, we focus mainly on a few dialogue acts relevant towards confidential internal applications - namely AFFIRM and NEGATE. Each section describes how we build the utterance and associated dialogue act pairs towards dialogue act recognition. The final statistics for each dataset is presented in Table 1.

3.1 Schema Guided Dialogue (SGD)

The Schema Guided Dialogue (SGD) dataset consists of over 20k annotated multi-domain, task-oriented conversations between a human and a virtual assistant, spanning 20 domains such as banks, events, media, calendar, travel, and weather (Shah et al., 2018; Rastogi et al., 2020). Figure 1a shows the distribution of dialogue lengths across single-domain (average 15.3 turns) and multi-domain dialogues (average 23 turns). Figure 1b shows the frequency of the different dialogue acts contained in the dataset. The dataset also contains a significant number of unseen domains/APIs in the dev and test sets. 77% of the dialogue turns in the test set and 45% of the turns in dev set contain at least one service not present in the training set.

Each utterance in the SGD dataset comes with relevant information including a breakdown of all the dialogue acts and slots present in the utterance. Our model predicts all the dialogue acts associated with each frame. The final statistics for the dataset thus built is presented in Table 1.

3.2 Confidential Internal Data

The confidential internal data we utilize for researching the transferability and generalizability of the SGD dataset follows the same structure as the SGD data. This data reflects the services built on our virtual assistant which are similar to SGD but are specific to our customer domains.

The training set for the internal data is synthetically generated using GPT-3. We used different prompts to generate synthetic data with a large variety of dialogue act patterns. We expect that this variety will help our dialogue act models generalize well to unseen domains and use cases. There is evidence of this as shown by experiments described in 5. Our test set, modeling real user traffic, is created separately and annotated by Subject Matter Expert (SME) linguists. The statistics for this dataset are presented in Table 1.

This dataset has a much greater variety on the dialogue acts we experiment with in this paper compared to SGD. For example, almost all AFFIRMs in the SGD dataset have a 'yes' or a very similar strong affirmative word. In our test set, we have a rich variety of patterns, including explicit affirmatives, implicit affirmatives using context from the

	Prompt Type	Prompt Prefix	Prompt Sub-type	Prompt Affix	Generated Text
Few-shot	Full context	Example 1: Bot: Here are the available rooms near you. Do you want to book selected conference room? User: [PROMPT AFFIX] *[2 more examples]* Example 4: *[conversation context]* Bot: Do you have the account number?	[with context]	Yes, please book the room	yes i do
			[without context]	Yes, please go ahead.	yes
			[only context]	Book selected room.	i have the number.
	Immediate context	Example 1: Question: Here are the available rooms near you. Do you want to book selected conference room? Affirm: [PROMPT AFFIX] *[2 more examples]* Example 4: Question: Do you have the account number?	[with context]	Yes, please book the room	yes
			[without context]	Yes, please go ahead.	yes
			[only context]	Book selected room.	yeah
Zero-shot	Full context	Generate multiple positive responses to the question using only words from the question. *[conversation context]* Bot: [QUESTION] User:	-	-	• Yes I do. • Yes, I have the account number. • Yes, I can give you the account number. • The account number is ___ .
	Immediate context	Generate multiple positive responses to the question using only words from the question. Bot: [QUESTION] User:	-	-	• Yes, I have the account number. • Great, what is the account number? • The account number is ___. • Thank you for providing the account number.

Table 2: Prompt experiments, listing all the types of prompts we used and samples from the text GPT3 generated

conversation with a virtual agent as well as a mix of the two. This is further described in 4.

3.3 Observations

As discussed earlier, we observe that there exist a few shortcomings in the SGD data, mainly related to the variety in the form of utterances in each dialogue act. Out of $15k$ utterances with AFFIRM or AFFIRM_INTENT as the sole dialogue acts, only $4k$ of them are unique. Moreover, over 70% of all AFFIRM utterances contain the word 'yes' or its variations like 'yup', 'yep', 'yeah' or start with 'sure'. Similarly, more than 80% of all NEGATE utterances start with 'no' or 'nope' and out of $2.7k$ utterances in NEGATE or NEGATE_INTENT, only $1.2k$ are unique. We see a similar distribution in test and validation sets as well, leading us to believe that the existence of this predictable pattern is what contributes to the strong performance baselines.

Acting on our findings, we experiment with adding synthetically generated data to our dataset. We choose this augmentation method since it allows us to contribute relevant yet original data, while generating varied forms and structures for each utterance. We first experiment with an SGD-fine-tuned data (Section 5.1, and find that this lack of variety does indeed lead to worse predictions on our rich SME linguist generated test set. We present methods and evaluation techniques used to overcome these shortcomings by generating synthetic data (Section 4).

4 Synthetic Data Generation

We aim to augment our dataset using synthetic data generated by prompting GPT-3, as described in Section 2. We detail our experiments and their results in this section.

4.1 Experiments

We utilize OpenAI's GPT-3 Completions API to generate synthetic data which could be useful towards mitigating the effects of the presence of patterns in the training data. We experiment with different kinds of prompts, following guidelines laid out by OpenAI[1] for text generation (detailed in Table 2).

The main prompt types we experiment with include few-shot and zero-shot. In the few-shot setting, the prompt consists of a few examples (3 to 5 examples) which can help demonstrate the completions we expect. In the zero-shot setting, the prompt includes an instruction along with the question. Additionally, we frame prompts so as to generate different kinds of responses for both AFFIRM and NEGATE. For example, each yes/no question (such as "Would you like to continue?") can be answered by a human in 3 different ways,

[1]https://beta.openai.com/docs/guides/completion

1) with-context (such as "Yes, I would like that"), 2) without-context (such as "Yes please"), and 3) only-context (such as "Please continue").

In addition to various framing, we also experiment with both the *Curie* and *Davinci* engines, although we conclusively find that *Davinci* performs better in initial experiments. Thus, the results included in this paper are all generations using the *Davinci* engine.

We find that some prompts perform better than others for different kinds of expected generations. We discuss our evaluation strategies next, and present our findings and takeaways in Section 4.3.

4.2 Evaluation

We employ multiple strategies for evaluating the generated synthetic data, consisting of both automatic and human evaluation methods. We employ custom automatic evaluation metrics, such as the presence of key words, to ensure that we generate different kinds of variations. For human evaluations, we work with subject matter experts (SMEs), who hand annotate each synthetic generation as good, alright, or bad generations, depending on our generation goal with a specific prompt. Further details for our evaluation strategies is presented in Table 3.

Tables 4 and 5 list the performance of our major experiments. We required fewer experiments for NEGATE since we were able to learn from our takeaways stemming from our experiments with AFFIRM.

For AFFIRM, the few-shot examples are listed in Table 2. With zero-shot prompts, Type 1 consisted of the instruction "Generate multiple positive responses as a human would to the following question asked by a bot:", Type 2 consisted of "Imagine a conversation between a bot and a human. Generate multiple positive responses to the following question asked by the bot:", Type 3 consisted of "Generate multiple positive responses as a human would to the following question asked by a bot:", Type 4 consisted of "Generate multiple affirmative responses as a human would to the following question asked by a bot:", and Type 5 consisted of "Generate multiple responses that agree with the question using only words from the question. Do not use the word "yes".". Evaluations for how well each of the generations perform are shown in Table 3. Few-shot, full context prompts do perform the best, however these require a heavy payload to the API and thus cost more (compared to zero-shot prompts). Thus, we focus more on improving the zero-shot prompts, and find that instructions which include multiple yet simple asks perform best. Further takeaways are discussed in the next section.

For NEGATE, Type 1 consisted of "Generate at least 5 negative responses as a human would to the following question asked by a bot. Do not generate positive responses:", while Type 2 consisted of "Generate at least 5 responses that disagree with the following question asked by a bot. Do not generate positive responses:". As shown, the performance is comparable for both prompts.

Combining the automatic and human evaluation metrics allows us to better gauge the effectiveness of our prompts. The SME linguists also provided us with deeper insights into patterns associated with prompt wording. In general, we find that utilizing both instructions and examples can help generate more relevant data.

4.3 Discussion

We observe that many data points in the SGD dataset consist of utterances which contain a keyword like 'yes' or 'yeah', which can become a pattern that signifies the dialogue act for AFFIRM, and similarly for NEGATE. Therefore, our prompts aim to generate data points which could serve as utterances which have the context of the preceding utterance (generally a REQUEST). Through our experiments, we observe a number of relevant takeaways for generation with GPT-3.

Firstly, we discover that if a REQUEST is posed as a statement and not a question, ie if the REQUEST does not end with a question mark, then the Completions API tends to hallucinate wildly, even if relevant contextual information (such as the preceding conversation) is available. For example, if a prompt asking for a laptop replacement ends with "requesting a loaner", the output first hallucinates and generates completions such as "vehicle of make and model?". We also experiment with removing question marks in a few cases where we observe good synthetic generations, and find that we are able to replicate this problem. Therefore, there is a need to ensure that prompts end with a question mark if the objective is to generate relevant responses.

Secondly, it is always better to show the completions API that a question was spoken by a bot,

Dialogue Act	Automatic	Human
Both	1. Word count 2. Jaccard similarity with REQUEST 3. GUSE similarity with REQUEST 4. All scores averaged	1. Grammaticality & Fluency 2. Follows dialogue constraints (ex, conversation flow) 3. Follows cooperative principle (effective communication)
AFFIRM	Presence of 'yes' and related words	Variety in form and linguistic features
NEGATE	Presence of 'no' and related words	Variety in form and linguistic features

Table 3: Evaluation metrics used for evaluating synthetically generated data

Prompt Type	Generation Type	Good Generations
Few-shot, full context	with-context	7
	without-context	37
	only-context	**75**
Zero-shot	Type 1	48
	Type 2	49
	Type 3	56
	Type 4	58
	Type 5	**67**

Table 4: AFFIRM prompts and performance for a total of 81 data points - bold text shows best performance

Prompt Type	Generation Type	Good Generations
Zero-shot	Type 1	48
	Type 2	47

Table 5: NEGATE prompts and performance for a total of 67 data points

rather than instruct the API to generate completions for questions posed by a bot. This becomes important for our use-case since we are aiming to generate responses that sound like they are coming from a user who is interacting with the bot. Therefore, we want succinct yet easy to understand responses which can be easily understood by a dialogue system, coming from the user's point of view. Thus, it is useful to have prompts such as "Generate responses to the following question. Bot: Would you like me to proceed? User:" as compared to "Generate responses for the following question asked by a bot. Would you like me to proceed?".

Lastly, we observe that using simple, small but multiple instructions works better than using long and complex instructions. For example, the prompt "Generate at least 5 negative response to the following question. Be polite. Do not use `no`" works better than "Generate multiple polite negative responses to the following question without saying `no`".

Overall, our findings echo many of the guidelines suggested by OpenAI while also showcasing that prompt design requires experimentation to fit into specific use-cases. Especially in scenarios where there is a need to report on which prompts worked better and to understand why, as well as a subjective view of which synthetic generations would be the best addition to training data, soft prompting and prompt tuning become difficult to implement. We therefore focus our efforts on understanding the underlying conditions and guidelines under which we are able to generate synthetic data which eventually can boost dialogue act recognition.

5 Dialogue Act Recognition

We show how our synthetically generated data can boost the capabilities of dialogue act recognition models in this section. We detail each step in our experiments as well as our findings.

5.1 Experimental Setup

We utilize the SGD training set, synthetic generations using OpenAI and a fraction of hand-written generations produced by our SME linguists as training data. For the synthetic data, we generate AFFIRM and NEGATE utterances using various prompts which are then filtered by human experts as relevant or not. Unless otherwise mentioned, we only use the relevant synthetic generations for training.

We evaluate the model on both SGD test set and gold standard SME linguist generated test data, specifically written to include several forms of utterances for each dialogue act, making it difficult to achieve perfect performance on them. We report the F1 score computed separately for each dialogue act, averaged across 3 training runs with different random seeds.

For all our experiments, we fine-tune the BERT-small model to predict dialogue acts. We train the model for 4 epochs with a learning rate of $1e$-5 and a batch size of 64. As input to the model, we concatenate the previous and current utterance with a [SEP] token. Predicting dialogue acts is a multi-label task and hence we use a sigmoid activation for the last layer and Binary Cross Entropy as the loss function.

5.2 Adding synthetic data to SGD

Table 6 shows the results from adding synthetic data to the training set. Here we use all of SME dataset for evaluation. `Synthetic-all` consists of all synthetic utterances whereas `Synthetic-Dis` is the subset of synthetic utterances taken from conversations which are disjoint from the ones used in SME dataset (test set). We see a significant increase in the performance upon adding just a few hundred synthetic utterances. The size of synthetic dataset is quite small when compared to the size of the SGD dataset which can inhibit the model from learning from the synthetic generations. Owing to this, we experiment with various sampling factors, where a sampling factor of k means we duplicate the synthetic dataset k times. As an example, an affirming utterance for the request "Do you want to setup okta mfa? I'd like to" gives no prediction when trained only on SGD, whereas SGD + `Synthetic-all` predicts AFFIRM. Similarly, a negating utterance to the same request "I'd like to skip" also gives no prediction for SGD, whereas SGD + `Synthetic-all` predicts NEGATE.

Table 7 shows how performance varies with the sampling factors. The performance increases with sampling factor up to a certain point after which it degrades, indicating that a balance between the SGD dataset and synthetic dataset is essential for good performance. More notably, we see that with adequate oversampling we can bridge the gap in performance between `Synthetic-dis` and `Synthetic-all` for NEGATE and bring F1 score for AFFIRM within 0.03 points.

5.3 Adding linguist data

Next, we check the performance upon adding a small amount of SME data to the training mix to get an idea of the gap between synthetic and human generated data. We use 20% of the SME data for training (`SME-train`) and use the remaining 80% for evaluation (`SME-test`). To have a fair comparison, we compare `SME-train` with `Synthetic-dis` since using `Synthetic-all` would have overlapping conversations with `SME-test`.

	SGD-test		SME	
	AFFIRM	NEGATE	AFFIRM	NEGATE
SGD-train	0.98	0.98	0.39	0.16
SGD-train, Synthetic-dis	0.98	0.98	0.71	0.46
SGD-train, Synthetic-all	0.98	0.98	0.76	0.62

Table 6: F1 scores for the Dialogue Act Recognition models with and without synthetic data

sampling factor	SGD-train, Synthetic-dis		SGD-train, Synthetic-all	
	AFFIRM	NEGATE	AFFIRM	NEGATE
1	0.71	0.46	0.76	0.62
2	0.73	0.51	0.78	0.65
4	0.75	0.53	0.79	0.69
8	0.76	0.58	**0.8**	**0.72**
16	0.76	0.62	0.78	0.71
32	0.77	0.64	0.77	0.69
64	0.77	0.66	0.76	0.71
128	**0.77**	**0.73**	0.77	0.71
256	0.76	0.71	0.75	0.69

Table 7: F1 scores for the Dialogue Act Recognition models with different oversampling factors applied to the synthetic training sets - bold text shows best performance

Table 8 shows that both with and without oversampling, using SME data performs better than synthetic data, especially for NEGATE. However, using both SME and synthetic data performs better than using just SME data, showing the value of augmenting human-generated data with synthetic data.

5.4 Filtered vs unfiltered data

So far we have used AFFIRM and NEGATE generations from various LLM prompts which have been vetted by humans. However, this approach is not scalable and we thus check the value of using synthetic generations without any human intervention.

We select 2 prompts for each AFFIRM and NEGATE which work the best according to human evaluation and take all generations from those prompts across all conversations. This covers more conversations but since we restrict the synthetic data to only 2 prompts per dialogue act, we end up with $1k$ (only 2 prompts each for AFFIRM and NEGATE) utterances as opposed to $1.9k$ (human annotated data from all prompts) earlier.

We report the results from the best oversam-

sampling factor	SGD-train, Synthetic-dis		SGD-train, SME-train		SGD-train, Synthetic-dis, SME-train	
	AFFIRM	NEGATE	AFFIRM	NEGATE	AFFIRM	NEGATE
1	0.73	0.54	0.69	0.78	0.86	0.84
2	0.75	0.58	0.77	0.83	0.88	0.88
4	0.77	0.58	0.81	0.86	0.88	0.87
8	0.78	0.62	**0.83**	**0.87**	**0.88**	**0.89**
16	0.79	0.67	0.80	0.86	0.86	0.86
32	0.79	0.66	0.80	0.83	0.88	0.87
64	0.79	0.68	0.80	0.84	0.85	0.84
128	**0.79**	**0.74**	0.77	0.80	0.83	0.84
256	0.79	0.72	0.75	0.79	0.83	0.83

Table 8: F1 scores for the Dialogue Act Recognition models with synthetic and SME data - bold text shows best performance

pling factor using filtered and noisy synthetic data in Table 9. With the disjoint synthetic dataset, noisy utterances give the same performance as filtered utterances. Using noisy utterances from just 2 good prompts we get significantly better performance than using filtered utterances across all prompts. This shows the importance of choosing good prompts for data generation. With careful prompt selection, LLMs can generate high quality data without the need for human intervention.

	sampling factor	AFFIRM	NEGATE
SGD-train, Synthetic-dis	256	0.77	0.73
SGD-train, Synthetic-dis-noisy	128	0.79	0.7
SGD-train, Synthetic-all	16	0.8	0.72
SGD-train, Synthetic-all-noisy	16	0.85	0.88

Table 9: F1 scores for the Dialogue Act Recognition models with filtered and unfiltered synthetic data. `Synthetic-dis`, `Synthetic-all` denote the filtered versions and `Synthetic-dis-noisy`, `Synthetic-all-noisy` denote the unfiltered versions

6 Conclusion

We present shortcomings of existing datasets utilized towards Dialogue Act Recognition, such as the Schema-Guided Dialogue (SGD) datasets and propose using LLMs to generate data for overcoming the issues. We find that data generated synthetically helps with generalization to new domains without the need for human labeling. Moreover, in presence of labeled domain data, the synthetically generated data complements the variety of forms and linguistic properties present in training data and improves performance for Dialogue Act Recognition.

We utilize OpenAI's GPT-3 Completions API to generate the synthetic data, and find some interesting general takeaways for †ext generation. We present our findings in detail in Section 4.3. Mainly, we find that 1) questions should end in a question mark; 2) instead of saying a question was posed by a bot, it is better to append "Bot:" to the beginning of an utterance; and 3) multiple, simple instructions work better than a single, long instruction.

We find that even a small number of synthetic generations which are more varied in forms lead to better generalizability and performance for dialogue act recognition. We detail the findings in Section 5. We find that adding synthetic data is helpful, especially once we are able to class balance with oversampling. Synthetic data also complements human generated well, and used together help with making a model more robust - we find that using a few good prompts for generation without filtering can perform as well as (or even better than) using multiple prompts with human filtering.

References

Ali Ahmadvand, Jason Ingyu Choi, and Eugene Agichtein. 2019. Contextual dialogue act classification for open-domain conversational agents. In *Proceedings of the 42nd international acm sigir conference on research and development in information retrieval*, pages 1273–1276.

Vevake Balaraman, Seyedmostafa Sheikhalishahi, and Bernardo Magnini. 2021. Recent neural methods on dialogue state tracking for task-oriented dialogue systems: A survey. In *Proceedings of the 22nd Annual Meeting of the Special Interest Group on Discourse and Dialogue*, pages 239–251.

Max Bartolo, Tristan Thrush, Robin Jia, Sebastian Riedel, Pontus Stenetorp, and Douwe Kiela. 2021.

Improving question answering model robustness with synthetic adversarial data generation. In *Proceedings of the 2021 Conference on Empirical Methods in Natural Language Processing*, pages 8830–8848.

Luiz Bonifacio, Hugo Abonizio, Marzieh Fadaee, and Rodrigo Nogueira. 2022. Inpars: Data augmentation for information retrieval using large language models. *arXiv preprint arXiv:2202.05144*.

Kristy Boyer, Eun Young Ha, Robert Phillips, Michael Wallis, Mladen Vouk, and James Lester. 2010. Dialogue act modeling in a complex task-oriented domain. In *Proceedings of the SIGDIAL 2010 Conference*, pages 297–305.

Tom Brown, Benjamin Mann, Nick Ryder, Melanie Subbiah, Jared D Kaplan, Prafulla Dhariwal, Arvind Neelakantan, Pranav Shyam, Girish Sastry, Amanda Askell, et al. 2020. Language models are few-shot learners. *Advances in neural information processing systems*, 33:1877–1901.

Zheqian Chen, Rongqin Yang, Zhou Zhao, Deng Cai, and Xiaofei He. 2018. Dialogue act recognition via crf-attentive structured network. In *The 41st international acm sigir conference on research & development in information retrieval*, pages 225–234.

Pierre Colombo, Emile Chapuis, Matteo Manica, Emmanuel Vignon, Giovanna Varni, and Chloe Clavel. 2020. Guiding attention in sequence-to-sequence models for dialogue act prediction. In *Proceedings of the AAAI Conference on Artificial Intelligence*, volume 34, pages 7594–7601.

Sergio Grau, Emilio Sanchis, Maria Jose Castro, and David Vilar. 2004. Dialogue act classification using a bayesian approach. In *9th Conference Speech and Computer*.

Han Guo, Bowen Tan, Zhengzhong Liu, Eric P Xing, and Zhiting Hu. 2021. Text generation with efficient (soft) q-learning. *arXiv preprint arXiv:2106.07704*.

Léo Jacqmin, Lina M Rojas-Barahona, and Benoit Favre. 2022. " do you follow me?": A survey of recent approaches in dialogue state tracking. *arXiv preprint arXiv:2207.14627*.

Harshit Kumar, Arvind Agarwal, Riddhiman Dasgupta, and Sachindra Joshi. 2018. Dialogue act sequence labeling using hierarchical encoder with crf. In *Proceedings of the aaai conference on artificial intelligence*, volume 32.

Bill Noble and Vladislav Maraev. 2021. Large-scale text pre-training helps with dialogue act recognition, but not without fine-tuning. In *Proceedings of the 14th International Conference on Computational Semantics (IWCS)*, pages 166–172.

Vipul Raheja and Joel Tetreault. 2019. Dialogue act classification with context-aware self-attention. In *Proceedings of the 2019 Conference of the North American Chapter of the Association for Computational Linguistics: Human Language Technologies, Volume 1 (Long and Short Papers)*, pages 3727–3733.

Abhinav Rastogi, Xiaoxue Zang, Srinivas Sunkara, Raghav Gupta, and Pranav Khaitan. 2020. Schema-guided dialogue state tracking task at dstc8. *arXiv preprint arXiv:2002.01359*.

Laria Reynolds and Kyle McDonell. 2021. Prompt programming for large language models: Beyond the few-shot paradigm. In *Extended Abstracts of the 2021 CHI Conference on Human Factors in Computing Systems*, pages 1–7.

Tulika Saha, Saurabh Srivastava, Mauajama Firdaus, Sriparna Saha, Asif Ekbal, and Pushpak Bhattacharyya. 2019. Exploring machine learning and deep learning frameworks for task-oriented dialogue act classification. In *2019 International Joint Conference on Neural Networks (IJCNN)*, pages 1–8. IEEE.

Pararth Shah, Dilek Hakkani-Tür, Gokhan Tür, Abhinav Rastogi, Ankur Bapna, Neha Nayak, and Larry Heck. 2018. Building a conversational agent overnight with dialogue self-play. *arXiv preprint arXiv:1801.04871*.

Taylor Shin, Yasaman Razeghi, Robert L Logan IV, Eric Wallace, and Sameer Singh. 2020. Autoprompt: Eliciting knowledge from language models with automatically generated prompts. In *Proceedings of the 2020 Conference on Empirical Methods in Natural Language Processing (EMNLP)*, pages 4222–4235.

Andreas Stolcke, Klaus Ries, Noah Coccaro, Elizabeth Shriberg, Rebecca Bates, Daniel Jurafsky, Paul Taylor, Rachel Martin, Carol Van Ess-Dykema, and Marie Meteer. 2000. Dialogue act modeling for automatic tagging and recognition of conversational speech. *Computational linguistics*, 26(3):339–373.

Maryam Tavafi, Yashar Mehdad, Shafiq Joty, Giuseppe Carenini, and Raymond Ng. 2013. Dialogue act recognition in synchronous and asynchronous conversations. In *Proceedings of the SIGDIAL 2013 Conference*, pages 117–121.

Dewayne Whitfield. 2021. Using gpt-2 to create synthetic data to improve the prediction performance of nlp machine learning classification models. *arXiv preprint arXiv:2104.10658*.

On Decoding and Discourse Structure in Multi-Modal Text Generation

Nikolai Ilinykh **Simon Dobnik**
Centre for Linguistic Theory and Studies in Probability (CLASP)
Department of Philosophy, Linguistics and Theory of Science (FLoV)
University of Gothenburg, Sweden
{nikolai.ilinykh,simon.dobnik}@gu.se

Abstract

This paper describes insights into how different inference algorithms structure discourse in image paragraphs. We train a multi-modal transformer and compare 11 variations of decoding algorithms. We propose to evaluate image paragraphs not only with standard automatic metrics, but also with a more extensive, "under the hood" analysis of the discourse formed by sentences. Our results show that while decoding algorithms can be unfaithful to the reference texts, they still generate grounded descriptions, but they also lack understanding of the discourse structure and differ from humans in terms of attentional structure over images.

1 Introduction

What are the properties of the well-generated text? This question has been in the centre of many debates in the natural language generation community (Dale and White, 2007; Gatt and Krahmer, 2018). While human evaluation has always been the gold standard in the quality assessment of generated texts, the field is often reluctant to run such evaluation due to the lack of standardisation in evaluation reports and generally high cost (Howcroft et al., 2020). Therefore, a number of simpler and cheaper *automatic metrics* were introduced, specifically in the field of machine translation, although their validity has been questioned (Reiter and Belz, 2009).

As computer vision and NLP started to merge, automatic metrics became an important part of the evaluation process of image descriptions. In general, image descriptions are evaluated with means of BLEU (Papineni et al., 2002), METEOR (Lavie and Agarwal, 2007), ROUGE (Lin, 2004), CIDEr (Vedantam et al., 2015) and WMD (Kusner et al., 2015). However, Kulkarni et al. (2011) and Elliott and Keller (2014) have demonstrated that such metrics only weakly correlate with human judgements in the context of image description generation task. The discrepancy between human and automatic evaluation is deeply rooted in the differences between the fields of machine translation which originally introduced aforementioned metrics and image captioning, which adopted them. In principle, text-only evaluation is highly constrained: the key requirement for high-quality translation is the perseverance of semantics between two parallel texts. In comparison, evaluation of texts generated in multi-modal tasks is influenced by many factors as the generated texts might mention a different set of objects, attributes and relations which are not described in reference texts. Such generations would cause low values from reference-based metrics, although they could be completely plausible and truthful to the image. As such, the tasks of machine translation and image captioning are inherently dissimilar in terms of evaluation. To mitigate this problem, metrics that directly compare texts against image objects have been proposed (Jiang et al., 2019; Madhyastha et al., 2019; Wang et al., 2021; Hessel et al., 2021). They are typically better than BLEU in that they assign a more accurate score to image-correct descriptions. A relatively recent trend has been to develop a set of metrics that would evaluate goal-oriented captions, produced with specific communicative intent (Inan et al., 2021) or for a specific group of users (Fisch et al., 2020), for example, if an image of a snowdrop is described as "the spring flower".

A notable feature of the aforementioned metrics is their sole focus on evaluation of image captions. Different from captions, **multi-sentence** image descriptions impose additional challenges for generation systems including understanding of the textual *discourse* in the multi-modal context. Analysis of discourse has been in the focus of both text-only (Poesio et al., 2004; Poesio, 2004) and language-and-vision tasks (Takmaz et al., 2020; Dobnik et al., 2022). However, given a huge interest in generation of longer image descriptions, e.g. image paragraphs (Kong et al., 2014; Krause

Proceedings of the 2nd Workshop on Natural Language Generation, Evaluation, and Metrics (GEM), pages 480 - 493
December 7, 2022

et al., 2017; Ilinykh and Dobnik, 2020), recipes (Nishimura et al., 2019) and stories (Huang et al., 2016), we believe it is important to gain a deeper insight into how humans and models *structure* and *realise* discourse in such descriptions. In this paper, we understand discourse as a match between linearisation of the semantic knowledge (e.g., a fit of non-linear concepts into linguistic linear order) and underlying planning (Reiter and Dale, 1997). We build on previous intuitions about evaluation in NLG and look under the hood of how different decoding algorithms build discourse in image paragraphs. We compare a number of decoding strategies for correspondence with how humans distribute and describe objects in longer texts. The main purpose of this study is to gain insights into whether decoding strategies generate texts *similar* to humans and whether these texts exhibit the corresponding discourse structure. There is a limitation on what and how things can be communicated and decoding algorithms have a direct control over it. The choice of decoding algorithm also has an effect on how information is expressed in the communicative channel (Shannon, 1948) and how successful its reconstruction by the perceiver will be (Lazaridou et al., 2017). Our results shed more light on the differences between decoding algorithms in terms of (i) the discourse structure, (ii) faithfulness to the reference texts, (ii) groundedness into the image and (iv) attentional structure.

2 On the importance of decoding

It is impossible to neglect the impact of the choice of the decoding on the structure of the generated texts[1]. Discourse in multi-modal descriptions can be affected by many factors, including scene structure (Linde and Goguen, 1980), the desire to have more accurate or more diverse texts (Massarelli et al., 2020; Zhang et al., 2021) and aspects of the task (Kiddon et al., 2016; Narayan et al., 2022). Other constraints include adherence to a specific topic as in poetry generation by controlling for content and form (Hopkins and Kiela, 2017) and incorporating pragmatic reasoning when describing images with text (Cohn-Gordon et al., 2018; Vedantam et al., 2017) or optimising model's predictions for a specific metric (Rennie et al., 2017; Gu et al., 2017; Zarrieß and Schlangen, 2018) in the spirit of reinforcement learning. Notably, Balakrishnan et al. (2019) have shown that using tree-structured semantic representations, similar to those used in traditional rule-based NLG systems, helps to evaluate generated texts during decoding for the specific discourse. In this work, we describe analysis on *what* and *when* different algorithms generate, comparing their outputs with the human gold standard.

3 Task and model

As our modelling task, we choose the task of image paragraph generation and the Tell-me-more corpus described in (Ilinykh et al., 2019). In this task, a human is given an image and five (5) text fields. The describer writes sentences about the image so that they help a potential listener to identify it within a set. The describer is also asked to write sentences in a sequence, keeping in mind that after each sentence the listener needs more information to identify the image, e.g. thus, tell-me-more. Ilinykh et al. (2019) show that collected multi-sentence descriptions have a fixed intentional structure, in the sense of Grosz et al. (1995), but attention structure demonstrates a different behaviour as supported by the analysis in (Dobnik et al., 2022).

As our model, we use the architecture of the object relation transformer proposed by Herdade et al. (2019)[2]. This is a two-stream multi-modal transformer, which consists of three self-attention blocks, operating on the image, text and across modalities. Each block has the standard parts of the transformer (Vaswani et al., 2017): multi-head self-attention followed by a feed-forward network, residual connection and layer normalisation.

On the vision side, the model takes the set of pre-extracted visual features of detected objects, which we receive by using the object detector released by Anderson et al. (2018)[3] and pre-trained on Visual Genome (Krishna et al., 2016). Specifically, every object o_j in the the set of detected image objects $\mathbf{O} = (o_1, \ldots, o_{|\mathbf{O}|})$ has a visual feature $v_n \in \mathbb{R}^{1 \times D}$, where $|\mathbf{O}| = 36$ and $D = 2048$. In addition, we store other outputs of the object detector, including object labels, attributes and confidence scores. They will be used in later stages to link paragraphs with objects in the image. The benefit of the object relation transformer is its ability to encode complex geometric relations between bounding boxes. Thus, we also extract the set of

[1]For a broader overview of the factors that influence inference in generation we refer the reader to Zarrieß et al. (2021).

[2]`https://github.com/yahoo/object_relation_transformer`

[3]`https://github.com/peteanderson80/bottom-up-attention`

geometric features $\mathbf{G} = \{x, y, w, h\}$, which are fused with visual features inside the model[4].

On the textual side, the model generates a paragraph word by word in auto-regressive fashion. Specifically, it takes the current token w_j and constructs its representation based on previously generated tokens $\mathrm{w}_1, \ldots, \mathrm{w}_{j-1}$. All the future tokens in the paragraph $\mathrm{w}_{j+1}, \ldots, \mathrm{w}_{|\mathbf{W}|}$ are replaced with the MASK token, framing the task as the classic next word prediction task. The generation starts with the START token and ends when either the maximum length of the paragraph $\mathcal{L}$ is reached or when the END token is generated. As the last step, representation from two self-attention blocks are processed by the cross-attention which outputs the probability of all tokens from the vocabulary $\mathcal{V}$.

In terms of model's parameters, we keep all of them untouched, thus they correspond to the original set of parameters described in Herdade et al. (2019). We train the model on the full Tell-me-more dataset, consisting of 3590 image-paragraph pairs in the train set and 410 pairs in both validation and test sets. The analysis in this paper is performed on the test set only.

4 Decoding algorithms

Given the model vocabulary $\mathcal{V}$ and $\mathcal{L}$ as the maximum length of the generated sequence, the space of possible sequences has $|\mathcal{V}|^{\mathcal{L}}$ members, thus, becoming intractable. Rather than traversing through such space, a number of different decoding methods are used to find the most likely sequence. The most straightforward heuristics is to take the most probable word w at timestamp j until either the maximum length of the generated sequence $\mathbf{w}$ is reached ($\mathcal{L} = 100$) or the END token is generated. We employ standard **greedy search**:

$$w_j = \underset{w'_j}{\operatorname{argmax}} \log p(w'_j \mid \mathbf{w}_{<j}, \mathbf{O}; \theta), \qquad (1)$$

where $\mathbf{w}_{<j} = (\mathrm{w}_1, \ldots, \mathrm{w}_{j-1})$ is the sequence of previously predicted words, $\mathbf{O} = (o_1, \ldots, o_{|\mathbf{O}|})$ is the set of detected image objects and θ is the set of model parameters. Despite its simplicity and low complexity, greedy search is known for its sub-optimality on the global sentence level (Gu et al., 2017; Chen et al., 2018), often leading to generation problems such as the garden path sentence issue (Gibson, 1991).

[4]We refer the reader to (Herdade et al., 2019) for more details.

A more popular and standardized approach is to use **beam search**, a version of the breadth-first search, that tracks multiple candidate sequences $\mathbf{W} = (\mathbf{w}_1, \ldots, \mathbf{w}_k)$ and chooses the one with the highest cumulative probability score, frequently computed as summation of word scores in each sequence. Typically, the most probable sequence is picked as the final one, but other sequences can also be considered. The search starts with the word sequence $\mathbf{w}_1 = \{\text{START}\}$ and continues until the length of every predicted sequence reaches the maximum length $\mathcal{L}$ or all of them are completed with the END token:

$$\mathbf{w}_j = \underset{\substack{\mathbf{w}'_j \subseteq \mathcal{B}_j, \\ |\mathbf{w}'_j| = k}}{\operatorname{argmax}} \log p(\mathbf{w}'_j \mid \mathbf{w}_{j-1}, \mathbf{O}; \theta). \qquad (2)$$

In beam search, the parameter k denotes the number of desired sequence candidates and $\mathcal{B}$ stands for the set of sequences currently under generation. Beam search is computationally more expensive, but it is also more efficient in finding the optimal sequence due to more sophisticated exploration of the word space. However, bigger k often leads to "safe" and generic texts and candidate generations themselves can resemble each other a lot, lacking diversity (Li et al., 2016) or becoming repetitive (Holtzman et al., 2020).

The problems of beam search have been addressed by many different approaches, mostly focused on increasing intra-set diversity of generated sequences (Kulikov et al., 2019; Meister et al., 2021). In one of such approaches, Vijayakumar et al. (2018) propose to extend beam search by incorporating a *dissimilarity* term in the objective function. Specifically, **diverse beam search** splits beam sets into G groups $W^1, \ldots, W^G$ and at each word generation timestamp j for every sequence in the current group $\mathbf{w}_j^g \in W^g$, it encourages diversity with sequences from previous groups $W^{h, h \leq g}$ using a metric of dissimilarity Δ:

$$W_j^g = \operatorname{argmax} \sum_{k \in [B']} \log p(\mathbf{w}^g_{k,[j]}) + \lambda \sum_{h=1}^{g-1} \Delta(\mathbf{w}^g_{k,[j]}, W^h_{[j]}), \qquad (3)$$

where B' is the number of beams in each group, λ is the parameter that controls the diversity, Δ is the Hamming distance, which negatively penalises sequences sharing identical n-grams. Diverse beam search has been specifically designed to boost diversity in the multi-modal description generation task, where focus is to mimic human texts with shifts between many objects, relations and specific details. However, as reported by the authors, the best results in terms of diversity are achieved by using a simple n-gram-based heuristics, which does not take the multi-modal nature of the task into account. In addition, diversity is encouraged between beam sets on the group level rather than between sentences within a single group, limiting the scope of diversity on the sentence level. Finally, the look-up over groups is constrained to the current word position at each generation step, shrinking the context window for the currently generated word and possibly capping the number of satisfactory generations at this timestamp.

A very different method to encourage more diverse output is to sample from the word distribution. For obvious reasons pure sampling leads to incoherent and grammatically incorrect texts. Therefore, **top-*k* sampling** has been proposed by Fan et al. (2018): the method cuts the probability distribution and keeps the distribution p' consisting of top k tokens with the highest probability:

$$w_j \sim \log p'(w_j \mid \mathbf{w}_{<j}, \mathbf{O}; \theta). \tag{4}$$

A known issues with the top-k sampling algorithm is that it is hard to find the optimal value for the parameter k since setting it too low could remove highly probable words or, on the contrary, keep the less probable words if it is too high.

Instead of relying on pre-defined number of tokens, **nucleus sampling** (Holtzman et al., 2020) takes words from the subset of the vocabulary in which the defined probability mass is concentrated:

$$p' = \sum_{w_j \in \mathcal{V}'} \log p(w_j \mid \mathbf{w}_{<j}, \mathbf{O}; \theta) \geq p, \tag{5}$$

where $\mathcal{V}'$ is the top-p part of the vocabulary $\mathcal{V}$, in which only the words that accumulate most of the probability mass are kept. Parameter p is typically used to define the maximum value of accumulated probability. The original distribution is then re-scaled and the next word is sampled from the new distribution P:

$$P = \begin{cases} \log p(w_j \mid \mathbf{w}_{<j}, \mathbf{O}; \theta)/p' & \text{if } w_j \in \mathcal{V}' \\ 0 & \text{otherwise.} \end{cases} \tag{6}$$

The main advantage of nucleus sampling is its ability to track the shape of the probability distribution, allowing for dynamic control of the number of candidates at each timestamp. A different, but related method to introduce controlled randomness is to use **temperature scaling**. The diversity is achieved by controlling the peaks in the distribution and dividing it by the parameter τ:

$$p(w_j \mid \mathbf{w}_{<j}, \mathbf{O}; \theta) = \frac{\exp(\varphi_j/\tau)}{\sum\limits_{w_j \in \mathcal{V}} \exp(\varphi_j/\tau)}, \tag{7}$$

where φ_j is the logit for a word w_j in the vocabulary. Lower temperatures are known to enforce the high probability events and choosing a proper value for this parameter can lead to better texts in terms of quality and diversity (Caccia et al., 2020).

We note that in this work we mainly focus on the most frequently used decoding strategies, excluding analysis of the result of more direct manipulations with texts such as length normalisation and coverage penalty (Wu et al., 2016), n-gram blocking or introduction of the noise model (Hill et al., 2016; Lample et al., 2018).

For our experiments with decoding algorithms, we set the following set of parameters. We set the beam size $k = 2$. Vijayakumar et al. (2018) argue that setting setting $G = k$ leads to the best results in terms of generation with diverse beam algorithm, therefore, we set $G = k = 2$ and λ equals 0.5. For top-k sampling, we try multiple values for k, aiming to investigate the impact of this parameter on generation. Specifically, we generate texts with k being the value from the following set: $\{25, 50, 75, 100\}$. For nucleus sampling, we set p to one of the following values: $\{25, 50, 95\}$. We also run pure sampling with $k = 100$ and temperature scaling with $\tau = 0.5$. Our parameters for different inference algorithms are chosen based on experiences from the corresponding research that introduces these algorithms. They also reflect our goal of evaluating how results generated by different searches can be affected by a single hyperparameter.

5 Linking

In the context of the image paragraph generation task, discourse structure in texts is affected by both

Metric	g	b2	s25	s50	s75	s100	st50	n25	n50	n95	db2
BLEU-1	**37.16**	30.79	33.82	34.57	33.84	33.91	36.48	34.11	34.36	33.61	*37.08*
BLEU-2	**23.90**	19.86	18.54	19.20	18.54	18.29	22.20	18.70	19.07	18.46	*23.85*
BLEU-3	**15.53**	13.13	10.07	10.77	10.09	9.99	13.67	10.30	10.67	10.25	*15.51*
BLEU-4	**9.54**	8.02	4.81	5.40	4.95	5.00	7.89	5.29	5.62	5.15	*9.52*
METEOR	**14.22**	12.97	12.53	12.79	12.53	12.46	14.00	12.67	12.80	12.58	*14.20*
ROUGE-L	*30.64*	**30.71**	23.86	23.77	23.56	23.29	28.48	23.15	23.75	23.79	30.55
CIDEr	*16.62*	12.30	10.48	11.30	9.78	9.54	16.51	10.54	10.76	10.56	**16.80**
WMD	39.80	39.10	38.40	38.41	38.17	38.06	**40.26**	38.28	38.34	38.33	*39.84*

Table 1: Scores of automatic metrics for different inference algorithms. The best scores per metric are in **bold**, while second best scores are in *italics*. The notation for searches should be read as follows throughout the paper: "g" - greedy, "b2" - beam search with the width $k = 2$, "s*k*" - sampling, where *k* is the top tokens from which the prediction is sampled, "st50" - sampling from the full probability distribution with temperature scaling $\tau = 0.5$, "n*p*" - nucleus sampling with *p* denoting the part of the vocabulary with the most probability mass, "db2" - diverse beam search with the width $k = 2$.

text and image. To evaluate such structure, we require a mapping between object descriptions and objects in the image. While images in the Tell-me-more corpus were originally annotated with objects as part of the ADE20k corpus of house environments (Zhou et al., 2017), the descriptions were collected separately, hence, there are no annotations between texts and images. We decided to map noun phrases and image objects automatically, using *linking*, which is based on similarity between object labels and noun phrases in texts[5].

Primarily, linking is performed by taking both attribute and object label from the object detector and merging them into a single string, e.g. "white couch". Next, spaCy (Honnibal et al., 2020) is used to extract noun phrases from image paragraphs, and we seek to connect each noun phrase with one of the objects in the image $o_n \in \mathbf{O}$ by embedding them both with a Sentence Transformer (Reimers and Gurevych, 2019) and comparing them based on the cosine similarity with the threshold of 0.5[6]. If there are multiple similarity values that exceed these threshold for a single noun phrase, we map this phrase with the object that has the highest similarity value. Otherwise, if the noun phrase is in plural form, we map multiple objects that also share the same lemma. We perform linking for both reference texts and texts generated by each of the decoding algorithms.

6 Automatic evaluation

Table 1 shows scores for the most common metrics in multi-modal automatic evaluation. As we can see, greedy search and diverse beam perform the best. The worst performance is demonstrated by a variety of sampling algorithms and, somewhat surprisingly, nucleus sampling. Beam performs relatively well, achieving the highest score in ROUGE-L. When looking at the example generations in Table 2, we see that beam search generates very short sentences with fewer mentions of different objects, which definitely has an effect on the performance with n-gram-based metrics. Top-*k* sampling generally performs worse when the sampling size is increasing: CIDEr score drops to 9.54 with sampling from the full distribution. Interestingly, setting *k* to 50 improves the performance, indicating that this value might be the optimal one for this parameter. Nucleus sampling has a very stable performance with n50 showing the best scores. We note that temperature scaling has a huge positive impact on the scores of sampling algorithm, pushing it towards the performance of greedy and diverse beam search. This might indicate that sampling and its randomness can be successfully controlled with the proper value for temperature.

The reason for a high performance of greedy search could be its ability to generate the "safest" words combined with the simplicity of the images and the lack of surprisal in them. For example, images in the dataset correspond to standard room types and thus contain standard objects. This is a blessing if we care about model's ability to generalise over the house environments, but also a curse since occasionally a highly salient and surprising object might appear in the images and searches will not be able to describe it. We believe that our results show the inadequacy of automatic metrics in measuring the sensitivity of inference algorithms

[5]We use the linking from Dobnik et al. (2022).

[6]Different methods of linking noun phrases and object labels have been evaluated in Ilinykh and Dobnik (2022).

ref	there is a very large well made bed on the left. this looks like a hotel room. two lamps are on a table on the right side. a window that you can barely see out of can be seen if you look straight ahead. there is a picture on the wall to the left and another on the right side wall.
g	this is a living room with a white couch and love seat. there is a white couch with a white and white pillow. there is a coffee table in front of the couch. there is a glass coffee table in the middle of the room. there is a picture hanging on the wall.
b2	this is a living room. there is a white couch. there is a white couch. there is a white coffee table. there is a couch.
s25	this is a tv in UNK. the couches match the couches and bedspread is white. there are two green UNK and there is a sofa table with pillows. there are two different decorative beige feet couch.
s50	a large room with a sofa for a coffee table. a four drawer rectangular coffee table sits full of glass roses loveseat. a fireplace is on the left hand wall. a large telephone is near the couch. there are two brown chairs sitting at the far end of the couch.
s75	its a formal living room. a glass sofa and ottoman. a glass table is behind the couch. the tv is behind the sofa. a patterned sofa is on the right side of the one sofa.
s100	living room with a black couch with white print pillows underneath. coffee table piece of 2 candles hang on the back wall. green coffe coffee table lobby is sitting in the middle of the couch by chair and books. decorative and an condition painted on the floor in color. light brown seat at the back end of the room.
st50	this is a living room. the couches are white. there is a white couch. there is a coffee table. there is a white couch.
n25	this room is very neat and space. the couches have orange felt UNK around the mantel. on the right side of the picture contains red flowers. theres a picture on the wall facing the sofa. theres a sofa on the wall.
n50	its a living room with a grey couch and upholstered sofa. theres a tv on the right side next to the couch. two dining chairs UNK facing the couch. theres a coffee table in front of the couch and chair. theres a glass coffee table cloth and robe hanging in the middle.
n95	there is a stone seat in the photo. the sofa is white with UNK upholstery. a beige chair and orange chair chair a round coffee table but its not sailboat. the couches fabric cover match the white accent pillows with a picture on the wall alongside them as the black chair and tan carpet.
db2	this is a living room with a white couch and love seat. there is a white couch with a white and white pillow. there is a coffee table in front of the couch. there is a glass coffee table in the middle of the room. there is a picture hanging on the wall.

Table 2: Example of the image and paragraphs generated with different inference algorithms.

		g			**b2**			**s50**			**st50**			**n50**			**db2**		
		P	*S*	*K*	*P*	*S*	*K*	*P*	*S*	*K*	*P*	*S*	*K*	*P*	*S*	*K*	*P*	*S*	*K*
R	BLEU_1	0.23	0.18	0.13	0.3	0.28	0.22	-0.01	-0.06	-0.03	-0.06	-0.03	-0.02	0.25	0.21	0.15	0.27	0.19	0.15
	BLEU_2	0.21	0.17	0.12	0.34	0.28	0.2	-0.04	-0.16	-0.1	-0.13	-0.15	-0.11	0.14	0.1	0.06	0.3	0.19	0.14
	BLEU_3	0.14	0.16	0.1	0.29	0.22	0.17	-0.05	-0.12	-0.07	-0.15	-0.2	-0.14	0.11	0.1	0.07	0.27	0.21	0.16
	BLEU_4	0.01	0.1	0.07	0.26	0.24	0.18	0.04	-0.1	-0.04	-0.12	-0.16	-0.12	0.19	0.11	0.08	0.2	0.22	0.16
	METEOR	-0.21	-0.18	-0.13	0.14	0.12	0.09	-0.21	-0.22	-0.16	-0.22	-0.32	-0.22	-0.05	-0.09	-0.06	-0.26	-0.24	-0.19
	ROUGE_L	0.18	0.15	0.11	0.22	0.23	0.16	0.06	0.02	0.02	-0.19	-0.22	-0.15	0.19	0.16	0.11	0.28	0.21	0.15
	CIDEr	0.02	0.15	0.1	0.33	0.17	0.12	-0.06	-0.17	-0.1	-0.15	-0.18	-0.11	0.23	0.23	0.17	0.16	0.19	0.14
	WMD	-0.0	0.0	-0.0	0.2	0.16	0.1	-0.14	-0.09	-0.06	-0.12	-0.14	-0.1	-0.09	-0.09	-0.06	-0.14	-0.12	-0.09
C	BLEU_1	0.14	0.13	0.09	0.11	0.12	0.09	0.02	0.01	0.0	0.06	0.11	0.07	0.22	0.19	0.13	0.19	0.18	0.12
	BLEU_2	0.12	0.08	0.06	0.15	0.15	0.12	-0.05	-0.12	-0.09	0.09	0.13	0.09	0.13	0.1	0.06	0.21	0.18	0.12
	BLEU_3	0.02	0.05	0.03	0.09	0.11	0.08	-0.09	-0.12	-0.09	0.11	0.13	0.08	0.12	0.1	0.06	0.18	0.18	0.13
	BLEU_4	-0.12	-0.02	-0.03	0.02	0.09	0.06	-0.0	-0.13	-0.1	0.1	0.14	0.09	0.22	0.15	0.11	0.17	0.22	0.16
	METEOR	-0.15	-0.13	-0.08	0.09	0.08	0.06	-0.19	-0.17	-0.13	-0.09	-0.1	-0.07	-0.16	-0.24	-0.16	-0.27	-0.27	-0.2
	ROUGE_L	0.13	0.19	0.14	0.06	0.08	0.05	-0.07	-0.09	-0.07	-0.02	0.02	0.02	0.22	0.19	0.14	0.16	0.17	0.11
	CIDEr	0.03	0.12	0.09	0.14	0.1	0.05	-0.0	-0.01	-0.01	-0.07	0.09	0.08	0.22	0.26	0.17	0.12	0.21	0.16
	WMD	-0.02	-0.03	-0.02	0.16	0.13	0.1	-0.22	-0.17	-0.12	-0.09	-0.07	-0.05	-0.22	-0.28	-0.21	-0.1	-0.09	-0.08
F	BLEU_1	0.41	0.37	0.27	0.42	0.4	0.31	-0.22	-0.24	-0.19	0.01	0.0	0.01	0.13	0.08	0.06	0.32	0.32	0.24
	BLEU_2	0.39	0.36	0.28	0.38	0.29	0.23	-0.18	-0.27	-0.21	-0.01	-0.04	-0.03	0.07	0.05	0.03	0.32	0.31	0.22
	BLEU_3	0.29	0.32	0.23	0.35	0.25	0.19	-0.22	-0.25	-0.18	0.01	-0.0	0.0	0.12	0.07	0.05	0.3	0.3	0.22
	BLEU_4	0.15	0.24	0.18	0.23	0.2	0.14	-0.01	-0.17	-0.12	0.03	0.05	0.03	0.19	0.06	0.04	0.22	0.24	0.17
	METEOR	-0.07	-0.07	-0.08	0.12	0.09	0.06	-0.11	-0.14	-0.1	-0.0	-0.06	-0.03	-0.12	-0.2	-0.16	-0.01	-0.01	-0.01
	ROUGE_L	0.31	0.29	0.22	0.24	0.24	0.18	-0.06	-0.1	-0.08	-0.08	-0.07	-0.05	0.16	0.12	0.09	0.28	0.29	0.19
	CIDEr	0.16	0.27	0.2	0.36	0.27	0.21	-0.35	-0.37	-0.28	0.01	0.02	0.02	0.02	0.1	0.07	0.13	0.29	0.23
	WMD	0.04	0.03	0.02	0.19	0.22	0.14	-0.14	-0.16	-0.12	-0.03	-0.02	-0.03	-0.02	-0.03	-0.03	0.1	0.05	0.03

Table 3: Correlation scores between automatic metrics and human judgements across three criteria. **R**, **C** and **F** on the left side stand for relevance, correctness and composition (flow), corresponding to the type of questions that the crowdworkers were provided with. *P*, *S* and *K* stand for Pearson's, Spearman's and Kendall's correlations. We report correlation scores per search and per correlation metric. The scores coloured in red have $p < 0.05$.

to the type of objects and their salience.

7 Human evaluation

To support our hypothesis that automatic metrics are not enough to measure fine-grained differences between various decoding algorithms, we conduct a human evaluation on Amazon Mechanical Turk. We randomly sample 10% of images from the test set, which equals 41 items. For each of these images, we take generated texts from the top-6 decodings based on the CIDEr score. We get 287 different image-text pairs to evaluate. During the evaluation, we provide workers with an image and its description and ask them to answer 3 (three) different questions, aiming to evaluate (i) relevance: does the text describe relevant and essential objects, (ii) correctness: does the text describe objects correctly (e.g., using correct words), (iii) composition: do object descriptions naturally follow each other. The example item for human evaluation is shown in Appendix A. Each judgement is a score on a scale between 1 and 5, where 1 is the lowest rank. We collect three different judgements per item and average them. We pay 0.17 US dollars for a single assignment and restrict the location of the workers to the US, the UK, Canada, Ireland or Australia. We also ran our experiments with Master workers only (25 different human participants). We follow

	ref	g	b2	s25	s50	s75	s100	st50	n25	n50	n95	db2
s1	2.9	0.9	0.3	1.0	1.1	1.1	1.0	0.9	1.1	1.1	1.1	0.9
s2	1.6	1.7	1.5	1.7	1.7	1.8	1.8	1.7	1.8	1.8	1.7	1.8
s3	1.4	1.6	1.4	1.7	1.8	1.8	1.8	1.6	1.8	1.8	1.8	1.6
s4	1.3	1.6	1.4	1.8	1.8	1.8	1.9	1.6	1.8	1.9	1.8	1.6
s5	1.2	1.7	1.4	1.8	1.8	1.8	1.7	1.6	1.7	1.8	1.7	1.7

Table 4: Average number of noun phrases generated by different inference algorithms. The numbers are given per sentence.

	g	b2	s25	s50	s75	s100	st50	n25	n50	n95	db2
s1	200.0	175.0	227.9	215.0	233.3	231.0	208.0	227.9	209.2	228.2	200.0
s2	205.2	215.8	207.6	215.8	218.1	220.1	207.5	228.2	231.1	206.1	206.5
s3	210.8	205.2	213.8	215.0	233.3	203.8	210.3	202.6	219.3	207.1	207.2
s4	197.4	196.0	216.4	206.5	200.0	208.9	208.9	205.9	201.3	216.4	197.5
s5	198.0	212.5	202.6	205.1	211.3	214.4	197.3	209.6	215.8	208.7	200.0

Table 5: Average proportion of noun phrases (in percent) when *more* are generated than present in the references.

	g	b2	s25	s50	s75	s100	st50	n25	n50	n95	db2
s1	20.3	8.5	18.8	18.9	19.6	18.6	18.9	19.6	18.8	20.7	20.3
s2	45.3	44.2	42.6	42.9	40.4	43.1	45.9	39.8	40.0	39.7	45.5
s3	45.9	45.6	42.0	45.9	44.4	44.5	45.5	42.7	41.2	44.4	47.1
s4	46.5	46.8	43.9	45.8	43.3	43.4	47.0	45.0	43.3	42.9	46.6
s5	49.3	43.7	41.4	42.5	37.6	40.7	46.2	38.3	40.0	39.9	49.0

Table 6: Average proportion of noun phrases (in percent) when *fewer* are generated than present in the references.

Kilickaya et al. (2017) and compute three different correlation scores: Pearson's correlation, Spearman's rank correlation and Kendall's correlation.

The correlation scores are presented in Table 3. In general, sampling-based methods do not significantly correlate with automatic metrics or correlate but negatively. More controlled decodings, such as greedy or beam search, correlate with automatic metrics more, especially for the composition question (**F**). This indicates that automatic metrics correlate more with decodings that introduce less randomness. Future work will need to examine whether randomness and diversity in such searches as top-*k* sampling is a suitable type of diversity since it is unclear from correlation scores alone. In terms of the relevance of objects, sampling with temperature generally has negative scores (similar to other sampling-based methods). Still, a significant negative correlation is found only with Spearman's rank correlation for METEOR. Beam, however, might produce more relevant objects as demonstrated by high correlation in terms of BLEU_2 and CIDEr. We do not observe any correlation for the correctness criterion. On the contrary, text composition (flow) shows that more controlled decodings correlate considerably more with human judgements, especially when looking at n-gram metrics. This might demonstrate that more specific automatic metrics better reflect whether the object descriptions naturally follow each other. Overall, we show that while most of the automatic metrics are not sufficient in providing us with information about the salience and correctness of object descriptions for many different decoding algorithms, their scores, somewhat surprisingly, might still tell us about the sentence-level discourse and flow of object descriptions.

8 Non-grounded evaluation

Next, we will look at the surface level of noun phrases and examine faithfulness of generated texts to the reference ones. Noun phrases in image descriptions typically depict image objects, thus we believe that direct comparison of noun phrases in different texts can help us to understand how much each decoding algorithm learns on the surface of descriptions. Table 4 shows the average number of noun phrases in each sentence across different searches and references. We see that there is a gradual decrease in the number of noun phrases in references throughout the paragraph. Such decrease is not observed in texts generated by all algorithms. On the contrary, the first sentence typically has the fewest number of noun phrases generated with other sentences containing mostly the same number. This could be a sign that on the surface level decoding algorithms do not capture discourse structure, reflected in gradual decrease of the number of noun phrases. Instead, search algorithms tend to generate the same number of noun phrases across sentences, treating each sentence equally.

We also observe that the algorithms generate more noun phrases per sentence than required rather then generate fewer of them. Specifically, across all image-paragraph pairs a fewer number of noun phrases is generated for 757 sentences, a bigger number for 955 sentences and the exact number as in the references was produced for 493 sentences. To closer identify the impact of over- and under-generation of noun phrases, we compute proportion of noun phrases for both cases. As Table 5 demonstrates, all searches tend to generate nearly two times more noun phrases than required in each sentence. The picture changes when the searches under-generate. According to Table 6, while most of the sentences lack at least half of the required noun phrases (in terms of quantity), the first sentence is affected the most by under-

	g	b2	s25	s50	s75	s100	st50	n25	n50	n95	db2
s1	0.18	0.10	0.10	0.13	0.11	0.08	0.14	0.12	0.10	0.13	0.18
s2	0.17	0.17	0.13	0.13	0.13	0.14	0.17	0.12	0.15	0.13	0.17
s3	0.13	0.12	0.10	0.10	0.09	0.11	0.11	0.10	0.11	0.10	0.13
s4	0.10	0.09	0.10	0.09	0.08	0.09	0.09	0.09	0.09	0.09	0.10
s5	0.10	0.10	0.07	0.07	0.08	0.07	0.08	0.07	0.07	0.08	0.10

Table 7: Dice similarity coefficient between the set of objects described in reference texts and texts generated by different decoding algorithms. The values are provided per sentence and averaged across all image-paragraph pairs.

generation. Coupled with the results in Table 4, we conclude that decoding algorithms do not learn the structure of discourse on the simplest surface level of descriptions reflected in the differences in the number of noun phrases. This result indicates that searches might generate a discourse that is different from the one observed in references. In the following analysis, we will move from the surface level to the grounding level, in which we will examine if the noun phrases that are generated can be linked with image objects. We will also compare whether the objects described by different searches overlap with the ones found in reference texts.

9 Grounded evaluation

Table 7 shows the degree of overlap between two object sets: the first set includes objects described in references, while the second set contains objects mapped with noun phrases in generated texts from different decodings algorithms. We use Sørensen–Dice coefficient $\frac{2|A \cap B|}{|A|+|B|}$ to measure the overlap. The closer the result to 0, the less overlap is present. The results demonstrate that searches describe a very different set of objects rather than the one mentioned in the references. The highest overlap is observed with greedy search and diverse beam. The scores indicate that either a different and correct set of objects is described or the noun phrases cannot be linked with objects because they are incorrect (could also be because of high randomness, leading to the lack of grammaticality).

We examine whether noun phrases in generated texts can be linked with any of the objects in the image. Table 8 shows the proportion of successful linking once we link noun phrases with image objects using cosine similarity. We set the similarity threshold to 0.5: if the similarity between the object label and noun phrase is higher than this value, we decide that this noun phrase is faithful to the image and can be grounded.

	g	b2	s25	s50	s75	s100	st50	n25	n50	n95	db2
s1	69.5	72.7	46.5	46.3	43.2	46.1	66.5	51.1	45.2	50.5	69.5
s2	65.6	65.1	47.2	49.0	43.8	46.6	58.8	44.7	50.3	47.7	65.5
s3	61.6	59.5	43.6	46.9	40.5	45.1	53.1	40.1	40.6	44.7	60.7
s4	55.4	57.6	43.7	42.7	44.7	41.0	52.5	45.0	43.7	38.3	55.7
s5	60.5	57.4	47.6	43.2	43.4	43.7	53.3	39.2	38.9	44.4	59.3

Table 8: Average proportion of successful linking (in percent) between noun phrases in generated texts and image objects.

The results demonstrate that half and more of the generated noun phrases can be linked with objects in the image. In general, sampling algorithms generate fewer number of grounded noun phrases, possibly due to the increased randomness. Greedy search, beam and diverse beam generate the highest number of noun phrases which are truthful to the image. We believe that while reference-correctness of generated texts can get worse, inference algorithms are still able to generate alternative descriptions of images which can be grounded. However, the structure of discourse reflected on the surface level and the level of grounding might not necessarily correspond to the one observed in references. In the next experiment, we look at the problem under the angle of attentional structure and examine spatial arrangement of linked objects and how these arrangements differ between decoding algorithms.

10 Attentional structure of discourse

Figure 1 demonstrates a number of the attention heatmaps across areas in the image for different sentences. At first glance, different inference algorithms look at similar locations in the image and also focus on parts which are attended by humans. However, there are relatively more areas described in the first sentence of the references, while a much smaller and fewer areas are described in generated texts. This could be directly related to the fewer number of objects and under-generation discussed previously. The second and third sentences describe specific areas of the image in all cases, mostly central ones. Interestingly, greedy and diverse beam have highly similar attention across the image. In sentence 4, human attention disperses over the full scene, while it is unclear whether the same pattern happens in generated texts. This could signal a possible *topic shift*, happening in later parts of the paragraph and inability of searches to capture that. To understand the differences on the level of sentences better, we measure the correlation between flattened heatmaps pixel by pixel.

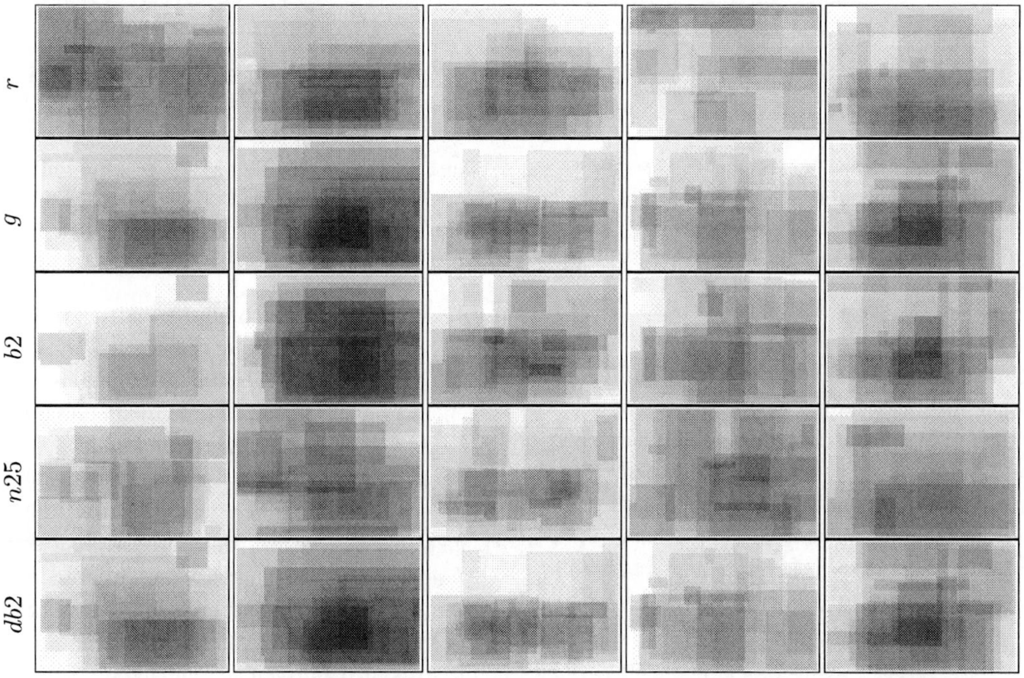

(a) Sentence 1 (b) Sentence 2 (c) Sentence 3 (d) Sentence 4 (e) Sentence 5

Figure 1: Attention heatmaps over objects, described in texts according to the results of linking. Results are shown per sentence and per search. The first row denotes attention in reference texts. We aggregate heatmaps across all images into the single image, therefore, darker colour denotes higher focus on the specific area in the image.

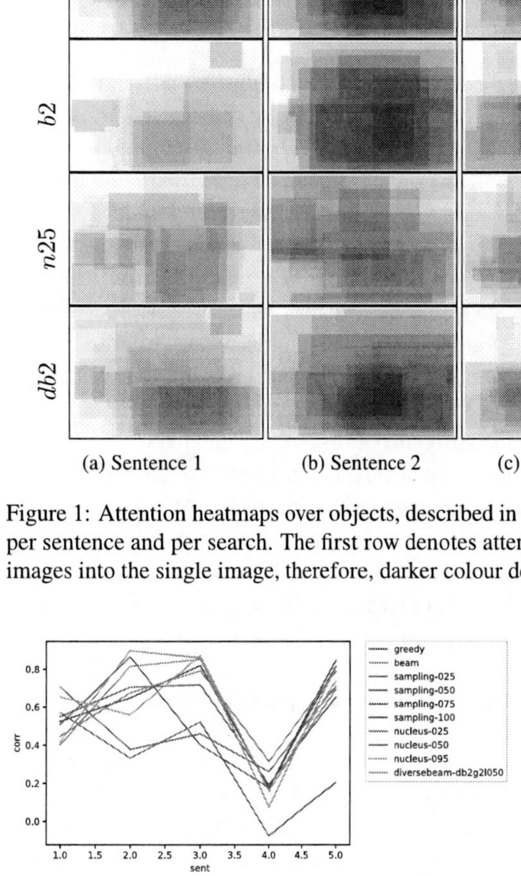

Figure 2: Correlation between heatmaps for different searches and reference paragraphs. X-axis is sentence in the paragraph (1-5), Y-axis is the correlation coefficient, pixel-by-pixel correlation between attention heatmaps.

We use Pearson product-moment correlation coefficient which can be applied to images across the channels. The results are shown in Figure 2. As we can see, in sentence 4 attentional structure on the image differs between searches and references, supporting the idea of topic shift. Sampling methods have the lowest correlation with the references, while nucleus with $p = 25$ is affected the least in sentence 4. Note that the correlation in the first sentence is lower than in the second and the third one for most of the searches. This could be related to the importance of the first sentence and a bigger number of noun phrases in it, which are not generated during the decoding stage.

11 Conclusion

In this paper we described our analysis of how decoding strategies structure discourse in multimodal longer image descriptions. We performed evaluation using intuitions from different evaluation perspectives: automatic, surface-based (non-grounded), image-based (grounded) and attention-based. The results suggest that for the task of image paragraph generation decoding algorithms diverge from humans in generating specific type of discourse. Although they might generate reference-incorrect but image-correct descriptions, it is unclear what kind of discourse is generated in the end. In general, algorithms which are less random construct discourse similar to the one in human references, while sampling-based methods generate a different type of discourse, which is hard to control for. We plan to use the insights described in this paper and build a metric that would evaluate the structure of longer image paragraphs, reflected in *both* object and relation descriptions as this is currently a much needed evaluation measure.

12 Limitations

There are several directions which can support the analysis in this paper. First, the automatic linking is not a perfect mechanism, prone to errors. The method that we use works better for shorter phrases which share the same lemmas and thus are less ambiguous. Second, using more models (Li et al., 2019) or more datasets (Krause et al., 2017) would potentially give us a broader picture of the type of discourses formed by humans and quality of representations used during decoding phase. We also consider our analysis preliminary with the opportunity of developing a separate metric to evaluate discourse in longer image descriptions.

Acknowledgements

The research reported in this paper was supported by a grant from the Swedish Research Council (VR project 2014-39) for the establishment of the Centre for Linguistic Theory and Studies in Probability (CLASP) at the University of Gothenburg.

References

Peter Anderson, Xiaodong He, Chris Buehler, Damien Teney, Mark Johnson, Stephen Gould, and Lei Zhang. 2018. Bottom-up and top-down attention for image captioning and visual question answering. In *2018 IEEE/CVF Conference on Computer Vision and Pattern Recognition*, pages 6077–6086.

Anusha Balakrishnan, Jinfeng Rao, Kartikeya Upasani, Michael White, and Rajen Subba. 2019. Constrained decoding for neural NLG from compositional representations in task-oriented dialogue. In *Proceedings of the 57th Annual Meeting of the Association for Computational Linguistics*, pages 831–844, Florence, Italy. Association for Computational Linguistics.

Massimo Caccia, Lucas Caccia, William Fedus, Hugo Larochelle, Joelle Pineau, and Laurent Charlin. 2020. Language gans falling short. In *8th International Conference on Learning Representations, ICLR 2020, Addis Ababa, Ethiopia, April 26-30, 2020*. OpenReview.net.

Yun Chen, Victor O.K. Li, Kyunghyun Cho, and Samuel Bowman. 2018. A stable and effective learning strategy for trainable greedy decoding. In *Proceedings of the 2018 Conference on Empirical Methods in Natural Language Processing*, pages 380–390, Brussels, Belgium. Association for Computational Linguistics.

Reuben Cohn-Gordon, Noah Goodman, and Christopher Potts. 2018. Pragmatically informative image captioning with character-level inference. In *Proceedings of the 2018 Conference of the North American Chapter of the Association for Computational Linguistics: Human Language Technologies, Volume 2 (Short Papers)*, pages 439–443, New Orleans, Louisiana. Association for Computational Linguistics.

Robert Dale and Michael White. 2007. Shared tasks and comparative evaluation in natural language generation. In *Proceedings of the Workshop on Shared Tasks and Comparative Evaluation in Natural Language Generation*.

Simon Dobnik, Nikolai Ilinykh, and Aram Karimi. 2022. What to refer to and when? reference and re-reference in two language-and-vision tasks. In *Proceedings of the 26th Workshop on the Semantics and Pragmatics of Dialogue - Full Papers*, pages 146–159, Dublin, Ireland. SEMDIAL.

Desmond Elliott and Frank Keller. 2014. Comparing automatic evaluation measures for image description. In *Proceedings of the 52nd Annual Meeting of the Association for Computational Linguistics (Volume 2: Short Papers)*, pages 452–457, Baltimore, Maryland. Association for Computational Linguistics.

Angela Fan, Mike Lewis, and Yann Dauphin. 2018. Hierarchical neural story generation. In *Proceedings of the 56th Annual Meeting of the Association for Computational Linguistics (Volume 1: Long Papers)*, pages 889–898, Melbourne, Australia. Association for Computational Linguistics.

Adam Fisch, Kenton Lee, Ming-Wei Chang, Jonathan Clark, and Regina Barzilay. 2020. CapWAP: Image captioning with a purpose. In *Proceedings of the 2020 Conference on Empirical Methods in Natural Language Processing (EMNLP)*, pages 8755–8768, Online. Association for Computational Linguistics.

Albert Gatt and E.J. Krahmer. 2018. Survey of the state of the art in natural language generation: Core tasks, applications and evaluation. *Journal of Artificial Intelligence Research*, 61(1):65–170.

Edward Albert Fletcher Gibson. 1991. *A Computational Theory of Human Linguistic Processing: Memory Limitations and Processing Breakdown*. Ph.D. thesis, Carnegie Mellon University, USA. UMI Order No. GAX91-26944.

Barbara J. Grosz, Aravind K. Joshi, and Scott Weinstein. 1995. Centering: A framework for modeling the local coherence of discourse. *Computational Linguistics*, 21(2):203–225.

Jiatao Gu, Kyunghyun Cho, and Victor O.K. Li. 2017. Trainable greedy decoding for neural machine translation. In *Proceedings of the 2017 Conference on Empirical Methods in Natural Language Processing*, pages 1968–1978, Copenhagen, Denmark. Association for Computational Linguistics.

Simao Herdade, Armin Kappeler, Kofi Boakye, and Joao Soares. 2019. Image captioning: Transforming objects into words. In *Advances in Neural Information Processing Systems*, volume 32. Curran Associates, Inc.

Jack Hessel, Ari Holtzman, Maxwell Forbes, Ronan Le Bras, and Yejin Choi. 2021. CLIPScore: A reference-free evaluation metric for image captioning. In *Proceedings of the 2021 Conference on Empirical Methods in Natural Language Processing*, pages 7514–7528, Online and Punta Cana, Dominican Republic. Association for Computational Linguistics.

Felix Hill, Kyunghyun Cho, and Anna Korhonen. 2016. Learning distributed representations of sentences from unlabelled data. In *Proceedings of the 2016 Conference of the North American Chapter of the Association for Computational Linguistics: Human Language Technologies*, pages 1367–1377, San Diego, California. Association for Computational Linguistics.

Ari Holtzman, Jan Buys, Li Du, Maxwell Forbes, and Yejin Choi. 2020. The curious case of neural text degeneration. In *8th International Conference on Learning Representations, ICLR 2020, Addis Ababa, Ethiopia, April 26-30, 2020*. OpenReview.net.

Matthew Honnibal, Ines Montani, Sofie Van Landeghem, and Adriane Boyd. 2020. spaCy: Industrial-strength Natural Language Processing in Python.

Jack Hopkins and Douwe Kiela. 2017. Automatically generating rhythmic verse with neural networks. In *Proceedings of the 55th Annual Meeting of the Association for Computational Linguistics (Volume 1: Long Papers)*, pages 168–178, Vancouver, Canada. Association for Computational Linguistics.

David M. Howcroft, Anya Belz, Miruna-Adriana Clinciu, Dimitra Gkatzia, Sadid A. Hasan, Saad Mahamood, Simon Mille, Emiel van Miltenburg, Sashank Santhanam, and Verena Rieser. 2020. Twenty years of confusion in human evaluation: NLG needs evaluation sheets and standardised definitions. In *Proceedings of the 13th International Conference on Natural Language Generation*, pages 169–182, Dublin, Ireland. Association for Computational Linguistics.

Ting-Hao Kenneth Huang, Francis Ferraro, Nasrin Mostafazadeh, Ishan Misra, Aishwarya Agrawal, Jacob Devlin, Ross Girshick, Xiaodong He, Pushmeet Kohli, Dhruv Batra, C. Lawrence Zitnick, Devi Parikh, Lucy Vanderwende, Michel Galley, and Margaret Mitchell. 2016. Visual storytelling. In *Proceedings of the 2016 Conference of the North American Chapter of the Association for Computational Linguistics: Human Language Technologies*, pages 1233–1239, San Diego, California. Association for Computational Linguistics.

Nikolai Ilinykh and Simon Dobnik. 2020. When an image tells a story: The role of visual and semantic information for generating paragraph descriptions. In *Proceedings of the 13th International Conference on Natural Language Generation*, pages 338–348, Dublin, Ireland. Association for Computational Linguistics.

Nikolai Ilinykh and Simon Dobnik. 2022. Attention as grounding: Exploring textual and cross-modal attention on entities and relations in language-and-vision transformer. In *Findings of the Association for Computational Linguistics: ACL 2022*, pages 4062–4073, Dublin, Ireland. Association for Computational Linguistics.

Nikolai Ilinykh, Sina Zarrieß, and David Schlangen. 2019. Tell me more: A dataset of visual scene description sequences. In *Proceedings of the 12th International Conference on Natural Language Generation*, pages 152–157, Tokyo, Japan. Association for Computational Linguistics.

Mert Inan, Piyush Sharma, Baber Khalid, Radu Soricut, Matthew Stone, and Malihe Alikhani. 2021. COSMic: A coherence-aware generation metric for image descriptions. In *Findings of the Association for Computational Linguistics: EMNLP 2021*, pages 3419–3430, Punta Cana, Dominican Republic. Association for Computational Linguistics.

Ming Jiang, Qiuyuan Huang, Lei Zhang, Xin Wang, Pengchuan Zhang, Zhe Gan, Jana Diesner, and Jianfeng Gao. 2019. TIGEr: Text-to-image grounding for image caption evaluation. In *Proceedings of the 2019 Conference on Empirical Methods in Natural Language Processing and the 9th International Joint Conference on Natural Language Processing (EMNLP-IJCNLP)*, pages 2141–2152, Hong Kong, China. Association for Computational Linguistics.

Chloé Kiddon, Luke Zettlemoyer, and Yejin Choi. 2016. Globally coherent text generation with neural checklist models. In *Proceedings of the 2016 Conference on Empirical Methods in Natural Language Processing*, pages 329–339, Austin, Texas. Association for Computational Linguistics.

Mert Kilickaya, Aykut Erdem, Nazli Ikizler-Cinbis, and Erkut Erdem. 2017. Re-evaluating automatic metrics for image captioning. In *Proceedings of the 15th Conference of the European Chapter of the Association for Computational Linguistics: Volume 1, Long Papers*, pages 199–209, Valencia, Spain. Association for Computational Linguistics.

Chen Kong, Dahua Lin, Mohit Bansal, Raquel Urtasun, and Sanja Fidler. 2014. What are you talking about? text-to-image coreference. In *Proceedings of the IEEE Conference on Computer Vision and Pattern Recognition (CVPR)*, pages 3558–3565.

Jonathan Krause, Justin Johnson, Ranjay Krishna, and Li Fei-Fei. 2017. A hierarchical approach for generating descriptive image paragraphs. In *Proceedings of the IEEE Conference on Computer Vision and Pattern Recognition (CVPR)*, pages 317–325.

Ranjay Krishna, Yuke Zhu, Oliver Groth, Justin Johnson, Kenji Hata, Joshua Kravitz, Stephanie Chen, Yannis Kalantidis, Li-Jia Li, David A Shamma, Michael Bernstein, and Li Fei-Fei. 2016. Visual genome: Connecting language and vision using crowdsourced dense image annotations.

Ilia Kulikov, Alexander Miller, Kyunghyun Cho, and Jason Weston. 2019. Importance of search and evaluation strategies in neural dialogue modeling. In *Proceedings of the 12th International Conference on Natural Language Generation*, pages 76–87, Tokyo, Japan. Association for Computational Linguistics.

Girish Kulkarni, Visruth Premraj, Sagnik Dhar, Siming Li, Yejin Choi, Alexander C Berg, and Tamara L Berg. 2011. Baby talk: Understanding and generating simple image descriptions. In *CVPR 2011*, pages 1601–1608.

Matt Kusner, Yu Sun, Nicholas Kolkin, and Kilian Weinberger. 2015. From word embeddings to document distances. In *Proceedings of the 32nd International Conference on Machine Learning*, volume 37 of *Proceedings of Machine Learning Research*, pages 957–966, Lille, France. PMLR.

Guillaume Lample, Alexis Conneau, Ludovic Denoyer, and Marc'Aurelio Ranzato. 2018. Unsupervised machine translation using monolingual corpora only. In *6th International Conference on Learning Representations, ICLR 2018, Vancouver, BC, Canada, April 30 - May 3, 2018, Conference Track Proceedings*. OpenReview.net.

Alon Lavie and Abhaya Agarwal. 2007. METEOR: An automatic metric for MT evaluation with high levels of correlation with human judgments. In *Proceedings of the Second Workshop on Statistical Machine Translation*, pages 228–231, Prague, Czech Republic. Association for Computational Linguistics.

Angeliki Lazaridou, Alexander Peysakhovich, and Marco Baroni. 2017. Multi-agent cooperation and the emergence of (natural) language. In *5th International Conference on Learning Representations, ICLR 2017, Toulon, France, April 24-26, 2017, Conference Track Proceedings*. OpenReview.net.

Guang Li, Linchao Zhu, Ping Liu, and Yi Yang. 2019. Entangled transformer for image captioning. In *Proceedings of the IEEE/CVF International Conference on Computer Vision (ICCV)*, pages 8928–8937.

Jiwei Li, Michel Galley, Chris Brockett, Jianfeng Gao, and Bill Dolan. 2016. A diversity-promoting objective function for neural conversation models. In *Proceedings of the 2016 Conference of the North American Chapter of the Association for Computational Linguistics: Human Language Technologies*, pages 110–119, San Diego, California. Association for Computational Linguistics.

Chin-Yew Lin. 2004. ROUGE: A package for automatic evaluation of summaries. In *Text Summarization Branches Out*, pages 74–81, Barcelona, Spain. Association for Computational Linguistics.

Charlotte Linde and J.A. Goguen. 1980. On the independence of discourse structure and semantic domain. In *18th Annual Meeting of the Association for Computational Linguistics*, pages 35–37, Philadelphia, Pennsylvania, USA. Association for Computational Linguistics.

Pranava Madhyastha, Josiah Wang, and Lucia Specia. 2019. VIFIDEL: Evaluating the visual fidelity of image descriptions. In *Proceedings of the 57th Annual Meeting of the Association for Computational Linguistics*, pages 6539–6550, Florence, Italy. Association for Computational Linguistics.

Luca Massarelli, Fabio Petroni, Aleksandra Piktus, Myle Ott, Tim Rocktäschel, Vassilis Plachouras, Fabrizio Silvestri, and Sebastian Riedel. 2020. How decoding strategies affect the verifiability of generated text. In *Findings of the Association for Computational Linguistics: EMNLP 2020*, pages 223–235, Online. Association for Computational Linguistics.

Clara Meister, Martina Forster, and Ryan Cotterell. 2021. Determinantal beam search. In *Proceedings of the 59th Annual Meeting of the Association for Computational Linguistics and the 11th International Joint Conference on Natural Language Processing (Volume 1: Long Papers)*, pages 6551–6562, Online. Association for Computational Linguistics.

Shashi Narayan, Gonçalo Simões, Yao Zhao, Joshua Maynez, Dipanjan Das, Michael Collins, and Mirella Lapata. 2022. A well-composed text is half done! composition sampling for diverse conditional generation. In *Proceedings of the 60th Annual Meeting of the Association for Computational Linguistics (Volume 1: Long Papers)*, pages 1319–1339, Dublin, Ireland. Association for Computational Linguistics.

Taichi Nishimura, Atsushi Hashimoto, and Shinsuke Mori. 2019. Procedural text generation from a photo sequence. In *Proceedings of the 12th International Conference on Natural Language Generation*, pages 409–414, Tokyo, Japan. Association for Computational Linguistics.

Kishore Papineni, Salim Roukos, Todd Ward, and Wei-Jing Zhu. 2002. Bleu: a method for automatic evaluation of machine translation. In *Proceedings of the 40th Annual Meeting of the Association for Computational Linguistics*, pages 311–318, Philadelphia, Pennsylvania, USA. Association for Computational Linguistics.

Massimo Poesio. 2004. Discourse annotation and semantic annotation in the GNOME corpus. In *Proceedings of the Workshop on Discourse Annotation*, pages 72–79, Barcelona, Spain. Association for Computational Linguistics.

Massimo Poesio, Rosemary Stevenson, Barbara Di Eugenio, and Janet Hitzeman. 2004. Centering: A parametric theory and its instantiations. *Computational Linguistics*, 30(3):309–363.

Nils Reimers and Iryna Gurevych. 2019. Sentence-BERT: Sentence embeddings using Siamese BERT-networks. In *Proceedings of the 2019 Conference on Empirical Methods in Natural Language Processing and the 9th International Joint Conference on Natural Language Processing (EMNLP-IJCNLP)*, pages 3982–3992, Hong Kong, China. Association for Computational Linguistics.

Ehud Reiter and Anja Belz. 2009. An investigation into the validity of some metrics for automatically evaluating natural language generation systems. *Computational Linguistics*, 35(4):529–558.

Ehud Reiter and Robert Dale. 1997. Building applied natural language generation systems. *Natural Language Engineering*, 3(1):57–87.

Steven J. Rennie, Etienne Marcheret, Youssef Mroueh, Jerret Ross, and Vaibhava Goel. 2017. Self-critical sequence training for image captioning. In *2017 IEEE Conference on Computer Vision and Pattern Recognition (CVPR)*, pages 1179–1195.

Claude Elwood Shannon. 1948. A mathematical theory of communication. *The Bell System Technical Journal*, 27:379–423.

Ece Takmaz, Mario Giulianelli, Sandro Pezzelle, Arabella Sinclair, and Raquel Fernández. 2020. Refer, Reuse, Reduce: Generating Subsequent References in Visual and Conversational Contexts. In *Proceedings of the 2020 Conference on Empirical Methods in Natural Language Processing (EMNLP)*, pages 4350–4368, Online. Association for Computational Linguistics.

Ashish Vaswani, Noam Shazeer, Niki Parmar, Jakob Uszkoreit, Llion Jones, Aidan N Gomez, Ł ukasz Kaiser, and Illia Polosukhin. 2017. Attention is all you need. In *Advances in Neural Information Processing Systems*, volume 30, pages 5998–6008. Curran Associates, Inc.

Ramakrishna Vedantam, Samy Bengio, Kevin Murphy, Devi Parikh, and Gal Chechik. 2017. Context-aware captions from context-agnostic supervision. In *2017 IEEE Conference on Computer Vision and Pattern Recognition (CVPR)*, pages 1070–1079.

Ramakrishna Vedantam, C. Lawrence Zitnick, and Devi Parikh. 2015. Cider: Consensus-based image description evaluation. In *2015 IEEE Conference on Computer Vision and Pattern Recognition (CVPR)*, pages 4566–4575.

Ashwin Vijayakumar, Michael Cogswell, Ramprasaath Selvaraju, Qing Sun, Stefan Lee, David Crandall, and Dhruv Batra. 2018. Diverse beam search for improved description of complex scenes. *Proceedings of the AAAI Conference on Artificial Intelligence*, 32(1).

Sijin Wang, Ziwei Yao, Ruiping Wang, Zhongqin Wu, and Xilin Chen. 2021. Faier: Fidelity and adequacy ensured image caption evaluation. In *2021 IEEE/CVF Conference on Computer Vision and Pattern Recognition (CVPR)*, pages 14045–14054.

Yonghui Wu, Mike Schuster, Zhifeng Chen, Quoc V. Le, Mohammad Norouzi, Wolfgang Macherey, Maxim Krikun, Yuan Cao, Qin Gao, Klaus Macherey, Jeff Klingner, Apurva Shah, Melvin Johnson, Xiaobing Liu, Lukasz Kaiser, Stephan Gouws, Yoshikiyo Kato, Taku Kudo, Hideto Kazawa, Keith Stevens, George Kurian, Nishant Patil, Wei Wang, Cliff Young, Jason Smith, Jason Riesa, Alex Rudnick, Oriol Vinyals, Greg Corrado, Macduff Hughes, and Jeffrey Dean. 2016. Google's neural machine translation system: Bridging the gap between human and machine translation. *CoRR*, abs/1609.08144.

Sina Zarrieß and David Schlangen. 2018. Decoding strategies for neural referring expression generation. In *Proceedings of the 11th International Conference on Natural Language Generation*, pages 503–512, Tilburg University, The Netherlands. Association for Computational Linguistics.

Sina Zarrieß, Henrik Voigt, and Simeon Schüz. 2021. Decoding methods in neural language generation: A survey. *Information*, 12(9).

Hugh Zhang, Daniel Duckworth, Daphne Ippolito, and Arvind Neelakantan. 2021. Trading off diversity and quality in natural language generation. In *Proceedings of the Workshop on Human Evaluation of NLP Systems (HumEval)*, pages 25–33, Online. Association for Computational Linguistics.

Bolei Zhou, Hang Zhao, Xavier Puig, Sanja Fidler, Adela Barriuso, and Antonio Torralba. 2017. Scene parsing through ade20k dataset. In *Proceedings of the IEEE Conference on Computer Vision and Pattern Recognition (CVPR)*.

A Appendix A

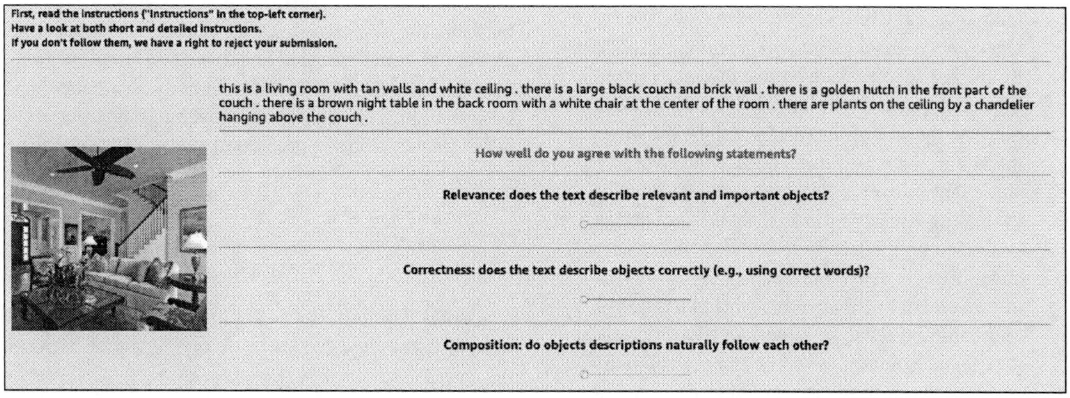

Figure 3: The example item for the workers on AMT for human evaluation.

20Q: Overlap-Free World Knowledge Benchmark for Language Models

Maxime De Bruyn, Ehsan Lotfi, Jeska Buhmann, Walter Daelemans
CLiPS Research Center
University of Antwerp, Belgium
maxime.debruyn@uantwerpen.be

Abstract

What do language models know about our world? This question is hard to answer but important to get right. To this end, we introduce 20Q, a novel benchmark using the Twenty Questions game to evaluate world knowledge and common sense of language models. Thanks to our overlap-free benchmark, language models learn the game of Twenty Questions without learning relevant knowledge for the test set. We uncover two intuitive factors influencing the world knowledge of language models: the size of the model and the topic frequency in the pre-training data. Moreover, we show that in-context learning is inefficient for evaluating language models' world knowledge — fine-tuning is necessary to show their true capabilities. Lastly, our results show room for improvement to enhance the world knowledge and common sense of large language models. A potential solution would be to up-sample unfrequent topics in the pre-training of language models.

1 Introduction

Transformers are omnipresent in today's Natural Language Processing. Using a simple training and inference procedure, they reach human-level performance on numerous benchmarks.

The scale of these models is hard to grasp. The most recent one, PaLM (Chowdhery et al., 2022), has 540 billion parameters. It has sixteen times more parameters than all words on Wikipedia, or sixty-eight times more parameters than the total population on Earth (Roser et al., 2013).

Much previous work focused on what these models can do: question-answering, mathematics, translation, or code generation (Wei et al., 2022; Chen et al., 2021; Cobbe et al., 2021; NLLB Team et al., 2022; Lewkowycz et al., 2022). Another exciting area of research is to focus on what these models know: common sense, world knowledge, or biases (Kejriwal et al., 2022; Kadavath et al., 2022; Lucy and Bamman, 2021; Abid et al., 2021).

Topic	Question	Answer
Gorilla	Is it alive?	Yes
Ball	Can we eat it?	No
Anchor	Is it heavy?	Yes
Pen	Can it fly?	No
Car	Can you drive it?	Yes
Satellite	It it furniture?	No

Table 1: Example questions and answers in our 20Q benchmark. We use simple questions to compare the amount of world knowledge between different language models. Despite its apparent simplicity, this benchmark is challenging for even the largest language models — GPT-3 makes a wrong prediction about 20% of the time.

Transformers (Vaswani et al., 2017) models do not store knowledge symbolically — they distribute the knowledge within their weights. As a result, researchers have to use proxy tasks to study it. Previous research used closed-book question-answering datasets to study how much knowledge language models can store (Roberts et al., 2020). They concluded that language models perform similarly with or without external information, thanks to a broad embedded knowledge.

Unfortunately, Lewis et al. (2021) later demonstrated that these datasets suffer from a significant overlap between the training and test set. For example, *who has scored more goals in the premier league* shares the same answer with *most goals scored by a premier league player*. Training on the first and evaluating on the second does not make sense. As a result, T5's (Raffel et al., 2020) performance dramatically dropped when Lewis et al. (2021) removed the overlap – invalidating the conclusion that these models performed equally with or without external knowledge. Our analysis reveals commonsense reasoning benchmarks also display major overlap between the training and test sets.

Proceedings of the 2nd Workshop on Natural Language Generation, Evaluation, and Metrics (GEM), pages 494 - 508
December 7, 2022 ©2022 Association for Computational Linguistics

Commonsense QA 2.0 Talmor et al. (2022) and Com2sense (Singh et al., 2021) have exact or close-to-exact duplicates between the training and test set.

In this work, we propose a new benchmark, free of any lexical and semantic overlap between the training and test set, to evaluate the world knowledge of large language models using the game of Twenty Questions – a popular yes/no guessing game. See Table 1 for example questions and answers.

We test two hypotheses using this benchmark. First, we test whether large models possess more world knowledge that smaller models. Second, we test our intuition that world knowledge is correlated with the frequency of the topic in language models' pre-training data.

Despite the massive size of GPT-3, it only reaches an F1 score of 82% on our benchmark. It is however much better than its smaller variants, which validates our first hypothesis that larger models possess more world knowledge than smaller models.

Our dataset's unique feature — a generic question and a topic — is ideal for testing our second hypothesis: does world knowledge correlate with topic frequency. Again, the results show our hypothesis is true as the bottom quartile of topics is associated with higher variability, whereas the other quartiles are not.

We conclude this introduction by summarizing our main contributions:

- We release a new benchmark to study the world knowledge of language models. It is free of any overlap between the training and test set.
- We show that large models possess more knowledge than smaller ones. However, the relationship is not linear.
- We show that the knowledgeability of language models on a specific topic depends on the relative frequency of the topic in the pre-training data.

We release our benchmark on the HuggingFace dataset hub (Lhoest et al., 2021) for anyone to use.[1]

[1] https://huggingface.co/datasets/clips/20Q

2 Related Work

Before the rise of deep learning, NLP stored commonsense and world knowledge using semantic networks such as WordNet (Miller, 1995) and later ConceptNet (Speer et al., 2017). These graphs have the advantage of using symbolic representations, facilitating their analysis. Contrary to Transformers-based models, they perform equally well on lower-frequency topics.

Commonsense and world knowledge of Transformers' based models is harder to evaluate, researchers resort to using proxy tasks to evaluate it. Several previous works studied the commonsense abilities of language models in multiple areas: pronoun resolution (Levesque et al., 2012; Sakaguchi et al., 2021), natural language generation (Lin et al., 2020), story understanding (Mostafazadeh et al., 2016), reading comprehension (Zhang et al., 2018; Huang et al., 2019; Ning et al., 2020), physical and social intelligence (Bisk et al., 2020; Sap et al., 2019), temporal reasoning (Zhou et al., 2019), numerical knowledge (Dua et al., 2019; Ravichander et al., 2019), and global commonsense reasoning (Singh et al., 2021; Talmor et al., 2022, 2019).

The remainder of this section focuses on two datasets evaluation the commonsense knowledge of language models using yes/no questions: Commonsense QA 2.0 (Talmor et al., 2022) and Com2Sense (Singh et al., 2021). For both of these datasets, we review the overlap between the training and test set and find troubling examples.

2.1 Commonsense QA 2.0

Talmor et al. (2022) provide a dataset of 14,343 yes/no questions on several commonsense skills: numerical reasoning, causal reasoning, world knowledge, temporal understanding. The authors used a human-in-the-loop approach to create a challenging benchmark for language models. We partially share the same seed data (AllenAI, 2018) as Commonsense QA 2.0, however we follow a stricter pre-processing and split formation procedure.

Overlap Analysis The authors split the training and test sets according to the topic of questions.[2] Our qualitative review of the overlap between the training and test reveals problematic examples. Some examples are almost duplicates: «

[2] For example the question « *an uncle has to have a brother or sister* » has the topic *uncle* even though it also is about the *brother* topic.

an electron holds a positive charge » and, « *an electron holds a positive charge and* »,[3] while others are lexically different but semantically similar: « *most happy meals include a toy* » and, « *happy meals almost always come with a toy* ». We provide more examples in Appendix A.

2.2 Com2sense

Com2sense (Singh et al., 2021) provides a comprehensive commonsense benchmark to test language models' understanding of everyday events and entities by answering yes/no questions. The authors classify their dataset on three axes: knowledge domain (physical, social, or temporal), reasoning scenario (comparative or causal) and numeracy.

Overlap Analysis The authors do not take any special care in the division of the data. However, a key feature of the dataset introduces a high overlap between the two. The authors use a simple technique to double the size of the dataset: edit a few words of each sentence to flip the answer: *to ~~read books~~ see stars at night, one should turn on the lights*. Our qualitative review of the overlap between the training and test reveals highly problematic examples. First, we found exact duplicates between the training and test sets. Second, some examples in the test set are simple negations of examples in the training set. For example « *[...] opening the blinds will help you see* » and, « *[...] opening the blinds will not help you see* ». Third, some examples only change one term between the test and training set, but are semantically similar. We provide more examples in Apppendix A.

2.3 Overlap Analysis Summary

Our qualitative review reveals both of these benchmarks do not properly check for training and test set overlap.

Unfortunately, Lewis et al. (2021) demonstrated that a high overlap between the training and test set can inflate the true performance of language models.

To summarize, we provide the first commonsense reasoning benchmark focused exclusively on world knowledge. Contrary to existing benchmarks, we take extensive measures to ensure there is no overlap between the training and test set. We compare 20Q against alternative benchmarks in Table 2.

[3]the *and* at the end of the sentence is not a typo.

3 Data

Data is a double-edged sword. On the one hand, more data is usually good. However, on the other hand, more data can also complicate the study of the generalization abilities of the model as it gets harder to find uncorrelated validation data.

Regarding world knowledge and common sense, two factors can contaminate the validation data: the training and pre-training data. Large language models can memorize their pre-training data. The bigger the model, the larger the probability of memorization (Chowdhery et al., 2022).

In this work, we take a novel approach and analyze the inner knowledge of large transformers models through the game of Twenty Questions — a popular yes/no guessing game. We take extra care to avoid lexical and semantic overlap between the training and validation sets.

3.1 Twenty Questions Game

Wikipedia describes Twenty Questions as a game that encourages deductive reasoning and creativity. In the traditional game, the answerer chooses a topic and does not reveal it to the questioners, whom themselves must find the hidden entity by asking yes/no questions to the answerer. Humans can play this game (or a variant of it like Guess Who) from a young age.

3.2 Twenty Questions Dataset

We do not generate a dataset ourselves. Instead, we rely on an existing dataset of Twenty Questions games developed by AllenAI, where they had humans play the game of Twenty Questions on Amazon Mechanical Turk. In total, they collected 78,890 questions in the style of Twenty Questions. The dataset is available on Github (AllenAI, 2018).[4]

3.2.1 Generic Questions

As the questioner does not know the topic, he mainly refers to the entity using "it". Therefore, we term these "generic questions." This disentangling of question and topic is helpful in two regards. First, we can use it to ensure no semantic and lexical overlap between the training and validation sets for both topics and questions. Second, we can measure the topic's knowledge by type of word, domain, or relative frequency in the pre-training data.

[4]https://github.com/allenai/twentyquestions

Dataset	Train	Valid.	Test	No Overlap	Focus	Example
CQA2.0	9,264	2,541	2,473	✗	Multiple	*A bus has at least two steering wheels.*
Com2sense	804	402	2,779	✗	Multiple	*As the weather was very cold he put on his jacket to protect himself.*
20Q (ours)	815	-	2,500	✓	World Knowledge	*Can [an acquittal] cheer you up?*

Table 2: Comparison of 20Q with other similar benchmarks. 20Q focuses solely on world-knowledge and is free of any overlap between the training and test set.

3.2.2 Fine-grained Answers

Reducing the world to yes and no can be challenging, even impossible. Instead of answering with yes or no, annotators[5] must answer with fine-grained answers: *never*, *rarely*, *sometimes*, *usually*, or *always*. Three annotators answer each question. With a Kappa score of 57%, the disagreement between annotators is high. However, converting the answers to *yes* or *no* instead of fine-grained answers resolves any disagreement between annotators. Using a binary answer also facilitates the analysis.

3.2.3 Quality Score

Annotators provide a quality score for each question and flag potential problems: questions that are not answerable by yes or no, questions that are not playing the game, or questions that refer to another turn. We only retain questions with the highest quality score (85% of the dataset).

3.3 Pre-processing

As with all data generated by humans, it can be noisy. The original dataset contains many sentences with orthographic errors, or even questions unrelated to the Twenty Questions game. Our goal is to understand the knowledge stored inside the language models, not their capacity to deal with noise. Therefore, we take extensive pre-processing steps to clean the dataset. We give further insight into our pre-processing in Annex B. First, we remove all questions below the maximum score of three (-15%). Next, we remove all questions which do not use "it" (-12%). Finally, we remove all duplicate questions (-3%) and answers where the topic is not in WordNet (-3%). Our pre-processing removes 34% of the initial dataset.

3.4 Training Set

The original authors performed a random split of questions into training, validation, and test set. The authors deal with training/test overlap by flagging questions where the topic is also present in the training set. We take a much stronger stance on train/test overlap and include the semantic overlap between topics and questions.

Our objective is to test the existing knowledge of language models — not to provide new knowledge. Therefore, the priority should be the size of the test set, not the training set. Our training set consists of 815 questions (500 generic questions) on 707 different topics.

3.5 Similarity Metrics

Before removing the overlap between the training and test set, we must first decide which similarity metric to use.

We use three methods to compute the similarity between two topics (words) or questions (sequence of words).

Bag-of-words The simplest method to compare two words or sequences of words is their bag-of-words representations. We first tokenize, remove stop-words, and finally stem the words. This method typically identifies close lexical duplicates such as *is it animal & is it an animal.*

WordNet Our second method uses the semantic graph WordNet (Miller, 1995). WordNet excels at identifying synonyms. For example, it will identify that *bike* is a synonym of *bicycle*.

Sentence Transformers Our last method uses Sentence Transformers (Reimers and Gurevych, 2019). It uses pre-trained encoder networks to compute vector representations of sentences (it also works for single words). We can compare the similarity of two sentences (resp. words) by looking at the cosine similarity of their vector representations. We use three different models.

3.6 Test Set

We follow three steps before including an example in the test set:

[5]We want to stress that we are referring to the annotation of the original dataset (AllenAI, 2018).

	Training	Test
Questions (total)	815	2,500
Generic Questions	500	1,250
Topics	707	1,436
Words	5.3	5.2
Yes	46%	42%
No	54%	58%

Table 3: Descriptive statistics. Our goal is not to learn new knowledge but to test existing knowledge. As a result, the training set is small compared to the validation set.

1. We ensure that the bag-of-words representation of the question and the topic is not present in the training set.
2. We check if the topic of the question is not a synonym of any topic in the training set.
3. Our last step removes any example with a cosine similarity larger than 0.8 with any topic or question in the training set.

After all these steps, we arrive at a test set of 4,201 examples. Given the high cost of evaluating very large language models, we only keep the first 2,500 examples. Given the limited size of the validation set, we did not implement a test set. Additional statistics about the dataset are available in Table 3. Our validation consists of only 4% of the clean dataset. However, as there is no overlap between the training and validation set, we can make safe conclusions on the generalization abilities of language models.

4 Overlap Exploration

Lewis et al. (2021) demonstrated the devastating effect of an uncontrolled overlap between the training and validation set. Therefore, this section uses different techniques to inspect the most similar items between the training and validation set.

4.1 Topic Overlap in 20Q

We start by analyzing the overlap in topics. For example, we want to avoid having questions about *cars* in the training set and about *automobiles* in the validation set.

N-grams Character n-grams are a good way to retrieve words sharing almost the same lexical form.[6]

[6]We use a character tri-grams

We show the five most similar pairs of topics between the training and validation set in Table 7 in Annex C. The most similar topics according to this method are *account* and *accountant*. This technique does not reveal problematic overlap between the two sets.

WordNet We use WordNet to compute the distance between two topics by following the hypernym or hyponym chain. Table 8 in Annex C shows this technique's most similar pair of topics. None of the retrieved pairs show a significant semantical or lexical overlap.

Sentence Transformers We finish our qualitative review of the topic overlap using Sentence Transformers. Table 9 in Annex C shows the five most similar pairs of topics. The most similar pairs are *costume* with *halloween*, *chlorophyll* and *chrysanthemum*, *bracelet* and *pendant*. All of these words are related, but none are synonyms of one another.

4.2 Question Overlap in 20Q

An overlap in terms of topics is only part of the story. We also want to avoid evaluating models on the same kind of answers used to train them. Therefore, we perform the same procedure to avoid lexical and semantic overlap between the questions in the training and validation set. The task is trickier than for topics. For example, *Does it make you cry* and *Does it make you laugh* only differ in a single token, but their meaning is opposite.

BM25 We use BM25 to retrieve similar questions between the two sets. The two most similar questions are *Can the human population fit on it?* and *Would it fit in the palm of a human hand?*. These questions share two important tokens: *fit* and *human*, but they do not have the same meaning. See table 4 for more examples. This clearly shows how semantically inequivalent even the most similar sentences in the train and validation set are.

Sentence Transformers Next, we perform the same analysis with Sentence Transformers. The most similar questions between the two sets are *does it have a steering wheel?* and *does it have gears or screws?*, indicating a sufficient amount of dissimilarity between the questions in the training and test set.

Train	Topic	Validation	Topic
Does it have a one time function?	knocker	Does it need to be one student at a time?	lettering
Would a parent want their child to do it?	soloist	Is it a category response, like parent or child?	cornea
Can the human population fit on it?	earth	Would it fit in the palm of a human hand?	keyboard
Does it rock?	brim	Is it some sort of precious, rare stone or rock?	emerald
Is it a turn?	heron	Is it something you turn on?	dice

Table 4: Qualitative review of the most similar pair of questions computed using BM25. Questions usually share a similar word (e.g., *child* or *rock*), however, it is used in a different context each time. Moreover, the topics are completely unrelated, reducing the risk of overlap even more.

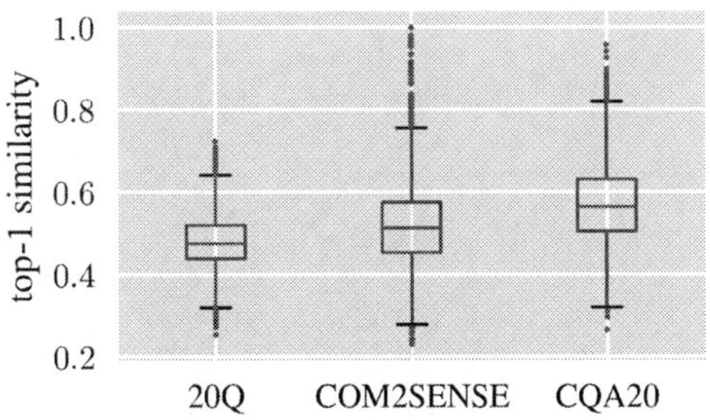

Figure 1: Distribution of top-1 similarity between examples in the training and test set. 20Q has the lowest similarity between the two (by design).

4.3 Comparison with Existing Benchmarks

We finish this section by comparing the train/test overlap of 20Q with two existing benchmarks presented in Section 2: Commonsense QA 2.0 and Com2sense. For each question in the test set, we look for the most similar one in the training set using Sentence Transformers. We summarize the results in Figure 1. The results are striking, 20Q has significantly less overlap with the training set than Com2sense and Commonsense QA 2.0. Our qualitative analysis of these results reveal dangerously close duplicates between the training and test of these two benchmarks. Even less expected, we uncover exact duplicates between the training and test of Com2sense. We provide a more detailed analysis in Annex A.

To summarize, our benchmark is free of any semantic and lexical overlap between the training and validation set regarding topics and questions. Moreover, despite the strict separation constraints, both sets stay semantically diverse.

5 Language Model

After reviewing that data, we review the language models. Although previous work used text-to-text models such as T5 (Raffel et al., 2020), T0 (Sanh et al., 2022), and BART (Lewis et al., 2020), in this work, we stick to GPT-3 (Brown et al., 2020), a general-purpose decoder-only Transformers language model. By sticking to a single model, we can ensure that the only differentiating factor between the models is the network size, not the pre-training data or model architecture.

5.1 GPT-3

GPT-3 (Brown et al., 2020) is an auto-regressive language model developed by OpenAI. The model weights are not publicly available, although the model's predictions are available through a paid API.

Size GPT-3 comes in four sizes: 2.7B, 6.7B, 13B and 175B. We use this feature to understand how the size of a model influences the amount of world knowledge it can store.

Pre-training Data The authors of GPT-3 did not release the pre-training data used to train the model. So instead, we use C4, the dataset used to train T5 (Raffel et al., 2019), as a proxy to estimate the frequency of each topic in our benchmark.

Prompting GPT-3 was never trained to answer yes/no questions. Instead, its objective is to predict the next token in a piece of text. The standard way to query a large language model is to use in-context learning, where one provides a few examples of the task in the prompt and asks the language model to complete the last example.

6 Experiments

Our experiments aim at understanding which models possess the best world knowledge. We believe large language models are ineffective at querying their internal knowledge using in-context learning. For this reason, we also fine-tune each model on the training set for a single epoch. The goal is not to teach new knowledge but to guide the model into learning the task. As we meticulously assembled

		F1			NLL		
Model	**Size**	**Z-S**	**F-S**	**F-T**	**Z-S**	**F-S**	**F-T**
GPT-3	2.7B	58.77	58.02	58.04	112.9	82.64	66.46
GPT-3	6.7B	58.45	54.53	66.35	140.5	80.56	55.41
GPT-3	13B	59.65	48.88	74.48	79.87	65.52	55.63
GPT-3	175B	61.10	67.14	**82.50**	69.86	62.23	**41.16**

Table 5: Results per model size and inference method: zero-shot (Z-S), few-shot (F-S), and fine-tune (F-T). According to F1 and NLL, the best method is the largest GPT-3 fine-tuned on our training set.

our training and validation splits, we are sure any performance gain will not come from the knowledge acquired during fine-tuning.

6.1 Zero-shot

The zero-shot approach is the simplest way to evaluate the knowledge of the language model. The model must predict the next token without any prior examples. We record the probability of the yes token and no token.

Prompt

```
You are playing a game of 20 questions.
Answer the following question
about with yes or no.

Topic: {{ question_topic_1 }}
Question: {{ question_example_1 }}
Answer:
```

6.2 Few-shot

This approach improves upon the previous one by providing multiple examples to steer the model in the right direction. The model learns the task *on the fly* using examples from the training set. We record the probability of the yes token and no token.

Prompt

```
Topic: {{ topic_example_1 }}
Question: {{ question_example_1 }}
Answer: {{ answer_example_1 }}
...
Topic: {{ topic_example_n }}
Question: {{ question_example_n }}
Answer:
```

Settings We provide four examples in a random order (two positives and two negatives) from the training set.

6.3 Fine-tuning

Understanding the task of answering yes/no questions using on the fly examples is hard. Therefore, we also tested another approach where we fine-tuned models on our training set.

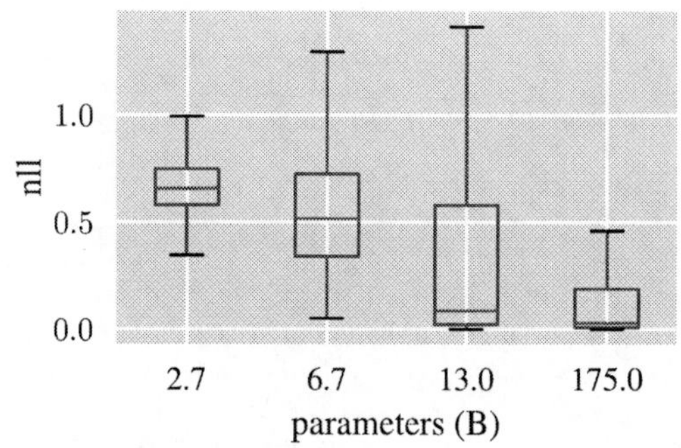

Figure 2: Box-plot of negative-likelihood (NLL) per model size.

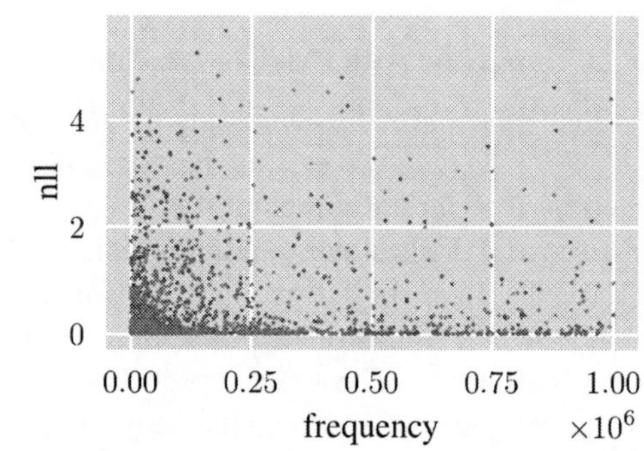

Figure 3: Scatter plot of NLL by topic frequency for the 13B (blue) and 175B (green) models.

Prompt

```
Topic: {{ topic_example }}
Question: {{ question_example }}
Answer:
```

Settings Each model is trained on a single epoch of the training set.

7 Results

We run all experiments and report binary-F1 and Negative Log-Likelihood (NLL) to the ground-truth answers in Table 5. We start by reviewing the effect of fine-tuning and then analyze our two hypotheses.

7.1 Fine-tuning

The benefit of fine-tuning is clear: fine-tuned models are systematically better than few-shot and zero-shot across model size and evaluation metrics. Moreover, thanks to our detailed review of the overlap, we can safely assume the out-performance does not come from learning any new knowledge but is due to better use of the world knowledge already present in the language models.

7.2 Size Effect

In theory, the larger the model, the more space it has to store world knowledge. Therefore, we expect to see better performance for large models. Figure 2 shows a box-plot of the negative log-likelihood of the fine-tuned results by the model size.

The results are somewhat unexpected. Although the median negative log-likelihood is steadily declining with the model size, the variability also increases with the model size, except for the largest one, which breaks the trend with a low median loss and low variability. In other words, the model's ability to know what it does not know diminishes with model size.

7.3 Frequency Effect

Previous research showed that the frequency of tokens in the pre-training data influences the ability of large language models to do numeric reasoning (Razeghi et al., 2022). We hypothesize that the same is true when it comes to world knowledge. Language models should have a harder time answering questions on topics they have rarely encountered during pre-training. Therefore, we collected the frequency count of each topic in a large pre-training corpus: C4 (Raffel et al., 2020). Our experiments revealed the high correlation of topic frequency with the perplexity of GPT-2 (XL) to generate the word. We use this metric as it scales to different word forms and is easier to collect. [7]

Figure 3 clearly shows the frequency effect. Topics associated with a lower frequency quartile have more variability in negative log-likelihood than higher quartiles. This effect is especially strong on the 13B model.

7.4 Question Bias

In this section, we try to uncover whether language models use statistical cues in the question rather than their internal knowledge to answer questions. To this end, we run the fine-tuned model (explained in Section 6.3) without the topic in the prompt. If language models use statistical patterns in questions, it should not matter whether the subject is present or not. The F1 score of GPT-3 (175B) drops from 82.50% to 59.40%, just over the performance of the smallest GPT-3 model. We conclude that language models use their internal knowledge rather than statistical cues in the questions.

[7] We use the cross-entropy loss (using a sum reduction) from a GPT-2 XL model as a measure of frequency

8 Conclusion

Previous research (Lewis et al., 2021) showed that language models do not have enough world knowledge to rival open-domain question-answering systems. We update this claim using larger models and a novel benchmark, 20Q. We find two factors influencing the world knowledge of language models: the model's size and the topic's frequency in the pre-training data. Thanks to careful attention to the overlap between the training and validation set, we can safely conclude that fine-tuning provides a better picture of the world knowledge possessed by language models. Our benchmark shows that even the largest language models (175 billion parameters) have room for improvement regarding world knowledge. We propose several areas of improvement for coping with a rapidly changing world as future work.

Acknowledgement

We thank the reviewers for their helpful feedback. This research received funding from the Flemish Government under the *Onderzoeksprogramma Artificiële Intelligentie (AI) Vlaanderen* programme.

References

Abubakar Abid, Maheen Farooqi, and James Zou. 2021. Persistent anti-muslim bias in large language models. In *Proceedings of the 2021 AAAI/ACM Conference on AI, Ethics, and Society*, AIES '21, page 298–306, New York, NY, USA. Association for Computing Machinery.

AllenAI. 2018. A web application for playing 20 questions to crowdsource common sense.

Yonatan Bisk, Rowan Zellers, Jianfeng Gao, Yejin Choi, et al. 2020. Piqa: Reasoning about physical commonsense in natural language. In *Proceedings of the AAAI conference on artificial intelligence*, volume 34, pages 7432–7439.

Tom Brown, Benjamin Mann, Nick Ryder, Melanie Subbiah, Jared D Kaplan, Prafulla Dhariwal, Arvind Neelakantan, Pranav Shyam, Girish Sastry, Amanda Askell, Sandhini Agarwal, Ariel Herbert-Voss, Gretchen Krueger, Tom Henighan, Rewon Child, Aditya Ramesh, Daniel Ziegler, Jeffrey Wu, Clemens Winter, Chris Hesse, Mark Chen, Eric Sigler, Mateusz Litwin, Scott Gray, Benjamin Chess, Jack Clark, Christopher Berner, Sam McCandlish, Alec Radford, Ilya Sutskever, and Dario Amodei. 2020. Language models are few-shot learners. In *Advances in Neural Information Processing Systems*, volume 33, pages 1877–1901. Curran Associates, Inc.

Mark Chen, Jerry Tworek, Heewoo Jun, Qiming Yuan, Henrique Ponde de Oliveira Pinto, Jared Kaplan, Harrison Edwards, Yuri Burda, Nicholas Joseph, Greg Brockman, Alex Ray, Raul Puri, Gretchen Krueger, Michael Petrov, Heidy Khlaaf, Girish Sastry, Pamela Mishkin, Brooke Chan, Scott Gray, Nick Ryder, Mikhail Pavlov, Alethea Power, Lukasz Kaiser, Mohammad Bavarian, Clemens Winter, Philippe Tillet, Felipe Petroski Such, Dave Cummings, Matthias Plappert, Fotios Chantzis, Elizabeth Barnes, Ariel Herbert-Voss, William Hebgen Guss, Alex Nichol, Alex Paino, Nikolas Tezak, Jie Tang, Igor Babuschkin, Suchir Balaji, Shantanu Jain, William Saunders, Christopher Hesse, Andrew N. Carr, Jan Leike, Joshua Achiam, Vedant Misra, Evan Morikawa, Alec Radford, Matthew Knight, Miles Brundage, Mira Murati, Katie Mayer, Peter Welinder, Bob McGrew, Dario Amodei, Sam McCandlish, Ilya Sutskever, and Wojciech Zaremba. 2021. Evaluating large language models trained on code. *ArXiv*, abs/2107.03374.

Aakanksha Chowdhery, Sharan Narang, Jacob Devlin, Maarten Bosma, Gaurav Mishra, Adam Roberts, Paul Barham, Hyung Won Chung, Charles Sutton, Sebastian Gehrmann, Parker Schuh, Kensen Shi, Sasha Tsvyashchenko, Joshua Maynez, Abhishek B Rao, Parker Barnes, Yi Tay, Noam M. Shazeer, Vinodkumar Prabhakaran, Emily Reif, Nan Du, Benton C. Hutchinson, Reiner Pope, James Bradbury, Jacob Austin, Michael Isard, Guy Gur-Ari, Pengcheng Yin, Toju Duke, Anselm Levskaya, Sanjay Ghemawat, Sunipa Dev, Henryk Michalewski, Xavier García, Vedant Misra, Kevin Robinson, Liam Fedus, Denny Zhou, Daphne Ippolito, David Luan, Hyeontaek Lim, Barret Zoph, Alexander Spiridonov, Ryan Sepassi, David Dohan, Shivani Agrawal, Mark Omernick, Andrew M. Dai, Thanumalayan Sankaranarayana Pillai, Marie Pellat, Aitor Lewkowycz, Erica Oliveira Moreira, Rewon Child, Oleksandr Polozov, Katherine Lee, Zongwei Zhou, Xuezhi Wang, Brennan Saeta, Mark Díaz, Orhan Firat, Michele Catasta, Jason Wei, Kathleen S. Meier-Hellstern, Douglas Eck, Jeff Dean, Slav Petrov, and Noah Fiedel. 2022. Palm: Scaling language modeling with pathways. *ArXiv*, abs/2204.02311.

Karl Cobbe, Vineet Kosaraju, Mohammad Bavarian, Jacob Hilton, Reiichiro Nakano, Christopher Hesse, and John Schulman. 2021. Training verifiers to solve math word problems. *ArXiv*, abs/2110.14168.

Dheeru Dua, Yizhong Wang, Pradeep Dasigi, Gabriel Stanovsky, Sameer Singh, and Matt Gardner. 2019. DROP: A reading comprehension benchmark requiring discrete reasoning over paragraphs. In *Proceedings of the 2019 Conference of the North American Chapter of the Association for Computational Linguistics: Human Language Technologies, Volume 1 (Long and Short Papers)*, pages 2368–2378, Minneapolis, Minnesota. Association for Computational Linguistics.

Lifu Huang, Ronan Le Bras, Chandra Bhagavatula, and Yejin Choi. 2019. Cosmos QA: Machine reading comprehension with contextual commonsense reasoning. In *Proceedings of the 2019 Conference on Empirical Methods in Natural Language Processing and the 9th International Joint Conference on Natural Language Processing (EMNLP-IJCNLP)*, pages 2391–2401, Hong Kong, China. Association for Computational Linguistics.

Saurav Kadavath, Tom Conerly, Amanda Askell, Tom Henighan, Dawn Drain, Ethan Perez, Nicholas Schiefer, Zac Hatfield Dodds, Nova DasSarma, Eli Tran-Johnson, Scott Johnston, Sheer El-Showk, Andy Jones, Nelson Elhage, Tristan Hume, Anna Chen, Yuntao Bai, Sam Bowman, Stanislav Fort, Deep Ganguli, Danny Hernandez, Josh Jacobson, Jackson Kernion, Shauna Kravec, Liane Lovitt, Kamal Ndousse, Catherine Olsson, Sam Ringer, Dario Amodei, Tom Brown, Jack Clark, Nicholas Joseph, Ben Mann, Sam McCandlish, Chris Olah, and Jared Kaplan. 2022. Language models (mostly) know what they know. *ArXiv*, abs/2207.05221.

Mayank Kejriwal, Henrique Santos, Alice M Mulvehill, and Deborah L McGuinness. 2022. Designing a strong test for measuring true common-sense reasoning. *Nature Machine Intelligence*, 4(4):318–322.

Hector J. Levesque, Ernest Davis, and Leora Morgenstern. 2012. The winograd schema challenge. In *Proceedings of the Thirteenth International Conference on Principles of Knowledge Representation and Reasoning*, KR'12, page 552–561. AAAI Press.

Mike Lewis, Yinhan Liu, Naman Goyal, Marjan Ghazvininejad, Abdelrahman Mohamed, Omer Levy, Veselin Stoyanov, and Luke Zettlemoyer. 2020. BART: Denoising sequence-to-sequence pre-training for natural language generation, translation, and comprehension. In *Proceedings of the 58th Annual Meeting of the Association for Computational Linguistics*, pages 7871–7880, Online. Association for Computational Linguistics.

Patrick Lewis, Pontus Stenetorp, and Sebastian Riedel. 2021. Question and answer test-train overlap in open-domain question answering datasets. In *Proceedings of the 16th Conference of the European Chapter of the Association for Computational Linguistics: Main Volume*, pages 1000–1008, Online. Association for Computational Linguistics.

Aitor Lewkowycz, Anders Andreassen, David Dohan, Ethan Dyer, Henryk Michalewski, Vinay Ramasesh, Ambrose Slone, Cem Anil, Imanol Schlag, Theo Gutman-Solo, Yuhuai Wu, Behnam Neyshabur, Guy Gur-Ari, and Vedant Misra. 2022. Solving quantitative reasoning problems with language models.

Quentin Lhoest, Albert Villanova del Moral, Yacine Jernite, Abhishek Thakur, Patrick von Platen, Suraj Patil, Julien Chaumond, Mariama Drame, Julien Plu, Lewis Tunstall, Joe Davison, Mario Šaško, Gunjan Chhablani, Bhavitvya Malik, Simon Brandeis, Teven Le Scao, Victor Sanh, Canwen Xu, Nicolas Patry, Angelina McMillan-Major, Philipp Schmid, Sylvain Gugger, Clément Delangue, Théo Matussière, Lysandre Debut, Stas Bekman, Pierric Cistac, Thibault Goehringer, Victor Mustar, François Lagunas, Alexander Rush, and Thomas Wolf. 2021. Datasets: A community library for natural language processing. In *Proceedings of the 2021 Conference on Empirical Methods in Natural Language Processing: System Demonstrations*, pages 175–184, Online and Punta Cana, Dominican Republic. Association for Computational Linguistics.

Bill Yuchen Lin, Wangchunshu Zhou, Ming Shen, Pei Zhou, Chandra Bhagavatula, Yejin Choi, and Xiang Ren. 2020. CommonGen: A constrained text generation challenge for generative commonsense reasoning. In *Findings of the Association for Computational Linguistics: EMNLP 2020*, pages 1823–1840, Online. Association for Computational Linguistics.

Li Lucy and David Bamman. 2021. Gender and representation bias in GPT-3 generated stories. In *Proceedings of the Third Workshop on Narrative Understanding*, pages 48–55, Virtual. Association for Computational Linguistics.

George A. Miller. 1995. Wordnet: A lexical database for english. *Commun. ACM*, 38(11):39–41.

Nasrin Mostafazadeh, Nathanael Chambers, Xiaodong He, Devi Parikh, Dhruv Batra, Lucy Vanderwende, Pushmeet Kohli, and James Allen. 2016. A corpus and cloze evaluation for deeper understanding of commonsense stories. In *Proceedings of the 2016 Conference of the North American Chapter of the Association for Computational Linguistics: Human Language Technologies*, pages 839–849, San Diego, California. Association for Computational Linguistics.

Qiang Ning, Hao Wu, Rujun Han, Nanyun Peng, Matt Gardner, and Dan Roth. 2020. TORQUE: A reading comprehension dataset of temporal ordering questions. In *Proceedings of the 2020 Conference on Empirical Methods in Natural Language Processing (EMNLP)*, pages 1158–1172, Online. Association for Computational Linguistics.

NLLB Team, Marta R. Costa-jussà, James Cross, Onur Çelebi, Maha Elbayad, Kenneth Heafield, Kevin Heffernan, Elahe Kalbassi, Janice Lam, Daniel Licht, Jean Maillard, Anna Sun, Skyler Wang, Guillaume Wenzek, Al Youngblood, Bapi Akula, Loic Barrault, Gabriel Mejia Gonzalez, Prangthip Hansanti, John Hoffman, Semarley Jarrett, Kaushik Ram Sadagopan, Dirk Rowe, Shannon Spruit, Chau Tran, Pierre Andrews, Necip Fazil Ayan, Shruti Bhosale, Sergey Edunov, Angela Fan, Cynthia Gao, Vedanuj Goswami, Francisco Guzmán, Philipp Koehn, Alexandre Mourachko, Christophe Ropers, Safiyyah Saleem, Holger Schwenk, and Jeff Wang. 2022. No language left behind: Scaling human-centered machine translation. *ArXiv*, abs/2207.04672.

Colin Raffel, Noam Shazeer, Adam Roberts, Katherine Lee, Sharan Narang, Michael Matena, Yanqi Zhou, Wei Li, and Peter J. Liu. 2019. Exploring the limits of transfer learning with a unified text-to-text transformer. *arXiv e-prints*.

Colin Raffel, Noam Shazeer, Adam Roberts, Katherine Lee, Sharan Narang, Michael Matena, Yanqi Zhou, Wei Li, and Peter J. Liu. 2020. Exploring the limits of transfer learning with a unified text-to-text transformer. *Journal of Machine Learning Research*, 21(140):1–67.

Abhilasha Ravichander, Aakanksha Naik, Carolyn Rose, and Eduard Hovy. 2019. EQUATE: A benchmark evaluation framework for quantitative reasoning in natural language inference. In *Proceedings of the 23rd Conference on Computational Natural Language Learning (CoNLL)*, pages 349–361, Hong Kong, China. Association for Computational Linguistics.

Yasaman Razeghi, Robert L. Logan, Matt Gardner, and Sameer Singh. 2022. Impact of pretraining term frequencies on few-shot reasoning.

Nils Reimers and Iryna Gurevych. 2019. Sentence-BERT: Sentence embeddings using Siamese BERT-networks. In *Proceedings of the 2019 Conference on Empirical Methods in Natural Language Processing and the 9th International Joint Conference on Natural Language Processing (EMNLP-IJCNLP)*, pages 3982–3992, Hong Kong, China. Association for Computational Linguistics.

Adam Roberts, Colin Raffel, and Noam Shazeer. 2020. How much knowledge can you pack into the parameters of a language model? In *Proceedings of the 2020 Conference on Empirical Methods in Natural Language Processing (EMNLP)*, pages 5418–5426, Online. Association for Computational Linguistics.

Max Roser, Hannah Ritchie, and Esteban Ortiz-Ospina. 2013. World population growth. *Our World in Data*.

Keisuke Sakaguchi, Ronan Le Bras, Chandra Bhagavatula, and Yejin Choi. 2021. Winogrande: An adversarial winograd schema challenge at scale. *Communications of the ACM*, 64(9):99–106.

Victor Sanh, Albert Webson, Colin Raffel, Stephen Bach, Lintang Sutawika, Zaid Alyafeai, Antoine

Chaffin, Arnaud Stiegler, Teven Le Scao, Arun Raja, et al. 2022. Multitask prompted training enables zero-shot task generalization. In *The Tenth International Conference on Learning Representations.*

Maarten Sap, Hannah Rashkin, Derek Chen, Ronan Le Bras, and Yejin Choi. 2019. Social IQa: Commonsense reasoning about social interactions. In *Proceedings of the 2019 Conference on Empirical Methods in Natural Language Processing and the 9th International Joint Conference on Natural Language Processing (EMNLP-IJCNLP)*, pages 4463–4473, Hong Kong, China. Association for Computational Linguistics.

Shikhar Singh, Nuan Wen, Yu Hou, Pegah Alipoormolabashi, Te-lin Wu, Xuezhe Ma, and Nanyun Peng. 2021. COM2SENSE: A commonsense reasoning benchmark with complementary sentences. In *Findings of the Association for Computational Linguistics: ACL-IJCNLP 2021*, pages 883–898, Online. Association for Computational Linguistics.

Robyn Speer, Joshua Chin, and Catherine Havasi. 2017. Conceptnet 5.5: An open multilingual graph of general knowledge. In *Proceedings of the Thirty-First AAAI Conference on Artificial Intelligence*, AAAI'17, page 4444–4451. AAAI Press.

Alon Talmor, Jonathan Herzig, Nicholas Lourie, and Jonathan Berant. 2019. CommonsenseQA: A question answering challenge targeting commonsense knowledge. In *Proceedings of the 2019 Conference of the North American Chapter of the Association for Computational Linguistics: Human Language Technologies, Volume 1 (Long and Short Papers)*, pages 4149–4158, Minneapolis, Minnesota. Association for Computational Linguistics.

Alon Talmor, Ori Yoran, Ronan Le Bras, Chandra Bhagavatula, Yoav Goldberg, Yejin Choi, and Jonathan Berant. 2022. Commonsenseqa 2.0: Exposing the limits of AI through gamification. *ArXiv*, abs/2201.05320.

Ashish Vaswani, Noam Shazeer, Niki Parmar, Jakob Uszkoreit, Llion Jones, Aidan N Gomez, Ł ukasz Kaiser, and Illia Polosukhin. 2017. Attention is all you need. In *Advances in Neural Information Processing Systems*, volume 30. Curran Associates, Inc.

Jason Wei, Xuezhi Wang, Dale Schuurmans, Maarten Bosma, Ed H. Chi, Quoc Le, and Denny Zhou. 2022. Chain of thought prompting elicits reasoning in large language models. *ArXiv*, abs/2201.11903.

Sheng Zhang, Xiaodong Liu, Jingjing Liu, Jianfeng Gao, Kevin Duh, and Benjamin Van Durme. 2018. Record: Bridging the gap between human and machine commonsense reading comprehension. *ArXiv*, abs/1810.12885.

Ben Zhou, Daniel Khashabi, Qiang Ning, and Dan Roth. 2019. "going on a vacation" takes longer than "going for a walk": A study of temporal commonsense understanding. In *Proceedings of the 2019 Conference on Empirical Methods in Natural Language Processing and the 9th International Joint Conference on Natural Language Processing (EMNLP-IJCNLP)*, pages 3363–3369, Hong Kong, China. Association for Computational Linguistics.

A Detailed Overlap Analysis

In this section, we review the most similar pairs of questions between the training and test for Commonsense QA 2.0, Com2sense, and 20Q (our benchmark). We use Sentence Transformers (Reimers and Gurevych, 2019) to compute the similarity between all pairs of questions in the training and test set.

A.1 Commonsense QA 2.0

The authors of Commonsense QA 2.0 used a topical split to divide the training and test set. We list the top 15 most overlapped questions between the training and test set in Table 11. A quick analysis of the table reveals a number of problematic pairs such as *« an electron holds a positive charge and »* is an almost duplicate to *« an electron hold a positive charge »*.

A.2 Com2sense

Our overlap analysis of com2sense reveals three *exact duplicates* between the training and test set of Com2sense. A number of examples are close duplicates and only change with one word or punctuation. For example *« if it is dark outside, opening the blinds will not help you see »* and *« if it is dark outside opening the blinds will help you see »*. We list the top fifteen overlap pairs in Table 12.

A.3 20Q

Our overlap analysis of 20Q does not reveal any overlap thanks to our strict pre-processing pipeline. We list the top fifteen overlap pairs in Table 10.

A.3.1 UMAP

Figure 4 and 5 provide a 2 dimension projection of the semantic of questions and subject in 20Q.

B Pre-processing

The original Twenty Questions dataset is generated by humans, and is thus extremely noisy. In this section, we expand upon Section 3.3 and go into the details of our pre-processing steps. We detail our pre-processing steps and the percentage of questions removed in Table 6.

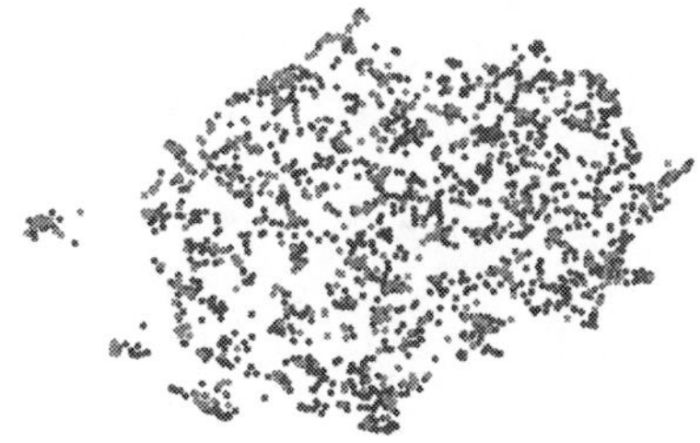

Figure 4: UMAP projection of the Sentence Transformers representation of the questions. Blue dots belong to the training set, red dots belong to the validation set.

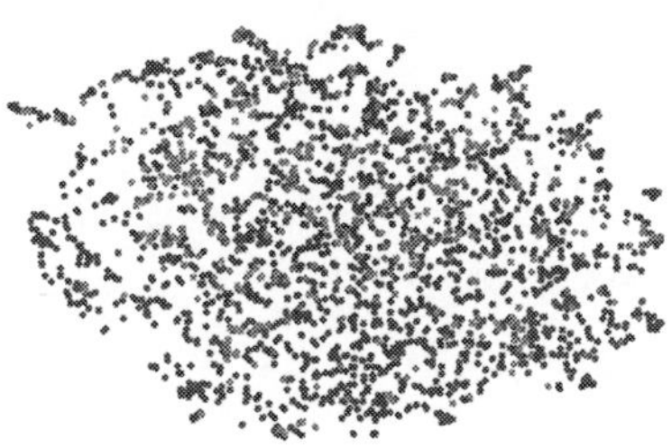

Figure 5: UMAP projection of the Sentence Transformers representation of the topics. Blue dots belong to the training set. Red dots belong to the validation set.

Step	Size (abs)	Size (%)
Initial dataset	78,890	100
Low scores	-12,396	-15.7
Do not use "it"	-9,665	-12.3
Duplicates	-2,708	-3.4
WordNet	-2,312	-2.9
Clean dataset	51,809	65.7

Table 6: Pre-processing of the original dataset. We are aggressive in our pre-processing as we prefer a small dataset of high quality to the reverse. First, we remove all questions with a score of 2 (the maximum is 3). We then remove all sentences that do not use "it." Next, we use a stemmed bag-of-words representation to remove close duplicates. Finally, we remove all questions where the answer is not in WordNet.

B.1 Quality Score

We start our pre-processing by removing all sentences with a score below three. These are questions which are not answerable with *yes* or *no*, or questions which are not playing the game of Twenty Questions. For example, questions such as « *so not an object, but tangible. is it edible* » which references the previous turn, or simple one word questions such as « *mountain?* »

B.2 Use of *it*

Our goal is to understand the world knowledge of language models. For some models such as T0 or T5, it may be easier to answer the question if the topic is part of the question, instead of having two separated parts. For example it is easier to answer: « *does a rock float* » than « *subject: rock, question: does it float* ». To make sure all questions are equally easy or difficult in terms of lexical information, we only keep questions of the latter format.

B.3 Duplicate Questions

Some questions may be close, but not exact, duplicates. We want to avoid such questions in the training or test set as these add very little information while artificially inflating the size of the dataset. We use a stemmed bag-of-words approach to detect these questions. For example, questions such as « *is it animal* » and « *is it an animal* ».

B.4 WordNet Filtering

We want to avoid having questions where the subject is not orthographically correct. We remove all questions where the subject is not present within WordNet. In effect, this will remove words such as *trex*, *chldren*, *voiceing*, or acronym words such as *potus* or *49ers*.

C Topic Overlap Exploration

In this section, we show the list the overlapping topics according to three different metrics.

C.1 N-grams

We show the five most similar pairs of topics between the training and validation set in Table 7.

C.2 WordNet

We use WordNet to compute the distance between two topics by following the hypernym or hyponym chain. Table 8 shows this technique's most similar pair of topics.

Train	Validation	Sim.
Account	Accountant	0.84
Thinking	Thing	0.79
Constitution	Institution	0.78
Extraction	Traction	0.78
Attraction	Traction	0.78

Table 7: Most similar pair of topics between the training and validation set using a character tri-gram method.

Train	Validation	Sim.
Vegetation	Galaxy	0.33
Purifier	Pendulum	0.33
Lambskin	Squirrel	0.33
Foil	Steel	0.33
Repellent	Menthol	0.33

Table 8: Most similar pair of topics between the training and validation set using the WordNet method.

C.3 Sentence Transformers

We finish our qualitative review of the topic overlap using Sentence Transformers. Table 9 shows the five most similar pairs of topics.

Train	Validation	Sim.
Costume	Halloween	0.60
Chlorophyll	Chrysanthemum	0.60
Housekeeper	Groomsman	0.60
Bracelet	Pendant	0.60
Forearm	Ankle	0.60

Table 9: Most similar pair of topics between the training and validation set using the Sentence Transformers method.

Test Set	Training Set
would it [a granite] be of rock material?	can it [a rock] be molded?
is it [a window] see through?	does it [a curtain] cover a window?
is it [a sweat] produced by the human body?	does it [an exercise] involve sweating?
does it [a hyacinth] have red flowers?	does it [a chrysanthemum] have a long stem?
is it [a ring] jewlery?	does it [a treasure] go on engagement rings?
is it [a bridge] larger than a car?	is it [a bumper] a bridge?
is it [a refuge] a type of campsite?	is it [a campground] the mountains?
is it [an ant] bigger than a honeybee?	does it [a honeybee] collect nectar?
is it [a marsupial] a kind of bear?	is it [a bear] long?
does it [a hyacinth] have white flowers?	does it [a chrysanthemum] have a long stem?
is it [a pendant] jeweled?	does it [a treasure] go on engagement rings?
does it [a hyacinth] have yellow flowers?	does it [a chrysanthemum] have a long stem?
is it [a ship] larger than a whale?	does it [a whale] have fins?
is it [a hurdle] made of stone or rock?	can it [a rock] be molded?
is it [a fly] a bug?	does it [an insect] have antennae?

Table 10: Top fifteen most similar pairs of questions between the training and test set of 20Q.

Test Set	Training Set
an electron holds a positive charge and	an electron holds a positive charge.
happy meals almost always come with a toy.	most happy meals include a toy.
april is larger than february	april is smaller than march
sunlight on the skin causes eye cancer	sunlight causes almost all skin cancer
thunder sounds before lightning strikes	noise of thunder is heard before the lightning.
the beginning of a story is part of the end	a story has a beginning and an end.
is there a feminine french word for a city hall?	in french is it true that there are feminine and masculine words for a city hall?
europe is considered to be the most wealthy and richest continent.	europe has the richest countries in the world
a grapefruit is a fruit larger than a watermelon?	is a watermelon smaller than an apple?
tree is always part of forest	trees are never part of forests
someone of the male gender cannot give birth.	an adult male cannot give birth
if you add two plus two you will always get four.	two plus two unfortunately cannot ever add up to anything but four.
you can return items to a store only if you have a receipt.	an item can be returned from a store only if it is sold by that store.
private is another way to say public	private almost never means public.
a letter can be written with invisible ink.	writing cannot be read if you use invisible ink.

Table 11: Top fifteen most similar pairs of questions between the training and test set of Commonsense QA 2.0.

Test Set	Training Set
john leaves work at 6 pm so that he is an unlikely suspect for theft that happened in the office at 8 pm.	john leaves work at 6 pm so that he is an unlikely suspect for theft that happened in the office at 8 pm.
while in a windy rainstorm, you should always point your umbrella away from the wind.	while in a windy rainstorm, you should always point your umbrella away from the wind.
while in a windy rainstorm, you should always point your umbrella into the wind.	while in a windy rainstorm, you should always point your umbrella into the wind.
since i want to improve my golf skill quickly, i spend 2 hours on the course every day.	since i want to improve my golf game, i spend 2 hours on the course every day.
if it is dark outside, opening the blinds will help you see.	if it is dark outside opening the blinds will not help you see.
because it was halloween eve and we had no candy, i decided to open the door and turn the porch light on.	because it was 6pm on halloween and we no candy, i decided to open the door and turn the porch light on.
having to teach a night class in thirty minutes, he should cook a three-course dinner instead of heating a frozen meal.	having to teach a night class in thirty minutes, he should make a three-course dinner instead of a frozen meal.
danny smokes a lot and drinks thirty beers per week while sarah doesn't smoke and doesn't drink, sarah will probably live longer.	danny smoke a lot and drink thirty beer per week while sarah dont smoke and dont drink, sarah will probably live longer.
if it is dark outside, opening the blinds will not help you see.	if it is dark outside opening the blinds will not help you see.
because it was halloween eve and we had plenty of candy, i decided to open the door and turn the porch light on.	because it was 6pm on halloween and we had plenty of candy, i decided to open the door and turn the porch light on.
having to teach a night class in thirty minutes, he should heat a frozen meal instead of cooking a three-course dinner.	having to teach a night class in thirty minutes, he should make a frozen meal instead of a three-course dinner.
danny smokes a lot and drinks thirty beers per week while sarah doesn't smoke and doesn't drink, danny will probably live longer.	danny smoke a lot and drink thirty beer per week while sarah dont smoke and dont drink, danny will probably live longer.
a spoon is more suitable for eating soup than a fork.	a spoon might be more suitable for eating soup than a fork.
it is easier to run one mile in 5 minutes than a half mile in 10 minutes.	it is easier to run two miles in five minutes than it is to run one mile in ten minutes.
a fork is more suitable for eating soup than a spoon.	a spoon might be more suitable for eating soup than a fork.

Table 12: Top fifteen most similar pairs of questions between the training and test set of Com2sense.

What Was Your Name Again? Interrogating Generative Conversational Models For Factual Consistency Evaluation

Ehsan Lotfi, Maxime De Bruyn, Jeska Buhmann, Walter Daelemans
CLiPS Research Center
University of Antwerp, Belgium
firstname.lastname@uantwerpen.be

Abstract

Generative conversational agents are known to suffer from problems like inconsistency and hallucination, and a big challenge in studying these issues remains evaluation: they are not properly reflected in common text generation metrics like perplexity or BLEU, and alternative implicit methods like semantic similarity or NLI labels can be misguided when few specific tokens are decisive. In this work we propose ConsisTest; a factual consistency benchmark including both WH and Y/N questions based on PersonaChat, along with a hybrid evaluation pipeline which aims to get the best of symbolic and sub-symbolic methods. Using these and focusing on pretrained generative models like BART, we provide detailed analysis on how the model's factual consistency is affected by variations in question and context.

Agent persona
my name is paul.
I live with my two sons in chicago.
my favorite color is green.
I am a professional golf player.
Utterances
user> hi! what's your name?
- my name is paul. how are you today?
user> I am good. my name is luna.
- nice to meet you luna. what do you do for work?
user> I am a journalist. are you married ?
- no I am not married. do you have any kids?
user> I don't. how about you?
- I have two sons. do you have any hobbies?
user> I like to read. what was your name again?.
- my name is luna. what is your favorite color?

Table 1: Example interaction with a pre-trained generative model fine-tuned on the PersonaChat dataset, which ends with an inconsistency.

1 Introduction

Although capable of producing fluent responses, generative conversational models have proved to be prone to problems like hallucination and self-contradiction, which do not go away with increasing model size (Roller et al., 2021; Adiwardana et al., 2020; Shuster et al., 2021b).

In knowledge-grounded conversation, the prominent issue is hallucination —i.e. generating plausible looking statements that are factually incorrect— and can be partly mitigated by improving the knowledge selection or retrieval module (Shuster et al., 2021a). In open-domain chitchat, where the grounding "knowledge" is mainly personal attributes and facts (preset before or said during the conversation), this manifests itself as inconsistency or forgetfulness (Table 1) where the conversational agent does not commit to its personal narrative although the facts are present in the conversational context. These self-contradictions immediately disrupt the conversational flow and cause the agents to fail in gaining user trust and their long-term communication confidence (Nie et al., 2021).

On a general level, open-domain conversational consistency can be defined with respect to persona, style, and context (Huang et al., 2020). When limited to persona and context (which is often the case in literature), due to the inherent logical aspect, consistency becomes a relatively objective and quantifiable attribute compared to most other conversational traits: While qualities like humanness, interestingness or engagingness (Li et al., 2019) usually need human evaluation for a reliable assessment, consistency can be fairly estimated using simplifying assumptions. In particular, identifying inconsistent utterances can be reduced to a classic NLI (natural language inference) problem by assuming that contradictions are contained in a sentence pair (Welleck et al., 2019). Following the NLI paradigm, many studies have tried to provide better and bigger datasets or models to train for detecting contradictions. These efforts how-

Proceedings of the 2nd Workshop on Natural Language Generation, Evaluation, and Metrics (GEM), pages 509 - 519
December 7, 2022 ©2022 Association for Computational Linguistics

ever mainly focused on the overall assessment at inference time —which allows for improving consistency by re-ranking response candidates—, and have not explored enough the fine-grained dependencies of consistency, subject to parameters like data and training.

In this work we try to get new insights into conversational consistency, via simplifying assumptions that allow to reduce the problem one step further, into a pseudo-QA case. To this end, we create an evaluation dataset following an interrogative approach; i.e. posing factual questions about the facts that are already mentioned in the conversation history or persona. This allows us to develop and use a hybrid evaluation method for precise performance assessment.

Our contribution is threefold:(1) We present ConsisTest: an interrogative conversational QA dataset with both WH and Y/N questions to assess factual consistency in open-domain conversational agents. (2) We develop a hybrid evaluation pipeline, tailored to our dataset which provides reliable consistency scores, highly correlated with human evaluation. (3) We use the benchmark to explore the effect of parameters like question source and question type on model's consistency[1].

2 Related Work

Consistency and factuality of responses has always been one of the main qualities in the assessment of conversational agents but framing it as an NLI problem by Welleck et al. (2019) opened the way for reliable automatic evaluations using models trained on labelled data: They introduced the DNLI dataset, comprising of premise-hypothesis pairs semi-automatically generated from the PersonaChat persona statements and showed that using the NLI model to re-rank generated responses, improves persona consistency in dialogue. Dziri et al. (2019) created InferConvAI, another dataset based on PersonaChat personas, and applied it for dialogue topic coherence evaluation. Li et al. (2020) employed such an evaluator for unlikelihood training and showed its effectiveness for improving logical consistency, while Mesgar et al. (2021) used it as a reward function in reinforcement learning with positive impact on the factual consistency between response and persona facts. To address the limitations of DNLI, Nie et al. (2021) introduced DECODE, a human-written fully-conversational dataset based on multiple datasets and covering logical and context-related reasoning beyond personal facts, which proved to result in significantly more robust consistency evaluation.

Another approach (besides the NLI-based methods) for automatic evaluation of consistency is asking and answering questions, which is more applicable to knowledge-grounded conversation. Originally proposed in abstractive summarization (Durmus et al., 2020; Wang et al., 2020), it assumes that factually equivalent or consistent texts should be interchangeably usable to generate factual questions and to answer them. Honovich et al. (2021) adapted it to introduce Q^2, to assess factual consistency in knowledge-grounded dialogues with significantly higher correlation with human judgement.

More related to our work, Li et al. (2020) applied a similar interrogative approach (but limited to WH questions on history) combined with NLI-based assessment, to provide a framework for evaluating consistency in open-domain conversational agents, and used it to compare chatbots in interactive setups. Finally, Rashkin et al. (2021) explored adding control code features (via special tokens) to inform a pretrained model about the groundedness of responses in knowledge-grounded conversations, and showed that by using these codes during the inference, the model can be effectively persuaded to generate more grounded responses.

3 ConsisTest

The ConsisTest benchmark is based on 'interrogative factual questioning': Since a consistent dialogue agent should commit to its personal narrative, to assess consistency, we ask the agent factual questions about previously stated or uttered facts, and demand accordance with them.

To create the benchmark, we apply this approach on the popular PersonaChat dataset (Zhang et al., 2018) which contains crowd-sourced conversations grounded in predefined "personas" (i.e. a set of 4–6 simple personal statements), and therefore allows us to study both the persona and history consistency. Figure 1 demonstrates the overall process in two steps: First, a PersonaChat persona+conversation pair (a) is studied to produce simple factual questions in both WH and Y/N formats (b). Then these questions are appended to conversation segments to create a benchmark sample (c).

Next we discuss the process in more detail.

[1]The dataset and evaluation code are available at: https://github.com/ELotfi/consistest

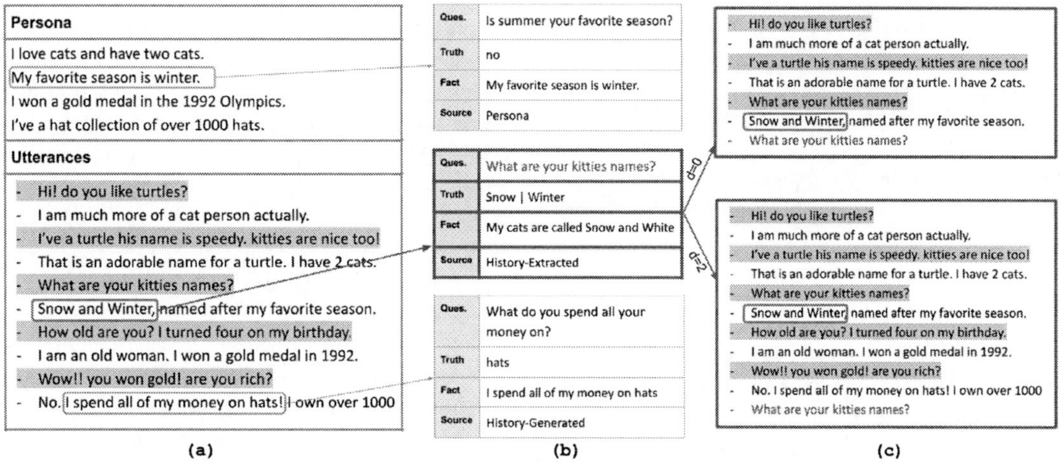

Figure 1: Creating ConsisTest: a) An (edited) example of a conversation from PersonaChat. Unshaded utterances are from the speaker with the mentioned persona (agent). b) Producing factual questions from Persona or History via generation or extraction. c) Creating ConsisTest samples by adding produced questions after the facts they are based on: immediately after (d=0), and with 2 turns in between (d=2).

3.1 Producing Questions

As mentioned above, the first step is to produce questions from a PersonaChat persona+conversation sample. The original validation set –which we use here– contains 1000 persona+conversation pairs, but a quick study shows that the 1000 persona sets are curated from 550 unique statements. We use three methods to acquire factual questions from these statements as well as utterances (more details in Appendix A):

- **Rule-based Generation:** Using a simple rule-based process and proper templates, we generate Y/N questions based on persona statements and (cleaned) factual utterances (Figure 1-(b)-top).
- **Neural Generation:** Using a T5 model (Raffel et al., 2020) finetuned on answer-agnostic question generation with SQuAD, we produce WH-questions based on persona statements and (cleaned) factual utterances. The outputs are then used to get answers from the context (as spans) via an extractive question answering model (Figure 1-(b)-bottom).
- **Extraction:** We extract question and answer pairs that already exist in the utterances (Figure 1-(b)-middle). We mark these History-Extracted, as opposed to History-Generated which are questions *generated* from history.

During the procedure, we annotate the question **Source** (Persona, History-Generated or History-Extracted), question **Type** (WH or Y/N), and —in the case of history-based questions— the **Turn** index in dialogue from which the QA has been generated or extracted. We also manually annotate the **Fact** (Figure 1-(b)) on which the question is based as a self-contained statement which can act as the gold long answer to the proposed question (as opposed to **Truth** which only contains the short answer keywords). At the end we obtain around 12k question-answer candidates which after manual cleaning and filtering (details in Appendix A) amount to 3125 samples. Table 2 shows the statistics of the final QA set[2].

Source	Total #	WH	Y/N	Extracted
Persona	1100	492	608	-
History	2025	1613	412	588
Total	3125	2105	1020	588

Table 2: Statistics of the final QA set. The "Extracted" column is already counted in WH and Y/N numbers.

3.2 Creating Benchmark Samples

Having the questions at hand, we now can append them to proper dialog segments (or contexts) to

[2]Since the persona-based and history-based questions have been created from 550 statements and 1000 dialogues respectively, these numbers mean that on average each persona statement has originated 2 questions, while the same is true for a whole dialogue. This difference in question density will manifest itself when constructing the final benchmark, as observed in the next section.

Source	Total #	WH	Y/N	Extracted
Persona	15088	7008	8080	-
History	3545	2818	727	1023
Total	18633	9826	8807	1023

Table 3: Distribution of samples in ConsisTest-02. The "Extracted" column is already counted in WH and Y/N numbers.

create benchmark samples (Figure 1-(c)). Since a question theoretically can be asked anywhere *after* its supporting fact, we examine two cases: $d = 0$; i.e. question comes right after the fact (c-top), and $d = 2$; i.e. question comes 2 turns after the fact (c-bottom).[3] Following these conventions, we get a set of 18633 conversational samples (context + question), which we call **ConsisTest-02** (referring to the chosen values for d or distance parameter). Table 3 shows the details.

The curated benchmark can now be used to assess a dialog agent's factual consistency if we have a reliable way to evaluate the agent's responses to the proposed context+question pair.

4 Evaluation Method

Evaluating generated text is a well-known challenge in NLP, situated between the inadequacies of automatic metrics and difficulties of human evaluation (van der Lee et al., 2019). When limited to answering questions, the task becomes more manageable and well-defined since there are often logically limited sets of correct or 'gold' answers that can act as reference. In particular, factual questions provide the possibility to formulate the problem as span extraction (e.g. SQuAD dataset (Rajpurkar et al., 2016)) which then can be evaluated with more confidence using token-level comparison methods like the F1-score. But the conversational aspect of our problem prevents us from directly and exclusively relying on token-level evaluation, since the overall semantic agreement between the response and reference fact is not guaranteed.

A common alternative, especially when dealing with consistency, is using NLI models (Welleck et al., 2019) which classify the relationship between a pair of phrases (corresponding to the reference fact and model response in our case) as one of Entailment, Neutral or Contradiction. This is quite helpful in identifying sharp inconsistencies but is less sensitive to token-level nuances that might be of interest in factual QAs. Regarding our benchmark, there are cases where the pure NLI method often falls short of a valid assessment, most notably:

- **Partial keyword coverage:** NLI models often are unable to check for the full coverage of important keywords. For example the `roberta-large-mnli` model (referred to as RobNLI in the rest of this section) identifies the [*'My cats are called snow and winter.'* , *'They are called winter.'*] pair as Entailment.
- **Neutralized judgement:** When the provided hypothesis goes beyond the premise content (which is quite common in conversational data), the model's verdict can shift towards "Neutral". For example, while RobNLI classifies [*'My cats are called snow and winter.'* , *'they are called snow and puffy.'*] as Contradiction, changing the hypothesis to *'they are called snow and puffy. I love them a lot.'* results in a Neutral verdict.
- **Y/N questions:** In our case, the included Y/N questions prove to bring new challenges. First, the agent might give brief answers (e.g. *I am.* or *Nope.*), which are not self-contained enough for an NLI model to do a solid judgment. Second, it turns out that agreement between the short and long answer is not a given in generated responses[4]. For example when asked 'Are you single?' (with Fact = 'I am married.'), models occasionally respond with phrases like 'yes I'm married.' which we consider to be wrong, while any NLI model would naturally classify the [*'I am married'* , *'yes I'm married.'*] pair as Entailment.

Fine-tuning the classic NLI model on conversational data (e.g. the DNLI dataset (Welleck et al., 2019)) leads to partial improvement but to achieve more accurate results we decide to develop a hybrid pipeline which tries to get the best of the symbolic and sub-symbolic methods.

4.1 The Hybrid Approach

Our hybrid method consists of 3 main components: 1) Rule-based assessment, 2) NLI model, and 3)

[3]Note that the context received by the conversational model is Persona+History. Therefore for Persona-based questions, the $d = 0$ case means that the conversation starts with the question (i.e. no History).

[4]We will revisit this observation later in the experiments.

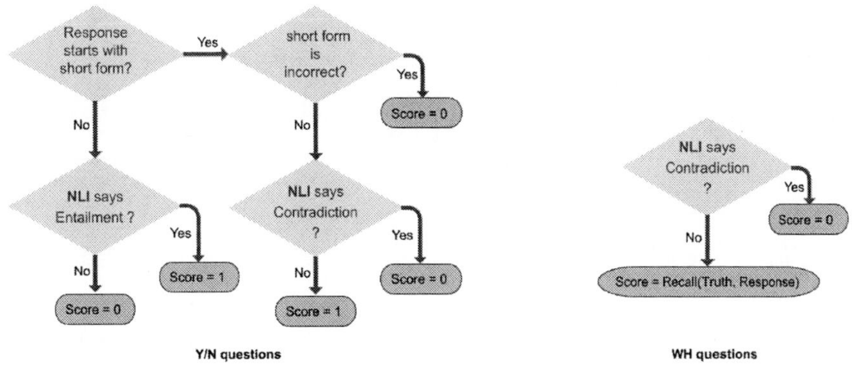

Figure 2: Our Hybrid evaluation pipeline for Y/N (left) and WH questions (right).

Token-level metrics. Figure 2 shows how these components are used based on the question type[5]:

- **Y/N questions**: Here the method tries to deal with the Y/N short-answer challenges (mentioned above) before using the NLI module. More specifically, it first checks (via templates) whether the response starts with a short-form answer like *no.* or *I do.*, in which case the short answer is assessed using rules. Then the NLI module is employed to compare the response with the reference fact.

- **WH questions**: Here the NLI module acts as a safeguard to make sure the response does not contradict the reference fact. If the response passes this check, it will be scored by the Recall of the Truth keywords.

Note that the token-level assessment, seemingly applies a more strict measure of consistency which demands grounding and punishes generic or irrelevant responses. However, since all questions have their supporting facts present in the context received by the conversational model: a) generic responses like *'I don't know.'* can be safely considered inconsistent, and b) completely irrelevant responses are almost non-existent.

To assess the pipeline, we compare the performance of the following methods with human evaluation:

- **F1**: F1-score of response with respect to Fact.

- **Recall**: Ratio of Truth keywords covered in response.

- **RobNLI**: Entailment score of response (ref.=Fact) according to RoBERTa-large model finetuned on MNLI data.

- **RobDNLI**: Entailment score of response (ref.=Fact) according to The RobNLI model finetuned on the DNLI dataset (Welleck et al., 2019).

- **Hybrid(RobNLI)**: Our Hybrid pipeline, with RobNLI as the NLI module.

- **Hybrid(RobDNLI)**: Our Hybrid pipeline, with RobDNLI as the NLI module.

For the evaluation set, we first generate responses to 1000 extra pairs of context+question using 4 pretrained models finetuned on PersonaChat, under slightly different settings. We then randomly sample 1000 instances to be manually scored following simple guidelines that are described in Appendix C. Finally, we apply the listed methods on the same set and compare their scores with human evaluation.

Method \Subset	All	WH	Y/N	MSE
F1	.517	.512	.520	.214
Recall	.553	.564	.538	.131
RobNLI	.511	.448	.599	.256
RobDNLI	.71	.709	.715	.220
Hyb (RobNLI)	.604	.545	.686	.071
Hyb (RobDNLI)	.640	.565	.743	.047
Human Eval	.645	.577	.739	0.0

Table 4: Consistency score obtained by different methods/baselines applied on the curated evaluation set. MSE is the mean square error against the human evaluation scores.

[5]More details can be found in Appendix B

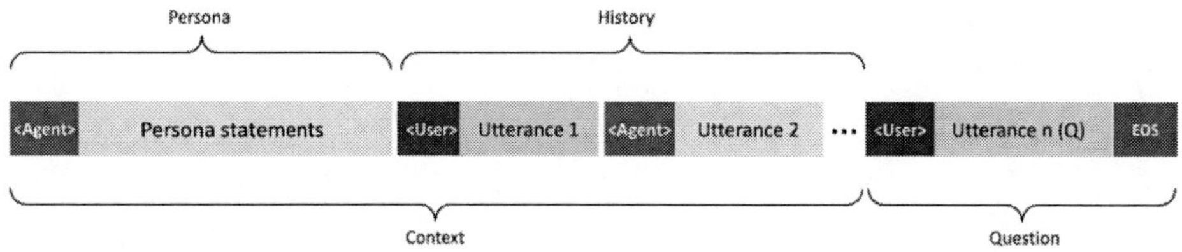

Figure 3: Punctuating a conversational input sequence (e.g. in ConsisTest) with special tokens to mark the speakers.

Table 4 shows the results on the curated set and its question-type subsets. The last column shows the mean square error against the human evaluation scores. As one can see, the Hybrid(RobDNLI) method achieves the best results (i.e. closest to human evaluation) on average and across all subsets, which agrees with the observation that RobDNLI and Recall —as the main components of this method— have very good performances on the Y/N and WH subsets, respectively. In other words the Hybrid method manages to benefit from the strengths of symbolic and sub-symbolic approaches by properly switching between them.

Based on these results, we pick the Hybrid(RobDNLI) method as our consistency evaluation approach for the rest of this paper. It should be mentioned however that the Hybrid method is tailored to the specifics of this problem and dataset and, although it might work well in other cases, it is not presented here as a generic evaluation method for consistency.

5 Experiments

Having a reliable evaluation method, we can now delve deeper to see how/if the consistency of a conversational model is affected by question properties (e.g. Source and Type) and training setups (e.g. input encoding scheme).

As the standard model, we pick the base version of BART (Lewis et al., 2020) which is a pretrained encoder-decoder transformer with a total number of 12 layers (6+6) and 140M parameters. To encode the inputs, we follow the standard practice of identifying the speakers via <user> and <agent> 'special tokens' (Wolf et al., 2019). Figure 3 shows the result of applying such an encoding to an arbitrary sample of ConsisTest or PersonaChat dataset.

We choose 3 full turns -or 6 utterances- for the memory size (maximum number of previous utterances kept in the context) and finetune the model on PersonaChat train set for 6 epochs (early-stopping) with an effective batch size of 128. We then use the finetuned model to do inference on ConsisTest-02; i.e. generating responses to the provided context+question pairs. To ease reproducibility, we implement the training and inference using the Trainer and generate methods from the HuggingFace Transformers library (Wolf et al., 2020). Table 5 shows the obtained scores.

All	**Persona**		**History**	
	WH	Y/N	WH	Y/N
.74	.86	.80	.35	.57

Table 5: Factual consistency scores on ConsisTest-02 for BART-base

5.1 Question Source

One interesting observation in Table 5 is the large gap in consistency score between the Persona- and History-based questions. To explain this gap, we consider three potential factors or hypotheses:

1. **Linguistic-Statistical**: The Persona-based questions (in our dataset) are essentially easier to answer than the History-based ones.

2. **Structural**: The supporting fact for Persona-based questions is clean and clear (a persona statement) whereas the History-based facts should be extracted or even induced from the utterances.

3. **Positional**: There is a positional bias at work which benefits Persona-based questions since their supporting fact comes in the beginning of the input.

To assess the first, we consider the ultimate case in which the model only receives the clean supporting statement (i.e. the Fact) as context. This eliminates the structural disparities and transforms the problem into a very straightforward Question-Answering with minimum noise (no irrelevant information in the context) whose results can be used

Model Input	Persona		History	
	WH	Y/N	WH	Y/N
Persona + History + Question (standard)	.86	.80	.35	.57
Fact + Question	.93	.82	.90	.82
Persona + Fact + History + Question	.86	.80	.66	.74
Fact + Persona + History + Question	.81	.76	.79	.80

Table 6: The effect of providing clean grounding context on model's consistency score under different combinations of input

as a proxy for 'average question difficulty'. Results (second row in Table 6) show that this modification almost fills the gap between the subset performances, and can be taken as an indication that the History-based questions —by themselves— are not significantly more challenging than the Persona-based ones.

To assess the second hypothesis, we do the inference and evaluation again, but this time for the History-based questions we add the Fact to the end of the Persona section and mask the grounding turn (i.e. the utterance containing the Fact) in History. The evaluation results (third row in Table 6) show an expected boost in the History-based subset which is more significant for WH questions (.35 to .66), but it does not fully eliminate the performance gap.

For the third hypothesis (positional bias), we repeat the previous experiment but this time we add the Fact to the beginning of Persona instead of its end. As the last row in Table 6 shows, this change not only results in a significant boost in the History-based performance, it also has a negative effect on the Persona-based performance, bringing them almost on par with each other[6]. We can therefore conclude that the structural and positional advantages are mainly responsible for the source-based performance gap.

5.2 Question Type

As foreshadowed in 4, one observation in model responses to Y/N questions is the frequent disagreement between the three (potential) parts of a Y/N response; i.e. yes/no, short answer, and long answer. In many cases, although the long answer is correct and consistent, the short answer or the yes/no part contradicts it, leading to examples like *yes I work at a school* in response to *do you work at a bar?*, asked based on the Fact :*I work at a school.*

To get a better idea of the weight of this issue, we look into the Persona-based subset which contains most of the Y/N questions. Table 7 shows the results. The included percentages are relative to the previous column; for example the first row shows that from the 5178 Y/N questions with positive Truth, 12% were answered incorrectly, of which 76% had incorrect short answers. From these we can see that:

1. Negation is significantly more challenging than confirmation (35% vs. 12% error rate).
2. Short-long-answer inconsistency accounts for the majority of Y/N mistakes (87% in total).
3. Short-long-answer inconsistency is more evident in negation cases 93% vs. 76%).

Truth	Total #	Wrong Ans.	Wrong Short Ans.
Yes	5178	621 (12%)	475 (76%)
No	2904	1007 (35%)	936 (93%)
All	8082	1628 (20%)	1411 (87%)

Table 7: Error analysis in the Persona-based Y/N question subset (BART-base-special). Percentages are relative to the previous column.

6 Conclusion and Future Work

In this work we tried to obtain new insights into one of the prominent issues in open-domain conversational modeling, i.e. consistency. Taking a factual questioning approach, we built a benchmark dataset (ConsisTest) based on PersonaChat, and developed a hybrid evaluation pipeline that takes advantage of both symbolic and sub-symbolic methods to achieve high correlation with human evaluation of factual consistency. Then, focusing on pretrained generative transformers (i.e. BART),

[6]To rule out the possibility of training bias (i.e. early persona statements are significantly more talked and asked about in the training set), we train a model with persona statement permutation, which does not result in any significant change in performance scores.

we studied how the consistency score varies in different subsets of our benchmark: We confirmed the intuition that in a persona-history setting, remaining consistent with respect to conversation history is significantly more challenging than commitment to persona, and we showed that this gap is mainly rooted in structural and positional advantages of the latter. We also observed that in the case of Y/N questions, agreement between the short and long answer is not a given with these models, and accounts for the majority of Y/N inconsistencies.

Many more aspects and dependencies of conversational consistency remain to be explored, including the difference between the History-Generated and History-Extracted questions, effect of insertion distance (d), importance of the base model (e.g. decoder-only models like GPT2 vs. encoder-decoders like BART), and the detailed dynamics behind the apparent positional bias observed in 5.1. These, along with the refinement and expansion of the dataset, provide interesting options for the future work.

7 Limitations

The choices we made in our study, come with their own limitations which should be acknowledged and –if possible– addressed in future work. Most importantly, is the statistical and linguistic properties of our benchmark dataset which only includes short, clear and straightforward question-answer pairs. While highly facilitating our evaluation method, we should keep in mind that challenges in conversational consistency are not limited to the factual aspect. The benchmark can also benefit from more instances and a better question-source balance, specially if discrepancies between the History-Generated and History-Extracted subset performances are to be explored. Finally, having access to fine-grained QA annotations (e.g. complexity proxies like whether the question can be answered by simple extraction, or does it need the employment of external common sense, multi-hop reasoning, coreference resolution etc.) enables us to make more reliable conclusions.

In the evaluation part, our hybrid pipeline demonstrates relatively accurate results, showing that it is well-suited to our data. But this comes at the cost of 'specificity' which makes it less robust to future modifications. Therefore the pipeline's scope of validity should be considered before its employment in new scenarios.

Acknowledgements

This research received funding from the Flemish Government under the "Onderzoeksprogramma Artificiële Intelligentie (AI) Vlaanderen" programme.

References

Daniel Adiwardana, Minh-Thang Luong, David R. So, Jamie Hall, Noah Fiedel, Romal Thoppilan, Zi Yang, Apoorv Kulshreshtha, Gaurav Nemade, Yifeng Lu, and Quoc V. Le. 2020. Towards a human-like open-domain chatbot.

Esin Durmus, He He, and Mona Diab. 2020. FEQA: A question answering evaluation framework for faithfulness assessment in abstractive summarization. In *Proceedings of the 58th Annual Meeting of the Association for Computational Linguistics*, pages 5055–5070, Online. Association for Computational Linguistics.

Nouha Dziri, Ehsan Kamalloo, Kory Mathewson, and Osmar Zaiane. 2019. Evaluating coherence in dialogue systems using entailment. In *Proceedings of the 2019 Conference of the North American Chapter of the Association for Computational Linguistics: Human Language Technologies, Volume 1 (Long and Short Papers)*, pages 3806–3812, Minneapolis, Minnesota. Association for Computational Linguistics.

Nouha Dziri, Hannah Rashkin, Tal Linzen, and David Reitter. 2021. Evaluating groundedness in dialogue systems: The begin benchmark.

Or Honovich, Leshem Choshen, Roee Aharoni, Ella Neeman, Idan Szpektor, and Omri Abend. 2021. q^2: Evaluating factual consistency in knowledge-grounded dialogues via question generation and question answering. In *Proceedings of the 2021 Conference on Empirical Methods in Natural Language Processing*, pages 7856–7870, Online and Punta Cana, Dominican Republic. Association for Computational Linguistics.

Minlie Huang, Xiaoyan Zhu, and Jianfeng Gao. 2020. Challenges in building intelligent open-domain dialog systems. *ACM Transactions on Information Systems*, 38:1–32.

Mike Lewis, Yinhan Liu, Naman Goyal, Marjan Ghazvininejad, Abdelrahman Mohamed, Omer Levy, Veselin Stoyanov, and Luke Zettlemoyer. 2020. BART: Denoising sequence-to-sequence pre-training for natural language generation, translation, and comprehension. In *Proceedings of the 58th Annual Meeting of the Association for Computational Linguistics*, pages 7871–7880, Online. Association for Computational Linguistics.

Margaret Li, Stephen Roller, Ilia Kulikov, Sean Welleck, Y-Lan Boureau, Kyunghyun Cho, and Jason Weston. 2020. Don't say that! making inconsistent dialogue unlikely with unlikelihood training. In *Proceedings of the 58th Annual Meeting of the Association for Computational Linguistics*, pages 4715–4728, Online. Association for Computational Linguistics.

Margaret Li, Jason Weston, and Stephen Roller. 2019. ACUTE-EVAL: improved dialogue evaluation with optimized questions and multi-turn comparisons. *CoRR*, abs/1909.03087.

Mohsen Mesgar, Edwin Simpson, and Iryna Gurevych. 2021. Improving factual consistency between a response and persona facts. In *Proceedings of the 16th Conference of the European Chapter of the Association for Computational Linguistics: Main Volume*, pages 549–562, Online. Association for Computational Linguistics.

Yixin Nie, Mary Williamson, Mohit Bansal, Douwe Kiela, and Jason Weston. 2021. I like fish, especially dolphins: Addressing contradictions in dialogue modeling. In *Proceedings of the 59th Annual Meeting of the Association for Computational Linguistics and the 11th International Joint Conference on Natural Language Processing (Volume 1: Long Papers)*, pages 1699–1713, Online. Association for Computational Linguistics.

Colin Raffel, Noam Shazeer, Adam Roberts, Katherine Lee, Sharan Narang, Michael Matena, Yanqi Zhou, Wei Li, and Peter J. Liu. 2020. Exploring the limits of transfer learning with a unified text-to-text transformer. *J. Mach. Learn. Res.*, 21:140:1–140:67.

Pranav Rajpurkar, Jian Zhang, Konstantin Lopyrev, and Percy Liang. 2016. SQuAD: 100,000+ questions for machine comprehension of text. In *Proceedings of the 2016 Conference on Empirical Methods in Natural Language Processing*, pages 2383–2392, Austin, Texas. Association for Computational Linguistics.

Hannah Rashkin, David Reitter, Gaurav Singh Tomar, and Dipanjan Das. 2021. Increasing faithfulness in knowledge-grounded dialogue with controllable features. In *Proceedings of the 59th Annual Meeting of the Association for Computational Linguistics and the 11th International Joint Conference on Natural Language Processing (Volume 1: Long Papers)*, pages 704–718, Online. Association for Computational Linguistics.

Stephen Roller, Emily Dinan, Naman Goyal, Da Ju, Mary Williamson, Yinhan Liu, Jing Xu, Myle Ott, Eric Michael Smith, Y-Lan Boureau, and Jason Weston. 2021. Recipes for building an open-domain chatbot. In *Proceedings of the 16th Conference of the European Chapter of the Association for Computational Linguistics: Main Volume*, pages 300–325, Online. Association for Computational Linguistics.

Kurt Shuster, Spencer Poff, Moya Chen, Douwe Kiela, and Jason Weston. 2021a. Retrieval augmentation reduces hallucination in conversation. In *Findings of the Association for Computational Linguistics: EMNLP 2021*, pages 3784–3803, Punta Cana, Dominican Republic. Association for Computational Linguistics.

Kurt Shuster, Jack Urbanek, Arthur Szlam, and Jason Weston. 2021b. Am i me or you? state-of-the-art dialogue models cannot maintain an identity.

Chris van der Lee, Albert Gatt, Emiel van Miltenburg, Sander Wubben, and Emiel Krahmer. 2019. Best practices for the human evaluation of automatically generated text. In *Proceedings of the 12th International Conference on Natural Language Generation*, pages 355–368, Tokyo, Japan. Association for Computational Linguistics.

Alex Wang, Kyunghyun Cho, and Mike Lewis. 2020. Asking and answering questions to evaluate the factual consistency of summaries. In *Proceedings of the 58th Annual Meeting of the Association for Computational Linguistics*, pages 5008–5020, Online. Association for Computational Linguistics.

Sean Welleck, Jason Weston, Arthur Szlam, and Kyunghyun Cho. 2019. Dialogue natural language inference. In *Proceedings of the 57th Annual Meeting of the Association for Computational Linguistics*, pages 3731–3741, Florence, Italy. Association for Computational Linguistics.

Thomas Wolf, Lysandre Debut, Victor Sanh, Julien Chaumond, Clement Delangue, Anthony Moi, Pierric Cistac, Tim Rault, Remi Louf, Morgan Funtowicz, Joe Davison, Sam Shleifer, Patrick von Platen, Clara Ma, Yacine Jernite, Julien Plu, Canwen Xu, Teven Le Scao, Sylvain Gugger, Mariama Drame, Quentin Lhoest, and Alexander Rush. 2020. Transformers: State-of-the-art natural language processing. In *Proceedings of the 2020 Conference on Empirical Methods in Natural Language Processing: System Demonstrations*, pages 38–45, Online. Association for Computational Linguistics.

Thomas Wolf, Victor Sanh, Julien Chaumond, and Clement Delangue. 2019. Transfertransfo: A transfer learning approach for neural network based conversational agents.

Saizheng Zhang, Emily Dinan, Jack Urbanek, Arthur Szlam, Douwe Kiela, and Jason Weston. 2018. Personalizing dialogue agents: I have a dog, do you have pets too?

A Appendix: Question Generation and Cleaning

PersonaChat's validation set contains 1000 dialogues and 7801 utterance pairs. Each dialogue comes with a persona set for the "self" speaker (which hereafter we refer to as "agent"), corresponding to even utterances. In total these sets amount to 4483 persona statements which are unseen in the training set but are not all unique; i.e. the 1000 persona sets are combinations of around 550 unique statements[7]. We distill these unique persona lines and use them as input for two question generation methods:

- **Deep Neural Generation pipeline** using a T5 model finetuned on answer-agnostic question generation with SQuAD. The outputs (questions) are then used to get answers from the context by a question answering model. Because of its extractive nature, this pipeline only produces WH questions.
- **Rule-based Generation pipeline** using a simple rule-based process which checks for the polarity of the statement (mainly based on the presence of negation) and then generates Y/N questions following proper templates. Here the simple and repetitive structure of persona statements comes in useful[8].

For the History-based questions we distinguish two ways to produce questions:

- **Generation**: Using the agent's utterances in the same way as personas (i.e. feeding them to the deep and rule-based generation pipelines to get WH and Y/N QA candidates). Since utterances are not single-sentence clean statements like personas, we first split each agent's utterance into sentences and filter out the interrogative ones (using question words and '?' as clues), as these rarely contain any information about the agent. We mark these questions as Hist_Gen.
- **Extraction**: In many cases, a Q&A pair already exists in the utterances but they often escape the previous approach due to short-form answers (e.g. the 3rd turn in Figure 1-(a)). To capture these we extract utterance pairs in which a question is asked from the agent (using question cues), and clean the pair by removing any possible non-interrogative parts from the first, and any interrogative parts from the second utterance. We mark these questions as Hist_Ext.

In the cleaning process we filter the produced QA pairs mainly by removing errors and duplicates, but also WH questions based on clearly non-exclusive facts. For example in Figure 1-(a) one candidate question about the first persona might be: *What animal do you love?* with the answer being 'cats'. We remove this QA since 'cats' is not necessarily the complete answer, as the agent might also love other animals![9]. This step allows us to safely apply the seemingly stricter consistency measure discussed in 4.1; i.e. with an exclusive fact, a general or uninformative response can be more fairly and confidently rejected as inconsistency.

B Appendix: Evaluation Method

The evaluation pipeline receives Truth, Fact and model's Response to perform a hybrid evaluation. It comprises of two main components:

Symbolic: which does token-level comparison between Response and Truth.

Sub-symbolic: which uses an NLI (Natural Language Inference) classifier to do sentence-level comparison between Response and Fact. Based on Table 4 we use RobDNLI which is the `roberta-large-mnli` model finetuned on the DNLI dataset (Welleck et al., 2019), and classifies the relationship between a pair of inputs as one of Entailment, Neutral or Contradiction.

Before using the pipeline, Response and Truth go through a pre-processing step which first removes the potential interrogative parts in Response (e.g. the second sentence in 'They are called snow and winter. Do you have any hobbies?'), using simple pattern matching. Then numeric words in Response and Truth (if any) are converted to digits using a rule-based code (e.g. twenty one -> 21). After this step, Response and Truth/Fact are compared based on the question type as was demonstrated in Figure 2:

- **Y/N Questions**: Using a lexicon, the pipeline first checks if the Response starts with a short form answer (e.g. *yes*, *I do.*, etc.). If so, it checks whether the short form is wrong (e.g. *yes* or *I do.* to a negative question) in which

[7] 670, considering contractions (e.g. *I'm* vs. *I am*)

[8] e.g. out of 550 statements, 148 start with *I am* or *I have*.

[9] However the Y/N question *Do you love cats?* is kept

	Fact	Question	Truth	Response
1	I'm 30.	how old are you?	30	I've a german shepherd named barnaby.
2	I like spawn and the x men	What comic books do you like?	spawn and the x men	I like all kinds of comic books.
3	I drive a bmw.	do you drive a mercedes?	no	I do. I drive a bmw.
4	I don't go to school anymore.	are you going to school at all?	no	no. I am a student. what do you do for fun?

Table 8: Examples of Inconsistency (score = 0) demonstrating annotation guidelines.

case the score will be 0. Otherwise (i.e. correct short answer), the Response receives full score (1) unless the NLI model identifies it as contradicting the Fact, in which case the score will be 0. If the Response does not start with a short form, the value of NLI(Response, Truth)==Entailment is used as the score.

- **WH Questions**: Here the recalled ratio of Truth tokens in Response is returned, unless the NLI model identifies the Response as contradicting the Fact, in which case the score will be 0.

C Appendix: Human Evaluation

We score the 1000-sample response set for consistency, following these guidelines:

- The response should be (partly or fully) grounded in the fact about which the agent is asked. Therefore —and using the taxonomy described in Dziri et al. (2021)— generic, off-topic, uncooperative or hallucinative responses are considered inconsistent or wrong. (rows 1–2 in Table 8)

- In Y/N questions, the label/score is binary (0 or 1), and a "correct" answer should be consistent across its parts. Therefore any disagreement between the Yes/No part, the short answer and the long answer (if present) results in score = 0. (rows 3–4 in Table 8)

- In WH questions, the response is labeled as inconsistent, partly consistent or fully consistent (corresponding to [0, .5, 1] scores) based on agreement with Truth/Fact. The score should take into account the recalled fraction of Truth keywords (positive) as well as any hallucinated ones (negative). The exact lexical match is not important as long as the same concept(s) are conveyed.

Then a second annotator was presented with the guidelines and the demonstrative examples, and asked to score a 500-sample subset. Table 9 shows the agreement results (Cohen's κ) for the Y/N and WH subsets which —not surprisingly— are quite high.

Subset	Cohen κ	Annot. 1 (avg. score)	Annot. 2 (avg. score)
Y/N QAs	.94	.69	.67
WH QAs	.88	.59	.58
All	-	.632	.618

Table 9: Agreement between annotators in labeling the Y/N and WH responses. The last two columns show the average values when labels are taken for their numeric values.

D Appendix: Training and inference parameters

We choose 3 turns (or 6 utterances) for the memory size (maximum number of previous utterances kept in the context) and do the finetuning with early-stopping w.r.t evaluation set, using an effective batch size of 128 and lr=2e-5. To ease the reproducibility, we implement the training and inference using the `Trainer` and `generate` methods from the HuggingFace Transformers library (Wolf et al., 2020). The inference is done in a greedy way unless stated otherwise. The BART-base, BART-large and RoBERTa-MNLI model are accessible from this library as `facebook/bart-base`, `facebook/bart-large` and `roberta-large-mnli` respectively.

Narrative Why-Question Answering: A Review of Challenges and Datasets

Emil Kalbaliyev
Institute of Computer Science
University of Tartu
Tartu, Estonia
emil.kalbaliyev@ut.ee

Kairit Sirts
Institute of Computer Science
University of Tartu
Tartu, Estonia
kairit.sirts@ut.ee

Abstract

Narrative Why-Question Answering is an important task to assess the causal reasoning ability of models in narrative settings. Further progress in this domain requires clear identification of challenges that question answering models need to address. Since Narrative Why-Question Answering combines the characteristics of both narrative understanding and why-question answering, we review the challenges related to these two domains. In the context of why-questions, we review the characteristics of causal relations and the sources of ambiguity in why-questions. In relation to narratives, we discuss the challenges posed by the implicitness and the length of the narrative texts. Furthermore, we identify suitable datasets for Narrative Why-Question Answering and outline both data-specific and task-specific challenges that can be utilized to test the performance of models. Additionally, we discuss some issues that can pose problems in benchmarking Narrative Why-Question Answering systems.

1 Introduction

Narrative Why-Question Answering is the task of answering why-questions in narrative settings. This task combines the challenging properties of both why-question answering and narrative understanding. As such, Narrative Why-Question Answering makes a suitable task for evaluating complex comprehension abilities of language models.

Why-question is one of the most challenging non-factoid question types (Bolotova et al., 2022) because it requires discovering explicitly or implicitly stated causal relations from text. As such, why-questions can be used to test the causal reasoning abilities of QA systems. On the other hand, narratives can be considered a desirable testbed for machine reading comprehension (MRC) tasks because narratives play a central role in the life of human beings, they have implicit nature and complex structure, and fictional narratives are self-contained (Dunietz et al., 2020).

Although humans can easily identify causal relations in narratives and make inferences by using their background knowledge and by paying close attention to the timeline, cause, and motivation of the events/entities, current QA systems have difficulties extracting correct relations and making such complex inferences in narratives (Lal et al., 2021, 2022). In order to make further progress in the Narrative Why-Question Answering, one should be knowledgeable about challenges that exist in this domain and in its datasets. These challenges can stem from both the properties of the narrative understanding and the specifics of why-question answering. Some previous works (Lal et al., 2021, 2022) have mentioned commonsense-related challenges. However, we are not aware of any previous work that has attempted to give a comprehensive list of challenges related to this topic.

In this paper, our goal is to give a wider overview of the potential challenges in Narrative Why-Question Answering that can help to inform the researchers working in this domain. Furthermore, in terms of datasets, the TellMeWhy dataset (Lal et al., 2021) is the only dataset that solely focuses on Narrative Why-Question Answering. In this paper, we also address why-questions in multiple-choice, free-form, and extractive narrative QA datasets in order to more fully identify the scope of challenges in this domain. We believe that considering other Narrative Why-Question Answering datasets can also help further development in this domain.

We start by reviewing the concepts and challenges of why-questions and narratives in sections 2 and 3. In section 4, we identify the datasets relevant to Narrative Why-Question Answering, and provide an overview of the commonly used evaluation measures. Finally, in section 5, we analyze the dataset- and task-specific challenges according to the concepts mentioned in previous sections.

Proceedings of the 2nd Workshop on Natural Language Generation, Evaluation, and Metrics (GEM), pages 520 - 530
December 7, 2022 ©2022 Association for Computational Linguistics

2 Why-Questions

A why-question is typically asked about a causal relation in the text. Causal questions can be constructed in several ways and they are not limited to why-questions only. Causal questions can be also asked with *what* (e.g., what is the cause of), *which* (e.g., which are the consequences of), and *how* (e.g., how dangerous is) (Girju, 2003). However, why-question is the only question type that solely represents causality and can be used to test causal reasoning (Grivaz, 2010; Dunietz et al., 2017; Tan et al., 2022). Furthermore, answering why-questions requires more complex reasoning than answering other types of causal questions because it is more difficult for QA-systems to decide directly from a why-question which type of information needs to be searched for in the text (Girju, 2003). In the following subsections, we start by elaborating on the notion of causality, including how causal relations are expressed in the texts, and then review what ambiguities why-questions hold in relation to causality.

2.1 Causality

Causality is a semantic relationship between events showing that an event occurs or holds due to another event (Mostafazadeh et al., 2016b). Mostafazadeh et al. (2016b) distinguish four types of lexical causality relations: *cause*, *enable*, *prevent*, and *cause-to-end* based on the works by Wolff and Song (2003), Wolff (2007), and Khemlani et al. (2014). Moreover, causality has temporal implications such that if an event A causes/enables/prevents an event B, then A should start before B, or if an event A causes an event B to end, then B should start before A. Causality relations can hold one of the three temporal implications: *before*, *overlaps*, and *during* (Mostafazadeh et al., 2016b). Thus, while answering a why-question, the temporal relation between the events should also be taken into account in addition to the causality relation.

A causal relation is constructed from two components: cause and effect. Based on how the cause and the effect are conveyed in a text, causation can be distinguished into the following categories: explicit vs implicit, marked vs unmarked, and ambiguous vs unambiguous.

Explicit vs Implicit. Causation is explicit if both the cause and the effect are present in the text. Causation is implicit if either the cause or the effect of both are missing from the text (Blanco et al., 2008). For instance, "She was accepted to a top university after receiving a high score in the state examination" is explicit, while "I did not attend the mandatory final exam." is implicit because the effect of "failing the course" is not explicitly stated.

Marked vs Unmarked. Causation is marked if the text contains the causal signal words that indicate the causal relation (Blanco et al., 2008). For example, "I was late *because of* traffic" is marked, but "Do not buy any bread. We have already got two at home" is unmarked.

Ambiguous vs Unambiguous. If the causal relation is presented in the text with causal keywords (e.g., *cause*, *effect*, *consequence*) or with causal signals (e.g., *because of*, *due to*, *as a result of*), it is considered unambiguous (Girju, 2003). On the other hand, if a causal relation is constructed in the form of an expression containing affect verbs (e.g., *affect*, *change*, *influence*) or link verbs (e.g., *link*, *lead*, *depend*), it is considered ambiguous. Furthermore, if a marked signal always refers to causation (e.g., *because*), it is unambiguous, while if a marked word occasionally signals causation (e.g., *since*), it is ambiguous (Blanco et al., 2008).

2.2 Why-Questions: Ambiguity

Why-questions are constructed based on explicit and implicit causal relations in the text. Such questions seek a reason/cause as an answer. However, it is not always clear which reason/cause can be an answer to a question. There are two types of ambiguity: question ambiguity and answer ambiguity.

2.2.1 Question ambiguity

Question ambiguity can occur because of the structural ambiguity in the syntax of the question (Verberne et al., 2006). Due to question ambiguity, it might be not clear what action the why-question refers to. For example, "Why did he say that he will not come to the party?" can be interpreted as "Why did he say it?" or "Why will he not come to the party?". Both "He was asked what he will wear to the party." and "He has other plans for that time." can be correct answers based on different interpretations of the question.

2.2.2 Answer ambiguity

Answer ambiguity occurs because most questions can have multiple answers belonging to different answer types and because often the desired type is not expressed in the question. Several partially overlapping taxonomies of reasons, which is the cause component of a causal relation, have been proposed (Verberne et al., 2006; Dunietz et al., 2017; Tan et al., 2022). Verberne et al. (2006) distinguish four types of reasons based on Quirk et al. (1985):

- *Cause* - a temporal and causal relation without the involvement of the human intention: an event mechanistically leads to another event;
- *Motivation* - a temporal and causal relation with an involvement of the human intention: a goal or a motivation of an agent leads to their action;
- *Circumstance* - a temporal and causal relation based on conditionality: one event is a condition for another event to occur;
- *Generic purpose* - a causal relation stemming from physical functions of the objects.

Similarly, Dunietz et al. (2017) defines three types of causalities while annotating causal relations: (1) Consequence: similar to the Cause type above, (2) Motivation and (3) Purpose: similar to the Motivation type above. Tan et al. (2022) defines four senses for causality based on Webber et al. (2019) for annotating causal relations: (1) Cause: similar to the Cause type above (2) Purpose: similar to the Motivation type above, (3) Condition and (4) Negative-Condition, which can fit into the Circumstance type above. Although the types of reasons introduced by Verberne et al. (2006) are broader than the taxonomies of Dunietz et al. (2017) and Tan et al. (2022), this list is not complete, as Verberne et al. (2006) demonstrated that not all why-questions can be classified into these categories.

Context: "He opened the box to take a slice of pizza." ***Question:*** "Why did he open the box?" ***Answers:*** (1) The pizza was in the box. (2) The box was closed. (3) He was hungry. (4) He wanted to eat pizza. (5) He wanted to take a slice of pizza.

Table 1: An example of answer ambiguity. Answers (1) and (2) refer to causal reasons, answers (3), (4) and (5) refer to motivational reasons.

Valid answers to a why-question about an event or a state can include at least one of the cause, motivation, circumstance, or generic purpose of an event or state according to the above taxonomy. Since a why-question can often be answered with answers falling into several type categories, the necessity to choose the correct answer type creates ambiguity since the desired type is typically not explicitly stated in the question. Furthermore, a why-question can be answered with several causes in the causal chain (Verberne et al., 2006), and in that case all these answers can be considered as correct. For instance, consider the example shown in Table 1. For this example question, several potential causes can be the basis for the answer. Consequently, this why-question can be answered according to both mechanistically causal (answers 1, 2) and motivational (answers 3, 4, 5) reasons.

3 Narratives

Narratives are texts in which events are causally or thematically linked and develop within a temporal framework (Brewer, 2017). Narratives are generally agent-oriented and their main scope is centered on characters, their actions, and motivations (Sang et al., 2022). In narrative QA, stories, fairytales, books, and (movie) scripts are commonly utilized as narrative texts. Characteristics of narrative texts, such as causality of events and motivations of agents, make narratives a suitable context for asking why-questions. Additionally, fictional narratives can ensure the test of comprehension because they are self-contained, meaning that all elements needed to understand the narrative, such as events, characters, and settings, are present in the text and QA models need to comprehend the narrative in order to answer questions (Dunietz et al., 2020; Richardson et al., 2013; Kočiský et al., 2018). Implicitness is a key feature of narratives that makes it different from other types of texts. Length is another characteristic dimension of narratives which is also very important for QA systems. In the following subsections, we will review these characteristics in more detail.

3.1 Implicitness: "Reading between the lines"

People often think and communicate with each other in the form of a narrative (story) (Dunietz et al., 2020). They assume that other people with whom they interact share a common ground with them, so they do not have to mention or specify commonly known knowledge (Ostermann et al., 2018a). Similar to the implicitness characteristic of the natural narrative-style communication, narrative texts tend to exclude common knowledge, such as commonsense and script (typical sequences of events to accomplish common tasks) knowledge, and assume that the reader has the background knowledge required to infer relevant implicit information (Schank and Abelson, 1975). For instance, not all causes of events and reasons for actions of agents are explicitly stated in narratives. Thus, the ability to "read between the lines" is necessary for properly understanding narratives (Norvig, 1987).

3.2 Short vs long narratives

Narratives can be short or long based on the scope of the text stream and the number of events it contains.

Short narratives cover a small number of events and briefly narrate the actions of fewer agents. The local structure of a longer narrative such as an individual scene can be also considered and used as a short narrative. In short narratives, the reader can make inferences by linking local narrative elements and creating a local narrative representation (Sang et al., 2022; Kintsch, 1988).

Long narratives, on the other hand, have large textual content, cover many events, and focus on the actions and interactions of many agents. Long narratives require the readers to comprehend the underlying deep structure of the narrative and analyze the high-level abstractions. Answering questions in this setting requires understanding the global narrative structure, such as the whole story (Sang et al., 2022; Kintsch, 1988) and the integration of various information stated in different parts of the long narrative by connecting individual scenes (McNamara and Magliano, 2009).

4 Narrative Why-Question Answering

Narrative Why-Question Answering task can be formulated as a special case of Why-QA where the context is a complex structured text—a narrative. Currently, there exists only one QA dataset (TellMeWhy) that solely consists of why-questions in narrative setting. Additionally, several other narrative QA datasets contain why-questions in various proportions. The subsets consisting of why-questions can be extracted from these datasets and used for training or testing Narrative Why-Question Answering systems. In the following subsections, we first review these potential datasets suitable for Narrative Why-QA, and then give an overview of common evaluation measures used to assess the performance of Narrative Why-Question Answering systems.

4.1 Datasets

We selected several multiple-choice, extractive, and free-form QA datasets that utilize narrative as their context. In order to identify why-questions in these datasets, we first extracted all questions including the word *why*. We then manually removed any non-why questions (e.g, "what did the king's son do after he wondered why the girl was crying") from the questions that do not start with *why*. The relevant statistics of all datasets are shown in Table 2.

TellMeWhy (Lal et al., 2021) dataset presents free-form why-questions over events in short narratives. It is the only existing dataset created with the Narrative Why-Question Answering task in mind. The questions were created using template-based transformations and the answers to questions were crowdsourced. Narratives were collected from ROCStories (Mostafazadeh et al., 2016a) and CATERS (Mostafazadeh et al., 2016b). The dataset has a total of 30,519 why-questions with three golden free-form answers for each question. According to data annotators, 28.82% of questions in the dataset cannot be answered explicitly based on the narrative (context).

MCTest (Richardson et al., 2013) is a multiple-choice MRC dataset based on fictional stories. The dataset is created via crowdsourcing and it is designed for the level of understanding of 7-year-old children. The fictional and basic comprehension nature of the dataset decreases the need for additional world knowledge and makes it possible to find the answer only based on the text.

MCScript (Ostermann et al., 2018a) is a multiple-choice MRC dataset based on stories about daily activities. It is created to evaluate machine comprehension using commonsense (script) knowledge (Ostermann et al., 2018b). Stories are collected by crowdsourcing new texts based on selected scenarios. Questions are crowdsourced based on scenarios independent of narratives and then matched with narratives randomly. Similar to MCTest, texts and questions are created according to the understanding level of a child. In general, 27.4% of questions require commonsense (script) knowledge to correctly infer the answer.

Dataset	# of Why	% of Why	Answer	Context	% of Implicit
TellMeWhy	30519	100	free-form	short	28.82
MCTest	329	12.5	multiple-choice	short	-
MCScript	1623	11.6	multiple-choice	short	27.4
MCScript2.0	136	0.6	multiple-choice	short	50
CosmosQA	12439	35	multiple-choice	short	93.8
NarrativeQA	4179	9	free-form	long/summaries	42
FairytaleQA	2864	27	span/free-form	short	25.5

Table 2: Statistics of the narrative why-QA datasets. # of Why shows the number of why-questions in the datasets. % of Why refers to the proportion of why-questions in the datasets. The percentage of implicit questions is taken from the respective dataset papers, except for the NarrativeQA for which this number is due to the analysis done by Bauer et al. (2018)

MCScript2.0 (Ostermann et al., 2019) is another multiple-choice MRC dataset focused on script knowledge. The stories were collected by reusing narratives from the MCScript, and crowdsourcing texts based on new scenarios. Questions were collected based on target sentences of stories rather than scenarios or complete stories. Similar to MCScript and MCTest, the texts and questions are created according to the understanding level of a child. Correct and incorrect answers were crowdsourced by showing questions and hiding the target sentences in the story. In total, 50% of the questions require commonsense knowledge to be answered.

Cosmos QA (Huang et al., 2019) is a multiple-choice commonsense-based reading comprehension dataset. 93.8% of the questions in the dataset require contextual commonsense reasoning. Context paragraphs were collected from the spinn3r blog story corpus Burton et al. (2009) and a dataset by Gordon and Swanson (2009). Both questions and answers were crowdsourced. Questions are based on the causes and effects of events, facts about entities, and counterfactuals.

NarrativeQA (Kočiský et al., 2018) is a narrative reading comprehension dataset based on books and movies. Books from the Project Gutenberg and movie scripts from the web are used as stories. Moreover, summaries for long narratives are obtained from Wikipedia. Questions and answers are crowdsourced based on summaries only. Since both original long stories and summaries exist for each question, this dataset can be used for two tasks: narrative QA based on long narratives (books and movie scripts) and short narratives (summaries). Manual analysis on the validation set by Bauer et al. (2018) showed that 42% of the questions need commonsense knowledge for inference.

FairytaleQA (Xu et al., 2022) is a narrative comprehension dataset designed for both question answering and question generation tasks. The narratives were collected from the Project Gutenberg by considering the reading difficulty up to the 10th-grade level. Small sections were extracted from fairytales as context paragraphs. Following the narrative comprehension frameworks by Paris and Paris (2003) and Alonzo et al. (2009), trained annotators created questions and answers for the contexts. The most common questions are about characters' behavior and causal relationships. 25.5% of the questions are implicit (free-form) and 74.5% of the questions are explicit (span-based).

The amount of why-questions in the reviewed datasets is reported in Table 2. Among the multiple-choice QA datasets, CosmosQA has a higher number of why-questions compared to others. Among the free-form QA datasets, TellMeWhy dataset contains approximately 4.5 times more why-questions than the other two free-form QA datasets combined. Considering the proportion of why-questions in these datasets (also shown in Table 2), why-questions are well-represented in the CosmosQA and FairytaleQA datasets where they make up a sizeable part of the whole dataset, while in the MCTest, MCScript, MCScript2.0, and NarrativeQA datasets, why-questions cover only a small portion of the whole dataset.

4.2 Evaluation measures

For multiple-choice QA datasets, accuracy is a commonly used metric to measure the performance of a model. For free-form QA datasets, both automatic and human evaluation measures are utilized to evaluate the capabilities of the QA model. Most commonly, ROUGE-L (Lin, 2004), Meteor (Denkowski and Lavie, 2011), BLEU (Papineni et al., 2002), BLEURT (Sellam et al., 2020) and

BertScore (Zhang et al., 2020) have been used to automatically evaluate the performance of the free-form QA models in narrative setting. Overall, F1 score of the ROUGE-L is the most commonly reported automatic evaluation measure.

In terms of human evaluation, Lal et al. (2021) proposed to assess the grammaticality and validity of the answers based on a 5-point Likert scale. The scale of the grammaticality ranges from strongly ungrammatical (1) to strongly grammatical (5), where a strongly grammatical answer must follow all the rules of the English grammar and a neutral score (3) is indicated when the meaning of the answer can be still inferred despite clear grammatical mistakes. The validity scale assesses whether the answer is valid and makes sense in the given context.

5 Challenges

In this section, we list challenges based on our analysis of the datasets and the characteristics of the Narrative Why-Question Answering. This section is divided into three parts. In the first part, we focus on the commonly addressed challenges in the Narrative Why-Question Answering. The existing datasets are created generally to test the abilities of models on these challenges. In the second part, we review some potential challenges that are not marked in existing datasets and that the current models thus cannot be tested on. Lastly, we review challenges that stem from both the datasets and the characteristics of the Narrative Why-Question Answering that can create problems on benchmarking models on this task.

5.1 Commonly focused challenges

In this subsection, we review the challenges that the creators of existing datasets have focused on, related to the implicit vs explicit questions and the length of the narrative.

5.1.1 Explicit vs implicit questions

Questions in the majority of datasets ask about both explicit and implicit causal relations stated in the narratives. The distinction between explicit vs implicit questions is based on the notions stated in sections 2.1 and 3.1:

- *Explicit questions* ask about clearly stated causal relations in the narratives. The answer can be found in the narrative, often as a span of the text. Answering explicit why-questions requires the model to identify affect, link, and causative verbs (e.g., *change*, *lead*, *cause*) or causal signals (e.g., *because of*, *as a result of*, *due to*, *so*) in the narratives (Mirza and Tonelli, 2014).
- *Implicit questions* ask about not explicitly stated causal relations in the narratives. Answering these questions requires filling in the gaps with additional background knowledge, such as commonsense or script knowledge (Norvig, 1987; Lal et al., 2021).

In Table 2, we can see that most reviewed datasets contain more explicit questions than implicit ones. The CosmosQA dataset is an exception here, as it was designed as a commonsense reasoning dataset with a focus on narratives, in which answers cannot be found using the text spans of the context only, and commonsense knowledge is required to answer most questions.

Generally, the inclusion of additional knowledge improves the performance of the QA models to answer implicit questions (Lal et al., 2022). However, in simple stories, such as in MCScript, the system can learn some amount of background knowledge also from the stories and the effect of using additional commonsense knowledge is small (Ostermann et al., 2018b).

5.1.2 Short vs Long narratives

All reviewed datasets have short narratives as their context. The NarrativeQA short texts have a more complex narrative structure than other datasets, since the short context versions of the NarrativeQA are summaries of the larger narratives, and not single scenes from the long narratives. In short narratives, if there is a common lexical pattern between the question and a part of the narrative, or a large lexical overlap between the answer and the narrative, sophisticated models can treat free-form QA as an extractive task. For example, models trained on the TellMeWhy dataset generally try to find the answer span in the text and copy a part of the narrative as an answer (Lal et al., 2021).

The NarrativeQA dataset is the only dataset that has long narratives as its context. Linking narrative elements to answer questions in large narratives is harder than in short narratives (see section 3.2). Typically, in order to reason about long narratives, the parts relevant to reasoning are retrieved first (Kočiský et al., 2018; Tay et al., 2019; Fremann, 2019; Mou et al., 2020, 2021). The retrieval is difficult even with the state-of-the-art models due to the characteristics of narratives and the necessity of high-level narrative comprehension (Mou et al., 2021).

5.2 Less focused challenges

In this subsection, we list some of the challenges that can be potentially relevant for why-question answering but that the current datasets do not concentrate on. In particular, we review different formats the why-questions can have, and discuss the unmarked and ambiguous causal relations.

5.2.1 Why-question formats

In why-questions, *why* can appear in different parts of the question and questions can be formulated in different ways. Based on the manual analysis of the questions in the datasets listed, we observed the following variations of why-questions.

- *Simple why-question:* the question starts with *why*. Most why-questions in the reviewed datasets follow this format.
- *Long why-question:* the why-question is formulated in a long format such as "What (is/was/may be) (the/a possible/a real) reason why ..." or "(Could/Can) you tell me why ...".
- *Specific why-question:* the question first limits the situation to a certain time/place/person and then formulates the why-question. For instance, "At the end of the story, surrounded by cameras and police, why does Norma think she is on set?" or "According to Bonnie, why is Blanche a constant danger to the gang's well-being?".
- *Statement+why question:* this is a differently formulated type of specific why-question that starts with a statement, which is followed by the one-word question "why?". For example, "When Gandhi was 23, he was thrown off a train in South Africa. Why?"
- *Question chain:* several questions including at least one why-question formulated in one sentence, e.g., "What is Gruul and why are they raiding?".

Most reviewed datasets contain simple why-questions, other variations of why-questions make up a very small portion of the datasets if any. For example, the TellMeWhy dataset contains only simple why-questions since the questions were constructed using question templates where *why* is always the first word of the question. It would be useful to have a fair portion of other why-question formats in the datasets as well in order to test how well the models can handle these other format types. One easy way to accomplish this would be to use templates to transform current simple why-questions into other formats.

5.2.2 Unmarked and ambiguous causality

As discussed in section 2.1, based on causality construction, causation can be categorized to marked vs unmarked and ambiguous vs unambiguous in addition to explicit vs implicit. The reviewed datasets only focus on explicit vs implicit causation nuance (see section 5.1.1) and further categorization is not annotated in these datasets. Thus, it is currently difficult to identify how the models' performance would differ in answering questions asked about marked vs unmarked or ambiguous vs unambiguous causal relations.

5.3 Challenges for benchmarking

In this subsection, we review some challenges that can occur during assessing the performance of models on the datasets. First, we look into what we call the general question problem and list its potential causes. Then, we discuss how the general question problem and the ambiguity of the why-questions can affect the evaluation of models on the Narrative Why-Question Answering task.

5.3.1 General question problem

Tasks designed on narrative QA datasets require systems to answer questions based on narrative (context). Questions, for which a context/narrative is available, should be correctly answerable only based on this context/narrative. If the question can be answered without the narrative, it does not meet the requirements of reading comprehension, especially in narrative QA. We distinguish between the context-specific and general questions as follows:

- *Context-specific questions* are questions that can be answered correctly only by using the information given in the context.
- *General questions* are questions that can be answered without the context.

Although we expect all why-questions in narrative settings to be context-specific, datasets still contain questions that can be answered both with and without the consideration of the context. This can happen due to the issues in data collection process and due to the characteristics of the causal questions.

If the questions are created without considering the context details, questions can end up being general. This is the case of the MCScript dataset, where questions were asked based on the general scenario description and not on the specific narrative. Thus, some questions that were created are answerable irrespective of the narrative (Ostermann et al., 2019).

When questions have several golden answers (i.e., in free-form QA datasets), a question is considered context-specific if all golden answers can be correctly inferred only by using the information given in the context. In some question-answer pairs, the question can be general because some of the answers do not contain context-specific information. For instance, in the example shown in Table 1, while answers (1), (3), (4), and (5) are specifically related to context, the answer (2) can be correct in any context such as "She opened the box to take out her shoes". A QA model can treat this example question both as context-specific or general, and any of the given five answers can be considered correct. So, in order avoid a question being general, context-specific information can be added to answers that make the question context-specific. In the example of Table 1, "The box was closed." can be converted to "The pizza box was closed." which contains the context-specific word "pizza"; this step makes the question context-specific for all the answers in the given set.

5.3.2 Evaluation

Evaluation of multiple-choice QA datasets. Evaluating answers of why-questions in multiple-choice datasets is a straightforward process. The presence of only one correct answer in multiple-choice questions helps to correctly assess the performance of the model without having to consider the potential answer ambiguity of why-questions. However, if question ambiguity is not addressed in the dataset, some of the questions can have more than one correct answer. Moreover, general why-questions can affect the accuracy of the overall assessment since these questions remove the necessity of the narrative understanding component of the task. Therefore, general questions should be identified and removed from the datasets in order to correctly assess the models' comprehension ability.

Evaluation of free-form QA datasets. General questions can affect the correct evaluation on free-form QA datasets as well. Thus, in order to increase the accuracy of the overall evaluation process, general questions should be identified and transformed to context-specific by adding contextual information to those answers that make the question general. Moreover, ambiguity in why-questions can cause additional problems with both automatic and human evaluations. Due to the question and answer ambiguities, why-questions can have more valid answers than the collected golden answers in the datasets, and collecting all valid answers to these questions is not feasible and is probably impossible. Consequently, automatic metrics can only evaluate the output of models against the set of golden answers, which is likely only a small subset of all valid answers, and thus these metrics cannot fully measure the capacity of the models.

Human evaluation is considered the gold standard in all text generation tasks, including free-form QA (Celikyilmaz et al., 2020). However, performing human evaluation is a costly and slow process (Lal et al., 2021), and the reliability of human judgments is questionable (Gatt and Krahmer, 2018), especially in why-question answering that possesses many ambiguities. For example, human evaluators can prefer one interpretation of the question over another in terms of question ambiguity (section 2.2.1) or consider some causes (e.g., motivational) in the causal chain more reasonable than other causes (e.g., mechanistically causal) in case of answer ambiguity (section 2.2.2). Thus, further instructions are needed in the evaluation process to resolve ambiguities in the why-questions.

6 Conclusion

In this paper, we reviewed challenges and datasets related to Narrative Why-Question Answering. The challenges that occur in this domain can stem from both the properties of narrative understanding and the specifics of why-question answering. The main challenges regarding narrative understanding are the exclusion of common knowledge, the necessity of understanding the local and global narrative structure, and high-level abstraction. The primary challenges of why-question answering are related to identifying causal relations, and ambiguities in questions and answers.

In order to understand data-specific challenges

and the implications of task-specific challenges in datasets, we reviewed seven datasets that can be suitable for this task. We listed challenges that models are tested on in these datasets. The implicitness of questions and the length of narratives are more tested challenges in the datasets. We outlined different why-question formats and questions about unmarked and ambiguous causal relations as other potential challenges that models can be tested on.

Finally, we argued that general questions, and answer and question ambiguities in why-questions can create challenges for benchmarking. We propose that removing general questions and resolving ambiguities in why-questions can lead to more accurate evaluation of systems. We hope that the review of this potential challenges and the analysis of the datasets listed in this paper will help to further the progress in Narrative Why-Question Answering.

Limitations

In the paper, we focus on free-form/span-based and multiple-choice question answering datasets and do not consider other types of QA datasets, such as the cloze test. We also do not focus on datasets that have a mix of narrative and expository contexts. Also, although we took the effort to carefully list the challenges relevant to Narrative Why-Question Answering, it is possible that we missed something; thus, the list of challenges presented in this paper should not be considered complete.

Ethics Statement

In this paper, we review existing datasets and literature related to the task of Narrative Why-Question Answering. The reviewed datasets are publicly available and do not contain sensitive data. We do not publish any new data or experimental results.

Acknowledgements

This work was supported by the Estonian Research Council grant PSG721 and the European Social Fund via the IT Academy programme.

References

Julie Alonzo, Deni Basaraba, Gerald Tindal, and Ronald S. Carriveau. 2009. They read, but how well do they understand?: An empirical look at the nuances of measuring reading comprehension. *Assessment for Effective Intervention*, 35(1):34–44.

Lisa Bauer, Yicheng Wang, and Mohit Bansal. 2018. Commonsense for generative multi-hop question answering tasks. In *Proceedings of the 2018 Conference on Empirical Methods in Natural Language Processing*, pages 4220–4230, Brussels, Belgium. Association for Computational Linguistics.

Eduardo Blanco, Nuria Castell, and Dan Moldovan. 2008. Causal relation extraction. In *Proceedings of the Sixth International Conference on Language Resources and Evaluation (LREC'08)*, Marrakech, Morocco. European Language Resources Association (ELRA).

Valeriia Bolotova, Vladislav Blinov, Falk Scholer, W. Bruce Croft, and Mark Sanderson. 2022. A non-factoid question-answering taxonomy. In *Proceedings of the 45th International ACM SIGIR Conference on Research and Development in Information Retrieval*, SIGIR '22, page 1196–1207, New York, NY, USA. Association for Computing Machinery.

William F. Brewer. 2017. Literary theory, rhetoric, and stylistics: Implications for psychology. In *In Theoretical issues in reading comprehension.*

Kevin R. Burton, Akshay Java, and Ian Soboroff. 2009. The icwsm 2009 spinn3r dataset. In *In Third Annual Conference on Weblogs and Social Media (ICWSM 2009).*

Asli Celikyilmaz, Elizabeth Clark, and Jianfeng Gao. 2020. Evaluation of text generation: A survey.

Michael Denkowski and Alon Lavie. 2011. Meteor 1.3: Automatic metric for reliable optimization and evaluation of machine translation systems. In *Proceedings of the Sixth Workshop on Statistical Machine Translation*, pages 85–91, Edinburgh, Scotland. Association for Computational Linguistics.

Jesse Dunietz, Greg Burnham, Akash Bharadwaj, Owen Rambow, Jennifer Chu-Carroll, and Dave Ferrucci. 2020. To test machine comprehension, start by defining comprehension. In *Proceedings of the 58th Annual Meeting of the Association for Computational Linguistics*, pages 7839–7859, Online. Association for Computational Linguistics.

Jesse Dunietz, Lori Levin, and Jaime Carbonell. 2017. The BECauSE corpus 2.0: Annotating causality and overlapping relations. In *Proceedings of the 11th Linguistic Annotation Workshop*, pages 95–104, Valencia, Spain. Association for Computational Linguistics.

Lea Frermann. 2019. Extractive NarrativeQA with heuristic pre-training. In *Proceedings of the 2nd Workshop on Machine Reading for Question Answering*, pages 172–182, Hong Kong, China. Association for Computational Linguistics.

Albert Gatt and Emiel Krahmer. 2018. Survey of the state of the art in natural language generation: Core tasks, applications and evaluation. *J. Artif. Int. Res.*, 61(1):65–170.

Roxana Girju. 2003. Automatic detection of causal relations for question answering. In *Proceedings of the ACL 2003 Workshop on Multilingual Summarization and Question Answering*, pages 76–83, Sapporo, Japan. Association for Computational Linguistics.

Andrew S. Gordon and Reid Swanson. 2009. Identifying personal stories in millions of weblog entries. In *In Third Annual Conference on Weblogs and Social Media (ICWSM 2009)*.

Cécile Grivaz. 2010. Human judgements on causation in French texts. In *Proceedings of the Seventh International Conference on Language Resources and Evaluation (LREC'10)*, Valletta, Malta. European Language Resources Association (ELRA).

Lifu Huang, Ronan Le Bras, Chandra Bhagavatula, and Yejin Choi. 2019. Cosmos QA: Machine reading comprehension with contextual commonsense reasoning. In *Proceedings of the 2019 Conference on Empirical Methods in Natural Language Processing and the 9th International Joint Conference on Natural Language Processing (EMNLP-IJCNLP)*, pages 2391–2401, Hong Kong, China. Association for Computational Linguistics.

Sangeet S. Khemlani, Aron K. Barbey, and Philip N. Johnson-Laird. 2014. Causal reasoning with mental models. *Frontiers in Human Neuroscience*, 8.

Walter Kintsch. 1988. The role of knowledge in discourse comprehension: A construction-integration model. *Psychological Review*, 95(2):163–182.

Tomáš Kočiský, Jonathan Schwarz, Phil Blunsom, Chris Dyer, Karl Moritz Hermann, Gábor Melis, and Edward Grefenstette. 2018. The NarrativeQA reading comprehension challenge. *Transactions of the Association for Computational Linguistics*, 6:317–328.

Yash Kumar Lal, Nathanael Chambers, Raymond Mooney, and Niranjan Balasubramanian. 2021. TellMeWhy: A dataset for answering why-questions in narratives. In *Findings of the Association for Computational Linguistics: ACL-IJCNLP 2021*, pages 596–610, Online. Association for Computational Linguistics.

Yash Kumar Lal, Horace Liu, Niket Tandon, Nathanael Chambers, Ray Mooney, and Niranjan Balasubramanian. 2022. Analyzing the contribution of commonsense knowledge sources for why-question answering. In *ACL 2022 Workshop on Commonsense Representation and Reasoning*.

Chin-Yew Lin. 2004. ROUGE: A package for automatic evaluation of summaries. In *Text Summarization Branches Out*, pages 74–81, Barcelona, Spain. Association for Computational Linguistics.

Danielle S. McNamara and Joe Magliano. 2009. Chapter 9 toward a comprehensive model of comprehension. In *The Psychology of Learning and Motivation*, volume 51 of *Psychology of Learning and Motivation*, pages 297–384. Academic Press.

Paramita Mirza and Sara Tonelli. 2014. An analysis of causality between events and its relation to temporal information. In *Proceedings of COLING 2014, the 25th International Conference on Computational Linguistics: Technical Papers*, pages 2097–2106, Dublin, Ireland. Dublin City University and Association for Computational Linguistics.

Nasrin Mostafazadeh, Nathanael Chambers, Xiaodong He, Devi Parikh, Dhruv Batra, Lucy Vanderwende, Pushmeet Kohli, and James Allen. 2016a. A corpus and cloze evaluation for deeper understanding of commonsense stories. In *Proceedings of the 2016 Conference of the North American Chapter of the Association for Computational Linguistics: Human Language Technologies*, pages 839–849, San Diego, California. Association for Computational Linguistics.

Nasrin Mostafazadeh, Alyson Grealish, Nathanael Chambers, James Allen, and Lucy Vanderwende. 2016b. CaTeRS: Causal and temporal relation scheme for semantic annotation of event structures. In *Proceedings of the Fourth Workshop on Events*, pages 51–61, San Diego, California. Association for Computational Linguistics.

Xiangyang Mou, Chenghao Yang, Mo Yu, Bingsheng Yao, Xiaoxiao Guo, Saloni Potdar, and Hui Su. 2021. Narrative question answering with cutting-edge open-domain QA techniques: A comprehensive study. *Transactions of the Association for Computational Linguistics*, 9:1032–1046.

Xiangyang Mou, Mo Yu, Bingsheng Yao, Chenghao Yang, Xiaoxiao Guo, Saloni Potdar, and Hui Su. 2020. Frustratingly hard evidence retrieval for QA over books. In *Proceedings of the First Joint Workshop on Narrative Understanding, Storylines, and Events*, pages 108–113, Online. Association for Computational Linguistics.

Peter Norvig. 1987. *A Unified Theory of Inference for Text Understanding*. Ph.D. thesis, EECS Department, University of California, Berkeley.

Simon Ostermann, Ashutosh Modi, Michael Roth, Stefan Thater, and Manfred Pinkal. 2018a. MCScript: A novel dataset for assessing machine comprehension using script knowledge. In *Proceedings of the Eleventh International Conference on Language Resources and Evaluation (LREC 2018)*, Miyazaki, Japan. European Language Resources Association (ELRA).

Simon Ostermann, Michael Roth, Ashutosh Modi, Stefan Thater, and Manfred Pinkal. 2018b. SemEval-2018 task 11: Machine comprehension using commonsense knowledge. In *Proceedings of The 12th International Workshop on Semantic Evaluation*, pages 747–757, New Orleans, Louisiana. Association for Computational Linguistics.

Simon Ostermann, Michael Roth, and Manfred Pinkal. 2019. MCScript2.0: A machine comprehension corpus focused on script events and participants. In *Proceedings of the Eighth Joint Conference on Lexical and Computational Semantics (*SEM 2019)*, pages 103–117, Minneapolis, Minnesota. Association for Computational Linguistics.

Kishore Papineni, Salim Roukos, Todd Ward, and Wei-Jing Zhu. 2002. Bleu: a method for automatic evaluation of machine translation. In *Proceedings of the 40th Annual Meeting of the Association for Computational Linguistics*, pages 311–318, Philadelphia, Pennsylvania, USA. Association for Computational Linguistics.

Alison H. Paris and Scott G. Paris. 2003. Assessing narrative comprehension in young children. *Reading Research Quarterly*, 38(1):36–76.

Randolph Quirk, Sidney Greenbaum, Geoffrey Leech, and Jan Svartvik. 1985. *A Comprehensive grammar of the English language*. Longman, London ; New York.

Matthew Richardson, Christopher J.C. Burges, and Erin Renshaw. 2013. MCTest: A challenge dataset for the open-domain machine comprehension of text. In *Proceedings of the 2013 Conference on Empirical Methods in Natural Language Processing*, pages 193–203, Seattle, Washington, USA. Association for Computational Linguistics.

Yisi Sang, Xiangyang Mou, Jing Li, Jeffrey Stanton, and Mo Yu. 2022. A survey of machine narrative reading comprehension assessments. In *Proceedings of the Thirty-First International Joint Conference on Artificial Intelligence, IJCAI-22*, pages 5580–5587. International Joint Conferences on Artificial Intelligence Organization. Survey Track.

Roger C. Schank and Robert P. Abelson. 1975. Scripts, plans, and knowledge. In *Proceedings of the 4th International Joint Conference on Artificial Intelligence - Volume 1*, IJCAI'75, page 151–157, San Francisco, CA, USA. Morgan Kaufmann Publishers Inc.

Thibault Sellam, Dipanjan Das, and Ankur Parikh. 2020. BLEURT: Learning robust metrics for text generation. In *Proceedings of the 58th Annual Meeting of the Association for Computational Linguistics*, pages 7881–7892, Online. Association for Computational Linguistics.

Fiona Anting Tan, Ali Hürriyetoğlu, Tommaso Caselli, Nelleke Oostdijk, Tadashi Nomoto, Hansi Hettiarachchi, Iqra Ameer, Onur Uca, Farhana Ferdousi Liza, and Tiancheng Hu. 2022. The causal news corpus: Annotating causal relations in event sentences from news.

Yi Tay, Shuohang Wang, Anh Tuan Luu, Jie Fu, Minh C. Phan, Xingdi Yuan, Jinfeng Rao, Siu Cheung Hui, and Aston Zhang. 2019. Simple and effective curriculum pointer-generator networks for reading comprehension over long narratives. In *Proceedings of the 57th Annual Meeting of the Association for Computational Linguistics*, pages 4922–4931, Florence, Italy. Association for Computational Linguistics.

Suzan Verberne, Lou Boves, Nelleke Oostdijk, and Peter-Arno Coppen. 2006. Data for question answering: The case of why. In *Proceedings of the Fifth International Conference on Language Resources and Evaluation (LREC'06)*, Genoa, Italy. European Language Resources Association (ELRA).

Bonnie Webber, Rashmi Prasad, Alan Lee, and Aravind Joshi. 2019. The Penn Discourse Treebank 3.0 Annotation Manual.

Phillip Wolff. 2007. Representing causation. *Journal of Experimental Psychology: General*, 136(1):82–111.

Phillip Wolff and Grace Song. 2003. Models of causation and the semantics of causal verbs. *Cognitive Psychology*, 47(3):276–332.

Ying Xu, Dakuo Wang, Mo Yu, Daniel Ritchie, Bingsheng Yao, Tongshuang Wu, Zheng Zhang, Toby Li, Nora Bradford, Branda Sun, Tran Hoang, Yisi Sang, Yufang Hou, Xiaojuan Ma, Diyi Yang, Nanyun Peng, Zhou Yu, and Mark Warschauer. 2022. Fantastic questions and where to find them: FairytaleQA – an authentic dataset for narrative comprehension. In *Proceedings of the 60th Annual Meeting of the Association for Computational Linguistics (Volume 1: Long Papers)*, pages 447–460, Dublin, Ireland. Association for Computational Linguistics.

Tianyi Zhang, Varsha Kishore, Felix Wu, Kilian Q. Weinberger, and Yoav Artzi. 2020. Bertscore: Evaluating text generation with bert. In *International Conference on Learning Representations*.

Exploring a POS-based Two-stage Approach for Improving Low-Resource AMR-to-Text Generation

Marco Antonio Sobrevilla Cabezudo and **Thiago Alexandre Salgueiro Pardo**
Interinstitutional Center for Computational Linguistics (NILC)
Institute of Mathematical and Computer Sciences, University of São Paulo
São Carlos/SP, Brazil
msobrevillac@usp.br, taspardo@icmc.usp.br

Abstract

This work presents a two-stage approach for tackling low-resource AMR-to-text generation for Brazilian Portuguese. Our approach consists of (1) generating a masked surface realization in which some tokens are masked according to its Part-of-Speech class and (2) infilling the masked tokens according to the AMR graph and the previous masked surface realization. Results show a slight improvement over the baseline, mainly in BLEU (1.63) and METEOR (0.02) scores. Moreover, we evaluate the pipeline components separately, showing that the bottleneck of the pipeline is the masked surface realization. Finally, the human revision suggests that models still suffer from hallucinations, and some strategies to deal with the problems found are proposed.

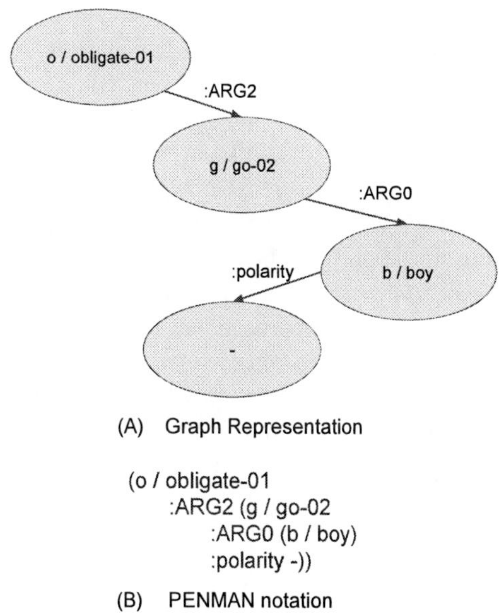

Figure 1: AMR example for the sentence "The boy must not go."

1 Introduction

Abstract Meaning Representation (AMR) is a semantic formalism that encodes the meaning of a sentence into a labeled directed and rooted graph (Banarescu et al., 2013). This representation comprises semantic information related to semantic roles, named entities, and co-references, among others.

AMR is a widely-studied research topic in the semantic representation field and has been proven helpful in many Natural Language Processing tasks (Liao et al., 2018; Song et al., 2019). Its success is partially based on its broad use of mature linguistic resources, such as PropBank (Palmer et al., 2005), and its attempt to abstract away from syntax. Figure 1 shows an example of an AMR graph and its corresponding PENMAN notation for the sentence "*The boy must not go.*".

AMR-to-text generation aims to "translate" an Abstract Meaning Representation graph into its corresponding text. This task has been widely tackled by diverse approaches, starting from statistical, transducer-based and transition-based ones (Pourdamghani et al., 2016; Flanigan et al., 2016; Lampouras and Vlachos, 2017), until end-to-end neural ones (Mager et al., 2020; Ribeiro et al., 2021a), recently.

In particular, end-to-end neural models -mainly those based on pre-trained models- have largely outperformed the initial methods, achieving state-of-the-art results (Ribeiro et al., 2021b). These models can generate fluent text. However, they are prone to generate hallucinations, i.e., texts that are irrelevant to or contradicted with the input (Reiter, 2018).

Another drawback is that these models are usually data-hungry, i.e., they need to be trained on a large dataset to achieve a good performance. It can be a problem when we deal with low-resource domains, languages, or tasks (Sobrevilla Cabezudo and Pardo, 2022). Even when the results may be better than those obtained by statistical methods,

Proceedings of the 2nd Workshop on Natural Language Generation, Evaluation, and Metrics (GEM), pages 531 - 538
December 7, 2022 ©2022 Association for Computational Linguistics

they are still far from good results. For example, Ribeiro et al. (2021b) show that fine-tuning T5 (Raffel et al., 2020) on a small portion of a big dataset ($\sim$500 instances) produces a $\sim$10-15 BLEU score.

In general, an approach to have more control over the decoding process (and avoid hallucinations) is to use a pipeline-based method in which the model of each pipeline's module is implemented with neural models (Castro Ferreira et al., 2019; Ma et al., 2019; Puduppully and Lapata, 2021). Another alternative is to use templates, infill concepts in these templates, and then define a strategy to transform them into sentences/paragraphs (Kasner and Dušek, 2020; Mota et al., 2020). Both approaches have proven to be helpful in text generation tasks. However, the main issue for the latter one is that it only can be applied in restricted domains as it is necessary to define a set of templates.

In this work, we approach the AMR-to-text generation task in two stages. Firstly, generating a masked surface realization in which some tokens are masked according to its Part-of-Speech (POS) classes. Then, finally, infilling the masked tokens according to the AMR graph and the previous masked surface realization[1].

The intuition for masking some tokens this way is that some POS classes are more difficult to be predicted during text decoding and can harm the performance. On the other hand, filling-in-the-blank is commonly used on current SotA architectures, such as T5 (Raffel et al., 2020) during the pre-training phase. This way, we can leverage the learned knowledge to infill the masked tokens in the previous stage adequately.

Experiments are conducted on low-resource an AMR-to-text generation task for Brazilian Portuguese (Inácio et al., 2022) to show how this method behaves even when a large dataset is unavailable.

In general, our main contributions are:

- we propose a simple two-stage method that consists of generating masked surface realization and infilling the masked tokens with a transformer-based architecture;
- we conduct a manual revision on the outputs of the best approaches and the end-to-end approach.

[1]The code is available at https://github.com/msobrevillac/DICO-AMR2Text.

2 Related Work

AMR-to-Text generation Modular approaches have been mainly focused on converting AMR graphs into syntax trees via transition-based methods (Lampouras and Vlachos, 2017), end-to-end methods (Cao and Clark, 2019) or rule-based graph-transducers (Mille et al., 2017) and use an off-the-shelf method (neural or statistical) to generate the text. These methods usually have got a low performance on test sets (May and Priyadarshi, 2017).

AMR is more open-ended than other datasets such as WebNLG (Gardent et al., 2017). This way, extracting templates can be a complex task. Some attempts to get templates in the form of rules are presented by Flanigan et al. (2016) and Song et al. (2017). However, these approaches need some manually created rules and have been surpassed by current models.

On the other hand, current neural models have achieved SotA results. However, they need a large dataset to get high performance. On the contrary, a small portion of an extensive dataset produces lower scores (Ribeiro et al., 2021a,b)[2].

Data-to-Text generation Currently, most data-to-text methods are based on end-to-end neural approaches. In particular, methods that fine-tunes a pre-trained model, such as BART (Lewis et al., 2020) or T5 (Raffel et al., 2020), on its specific generation task have achieved SotA results.

Other works have tried to approach this kind of tasks using pipeline approaches (Castro Ferreira et al., 2019; Ma et al., 2019; Puduppully and Lapata, 2021) and template-based approaches (Kasner and Dušek, 2020; Mota et al., 2020). In particular, pipeline approaches have advantages in low-resource settings and unseen domains. On the other hand, template-based approaches tend to infill the templates with concepts and then use them to generate the complete sentence.

3 Experimental Setup

3.1 Dataset

We conduct all experiments on the journalistic section of the AMR-PT corpus (Inácio et al., 2022) (named AMRNews)[3]. The AMRNews corpus comprises 870 sentences with up to 23 tokens each from

[2]Ribeiro et al. (2021b) show an impressive improvement using structural adapters. However, this is not part of this study.

[3]AMRNews is freely available at https://github.com/nilc-nlp/AMR-BP/tree/master/AMRNews.

Brazilian news texts manually annotated according to adapted AMR guidelines (Sobrevilla Cabezudo and Pardo, 2019). Besides, it is divided into 402, 224, and 244 instances for training, development, and testing, respectively.

3.2 Architecture

Aiming to leverage the "fill-in-the-blank" potential of current pre-trained neural models, we propose a two-stage approach consisting of generating a masked surface realization and then infilling the masked tokens using a pre-trained model. Figure 2 shows an example of the whole process.

3.2.1 Masked Surface Realisation

The first stage involves generating a sentence corresponding to an AMR graph in which some tokens are masked. The idea behind this is that some tokens can be more difficult to be predicted. This way, we can mask them and let the next stage complete the masked tokens.

To decide what tokens should be masked, we use Part-of-Speech-based criteria. This way, we group all Part-of-Speech (POS) classes into main classes according to their function. For example, pronouns, nouns, and proper nouns are usually actors/places in a sentence, while verbs represent relations. This way, the main classes are: "*substantivos*" (nouns), "*verbos*" (verbs), "*qualificadores*" (qualifiers), and "*outros*" (others). Table 1 shows the main and POS classes included in each.

Main Class	Part-of-Speech
Substantivos (nouns)	pronoun, noun, proper noun
Verbos (verbs)	auxiliary verb, verb
Qualificadores (qualifiers)	adverb, adjective
Outros (others)	other Part-of-Speech

Table 1: Main and POS classes used in experiments

We train a model for each main class separately. Besides, we train a model for all main classes together. The input consists of a prefix and an AMR graph in the PENMAN notation (eliminating the frameset numbers). We use the expression "*mascarar **X** desde amr:*" ("Mask **X** from amr:") as prefix for each instance, where "*X*" is an specific main class. The output is the corresponding sentence, but words that belong to the target main class are masked. Box 1 from Figure 2 shows an example of this sub-task.

For experiments, we fine-tune the Portuguese T5 (PTT5) (Carmo et al., 2020)[4] on our corpus. Among the hyperparameters, we use AdamW optimizer with a learning rate of 5e-4, a max source and target length of 120 and 80 tokens, a batch size of 8, and a gradient accumulation of 4. The model trains by 12 epochs and is evaluated after each epoch. We use perplexity as evaluation criteria, and the training is halted if the model does not improve after 4 epochs.

3.2.2 Word Infilling

The second stage in the pipeline consists of infilling the masked tokens. In general, the task can be defined as follows: given an AMR graph in a similar format to the one used at the previous stage and a masked sentence, the model predicts the masked words.

Each instance in the corpus is formatted as follows: a prefix, the AMR graph similar to the one used in the previous stage, the word "*contexto*:" (context), and the masked sentence. Box 2 from Figure 2 shows an example of the input and output. We use the expression "*preencher amr:*" ("fill amr:") as prefix and train a model for each main class separately and another model for all main classes together.

Similar to the previous stage, we fine-tune PTT5 on our task. The main reason use PTT5 is that it was pre-trained for a similar task ('filling-in-the-blank') (Carmo et al., 2020; Raffel et al., 2020). This way, we aim to leverage the learned knowledge in our use case. We use the same hyperparameters as the used ones in the first stage; however, we modify the source length to 200 tokens.

4 Results and Discussion

Table 2 shows the overall results for all the trained models on test set in terms of BLEU (Papineni et al., 2002), METEOR (Lavie and Agarwal, 2007), chrF++ (Popović, 2017), and BERTScore (Zhang et al., 2020) evaluation metrics[5][6]. In addition, we report the results for a baseline that generates sentences with no masked tokens. This baseline is obtained by fine-tuning PPT5 on our task. However, the input consists of a prefix "*gerar texto desde amr:*" ("generate text from amr:"), followed

[4]Available at https://huggingface.co/unicamp-dl/ptt5-base-portuguese-vocab.

[5]We execute 4 runs for each experiment and show the mean and standard deviation.

[6]Metrics are calculated by using the code available at `https://github.com/WebNLG/GenerationEval`.

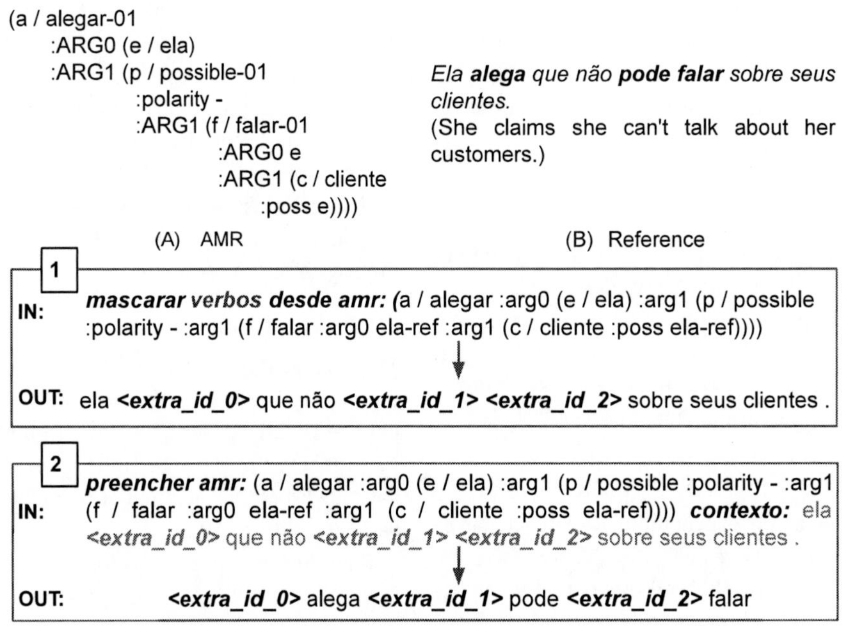

Figure 2: Pipeline Example. Box 1 describes the input and output for the masked surface realization module, and Box 2 illustrates the input and output for the word infilling module.

by an AMR graph represented by the PENMAN notation in a similar way as all already mentioned models, and the output is the original sentence.

Overall, results show a slight improvement over the baseline when we use the model trained on all main classes, mainly in BLEU (+1.63) and METEOR (+0.02) scores. Moreover, the best main classes to be masked seem to be "verb" and "qualifier". On the other hand, masking nouns and other POS classes harm the decoding performance. We might interpret this result as the characters in a sentence, and some connections between chunks are the most important in the realization of a sentence.

Another point to note is that it is better to train models on all main classes together instead of separately. A possible explanation is that more data can lead to better results. Also, examples from other main classes serve as negative examples for a specific main class, and it helps to improve its performance.

In order to verify which stage of the pipeline is affecting the overall performance, we evaluate each module separately. Table 3 and 4 shows the performance on both modules in terms of BLEU, METEOR and chrF++. However, for word infilling, we only evaluate BLEU-2 and BLEU-3, as the number of tokens to be predicted is three as most. In addition, we evaluate METEOR.

Concerning the Mask Surface Realization task, Table 3 indicates that verb masking leads to the best performance. A possible explanation for this result is that, as mentioned before, participants, situations, or locations in a sentence and connections between chunks are the most important and the easiest classes to predict during decoding. Also, it is worth noting that the verbs and qualifiers are less frequent in our dataset, as we can find 1.37-1.47 verbs/qualifiers per sentence. Therefore, it can make decoding easier than nouns (2.23 nouns per sentence).

Table 4 shows the opposite result, as the verb infilling is the most challenging task. However, we note that the values for BLEU-3 in the case of nouns and others are small. This way, it can confuse the infilling order in sentences with more tokens belonging to these classes. Moreover, we note that METEOR score for verbs less penalizes the performance (in comparison with BLEU), suggesting that the model can predict a different conjugation of the expected word.

It is worth noting that, in general, the bottleneck of the whole pipeline is the masked surface realization task, as values are similar to the overall performance. Even the verb-focused decoding,

		BLEU	METEOR	chrF++	BERTScore
Baseline		10.39 ± 0.48	0.29 ± 0.01	0.41 ± 0.01	0.82 ± 0.00
SEP	Noun	5.32 ± 0.56	0.22 ± 0.01	0.35 ± 0.01	0.80 ± 0.01
	Verb	8.95 ± 1.46	0.27 ± 0.01	0.39 ± 0.02	0.81 ± 0.00
	Qualifier	9.44 ± 0.87	0.27 ± 0.01	0.39 ± 0.01	0.81 ± 0.00
	Other	8.21 ± 0.99	0.27 ± 0.01	0.39 ± 0.02	0.81 ± 0.01
ALL	Noun	8.87 ± 0.69	0.28 ± 0.01	0.40 ± 0.02	0.81 ± 0.01
	Verb	**12.02 ± 2.13**	**0.31 ± 0.03**	0.42 ± 0.03	0.83 ± 0.01
	Qualifier	10.34 ± 1.34	0.30 ± 0.02	0.42 ± 0.02	0.83 ± 0.01
	Other	7.74 ± 1.71	0.28 ± 0.01	0.42 ± 0.02	0.81 ± 0.00

Table 2: Overall Results on test set. Experiments in block "SEP" are the ones in which a model is trained on each main class separately, and "ALL" are the ones in which a model is trained on all main classes together, but we evaluate it individually.

having the worst performance on the word infilling task, achieves the highest performance because the previous task gets the best one. A possible explanation for this problem is how the generation is performed. We use an encoder-decoder architecture in which the generation of a token depends on the previously generated tokens. This way, adding mask tokens in training could make it more difficult as the pre-trained model never saw these tokens in a generation task (these were used for training the blank infilling task). Among the alternatives to solve this issue, we could explore other strategies to determine the less confident tokens in a generated sentence and mask them for the next stage. Also, we could try a non-autoregressive model that can overcome the problem of dependency mentioned before (Su et al., 2021).

		BLEU	METEOR	chrF++
SEP	Noun	6.90 ± 1.05	0.45 ± 0.02	0.48 ± 0.02
	Verb	10.91 ± 0.48	0.42 ± 0.02	0.47 ± 0.02
	Qualifier	8.43 ± 0.82	0.30 ± 0.01	0.39 ± 0.01
	Other	10.11 ± 0.74	0.53 ± 0.03	0.56 ± 0.03
ALL	Noun	9.41 ± 1.65	0.49 ± 0.03	0.51 ± 0.03
	Verb	12.31 ± 1.52	0.45 ± 0.03	0.49 ± 0.04
	Qualifier	10.31 ± 1.27	0.32 ± 0.03	0.40 ± 0.03
	Other	10.22 ± 2.67	0.54 ± 0.04	0.56 ± 0.04

Table 3: Results on Mask Surface Realisation on dev test.

5 Manual Revision

We conduct a manual revision of the outputs for each model in order to check the main and most common errors. In particular, we select the two best models in our experiments, i.e., the ones trained on all main classes but focusing on masking/filling verbs and qualifiers.

		BLEU-2	BLEU-3	METEOR
SEP	Noun	33.80 ± 3.83	11.45 ± 3.33	0.46 ± 0.03
	Verb	18.53 ± 2.22	-	0.41 ± 0.01
	Qualifier	44.98 ± 9.12	-	0.57 ± 0.01
	Other	40.35 ± 3.99	18.48 ± 4.02	0.52 ± 0.02
ALL	Noun	41.20 ± 3.07	22.20 ± 3.43	0.57 ± 0.02
	Verb	20.95 ± 3.77	-	0.50 ± 0.02
	Qualifier	39.05 ± 10.21	-	0.65 ± 0.01
	Other	40.90 ± 4.70	19.55 ± 4.13	0.53 ± 0.03

Table 4: Results on Word Infilling on dev set

We analyze 35 instances from the test set and classify the outputs into four classes: (1) Accurate ("Acc"), for accurate outputs,(2) Hallucination ("Hall"), for outputs that are not related to the reference, (3) Cut chunk, for outputs that contains only a portion of the reference, and (4) Small Changes, for outputs with slightly different from the reference (some tokens are different). Table 5 shows the frequency of each class for all evaluated models.

In general, the model trained on all main classes, but focusing on verbs got the best results. It is worth noting the high number of hallucinations in all models, mainly when longer sentences are evaluated. Also, the cut chunks happen in the same cases. Moreover, there are several instances where only changing a simple word (or two) would be necessary to make the output similar to the reference. This problem happens mainly with connectors such as "*em*" ("in" or "at") or "*de*" ("of") (words highlighted in red in Figure 3) and with bad conjugations in the case of the verbs.

Figure 3 shows three examples. The first example shows that the model focused on verbs gets an accurate output (example 1). The second example shows that the outputs for models focused on verbs and qualifiers can generate paraphrases instead of

	Acc	Hall	Cut Chunk	Small Changes
Baseline	9	16	4	6
ALL-Verb	14	12	1	8
ALL-Qualifier	9	18	1	7

Table 5: Number of accurate outputs ("Acc") and errors in the human evaluation.

the same sentence; however, these are accurate too. Finally, the third example is a case in which the models generate hallucinations (*"eua investiram em 2010."*), outputs with cut chunks (*"investir em os eua."*) or small changes.

Reference	*nada disso é criminoso .* none of this is criminal.
Baseline	*nada de isso .* none of that.
ALL-Verb	***nada de isso é criminoso .*** none of this is criminal.
ALL-Qualifier	*nada de criminoso .* nothing criminal.
Reference	*no vestiário , passou mal .* in the locker room , he felt sick .
Baseline	*passou mal .* he was feeling sick
ALL-Verb	***ele passou mal no vestiário .*** he got sick in the locker room.
ALL-Qualifier	***passou mal no vestiário .*** he got sick in the locker room.
Reference	*desde 2010 , o empresário investe nos eua .* since 2010, the businnessman invests in the usa.
Baseline	*eua investiram em 2010 .* usa invested in 2010.
ALL-Verb	*investir em os eua .* invest in the usa.
ALL-Qualifier	*em 2010 , o empresário não investiu no eua .* in 2010, the businessman did not invest in the usa.

Figure 3: Outputs comparison between the reference, the baseline, and the two best models in our experiments. The first lines for each model are the sentences generated in Brazilian Portuguese, and the next ones are the corresponding English translations.

6 Conclusion and Further Work

This work presents a simple two-stage approach to the low-resource AMR-to-text generation task. The approach consists of generating a masked surface realization in which some tokens are masked according to a POS class criteria and infilling the masked tokens according to the AMR graph and the previous masked surface realization.

Results show a slight improvement over the baseline, mainly in BLEU (1.63) and METEOR (0.02) scores. However, it is necessary to fine-tune the model on all the sub-corpus created together. Besides, we can note that verb masking seems to be the best strategy in this approach.

On the other hand, we note that the bottleneck of this approach is the masked surface realization model, as some generated tokens are different and unrelated to the original reference (hallucinations), and some tokens are omitted from the original reference. Some possible explanations for this problem are how the generation is performed -as each output word is conditioned on previously generated outputs-and the need to constrain the decoding process.

As further work, we plan to explore strategies to enforce the model to cover all the AMR concepts in the masked generated sentence and non-autoregressive text generation with pre-trained models, similar to Su et al. (2021). Besides, we plan to explore other strategies to mask tokens according to its confidence in decoding instead of using a POS-based one as the later can add more complexity to the task. Finally, we plan to extend this work to English AMR corpus, in order to make a better comparison in terms of generalization.

Limitations

This work tackles the AMR-to-Text generation task with a pipeline approach, and the results are similar to those obtained for previous work with the same amount of data (~10-15 BLEU score). However, the performance could be different as the lengths of the sentences in our task are up to 23 tokens, and the sentences evaluated in works for English are longer.

Other limitation is related to the criteria used for masking some tokens as it can introduce more complexity, mainly for low-resource languages.

Acknowledgments

The authors of this work would like to thank the Center for Artificial Intelligence (C4AI-USP) and the support from the São Paulo Research Foundation (FAPESP grant 2019/07665-4) and from the IBM Corporation. Besides, this research carried out using the computational resources of the Center for Mathematical Sciences Applied to Industry (CeMEAI) funded by FAPESP (grant 2013/07375-0).

References

Laura Banarescu, Claire Bonial, Shu Cai, Madalina Georgescu, Kira Griffitt, Ulf Hermjakob, Kevin Knight, Philipp Koehn, Martha Palmer, and Nathan Schneider. 2013. Abstract meaning representation for sembanking. In *Proceedings of the 7th Linguistic*

Annotation Workshop and Interoperability with Discourse, pages 178–186, Sofia, Bulgaria. Association for Computational Linguistics.

Kris Cao and Stephen Clark. 2019. Factorising AMR generation through syntax. In *Proceedings of the 2019 Conference of the North American Chapter of the Association for Computational Linguistics: Human Language Technologies, Volume 1 (Long and Short Papers)*, pages 2157–2163, Minneapolis, Minnesota. Association for Computational Linguistics.

Diedre Carmo, Marcos Piau, Israel Campiotti, Rodrigo Nogueira, and Roberto Lotufo. 2020. Ptt5: Pretraining and validating the t5 model on brazilian portuguese data. *arXiv preprint arXiv:2008.09144*.

Thiago Castro Ferreira, Chris van der Lee, Emiel van Miltenburg, and Emiel Krahmer. 2019. Neural data-to-text generation: A comparison between pipeline and end-to-end architectures. In *Proceedings of the 2019 Conference on Empirical Methods in Natural Language Processing and the 9th International Joint Conference on Natural Language Processing (EMNLP-IJCNLP)*, pages 552–562, Hong Kong, China. Association for Computational Linguistics.

Jeffrey Flanigan, Chris Dyer, Noah A. Smith, and Jaime Carbonell. 2016. Generation from abstract meaning representation using tree transducers. In *Proceedings of the 2016 Conference of the North American Chapter of the Association for Computational Linguistics: Human Language Technologies*, pages 731–739, San Diego, California. Association for Computational Linguistics.

Claire Gardent, Anastasia Shimorina, Shashi Narayan, and Laura Perez-Beltrachini. 2017. Creating training corpora for NLG micro-planners. In *Proceedings of the 55th Annual Meeting of the Association for Computational Linguistics (Volume 1: Long Papers)*, pages 179–188, Vancouver, Canada. Association for Computational Linguistics.

Marcio Lima Inácio, Marco Antonio Sobrevilla Cabezudo, Renata Ramisch, Ariani Di Felippo, and Thiago Alexandre Salgueiro Pardo. 2022. The amr-pt corpus and the semantic annotation of challenging sentences from journalistic and opinion texts. *SciELO Preprints*.

Zdeněk Kasner and Ondřej Dušek. 2020. Data-to-text generation with iterative text editing. In *Proceedings of the 13th International Conference on Natural Language Generation*, pages 60–67, Dublin, Ireland. Association for Computational Linguistics.

Gerasimos Lampouras and Andreas Vlachos. 2017. Sheffield at SemEval-2017 task 9: Transition-based language generation from AMR. In *Proceedings of the 11th International Workshop on Semantic Evaluation (SemEval-2017)*, pages 586–591, Vancouver, Canada. Association for Computational Linguistics.

Alon Lavie and Abhaya Agarwal. 2007. METEOR: An automatic metric for MT evaluation with high levels of correlation with human judgments. In *Proceedings of the 2nd Workshop on Statistical Machine Translation*, pages 228–231, Prague, Czech Republic. Association for Computational Linguistics.

Mike Lewis, Yinhan Liu, Naman Goyal, Marjan Ghazvininejad, Abdelrahman Mohamed, Omer Levy, Veselin Stoyanov, and Luke Zettlemoyer. 2020. BART: Denoising sequence-to-sequence pre-training for natural language generation, translation, and comprehension. In *Proceedings of the 58th Annual Meeting of the Association for Computational Linguistics*, pages 7871–7880, Online. Association for Computational Linguistics.

Kexin Liao, Logan Lebanoff, and Fei Liu. 2018. Abstract meaning representation for multi-document summarization. In *Proceedings of the 27th International Conference on Computational Linguistics*, pages 1178–1190, Santa Fe, New Mexico, USA. Association for Computational Linguistics.

Shuming Ma, Pengcheng Yang, Tianyu Liu, Peng Li, Jie Zhou, and Xu Sun. 2019. Key fact as pivot: A two-stage model for low resource table-to-text generation. In *Proceedings of the 57th Annual Meeting of the Association for Computational Linguistics*, pages 2047–2057, Florence, Italy. Association for Computational Linguistics.

Manuel Mager, Ramón Fernandez Astudillo, Tahira Naseem, Md Arafat Sultan, Young-Suk Lee, Radu Florian, and Salim Roukos. 2020. GPT-too: A language-model-first approach for AMR-to-text generation. In *Proceedings of the 58th Annual Meeting of the Association for Computational Linguistics*, pages 1846–1852, Online. Association for Computational Linguistics.

Jonathan May and Jay Priyadarshi. 2017. SemEval-2017 task 9: Abstract Meaning Representation parsing and generation. In *Proceedings of the 11th International Workshop on Semantic Evaluation (SemEval-2017)*, pages 536–545, Vancouver, Canada. Association for Computational Linguistics.

Simon Mille, Roberto Carlini, Alicia Burga, and Leo Wanner. 2017. FORGe at SemEval-2017 task 9: Deep sentence generation based on a sequence of graph transducers. In *Proceedings of the 11th International Workshop on Semantic Evaluation (SemEval-2017)*, pages 920–923, Vancouver, Canada. Association for Computational Linguistics.

Abelardo Vieira Mota, Ticiana Linhares Coelho da Silva, and José Antônio Fernandes De Macêdo. 2020. Template-based multi-solution approach for data-to-text generation. In *Advances in Databases and Information Systems: 24th European Conference, ADBIS 2020, Lyon, France, August 25–27, 2020, Proceedings*, page 157–170, Berlin, Heidelberg. Springer-Verlag.

Martha Palmer, Daniel Gildea, and Paul Kingsbury. 2005. The proposition bank: An annotated corpus of semantic roles. *Computational Linguistics*, 31(1):71–106.

Kishore Papineni, Salim Roukos, Todd Ward, and Wei-Jing Zhu. 2002. Bleu: a method for automatic evaluation of machine translation. In *Proceedings of the 40th Annual Meeting of the Association for Computational Linguistics*, pages 311–318, Philadelphia, Pennsylvania, USA. Association for Computational Linguistics.

Maja Popović. 2017. chrF++: words helping character n-grams. In *Proceedings of the Second Conference on Machine Translation*, pages 612–618, Copenhagen, Denmark. Association for Computational Linguistics.

Nima Pourdamghani, Kevin Knight, and Ulf Hermjakob. 2016. Generating English from abstract meaning representations. In *Proceedings of the 9th International Natural Language Generation conference*, pages 21–25, Edinburgh, UK. Association for Computational Linguistics.

Ratish Puduppully and Mirella Lapata. 2021. Data-to-text Generation with Macro Planning. *Transactions of the Association for Computational Linguistics*, 9:510–527.

Colin Raffel, Noam Shazeer, Adam Roberts, Katherine Lee, Sharan Narang, Michael Matena, Yanqi Zhou, Wei Li, and Peter J. Liu. 2020. Exploring the limits of transfer learning with a unified text-to-text transformer. *Journal of Machine Learning Research*, 21(140):1–67.

Ehud Reiter. 2018. Hallucination in neural NLG.

Leonardo F. R. Ribeiro, Martin Schmitt, Hinrich Schütze, and Iryna Gurevych. 2021a. Investigating pretrained language models for graph-to-text generation. In *Proceedings of the 3rd Workshop on Natural Language Processing for Conversational AI*, pages 211–227, Online. Association for Computational Linguistics.

Leonardo F. R. Ribeiro, Yue Zhang, and Iryna Gurevych. 2021b. Structural adapters in pretrained language models for AMR-to-Text generation. In *Proceedings of the 2021 Conference on Empirical Methods in Natural Language Processing*, pages 4269–4282, Online and Punta Cana, Dominican Republic. Association for Computational Linguistics.

Marco A. Sobrevilla Cabezudo and Thiago A.S. Pardo. 2022. Low-resource amr-to-text generation: A study on brazilian portuguese. *Procesamiento del Lenguaje Natural*, 68.

Marco Antonio Sobrevilla Cabezudo and Thiago Pardo. 2019. Towards a general abstract meaning representation corpus for Brazilian Portuguese. In *Proceedings of the 13th Linguistic Annotation Workshop*, pages 236–244, Florence, Italy. Association for Computational Linguistics.

Linfeng Song, Daniel Gildea, Yue Zhang, Zhiguo Wang, and Jinsong Su. 2019. Semantic neural machine translation using amr. *Transactions of the Association for Computational Linguistics*, 7:19–31.

Linfeng Song, Xiaochang Peng, Yue Zhang, Zhiguo Wang, and Daniel Gildea. 2017. AMR-to-text generation with synchronous node replacement grammar. In *Proceedings of the 55th Annual Meeting of the Association for Computational Linguistics (Volume 2: Short Papers)*, pages 7–13, Vancouver, Canada. Association for Computational Linguistics.

Yixuan Su, Deng Cai, Yan Wang, David Vandyke, Simon Baker, Piji Li, and Nigel Collier. 2021. Non-autoregressive text generation with pre-trained language models. In *Proceedings of the 16th Conference of the European Chapter of the Association for Computational Linguistics: Main Volume*, pages 234–243, Online. Association for Computational Linguistics.

Tianyi Zhang, Varsha Kishore, Felix Wu, Kilian Q. Weinberger, and Yoav Artzi. 2020. Bertscore: Evaluating text generation with bert. In *International Conference on Learning Representations*.

What Makes Data-to-Text Generation Hard for Pretrained Language Models?

Moniba Keymanesh[1*] **Adrian Benton**[1†] **Mark Dredze**[1,2]
[1] Bloomberg, New York, NY USA
[2] Computer Science, Johns Hopkins University, Baltimore, MD USA
mkeymanesh1@bloomberg.net, adbenton@google.com, mdredze@cs.jhu.edu

Abstract

Expressing natural language descriptions of structured facts or relations – data-to-text generation (D2T) – increases the accessibility of structured knowledge repositories. Previous work (Nan et al., 2020) shows that pre-trained language models (PLMs) perform remarkably well on this task after fine-tuning on a significant amount of task-specific training data. On the other hand, while auto-regressive PLMs can generalize from a few task examples, their efficacy at D2T is largely unexplored. Furthermore, we have an incomplete understanding of the limits of PLMs on D2T. In this work, we conduct an empirical study of both fine-tuned and auto-regressive PLMs on the DART multi-domain D2T dataset. We consider their performance as a function of the amount of task-specific data and how the data is incorporated into the models: zero and few-shot learning, and fine-tuning of model weights. In addition, we probe the limits of PLMs by measuring performance on subsets of the evaluation data: novel predicates and abstractive test examples. To improve the performance on these subsets, we investigate two techniques: providing predicate descriptions in the context and re-ranking generated candidates by information reflected in the source. Finally, we conduct a human evaluation of model errors and show that D2T generation tasks would benefit from datasets with more careful manual curation.

1 Introduction

Structured data repositories, or knowledge bases, contain a wealth of information organized to facilitate automated access and analysis. Automated data-to-text (D2T) generation systems can transform and organize this knowledge into natural language text snippets that enable broader access (Gatt and Krahmer, 2018). These systems take as input a set of relations, where each relation is a (subject, predicate, object) triple. Applications of this technology include story or dialogue generation (Moon et al., 2019), open-domain question-answering (Ma et al., 2021; Fan et al., 2019), and text summarization (Wiseman et al., 2017). Domains span journalism (Leppänen et al., 2017), weather (Ramos-Soto et al., 2014; Mei et al., 2015), finance, sports (Plachouras et al., 2016; Chen and Mooney, 2008; van der Lee et al., 2017), and summarizing patient medical histories (Portet et al., 2009).

Historically, D2T systems included pipeline approaches with customized models (Gardent et al., 2017), but have now shifted to pretrained Transformer-based language models (PLMs) (Devlin et al., 2018; Liu et al., 2019; Radford et al., 2019). Recent examples include Mager et al. (2020) and Kale and Rastogi (2020), who use models like GPT-2 (Radford et al., 2019) and T5 (Raffel et al., 2019) to generate natural language descriptions for relations. To support these types of systems, Nan et al. (2020) introduced DART, a large open-domain data-to-text generation corpus. Models trained on DART, both larger and more diverse than previous corpora, improve the performance of BART (Lewis et al., 2019) and T5 on the standard WebNLG challenge (Gardent et al., 2017). This approach requires a PLM to be fine-tuned on a task-specific in-domain dataset (Howard and Ruder, 2018; See et al., 2019; Keskar et al., 2019). The promising results achieved by fine-tuning on DART belie the reality – in spite of DART's aspirations, most domains and relations that one could express fail to appear in DART.

A variety of methods have emerged within PLM research to address domain or task adaptation. For example, auto-regressive models, like GPT, have demonstrated improved performance on a wide range of tasks via few-shot learning from a handful of examples (Chen et al., 2019). Other strategies, such as prompt tuning (Lester et al., 2021), can adapt PLMs to specific down-stream tasks by up-

*Work done during an internship at Bloomberg.
†Now at Google Research.

Proceedings of the 2nd Workshop on Natural Language Generation, Evaluation, and Metrics (GEM), pages 539 - 554
December 7, 2022 ©2022 Association for Computational Linguistics

dating only a small subset of model parameters.

While great progress has been made in utilizing PLMs for D2T generation, the path forward is unclear, as we have an incomplete understanding as to which examples they fall short on and the quantity of training resources they need to achieve acceptable performance. More specifically, it is not clear which classes of D2T examples are challenging for these models. In addition, we do not fully understand what classes of errors PLMs are prone to and how the adaptation mechanism (e.g., k-shot learning, fine-tuning) affects the prevalence of these errors.

In this work, we conduct an evaluation of PLMs for D2T generation, focusing on two classes of challenging examples: examples with novel (*unseen*) relations (*predicates*) and examples where the source and target sequences are lexically very different (not amenable to purely extractive D2T systems). We consider how GPT-2, adapted with few-shot learning, prompt tuning, and the addition of predicate descriptions, performs on these example classes as compared to a state-of-the-art fine-tuned T5. We show that while GPT-2 performs poorly on DART in the 0-shot setting, its performance can be drastically improved by employing the above techniques. We make the following contributions:

- We evaluate GPT2-XL and fine-tuned T5 for D2T generation. While the 0-shot GPT model performs poorly, we evaluate several strategies to improve performance, including few-shot learning and prompt tuning. Both provide significant improvements on the DART dataset.

- We compare model performance on two classes of difficult examples: examples with unseen predicates, and abstractive examples (examples where source and target sequences are lexically dissimilar). We investigate whether including predicate descriptions in the prompt can improve the ability of PLMs on these classes.

- We conduct a human evaluation of PLMs to quantify the prevalence of hallucination and missing information in generations as a function of the model adaptation technique. We find that a re-ranking strategy for few-shot GPT2-XL, despite having little effect on automatic metrics like BLEU, reduces the incidence of missing information, without requiring additional training data.

Finally, we provide recommendations for future model and dataset research in D2T generation.

2 Background and Related Work

In the task of data-to-text generation, we are provided a set of triples that include a predicate, subject, and object. The system then produces a text snippet expressing the predicate in natural language. Figure 2 shows examples of predicates about sports. The system can be given a set of triples with related predicates (e.g., CLUB, LEAGUE, FORMER_TEAM) and must generate text that expresses the facts encoded by these relations. The resulting text is typically evaluated by comparison to a set of reference texts, which represent various ways of expressing this triple set.

Variations in the formulation of this task depend on the structure of the relations (e.g., tables, triples), the domain of the task (single or open domain), and the source of the data (manually created, automatically derived).

Harkous et al. (2020) follow a generate-and-rerank paradigm to improve the semantic fidelity of the generated text by fine-tuned GPT-2 model. More recently, Ribeiro et al. (2020) propose a new task-adaptive pretraining strategy to adapt BART (Lewis et al., 2019) and T5 (Raffel et al., 2019) models for data-to-text generation. They show that adding an intermediate task-adaptive pretraining step between the task-independent pretraining and fine-tuning further improves the performance of these models on data-to-text generation.

Despite the progress of these models, it is not clear which types of D2T examples are most challenging for PLMs or what errors are prevalent in generations. Futhermore, how does PLM adaptation (tuning/prompting) interact with the occurrence of these errors. On the other hand, D2T datasets are not readily available in many domains. Weakly supervised annotation methods (e.g., based on identifying sentences in a corpus that are likely to express a data record) require significant manual effort and often result in annotations with low fidelity between data records and the corresponding textual expression (Mintz et al., 2009). Training NLG models on such data can result in generations with missing information or hallucination (Dušek et al., 2019; Dziri et al., 2022a,b). These issues render the path forward for D2T generation research

Zero-shot Prompt

Translate Graph to English:

Graph: <H> Alan Martin (footballer) <R> CLUB <T> Hamilton Academical F.C.

English:

Zero-shot Prompt + Relation Description

Translate Graph to English:

Definition: club is an organization of players and managers associated with a particular football team.

Graph: <H> Alan Martin (footballer) <R> CLUB <T> Hamilton Academical F.C.

English:

Figure 1: A customized 0-shot prompt for GPT

Few-shot Prompt

Translate Graph to English:

Graph: <H> Paulo Sousa <R> CLUB <T> ACF Fiorentina

English: Paulo Sousa plays for ACF Fiorentina.

###

Graph: <H> Dave Challinor <R> CLUB <T> Colwyn Bay F.C.

English: Dave Challinor plays for Colwyn Bay F.C.

###

Graph: <H> Alan Martin (footballer) <R> CLUB <T> Hamilton Academical F.C.

English:

Figure 2: A customized 3-shot prompt for GPT

unclear.

3 Model Adaptation

As a supervised task, D2T generation systems rely on previously observed examples to learn the correct generation or level of required "re-writing" for a predicate. On the other hand, large auto-regressive PLMs (such as GPT2-XL) are able to perform D2T generation without any explicit fine-tuning at all. However, their efficacy on D2T and potential shortcomings are largely unexplored. How well do PLMs perform on relations with a novel predicate? Do PLMs overly rely on copying verbatim from the input or are they capable of abstraction when required? What classes of errors are prevalent in the generations and how do they interact with the choice of adaptation mechanism? Our focus is on the analysis of PLMs for D2T generation.

We study this problem using two types of PLMs: auto-regressive models like GPT-2 and "supervised" models like T5 (Raffel et al., 2019). While prior work has demonstrated that T5 achieves state-of-the-art results on D2T, these "supervised" models[1] expect task-specific training data, whereas generative PLMs excel at adapting to new tasks. Since auto-regressive models have not been fully benchmarked for D2T, we will evaluate them in multiple settings and compare to T5. For both, we will explore the effect of varying training size and their pathological behaviors.

While PLMs can be fine-tuned, their increasing size and training requirements disfavors this approach. Instead, current work assumes a single PLM capable of performing multiple downstream tasks (Lester et al., 2021). We adopt GPT2-XL, a decoder-only Transformer (Vaswani et al., 2017) with 1.5B parameters pre-trained for language modeling (Radford et al., 2019).[2] We utilize GPT2-XL as a D2T generation model by varying the amount of supervised information available. Instead of fine-tuning GPT2-XL, we investigate both few-shot learning (Radford et al., 2019), which is better suited to settings where little training data is available, and prompt tuning, which enables us to tractably update a subset of model weights in spite of GPT2-XL's large parameter count.

3.1 0-shot Setting

We start by evaluating GPT2-XL in the 0-shot setting, an especially challenging setting due to a lack of coverage in the training data of pairings between structured records and unstructured text (Gong et al., 2020). Ribeiro et al. (2020) handled this by including an additional pretraining step. Our focus is on an off-the-shelf GPT2-XL model. We format the input data using the D2T generation infix and prefix formatting of Ribeiro et al. (2020) (example in Figure 1). We provide no additional context or task-specific training.

[1]We note that new findings (Sanh et al., 2021) has demonstrated T5 can handle 0-shot task adaptation with the right prompts; this is an evolving research area.

[2]WebText (the training dataset) includes the content of more than 8 million documents with outbound links from Reddit, a social media platform. Wikipedia (the main data source for DART) is excluded.

3.2 Few-shot Setting

We next consider a few-shot setting by augmenting the format of the 0-shot input with reference generations from the training corpus. We evaluate GPT2-XL under the 3-shot learning setting (example in Figure 2). For predicates "seen" in the training set, we select three shots with the same predicate uniformly at random from the training set. For "unseen" predicates – predicates not covered in the training set – we randomly select any three examples. Previous work has found that careful shot selection based on input text similarity can be beneficial (Liu et al., 2021a). However, it's less clear how this would apply to unseen predicates. We leave this for future work.

3.3 Prompt Tuning

The expected task for a PLM is indicated by the choice of prompt; ours (Figure 1) follows prior work (Ribeiro et al., 2020; Nan et al., 2020). The prompt includes a prefix ("Graph") and an infix token ("English") that indicate the start of the input and the start of the expected output. Autoregressive language models are sensitive to the choice of prompt, and significant effort is needed to craft effective prompts (Liu et al., 2021b).

Lester et al. (2021) proposed an alternate method: prompt tuning. Instead of using discrete prompt tokens, they use "soft-prompts" which are pseudo-token embeddings that are learned during fine-tuning, with all other model parameters held fixed. We follow previous work (Lester et al., 2021; Chowdhury et al., 2022) and use a generic sequence of tokens to denote the prompt prefix $p_{1:s} = (p_1, p_2, ...p_s)$ and infix $q_{1:t} = (q_1, q_2, ...q_t)$. The PLM is provided the input sequence $p_{1:s}$ *<H>* x_1 *<R>* x_2 *<T>* x_3 $q_{1:t}$, where x_1, x_2 and x_3 are head, predicate (relation), and tail strings from the example.

The objective during prompt tuning is to maximize the probability of output sequence $y_{1:m}$ given input data record, prefix $p_{1:s}$, and infix $q_{1:t}$. During training, however, only the embedding of the prompt tokens can be updated. Unlike fine-tuning which updates all model parameters on the target task, prompt tuning tunes a small number of parameters (less than 0.01% of all parameters) while keeping most of the language model fixed. While this requires the use of the full training set, as opposed to few-shot learning, it illuminates the abilities of GPT2-XL given access to such data.

3.4 Domain Knowledge

We explore another way of improving model performance for novel predicates and for examples where significant re-writing is needed: providing definitions for predicates. In many domains, we may find a knowledge base containing many predicates, and definitions for those relations, but no examples of sentences expressing those relations. In these cases, we want to enhance the context of the PLM with predicate definitions. For example, for the tuple *<H> Genuine Parts <R> DISTRIBUTOR <T> automotive and industrial replacement parts* we may know that DISTRIBUTOR means *"someone who markets merchandise"*. This definition can be helpful to a model that was never exposed to this predicate at training time.

We source predicate definitions for our data from WordNet, a lexical database in English (Miller, 1995), and WikiData.[3] We use WikiData since Wikipedia was the source of many relations in the DART data.[4] An example of the input prompt enhanced with the predicate definition appears in Figure 1. We also consider using predicate descriptions in combination with prompt tuning.

3.5 Fine-tuned PLM

Our second model type is $T5_{large}$ (Raffel et al., 2019), a Transformer encoder-decoder architecture with 770M parameters for text generation. The model is pretrained with a denoising objective on a variety of NLP tasks and web-extracted C4 corpus. Unlike GPT2-XL, the denoising objective means an off-the-shelf model performs poorly on unseen tasks, such as D2T generation (Raffel et al., 2019; Lester et al., 2021). We follow Nan et al. (2020) and fine-tune $T5_{large}$ on the DART training set. While this model requires a large amount of supervised examples, it attains state of the art performance on this task.

4 Dataset

For our experiments we use DART (Nan et al., 2020), the largest publicly available open-domain data-to-text generation corpus. DART relies on data from Wikipedia as well as two other commonly used data sets for this task: WebNLG (Gar-

[3] wikidata.org

[4] DART includes predicates such as *MARGIN_OF_VICTORY* and *INTERMEDIATE_(SOUTH)_WINNERS*. Since descriptions for such relations cannot be found verbatim in WordNet or WikiData, no description is added to those cases.

	Train	Dev	Test
Size	30,526	2,768	5,097
#Unique relation types	4,221	419	494
#Ref per example min/avg/max	1/2.0/48	1/2.5/33	1/2.4/35
#Triples per record min/avg/max	1/3.3/10	1/3.7/8	1/3.6/7

Table 1: Descriptive statistics of the DART version 1.1.1

dent et al., 2017) and E2E (Novikova et al., 2017). Each instance includes a triple set (a set of one or more predicates and their labels) and a natural language reference that expresses the facts in the triple set. We choose DART due to its size and wide coverage of predicate types. Relevant DART statistics appear in Table 1. We use the original train, development, and test splits.[5] [6]

Data Splits The DART test set includes 5,097 examples, of which 4,826 (94.4%) include at least one relation type that appears in the training set. We refer to this subset as the SEEN partition. The remaining 271 instances (5.3%) are considered UNSEEN.[7] To support additional system analysis, we create another partition of the test data: EASY and HARD. HARD examples are identified by similarity of the input triple to the reference text. In many cases, the reference has high lexical overlap with and similar meaning to the input, while in other cases the generation is non-trivial (see Appendix A for examples). To create the EASY and HARD partitions, we use BERTScore (Zhang et al., 2019) to compute similarity of the input triple with respect to the reference. Examples are ranked based on BERTScore (F1) and the top 10% (510 examples) comprise the EASY partition, while the bottom 10% comprise the HARD partition. By using BertScore to separate EASY and HARD examples, we are not relying purely on lexical overlap to score the difficulty of an example.

5 Experimental Setup

Model Training We use the pretrained models GPT2-XL and T5_{large} released by Hugging Face (Wolf et al., 2019), along with their respective tokenizers, for all experiments.

We use beam search with beam size of three for decoding in all models, lightly post-processing the generated text by truncating generations at the newline character. We set maximum generated tokens to 100 and repetition penalty to 1.01 for all experiments.

We used a single V100 GPU with 32GB of memory for all prompt tuning experiments, tuning for a single epoch on the DART train set with prefix and infix length both set to 8 tokens. We use the Adam optimizer (Kingma and Ba, 2014) with a maximum learning rate of 0.1 and 100 warm-up steps for the linear learning rate schedule. The training batch size was fixed to 2, with 32 gradient accumulation steps (effective batch size of 64 examples).

We use the scripts from Ribeiro et al. (2020) to fine-tune T5 on DART, using identical hyperparameter settings.[8] We use the Adam optimizer with an initial learning rate of 3e-5 and a linearly decreasing learning rate schedule. We fine-tune the model on four GPUs for a maximum of 100 epochs and stop training early if the performance does not improve on the dev set for 15 epochs. Each training epoch takes approximately two hours for each model.

Finally, we include a baseline system to benchmark the performance of our machine learning models. In a "copy baseline" we simply copy the input text and remove the prefix tokens (<H>, <R>, <T>) as well as special characters (e.g., underscores) common in DART predicates. This baseline performs well for examples with high lexical overlap between input triple set and reference.

Evaluation Metrics Following previous work, we use automated metrics such as BLEU (Papineni et al., 2002), METEOR (Denkowski and Lavie, 2014), translation edit rate (TER) (Snover et al., 2006), and chrF++ (Popović, 2015) for evaluating our generation results. In addition, we also report BERTScore (Zhang et al., 2019) and BLEURT (Sellam et al., 2020). These metrics go beyond surface form similarities and use contextual embeddings to measure semantic similarity between the generated and reference text.[9]

[5]Nan et al. (2020) use version v1.0.0 of DART, whereas we use the publicly available version, v1.1.1.

[6]In the DART dataset, some data records are paired with more than 30 references. Nan et al. (2020) do not report the number of references used for their experiments. However in their adaptation of Ribeiro et al. (2020)'s fine-tuning script they only use three references. We follow their methodology and only use up to three references per example.

[7]Note that Nan et al. (2020) report performance on the "unseen" portion of WebNLG. "Unseen", in this case, means that the relations do not appear in the WebNLG training data; there is no guarantee that they do not appear in the DART training data. Our splits ensure that the UNSEEN partition only contains predicates not seen during DART training.

[8]`https://github.com/UKPLab/plms-graph2text` (Apache 2.0 license)

[9]We use the evaluation scripts provided in the official WebNLG challenge: `https://github.com/WebNLG/GenerationEval` (MIT license)

ID	Model	BLEU ↑			METEOR ↑			TER ↓		
		SEEN	UNSEEN	ALL	SEEN	UNSEEN	ALL	SEEN	UNSEEN	ALL
1	copy baseline	4.48	5.07	4.50	0.28	0.31	0.28	0.92	0.86	0.92
2	GPT2-XL (0-shot)	13.13	13.88	13.26	0.23	0.27	0.23	0.69	0.78	0.70
3	GPT2-XL(3-shot)	26.74	23.72	26.65	0.29	0.28	0.29	0.85	0.78	0.84
4	GPT2-XL-PT	33.55	29.86	33.41	0.24	0.28	0.24	0.65	0.61	0.65
5	GPT2-XL-PT + Reranking	31.03	31.67	31.09	0.28	0.30	0.28	0.63	0.58	0.63
6	$T5_{large}$	48.41	43.48	48.25	0.39	0.40	0.39	0.46	0.44	0.46
+Descriptions										
7	GPT2-XL(0-shot)	11.45	8.05	11.4	0.20	0.19	0.20	0.70	1.00	0.72
8	GPT2-XL(3-shot)	26.32	21.30	26.14	0.28	0.27	0.28	0.83	0.89	0.83
9	GPT2-XL-PT	33.96	31.37	33.85	0.24	0.28	0.24	0.66	0.59	0.66
10	$T5_{large}$	48.56	43.82	48.4	0.39	0.39	0.39	0.46	0.45	0.46

Table 2: Model results on test set of the DART dataset. ↑: Higher is better. ↓: Lower is better.

ID	Model	BLEU ↑		METEOR ↑		chrF++ ↑		TER ↓		BERTScore(F1) ↑		BLEURT ↑	
		EASY	HARD	EASY	HARD	EASY	HARD	EASY	HARD	EASY	HARD	EASY	HARD
11	copy baseline	18.00	2.01	0.41	0.23	0.45	0.32	0.79	0.99	0.88	0,80	0.12	-1.00
12	GPT2-XL (0-shot)	22.20	6.92	0.34	0.18	0.47	0.31	0.83	0.64	0.90	0.88	-0.09	-0.54
13	GPT2-XL (3-shot)	34.97	1.88	0.34	0.06	0.54	0.07	0.82	0.38	0.92	0.93	-0.09	-0.11
14	GPT2-XL-PT	42.81	31.78	0.35	0.23	0.57	0.39	0.48	0.69	0.94	0.92	0.31	-0.17
15	GPT2-XL-PT + Reranking	43.35	25.79	0.37	0.29	0.60	0.48	0.47	0.66	0.94	0.93	0.34	-0.04
16	$T5_{large}$	70.54	38.34	0.51	0.35	0.80	0.57	0.23	0.59	0.97	0.94	0.70	0.20
+Descriptions													
17	GPT2-XL (0-shot)	19.00	6.43	0.30	0.17	0.42	0.31	0.93	0.65	0.89	0.88	-0.20	-0.54
18	GPT2-XL (3-shot)	34.19	20.54	0.38	0.26	0.61	0.44	0.92	0.81	0.93	0.91	0.07	-0.26
19	GPT2-XL-PT	42.52	33.1	0.34	0.23	0.56	0.39	0.5	0.69	0.93	0.91	0.28	-0.21
20	$T5_{large}$	70.06	38.49	0.51	0.34	0.80	0.57	0.23	0.60	0.97	0.94	0.69	0.20

Table 3: Model results on EASY and HARD partitions of the DART test set. ↑: Higher is better. ↓: Lower is better.

6 Experiments

We evaluate PLMs with various input types and training regimes to answer the following empirical questions:

- How do the adaptation mechanism and level of supervision at train time affect PLM performance on the D2T task?
- What classes of D2T examples are particularly challenging for each PLM? How well do PLMs perform on out-of-sample predicates and examples that are more abstractive (dissimilar source and target sequences)?
- Can we improve performance on examples with unseen predicates by including predicate descriptions in the prompt, as mentioned in §3.4?
- Qualitatively, what kinds of errors do PLMs make on the D2T task? Are some adaptation techniques more susceptible to classes of errors than others?
- Can we mitigate some of these errors by reranking the decoding results?

6.1 Results

Table 2 presents model performance on the entire DART dataset (ALL), as well as the SEEN and UNSEEN partitions. See Appendix B for chrF++, BERTScore, and BLEURT results. Table 3 shows model performance on the EASY and HARD partitions.

Level of Supervision We first turn to GPT2-XL, which is evaluated on this task without any training data. Following previous work we find that GPT2-XL makes an effective 0-shot model, outperforming the copy baseline according to BLEU and METEOR (row 2). Examining the output more closely, we find that GPT2-XL mostly copies the input; while it outperforms the copy baseline, its strategy is largely the same. We include example generations in Appendix C. 3-shot GPT2-XL (row 3) does much better than the 0-shot case. Note that in this setting, no model parameters are updated. In addition, the amount of annotated data used for creating 3-shot prompts is much less than what is used for prompt tuning and fine-tuning. While few-shot prompting leads to a boost in BLEU and METEOR, TER increases by 0.14 point. We conjecture that this is due to an increase in hallucinated content in this setting. We take a closer look at these pathological behaviors in our human evaluation.

Both GPT2-XL models prompt tuned on the entire DART dataset (rows 4 and 5) outperform the 3-shot model by a wide margin. As reported previously (Nan et al., 2020), we also notice that fine-tuned T5 (row 6) performs well on this task surpassing either prompt-tuned GPT2-XL model.

Consistent with previous findings, we also notice that the more training data that is used to adapt the model (either by few-shot learning or training model weights), the better PLMs perform. However, in a resource-constrained setting, few-shot GPT2-XL achieves reasonable performance. Few-shot adaptation might be a good choice for D2T when the number of unique predicates in the test set is small, and only very few examples can be manually annotated. On the other hand, if more data is available, fine-tuning T5 leads to better results for D2T. In fact, our experiments show that T5 can surpass the 3-shot GPT2-XL after fine-tuning on only 200 examples. See Appendix B for details.

Predicate Novelty As expected, the copy baseline (row 1) performs poorly across all conditions, but consistent for both the SEEN and UNSEEN partitions. 0-shot GPT2-XL also performs similarly on both partitions, since it was not trained on any task data. GPT2-XL with a 3-shot prompt (row 3) outperforms 0-shot on both partitions, despite the unseen prompts including unrelated predicates; the model still benefits from multiple shots even if they do not contain the same predicates (+9.84 BLEU points).

Prompt tuning and re-ranking generated samples by overlap with the triple set entities both improve the performance of GPT2-XL on novel predicates. Overall, GPT2-XL performs consistently across SEEN and UNSEEN partitions, while T5 performance is more sensitive to whether the predicate was observed during training (e.g., difference of 4.93 points BLEU in row 6).

We next turn to evaluating the impact of augmenting prompts with predicate descriptions for unseen predicates. This process is described in §3.4. We evaluate this augmentation in the 0-shot (row 7), 3-shot (row 8) and prompt tuning (row 9) settings, as well as in T5 fine-tuning (row 10). We observe very small improvements on the UNSEEN partition and only in cases where model parameters are updated (rows 9 and 10). We suspect that as descriptions are sourced from WordNet and Wiki-Data, either many predicates could not be resolved to a description in these tables, or the predicates that could be resolved were largely self-explanatory. We conjecture that in the 0-shot setting, conditioning the generation on descriptions might distract the model from the head and tail entity. On the other hand, many of the unseen predicates in DART are not words that can be easily resolved. However, we suspect that if they were to be reliably resolved, specialized domains such as finance or medicine would benefit from adding predicate descriptions.

Generation Difficulty Table 3 shows the performance of all models on the EASY and HARD partitions. All models have noticeably worse performance on HARD examples, where more abstraction is needed. The best performing model, T5 (row 16), has a gap of 0.16 METEOR between the EASY and HARD partition, while the prompt tuned GPT2-XL (row 14) has the smallest difference in performance between the partitions. It is clear that these models perform well overall when copying from the input suffices, but do poorly when significant rewriting is required. In many domains, we may prefer models with more diverse, creative generations, a task at which these models do not do well. On the other hand, DART is a mostly automatically derived dataset, with significant errors in some examples, where the reference text may contain information that is unsupported by the input triple. These examples may pervade the HARD partition.

Next, we investigate the impact of adding predicate descriptions on D2T of the HARD partition. In the few-shot setting, adding predicate descriptions improves the BLEU score to 20.54 on the HARD partition (row 18). Conditioning the model on predicate descriptions significantly enhances its re-writing ability. For the prompt tuned GPT2-XL, BLEU score improves to 33.1 (row 19). However, we do not see any gains for 0-shot GPT or T5 (rows 17 and 20). Overall, GPT2-XL benefits from predicate descriptions on examples where significant re-writing is needed, even when additionally prompt tuned. GPT2-XL with prompt tuning achieves competitive results with benchmark T5 on the HARD partition (33.1 vs 38.49 BLEU).

Human Evaluation To further examine the pathological behaviors of the models, we randomly sampled 50 examples from the DART test set for human evaluation. For each example, the output

Source	Hallucination ↓	Missing Info ↓	Fluency ↑
Reference	1.53	1.19	4.51
GPT2-XL(3-shot)	3.26	3.61	3.17
GPT2-XL-PT	1.73	3.35	4.64
GPT2-XL-PT + Ranking	1.73	2.79	4.75
$T5_{large}$	1.16	1.23	4.79
Agreement	0.64	0.77	0.50

Table 4: Results of the qualitative evaluation. ↓: Lower is better. ↑: Higher is better. Inter-annotator agreement is measured by Kendall's τ rank correlation coefficient.

of T5 and GPT2-XL in the 3-shot, prompt tuned, and re-ranked settings were presented to two annotators.[10] We also showed the reference text as another candidate, with the generating model identity hidden. Annotators evaluated output quality based on three criteria: (1) whether it contains hallucinated content *(hallucination)* (2) whether the text is missing information from the input records *(missing info)*, and (3) *fluency*. Annotators indicated agreement with each of these Likert items on an ordinal scale from 1 (strongly disagree) to 5 (strongly agree).

Table 4 presents the average annotator score according to each of these Likert items. GPT2-XL in the 3-shot setting often misses information. Notably, both prompt-tuned variations generate very fluent text. Re-ranking improves the quality of the generations by decreasing the amount of missing information and improving fluency. While the best GPT2-XL model does very similar to $T5_{large}$ in terms of fluency, on average it hallucinates or misses information more often.

Re-ranking GPT2-XL prompt tuned is both parameter efficient and generalizes very well to novel predicates. It also does very well on examples that require more re-writing. It approaches the performance of fine-tuned $T5_{large}$ according to avoiding hallucinations and fluency. During the human evaluation, we observe that this model would often miss the subject or object of the predicate in its generations (see our human evaluation for details). We can mitigate this problem without additional model training through a re-ranking strategy to ensure that the selected generation contains all relevant information.

We first create multiple candidate generations by increasing beam size during decoding. Next, we compute the percentage of head and tail entities covered in the text. Finally, we pick the candidate that contains the highest percentage of entity spans from the input triple.[11] Rows 5 and 15 show the results of re-ranking a GPT2-XL prompt tuned model. Re-ranking modestly improves performance on all partitions, and across all metrics except BLEU.

[10]Two of the paper authors.

7 Conclusion and Future Work

In this work, we systematically analyze the performance of two PLMs – T5 and GPT2-XL – for D2T generation by examining performance based on the choice of adaptation mechanism: fine-tuning, prompt tuning, and few-shot learning. We observe that while fine-tuning on more data leads to better performance, when no training data is available, GPT2-XL (0-shot) outperforms T5. With a small number of training examples, few-shot GPT2-XL is a more appropriate solution for D2T.

We also conduct a thorough investigation of D2T challenges for PLMs by evaluating them on two divisions of the DART test set: novel predicates and abstractive examples. We show that the performance of fine-tuned T5 drops significantly on unseen predicates. On the other hand, the performance of few-shot GPT2-XL on unseen predicates can be enhanced even with shots containing unrelated predicates. We also notice that T5 and GPT2-XL both do well at D2T by copying the input. However, they do noticeably worse on examples where significant re-writing is needed. Adding domain knowledge (predicate descriptions) to the prompts can improve the performance of few-shot GPT2-XL on this subset by a large amount. We also conduct a human evaluation of the generations and find that prompt tuned GPT2-XL generations can be improved by re-ranking generations by overlap with the input entity spans.

Future work in D2T generation should consider more challenging examples, and should consider ways in which to generate more diverse variations for expressing a given predicate. This should include more challenging and disparate domains, such as finance or medicine. In these cases, one may see benefits from including predicate descriptions, which performed well on the most abstractive examples.

Limitations

An important challenge for D2T is how to train models that can generalize to new domains. While

[11]We use a beam size of 20 during decoding. Prior to measuring the entity coverage in the candidates, we normalize the text by lower casing and removing special characters.

this work looked at a related class of examples (instances with unseen predicates), it would be interesting to investigate how PLMs trained on one domain can be efficiently adapted to perform D2T on another unrelated domain (e.g., sports to finance). This would require creating domain-specific datasets for D2T.

Moreover, we observed that adding domain knowledge (predicate descriptions) to prompts can improve the performance of few-shot GPT2-XL on abstractive examples. We suspect that this idea may work better on specialized domains, with better relation descriptions, or with a larger language model; we could not test this without a specialized D2T dataset with better task relation descriptions.

Finally, many applications prefer generating novel or interesting descriptions for a data record over "safe" and "generic" ones, which are predominant in our training data (Li et al., 2015, 2016; Baheti et al., 2018; Shao et al., 2021). Evaluating PLMs for diversity of generated text is an orthogonal and promising future direction.

References

Ashutosh Baheti, Alan Ritter, Jiwei Li, and Bill Dolan. 2018. Generating more interesting responses in neural conversation models with distributional constraints. In *Proceedings of the 2018 Conference on Empirical Methods in Natural Language Processing*, pages 3970–3980, Brussels, Belgium. Association for Computational Linguistics.

David L Chen and Raymond J Mooney. 2008. Learning to sportscast: a test of grounded language acquisition. In *Proceedings of the 25th international conference on Machine learning*, pages 128–135.

Zhiyu Chen, Harini Eavani, Wenhu Chen, Yinyin Liu, and William Yang Wang. 2019. Few-shot NLG with pre-trained language model. *arXiv preprint arXiv:1904.09521*.

Jishnu Ray Chowdhury, Yong Zhuang, and Shuyi Wang. 2022. Novelty controlled paraphrase generation with retrieval augmented conditional prompt tuning. In *Association for the Advancement of Artificial Intelligence (AAAI)*. AAAI.

Michael Denkowski and Alon Lavie. 2014. Meteor universal: Language specific translation evaluation for any target language. In *Proceedings of the ninth workshop on statistical machine translation*, pages 376–380.

Jacob Devlin, Ming-Wei Chang, Kenton Lee, and Kristina Toutanova. 2018. Bert: Pre-training of deep bidirectional transformers for language understanding. *arXiv preprint arXiv:1810.04805*.

Ondřej Dušek, David M Howcroft, and Verena Rieser. 2019. Semantic noise matters for neural natural language generation. *arXiv preprint arXiv:1911.03905*.

Nouha Dziri, Ehsan Kamalloo, Sivan Milton, Osmar Zaiane, Mo Yu, Edoardo M Ponti, and Siva Reddy. 2022a. FaithDial: A faithful benchmark for information-seeking dialogue. *arXiv preprint arXiv:2204.10757*.

Nouha Dziri, Sivan Milton, Mo Yu, Osmar Zaiane, and Siva Reddy. 2022b. On the origin of hallucinations in conversational models: Is it the datasets or the models? *arXiv preprint arXiv:2204.07931*.

Angela Fan, Claire Gardent, Chloé Braud, and Antoine Bordes. 2019. Using local knowledge graph construction to scale seq2seq models to multi-document inputs. *arXiv preprint arXiv:1910.08435*.

Claire Gardent, Anastasia Shimorina, Shashi Narayan, and Laura Perez-Beltrachini. 2017. The WebNLG challenge: Generating text from RDF data. In *Proceedings of the 10th International Conference on Natural Language Generation*, pages 124–133.

Albert Gatt and Emiel Krahmer. 2018. Survey of the state of the art in natural language generation: Core tasks, applications and evaluation. *Journal of Artificial Intelligence Research*, 61:65–170.

Heng Gong, Yawei Sun, Xiaocheng Feng, Bing Qin, Wei Bi, Xiaojiang Liu, and Ting Liu. 2020. Tablegpt: Few-shot table-to-text generation with table structure reconstruction and content matching. In *Proceedings of the 28th International Conference on Computational Linguistics*, pages 1978–1988.

Hamza Harkous, Isabel Groves, and Amir Saffari. 2020. Have your text and use it too! End-to-end neural data-to-text generation with semantic fidelity. *arXiv preprint arXiv:2004.06577*.

Jeremy Howard and Sebastian Ruder. 2018. Universal language model fine-tuning for text classification. *arXiv preprint arXiv:1801.06146*.

Mihir Kale and Abhinav Rastogi. 2020. Text-to-text pre-training for data-to-text tasks. In *Proceedings of the 13th International Conference on Natural Language Generation*, pages 97–102, Dublin, Ireland. Association for Computational Linguistics.

Nitish Shirish Keskar, Bryan McCann, Lav R Varshney, Caiming Xiong, and Richard Socher. 2019. Ctrl: A conditional transformer language model for controllable generation. *arXiv preprint arXiv:1909.05858*.

Diederik P Kingma and Jimmy Ba. 2014. Adam: A method for stochastic optimization. *arXiv preprint arXiv:1412.6980*.

Leo Leppänen, Myriam Munezero, Mark Granroth-Wilding, and Hannu Toivonen. 2017. Data-driven news generation for automated journalism. In *Proceedings of the 10th International Conference on Natural Language Generation*, pages 188–197.

Brian Lester, Rami Al-Rfou, and Noah Constant. 2021. The power of scale for parameter-efficient prompt tuning. *arXiv preprint arXiv:2104.08691*.

Mike Lewis, Yinhan Liu, Naman Goyal, Marjan Ghazvininejad, Abdelrahman Mohamed, Omer Levy, Ves Stoyanov, and Luke Zettlemoyer. 2019. Bart: Denoising sequence-to-sequence pre-training for natural language generation, translation, and comprehension. *arXiv preprint arXiv:1910.13461*.

Jiwei Li, Michel Galley, Chris Brockett, Jianfeng Gao, and Bill Dolan. 2015. A diversity-promoting objective function for neural conversation models. *arXiv preprint arXiv:1510.03055*.

Jiwei Li, Will Monroe, and Dan Jurafsky. 2016. A simple, fast diverse decoding algorithm for neural generation. *arXiv preprint arXiv:1611.08562*.

Jiachang Liu, Dinghan Shen, Yizhe Zhang, Bill Dolan, Lawrence Carin, and Weizhu Chen. 2021a. What makes good in-context examples for GPT-3? *arXiv preprint arXiv:2101.06804*.

Xiao Liu, Yanan Zheng, Zhengxiao Du, Ming Ding, Yujie Qian, Zhilin Yang, and Jie Tang. 2021b. GPT understands, too. *arXiv preprint arXiv:2103.10385*.

Yinhan Liu, Myle Ott, Naman Goyal, Jingfei Du, Mandar Joshi, Danqi Chen, Omer Levy, Mike Lewis, Luke Zettlemoyer, and Veselin Stoyanov. 2019. Roberta: A robustly optimized bert pretraining approach. *arXiv preprint arXiv:1907.11692*.

Kaixin Ma, Hao Cheng, Xiaodong Liu, Eric Nyberg, and Jianfeng Gao. 2021. Open domain question answering over virtual documents: A unified approach for data and text. *arXiv preprint arXiv:2110.08417*.

Manuel Mager, Ramón Fernandez Astudillo, Tahira Naseem, Md Arafat Sultan, Young-Suk Lee, Radu Florian, and Salim Roukos. 2020. GPT-too: A language-model-first approach for amr-to-text generation. *arXiv preprint arXiv:2005.09123*.

Hongyuan Mei, Mohit Bansal, and Matthew R Walter. 2015. What to talk about and how? selective generation using lstms with coarse-to-fine alignment. *arXiv preprint arXiv:1509.00838*.

George A Miller. 1995. Wordnet: a lexical database for English. *Communications of the ACM*, 38(11):39–41.

Mike Mintz, Steven Bills, Rion Snow, and Dan Jurafsky. 2009. Distant supervision for relation extraction without labeled data. In *Proceedings of the Joint Conference of the 47th Annual Meeting of the ACL and the 4th International Joint Conference on Natural Language Processing of the AFNLP*, pages 1003–1011.

Seungwhan Moon, Pararth Shah, Anuj Kumar, and Rajen Subba. 2019. Opendialkg: Explainable conversational reasoning with attention-based walks over knowledge graphs. In *Proceedings of the 57th Annual Meeting of the Association for Computational Linguistics*, pages 845–854.

Linyong Nan, Dragomir Radev, Rui Zhang, Amrit Rau, Abhinand Sivaprasad, Chiachun Hsieh, Xiangru Tang, Aadit Vyas, Neha Verma, Pranav Krishna, et al. 2020. Dart: Open-domain structured data record to text generation. *arXiv preprint arXiv:2007.02871*.

Jekaterina Novikova, Ondřej Dušek, and Verena Rieser. 2017. The E2E dataset: New challenges for end-to-end generation. *arXiv preprint arXiv:1706.09254*.

Kishore Papineni, Salim Roukos, Todd Ward, and Wei-Jing Zhu. 2002. Bleu: a method for automatic evaluation of machine translation. In *Proceedings of the 40th annual meeting of the Association for Computational Linguistics*, pages 311–318.

Vassilis Plachouras, Charese Smiley, Hiroko Bretz, Ola Taylor, Jochen L Leidner, Dezhao Song, and Frank Schilder. 2016. Interacting with financial data using natural language. In *Proceedings of the 39th International ACM SIGIR conference on Research and Development in Information Retrieval*, pages 1121–1124.

Maja Popović. 2015. chrF: character n-gram F-score for automatic MT evaluation. In *Proceedings of the Tenth Workshop on Statistical Machine Translation*, pages 392–395.

François Portet, Ehud Reiter, Albert Gatt, Jim Hunter, Somayajulu Sripada, Yvonne Freer, and Cindy Sykes. 2009. Automatic generation of textual summaries from neonatal intensive care data. *Artificial Intelligence*, 173(7-8):789–816.

Alec Radford, Jeffrey Wu, Rewon Child, David Luan, Dario Amodei, Ilya Sutskever, et al. 2019. Language models are unsupervised multitask learners. *OpenAI blog*, 1(8):9.

Colin Raffel, Noam Shazeer, Adam Roberts, Katherine Lee, Sharan Narang, Michael Matena, Yanqi Zhou, Wei Li, and Peter J Liu. 2019. Exploring the limits of transfer learning with a unified text-to-text transformer. *arXiv preprint arXiv:1910.10683*.

Alejandro Ramos-Soto, Alberto Jose Bugarin, Senén Barro, and Juan Taboada. 2014. Linguistic descriptions for automatic generation of textual short-term weather forecasts on real prediction data. *IEEE Transactions on Fuzzy Systems*, 23(1):44–57.

Leonardo FR Ribeiro, Martin Schmitt, Hinrich Schütze, and Iryna Gurevych. 2020. Investigating pretrained language models for graph-to-text generation. *arXiv preprint arXiv:2007.08426*.

Victor Sanh, Albert Webson, Colin Raffel, Stephen H Bach, Lintang Sutawika, Zaid Alyafeai, Antoine Chaffin, Arnaud Stiegler, Teven Le Scao, Arun Raja, et al. 2021. Multitask prompted training enables zero-shot task generalization. *arXiv preprint arXiv:2110.08207*.

Abigail See, Aneesh Pappu, Rohun Saxena, Akhila Yerukola, and Christopher D Manning. 2019. Do massively pretrained language models make better storytellers? *arXiv preprint arXiv:1909.10705*.

Thibault Sellam, Dipanjan Das, and Ankur P Parikh. 2020. BLEURT: Learning robust metrics for text generation. *arXiv preprint arXiv:2004.04696*.

Huajie Shao, Jun Wang, Haohong Lin, Xuezhou Zhang, Aston Zhang, Heng Ji, and Tarek Abdelzaher. 2021. Controllable and diverse text generation in e-commerce. In *Proceedings of the Web Conference 2021*, pages 2392–2401.

Matthew Snover, Bonnie Dorr, Richard Schwartz, Linnea Micciulla, and John Makhoul. 2006. A study of translation edit rate with targeted human annotation. In *Proceedings of the 7th Conference of the Association for Machine Translation in the Americas: Technical Papers*, pages 223–231.

Chris van der Lee, Emiel Krahmer, and Sander Wubben. 2017. PASS: A dutch data-to-text system for soccer, targeted towards specific audiences. In *Proceedings of the 10th International Conference on Natural Language Generation*, pages 95–104.

Ashish Vaswani, Noam Shazeer, Niki Parmar, Jakob Uszkoreit, Llion Jones, Aidan N Gomez, Łukasz Kaiser, and Illia Polosukhin. 2017. Attention is all you need. In *Advances in neural information processing systems*, pages 5998–6008.

Sam Wiseman, Stuart M Shieber, and Alexander M Rush. 2017. Challenges in data-to-document generation. *arXiv preprint arXiv:1707.08052*.

Thomas Wolf, Lysandre Debut, Victor Sanh, Julien Chaumond, Clement Delangue, Anthony Moi, Pierric Cistac, Tim Rault, Rémi Louf, Morgan Funtowicz, et al. 2019. Huggingface's transformers: State-of-the-art natural language processing. *arXiv preprint arXiv:1910.03771*.

Tianyi Zhang, Varsha Kishore, Felix Wu, Kilian Q Weinberger, and Yoav Artzi. 2019. Bertscore: Evaluating text generation with bert. *arXiv preprint arXiv:1904.09675*.

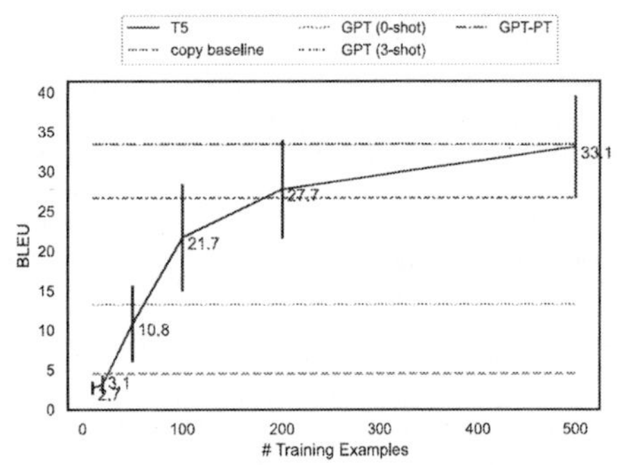

Figure 3: Impact of fine-tuning data size on performance of T5. Numbers reflect average performance over 5 different data samples, with standard error of the mean indicated by bars.

Appendices

A Data Splits

Examples from the EASY and HARD partitions are shown in Figure 4. The copy baseline achieves good results on the EASY examples. On the other hand, the examples from the HARD partition are more abtractive – generating descriptions for these examples requires substantial rewriting. In several cases, the reference text has a low fidelity with respect to the input record. For example, when one or more triples in the input are not described in the reference text. This is a data quality issue and is a common occurrence in DART.

B Results

Experimental results on SEEN and UNSEEN partitions are presented in Table 5. As reported in § 6, T5 performs well on this task (row 6). The 0-shot GPT2-XL outperforms the copy baseline in terms of all metrics except for chrF++ (row 2). GPT2-XL with a 3-shot prompt does much better than the 0-shot case. Prompt tuning improves the results both in terms of BertScore and BLEURT (row 4). We see another gain in the performance by adding re-ranking (row 5). These trends are consistent with what we observed for BLEU, METEOR, and TER in Table 2.

We do not see a consistent performance drop going from SEEN to the UNSEEN partition when looking at chrF++, BertScore, and BLEURT. This is somewhat surprising, but also hard to interpret given that chrF++ relies on character n-gram and BertScore and BLEU rely in contextualized embeddings.

Training Curves In this experiment, we seek to answer that how much data does T5 require to do well on this task? Specifically, how many examples are required for T5 to exceed the performance of the few-shot GPT2-XL? We fine-tune T5 on increasingly larger amounts of training data. We start off with an off-the-shelf T5 model with no additional training. We then vary the number of training examples in $\{10, 20, 50, 100, 200, 500\}$.[12] We repeat each setting five times by resampling a training set and fine-tuning T5, and report results for each training set size averaged cross all test partitions. Figure 3 shows the BLEU performance (y-axis) of T5 as a function of number of training examples (x-axis). Performance of the copy baseline, 0-shot, 3-shot, and prompt tuned GPT2-XL are indicated by horizontal lines. Without any task-specific fine-tuning, T5 does slightly worse than the copy baseline, easily outperformed by 0-shot GPT2-XL. In settings without training data, GPT2-XL is the clear choice. T5 continues to lag behind GPT2-XL 3-shot until trained on at least 200 examples, and meets the performance of GPT2-XL prompt tuned after training on 500.

C Sample Model Output

In this section, we share a few samples from the DART test set as well as outputs generated by different models. We qualitatively compare different models and highlight a few of their common errors.

Task Prompting As seen in Examples 1 and 2, GPT2-XL in the 0-shot setting often copies the input. GPT2-XL with a 3-shot prompt generates a much more fluent text than the 0-shot case. This can be seen in Examples 2, 4, and 5. Although GPT2-XL with few-shot prompting generates more fluent text, it often generates hallucinated content (see Example 3).

We see that prompt tuning further boosts our performance and generates a more coherent text in comparison to few-shot GPT2-XL (see Example 1 and 3). Moreover, it hallucinates much less than the few-shot setting (e.g. see Example 3). We also saw this previously in Table 2, as the prompt tuned GPT2-XL achieved lower TER score. In contrast to T5 training, in which all model parameters are updated, prompt tuning adapts only a small fraction

[12]We use the same hyper-parameters as before except for the number of training epochs and batch size. To avoid over-fitting on small data, we only fine-tune for 1 epoch. We use batch size of 2.

ID	Model	chrF++ ↑			BERTScore(F1) ↑			BLEURT ↑		
		SEEN	UNSEEN	ALL	SEEN	UNSEEN	ALL	SEEN	UNSEEN	ALL
1	copy baseline	0.33	0.34	0.33	0.83	0.85	0.83	-0.59	-0.29	-0.58
2	GPT2-XL (0-shot)	0.34	0.34	0.34	0.88	0.87	0.88	-0.46	-0.30	-0.46
3	GPT2-XL (3-shot)	0.48	0.44	0.48	0.91	0.91	0.91	-0.19	-0.17	-0.19
4	GPT2-XL-PT	0.40	0.44	0.40	0.92	0.92	0.92	-0.11	0.06	-0.10
5	GPT2-XL-PT + Reranking	0.46	0.47	0.46	0.92	0.92	0.92	-0.01	0.12	0.00
6	$T5_{large}$	0.64	0.64	0.64	0.95	0.95	0.95	0.38	0.44	0.39
	+ Description									
7	GPT2-XL (0-shot)	0.31	0.23	0.30	0.88	0.86	0.88	-0.46	-0.54	-0.46
8	GPT2-XL (3-shot)	0.47	0.42	0.46	0.91	0.90	0.91	-0.19	-0.16	-0.19
9	GPT2-XL-PT	0.39	0.45	0.39	0.91	0.92	0.91	-0.14	0.09	-0.13
10	$T5_{large}$	0.64	0.63	0.64	0.95	0.95	0.95	0.38	0.43	0.38

Table 5: Performance on the DART test set, partitioned by whether predicates are SEEN, UNSEEN, and overall. ↑: Higher is better.

of the model parameters. However, in many cases the generated text is as good as the benchmark T5 (see Example 2). Despite generating very fluent text, prompt tuned GPT2-XL often misses information from one or more relations (Examples 1, 3, and 4).

Re-ranking Re-ranking based on entity coverage solves the missing information issue in several cases. For example, in Example 3, the entity *Alvis Speed 25* which is missed by the prompt tuned GPT2-XL, is covered after re-ranking. The benefit of re-ranking also can be seen in Example 4. On the other hand, in Example 2, ranking does not solve the missing information issue. This is because argument "yes" of "family-friendly" probably would not naturally appear in generated text (e.g., "Yes, this is a family-friendly restaurant"). For such cases, the re-ranking heuristic will not provide useful feedback.

Predicate Descriptions As mentioned in Section 6.1, in several cases, the description extracted from WordNet and WikiData are trivial. In Example 2, the definition of relations *food*, *area*, and *near* add no information beyond the word itself, and therefore not helpful for the model. On the other hand, it seems like defining relation *MANUFACTURER* in Example 3 has improved generations of GPT2-XL in both the few-shot and prompt-tuned settings. In some cases, while the predicate description can be potentially useful, the model ignores the augmented description. For example, in 4, the definition of relation *GENRE* is not covered in the generated text of any of models.

EASY Examples

Input: <H> Adolfo Suárez Madrid–Barajas Airport <R> LOCATION <T> Madrid, Paracuellos de Jarama, San Sebastián de los Reyes and Alcobendas

Reference: Adolfo Suárez Madrid–Barajas Airport can be found in Madrid, Paracuellos de Jarama, San Sebastián de los Reyes and Alcobendas.'

###

Input: <H> Alaa Abdul-Zahra <R> CLUB <T> Sanat Mes Kerman F.C.

Reference: Alaa Abdul-Zahra's club is Sanat Mes Kerman F.C.

###

Input: <H> Alderney Airport <R> RUNWAY_NAME <T> "14/32"

Reference: Alderney Airport runway name is 14/32

###

Input: <H> Asunción <R> IS_PART_OF <T> Gran Asunci6n

Reference: Asunción is a part of Gran Asunci6n.

###

Input: <H> Airey Neave <R> AWARD <T> Military Cross

Reference: Airey Neave was awarded the Military Cross.

HARD Examples

Input: <H> 2004 <R> MOVEMENTS <T> Promotion Playoffs - Promoted <H> 2004 <R> POSITION <T> 1st

Reference: Sports stats for Ljungskile SK

###

Input: <H> Khokhan Sen <R> MATCHES <T> 14 <H> Khokhan Sen <R> INNINGS <T> 21 <H> Khokhan Sen <R> RANK <T> 9 <H> Khokhan Sen <R> CAUGHT <T> 20 <H> Khokhan Sen <R> STUMPED <T> 11 <H> Khokhan Sen <R> DISMISSALS <T> 31

Reference: The innings when caught was 20 was 21

###

Input: <H> thierry morin <R> POSITION <T> defender <H> [TABLECONTEXT] <R> NAME <T> thierry morin <H> [TABLECONTEXT] <R> [TITLE] <T> Players

Reference: Thierry Morin was a defender for Paris Saint-Germain.

###

Input: <H> ALV X-1 <R> COUNTRY_ORIGIN <T> United States <H> United States <R> ETHNIC_GROUP <T> African Americans <H> United States <R> DEMONYM <T> Americans

Reference: Originating in the United States and by Americans, some of African decent is the ALVX-1.', 'ALVX-1 comes from the US where Americans live and African Americans are an ethnic group

###

Input: <H> past tense <R> SEASON_# <T> 4 <H> past tense <R> ORIGINAL_AIR_DATE <T> october29,2008 <H> past tense <R> NO._IN_SERIES <T> 13 <H> past tense <R> U.S._VIEWERS_(MILLIONS) <T> 7.93 <H> past tense <R> DIRECTED_BY <T> michael pressman <H> past tense <R> WRITTEN_BY <T> craig turk

Reference: Past Tense was the 13th episode in the series.

Figure 4: Examples from the EASY and HARD partition

Example #1

Input: <H> Aleksey Chirikov (icebreaker) <R> SHIP_BEAM <T> 21.2 <H> Aleksey Chirikov (icebreaker) <R> STATUS <T> ""In service"" <H> Aleksey Chirikov (icebreaker) <R> BUILDER <T> Helsinki <H> Aleksey Chirikov (icebreaker) <R> BUILDER <T> Arctech Helsinki Shipyard

Reference: The icebreaker Aleksey Chirikov was built at the Arctech Helsinki Shipyard in Helsinki. The Aleksey Chirikov (icebreaker) is in service and its ship beam is 21.2

Description: BUILDER means a person who constructs something

GPT2-XL (0-shot): <H> Aleksey Chirikov (icebreaker) <R> SHIP_BEAM <T> 21.2 <H> Aleksey Chirikov (icebreaker) <R> STATUS <T> "In service" <H> Aleksey Chirikov (icebreaker) <R> BUILDER <T> Helsinki <H> Aleksey Chirikov (icebreaker) <R> BUILDER <T>

GPT2-XL (3-shot): Aleksey Chirikov (icebreaker) is of type 21.2.

GPT2-XL (3-shot) + Description: Aleksey Chirikov (icebreaker) was a Russian icebreaker.

GPT2-XL-PT: Aleksey Chirikov (icebreaker) was built by Arctech Helsinki Shipyard.

GPT2-XL-PT + Description: Aleksey Chirikov (icebreaker) was built by Arctech Helsinki Shipyard.

GPT2-XL-PT + Reranking: Aleksey Chirikov (icebreaker) is in service at Arctech Helsinki Shipyard.

$T5_{large}$: The ship Aleksey Chirikov was built by Arctech, Helsinki Shipyard and has a ship beam of 21.2 metres. It is currently in service.

Example #2

Input: <H> The Mill <R> eatType <T> pub <H> The Mill <R> food <T> Fast food <H> The Mill <R> area <T> city centre <H> The Mill <R> familyFriendly <T> no <H> The Mill <R> near <T> Café Sicilia

Reference: The Mill pub is near Café Sicilia in the city centre that isn't family friendly, is average and has Fast food.

Description: eatType means type of food served by a restaurant or restaurant chain. food means any substance that can be metabolized by an animal to give energy and build tissue. area means area occupied by an object. near means move towards.

GPT2-XL (0-shot): Graph: <H> The Mill <R> eatType <T> pub <H> The Mill <R> food <T> Fast food <H> The Mill <R> area <T> city centre <H> The Mill <R> familyFriendly <T> no <H> The Mill <R> near <T> Café Sicilia
English:

GPT2-XL (3-shot): The Mill is located in the city centre near Café Sicilia. It serves fast food in the price range of £20-25 with a moderate customer rating

GPT2-XL (3-shot) + Description: The fast food restaurant, The Mill, has an average rating of 3 out of 5 perhaps as it is not friendly to kids. The Mill is located in the city centre area near Café Sicilia.

GPT2-XL-PT: The Mill is a fast food pub in the city centre near Café Sicilia.

GPT2-XL-PT + Description: The Mill is a family friendly pub near Cafe Sicilia.

GPT2-XL-PT + Reranking: The Mill is a fast food pub in the city centre near Café Sicilia.

$T5_{large}$: The Mill is a fast food pub in the city centre near Café Sicilia.

Example #3

Input: <H> Alvis Speed 25 <R> MANUFACTURER <T> Alvis Car and Engineering Company <H> Alvis Car and Engineering Company <R> LOCATION_CITY <T> Coventry

Reference: Alvis Speed 25 was made by the Alvis Car and Engineering Company of Coventry.

Description: MANUFACTURER means manufacturer or producer of this product.

GPT2-XL (0-shot): <H> Alvis Speed 25 <R> MANUFACTURER <T> Alvis Car and Engineering Company <H> Alvis Car and Engineering Company <R> LOCATION_CITY <T> Coventry

GPT2-XL (3-shot): Alvis Speed 25 won the race in Coventry on April 25, 1996.

GPT2-XL (3-shot) + Description: Alvis Speed 25 is a car manufactured by Alvis Car and Engineering Company in Coventry, England

GPT2-XL-PT: Alvis Car and Engineering Company is located in Coventry.

GPT2-XL-PT + Description: Alvis Speed 25 is manufactured in Coventry.

GPT2-XL-PT + Reranking: Alvis Speed 25 is manufactured by Alvis Car and Engineering Company in Coventry.

$T5_{large}$: Alvis Car and Engineering Company is located in Coventry and manufactures the Alvis Speed 25.

Example #4

Input: <H> Anders Osborne <R> ASSOCIATED_BAND_ASSOCIATED_MUSICAL_ARTIST <T> Galactic <H> Anders Osborne <R> ASSOCIATED_BAND_ASSOCIATED_MUSICAL_ARTIST <T> Tab Benoit <H> Anders Osborne <R> GENRE <T> Blues <H> Anders Osborne <R> ASSOCIATED_BAND_ASSOCIATED_MUSICAL_ARTIST <T> Billy Iuso <H> Anders Osborne <R> ACTIVE_YEARS_START_YEAR <T> 1989

Reference: Anders Osborne musical career began in 1989. His career began in the blue's genre. He has been associated with the band, Galactic as well as Tab Benoit. Osborne also has ties to fellow musician Billy Iuso.

Description: GENRE means creative work's genre or an artist's field of work

GPT2-XL (0-shot): <H> Anders Osborne <R> ASSOCIATED_BAND_ASSOCIATED_MUSICAL_ARTIST <T> Galactic <H> Anders Osborne <R> ASSOCIATED_BAND_ASSOCIATED_MUSICAL_ARTIST <T> Tab Benoit <H> Anders Osborne <R> GENRE <T> Blues <H> Anders Osborne <R> ASSOCIATED_BAND_ASSOCIATED_M

GPT2-XL (3-shot): Anders Osborne is an English singer, songwriter and guitarist.

GPT2-XL (3-shot) + Description: Anders Osborne is an active musician and composer.

GPT2-XL-PT: Tab Benoit and Anders Osborne are associated with Galactic.

GPT2-XL-PT + Description: Tab Benoit and Anders Osborne are associated with Galactic.

GPT2-XL-PT + Reranking: Tab Benoit is associated with Galactic and Anders Osborne is associated with Billy Iuso.

$T5_{large}$: Anders Osborne is associated with the band Galactic, Billy Iuso, Tab Benoit and the genre of Blues. His active years start in 1989.

Example #5

Input: <H> Nurburgring <R> FASTEST_LAP <T> PSV Eindhoven <H> Nurburgring <R> WINNING_CLUB <T> A.C. Milan

Reference: PSV Eindhoven had the fastest lab on the Nurburgring, and A.C. Milan was the winning club at that race.

Description: FASTEST_LAP means person who does the fastest lap during a motorsport race.

GPT2-XL (0-shot): <H> Nurburgring <R> FASTEST_LAP <T> PSV Eindhoven <H> Nurburgring <R> WINNING_CLUB <T> A.C. Milan

GPT2-XL (3-shot): A.C. Milan had the fastest lap in the race won by PSV Eindhoven.

GPT2-XL (3-shot) + Description: A.C. Milan set the fastest lap at the Nurburgring when the winning team was PSV Eindhoven.

GPT2-XL-PT: Nurburgring is the fastest lap at A.C. Milan.

GPT2-XL-PT + Description: PSV Eindhoven is the winning club at the Nurburgring.

GPT2-XL-PT + Reranking: Nurburgring is the fastest lap at A.C. Milan

$T5_{large}$: A.C. Milan won the race where PSV Eindhoven had the fastest lap.

Don't Say What You Don't Know: Improving the Consistency of Abstractive Summarization by Constraining Beam Search

Daniel King[*†] **Zejiang Shen**[*‡] **Nishant Subramani**[⋆,♢] **Daniel S. Weld**[⋆,♡]
Iz Beltagy[⋆] **Doug Downey**[⋆,♣]

[†]MosaicML [‡]MIT [⋆]Allen Institute for AI [♢]Masakhane
[♡]University of Washington [♣]Northwestern University

daking@hey.com zjshen@mit.edu {nishants, danw, beltagy, dougd}@allenai.org

Abstract

Abstractive summarization systems today produce fluent and relevant output, but often "hallucinate" statements not supported by the source text. We analyze the connection between hallucinations and training data, and find evidence that models hallucinate because they train on target summaries that are unsupported by the source. Based on our findings, we present PINOCCHIO, a new decoding method that improves the consistency of a transformer-based abstractive summarizer by constraining beam search to avoid hallucinations. Given the model states and outputs at a given step, PINOCCHIO detects likely model hallucinations based on various measures of attribution to the source text. PINOCCHIO backtracks to find more consistent output, and can opt to produce no summary at all when no consistent generation can be found. In experiments, we find that PINOCCHIO improves the consistency of generation by an average of 68% on two abstractive summarization datasets, without hurting recall.

Method	Text
Source	...The PSNI said the tablets were "as yet unidentified" but warned of the "potential dangers" they posed...
BART	A 17-year-old boy has been charged after a teenager was taken ill after taking what police have described as *"potentially lethal" ecstasy tablets.*
PINOCCHIO	A 17-year-old teenager has been charged with drugs offences after a teenager was treated in hospital after taking what police described as an "unidentified" drug.

Table 1: An example of hallucination. Inconsistent words are highlighted in *red italic* fonts. In this case, PINOCCHIO corrects the inconsistent detail in the BART output.

1 Introduction

Abstractive text generation is an important task with the promise of compressing lengthy source material into concise summaries, satisfying application or user needs. Pretrained abstractive summarizers (e.g. BART (Lewis et al., 2020)) have recently achieved new state-of-the-art (SOTA) across multiple datasets (Fabbri et al., 2020). However, these systems remain unusable in most real world scenarios, because they frequently hallucinate information that is inconsistent with the input (Maynez et al., 2020).

Many researchers have proposed methods to assess and improve the consistency[1] of summarization systems. Two popular approaches are 1) incorporating extracted knowledge (Zhu et al., 2021) (possibly in the form of questions (Durmus et al., 2020)), and 2) incorporating a consistency text classifier (Kryscinski et al., 2020) (often based on natural language inference (NLI) (Falke et al., 2019)). These methods tend to reduce the problem of generating consistent text to another difficult problem (e.g. information extraction (IE) or NLI). Given a strong IE system or a structured representation of the source information, it is possible to dramatically improve the consistency of generated text (Zhang et al., 2020b; Tian et al., 2019), but such resources are only available in a narrow subset of domains.

We propose a different approach for generating more consistent summaries. It is based on the observation that today's abstractive summarizers are often trained on target summaries that contain statements unsupported by the source text (Matsumaru et al., 2020). This disconnect arises because the training datasets are acquired from noisy "silver" sources in order to scale, e.g. treating a news headline as a summary of its article or an encyclopedia entry as a summary of a portion of its references. We conjecture that a model optimized for likelihood and trained on target summaries containing unsupported statements will have a strong tendency

*Both authors contributed equally. The first author's work was performed while at the Allen Institute for AI.

[1]We use the terms "consistent" and "hallucinated" as antonyms, and avoid "factual". Check Section 2 for details.

Proceedings of the 2nd Workshop on Natural Language Generation, Evaluation, and Metrics (GEM), pages 555 - 571
December 7, 2022 ©2022 Association for Computational Linguistics

to hallucinate information rather than say something less "likely," but supported (§3). Further, common automatic evaluation metrics like ROUGE *reward* lexical similarity significantly more than consistency, preferring hallucinated lexically similar summaries to completely consistent lexically different ones.

Our method, called PINOCCHIO, is a novel decoding algorithm that constrains beam search to only consider predicted tokens that are likely to be supported by the source text. PINOCCHIO estimates which tokens are likely supported using simple but effective heuristics based on the model's confidence and attention distribution, and word frequency. When PINOCCHIO reaches a state where no supported token can be generated, it backtracks the search. It can also opt-out from generating a summary at all, rather than produce one expected to be hallucinated. We show how PINOCCHIO significantly improves consistency on two abstractive summarization datasets with only a small decrease in fluency, measured using careful human evaluations.

To test PINOCCHIO on diverse domains, we also develop a new abstractive summarization dataset called Scientific Concept Description (SCD). Inspired by the WikiSum (Liu* et al., 2018) dataset, SCD uses Wikipedia descriptions as the target summaries and the referenced papers as the source documents, detailed in (§5). SCD is motivated by the goal of automatically generating a high-quality encyclopedia for the long tail of scientific concepts described in papers, and presents a challenging workload for abstractive summarization. It comes with a total of 60k samples of scientific concepts and 118k corresponding paper identifiers, with full text for 8k of the papers.

We make the following contributions:

1. We analyze the relationship between hallucination and training on targets that are not fully supported by the source.
2. We introduce PINOCCHIO, a decoding algorithm that improves generation consistency by constraining beam search to focus on input-supported tokens. It improves consistency by an average of 68% in two abstractive summarization datasets at the expense of a minor decrease to fluency.
3. We introduce Scientific Concept Description, a challenging new abstractive summarization task, and release a dataset.

The SCD dataset, along with our code, trained models, and human evaluations, is available at `https://github.com/allenai/pinocchio`.

2 Related work

Pretrained language models have recently taken the top spots on summarization leaderboards (Fabbri et al., 2020; Huang et al., 2020). This includes models like BART (Lewis et al., 2020), PEGASUS (Zhang et al., 2020a), and UniLM (Dong et al., 2019). In a recent large scale evaluation of summarization models, Fabbri et al. (2020) found BART and PEGASUS to be the top performing models. We choose to focus on BART in this work.

It is widely known that SOTA summarization models tend to hallucinate facts (Maynez et al., 2020), and the most closely related works to ours are those on factual summarization. However, we avoid the term "factuality" and instead use "consistency" to denote that the generated summary is supported by the input text. As noted in Maynez et al. (2020), a summary could be hallucinated but still be factually correct. In this work, we aim to improve consistency and reduce hallucinations, which indirectly improves factuality, without directly optimizing for it.

Prior works attempt to improve consistency by correcting already-generated summaries (Dong et al., 2020; Zhu et al., 2021), using a knowledge graph (Zhu et al., 2021), filtering training data (Nan et al., 2021), constraining generation with keywords (Mao et al., 2020), using NLI models (Barrantes et al., 2020; Mishra et al., 2020), among others. Some have focused on the data-to-text setting, which presupposes structured input (Tian et al., 2019; Wang et al., 2020b). Some works control the extractiveness of generations (Song et al., 2020). There have also been multiple works on automatically measuring consistency (Durmus et al., 2020; Kryscinski et al., 2020; Wang et al., 2020a). Matsubara and Singh (2020) noted that hallucinations come from a source-target discrepancy, where many training targets are not fully supported by their source text, and suggested to address it by removing samples with unsupported summaries. We extend their empirical findings with similar measurements on three additional datasets, conjecture that hallucination is unavoidable in such settings, and provide evidence for the conjecture in terms of the lexical statistics of output summaries.

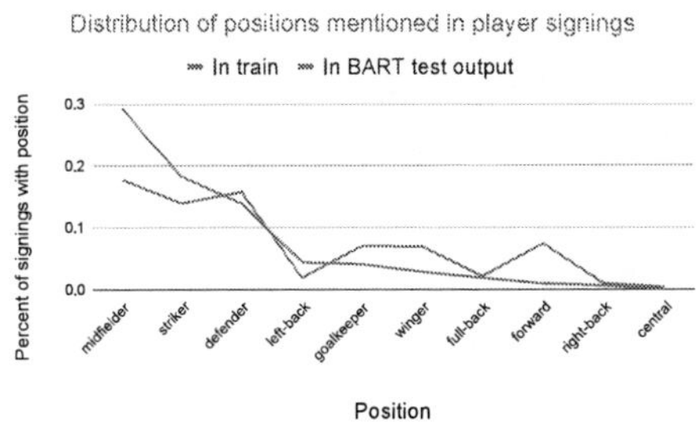

Figure 1: Distribution of positions in summaries about player signings in train vs. BART output. BART output is more peaked at positions more common in train, suggesting BART defaults to these when no position is supported by the source.

We use beam search for decoding, which has become standard practice for neural seq2seq models (Graves, 2012; Sutskever et al., 2014). Our approach can be viewed as a version of constrained decoding (Hokamp and Liu, 2017) but with dynamically identified constraints and the ability to backtrack. Our constraints come from various model internal signals that indicate attribution to the source text. One such signal is entropy, where Xu et al. (2020) found that low next token entropy indicates the model is copying. Unlike previous work, we do not attempt to imbue models with a new level of textual understanding, but rather show that we can improve consistency of generated text using simple signals based on model internals.

3 Why Do Models Generate Inconsistent Summaries?

In this section, we analyze why models generate inconsistent summaries. Here, we use the definition of *consistent* from Fabbri et al. (2020), i.e., the factual alignment between the summary and the summarized source.

We hypothesize that there are two factors that contribute to inconsistency: 1) the maximum likelihood training and generation strategy used in summarization models, and 2) imperfect training datasets that contain many instances where the target is difficult or impossible to deduce from the source. Specifically, we conjecture that in the presence of these two factors, models are guaranteed to hallucinate because they either 1) default to a background distribution of the most common relevant terms during generation or 2) learn spurious correlations between the source and target texts. In either case, the model generates text that is often inconsistent with the inputs.

We present our analysis in terms of a motivating example below, and provide empirical support for it in Sec. 7. The analysis inspires the design of the PINOCCHIO method in Sec. 4.

3.1 Motivating example

Consider the target summary of an article about a team signing a football player, from XSUM:

```
'League Two club Cheltenham Town have
signed Hibernian striker Brian Graham on
a free transfer.'
```

Many of the details in this summary are difficult for a model to predict because they are *not* supported directly by the input passage.[2] For example, the player's first name ("Brian") and position ("striker"), and the lack of signing fee ("free transfer") are nowhere mentioned. This mismatch between typical summary fields and the text available in the input passage is not restricted to summaries about player signings, but is more generally observed across a variety of article types in XSUM and also our new SCD data set.

Achieving a high likelihood on the training dataset requires that the trained models output the aforementioned fields anyway: e.g., in summaries of player signings, from a sample of 43 summaries, 100% mention the player's full name, 88% the player's position, 78% the length of the signing, etc, even though they are often not supported in the source. As a result, the BART summarizer outputs the following summary for the example:

```
'League Two side Cheltenham Town have
signed Hibernian midfielder Scott Graham
on loan until the end of the season.'
```

This summary begins nearly identically to the target, but then outputs the three field values incorrectly (first name, position, and length of the contract).

The errors make sense when you consider the model's calculus for choosing a summary. Consider a single field that can be present or absent in a summary, and make the simplifying assumption[3] that the probability of the most-likely summary with a field value is strictly monotonic in the probability of the field value (see App. B for formal details). In that case, a model that maximizes likelihood will output the field if and only if its best

[2]The full input passage summarized in this example is in App. C.2.

[3]Note that the PINOCCHIO *method* (Sec. 4) does not depend on this assumption, it is only used here for intuition and ease of analysis.

guess of the field value is more probable than the field's absence. In practice, the probability of field absence is often low because training summaries of certain topics reliably cover certain fields, and the best guess probabilities are often higher because the model can do *some* inference to narrow the choice set to a limited and typically peaked distribution (e.g., to a small number of football player positions). Thus, hallucinating a best guess is often preferred by the model—even, in some cases, when the model estimates that the guess is less likely than chance to be correct. In the example, since the estimated probability that the player is a "midfielder" is relatively high ("midfielder" is relatively common, shown in Fig. 1), and position going unmentioned is rare (about 12% of the time), the model chooses to incorrectly output "midfielder."

Of course, the assumptions in our analysis may not always hold, and hallucination is likely more complex than the single phenomenon analyzed here. But our approach, motivated by the above conjecture, can improve the consistency of summaries in practice. Further, in Section 7 we validate two aspects of our analysis empirically, showing that ground truth training summaries for abstractive summarization do contain unsupported statements, and that summarizers do disproportionately produce more common terms in their output.

4 PINOCCHIO: Constraining Beam Search to Improve Consistency

Inspired by the previous analysis, we introduce PINOCCHIO; a modification to standard beam search for **supported-decoding** (Alg. 1).

Beam search for text generation typically works by adding to a small set of candidate generations one token at a time, keeping the top B generations according to model-predicted likelihood after each prediction timestep. After <end> has been predicted in B beams, those B candidates are rescored with a length penalty (Wu et al., 2016), and the best one is chosen as the final output. PINOCCHIO differs from regular beam search only in its use of the set R, which holds a set of disallowed generation paths; if R is always empty, Alg. 1 simplifies to standard beam search. PINOCCHIO modifies the model predicted token scores to avoid inconsistent predictions.

In particular, PINOCCHIO applies a function $f_c(\text{model state, candidate next generation})$ to the predicted likelihood of the top predicted tokens. If

Algorithm 1: Supported-decoding

```
Input: beam size B, generative model M,
       consistency function f_c, vocab V,
       maximumly allowed backtrack count N
priority queue PQ = ["<start>"]*B;
completed generations CG = {};
rejected paths R = {};
backtrack count η = 0;
while |CG| < B do
    C := {x + v : x ∈ PQ, v ∈ V} − R;
    T := top 2B items of C scored by M;
    R := R ∪ {d ∈ T : f_c(M, d) = 0};
    if T − R == ∅ then
        if η ≥ N then
            // Stop Generation
            return {};
        end
        R := R ∪ {x[: −1] : x ∈ T};
        PQ := {x[: −1] : x ∈ PQ};
        η := η + 1;
        continue;
    end
    T := T − R;
    PQ := top B elements of T according to M not
      ending in "<end>";
    CG := CG ∪ {d ∈ T : d scores higher than
      min in PQ and ends in "<end>"};
end
return top-ranked element of CG;
```

all top predicted tokens for a given timestep are inconsistent according to f_c, PINOCCHIO backtracks by removing the last predicted token from each beam, and predicts again without the ability to predict the removed tokens. The number of times this backtracking occurs η, combined with the average entropy of the token predictions in the final output is a good indicator of whether the model succeeded in producing a good summary or not. Thus, we eliminate generations with multiple backtracks (e.g., $\eta > 2$) and high entropy, as well as individual sentences with high entropy (>2.75) from multi-sentence outputs.

Within this framework, we present an instantiation of f_c based on a set of carefully curated heuristics, determining if a token is allowed to be predicted or not.

The function f_c consists of a series of binary checks, which take into account both model internals as well as language features. If any of the checks succeeds, f_c is 1 and the model continues generating, but if all of the checks fail $f_c = 0$ and the model disallows the generation path. First, we consider the *model confidence* for the current prediction—based on the intuition that a low entropy of the token prediction probability distribution corresponds to more certain, and potentially

Method	Dataset	% Cons.=5	% Cons.= 4/5	Cons.	Flue.	Rele.	Cohe.
BART (n=282)	XSUM	0.287	0.709	3.908	**4.794**	4.887	-
PINOCCHIO (n=211)	XSUM	0.422	0.82	**4.19**	4.649	4.886	-
BART (n=268)	SCD	0.209	0.552	3.612	**4.537**	**4.925**	4.619
PINOCCHIO (n=207)	SCD	0.396	0.768	**4.082**	4.338	4.816	4.585

Table 2: Human evaluation of models. PINOCCHIO improves consistency significantly, while decreasing fluency slightly. For the 4 evaluation metrics, significant (Mann–Whitney U test, p<0.01) differences are bolded. Cons.=Consistency, Flue.=Fluency, Rele.=Relevance, Cohe.=Coherence. For each row, n denotes the number of examples output, which is lower for PINOCCHIO than for BART because PINOCCHIO elects to skip certain cases.

more correct, predictions. Second, we keep track of the source text with high *attention* scores during the generation process: when the attended texts are semantically or lexically similar to the token to be generated, that suggests that the token may be supported by the source. Third, PINOCCHIO also allows tokens that are especially *common* (such as stopwords), as we expect these are less likely to be hallucinations. We develop a total of 8 different binary functions within the three categories above (details in §D.1).

The heuristics do not require additional training steps, and all the associated thresholds or hyperparameters were determined by manual inspection on a small number of samples (e.g., n=20) from each dataset. Different from prior work Matsubara and Singh (2020), this non-machine learning approach is based on scrutiny of the model generation process. It is easy to execute and more explainable compared to black-box models.

5 Tasks and Datasets

We evaluate PINOCCHIO on two distinct summarization tasks: news summarization (XSUM and CNN / Daily Mail) and scientific concept description (the newly proposed SCD dataset).

5.1 News Summarization

XSUM (Narayan et al., 2018) is a popular abstractive news summarization dataset. XSUM is a challenging dataset; the source text frequently does not entail the target text, the target task is not exactly summarization (XSUM is closer to headline generation than summarization), and data is noisy (e.g. there are articles in another language, Welsh). Challenges aside, XSUM is highly regular, as mentioned in Sec. 3. Although this seems to make the task easier, a strong pattern matcher will reproduce dataset patterns (see Appendix G and Tab. 7 for example patterns), *whether or not* it is able to fill in all the details in the pattern correctly.

CNN / Daily Mail Dataset (Nallapati et al., 2016) is another commonly used dataset for news summarization. Different from XSUM, the summaries are relatively longer (one sentence vs more than 2 sentences) and are considered to be nearly extractive (see Sharma et al. (2019) and our results in Tab. 6) as the summaries are based on summary bullets from the original news article.

5.2 Scientific Concept Description

We introduce the novel task of *scientific concept description* (SCD): automatically generating a brief description of a scientific concept, given the concept name and some papers discussing the concept. Test data has been manually evaluated to ensure quality.

SCD training corpus Training an SCD system requires a large set of ground-truth descriptions. Inspired by the WikiSum dataset (Liu* et al., 2018), we construct our training set using Wikipedia intro sections[4] as the target descriptions,[5] with the papers cited in each description as source text. To remove intractable examples, we filter out those with lower than 0.15 ROUGE-1 recall between the cited papers and the target Wikipedia description. The dataset is split into train/dev/test with 47570/5989/5839 examples. Examples have 2.4 source documents with a total of 319 sentences on average and target descriptions averaging 6 sentences each. We are able to extract body text for ~57% of the cited papers, and use just the titles and abstracts of the remainder.

[4]Specifically, we use the first section for the concept, and also include sections with definitional headers (Introduction, Definition, Uses, Description, Function, Overview).

[5]English Wikipedia 4/1/20 dump processed with `https://github.com/spencermountain/dumpster-dive`

Method	Dataset	# Samples	R1	R2	RL
BART	XSUM	11333	0.444	0.210	0.354
BART*	XSUM	8345[1]	0.442	0.207	0.349
PINOCCHIO	XSUM	8345	0.431	0.196	0.338
BART	SCD	5839	0.380	0.167	0.270
BART*	SCD	2335	0.398	0.189	0.291
PINOCCHIO	SCD	2335	0.391	0.181	0.284
BART	CNN/DM	10990	0.438	0.209	0.372
BART*	CNN/DM	10943	0.438	0.209	0.372
PINOCCHIO	CNN/DM	10943	0.438	0.209	0.372

[1] Because PINOCCHIO can elect to skip in certain cases, we report two scores for BART model outputs: for all test samples, and for the samples where PINOCCHIO generates results.

Table 3: Rouge scores on different datasets with and without using PINOCCHIO. Datasets with higher abstractiveness (e.g., XSUM and SCD) may suffer from higher ROUGE drops when PINOCCHIO is used.

Manually-evaluated SCD test corpus The motivating use case for the SCD task is automatically generating a high-quality encyclopedia for the long tail of scientific knowledge presented in papers. As a result, we construct a second test set of SCD evaluation examples not from Wikipedia, but instead from a much broader set of scientific concepts mined from computer science papers using ForeCite (King et al., 2020). This set lacks target descriptions, so it requires manual evaluation.

Training on surrogate data that differs somewhat from the intended use case but can be obtained at scale is common in summarization research (e.g. abstracts as paper summaries (Cohan et al., 2018); headlines as news summaries (Narayan et al., 2018)). In our case there are two major discrepancies between train and test: the textual domain (train is mostly biomedical, test is largely computer science), and the level of supporting text (the Wikipedia-cited training inputs often have less support for the concept description than the ForeCite-mined test inputs do, as ForeCite pairs concepts with their likely introducing paper(s)).

6 Experiments

6.1 Metrics

We rely on human evaluation, as current automatic metrics are unreliable for evaluating factuality (see §6.4). We are not targeting ROUGE metrics (Lin, 2004), but present them for completeness.[6]

For human evaluation, we use standard dimensions of consistency (does the source entail the target?), fluency (is the target grammatical, understandable English?), relevance (does the target contain important information for understanding the source?), and coherence (do the sentences flow together coherently?)[7], with definitions adapted slightly from (Fabbri et al., 2020) via calibration with our annotators. We also decided to rate consistency and fluency on a five-point 1-5 scale, but relevance and coherence on a coarser three-point 1,3,5 scale. See App. E for annotation guidelines.

Metric	Dataset	Cons.	Flue.	Rele.	Cohe.
tau	XSUM	0.60	0.84	-	-
exact	XSUM	0.66	0.89	0.96	-
compare	XSUM	0.69	0.82	1.0	-
compare~	XSUM	1.0	1.0	1.0	-
tau	SCD	0.55	0.43	0.20	0.53
exact	SCD	0.55	0.69	0.93	0.80
compare	SCD	0.67	0.64	0.86	0.64
compare~	SCD	0.95	0.98	1.0	0.98

Table 4: Mean agreement metrics between all pairs of annotators. tau=Kendall's tau, exact=exact agreement, see §6.5 for compare and compare~. The very low/null correlation values are due to low variance in relevance.

6.2 Manual evaluation

In Tab. 2, we report manual evaluation results, with each example annotated by one annotator (inter-annotator agreement is reported in Section 6.5). PINOCCHIO improves overall consistency. Expressing the results in terms of precision and recall, treating perfectly consistent output (i.e., a consistency score of 5) as a true positive, Table 2 shows that PINOCCHIO improves precision by 68% on average (47% on XSUM, and 89% on SCD) without hurting recall, yielding an F1 improvement from 0.209 to 0.345 and 0.287 to 0.361 on SCD and XSUM respectively. The improvements in consistency arise from two cases: first, when PINOCCHIO produces output, it is rated more consistent than BART on 44% and 24% of the examples from SCD and XSUM respectively, whereas BART is more consistent for only 16% and 13% (in the remaining cases, the two systems are equallly consistent). Second, on the examples where PINOCCHIO produces no output, BART's output is tends to be less factually consistent than its average, scoring 0.30 and 0.44 points lower (on the 5-point consistency scale) than its average for SCD and XSUM respectively.

We see that PINOCCHIO *does* reduce fluency with respect to the base BART model, and further that the sentence level entropy filter applied

[6] https://github.com/Yale-LILY/SummEval

[7] Coherence not used on XSUM as targets are 1 sentence

Metric	FactCC	FEQA
tau	-0.02	0.233
compare$\neq$	0.528	0.585
mean/σ pairwise ties	1.354/1.464	0.108/0.096
mean/σ pairwise not ties	1.699/1.518	0.113/0.1

Table 5: Agreement between automated metrics and our annotations. tau represents Kendall's tau, compare$\neq$ denotes agreement with the annotator on which model is better, *when the annotator did not rate the models as equivalent*, "Mean/σ pairwise ties" gives the mean/std of absolute value of difference between the metric's rating for each model, for pairs where the annotator rated the models as the same, and "Mean/σ pairwise not ties" is the same but for pairs where the annotator rated the models as different. A well-calibrated metric should have mean near zero and low standard deviation when the models are annotated as equivalent. We find the automated metrics exhibit low agreement with our annotators.

in PINOCCHIO sometimes removes the key first sentence that defines the entity in SCD, resulting in a decrease in relevance. Pretrained language models are capable of producing incredibly fluent text and prior work on steering them over-optimizes for maximizing the highest likelihood output (Subramani et al., 2019; Subramani and Suresh, 2020). As a result, steering them away from their highest likelihood output as PINOCCHIO does is bound to reduce fluency. Our results suggest that some of this fluency is coming at the cost of factual consistency, as the model has learned how to follow patterns to produce plausible sentences, but not necessarily while sticking to the source text (see §3 and Appendix §G).

6.3 Automatic evaluation

For completeness, we report ROUGE 1, 2 and L (Tab. 3), for the two tasks along with results on the CNN/Daily Mail dataset (Hermann et al., 2015a) for reference. We note that PINOCCHIO elects not to generate for a much higher portion of samples in SCD. This can be partially explained by the abstractiveness of these datasets, which we detail in Section 7.1. For the examples where PINOCCHIO generates, PINOCCHIO lowers ROUGE moderately for the two abstractive datasets compared to BART, and by somewhat more on XSUM than on SCD. We analyze the ROUGE drop in XSUM in Appendix §G). By contrast, PINOCCHIO fires only rarely for the extractive CNN/DM dataset, and therefore its ROUGE scores are unchanged from BART.

6.4 Comparison against existing correctors and factuality metrics

We also compare with three recent methods for automatically correcting summaries or measuring their factuality. Here we evaluate on XSUM, which we expect to be more suitable for these methods (each were evaluated on XSUM in previous work, whereas SCD is out of domain). First, we compare against Zhu et al. (2021), a recent seq2seq fact corrector (FC) that incorporates OpenIE (Angeli et al., 2015) and knowledge graph embedding. We take the output of their strongest model (UniLM (Dong et al., 2019)+FC) on the XSUM test set and find that it changes only ~5% of examples, and that the net improvement rate of the changes is 15% (see App. F for details). This corresponds to an improvement on <1% of the full XSUM test set. By contrast, our experiments in the previous section show that PINOCCHIO yields an improvement on ~8.5% of XSUM, more than a factor of eight higher.

Finally, we assess two representative automatic factuality metrics, FactCC (Kryscinski et al., 2020) and FEQA (Durmus et al., 2020). FactCC trains a <source, summary sentence> classifier; FEQA generates/answers questions from the summary, checking if answers are the same when using the source. We find neither metric suitable for our highly abstractive setting; each has low agreement with our XSUM annotations (Tab. 5), a result in line with a very recent evaluation of factuality measures (Pagnoni et al., 2021).

6.5 Inter-annotator agreement

In Tab. 4, we report various inter-annotator agreement measures. We had three expert annotators, and the agreement stats are averaged between all pairs of annotators, on a set of 30 examples (15 from each model) from each dataset. For model comparison, the most important metrics are the "compare" metrics, which measure how often the annotators agree on which model's output is better for a given example. The "compare" metric is the fraction of examples for which the pair of annotators agree on which model's output is better or both say the outputs are equivalent. The "compare~" metric is similar but more lenient, as it only counts as disagreement the examples where one annotator says one model is better, and the other annotator says the opposite. These kinds of strong disagreements are very rare in our data, suggesting that the relative comparisons between models in

	Dataset Abstractiveness					Human Annotated Unsupported Words		BART+PINOCCHIO
Dataset	1-gram	2-gram	3-gram	4-gram	Avg.	% Unsupported Words	IAA - Cohen κ	Avg. η per Successful Generation
CNN/DM[1]	17.18%	58.44%	78.06%	86.71%	60.10%	1.57%	0.571	0.0003
XSUM	49.88%	89.65%	98.13%	99.60%	84.31%	17.78%	0.728	0.1541
SCD	60.16%	88.97%	96.81%	98.61%	86.14%	23.84%	0.414	0.2300

[1] We report the scores for the CNN / Daily Mail dataset (See et al., 2017; Hermann et al., 2015b) for comparison because it is highly extractive.

Table 6: Analysis of the abstractiveness of three summarization datasets. The abstractive XSUM and SCD datasets contain a substantial fraction of unsupported words, measured in terms of either automated n-gram overlap measures or manual annotation. BART+PINOCCHIO performs more backtracks η on more abstractive datasets.

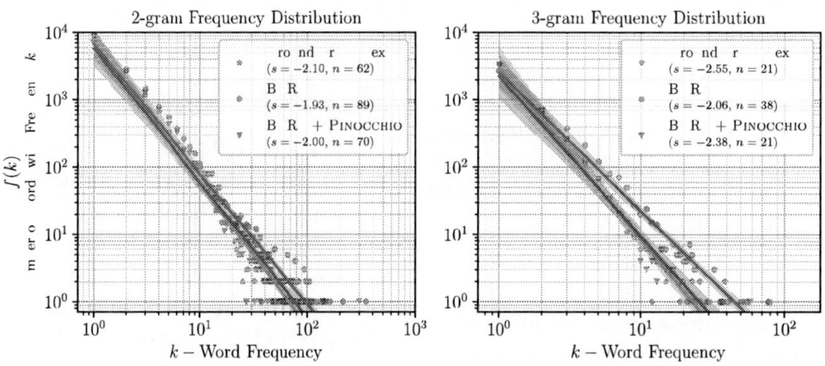

Figure 2: Comparing the n-gram frequency distribution on the XSUM Dataset for generated, versus ground truth sources. The default BART model outputs (in green) over-represent frequent n-grams (bottom right of the distribution), but PINOCCHIO is closer to the ground-truth. Results in the SCD dataset are similar. The slope of the linear fits for ground-truth text and BART generations are significantly different ($p \ll 0.05$, ANCOVA) while those between ground-truth and BART + PINOCCHIO generations are not ($p > 0.05$) for both 2-gram and 3-grams.

our experiments are reliable.

7 Discussion

7.1 Empirical validation of the intuition motivating PINOCCHIO

We now present two empirical analyses to verify the intuition sketched in Section 3. First, we verify our claim that the ground truth summaries in our data sets contain unsupported terms (Table 6). We define *Dataset Abstractiveness* as the ratio of n-grams that appear in the summary but not in the source text. The two abstractive datasets (XSUM and SCD) show high abstractiveness, with approximately half or more of the terms in the summaries not appearing in the source. Of course, a lack of lexical overlap could arise from summaries stating supported information but in different terms from the source. Thus, we also manually examine twenty examples for XSUM and CNNDM and ten for SCD and measure the fraction that are not directly supported by the source.[8] This fraction is substantial (18-24%) for the abstractive datasets, but much smaller (2%) for the more extractive CNN/DM dataset. Finally, η, the number of times our proposed method BART + PINOCCHIO *backtracks*, which is a measure of how often the method estimates that generated tokens are unsupported, also correlates with the abstractiveness measures.

We also verify one expected consequence of our hypothesized mechanism of hallucination. If indeed BART is defaulting to a background distribution of field values (based on frequency in the training summaries), then we would expect the more frequent training values to become even more probable in BART's output, as the model defaults to these as best guesses. We observe this effect for positions in player signings, as shown in Fig. 1. It is notable that while this distribution is more peaked, it is not entirely concentrated on the most-likely field value, suggesting that the model has learned spurious correlations that lead it to output other more rare field values, even when unsupported.

More generally, we also observe a similar bias across all n-grams; compared to the original ground truth summaries, the BART output tends to be less heavy-tailed, including disproportionately more of

[8] This annotation task can be challenging and subjective especially for the SCD dataset, see appendix §C for details.

the high-likelihood n-grams. We show this by plotting the n-gram frequency distributions (which follow a power law) on a log-log scale in Fig. 2. The BART output generally has a less negative slope than the ground truth distribution on these plots. BART + PINOCCHIO method results in a distribution that is closer to the ground truth for 2- and 3-grams.

7.2 Errors analysis

To provide insight into dominant error types, we sample 20 PINOCCHIO generations from the SCD evaluation with inconsistent outputs, and identify three common error causes that each occur in ~20% of the samples: 1) Incorrect paraphrasing or omission of meaning-changing information (e.g. X has a long history of being used for Y vs. X is the model of choice for Y) 2) Incorrect treatment of entities as coreferent/synonymous 3) Difficulty with heavy mathematical notation.

We also provide additional qualitative analysis on the generated outputs in Appendix G. We conclude that BART tends to exploit specific patterns in the dataset that contribute to its better ROUGE scores, but it fails to reliably apply commonsense or facts learned during training. Targeting these challenges in generative models is a promising future direction.

8 Conclusion

In this work, we present PINOCCHIO, a simple, no-additional-machine-learning required, method for reducing hallucination in generative encoder-decoder models. PINOCCHIO provides a substantial lift in consistency, with only a small decrease in fluency. We analyze why existing summarizers hallucinate, showing that silver abstractive summarization datasets can contain unsupported target summaries, and presenting evidence for our conjecture that models that maximize likelihood trained on such data will tend to hallucinate. We also show that existing factuality metrics are insufficient, and further explore how patterns in the training dataset can produce misleading results on the test test. We also introduce the task of scientific concept description and release a Wikipedia-based dataset for it.

We would like to clearly acknowledge the limitations of our approach. PINOCCHIO does not add new learned behavior to the model, using simple heuristics and single-step backtracking to steer the model towards more consistent output. The heuristics have settings that require some adaptation for each data set, and while limited manual tuning was sufficient for the two data sets in our experiments, further experiments with additional data sets are necessary. Further, preliminary experiments suggest that the settings that were effective for BART do not simply work out of the box for another summarizer, PEGASUS. We also acknowledge that while PINOCCHIO offers improvements in consistency, the results are still far from perfect, and thus the system is not suitable for certain applications. We hope the approach and insights in this paper help spur further development of models that generate consistent text.

References

Gabor Angeli, M. Johnson, and Christopher D. Manning. 2015. Leveraging linguistic structure for open domain information extraction. In *ACL*.

Mario Barrantes, Benedikt Herudek, and R. Wang. 2020. Adversarial nli for factual correctness in text summarisation models. *ArXiv*, abs/2005.11739.

Iz Beltagy, Kyle Lo, and Arman Cohan. 2019. SciBERT: A pretrained language model for scientific text. In *Proceedings of the 2019 Conference on Empirical Methods in Natural Language Processing and the 9th International Joint Conference on Natural Language Processing (EMNLP-IJCNLP)*, pages 3615–3620, Hong Kong, China. Association for Computational Linguistics.

Arman Cohan, Franck Dernoncourt, Doo Soon Kim, Trung Bui, Seokhwan Kim, Walter Chang, and Nazli Goharian. 2018. A discourse-aware attention model for abstractive summarization of long documents. In *Proceedings of the 2018 Conference of the North American Chapter of the Association for Computational Linguistics: Human Language Technologies, Volume 2 (Short Papers)*, pages 615–621, New Orleans, Louisiana. Association for Computational Linguistics.

Li Dong, Nan Yang, Wenhui Wang, Furu Wei, Xiaodong Liu, Yu Wang, Jianfeng Gao, Ming Zhou, and Hsiao-Wuen Hon. 2019. Unified language model pre-training for natural language understanding and generation. In *Advances in Neural Information Processing Systems*, volume 32. Curran Associates, Inc.

Yue Dong, Shuohang Wang, Zhe Gan, Yu Cheng, Jackie Chi Kit Cheung, and Jingjing Liu. 2020. Multi-fact correction in abstractive text summarization. In *Proceedings of the 2020 Conference on Empirical Methods in Natural Language Processing (EMNLP)*, pages 9320–9331, Online. Association for Computational Linguistics.

Esin Durmus, He He, and Mona Diab. 2020. FEQA: A question answering evaluation framework for faithfulness assessment in abstractive summarization. In *Proceedings of the 58th Annual Meeting of the Association for Computational Linguistics*, pages 5055–5070, Online. Association for Computational Linguistics.

Alexander R Fabbri, Wojciech Kryściński, Bryan McCann, Caiming Xiong, Richard Socher, and Dragomir Radev. 2020. Summeval: Re-evaluating summarization evaluation. *arXiv preprint arXiv:2007.12626*.

Tobias Falke, Leonardo F. R. Ribeiro, Prasetya Ajie Utama, Ido Dagan, and Iryna Gurevych. 2019. Ranking generated summaries by correctness: An interesting but challenging application for natural language inference. In *Proceedings of the 57th Annual Meeting of the Association for Computational Linguistics*, pages 2214–2220, Florence, Italy. Association for Computational Linguistics.

Alex Graves. 2012. Sequence transduction with recurrent neural networks. *ArXiv*, abs/1211.3711.

K. Hermann, Tomás Kociský, Edward Grefenstette, Lasse Espeholt, Will Kay, Mustafa Suleyman, and P. Blunsom. 2015a. Teaching machines to read and comprehend. In *NIPS*.

Karl Moritz Hermann, Tomás Kociský, Edward Grefenstette, Lasse Espeholt, Will Kay, Mustafa Suleyman, and Phil Blunsom. 2015b. Teaching machines to read and comprehend. In *NIPS*, pages 1693–1701.

Chris Hokamp and Qun Liu. 2017. Lexically constrained decoding for sequence generation using grid beam search. In *Proceedings of the 55th Annual Meeting of the Association for Computational Linguistics (Volume 1: Long Papers)*, pages 1535–1546, Vancouver, Canada. Association for Computational Linguistics.

Matthew Honnibal, Ines Montani, Sofie Van Landeghem, and Adriane Boyd. 2020. spaCy: Industrial-strength Natural Language Processing in Python.

Dandan Huang, Leyang Cui, Sen Yang, Guangsheng Bao, Kun Wang, Jun Xie, and Yue Zhang. 2020. What have we achieved on text summarization? In *Proceedings of the 2020 Conference on Empirical Methods in Natural Language Processing (EMNLP)*, pages 446–469, Online. Association for Computational Linguistics.

Daniel King, Doug Downey, and Daniel S. Weld. 2020. High-precision extraction of emerging concepts from scientific literature. *Proceedings of the 43rd International ACM SIGIR Conference on Research and Development in Information Retrieval.*

Wojciech Kryscinski, Bryan McCann, Caiming Xiong, and Richard Socher. 2020. Evaluating the factual consistency of abstractive text summarization. In *Proceedings of the 2020 Conference on Empirical Methods in Natural Language Processing (EMNLP)*, pages 9332–9346, Online. Association for Computational Linguistics.

Mike Lewis, Yinhan Liu, Naman Goyal, Marjan Ghazvininejad, Abdelrahman Mohamed, Omer Levy, Veselin Stoyanov, and Luke Zettlemoyer. 2020. BART: Denoising sequence-to-sequence pre-training for natural language generation, translation, and comprehension. In *Proceedings of the 58th Annual Meeting of the Association for Computational Linguistics*, pages 7871–7880, Online. Association for Computational Linguistics.

Chin-Yew Lin. 2004. Rouge: A package for automatic evaluation of summaries. In *ACL 2004*.

Peter J. Liu*, Mohammad Saleh*, Etienne Pot, Ben Goodrich, Ryan Sepassi, Lukasz Kaiser, and Noam Shazeer. 2018. Generating wikipedia by summarizing long sequences. In *International Conference on Learning Representations*.

Yang Liu and Mirella Lapata. 2019. Hierarchical transformers for multi-document summarization. In *Proceedings of the 57th Annual Meeting of the Association for Computational Linguistics*, pages 5070–5081, Florence, Italy. Association for Computational Linguistics.

I. Loshchilov and F. Hutter. 2017. Fixing weight decay regularization in adam. *ArXiv*, abs/1711.05101.

Yuning Mao, X. Ren, Huai zhong Ji, and Jiawei Han. 2020. Constrained abstractive summarization: Preserving factual consistency with constrained generation. *ArXiv*, abs/2010.12723.

Yoshitomo Matsubara and Sameer Singh. 2020. Citations beyond self citations: Identifying authors, affiliations, and nationalities in scientific papers. In *Proceedings of the 8th International Workshop on Mining Scientific Publications*, pages 9–20, Wuhan, China. Association for Computational Linguistics.

Kazuki Matsumaru, Sho Takase, and Naoaki Okazaki. 2020. Improving truthfulness of headline generation. In *Proceedings of the 58th Annual Meeting of the Association for Computational Linguistics*, pages 1335–1346, Online. Association for Computational Linguistics.

Joshua Maynez, Shashi Narayan, Bernd Bohnet, and Ryan McDonald. 2020. On faithfulness and factuality in abstractive summarization. In *Proceedings of the 58th Annual Meeting of the Association for Computational Linguistics*, pages 1906–1919, Online. Association for Computational Linguistics.

Anshuman Mishra, Dhruvesh Patel, Aparna Vijayakumar, Xiang Li, Pavan Kapanipathi, and Kartik Talamadupula. 2020. Looking beyond sentence-level natural language inference for downstream tasks. *ArXiv*, abs/2009.09099.

Ramesh Nallapati, Bowen Zhou, Caglar Gulcehre, Bing Xiang, et al. 2016. Abstractive text summarization using sequence-to-sequence rnns and beyond. *arXiv preprint arXiv:1602.06023*.

Feng Nan, Ramesh Nallapati, Zhiguo Wang, Cicero Nogueira dos Santos, Henghui Zhu, Dejiao Zhang, Kathleen McKeown, and Bing Xiang. 2021. Entity-level factual consistency of abstractive text summarization. In *Proceedings of the 16th Conference of the European Chapter of the Association for Computational Linguistics: Main Volume*, pages 2727–2733, Online. Association for Computational Linguistics.

Shashi Narayan, Shay B. Cohen, and Mirella Lapata. 2018. Don't give me the details, just the summary! topic-aware convolutional neural networks for extreme summarization. In *Proceedings of the 2018 Conference on Empirical Methods in Natural Language Processing*, pages 1797–1807, Brussels, Belgium. Association for Computational Linguistics.

Artidoro Pagnoni, Vidhisha Balachandran, and Yulia Tsvetkov. 2021. Understanding factuality in abstractive summarization with frank: A benchmark for factuality metrics. *ArXiv*, abs/2104.13346.

Abigail See, Peter J Liu, and Christopher D Manning. 2017. Get to the point: Summarization with pointer-generator networks. *arXiv preprint arXiv:1704.04368*.

Eva Sharma, Chen Li, and Lu Wang. 2019. BIGPATENT: A large-scale dataset for abstractive and coherent summarization. In *Proceedings of the 57th Annual Meeting of the Association for Computational Linguistics*, pages 2204–2213, Florence, Italy. Association for Computational Linguistics.

Kaiqiang Song, Bingqing Wang, Zhe Feng, Ren Liu, and Fei Liu. 2020. Controlling the amount of verbatim copying in abstractive summarization. In *The Thirty-Fourth AAAI Conference on Artificial Intelligence, AAAI 2020, The Thirty-Second Innovative Applications of Artificial Intelligence Conference, IAAI 2020, The Tenth AAAI Symposium on Educational Advances in Artificial Intelligence, EAAI 2020, New York, NY, USA, February 7-12, 2020*, pages 8902–8909. AAAI Press.

Nishant Subramani, Samuel R. Bowman, and Kyunghyun Cho. 2019. Can unconditional language models recover arbitrary sentences? In *NeurIPS*.

Nishant Subramani and Nivedita Suresh. 2020. Discovering useful sentence representations from large pretrained language models. *ArXiv*, abs/2008.09049.

Ilya Sutskever, Oriol Vinyals, and Quoc V. Le. 2014. Sequence to sequence learning with neural networks. In *NIPS*.

Ran Tian, Shashi Narayan, Thibault Sellam, and Ankur P. Parikh. 2019. Sticking to the facts: Confident decoding for faithful data-to-text generation. *ArXiv*, abs/1910.08684.

Alex Wang, Kyunghyun Cho, and Mike Lewis. 2020a. Asking and answering questions to evaluate the factual consistency of summaries. In *Proceedings of the 58th Annual Meeting of the Association for Computational Linguistics*, pages 5008–5020, Online. Association for Computational Linguistics.

Zhenyi Wang, Xiaoyang Wang, Bang An, Dong Yu, and Changyou Chen. 2020b. Towards faithful neural table-to-text generation with content-matching constraints. In *Proceedings of the 58th Annual Meeting of the Association for Computational Linguistics*, pages 1072–1086, Online. Association for Computational Linguistics.

Yonghui Wu, Mike Schuster, Zhifeng Chen, Quoc V. Le, Mohammad Norouzi, Wolfgang Macherey, Maxim Krikun, Yuan Cao, Qin Gao, Klaus Macherey, Jeff Klingner, Apurva Shah, Melvin Johnson, Xiaobing Liu, Łukasz Kaiser, Stephan Gouws, Yoshikiyo Kato, Taku Kudo, Hideto Kazawa, Keith Stevens, George Kurian, Nishant Patil, Wei Wang, Cliff Young, Jason Smith, Jason Riesa, Alex Rudnick, Oriol Vinyals, Greg Corrado, Macduff Hughes, and Jeffrey Dean. 2016. Google's neural machine translation system: Bridging the gap between human and machine translation. *CoRR*, abs/1609.08144.

Jiacheng Xu, Shrey Desai, and Greg Durrett. 2020. Understanding neural abstractive summarization models via uncertainty. In *Proceedings of the 2020 Conference on Empirical Methods in Natural Language Processing (EMNLP)*, pages 6275–6281, Online. Association for Computational Linguistics.

Jingqing Zhang, Y. Zhao, Mohammad Saleh, and Peter J. Liu. 2020a. Pegasus: Pre-training with extracted gap-sentences for abstractive summarization. In *ICML*.

Yuhao Zhang, Derek Merck, Emily Tsai, Christopher D. Manning, and Curtis Langlotz. 2020b. Optimizing the factual correctness of a summary: A study of summarizing radiology reports. In *Proceedings of the 58th Annual Meeting of the Association for Computational Linguistics*, pages 5108–5120, Online. Association for Computational Linguistics.

Chenguang Zhu, William Hinthorn, Ruochen Xu, Qingkai Zeng, Michael Zeng, Xuedong Huang, and Meng Jiang. 2021. Enhancing factual consistency of abstractive summarization. In *NAACL*.

A Example Full Text

A.1 Example from Table 1

Police said the 14-year-old reported feeling unwell and required hospital treatment. He was later discharged from hospital and is recovering at home. The incident happened in Holywood, County Down, on Saturday. The PSNI said the tablets were "as yet unidentified" but warned of the "potential dangers" they posed. The 17-year-old, has been charged with possessing a Class A controlled drug with intent to supply; possessing a Class B controlled drug with intent to supply; possession of a Class A controlled drug; possession of a Class B controlled drug and supplying a Class A controlled drug. He is due to appear at Newtownards Youth Court on 14 February.

A.2 Player signings

The 29-year-old Scot has signed a two-year contract with the Gloucestershire outfit. Prior to joining Hibs in August 2016, Graham had spells at six other Scottish sides, including Dundee United, St Johnstone and Ross County. He will be available for Saturday's league visit of Crawley Town, subject to receiving international clearance. Find all the latest football transfers on our dedicated page.

B Mathematical Details of Hallucination Analysis

Formally, a summarization model is defined by a distribution $P(S|P)$ over output textual summaries S conditioned on an input passage P. We assume that the summarization system aims to maximize the probability of the summary S given the text passage, i.e. it outputs $\arg\max_S P(S|P)$. While in practice (including in our experiments), summarization models use imperfect search procedures like beam search to find high-likelihood generations, and may rescore complete generations using factors other than likelihood (like length), in this analysis we ignore these details and assume the generator simply maximizes likelihood. Analyzing the impact of more complex generation aspects is an item of future work.

Let $F(S)$ be a function denoting the value of a given "field" in the summary S, equal either to some string value or to $\emptyset$ if the field does not occur in S. A "field" is a typical piece of information that is often mentioned in a summary of a given topic (e.g., participating teams, in a summary of a sporting event; or the university where an idea was developed, in a scientific concept description). Then the model's distribution over a field value for a given passage is $P(F = \mathbf{f}|P) = \sum_S P(F(S) = \mathbf{f}|P)$.

Our analysis uses the following assumption:

Assumption **A1**: The model's most likely summary probability is strictly monotonic in the probability of its included field values. That is, whenever:

$$P(F = \mathbf{f}|P) > P(F = \mathbf{f}'|P) \quad (1)$$

then

$$\max_S P(S, F(S) = \mathbf{f}|P) > \max_S P(S, F(S) = \mathbf{f}'|P) \quad (2)$$

That is, when the model thinks a field value is more likely in a summary for a given passage, then it can find a more likely summary that uses that field value. This assumption seems likely to hold often in practice (for example, we would expect that by simply swapping out a less likely field value in a summary for a more likely one, we would often arrive at a more probable summary).

The observation used in the analysis in Section 3 is then: given a passage p, a field F, and a summarization model $P(S|P)$, if assumption A1 holds, then a generator that maximizes likelihood will choose to output $\mathbf{f} = \arg\max_{\mathbf{f}} P(F = \mathbf{f}|P)$ for the field's value (or omit the field, if $\mathbf{f} = \emptyset$). This fact is straightforward from the definitions.

C Manual Examination of the Unsupported Dataset Samples

Identifying parts of a summary that are not supported by the source document is a challenging annotation task. In this section, we explain how we formalize this task as a binary token tagging problem, and we show one example that illustrate the difficulty of annotation.

C.1 Annotating unsupported words

Naturally, words that appear only in the summary but not the source document tend to have a higher chance of being "hallucinated", and vice versa. Hence, we select such words from the summary, and the goal is try to identify whether the meaning of these words can be deduced from the source documents. Compared to the automated measurements, the manually inspected labels are considered to be a better approximation of the true abstractiveness of the dataset or the samples.

C.2 One challenging example

In practice, understanding the source document involves multiple (common sense) reasoning steps and subjective judgements.

Considering the following document text:

`'ABC of allergies: Venom allergy Stings from bees and wasps, the most common stinging insects in Britain, can cause severe allergic reactions, including anaphylaxis. Coroners' data suggest that an average of four deaths from bee or wasp stings occur each year in the United Kingdom, but this is almost certainly an underestimate because venom anaphylaxis is not always recognised as the cause of death'`

For one sentence in the summary, we highlight the words that do not appear in the source in red:

`'The stings of most of these species (Bees) can be quite painful, and are therefore keenly avoided by many people.'`

The source text mentions several dangerous aspects of bee stings, but whether it can be concluded that they are avoided by many people (a plausible commonsense implication) is subjective to judge, and annotators often had differing opinions on these judgments.

D PINOCCHIO Details

D.1 Heuristics in f_c

We develop 8 binary checks that constitute the heuristics for f_c, which fall into three categories. Two categories use model internals, *model confidence* and *source text attribution* for the predicted token. The third category uses language features, allowing generations that are *common words*.

Model confidence

- entropy of next-token distribution $< \tau$ for a token in the top 2 predictions
- from the top 10 predicted next tokens, the number that match a top 5 attended-to piece of source text[9] is $>= \frac{1}{2}(10-$the number that are stopwords)

Source text attribution

- the most attended-to piece of the source text contains the predicted token
- 3 out of the top 5 attended-to pieces of the source text contain the predicted token
- sum of the attention scores of the attended-to pieces of source text (out of the top 5) that contain the predicted token is greater than $\frac{1}{3}$ of the sum of the top 5 attention scores
- max cosine similarity between the embedding of the predicted token and that of any word in the top 5 attended-to pieces of source text is greater than 0.15 (and the word is not capitalized or a number word)*[10]

Common word

- predicted token is a stopword*
- prediction matches[11] one of the top 5 predictions of roberta-base[12]

All of the components and hyperparameters above were determined via inspection on a small number of samples (e.g., n=20) from the XSUM and SCD dataset. In the subsequent sections we detail the configurations of the parameters on each dataset.

D.2 XSUM modeling details

For configuration of PINOCCHIO for XSUM, we set $\tau = 1.0$ and do not use the optional stopword condition, in order to accommodate the highly abstractive nature of the XSUM dataset and attempt to prevent the use of stopwords in hallucinations.

One other important detail is that XSUM has a surprising property with respect to first names. If a person appears in the source as "Mr/Ms" X, and also in the headline, they *always* appear as <FIRST NAME> X in the headline. This leads to BART *always* guessing the first name of a person, frequently incorrectly. Our f_c often identifies the first name as unsupported, but because BART is essentially unable to predict anything other than a first name in this situation, it is unable to recover from this error. For this reason, when an unsupported token is identified as a name using spaCy (Honnibal et al., 2020), we deterministically replace it with Mr/Ms.[13]

[9]All reference to "top attended-to pieces of the source text" means a max across locations in the source text across attention heads in the final layer of the decoder's cross-attention, and a 10-wordpiece window around the attended-to location.

[10]Items marked with an asterisk * are optional.

[11]For all string matching, we lemmatize first.

[12]`https://huggingface.co/roberta-base`

[13]For real applications, we suggest using a gender neutral honorific, as gender is not possible to infer using first names

D.3 SCD modeling details

For SCD, the source consists of full papers and is too long to input to BART directly, so we train a separate BERT-based model to extractively rank chunks of the input text based on predicted ROUGE-L F1 score against the target text. This setup of ranking extractive chunks and then passing them to an abstractive model is similar to prior work on long text summarization (Liu and Lapata, 2019). We pass the concept name/aliases and each chunk of text to rank to SciBERT-base (Beltagy et al., 2019), with a final linear layer to predict the ROUGE-L score. We then finetune BART, with the ranked extractive chunks as source, again concatenated with the concept name/aliases. For inference, we also filter the chunks to those that include the concept name or an alias.

Beam search parameters We use standard parameters for the beam search of min_length=5, max_length=500, no_repeat_ngram_size=3, length_penalty=2.0, and num_beams=6.

Extractive ranker for descriptions The extractive ranker uses SciBERT[14], followed by a linear layer, and is trained with MSE loss. We also use dropout of 0.1. We train on chunks containing three sentences, and use the average ROUGE-L as the label. To reduce the size of the training set, for each target description, we select the top 5 and bottom 5 chunks by ROUGE-L, and an additional 5 random chunks from the middle. We train for 3 epochs, with a batch size of 1, 8 gradient accumulation steps, and the AdamW (Loshchilov and Hutter, 2017) optimizer, with weight decay 0.01, and a slanted triangular learning rate scheduler with peak learning rate 5e-5.

D.4 Finetuning BART on descriptions

BART was finetuned with the standard settings,[15] a batch size of 4 with 8 gradient accumulation steps, for 10 epochs, selecting the epoch 5 model based on validation loss. The same optimizer as above was used, with 500 warmup steps. The model was trained for 5.5 hours on 3 NVIDIA Quadro RTX 8000s. We additionally filter out examples that have a target length less than 150 characters, and examples where the source and target have less than 0.2 token overlap.

[14] `https://huggingface.co/allenai/scibert_scivocab_uncased`

[15] `https://huggingface.co/facebook/bart-large/blob/main/config.json`

For configuration of PINOCCHIO for SCD, we set τ=0.75 and do not use the optional cosine similarity condition, to encourage more extractiveness.

E Annotation Instructions

- Consistency
  - 1: completely made up
  - 2: some phrases supported, but largely made up
  - 3: some full details correct, but key details made up
  - 4: minor details not fully supported (e.g. acronym wrong, location abstracted a bit wrong)
  - 5: fully supported
  - Other notes: An unresolved "it" should be assumed to refer to the main concept. If this makes it not factual, that counts against consistency, otherwise it counts against coherence.
- Coherence
  - 1: all sentences/phrases don't make sense together
  - 3: some sentences/phrases don't make sentence together, separate from whether they are factual
  - 5: no issues with how phrases/sentences are put together
- Fluency (at the sentence level)
  - 1: not fluent English to the point that it is impossible to understand/meaningless
  - 2: not fluent English to the point that it is very hard to understand
  - 3: semi fluent English (including major fluency errors resulting from copying source text), but still largely understandable
  - 4: Mostly fluent English (including minor fluency errors resulting from source text), does not impact understanding
  - 5: Fluent English
- Relevance
  - 1: off-topic
  - 3: mostly on-topic or seems to be missing an actual statement of what the concept is (or for news, what the article is about)
  - 5: on-topic and contains the key statement of what the concept is (or for news, what the article is about)

F UniLM+FC Comparison Details

Model output downloaded from `https://drive.google.com/file/d/1blmmJvniToN1yedoWUH3u0SNtXnMVDAs/view?usp=sharing` on 03/23/21. We consider an output "changed" by FC if it is not a prefix match for the original UniLM output, after lowercasing and removing spaces and apostrophes. Many FC-corrected examples seem to simply cutoff the end of the generated text. We choose to not count these as "changed." There are 579 such cases. Given this criteria, FC changes 594 examples in the XSUM test set, and we sample 100 of these for evaluation. FC makes very minimal edits, so it is straightforward to identify whether the edit is an improvement or not. The net improvement is the number of increases in consistency minus the number of decreases in consistency.

G Patterns and Hallucination

We provide additional discussions for some qualitative aspects of our results. First, we need to discuss the substantial drop in ROUGE on XSUM. As alluded to in §3, we believe this is due to a pervasive regularity in the XSUM dataset, which BART is able to capture very well. In Tab. 7, we show the top examples sorted by ROUGE-L difference between BART and PINOCCHIO, along with a hand-crafted regex matching the example, how many times it matches target outputs from the training and validation set, how many times it matches BART predictions on the test set, and how many of those predictions are completely factually consistent. Most of these examples straightforwardly map to patterns of text that occur in the training data. We also see that test set predictions matching these patterns are largely not consistent. As discussed in §3, this is because BART assigns high likelihood to the general pattern, but guesses to fill in the details. Some of these patterns are straightforward to identify, but many are likely to be more complicated. Broadly speaking, XSUM contains a lot of regularity in the mapping between the source topic, phrases, and vocabulary used in the target summary. BART exploits this, whereas PINOCCHIO steers the model away from the patterns, which are often not supported by the source text, which lowers ROUGE.

A related question is if BART trained on XSUM applies facts learned during training correctly. Does it learn that Antonio Conte is the coach of the Italian football team, thus someone named "Conte" who coaches the Italian team is Antonio Conte? Or does it merely learn the first name most commonly associated with "Conte" in train is "Antonio", and so everyone named "Conte" is Antonio Conte? [16] It is difficult to assess this automatically, so we present an example of BART's tendency to guess world knowledge. We create one three-sentence source, "Sometime last week, a fire burned down a <BUILDING>, killing a number of people. The fire took place in <LOCATION>. Investigators believe at least four people to be missing.", filling in the blanks with three made up locations and three building types. BART produces plausible but inconsistent summaries. Nine out of nine outputs hallucinate the location, eight discuss arrests or hospitalizations, and three mention the police or fire service reporting the details of the situation. These characteristics are all due to biases present in the training data. Locations are often abstracted, reported fires often result in someone being arrested or hospitalized, and they are usually reported by authorities. We present this example as evidence that BART is not learning how to reliably apply commonsense and learned facts, but rather, is naively reproducing patterns and word associations.

H Comparing Generated Summaries with and without PINOCCHIO

In Tab. 8 and 9, we include example summaries generated with and without PINOCCHIO. We additionally include the annotator ratings and their comments to illustrate how PINOCCHIO improves the quality of the summaries.

[16] Experiments with this example strongly suggest the latter.

BART generation	Manual pattern	Train/val	Predicted	Consistent
A 70-year-old man who died after being hit by a car in Monmouthshire has been named by police.	.*year-old.*who died.*named.*	47	4	0
Chinese businessman Dr Tony Xia has completed his £52m takeover of Championship club Aston Villa.	.*Tony Xia.*Aston Villa.*| .*Aston Villa.*Tony Xia.*	7	1	0
All pictures are copyrighted.	.*All pictures are copyrighted.*	44	4	4
Forfar Athletic extended their lead at the top of Scottish League Two to five points with a 3-0 win over Berwick Rangers.	.*extended.*top.*points.*win.* .*Forfar Athletic.*top of Scottish League Two.*	9 10	3 1	0 0

Table 7: Top-5 BART generations, by ROUGE-L gain over PINOCCHIO (#2 is excluded; it doesn't match an obvious pattern and is factually consistent). In all examples, BART clearly memorized training patterns and guesses the details in at least 3 (the 3rd output is memorized from noise in XSUM), which is not strongly penalized by ROUGE.

Table 8: Side-by-side comparison of the generated summaries with and without PINOCCHIO – Example 1 in XSUM.

Source	Tourism NI said it expects a strategy to be in place by early next year. Janice Gault from the Hotels Federation told the BBC's Inside Business programme it was crucial for the industry. She said a "partnership" approach was essential. "I mean we've really urged people to get a strategy at sort of quite a high level so that everybody can buy into that," she said. "Hotels have probably spent about a billion pounds in the last decade and are set to spend more." Ms Gault said another big boom was expected in the hotel market which would probably generate another half a billion pounds. "The funny thing about the strategy is we still have the target, but we don't have the strategy. We only have one way to go and that's growth and the way for us to get that is to partnership," she added.	
Generation	**BART**	**BART+PINOCCHIO**
	The Northern Ireland Hotels Federation has called on the Northern Ireland Executive to set out a strategy for growth in the hotel industry.	A new strategy for Northern Ireland's hotel industry has been urged by the Hotels Federation and Tourism NI as the industry is set for another big year.
Ratings	Consistency: 3 Fluency: 5 Relevance: 5	Consistency: 5 Fluency: 5 Relevance: 5
Annotator Comment	*Executive abstracted; didn't call on her; strategy is not to "grow" the industry*	

Table 9: Side-by-side comparison of the generated summaries with and without PINOCCHIO – Example 2 in XSUM.

Source	The University and College Union says the 1.1% rise offered by the universities is "an insult". But the Universities and Colleges Employers Association said the walkout was "disappointing given the very good pay offer". Unions representing university support staff are balloting on the offer, with strike action possible in the autumn. UCU says its members have suffered a real-terms pay cut of 14.% since 2009 and complains the squeeze on staff salaries has come as university leaders enjoyed hefty increases. "A 1.1% pay offer is an insult to hardworking staff, especially in light of the 5% pay rise vice-chancellors have enjoyed while holding down staff pay," said general secretary Sally Hunt. "Industrial action which impacts on students is never taken lightly, but members feel that they have been left with no alternative. "If the employers wish to see a swift end to this dispute, and avoid further disruption, they need to come back to the table with a much-improved offer." Summer exams are still running at some universities, though many have finished. A spokesman for the employers anticipated only "minor impact and minimal student disruption". "Even for examinations which are still taking place at some higher education institutions, more than nine out of 10 report that a no to low impact is anticipated," said the spokesman. "We would like to see the UCU consulting its members on the final offer." The employers say the offer is "at, and, for some, beyond, a limit of affordability for higher education institutions and the very best offer that will be available this year". They maintain the weighting of the offer means the worst paid university staff will get a rise of more than 5%. They say they have also offered talks on zero-hours contracts and on improving lower pay for female academics. But UCU says it rejected the 1.1% offer as it was only a marginal improvement on the original 1% on which it had balloted members. Ballots of university support staff represented by Unison and Unite are also under way on the improved offer, with both unions recommending it be rejected. Any action would take place during the autumn term, said a Unison spokeswoman. UCU is planning strike rallies in: Staff are also working to contract from Wednesday - refusing to set extra work, cover for absent colleagues or work overtime.	
Generation	**BART**	**BART+PINOCCHIO**
	University staff in England are to stage a one-day strike on Wednesday in a row over pay, in a dispute that could lead to further industrial action.	Universities have warned of "minor disruption" for students in England after staff rejected an improved pay offer in a dispute over a pay rise.
Ratings	Consistency: 3 Fluency: 3 Relevance: 5	Consistency: 4 Fluency: 5 Relevance: 3
Annotator Comment	*consistency: location abstracted; "one day" on Wednesday not true* *fluency: "in a" twice in same sentence, doesn't flow*	*consistency: quoted text is not an actual quote; location abstracted* *relevance: "improved pay" is misleading, missing key information: "1.1% marginal improvement"*

Author Index

Association for Computational Linguistics
209 N. Eighth Street
Stroudsburg, Pennsylvania 18360

ISBN 978-1-7138-9111-6
9 781713 891116

CURRAN ASSOCIATES INC.
proceedings.com